DISTRICT OF COLUMBIA
Interments (Index to Deaths)
January 1, 1855 to July 31, 1874

GRAVE OF JOHN HOWARD PAYNE AT OAK HILL CEMETERY

Wesley E. Pippenger

HERITAGE BOOKS
2007

HERITAGE BOOKS
AN IMPRINT OF HERITAGE BOOKS, INC.

Books, CDs, and more—Worldwide

For our listing of thousands of titles see our website
at
www.HeritageBooks.com

Published 2007 by
HERITAGE BOOKS, INC.
Publishing Division
65 East Main Street
Westminster, Maryland 21157-5026

Copyright © 1999 Wesley E. Pippenger

All rights reserved. No part of this book may be reproduced or transmitted in any form or by any means, electronic or mechanical, including photocopying, recording or by any information storage and retrieval system without written permission from the author, except for the inclusion of brief quotations in a review.

International Standard Book Number: 978-1-58549-154-4

DISTRICT OF COLUMBIA
Interments (Index to Deaths)
January 1, 1855 to July 31, 1874

Other Heritage Books by Wesley E. Pippenger:

Alexandria (Arlington) County, Virginia Death Records, 1853-1896

Alexandria City and Arlington County, Virginia Records Index: Vol. 1

Alexandria City and Arlington County, Virginia Records Index: Vol. 2

Alexandria County, Virginia Marriage Records, 1853-1895

Alexandria Virginia Marriage Index, January 10, 1893 to August 31, 1905

Alexandria, Virginia Marriages, 1870-1892

Alexandria, Virginia Town Lots, 1749-1801, Together with the Proceedings of the Board of Trustees, 1749-1780

Alexandria, Virginia Wills, Administrations and Guardianships, 1786-1800

Alexandria, Virginia 1808 Census (Wards 1, 2, 3, and 4)

Alexandria, Virginia Death Records, 1863-1896

Alexandria, Virginia Hustings Court Orders, Volume 1, 1780-1787

Connections and Separations: Divorce, Name Change and Other Genealogical Tidbits from the Acts of the Virginia General Assembly

Daily National Intelligencer *Index to Deaths, 1855-1870*

Daily National Intelligencer, *Washington, District of Columbia Marriages and Deaths Notices (January 1, 1851 to December 30, 1854)*

Dead People on the Move: Reconstruction of the Georgetown Presbyterian Burying Ground,
Holmead's (Western) Burying Ground, and other Removals in the District of Columbia

Death Notices from Richmond, Virginia Newspapers, 1841-1853

District of Columbia Ancestors, A Guide to Records of the District of Columbia

District of Columbia Death Records: August 1, 1874-July 31, 1879

District of Columbia Foreign Deaths, 1888-1923

District of Columbia Guardianship Index, 1802-1928

District of Columbia Interments (Index to Deaths), January 1, 1855 to July 31, 1874

District of Columbia Marriage Licenses, Register 1: 1811-1858

District of Columbia Marriage Licenses, Register 2: 1858-1870

District of Columbia Marriage Records Index, 1877-1885

District of Columbia Marriage Records Index, October 20, 1885 to January 20, 1892: Marriage Record Books 21 to 30

District of Columbia Probate Records, 1801-1852

District of Columbia: Original Land Owners, 1791-1800

Early Church Records of Alexandria City and Fairfax County, Virginia

Georgetown, District of Columbia 1850 Federal Population Census (Schedule I) and 1853 Directory of Residents of Georgetown

Georgetown, District of Columbia Marriage and Death Notices, 1801-1838

Husbands and Wives Associated with Early Alexandria, Virginia
(and the Surrounding Area), 3rd Edition, Revised

Index to Virginia Estates, 1800-1865
Volumes 4, 5 and 6

John Alexander, a Northern Neck Proprietor, His Family, Friends and Kin

Legislative Petitions of Alexandria, 1778-1861

Pippenger and Pittenger Families

Proceedings of the Orphan's Court, Washington County, District of Columbia, 1801-1808

The Georgetown Courier *Marriage and Death Notices:*
Georgetown, District of Columbia, November 18, 1865 to May 6, 1876

The Georgetown Directory for the Year 1830: to which is appended, a Short Description of
the Churches, Public Institutions, and the Original Charter of Georgetown, and
Extracts of the Laws Pertaining to the Chesapeake and Ohio Canal Company

The Virginia Gazette and Alexandria Advertiser:
Volume 1, September 3, 1789 to November 11, 1790

The Virginia Journal and Alexandria Advertiser:
Volume I (February 5, 1784 to January 27, 1785)

Volume II (February 3, 1785 to January 26, 1786)

Volume III (March 2, 1786 to January 25, 1787)

Volume IV (February 8, 1787 to May 21, 1789)

The Washington and Georgetown Directory of 1853

Tombstone Inscriptions of Alexandria, Volumes 1-4

Introduction

The purpose of this work is to provide an index to the Interment Register which covers the period January 1, 1855 to July 31, 1874. The Register is not complete, as there are no records for the periods June 27, 1861 to June 3, 1862, and August 1, 1862 to January 1, 1866. The original volume is in a deteriorating condition and is kept by the District of Columbia Department of Health, Vital Records Division. The original record was used only briefly to verify information that the compiler had difficulty interpreting from a microfilm copy (LDS #1994617) of the Register. Although the Register begins with January 1855, the first two pages for this month which were fragmented and in poor condition when the film was made, cannot now be located. A number of pages on the microfilm are almost entirely illegible. Those which cannot be read easily include pages 1-2 (January 1855), and 9-24 (June-September 1855). The microfilm copy omits pages 104, 20, 401, 452, 453 and 706 which each contain information in the original record. Most pages in the Register are loose, missing pieces around the edges, and are brittle. When this deterioration affects record content it is indicated here in a record entry as "[torn]."

Columns in the original record provide space for inserting: (a) date; (b) name of the deceased; (c) age in years, months and days; (d) color; (e) sex; (f) occupation; (g) nativity; (h) [length of] residence in Washington; (i) primary disease; (j) duration; (k) secondary disease; (l) duration; (m) married or single; and (n) burial ground. As is unfortunately true with many public records of this type, information about deaths was not received, recorded, or recorded completely. This work presents the: (a) Register page number; (b) name of the deceased; (c) occupation; (d) age in years, months, days, weeks, hours or minutes; (e) race; (f) nativity; (g) date of death; and (h) burial place.

Users should be aware that the date listed in the interment register is virtually always the date of death, and is oftentimes much earlier than the date of actual burial that may be found in a cemetery record. The handwriting within the Register is not always the same, and it is obviously grouped by different scribes. A difficult handwriting begins in 1871. Particularly disturbing is in records of September 1871 where, presumably in error, the majority of deaths are recorded on but a few days. One will occasionally find an occupation given for an infant, or an age figure that is seemingly recorded in the wrong column.

In addition to the Register data, the compiler has checked data from outside sources—primarily cemetery records. Entries that reflect information from cemetery records include an asterisk (*) after the place of burial. Staff at local cemetery offices were extremely supportive in assisting the compiler in making such verifications.

Every effort has been made to correctly interpret the sometimes illegible and frequently difficult handwriting that is found in the Register. The compiler was often suspicious that the record creator could not spell, or did not in some way obtain correct and/or complete information about the decedent. Particularly questionable portions are underscored in this work.

Finally, the compiler suggests that this work be used as a finding aid for researchers and not a replacement for original records. The end product comes to you with the support and assistance from Joseph and Ella S. Pozell, Oak Hill Cemetery; Jim Oliver, Congressional Cemetery; Urbane Bass, Vital Records Division; and Dorothy Provine, former Archivist at the D.C. Archives.

Wesley E. Pippenger
Arlington, Virginia
September 1999

Statistical Analysis

The Register contains 22,835 records. In studying these, some interesting conclusions can be made from records that contain data in a particular field.

AGE

DEATHS BY AGE GROUP	
Still/Premature	607
under 1 year	7,244
1-10 years	3,255
11-20 years	1,086
21-30 years	2,378
31-40 years	1,907
41-50 years	1,492
51-60 years	1,309
61-70 years	1,187
71-80 years	960
81-90 years	320
91-99 years	61
100 and over	38
Unidentified	991
TOTAL	22,835

YEAR

DEATHS BY YEAR	
1855	1,061
1856	957
1857	922
1858	1,049
1859	932
1860	637
1861	177
1862	40
1866	1,264
1867	1,236
1868	2,764
1869	2,064
1870	1,945
1871	1,563
1872	2,498
1873	2,272
1874	1,454
TOTAL	22,835

RACE

DEATHS BY RACE	
Black	193
Colored	7,080
Mulatto	13
Yellow	5
Indian	12
White	14,991
Other	10
Unidentified	531
TOTAL	22,835

PLACE OF BURIAL

Burial numbers for the most active cemeteries for the period, 1855-1874, are:

Congressional	4,140	Freedmen's (Bureau, Hospital)	194
Mt. Olivet	2,646	Potters Field	169
Glenwood	1,834	Beckett's	167
Washington Asylum	1,325	Union	155
Young Mens	928	German	154
Holmead (Western)	722	St. Matthews	145
Oak Hill	647	Rock Creek	136
Prospect Hill	634	Holy Rood (Trinity)	122
St. Patricks	590	Alexandria, Va.	86
Columbian Harmony	588	Mt. Pleasant [Plains]	79
Small Pox	556	Asylum	53
Ebenezer	548	(Washington) Hebrew	51
Alms/Poor House	387	Eastern Methodist	48
Methodist (not specific)	335	Catholic (not specific)	38
St. Marys (German Catholic)	276	Presbyterian	31
Foundry (Western Methodist)	229	Mt. Zion	31
St. Peters	216	Graceland	27

Frequently the place of burial is listed in a distant location, for example: Alexandria, Va. (68); Annapolis, Md. (8); Arlington, Va. (6); Baltimore, Md. (204); Fairfax County, Va. (8); Boston, Mass. (20); Philadelphia, Pa. (71); Richmond, Va. (11), or New York (75). Many other burial locations are scattered throughout this work. The winter 1872-1873 brought to the District a widespread small pox epidemic which resulted in hundreds of burials in the local small pox burying ground.

NATIVITY

PLACE OF BIRTH BY LOCATION (WHEN IDENTIFIED)							
Alabama	9	Foreign	1	Missouri	10	Scotland	69
American	122	France	39	North Carolina	46	At Sea	1
Arkansas	1	Georgia	10	New Hampshire	41	Sicily	1
Austria	1	Germany	569	New Jersey	65	Spain	4
Baden	1	Illinois	14	New Mexico	1	Sweden	2
Bavaria	9	Indiana	10	New York	279	Switzerland	16
Belgium	4	Iowa	4	Nova Scotia	4	Tennessee	9
Berumda	1	Ireland	1,148	Nebraska	2	Texas	2
Bolivia	1	Italy	25	Norway	1	Tuscany	1
Brazil	1	Kansas	2	Ohio	53	U.S.	4,432
California	2	Kentucky	23	Puerto Rico	1	Vermont	31
Canada	13	Long Island	1	Pennsylvania	258	Virginia	1,447
Connecticut	39	Louisiana	13	Poland	9	Alexandria	78
D.C.	7,672	Massachusetts	94	Portugal	2	Wales	6
Georgetown	112	Maryland	1,747	Prussia	24	West Indies	7
Delaware	20	Maine	42	Rhode Island	11	West Virginia	5
Denmark	4	Mexico	1	Russia	4	Wisconsin	6
England	244	Michigan	14	South Carolina	25	Würtemberg	2
Europe	7	Minnesota	2	South Wales	1	York	1
Florida	4	Mississippi	6	Saxony	4		

Cemeteries and Burial Grounds

On May 15, 1820,[1] a former Act of 1804 was amended to contain provisions that affected the regulation and care of burial grounds within the city limits, and for registering births, deaths, and marriages. On March 30, 1822, the D.C. Board of Health was established.[2] The Board supervised nuisances or sources of disease, and required the keeping of a register of deaths in the city. Three Commissioners were appointed to oversee activities for the eastern and western burial grounds. They were "appointed for the purpose of dividing the burial grounds into suitable sites for graves, and to dispose of the same, in the manner prescribed by the laws of the Corporation." The Commissioners were also authorized to apply the money arising from the sale of sites for graves, to the improvement and repairs of the fences and burial grounds, and to the purchase of a lot, and the erection of a house thereon, in the neighborhood of each, for the accommodation of the sextons.[3] One sexton was appointed for each burial ground by the Mayor. The sextons or their deputies were the only persons allowed to dig graves in the burial grounds to which they were respectively attached. The sextons were required to keep an exact account of all interments made by them, and make a return thereof to the Register of the city every three months. The 1822 city directory lists the commissioners of the eastern burial ground as John Chalmers, Daniel Rapine and John Crabb, with John L. Brightwell as sexton.[4] The commissioners in 1822 for the western burial ground (Holmead's) were David Easton, Robert King and Benjamin M. Belt, with Phillip Williams as sexton.

By city ordinance passed in June 1852, no new burial ground could be established within the Boundary Street (Florida Avenue to the north) city limits. In 1853, the city council ordered that the remains buried at the old poorhouse, located between 6th and 7th streets, and on the north side of M Street, N.W., be removed to a new potters field. The latter was located just north of present Congressional cemetery. In the 1850's, the Board of Health urged physicians and undertakers to comply with requirements to return to the Board information regarding cause of death and interment.[5] In 1866,[6] the Board recommended updated legislation on the reporting of births, marriages and deaths. The resulting Act can be found transcribed elsewhere in this work.

In March and April 1909, the Corps of Engineers and others inquired of the District of Columbia Health Officer of a proposed bill to remove bodies from abandoned cemeteries in the District. The legislation would enable a purchaser of ground formerly used as a cemetery, but which was abandoned for that use, to have the bodies removed and reinterred in another cemetery so that the purchaser could extend streets through the ground and sell it for building purposes. At the time city officials voiced no intention to require the general removal of remains from family vaults or private burial places. It was explained that if one should sell the property on which their family vault was located, and the purchaser should desire to remove the remains therein for purposes of developing the land, the proposed law would enable that person to do so, but would not affect the present status of the land.[7] Approvals were advertised 27 MAR 1909 in the Washington Post, describing how the Commissioners approved recommendations that provided for removing remains from abandoned cemeteries in the District of Columbia.

Many family or private burial grounds vanished from properties once configured as residences—sometimes of prominent individuals. For instance, the grave of Gen. Robert Brent, U.S. Army Paymaster General and first Mayor of the City of Washington, was known to be at "Brentwood" (see discussion of Carroll Family burial

---

[1] "Charter of Washington," to incorporate the inhabitants of the City of Washington, and to repeal all acts heretofore passed for that purpose. Approved May 15, 1820. Also see The Charter of Washington... (Washington, D.C.: John T. Towers, Printer, 1848), p. 10.

[2] Surviving written procedures of the Board of Health, beginning April 13, 1822, may be found at the D.C. Archives. At the first meeting, Dr. Frederick May was elected president of the Board, with chairman Charles W. Goldsborough, and secretary Dr. Henry Huntt.

[3] The Register documents the deaths of the following sextons: John P. Duvall (3 APR 1855), John Farrell (20 FEB 1874), Richard Furtner (19 AUG 1857), John Lainharendt (1 OCT 1870), and Jonathan Mullan (20 JAN 1869).

[4] The Washington Directory... (Washington, D.C.: R.L. Polk & Co., 1822), p. 104.

[5] D.C. Board of Health Minutes, 1848-1871, July 1, 1855, no page.

[6] Ibid., September 17, 1866, no page.

[7] Engineer Department records, file #77872, L.S. Vol. 218, p. 468.

ground). The last family interment there was made about July 1874, making 15 known graves. The location was described as being *1-3/4 miles northeast of the capitol building (as the bird flies), just in the rear of the Deaf and Dumb Asylum.* An inspector of the property in the 20th century found:

> "The tomb was constructed, so far as can be learned, in the year 1819, and was used from time to time as a receptacle for such members of the family as desired to be interred within it. It is constructed of solid granite blocks, almost square in shape, and surmounted by an arched roof set off by a heavy projecting cornice, resembling somewhat those used by the ancient Egyptians at Luxor and Karnak. An ivy vine, with thick roots and branches, nearly covers the sides and roof of the tomb, while the immediate surroundings are heavily grown with deep underbrush and trees. Just over the doorway is the Latin quotation: *requiescat in pace*. This is the only inscription to be seen."

Such fate of neglect was commonplace among burial grounds in the District of Columbia. Contrary to what one finds today, a surprising number of private burial grounds once dotted the city landscape. It has been said that between the years 1890 and 1940, over 30 burial places were condemned and the remains therein moved out of the city limits.

The Register mentions numerous different public cemeteries and a number of private burial grounds. The list below contains descriptive details for many of the cemeteries and burial grounds which can be identified. Sources for this information include city directories, personal accounts of the city, and records of the D.C. Engineer Department.

List of Cemeteries and Burial Grounds

We continue to learn more about burial places that once scattered the District of Columbia area. As the area developed, location names changed and became more specific. Following is a list of known burial places with descriptions found in death records, city directories, maps, or other documents.

A

Adams (Family) Farm. The certificate of death for Robert Adams (#5985) describes the place of burial as Mr. Adams' Farm, 3 miles from Bladensburg. Located on property owned by Josiah Adams (d. 1884), said to be a gardener for the Calvert family. Located in Beacon Heights, Prince George's County, Maryland. Later known as Cherry Hill cemetery.

Adas Israel. First appears under this name in the 1887 city directory (formerly Jews Burial Ground). Described in 1871 as being located about 1½ miles from the Government Insane Asylum. The cemetery office is located off Stanton Road at 1400 Alabama Avenue, S.E., Washington, DC 20032. Burial records, 1870 to 1919, are found on microfiche at the Library of Congress, LC Call Number Microfiche 96/79F.

Addison (Family). In 1879 and 1883, located on the farm of Reason Addison near Tennallytown.

Addison's Chapel (Private). Bunker Hill Road (1889, 1890), in Prince George's County, Maryland (1875), near the District line at Chesapeake Junction. Buried here were Mr. and Mrs. Benjamin Stoddert. Burials as late as 1942 were primarily white persons.

Alms House (see Washington Asylum).

Aurora. In 1899, on Brentwood Road.

B

Baptist. There were several Baptist burial grounds in the area. A Baptist ground was located in Potomac City (1876). One is described on certificate of death #10395 as being near Chain Bridge (1877). Located on Conduit Road near Drovers' Rest (1882, 1890), outside of Georgetown. Edward Palmer, sexton (1883-1887).

Baptist. Tennallytown (1885).

Barlow (Family). In 1807, the remains of Abraham Baldwin were interred on the family estate "Kalorama," located off Massachusetts Avenue, N.W. at Boundary (Florida) Avenue. "Kalorama" was a portion of the large Holmead estate known as "Rock Hill." In a mausoleum at "Kalorama," were found a cenotaph to Joel Barlow who was buried in Poland in 1812, the remains of his wife Ruth Baldwin (d. 1818), her sister Clara (Mrs. George Bomford), George Bomford, and Henry Baldwin. Captain Stephen Decatur was initially buried here in 1820. The mausoleum remained here until 1892.[8] Removals were made to Rock Creek cemetery; Decatur's remains were removed to St. Peter's churchyard in Philadelphia where his parents were buried.

Barnabas Church (see St. Barnabas).

Barnes Hospital (see Soldier's Home).

Barry Chapel. A small place of worship built by James Barry, located at O and ½ streets, S.E. Barry, his wife and daughters are said to have been buried here.

Battle Ground (National). The city directory for 1880 shows location at 7th Street Road near Brightwood — a neighborhood in the upper part of the District across from Takoma Park, Maryland. The cobblestone guttering in front of the cemetery has never been relaid since a retaining wall was set back last summer, making the street muddy (1901). Gutters were cleaned but are in need of repair, and the entrance gate along Brightwood Avenue contains many deep holes (1907). A wall on Georgia Avenue, N.W. was repaired in 1916. Area covers an acre, contains bodies of Union soldiers who died at the Battle of Fort Stevens in 1864. Early Superintendents were Aug. Armbrecht (1879-1881), Stephen S. Cole (1883), and Ernest Rittenhouse (1885-1887). Current address is 6625 Georgia Avenue, N.W.

Beachdale. Records of the Joseph F. Birch funeral home show this burial location in 1903 on Conduit Road.

---

[8] Records of the Columbia Historical Society, Vol. XIII, p. 107, monument inscriptions are detailed.

Beall (Family). Records of Oak Hill cemetery note removals to Lot 754 of that location in April 1873, a "Quantity of remains from the private Burial Place of the Beall family on Gay Street, Georgetown."

Beckett's. The 1858-1859 map of Washington City, by A. Boschke, shows a cemetery in Square 1089, surrounded by C and D, and 16th and 17th streets, S.E. The proprietor in 1876 was William Beckett. Described in the 1880 city directory as being on C Street between 16th and 17th streets S.E. Not listed as Beckett's in city directories after 1882. Found in the 1881 city directory as "Union Beneficial Association Cemetery" at the same location, with William Beckett, sexton. In 1882, Mr. Beckett resided at 908 E St., S.W. Occasionally one finds entries of Beckett's and Ebenezer confused, because they were at the same street intersection. Later entries simply note "Union" cemetery.

Bell (Family). The certificate of death for Alexander McCormick (#78311), 1891, shows burial in Bell Burying Ground near Bennings.

Belt (Family) Farm. Located north of Tennallytown (1880, 1882, 1890). An 1880 map shows Belt family property at the end of Brookville Road. Sprigg Belt, sexton (1884-1887). Burials were primarily of black persons. In 1881, Charles R. Belt, white, was buried there (#30638); however, his remains were removed to Montgomery County, Maryland in 1907.

Berry (Family) Farm. Owned by Richard L. Berry (1883-1888), and earlier the property of Zachariah Berry. Hillsdale (1890). Identified burials here in 1881 and 1882 were for black persons.

Berry (Family) Farm. Identified in 1875 as being near Tennallytown.

Blue Plains. In 1901, the D.C. Commissioners bought land at Blue Plains, across the Anacostia in the southern part of the District. In 1907 requested that additional land there be "condemned for a site for a municipal alms house and a burial place for the indigent dead [as] authorized...by Act of Congress, June 27, 1906."[9] In September 1942, an administrative assistant of the D.C. Water Department was granted a disinterment permit to remove 10 bodies, more or less, from the Georgetown Presbyterian cemetery, and reinter them at Blue Plains. See also information at "Hillsdale."

Bomford (Family). Part of the "Widow's Mite" tract, as conveyed to Thomas R. Lovett by George Bomford and wife on June 6, 1846 (Deeds, Bk. W.B. 126, p. 154), is described on a plat as "one are of ground reserved to Geo. Bumford [sic] and his heirs as a family vault." No metes and bounds are given, but the burial place is shown to be opposite the end of Massachusetts Avenue at Boundary Street. This is the burial place of "Kalorama," the residence of the Bomford and Barlow families (see Barlow Family).

Bradley (Family). In September 1887, the remains of Abraham, Hannah S. and Thomas Bradley were removed from a private cemetery in Montgomery County, Maryland, to Oak Hill cemetery (Lot 465).

Brent (Family). (see Carroll Family).

Bridge Street Presbyterian. Georgetown. The location of the church burial ground is uncertain, but may have surrounded the church building. The congregation was founded in 1780 by Rev. Stephen Bloomer Balch who was first buried at the front of his beloved church. His remains were removed to the Presbyterian church burial ground on Market Street, then to Oak Hill cemetery. The building that dates from 1820 was located at the corner of M and 30th streets, N.W., and was razed in 1872. The remains from the Bridge Street Church graveyard were transferred in 1873 to the Presbyterian burial ground on Market Street.[10]

Brightwood. Located in the Brightwood neighborhood (1882, 1890). Hilleary Green, sexton (1882-1887). Dozens of burials here between 1875 and 1879 were for black persons.

Broad Creek. Located in Prince George's County, Maryland (1882).

Brooks (Family). Evidently located near the line between the District and Prince George's County, Maryland. Specific location undetermined for burials of black persons between 1880 and 1885.

Brown (Family) (see Hillsdale).

Burnes (Family). The graveyard of the Thomas Burnes family (Van Ness' mausoleum) was located on the south side of H Street between 9th and 10th streets west.[11] The remains of David Burnes are now found interred in Rock Creek cemetery.

Burrows (Family). The certificate of death for John H. Burrows (#34486), September 12, 1882, notes place of burial as "On Farm, Family Ground." He died near Tennallytown.

Butler (Family). The certificate of death for an infant of L.A. Shamwell (#21700), September 15, 1879, notes place of burial as "Butler's." The infant died in Brightwood.

---

[9] Records of the Columbia Historical Society, 1963-1965, p. 29, "Blue Plains and Bellevue."
[10] James M. Goode, Capital Losses: A Cultural History of Washington's Destroyed Buildings (Washington, D.C.: Smithsonian Institution Press, 1979), p. 208.
[11] Christian Hines, Early Recollections of Washington City (Washington, D.C., 1866), p. 39; Records of the Columbia Historical Society, Vol. 22, pp. 158, 193.

C

Calvin (Family). The certificate of death for Jackson Powell (#38852), September 7, 1883, notes place of burial as "Calvin farm, family grounds." He died near Drover's Rest in Washington County, on Ridge Road above the junction of the railroad and north creek road.

Capital Orthodox Christian. Located on Benning Road, S.E., north of F Street, where a cemetery was ordered to be laid out in 1934.[12]

Carroll (Family). The last known interment was made here in July 1874, after which time the vault at Brentwood remained in good condition. An undated newspaper article describes the scene: "In visiting the family vault at the end of the garden walk at Brentwood some two years ago, some one has written: The tomb was constructed, so far as can be learned, in the year 1819, and was used from time to time as a receptacle for such members of the family as desired to be interred within it. It was constructed of solid granite blocks, almost square in shape, and surmounted by an arched roof set off by a heavy projecting cornice, resembling somewhat those used by the ancient Egyptians at Luxor and Karnak. An ivy vine, with thick roots and branches, nearly covers the sides and roof of the tomb, while the immediate surroundings are heavily grown with deep underbrush and trees. Just over the doorway is the Latin quotation: 'Requiescat in pace.' This is the only inscription to be seen. In this vault rest the remains of Robert Brent." In 1915, the remains of Elizabeth Carroll, Catherine W. Brent, Robert Brent, John Farley, Eleanor Pearson, and Ellen P. Farley were removed from a private vault at Brentwood, D.C. (except the Farley's being cremated) to Forest Glen, Md. See D.C. disinterment permits #8429-8434. Correspondence of the D.C. Engineer Commissioner show us that in 1909 plans were underway to extend streets through what was an abandoned burial ground. Brig. General Joseph P. Farley, Ft. Monroe, Virginia, great-grandson of Robert Brent, was notified that should he sell the property on which his family vault was located, and the purchaser should desire to remove the bodies for the purpose of developing the land, a proposed law would enable him to do so, but would not affect the present status of the land. In Farley's inquiry to officials he characterized the family vault at Brentwood as being about 1¾ miles northeast of the Capitol building (as the bird flies), and just in the rear of the Deaf and Dumb Asylum. At least 14 burials were made here according to Farley.

Carroll Chapel. Also known as Nancy Carroll's Chapel. Located in Forest Glen, Montgomery County, Maryland, at the corner of Forest Glen and Rosensteel roads. 19th Century burials are primarily white persons.

Cathedral Cemetery Association. By January 1910, an application was made to the D.C. Health Department to establish a cemetery in the name of the Cathedral Cemetery Association, on parcels 7/3, 14/7 and 14/6 of Murdock's Subdivision of Friendship Heights. A letter of March 10, 1910 orders that such application not be granted for reason that the proposed cemetery adjoins the government reservation protecting and is immediately within the drainage area of the Conduit Road Receiving Reservoir.

Catholic. The 1822 and 1827 city directories describe the location of the catholic burying ground as near the north end of 3rd Street West, outside the city limits.

Catholic Orthodox. In summer 1926, application was made to establish a cemetery at the District line, within 1½ miles from the boundaries of the City of Washington. The request was denied because the Commissioners determined there should be no more cemeteries within the District of Columbia. The proposed location was at the corner of Fitch and St. Louis streets, near Benning Road and Central Avenue. The land in question was part of a tract called "Stony Hill," in an area called Deanwood, and was owned by J.C. Rosenthall.

Causin (Family). The certificate of death for Nathaniel Pope Causin (#36384), March 5, 1883, notes place of burial as "Causin Farm, D.C." Causin, an insurance agent, died at the West End Hotel.

Cedars. Once the property of Colonel John Cox. Located where recently stood the Western High School, Georgetown.[13] The certificate of death for Richard Young (#26019), September 29, 1881, notes place of burial as "Cedar Grove, Montgomery Co., Md." He died at 86 Bridge Street, Georgetown.

Cedar Hill. Located at Pennsylvania Avenue and Alabama Avenue, S.E.

Cephas (Family). John Cephas, proprietor (1882-1888). Located on Conduit Road near Drovers' Rest (1882, 1890). Known burials are for black persons.

Chapman (Family). Location undetermined (1878). See certificate of death for John Taylor (#16107).

Chappel's (Family) Farm (see also Christian). J.E. Chappel, owner (1882-1888). Located on a private farm one mile northeast of Tennallytown (1882, 1890).

Cherry Hill (see Adams Family).

---

[12] See D.C. Engineer's Department records, #240250, D.C. Archives.
[13] Harold Donaldson Eberlein and Cortlandt Van Dyke Hubbard, Historic Houses of George-town & Washington City (Richmond, Va.: The Dietz Press, Inc., 1958), pp. 64-65; Records of the Columbia Historical Society, Vol. 21, p. 142.

(Georgetown) College Burial Ground. Private, Georgetown (1890). On the present campus of Georgetown University. Graves for those identified as "College" on certificates of death may be found in what is now known as the Jesuit community cemetery. The *Georgetown Courier*, March 22, 1873, noted a recent fire in the old cemetery, on the college grounds and just beyond the convent enclosure. The blaze destroyed the fence of the graveyard.

Christian. Located on the Chappel Farm near Tennallytown (1883). R. Dorsey, sexton (1883-1887). The certificate of death for Sarah Thomas (#36181), February 15, 1883, notes place of burial as "Christian cem., Chapel's Farm." Her place of death was the Rosedale farm near Tennallytown. The location has been described as being on a hill west of the intersection of Fessenden Street and Reno Road.

Christian Brothers. In 1947, disinterment permits (#19432 and #19433) were issued to undertaker Chambers to remove the remains of Brother John and Brother Fidelis from Mt. Olivet cemetery to Christian Brothers cemetery of Ammendale Normal Institute, Beltsville P.O., Maryland.

Columbian Harmony Burial Ground. Founded in 1825 by a society composed of freedmen. First situated where it was bounded by 5th, 6th, S and Boundary streets, N.W. Mentioned in the 1850 city directory as the African cemetery, located at the above coordinates, in Square 475. Relocated in 1856 to Youngsborough, about 1 mile north of the intersection of H Street North and the Baltimore railroad. Superintendents were John F. Cook (1874), Benjamin McCoy (1880-1884), and Lavina McCoy (1885-1886). The 1890 city directory describes it as the Harmonia Burial Ground at Brentwood Road, 2 miles from the city. This site is now the Rhode Island Metro Station.[14] In 1959, Columbian Harmony moved to a new location in Landover, Prince George's County, Maryland, and is now known as the National Harmony Memorial Park.[15]

Congressional. Officially named Washington Parish Burial Ground, was established in 1807 on Square 1115. In 1848, it was expanded to Square 1116 to the south. In 1853, it also encompassed Square 1104 to the west.[16] Range locations changed from an alphabetic series to numbers in 1854. It is commonly noted in records as "Congress" burial ground. City directories describe the location as "situated on the eastern branch of the Potomac River, about 1½ miles from the Capitol.," or at 18th Street, S.E. (1890). Early Superintendents were Charles F. Smith (1874-1882), and J.B. Cross (1883-1887). Comprises about 30 acres. Details on the early particulars of the original cemetery may be obtained from the cemetery office.[17]

Convent, Georgetown Visitation. Private, located at 35th and P streets N.W. (1890), on the present Convent of the Georgetown Visitation. Several burial places are in the immediate area. Graves for those identified on certificates of death as being buried at the "convent" may be found at what is now called the monastery garden. The present convent visitation cemetery is more modern.

Cox's Station (Family). Located in Maryland, 1875-1877.

Custer (Family) Farm. The certificate of death for Thomas Hedgman (#25382), August 12, 1880, notes burial at "Custer Farm, Co." He died on Ridge Road.

D

Danford (Family) Farm. Located on River Road, 1875-1876. See certificate of death for Joseph P. Sayles (#5047a), and that for Mary A. Brackson (#6371).

Dangerfield (Family). Henry Dangerfield, superintendent (1884-1886), and John W. Dangerfield, superintendent (1887-1891). No location given in city directories; however, death records show this burial ground was in Hillsdale. The death certificate for James H. Dangerfield (#31191), December 6, 1881, notes place of burial as "Family Ground." He died in Hillsdale, Washington County.

Davidson (Family). In his 1805 will, Samuel Davidson requested burial in his intended burying ground at "Evermay."[18] The Davidson burial ground is now part of Oak Hill cemetery.

Dean (Family). Described on certificate of death #7919 as "Dr. Deans Family Ground, Bennings Station." On Sheriff Road (1882, 1890, 1891). Julius Dean was Superintendent (1882-1886), and Julian W. Dean (1887). More information under Sheriff (Family) Farm.

Donaldson (Family) Farm. Records of the Joseph F. Birch funeral home describe the place of burial in June 1925 for W.C. Donaldson as the "Donaldson Farm." Location undetermined, and may be in Virginia.

---

[14] Washington Post, 23 JUN 1982, "Dispute Surrounds Memorial To Veterans."
[15] Washington Post, 13 FEB 1986, District Weekly, "Learning History From Tombstones of 19th Century."
[16] Records of the Columbia Historical Society, Vol. 11, p. 365.
[17] U.S. Senate, 59th Congress, 2nd Session, Senate Document No. 72, to accompany report H.R. 5972, reprinted as "History of the Congressional Cemetery."
[18] D.C. Wills, Bk. 1, pp. 320-323(178-180); file O.S. 411 in Record Group 21 at the National Archives; original in Box 3 at the D.C. Archives.

E

Eastern. Established on February 28, 1798, by the Commissioners of Washington as a public burial ground. The 1827 city directory describes the location as Square 1026, between H and I streets North, and 13th and 14th streets East— just north of where Maryland Avenue exited the city limits. By 1835, the burial ground was described as being much ornamented and well enclosed. "The numerous handsome monuments and vaults already make this place worthy to be visited by strangers."[19] In 1860, the eastern graveyard, located in the sixth ward of the city, was extended to the west and improved.[20] Marsh conditions led to discontinued use. The 1822 city directory lists the commissioners of the eastern burial ground as John Chalmers, Daniel Rapine, John Crabb, with John L. Brightwell as sexton.[21] Nothing is known about any surviving records.

Eastern Methodist (see Methodist (Ebenezer)).

Eaton (Family). Location undetermined.

Ebenezer African M.E. Church. Established shortly after 1825 when property was transferred by J. Elgar to Israel Little and others as trustees of the Methodist Society.[22] The 1858-1859 map of the City of Washington, by A. Boschke, shows this burial ground in Square 1102, bounded by E and D, and 17th and 18th streets, S.E., immediately across from the front gate of Congressional cemetery. A majority of the remains were removed to Congressional cemetery. See Methodist (Ebenezer) for more information.

Eckton (Family). Location undetermined.

Eldbrooke Methodist (see Methodist (Tennallytown)). Located adjacent to the Eldbrooke United Methodist Church, 4100 River Road, N.W.

Elesavetgrad. Located in Square 5886, at 3217 15th Place, S.E. In 1911, the Elesavetgrad Benevolent Society changed its name to the Elesavetgrad Cemetery Association. Typical burial lots here measured 3 by 8 feet, and were described in December 1911 as being "one jammed against the other, there being no space between the burial lots, nor is there any provision for reaching the interior lots from the walks without passing over the lots." The location is "peculiarly suited for cemetery purposes as it is almost entirely surrounded by other cemeteries." About 1933, the cemetery was granted permission to use additional land for burial purposes.

Episcopal. The 1822 and 1827 city directories describe the location as near the Eastern branch, upper bridge (see Congressional).

Episcopal (New). The 1827 city directory describes the location of the new Episcopal burying ground as being in Square 276, between 12th and 13th streets West, and R and S streets North (see St. John's Episcopal).

Evans (Family). The certificate of death for Howard Johnson (#44176), October 18, 1884, notes place of burial as "Evans, Private grounds." He died in Stantontown, Anacostia.

"Evermay" (see Davidson Family).

F

"Flint Hill" Burial Ground. Located near Fairfax Courthouse, Virginia. (1876).

Forrest (Family) Farm. Owned by Catharine Forrest in 1878. See certificate of death for Mauna Bailey (#16259).

Fort Lincoln. Located at 3201 Bladensburg Road, N.E.

Foundry (see Methodist Episcopal (Foundry)).

Foxall (Family). Records of Oak Hill cemetery, Georgetown, note the remains for six burials of the Harkness and Blake families were removed in 1870 to that location from the Foxall Burying Ground. John C. Harkness was a member of First Foundry Church. Henry Foxall, a native of England, owned a farm tract called "Spring Hill," outside of Georgetown in Washington County. He also maintained a residence in Georgetown.[23]

Francis DeSales. Sometimes referred to as Queens Chapel Roman Catholic, located on Evarts Street, N.E., just off Queens Chapel Road, near the Langdon neighborhood. Richard Queen built a chapel at Langdon (near today's 20th and Evarts Street, N.E.), that included a burial ground.

Franciscan Monastery. Brookland (1900). Located on the grounds of the Franciscan Monastery at 14th and Quincy streets, N.E. The Report of the D.C. Health officer for 1901 notes this newly-created cemetery near the Franciscan Monastery, near Brookland.

---

[19] Records of the Columbia Historical Society, Vol. 11, p. 308.
[20] Records of the Columbia Historical Society, Vol. 11, p. 383.
[21] The Washington Directory... (Washington, D.C.: R.L. Polk & Co., 1822), p. 104.
[22] D.C. Deeds, Liber W.B. 13, folio 192 (old) 143 (new), dated 2 DEC 1824, for the purpose of a public burying ground subject to such regulations as the Methodist Society shall lawfully ordain.
[23] Records of the Columbia Historical Society, Vol. 11, pp. 47-49.

Furlong (Family) Farm. Records of the Joseph F. Birch funeral home show the burial of Sarah A. Hall in February 1908 at the Furlong Farm. Location not determined.

G

Gaines (Family) Farm. The certificate of death for Margaret Brown (#5150), September 24, 1875, notes place of burial as the "Gaines farm, near Tennallytown, D.C."

Garden (Family). Colored. It might be confused with Gardner's Farm, near Uniontown, as shown on the certificate of death for William Sales (#5233), October 21, 1875.[24] Alexander Garden, proprietor (1882-1888). Private, Anacostia Road (1890, 1891). In 1886, the former Uniontown was named Anacostia. The 1890 will of Alexander Garden describes his farm property in Chichester on the Eastern Branch of the Potomac River, in the County of Washington, lying on the west side of the center of the farm road which runs from the big gate at the public road to the river.

German (or German Presbyterian). Brentwood Road. So described as the place of burial for Elizabeth Brandt (#21760) who died September 22, 1879 on Brentwood Road near the entrance to the National Fair Grounds.

German Catholic (see St. Marys).

German Lutheran. The German Lutheran Church, situated at the corner of High and Fourth streets, Georgetown, was founded soon after land for its purpose was set aside in 1769 by Col. Charles Beatty. The German Lutherans are said to have constructed a school-house here, and surrounding land was used as a burying ground for upwards of 50 years. The certificate of death for Joseph McCoy (#24320), May 23, 1880, notes place of burial as "Luther Burrial Grn., Georgetown, D.C."

Glenwood. Situated north of the Capitol, about 1½ miles from City Hall (1874). This cemetery was established in 1854 and laid out on the plan of the celebrated Greenwood cemetery in New York City, of which it is said by travelers to excel in beauty and arrangement anything of the kind in Europe or America. It now comprises about 43 acres. Chronological burial records begin in June 1878 when a group of lot owners gained control of cemetery management. Prior to that time, only a cash book and an alphabetical index are known to exist. Glenwood is situated on the high ground overlooking the City of Washington, and on a direct line with North Capitol Street. Andrew J. Deming was Superintendent (1879-1881), and Alexander McKerichar (1883-1889). The cemetery was chartered by Congress, and the plots were not liable for debt, taxes or any other invasion (1874). On Lincoln Avenue (1890, 1891).

Good Hope. The community of Good Hope is in Anacostia, on the Eastern Branch. Much of the area property was owned by the Naylor family. William Batson, proprietor (1882-1886), and Samuel Patterson (1887). The Good Hope cemetery was located on Hamilton Road (1890, 1891). The certificate of death for Mary Jackson (#43277), August 13, 1884, notes place of burial as "Good Hope, D.C. (Baptist)."

In October 1940, the Alley Dwelling Authority was granted permission to disinter a number of bodies from an abandoned burying ground not recorded as a public cemetery, in the vicinity of Alabama Avenue and 20th Street, S.E. This came about in connection with the development of the Frederick Douglass dwelling project. The remains of about 22 bodies were removed to Payne's cemetery.

Graceland. Established in 1872, and comprised about 25 acres.[25] Discontinued in July 1894, because of its location on marsh land. William H. Gafford, superintendent (1874-1891). Located at the terminus of H Street Northeast (1871, 1883); at 15th and H Street Northeast (1890, 1891). Woodlawn cemetery essentially replaced Graceland. Debate went on between 1907 and 1912, whether the tract was suitable for a park (Anacostia Water Park) or if it should be divided for development as housing.[26] The location is recently occupied by Hechinger Mall at Benning Road, H Street, and Bladensburg Road, N.E.

"Grassland" (see Loughborough Family).

Green Vale. Ruth Davis in charge (1883-1887). Located near Tennallytown (1883, 1890, 1891).

Green (Family) Farm. Location undetermined. See certificate of death for William Green (#20679).

H

Hardy (Family). The certificate of death for Maria Willis (#27218), January 16, 1881, notes place of burial as "Hardy's Family, P.G. C., Md."

Harmonia, Harmoneon, or Harmony (see Columbian Harmony).

---

[24] Attached to the certificate is a note from E.M. Boteler, undertaker, stating "the relatives of Wm. Sales wishes to bury him on Mr. Gardner's place near the River Road leading from Uniontown to Bennings Bridge if they can get a permit to do so."

[25] D.C. Engineer Department Records, D.C. Archives, #10819/26.

[26] See 60th Congress, 1st Session, proposed bill to in part authorize the purchase for $150,000 the cemetery site.

Havenner (Family). The certificate of death for Ellen A. Havener [sic] (#27277), January 23, 1881, notes place of burial as "Havenner's Family Ground, MD."

Hebbon (Family). Eliza Hebbon, proprietor (1882-1888). The certificate of death for Eliza Johnson (#43679), September 9, 1884, notes place of burial as "Hebbons family, Country, near Tennallytown." Broad Branch Road (1890, 1891). Located in Chevy Chase according to the 1900 city directory.

Hebrew (see Washington Hebrew).

Hillbrook. In August 1907, permission was requested of the Engineer Department to establish a cemetery for the Jewish society, to be located in Square 5145, Hillbrook, D.C.[27]

Hillsdale. A community earlier known as Barry's Farm[28] (or Potomac City as it was sometimes called), and in 1872 renamed "Hillsboro," and by 1874, called "Hillsdale." Solomon G. Brown (1831-d. June 26, 1906), proprietor (1882-1885), John Cook, sexton (1886-1887). Located on Elvans Avenue, Hillsdale (1891), a portion of Anacostia (1890). Frederick Douglass (d. 1895) in 1879 purchased Lot 4 in Section 1. In January 1967, a blanket disinterment permit (No. 67-1) was issued by the D.C. Department of Public Health for Stanton Courts Joint Venture, Inc. to disinter and remove the bodies from those parts of old Hillsdale cemetery belonging in the District of Columbia.[29] Reinterments were to be made at a District cemetery located at Blue Plains.

Hines (Family). As near as can be ascertained, the burial plot of the Hines family was located around the rear of the stores at 2440 to 2444 18th Street, N.W., and adjoining the southern wall of Crandall's Knickerbocker Theater.[30]

Hokoo Scholene Hebrew. Located at 15th Place and Congress Street, S.E. (1935).

Holmead's (also known as the Western Burial Ground). Established in 1798 on land patented by James Holmead. Occupied Square 109, bound by 19th, 20th, S, and Boundary (now Florida Avenue) streets. The 1822 city directory describes the location as Square 109, bounded by S and T north, and 19th and 20th streets west. The commissioners in 1822 for the western burial ground (Holmead's) were David Easton, Robert King, Benjamin M. Belt, with Phillip Williams as sexton. Buried here were Rev. Lorenzo Dow; William Seaton, journalist; James Hoban, architect; and Andrew Way, printer. Joseph Meigs, father of Gen. Meigs, was first buried at Holmead, but removed to Oak Hill.[31] By 1855, the western graveyard had a new substantial fence.[32] In 1881, the D.C. Engineer Commissioner was authorized to advertise for proposals for removal of bodies from Holmead.[33] In disrepair by 1884, when the remains for over 3,000 dead were relocated to other cemeteries. Destroyed.

Holt (Family) Farm. The certificate of death for John T. Tucker (#22999), January 26, 1880, notes place of burial at "Dr. H. Holt's farm." He died at Jackson Mill, in Washington County.

Holy Rood. Georgetown. Established by Holy Trinity Catholic Church by 1832. On 32nd (High) Street extension (1890). John A. Heenan, sexton (1880-1891). Also called Georgetown Catholic cemetery. In 1942, Georgetown University inherited management responsibilities for the cemetery and maintained the applicable burial records. By 1984, the university wanted to get out of the cemetery business and close the cemetery.[34] Over 7,000 known burials. Records are kept at Lauinger Library of Georgetown University.

Homedale. Records of Oak Hill cemetery, Georgetown, note removal in September 1869 of Francis Q. Rowzea and Thomazine Rowzee to Oak Hill from Homedale cemetery, D.C. Location not determined.

Homewood Farm. The certificate of death for Bryan B.K. Carpenter (#38804), September 3, 1883, notes the initial place of burial was "Homewood Farm, about half way from Benning and Anacostia bridges on River Road, east side, formerly S.J. Bowens." Carpenter died at "Homewood, D.C., near Anacostia." In January 1884, the remains were removed to Kittanning, Pennsylvania.

Honesty (Family). The certificate of death for James Walter Honesty (#51397), April 11, 1886, notes place of burial as "Family Grounds." He died near Conduit Road in Washington County. The certificate of death for Bessie Nero (#52180) notes place of burial as "Honesty (Family Ground)."

Hospital (see Washington Asylum). Often refers to the Government Hospital, later Gallinger Hospital, later D.C. General Hospital. Several hospitals were associated with the Washington Asylum. A burial

---

[27] D.C. Engineer Department Records, D.C. Archives, #67544.
[28] Plat recorded in Liber Levy Court No. 2, Folio 1, of the records of the Office of the Surveyor of the District of Columbia, showing location in parts of original lots 13 and 14 in Section 5, of "Barry Farm."
[29] The order for disinterment, filed December 13, 1966, described the location as being Lots 13 and 14 which lie within Bruce Place, S.E., and Jasper Place, S.E., and part of Lot 13 which formerly lay within 13th Street, S.E. The cemetery has been abandoned for at least 40 years, and probably for 65 years.
[30] Records of the Columbia Historical Society, Vol. 22, p. 39.
[31] Helen W. Ridgely, Historic Graves of Maryland and the District of Columbia (Grafton Press, 1908), p. 260, gives a partial list of notables once buried at Holmead's.
[32] Records of the Columbia Historical Society, Vol. 11, p. 365.
[33] Report of the Commissioners of the District of Columbia, Fiscal Year 1881, p. 19.
[34] Washington Post, 11 NOV 1984, Metro Scene, "GU to Close Cemetery."

place at the small pox hospital was frequently described as the small pox grounds. The small pox hospital site was due east of the alms house, and practically at the river. This grouping of facilities is adjacent to Congressional cemetery.[35]

Howard (Family). Robert Howard was Superintendent (1882-1886), and Robert S. Howard (1887-1888). Private, Anacostia Road (1890, 1891). The earliest burial record found for this location is August 1874.

Hurdle (Family). The certificate of death for Etha Hurdle (#37651), June 15, 1883, notes place of burial as "Hurdle (Family)." She died in Tennallytown. Other Hurdle family burials in this ground were for deaths that occurred in Tennallytown.

I

Insane Asylum (see St. Elizabeth's).

Israelite. The certificate of death for Henry Coopper (#25136), July 13, 1880, notes place of burial here. He died at 154 Bridge Street, Georgetown. Location not determined.

J

Jail. The certificate of death for Charles Julius Guiteau (#33577), June 30, 1882, notes place of burial as "U.S. Jail, D.C." where he died.

Jenkins (Family). Thomas Jenkins, proprietor (1882-1886), and Henry J. Hoyle (1887). Private, on Jenkins Family farm (1890). The certificate of death for Eliza Jenkins (#21512), August 28, 1879, notes place of burial as "Jenkins family ground, Good Hope."

Jewish. In 1907, the Jewish society requested permission to locate a cemetery in Square 5145, in Hillbrook (see also Hillbrook).

Jewish (see Adas Israel, Washington Hebrew).

Jewish (Ohev Sholom Talmud Torah). The cemetery of the Congregation Talmud Torah, was located at 3237 15th Place, S.E. and Alabama Avenue, S.E.

Jews Burial Ground (see Adas Israel after 1887). About 1½ miles from the Government Insane Asylum (1874, 1876). George Groner, sexton (1883-1887).

Jones Chapel. William Henson was Superintendent (1882-1886), and Frederick Jackson (1887). Bennings Station (1876), Bennings Road (1890, 1891). The earliest burial here as found in death records is January 2, 1875.

K

"Kalorama" (see Barlow Family).

Kengla (Family) Farm. The certificate of death for James Henry Mathews (#32646), April 11, 1882, notes place of burial as "Kengla's Farm, Private." The Kengla family owned property between Tennallytown and Georgetown.

L

Lacy (Family) Farm. Location undetermined.

Loughborough (Family). Nathan Loughborough died in 1852 and was buried at "Grassland."[36]

Lutheran. Square 1272 (1899). Discontinued.

M

Macedonia, or Macedonian. Henry Waddy, sexton (1882-1886), and William Ellis (1887). Macedonian is given on the certificate of death for Harriet Lyons (#1857) as being in Uniontown. On the certificate of death for Rose Dobbs (#10500), this place of burial is noted as being located in Potomac City. Described in city directories for 1882 and 1890 as being near Sheridan Avenue in Hillsdale. A number of persons buried here died in the Stanton/Hillsdale Village area. The earliest death record for a burial here is for Ellen Carvalho, August 11, 1874.

Macpelah (Hebrew). George Graner was Superintendent (1886-1887). Located on Hamilton Road (1890).

Maddox (Family). Near Good Hope, probably in Prince George's County, Maryland (1881).

Marlow (Family) Farm. The certificate of death for Stepny Marlow (#4220), July 20, 1875, notes place of burial as "Marlow's Farm near Good Hope."

---

[35] D.C. Engineer Department Records, D.C. Archives, E.D. plat attached to #31362/6.
[36] Records of the Columbia Historical Society, Vol. 24, p. 5. The bodies of Mr. and Mrs. Loughborough (1st wife) were removed to Oak Hill.

Mason (Family) Farm. The certificate of death for Randall Johnson (#43351), August 18, 1884, notes place of burial as "Mason Farm." He died in Stantontown, Anacostia.

McPherson (Family). William Pinney, sexton (1882-1886), and D. Tinney (1887). Private, located in Hillsdale (1890, 1891).

Methodist (Ebenezer), or Eastern Methodist. Early city directories show the church of this congregation to be located on the east side of 4th Street East, between F and G Streets North. The cemetery was located between 16th and 17th streets East, and C and D streets South, near the Congressional burial ground. This is the same location often given for Beckett's cemetery; however, the two burial grounds were across corner from each other. Sexton is Wm. Brown (1871, 1874). The city directory for 1876 gives location as E Street between 17th and 18th streets, S.E., with sexton John H. Shelton (1876-1877), and G.C.H. Better (1880-1881). By 1890 a decision was made to discontinue use of this tract as a burial ground. In July 1891, Congress released Ebenezer Church from conditions in the original deed that stated the land must remain exclusively a burial ground. The governing body of the cemetery was the 4th Street Presbyterian Church. A majority of the remains from Ebenezer were removed to nearby Congressional cemetery where the office maintains records that survived from Ebenezer. Fragments of the sexton's journal have pages headed "Eastern M.E. Burial Ground." Records begin in 1823.

    A notice of 27 MAR 1909, in the <u>Washington Post</u>, stated that attorney A.A. Lipscomb, on behalf of Henry G. Freitag, owner of a lot at 16th and C streets, S.E., formerly the cemetery of the Ebenezer African Church, took action regarding the state of the burial ground. Lipsomb's letter stated that the ground is filled with bodies, and that no interments have been made there since 1879.

Methodist (Georgetown) (see Mt. Zion).

Methodist (Tennallytown). Located on 42nd Street, N.W. It was initially set aside in 1855 by deed from William D.C. Murdock and wife to trustees of the Methodist church for $50. Used from 1855 through the 1890's by members of both St. Alban's and its Tennallytown mission, St. Columba's. Located on Murdock Mill Road, N.W., immediately behind Eldbrooke Methodist Church at River Road, Tennallytown (1890). W.H. Walker, sexton (1883-1886). Here was interred John "Bull" Frizzell in 1879.[37] Later known as the Tennallytown Methodist cemetery. Today, the neighborhood is called Tenleytown. In 1929, the cemetery was affected by the extension of Albemarle Street.

Methodist Episcopal (Foundry), also called the Western Methodist. Named after the foundry of the church's chief benefactor, Henry Foxall. The church building was in 1822 located at the corner of G Street North and 14th Street West. The burial ground associated with Foundry Methodist Episcopal Church was once located in Square 235, bounded by V, W, 13th and 14th streets, N.W., in Square 235. The property was sold to real estate developers for $18,000 and the 1,800 graves moved to Glenwood cemetery.[38] This burial ground was adjacent to that of St. Matthew's Catholic Church.

Metropolis View. Records of Rock Creek cemetery note the removal from Metropolis View, D.C., the remains of Mary L. Berry and Elenor D. Berry.

Moore's (Family). Established c.1850 by Jacob Moore, near "T" Street Hill (now Stanton Road and Suitland Parkway). John Gales, sexton (1886-1887). In Hillsdale at 3134 Stanton Road, S.E. An 1881 map by Griffith M. Hopkins shows Jacob Moore having 6.75 acres just east of the bend in Stanton Road. The city directory for 1899 describes the location as Barry Farm, Potomac City. The certificate of death for Hester Diggs (#6951), 1876, gives location as Union Town; another for Thomas Barton (#10,430) gives location as Stanton Hill. Moore's was renamed c.1927 to Rosemont cemetery. "Many years after the abandonment of this burying ground, the remains of residents of the old Barry Farm/Hillsdale community were reinterred in National Harmony Memorial Park, Landover, Maryland, in October 1965."[39]

Moreland (Family) Farm. The certificate of death for Jacob Groves, a white person (#24222), May 15, 1880, notes place of burial as "Moreland Farm."

Morgan (Family) Farm. The certificate of death for John Wendel Morgan, a white person (#54596), December 17, 1886, notes place of burial as "family burial ground on farm." According to the same record, Morgan was born and died on Grant Road, Washington County.

Moses. A burial ground was operated by Moses Lodge of Tennallytown. Location undetermined.

Mount Airy. The certificate of death for Ann M. Biscoe (#28380), April 28, 1881, notes place of burial as "Mt. Airy, Md., near Marlboro."

Mount Olivet (Catholic). Situated at 1300 Bladensburg Road, N.E., about a half mile beyond the tollgate (1874). Early Superintendents were Patrick Duffy (1874-1880), and Philip J. McHenry (1881-1889).

---

[37] Judith Beck Helm, <u>Tenleytown, D.C.: Country Village Into City Neighborhood</u> (Washington, D.C.: Tenleytown Press, 1981), p. 309.

[38] James M. Goode, <u>Capital Losses: A Cultural History of Washington's Destroyed Buildings</u> (Washington, D.C.: Smithsonian Institution Press, 1979), pp. 206-207..

[39] <u>Hutchinson</u>, p. 132.

Mount Pleasant Plain(s). Located on Adams Mill Road (1899) at Calvert Street, N.W., in the Mount Pleasant neighborhood. Established by the Colored Union Benevolent Association, and was first located between 12th, 13th, V and W streets, N.W. Also known as the Free Young Mens Burial Ground. The ground became marshy due to proximity of the headwaters of Reedy Branch. Superintendents were Joseph Shorter (1876, 1877), Aaron Talbert (1878-1881), James Talbert (1883), Isaac Talbert (1884), and James F. Herbert (1885-1887). Near Mount Pleasant (1890, 1891). Inactive by 1890, some reinterments made in Columbian Harmony. In 1897, a portion of the Association's property was purchased for the zoo. Between October and December 1939[40], extant remains of about 500 bodies were removed to Woodlawn cemetery. Discontinued.

Mount Zion. The ground was conveyed by Thomas Beall to Ebenezer Eliason and others, by deed of October 13, 1808. Care was turned over to Mt. Zion church.[41] Located on property purchased by the Montgomery Street Church (known as the Dumbarton Methodist Church after 1850).[42] Henry Bolles, sexton (1883-1887). Located on [Lyons] Mill Road near P Street, N.W. (1890, 1891). It was actually located on the creek side of Q Street.[43] The remains of Dr. James Heighe Blake, who died July 29, 1819, were first interred in the Methodist Episcopal Burial Ground of Georgetown, and were removed November 2, 1870 to the William A. Gordon lot in Oak Hill.[44] The Old Methodist Burying Ground, Mt. Zion cemetery and the Female Union Band Society Burying Ground are located collectively in Squares 1288 and 1289, just east of Oak Hill cemetery in Georgetown. About 1879, a portion of the Old Methodist Burying Ground was set aside for use by the Mt. Zion Church. Black persons were buried on the west side. By 1898, the Rittenhouse family heirs became involved in configuring land for use of the burial ground, and opening of Q Street, both of which were adjacent to their property. Also described as being located off 27th and Q streets, N.W. near Rock Creek Park.[45]

Murdock (Family) Farm. The certificate of death for George Mason (#30223), September 21, 1831, notes place of burial at "Murdock Farm." He died near Tennallytown.

N

National Capital Hebrew. Located at Benning Road and Central Avenue, and is partially in the District and Maryland. Hearings were held in February 1911 involving hundreds of Jewish families wanting to establish a Jewish cemetery. At the time, one deponant noted that seven acres remained unused in the other Jewish cemetery, Adas Israel.

Nonesuch Farm. The "Nonesuch" property, established in 1793, was east of the Good Hope tavern. The certificate of death for Maria Lewis (#433), September 5, 1874, notes place of burial as "Nunsuch Farm, Good Hope hill."

O

Oak Hill. An old citizen of Georgetown penned an editorial on how the town needed a town cemetery.[46] Shortly thereafter, Oak Hill was established by charter of March 3, 1849. On property formerly known as "Parrott's Woods." Entrance (1874) to the cemetery was on Road Street at the head of Washington Street in Georgetown. President (1874) was W.W. Corcoran. James Walker, assistant superintendent of Oak Hill cemetery died Tuesday night, October 19, 1875 at the General Hospital, "from the effects of a leg injury, which he received some time since while erecting a wall for a grave. His limb was amputated on Tuesday." The office of the cemetery's superindendent maintains records from 1849.

Offutt (Family). The certificate of death for William A. Offutt (#26449), November 6, 1880, notes place of burial as "Offutt's X Roads, Md." He died at 43½ Gay Street, Georgetown.

Old Ebenezer (see Methodist).

---

[40] As a result of Public Law 526 of the 67th Congress, H.R. 13617. See D.C. disintermit permit #17636 at the D.C. Archives. "An old abandoned colored cemetery on Adams Mill Road, N.W. is the subject of a real estate deal of considerable proportions. It may become necessary to disinter and move all the bodies buried here to another cemetery. The number of bodies has been estimated as high as 1,500. The people interested in the deal desire to know the particulars as regards the Health Department's concern in the matter..." "Quaker Cemetery owned part of this land previously, Mary [Shreve?] tombstone was found."

[41] Richard P. Jackson, The Chronicles of Georgetown, D.C., From 1751 to 1878 (Washington, D.C.: R.O. Polkinhorn, Printer, 1878), p. 270.

[42] The 1823 will of Henry Foxall provides for a gift to the trustees of the Methodist Episcopal Church in Georgetown, a lot of ground situate in Georgetown, fronting 30 feet on Montgomery Street, and running back 120 feet, and adjoining the Methodist church, to be used as a residence for the minister of that church. At the time of Foxall's death he was carrying on a baking business in Georgetown.

[43] D.C. Engineer Department Records, D.C. Archives, #14884/5.

[44] Records of the Columbia Historical Society, Vol. 24, pp. 160-161.

[45] Washington Post, 16 NOV 1989, "A Plot of History Crumbling: In Georgetown, Nature Overrunning D.C.'s Oldest Black Cemetery."

[46] The Georgetown Advocate, Monday, November 3, 1846, p. 2, "Town Cemetery."

Old Methodist Burying Ground (see Mt. Zion). Located just east of Oak Hill cemetery in Georgetown. Established on property owned by the Montgomery Street Church, known after 1850 as the Dumbarton Methodist Church. A portion was set aside for Mt. Zion church to bury blacks.

P

Payne (Family). Founded c.1851; John Payne's Burial Ground (1879), near the Bennings bridge. Mary Payne, sexton (1884), and Henry Speeks (1885-1887). Located in the Bennings neighborhood (1890, 1891), at 4600 Benning Road, S.E., just opposite Woodlawn. Boundaries were extended in 1929. In October 1940, a number of unidentified remains were brought to Payne's from a Good Hope cemetery in the vicinity of Alabama Avenue and 20th Street, S.E. The last removals at Payne's were made in the 1960's to the National Harmony Memorial Park.

Pearce (Family). Situated on the north side of Pennsylvania Avenue, opposite the President's House, between the southwest corner and south gate of Lafayette Square. About 30 feet square.[47]

Peltz (Family) Farm. Located in Silver Hill, Prince George's County, Maryland. Rosa Peltz was buried here in October 1875 (#5065).

Point of Rocks. The certificate of death for Charles Nichols (#47927), July 14, 1885, notes place of burial as "Point of Rocks." He died at the canal at the Aqueduct bridge. Location undetermined.

Poor House (see also Washington Asylum). The first charitable institution in the District was established by law of the corporation passed October 31, 1806. It's official name was the Washington Infirmary, and was located in the square bounded by 6th and 7th streets, and M and N streets. About 1846, it was merged with the Washington Asylum, built on the banks of the Anacostia.[48] In 1853, the city council ordered that the remains buried at the old poorhouse, located between 6th and 7th streets, and on the north side of M Street, N.W., be removed to a new potters field. The Infirmary was taken over by the Columbian College, relinquished to government control in April 1861, and in November that year, the building was totally destroyed by fire.

Posey (Family) Farm. The certificate of death for Emma Green (#33864), July 17, 1882, notes place of burial as "Posey's Farm, Mont. Co., Md."

Potters Field. At the Washington Asylum (1890), and is the same burial place as when "Washington Asylum" is given in the Register. Established for use in burying indigents. Located at the site recently occupied by D.C. General Hospital.[49] A former potters field is said to have been located until 1846 in the northeast corner of an almshouse square that was on the north side of M Street, N.W., between 6th and 7th streets. W.H. Stoutenburg was the superintendent here between 1883 and 1888.

In May 1904, the D.C Engineer's Department noted that a plat of the cemetery was on file,[50] and that a plat was to be ordered of the new potters field at the Washington Asylum.[51] At the D.C. Archives one will find a volume which begins in the 1890's that is entitled "Record of Coffins Furnished and Burials in Potter's Field."

In January 1917, a city official recommended that "the piece of ground known as old Potters Field, and abandoned as a burial ground for paupers many years ago, be turned over to his department to be used as a nursery for the raising of sod to be used in connection with the improvement of various reservations and parkings under the D.C. Department of Trees and Parkings.[52]

A potters field was also located at Blue Plains.

The certificate of death for Randall Fish (#5167), October 16, 1875, notes place of burial as "Potters Field (Dead House)."

Presbyterian. Located between 4th, 5th, Market and Frederick streets in Georgetown. Once buried here were the remains of Robert Peter (d. 1806), first mayor of Georgetown; John Barnes (d. 1826), collector of the port of Georgetown for 20 years, and founder of the poor house; James Gillespie (d. 1805), member of Congress from North Carolina; Mary Bohrer (d. 1844), wife of John P. Bohrer; Elizabeth Thompson (d. 1847); William Waters (d. 1859), a soldier of the Revolutionary War; Col. George Beall (d. 1807), grandson of Ninian Beall. The 1890 and 1891 city directories give the location as 34th Street and Q Street, N.W., Georgetown; Square 1273 (1899). Discontinued by 1896.

---

[47] Hines, pp. 39-40; Records of the Columbia Historical Society, Vol. 28, p. 136.
[48] Charles Moore, Joint Select Committee to Investigate the Charities and Reformatory Institutions in the District of Columbia (Washington: Government Printing Office, 1898), pp. 2-3.
[49] City Paper, 30 MAY-5 JUN 1986, pp. 1, 16, "Dead Broke..."; Washington Star, 1 DEC 1912, "In Potter's Field, Where Sleep the City's Unknown and Pauper Dead."
[50] D.C. Engineer Department Records, D.C. Archives.
[51] D.C. Engineer Department Records, D.C. Archives, #80225.
[52] The letter also recommended that the barn be used by the Superintendent of the jail and Washington Asylum for housing eight horses (although having capacity to house about thirty).

Purchased as public park in 1903, although remains had not been removed.[53] In 1897, the city taxed for a sewer line adjacent to the burial ground.[54] In 1907, much discussion was made about removal of remains and grading of the burial ground.[55] By October 31, 1907, it was described that the monuments and stones through the entire cemetery, except that part covered by lot P, "are entirely gone and none of the remains have been removed as provided by our contract with Mr. Malley." In September 1942, an administrative assistant of the D.C. Water Department was granted a disinterment permit (#18,419) to remove 10 bodies, more or less, from the Georgetown Presbyterian cemetery, and reinter them at Blue Plains, D.C. Human bones were encountered while digging a ditch of about 100 feet long and 30 inches wide, and between 5 and 6 feet deep. At that time, the location of the Presbyterian burial ground was described as being in Square 1273, between 33rd and 34th streets, Volta Place, and Q Street, N.W.

Prospect Hill Farm. In 1901, Rev. R.W. Lowrie submitted to the D.C. Engineer Department a plat of a family burial ground called "Prospect Hill Farm."[56]

Prospect Hill (German Lutheran). 2201 North Capitol Street, N.E. Adjoining Glenwood cemetery on the west. Early Superintendents were Gustav Hartig (1874, 1876, 1877), George C. Walker (1878-1883), Christian Bucheler (1884-1885), and J.A. Griesbauer (1886). Records begin in 1858, and were once maintained by the overseers of the adjacent Glenwood cemetery. The current proprietor of Prospect Hill is not kind to genealogists and is unwilling to consider assisting with inquiries of any kind without a payment of fees or "donation."

Q

Quaker. Established in March 1807[57] on land provided by Jonathan Shoemaker, with a stipulation that the land be used forever as a Friends burial ground. Located on Adams Mill Road (1899), adjacent to the Free Young Mens Burial Ground. The certificate of death for Percy Akers Towne (#34275), August 22, 1882, notes place of burial as "Friends Cemetery." He died in Mt. Pleasant. By 1953, city officials decided that the seemingly abandoned property could be taxed. Recently configured as a ball diamond and city park.[58]

Queen (Family) Farm. Interments in the Queen family farm of Pleasant Vale, Washington, D.C., were removed to Rock Creek. Destroyed.

Queens Chapel. Located on Queens Chapel Road (1899), or Evarts Street, N.E.,[59] and near the Langdon School playground. Also known as the Francis DeSales cemetery. In 1901, a survey of the old Queen's Chapel burying ground was submitted to the D.C. Engineer Department. This survey which was a result of interest by the Lutheran Church in the property, has not been located.[60] Destroyed and remains removed in 1936 to Mt. Olivet cemetery.

R

Reform School. Located at South Dakota Avenue and 33rd Street, N.E. The earliest death record found for burial in this location was that of George Johnson, September 6, 1875 (#4931). The 1871 city directory describes that a Reform School was created by Act of Congress, July 25, 1866, as a house of correction; however, this one was at the time located on a government farm near Georgetown.

---

[53] D.C. Engineer Department Records, D.C. Archives, #51648-43, letter dated October 28, 1907 from Wm. H. Manogue to H.L. West, "I beg to invite your attention to the fact that some parties are grading the presbyterian Burial Grounds in Georgetown recently purchased by the Commissioners for Play Grounds, and are doing so in violation of the express terms of the contract of sale which required the removal of the remains enterred [sic] therein prior to settlement or sale. ...I respectfully protest against the ruthless manner in which the land is being plowed over, and the location of the dead forever destroyed."

[54] D.C. Engineer Department Records, D.C. Archives, #2313, letter of S. Thomas Brown in protest against assessments for sewer laid front of Lot P, Square 1273, on 34th Street. Mr. Brown describes that the lot was donated to the church for a burial ground many years ago and has been held as such up to this time--it was supposed that it was not subject to any taxes.

[55] D.C. Engineer Department Records, D.C. Archives, #51648-43, letter dated October 28, 1907, from the Corps of Engineers to Mr. William H. Manogue, "In reply to your letter of this date, relative to the grading being done by the trustees of the West Street Presbyterian Church in the old burial ground in Georgetown, I would state that I have, since talking with you, conferred with Mr. Malery, representing the trustees, and he authorizes me to state that the church stands ready to disinter the remains of any of the deceased members of the families of the heirs which you represent if the graves will be pointed out to him, and that it is their intention to disinter and re-inter any remains that may be found in the grading operations." Another letter, dated the same day, infers involvement of the Beatty family.

[56] D.C. Engineer Department Records, D.C. Archives, #35691-3.

[57] Records of the Columbia Historical Society, Vol. 40-41, p. 37.

[58] Washington Post, 30 DEC 1986, "Lawsuit Revives Dispute Over Quaker Cemetery."

[59] The Sunday Star (Washington), March 29, 1936, "Cemetery Bars Building of Sidewalk: Loophole in Act of Congress Prevents Removal of Graves on Evarts Street Northeast."

[60] D.C. Engineer Department Records, D.C. Archives, #35691, letter dated June 7, 1901, indicates that a careful study of the description of the original deed has been made as well as of a survey made by Howell & Taylor for the Lutheran people. "Our survey is very similar to that Mr. Howell made them, but I think is somewhat better in view of the fact that it ties up to at least one definite monument still standing, and which appears to be very ancient."

Rock Creek. Located immediately north of the Soldiers' Home on Rock Creek Church Road. On the premises is St. Paul's Episcopal Church. Charles W. Neale, sexton (1881). The tract became part of Prince George's Parish of the Episcopal Church in 1726.

Rosemont (see Moore's). Once located at 3134 Stanton Road, S.E., and occupied Square 5879.

Russian Hebrew. Located in Congress Heights in the 1900 city directory.

S

St. Albans (Episcopal). Described in the 1890 and 1891 city directories as being on the Rockville Turnpike. In 1940, we find that in connection with the extension of 42nd Street, N.W., the Health Officer authorized Geo. W. Wise, undertaker, to remove 63 or more remaining bodies from St. Alban's cemetery (or Episcopal Cemetery), and the Methodist cemetery. If may be that only 50 of these were from St. Alban's. The place of reinterment is unknown. See more information under Methodist (Tennallytown).

St. Albans (Episcopal). In Cathedral close on the heights above Georgetown, and on Wisconsin Avenue. The Report of the D.C. Health Officer for 1901 notes the new cemetery in the lands of the Protestant Episcopal Cathedral Foundation on Wisconsin avenue, established by an act of Congress of March 1, 1901. Disinterment permit #17231 was issued in June 1938 for removal of the body of Edith Morgan Millett from the Washington Cathedral for reinterment in St. John in the Wilderness, Flat Rock, North Carolina. Other removals from the Cathedral grounds were made in 1935.

St. Aloysius. Burials here in 1868. Location not determined.

St. Barnabas. Located about 5 miles from Upper Marlborough, in Oxen Hill, Maryland.

St. Columba (see Methodist (Tennallytown)).

St. Elizabeth's Hospital. Located on Nichols Avenue beyond the Anacostia river. The organizational outlines for the government's hospital for the insane were established by an Act in March 1855 (10 Stat. 682). The institution was in 1916 officially named St. Elizabeth's Hospital after the name of the property on which it stands. Two lists are known to exist, giving the name of the hospital patient buried, case number, grave number or letter, admission and death date, and rank and military company. These lists were compiled in 1964, and are to be part of Record Group 418 at the National Archives.

St. Ignatius. Located in Prince George's County, Maryland.

St. Johns. A burial ground by this name is located in Montgomery County, Maryland.

St. Johns Episcopal. Established c.1796 on land given by Col. William Deakins. Once described as being located somewhere near Franklin Row.[61] John Clagett Proctor described the location of St. John's cemetery as being between R and S streets, between 12th and 13th streets, N.W. (Square 276). Remains of several hundred bodies were removed in July 1860 from St. John's to Congressional cemetery. The Redfern family graves, once at St. John's were removed to Rock Creek cemetery.

St. Marys German Catholic. Established in 1846, and located at 3rd and H streets, N.W. In 1862, St. Mary's abandoned the site in favor of land they purchased from Georgetown College at North Capitol and O streets. They once again moved about 8 years later to Lincoln Road near Prospect Hill (1890, 1891). Described on certificate of death #5843 as "Father Ailig's German Catholic cemetery near Glenwood" [cemetery]. Rev. Mathias Alig, who died June 9th 1883, was buried here. Early Superintendents were John W. Cord (1881-1883, 1887) and W.P Cord (1884-1886).

St. Matthews Catholic. The parish was established in 1840, and the congregation held services at 15th and H streets, N.W. The present building on Rhode Island Avenue was begun in 1893. The cemetery opened in 1848 in the west half of Square 236, between U and V streets, and between 13th and 14th streets, N.W., on land donated by William Easby. This was adjacent to Foundry Methodist cemetery. The cemetery plat shows lots numbered 1 through 280 in a grid that was crossed by two alleys 20-feet wide. Lot No. 1 was in the southwest corner of the area, and numbers ran in a zig-zag fashion parallel to 14th Street. Based on the plan, the cemetery could accommodate 2,360 burials. The cemetery vault was in the center of the ground that fronted V Street. The property was sold by act of Congress in February 1861,[62] and the graves were removed in 1866 to the new Mt. Olivet

---

[61] Hines, p. 40. The 1832 will of Dr. Thomas Sim, of Washington, D.C., requested the doctor's desire to be decently interred in the site of the burial ground attached to St. John's Episcopal Church, in the City of Washington, parallel with the remains of his beloved wife Hannah L. Sim.

[62] Private Act 26, approved February 16, 1861, filed February 23, 1861 at the Department of State, "For the relief of the Parish of Saint Matthew's Church, of the City of Washington..." that Charles J. White, parish priest of St. Matthew's Church, is authorized to sell certain lots of ground deeded to the priest of said parish by the late William Easby, Commissioner of Public Buildings and Grounds, and known in the plat of the said Washington city as lots numbered five, six, seven, eight, nine, ten, eleven, twelve, thirteen and fourteen, in square numbered two hundred and thirty-six; the proceeds of such sale to be applied to the uses and benefit of the said parish.

cemetery.[63] After the sale of St. Matthew's cemetery, pastors of St. Matthew's, St. Patrick's, St. Peter's and St. Dominic's parishes purchased about 40 acres of the Fenwick farm for the first section of Mt. Olivet cemetery, a half mile from the toll-gate on the Bladensburg Road.[34] St. Matthew's cemetery was destroyed. A burial register for the period 1863-1876 is maintained by the archivist of St. Matthew's Cathedral, Rhode Island Avenue. The Register records the interment of parishioners in burial places other than St. Matthew's, and primarily in Mt. Olivet cemetery.

St. Patricks Catholic. Located on Boundary (Florida Avenue) off North Capitol between 1st and 3rd streets, N.W.,[65] north of Square 551, was the burial ground for St. Patrick's Church.[66] The property was donated by Ann, daughter of Notley Young. Although the church was organized in 1797, the burial ground did not begin use until 1810. In his will of 1850, David Fitzgerald wished to be buried at St. Patrick's to be with the remains of his late mother. In the late 1850's, remains at St. Patrick's were exhumed and reinterred at Mt. Olivet, as were others from St. Peter's and St. Matthew's. Discontinued.

St. Peters Catholic. Located on property donated by Nicholas, son of Notley Young. The 1850 city directory describes the location in Square 808, between 4th, 5th, H and I streets, N.E. It is said that the cemetery was at a steep hill—proving especially troublesome during bad whether. Pallbearers often found it necessary to slide coffins down the slippery dirt road on a skid or sled. Daniel Carroll of "Duddington," who died May 9, 1849, was buried here. Closed in 1862, remains were reinterred at Mt. Olivet. Destroyed.

Scaggs (Family). Sarah Scaggs was Superintendent (1882-1887). Located on Anacostia Road (1890, 1891), Bennings. The certificate of death for Selby Brinker Scaggs (#26200), October 13, 1880, notes place of burial as "Scaggs, Piney Grove Chapel near Bennings." Other certificates (#45790, #50501) have stricken the place of burial of Piney Grove Church as replaced with Scaggs. An 1880 map of the area shows the Scaggs family were property owners on both sides of the railroad and south of where it crosses the road from the Bennings bridge.

Scottish Rite Temple. Burials have occurred within the House of the Temple, Scottish Rite Temple, located at 1733 16th Street, N.W. The remains of Gen. Albert Pike, who died at 433 3rd St., N.W. on April 2, 1891, were removed from Oak Hill cemetery to the Temple at the end of December 1944.

Sears (Family). The certificate of death for an infant of Pauline Nelson (#47944), July 15, 1885, notes place of burial as "Sears, Private."

Shaw (Family). Resin Shaw operated a burial ground in Washington County. The remains of Nicholas Snethen Shaw (#1978), who died January 28, 1875, were buried here.

Sheriff (Family) Farm. Established in 1850 on the farm of Levi Sheriff, and located north of Benning Road, N.E., east of the Anacostia River. Levi Sheriff, a prosperous merchant of Bladensburg, Maryland, died in 1853. Here were buried members of the Sheriff, Dean(e) and McCormick families. Levi Sheriff's daughter Mary Cornelia Sheriff was the wife of John T.W. Dean, associate judge of the 2nd election district of Prince George's County, Maryland. Elizabeth T.B. McCormick and Alexander McCormick were removed from here and reinterred in Congressional cemetery in October 1930. The Sheriff family graves were removed in June and July 1930 to Rock Creek cemetery. The oldest death found on a disinterment permit (#14434) for a person buried here was for Dr. Lemuel Sheriff who died August 10, 1843 at "Beall's Pleasure" near Bladensburg. We know that Mrs. Matilda Wilson Sheriff, consort of Levi Sheriff of Bladensburg, died April 11, 1827, age 31 years, leaving eight children. Also associated with this property was Rev. R.W. Lowrie who was at times shown as the proprietor of the burial ground on the "Prospect Hill" farm at this location. Destroyed.

Shoemaker (Family) Farm. Pierce Shoemaker, owner (1882-1888). Private, near Pierce's Mill (1890, 1891), on Pierce Mill Road in 1899.

Shoemaker (Family). Burial ground on the property of Isaac Shoemaker near Tennallytown (1890, 1891). David Shoemaker was owner (1883-1888). Christian D. Shoemaker, who died July 21, 1832, was buried here. David Shoemaker died at the age of 79 years, December 6, 1886, on his farm near Tennallytown (#54486), and was buried here.

Shoemaker (Family). The certificate of death for Samuel W. Collins (#2155 foreign), August 14, 1896, note place of burial as "Chas. Shoemaker's farm, Montgomery Co., Md." He died in Leavenworth, Kansas.

---

[63] Helene, Estelle and Imogene Philibert, Saint Matthew's of Washington, 1840-1940 (Baltimore, Md.: A. Hoen & Co., 1940, pp. 50-51. The original lot owners of the catholic burial ground included: Benjamin G. Clements, George Vondelehr, Mr. Holmead, Richard Barry, Mr. Newton, William F. Dove, Lucius M. Clements, Jno. F. Bridget, and Col. P. Taylor.

[64] Philibert, p. 51.

[65] Records of the Columbia Historical Society, Vol. 24, p. 123, describe the location of St. Patrick's burying ground at the corner of 10th and F streets.

[66] One monument that survived: "Mary E. Griner is my name / And Heaven is my station / Washington City was my dwelling place / And Christ is my salvation / When I am dead and in my grave / And all my bones are rotten / When this you see / Remember me / That I may never be forgotten." She died April 16, 1843, in her 28th year.

The Joseph F. Birch funeral home made several burials here between 1905 and 1907.

Sibley (Family) Farm. Located in Montgomery County, Maryland. Interments from the Sibley farm grounds were removed in October 1879 to Rock Creek cemetery. These include William Sibley (d. 1831) and his wife Elizabeth Sibley (d. 1867). Destroyed.

Simpson (Family). Located in Montgomery County, Maryland. Six interments from the Simpson family grounds were removed to Rock Creek cemetery.

Small Pox Grounds (see also Washington Asylum). Located along the north perimeter of the Washington Asylum and at the river. There was a small pox epidemic in the District in the winter of 1872-1873. A small pox hospital was separate from the Washington Asylum hospital, and was on the east side of the asylum grounds. It was surrounded by a wall. A parking lot presently covers the general area.

Smith (Family). Located in the vicinity of Congress Street and Savannah Place, S.E., variously known as the Mathilda Smith cemetery, Smith's cemetery of Anacostia, Smith's cemetery of Good Hope Hill, Good Hope Hill cemetery, and Smith's cemetery of Hamilton Road.[67] A plat of the family cemetery belonging to the heirs of the late Matilda Smith, dated 1900, notes that the old graves were very irregular.[68] Matilda was the daughter of Tobias Henson, a freed slave. In 1813, Henson acquired a 24-acre tract called "The Ridge," located in the community now known as Congress Heights. Richard Smith, sexton (1882-1888). The city directory of 1879 gives the Smith burial ground location as Good Hope, and on Hamilton Road in the directories for 1890 and 1891. Burials here were more than one might expect, at least 100 could be identified. An order was made February 3, 1950 for all remains to be disinterred — many reinterments were made in Lincoln Memorial cemetery (Section G, Row 29-A, sites 30-33).

Soldiers Home (National). Mathias Glynn, superintendent (1880-1887). Harewood Road (1890, 1891); Barnes Hospital. South of Rock Creek cemetery.

Springdale. The certificate of death for Addie Sherritt (#897 foreign), April 2, 1888, notes place of burial in "Springdale, D.C." She died in Fairbault, Minnesota.

Springland Farm. Records of the Joseph F. Birch funeral home show in August 1915 the burial of an infant of John A. Sterrett in Springland Farm, D.C.

Swartz (or Swarts) Farm (Family). B.T. Swartz, owner (1883-1888). In Washington County near Brightwood (1890, 1891). At least 16 known burials here.

T

Tennallytown (also Tenleytown and other spellings). See information for Methodist, and Presbyterian cemeteries.

Thomas (Family). Proprietor Thomas Thomas. Location described in 1879 as being in Good Hope. At least two dozen burials here. A Thomas cemetery is in Prince George's County, Maryland in 1882.

U

Union Baptist. Established after 1868, northeast of the intersection of MacArthur Boulevard and Chain Bridge Road, N.W. Discontinued.

Union Beneficial Association (see Beckett's). John F.N. Wilkinson, superintendent (1883).

Union Benevolent Association (see Mount Pleasant). Located on Adams Mill Road, N.W.

Unknown. A graveyard was on 24th Street west, between H and I streets north. According to Christian Hines, it was said by some to have been the burial ground of soldiers who were quartered in that neighborhood prior to 1800.[69]

Unknown. Possibly located between E and F streets north, and not far from Easby's ship yard. This is said to have been the place where there were interred bodies found floating down the river.[70]

Unknown. A "tolerably large grave yard," on the eastern slope of Observatory Hill.[71] The 1843 city directory describes that the observatory was located on the south side of Pennsylvania Avenue, between 24th and 25th Streets West, near 25th Street.

Unknown. Along and partly in F Street north, possibly between 22nd and 23rd streets. May have contained the grave for Casper Yost.[72]

Unknown. Located where "the old race-course used to be," on a farm occupied by a Mr. Myers, near Boundary Street, and nearly south of Commodore Porter's estate.[73]

---

[67] See D.C. Engineer Department records, #262024, at the D.C. Archives.
[68] Louise Daniel Hutchinson, The Anacostia Story: 1806-1930 (Washington, D.C.: Smithsonian Institution Press, 1977), p. 45.
[69] Christian Hines, Early Recollections of Washington City (Washington, D.C., 1866), p. 38.
[70] Hines, p. 38.
[71] Hines, pp. 38-39.
[72] Hines, p. 39.
[73] Hines, p. 39.

V

Vanburia. The certificate of death for Maria Abel (#25077), July 9, 1880, notes place of burial as "Vanburia." She died in Hillsdale.

Veitch (Family). Founded by John Veitch (d. 1864), the grandson of John Veitch who in 1719 married a daughter of Rev. Hugh Conn. About 10 graves of the Veitch family were located at a distance from graves for at least 30 others. On grounds of the Reform School (1899). The property was acquired in 1913 by the government for use as the National Training School for Boys. The last interment was made in 1919.[74] Located northeast of South Dakota Avenue at 33rd Street, N.E. By the 1970's the area was part of the Fort Lincoln Urban Renewal project. In July 1978, remains from about 40 grave sites once in the Veitch family burial ground were relocated to Ft. Lincoln cemetery, Bladensburg Road, Prince George's County, Maryland. The contract for the removal required that the monuments be set aside and picked up and disposed of by others.

Vincent (Family) Farm. The remains of Catherine F. Alexander (#2148 foreign), d. November 27, 1847, were removed from the Vincent farm in Virginia (Alexandria County) to Oak Hill cemetery, on April 26, 1897. Those for her husband Walter S. Alexander (#2149 foreign), d. March 9, 1856, were also removed as above.

W

Walker (Family) Farm. The certificate of death for Elizabeth Smith (#52342), June 30, 1886, notes place of burial as "Walker's family grown."

Washington Asylum (also see Potters Field). The 1822 and 1827 city directories describe the location of an asylum in Square 448, bounded by 6th and 7th streets West, between M and N streets North. Later, the location was on the tract at B and 19th streets, S.E. There were numerous different asylums in the area, e.g. insane asylum, orphan asylums, foundling asylums. However, the Washington Asylum is the only one known by this compiler to have maintained a burial ground. One burial ground here was along the Eastern Branch (Anacostia) River, and near the small pox hospital. The Washington Asylum Hospital, founded in 1832, occupied a portion of the grounds belonging to the asylum. It was renamed Gallinger Hospital, and later became D.C. General Hospital. The original Municipal alms house had its name changed to the Home for Aged and Infirm, and in 1954, to the D.C. Village. A volume inscribed "Record of Interments in the Washington Asylum Burial Ground, District of Columbia," can be found at the D.C. Archives. It is volume three of a series, and covers the period September 18, 1875 to December 18, 1903.

Washington Hebrew (see Adas Israel).

Weems (Family). A history of Tenleytown, D.C., by Judith Beck Helm, page 119, describes that the Weems family burial plot was on the hill (close to what later became the Ft. Reno water pumping station) and was situated in Giles Dyer's garden. The Weems tombstones were standing before the Civil War, but construction of the fort destroyed all trace of the graveyard.

West or Western Burial Ground (see Holmead's).

Western Methodist (see Foundry).

White's Tabernacle. A note in the D.C. Engineer Department records (#117438) indicates that a bill was passed in 1914 which prohibited the interment of the body of any person in the cemetery of the White's Tabernacle #39 of the Ancient United Order of Sons and Daughters, Brethren and Sisters of Moses in the District of Columbia. Location not determined.

Whitehaven. On September 23, 1893, removals were made from Whitehaven, D.C. to Oak Hill cemetery (Lot 621E), Georgetown. A single monument marked the graves of the Baker, Chew and Pratt families.

Wighht (Family). Located near what is now 12th and Monroe streets, N.E. The Wightt, Queen, Brooks tract was divided to form the Brookland neighborhood.[75]

Wilson (Family) Farm. The certificate of death for William C. Bryant (#4344), July 28, 1875, notes the place of burial as "Wilson's Farm, Good Hope, D.C."

Wood (Family) Farm. A return of a still birth for an infant of William and Frances Wood (#1966), January 18, 1875, notes the place of burial as "Wood's Farm." The residence of the parents is Anacostia.

Woodlawn. Woodlawn Cemetery Association was incorporated on 8 JAN 1895. The cemetery was founded the same year at 4611 Benning Road, S.E. Remains from more than 6,000 burials were reinterred here from the now destroyed Graceland cemetery. Closed between 1972 and 1975.[76] Reopened for

---

[74] The News Leader (Laurel, Md.), 10 JAN 1968, "Final Notes on the Veitch Family," final part in a series of three articles. See also The News Leader, 27 DEC 1867, "County History Unconfined." As of October 1973, a monument for Isabella Veitch, 1826-1919 could be found.

[75] Records of the Columbia Historical Society, Vol. 22, pp. 193-194; Vol. 50, p. 114.

[76] Washington Star, 4 MAR 1973, "Sad Story of a Cemetery"; Washington Times, 16 APR 1987, "Woman Wages Lonely Battle to Preserve Black Cemeteries."

burials,[77] but conditions deteriorated further.[78] In 1997, members of the AmeriCorps national service program worked to remove brush at Woodlawn.[79]

Woodley. The "Register of Interments in the Cemetery of Oak Hill" shows that on November 2, 1869, Oak Hill received removals from Woodley, D.C. These reinterments were for the Ridgely, Gough, Hollingsworth, Chase, Forbes, and Key families—each indicating that the last place of residence was Georgetown. Death dates of the deceased range between 1815 and 1862, and the reinterments include that of Philip Barton Key who died July 28, 1815.

Y

Young (Family). Remains of Notley Young were interred in the family lot on Square 390. They were subsequently disinterred and buried by Robert Brent in Carroll Chapel graveyard, Forest Glen, Maryland.[80]

Young Mens (see also Mt. Pleasant Plain(s), and Free Young Mens Burying Ground). Located at 12th and V streets, N.E. Also described as being about one half mile northwest of Columbian College. Sexton is Mr. Talbert (1874). Mount Pleasant (1899). Discontinued, reinterments after 1890 to Woodlawn.

Z

Zachman (Family). The certificate of death for Letitia Harshman (#22647), December 25, 1879, notes the place of burial as "Zachman family Cemetery." She died near Anacostia.

---

[77] Washington Star, 27 FEB 1975, "New School Helps Renewal of Old Cemetery."
[78] Washington Post, 13 DEC 1980, "Are Our Dead Truly Gone and Forgotten?"
[79] Washington Post, 6 FEB 1997, "New Life for a Neglected Cemetery."
[80] Records of the Columbia Historical Society, Vol. 21, pp. 148-149.

Abbreviations

A number of routine abbreviations that are used in the Register are used in this work. In addition, this compiler has used an asterisk (*) to indicate: (1) additional information about locations that cannot be inserted here due to space constraints, or (2) when the place of burial is blank in the Register but has been confirmed by cemetery records, or is different in cemetery records. Further explanation is given below. Regular abbreviations include:

B	Black
C	Colored
D.C.*	Georgetown, D.C.
I	Indian
M	Mulatto
Va.*	Alexandria, Va.
W	White
Y	Yellow

CLARIFICATION FOR THE "BURIAL GROUND" COLUMN

Not many records have survived for the destroyed burial grounds given in the Register. However, the compiler has tried to compare burial records of a few large cemeteries with Register entries. When the place of burial is not given in the Register, but the compiler has identified it from cemetery records, the burial ground entry in this work is followed by an asterisk (*). For example, in cases where the Register gives "Washington" as the burial ground, and it is known the burial took place in Congressional cemetery (Washington Parish), the entry is provided as "Congressional*."

Requirement for Registering Deaths

During the 1850's, the minutes of the District of Columbia Board of Health show concern over practices of reporting deaths.[81] The Act that regulated the reporting of such information contained no provision for the enforcement of its requirements, and had been almost entirely disregarded by those who should make returns. It was left to the wisdom of the City Councils to say whether the subject is one of sufficient importance to occupy their attendance and if so, to devise the most effectual method of securing correct and regular returns. The Councils lingered to act, and the Board felt their concerns remained unaddressed.

Legislation which was finally passed June 3, 1853, caused the creation of the subject Register. Text of the Act, entitled "An ACT to provide for the registry of births, marriages, and deaths," appeared in the newspaper, as follows:[82]

> *Be it enacted, &c.* That whenever hereafter any child shall have been born in the said city, it shall be the duty of the head of the family in which such child shall have been born, or such person as may for the time being have the principal charge or superintendence of the affairs of such family, to cause to be made out and delivered, within six days after such birth, to one of the members of the Board of Health of the ward in which such birth may have happened, a certificate thereof, stating distinctly the date of such birth, the sex and color of such child, and whether still-born or not; which certificate it shall be the duty of the said commissioner to deliver to the health officer of the city for the time being, within six days after the receipt of the same.
>
> Sec. 2. *And be it enacted*, That it shall be the duty of every clergyman or other person who may be legally authorized to celebrate the rites of matrimony in this city to keep a record of all marriages celebrated by him therein, which shall plainly exhibit the Christian and surnames of the parties married, the reputed residence of each, and the authority under which such marriage was solemnized; and shall moreover, within three months after the celebration of any marriage by him, transmit to the Register a correct and full transcript of the record required to be kept as aforesaid; and it shall be the duty of the Register, upon receipt of any such exemplification or transcript, or within thirty days thereafter, to record the same in a bound book, to be kept by him for that purpose.
>
> Sec. 3. *And be it enacted*, That if any clergyman or other person authorized to celebrate the rites of matrimony in this city, or the Register, shall refuse, fail, or neglect to observe, fulfil, and perform the several duties enjoined on them respectively by the preceding section, shall for each offence or failure forfeit and pay the sum of twenty dollars, to be recovered and applied as other fines are by the laws of this Corporation.
>
> Sec. 4. *And be it enacted*, That from and after the first day of July next [July 1, 1854], it shall not be lawful for any person, without a permission in writing from the Register of the city, to remove the body of a human being who died or was found dead within the limits of this Corporation, for the purpose of interment either within or without the said limits; and any person offending against this provision shall forfeit and pay a fine of ten dollars for each and every such offence.
>
> Sec. 5. *And be it enacted*, That in every case of the death of a human being within the limits of this Corporation, it shall be incumbent on some one interested in the interment, or whose duty it may be otherwise made to cause the interment of the dead body, to procure from the attending physician, if there had been one, or if not, from the coroner of the district, or from some respectable and responsible person cognizant of the circumstances attending the death of the individual, a certificate setting forth, as near as possible, the age, sex, and color of the deceased; the place of his or her nativity; the length of time he or she had been a resident of this city; the

---

[81] District of Columbia Board of Health, Minutes, 1848-1871, August 28, 1852. Record keeping of other vital records was not any easier, as we read here, "so few returns of marriages and births have been made to the Board that no practical benefit would be gained by reporting them."
[82] National Intelligencer (Washington, 20 JUN 1853), supplement.

occupation or business pursuit; whether married or unmarried, a widower or widow at the time of death; and the nature of the disease or other cause of his or her death; which certificate shall be presented to the Register of the city as an application for and the foundation of the permission he shall thereon give for the removal of the dead body to the place of interment.

Sec. 6. *And be it enacted*, That the Register of the city shall keep a register in detail of the certificates thus presented to him and the permits thereon granted in chronological order; and shall, at the close of each month, transmit the same to the President of the Board of Health.

Sec. 7. *And be it enacted*, That the sextons or persons having charge of the several grave yards and burying grounds within the city of Washington be and they are hereby required to make monthly returns on the first day of every month to the President of the Board of Health of said city of the permits of the Register for interments of deceased persons in the respective burying grounds under their charge during the preceding month; and in case any sexton or person having charge of burying grounds or grave yards shall refuse or neglect to make said return by the fifth day of every month after the passage or promulgation of this act, or shall permit, suffer, or allow any interment in their respective grave yards or burial places without the written permission of the Register as aforesaid, he shall forfeit and pay in either case the sum of two dollars for each and every offence, to be recovered and appropriated as are other fines and penalties imposed by the acts of this Corporation.

Sec. 8. *And be it enacted*, That the act requiring sextons to make monthly returns of interments of deceased persons, approved August 10th 1836, and the act to provide for the registry of births, deaths, and marriages, approved April 14th 1821, be and the same are hereby repealed.

Approved, June 3, 1853.

By 1855, the lack of reporting of information about deaths had not improved. Minutes of the Board of Health show that for the year ending June 30, 1855, the mortality report was defective in regard to causes of death. For 72 cases of 1,188, the causes of death were not reported and it *must be at once apparent that the interest and value of the statistical statements hereto appended are materially lessened.*[83] The Board found that the neglect is:

> entirely with the physician who, tho appealed to through former annual reports upon the grounds of scientific interests in correct statistical tables, embodying such information as is called for by the certificates of death which they are desired to fill up and sign, yet continued, some of them, practically to deny all interest in them by neglecting and in some cases we are assured by the undertakers positively refusing to give the information over their signatures. It consequently devolves upon the undertakers who are required by law under penalty of fine to return to the Board of Health a certificate for each interment made by them, to obtain such information as they can from the friends; and a large number of certificates come to [the] Board filled up and signed by them as persons cognizant of the circumstances of death.[34]

The minutes state that although the whole number of deaths in the city during 1855 was 1,188, it was rather less than during the preceding year. Of this number, the minutes show that 46 percent were under age 5 years, 8 percent from 5 to 20 years, 20 percent from 20 to 40 years, 12 percent from 40 to 60 years, 12 percent over 60 years, and about 2 percent not reported.

The rules were clarified in 1868 to cover learning experiences from the 1853 legislation. The following Act specifically addressed keeping death records in the District of Columbia:

AN ACT to provide for the Registry of Deaths and for other purposes.

Be it enacted by the Board of Aldermen and Board of Common Council of the City of Washington, That whenever any person shall die within the limits of the City of Washington, it shall be the duty of the physician who attended during his or her last sickness, or of the Coroner of Washington County, when the case comes

---

[83] District of Columbia Board of Health, Minutes, 1848-1871, July 1, 1855.
[84] Ibid.

under his notice, to furnish and deliver to the family of the deceased, or to the undertaker or other person having charge of or superintending the burial of the said deceased, a certificate setting forth, as far as the same can be ascertained, the name, sex, color, nativity, occupation, probable age, place of decease, time of, and supposed cause of death, of the person deceased. And it shall be the duty of the physician or coroner, as above stated, to deliver or cause to be delivered the above-named certificate to the party or parties above named, within forty-eight hours after the death of said deceased shall come to their knowledge, and they deliver said certificate sooner if possible, if requested so to do.

SEC. 2. *And be it further enacted,* That no person having the charge, as sexton or otherwise, of any vault, burial-ground, or cemetery within the City of Washington, (including the Intendant of the Washington Asylum,) shall inter or allow to be interred, place or allow to be placed in any vault, burial-ground, or cemetery under their control, the dead body of any person, unless there shall have been delivered to them by the person or persons ordering the said interment, or the placing of a dead body in a vault, a certificate as hereinbefore, or as may be hereafter provided for.

SEC. 3. *And be it further enacted,* That any undertaker or other person removing the dead body of a person who has died in said city, (and which dead body shall not have been previously buried, or been placed in a vault or other receptacle for the temporary deposit of the dead,) to any place beyond the limits of said city, shall deliver or cause to be delivered, the hereinbefore or as may be hereinafter required certificate to the Secretary of the Board of Health, to be left at his residence or place of business on or before the tenth of the succeeding month, to which certificate the date and place of interment shall be attached.

SEC. 4. *And be if further enacted,* In case any person shall die without the attendance of a physician, or if the physician who did attend at the time of the death of said person refuses or neglects to deliver the certificate as hereinbefore required, then the said certificate may be furnished by the Secretary of the Board of Health, any member of the Board of Health, or by any respectable citizen cognizant of the circumstances and causes of death, and should there be no physician, and an inquest be held, and the Coroner refuses or neglects to furnish the certificate as hereinbefore required, then the said certificate may be furnished by either of the parties above enumerated in this section.

SEC. 5. *And be it further enacted,* That every sexton or other person having charge of any vault, burial-ground, or cemetery within the limits of the City of Washington, shall return each and every certificate of death coming into his or their hands, in accordance with the foregoing provisions of this act, and shall deliver or cause such certificate or certificates to be delivered at the residence or office of the Secretary of the Board of Health on or before the tenth of the month following that in which said death shall have occurred.

SEC. 6. *And be it further enacted,* That it shall be the duty of the Secretary of the Board of Health to furnish each and every undertaker within the limits of the City of Washington, with a list, containing the name and residence of each and every member of the Board of Health, and he shall promptly communicate to the aforesaid undertakers any change that may be made therein; he shall also keep on hand, and promptly furnish to undertakers, physicians, and such other persons as may require them, blank forms for such certificates as are hereinbefore required; he shall also furnish each and every physician and undertaker, and also every sexton or other person in charge of any vault, burial-ground, or cemetery within the limits of the City of Washington, with a printed copy of this act, and he shall publish a statistical report of all certificates coming into his hands, on or before the fifteenth of each month, giving numbers of deaths, various causes, ages, &c., and shall also perform such other duties as may be necessary to facilitate a compliance with the provisions of this act.

SEC. 7. *And be it further enacted,* That in case any physician or coroner shall refuse or neglect to deliver such certificates, and at the time and in the manner hereinbefore required, he or they shall forfeit and pay the sum of ten dollars for each and every such neglect, or refusal; said fines to be recovered as other fines for the use and benefit of the Corporation of Washington City; and it is hereby made the duty of the Secretary of the Board of Health to see that the provisions of this section are rigidly enforced.

SEC. 8. *And be it further enacted,* That every undertaker, sexton, or other person removing the dead body of any person beyond the city limits, who shall have died within the City of Washington, except as provided for in section three of this act, or having charge of any vault, burial-ground, or cemetery, within the limits of said city, who refuses or neglects to perform any of the duties required of them by the provisions of this act, shall, for each and every such refusal or neglect, forfeit and pay the sum of two dollars; and the Secretary of the Board of Health, for each and every refusal or neglect to perform the duties as hereinbefore required of him shall forfeit and pay the sum of five dollars; said fines as enumerated in this section to be recovered as are other fines for the use and benefit of the Corporation of Washington City.

SEC. 9. *And be it further enacted,* That all acts or parts or acts inconsistent with the provisions of this act be, and the same are hereby, repealed.

Approved January 8, 1868.

RULES, REGULATIONS, AND INSTRUCTIONS FOR THE PREVENTION OF THE SPREAD OF EPIDEMIC, INFECTIOUS AND CONTAGIOUS DISEASES IN THE DISTRICT OF COLUMBIA

5. That all undertakers, or persons acting as undertakers, in the city of Georgetown are hereby required to report to the Board of Health, on or before the tenth day of each month, until otherwise ordered, all interments made by them, together with a certificate from the physician or other responsible person cognizant of the circumstances attending the death of any individual, setting forth the name, sex, color, age, time of and cause of death, and also the place of interment, together with such other facts as may serve to identify the individual and be of service to the Board in preventing the spread of epidemic, infectious or contagious disease.

These regulations the Board of Health will, to conserve the public health, rigidly enforce according to the law conferring the authority and making it the duty of the Board of Health to issue orders, regulations, and instructions as aforesaid.

Chris. C. Cox, M.D.,
President Board of Health, District of Columbia

Attest: D.W. Bliss, M.D., Secretary
Approved: H.D. Cooke, Governor

DISTRICT OF COLUMBIA
Interment (Index to Deaths)
January 1, 1855 to July 31, 1874

Page	Name	Age	Race	Birth	Death Date	Burial Place
	A					
077	A__, Wm.	1y	W	D.C.	01 MAY 1857	Glenwood
690	Abbot, Albert, sailor	52y	W	U.S.	14 MAY 1873	
492	Abbot, Dora	9y	W	U.S.	20 DEC 1870	Congressional
293	Abbot, Mary D.	53y	W	D.C.	27 FEB 1868	Oak Hill
198	Abbot, [blank]	37y	W		31 JAN 1861	Oak Hill
596	Abbott, Elisabeth	73y	W	Eng.	08 APR 1872	
039	Abbott, George, clerk	45y	W	N.H.	13 MAR 1856	Not Reported
337	Abbott, James Sty.	5d	C	U.S.	15 AUG 1868	Washington Asylum
202	Abbott, Joseph	74y	W	Eng.	01 APR 1861	Oak Hill
046	Abbott, Lara Ida	5m	W	Va.	17 JUN 1856	St. Matthews
365	Abbott, Letha Ann	18y	B	Va.	23 DEC 1868	Young Mens
637	Abbott, Lousia		C	U.S.	12 NOV 1872	
664	Abell, Ella S.P.	9y	W	U.S.	13 JAN 1873	Small Pox*
262	Abercrombie, Mary F.	71y	W	Md.	08 JUN 1867	Congressional
326	Able, Annie E.	8m	W	D.C.	12 JUL 1868	Congressional
351	Abner, Hermann	4y	W		26 SEP 1868	Prospect Hill
344	Abner, Louise	1y	W	D.C.	20 AUG 1868	Prospect Hill
666	Abott, Roselee	28y	W	U.S.	07 FEB 1873	Glenwood
310	Abrew, Joanna	38y	W	Ire.	27 APR 1868	Mt. Olivet
732	Achenback, L.C.	19d	W	U.S.	29 NOV 1873	Prospect Hill
457	Acker, Eva M.	1y	W	D.C.	05 JUN 1870	Congressional
482	Acker, Rose A.	3y	W	D.C.	30 OCT 1870	Mt. Olivet
430	Ackerman, Nellis A.	7d	W		15 DEC 1869	Glenwood
547	Ackman, Charles	18y	W	Md.	08 DEC 1871	German
357	Actis, Anna	45y	B	Va.	18 OCT 1868	Washington Asylum
127	Acton, Charles	6y	W	D.C.	15 SEP 1858	Congressional
070	Acton, Emily	45y	W	Md.	09 FEB 1857	Congressional
778a	Acton, Mary	41y	W	U.S.	26 JUL 1874	Congressional
215	Acton, Nelly				19 MAR 1866	Western
342	Acton, Saml. J.	5m	W	D.C.	01 AUG 1868	Congressional
434	Acton, W. Osborne	40y	W		30 JAN 1870	Congressional
013	Acton, Wm. E.	2y	W	D.C.	26 JUL 1855	Congressional
349	Adair, Margaret	33y	W	Ire.	22 SEP 1868	Glenwood
250	Adair, Sarah E.	3y	W	D.C.	01 JAN 1867	Glenwood
266	Adam, Frank	4m	C	D.C.	14 JUL 1867	Young Mens
138	Adams, Alexander, grocer	56y	W		23 JAN 1859	Congressional
592	Adams, Anny, cook	76y	W	D.C.	01 APR 1872	Mt. Olivet
730	Adams, C.H., lady	65y	W	U.S.	17 NOV 1873	Congressional
250	Adams, Caleb	37y	C	Md.	21 JAN 1867	Harmony
057	Adams, Caroline	50y	W	Mass.	04 SEP 1856	Congressional
613	Adams, Clinton A.	1y	C	U.S.	17 JUL 1872	
451	Adams, David, laborer	22y	C	Va.	02 APR 1870	Washington Asylum
367	Adams, Delilia	90y	B	N.C.	15 DEC 1868	Washington Asylum
335	Adams, E.H., son of	4m	C		14 JUL 1868	
508	Adams, Edgar, soldier	26y	C	D.C.	08 FEB 1871	Ebenezer
362	Adams, Edward	2y	C	D.C.	05 NOV 1868	Ebenezer
300	Adams, Eliza	14y	C	Va.	08 MAR 1868	Alms House
482	Adams, Elizabeth		W		19 OCT 1870	Methodist
778a	Adams, Florence A.	2h	C	U.S.	18 JUL 1874	
350	Adams, Francis	1y	C	D.C.	17 SEP 1868	Young Mens
308	Adams, Geo. M.	6m	W	D.C.	16 APR 1868	Methodist
045	Adams, Geo. T.	7y	C	D.C.	21 MAY 1856	Harmony
645	Adams, George A., painter	27y	W	U.S.	26 DEC 1872	Congressional
122	Adams, Georgianna	8m	W	D.C.	22 JUL 1858	Congressional

District of Columbia Interments (Index to Deaths), 1855-1874

Page	Name	Age	Race	Birth	Death Date	Burial Ground
150	Adams, Henry	33y	C	D.C.	06 JUN 1859	St. Patricks
384	Adams, Henry	4y	C	D.C.	17 MAR 1869	Washington Asylum
544	Adams, Henry, laborer	75y	C	Va.	08 NOV 1871	Washington
317	Adams, J.F. Virginia	7m	W		19 JUN 1868	Congressional
423	Adams, Jane A.	16y	C		21 OCT 1869	Washington Asylum
487	Adams, Jesse	6y	W	U.S.	25 NOV 1870	Congressional
499	Adams, John, rigger	58y	W		01 JAN 1871	Congressional
18	Adams, John S.	4y	C	U.S.	02 AUG 1872	Beckett's
137	Adams, John, waiter	40y	C	D.C.	17 JAN 1859	Young Mens
174	Adams, Joseph Moody, clerk	26y	W	D.C.	10 MAR 1860	Congressional
216	Adams, Josias, Asylum attendant	58y	W	Md.	30 MAR 1866	Congressional
039	Adams, Leonard, messenger	83y	W	Mass.	03 MAR 1856	Alexandria, Va.
456	Adams, Louis B., clerk	52y	W	N.Y.	28 JUN 1870	Constantine, Mich.
370	Adams, Louisa C.	45y	W		12 JAN 1869	Oak Hill
617	Adams, Margaret	6y	C	U.S.	30 AUG 1872	
758	Adams, Marshall, laborer	40y	C	U.S.	30 APR 1874	Beckett's
191	Adams, Mary		W		09 OCT 1860	Congressional
305	Adams, Mary	22y	W	U.S.	31 MAR 1868	Congressional
300	Adams, Mary	25y	C	D.C.	11 MAR 1868	Mt. Olivet
409	Adams, Mary G.	22y	W		15 AUG 1869	Glenwood
750	Adams, Mary, infant of	1d	C	U.S.	04 FEB 1874	
363	Adams, Milly	9m	C	D.C.	28 NOV 1868	Washington Asylum
244	Adams, Mrs.	65y	C		07 NOV 1866	Young Mens
102	Adams, Notley L.	70y	W	Md.	21 JAN 1858	Congressional
524	Adams, Priscilla	85y	W		20 JUN 1871	Congressional*
091	Adams, Rebecca	86y		Md.	16 SEP 1857	
250	Adams, Sarah	7m	C	D.C.	07 JAN 1867	Ebenezer
063	Adams, Sheldon G., soldier	59y	W	U.S.	02 NOV 1856	Marine
191	Adams, Thomas, turner	84y	W		01 OCT 1860	Congressional
717	Adams, Thos. Nelson, clerk	52y	W	D.C.	06 SEP 1873	Glenwood
738	Adams, W.H., Jr.	2y	W	U.S.	30 DEC 1873	Oak Hill
288	Adams, William	1y	W	D.C.	19 DEC 1867	Glenwood
257	Adams, Wilmuth, Mrs.	41y	W	Va.	02 MAR 1867	Glenwood
667	Adams, Wm., laborer	50y	C	U.S.	10 FEB 1873	Harmony
282	Adams, [blank]		W		03 NOV 1867	Congressional
131	Adams, [blank], Mr.	60y	C		31 OCT 1858	Mt. Olivet
317	Adamson, Thos. J.	9m	W	D.C.	11 JUN 1868	Congressional
016	Addams, Ellen Ann	3y	C	D.C.	27 JUL 1855	Navy Yard (Col'd)
600	Addella, Casia	11y	C	U.S.	28 MAY 1872	Ebenezer
730	Addis, Robert W., artist	45y	W	U.S.	15 NOV 1873	Congressional*
733	Addis, Robt. W., photographer	45y	W	U.S.	15 NOV 1873	
386	Addison, Amelia	3d		D.C.	17 APR 1869	Mt. Olivet
268	Addison, Caroline E.	1y	W	D.C.	14 AUG 1867	Congressional
746	Addison, Charles	1y	C	U.S.	04 FEB 1874	
708	Addison, Daniel D., attorney	63y	W	U.S.	01 JUL 1873	Oak Hill
265	Addison, Eliza	45y	C	Va.	18 JUL 1867	Young Mens
026	Addison, Henry S., clerk	40y	W	Md.	13 OCT 1855	Glenwood
502	Addison, Hester Jane	6d			03 JAN 1871	
213	Addison, James H.	26y	W	Va.	25 FEB 1866	Congressional
089	Adenwald, Fanny	7m	W	D.C.	31 AUG 1857	Hebrew
083	Adesar, Christian	4y	W	D.C.	12 JUL 1857	German
335	Adkins, John	10m	C		13 JUL 1868	Ebenezer
602	Adkins, Wm.	8y	C	D.C.	02 MAY 1872	Asylum
758	Adley, Mary	2y	W	U.S.	03 APR 1874	Holyrood
528	Adolph, Daniel	7m	W	D.C.	21 JUL 1871	Congressional
107	Adrian, F., laborer	26y	W	Ger.	10 MAR 1858	German Catholic
215	Adult		C		16 MAR 1866	Alms House
214	Adult		W		02 MAR 1866	Deliver to Government

District of Columbia Interments (Index to Deaths), 1855-1874

Page	Name	Age	Race	Birth	Death Date	Burial Ground
209	Adult Male		C		10 JAN 1866	Alms House
778a	Aenning, Allen W.	9m	W		02 JUL 1874	Oak Hill
344	Agnes, Mary	10m	W	D.C.	15 AUG 1868	St. Aloysius
015	Agney, Jane S.	59y	W	Pa.	01 JUL 1855	Congressional
215	Ah-Moose	66y	I	Wisc.	17 MAR 1866	Congressional
483	Aheren, James	1m	W	D.C.	22 OCT 1870	Mt. Olivet
620	Ahern, Bridget	36y	W	U.S.	09 AUG 1872	Mt. Olivet
695	Ahern, Wm. C.	14y	W	Md.	07 JUN 1873	Mt. Olivet
487	Aherns, Jno., laborer	42y	W	Ire.	14 NOV 1870	Mt. Olivet
371	Aigler, Andrew	47y	W	Ger.	31 JAN 1869	Glenwood
634	Aigler, Jacob, confectioner	52y	W	Ger.	20 OCT 1872	
136	Aiken, Charles F., travelling agent	22y	W	Mass.	29 DEC 1858	Lowell, Mass.
260	Aiken, Matilda A.	65y	W	D.C.	10 MAY 1867	Congressional
260	Aiken, Prudence	75y	W	Pa.	19 MAY 1867	Congressional
339	Aikens, Henry, watchman	57y	W	Pa.	28 AUG 1868	Methodist, East
152	Ailier, Catharine	76y	W	Ger.	15 JUN 1859	Mt. Olivet
463	Ainett, Wm. Conrad	1m	W	D.C.	15 JUL 1870	Prospect Hill
435	Ainson, Catharine	1y	C		09 JAN 1870	
047	Aisquith, Wm. E., watchman	45y	W	Va.	29 JUN 1856	Congressional
736	Akers, G.W.	32y	W	U.S.	19 DEC 1873	
135	Albert, [blank]	Still			11 DEC 1858	German
279	Alburger, Emma J.	3y	W	Pa.	28 OCT 1867	Philadelphia, Pa.
477	Alcorn, Sarah	14d	W	D.C.	28 SEP 1870	Congressional
299	Alden, J.M., infant of	13d	W	D.C.	22 MAR 1868	Oak Hill
555	Alden, Louis D.	13d	W	U.S.	25 JAN 1872	
276	Alden, Mary V.	11m	W	D.C.	26 SEP 1867	Glenwood
595	Aldolph, Sarah A.	4y	W	D.C.	10 APR 1872	Presbyterian
230	Aldrich, Lottie	1y	W		09 JUL 1866	Glenwood
642	Aldrick, Caroline L.	35y	W	U.S.	02 DEC 1872	North Attleboro
605	Aldrige, Hiram, laborer	25y	C	Md.	20 JUN 1872	Asylum
230	Alexander, Beverly	20y			24 JUL 1866	Young Mens
365	Alexander, Caroline	26y	B		07 DEC 1868	Union
615	Alexander, Celia	35y	C	U.S.	15 JUL 1872	
684	Alexander, Charles	22y	C	U.S.	25 APR 1873	Small Pox
434	Alexander, Charles A., Col., lawyer	68y	W	Va.	28 JAN 1870	Congressional
555	Alexander, Chas. P.	14y	W	U.S.	30 JAN 1872	Congressional
210	Alexander, Col., child of				17 JAN 1866	Silver Spring, Md.
016	Alexander, Danl.	15d	C	D.C.	19 JUL 1855	Harmony
531	Alexander, David, clerk	43y	W	Scot.	05 AUG 1871	Washington
594	Alexander, Francis	35y	C	Va.	25 APR 1872	Washington
589	Alexander, Isaac	2y	C	Ky.	30 MAR 1872	Western
029	Alexander, J.H., clerk	26y	W	Fra.	19 NOV 1855	Oak Hill
495	Alexander, John H.	21d	C	D.C.	19 DEC 1870	Potters Field
372	Alexander, Julia	Still	C		12 JAN 1869	Washington Asylum
352	Alexander, Leland	2y	C	D.C.	07 SEP 1868	Washington Asylum
642	Alexander, Lewis E.	19y	C	U.S.	28 DEC 1872	Small Pox
014	Alexander, M.E.	26y	C	Va.	08 JUL 1855	Young Mens
499	Alexander, Mary	80y	W	U.S.	31 JAN 1871	Congressional
497	Alexander, Mary	80y	W	U.S.	31 DEC 1870	Congressional
591	Alexander, Mary	3y	C	U.S.	27 APR 1872	Small Pox
603	Alexander, Mary	73y	C	Va.	06 JUN 1872	Union
185	Alexander, Mary	14y	C	D.C.	21 JUL 1860	Western
328	Alexander, Robert	1y	C	D.C.	12 JUL 1868	Alms House
704	Alexander, Saml.	14m	C	D.C.	21 JUL 1873	Harmony
276	Alexander, Seymour	7y	C		30 SEP 1867	Freedmen's Hospital
703	Alexander, Virginia	2y	W	D.C.	04 JUL 1873	Mt. Olivet
508	Alexander, Wm. W.	2y	C	D.C.	16 FEB 1871	Union
094	Alexander, [blank]	1y	W	Ind.	23 OCT 1857	Congressional

Page	Name	Age	Race	Birth	Death Date	Burial Ground
346	Alexandria, Frances	1y	C	Va.	02 AUG 1868	Young Mens
279	Algerine, Henry	3y	C	Mass.	11 OCT 1867	Harmony
182	All, Jackson	8m	W	D.C.	23 JUN 1860	Washington Asylum
334	Allard, Emma P.	10m	W		08 JUL 1868	Baltimore, Md.
778a	Allen, Albert	8m	W	U.S.	26 JUL 1874	Congressional
711	Allen, Albert G., editor	55y	W	N.H.	10 AUG 1873	Congressional*
400	Allen, Aloysius	1y	C		— JUL 1869	Mt. Olivet
336	Allen, Amelia	1y	C	D.C.	03 AUG 1868	
317	Allen, Ann	65y	W	D.C.	08 JUN 1868	Congressional
412	Allen, Anna Kerdelen	7m	C		22 AUG 1869	
299	Allen, Charles T., printer	43y	W	Me.	26 MAR 1868	Glenwood
611	Allen, Chas.	3m	C	U.S.	21 JUL 1872	
540	Allen, Chas. R.	8y	W	Wisc.	08 OCT 1871	Congressional
684	Allen, Christopher	8m	C	U.S.	10 APR 1873	Small Pox*
457	Allen, Edward S., lime/cement dlr.	41y	W	D.C.	17 JUN 1870	Oak Hill
668	Allen, Eliza E.	66y	W	U.S.	22 FEB 1873	Glenwood
435	Allen, Ellen	13y	W	Mass.	16 JAN 1870	Fall River, Mass.
778a	Allen, Ellen	48y	C	U.S.	29 JUL 1874	Harmony
350	Allen, George	3y	C	D.C.	06 SEP 1868	Washington Asylum
445	Allen, George F., merchant	53y	W		06 MAR 1870	Mt. Olivet*
409	Allen, Goodwin/Mary E., child of	P.B.			25 AUG 1869	Mt. Olivet
684	Allen, Henry	6y	C	U.S.	28 APR 1873	Small Pox*
035	Allen, Hiram				13 FEB 1856	Methodist, East
319	Allen, J.C. & Annie, child of	1m	W	U.S.	30 JUN 1868	Western
043	Allen, James	89y	C	Va.	05 APR 1856	Colored, Methodist
237	Allen, John	76y	W	Ire.	05 SEP 1866	Mt. Olivet
197	Allen, John	48y	W	Va.	25 JAN 1861	Washington Asylum
557	Allen, John	9m	C	D.C.	02 FEB 1872	Young Mens
216	Allen, John C., shoemaker	41y	W		21 MAR 1866	Congressional
248	Allen, John, infant of		C	D.C.	25 DEC 1866	Beckett's
499	Allen, Julia M.	30h	W	D.C.	30 JAN 1871	Congressional
381	Allen, Katie Lucina	6m	W	Ill.	25 MAR 1869	Chicago, Ill.
532	Allen, Lloyd	1y	C		17 AUG 1871	Mt. Olivet
035	Allen, Lydia	65y	W	Va.	16 FEB 1856	Not Reported
625	Allen, Marg.	13m	W	U.S.	16 SEP 1872	
778a	Allen, Margaret T.	9m	C	U.S.	03 JUL 1874	
710	Allen, Maria	16m	C	D.C.	01 AUG 1873	Beckett's
336	Allen, Mary	1y	C	D.C.	06 AUG 1868	Alms House
337	Allen, Mary				07 AUG 1868	Washington Asylum
363	Allen, Mary	20y	C	Va.	20 NOV 1868	Washington Asylum
235	Allen, Mary A.	1m	W	Va.	16 SEP 1866	Va.
541	Allen, Mary B.	50y	W	Va.	14 OCT 1871	W.Va.
401	Allen, Mary Jane	1y	C	D.C.	27 JUL 1869	Young Mens
314	Allen, Oliver E., blacksmith	31y	W	D.C.	06 MAY 1868	Congressional
325	Allen, Richard, Rev.	69y	W	D.C.	23 JUL 1868	Congressional
778a	Allen, Robert	76y	W	U.S.	07 JUL 1874	Glenwood
387	Allen, Robert E.	7y	C	Md.	02 APR 1869	Harmony
476	Allen, Rose	4d	W	Amer.	14 SEP 1870	Mt. Olivet
351	Allen, Sam	1y	C	D.C.	24 SEP 1868	Young Mens
276	Allen, Spencer	12y	C	Va.	16 SEP 1867	Ebenezer
514	Allen, T. Dwight, bookkeeper	33y	W	N.Y.	17 MAR 1871	Mt. Olivet
641	Allen, Teresa E., servant	25y	C	U.S.	10 DEC 1872	Small Pox
157	Allen, W.C., clerk	65y	W	U.S.	12 AUG 1859	York Co., Me.
703	Allen, W.H., shoemaker	54y	W	Va.	21 JUL 1873	Glenwood
402	Allen, William	3m	W	D.C.	22 JUL 1869	Mt. Olivet
239	Allen, William B., laborer	59y	W	Md.	29 OCT 1866	Alms House
292a	Allen, William, laborer	45y	W		01 JAN 1868	Oak Hill
507	Allen, [blank]	1m	W	D.C.	19 FEB 1871	Congressional

District of Columbia Interments (Index to Deaths), 1855-1874

Page	Name	Age	Race	Birth	Death Date	Burial Ground
742	Allison, Geo. H., laborer	23y	C	U.S.	16 JAN 1874	Washington Asylum
241	Allyn, Mary M.	54y	W	Me.	18 OCT 1866	Glenwood
344	Alman, Margaret	23y	W	Ire.	30 AUG 1868	Mt. Olivet
033	Almond, Sarah	45y	C	D.C.	27 JAN 1856	Asylum
332	Almore, Johana	1y	W	D.C.	16 JUL 1868	Mt. Olivet
548	Almy, Sarah G.	44y	W	U.S.	09 DEC 1871	Congressional
492	Alshlager, Amelia	6y	W		29 DEC 1870	Prospect Hill
079	Alsten, Christopher H.	55y	W		01 JUN 1857	Congressional
181	Alston, Mrs. [Sarah]	50y	W	Md.	19 JUN 1860	Congressional*
321	Alston, Thomas	30y	C	Conn.	23 JUN 1868	Harmony
778a	Altemus, Andrew F., clerk	29y	W	U.S.	02 JUL 1874	Congressional
189	Altemus, Samuel	7m	W	D.C.	08 SEP 1860	Congressional
738	Altmanburger, Chas., brewer	39y	W	Ger.	20 DEC 1873	
182	Altmannsperger, Peter W.	1m	W		24 JUN 1860	Glenwood
616	Altmansperger, Anna	9m	W	U.S.	01 JUL 1872	
319	Alvan, Bridget	10m	W		25 JUN 1868	Mt. Olivet
526	Alvey, Albert	11m	W	U.S.	06 JUL 1871	
234	Alwath, John	1y	W	D.C.	10 SEP 1866	Mt. Olivet
229	Alworth, Mary	80y	W	Ire.	21 JUL 1866	Mt. Olivet
550	Aman, Clifford S.	4y	W	D.C.	27 DEC 1871	Glenwood
729	Aman, Ella Kobb	27y	W	Ger.	02 NOV 1873	Glenwood
475	Aman, Julia A.	1y	W	D.C.	09 SEP 1870	Glenwood
531	Ambrose, Frank, farmer	50y	W	Va.	05 AUG 1871	Washington
296	Ambrose, William	27y	C	Pa.	19 FEB 1868	Freedmen's Hospital
456	Ambus, Katy	4m	C	D.C.	17 JUN 1870	Union
377	Ambush, Henrietta, seamstress	66y	C	Md.	16 FEB 1869	
625	Ambush, Hiram	7y	C	U.S.	03 OCT 1872	
416	Ambush, John, laborer	70y	C	Md.	19 SEP 1869	Beckett's
263	Ambush, Louvillas Edmonia	1m	C	D.C.	29 JUN 1867	Union Beneficial
495	Ambush, Lucy	55y	C	Me.	05 DEC 1870	Potters Field
273	Ambush, Sarah	9m	C	D.C.	27 SEP 1867	Harmony
243	Ambush, Thomas B.S.	12y	C	D.C.	18 NOV 1866	Young Mens
092	Amendt, Geo., sgtone cutter	50y	W	Ger.	24 SEP 1857	German
682	America, Maggie	4y	W		28 APR 1873	Congressional*
261	Ames, John	6m	C	D.C.	03 MAY 1867	Rock Creek
496	Ames, Reason, soldier	25y	C	Md.	09 DEC 1870	Potters Field
088	Ames, W.	60y	C		20 AUG 1857	Potters Field
430	Amidon, Margaret Agnes, teacher	43y	W		03 DEC 1869	Glenwood
545	Amman, Mary	11m	W	D.C.	19 NOV 1871	Congressional
730	Ammon, C.	5y	W	U.S.	17 NOV 1873	
133	Ammon, George, carpenter	42y	W	Ger.	20 NOV 1858	German
050	Ammon, Gustav	1y			19 JUL 1856	German
475	Amos, Andrew J., engineer	42y	W	Va.	14 SEP 1870	Glenwood
746	Amos, Joseph F.	5m	C	U.S.	25 FEB 1874	Young Mens
336	Amrein, John, shoemaker	34y	W	Ger.	04 AUG 1868	German Lutheran
278	Anadale, John W.	1y	W	D.C.	23 OCT 1867	Glenwood
624	Anderman, H.T., Rev.	60y	W	U.S.	19 SEP 1872	
317	Anderman, [blank]		W		20 JUN 1868	Prospect Hill
423	Anderson, A.	1d	C	D.C.	20 OCT 1869	Washington Asylum
681	Anderson, Ada	6m	C	U.S.	15 APR 1873	
732	Anderson, Adeline	70y	W	U.S.	29 NOV 1873	Congressional*
462	Anderson, Barbara E.	1y	W	D.C.	04 JUL 1870	Congressional
392	Anderson, Brown, blacksmith	30y	C		29 MAY 1869	
616	Anderson, C., housekeeper	35y	C	U.S.	15 JUL 1872	
608	Anderson, C.J.	11m	W	D.C.	21 JUN 1872	Congressional*
148	Anderson, Casselia	8m	C	D.C.	06 MAY 1859	Young Mens
741	Anderson, Catharine	50y	W	U.S.	14 JAN 1874	Congressional
342	Anderson, Charles Lybrun	5m	W	D.C.	08 AUG 1868	Congressional

Page	Name	Age	Race	Birth	Death Date	Burial Ground
021	Anderson, E.D.	1y	W	D.C.	28 AUG 1855	Washington
601	Anderson, Eliza E.	24y	W	U.S.	09 MAY 1872	Congressional
031	Anderson, Eliza J.	18y	W	D.C.	10 DEC 1855	Glenwood
017	Anderson, Eliza S.	34y	W	D.C.	15 JUL 1855	Washington
017	Anderson, Ellen	45y	C	Va.	18 JUL 1855	Harmony
525	Anderson, Emma T.		C	D.C.	27 JUN 1871	
392	Anderson, Geo.	1m	C		26 MAY 1869	
084	Anderson, George W.	4m	C	D.C.	25 JUL 1857	Young Mens
541	Anderson, Henry	50y	C	D.C.	13 OCT 1871	Washington
325	Anderson, Hezekiah	72y	W		17 JUL 1868	Washington
230	Anderson, J.	58y	W		30 JUL 1866	Glenwood
083	Anderson, Jane		W		15 JUL 1857	Congressional
724	Anderson, Jane	27y	W	Md.	13 OCT 1873	Methodist, East
337	Anderson, Jessie	2y	C	Va.	05 AUG 1868	Washington Asylum
555	Anderson, Jessie B., grocer	42y	W	D.C.	30 JAN 1872	Congressional
589	Anderson, John	6y	C	D.C.	14 MAR 1872	
039	Anderson, John G.	33y	W	Va.	11 MAR 1856	Holmead
451	Anderson, John, servant	23y	C	Md.	26 APR 1870	Washington Asylum
182	Anderson, John Thos.	4m	C	D.C.	29 JUN 1860	Foundry
764	Anderson, Joseph	51y	C	U.S.	02 MAY 1874	Washington Asylum
021	Anderson, Josephine	16y	W	N.Y.	01 AUG 1855	N.Y.
239	Anderson, Kate	6m	C	D.C.	25 OCT 1866	Young Mens
548	Anderson, Katrina	30y	W	Ky.	17 DEC 1871	Prospect Hill
688	Anderson, Laurence W.	1y	W	U.S.	10 MAY 1873	Oak Hill
416	Anderson, Lilly V.	2y	C		2- SEP 1869	Harmony
595	Anderson, Margret B.	22y	W	D.C.	24 APR 1872	Congressional
257	Anderson, Martha E.	7y	C	Mass.	01 MAR 1867	Ebenezer
328	Anderson, Martha Ellen	3y	W	D.C.	25 JUL 1868	Western
547	Anderson, Mary	52y	W	Ire.	07 DEC 1871	Mt. Olivet
752	Anderson, Mary A.	10m	C	U.S.	04 MAR 1874	
214	Anderson, Mary A., seamstress	51y	W	Del.	12 MAR 1866	Congressional
404	Anderson, Mary E.	9m	W	D.C.	08 JUL 1869	
590	Anderson, Mary J.		W	D.C.	02 APR 1872	Mt. Olivet
611	Anderson, Mary R.	1m	C	U.S.	04 JUL 1872	
281	Anderson, Miss	23y	W	D.C.	29 OCT 1867	Glenwood
259	Anderson, Mr., child of	6d	W		02 APR 1867	Congressional
181	Anderson, Mrs.	68y	W		05 JUN 1860	Western
276	Anderson, Mrs., child of	Still	W	D.C.	17 SEP 1867	Mt. Olivet
307	Anderson, Mrs., child of	2h	W	D.C.	02 APR 1868	Western
521	Anderson, Nelly	3y	C	D.C.	07 JUN 1871	Western
458	Anderson, Peggy	6m	C	D.C.	19 JUN 1870	Potters Field
727	Anderson, Polly J.	9y	W	Eng.	31 OCT 1873	Congressional
508	Anderson, Rebecca	18y	C	Va.	18 FEB 1871	Union
328	Anderson, Robert	7d	C	D.C.	21 JUL 1868	Congressional
312	Anderson, Robt. L.	21d	W	D.C.	12 MAY 1868	Western
624	Anderson, S.	1y	C	U.S.	14 SEP 1872	
143	Anderson, Saml. C.	7m	W	D.C.	08 MAR 1859	Congressional*
435	Anderson, Stephen Ellwood	3y	W		16 JAN 1870	Brookville, Md.
690	Anderson, Thomas	6y	C	U.S.	29 MAY 1873	Small Pox
585	Anderson, Virginia	6y	C	D.C.	08 MAR 1872	Ebenezer
770	Anderson, W. Stanley	3m	W	U.S.	14 JUN 1874	
524	Anderson, Walter	2y	C	D.C.	22 JUN 1871	Western
548	Anderson, Wm.	11y	W	Va.	10 DEC 1871	Congressional
131	Anderson, Wm.	7y	W	D.C.	23 OCT 1858	Western
031	Anderson, Wm. E.	1y	W	Md.	02 DEC 1855	Md.
416	Anderson, Wm. Henry	1y	C		20 SEP 1869	
546	Anderson, Wm., laborer	50y	C	Va.	24 NOV 1871	Washington
010	Anderson, [blank]	1y	W	D.C.	28 JUN 1855	Catholic, Georgetown

District of Columbia Interments (Index to Deaths), 1855-1874

Page	Name	Age	Race	Birth	Death Date	Burial Ground
003	Anderson, [blank]	Still	W	D.C.	01 FEB 1855	Western
337	Andrew, Rich.	1y	C	U.S.	15 AUG 1868	Washington Asylum
245	Andrews, Christopher, paymstr USA	66y	W	Ire.	11 NOV 1866	Congressional
150	Andrews, Elizabeth	1y	W	D.C.	12 JUN 1859	German Catholic
182	Andrews, Eva	18y	W	D.C.	27 JUN 1860	Glenwood
101	Andrews, J.	1y	W	D.C.	10 JAN 1858	Glenwood
674	Andrews, Louisa	37y	W	U.S.	13 MAR 1873	Glenwood
640	Andrews, Saml.	21y	W	U.S.	15 DEC 1872	Small Pox*
301	Andrews, Timothy P., Col. USA	74y	W	Ire.	11 MAR 1868	Rock Creek
440	Angel, H. Scofield	2m	W		04 FEB 1870	Methodist
172	Angel, John, cabinet maker		W	U.S.	11 FEB 1860	Congressional*
645	Angel, Maria	65y	W	U.S.	26 DEC 1872	Methodist
764	Angel, Minnie B.	3d	W	U.S.	29 MAY 1874	
335	Anison, Martha	1y	C	D.C.	12 JUL 1868	Ebenezer
018	Anthoney, L.B.	65y	W	N.Y.	13 AUG 1855	Methodist
364	Anthony, Clara B.	2m	W	D.C.	24 DEC 1868	Congressional*
312	Anthony, John, laborer	28y	C	Va.	15 MAY 1868	Alms House
395	Anthony, [blank]	Still	W		12 JUN 1869	Mt. Olivet
736	Antionatte, C.E.	22y	W	U.S.	19 DEC 1873	Prospect Hill
055	Antonie, Harriet	25y	W	Md.	08 AUG 1856	5th St. Catholic
120	Appelby, Jane	1m	W	D.C.	02 JUL 1858	Foundry
439	Appeldias, Mina Christina	4y	W		17 FEB 1870	Prospect Hill
070	Appleby, Emma S.	1y	W	D.C.	05 FEB 1857	Glenwood
010	Appleby, Jas. H.	4m	W		29 JUN 1855	Foundry
107	Appleton, D. Edward	1y	W	D.C.	09 MAR 1858	Oak Hill
496	Archer, Elizabeth	25y	C	Va.	27 DEC 1870	Harmony
682	Archer, Henry, laborer	30y	C	U.S.	27 APR 1873	
053	Archer, William, archtect	70y	W	Scot.	12 AUG 1856	Glenwood
677	Archy, Jackson	13y	C	U.S.	14 MAR 1873	Small Pox
495	Ard, Wilhelm	60y	W	Ger.	17 DEC 1870	Potters Field
705	Ardeesar, Chas.	18m	W	Md.	11 JUL 1873	St. Marys
359	Aren, Georgia	Still	W		08 NOV 1868	Congressional
334	Arle, Gertrude Maria	1y	W	D.C.	06 JUL 1868	German Catholic
633	Armour, Wm.	57y	W	Eng.	10 OCT 1872	
155	Armstead, Jane	1m	W	D.C.	28 JUL 1859	Methodist
236	Armstead, Saml., mechanic	46y	W	D.C.	02 SEP 1866	Congressional
580	Armstrong, Catharine D.	47y	W	N.Y.	11 FEB 1872	Congressional
335b	Armstrong, Frank	3m	B	D.C.	01 JUL 1868	Washington Asylum
339	Armstrong, James Francis	11m	W	D.C.	05 AUG 1868	Mt. Olivet
107	Armstrong, John T.	9m	W	D.C.	01 MAR 1858	St. Matthews
523	Armstrong, Joshua	1y	C	Md.	18 JUN 1871	
049	Armstrong, Mary	35y	C	Va.*	08 JUL 1856	Alexandria, Va.
335b	Armstrong, Phebe L.				14 JUL 1868	Washington Asylum
174	Armstrong, Thomas	1m	W	D.C.	12 MAR 1860	Western
458	Armstrong, Wm.	3m	C	D.C.	23 JUN 1870	Potters Field
513	Arnold, Aquilla, J.P.	75y	W	Amer.	13 MAR 1871	Oak Hill
518	Arnold, Elisabeth	40y	W	Md.	02 MAY 1871	Washington
676	Arnold, Fred H.	1m	W	U.S.	31 MAR 1873	Glenwood
325	Arnold, Hattie B.	3m	W	D.C.	01 JUL 1868	Congressional
185	Arnold, James, hackman	52y	W	Va.	27 JUL 1860	Congressional
359	Arnold, Jay H., child of	Still	W	D.C.	21 NOV 1868	Congressional
061	Arnold, Julia Ann	30y	W	D.C.	05 OCT 1856	Congressional
179	Arnold, Lydia	24y	W		22 MAY 1860	Congressional
445	Arnold, Mary	4y	W		28 MAR 1870	Prospect Hill
313	Arnold, Mary Barbara	77y	W	Ger.	27 MAY 1868	German Catholic
724	Arnold, Mary, fancy goods dealer	51y	W	U.S.	15 OCT 1873	St. Marys
741	Arnold, Mary, housekeeper		W	U.S.	11 JAN 1874	Mt. Olivet
529	Arnold, Rezin, farmer	74y	W	U.S.	27 JUL 1871	Congressional

Page	Name	Age	Race	Birth	Death Date	Burial Ground
536	Arnold, Sarah, servant	69y	W	Md.	18 SEP 1871	Congressional*
550	Arnold, Wm.	8y	W		31 DEC 1871	
335	Arnold, [blank]	10m	C	D.C.	27 JUL 1868	Congressional
364	Arnold[85], Isabella	50y	W	Eng.	29 DEC 1868	Congressional*
399	Arnolds, Emma R.	3y	W		10 JUL 1869	Congressional
466	Aron, Daniel	1y	C	Va.	11 JUL 1870	Holmead
360	Arth, Geo. W.	4y	W	D.C.	30 NOV 1868	Mt. Olivet
420	Arth, Julius	1y	W		07 OCT 1869	Mt. Olivet
347	Arth, Miama	6m	W	D.C.	05 SEP 1868	Congressional
603	Artherton, H., huckster	62y	C	D.C.	07 JUN 1872	Small Pox
228	Arthur, Richard	35y	W	Md.	14 JUL 1866	Alms House
446	Arthur, William	44y	W	N.Y.	17 MAR 1870	Laurel, Md.
308	Arundel, John, child of	Still	W	D.C.	19 APR 1868	Congressional
293	Asbury, William	5m	C	D.C.*	22 MAR 1868	Holy Rood
184	Aschenbach, Henry L.	20d	W	D.C.	08 JUL 1860	Prospect Hill
450	Aschenbach, Sebastian, p. hanger	19y	W	Ger.	23 APR 1870	Prospect Hill
731	Ash, Jacob R., baggage master	65y	W	U.S.	24 NOV 1873	Congressional
331	Ash, James	1y	W	D.C.	17 JUL 1868	Mt. Olivet
046	Ashberry, D.P., farmer	39y	I	Ala.	01 JUN 1856	Congressional
516	Ashdown, Maggie V.	25y	W	D.C.*	05 MAR 1871	Congressional
210	Ashdown, Mary Ann	65y	W	N.Y.	16 JAN 1866	Congressional
506	Ashdown, Wm.	11d	W	D.C.	11 FEB 1871	Congressional
001	Ashley, Harriet	27y		D.C.	18 JAN 1855	
213	Ashley, Thomas K., disc. soldier		W		15 FEB 1866	Pittsburgh, Pa.
452	Ashmore, Mary	95y	W	Md.	12 APR 1870	Washington Asylum
584	Ashton, Alexander	60y	W	Va.	05 MAR 1872	Congressional
261	Ashton, Charles H.	30y	W	Del.	31 MAY 1867	Wilmington, Del.
314	Ashton, Child	Still	W	D.C.	16 MAY 1868	Congressional
398	Ashton, Henry	Still	B		07 JUN 1869	Washington Asylum
394	Ashton, John W.	70y	W	U.S.	19 JUN 1869	Congressional
758	Ashton, Kitty	1y	W	U.S.	08 APR 1874	Oak Hill
374	Ashton, Lela	3m	W		15 FEB 1869	Congressional
046	Ashton, Lillian V.	7m	W	D.C.	19 JUN 1856	Congressional
244	Ashton, Mary V.	17y	W	D.C.*	19 NOV 1866	Congressional
455	Ashton, Sydney	17y	C	Va.	17 MAY 1870	Ebenezer
675	Ashton, Thomas	50y	W	U.S.	27 MAR 1873	Washington Asylum
379	Ashton, Wm., stone polisher	39y	W	Eng.	25 MAR 1869	Congressional
160	Ashton, [blank]	1y	C	D.C.	12 AUG 1859	Holmead
135	Atcheson, Ida	1y	W	D.C.	04 DEC 1858	Congressional
406	Atchinson, Ada	1y	W		19 JUL 1869	Methodist
630	Atchinson, Emma M.	10y	W	U.S.	13 OCT 1872	Small Pox
013	Atchison, A.V.	2y	W	D.C.	14 JUL 1855	Congressional
515	Atchison, Sarah C., housewife	53y	W	Md.	01 MAR 1871	Congressional
617	Atchison, Warren	10m	W	U.S.	22 AUG 1872	Mt. Olivet*
542	Ates, Robert Henry	7m	C		17 OCT 1871	
290	Atkins, Charles	35y	C		15 JAN 1868	Freedmen's Hospital
209	Atkins, David	75y	C		01 JAN 1866	Mt. Olivet
421	Atkins, Edmund, cooper	60y	C	Va.	07 OCT 1869	Young Mens
373	Atkins, Maria	30y	C	Md.	05 JAN 1869	Young Mens
446	Atkins, Ratcliffe, laborer	50y	C	Va.	13 MAR 1870	Holmead
451	Atkinson, Henry	40y	C	Va.	13 APR 1870	Washington Asylum
354	Atkinson, Henry, iron moulder	38y	W	Md.	22 OCT 1868	Congressional
730	Atkinson, Mary E.	1m	W	U.S.	17 NOV 1873	Glenwood
413	Atkinson, Moses, laborer	30y	C	Md.	18 AUG 1869	Washington Asylum
631	Atlee, R.A.	6m	W	U.S.	11 OCT 1872	Mt. Olivet

---

[85] The Register gives surname as "Annall."

District of Columbia Interments (Index to Deaths), 1855-1874

Page	Name	Age	Race	Birth	Death Date	Burial Ground
746	AtLee, Robert W.	5m	W	U.S.	11 FEB 1874	Mt. Olivet
581	Attemus, Geo. C., clerk	20y	W	Pa.	17 FEB 1872	Congressional
140	Atwell, Emeline	16y	W	Va.*	10 FEB 1859	Congressional
587	Atwell, James V., officer	31y	W	Va.	20 MAR 1872	Congressional
355	Auchmoody, Julia A., Mrs.	34y	W	N.Y.	18 OCT 1868	Fairfax Co., Va
124	Auerochs, Louisa	1y	W	D.C.	12 AUG 1858	German
344	Auferd, Paufina	2y	C	D.C.	06 AUG 1868	Western
341	Auffort, George F.	8m	W	D.C.	23 AUG 1868	Congressional
398	Aufman, John K., paper hanger	35y	W	Ger.	05 JUN 1869	Prospect Hill
770	Augherton, Almira J.	39y	W	U.S.	05 JUN 1874	Congressional*
397	August, H.W.	9d	W	Ger.	21 JUN 1869	
098	Augustiffle, Charles W.	26d	W	D.C.	16 DEC 1857	German Catholic
723	Aukward, Horatio F.	1y	W	D.C.	08 OCT 1873	Congressional*
340	Aukward, Nina Elizabeth	10m	W	D.C.	05 AUG 1868	Congressional
506	Aukward, Robt. M.	4m	W	D.C.	09 FEB 1871	Congressional
044	Auld, Lavinia	13y	W		09 MAY 1856	Glenwood
114	Auld, Virginia T.	48y	W	Va.	16 MAY 1858	Glenwood
237	Aulick, Comm., Mrs. [Mary F.]	68y	W		19 SEP 1866	Congressional*
682	Aulick, John Hy., Com. U.S.N.	85y	W	U.S.	27 APR 1873	Congressional*
319	Aulick, Richmond, Com. USA	42y	W	Conn.	08 JUN 1868	Congressional
303	Ausley, Mary		C		25 MAR 1868	Alms House
090	Austin, James G., land agent	64y	W	N.Y.	10 SEP 1857	Glenwood
014	Austin, Maria	2y	W	D.C.	14 JUL 1855	St. Patricks
257	Austin, S.C.	27y	W	Mich.	08 MAR 1867	Mich.
275	Austin, [blank]	2m	W		14 SEP 1867	Mt. Olivet
540	Auth, Lina	3m	W	D.C.	03 OCT 1871	Mt. Olivet
608	Averdon, Mary M.	1y	W	D.C.	01 JUN 1872	Glenwood
103	Avery, George, painter	20y	W	D.C.	28 JAN 1858	Holmead
375	Avery, Hatie C., Mrs.		W		16 FEB 1869	Glenwood
028	Avery, Thos.	36y	W		01 OCT 1855	Congressional
435	Aves, Julia Irene	3y	C		19 JAN 1870	Harmony
682	Avis, Caroline	21y	C	U.S.	22 APR 1873	
483	Awkward, Maggie	24y	W	Md.	04 OCT 1870	Congressional
244	Axtell, Catherine Ann	23y	W	Md.	10 NOV 1866	Annapolis, Md.
609	Ayer, Wm. C.	1y	W	U.S.	14 JUN 1872	Congressional*
299	Aylmer, Robert R., grocer	47y	W	Va.	10 MAR 1868	Holyrood
536	Ayres, Mary E.	1y	W	D.C.	17 SEP 1871	Mt. Olivet

District of Columbia Interments (Index to Deaths), 1855-1874

Page	Name	Age	Race	Birth	Death Date	Burial Ground
B						
588	Babbington, Nancy	76y	W	D.C.	25 MAR 1872	Mt. Olivet
292	Babcock, Benj. B., Dr.	31y	W	U.S.	21 JAN 1868	Congressional
542	Babel, Gustavus	51y	W	Prus.	25 OCT 1871	Prospect Hill
016	Babet, Elizabeth	1y	W	Md.	13 JUL 1855	German Evangelic
628	Babington, Wm., contractor	48y	W	Ire.	04 SEP 1872	
737	Babson, Donn H.	2y	W	U.S.	26 DEC 1873	Congressional
513	Bachman, J.D., clerk	43y	W	Pa.	04 MAR 1871	Lancaster, Pa.
323	Backan, Amey C.	18m	W	Amer.	21 JUL 1868	Mt. Olivet
071	Backman, James E.	10m	C	D.C.	13 FEB 1857	St. Matthews
495	Bacon, Augustus M.	35y	W		20 DEC 1870	Potters Field
157	Bacon, Henry Clay	7y	W	D.C.	11 AUG 1859	Congressional
393	Bacon, Susan	70y	C	Md.	24 MAY 1869	Harmony
636	Bacon, Washington	65y	W	U.S.	21 NOV 1872	Congressional*
249	Baden, Eleanor	69y	W	Md.	08 JAN 1867	Congressional
733	Baden, John, farmer	43y	W	U.S.	18 NOV 1873	
741	Baden, John W., clerk	51y	W	U.S.	10 JAN 1874	Congressional
326	Baden, Mary Louise	3m	W	N.Y.	10 JUL 1868	Congressional
234	Baden, Maude	7m			12 SEP 1866	Congressional
770	Baeschlin, John	74y	W	Switz.	21 JUN 1874	Congressional
587	Baeschlin, Madaline	37y	W	D.C.	22 MAR 1872	Congressional*
488	Bagley, H.Z.	1y	W	D.C.	10 NOV 1870	Congressional
335	Bagman, Samuel	7m	C		17 JUL 1868	
013	Bahrs, Mary	1y	W		02 JUL 1855	Congressional
274	Bailen, Mrs. [Ellen]	63y	W	Ger.	02 SEP 1867	Congressional*
670	Bailey, Anna	1y	C	U.S.	22 FEB 1873	Small Pox
345	Bailey, Annie I.	3y	W	Md.	13 AUG 1868	Mt. Olivet
727	Bailey, Chas. E.	1y	B	U.S.	30 OCT 1873	Young Mens
631	Bailey, Cornelia Y., teacher	20y	W	U.S.	08 OCT 1872	Congressional*
704	Bailey, E.R.	6m	W	D.C.	15 JUL 1873	Congressional*
770	Bailey, Eva M.	7m	W	U.S.	30 JUN 1874	Congressional
520	Bailey, Frederick, blacksmith	20y	W	Amer.	31 MAY 1871	Congressional*
730	Bailey, Goerge	9d	C	U.S.	13 NOV 1873	Cincinnati, Ohio
386	Bailey, Helen V.	10d	W		08 APR 1869	Oak Hill
367	Bailey, James	23y	B	U.S.	12 DEC 1868	Washington Asylum
659	Bailey, Jas. C., brick maker	61y	C	U.S.	14 JAN 1873	Harmony
704	Bailey, John	14d	W	D.C.	26 JUL 1873	Ebenezer
221	Bailey, John, laborer	65y	W	Md.	24 MAY 1866	Mt. Olivet
617	Bailey, John W.	1y	W	U.S.	09 AUG 1872	
521	Bailey, Joseph S.	4m	W	D.C.	01 JUN 1871	Oak Hill
682	Bailey, Julia E.	29y	W	U.S.	29 APR 1873	Congressional
058	Bailey, Julia E.	5y	W	D.C.	28 SEP 1856	Methodist, East
532	Bailey, Laura M.	1y	W	D.C.	16 AUG 1871	Glenwood
287	Bailey, Lewis		C		c.28 DEC 1867	Alms House
217	Bailey, Lillie	10y	C	Md.	06 APR 1866	Union Beneficial
355	Bailey, Lizzie	1d	W	D.C.	07 OCT 1868	Congressional
350	Bailey, Louisa	1m	W	D.C.	28 SEP 1868	Young Mens
251	Bailey, Mary	63y	C	Md.	12 JAN 1867	Beckett's
613	Bailey, Mary A.	14d	C	U.S.	16 JUL 1872	
584	Bailey, Mary E.	21y	W	D.C.	04 MAR 1872	Mt. Olivet
741	Bailey, Mary E.	7d	C	U.S.	10 JAN 1874	Young Mens
069	Bailey, Phinela	25y	W	Va.	29 JAN 1857	Washington Asylum
046	Bailey, Rebecca	27y	W	Md.	16 JUN 1856	Va.
444	Bailey, Robert	31y	W		04 MAR 1870	Congressional
332	Bailey, Robert	7m	W	D.C.	18 JUL 1868	Glenwood
401	Bailey, Robert H.	14d	C	D.C.	25 JUL 1869	Young Mens
515	Bailey, Saml. R.	1y	W	U.S.	01 MAR 1871	Congressional
262	Bailey, Samuel H., painter	23y	W	Va.	19 JUN 1867	Congressional

District of Columbia Interments (Index to Deaths), 1855-1874

Page	Name	Age	Race	Birth	Death Date	Burial Ground
691	Bailey, W.W.	1y	W	U.S.	27 MAY 1873	Congressional
463	Bailey, Walter S.	12y	W	D.C.	13 JUL 1870	Newport, Conn.
336	Bailey, William	1y	C	D.C.	03 AUG 1868	Young Mens
079	Bailey, William B.	6m	W	D.C.	11 JUN 1857	
429	Bailey, Wm. H., bookbinder	35y	W	Pa.	22 DEC 1869	Congressional
684	Bailey, Wm. W., ice dealer	37y	W	U.S.	26 APR 1873	Congressional
714	Bailey, [blank]	3y	W	D.C.	31 AUG 1873	Congressional
330	Bailey, [blank]	10d	C	D.C.	29 JUL 1868	Young Mens
073	Bain, James, marble worker	45y	W	Ire.	10 MAR 1857	Richmond, Va.
741	Bain, John, stone cutter	68y	W	Ire.	10 JAN 1874	Glenwood
606	Baird, Fannie	1y	W	D.C.	15 JUN 1872	Congressional*
694	Baird, John, laborer	73y	C	Va.	10 JUN 1873	Beckett's
053	Baird, Mary Lizzie	6d	W	D.C.	22 AUG 1856	Congressional
475	Baiter, Ione T.	1y	W	D.C.	06 SEP 1870	Congressional
384	Baker, Aaron	65y	C	Md.	31 MAR 1869	Washington Asylum
222	Baker, Butler, carpenter	67y	W	Va.	27 MAY 1866	Congressional
717	Baker, Chas. P., clerk	24y	W	Me.	03 SEP 1873	Portland, Me.
682	Baker, Clarance	40y	W	U.S.	27 APR 1873	Glenwood
430	Baker, Eliza, Mrs.	54y	W	Eng.	01 DEC 1869	Glenwood
355	Baker, Elizabeth	83y	W	W.I.	28 OCT 1868	Congressional
216	Baker, Emily D., clerk	35y	W	N.Y.	25 MAR 1866	N.Y.
281	Baker, Eva Frances	23y	W	N.Y.	18 OCT 1867	Oak Hill
636	Baker, Geo. C., printer	36y	W	U.S.	23 NOV 1872	Congressional*
399	Baker, Grace A.	3y	W		23 JUL 1869	Congressional
395	Baker, Hattie	6m	W	D.C.	19 JUN 1869	Glenwood
250	Baker, Henry	3y	C	D.C.	07 JAN 1867	
734	Baker, Henry J.	43y	W	Ger.	05 DEC 1873	
540	Baker, Jack	1m	W	D.C.	05 OCT 1871	Congressional
778a	Baker, Jacob H., cigar maker	28y	W	U.S.	05 JUL 1874	Congressional
471	Baker, Jane	66y	W	Eng.	11 AUG 1870	Congressional
453	Baker, John A.	10d	W		15 MAY 1870	Congressional
070	Baker, John E.	3y	W	D.C.	01 FEB 1857	Glenwood
036	Baker, John Thos.	8y	W	D.C.	15 FEB 1856	Foundry
603	Baker, Julian	5y	W	D.C.	28 JUN 1872	
712	Baker, Lethie	25y	C	D.C.	16 AUG 1873	Washington Asylum
550	Baker, Lola	1y	W	D.C.	27 DEC 1871	Holy [Rood]
736	Baker, Lottie A.	1y	W	U.S.	20 DEC 1873	
403	Baker, Margaret S.	78y	W		11 JUL 1869	Oak Hill
764	Baker, Mary A., teacher	60y	W	U.S.	06 MAY 1874	Georgetown College
256	Baker, Mary M.	3y	W	D.C.	23 MAR 1867	Glenwood
014	Baker, Penelope	9m	W		11 JUL 1855	Congressional
250	Baker, Quintin	66y	W	Va.	29 JAN 1867	Glenwood
461	Baker, Stephen M., painter	57y	W	Amer.	27 JUL 1870	Congressional
720	Baker, Terener	50y	C	D.C.	26 SEP 1873	Washington Asylum
098	Baker, Thomas, cart man	20y	C	Va.	03 DEC 1857	
292a	Baker, Virginia	35y	W	D.C.*	10 FEB 1868	Holy Rood
606	Baker, Wm. H., clerk	21y	W	D.C.	22 JUN 1872	Campton, N.H.
402	Balback, Arthur, engineer/draught.	45y	W	Ger.	12 JUL 1869	Mt. Olivet
008	Balch, Wm., servant of		C	Va.	05 MAY 1855	Young Mens
719	Baldman, Jno. H., laborer	65y	W	Ger.	17 SEP 1873	Prospect Hill
764	Baldwin, Almon	82y	W	U.S.	03 MAY 1874	Congressional
736	Baldwin, Ann W.	42y	W	U.S.	18 DEC 1873	
228	Baldwin, Annie	3m	W	D.C.	14 JUL 1866	Congressional
779	Baldwin, Annie	9d	W	U.S.	27 JUL 1874	Potters Field
210	Baldwin, E. Gilman	10y	W	D.C.	— JAN 1866	Congressional
148	Baldwin, Elizabeth	24y	W		13 MAY 1859	Kalorama
417	Baldwin, Elizabeth, infant of	Still	C		04 SEP 1869	
547	Baldwin, Geo. D., engraver	61y	W	D.C.	06 DEC 1871	N.Y.

District of Columbia Interments (Index to Deaths), 1855-1874

Page	Name	Age	Race	Birth	Death Date	Burial Ground
070	Baldwin, Henry E.	41y	W	N.H.	12 FEB 1857	N.H.
300	Baldwin, Henry, lawyer	64y	W	Pa.	01 MAR 1868	Kalorama
687	Baldwin, Howard	8y	W	U.S.	03 MAY 1873	Oak Hill
022	Baldwin, James, laborer	55y	W	Ire.	20 AUG 1855	St. Peters
449	Baldwin, Jane, Mrs.	60y	W	La.	20 APR 1870	Congressional
704	Baldwin, Jos.	1½m	C	D.C.	06 JUL 1873	Ebenezer
737	Baldwin, Kingley	5m	C	U.S.	23 DEC 1873	Ebenezer
213	Baldwin, Mrs. [Nellie]	19y	W		27 FEB 1866	Congressional*
154	Baldwin, William	7y	W	U.S.	18 JUL 1859	
425	Balenger, Augustus	Still	W		08 NOV 1869	Congressional
049	Balestin, W.J.	35y	W	La.	05 JUL 1856	Congressional
247	Baley, William T.	60y	W		09 DEC 1866	Congressional
168	Ball, A. Virginia	5y	W	Md.	22 DEC 1859	Baltimore, Md.
005	Ball, Ann C.	38y	W	Va.	02 MAR 1855	Congressional
434	Ball, Benjamin F.	6m	W	D.C.	20 JAN 1870	Congressional
020	Ball, Chs. C.	2m	W	D.C.	09 AUG 1855	Glenwood
079	Ball, D.	67y	W		06 JUN 1857	Fairfax Co., Va.
020	Ball, Ellen	1y	W	D.C.	22 AUG 1855	St. Patricks
318	Ball, Geo. P.	3y	W	Md.	09 JUN 1868	Congressional
007	Ball, Henry W., city surveyor	38y	W		20 APR 1855	Glenwood
419	Ball, Isaac N.	55y	W	Mass.	31 OCT 1869	Congressional
752	Ball, Jerry	5d	C	U.S.	09 MAR 1874	Mt. Olivet
006	Ball, John T., clerk	35y	W		— APR 1855	Congressional*
613	Ball, John W.	1y	W	U.S.	22 JUL 1872	
243	Ball, John William, clerk	17y	W	D.C.	26 NOV 1866	Glenwood
031	Ball, William, wheelwright	51y	W	Va.*	06 DEC 1855	Balls X Roads, Va.
160	Ball, [blank]	1y	W	D.C.	13 AUG 1859	Glenwood
340	Ballanger, A.A.M.	1y	W	D.C.	06 AUG 1868	Congressional
444	Ballanger, George W.	1y	W		11 MAR 1870	Congressional
374	Ballanger, Richd.		W		20 FEB 1869	Congressional
283	Ballenger, Asa	6d	W	D.C.	30 NOV 1867	Alexandria, Va.
439	Ballenger, Clarence L.	6m	W	D.C.	05 FEB 1870	Congressional
636	Ballenger, G.R.	2y	W	U.S.	14 NOV 1872	Congressional*
475	Ballenger, S.F.	26y	W	D.C.	27 SEP 1870	Congressional
439	Ballenger, Wm. F.	4y	W		18 FEB 1870	Congressional
483	Ballinger, Richard		W		22 OCT 1870	Congressional
721	Ballinger, [blank]	4m	W	D.C.	29 SEP 1873	Congressional*
082	Ballman, Henry H.	1y		D.C.	10 JUL 1857	Congressional
681	Ballock, Herbert W.	14y	W	U.S.	19 APR 1873	Glenwood
325	Balmain, Andrew	23y	W	D.C.	12 JUL 1868	Congressional
585	Balmain, Nancy	71y	W	Va.	05 MAR 1872	Congressional
381	Baltey, M.C., Mrs.	27y	W		09 MAR 1869	N.J.
073	Baltimore, A.C.	18y	C	D.C.	02 MAR 1857	Washington Asylum
634	Baltimore, G., servant	22y	C	U.S.	18 OCT 1872	
236	Baltimore, Hannah	45y	C	Md.	29 SEP 1866	Ebenezer
144	Baltimore, [blank]	Still	C	D.C.	22 MAR 1859	Georgetown
280	Balton, [blank]	1y	C	D.C.	09 OCT 1867	
058	Baltza, Alberta F.	8y	W	D.C.	14 SEP 1856	St. Matthews
006	Baltzer, Louisa	57y	W	D.C.*	03 APR 1855	Oak Hill
150	Baltzer, Mary A.	52y	W	D.C.*	02 JUN 1859	Glenwood
113	Baltzier, Jane	12d	C	D.C.	10 MAY 1858	Young Mens
176	Balz, Edward	17y	W	D.C.	14 APR 1860	Glenwood
326	Bamberger, George C.	3y	W	D.C.	13 JUL 1868	Glenwood
402	Bamberger, Henry C., bricklayer	35y	W	Md.	28 JUL 1869	Mt. Olivet
477	Bamberger, John E.	9y	W	D.C.	28 SEP 1870	Glenwood
062	Bamberger, John H.	2y	W	D.C.	09 NOV 1856	Glenwood
359	Bamberger, May Irene	1y	W	D.C.	10 NOV 1868	Glenwood
738	Bandergrift, Mary, housekeeper	45y	W	U.S.	30 DEC 1873	

District of Columbia Interments (Index to Deaths), 1855-1874

Page	Name	Age	Race	Birth	Death Date	Burial Ground
381	Bandon, James P., carpenter	54y	W	Va.	27 MAR 1869	Congressional
731	Banett, Mary	1y	W	U.S.	24 NOV 1873	Prospect Hill
356	Bang, Margaret	1y	W	D.C.	17 OCT 1868	Mt. Olivet
166	Bangs, Wm. Howell, clerk	31y	W	U.S.	03 NOV 1859	Oak Hill*
253	Bank, Jane, infant of	21d	C	D.C.	18 FEB 1867	Ebenezer
465	Banket, Charlotte	11m	C	D.C.	16 JUL 1870	
409	Banket, Sarah	1y	C		15 AUG 1869	Young Mens
373	Bankett, Edward	2m	C	D.C.	31 JAN 1869	
335a	Bankhead, Jas.				29 JUL 1868	Washington Asylum
710	Bankitt, Mary Ella	3y	W	D.C.	04 AUG 1873	
320	Banks, Anderson, laborer	65y	C	Md.	28 JUN 1868	
624	Banks, Anthony	15m	C	U.S.	01 SEP 1872	
534	Banks, Bella	2y	C	D.C.	30 AUG 1871	Union
733	Banks, Betsey, servant	70y	C	U.S.	10 NOV 1873	
532	Banks, Fannie	3y	C	D.C.	10 AUG 1871	
546	Banks, Fanny	80y	C	Va.	23 NOV 1871	Washington
378	Banks, Fanny	6y	C	U.S.	21 FEB 1869	Washington Asylum
708	Banks, George	20y	C	Md.	14 JUL 1873	Washington Asylum
381	Banks, Henry	1m	W		07 MAR 1869	Rock Creek
367	Banks, Jennie	2y	B	D.C.	04 DEC 1868	Washington Asylum
431	Banks, John	10m	C	Va.	24 DEC 1869	
670	Banks, John	8m	C	U.S.	23 FEB 1873	Small Pox
733	Banks, Julia E.	3m	C	U.S.	19 NOV 1873	
671	Banks, Mary	25y	C	U.S.	12 FEB 1873	Small Pox*
441	Banks, Miss	5y	C		26 FEB 1870	Western
446	Banks, Nelly	8m	C		26 MAR 1870	Western
357	Banks, Rosetta	31y	B	Va.	02 OCT 1868	Washington Asylum
127	Banks, Susan	46y	W		06 SEP 1858	Glenwood
342	Banks, Viny	8m	C	D.C.	16 AUG 1868	Union
695	Banks, Willy	6m	C	D.C.	11 JUN 1873	Washington Asylum
752	Banks, Wm. B.	1y	C	U.S.	14 MAR 1874	
714	Bannam, Frank	56y	C	Va.	01 AUG 1873	Holmead
599	Bannerman, Wm. C., clerk	41y	W	U.S.	10 MAY 1872	Glenwood
758	Bannister, George	2y	C	U.S.	21 APR 1874	
758	Bannister, William	2y	C	U.S.	22 APR 1874	Mt. Pleasant
770	Bannvart, Louis O.C.	7m	W	U.S.	21 JUN 1874	Congressional
430	Barbara, Mary E.E.	2y	W		30 DEC 1869	Prospect Hill
682	Barber, Henry, laborer	22y	C	U.S.	24 APR 1873	Brookes, Maj. Ed
387	Barber, J.	3m	C		— APR 1869	Young Mens
605	Barber, John, laborer	20y	C	Md.	23 JUN 1872	Asylum
600	Barber, Lillie A.	11m	C	U.S.	05 MAY 1872	Harmony
309	Barber, Mary Louise	1½d	W	D.C.	26 APR 1868	Glenwood
344	Barber, Orange, dyer	50y	C	Va.	07 AUG 1868	Western
191	Barber, [blank]		W	D.C.	08 OCT 1860	Methodist
345	Barbon, [blank]				30 AUG 1868	
446	Barbor, Frank	15y	C		30 MAR 1870	
110	Barbour, Anna C.	5d	W	D.C.	04 APR 1858	Methodist
245	Barbour, Annette, cook		C		01 NOV 1866	Mt. Olivet
216	Barbour, Elvina N.	28y	W	D.C.	31 MAR 1866	Congressional
220	Barbour, Nellie	1y	W	D.C.	06 MAY 1866	Mt. Olivet
494	Barbour, Thomas	5m	W	U.S.	06 DEC 1870	Mt. Olivet
146	Barbour, [blank]	Still	W	D.C.	02 APR 1859	St. Patricks
583	Barcia, Susan R.	54y	W	Va.	26 FEB 1872	Congressional
218	Barclay, George W., merchant	75y	W	Md.	26 APR 1866	
330	Barclay, Maria	6m	W	D.C.	14 JUL 1868	Oak Hill
292	Barclay, Nannie W.	17y	W	Pa.	09 JAN 1868	Pittsburgh, Pa.
410	Barclay, William	19d	W		22 AUG 1869	Oak Hill
519	Barcley, Dave	26y	C	Md.	17 MAY 1871	Potters Field

District of Columbia Interments (Index to Deaths), 1855-1874

Page	Name	Age	Race	Birth	Death Date	Burial Ground
410	Bares, Elizabeth	42y	W		29 AUG 1869	Methodist
346	Barghausen, Catherine L.	1y	W	D.C.	01 AUG 1868	
680	Bargluff, Mary, housekeeper	52y	W	U.S.	01 APR 1873	Congressional
534	Barker, Ada F.	10m	W	U.S.	28 AUG 1871	Congressional
051	Barker, Amelia	6y	C	D.C.	24 JUL 1856	Washington Asylum
746	Barker, Balinda	31y	W	U.S.	06 FEB 1874	Congressional
098	Barker, Florence B.	11m	W	D.C.	23 DEC 1857	Glenwood
128	Barker, Hayward	9m	C	D.C.	29 SEP 1858	Foundry
057	Barker, Jeannet	25y	W	Md.	06 SEP 1856	Glenwood
449	Barker, John E.	9m	W		01 APR 1870	Congressional
130	Barker, Malinda	40y	W	Va.	13 OCT 1858	Congressional
724	Barker, Matilda	50y	B	Md.	15 OCT 1873	Young Mens
519	Barker, Rebecca D.	43y	W		16 MAY 1871	Congressional*
326	Barker, Rufus	3m	W	Md.	20 JUL 1868	Congressional
689	Barker, Sarah	35y	W	U.S.	24 MAY 1873	Mt. Olivet
770	Barker, Tabbie	10m	W	U.S.	18 JUN 1874	Oak Hill
257	Barker, Will Spencer	12y	C	D.C.	14 MAR 1867	Young Mens
624	Barker, Wm. K.	22m	W	U.S.	09 SEP 1872	
614	Barker, Wm. N.	54y	W	U.S.	03 JUL 1872	
442	Barkett, A., Mrs.	27y	C	Va.	24 FEB 1870	
735	Barkley, Clara	60y	C	U.S.	12 DEC 1873	Washington Asylum
177	Barkley, George	3m	W	D.C.	24 APR 1860	Md.
356	Barks, Mary	4m	C	D.C.	18 OCT 1868	
078	Barler, Jurey	14d		D.C.	27 MAY 1857	
736	Barley, Jerry	41y	C	U.S.	17 DEC 1873	Washington Asylum
632	Barley, Wm. H.H.	42y	W	U.S.	30 OCT 1872	
098	Barlow, James, clerk	50y	W	N.Y.	08 DEC 1857	Congressional
114	Barlow, John, laborer	62y	C	Md.	18 MAY 1858	Foundry
681	Barnacloe, Thomas	9m	W	U.S.	12 APR 1873	Mt. Olivet
269	Barnard, Caroline	1y	W	D.C.	06 AUG 1867	Congressional
544	Barnard, Hansom	2d	W	D.C.	08 NOV 1871	Oak Hill
378	Barnard, Henry D., soldier	42y	W	N.Y.	14 FEB 1869	Mt. Olivet
279	Barnard, Ida	2y	W	D.C.	05 OCT 1867	Oak Hill
465	Barnard, Moses	4m	C	D.C.	20 JUL 1870	Young Mens
044	Barnard, Rachel B.	50y	W	Md.	16 MAY 1856	Oak Hill
617	Barnard, [blank]	1m	W	U.S.	02 AUG 1872	
113	Barneclo, George	1y	W	D.C.	03 MAY 1858	Oak Hill
099	Barnecloe, Catherine	25y	W	D.C.	26 DEC 1857	Oak Hill
085	Barnel, Susa	6m	C	D.C.	31 JUL 1857	German
736	Barnes, B.A., clerk	48y	W	U.S.	19 DEC 1873	Monson, Mass.
220	Barnes, Caroline	15y	C	Md.	01 MAY 1866	
436	Barnes, Charity	80y	C		22 JAN 1870	Washington Asylum
407	Barnes, Charles E.	1y	W		03 AUG 1869	Congressional
289	Barnes, Charlotte	50y	C	Md.	23 JAN 1868	Alms House
327	Barnes, Edward	10m	W	D.C.	22 JUL 1868	Western
530	Barnes, Frank	5m	W	D.C.	31 JUL 1871	Congressional*
125	Barnes, Geo. H.	1y	C	D.C.	19 AUG 1858	Young Mens
340	Barnes, Harriet	1y	W	D.C.	04 AUG 1868	Congressional
705	Barnes, Henry	2m	W		14 JUL 1873	Congressional*
729	Barnes, Henry	54y	C	U.S.	02 NOV 1873	Washington Asylum
542	Barnes, Henry, laborer	60y	C	Md.	17 OCT 1871	Washington
339	Barnes, Henry S., butcher	30y	W	D.C.*	06 AUG 1868	Oak Hill
752	Barnes, Hester	70y	C	U.S.	15 MAR 1874	Washington Asylum
707	Barnes, Jane	Still	C	D.C.	19 JUL 1873	
695	Barnes, Jane	Still	C	D.C.	19 JUN 1873	
695	Barnes, Jane, servant	27y	C	Md.	17 JUN 1873	
370	Barnes, M.	80y	W	Ire.	15 JAN 1869	Mt. Olivet
778a	Barnes, Margaret	86y	W	unk.	15 JUL 1874	Congressional

District of Columbia Interments (Index to Deaths), 1855-1874

Page	Name	Age	Race	Birth	Death Date	Burial Ground
123	Barnes, Martha	1y	W		27 JUL 1858	Ebenezer
023	Barnes, Mary C.	1y		D.C.	11 SEP 1855	St. Patricks
282	Barnes, Mary Jane		C		— NOV 1867	Harmony
705	Barnes, Minnie	4y	W		15 JUL 1873	Congressional*
659	Barnes, Oscar, laborer		C	U.S.	10 JAN 1873	
634	Barnes, Ralph	13m	W	U.S.	13 OCT 1872	Vienna, Va.
711	Barnes, Reberta	25y	C	Va.	12 AUG 1873	Beckett's
711	Barnes, Richard	2y	C	U.S.	09 AUG 1873	Washington Asylum
615	Barnes, Robt.	40y	C	U.S.	03 JUL 1872	
234	Barnes, Saml.	14m	C	D.C.	11 SEP 1866	Young Mens
638	Barnes, Sarah	4y	C	U.S.	22 NOV 1872	
635	Barnes, Sarah	4y	C	U.S.	22 NOV 1872	Small Pox
118	Barnes, Sarah A.	1y	W	D.C.	10 JUN 1858	Congressional
746	Barnes, Susan, servant	50y	C	U.S.	19 FEB 1874	
103	Barnes, Thomas	65y	W	Ire.	01 JAN 1858	St. Patricks
530	Barnes, Walter B.	1y	W	D.C.	28 JUL 1871	Washington
663	Barnes, William	24y	C	U.S.	16 JAN 1873	Small Pox
738	Barnes, Wm. F., brakeman	28y	W	U.S.	04 DEC 1873	
108	Barnes, Wm. H.	6m	C	D.C.	17 MAR 1858	Young Mens
289	Barnett, Thomas, soldier 44th Inf.	53y	W	Eng.	30 JAN 1868	to officers of reg't.
529	Barney, Henrietta	2m	C	D.C.	27 JUL 1871	Young Mens
607	Barney, M.C.	88y	W	Md.	30 JUN 1872	
403	Barnhardt, George F.	12d	W		01 JUL 1869	German
091	Barnhill, Abigail	74y	W	Pa.	18 SEP 1857	Holmead
220	Barnhill, Gabriel, printer	72y	W	Ire.	02 MAY 1866	Holmead
125	Barnhouse, Susan	8y	W	D.C.	26 AUG 1858	Foundry
738	Barnodi, Frank L.	2y	W	U.S.	31 DEC 1873	Congressional
089	Barns, Alice Ann	3y	W	Md.	27 AUG 1857	St. Patricks
643	Barns, Elizabeth	1m	W	U.S.	08 DEC 1872	Mt. Olivet
499	Barns, Elizabeth B.	2y	W	D.C.	08 JAN 1871	Congressional
083	Barns, Mary	10m	W		17 JUL 1857	St. Patricks
274	Barns, [blank]	10m	W	D.C.	15 SEP 1867	
764	Barnswell, Chas.	7d	C	U.S.	18 MAY 1874	Mt. Olivet
418	Barnum, Wm.	80y	C	Va.	23 SEP 1869	
410	Barr, Edward	19y	W		29 AUG 1869	Oak Hill
717	Barr, Ida A.	14m	W	U.S.	01 SEP 1873	
432	Barr, James	22y	C	N.C.	02 DEC 1869	
368	Barr, James	22y	C	N.C.	02 DEC 1868	Freedmens Hospital
664	Barr, James A.	12y	W	U.S.	23 JAN 1873	Small Pox*
086	Barr, Julia J.	2y	W	D.C.	06 AUG 1857	Congressional
586	Barr, Margret E.	6m	W	D.C.	14 MAR 1872	Glenwood
071	Barr, Richard A.	3y	W	D.C.	25 FEB 1857	Oak Hill
174	Barr, Thomas	3y	W	D.C.	13 MAR 1860	Washington Co.
361	Barrett, Agnes May	2y	W		07 NOV 1868	Glenwood
229	Barrett, Edward S., clerk	56y	W	Ver.	18 JUL 1866	Proctorsville, Ver.
271	Barrett, Margaret	30y	W	Ire.	22 AUG 1867	Mt. Olivet
688	Barrett, Margaret J.	37y	W	U.S.	10 MAY 1873	Mt. Olivet
007	Barrett, Mary Ann	3y	W	D.C.	14 MAY 1855	St. Patricks
615	Barrett, Pauline	15y	C	U.S.	28 JUL 1872	
319	Barrett, Robert Henry	11y	W	D.C.	26 JUN 1868	Congressional
391	Barrett, Thomas	3y	W	D.C.	12 MAY 1869	Mt. Olivet
673	Barrett, Thomas, grave digger		W	Ire.	01 MAR 1873	Mt. Olivet
544	Barrett, Wm., baker	40y	W	Ire.	10 NOV 1871	Mt. Olivet
199	Barrett, [blank]	65y	W	Md.	07 FEB 1861	Rock Creek
764	Barrick, Mary A., housekeeper	59y	W	U.S.	20 MAY 1874	Mt. Olivet
388	Barrie, Charlton E.	1y	W		16 APR 1869	Prospect Hill
227	Barroll, Mary E.	1y	W	D.C.	01 JUL 1866	Glenwood
758	Barron, Daniel R., engineer	48y	W	U.S.	22 APR 1874	Mt. Olivet

Page	Name	Age	Race	Birth	Death Date	Burial Ground
298	Barron, James	63y	W	Ire.	11 FEB 1868	Mt. Olivet
125	Barron, James, bricklayer	63y	W	Md.	24 AUG 1858	Congressional*
347	Barron, Laura	9m	W		13 SEP 1868	Congressional
090	Barron, Sarah Agnes	1y	W	D.C.	11 SEP 1857	St. Patricks
519	Barrow, Dasie	1y	W	D.C.	15 MAY 1871	Congressional*
616b	Barrow, Henry, carpenter	73y	W	U.S.	12 JUL 1872	Congressional
252	Barrow, J. Denwood, banker	46y	W		09 FEB 1867	Glenwood
213	Barrow, John Henry	1y	W	D.C.	26 FEB 1866	Glenwood
770	Barrow, Margaret Susan	5m	W	U.S.	20 JUN 1874	Oak Hill
719	Barry, Ann, Mrs.	60y	W	Ire.	20 SEP 1873	Mt. Olivet*
734	Barry, Catharine	40y	W	Scot.	02 DEC 1873	
169	Barry, Daniel P., famer	32y	W	D.C.	13 JAN 1860	Congressional
419	Barry, David, farmer	58y	W	D.C.	23 OCT 1869	Congressional
253	Barry, Edmund, late capt. CA	48y	W	D.C.	01 FEB 1867	Congressional
770	Barry, Ellen	1d	W	U.S.	21 JUN 1874	Mt. Olivet
758	Barry, Garrett, Sr., sculptor	65y	W	Ire.	25 APR 1874	Boston, Mass.
417	Barry, George, butcher	26y	W		24 SEP 1869	Mt. Olivet
177	Barry, James C.		W	D.C.	20 APR 1860	Congressional
046	Barry, James, druggist	40y	W	Pa.	19 JUN 1856	Congressional
764	Barry, Johanna, housekeeper	70y	W	U.S.	07 MAY 1874	
026	Barry, John F.	23y	W		08 OCT 1855	St. Matthews
541	Barry, John H.	1y	W	D.C.	08 OCT 1871	Mt. Olivet
444	Barry, Maria, Mrs.	73y	W	Ire.	22 MAR 1870	Congressional
729	Barry, Mary C.	3y	W	U.S.	10 NOV 1873	Mt. Olivet
731	Barry, Michael, paver	23y	W	Ire.	19 NOV 1873	Mt. Olivet
380	Barry, Morris	54y	W	Ire.	23 MAR 1869	Holyrood
770	Barry, Patrick	9m	W	U.S.	29 JUN 1874	Mt. Olivet
028	Barry, Patrick	1y	W		11 OCT 1855	St. Patricks
087	Barry, Robert T., Dr., surgeon	48y	W	D.C.	14 AUG 1857	St. Peters
393	Barry, Washington	36y	W	D.C.	08 MAY 1869	Washington Asylum
229	Barry, William, printer	29y	W	Ire.	21 JUL 1866	Mt. Olivet
182	Barry, [blank]	8d	W	D.C.	30 JUN 1860	St. Patricks
176	Barsell, O.K., clerk	53y	W	Del.	10 APR 1860	Congressional*
724	Barstow, Mary Eloise	21d	W	D.C.	12 OCT 1873	Congressional
673	Bart, Paul, cook	66y	W	Fra.	02 MAR 1873	Mt. Olivet
606	Bartell, Frank, bartender	42y	W	D.C.	10 JUN 1872	Congressional*
169	Bartelo, Geo. Wm. J.A.	2y	W	Md.	01 JAN 1860	Prospect Hill
283	Bartely, William, gardener	66y	W	Prus.	28 NOV 1867	Prospect Hill
067	Barter, [blank]		W		28 DEC 1856	Methodist
236	Barth, Annie V.	9m	W	D.C.	28 SEP 1866	Mt. Olivet
442	Barth, Francis	70y	W	Ger.	13 FEB 1870	Washington Asylum
778a	Barth, William, Supt. B.P.W.	66y	W	U.S.	12 JUL 1874	
527	Bartham, Jennie Y.		W	D.C.	10 JUL 1871	Washington
179	Barthell, John	8m	W	D.C.	14 MAY 1860	Prospect Hill
396	Barthels, Antonia	3y	W	D.C.	07 JUN 1869	Prospect Hill
320	Barthol, William	5y	W	Va.	01 JUN 1868	Prospect Hill
764	Bartholomew, Geo. A.	8y	W	U.S.	19 MAY 1874	St. Marys
528	Bartlett, Louisa M.	45y	W	D.C.	16 JUL 1871	Glenwood
128	Bartlett, Mary	6m	W	D.C.	19 SEP 1858	Methodist
027	Bartlett, Sarah F.	25y	W	D.C.*	23 OCT 1855	Glenwood
359	Bartlett, Thomas	63y	W	Mass.	11 NOV 1868	Congressional
262	Bartlett, Walter, blockmaker	53y	W	Md.	06 JUN 1867	Congressional
622	Bartlette, Geo. W.	19m	W	U.S.	09 AUG 1872	
308	Bartley, William, laborer	27y	W	U.S.	16 APR 1868	Congressional
465	Barton, Eva Ann	1y	C		17 JUL 1870	Ebenezer
629	Barton, L.F.	35y	W	U.S.	25 OCT 1872	
409	Barton, Mary	8m	W	D.C.	02 AUG 1869	St. Patricks
123	Barton, Seth W.	16y	W	Mass.	29 JUL 1858	Foundry

District of Columbia Interments (Index to Deaths), 1855-1874

Page	Name	Age	Race	Birth	Death Date	Burial Ground
296	Barton, William	45y	C	Md.	23 FEB 1868	Freedmen's Hospital
615	Barton, Wm.	75y	C	U.S.	22 JUL 1872	
296	Baruch, John W.	15y	C	Md.	12 FEB 1868	Freedmen's Hospital
383	Barwald, Bernard	1y	W	D.C.*	25 MAR 1869	Washington Hebrew
284	Bary, Richard	73y	W	Md.	07 NOV 1867	
523	Bash, Hannah	45y	C	Md.	18 JUN 1871	Holmead
387	Bash, Hannohen	38y	W	Ger.	10 APR 1869	Washington Hebrew
758	Bassett, A.V.	43y	W	U.S.	25 APR 1874	Congressional
675	Bassett, Cora Ann	2y	C	U.S.	25 MAR 1873	
688	Bassett, David, clerk	52y	W	U.S.	15 MAY 1873	Glenwood
379	Bassett, Effie E., Mrs.	74y	W	Ire.	24 MAR 1869	Congressional
045	Bassitt, Sidney D., mechanic	30y	W	D.C.	24 MAY 1856	Congressional
535	Basswood, Charlotte	78y	C	Va.	03 SEP 1871	Washington
144	Bastable, Emma Maria	1y	W	D.C.	23 MAR 1859	Mt. Olivet
207	Bastable, Mary Rebecca	9y	W	Md.	26 JUL 1862	Mt. Olivet
714	Batching, John, bar keeper	23y	W	Ger.	31 AUG 1873	Baltimore, Md.
249	Bateman, A.		C		05 JAN 1867	Young Mens
015	Bateman, Charles	7y	W		01 JUL 1855	Baltimore, Md.
059	Bateman, Edward	25y	C	D.C.	29 SEP 1856	Young Mens
387	Bateman, Emaline, laundress	60y	C	D.C.	06 APR 1869	
273	Bates, Amelia	28y	W	N.J.	28 SEP 1867	Newark, N.J.
484	Bates, Ann Louisa	59y	W		13 OCT 1870	Congressional
006	Bates, Edda	6y	W		14 APR 1855	Congressional
484	Bates, Elizabeth A.	59y	W	Amer.	21 OCT 1870	Congressional
425	Bates, Emma Richardson	7y	W	N.J.	01 NOV 1869	Congressional
658	Bates, Eugene	6m	W	U.S.	08 JAN 1873	Glenwood
425	Bates, Frank	4y	W	D.C.	10 NOV 1869	Congressional
659	Bates, Geo. H.	1y	W	U.S.	11 JAN 1873	Congressional
304	Bates, Grace S.	11m	W	D.C.	06 MAR 1868	Congressional
168	Bates, H. Clay	14y	W	D.C.	29 DEC 1859	Congressional
260	Bates, Henry, moulder	55y	W		23 MAY 1867	Congressional
006	Bates, Jessy	4y	W		01 APR 1855	Congressional
695	Bates, John	1y	C	D.C.	18 JUN 1873	Ebenezer
303	Bates, Josephine	4m	W	D.C.	28 MAR 1868	Congressional
616	Bates, Mary	1m	W	U.S.	18 JUL 1872	
143	Bates, Mary, servant	22y	C	Va.	12 MAR 1859	Foundry
628	Bates, Millard [corrected]	10y	W	U.S.	04 SEP 1872	
182	Bates, Richard, laborer	50y	C	Va.	27 JUN 1860	Harmony
555	Bates, Sarah F.	28y	W	U.S.	28 JAN 1872	Congressional
752	Bates, [blank]	4d	C	U.S.	13 MAR 1874	
005	Bates, [blank]	15m	W		25 MAR 1855	Congressional
274	Bates, [blank]	1d	W	D.C.	11 SEP 1867	Congressional*
250	Bathan, Jane		W		25 JAN 1867	Congressional
545	Batrow, D.	1y			12 NOV 1871	
338	Batson, Frank	14y	C		27 AUG 1868	Washington Asylum
306	Batson, Henry	3y	C	D.C.	14 APR 1868	Young Mens
173	Battersby, Mrs.	82y	W	Eng.	25 FEB 1860	Congressional*
427	Battles, Andrew	2y	C		02 NOV 1869	Washington Asylum
464	Batto, Rosie	4y	W	D.C.	30 JUL 1870	German Catholic
660	Baudon, Clora	4m	C	U.S.	18 JAN 1873	
255	Bauer, Anton, wheelwright	33y	W	Ger.	13 MAR 1867	German Catholic
587	Bauer, Martin, baker	31y	W	Ger.	20 MAR 1872	Prospect Hill
057	Bauer, Mary	9m	W	D.C.	04 SEP 1856	German
430	Bauer, Mary C.	1m	W		26 DEC 1869	
465	Baum, Alice	1y	C	D.C.	28 JUL 1870	Ebenezer
225	Baum, Andrew Johnson	2m	W	D.C.	24 JUN 1866	Glenwood
156	Baum, Charles, carpenter	47y	W	D.C.	09 JUL 1859	Glenwood
622	Baum, Chas. L.	54y	W	U.S.	24 AUG 1872	

Page	Name	Age	Race	Birth	Death Date	Burial Ground
582	Baum, Leonard	65y	W	D.C.	22 FEB 1872	
393	Baum, Rebecca, infant of	7m	C		13 MAY 1869	Ebenezer
224	Bauman, Caroline	30y	W	Ger.	16 JUN 1866	Alms House
296	Bauman, Mary Emilie Eliz.	28d	W	D.C.	13 FEB 1868	Prospect Hill
040	Baumann, Charles	1y	W	D.C.	13 MAR 1856	German
456	Baumann, Mary	11m	W	D.C.	08 JUN 1870	Prospect Hill
395	Baumen, Catherina	45y	W	Ger.	30 JUN 1869	Mt. Olivet
154	Baurer, C.A.	1y	W	D.C.	20 JUL 1859	German Catholic
019	Bauthman, Martha	27y	W	D.C.*	15 AUG 1855	Washington Asylum
179	Bawn, Mary		C	Md.	10 MAY 1860	Washington Asylum
610	Baxter, Blanche	1y	W	U.S.	13 JUL 1872	
740	Baxter, Charles	2y	W	U.S.	04 JAN 1874	Congressional*
726	Baxter, Elizabeth	6y	W	U.S.	28 OCT 1873	Methodist
553	Baxter, Geo. M., cabinet maker	44y	W	U.S.	11 JAN 1872	Glenwood
670	Baxter, George	43y	C	U.S.	17 FEB 1873	Small Pox
529	Baxter, Ida	5m	W	D.C.	28 JUL 1871	Congressional*
689	Baxter, Jno. Ira	15y	W	U.S.	26 MAY 1873	Glenwood
726	Baxter, Lewis A., carpenter	33y	B	U.S.	23 OCT 1873	Alexandria, Va.
361	Baxter, Louis R.	10m	C	D.C.	24 NOV 1868	Young Mens
301	Baxter, Portus, gentleman	61y	W	Ver.	04 MAR 1868	Oak Hill
334	Baxter, Wm. A.	9m	W	D.C.	12 JUL 1868	German Catholic
169	Baxter, [blank]	Still	W	D.C.	17 JAN 1860	Methodist
327	Bayet, Maggie	1y	C		28 JUL 1868	Western
016	Bayhaw, [blank]	9m	W	D.C.	13 JUL 1855	German
218	Bayington, Harriet	29y	W	Ire.	16 APR 1866	Mt. Olivet
746	Bayless, Chas. E.	1y	W	U.S.	20 FEB 1874	Congressional
606	Bayless, John R.	3y	W	D.C.	12 JUN 1872	Congressional*
273	Bayley, Margaret	1y	W	D.C.	19 SEP 1867	Congressional
455	Bayley, Margaret	17y	C	Va.	14 MAY 1870	Young Mens
778a	Bayliss, Buckner, real estate	68y	W	U.S.	09 JUL 1874	Mt. Olivet
778a	Bayliss, Edward S.	3m	W	U.S.	09 JUL 1874	Congressional*
531	Bayliss, Wm.	1y	C	D.C.	08 AUG 1871	Unknown
714	Baylor, Daniel	unk.	C	U.S.	31 AUG 1873	Beckett's
625	Baylor, Sarah	19y	C	U.S.	06 SEP 1872	
364	Bayly, Benjamin S., merchant	68y	W	Md.	04 DEC 1868	Congressional
603	Bayly, Laura C.	6m	W	D.C.	02 JUN 1872	Glenwood
604	Bayly, Laura C.	6m	W	D.C.	02 JUN 1872	Glenwood
681	Bayly, Mary	32y	W	U.S.	18 APR 1873	Glenwood
080	Bayman, Mary F.	2y	W	D.C.	17 JUN 1857	St. Patricks
726	Bayne, Harriet	70y	W	U.S.	25 OCT 1873	Congressional*
388	Bayne, John D., printer	32y	W	Scot.	12 APR 1869	Glenwood
621	Bayne, Lydia	39y	C	U.S.	07 AUG 1872	
447	Bayne, Samuel	1y	C	D.C.	30 MAR 1870	Washington Asylum
098	Beach, Amanda	5y	W	Va.	19 DEC 1857	Glenwood
663	Beach, Levy	70y	W	U.S.	04 JAN 1873	Small Pox*
582	Beach, Mrs., housekeeper	87y	W	D.C.	20 FEB 1872	
204	Beach, Silas W., tinner	29y	W	D.C.	23 JUN 1861	Glenwood
482	Beacham, John, waterman	60y	W	Va.	29 OCT 1870	Va.
084	Beack, William E., tinner	32y	W		26 JUL 1857	Glenwood
342	Beadle, Robert Allan	15y	W	D.C.	31 AUG 1868	Congressional
262	Beagle, Edward	12y	W	D.C.	04 JUN 1867	Congressional
172	Beahan, Michael I.	58y	W		14 FEB 1860	
519	Beal, Eugene	10m	W	D.C.	15 MAY 1871	Congressional
302	Beal, William	28y	W	Va.	17 MAR 1868	Alms House
139	Beale, Elizabeth		W		24 JAN 1859	Congressional
223	Beale, Robert M., lawyer	26y	W	D.C.	08 JUN 1866	Congressional
180	Beale, Sarah	10y	C	D.C.	29 MAY 1860	
493	Beale, Truxton D., clerk	55y	W	D.C.	25 DEC 1870	Congressional

District of Columbia Interments (Index to Deaths), 1855-1874

Page	Name	Age	Race	Birth	Death Date	Burial Ground
143	Bealer, Henry W., cartman	23y	W		10 MAR 1859	St. Patricks
267	Beall, Ada Rebecca	10y	W	D.C.	23 JUL 1867	Congressional
051	Beall, Alice	5m	W	D.C.	26 JUL 1856	Glenwood
587	Beall, Amy O.	1y	W	D.C.	22 MAR 1872	Congressional*
320	Beall, Ann E.	4m	W	D.C.	16 JUN 1868	Glenwood
035	Beall, Elana	63y	W	Md.	28 FEB 1856	Glenwood
083	Beall, Eliza	55y	W	D.C.	20 JUL 1857	Holmead
270	Beall, Elizabeth A.	43y	W	D.C.	04 AUG 1867	Oak Hill
707	Beall, Ernest	16m	W	D.C.	17 JUL 1873	
030	Beall, G.W.	37y	W		13 NOV 1855	Glenwood
038	Beall, Ida M.	5m	W	D.C.	28 MAR 1856	Congressional
113	Beall, James	10y	C	D.C.	02 MAY 1858	Harmony
770	Beall, Jane E.	32y	W	U.S.	21 JUN 1874	Glenwood
218	Beall, John L.	2y	W	D.C.	19 APR 1866	Glenwood
553	Beall, John, laborer	50y	C	Va.	09 JAN 1872	Washington
101	Beall, L.	25y	C	D.C.	— JAN 1858	
060	Beall, Louisa	4y	C	D.C.	13 OCT 1856	Harmony
524	Beall, Margaret				21 JUN 1871	Mt. Zion
033	Beall, Martha E.	3m	W	D.C.	04 JAN 1856	Glenwood
115	Beall, Mary A.	56y	W		07 JUN 1858	Oak Hill
041	Beall, Sarah J.	31y	W	D.C.	10 APR 1856	Glenwood
642	Beall, Virginia H.	28y	W	U.S.	03 DEC 1872	Oak Hill
521	Beall, Willie Alpho.	6m	W	Amer.	08 JUN 1871	Glenwood
770	Beam, Saml.	2y	W	U.S.	29 JUN 1874	Congressional
496	Beaman, Chas. M.	6m	W	D.C.	24 DEC 1870	Baltimore, Md.
091	Beams, Mary	57y	C	Va.	15 SEP 1857	St. Patricks
550	Bean, Ann	79y	W	Md.	29 DEC 1871	Congressional*
054	Bean, Colby	2y	W		15 AUG 1856	Congressional
169	Bean, Colmore	70y	W	U.S.	05 JAN 1860	Methodist
054	Bean, Emmeline	30y	W	Md.	06 AUG 1856	Congressional
473	Bean, Francis	10d	C	D.C.	07 AUG 1870	Holmead
642	Bean, Henry	11y	C	U.S.	22 DEC 1872	Small Pox
546	Bean, Hester Ann	27y	W	N.J.	24 NOV 1871	
260	Bean, John W., hack driver	38y	W	Md.	08 MAY 1867	Congressional
624	Bean, Thos. E., butcher	31y	W	U.S.	21 SEP 1872	Congressional*
308	Bean, William Seaman, clerk	45y	W	N.Y.	21 APR 1868	Congressional
024	Bean, Wm. S.	33y	W	Pa.	17 SEP 1855	Congressional
437	Beans, Geo. Ed.	4m	C	D.C.	30 JAN 1870	Washington Asylum
640	Beans, Henry, Sr.	60y	C	U.S.	24 DEC 1872	Small Pox*
640	Beans, James R.	11y	C	U.S.	20 DEC 1872	Small Pox*
531	Beans, Mary E.	8m	C	D.C.	04 AUG 1871	Unknown
615	Bear, Wm.	7y	C	U.S.	14 JUL 1872	
142	Beardsley, James S.	2y	W	D.C.	26 FEB 1859	Congressional*
023	Beark, Ellen	9m	W	D.C.	13 SEP 1855	St. Patricks
300	Bearsley, Fred.	45y	C	Va.	24 MAR 1868	Alms House
354	Bearsley, Henry, miner	36y	W	Eng.	29 OCT 1868	Congressional
096	Beasant, Mary Anna	41y	W	Eng.	02 NOV 1857	Congressional
113	Beasly, George, hackman	41y	W	Eng.	04 MAY 1858	Congressional
338	Beattie, Mary Elizabeth	8m	W		12 AUG 1868	Georgetown
309	Beattie, Walter L.	2m	W	D.C.	06 APR 1868	Presbyterian
341	Beatty, John A., printer	54y	W	Ohio	19 AUG 1868	Congressional
070	Beaumann, Mary Louisa	1y	W	U.S.	02 FEB 1857	German
033	Beaumont, Jno., hatter	41y	W	Eng.	13 JAN 1856	Asylum
623	Beauregard, Ann M.	3m	W	U.S.	24 JUL 1872	
622	Beavers, Jas. H.	23m	W	U.S.	04 AUG 1872	
247	Beavin, Louisa	18y	C	Va.	12 DEC 1866	Young Mens
758	Becher, Adolph, druggist	72y	W	Ger.	03 APR 1874	
746	Bechtold, Cuntus, baker	38y	W	Ger.	02 FEB 1874	St. Marys

District of Columbia Interments (Index to Deaths), 1855-1874

Page	Name	Age	Race	Birth	Death Date	Burial Ground
585	Beck, A.	4m	W	D.C.	09 MAR 1872	Prospect Hill
058	Beck, Augustus	2m	W		15 SEP 1856	German
088	Beck, Elizabeth O.	63y	W	Scot.	24 AUG 1857	Congressional
519	Beck, Ella	3y	W	D.C.	16 MAY 1871	Congressional*
536	Beck, Emiline	40y	W	Pa.	17 SEP 1871	Congressional*
316	Beck, James S.	10m	C	D.C.	25 MAY 1868	Harmony
396	Beck, L.	4m	W	D.C.	16 JUN 1869	Prospect Hill
671	Beck, Mary C.	24y	W	U.S.	16 FEB 1873	Small Pox*
063	Beck, Matilda, seamstress	27y	W	Va.	09 NOV 1856	Washington Asylum
184	Beck, Rezin, teacher	63y	W	U.S.	05 JUL 1860	Congressional
255	Beckelf, Elizabeth	50y	W	Ger.	20 MAR 1867	Congressional
041	Beckenhan, Johanah	8m	W	D.C.	07 APR 1856	St. Peters
487	Becker, Ann	13y	W	D.C.	04 NOV 1870	Mt. Olivet
087	Becker, Christina	3m	C		10 AUG 1857	Young Mens
114	Becker, George A.	5y	W	D.C.	25 MAY 1858	St. Peters
553	Becker, John G.	1y	W	D.C.	12 JAN 1872	Prospect Hill
062	Beckert, Francis	10m	W		04 NOV 1856	German
159	Beckert, George, plasterer	58y	W	Ger.	29 AUG 1859	Congressional
354	Beckert, John	49y	W	Ger.	13 OCT 1868	Congressional
166	Beckert, Rosa	1y	W	D.C.	29 NOV 1859	Prospect Hill
036	Becket, Charles H.	9m	C		15 FEB 1856	Harmony
319	Becket, Frances	1y	C	D.C.	29 JUN 1868	Young Mens
452	Becket, Hezekiah	2y	C		26 APR 1870	
353	Becket, J.H.	49y	C	S.C.	01 SEP 1868	Freedmen's Hospital
055	Becket, Mary Ellen	1y	C	D.C.	22 AUG 1856	Foundry
310	Becket, Romeo	6y	C		c.13 APR 1868	Mt. Olivet
343	Beckett, Andrew	7m	C	D.C.	17 AUG 1868	
069	Beckett, [blank]	2y	C		20 JAN 1857	Young Mens
308	Beckley, Julia	1y	W	D.C.	17 APR 1868	Congressional
764	Beckman, Sarah	49y	C	U.S.	19 MAY 1874	Mt. Olivet
727	Beckner, L.A.	35y	W	U.S.	20 OCT 1873	Oak Hill
332	Beckwith, Oscar L.	5m	W	D.C.	22 JUL 1868	
202	Beckwith, Sarah, washerwoman	37y	C	D.C.	27 APR 1861	Mt. Olivet
441	Beckworth, Julian	70y	C	Va.	26 FEB 1870	Young Mens
366	Bede, Jane	62y	W	D.C.	06 DEC 1868	Congressional*
062	Beebet, Frank, messenger	29y	W	D.C.	16 NOV 1856	Holmead
482	Beech, Adelide	5y	W	D.C.	07 OCT 1870	Mt. Olivet
696	Beedle, Leanora	81y	W	D.C.	18 JUN 1873	
675	Beem, Melvina	25y	W	U.S.	21 MAR 1873	Methodist
662	Been, Harrison	31y	C	U.S.	04 JAN 1873	Small Pox
677	Been, Lizzie	7y	C	U.S.	23 MAR 1873	Small Pox
147	Beener, Charles	62y	C		25 APR 1859	Mt. Olivet
471	Beer, Konrad	45y	W		07 AUG 1870	Prospect Hill
240	Beers, George H., clerk	22y	W	Md.	27 OCT 1866	Baltimore, Md.
175	Beers, Millie A.	57y	W	U.S.	31 MAR 1860	Congressional
364	Behrend, Sophia, housewife	22y	W	N.Y.	30 DEC 1868	Congressional
680	Behrens, John E., cigar maker		W	Ger.	10 APR 1873	Prospect Hill
344	Behrens, Margaretha	58y	W	Ger.	10 AUG 1868	Prospect Hill
241	Behrens, Mrs.		W		16 OCT 1866	Alms House
275	Beinletch, Henry V.	9m	W	D.C.	19 SEP 1867	Glenwood
382	Belfour, Louise	38y	C	Va.	31 MAR 1869	Young Mens
495	Belker, Sarah	72y	W	Md.	14 DEC 1870	Glenwood
496	Belknap, Carita T.	31y	W	Ky.	29 DEC 1870	Oak Hill
475	Bell, Alexander	5y	W		16 SEP 1870	Congressional
173	Bell, Alexander, merchant	60y	W	Tenn.	21 FEB 1860	
063	Bell, Alice	1y	C	D.C.	21 NOV 1856	
065	Bell, Ann	48y	W	D.C.	06 DEC 1856	Glenwood
465	Bell, Ann P.	60y	W	Md.	11 JUL 1870	Congressional

District of Columbia Interments (Index to Deaths), 1855-1874

Page	Name	Age	Race	Birth	Death Date	Burial Ground
584	Bell, Anna	25y	C	U.S.	01 MAR 1872	
687	Bell, Anna	76y	C	U.S.	03 MAY 1873	Congressional
586	Bell, Anna	22y	C	U.S.	12 MAR 1872	Mt. Zion
543	Bell, Anna	7m	C	D.C.	29 OCT 1871	Unknown
082	Bell, Benj. F., carpenter	21y	W	Va.	02 JUL 1857	Glenwood
608	Bell, Benja.	36y	W		20 JUN 1872	
475	Bell, Blanch	1m	W	Amer.	27 SEP 1870	Congressional
610	Bell, Caroline	40y	C		03 JUN 1867	Young Mens
078	Bell, Caroline, washerwoman	40y	C	Md.	28 MAY 1857	
589	Bell, Charlotte	57y	W	N.Y.	29 MAR 1872	
049	Bell, Chas.	37y	W	Ger.	04 JUL 1856	German
665	Bell, Chas.	7y	C	U.S.	26 JAN 1873	Small Pox*
330	Bell, Clara	4m	C	D.C.	08 JUL 1868	Young Mens
779	Bell, Eliza	50y	C	U.S.	31 JUL 1874	Harmony
124	Bell, Eliza Jane	4y	C	D.C.	10 AUG 1858	Young Mens
416	Bell, Elizabeth	1y	C		08 SEP 1869	
035	Bell, Elizabeth	45y	C	Md.	25 FEB 1856	St. Patricks
070	Bell, Elizabeth A.	37y	W	N.Y.	11 FEB 1857	Congressional
006	Bell, Eugene	10m	C		03 APR 1855	Foundry
542	Bell, Eva Moss	8y	W	U.S.	23 OCT 1871	Glenwood
741	Bell, Ezra, clerk	36y	W	U.S.	06 JAN 1874	N.H.
764	Bell, Frank E.	5m	W	U.S.	26 MAY 1874	Oak Hill
174	Bell, Geo. Washington	23d	W	D.C.	11 MAR 1860	Washington Asylum
529	Bell, George W.	5m	C	D.C.	23 JUL 1871	
703	Bell, Henrietta	20y	C	D.C.	16 JUL 1873	Mt. Pleasant
623	Bell, Isaac	1y	C	U.S.	04 AUG 1872	Mt. Zion
381	Bell, James M., bdg. hse. kpr.	58y	W	N.C.	14 MAR 1869	Harmony
631	Bell, Jane	4y	C	U.S.	03 OCT 1872	
372	Bell, Jane	4y	C	D.C.	22 JAN 1869	Young Mens
373	Bell, Jane	25y	C	Va.	15 JAN 1869	Young Mens
164	Bell, Jas. Marcellus	1y	C	D.C.	11 OCT 1859	Harmony
323	Bell, John	5m	B	D.C.	05 JUL 1868	Harmony
664	Bell, John	7m	C	U.S.	17 JAN 1873	Small Pox*
133	Bell, John	25y	C		19 NOV 1858	Young Mens
428	Bell, John	1d	C		23 NOV 1869	Young Mens
527	Bell, Joseph	47y	W	Ala.	12 JUL 1871	Washington
658	Bell, Laura B.	75y	W	U.S.	01 JAN 1873	Haverhill, N.H.
387	Bell, Lellitia	4m	C	D.C.	17 APR 1869	Harmony
231	Bell, Margaret	25y	C	Md.	18 AUG 1866	Methodist
413	Bell, Margaret	75y	C	Va.	18 AUG 1869	Washington Asylum
673	Bell, Maria	60y	C	U.S.	10 MAR 1873	Holmead
062	Bell, Mary	1y	C	D.C.	18 NOV 1856	Harmony
436	Bell, Mary Virginia	59y	C	Va.	27 JAN 1870	Harmony
645	Bell, Moses	84y	C	U.S.	25 DEC 1872	Washington Asylum
152	Bell, Mrs.	103y	W	Md.	05 JUN 1859	Country
726	Bell, Rebecca	39y	B	U.S.	24 OCT 1873	
541	Bell, Richd.		C	Md.	08 OCT 1871	Washington
125	Bell, Robert	3y	C		24 AUG 1858	Foundry
399	Bell, Robert Townsend	3d	W	D.C.	06 JUL 1869	Congressional
079	Bell, Robert W., waiter	24y	C	Md.	13 JUN 1857	Freeman Union
247	Bell, Saml. Campbell	5y	W	D.C.	16 DEC 1866	Congressional
412	Bell, Samuel	70y	C	Md.	22 AUG 1869	Harmony
582	Bell, Sarah E.	30y	C	D.C.	24 FEB 1872	Ebenezer
152	Bell, Simon	80y	C	D.C.	28 JUN 1859	Van Ness'
596	Bell, Sophie	76y	C	Md.	07 APR 1872	
226	Bell, Susan	6m	C	D.C.	27 JUN 1866	Moore's
729	Bell, Susan, housewife	37y	C	U.S.	04 NOV 1873	
475	Bell, Thomas C., tailor	53y	W	Scot.	06 SEP 1870	Congressional

Page	Name	Age	Race	Birth	Death Date	Burial Ground
088	Bell, Virginia	7d	C		20 AUG 1857	Young Mens
674	Bell, Willie T.	7m	W	U.S.	14 MAR 1873	Congressional
670	Bell, Wm.	6m	C	U.S.	09 FEB 1873	Small Pox*
214	Bell, [blank]		C		07 MAR 1866	Alms House
518	Bell, [blank]	2m	W	D.C.	12 MAY 1871	Congressional
585	Bell, [blank]	2y	W	D.C.	08 MAR 1872	Glenwood
096	Bell, [blank]	6d	W	D.C.	03 NOV 1857	St. Matthews
208	Bell, [blank]		C		29 JUL 1862	Western
713	Beller, Pauline S.	6m	W	D.C.	26 AUG 1873	Mt. Pleasant
346	Bellfield, John A.		C		08 AUG 1868	Freedmen's Hospital
597	Bellford, Lizzie	3y	C	U.S.	16 MAY 1872	Small Pox
706	Bellis, Clinton	8m	C	D.C.	29 JUL 1873	Ebenezer
420	Belt, Alfred C., carpenter	52y	W		14 OCT 1869	Oak Hill
020	Belt, Chas. E.	9m	C	D.C.	09 AUG 1855	
546	Belt, Christine	1d	W	D.C.	24 NOV 1871	Mt. Olivet*
317	Belt, Ed. Col.	2y	W	D.C.	29 JUN 1868	Oak Hill
331	Belt, Eliza	21d	C	D.C.	27 JUL 1868	Freedmen's Hospital
738	Belt, Eliza C.	6y	W	U.S.	30 DEC 1873	Oak Hill
326	Belt, Emma Nailor	1y	W	D.C.	11 JUL 1868	Mt. Olivet*
415	Belt, H., infant of	Still	W		02 SEP 1869	Glenwood
557	Belt, Henrietta	80y	C	Md.	03 FEB 1872	Holy Rood
707	Belt, Henry G.	2m	C	D.C.	19 JUL 1873	Mt. Pleasant
385	Belt, Kate, domestic	14y	C	Md.	05 APR 1869	Mt. Olivet
396	Belt, Mary F.	1y	W	D.C.	19 JUN 1869	Oak Hill
745	Belt, Thomas	5m	C	U.S.	07 JAN 1874	
395	Belt, Thomas McGill	3m	W	D.C.	— JUN 1869	Glenwood
580	Bemans, I.C.	1m	W	D.C.	10 FEB 1872	Congressional*
528	Benda, Carl W.C.	8m	W	D.C.	c.21 JUL 1871	Congressional
231	Bender, Anna E.	1y	C	D.C.	11 AUG 1866	Young Mens
779	Bender, Mary M.	11m	W	U.S.	27 JUL 1874	Mt. Olivet
283	Bendz, Emma Belinda	6h	W	D.C.	01 NOV 1867	Congressional
636	Benette, Alex., saloon keeper	58y	W	U.S.	20 NOV 1872	
288	Benezet, H.	54y	W	Pa.	22 DEC 1867	Congressional
588	Benham, Edw. M.	1m	W	D.C.	25 MAR 1872	Congressional*
252	Benhard, Rosae	2y	W	D.C.	23 FEB 1867	
121	Benin, Geo. L.	18d	W	D.C.	14 JUL 1858	Congressional
381	Benisch, John	46y	W	Hung.	15 MAR 1869	Mt. Olivet
177	Benjamin, Fanny	22y	W	Va.	26 APR 1860	Washington Asylum
688	Benjamin, Leonard H.	7m	W	U.S.	21 MAY 1873	
397	Benman, Joseph C.	2m	D		24 JUN 1869	
634	Benner, J.R., clerk	40y	W	U.S.	01 OCT 1872	Congressional*
499	Bennet, Ann	3y	W	Pa.	24 JAN 1871	Congressional
425	Bennett, Andrew R., boat captain	40y	W		12 NOV 1869	Congressional
090	Bennett, Benj. F.	4y	C	D.C.	08 SEP 1857	Holmead
166	Bennett, Ellie	3y	W	D.C.	29 NOV 1859	Glenwood
029	Bennett, James	1m	W	D.C.	16 NOV 1855	Foundry
253	Bennett, Julia Ann	3y	C	D.C.	24 FEB 1867	Holmead
740	Bennett, M.H.	2y	W	U.S.	01 JAN 1874	Graceland
239	Bennett, Margaret		W	Ire.	02 OCT 1866	Alms House
187	Bennett, Margaret	4m	W	D.C.	06 AUG 1860	Western
474	Bennett, Mary	14d	C		07 AUG 1870	Washington Asylum
622	Bennett, Peter, turner	18y	W	Ire.	26 AUG 1872	
489	Bennett, Wm. W., clerk	29y	W	N.Y.	02 NOV 1870	
493	Bennigan, [blank]	2y	W	D.C.	31 DEC 1870	Mt. Olivet
591	Bennum, Lewis E.	4m	C	D.C.	19 APR 1872	Small Pox
132	Bensen, Eliza	65y	W		16 NOV 1858	Glenwood
371	Benser, George	6y	W		17 JAN 1869	Baltimore, Md.
370	Benser, Martha W.	3y	W		26 JAN 1869	Baltimore, Md.

Page	Name	Age	Race	Birth	Death Date	Burial Ground
402	Bensinger, Simon, butcher	47y	W	Ger.	26 JUL 1869	Hebrew
014	Benson, B., Mrs., child of		W		24 JUL 1855	
430	Benson, Hepburn S., prop. Nat. Hotel	55y	W	Del.	22 DEC 1869	Philadelphia, Pa.
014	Benson, Ida Ella	15m	W	D.C.	07 JUL 1855	Pr. Geo. Co., Md.
331	Benson, Margaret	1y	C	D.C.	31 JUL 1868	
481	Benson, Wm. B.	84y	W	Md.	21 OCT 1870	Glenwood
478	Bent, Mary	70y	C	Va.	27 SEP 1870	Young Mens
235	Bentley, Lilie C.	30y	W		15 SEP 1866	Oak Hill
457	Bentley, Nettie	4m	W		08 JUN 1870	Mt. Olivet
022	Bently, Florence [of Thomas]	9m	W	D.C.	21 AUG 1855	Congressional
084	Bently, John P.	8y	W		26 JUL 1857	Oak Hill
397	Bentney, Saml. W.	5m	B	Amer.	07 JUN 1869	
063	Bentoli, Luigi, soldier	25y	W	Italy	02 NOV 1856	Congressional
253	Benton, Christina	63y	W	Ger.	27 FEB 1867	Alms House
778a	Benton, Clara	9m	W	U.S.	02 JUL 1874	Mt. Olivet
111	Benton, Thomas H., lawyer	76y	W	N.C.	10 APR 1858	St. Louis, Mo.
582	Bentzly, Goldie	28d	W	D.C.	19 FEB 1872	
146	Bequin, Mary Florence	3y	W	D.C.	03 APR 1859	Mt. Olivet
024	Berdine, Geo.	2y	W	D.C.	09 SEP 1855	Congressional
612	Berens, Henry	1y	W	U.S.	29 JUL 1872	
150	Bergeman, Charles	3y	W	D.C.	07 JUN 1859	Glenwood
020	Bergenhanzen, John	21d	W		27 AUG 1855	German Catholic
627	Berger, Carl H.	59y	W	Ger.	02 SEP 1872	German
265	Berger, Viola A.	3y	W	N.Y.	13 JUL 1867	N.Y.
346	Bergliez, Lewis	1y	W	D.C.	30 AUG 1868	German Catholic
095	Bergman, Bernard	70y	W	Ger.	31 OCT 1857	German Catholic
355	Bergman, Charles C.	11m	W	D.C.	28 OCT 1868	Glenwood
664	Bergman, Conrad	21y	W	U.S.	24 JAN 1873	Small Pox*
396	Bergman, Emelia (twin)	27d	W	D.C.	26 JUN 1869	Prospect Hill
078	Bergman, Gehard, carpenter	72y	W	Ger.	21 MAY 1857	German
038	Bergman, Henry, laborer	43y	W	Ger.	28 MAR 1856	German
543	Bergman, Peter, wheelwright	80y	W	Pa.	29 OCT 1871	Unknown
155	Bergman, Robert	4m	W	D.C.	30 JUL 1859	Holmead
396	Bergman, William (twin)	25d	W	D.C.	24 JUN 1869	Prospect Hill
267	Bergman, [blank]		W		— JUL 1867	Glenwood
526	Bergstun, Maria	78y	W	D.C.	01 JUL 1871	Glenwood
387	Berhard, Mrs.	81y	W		28 APR 1869	Prospect Hill
532	Berkley, Aleck	11y	C	Va.	12 AUG 1871	
096	Berkley, Chloe	83y	W	Md.	15 NOV 1857	Methodist
719	Berkley, Edwd.	1½m	W	D.C.	16 SEP 1873	
737	Berkley, Elizabeth	77y	W	U.S.	28 DEC 1873	Congressional
717	Berkley, Geo.	1m	W	D.C.	06 SEP 1873	Congressional
640	Berkley, Ida May	6m	W	U.S.	19 DEC 1872	Small Pox*
169	Berkley, Jas. Wesley, butcher	18y	W	D.C.	11 JAN 1860	Methodist
341	Berkley, Julian Ernest	10m	W	D.C.	24 AUG 1868	Congressional
347	Berkley, Minnie M.	1y	W		24 SEP 1868	Congressional
664	Berkley, Rachell	7y	C	U.S.	20 JAN 1873	Small Pox*
663	Berkley, Rose	6y	C	U.S.	04 JAN 1873	Small Pox*
185	Berkly, James	35y	W	Md.	25 JUL 1860	Washington Asylum
309	Bernard, Caroline A.	2y	W	U.S.	17 APR 1868	Mt. Olivet
519	Bernard, Edgar	5y	W	U.S.	21 MAY 1871	Prospect Hill
764	Bernard, Harriet J.	65y	W	U.S.	23 MAY 1874	Adrian, Mich.
290	Bernard, Ursula	31y	W	Switz.	28 JAN 1868	German Catholic
160	Berney, Woodburn	9m	W	D.C.	05 AUG 1859	
674	Bernhard, Mary	4m	W	U.S.	12 MAR 1873	Prospect Hill
464	Bernhardt, Louisa Maria	4y	W	D.C.	11 JUL 1870	Prospect Hill
212	Bernsford, F.	22y	W	Va.	13 FEB 1866	Richmond, Va.
736	Berret, Harry A., clerk	27y	W	U.S.	20 DEC 1873	Congressional

Page	Name	Age	Race	Birth	Death Date	Burial Ground
285	Berry, A.F., tinner	40y	W	Md.	16 DEC 1867	Congressional
153	Berry, Ann	51y	W	Va.	07 JUL 1859	Glenwood
379	Berry, Ann B.	52y	W	Va.	01 MAR 1869	Congressional
015	Berry, Charles	2y	W	Md.	05 JUL 1855	Congressional
671	Berry, Clara	2y	W	U.S.	25 FEB 1873	Small Pox*
534	Berry, E. Alexander		C	D.C.	27 AUG 1871	Holmead
050	Berry, Eliza, servant	50y	C	Md.	10 JUL 1856	Md.
231	Berry, Eliza V.	8m	W		14 AUG 1866	Harmony
013	Berry, Emma	1y	W	D.C.	02 JUL 1855	
645	Berry, Florence	22m	C	U.S.	29 DEC 1872	
497	Berry, Fredk.	43y	W	Ger.	03 DEC 1870	Prospect Hill
726	Berry, Isabella	39y	B	U.S.	24 OCT 1873	Beckett's
236	Berry, Jane L.	49y	W	Md.	28 SEP 1866	Piscataway, Md.
662	Berry, Jefferson	55y	C	U.S.	05 JAN 1873	Small Pox
272	Berry, Jennie	60y	C		15 AUG 1867	Freedmen's Bureau
677	Berry, John	2y	C	U.S.	08 MAR 1873	Congressional
290	Berry, John	30y	C		23 JAN 1868	Freedmen's Hospital
185	Berry, John	51y	W	Ger.	22 JUL 1860	German Catholic
070	Berry, Laura V.	8m	W	D.C.	11 FEB 1857	Methodist
391	Berry, Maria, Mrs.	29y	W	Me.	01 MAY 1869	Bath, Me.
061	Berry, Martha A.	13y	C	Va.	22 OCT 1856	Colored, Georgetown
658	Berry, Mary	4y	W	U.S.	02 JAN 1873	Mt. Olivet
010	Berry, Mary A.	14m	W	D.C.	20 JUN 1855	St. Patricks
014	Berry, Mary, Mrs., child of		W		29 JUL 1855	St. Patricks
527	Berry, Michael R., bookkeeper	75y	W	Md.	07 JUL 1871	Congressional
161	Berry, Mrs.	41y	W	Ger.	— SEP 1859	Prospect Hill
057	Berry, Sarah	44y	W	Md.	09 SEP 1856	Glenwood
638	Berry, Thornton	80y	C	U.S.	06 NOV 1872	Washington Asylum
548	Berry, Vive J.	10y	C	D.C.	08 DEC 1871	
164	Berry, William	45y	W	Va.	06 OCT 1859	Washington Asylum
074	Berry, William, engineer	34y	W	Md.	27 MAR 1857	Methodist
604	Berry, Wm.	11y	C	D.C.	19 JUN 1872	Ebenezer
213	Berry, [blank]	1y	W		20 FEB 1866	
337	Berryman, Maria	1y	C	U.S.	13 AUG 1868	Washington Asylum
314	Berryman, Mary A.		C		01 MAY 1868	Alms House
638	Bertin, Wm.	36y	C	U.S.	19 NOV 1872	Washington Asylum
582	Bessler, Charles	7m	W	D.C.	22 FEB 1872	German/Glenwood
517	Best, Bernard	5m	W	D.C.	30 APR 1871	Glenwood
590	Best, Bernard	5m	W	D.C.	24 APR 1872	Glenwood
601	Bestor, George, contractor	66y	W	U.S.	12 MAY 1872	Ill.
733	Bestor, Witman C., banker	51y	W	U.S.	14 NOV 1873	
448	Betout, Eugene Jos., hair dresser	49y	W	Fra.	20 MAR 1870	Mt. Olivet
545	Bets, John M.	34y	W	Ger.	16 NOV 1871	Prospect Hill
638	Better, Ann	15m	C	U.S.	05 NOV 1872	
336	Better, Wm. T.	5m	C	D.C.	15 AUG 1868	Ebenezer
690	Betters, Alice	6y	C	U.S.	28 MAY 1873	Small Pox
620	Betters, Mary S.	2y	W	U.S.	26 AUG 1872	
689	Betthold, M.V.	8m	W	U.S.	29 MAY 1873	St. Marys
444	Betts, Rosa Adella	1y	W		17 MAR 1870	Congressional
604	Bettz, L.W.	6m	W	D.C.	05 JUN 1872	Prospect Hill
430	Betz, Anna Maria	7m	W	D.C.	12 DEC 1869	Prospect Hill
477	Betz, Barly	1y	W	D.C.	15 SEP 1870	Prospect Hill
588	Betz, Fred. W.	1y	W	D.C.	24 MAR 1872	Prospect Hill
434	Betz, Louisa Cathrina	3y	W	D.C.	07 JAN 1870	Prospect Hill
778a	Betz, Rosa Emilia	8m	W	U.S.	22 JUL 1874	Prospect Hill
430	Betz, Susan Chr.	5y	W	D.C.	20 DEC 1869	Prospect Hill
464	Beuchart, Josephine	23y	W	Ger.	23 JUL 1870	St. Marys
516	Bevan, Mary	80y	W	Wales	09 MAR 1871	Congressional

District of Columbia Interments (Index to Deaths), 1855-1874

Page	Name	Age	Race	Birth	Death Date	Burial Ground
506	Bevans, Adele V.	6y	W	D.C.	28 FEB 1871	Congressional
239	Bevans, Catherine E.	32y	W	D.C.	28 OCT 1866	Congressional
039	Bevans, Delilah	28y	W	Md.	02 MAR 1856	St. Peters
744	Bevans, Margaret E.	3m	W	U.S.	29 JAN 1874	Congressional
641	Bevealy, Henry	11y	C	U.S.	11 DEC 1872	Small Pox
404	Beverige, Mary Jane	3y	W	Pa.	11 JUL 1869	Baltimore, Md.
495	Beverly, Harris	80y	C	Va.	26 DEC 1870	Potters Field
296	Beverly, Isabella	3d	C		12 FEB 1868	Alms House
295	Beverly, Isabella, domestic	35y	C	Va.	14 FEB 1868	Alms House
615	Beverly, Martha	20y	C	U.S.	16 JUL 1872	
442	Beverly, Nancy	80y	C	Va.	28 FEB 1870	Washington Asylum
496	Beverly, Wm., laborer	38y	C	Va.	01 DEC 1870	Beckett's
320	Beyman, Minna	2y	W		16 JUN 1868	Prospect Hill
177	Bias, Ann, domestic	40y	C	D.C.	18 APR 1860	Harmony
147	Bias, Eleather, washerwoman	61y	C		29 APR 1859	Georgetown
098	Bibby, Monroe L., child of		W	D.C.	11 DEC 1857	Glenwood
444	Bichter, Mary C.	8m	W		01 MAR 1870	Congressional
429	Bickford, E.E.	20y	W		22 DEC 1869	Congressional
681	Bickford, Mary H.	6y	W	U.S.	14 APR 1873	Rehrersburg, Pa.
165	Bicksler, Mary	34y	W	Va.	10 NOV 1859	Va.
414	Bickster, Leroy	21d	W	D.C.	29 SEP 1869	Congressional
018	Biddle, Ada B.	10m	W	D.C.	17 AUG 1855	Beltsville, Md.
046	Biddle, George E.	2y	W	D.C.	16 JUN 1856	Country
250	Bielaski, Victor E., clerk	20y	W	Ill.	24 JAN 1867	Congressional
222	Biesching, Henrietta Dorothea	8m	W	D.C.	31 MAY 1866	Prospect Hill
135	Bigg, Alvert A.	4m	W	D.C.	07 DEC 1858	Western
478	Biggan, Jeremiah, grocer	43y	W	Ire.	29 SEP 1870	Mt. Olivet
467	Biggs, Albert D.	8m	W	D.C.	31 JUL 1870	Western
778a	Biggs, Catherine E.	11m	W	unk.	16 JUL 1874	
382	Biggs, Daniel	36y	C	N.Y.	09 MAR 1869	Harmony
440	Biggs, John, infant of	4d	W		25 FEB 1870	
068	Biggs, John T.			Md.	06 JAN 1857	Congressional
488	Biggs, Rebecca	40y	W	D.C.	05 NOV 1870	Congressional
080	Biggs, [blank]	8m	W	D.C.	17 JUN 1857	Methodist
120	Biggs, [blank]	6d	W	D.C.	03 JUL 1858	St. Matthews
057	Billenger, Elizabeth	55y	W	Md.	02 SEP 1856	Congressional
197	Billings, Augustus	4y	C	D.C.	14 JAN 1861	Colored
387	Billis, Rebecca	1y	W	Md.	16 APR 1869	Annapolis, Md.
341	Billup, Wm. Franklin	9h	W		27 AUG 1868	Congressional
323	Binckley, Francis Macartney	21d	W	D.C.	09 JUL 1868	Oak Hill
660	Binger, Anna O., cook	70y	W	Ger.	19 JAN 1873	Mt. Olivet
274	Bingham, Anna P.	1m	W	D.C.	11 SEP 1867	Mt. Olivet
144	Bingham, Jno. Harry, clerk	78y	W	Mass.	31 MAR 1859	
618	Bingham, John, Jr.	3m	W	U.S.	22 AUG 1872	Mt. Olivet
408	Bingham, Mary B.	9m	W		14 AUG 1869	Glenwood
538	Binkley, Indiana	5y	W	U.S.	29 SEP 1871	Methodist
675	Birch, Eva	14d	W	U.S.	27 MAR 1873	Congressional
062	Birch, Frederick, laborer	70y	C	Md.	01 NOV 1856	Foundry
531	Birch, Geo. A., plasterer	56y		D.C.	08 AUG 1871	Unknown
492	Birch, George F.	1m	W		03 DEC 1870	Congressional
093	Birch, Henry	2y		D.C.	15 OCT 1857	
493	Birch, James H.	67y	W	Va.	20 DEC 1870	Congressional
061	Birch, Jane	46y	W	Va.	31 OCT 1856	Va.
094	Birch, John	1y	W	D.C.	20 OCT 1857	
053	Birch, Mary	27y	W	Md.	13 AUG 1856	Methodist
492	Birch, Sarah	34y	W	D.C.	07 DEC 1870	Congressional
094	Birch, [blank]	3d	W	D.C.	23 OCT 1857	Congressional
482	Birch, [blank]	Still	W	Amer.	19 OCT 1870	Va.

Page	Name	Age	Race	Birth	Death Date	Burial Ground
730	Birchhead, Rebecca	84y	W	U.S.	11 NOV 1873	Congressional
046	Bird, Ann M.	65y	W	D.C.	04 JUN 1856	Methodist
630	Bird, Dora	7y	C	U.S.	27 OCT 1872	
253	Bird, Frederick	1m	W	D.C.	08 FEB 1867	Glenwood
717	Bird, Jno. H.	21d	W	D.C.	03 SEP 1873	Glenwood
311	Bird, Mary		C		c.15 APR 1868	Alms House
006	Bird, William, carpenter	56y	W	Va.	27 APR 1855	Methodist, West
012	Bird, Wm.	10y	W	D.C.	05 JUN 1855	14th Street
032	Bird, [blank], Mr.	60y	W		20 DEC 1855	Young Mens
041	Birnie, Robt. E., clerk	22y	W		07 APR 1856	Oak Hill
731	Birth, E.J.		W	U.S.	19 NOV 1873	Congressional
347	Bischoff, Jane, cook	22y	W	Eng.	09 SEP 1868	Congressional
464	Bishof, Aloysius	6m	W	D.C.	28 JUL 1870	German Catholic
303	Bishop, Charles, child of	P.B.	W	D.C.	07 MAR 1868	Congressional
740	Bishop, Eliza V.	4y	W	U.S.	02 JAN 1874	Congressional*
149	Bishop, Frances H.	7m	W	D.C.	18 MAY 1859	Congressional
519	Bishop, Joane	79y	W	Amer.	22 MAY 1871	Glenwood
680	Bishop, Lewis B.	4y	W	U.S.	03 APR 1873	Congressional
060	Bishop, Luke	9m	W	D.C.	12 OCT 1856	Congressional
339	Bishop, Maria	38y	W	D.C.	11 AUG 1868	Glenwood
060	Bishop, Mark	9m	W	D.C.	17 OCT 1856	Congressional
184	Bishop, Mary M.	5m	W	D.C.	08 JUL 1860	Glenwood
076	Bishop, Mary, seamstress	54y	W	Ire.	28 APR 1857	Holmead
033	Bishop, Mathew	2m	W	D.C.	27 JAN 1856	Congressional
529	Bishop, Raymond	1m	C	D.C.	27 JUL 1871	Oak Hill
764	Bishop, William, Dr.	56y	W	U.S.	26 MAY 1874	Strausburg, Pa.
547	Bishops, Henry	19y	W	D.C.	05 DEC 1871	St. Marys
711	Bissler, Matilda	20y	W	D.C.	11 AUG 1873	St. Marys
439	Black, C.W., instrument maker	25y	W	D.C.	26 FEB 1870	Congressional
661	Black, Charles	9m	W	U.S.	25 JAN 1873	
235	Black, Cornelia	45y	C		13 SEP 1866	Ebenezer
622a	Black, Elizabeth	40y	W	Ire.	13 AUG 1872	
329	Black, Emma A.	5m	W	D.C.	13 JUL 1868	Oak Hill
170	Black, James A., huckster	35y	W	Me.	24 JAN 1860	Congressional
144	Black, Joseph S.	1y	W		20 MAR 1859	Congressional*
066	Black, M.	27y	W	D.C.	25 DEC 1856	Foundry
515	Black, Moses, laborer	80y	C	Md.	13 MAR 1871	Ebenezer
282	Black, Owen, storekeeper	35y	W	Ire.	08 NOV 1867	Mt. Olivet
011	Black, [blank]	38y	C	Md.	02 JUN 1855	
291	Blackburn, Mary, domestic	45y	C	D.C.	27 JAN 1868	Colored
671	Blackburn, Wm.	7y	C	U.S.	24 FEB 1873	Small Pox*
459	Blackby, Mary Ann	3y	C	U.S.	07 JUN 1870	
373	Blackey, Douglass	2y	C		21 JAN 1869	Holmead
288	Blackfan, Catherine C.	41y	W	N.J.	07 DEC 1867	Trenton, N.J.
778a	Blackford, Ernest	28d	W	U.S.	04 JUL 1874	Oak Hill
589	Blackford, Grace	1y	W	D.C.	26 MAR 1872	
589	Blackford, John W.	3y	W	D.C.	20 MAR 1872	
609	Blackford, Katie	1m	W	U.S.	11 JUN 1872	
295	Blackie, Emily	26y	W	D.C.	09 FEB 1868	Congressional
770	Blacklock, Geo. McC.	8m	W	U.S.	09 JUN 1874	Alexandria, Va.
118	Blackstock, Mary A.R.	1m	W	D.C.	18 JUN 1858	St. Patricks
182	Blackston, Rebecca	104y	C	Va.	25 JUN 1860	Mt. Olivet
479	Blackston, Sarah J.	14y	C	D.C.	28 SEP 1870	Washington Asylum
030	Blackstone, Alfred	22y	C	D.C.	23 NOV 1855	Harmony
777a	Blackstone, Anna	14d	C	U.S.	15 JUN 1874	
770	Blackstone, Anna	15d	C	U.S.	15 JUN 1874	Poors Grounds
458	Blackwell, Fannie	6m	C	D.C.	29 JUN 1870	Potters Field
601	Blackwell, L.M., clerk	29y	W	U.S.	10 MAY 1872	Congressional

District of Columbia Interments (Index to Deaths), 1855-1874

Page	Name	Age	Race	Birth	Death Date	Burial Ground
592	Blackwell, Liberna	1y	C	U.S.	08 APR 1872	
683	Blackwell, Louisa	4y	C	U.S.	12 APR 1873	
674	Blackwell, Mary	36y	C	U.S.	15 MAR 1873	
710	Blackwell, Mary E.	20y	C	Va.	08 AUG 1873	Beckett's
330	Blackwell, Moses	5m	C	D.C.	24 JUL 1868	
010	Blackwell, Mrs.		W		25 JUN 1855	West
619	Blackwell, Saml.	55y	C	U.S.	21 AUG 1872	Young Mens
630	Blackwell, Thos.	25y	C	U.S.	22 OCT 1872	Small Pox
764	Blackwell, Victoria	6y	C	U.S.	24 MAY 1874	
301	Blackwell, Winnie, servant	24y	C	Va.	30 MAR 1868	Young Mens
740	Bladen, Effie A.	1y	W	U.S.	03 JAN 1874	Congressional
133	Bladen, Sarah Ann	3y	W	D.C.	23 NOV 1858	Congressional
456	Blagden, Danl.	5m	C		24 JUN 1870	
308	Blain, Fannie S.	25y	W	N.Y.	18 APR 1868	Congressional
673	Blair, Jno. T., blacksmith	60y	C	U.S.	04 MAR 1873	
479	Blair, Lutz L.	1y	W	D.C.	27 SEP 1870	Congressional
490	Blair, Mary M.	9d	C	D.C.	04 NOV 1870	Ebenezer
280	Blake, Alice	4y	C		09 OCT 1867	Freedmen's Hospital
630	Blake, Ann L.	35y	C	U.S.	27 OCT 1872	Small Pox
232	Blake, Bridget	2y	W	D.C.	22 AUG 1866	Mt. Olivet
779	Blake, Catharine	29y	W	U.S.	30 JUL 1874	Presbyterian
541	Blake, Catharine, housewife	35y	W	D.C.	08 OCT 1871	Congressional*
228	Blake, Franklin	6m	W	D.C.	11 JUL 1866	Congressional
668	Blake, Mary E.	48y	W		17 FEB 1873	Mt. Olivet
395	Blake, Michael	16y	W	D.C.	30 JUN 1869	Mt. Olivet
122	Blake, [blank]	1d	W	D.C.	20 JUL 1858	Rock Creek
638	Blaking, Lillian S.	12y	W	U.S.	05 NOV 1872	Congressional
282	Blakney, Jessie May	3y	W	D.C.	10 NOV 1867	Congressional
744	Blan, Cornelia	22y	W	U.S.	31 JAN 1874	Congressional*
217	Blan, J. Augustus, stair builder	37y	W	Fra.	12 APR 1866	Glenwood
337	Blanchard, Anna F.	1y	C	D.C.	05 AUG 1868	Washington Asylum
513	Blanchard, Anne	86y	W	Eng.	11 MAR 1871	Oak Hill
029	Blanchard, J.A.	3y		D.C.	07 NOV 1855	
246	Bland, Alice	6m	C	D.C.	26 DEC 1866	Beckett's
144	Bland, Annie	12y	W	D.C.	31 MAR 1859	Congressional
029	Bland, Delilah	64y	W	Md.	02 NOV 1855	Congressional
144	Bland, Elizabeth M.	5y	W	D.C.	25 MAR 1859	Congressional
527	Bland, Hezekiah	6y	C	D.C.	11 JUL 1871	Ebenezer
683	Bland, John	13y	C	U.S.	12 APR 1873	Small Pox
273	Bland, Mary	2m	C		06 SEP 1867	Freedmen's Bureau
342	Bland, Mary	35y	C		23 AUG 1868	Young Mens
519	Blandford, Emma	2y	W		20 MAY 1871	Congressional*
617	Blanton, Henrietta	49y	C	U.S.	29 AUG 1872	
777a	Blencherd, Adam, tailor	22y	W	Ger.	04 JUN 1874	
179	Blendingham, Elizabeth	32y	W	Va.	28 MAY 1860	Washington Asylum
034	Blick, G., laborer	56y	W	Ger.	06 JAN 1856	German
725	Bligh, James, stone cutter	50y	W	Ire.	17 OCT 1873	Mt. Olivet
726	Bligh, Margaret	42y	W	Ire.	30 OCT 1873	Mt. Olivet
230	Bligh, Mr., child of	4m			13 JUL 1866	Young Mens
209	Blinthorn, John, Mrs.	28y	W	D.C.	09 JAN 1866	Mt. Olivet
158	Bliss, Samuel	5m	W	D.C.	18 AUG 1859	Glenwood
492	Blitts, Anna	7d	W	D.C.	11 DEC 1870	Prospect Hill
523	Block, W.	19y	W	Ger.	14 JUN 1871	Congressional
125	Bloecher, John, tailor	58y	W	Ger.	25 AUG 1858	Glenwood
386	Bloomer, Elizabeth	60y	W	Ger.	21 APR 1869	Congressional
724	Bloomer, Laura Va.	1y	W	D.C.	10 OCT 1873	Congressional
547	Bloor, Catharine M., lady	34y	W		01 DEC 1871	Glenwood
230	Blow, C.	4d	W		24 JUL 1866	Oak Hill

District of Columbia Interments (Index to Deaths), 1855-1874

Page	Name	Age	Race	Birth	Death Date	Burial Ground
553	Blow, Rosa, servant	36y	C	Va.	08 JAN 1872	Washington
383	Blue, Franalia	1y	C		31 MAR 1869	Harmony
588	Blum, Blanshett	8m	W	U.S.	27 MAR 1872	N.Y.
439	Blumer, John H.	2y	W	D.C.	12 FEB 1870	Congressional
042	Blunden, Patrick, laborer	50y	W	Ire.	19 APR 1856	St. Patricks
778a	Blundon, Mary E.	26y	W	U.S.	21 JUL 1874	Oak Hill
532	Boans, George E.	8m		D.C.	10 AUG 1871	
541	Boardman, Almira	26y	W	Md.	13 OCT 1871	Congressional*
106	Boarman, Charlotte	40y	W	Md.	04 FEB 1858	Methodist
518	Boarman, Joseph	4m	C	D.C.*	06 MAY 1871	Holy Rood
494	Boarman, Joseph	4y	W	D.C.	31 DEC 1870	Mt. Olivet
084	Boarman, Mary J., servant	26y	C	Md.	27 JUL 1857	St. Matthews
484	Boast, Frank	45y	W	D.C.	20 OCT 1870	Potters Field
221	Boch, John	9y	W		17 MAY 1866	
487	Bock, Sophie, lady	15y	W	Ger.	27 NOV 1870	Congressional
362	Boddy, Elizabeth Ann	9d	W	D.C.	10 NOV 1868	Holmead
522	Bodely, Joshua	5m	C		13 JUN 1871	Union
127	Bodien, Eliza Jane	1y	W	D.C.	07 SEP 1858	Glenwood
340	Bodine, Nellie L.	1y	W	D.C.	07 AUG 1868	Congressional
616	Body, Cora	9m	C	U.S.	05 JUL 1872	
673	Boecheres, Joseph	10d	W	U.S.	04 MAR 1873	Mt. Olivet
005	Boegler, Josephine	10y	W		24 APR 1855	
137	Boemer, Josephine	1y	W	N.Y.	21 JAN 1859	German
726	Boernstein, Fredk., M.D.	37y	W	U.S.	28 OCT 1873	Congressional
270	Boernstein, Ida	5m	W	D.C.	02 AUG 1867	Congressional
351	Boettcher, Margaret, Mrs.	41y	W	Ger.	06 SEP 1868	Prospect Hill
122	Boff, Elizabeth D.	1y	W	D.C.	22 JUL 1858	Congressional
622	Boffy, Cornelius	3y	W	U.S.	22 AUG 1872	
488	Bogan, Joseph Borrows	Still	W	D.C.	23 NOV 1870	Va.
554	Bogan, V.P.	4y	W	D.C.	17 JAN 1872	Glenwood
375	Bogert, George, paper hanger	19y	W	Md.	05 FEB 1869	Factory vault
247	Boggs, Cornelius M.	3m	W	D.C.	28 DEC 1866	Glenwood/Graceland
275	Bohanna, Martha		C		17 SEP 1867	Young Mens
583	Bohannan, H.W.	1y	W	D.C.	25 FEB 1872	Congressional*
592	Bohlayer, John, blacksmith	60y	W	Ger.	21 APR 1872	Congressional*
226	Bohrer, Abrhaam Kenvale	15y	W	D.C.	24 JUN 1866	Congressional
550	Bohrer, Andrew A.	3y		D.C.	28 DEC 1871	
036	Boiling, Saml.		W		15 FEB 1856	St. Patricks
405	Boings, Jno. F.	9m	C	D.C.	27 JUL 1869	Washington Asylum
174	Bokee, David A., lawyer	55y	W	N.Y.	16 MAR 1860	Brooklyn, N.Y.
524	Boland, Annie	6y	W	D.C.	20 JUN 1871	Mt. Olivet
349	Boland, Julia	1y	W		12 SEP 1868	Mt. Olivet
778a	Boland, Sophia	63y	W		07 JUL 1874	Holyrood
469	Boland, Wm. E.	2d	W	D.C.	11 AUG 1870	Mt. Olivet
607	Bolart, M.E.	4m	W	D.C.	20 JUN 1872	Methodist
430	Bold, Mary P.A.	10m	W		17 DEC 1869	Mt. Olivet
431	Bolden, A.F.	10m	C		22 DEC 1869	Mt. Olivet
588	Bolden, Charlotte	58y	W	D.C.	25 MAR 1872	Holmead
465	Bolden, Isaiah, clerk	30y	C	Md.	04 JUL 1870	Mt. Olivet
351	Bolden, John T.	3m	C	D.C.	15 SEP 1868	Young Mens
533	Bolden, Sarah	22y	C	Md.	21 AUG 1871	Young Mens
485	Boldin, Sarah E.	3m	C	D.C.	24 OCT 1870	Ebenezer
255	Boldin, Thomas, laborer	38y	W	Ire.	31 MAR 1867	Mt. Olivet
475	Boldin, Wm. H., laborer	23y	C	Va.	12 SEP 1870	Freedmen's Hospital
262	Bolding, Harriett, seamstress	21y	C	Md.	07 JUN 1867	Ebenezer
619	Boles, F.F.	7m	C	U.S.	13 AUG 1872	
619	Boles, Luke	3y	C	U.S.	05 AUG 1872	Young Mens
642	Boles, Sarah E.	6y	C	U.S.	01 DEC 1872	

District of Columbia Interments (Index to Deaths), 1855-1874

Page	Name	Age	Race	Birth	Death Date	Burial Ground
063	Bolin, Mary M., servant	19y	C	Md.	02 NOV 1856	St. Peters
599	Boloch, [blank]	Still		U.S.	30 MAY 1872	Prospect Hill
327	Bolsch, [blank]				31 JUL 1868	Prospect Hill
248	Bomke, Edwd. William	1y	W	D.C.	08 DEC 1866	Baltimore, Md.
495	Bonce, Geo. A.	35y	W	N.Y.	22 DEC 1870	Waterford, N.Y.
367	Bond, Amelia	Still	B	D.C.	30 DEC 1868	Washington Asylum
419	Bond, Edith May	2d	W		27 OCT 1869	Congressional
666	Bond, Erens	17y	C	U.S.	03 FEB 1873	Washington Asylum
681	Bond, Frank O.	5y	W	U.S.	18 APR 1873	Sandy Spring, Md.
317	Bond, Harriet, worker	50y	C	Md.	08 JUN 1868	Ebenezer
764	Bond, John H., merchant	51y	W	Eng.	09 MAY 1874	Oak Hill
627	Bond, Nancy L.	16y	C	U.S.	10 SEP 1872	
458	Bond, Oscar	Still	C	D.C.	17 JUN 1870	Potters Field
599	Bond, Richd. W.	12y	C	U.S.	26 MAY 1872	Unknown
398	Bond, Willie	6m	B	D.C.	21 JUN 1869	Washington Asylum
617	Bond, Wm., laborer	24y	C	U.S.	17 AUG 1872	Ebenezer
006	Boner, Mary	95y	C	Md.	09 APR 1855	St. Matthews
137	Bones, Mrs.		W		17 JAN 1859	Washington Asylum
162	Boninni, John	10m	W	D.C.	17 SEP 1859	Congressional
055	Bonnahan, Patrick	8y	W	Ire.	29 AUG 1856	St. Peters
470	Bonnell, Mary A.	1y	W	D.C.	01 AUG 1870	Oak Hill
356	Bonner, Adda	4m	D	D.C.	02 OCT 1868	Union
764	Bonner, Isabella	1y	C	U.S.	23 MAY 1874	
240	Bonsall, Lydia E.	26y	W	Pa.	08 OCT 1866	Philadelphia, Pa.
170	Bontz, Jacob, tobacconist	80y	W	Va.*	31 JAN 1860	
257	Bontz, Laura	14d	W	D.C.	13 MAR 1867	Congressional
232	Bontz, Sarah E.	9m	W	D.C.	22 AUG 1866	Glenwood
237	Booker, Mary M.	1y	C		26 SEP 1866	Harmony
284	Booker, Nathan	19y	C		30 NOV 1867	
372	Boon, Barney	Still	C	D.C.	28 JAN 1869	Washington Asylum
297	Boon, Emma		C		c.13 FEB 1868	Alms House
493	Boone, Hannah	9m	C	D.C.	18 DEC 1870	Eastern Branch, over
154	Boone, John B., merchant	55y	W	Md.	14 JUL 1859	Mt. Olivet
379	Booth, Catharine V.	40y	W	D.C.	12 MAR 1869	Congressional
197	Booth, Edward	18d	W	D.C.	22 JAN 1861	Congressional
720	Booth, Jas., blacksmith	58y	W	D.C.	27 SEP 1873	Congressional
078	Booth, Mrs.	80y	W		20 MAY 1857	St. Patricks
545	Booth, Ward, blacksmith	49y	W	D.C.	19 NOV 1871	Congressional*
359	Boph, Frederick E.	1y	W	D.C.	12 NOV 1868	Congressional
524	Bopp, Anna L.	28y	W	Va.	21 JUN 1871	Congressional*
359	Bopp, Ida L.	4y	W		01 NOV 1868	Congressional
526	Bopp, Jane E.E.	18d	W	D.C.	02 JUL 1871	Congressional*
453	Bopp, Joseph E.	3m	W		09 MAY 1870	Congressional
461	Bopp, Susan	31y	W	D.C.	13 JUL 1870	Congressional
160	Bopst, [blank]	1y	W	D.C.	05 AUG 1859	Glenwood
326	Borden, John	9m	W	D.C.	10 JUL 1868	Congressional
227	Borden, Wm. F.	3m	W	D.C.	08 JUL 1866	Glenwood
644	Borland, Alex	83y	W	Ire.	20 DEC 1872	Oak Hill
240	Borland, Armstead, Rev.	40y	C	Va.	07 OCT 1866	Harmony
290	Borland, Charles Alex	1y	W	D.C.	07 JAN 1868	Oak Hill
696	Borland, Chas. H.	1y	W	D.C.	30 JUN 1873	
107	Borland, Id M.	2y	W	D.C.	07 MAR 1858	Glenwood
115	Borland, James	5y	W	Md.	07 JUN 1858	St. Peters
121	Borland, Jno. Alex.	7½m	W	D.C.	10 JUL 1858	Glenwood
615	Borland, Mary	82y	W	U.S.	23 JUL 1872	
066	Borland, Michael, laborer	35y	W	Ire.	26 DEC 1856	Washington Asylum
477	Borman, Fredk., soldier	50y	W	Ger.	24 SEP 1870	Holmead
233	Borman, H.	61y	W	Ger.	18 AUG 1866	

District of Columbia Interments (Index to Deaths), 1855-1874

Page	Name	Age	Race	Birth	Death Date	Burial Ground
053	Borne, Mary A.	1y		N.C.	05 AUG 1856	St. Matthews
385	Borstwell, William, private marine	23y	W	Scot.	12 APR 1869	Congressional
091	Borwell, Barbary	90y	W	Md.	18 SEP 1857	Frederick, Md.
071	Boscow, Arthur, grocer	45y	W	Eng.	16 FEB 1857	Glenwood
248	Boscow, Emma	50y	W	Eng.	07 DEC 1866	Glenwood
492	Bosenberg, William	3m	W	D.C.	01 DEC 1870	Prospect Hill
500	Bosensberg, Kathrena	33y	W	Ger.	06 JAN 1871	Prospect Hill
011	Bosey, Elijah	60y	C	Va.	01 JUN 1855	Harmony
596	Boss, A.E.	8y	W	D.C.	21 APR 1872	Glenwood
229	Boss, Amy Sophia	3y	W	D.C.	26 JUL 1866	Congressional
496	Boss, Ann D.	78y	W		31 DEC 1870	Glenwood
659	Boss, Ann Sophia	49y	W	U.S.	16 JAN 1873	Congressional*
122	Boss, Henry	8y	W	Ger.	24 JUL 1858	Congressional
065	Boss, Margaret R.	6y	W	D.C.	14 DEC 1856	Congressional
249	Bosse, Amelia	66y	W		08 JAN 1867	Glenwood
071	Bosse, Martin, wheelwright	62y	W	Ger.	13 FEB 1857	Glenwood
147	Bostal, [blank]	3m	C	D.C.	26 APR 1859	Foundry
307	Bostic, Abram	18y	C	S.C.	14 APR 1868	Freedmen's Hospital
473	Boston, Daniel	1y	C	D.C.	04 AUG 1870	Harmony
605	Boston, Danl.	9y	C	U.S.	25 JUN 1872	
764	Boston, Infant	5d	C	U.S.	11 MAY 1874	
557	Boston, Rose L.	1y	W		05 FEB 1872	Congressional*
663	Boston, Samuel	40y	W	U.S.	31 JAN 1873	Small Pox
494	Boswell, Amanda S.	32y	W	D.C.	29 DEC 1870	Glenwood
033	Boswell, Ann E.	8d	W		27 JAN 1856	Glenwood
280	Boswell, Arabella	79y	W	Md.	26 OCT 1867	Glenwood
038	Boswell, F.A.K.	2y	W	D.C.	29 MAR 1856	Glenwood
233	Boswell, Francis L.	5d	W	D.C.	25 AUG 1866	Glenwood
348	Boswell, Geo.	11m	W	D.C.	21 SEP 1868	Congressional
635	Boswell, Hellen	31y	W	U.S.	26 NOV 1872	Small Pox
743	Boswell, Henry T., clerk	68y	W	U.S.	26 JAN 1874	Methodist
631	Boswell, Ida	5m	W	U.S.	24 OCT 1872	Congressional
340	Boswell, Ida Rebecca	1y	W		08 AUG 1868	Congressional
326	Boswell, J.V.	10m	W	D.C.	30 JUL 1868	Congressional
538	Boswell, James W.	9d	C	D.C.	29 SEP 1871	Ebenezer
464	Boswell, Jas. E.	54y	W	Md.	19 JUL 1870	Baltimore, Md.
639	Boswell, Jas. H.	35y	W	U.S.	07 DEC 1872	Small Pox*
531	Boswell, John H.	1y	C	D.C.	05 AUG 1871	Washington
595	Boswell, M.	30y	W	Md.	14 APR 1872	Md.
347	Boswell, Maria	68y	W	D.C.	30 SEP 1868	Congressional
216	Boswell, Mary A.	34y	W		21 MAR 1866	Glenwood
329	Boswell, Mathew, plasterer & bklyr.	28y	C	Va.	03 JUL 1868	Alms House
499	Boswell, Phillip	2y	W	D.C.	12 JAN 1871	Congressional
362	Boswell, Thornton	1y	C		04 NOV 1868	
110	Boswell, Thos. P., cabinet maker	34y	W	Md.	09 APR 1858	Glenwood
635	Boswell, W.G.	7y	W	U.S.	27 NOV 1872	Small Pox
485	Bosworth, Carrie V.	1y	W	D.C.	28 OCT 1870	Mt. Olivet
309	Bosworth, Sarah V.	19y	W	D.C.	14 APR 1868	Prospect Hill
322	Bosworth, Sarah V.	2y	W	D.C.	24 JUN 1868	Prospect Hill
075	Boteler, Charles, ostler	24y	W	D.C.	10 APR 1857	Foundry
440	Boteler, Charles W., merchant	49y	W	D.C.	22 FEB 1870	Glenwood
210	Boteler, Chas. W., merchant	68y	W	Md.	16 JAN 1866	Glenwood
601	Boteler, Mary	76y	W	U.S.	24 MAY 1872	Glenwood
107	Boteler, Richard W.	5y	W	D.C.	06 MAR 1858	Congressional
531	Boteler, Sarah A.	55y		Md.	08 AUG 1871	Congressional*
483	Boteler, [blank]	11y	C	D.C.	15 OCT 1870	Mt. Olivet
666	Bothe, Herman, barber	32y	W	Prus.	03 FEB 1873	Mt. Olivet
746	Botsford, Marian	33y	W	U.S.	03 FEB 1874	N.Y.

Page	Name	Age	Race	Birth	Death Date	Burial Ground
179	Botts, Alexander L.	61y	W	Va.	16 MAY 1860	Greenwood, N.Y.
276	Botts, William H.	44y	W	Va.	02 SEP 1867	Congressional
501	Boucher, Alfred, merchant	78y	W		30 JAN 1871	Mt. Olivet
778a	Boucher, Joseph W., merchant	47y	W	unk.	16 JUL 1874	Mt. Olivet
237	Bouder, Peter, brewer	22y	W	Ger.	29 SEP 1866	Prospect Hill
339	Bouis, Robt. Edwin		W	D.C.	06 AUG 1868	Baltimore, Md.
523	Bouldin, Gertrude	6d		D.C.	19 JUN 1871	Young Mens
533	Boules, Granson, driver	63y	C	Va.	26 AUG 1871	Ebenezer
601	Boulton, Mary J.	5y	C	U.S.	26 MAY 1872	Union
082	Boulware, Ben., laborer	50y	W	Va.	07 JUL 1857	Washington Asylum
476	Bouly, F.M.	1y	C		28 SEP 1870	
542	Bouman, Edw., contractor	48y	W	Ver.	17 OCT 1871	N.Y.
209	Bounet, Eugene	61y	W	Fra.	04 JAN 1866	Mt. Olivet
642	Boutright, Eugene, laborer	19y	C	U.S.	31 DEC 1872	Small Pox
326	Bowbeen, Alice G.	1y	W	D.C.	12 JUL 1868	Congressional
247	Bowbeer, Mary	1y	W	D.C.	12 DEC 1866	Methodist
379	Bowbier, Isaac, child of	4d	W		30 MAR 1869	Congressional
630	Bowels, Nelson	1y	C	U.S.	05 OCT 1872	
590	Bowen, Ann E.	19y	C	D.C.	03 APR 1872	Young Mens
033	Bowen, Benjn. F.	7d	W	D.C.	01 JAN 1856	Congressional
227	Bowen, Charles Henry	5m	W	D.C.	02 JUL 1866	Glenwood
008	Bowen, Charles V.	3y	W	Md.	07 MAY 1855	Congressional
389	Bowen, Chas.	19y	C	U.S.	12 APR 1869	Washington Asylum
103	Bowen, Ella Frances	1y	W	D.C.	20 JAN 1858	
204	Bowen, George, barber	80y	C		26 JUN 1861	Young Mens
412	Bowen, Grace	1y	C		18 AUG 1869	
263	Bowen, Helen C.	9y	W	D.C.	13 JUN 1867	Glenwood
368	Bowen, Henry, printer	33y	W	D.C.	31 DEC 1868	Glenwood
031	Bowen, James	1y	W	D.C.	16 DEC 1855	St. Peters
674	Bowen, Jno. W., Dr.	68y	W	U.S.	17 MAR 1873	Congressional
304	Bowen, Joseph O'D., printer	53y	W	D.C.	10 MAR 1868	Congressional
167	Bowen, Leonidas, clerk	37y	W	D.C.	10 DEC 1859	Congressional
514	Bowen, Lucy A., cook	38y	C		15 MAR 1871	Ebenezer
308	Bowen, Maria, Mrs.	51y	W		22 APR 1868	Congressional
527	Bowen, Mary Ann	68y	W	Md.	07 JUL 1871	Glenwood
368	Bowen, Mary, book folder	26y	W	D.C.	12 DEC 1868	Glenwood
227	Bowen, Mary E.	27y	W	D.C.	07 JUL 1866	Glenwood
021	Bowen, Mary L.	3m	C	D.C.	27 AUG 1855	St. Matthews
174	Bowen, Peter	2y	C	D.C.	15 MAR 1860	Mt. Olivet
025	Bowen, Rosanna	73y	W	Pa.	27 SEP 1855	Congressional
538	Bowen, Sarah	70y		D.C.	24 SEP 1871	Beckett's
235	Bowen, Sydney A. Robinson	23y	W	D.C.	13 SEP 1866	Glenwood
438	Bowen, Theodore L., stone cutter	33y	W		09 JAN 1870	Glenwood
612	Bowen, W.	7m	C	U.S.	29 JUL 1872	
182	Bowen, Wm. D.	7m	C	D.C.	23 JUN 1860	Young Mens
427	Bower, George	3m	C		28 NOV 1869	Young Mens
742	Bower, Jacob	74y	W	U.S.	20 JAN 1874	Congressional
521	Bowie, Albert	2y	W	D.C.	09 JUN 1871	Glenwood
242	Bowie, Alethae, servant	50y	C	Md.	26 OCT 1866	Colored Methodist
290	Bowie, Betsy, servant	85y	C	Va.	03 JAN 1868	St. Patricks
778a	Bowie, Cathran T.P.	7m	C	U.S.	11 JUL 1874	Mt. Olivet
661	Bowie, Charity, midwife	100y	C	U.S.	30 JAN 1873	Mt. Olivet
003	Bowie, Emily	10y	C		01 FEB 1855	
057	Bowie, Emma A.	1y	C	D.C.	12 SEP 1856	Harmony
437	Bowie, Fredk.	6y	C	D.C.	22 JAN 1870	Washington Asylum
053	Bowie, H. Ray				29 AUG 1856	Baltimore, Md.
617	Bowie, Henry, laborer	30y	C	U.S.	14 AUG 1872	Harmony
380	Bowie, J. Orlando	1m	W		14 MAR 1869	Mt. Olivet

District of Columbia Interments (Index to Deaths), 1855-1874

Page	Name	Age	Race	Birth	Death Date	Burial Ground
432	Bowie, Julia	9m	C	D.C.	31 DEC 1869	Washington Asylum
083	Bowie, Linnie, servant	75y	C	Md.	12 JUL 1857	St. Patricks
737	Bowie, Lottie M.	15d	C	U.S.	29 DEC 1873	Young Mens
457	Bowie, Louisa	9m	C	D.C.	21 JUN 1870	Mt. Olivet
139	Bowie, Mary	6y	C	D.C.	30 JAN 1859	Colored
288	Bowie, Mary	85y			31 DEC 1867	Freedmen's Hospital
770	Bowie, Mary R.	3½m	W	U.S.	12 JUN 1874	
201	Bowie, Mollie		W		22 MAR 1861	Congressional
778a	Bowie, Thomas I.	7m	C	U.S.	14 JUL 1874	
118	Bowie, W. Arnel, cart driver	17y	C	D.C.	02 JUN 1858	Holmead
694	Bowin, Mary Cordelia	20m	W	D.C.	12 JUN 1873	
374	Bowles, Ella	5y	W		20 FEB 1869	Congressional
347	Bowles, Lilly May	1y	W		08 SEP 1868	Congressional
372	Bowlin, Agnes, servant	23y	C	Md.	02 JAN 1869	Freedmen's Hospital
778a	Bowling, [blank]	3h	W	U.S.	01 JUL 1874	Congressional
068	Bowman, Adeline, cook	77y	C	Md.	10 JAN 1857	St. Matthews
717	Bowman, Augustus	50y	C	Md.	01 SEP 1873	Washington Asylum
409	Bowman, Charles	1y	W		04 AUG 1869	Prospect Hill
758	Bowman, Hannah S.	73y	W	U.S.	08 APR 1874	Oak Hill
285	Bowman, Henry, laborer	29y	C	Va.	01 DEC 1867	Mt. Olivet
603	Bowman, Mary	25y	C	W.I.	13 JUN 1872	Asylum
369	Bowman, Richard	62y	W	Md.	12 JAN 1869	Congressional
019	Bowman, [blank], nurse	22y	C		09 AUG 1855	St. Patricks
609	Bowser, Elizabeth	7m	C	U.S.	24 JUN 1872	
148	Bowyer, Alice	13y	W	Va.	13 MAY 1859	Va.
676	Bowyer, Jefferson	7y	C	U.S.	06 MAR 1873	Small Pox
088	Boxx Joshua Clay	4m	W	D.C.	18 AUG 1857	Glenwood
365	Boy, James	21d	C	D.C.	12 DEC 1868	Young Mens
238	Boyce, Andrew H.	14y	W	D.C.	22 SEP 1866	
463	Boyce, Annie	30y	W	Ire.	04 JUL 1870	Mt. Olivet
335b	Boyce, Benj.	5m	B		04 JUL 1868	Washington Asylum
470	Boyce, Clara F.	1y	W		06 AUG 1870	Congressional
461	Boyce, Freddie B.	6m	W	N.H.	06 JUL 1870	Congressional
222	Boyce, Horace W.	2y	W		29 MAY 1866	Congressional
675	Boyd, Alfred	21y	C	U.S.	20 MAR 1873	Waterford, Va.
279	Boyd, Annie C.	17y	C	Va.	17 OCT 1867	Leesburg, Va.
256	Boyd, E.A.	29y			23 MAR 1867	R.I.
256	Boyd, E.A., child of				23 MAR 1867	R.I.
344	Boyd, Edwin Walter	8m	W	D.C.	08 AUG 1868	Western
591	Boyd, Frank, laborer	20y	C	Va.	10 APR 1872	
496	Boyd, George, hackman	45y	W	Ire.	21 DEC 1870	Glenwood
382	Boyd, Hester	10y	C	Md.	09 MAR 1869	Union
516	Boyd, Jeremiah	65y	W	Pa.	23 MAR 1871	Congressional
516a	Boyd, Jeremiah	65y	W	Pa.	30 MAR 1871	Washington Asylum
341	Boyd, John D.	1y	W	D.C.	06 AUG 1868	Congressional
301	Boyd, John, laborer	22y	C	D.C.	31 MAR 1868	Young Mens
314	Boyd, Martha Jane	21y	W	D.C.	13 MAY 1868	Congressional
024	Boyd, Mary	30y	W	Ire.	16 SEP 1855	St. Patricks
398	Boyd, N.	Still	B	D.C.	02 JUN 1869	Washington Asylum
481	Boyd, Nannie M.	5m	W	D.C.	17 OCT 1870	Glenwood
496	Boyd, Rueben A., agent	24y	W		18 DEC 1870	
469	Boyd, S.V., farmer	48y	W	N.Y.	29 AUG 1870	Albany, N.Y.
695	Boyd, Sam	7y	C	D.C.	03 JUN 1873	Washington Asylum
258	Boyd, Virginia, seamstress	39y	W	D.C.	04 APR 1867	Mt. Olivet
107	Boyd, [blank]	Still	W		11 MAR 1858	Congressional*
295	Boyde, James				11 FEB 1868	
327	Boyden, Cornelia M.	53y	W	N.Y.	06 JUL 1868	Boston, Mass.
663	Boyed, Donaldson	18y	C	U.S.	27 JAN 1873	Small Pox

Page	Name	Age	Race	Birth	Death Date	Burial Ground
212	Boyer, Francis	27y	W	D.C.	21 FEB 1866	Congressional
626	Boyer, Henriette	1y	W	U.S.	05 SEP 1872	Glenwood
540	Boyer, Mary C.	25y	W	Md.	03 OCT 1871	Congressional
508	Boyer, Sophia	2y	C	D.C.	15 FEB 1871	Prospect Hill
488	Boylan, Andrew, laborer	49y	W	Ire.	22 NOV 1870	Mt. Olivet*
005	Boylan, Ellen	9m	W	D.C.	05 APR 1855	
457	Boylan, Michael, laborer	34y	W	Ire.	30 JUN 1870	Mt. Olivet
124	Boyle, Eugene	4d	W	D.C.	15 AUG 1858	Glenwood
365	Boyle, Frederick J.	2y	W	D.C.	16 DEC 1868	Mt. Olivet
154	Boyle, Henry	2y	W	D.C.	19 JUL 1859	Mt. Olivet
488	Boyle, James Hash	17y	W	Amer.	09 NOV 1870	Congressional*
426	Boyle, John	5m	W		02 NOV 1869	Mt. Olivet
240	Boyle, Lavinia	54y	W	Md.	03 OCT 1866	St. Patricks
315	Boyle, Mary	2y	W		c.23 MAY 1868	Mt. Olivet
365	Boyle, Mrs., storekeeper	38y	W	Ire.	05 DEC 1868	Mt. Olivet
752	Boyle, Terance, laborer	76y	W	Ire.	19 MAR 1874	Mt. Olivet
705	Boyle, Walter A.	11m	W	D.C.	24 JUL 1873	
031	Boyne, Catharine A.	5y	W	Md.	01 DEC 1855	Baltimore, Md.
104	Boyne, Thomas I.	3y	W	D.C.	02 FEB 1858	Baltimore, Md.
118	Boynton, Louis Pinkney	1y	W	D.C.	23 JUN 1858	Congressional
513	Boynton, Theodore	70y	C	Md.	18 MAR 1871	Washington Asylum
234	Brachman, Mary	51y	W	Va.*	03 SEP 1866	Alexandria, Va.
144	Brackam, Ellen, domestic	40y	W	Ire.	29 MAR 1859	Washington Asylum
431	Bracker, John, boatman	57y	C	Md.	19 DEC 1869	Union
335a	Brackett, Maria				22 JUL 1868	Washington Asylum
465	Brackston, Willie	10y	C	Va.	27 JUL 1870	Union
296	Brackwell, Balina	95y	C	Va.	26 FEB 1868	Alms House
257	Bradbury, John W.	1y	W	D.C.	10 MAR 1867	Congressional*
351	Bradengeir, Chas. H.	10m	W	D.C.	28 SEP 1868	Prospect Hill
130	Bradford, Adelade	24y	W	D.C.	05 OCT 1858	Oak Hill
502	Bradford, Cassie	7m	W	D.C.	13 JAN 1871	Glenwood
034	Bradford, Edmund, clerk	56y	W	Va.	20 JAN 1856	Georgetown
146	Bradford, Jane	19y	W	D.C.*	13 APR 1859	Oak Hill
190	Bradford, William A., clerk	52y	C		29 SEP 1860	Glenwood
259	Bradford, William R., Hon.	53y	W	Ky.	05 APR 1867	Oak Hill
601	Bradley, Arthur W.	1y	W	U.S.	08 MAY 1872	Unknown
305	Bradley, Eliza	73y	W	Md.	29 MAR 1868	Congressional
143	Bradley, Eliza	21y	W	Md.	12 MAR 1859	Oak Hill
409	Bradley, Eliza Ann	3m	C		11 AUG 1869	
214	Bradley, H.		C		09 MAR 1866	Mt. Olivet
465	Bradley, John	77y	W	Conn.	09 JUL 1870	Conn.
361	Bradley, John T., clerk Int. Dept.	52y	W	Pa.	09 NOV 1868	Glenwood
622a	Bradley, Maria	60y	W	U.S.	28 AUG 1872	
188	Bradley, Mary	14y	C	D.C.	31 AUG 1860	Congressional
742	Bradley, Mary C.	19y	W	U.S.	19 JAN 1874	Mt. Olivet
580	Bradley, Mary P.	2y	W	Md.	07 FEB 1872	Oak Hill
213	Bradley, Mr., child of				21 FEB 1866	Western
213	Bradley, Mr., infant of		W		22 FEB 1866	
130	Bradley, Patrick	3d	W	D.C.	06 OCT 1858	St. Patricks
386	Bradley, Patrick, laborer	30y	W	Ire.	17 APR 1869	Mt. Olivet
031	Bradley, Reed, clerk in post office	40y	W	Mass.	03 DEC 1855	Congressional*
082	Bradley, Saml.		W		01 JUL 1857	Methodist
271	Bradley, William A., gentleman	73y	W		28 AUG 1867	Glenwood
188	Bradly, Catharine	14y	W	D.C.	31 AUG 1860	Congressional
627	Bradshaw, Hannah	75y	C	U.S.	30 SEP 1872	
395	Brady, Annie	19y	W	Ire.	19 JUN 1869	Mt. Olivet
502	Brady, Jasper E., lawyer	75y	W	Pa.	23 JAN 1871	Pittsburgh/Rock Creek
151	Brady, Julia	11y	W	D.C.	24 JUN 1859	Methodist

Page	Name	Age	Race	Birth	Death Date	Burial Ground
538	Brady, Matt, shoemaker	45y	W	Ire.	27 SEP 1871	Mt. Olivet
230	Brady, Mrs., child of	Still	W		16 JUL 1866	Western
207	Brady, P.	35y	W		09 JUL 1862	
229	Brady, P.F., contractor	40y	W	Pa.	19 JUL 1866	Philadelphia, Pa.
108	Brady, Patrick	3y	W	D.C.	19 MAR 1858	St. Peters
036	Brady, Peter, clerk, pen. ofc.	63y	W	Ire.	08 FEB 1856	St. Peters
127	Brady, Silas	Still	W	D.C.	09 SEP 1858	Western
212	Brady, Susannah	83y	W	Md.	11 FEB 1866	Methodist
299	Brahen, Eliza	2y	C		02 MAR 1868	Young Mens
698	Brahler, F.	1y	W	D.C.	28 JUN 1873	Prospect Hill
008	Brahler, Wm.	1y	W	D.C.	26 MAY 1855	German
524	Brahler, Wm. H.	1y	W	D.C.	25 JUN 1871	Prospect Hill
061	Braider, Elizabeth, lady	80y	W		24 OCT 1856	Congressional
291	Braig, Susan		C		06 JAN 1868	Alms House
472	Braigart, Mary	14d	W	D.C.	02 AUG 1870	St. Marys
256	Bramhall, [blank]	1y	W	Mass.	28 MAR 1867	Boston, Mass.
626	Branan, Eliza E.	100y	W	U.S.	09 SEP 1872	
120	Branaugh, Chas. N.	1m	W	D.C.	07 JUL 1858	Congressional
124	Branaugh, Sergnatt B.	15y	W	Va.	03 AUG 1858	Va.
583	Branch, John	10y	W	Md.	25 FEB 1872	
271	Brand, Catherine, domestic	38y	W	Ire.	21 AUG 1867	Mt. Olivet
770	Brandenburg, Wm. D.	17y	W	U.S.	28 JUN 1874	Oak Hill
140	Brandt, Frank I.	8y	W	D.C.	12 FEB 1859	Congressional
088	Brandt, John	2m	W	D.C.	25 AUG 1857	Congressional
141	Brandt, John A.D.	3y	W	D.C.	19 FEB 1859	Congressional
477	Brandt, John F., music professor	61y	W	Swe.	18 SEP 1870	Congressional
091	Braner, Mary	1y	W	D.C.	15 SEP 1857	German
668	Brannam, Mary A.	35y	W	Ire.	21 FEB 1873	Mt. Olivet
698	Brannan, Helena Effie	15y	W	D.C.	20 JUN 1873	Mt. Olivet*
250	Brannan, Josephine	1y			26 JAN 1867	Mt. Olivet*
117	Brannan, [blank]	64y	C		26 JUN 1858	Colored
291	Branner, Adam W., seaman		W		10 JAN 1868	Congressional
623	Brannon, Sarah L.	16m	W	U.S.	11 JUL 1872	Holy Rood
026	Brannson, Marshal	10y	W	Md.	29 OCT 1855	St. Peters
107	Branson, Charles	9m	W	D.C.	04 MAR 1858	St. Peters
627	Branson, Jas.	7y	C	U.S.	03 SEP 1872	Small Pox
395	Branson, Mary	28y	W	D.C.	10 JUN 1869	Mt. Olivet
003	Branson, Susan	65y	C	Va.	01 FEB 1855	
547	Branson, Thos. C.	2m	C	D.C.	03 DEC 1871	Harmony
671	Branson, Wm.	45y	W	U.S.	14 FEB 1873	Small Pox*
498	Branson, Wm. H., pauper	8d	B		03 JAN 1871	Washington Asylum
215	Branzell, George	1m		D.C.	19 MAR 1866	Mt. Olivet
746	Brase, Ernest, tailor	74y	W	Ger.	06 FEB 1874	Prospect Hill
167	Brashears, Mary	72y	W		08 DEC 1859	Congressional*
350	Brasley, [blank]	1m	C		02 SEP 1868	Young Mens
470	Brassing, M.A.P.	62y	W	Amer.	07 AUG 1870	Congressional
435	Brauer, Henry, model maker	30y	W	Ger.	09 JAN 1870	Prospect Hill
283	Brauman, Adam	1y	W	D.C.	03 NOV 1867	German Catholic
282	Brauman, Adam	10m	W	D.C.	02 NOV 1867	German Catholic
612	Braumann, Annie	11m	W	U.S.	14 JUL 1872	
545	Braun, Minnie E.	2y	W	D.C.	14 NOV 1871	Mt. Olivet
471	Braund, Agnes	33y	W	Eng.	27 AUG 1870	Congressional
407	Braund, Charles S.P.	3y	W		30 AUG 1869	Congressional
483	Braund, Mary Agnes	4m	W	D.C.	08 OCT 1870	Congressional
431	Brawer, Louis	3y	W		21 DEC 1869	Prospect Hill
315	Brawner, Louis	65y	C		c.19 MAY 1868	Mt. Olivet
376	Braxton, Albert, laborer	16y	C		06 FEB 1869	Young Mens
553	Braxton, Eveline	22y	C	Va.	08 JAN 1872	Washington

Page	Name	Age	Race	Birth	Death Date	Burial Ground
615	Braxton, Geo.	7y	C	U.S.	03 JUL 1872	
778a	Braxton, Richard F.	18y	W	U.S.	08 JUL 1874	Congressional
606	Braxton, Sarah	65y	C	Va.	20 JUN 1872	Asylum
373	Bray, Clive	7m	C	D.C.	22 JAN 1869	
296	Brayden, Sophia	20y	C		03 FEB 1868	Alms House
244	Brayton, James H., plasterer	26y	C	Va.	23 NOV 1866	Ebenezer
489	Breashear, William H.	4m	W	D.C.	05 NOV 1870	Glenwood
260	Brecht, Louisa	24y	W	D.C.	30 MAY 1867	Oak Hill
734	Brecht, Rose C.	9m	W	U.S.	03 DEC 1873	Oak Hill
590	Breck, John, bar tender	48y	W	Ger.	02 APR 1872	Prospect Hill
239	Breed, Mrs.		W		19 OCT 1866	Oak Hill
239	Breen, Mary	30y	W	Ire.	05 OCT 1866	Alexandria, Va.
239	Breen, Mary, child of	1d	W	D.C.	05 OCT 1866	Alexandria, Va.
487	Brelsford, Hiram W., child of	Still	W		12 NOV 1870	Congressional
544	Bremmer, Wm., tailor	81y	W	Ger.	08 NOV 1871	Prospect Hill
116	Brenard, Florence	4m	W	D.C.	17 JUN 1858	Holmead
481	Breneman, E. deW., Dr.	31y	W	Pa.	10 OCT 1870	Oak Hill
739	Brener, Harriet H.	28y	W	U.S.	15 DEC 1873	Graceland
083	Brennan, Chas. C., Rev.	44y	W	Ire.	17 JUL 1857	St. Peters
544	Brennan, Lizzie	1y	W	D.C.	01 NOV 1871	Mt. Olivet
395	Brennan, M.	16m	W	D.C.	12 JUN 1869	Mt. Olivet
439	Brennan, Mary	1y	W		02 FEB 1870	Holyrood
066	Brennan, Mary A.	3d	W	D.C.	25 DEC 1856	Washington Asylum
731	Brennan, Mary, nurse	79y	W	Ire.	25 NOV 1873	Mt. Olivet
770	Brennan, Patrick	7d	W	U.S.	17 JUN 1874	Mt. Olivet
339	Brenner, Anthony	42y	W	D.C.	16 AUG 1868	Glenwood
350	Brenner, Patrick	7y	W	D.C.	06 SEP 1868	Mt. Olivet
279	Brennerman, Julia A.	72y	W	Va.	20 OCT 1867	Glenwood
446	Brent, David, laborer	40y	C	Va.	28 MAR 1870	Western
241	Brent, Elizabeth, nurse		C	D.C.	28 OCT 1866	Young Mens
689	Brent, Gertrude	2y	C	U.S.	29 MAY 1873	Young Mens
594	Brent, Henry	80y	C	Va.	02 APR 1872	Washington
350	Brent, Jane	17y	C	Md.	25 SEP 1868	Young Mens
361	Brent, John, waiter	30y	C	Md.	05 NOV 1868	Young Mens
522	Brent, Joseph	8m	C	D.C.	10 JUN 1871	Good Hope
736	Brent, Julia A., servant	21y	C	U.S.	21 DEC 1873	Young Mens
182	Brent, Mary	1y	C	Md.	27 JUN 1860	
758	Brent, Minnie	1y	C	U.S.	15 APR 1874	Young Mens
018	Brent, Mrs.	84y	C		17 AUG 1855	West
204	Brent, Sarah T.	33y	W	D.C.	04 JUN 1861	Mt. Olivet
627	Brent, Sylvia, cook	24y	C	U.S.	06 SEP 1872	
627	Brent, Warren	19m	C	U.S.	01 SEP 1872	
189	Brent, William C., lawyer	36y	W	Md.	13 SEP 1860	Carroll Chapel
125	Brent, [blank]	2y	C	D.C.	19 AUG 1858	Young Mens
207	Brent, [blank], Mr.	65y	C		04 JUL 1862	Harmony
165	Brereton, Patrick	2m	W	D.C.	23 NOV 1859	Mt. Olivet
177	Breshenhan, Daniel	10m	W	D.C.	28 APR 1860	Mt. Olivet
661	Breshlin, Elizabeth	34y	W	Ire.	25 JAN 1873	Mt. Olivet
065	Breslyn, Dianna	45y	W	D.C.	09 DEC 1856	Congressional
039	Breslyn, Michael, blacksmith	49y	W	Va.	01 MAR 1856	Congressional
035	Breslyn, Michael, blacksmith	43y	W	N.Y.	29 FEB 1856	Congressional
769	Bresnaha, Willie	11y	W	U.S.	09 MAY 1874	
214	Bresnahan, Amos C.	1y	W	D.C.	03 MAR 1866	Mt. Olivet
185	Bresnahan, Mary	6m	W	D.C.	15 JUL 1860	Mt. Olivet
222	Bresnahan, Michael	1y	W	D.C.	29 MAY 1866	Mt. Olivet
233	Bresnahan, Michael	9m	W	D.C.	28 AUG 1866	Mt. Olivet
323	Bresnahan, Willie	13m	W	D.C.	16 JUL 1868	Mt. Olivet
717	Bresnahen, Jas., laborer	27y	W	Ire.	04 SEP 1873	Mt. Olivet

Page	Name	Age	Race	Birth	Death Date	Burial Ground
623	Brest, Jno. H.	12d	W	U.S.	10 JUL 1872	Holy Rood
278	Brest, Salena	4m	W	D.C.	29 OCT 1867	Congressional
719	Bret, Eddie	11m	C	D.C.	15 SEP 1873	Holmead
436	Brewer, Chas.	11m	C		19 JAN 1870	Young Mens
326	Brewer, E.B.	2m	W	D.C.	09 JUL 1868	Congressional
354	Brewer[86], Jonathan, merchant	27y	W	Va.	24 OCT 1868	Congressional*
364	Brewton, [blank]	2d	W	D.C.	15 DEC 1868	Congressional
063	Breyer, Rosena C.	28y	W	Ger.	04 NOV 1856	Congressional
017	Brian, Hannah	16m	W	D.C.	14 JUL 1855	St. Patricks
520	Brice, Mary E.	1y	C	D.C.	24 MAY 1871	Ebenezer
352	Brice, Wm.	2y	C		24 SEP 1868	Washington Asylum
307	Briches, John	2y	W	D.C.	04 APR 1868	German Catholic
375	Brick, Sarah O.	Still	W		26 FEB 1869	E. Cumberland
005	Bridge, Marrian	5y	W	Mass.	30 MAR 1855	Oak Hill
159	Bridget, Francis Albert	10m	W	D.C.	01 AUG 1859	
770	Bridget, Thornton, laborer	82y	C	U.S.	14 JUN 1874	Washington Asylum
488	Bridwell, Martha J.	48y	W	Va.	08 NOV 1870	Congressional
041	Brigett, Henrietta, midwife	104y	C	Va.	08 APR 1856	Harmony
471	Briggs, Elizabeth	74y	W	Ire.	10 AUG 1870	Congressional
610	Briggs, J.F.	6y	W		10 JUN 1867	Western
239	Briggs, John	46y	W	Pa.	18 OCT 1866	Alms House
423	Briggs, John	4m	C		15 OCT 1869	Washington Asylum
642	Briggs, John R., clerk	49y	W	U.S.	03 DEC 1872	Chicago, Ill.
407	Briggs, Jos. H., dyer	43y	W	Eng.	25 AUG 1869	Congressional
331	Briggs, Lewis	70y	C		21 JUL 1868	Freedmen's Hospital
673	Briggs, Maria	24y	C	U.S.	08 MAR 1873	Washington Asylum
096	Briggs, Mary	4y	W	D.C.	03 NOV 1857	Congressional*
451	Briggs, Nelly	72y	C	Va.	23 APR 1870	Washington Asylum
518	Briggs, Thomas, clerk	66y	W	Mich.	04 MAY 1871	Washington
487	Brigham, Henry A., capt. USA	55y	W	Eng.	15 NOV 1870	Troy, N.Y.
343	Brigham, Josiah Q.	42y	W	Mass.	19 AUG 1868	Mass.
527	Bright, Anna M.	74y	W	Ger.	08 JUL 1871	Glenwood
027	Bright, Annie E.	1y	W	D.C.	26 OCT 1855	St. Peters churchyard
484	Bright, Fanny M.	11m	W	D.C.	21 OCT 1870	Congressional
080	Bright, Geneva Ann	9m	W	D.C.	29 JUN 1857	Congressional
228	Bright, George W.	1y	W	D.C.	12 JUL 1866	Methodist
104	Bright, John Edward	3y	W	D.C.	12 FEB 1858	Congressional
470	Bright, Julia B.	1y	W	D.C.	17 AUG 1870	Congressional
224	Bright, Julia L.	6m	W	D.C.	15 JUN 1866	Congressional
339	Bright, Malinda A.	43y	W	D.C.	04 AUG 1868	Mt. Olivet
764	Bright, Maud B.	10m	W	U.S.	06 MAY 1874	Congressional
230	Bright, May Washington	6m			30 JUL 1866	Moore's
580	Bright, Walter	1y	W	U.S.	06 FEB 1872	Congressional
414	Brightwell, James, teamster	29y	W	U.S.	26 SEP 1869	Congressional
515	Briles, Betty, servant	30y	C	Va.	21 MAR 1871	Union
151	Brimmer, Ardenia	8m	W	D.C.	17 JUN 1859	Congressional
001	Brimmer, Charles		W	D.C.	10 JAN 1855	Congressional
260	Brink, Mary	9m	W		08 MAY 1867	Mt. Olivet
677	Brinkley, Anna	24y	C	U.S.	c.24 MAR 1873	Ebenezer
677	Brinkley, Jno. H.	25y	C	U.S.	c.10 MAR 1873	Ebenezer
778a	Brinkley, Laura	10m	W	U.S.	26 JUL 1874	Methodist
116	Brinkman, John	1m	W		24 JUN 1858	St. Patricks
421	Brintnall, Sewall, gov. official	70y	W	Mass.	16 OCT 1869	Glenwood/Rock Creek
320	Brisbee, George W., eating house	34y	W	N.Y.	17 JUN 1868	
684	Brisco, Edward	2m	C	U.S.	28 APR 1873	Small Pox*

---

[86] The Register clearly (and incorrectly) gives surname as "Bruce."

Page	Name	Age	Race	Birth	Death Date	Burial Ground
611	Brisco, G.E.	1y	C	U.S.	06 JUL 1872	
098	Brisco, Richard G., merchant	55y	W	Md.	07 DEC 1857	St. Patricks
422	Briscoe, Adelia	3y	C		31 OCT 1869	Harmony
215	Briscoe, Ann	107y	C		19 MAR 1866	Young Mens
691	Briscoe, Annie	9y	C	U.S.	12 MAY 1873	Small Pox*
717	Briscoe, Edgar	28y	C	Va.*	05 SEP 1873	
635	Briscoe, Ellen	35y	C	U.S.	03 NOV 1872	Small Pox
384	Briscoe, Harriet	Still	C	D.C.	23 MAR 1869	Washington Asylum
500	Briscoe, Henry, laborer	70y	C	U.S.	31 JAN 1871	Young Mens
715	Briscoe, Jos. F.	4y	C	Mass.	08 AUG 1873	
384	Briscoe, Julia A.	35y	C	Md.	11 MAR 1869	Washington Asylum
355	Briscoe, Julia Ann	9y	C	D.C.	31 OCT 1868	Ebenezer
441	Briscoe, Louisa, laundress	35y	C	Md.	15 FEB 1870	Union
087	Briscoe, Mary		C		11 AUG 1857	Harmony
501	Briscoe, P., scavenger	53y	C	D.C.	01 JAN 1871	Harmony
522	Briscoe, Spencer	61y	C	Md.	10 JUN 1871	Ebenezer
202	Briscoe, Theodore	20y	W	D.C.	09 APR 1861	Mt. Olivet
204	Briscoe, William	13y	C	D.C.	15 JUN 1861	Mt. Olivet
101	Briscoe, William	24y	C	Va.*	11 JAN 1858	Young Mens
741	Bristed, Chas. A., gentleman	53y	W	U.S.	14 JAN 1874	Stockbridge, Mass.
331	Bristoe, John	22y	C	Va.	22 JUL 1868	Freedmen's Hospital
094	Britter, John	1y	C	D.C.	22 OCT 1857	Ebenezer
120	Brittley, John	1y	W	D.C.	06 JUL 1858	Methodist, East
449	Britton, James	24d	W		06 APR 1870	Congressional
340	Brixley, A.S.	2m	W	D.C.	10 AUG 1868	Congressional
268	Brixley, Elmira Josephine	2m	W	D.C.	13 AUG 1867	Congressional
581	Broadas, Mary S.	1y	C	D.C.	15 FEB 1872	
392	Broadice, Ella	7d	C		06 MAY 1869	Union
758	Broadis, John	50y	C	U.S.	22 APR 1874	
377	Brock, Margaret	3y	C		03 FEB 1869	Washington Asylum
622	Brock, Sarah J.	4m	C	U.S.	21 AUG 1872	
377	Brock, Walter	50y	C	Va.	09 FEB 1869	Washington Asylum
605	Brocks, Mary F.	44y	W	Md.	13 JUN 1872	Oak Hill
280	Brodegain, William	1m	W	D.C.	17 OCT 1867	Mt. Olivet
542	Broden, Patrick	18y	W		17 OCT 1871	Mt. Olivet
401	Broden, Willie	1y	W		18 JUL 1869	Mt. Olivet
376	Broden, [blank]	4y	W		18 FEB 1869	Mt. Olivet
633	Broders, Eliza	69y	W	U.S.	21 OCT 1872	
501	Brodis, John	3m	C	D.C.	25 JAN 1871	Young Mens
739	Brodis, John, laborer	23y	C	U.S.	18 DEC 1873	
746	Brodlay, Katerine	73y	W	Ger.	22 FEB 1874	Prospect Hill
620	Brodon, Anna	16m	W	U.S.	28 AUG 1872	Mt. Olivet
719	Brody, Thos. A.	1y	W	D.C.	19 SEP 1873	Mt. Olivet
520	Brogan, Mary A.	46y	W	Md.	25 MAY 1871	Congressional*
276	Brokenberry, Alice	1y	C	D.C.	01 SEP 1867	Ebenezer
008	Bron, Estell	8y	W	D.C.	29 MAY 1855	Congressional
292a	Bronaugh, Anne E.	87y	W	Va.	02 FEB 1868	Congressional
541	Bronaugh, Jennie	40y	W	U.S.	09 OCT 1871	Congressional
036	Bronaugh, Jeremh. W., clerk	76y	W	Va.	03 FEB 1856	Congressional
077	Brone, J.B.	12d		D.C.	10 MAY 1857	St. Peters
197	Bronson, [blank]	29y	W		09 JAN 1861	Mt. Olivet
746	Brook, Elizabeth	4d	W	U.S.	05 FEB 1874	
218	Brook, Robt. C.	75y	W	Md.	27 APR 1866	Glenwood
472	Brook, Sml.		C	D.C.	14 AUG 1870	Young Mens
133	Brooke, Benj. C., officer USN	59y	W	Pa.	28 NOV 1858	Congressional
440	Brooke, Euell, Mrs.	71y	W		07 FEB 1870	Mt. Olivet
546	Brooke, Joseph	11m	W	D.C.	30 NOV 1871	Washington
015	Brooke, Louisa	23y	C	D.C.	10 JUL 1855	Young Mens

District of Columbia Interments (Index to Deaths), 1855-1874

Page	Name	Age	Race	Birth	Death Date	Burial Ground
035	Brooke, Lucy	84y	W	Va.	28 FEB 1856	Congressional
167	Brooke, Mary	73y	W	Md.	17 DEC 1859	Glenwood
232	Brooke, Mary Elizabeth	1y	C	D.C.	28 AUG 1866	Young Mens
165	Brooke, Robert C., clerk	27y	W	Md.	19 NOV 1859	Glenwood
159	Brooke, Rose C.	4y	W	D.C.	01 AUG 1859	
770	Brooke, Sarah V.	2y	W	U.S.	05 JUN 1874	Holyrood
662	Brookenburg, Ernest	3m	C	U.S.	09 JAN 1873	
431	Brookes, Jenifer	11y	C	Va.	02 DEC 1869	Young Mens
691	Brookes, Wm. M.	7y	W	U.S.	16 MAY 1873	Congressional*
357	Brookheise, [blank]	Still	W	D.C.	03 OCT 1868	Washington Asylum
708	Brooks, Aelia E.	7m	C	D.C.	04 JUL 1873	
737	Brooks, Albert, laborer	50y	C	U.S.	26 DEC 1873	
718	Brooks, Albert, watchman	46y	C	Md.	10 SEP 1873	Harmony
292a	Brooks, Allen T.	1y	C	Va.	16 JAN 1868	Methodist
149	Brooks, Amelia	62y	C		20 MAY 1859	Western
223	Brooks, Andrew	3y	C	D.C.	03 JUN 1866	Harmony
723	Brooks, Annie	35y	B	Va.	07 OCT 1873	Beckett's
546	Brooks, Ben	80y	C	Va.	28 NOV 1871	Washington
529	Brooks, Caroline A.	34y	W	D.C.	24 JUL 1871	Glenwood
383	Brooks, Catharine	3y	C	Va.*	14 MAR 1869	Harmony
770	Brooks, Catherine, house servant	23y	C	U.S.	20 JUN 1874	Mt. Olivet
397	Brooks, Clarance	1y	B	Amer.	11 JUN 1869	Ebenezer
779	Brooks, Cleas	2y	C	U.S.	31 JUL 1874	Beckett's
724	Brooks, Cordelia	13y	B	Md.	16 OCT 1873	Beckett's
382	Brooks, Cornelius, driver	31y	C		23 MAR 1869	Mt. Zion
658	Brooks, Daniel	18d	C	U.S.	07 JAN 1873	Young Mens
328	Brooks, Dennis	28y	C	D.C.	31 JUL 1868	Washington
162	Brooks, Edwd., clerk	75y	W	N.J.	19 SEP 1859	Glenwood
412	Brooks, Edwin	1y	C	D.C.	11 AUG 1869	Washington Asylum
660	Brooks, Eliza	25y	C	U.S.	17 JAN 1873	Harmony
553	Brooks, Eliza	13y	C	Ky.	08 JAN 1872	Washington
514	Brooks, Eliza Jane, teacher	33y	C	U.S.	15 MAR 1871	Beckett's
155	Brooks, Eliza, nurse	17y	C	D.C.	24 JUL 1859	Western
630	Brooks, Enoch	20y	C	U.S.	13 OCT 1872	
244	Brooks, Ernest Perry	2y	C	N.Y.	13 NOV 1866	Harmony
122	Brooks, Flora	60y	C	Md.	23 JUL 1858	Ebenezer
335a	Brooks, Franklin				24 JUL 1868	Washington Asylum
498	Brooks, George, pauper	12y	B	Md.	29 JAN 1871	Washington Asylum
673	Brooks, Hanson, carman	67y	C	U.S.	11 MAR 1873	Harmony
409	Brooks, Harriet	1y	C	D.C.	27 AUG 1869	Harmony
778a	Brooks, Harry	3m	C	U.S.	01 JUL 1874	Harmony
634	Brooks, Harry Aloysius	4y	W	U.S.	21 OCT 1872	Mt. Olivet
217	Brooks, Henry	10m	W	D.C.	03 APR 1866	Congressional
778a	Brooks, Ida	8m	C	U.S.	19 JUL 1874	
660	Brooks, Isaiah	5m	C	U.S.	20 JAN 1873	Ebenezer
682	Brooks, James, editor	62y	W	U.S.	30 APR 1873	Greenwood, N.Y.
131	Brooks, Jno. Henry	9h	C	D.C.	27 OCT 1858	Foundry
495	Brooks, John	1d	C	D.C.	10 DEC 1870	Potters Field
362	Brooks, John	25y	C	U.S.	10 NOV 1868	Washington Asylum
518	Brooks, John C.	61y	W	Me.	01 MAY 1871	Portland, Me.
083	Brooks, John H.	4m	C	D.C.	18 JUL 1857	Young Mens
697	Brooks, Jos. S.		C	D.C.	21 JUN 1873	Graceland
489	Brooks, Joseph	2m	C	D.C.	04 NOV 1870	Ebenezer
429	Brooks, Joseph H.	2y	W	D.C.	12 DEC 1869	Congressional
434	Brooks, Laura L.	4y	W	D.C.	14 JAN 1870	Congressional
287	Brooks, Lewis		C		c.21 DEC 1867	Alms House
538	Brooks, Lilly	1y	C	D.C.	26 SEP 1871	
278	Brooks, Lucy, servant	80y	C	Md.	26 OCT 1867	Mt. Olivet

District of Columbia Interments (Index to Deaths), 1855-1874

Page	Name	Age	Race	Birth	Death Date	Burial Ground
335b	Brooks, M.C.	2m	B	D.C.	13 JUL 1868	Washington Asylum
625	Brooks, M.E.	1y	C	U.S.	19 SEP 1872	
752	Brooks, Margarett A., servant	24y	C	U.S.	03 MAR 1874	
446	Brooks, Martha A.	2y	C		23 MAR 1870	Young Mens
373	Brooks, Mary	2y	C		05 JAN 1869	
408	Brooks, Mary	28y	C	Md.	14 AUG 1869	
212	Brooks, Mary	68y	W		05 FEB 1866	Congressional
770	Brooks, Mary E.G., teacher	23y	C	U.S.	29 JUN 1874	Baltimore, Md.
265	Brooks, Mary Emeline	10m	C		25 JUL 1867	
621	Brooks, Mary F.	4m	W	U.S.	17 AUG 1872	Oak Hill
055	Brooks, Mary V.	10d	C	D.C.	27 AUG 1856	Potters Field
777a	Brooks, Nancy, child of	6d	C	U.S.	08 JUN 1874	
110	Brooks, Oliver, book agent	60y	W	Va.	04 APR 1858	Washington Asylum
603	Brooks, Peter, laborer	45y	C	D.C.	13 JUN 1872	
604	Brooks, Peter, laborer	45y	C	Va.	13 JUN 1872	Small Pox
752	Brooks, Philip	70y	C	U.S.	17 MAR 1874	Washington Asylum
538	Brooks, Richard, blacksmith	72y	W	Md.	30 SEP 1871	Congressional*
638	Brooks, Richd.	25y	C	U.S.	28 NOV 1872	
733	Brooks, Robert	32y	C	U.S.	06 NOV 1873	
552	Brooks, Robert	75y	C	Va.	08 JAN 1872	Washington
618	Brooks, Robt.	36y	C	U.S.	06 AUG 1872	Washington Asylum
438	Brooks, Samuel	72y	C	Va.	30 JAN 1870	Mt. Olivet
778a	Brooks, Samuel	25y	C	U.S.	12 JUL 1874	Potters Field
474	Brooks, Sarah A.	1d	C		23 AUG 1870	Washington Asylum
552	Brooks, Stephen, laborer	80y	C	Va.	03 JAN 1872	Washington
442	Brooks, Susan	2y	C	Md.	14 FEB 1870	Washington Asylum
034	Brooks, Teresa	60y	C	Md.	29 JAN 1856	Colored, East
452	Brooks, Thomas	76y	C	Md.	21 APR 1870	Washington Asylum
703	Brooks, W.W.	78y	C	D.C.	22 JUL 1873	Mt. Pleasant
048	Brooks, William	12y			23 JUN 1856	
176	Brooks, Wm., child of	Still	W	D.C.	07 APR 1860	Congressional
127	Brooks, [blank]	1½h	C	D.C.	12 SEP 1858	Foundry
221	Brooks, [child]				21 MAY 1866	Western
622a	Broom, M.E.	72y	W	U.S.	14 AUG 1872	Congressional*
123	Broome, Maria M.	36y	W	D.C.	30 JUL 1858	Congressional
458	Brosnahan, Francis	3m	W	D.C.	27 JUN 1870	Mt. Olivet
469	Brosnahan, Josehpine	5m	W	D.C.	19 AUG 1870	Mt. Olivet
580	Brosnan, John	2y	W	D.C.	07 FEB 1872	Mt. Olivet
689	Brosran, Mary Agnes	4m	W	U.S.	12 MAY 1873	Mt. Olivet
742	Brother, John, teacher	20y	W	U.S.	18 JAN 1874	Mt. Olivet
124	Brousa, Edward, painter	31y	W	Ger.	16 AUG 1858	Congressional
489	Broushig, Simon	3m	W	D.C.	06 NOV 1870	Hebrew
374	Brower, Abraham K., clerk	33y	W	Pa.	05 FEB 1869	Congressional
143	Brown, Aaron V., postmaster gen.	63y	W	Va.	08 MAR 1859	Congressional
040	Brown, Abitha	104y	W	Md.	16 MAR 1856	Georgetown, Catholic
452	Brown, Abraham	6m	C	D.C.	11 APR 1870	Washington Asylum
337	Brown, Ada	6m	C	U.S.	11 AUG 1868	Washington Asylum
708	Brown, Adair, laborer	72y	C		14 JUL 1873	Washington Asylum
242	Brown, Adalaide	3m	W	D.C.	10 OCT 1866	Methodist
187	Brown, Adalina	25y	C	D.C.	12 AUG 1860	Young Mens
580	Brown, Addison, shoemaker	52y	W	Md.	05 FEB 1872	Holy Rood
382	Brown, Alfred	1y	C		16 MAR 1869	Young Mens
336	Brown, Alice	1y	C	R.I.	11 AUG 1868	
441	Brown, Allen	1y	C		22 FEB 1870	
204	Brown, Alphonso	8m	C	D.C.	18 JUN 1861	Young Mens
506	Brown, Ambrose, gas fitter	20y	W		16 FEB 1871	Congressional
684	Brown, Amelia	25y	C	U.S.	02 APR 1873	Small Pox*
764	Brown, Amelia	20y	C	U.S.	14 MAY 1874	Washington Asylum

District of Columbia Interments (Index to Deaths), 1855-1874

Page	Name	Age	Race	Birth	Death Date	Burial Ground
758	Brown, Amelia A.	9m	C	U.S.	02 APR 1874	
091	Brown, Andrew, child of		W		14 SEP 1857	Congressional
280	Brown, Andrew J.	11m	W	D.C.	08 OCT 1867	
002	Brown, Andrew, laborer	80y	C	Md.	— JAN 1855	Washington Asylum
752	Brown, Ann E.	5y	W	U.S.	25 MAR 1874	Mt. Olivet
140	Brown, Ann M.J.	7m	C	D.C.	04 FEB 1859	Foundry
725	Brown, Anna Eliz.	3y	W	D.C.	18 OCT 1873	Congressional*
131	Brown, Annie	1y	C	D.C.	27 OCT 1858	Harmony
597	Brown, Archer, laborer	80y	C	U.S.	17 MAY 1872	Unknown
538	Brown, Arelia	21y	W	Pa.	30 SEP 1871	Congressional*
343	Brown, August W., child of		C		— AUG 1868	
461	Brown, Augusta	38y	W		16 JUL 1870	Congressional
550	Brown, Auguste	8y	C	D.C.	28 DEC 1871	
545	Brown, Basil, laborer	27y	C	Md.	19 NOV 1871	Washington
256	Brown, Bedford, Dr., child of	4m	W	D.C.	14 MAR 1867	Congressional
677	Brown, Ben	19y	C	U.S.	10 MAR 1873	Small Pox
390	Brown, Bettie C.	27y	W	Va.	16 MAY 1869	Fairfax Co., Va.
282	Brown, C., Mrs.		W	Md.	29 NOV 1867	Montgomery Co., Md.
309	Brown, Caroline	22y	C		20 APR 1868	Mt. Olivet
691	Brown, Carrie	7y	C	U.S.	19 MAY 1873	Small Pox*
421	Brown, Catharine R.	1y	W		11 OCT 1869	Mt. Olivet
244	Brown, Charity	30y	C	Md.	08 NOV 1866	Young Mens
295	Brown, Charles	3y	C	D.C.	23 FEB 1868	Alms House
049	Brown, Charles	7d	W	D.C.	06 JUL 1856	Ebenezer
071	Brown, Charles	8y	W		20 FEB 1857	Foundry
584	Brown, Charles	33y	W	D.C.	01 MAR 1872	Holy Rood
258	Brown, Charles	28y	C		25 APR 1867	Young Mens
501	Brown, Charles	1y	C	Va.	19 JAN 1871	Young Mens
436	Brown, Charles A.	9m	C		12 JAN 1870	Union
004	Brown, Charles C.	3d	C		21 MAR 1855	Harmony
222	Brown, Charlotte	11m	W	D.C.	27 MAY 1866	Mt. Olivet
642	Brown, Chas.	26y	C	U.S.	24 DEC 1872	Small Pox
188	Brown, Chas. Henry	8m	W	D.C.	28 AUG 1860	Western
501	Brown, Chas., laborer	33y	C	Md.	10 JAN 1871	Potters Field
039	Brown, Child of And.		W	D.C.	28 MAR 1856	Congressional
758	Brown, Clara	1y	C	U.S.	03 APR 1874	
454a	Brown, Clara A., pauper	29y	C	Va.	15 MAY 1870	Washington Asylum
373	Brown, Claud	11m	C		31 JAN 1869	Harmony
696	Brown, Cora	8y	C	D.C.	05 JUN 1873	Washington Asylum
195	Brown, Daniel	1y	C	D.C.	17 DEC 1860	
264	Brown, Daniel	2y	C	D.C.	28 JUL 1867	Union
243	Brown, Daniel		C		07 NOV 1866	Young Mens
012	Brown, Daniel, laborer	35y	W	Ire.	22 JUN 1855	St. Peters
006	Brown, Danl.	7m	C	D.C.	26 APR 1855	Foundry
724	Brown, David, laborer	49y	B	Md.	15 OCT 1873	St. Patricks
690	Brown, David P., messenger	58y	W	Pa.	30 MAY 1873	
674	Brown, Dora	23y	C	U.S.	14 MAR 1873	Washington Asylum
735	Brown, Edmund F., notary public	66y	W	U.S.	10 DEC 1873	Congressional*
115	Brown, Edward	4y	C	D.C.	09 JUN 1858	St. Matthews
154	Brown, Edward K.	5m	W	D.C.	16 JUL 1859	Congressional
026	Brown, Edwd.	10m	W		21 OCT 1855	Congressional
208	Brown, Edwin L.	7m	W	D.C.	31 JUL 1862	Congressional
445	Brown, Elias Albert	6y	W		13 MAR 1870	Glenwood
305	Brown, Eliza	84y	C	Md.	25 MAR 1868	St. Patricks
737	Brown, Eliza, cook	16y	C	U.S.	26 DEC 1873	Mt. Pleasant
778a	Brown, Elizabeth	9d	C	U.S.	08 JUL 1874	
029	Brown, Elizabeth	20d	C		29 NOV 1855	Alms House
255	Brown, Elizabeth	66y	C	D.C.	10 MAR 1867	Beckett's

District of Columbia Interments (Index to Deaths), 1855-1874

Page	Name	Age	Race	Birth	Death Date	Burial Ground
690	Brown, Elizabeth	45y	C	U.S.	29 MAY 1873	Small Pox
353	Brown, Elizabeth	76y	W		25 SEP 1868	Washington Asylum
506	Brown, Elizabeth M.	63y	W	Md.	09 FEB 1871	Congressional
006	Brown, Elizabeth M.	4y	C	D.C.	11 APR 1855	Poor House
602	Brown, Ellen	55y	W	Ire.	04 MAY 1872	Mt. Olivet
403	Brown, Ellen	1y	C	D.C.	04 JUL 1869	St. Patricks
689	Brown, Ellen C.	45y	C	U.S.	28 MAY 1873	Germantown, Pa.
694	Brown, Ellen Jenie	10m	W	D.C.	11 JUN 1873	Glenwood
518	Brown, Ellen M.	6m			06 MAY 1871	Methodist
710	Brown, Emily Francis		W	D.C.	02 AUG 1873	
735	Brown, Emily, laundress	50y	C	U.S.	13 DEC 1873	Ebenezer
465	Brown, Emma	3m	C		02 JUL 1870	Ebenezer
248	Brown, Emma	1y	C	D.C.	02 DEC 1866	Young Mens
079	Brown, Ferdinand	4m	W	D.C.	14 JUN 1857	Holmead
207	Brown, Fillmore	5y	W	D.C.	16 JUL 1862	Methodist
243	Brown, Frances	24y	W	D.C.	02 NOV 1866	Alms House
752	Brown, Francis	44y	C	U.S.	26 MAR 1874	Washington Asylum
298	Brown, Francis	1m	C	D.C.	16 FEB 1868	Young Mens
552	Brown, Frank	13y	C	D.C.	05 JAN 1872	Washington
106	Brown, Franklin P.	3y	W	D.C.	26 FEB 1858	Foundry
008	Brown, Fredk., waiter	37y	C	Md.	09 MAY 1855	Harmony
590	Brown, Geo. W.	9m	W	D.C.	01 APR 1872	
459	Brown, George	2y	C		01 JUN 1870	
680	Brown, George	30y	C	U.S.	04 APR 1873	Washington Asylum
342	Brown, George	4y	C	D.C.	17 AUG 1868	Young Mens
642	Brown, George, laborer	65y	C	U.S.	01 DEC 1872	Mt. Olivet
494	Brown, George W., architect		W	Eng.	21 DEC 1870	Richmond, Va.
408	Brown, George Washington	10y	C	D.C.	25 AUG 1869	Holmead
270	Brown, Georgena	1y	C	D.C.	14 AUG 1867	Young Mens
177	Brown, Georgiana	20y	C	Va.	18 APR 1860	Foundry
337	Brown, Harriet	6y	C	U.S.	05 AUG 1868	Washington Asylum
528	Brown, Harriet	2y	C	Va.	17 JUL 1871	Young Mens
778a	Brown, Harry	1m	C	U.S.	02 JUL 1874	
158	Brown, Harry Eugene	11m	W	D.C.	20 AUG 1859	
066	Brown, Hennee	25y	C	D.C.	20 DEC 1856	Washington Asylum
758	Brown, Henry	4m	C	U.S.	18 APR 1874	
273	Brown, Henry, cobbler	45y	C	Va.	19 SEP 1867	Ebenezer
732	Brown, Henry P., clerk	27y	W	U.S.	26 NOV 1873	Auburn, N.Y.
515	Brown, Henry, waiter	60y	C	D.C.	03 MAR 1871	Congressional
404	Brown, I.	Still	C	D.C.	01 JUL 1869	Washington Asylum
330	Brown, Ida Rebecca	28d	C	D.C.	07 JUL 1868	Union
664	Brown, Ignatius	32y	W	U.S.	21 JAN 1873	Small Pox*
662	Brown, Jacob	35y	C	U.S.	10 JAN 1873	Small Pox
239	Brown, James	4y	W	D.C.	02 OCT 1866	Mt. Olivet
109	Brown, James B.	3y	W	D.C.	28 MAR 1858	Foundry
222	Brown, James P.				05 MAY 1866	Philadelphia, Pa.
063	Brown, James, slave	65y	C	Md.	20 NOV 1856	Foundry
717	Brown, Jane, Mrs., domestic	72y	C	Md.	05 SEP 1873	
079	Brown, Jeremiah				16 JUN 1857	Harmony
351	Brown, Jim	1y	C	D.C.	20 SEP 1868	Young Mens
243	Brown, Joanna C.	62y	W	D.C.	24 NOV 1866	Glenwood
303	Brown, John		C		24 MAR 1868	Alms House
302	Brown, John		C		23 MAR 1868	Alms House
001	Brown, John	64y	W	D.C.*	09 JAN 1855	Congressional
161	Brown, John	60y	W	Ire.	05 SEP 1859	Mt. Olivet
764	Brown, John	35y	W	Unk.	16 MAY 1874	Washington Asylum
009	Brown, John Alexr.	3y	W	La.	17 MAY 1855	Baltimore, Md.
538	Brown, John E.	7y	C	D.C.	29 SEP 1871	

Page	Name	Age	Race	Birth	Death Date	Burial Ground
054	Brown, John Elliot	6m	W	D.C.	21 AUG 1856	St. Peters
627	Brown, John, laborer	97y	C	U.S.	01 SEP 1872	
723	Brown, John, servant	32y	B	Va.	08 OCT 1873	Young Mens
112	Brown, John T., carpenter	34y	W	Md.	25 APR 1858	Foundry
770	Brown, Jos.	9m	C	U.S.	28 JUN 1874	
372	Brown, Josehpine	6y	C	D.C.	17 JAN 1869	Washington Asylum
712	Brown, Joseph	14d	C	D.C.	20 AUG 1873	Mt. Olivet
663	Brown, Joseph	70y	C	U.S.	06 JAN 1873	Small Pox*
158	Brown, Julia	42y	C	U.S.	19 AUG 1859	
288	Brown, Julia	35y	C	D.C.	29 DEC 1867	Freedmen's Hospital
286	Brown, Julia, child of	Still	C	D.C.	14 DEC 1867	Freedmen's Hospital
377	Brown, Julia, nurse [sic]	6y	C	Md.	08 FEB 1869	Mt. Olivet
458	Brown, Kate	Still	C	D.C.	28 JUN 1870	Potters Field
432	Brown, Kate	18y	C	Va.	21 DEC 1869	Washington Asylum
590	Brown, Kate (Jacobs)	25y	C	D.C.	02 APR 1872	Young Mens
495	Brown, Kemp	34y	C	U.S.	11 DEC 1870	Potters Field
055	Brown, Larry	1y	C	D.C.	12 AUG 1856	Western
557	Brown, Letha	85y	C	Md.	02 FEB 1872	
176	Brown, Leuellen A.	14y	W	D.C.	16 APR 1860	Glenwood
404	Brown, Levi	9m	C		15 JUL 1869	
185	Brown, Lewis H., shoemaker	48y	C	D.C.	25 JUL 1860	Mt. Olivet
400	Brown, Lillian Belle	Still	W		05 JUL 1869	Congressional
386	Brown, Lillie M.	3y	W	D.C.	18 APR 1869	Congressional
555	Brown, Lilly	1y	C	D.C.	28 JAN 1872	
501	Brown, Lilly B.	1y	C	D.C.	16 JAN 1871	Harmony
441	Brown, Lincoln	2y	C		25 FEB 1870	Holmead
306	Brown, Lizza, domestic	22y	C	D.C.	09 APR 1868	Alms House
297	Brown, Lizzie		C		c.25 FEB 1868	Alms House
435	Brown, Lizzie R.	5y	W		11 JAN 1870	Mt. Olivet
752	Brown, Louisa	1y	C	U.S.	19 MAR 1874	
292	Brown, Louisa		C		13 JAN 1868	Alms House
378	Brown, Lucinda, cook	45y	C	Md.	09 FEB 1869	Harmony
778a	Brown, Lucinda E.	1y	C	U.S.	22 JUL 1874	Beckett's
493	Brown, Lucy	10y	C	Va.	25 DEC 1870	Ebenezer
209	Brown, Lucy	3y	W	D.C.	01 JAN 1866	Holmead
328	Brown, Lucy	11m	C	D.C.	13 JUL 1868	Western
083	Brown, Lucy C.	1y	C	D.C.	19 JUL 1857	
305	Brown, Lucy, domestic	83y	C	Md.	13 MAR 1868	Carroll Chapel
469	Brown, Lucy F.	10y	W	Pa.	19 AUG 1870	Germantown, Pa.
746	Brown, Magdalena, dressmaker	29y	W	Ger.	22 FEB 1874	Prospect Hill
778a	Brown, Maggie I.	5d	W	U.S.	04 JUL 1874	Glenwood
711	Brown, Manda Ann	16m	C	D.C.	09 AUG 1873	
732	Brown, Margaret	73y	W	Ire.	28 NOV 1873	Flat Bush, N.Y.
117	Brown, Margaret	37y	W	D.C.	27 JUN 1858	Potters Field
351	Brown, Maria, infant of	13d	W		04 SEP 1868	
493	Brown, Maria, laborer	90y	C	Va.	18 DEC 1870	Ebenezer
074	Brown, Martha	1y	C	D.C.	22 MAR 1857	Young Mens
372	Brown, Martha A.	26y	C	Va.	29 JAN 1869	Washington Asylum
477	Brown, Martha E.	22y	W	Pa.	05 SEP 1870	Congressional
644	Brown, Mary		C	U.S.	19 DEC 1872	
153	Brown, Mary	4m	W	D.C.	03 JUL 1859	Congressional
347	Brown, Mary	33y	W	Ger.	21 SEP 1868	Congressional
758	Brown, Mary	52y	W	U.S.	22 APR 1874	Congressional
514	Brown, Mary	52y	W		17 MAR 1871	Glenwood
157	Brown, Mary	35y	C	D.C.	10 AUG 1859	Harmony
086	Brown, Mary	10m	C		09 AUG 1857	Harmony
231	Brown, Mary	5m	C		19 AUG 1866	Holmead
174	Brown, Mary	5m	C	D.C.	09 MAR 1860	Mt. Olivet

Page	Name	Age	Race	Birth	Death Date	Burial Ground
107	Brown, Mary	61y	W		06 MAR 1858	Oak Hill
683	Brown, Mary	5m	C	U.S.	08 APR 1873	Small Pox
060	Brown, Mary	22y	C	N.C.	16 OCT 1856	St. Patricks
366	Brown, Mary	4y	B	D.C.	21 DEC 1868	Union
423	Brown, Mary	2y	C	D.C.	26 OCT 1869	Washington Asylum
204	Brown, Mary	8m	C		23 JUN 1861	Young Mens
764	Brown, Mary A.	4y	W	U.S.	03 MAY 1874	Mt. Olivet
068	Brown, Mary A.	17y	C	D.C.	10 JAN 1857	Young Mens
086	Brown, Mary E.	5m	C	D.C.	04 AUG 1857	Colored
370	Brown, Mary E., housekeeper	44y	C	N.Y.	28 JAN 1869	Mt. Olivet
395	Brown, Mary E.	4y	Y	U.S.	15 JUN 1869	Mt. Olivet
340	Brown, Mary Ella	1y	W	D.C.	12 AUG 1868	Congressional
010	Brown, Mary Jane	9m	W	D.C.	02 JUN 1855	Foundry
334	Brown, Mary Jane, servant	20y	C		01 JUL 1868	Freedmen's Hospital
248	Brown, Mary Jane	45y	W	Va.	03 DEC 1866	Rock Creek
393	Brown, Mary, Miss	88y	W		22 MAY 1869	Holmead
370	Brown, Mary Virginia	2m	W		27 JAN 1869	Baltimore, Md.
283	Brown, Matilda	1y	C	D.C.	19 NOV 1867	Potters Field
383	Brown, Matilda	14d	C	D.C.	05 MAR 1869	Washington Asylum
078	Brown, Michael, laborer	40y	W	Ire.	22 MAY 1857	St. Patricks
315	Brown, Mrs.	54y	C	Md.	24 MAY 1868	Harmony
063	Brown, Nancy, cook	19y	C	U.S.	27 NOV 1856	Young Mens
074	Brown, Nathaniel	9m	C	D.C.	19 MAR 1857	Young Mens
599	Brown, Nelly	2y	C	U.S.	28 MAY 1872	Unknown
546	Brown, Nelson	9m	C	D.C.	22 NOV 1871	
658	Brown, Nelson	60y	C	U.S.	02 JAN 1873	Washington Asylum
083	Brown, Octavia	35y	C	Va.	21 JUL 1857	Foundry
441	Brown, Oelistius	60y	C	Md.	21 FEB 1870	Mt. Olivet
045	Brown, Peggy	80y	C	Md.	22 MAY 1856	Harmony
015	Brown, Pricilla, slave	70y	C	Va.	14 JUL 1855	Foundry
438	Brown, R., infant of Mrs.	Still	C		14 JAN 1870	Young Mens
536	Brown, Rachel A.	90y	W	Md.	18 SEP 1871	Glenwood
157	Brown, Richard, blacksmith	60y	W	Md.	13 AUG 1859	Congressional
185	Brown, Robert	7y	W	D.C.	25 JUL 1860	Carroll Chapel
354	Brown, Robert	84y	W	Scot.	02 OCT 1868	Congressional
538	Brown, Robert	5d	C	D.C.	28 SEP 1871	Young Mens
347	Brown, Robert M., clerk	26y	W	Md.	07 SEP 1868	Congressional
544	Brown, Robt. H.	7m	C	D.C.	04 NOV 1871	
689	Brown, Rolins	9m	C	U.S.	25 MAY 1873	
444	Brown, Rosa	51y	W	Md.	25 MAR 1870	Congressional
465	Brown, Rosa Bell	6m	C		06 JUL 1870	Ebenezer
485	Brown, Rose	9m	C	D.C.	09 OCT 1870	Ebenezer
069	Brown, Ruben, huckster	45y	W	Md.	29 JAN 1857	Foundry
488	Brown, Sally	70y	C	Va.	17 NOV 1870	Washington Asylum
144	Brown, Saml. L.	5m	W	D.C.	18 MAR 1859	Glenwood
132	Brown, Samuel, grocer	28y	W	Pa.	15 NOV 1858	Glenwood
742	Brown, Samuel, laborer	80y	C	U.S.	15 JAN 1874	
071	Brown, Sarah	38y	W		21 FEB 1857	Glenwood
742	Brown, Sarah	50y	C	U.S.	19 JAN 1874	Washington Asylum
598	Brown, Scarlet	8y	C	U.S.	13 MAY 1872	Small Pox
397	Brown, Sidney	10m	W		27 JUN 1869	Georgetown, Catholic
618	Brown, Spencer	78y	C	U.S.	12 AUG 1872	Washington Asylum
213	Brown, Sraah	20y	W	D.C.	22 FEB 1866	
288	Brown, Stanley, dentist	26y	W	D.C.	16 DEC 1867	Baltimore, Md.
354	Brown, Stell	Still	W		19 OCT 1868	Mt. Olivet
490	Brown, Susan	75y	C	Va.	27 NOV 1870	Ebenezer
479	Brown, Susan	90y	C	Md.	09 SEP 1870	Washington Asylum
706	Brown, Susan	70y	C	Md.	09 JUL 1873	Washington Asylum

Page	Name	Age	Race	Birth	Death Date	Burial Ground
627	Brown, Susan, servant	20y	C	U.S.	08 SEP 1872	
631	Brown, Susan, servant	24y	C	U.S.	07 OCT 1872	
707	Brown, Susie	9m	C	D.C.	29 JUL 1873	Holmead/Mt. Pleasant
283	Brown, Sylvester	5y	C	Md.	20 NOV 1867	Potters Field
147	Brown, T.	65y	W		20 APR 1859	Western
078	Brown, T., Mrs., child of		W		24 MAY 1857	Foundry
717	Brown, T.J.	2m	C	D.C.	01 SEP 1873	Young Mens
048	Brown, Thomas	50y	C		21 JUN 1856	Alms House
362	Brown, Thomas	25y	C	U.S.	09 NOV 1868	Washington Asylum
362	Brown, Thomas B., clerk	51y	W		29 NOV 1868	Glenwood
138	Brown, Thomas C., barber	19y	C	D.C.	06 JAN 1859	Colored
057	Brown, Thomas, laborer	54y	C	Del.	01 SEP 1856	Washington Asylum
581	Brown, Thornton	4y	W	D.C.	18 FEB 1872	Washington
017	Brown, Verginius	4m	C	D.C.	22 JUL 1855	Harmony
396	Brown, Virginia	10y	C	Va.	08 JUN 1869	
474	Brown, Virginia	11m	C		20 AUG 1870	Washington Asylum
764	Brown, Virginia, domestic	30y	C	U.S.	03 MAY 1874	
636	Brown, W.C.	9y	W	U.S.	22 NOV 1872	Oak Hill
729	Brown, W.G.	2m	W	U.S.	09 NOV 1873	Prospect Hill
244	Brown, W.H.G.	32y	C		19 NOV 1866	Young Mens
638	Brown, Wallace, laborer	27y	C	U.S.	04 NOV 1872	Washington Asylum
710	Brown, Wilie	4m	W	D.C.	08 AUG 1873	Glenwood
764	Brown, William	1y	C	U.S.	01 MAY 1874	
712	Brown, William	8m	C	D.C.	17 AUG 1873	Potters Field
495	Brown, William	20y	W	N.H.	09 DEC 1870	Potters Field
442	Brown, William	11m	C		09 FEB 1870	Young Mens
248	Brown, William E., paver	29y	W	Md.	12 DEC 1866	Glenwood
246	Brown, William H.	2y	W	D.C.	22 DEC 1866	Glenwood
764	Brown, William L., plate printer	29y	W	U.S.	23 MAY 1874	Glenwood
417	Brown, William T.				03 SEP 1869	Glenwood
068	Brown, Willie G.	1y	W	Va.	03 JAN 1857	St. Matthews
615	Brown, Wm.	65y	C	U.S.	18 JUL 1872	
604	Brown, Wm.	5y	C	Va.	06 JUN 1872	Ebenezer
272	Brown, Wm.	60y	C		21 AUG 1867	Freedmen's Bureau
546	Brown, Wm.	75y	W	Eng.	31 NOV 1871	Glenwood
719	Brown, Wm.	57y	W	Scot.	20 SEP 1873	Mt. Olivet
536	Brown, Wm. A.	1y	W		18 SEP 1871	Methodist
515	Brown, Wm. H.	3y	C	D.C.	05 MAR 1871	Union
357	Brown, Wm. H.	3m	B	D.C.	16 OCT 1868	Washington Asylum
513	Brown, Wm. H.	3y	C	D.C.	07 MAR 1871	Young Mens
394	Brown, Wm. Henry, marine drummer	15y	W	Pa.	29 JUN 1869	Congressional
586	Brown, Wm., messenger	18y	C	Va.	13 MAR 1872	Western
595	Brown, Wm., sailor	28y	W	Ire.	16 APR 1872	Congressional
592	Brown, Wm., seaman	28y	W	Ire.	17 APR 1872	
141	Brown, Wm. W.	1y	C	D.C.	20 FEB 1859	Harmony
141	Brown, [blank]	Still	C	D.C.	20 FEB 1859	Colored Methodist
141	Brown, [blank]	Still	C	D.C.	20 FEB 1859	Colored Methodist
028	Brown, [blank]	8m	W		16 OCT 1855	Georgetown
059	Brown, [blank]	Still	C	D.C.	22 SEP 1856	Harmony
071	Brown, [blank]		W	D.C.	23 FEB 1857	Holmead
197	Brown, [blank]	54y	C		20 JAN 1861	Mt. Olivet
451	Brown, [blank]	Still	C		05 APR 1870	Washington Asylum
122	Brown, [blank]	6m	C		21 JUL 1858	Western
091	Brown, [blank]	28y	C		15 SEP 1857	Young Mens
012	Brown, [blank]	6m	W		27 JUN 1855	West
204	Brown, [blank]	Still	C	D.C.	14 JUN 1861	Young Mens
492	Brown, [blank]	2m	C	D.C.	10 DEC 1870	Young Mens
235	Brown, [blank], child of	5y	C	D.C.	12 SEP 1866	Young Mens

Page	Name	Age	Race	Birth	Death Date	Burial Ground
032	Brown, [blank], Mr.	6m	W		07 DEC 1855	Western
002	Brown, [premature infant]		C		— JAN 1855	Young Mens
051	Browne, Anna M.	18y	C	D.C.	28 JUL 1856	Harmony
313	Browne, Hattie P.	4y	W	D.C.	28 MAY 1868	Glenwood
289	Browne, Hiram T., student	16y	W	N.Y.	02 JAN 1868	Glenwood
534	Browne, John M.	38y	C	D.C.	27 AUG 1871	Harmony
097	Browne, Maria, seamstress	67y	C	Va.	26 NOV 1857	Harmony
054	Browne, Martha	6m	C	D.C.	02 AUG 1856	Harmony
682	Browne, Wm. H.	65y	W	U.S.	29 APR 1873	Fredericksburg, Va.
374	Browning, Ellen	40y	W	Md.	11 FEB 1869	Congressional
544	Browning, M.R.	1y	W		08 NOV 1871	Methodist
170	Brownman, I.	2m	W	D.C.	29 JAN 1860	German
667	Broxton, Frank	3y	C	U.S.	08 FEB 1873	Orphans Asylum, Col.
306	Bruce, Ann Amelia, monthly nurse	38y	C	Pa.	14 APR 1868	Harmony
264	Bruce, Celia, cook	82y	C	Md.	11 JUL 1867	Harmony
442	Bruce, Ferguson	14y	C	Md.	11 FEB 1870	Washington Asylum
268	Bruce, Henrietta	2y	C	D.C.	09 AUG 1867	
074	Bruce, J. Samuel	8y	W	Md.	28 MAR 1857	Congressional
032	Bruce, John	78y	W	Va.	23 DEC 1855	Congressional*
138	Bruce, John, stone cutter	45y	W	Ire.	14 JAN 1859	Congressional
604	Bruce, Lulie	4y	C	D.C.	09 JUN 1872	Ebenezer
337	Bruce, Martha	9m	C	U.S.	14 AUG 1868	Washington Asylum
725	Bruce, Mary, waiting maid	30y	B	U.S.	22 OCT 1873	Harmony
236	Bruce, Susan B.	15y	C	D.C.	24 SEP 1866	Harmony
270	Bruce, Susan, washerwoman	75y	C	D.C.*	04 AUG 1867	Harmony
604	Bruce, West B.	4y	C	D.C.	14 JUN 1872	Ebenezer
710	Brucheisen, Mrs.	35y	W	Ger.	01 AUG 1873	Prospect Hill
691	Bruff, Ella	18y	W	U.S.	16 MAY 1873	Congressional
157	Bruff, Rich.	1y	W	D.C.	10 AUG 1859	Methodist
341	Bruff, Wm. I.	1y	W	D.C.	02 AUG 1868	Congressional
387	Bruhan, George A.	3y	C		24 APR 1869	Young Mens
379	Brumagin, Mrs., child of	Still	W		31 MAR 1869	Congressional
541	Brumbrey, Wm.	17y	C	Va.	14 OCT 1871	Potters Field
434	Brumerger, Jackson	4y	W		08 JAN 1870	Congressional
402	Brumlar, Francis	1y	W		03 JUL 1869	Mt. Olivet
347	Brun, Jane E., Mrs.	64y	W		26 SEP 1868	Congressional
070	Brun, Michael	50y	W	Ire.	12 FEB 1857	St. Patricks
533	Brundage, Ada	6m	W	D.C.	19 AUG 1871	Glenwood
420	Brundage, Zebulon, machinist	60y	W	N.Y.	11 OCT 1869	Glenwood
314	Brunell, Charles, laborer	43y	W	N.Y.	18 MAY 1868	Congressional
641	Brunell, Sarah	10y	W	U.S.	16 DEC 1872	Small Pox
033	Brunett, Mary J.	30y	W	D.C.	21 JAN 1856	St. Patricks
029	Brunner, Kate E.	1y	W	D.C.	26 NOV 1855	Oak Hill
670	Brunnet, Edward	18y	C	U.S.	17 FEB 1873	Small Pox
336	Brunswick, Alexander	8m	W	D.C.	02 AUG 1868	Washington Hebrew
443	Brunt, Joe, laborer	20y	C	Md.	07 FEB 1870	Washington Asylum
248	Brusmer, Geo. W., reporter	25y	W	Pa.	06 DEC 1866	Philadelphia, Pa.
680	Bruster, Henry A., Indian agent	71y	W	U.S.	08 APR 1873	Rochester, N.Y.
355	Bryan, Anna	6y	W		09 OCT 1868	Congressional
506	Bryan, Benj. H., child of	Still	W	D.C.	10 FEB 1871	Congressional
074	Bryan, Elizabeth A.	4y	W	D.C.	24 MAR 1857	Methodist
661	Bryan, Florance E.	9m	W	U.S.	23 JAN 1873	Glenwood
764	Bryan, Joseph	79y	W	U.S.	20 MAY 1874	Glenwood
207	Bryan, Mary	42y	W	Va.	13 JUL 1862	Glenwood
165	Bryan, Mary	84y	W	N.C.	08 NOV 1859	Methodist
770	Bryan, Raphael	20m	W	U.S.	20 JUN 1874	Congressional*
660	Bryan, Wm. F.	10y	W	U.S.	17 JAN 1873	Glenwood
094	Bryan, Wyatt, drover	63y	C	Va.	24 OCT 1857	Harmony

Page	Name	Age	Race	Birth	Death Date	Burial Ground
087	Bryant, A.	1m	C		16 AUG 1857	Western
470	Bryant, Ann	2y	W	D.C.	21 AUG 1870	Congressional
425	Bryant, Charles D.	1y	W	D.C.	27 NOV 1869	Mt. Olivet
077	Bryant, J., child of	12d			07 MAY 1857	Western
377	Bryant, John	50y	C		28 FEB 1869	Washington Asylum
042	Bryant, John H.	7y	C	D.C.	14 APR 1856	West
351	Bryant, Joseph	4y	C	D.C.	20 SEP 1868	
528	Bryant, Lily M.	7m	C	D.C.	15 JUL 1871	Congressional*
306	Bryant, Mary	1y	C	D.C.	02 APR 1868	Young Mens
779	Bryant, Mary J.	17m	W	U.S.	28 JUL 1874	
351	Bryant, William Ward	9y	C	D.C.	10 SEP 1868	Good Hope, Md.
174	Bryant, [blank]	11m	C	D.C.	06 MAR 1860	Western
111	Bryant, [blank]	12d	C		15 APR 1858	Western
104	Bryant, [blank]	14d	C		12 FEB 1858	Western
314	Bryce, John	52y	W	N.Y.	15 MAY 1868	Alms House
071	Bryon, Elizabeth	61y	W	Md.	14 FEB 1857	Methodist
036	Bucacy, Ann, house servant	78y	C	Md.	26 FEB 1856	Young Mens
690	Buchanan, Anna, servant	25y	C	Md.	31 MAY 1873	
744	Buchanan, Henry, hackman	33y	C	U.S.	04 JAN 1874	
174	Buchanan, Mary, cook	50y	C	Va.	12 MAR 1860	Harmony
117	Buchanan, Polly	48y	C	Va.	26 JUN 1858	Washington Asylum
551	Buchanan, Robt., laborer	50y	C	Md.	— DEC 1871	
522	Buchanan, Sarah	3m	C	D.C.	09 JUN 1871	
613	Bucheler, Sophia	9m	W	U.S.	27 JUL 1872	
236	Buchenough, William, soldier	20y	W	Eng.	19 SEP 1866	Marine
057	Bucheur (alias Bitner), [blank]	40y	W	Ger.	10 SEP 1856	Washington Asylum
616	Buchholtz, Fredk., soldier	32y	W	Ger.	14 JUL 1872	
677	Buchley, Henry	9y	C	U.S.	27 MAR 1873	Small Pox
016	Buchley, Wm. S.	1m	W	D.C.	14 JUL 1855	Congressional
153	Buchly, John	21d	W	D.C.	11 JUL 1859	Congressional
553	Buchly, Rudolph E.	9d	W	D.C.	11 JAN 1872	Congressional
531	Buck, Dennis, clerk	54y	W	Ver.	05 AUG 1871	Congressional*
313	Buckinan, Alice	35y	C	Md.	12 MAY 1868	Freedmen's Hospital
324	Buckingham, Ada	3m	W	D.C.	26 JUL 1868	Mt. Olivet
557	Buckingham, Cabel, whitesmith	76y	W	Md.	02 FEB 1872	Congressional
031	Buckingham, E.F., child of	1d	W		11 DEC 1855	Congressional
487	Buckingham, Lydia F.	79y	W	D.C.	18 NOV 1870	Congressional
599	Buckland, Andw., shoemaker	40y	C	U.S.	11 MAY 1872	Unknown
407	Buckle, Charles H.	1y	W		15 AUG 1869	Congressional
548	Buckley, Bridget	55y	W	Ire.	12 DEC 1871	Mt. Olivet
153	Buckley, Dennis, laborer	35y	W	Ire.	05 JUL 1859	
154	Buckley, E., laborer	35y	W	Ire.	17 JUL 1859	Mt. Olivet
011	Buckley, Honora	25y	W	Ire.	20 JUN 1855	St. Patricks
770	Buckley, Mary	40y	W	Ire.	20 JUN 1874	Mt. Olivet*
403	Buckley, Mary Eliza	23d	W	D.C.	25 JUL 1869	Methodist
552	Buckley, Michael, laborer	72y	W	Ire.	— JAN 1872	Mt. Olivet
553	Buckley, Michael, laborer	72y	W	Ire.	09 JAN 1872	Mt. Olivet
746	Buckley, Millie	40y	C	U.S.	03 FEB 1874	Beckett's
201	Buckly, Geo. Warren	1m	W	D.C.	16 MAR 1861	Congressional
423	Buckner, Mary	14d	C	D.C.	19 OCT 1869	Washington Asylum
526	Buckner, Sallie	80y		Va.	02 JUL 1871	
472	Buckner, Thom, laborer	60y	C	Md.	28 AUG 1870	Freedmen's Hospital
675	Buckner, Wm., carpenter	45y	C	U.S.	28 MAR 1873	Ebenezer
296	Buckstine, Joseph	68y	C	Md.	04 FEB 1868	Freedmen's Hospital
466	Budd, Martha	35y	C	Md.	07 JUL 1870	Young Mens
590	Budd, Peter, laborer	22y	C	Md.	03 APR 1872	Young Mens
065	Budd, Viola	2y	W	Va.	08 DEC 1856	Philadelphia, Pa.
466	Budd, Willa	8m	C	D.C.	05 JUL 1870	Young Mens

District of Columbia Interments (Index to Deaths), 1855-1874

Page	Name	Age	Race	Birth	Death Date	Burial Ground
169	Buddy, William, slave	56y	C	Va.	17 JAN 1860	Alms House
212	Buel, Rufus F., clerk	3y	W		20 FEB 1866	Glenwood
093	Buelman, Nancy		C		11 OCT 1857	
003	Buery, [blank]	8y	C	D.C.	01 FEB 1855	Freedmen's
146	Buete, John Joseph	1y	W	D.C.	18 APR 1859	German
506	Buie, Elizabeth F.	23y	W	D.C.	20 FEB 1871	Congressional
366	Builleul, Mary A.	30y		D.C.	06 DEC 1868	
121	Bukpert, Henry	11m	W	D.C.	13 JUL 1858	German
010	Bull, John, pilot	65y	C		16 JUN 1855	Alms House
169	Bulley, Eleanor C.	62y	W	Del.	08 JAN 1860	Congressional
548	Bullman, Geo. M.	42y	W	N.J.	11 DEC 1871	Methodist
664	Buly, Richard	2y	C	U.S.	19 JAN 1873	Small Pox*
540	Bumber, Mrs.	35y	W	D.C.	05 OCT 1871	Glenwood
678	Bumberry, Horace	24y	C	U.S.	15 MAR 1873	Small Pox
492	Bumbray, Thomas	9y	C	Va.	10 DEC 1870	Ebenezer
640	Bumbrey, Jno. N.	13y	C	U.S.	26 DEC 1872	Small Pox*
663	Bumby, Wm.	25y	C	U.S.	07 JAN 1873	Small Pox*
369	Bumday, J.F., infant of	Still	W		05 JAN 1869	Congressional
589	Bumers, Richd.	4y	C	D.C.	31 MAR 1872	
234	Bumray, George, laborer	35y	C	Va.	08 SEP 1866	Holmead
001	Bunce, Maria	17y			17 JAN 1855	
581	Bunce, Milfred, seaman	23y	W	Eng.	18 FEB 1872	Congressional*
542	Bundey, Nat.	1d	C	D.C.	21 OCT 1871	
432	Bundy, Bertie E.	4m	C	D.C.	27 DEC 1869	Washington Asylum
363	Bundy, Grandison	2m	C	D.C.	20 NOV 1868	Washington Asylum
442	Bundy, Wm. H.	3y	C		15 FEB 1870	Washington Asylum
629	Bunell, F.R., clerk	20y		U.S.	20 OCT 1872	
706	Bunell, James		C	D.C.	14 JUL 1873	Holmead
636	Bunell, John, plumber	26y	W	U.S.	16 NOV 1872	
120	Bunn, Mary	3m	C	D.C.	04 JUL 1858	Young Mens
501	Bunson, Maria	56y	C	D.C.	29 JAN 1871	Potters Field
401	Bunty, John	54y	W	Md.	17 JUL 1869	Mt. Olivet
295	Buoy, Mary E.	11m	C	D.C.	18 FEB 1868	
051	Buoz, Wm. Thos.	5m	W	D.C.	25 JUL 1856	Glenwood
613	Burch, Anna R.	8m	C	U.S.	16 JUL 1872	
117	Burch, Edward	6m	W	D.C.	27 JUN 1858	Foundry
036	Burch, Elizabeth	70y	W	Md.	13 FEB 1856	Foundry
102	Burch, Fielder	63y	W	Md.	26 JAN 1858	St. Patricks
415	Burch, Geo. J.	1m	W		27 SEP 1869	Glenwood
191	Burch, Jane E.	23y	W	D.C.	19 OCT 1860	Glenwood
024	Burch, Joseph	2y	W	D.C.	14 SEP 1855	Methodist, East
226	Burch, Thomas W., corp. ofcr.	49y	W	D.C.	27 JUN 1866	Mt. Olivet
440	Burch, Verlinda, Miss	49y	W		12 FEB 1870	Glenwood
224	Burch, W.H.	14y	W	D.C.	13 JUN 1866	Congressional
380	Burch, William S.	50y	W		01 MAR 1869	Congressional
038	Burch, William, tinner	22y	W	D.C.	28 MAR 1856	Congressional
182	Burch, Wm. Joseph	8m	W	D.C.	20 JUN 1860	Congressional
611	Burchard, Wm.	1y	W	U.S.	07 JUL 1872	
102	Burche, George W., stone cutter	20y	W	D.C.	23 JAN 1858	St. Patricks
135	Burche, James B.	2y	W	D.C.	03 DEC 1858	Glenwood
118	Burche, James, soldier	28y	W		29 JUN 1858	Foundry
188	Burchell, Anna	2m	W	D.C.	23 AUG 1860	Congressional
661	Burck, Adolph, topographer	41y	W	Ger.	25 JAN 1873	Congressional*
404	Burd, Lusener	1y	C		— JUL 1869	
620	Burden, Amy	7m	W	U.S.	10 AUG 1872	Glenwood
684	Burden, Lavenia	18y	C	U.S.	23 APR 1873	Small Pox
626	Burden, Wm. R.	5y	W	U.S.	23 SEP 1872	
074	Burdett, James E.	1y	W	D.C.	20 MAR 1857	Congressional

District of Columbia Interments (Index to Deaths), 1855-1874

Page	Name	Age	Race	Birth	Death Date	Burial Ground
621	Burdett, Robt., student	14y	W	U.S.	02 AUG 1872	
521	Burdette, Clara Belle	5m	W	D.C.	04 JUN 1871	Congressional
741	Burdine, Margret	84y	W	U.S.	11 JAN 1874	Congressional*
741	Burdine, Margret E.	32y	W	U.S.	10 JAN 1874	Congressional*
189	Burdine, Reuben	64y	W	Ga.	10 SEP 1860	St. Marys
133	Burdine, William, joiner	74y	W	Va.	28 NOV 1858	Methodist
390	Burdon, Mary	5m	W	D.C.	29 MAY 1869	Congressional
639	Burfitt, Lizzie	6y	C	U.S.	12 DEC 1872	Small Pox*
407	Burgdorf, Annie R.	4m	W		05 AUG 1869	Congressional
252	Burgdorff, Annie R.	23y	W	D.C.	20 FEB 1867	Congressional
247	Burgee, Clara M.	1y	W	D.C.	26 DEC 1866	Glenwood
251	Burges, Catherine T.	1y	W	D.C.	11 JAN 1867	Mt. Olivet
162	Burgess, Andrew	19d	W	D.C.	19 SEP 1859	Congressional
220	Burgess, Annie, Mrs.	52y	W	Md.	05 MAY 1866	Piscataway, Md.
675	Burgess, Elizabeth	65y	W	U.S.	27 MAR 1873	Congressional*
673	Burgess, Emma, seamstress	30y	C	U.S.	08 MAR 1873	Mt. Olivet
229	Burgess, Franklin	9m	W	D.C.	21 JUL 1866	Congressional
011	Burgess, James	3y	W	D.C.	13 JUN 1855	Congressional
547	Burgess, John F.	1y	W	D.C.	04 DEC 1871	Congressional*
451	Burgess, Mary	1m	C	D.C.	03 APR 1870	Washington Asylum
419	Burgess, Mary Elizabeth	23y	W	D.C.	24 OCT 1869	Congressional
552	Burgess, Polly	75y	C	D.C.	03 JAN 1872	Washington
407	Burgess, Robert	1y	W		12 AUG 1869	Congressional
310	Burgess, Saml., child of	Still	W		c.14 APR 1868	Mt. Olivet
493	Burgess, Samuel S.	1y	C	U.S.	19 DEC 1870	Ebenezer
474	Burgess, William	8m	C		13 AUG 1870	Washington Asylum
185	Burgess, [blank], Mr.	35y	W		14 JUL 1860	Oak Hill
303	Burgesser, Saml. S., lawyer	49y	W	Md.	23 MAR 1868	Congressional
249	Burgis, Mary A.	3y	W	D.C.	03 JAN 1867	Mt. Olivet
165	Burgoyne, William, engineer	35y	W	Va.	25 NOV 1859	Congressional*
593	Burieseger, Louisa	2y	W	Va.	29 APR 1872	Mt. Olivet
122	Burk, Francis	3y	W	D.C.	25 JUL 1858	St. Peters
020	Burk, Infant	1y	C		12 AUG 1855	
199	Burk, Isabella	15y	C		11 FEB 1861	Western
133	Burk, Mary Ann	1y	W	D.C.	29 NOV 1858	Mt. Olivet
177	Burk, Thos., child of	Still	W	D.C.	16 APR 1860	Mt. Olivet
105	Burk, [blank], Mr.	70y	C		22 FEB 1858	Western
484	Burkart, Mary Ann	44y	W	Va.	25 OCT 1870	Congressional
265	Burke, Anastasia	68y	W	Ire.	06 JUL 1867	Mt. Olivet*
391	Burke, Bridget	40y	W	Ire.	17 MAY 1869	Mt. Olivet
707	Burke, E.	68y	W	Ire.	06 JUL 1873	Mt. Olivet
122	Burke, Fanny	1y	W	D.C.	26 JUL 1858	St. Peters
421	Burke, Hannorah	45y	C	Ire.	20 OCT 1869	Mt. Olivet
706	Burke, Herbert	22y	C	Va.	19 JUL 1873	Washington Asylum
600	Burke, Isaac, laborer	1y	C	U.S.	28 MAY 1872	Unknown
275	Burke, James	12y	W	D.C.	21 SEP 1867	Alms House
532	Burke, James	40y	W	Ire.	10 AUG 1871	Mt. Olivet*
256	Burke, John	79y	W	Ire.	29 MAR 1867	Mt. Olivet
549	Burke, John B., bar keeper	35y	W	Ire.	19 DEC 1871	Mt. Olivet*
140	Burke, John, laborer	28y	W	Ire.	10 FEB 1859	Mt. Olivet
555	Burke, M.F., shoolmaster	45y	W	Ire.	30 JAN 1872	Mt. Olivet
137	Burke, Margaret		W	Ire.	08 JAN 1859	Mt. Olivet
086	Burke, Michael, soldier		W	Ire.	04 AUG 1857	St. Peters
498	Burke, Michl., pauper	60y		Ire.	10 JAN 1871	Washington Asylum
088	Burke, Nathaniel	10m	C	D.C.	22 AUG 1857	Young Mens
061	Burke, Sarah, laundress	21y	C	D.C.	09 OCT 1856	Methodist, East
137	Burke, Simon, child of	Still	W	D.C.	08 JAN 1859	Mt. Olivet
272	Burke, Sukey	75y	C		04 AUG 1867	Freedmen's Bureau

District of Columbia Interments (Index to Deaths), 1855-1874

Page	Name	Age	Race	Birth	Death Date	Burial Ground
341	Burke, Wm. F.	3m	W	D.C.	07 AUG 1868	Congressional
210	Burke, [blank]	66y	C	Va.	17 JAN 1866	Western
133	Burke, [blank]	1y	C	D.C.	22 NOV 1858	Western
351	Burkhardt, N.	40h	W	D.C.	28 SEP 1868	Prospect Hill
533	Burkheart, Mary		W	D.C.	21 AUG 1871	Prospect Hill
770	Burks, L.	42y	C	U.S.	24 JUN 1874	Young Mens
334	Burley, George	6m	W	D.C.	30 JUL 1868	Young Mens
365	Burn, Mary	19y	W	Ire.	22 DEC 1868	Mt. Olivet
591	Burne, Betsey		C	Md.	15 APR 1872	Young Mens
148	Burnes, Mary	26y	W	Ire.	09 MAY 1859	Mt. Olivet
048	Burnes, Thomas	11y	W	N.Y.	10 JUN 1856	St. Patricks
477	Burnett, Albert	2y	W	D.C.	04 SEP 1870	Prospect Hill
735	Burnett, E., painter	56y	C	U.S.	08 DEC 1873	
624	Burnett, Eliza	4y	C	U.S.	11 SEP 1872	
321	Burnett, Elizabeth	3m	W		c.08 JUN 1868	Alms House
465	Burnett, Harry	10m	B		20 JUL 1870	
646	Burnett, James, laborer		C	U.S.	04 DEC 1872	
678	Burnett, Julius	14y	C	U.S.	28 MAR 1873	Small Pox
019	Burnett, Mary E.	16m	W		18 AUG 1855	St. Patricks
523	Burnett, Reburta	5m	C		17 JUN 1871	
489	Burney, John	1y	W	D.C.	10 NOV 1870	Mt. Olivet
667	Burnham, Caroline	37y	W	U.S.	08 FEB 1873	Mt. Olivet
252	Burnhansen, Joseph	7m	W	D.C.	23 FEB 1867	Mt. Olivet
266	Burniff, Jane	64y	W	Va.	21 JUL 1867	Congressional
416	Burnory, Elle	1y	C		10 SEP 1869	Holmead
257	Burns, Austin A.	2y	W	Pa.	11 MAR 1867	Glenwood/Arlington
428	Burns, Catharine	9m	W		04 NOV 1869	Mt. Olivet
720	Burns, Chas., clerk	23y	W		25 SEP 1873	Congressional*
550	Burns, Daniel, sailor	50y	W	Md.	28 DEC 1871	Congressional*
778a	Burns, David Silas	1y	W	U.S.	18 JUL 1874	Mt. Olivet
289	Burns, Elizabeth L.	6m	W	U.S.	30 JAN 1868	Arlington, Va.
477	Burns, Ellen L.	48y	W	Eng.	16 SEP 1870	Congressional
412	Burns, Ellenora	1y	C		10 AUG 1869	
501	Burns, Ignatius	1m	W	D.C.	12 JAN 1871	Mt. Olivet
027	Burns, John	2y	W	D.C.	02 OCT 1855	Foundry
018	Burns, John		W	D.C.	21 AUG 1855	St. Patricks
165	Burns, Lawrence, laborer	21y	W	Md.	23 NOV 1859	Washington Asylum
027	Burns, Margaret	40y			25 OCT 1855	Western
055	Burns, Mary, child of	Still	W		26 AUG 1856	St. Peters
705	Burns, Minnie H.	11m	W	D.C.	10 JUL 1873	Congressional
282	Burns, Miss, servant	25y	W	Ire.	02 NOV 1867	Mt. Olivet
141	Burns, Patrick	6m	W		12 FEB 1859	St. Patricks
663	Burns, Peter	24y	C	U.S.	18 JAN 1873	Small Pox
394	Burns, Thomas	5y	W	D.C.	04 JUN 1869	Mt. Olivet
467	Burns, Thomas I.	8m	W	D.C.	08 JUL 1870	Mt. Olivet
394	Burns, Wm. H.	3m	W	D.C.	22 JUN 1869	Mt. Olivet
721	Burns, Wm. Henry, plasterer	50y	W	Va.	21 SEP 1873	
016	Burns, [blank]	1d	W		24 JUL 1855	Holmead
758	Burntt, Margret E., seamstress	23y	C	U.S.	25 APR 1874	Harmony
758	Burr, Benjamin	22y	C	U.S.	13 APR 1874	Washington Asylum
778a	Burr, Ellen	23y	W	U.S.	26 JUL 1874	Glenwd./Mt. Holly, N.J.
092	Burr, Eugene, engineer	18y	W	D.C.	27 SEP 1857	Oak Hill
430	Burr, Fannie	24y	W		14 DEC 1869	Oak Hill
537	Burr, Franklin A., clerk	42y	W	U.S.	22 SEP 1871	Glenwood
627	Burr, John	1y	C	U.S.	22 SEP 1872	Small Pox
138	Burr, Mattie	20y	W	D.C.	12 JAN 1859	
392	Burr, Wm. N.	3m	C		02 MAY 1869	Washington Asylum
069	Burr, Wm. Waters, clerk	24y	W	Me.	25 JAN 1857	N.H.

Page	Name	Age	Race	Birth	Death Date	Burial Ground
501	Burrell, Jane, servant	17y	C	Va.	07 JAN 1871	Potters Field
207	Burrell, Marian Roberta	2y	C	D.C.	25 JUL 1862	Holmead
294	Burrell, Winnie	72y	C	Va.	20 FEB 1868	Western
263	Burress, Jane S.	78y	W	Md.	20 JUN 1867	Congressional
068	Burrill, Child of Mary		C		01 JAN 1857	Harmony
284	Burroughs, William, wood measr.	70y	W	Md.	25 NOV 1867	Congressional
292a	Burrows, Chas. H.		W	D.C.*	21 FEB 1868	
527	Burrows, Ezra	28y	W	Eng.	10 JUL 1871	German Catholic
417	Burrows, Jane	1d	C		28 SEP 1869	Washington Asylum
752	Burrows, Joshua	28y	C	U.S.	07 MAR 1874	Washington Asylum
239	Burrows, Rebecca	59y	W	Md.	27 OCT 1866	Alms House
292	Burrows, Robert, child of	21d	C	D.C.	16 JAN 1868	Young Mens
293	Burrows, [blank]		W		16 MAR 1868	Presbyterian
088	Burry, Edward	8m	W	D.C.	24 AUG 1857	St. Patricks
407	Bursley, Minda	2y	W		23 AUG 1869	Congressional
483	Burt, William	1y	W	D.C.	12 OCT 1870	Mt. Olivet
154	Burt, [blank]	½d	W	D.C.	14 JUL 1859	Congressional
401	Burten, Mary				29 JUL 1869	Young Mens
682	Burtin, Jean, cook	36y		Fra.	27 APR 1873	Mt. Olivet
589	Burton, Dennis E.	33y	W	D.C.	30 MAR 1872	Oak Hill
399	Burwell, Mary	76y	W		28 JUL 1869	Congressional
315	Buryman, Mary		C		c.01 MAY 1868	Alms House
440	Buschell, George, stone cutter	50y	W	Eng.	02 FEB 1870	Mt. Olivet
743	Buscher, Matilda	41y	W	Ger.	26 JAN 1874	St. Marys
410	Busching, Henry J.	2y	W		10 AUG 1869	Prospect Hill
086	Buschn, Catharine	44y	W	Ger.	04 AUG 1857	German Catholic
778a	Busey, Charles D.	6m	W	U.S.	18 JUL 1874	Glenwood
431	Busey, Henry	65y	W	Md.	28 DEC 1869	Glenwood
318	Busey, Minnie	6y	W	D.C.	06 JUN 1868	Congressional
675	Busey, Warren	15m	W	U.S.	29 MAR 1873	Glenwood
240	Busey, [Julia A.]	40y	W	Va.	13 OCT 1866	Congressional*
375	Bush, Christina	67y	W	Ger.	22 FEB 1869	German Catholic
750	Bush, G.P., watchman	42y	W	U.S.	01 FEB 1874	Congressional*
096	Bush, I.	4y	C		17 NOV 1857	Young Mens
176	Bush, James, child of	2m	C	D.C.	06 APR 1860	Young Mens
449	Bush, Martha	73y	W	Md.	06 APR 1870	Congressional
779	Bush, Mary	1m	W	U.S.	27 JUL 1874	Holyrood
059	Bush, Mary	28y	W	Ire.	29 SEP 1856	St. Peters
220	Bush, Mary E.	20y	C	D.C.	13 MAY 1866	Ebenezer
360	Bush, Mary T.	17y	W	D.C.	25 NOV 1868	Mt. Olivet
221	Bush, Mrs., child of				25 MAY 1866	Young Mens
380	Bushby, Sarah, Mrs.	79y	W	Va.	05 MAR 1869	Glenwood
730	Busher, Annie C.	3m	W	U.S.	17 NOV 1873	
626	Busher, Mary	76y	W	Ger.	28 SEP 1872	St. Marys
434	Buskirk, Mrs. [Saray]	18y	W		31 JAN 1870	Congressional*
704	Butcher, Annie L.	1y	C	D.C.	28 JUL 1873	Harmony
624	Butcher, E.	8m	C	U.S.	16 SEP 1872	
779	Butcher, Elizabeth	66y	C	U.S.	31 JUL 1874	Mt. Pleasant
173	Butcher, Joseph		C	U.S.	27 FEB 1860	Washington Asylum
141	Buthman, Jas. H., merchant	53y	W	Ger.	12 FEB 1859	Congressional
068	Butler, Ann	45y	W	D.C.*	15 JAN 1857	Foundry
778a	Butler, Anna	1m	C	unk.	07 JUL 1874	
638	Butler, Catharine	95y	C	U.S.	23 NOV 1872	
352	Butler, Cecelia	1y	C		22 SEP 1868	Washington Asylum
306	Butler, Charles Henry, laborer	52y	C	Md.	05 APR 1868	Young Mens
667	Butler, Charles M., clerk	28y	W	U.S.	12 FEB 1873	No. Berwick, Me.
269	Butler, Edward P.	11d	C	D.C.	08 AUG 1867	Holmead
140	Butler, Eliza	12y	C	D.C.	09 FEB 1859	Colored

District of Columbia Interments (Index to Deaths), 1855-1874

Page	Name	Age	Race	Birth	Death Date	Burial Ground
451	Butler, Eliza, nurse	66y	C	Va.	15 APR 1870	Harmony
043	Butler, Elizabeth	38y	C	Md.	15 APR 1856	Alms House
333	Butler, Ella	1y	C		18 JUL 1868	Alms House
335a	Butler, Ella				17 JUL 1868	Washington Asylum
473	Butler, Ellen C.	1y	C	D.C.	30 AUG 1870	Mt. Olivet
466	Butler, Emma	3m	C	D.C.	03 JUL 1870	Young Mens
353	Butler, Fanny	30y	C	Va.	09 SEP 1868	Freedmen's Hospital
007	Butler, Frances	47y	W	Va.	04 MAY 1855	St. [Patrick's]
623	Butler, H.	2m	C	U.S.	22 AUG 1872	Mt. Zion
625	Butler, Harriet	21y	C	U.S.	03 SEP 1872	
270	Butler, Harriet E.	18y	C	D.C.	03 AUG 1867	Holmead
616	Butler, Hennie	75y	C	U.S.	05 JUL 1872	
249	Butler, Henry		C		— JAN 1867	Mt. Olivet
732	Butler, Ida F.	29y	W	U.S.	30 NOV 1873	Oak Hill
550	Butler, J.	69y	W	Va.	27 DEC 1871	Congressional
335	Butler, James, child of	3d	C	D.C.	14 JUL 1868	
146	Butler, James, laborer	86y	C	Md.	04 APR 1859	Ebenezer
309	Butler, James T.	9m	C	D.C.	25 APR 1868	Harmony
752	Butler, Jane	7d	C	U.S.	04 MAR 1874	
617	Butler, Jas.	1y	C	U.S.	16 AUG 1872	
020	Butler, Jas.	5m	C		18 AUG 1855	Harmony
644	Butler, Jno. H.	5y	C	U.S.	15 DEC 1872	Mt. Olivet
054	Butler, John	3m	C	D.C.	01 AUG 1856	Ebenezer
421	Butler, John E., laborer	80y	C	Md.	30 OCT 1869	Mt. Olivet
046	Butler, John Fleming, printer	49y	W	Va.	09 JUN 1856	Congressional
172	Butler, Joseph, printer	69y	W	Va.	15 FEB 1860	Congressional*
474	Butler, Lewis	2y	C		31 AUG 1870	Washington Asylum
353	Butler, Louisa	4y	C	D.C.	01 SEP 1868	
116	Butler, Lucy	2m	C		21 JUN 1858	Harmony
115	Butler, Lucy	3m	C	D.C.	01 JUN 1858	St. Peters
526	Butler, Margaret	24y	C	Va.	01 JUL 1871	Washington
295	Butler, Maria	65y	W	Va.	26 FEB 1868	Ebenezer
222	Butler, Martha	35y	C		29 MAY 1866	Ebenezer
663	Butler, Martha E.	4y	C	U.S.	19 JAN 1873	Small Pox
617	Butler, Mary	3y	C	U.S.	01 AUG 1872	
139	Butler, Mary	70y	C		29 JAN 1859	Mt. Olivet
306	Butler, Mary	50y	C	Md.	15 APR 1868	Mt. Olivet
496	Butler, Mary	34y	W	Ire.	18 DEC 1870	Mt. Olivet
436	Butler, Mary Ann	3y	C		09 JAN 1870	Harmony
170	Butler, Mary, cook	43y	C	D.C.	20 JAN 1860	Holmead
413	Butler, Mary E.	1y	C		— AUG 1869	Ebenezer
413	Butler, Mary E.	1y	C		02 AUG 1869	Ebenezer
718	Butler, Mary Ellen	4y	W	D.C.	08 SEP 1873	
531	Butler, Mary H.			Md.	09 AUG 1871	Mt. Olivet
752	Butler, Matilda	40y	C	U.S.	15 MAR 1874	Ebenezer
016	Butler, Matilda	28y	C	Va.	27 JUL 1855	Montgomery Co., Md.
533	Butler, Milly	30y	C	D.C.	22 AUG 1871	Washington
770	Butler, Molly	32y	B	U.S.	08 JUN 1874	
159	Butler, Monacha	96y	C	U.S.	29 AUG 1859	Mt. Olivet
704	Butler, Nancy	70y	C	D.C.	03 JUL 1873	
372	Butler, Patrick, laborer	60y	C	Va.	25 JAN 1869	Freedmen's Hospital
758	Butler, Philip	1y	W	U.S.	20 APR 1874	Graceland
260	Butler, Richard	5d	W	D.C.	27 MAY 1867	Ebenezer
141	Butler, Rodgers, waiter	19y	C	D.C.	20 FEB 1859	Colored
619	Butler, Sarah	14m	C	U.S.	17 AUG 1872	
758	Butler, Sarah	50y	C	U.S.	19 APR 1874	Washington Asylum
752	Butler, Sarah	68y	C	U.S.	19 MAR 1874	Young Mens
530	Butler, Stuart	1y	C	D.C.	31 JUL 1871	

Page	Name	Age	Race	Birth	Death Date	Burial Ground
495	Butler, Ward, laborer	27y	C	Md.	20 DEC 1870	Beckett's
441	Butler, William, boatman	61y	C		22 FEB 1870	Holmead
280	Butler, Winnie	107y	C	Md.	12 OCT 1867	Mt. Olivet
111	Butler, Wm.	36y	C		16 APR 1858	
332	Butler, Wm.	2y	C	D.C.	25 JUL 1868	Alms House
335a	Butler, Wm.				25 JUL 1868	Washington Asylum
047	Butler, Wm.		C		24 JUN 1856	Young Mens
352	Butler, Wm. A.	40y	W		22 SEP 1868	Washington Asylum
002	Butler, Wm. Hanson	3y	C	D.C.	— JAN 1855	Harmony
108	Butler, Wm., servant	16y	C	Md.	26 MAR 1858	St. Patricks
098	Butler, [blank]	3y	C		03 DEC 1857	Methodist
215	Butler, [blank]		C		14 MAR 1866	Young Mens
770	Butterfield, [blank]	3d	W	U.S.	23 JUN 1874	
417	Button, Jane	Still	C		07 SEP 1869	Washington Asylum
779	Butts, Hattie C.	3y	W	U.S.	31 JUL 1874	
537	Butts, Ross	28d	W	D.C.	20 SEP 1871	Va.
507	Buxton, Clarence O	17y	W	N.Y.	23 FEB 1871	Warsaw, N.Y.
300	Buxton, James F.	76y	W	Mass.	05 MAR 1868	Nashua, N.H.
501	Buxton, Nelson, laborer	60y	C	Va.	— JAN 1871	Young Mens
309	Buyer, Anna	22d	W	D.C.	02 APR 1868	Baltimore, Md.
090	Byans, E.A.	6m	W	D.C.	06 SEP 1857	St. Patricks
381	Byram, Clark E.	1y	W		05 MAR 1869	
221	Byrne, Ann	2y	W	D.C.	15 MAY 1866	Mt. Olivet*
355	Byrne, Charles	86y	W	Ire.	24 OCT 1868	Mt. Olivet
326	Byrne, Elizabeth	1y	W	D.C.	25 JUL 1868	Mt. Olivet*
547	Byrne, George F.	40y	W	Md.	04 DEC 1871	Glenwood
233	Byrne, James				31 AUG 1866	Mt. Olivet
633	Byrne, Mary	34y	W	U.S.	07 OCT 1872	
601	Byrne, Matthew, grocer	42y	W	Ire.	25 MAY 1872	Mt. Olivet*
312	Byrne, Thomas, grocer	45y	W	Ire.	27 MAY 1868	Mt. Olivet*
107	Byrnes, A.W., servant	35y	W	Va.	11 MAR 1858	St. Matthews
259	Byrnes, Sarah E.	24y	W	Va.	05 APR 1867	Glenwood
108	Byrnes, Willie	9m	W	D.C.	20 MAR 1858	
640	Byron, Effie Jane	10m	W	U.S.	27 DEC 1872	Small Pox*
640	Byron, Geo. W.	5y	W	U.S.	27 DEC 1872	Small Pox*
475	Byron, Hattie Lee	1y	W	D.C.	21 SEP 1870	Congressional
341	Byron, Jessie T.	7m	W	D.C.	30 AUG 1868	Congressional
071	Byron, John, laborer	38y	W	Ire.	24 FEB 1857	St. Patricks
128	Byvus, Benjamin	3y	C		19 SEP 1858	West River, Md.

District of Columbia Interments (Index to Deaths), 1855-1874

Page	Name	Age	Race	Birth	Death Date	Burial Ground
C						
183	Caden, James, teacher	81y	W	Ire.	28 JUN 1860	Mt. Olivet
309	Cadin, Mary	21y	W	Ire.	10 APR 1868	Mt. Olivet
132	Cady, Edward	53y	W	Ire.	05 NOV 1858	Baltimore, Md.
010	Cady, John, laborer	20y	W	Ire.	18 JUN 1855	Catholic
312	Cady, P., child of	Still	W	D.C.	03 MAY 1868	Mt. Olivet
696	Caesar, Thomas, student	8y	W	D.C.	07 JUN 1873	
236	Cahan, Matilda R.	27y	W	N.Y.	28 SEP 1866	Holmead
415	Cahill, Jno.	1y	W		17 SEP 1869	Mt. Olivet
608	Cahill, John	1y	W	D.C.	13 JUN 1872	
470	Cahill, Mary Agnes	3m	W	D.C.	17 AUG 1870	Mt. Olivet
320	Cahill, [blank]	10y	W	U.S.	17 JUN 1868	Mt. Olivet
500	Cain, Edward H.	9m	W	D.C.	26 JAN 1871	Mt. Olivet
314	Calafornia, Gabriel, child of	Still	W	D.C.	14 MAY 1868	Congressional
144	Calahan, Eliza	62y	W	D.C.	22 MAR 1859	Mt. Olivet
752	Calahan, Jerome, bricklayer	45y	W	U.S.	13 MAR 1874	Mt. Olivet
148	Calahan, Mary	11m	W	D.C.	03 MAY 1859	Mt. Olivet
391	Caldin, Jas. M., infant of		W		12 MAY 1869	Oak Hill
696	Caldwell, A.M., messenger	44y	W	U.S.	27 JUN 1873	Glenwood
289	Caldwell, Catherine	33y		D.C.	10 JAN 1868	Oak Hill
290	Caldwell, Charity M.A., student	16y	W	N.Y.	15 JAN 1868	Mt. Olivet
436	Caldwell, Charles F.	13y	W		25 JAN 1870	Glenwood
298	Caldwell, John, plasterer	30y	W	Ire.	01 FEB 1868	St. Patricks
166	Caldwell, Josiah F.	86y	W	N.J.	15 NOV 1859	Congressional*
680	Caldwell, Thompson B.	50y	C	U.S.	04 APR 1873	
148	Caldwell, [blank]	2d	W	D.C.	06 MAY 1859	Western
302	Calhoun, Lewis A., laborer	22y	W	U.S.	28 MAR 1868	Western
637	Call, Michael	2m	W	U.S.	14 NOV 1872	Washington
155	Callagan, James	9y	W	D.C.	21 JUL 1859	St. Patricks
673	Callaghan, Bridget, housekeeper	34y	W	Ire.	02 MAR 1873	Mt. Olivet
402	Callaghan, John, laborer	50y	W	Ire.	26 JUL 1869	Mt. Olivet
400	Callaghan, Mary, Mrs., matron	55y	W	Md.	29 JUL 1869	Mt. Olivet
062	Callaghan, Patrick, laborer	79y	W	Ire.	06 NOV 1856	St. Peters
137	Callahan, Eliza	1y	W	D.C.	11 JAN 1859	St. Peters
249	Callahan, Elizabeth	30y	W	Ire.	07 JAN 1867	Mt. Olivet
238	Callahan, Mary	8d	W	D.C.	30 SEP 1866	Mt. Olivet
324	Callahan, Mary Teresa	1y	W	D.C.	29 JUL 1868	Mt. Olivet
544	Callahan, Wm. R.	3d	W	D.C.	04 NOV 1871	Congressional
617	Callan, A.H.	1y	W	U.S.	16 AUG 1872	
094	Callan, Abert G.	5y	W	D.C.	23 OCT 1857	St. Matthews
426	Callan, Alphonsus Lee	5y	W	Md.	14 NOV 1869	Georgetown, Catholic
408	Callan, George Thomas	5d	W		12 AUG 1869	Mt. Olivet
635	Callan, Ida	2y	W	U.S.	22 NOV 1872	Small Pox
609	Callan, Ida V.	8m	W	U.S.	14 JUN 1872	
426	Callan, Mary L.	4y	W	D.C.	08 NOV 1869	Mt. Olivet
742	Callan, Roberta L.	3m	W	U.S.	21 JAN 1874	Mt. Olivet
091	Caller, Alphonsus	3y	W	D.C.	12 SEP 1857	Georgetown
450	Callinane, Johanna, Mrs.	72y	W		01 APR 1870	Mt. Olivet
450	Callisher, Elizabeth	3y	W	D.C.	21 APR 1870	Washington Hebrew
450	Callishir, Adolphus S.	4y	W		24 APR 1870	Washington Hebrew
422	Calnion, George A.	2y	C		14 OCT 1869	
771	Calvert, Florence Mabel	7m	W	U.S.	12 JUN 1874	Glenwood
047	Calvert, George, slave	48y	C	Md.	30 JUN 1856	Harmony
102	Calvert, Julia	31y	W		20 JAN 1858	Philadelphia, Pa.
061	Calvert, Lucy, slave	22y	C	D.C.	15 OCT 1856	Colored, East
608	Calvert, Wm. H.	34y	W	D.C.	01 JUN 1872	
114	Calvert, [blank]	24y		Md.	23 MAY 1858	Methodist
143	Calvert, [blank]	21y	C		04 MAR 1859	Young Mens

Page	Name	Age	Race	Birth	Death Date	Burial Ground
394	Cambell, Mary	10m	W	D.C.	28 JUN 1869	Congressional
398	Cambell, Mary	7d	B	D.C.	23 JUN 1869	Washington Asylum
077	Cambell, [blank]	20y	C		09 MAY 1857	Western
342	Cambilard, Letty C.	1y	C	D.C.	10 AUG 1868	Young Mens
365	Camel, Douglas	3y	C	D.C.	— DEC 1868	Young Mens
201	Camer, Catherine	4y	W	D.C.	09 MAR 1861	Mt. Olivet
743	Cameron, John L., coal dealer	29y	W	Scot.	24 JAN 1874	Congressional*
457	Cameron, John, stone cutter	55y	W	Scot.	14 JUN 1870	Congressional
613	Cameron, Lillie	10m	C	U.S.	26 JUL 1872	
152	Cameron, Mary	1y	W	D.C.	03 JUN 1859	Mt. Olivet
688	Cameron, Wm. A.	32y	W	Eng.	20 MAY 1873	Oak Hill
299	Camfer, Mary H., Mrs.	74y	W	Md.	07 MAR 1868	Baltimore, Md.
626	Cammack, Chris.	76y	W	Eng.	08 SEP 1872	
779	Cammack, Ellen	80y	W	U.S.	21 JUL 1874	Oak Hill
039	Cammel, Jane	19y	C		18 MAR 1856	Alms House
312	Cammell, Hannah, domestic	40y	C	Va.	05 MAY 1868	Alms House
553	Camp, Allie	15y	W	Ill.	09 JAN 1872	Glenwood
165	Camp, Edward, clerk	47y	W	Conn.	25 NOV 1859	Conn.
271	Camp, Elisha E., Col. USA	42y	W	N.Y.	04 AUG 1867	Congressional
057	Camp, John	--			c.18 SEP 1856	Congressional
537	Campbell, Anna	57y	C	Va.	19 SEP 1871	Young Mens
737	Campbell, Bridget	50y	W	Ire.	25 DEC 1873	Mt. Olivet
771	Campbell, Catherine	41y	W	U.S.	20 JUN 1874	Mt. Olivet
456	Campbell, Charles	4m	W	D.C.	17 JUN 1870	Alexandria, Va.
779	Campbell, Charles	8m	C	U.S.	02 JUL 1874	
365	Campbell, Douglass	31y	B	D.C.	12 DEC 1868	Young Mens
698	Campbell, Ed Albert	7y	W		27 JUN 1873	Graceland
401	Campbell, Fanny	7m	C		14 JUL 1869	Young Mens
051	Campbell, Ida B.	3y	W	D.C.	21 JUL 1856	Glenwood
316	Campbell, James		C		c.15 MAY 1868	Alms House
428	Campbell, Jane, servant	10y	C	Va.	26 NOV 1869	Washington Asylum
621	Campbell, Jas., barber	34y	C	U.S.	13 AUG 1872	
756	Campbell, John	3m	C	U.S.	27 MAR 1874	
410	Campbell, John	2m	C		10 AUG 1869	Union
478	Campbell, Judy, laborer	50y	C	Va.	19 SEP 1870	Ebenezer
346	Campbell, Kezia	65y	C		30 AUG 1868	Freedmen's Hospital
756	Campbell, Mary	3y	C	U.S.	27 MAR 1874	
461	Campbell, Mary	55y	W	Va.	22 JUL 1870	Congressional
085	Campbell, Mary C.	6m	W	D.C.	28 JUL 1857	
372	Campbell, Mary C.	2y	C	D.C.	28 JAN 1869	Washington Asylum
682	Campbell, Matilda, housekeeper	57y	C	U.S.	23 APR 1873	Brightwood
671	Campbell, Milly	80y	C	U.S.	18 FEB 1873	Small Pox*
407	Campbell, Nancy	78y	W	Ire.	27 AUG 1869	Congressional
532	Campbell, Naomi, house servant	16y	C	Md.	16 AUG 1871	Prospect Hill
278	Campbell, Richard	10m	W	D.C.	07 OCT 1867	Congressional
365	Campbell, Sarah	1y	B	D.C.	18 DEC 1868	Young Mens
404	Campbell, Sarah Caroline	36y	W		16 JUL 1869	
329	Campbell, Spencer, laborer	65y	C	Va.	06 JUL 1868	
300	Campbell, Susan	35y	C	Va.	24 MAR 1868	Alms House
002	Campbell, Susan	19y	C	D.C.	2_ JAN 1855	Young Mens
390	Campbell, Thomas B.	7m	W	D.C.	29 MAY 1869	N.Y.
261	Campbell, Thomas F., clerk	47y	W	N.Y.	10 MAY 1867	N.Y.
076	Campbell, William	8m	W	D.C.	22 APR 1857	Congressional
051	Campbell, William H.	28d	W	D.C.	26 JUL 1856	St. Matthews
189	Campbell, William, oysterman	67y	C	Va.	11 SEP 1860	Young Mens
407	Campmere, George H.	1y	W		07 AUG 1869	Congressional
379	Campmire, Rosa	27y	W	D.C.	02 MAR 1869	Congressional
270	Canaby, Dennis	7m	W	D.C.	17 AUG 1867	Trinity, Georgetown

District of Columbia Interments (Index to Deaths), 1855-1874

Page	Name	Age	Race	Birth	Death Date	Burial Ground
762	Canal, David, laborer	52y	W	Ire.	03 APR 1874	
275	Canning, Amelia C.	18y	W	D.C.	08 SEP 1867	Congressional
453	Cannon, Laura	1y	W		06 MAY 1870	Congressional
734	Cannon, Margaret	76y	W	U.S.	05 DEC 1873	Congressional
582	Cannon, Mary J.	1y	W	D.C.	23 FEB 1872	Mt. Olivet
399	Cannon, Mary M.	7m	W	D.C.	26 JUL 1869	Congressional
482	Cansis, Jane	1y	C		26 OCT 1870	Young Mens
063	Cantine, Ruth	48y	W	N.Y.	24 NOV 1856	Congressional
603	Canton, Cressie	75y	C	U.S.	13 JUN 1872	Asylum
130	Cantwell, James	5m	W		20 OCT 1858	St. Patricks
456	Cantwell, Michael	1y	W		23 JUN 1870	Mt. Olivet
623	Caperton, Jennie	21y	W	U.S.	09 AUG 1872	Holy Rood
155	Carberry, Catharine	1m	W	D.C.	22 JUL 1859	St. Patricks
391	Carberry, Ruth, Miss	89y	W		19 MAY 1869	St. Patricks
689	Carbin, Mary	29y	C	U.S.	26 MAY 1873	Beckett's
758	Carbine, Joseph	73y	W	Tusc.	29 APR 1874	Congressional
770	Carey, Emily, child of	3m	C	U.S.	07 JUN 1874	Ebenezer
125	Carey, Larraden	14d	W	D.C.	25 AUG 1858	Congressional
746	Carey, Susan	12y	C	U.S.	03 FEB 1874	Washington Asylum
247	Carl, Louise	30y	W	D.C.	07 DEC 1866	Glenwood
589	Carle, John	85y	C	D.C.	31 MAR 1872	
719	Carlin, John	18m	C	D.C.	17 SEP 1873	Beckett's
752	Carlin, Mary	11m	C	U.S.	27 MAR 1874	Beckett's
758	Carlin, Mary Jane, dressmaker	45y	W	U.S.	20 APR 1874	Washington Asylum
385	Carlin, Peter J.	9m	W		04 APR 1869	Mt. Olivet*
027	Carlisle, Emeline	13m	W	D.C.	19 OCT 1855	Rock Creek
074	Carlisle, Emmeline	31y	W	Scot.	22 MAR 1857	Rock Creek
074	Carlisle, [blank]	4d	W	D.C.	21 MAR 1857	Rock Creek
258	Carlton, Edwd.	38y	C		26 APR 1867	Young Mens
588	Carlymph, Mary	1m	W	D.C.	26 MAR 1872	Mt. Olivet
588	Carmel, Leanna	45y	C	Va.	27 MAR 1872	Western
494	Carmen, Jane M.	80y	W	U.S.	26 DEC 1870	Mt. Olivet
771	Carmody, Wm.	4m	W	U.S.	30 JUN 1874	Mt. Olivet
080	Carmony, Margaret	10y	W	Eng.	22 JUN 1857	St. Patricks
273	Carne, Mary Ann, seamstress	45y	W	D.C.*	25 SEP 1867	Mt. Olivet
008	Carney, E., child of	Still	W	D.C.	14 MAY 1855	St. Patricks
644	Carney, Edward S.	3m	W	U.S.	19 DEC 1872	Mt. Olivet
058	Carney, Elizabeth	7d	W		25 SEP 1856	Harmony
463	Carney, Frederick	3m	W		26 JUL 1870	Mt. Olivet
456	Carney, Frederick	3m	W		26 JUN 1870	Mt. Olivet
024	Carney, J.H.	4m	C	D.C.	01 SEP 1855	Harmony
003	Carney, Johanna, housekeeper	47y	W	Ire.	28 FEB 1855	St. Patricks
220	Carney, Philip	2y	W	D.C.	13 MAY 1866	Mt. Olivet
117	Carney, Richard A.	11m	C		28 JUN 1858	St. Patricks
735	Carney, Winford	1y	W	U.S.	12 DEC 1873	Mt. Olivet
587	Carnol, T.	9y	W	Va.	20 MAR 1872	Mt. Olivet
765	Caron, Flora	3m	W	U.S.	29 MAY 1874	Prospect Hill
016	Carpenter, Ellen	16m	W		06 JUL 1855	St. Patricks
680	Carpenter, Ellen, Miss	45y	W	U.S.	10 APR 1873	Caroline Co., Va.
737	Carpenter, Emeline	63y	W	U.S.	29 DEC 1873	Congressional
290	Carpenter, Geo.	43y	C		01 JAN 1868	Freedmen's Hospital
627	Carpenter, Jas. P.	8y	W	U.S.	26 SEP 1872	
027	Carpenter, Mary	5m	W		14 OCT 1855	St. Patricks
493	Carpenter, Mary E.	20y	W	Ohio	27 DEC 1870	Congressional
349	Carpenter, W.L., printer	56y	W	N.Y.	02 SEP 1868	N.Y.
068	Carpenter, [blank]	62y	W		16 JAN 1857	Congressional
379	Carr, Edmund, child of	Still	W		13 MAR 1869	Congressional
616a	Carr, Elenora	23d	W	U.S.	17 JUL 1872	Congressional

Page	Name	Age	Race	Birth	Death Date	Burial Ground
617	Carr, Ella	19y	C	U.S.	20 AUG 1872	
248	Carr, Grace E.		W	D.C.	29 DEC 1866	Glenwood
726	Carr, Jennie, Mrs., lady	21y	W	U.S.	30 OCT 1873	Mt. Olivet
746	Carr, John	4y	W	U.S.	21 FEB 1874	Holyrood
585	Carr, Lena	36y	C	Md.	11 MAR 1872	Young Mens
355	Carr, Patrick	68y	W	Ire.	09 OCT 1868	Mt. Olivet*
417	Carr, Thomas	7y	C	Md.	07 SEP 1869	Washington Asylum
637	Carr, Thomas	27y	W	U.S.	25 NOV 1872	Young Mens
514	Carr, William	9m	W	D.C.	27 MAR 1871	Glenwood
124	Carr, William	5m	W	D.C.	16 AUG 1858	Oak Hill
770	Carr, Wm. T.	8m	W	U.S.	07 JUN 1874	Mt. Olivet
602	Carrey, Jane	47y	C	Ky.	01 MAY 1872	Asylum
381	Carrick, Ellen	68y	W		16 MAR 1869	Md., the country
093	Carrico, John	87y	W	Md.	15 OCT 1857	Congressional
098	Carrico, Wm. B., watchman	76y	W	Md.	06 DEC 1857	Congressional
718	Carridon, James, laborer	73y	W	Ire.	08 SEP 1873	Mt. Olivet
421	Carrier, James Alpy	10m	W		06 OCT 1869	Glenwood
378	Carrigan, John	3y	W	U.S.	16 FEB 1869	Mt. Olivet
720	Carrihan, James, laborer	27y	W	Eng.	25 SEP 1873	Mt. Olivet
184	Carrington, Charles	61y	W	Wales	07 JUL 1860	Washington Asylum
641	Carrol, George	24y	C	U.S.	04 DEC 1872	Small Pox
354	Carrol, Joseph H.	1d	W	D.C.	19 OCT 1868	Congressional
473	Carrol, Mary	41y	C	Md.	06 AUG 1870	Harmony
448	Carroll, Bryan, laborer	75y	W	Ire.	04 MAR 1870	Mt. Olivet
075	Carroll, Caroline, slave	45y	C	Md.	12 APR 1857	Methodist, East
071	Carroll, Carroll	5y	W	D.C.	21 FEB 1857	Oak Hill
496	Carroll, Catharine, servant	70y	C	Md.	26 DEC 1870	Harmony
348	Carroll, Charles		W	D.C.	29 SEP 1868	Congressional
459	Carroll, Daniel	2m	C	Amer.	15 JUN 1870	Harmony
257	Carroll, Daniel	6y	W	D.C.	05 MAR 1867	Mt. Olivet
204	Carroll, Darkey	53y	W		22 JUN 1861	Congressional
049	Carroll, Edward, laborer	23y	W	Ire.	— JUL 1856	
666	Carroll, Eliza	23y	C	U.S.	07 FEB 1873	Ebenezer
236	Carroll, Eliza, domestic	75y	C	Md.	23 SEP 1866	Mt. Olivet
159	Carroll, Elizabeth	58y	W	Md.	31 AUG 1859	Congressional
163	Carroll, Elizabeth		C	D.C.	27 OCT 1859	Harmony
240	Carroll, Ellen, washerwoman	45y	W	Ire.	10 OCT 1866	Mt. Olivet
338	Carroll, Fannie	2y	C	D.C.	27 AUG 1868	Young Mens
248	Carroll, Henrietta	26y	W	D.C.	20 DEC 1866	Trinity
713	Carroll, Henrietta, servant	65y	C	Md.	24 AUG 1873	
764	Carroll, Henry	75y	C	unk.	03 MAY 1874	Harmony
039	Carroll, Henry	11y	C	D.C.	26 MAR 1856	St. Peters
680	Carroll, Jas. T.	2y	W	U.S.	04 APR 1873	
223	Carroll, John, laborer	52y	W	Ire.	08 JUN 1866	Alms House
592	Carroll, John Lewis	3y	C	D.C.	11 APR 1872	
253	Carroll, Leonora C.	2m	W	D.C.	21 FEB 1867	Methodist
357	Carroll, Lewis H.	4d	B	D.C.	15 OCT 1868	Washington Asylum
355	Carroll, Maggie	1m	W	D.C.	20 OCT 1868	Congressional
161	Carroll, Margaret	57y	W	Md.	02 SEP 1859	Congressional
484	Carroll, Mary	22y	W	Va.	11 OCT 1870	Congressional
770	Carroll, Mary	47y	W	U.S.	07 JUN 1874	Mt. Olivet
047	Carroll, Mary, housekeeper	64y	W	Ire.	29 JUN 1856	St. Patricks
018	Carroll, Michael	11m	W	D.C.	11 AUG 1855	St. Patricks
135	Carroll, Nicholas, laborer	35y	W	Ire.	03 DEC 1858	Washington Asylum
123	Carroll, Owen	8m	W	Va.*	29 JUL 1858	Alexandria, Va.
454	Carroll, Peter, messenger	21y	W		31 MAY 1870	Mt. Olivet
591	Carroll, Rosa	1y	C	U.S.	12 APR 1872	Mt. Pleasant
386	Carroll, Susan A.	21y	W	Amer.	02 APR 1869	Congressional

District of Columbia Interments (Index to Deaths), 1855-1874

Page	Name	Age	Race	Birth	Death Date	Burial Ground
158	Carroll, Susan B.	24y	C	D.C.	16 AUG 1859	Harmony
723	Carroll, Thos. Lewis	2y	W	D.C.	08 OCT 1873	Congressional*
077	Carroll, Walter	49y	W	Md.	15 MAY 1857	Congressional
223	Carroll, William, laborer	45y	W	Ire.	10 JUN 1866	Alms House
008	Carroll, Wm., porter	50y	C		02 MAY 1855	14th St.
068	Carroll, Wm. Thos.	23y	C	D.C.	19 JAN 1857	Oak Hill
036	Carroll, [blank]	21d	W		17 FEB 1856	West
514	Carson, Georgiana	26y	W	Amer.	27 MAR 1871	Glenwood
771	Carson, Ida E., seamstress	18y	W	U.S.	17 JUN 1874	Congressional
453	Carson, Laurie Annie	1y	W		05 MAY 1870	Congressional
515	Carson, Mary E., housewife	22y	W	Pa.	29 MAR 1871	Congressional
390	Carson, [blank]	7m			16 MAY 1869	Congressional
676	Carter, Albert	22y	C	U.S.	05 MAR 1873	Small Pox
403	Carter, Ann	48y	C	Va.	11 JUL 1869	Beckett's
501	Carter, Ann	40y	C	Va.	19 JAN 1871	Potters Field
286	Carter, Arthur	23y	C		12 DEC 1867	Freedmen's Hospital
157	Carter, Austin T., slave	1y	C	D.C.	05 AUG 1859	Foundry
643	Carter, Blanche	17m	C	U.S.	09 DEC 1872	
604	Carter, Charles	3y	C	D.C.	16 JUN 1872	Ebenezer
114	Carter, Charles, laborer	65y	C		16 MAY 1858	Harmony
237	Carter, Daphne	90y			08 SEP 1866	Western
606	Carter, David	5m	C	D.C.	10 JUN 1872	Mt. Pleasant
639	Carter, Dennis, laborer	50y	C	U.S.	10 NOV 1872	
742	Carter, Edward	2y	C	U.S.	19 JAN 1874	
469	Carter, Eliza	21d	C	U.S.	04 AUG 1870	
368	Carter, Emily A.	55y	W	Md.	20 DEC 1868	Mt. Olivet
036	Carter, Enoch, wood sawyer	70y	C	Ohio	09 FEB 1856	Alms House
529	Carter, Fanny	1y	C	D.C.	26 JUL 1871	Young Mens
209	Carter, Fitzhugh Lee	2y	W	D.C.	09 JAN 1866	sent to the co[tton]
300	Carter, Frances	14y	C	U.S.	16 MAR 1868	Alms House
630	Carter, Geo.	40y	C	U.S.	30 OCT 1872	Small Pox
120	Carter, George H.	1m	W	D.C.	03 JUL 1858	Congressional
696	Carter, George, laborer	42y	C	Va.	25 JUN 1873	
321	Carter, Harriet	13y	C	D.C.	18 JUN 1868	Alms House
331	Carter, Harriet	23y	C		29 JUL 1868	Freedmen's Hospital
337	Carter, Harriet A.	4y	C	U.S.	06 AUG 1868	Washington Asylum
688	Carter, Harry	2y	C	U.S.	17 MAY 1873	
604	Carter, Henrietta	30y	C	D.C.	08 JUN 1872	Ebenezer
676	Carter, Henry	27y	C	U.S.	03 MAR 1873	Small Pox
384	Carter, Hualgia	9m	C	D.C.	24 MAR 1869	Washington Asylum
594	Carter, Isaac, waiter	29y	W	Miss.	23 APR 1872	Washington
770	Carter, Jacob	6m	W	U.S.	06 JUN 1874	Congressional
641	Carter, James	22y	C	U.S.	27 DEC 1872	Small Pox*
770	Carter, Jennie	25y	C	U.S.	07 JUN 1874	Washington Asylum
287	Carter, John		C		c.08 DEC 1867	Alms House
473	Carter, John	21d	C	D.C.	04 AUG 1870	Washington Asylum
069	Carter, John Charles	13y	W	Md.	21 JAN 1857	Congressional
607	Carter, John F., brick burner	75y	C	D.C.	19 JUN 1872	Harmony
403	Carter, John F.	21d	C		16 JUL 1869	Union
632	Carter, John H.	15m	W	U.S.	19 OCT 1872	
184	Carter, John T.	11y	C	D.C.	05 JUL 1860	Western
261	Carter, Julia	107y	C	Md.	05 MAY 1867	Young Mens
537	Carter, Lettie	17y	C	D.C.	19 SEP 1871	Washington
615	Carter, Louisa	50y	C	U.S.	08 JUL 1872	
276	Carter, Lucy	16y	C		07 SEP 1867	Freedmen's Hospital
273	Carter, Lucy	16y	C		07 SEP 1867	Freedmen's Bureau
088	Carter, Luke	84y	C		17 AUG 1857	Young Mens
664	Carter, Martha	5y	C	U.S.	17 JAN 1873	Small Pox*

Page	Name	Age	Race	Birth	Death Date	Burial Ground
473	Carter, Martha	2y	C	D.C.	28 AUG 1870	Western
409	Carter, Mary		C		04 AUG 1869	Holmead
394	Carter, Mary A.	4m	W	U.S.	27 JUN 1869	Congressional
272	Carter, Mary A.	4m	C		07 AUG 1867	Freedmen's Bureau
029	Carter, Mary Ann	6d	C	D.C.	04 NOV 1855	Wester
742	Carter, Mathew	7m	C	U.S.	16 JAN 1874	
013	Carter, Matilda, servant	32y	C	D.C.	01 JUL 1855	
534	Carter, Morgan E.	3y	W	D.C.	31 AUG 1871	Glenwood
674	Carter, Moses	22y	C	U.S.	13 MAR 1873	
365	Carter, Nancy W.	19y	C	Va.	— DEC 1868	Young Mens
631	Carter, Nathan	2y	C	U.S.	27 OCT 1872	
088	Carter, Nathan	11m	C	D.C.	20 AUG 1857	Foundry
501	Carter, Remus	70y	C	Md.	22 JAN 1871	Potters Field
203	Carter, Robert, refectory keeper	49y	C	Va.	27 MAY 1861	Young Mens
311	Carter, Saml.		C		c.24 APR 1868	Alms House
705	Carter, Sarah	6m	C	D.C.	25 JUL 1873	
287	Carter, Sarah		C		c.15 DEC 1867	Alms House
779	Carter, Sarah E.	1y	C	U.S.	01 JUL 1874	Ebenezer
300	Carter, Suberte	1y	C	D.C.	25 MAR 1868	Alms House
544	Carter, Thomas	30y	C	Md.	04 NOV 1871	Washington
592	Carter, Walter	3m	C	D.C.	05 APR 1872	Ebenezer
730	Carter, Washington, laborer	45y	C	U.S.	15 NOV 1873	Beckett's
389	Carter, William	3w	C	D.C.	05 APR 1869	Washington Asylum
327	Carter, Willie Arthur	1y	C	D.C.	09 JUL 1868	Harmony
405	Carter, Wm. E.	1m	C	D.C.	22 JUL 1869	Washington Asylum
209	Carter, [blank]				— JAN 1866	Western
215	Carter, [blank]	50y	C		15 MAR 1866	Young Mens
240	Carthy, Charles, carpenter	50y	W	Ire.	20 OCT 1866	Mt. Olivet
159	Cartis, Alice	21y	W	Eng.	23 AUG 1859	Rock Creek
159	Cartis, [blank]	13d	W	D.C.	27 AUG 1859	Rock Creek
257	Cartner, John, blacksmith	60y	C	D.C.	19 MAR 1867	Young Mens
538	Cartriett, Mary	35y	W	Ire.	25 SEP 1871	Mt. Olivet
521	Cartright, Violetta	19y	C	D.C.	01 JUN 1871	Congressional*
140	Cartwright, Annette	4m	C	D.C.	05 FEB 1859	Foundry
712	Cartwright, L.	1y	C	D.C.	17 AUG 1873	
266	Cartwright, R, Mrs..	67y	W	Md.	24 JUL 1867	Glenwood
221	Carusi, Arthur S.	2y	W	D.C.	19 MAY 1866	Mt. Olivet*
616b	Carvello, C.C.	1y	W	U.S.	21 JUL 1872	Congressional
532	Carver, Alice C.	7y	W	Va.	14 AUG 1871	Glenwood
720	Cary, Henry Oxtell, carpenter	56y	W	N.J.	25 SEP 1873	Glenwood, near
300	Cary, Mary, serving girl	22y	W	Ire.	09 MAR 1868	Mt. Olivet
327	Casassi, Joseph	1y	W	D.C.	24 JUL 1868	St. Marys
396	Case, Susan	18y	C	Va.	08 JUN 1869	Young Mens
132	Casen, [blank]	Still	W	D.C.	16 NOV 1858	Mt. Olivet
398	Casey, Edmond	3m	W		28 JUN 1869	Mt. Olivet
536	Casey, Ellen M.	33y	W	Can.	18 SEP 1871	Mt. Olivet*
256	Casey, Isaac K., officer USA	23y	W	Pa.	05 MAR 1867	Oak Hill
769	Casey, James	6y	C	U.S.	19 MAY 1874	
391	Casey, Julia	1y	W		23 MAY 1869	Mt. Olivet
064	Casey, Mary	25y	W	Ire.	03 NOV 1856	St. Peters
704	Casey, Wm.	3y	W	D.C.	26 JUL 1873	Mt. Olivet
055	Casey, [blank]	10m	W	D.C.	23 AUG 1856	St. Peters
509	Cash, Lelia W.	16y	W	Amer.	02 FEB 1871	Glenwood
720	Cashman, Wm., carpenter	59y	W	Ire.	25 SEP 1873	Mt. Olivet
285	Casidy, Mary Jane	1y	W		17 DEC 1867	Congressional
426	Caspari, Henry	9d	W		05 NOV 1869	German Catholic
379	Casparis, James, hotel propr.	56y	W	Switz.	23 MAR 1869	Congressional
610	Cassasa, John	60y	W	Italy	28 JUL 1872	

District of Columbia Interments (Index to Deaths), 1855-1874

Page	Name	Age	Race	Birth	Death Date	Burial Ground
481	Cassassa, John, merchant	47y	W	Italy	29 OCT 1870	St. Marys
415	Cassedy, Henry, constable	62y	W	Ire.	29 SEP 1869	Mt. Olivet
065	Cassell, Clotilda V.	21y	W	D.C.	13 DEC 1856	St. Patricks
067	Cassell, James B.	1m	W	D.C.	30 DEC 1856	St. Patricks
146	Cassell, Jno. A., bricklayer	52y	W		— APR 1859	Mt. Olivet
181	Cassell, Jno. T.	2m	W	D.C.	10 JUN 1860	Congressional
203	Cassell, Sallie A.E.	22y	W	Va.	02 MAY 1861	Congressional
481	Cassiday, Andrew P.	14y	W	D.C.	06 OCT 1870	Mt. Olivet
249	Cassidy, Mary	28y	W	Pa.	18 JAN 1867	Congressional
322	Cassidy, Walter	3m	W	D.C.	25 JUN 1868	Mt. Olivet
240	Cassin, Alice V.	24y	W	Md.	02 OCT 1866	Piscataway, Md.
584	Cassins, Thomas	7y	C	D.C.	04 MAR 1872	Western
078	Casson, Mrs., infant of	1m	W	D.C.	21 MAY 1857	Washington Asylum
019	Cassy, John	10m	W	D.C.	20 AUG 1855	St. Patricks
152	Castel, William E.	15y	W	D.C.	05 JUN 1859	Congressional*
188	Castleman, Jan	41y	W	D.C.	17 AUG 1860	Oak Hill
678	Castor, Robt. I.	6y	C	U.S.	27 MAR 1873	Small Pox
282	Caswell, A.B., lawyer	65y	W	Me.	10 NOV 1867	Farmington, Me.
771	Caswell, Alex Mahon	7m	W	U.S.	28 JUN 1874	Congressional
746	Caswell, Mary C.	26y	W	U.S.	08 FEB 1874	Congressional*
386	Caswell, Thomas, stone polisher	39y	W	Ire.	25 APR 1869	Mt. Olivet
524	Casy, Henry	11y	C	Ire.	22 JUN 1871	
093	Catalana, Martha	75y	W	Md.	03 OCT 1857	St. Patricks
236	Cataline, Julia	66y	W	Pa.	19 SEP 1866	Congressional
193	Cathcart, Thomas, clerk	35y	W	D.C.	26 NOV 1860	Western
270	Catlet, Henry E.	8m	W	D.C.	21 AUG 1867	Congressional
101	Caton, Bridget	84y	W	Ire.	13 JAN 1858	St. Patricks
243	Caton, George S., printer	32y	W	D.C.	15 NOV 1866	Mt. Olivet
220	Caton, Mrs.		W		03 MAY 1866	Mt. Olivet
325	Caton, Susan	69y	W	Md.	24 JUL 1868	Mt. Olivet
204	Caton, Thomas, printer	38y	W	D.C.	03 JUN 1861	St. Peters
157	Cator, Mary C.	1y	W	D.C.	06 AUG 1859	Mt. Olivet
705	Catrut, Barbera	9m	W	D.C.	06 JUL 1873	
324	Catuson, Mary	1y	W	D.C.	19 JUL 1868	Glenwood
084	Cauder, Caroline B.	57y	W	Md.	23 JUL 1857	Lutheran
721	Caulet, Caroline E.	1y	W	D.C.	29 SEP 1873	Prospect Hill
584	Caulvert, Frank	12y	W	Md.	02 MAR 1872	
418	Caunnell, Joseph, laborer	34y	C	Va.	26 SEP 1869	
596	Caushens, Emerich	12y	W	Ger.	28 APR 1872	Glenwood
051	Causten, Eliza, lady	64y	W	Md.	27 JUL 1856	Congressional
387	Caux, Thomas, messenger	71y	W	Eng.	18 APR 1869	Glenwood
764	Cavagnard, Antonio, fruit dealer	34y	W	Italy	05 MAY 1874	St. Marys
607	Cavanaugh, Frank	8m	W	D.C.	17 JUN 1872	Mt. Olivet
324	Cavanaugh, Wm. H.	14d	W	D.C.	22 JUL 1868	Mt. Olivet
509	Cavanaugh, [blank]	Still	W		09 FEB 1871	Methodist
252	Cave, Sarah C.	25y	W		19 FEB 1867	Mt. Olivet
375	Cavender, Kate, Mrs.	48y	W	Pa.	13 FEB 1869	Philadelphia, Pa.
514	Cavis, Phebe Paine	2y	W	D.C.	13 MAR 1871	Glenwood
091	Cawood, Geo. Thomas, turner	28y	W	Md.	18 SEP 1857	Broad Creek, Md
587	Cawood, H.R.V.	73y	W	Va.	19 MAR 1872	Md.
587	Cayrer, James L.	9m	W	D.C.	21 MAR 1872	Glenwood
175	Cazanave, Peter, wood merchant	64y	W	D.C.	16 MAR 1860	St. Matthews
639	Ceaton, Johnson F., Dr.	47y	W	U.S.	24 NOV 1872	Glenwood
746	Cemtutore, G.B.	53y	W	Italy	19 FEB 1874	Mt. Olivet
373	Cer, William H.	47y	C		27 JAN 1869	Harmony
137	Cevert, Rosa	8d	W	D.C.	07 JAN 1859	German Catholic
189	Chace, Elizabeth	1y	W	D.C.	19 SEP 1860	Glenwood
466	Chace, George A.	1y	C	D.C.	19 JUL 1870	Young Mers

District of Columbia Interments (Index to Deaths), 1855-1874

Page	Name	Age	Race	Birth	Death Date	Burial Ground
752	Chadman, Hellen, domestic	22y	C	U.S.	11 MAR 1874	
607	Chadwick, Saml., clerk	45y	W	Mich.	30 JUN 1872	Mich.
114	Chafford, Elizabeth	77y	W	Va.	23 MAY 1858	Holmead
350	Chalk, Mrs., housekeeper	23y	W	Md.	21 SEP 1868	Md.
608	Chamber, [blank]	4m	C	D.C.	10 JUN 1872	Mt. Pleasant
284	Chamberlain, J.G., clerk	29y	W	Pa.	02 NOV 1867	Pa.
677	Chamberlain, Wm.	4y	W	U.S.	14 MAR 1873	Presbyterian
764	Chamberlin, Catherine	66y	W	U.S.	11 MAY 1874	Rock Creek
531	Chamberlin, Chas. T.	4d	W	D.C.	05 AUG 1871	Unknown
737	Chamberlin, E.W.	11y	W	U.S.	27 DEC 1873	Oak Hill
350	Chamberlin, James A.	1y	W	D.C.	28 SEP 1868	Holmead
725	Chamberlin, L.L.	1y	W	U.S.	22 OCT 1873	
209	Chamberlin, Sarah	1y	W	D.C.	— JAN 1866	sent to Me.
502	Chambers, Benj., engraver	82y	W	N.C.	07 JAN 1871	Congressional
499	Chambers, Benjn., engraver	82y	W	N.C.	07 JAN 1871	Congressional
123	Chambers, Catharine	4m	W	Va.	30 JUL 1858	St. Patricks
327	Chambers, Charles Edward	3m	C	D.C.	25 JUL 1868	Holmead
545	Chambers, Edw., laborer	70y	C	Va.	17 NOV 1871	Washington
476	Chambers, Edward O.	12y	W	D.C.	26 SEP 1870	Congressional
738	Chambers, John C.	42y	W	U.S.	21 DEC 1873	
604	Chambers, M.J.	7y	C	D.C.	05 JUN 1872	Ebenezer
187	Chambers, Robert	1y	W	D.C.	01 AUG 1860	Mt. Olivet
023	Chambers, Sarah N.	1y	W	D.C.	31 SEP 1855	St. Patricks
181	Chambers, [blank]	2m	W	D.C.	17 JUN 1860	Congressional
426	Champ, Charlotte A.	1y	C		06 NOV 1869	Union
086	Champion, Laura J.	2y	W	D.C.	08 AUG 1857	Congressional
078	Champion, Saml.	48y	W		23 MAY 1857	Congressional
637	Champlain, Clara	4y	W	U.S.	16 NOV 1872	Congressional*
296	Chan, Catherine, child of	Still	C	D.C.	14 FEB 1868	Alms House
046	Chan, Child of Jane		C		19 JUN 1856	Young Mens
472	Chancellor, Florence	9m	C	D.C.	13 AUG 1870	Young Mens
457	Chandler, Carrie	4m	W		23 JUN 1870	Congressional
629	Chandler, E.L.	18y	W	U.S.	13 OCT 1872	
637	Chandler, Gracie	28y	W	U.S.	26 NOV 1872	
687	Chandler, Robert, Capt. 7th Inf.	46y	W	N.Y.	10 MAY 1873	Batavia, N.Y.
513	Chandler, W.E., child of	Still	W	D.C.	19 MAR 1871	Concord, N.H.
513	Chandler, Wm. E., Mrs.	35y	W	Mass.	20 MAR 1871	N.H.
406	Chandone, Angeline	44y	W	Fra.	20 JUL 1869	Methodist
031	Chaney, Emily	1y	W	D.C.	20 DEC 1855	Foundry
225	Chaney, Frances	21y	W	Md.	22 JUN 1866	Mt. Olivet*
159	Chaney, Samuel	1y	C	D.C.	26 AUG 1859	Bladensburg, Md.
771	Chapan, George, laborer	18y	C	U.S.	13 JUN 1874	
298	Chapin, Heman L., merchant	45y	W	Me.	28 FEB 1868	Congressional
680	Chapin, W.O.	59y	W	U.S.	06 APR 1873	Washington Asylum
516a	Chapman, Ann, pauper	8y	B	Md.	31 MAR 1871	Washington Asylum
622	Chapman, B.D., student	9y	W	U.S.	28 AUG 1872	
454	Chapman, Betsey Austin	71y	W	Ver.	28 MAY 1870	Ver.
744	Chapman, Chas. E.	2y	C	U.S.	28 JAN 1874	
492	Chapman, Edward	1y	C	D.C.	10 DEC 1870	Young Mens
094	Chapman, Infant		W		30 OCT 1857	Va.
329	Chapman, James, mason		W	Ire.	12 JUL 1868	Mt. Olivet
643	Chapman, Jno.	25y	C	U.S.	06 DEC 1872	Washington Asylum
263	Chapman, John Edwin	3m			27 JUN 1867	Mt. Olivet
058	Chapman, Jonathan, soldier	66y	W	Md.	23 SEP 1856	Washington Asylum
664	Chapman, Maria	12y	C	U.S.	21 JAN 1873	Small Pox*
449	Chapman, Thomas H.N.	1y	W		07 APR 1870	Congressional/Oak Hill
498	Chapman, [blank], pauper	2m	B	D.C.	29 JAN 1871	Washington Asylum
611	Chappell, Eliza	2m	W	U.S.	07 JUL 1872	

District of Columbia Interments (Index to Deaths), 1855-1874

Page	Name	Age	Race	Birth	Death Date	Burial Ground
600	Chappellar, Cath.	80y	W	U.S.	14 MAY 1872	Oak Hill
688	Chapple, Rosanna, dress maker	42y	W	Ire.	12 MAY 1873	Mt. Olivet
068	Charles, Ann V.	24y	W	Va.	01 JAN 1857	Rock Creek
311	Charles, Frank		W		c.12 APR 1868	Alms House
314	Charles, James, printer	56y	W	D.C.	03 MAY 1868	Congressional
667	Charllors, Wm.	27y	W	Eng.	11 FEB 1873	
599	Charmlin, Jordan, laborer	30y	C	U.S.	08 MAY 1872	Unknown
736	Chary, John C., watch maker	35y	W	U.S.	19 DEC 1873	Glenwood
502	Chase, Ada	9m	C		30 JAN 1871	Mt. Olivet
410	Chase, Amelia A.	19y	C	Md.	20 AUG 1869	Mt. Olivet
404	Chase, Anna M.	11y	C	Md.	27 JUL 1869	
304	Chase, Annie Phoebe	27y	W	Pa.	12 MAR 1868	Congressional
446	Chase, Cathrine	6d	C	D.C.	16 MAR 1870	Washington Asylum
522	Chase, Colfax F.	10m	W	D.C.	10 JUN 1871	Glenwood
107	Chase, Daniel, brick maker	19y	C	D.C.	04 MAR 1858	Young Mens
003	Chase, Danl.	38y	C	Md.	20 FEB 1855	Harmony
140	Chase, Edward	1y	C	D.C.	12 FEB 1859	Harmony
603	Chase, Ella	15d	W	D.C.	28 JUN 1872	Small Pox
372	Chase, Emeline	9m	C	D.C.	27 JAN 1869	Washington Asylum
779	Chase, Frank A., vocalist	43y	W	U.S.	07 JUL 1874	Congressional*
729	Chase, Geo. H.	10m	W	U.S.	01 NOV 1873	Hanover, N.H.
222	Chase, Hannah	80y	C	Md.	28 MAY 1866	Harmony
602	Chase, Harriet	35y	C	Va.	21 MAY 1872	Asylum
752	Chase, Harriet A.	2y	C	U.S.	11 MAR 1874	
777a	Chase, Henry, laborer	26y	C	U.S.	23 JUN 1874	
641	Chase, John	18y	C	U.S.	31 DEC 1872	Small Pox*
593	Chase, John	2y	C	D.C.	25 APR 1872	Young Mens
387	Chase, John W.	3m	C	D.C.	25 APR 1869	Union
197	Chase, Margaret, servant	83y	C	Md.	27 JAN 1861	Colored
600	Chase, Martha A.	4y	C	U.S.	03 MAY 1872	Young Mens
489	Chase, Mary	3y	C		03 NOV 1870	Harmony
086	Chase, Mary, servant	30y	C	D.C.	08 AUG 1857	Foundry
037	Chase, Milken, cook		C	D.C.	28 FEB 1856	Young Mens
440	Chase, Samuel	81y	W	Ver.	20 FEB 1870	Oswego Co., N.Y.
619	Chase, Thos. W.	19m	C	U.S.	19 AUG 1872	Young Mens
509	Chase, Virginia	18y	C	Va.	03 FEB 1871	Washington Asylum
047	Chasier, C.	86y	W	Va.	29 JUN 1856	Foundry
494	Chatelien, Antone	45y	W	Fra.	16 DEC 1870	Mt. Olivet
066	Chauncey, Wm. S.	5m	W	D.C.	26 DEC 1856	Congressional
310	Chauvin, H., Mrs.	50y	W		c.19 APR 1868	Mt. Olivet
528	Chaves, C.	7d	W	D.C.	14 JUL 1871	Mt. Olivet
548	Cheek, Henry N.	1y	W	D.C.	15 DEC 1871	Congressional
621	Cheeseman, Saml. M., ice recker	48y	W	U.S.	14 AUG 1872	
606	Cheesman, Hannah	65y	C	Va.	04 JUN 1872	Asylum
023	Cheney, Susan	3y	W	D.C.	26 SEP 1855	N.H.
718	Chenning, James	70y	W	Va.	13 SEP 1873	Washington Asylum
105	Cherlott, [blank], slave, nurse	65y	C	Va.	24 FEB 1858	Holmead
044	Cherry, Martin, dentist	56y	W	N.Y.	03 MAY 1856	Congressional
744	Cherry, Wm. C.	8y	W	U.S.	07 JAN 1874	
439	Cheshire, Rosina	81y	W		24 FEB 1870	Congressional
544	Chesley, Elisabeth B.	21y	W	Md.	11 NOV 1871	Aquia Creek
712	Chesley, Richard	18y	C	Va.	19 AUG 1873	Washington Asylum
229	Chessins, Thomas, clerk	32y	W	Nor.	21 JUL 1866	Congressional
373	Chestney, James	69y	W	S.C.	29 JAN 1869	Congressional
404	Chew, Alice	1y	C	Md.	09 JUL 1869	Washington Asylum
207	Chew, E.	16y	W		08 JUL 1862	Oak Hill
028	Chew, Ellen	13y	C	D.C.	10 OCT 1855	Harmony
263	Chew, Ida	11y	C	D.C.	30 JUN 1867	Harmony

District of Columbia Interments (Index to Deaths), 1855-1874

Page	Name	Age	Race	Birth	Death Date	Burial Ground
039	Chew, Nancy	70y	C	Md.	08 MAR 1856	Foundry
050	Chew, [blank]	5m	C	D.C.	18 JUL 1856	Harmony
050	Chews, Mary, child of	Still	W		15 JUL 1856	Harmony
294	Child	8d	C		08 FEB 1868	
322	Child	Still	W	U.S.	27 JUN 1868	
317	Child		C		22 JUN 1868	
287	Child		C		c.13 DEC 1867	Alms House
291	Child	Still	C		12 JAN 1868	Alms House
287	Child		C		c.20 DEC 1867	Alms House
287	Child		W		c.09 DEC 1867	Alms House
292	Child	Still	C		13 JAN 1868	Alms House
296	Child	7d	C	D.C.	25 FEB 1868	Alms House
292	Child	Still	C		13 JAN 1868	Alms House
316	Child	Still	C		c.22 MAY 1868	Alms House
291	Child	Still	W		04 JAN 1868	Alms House
296	Child	Still	C	D.C.	14 FEB 1868	Alms House
291	Child	Still	C		12 JAN 1868	Alms House
292	Child	Still	C		14 JAN 1868	Alms House
287	Child		C		c.23 DEC 1867	Alms House
287	Child		C		c.21 DEC 1867	Alms House
316	Child	Still	C		c.24 MAY 1868	Alms House
287	Child		C		c.21 DEC 1867	Alms House
316	Child	Still	C		c.22 MAY 1868	Alms House
311	Child	Still	W		c.30 APR 1868	Alms House
315	Child	Still	C		c.01 MAY 1868	Alms House
311	Child	Still	C		c.12 APR 1868	Alms House
297	Child	Still	C		c.27 FEB 1868	Alms House
316	Child	Still	C		c.08 MAY 1868	Alms House
297	Child	Still	C		c.08 FEB 1868	Alms House
287	Child		C		c.21 DEC 1867	Alms House
316	Child	Still	C		c.11 MAY 1868	Alms House
311	Child	Still	C		c.24 APR 1868	Alms House
297	Child	Still	C		c.26 FEB 1868	Alms House
311	Child	Still	C		c.14 APR 1868	Alms House
311	Child	Still	C		c.25 APR 1868	Alms House
311	Child	Still	C		c.26 APR 1868	Alms House
311	Child	Still	W		c.20 APR 1868	Alms House
311	Child	Still	C		c.13 APR 1868	Alms House
316	Child	Still	C		c.15 MAY 1868	Alms House
287	Child		C		c.27 DEC 1867	Alms House
311	Child	Still	C		c.14 APR 1868	Alms House
311	Child	Still	C		c.14 APR 1868	Alms House
311	Child	Still	C		c.12 APR 1868	Alms House
316	Child	Still	W		c.06 MAY 1868	Alms House
291	Child	Still	C	D.C.	21 JAN 1868	Beckett's
290	Child	Still	W	D.C.	11 JAN 1868	Congressional
334	Child	3m			12 JUL 1868	Ebenezer
038	Child		W		24 MAR 1856	Glenwood
310	Child	Still	W	D.C.	29 APR 1868	Glenwood
328	Child	3m	C		17 JUL 1868	Harmony
334	Child	5½m	C		20 JUL 1868	Harmony
290	Child	Still	C	D.C.	20 JAN 1868	Harmony
086	Child	20d	C	D.C.	09 AUG 1857	Methodist
267	Child	8m	C	D.C.	28 JUL 1867	Moore's
310	Child	Still	W		c.15 APR 1868	Mt. Olivet
267	Child	17d			19 JUL 1867	Prospect Hill
101	Child			D.C.	— JAN 1858	Washington Asylum
337	Child	Still	C	D.C.	04 AUG 1868	Washington Asylum

Page	Name	Age	Race	Birth	Death Date	Burial Ground
337	Child	Still	C	D.C.	03 AUG 1868	Washington Asylum
350	Child	8d	C	D.C.	25 SEP 1868	Washington Asylum
362	Child	Still	C	D.C.	09 NOV 1868	Washington Asylum
226	Child		C		27 JUN 1866	Young Mens
078	Child	18d	C		24 MAY 1857	Western
350	Child	14d	C	D.C.	19 SEP 1868	Young Mens
312	Child	P.B.	W	D.C.	26 MAY 1868	Western
303	Child at 404 11th St.	Still	W		11 MAR 1868	Congressional
207	Child at Catholic Asylum				14 JUL 1862	Mt. Olivet
207	Child at Catholic Asylum				15 JUL 1862	Mt. Olivet
207	Child at Catholic Asylum				11 JUL 1862	Mt. Olivet
250	Child, at infant asylum				03 JAN 1867	Mt. Olivet
191	Child, Qualls	2y	C	D.C.	05 OCT 1860	Western
345	Childs, Alberta	2y	W	D.C.	10 AUG 1868	Congressional
609	Childs, Emma N.	6y	W	U.S.	08 JUN 1872	
731	Childs, George N.	4m	W	U.S.	23 NOV 1873	Congressional
387	Childs, Harry M.	7m	W	D.C.	27 APR 1869	Glenwood
585	Childs, Jane	1y	W	D.C.	10 MAR 1872	Congressional*
708	Childs, Jno. B., bar keeper	34y	W	Va.	12 JUL 1873	
341	Childs, Lawrence H.	1y	W	D.C.	01 AUG 1868	Congressional
285	Childs, Lindsly, laborer	40y	C	Va.	19 DEC 1867	Young Mens
245	Childs, Mary Elizabeth	6y	W	D.C.	29 NOV 1866	Glenwood
507	Childs, Sarah P.	70y	W	N.H.	24 FEB 1871	Rock Creek
606	Childs, Susie B.	5y	W	Ga.	02 JUN 1872	Congressional
195	Childs, Wentworth L., M.G.	33y	W	N.H.	14 DEC 1860	Rock Creek
694	Chiles, Jane	68y	W	Md.	12 JUN 1873	Charles Co., Md.
315	Chilton, Stephen	1y	C		c.27 MAY 1868	Mt. Olivet
054	Chin, Elizabeth	35y	C	Va.	30 AUG 1856	Harmony
729	Chin, Harriet, laborer	48y	C	U.S.	01 NOV 1873	
373	Chin, Henry, laborer	27y	C	Va.	26 JAN 1869	Young Mens
373	Chin, Samuel, laborer	72y	C	Va.	15 JAN 1869	Young Mens
199	Chinchilla, Pascuel F.	1y	W	D.C.	12 FEB 1861	Congressional
606	Chinn, Fred.	14y	C	Del.	26 JUN 1872	
764	Chinn, Gertrude	11m	C	U.S.	06 MAY 1874	
624	Chinn, John, wood sawyer	22y	W	U.S.	25 SEP 1872	
526	Chinn, Sarah	91y	W	Va.	02 JUL 1871	Congressional*
463	Chipley, Sarah M.	62y	W	Va.	18 JUL 1870	Alexandria, Va.
771	Chipley, Wm., laborer	39y	C	U.S.	25 JUN 1874	Mt. Olivet
430	Chipman, George, gov. clerk	70y	W	Ver.	17 DEC 1869	Ver.
217	Chipman, Robert H.	4m	W	D.C.	10 APR 1866	Congressional
058	Chisely, Elizabeth	82y	C	U.S.	21 SEP 1856	Trinity
615	Chisholm, Catharine	74y	W	U.S.	08 JUL 1872	
758	Chisholm, Charlotte	85y	W	U.S.	15 APR 1874	Congressional
770	Chisley, Levi, hod carrier	49y	C	U.S.	06 JUN 1874	
265	Chisly, Nancy	60y	W	Md.	22 JUL 1867	Young Mens
023	Chism, Geo. W.	2y	W	D.C.	10 SEP 1855	Holmead
031	Chism, John W.	1y	W	D.C.	05 DEC 1855	Holmead
125	Chism, Thomas B.	6m	W	D.C.	28 AUG 1858	Western
174	Chisseltine, Elexius	65y	C	U.S.	01 MAR 1860	Mt. Olivet
494	Chitman, Mary C.	5m	C	U.S.	27 DEC 1870	Mt. Olivet
408	Chittens, Charles	3m	C	D.C.	20 AUG 1869	Mt. Olivet
105	Chou, [blank]	1y	W	D.C.	21 FEB 1858	Glenwood
732	Chreester, Luther	3y	C	U.S.	28 NOV 1873	Mt. Olivet
764	Chrestafee, Joseph	25y	C	U.S.	08 MAY 1874	Washington Asylum
182	Chrismond, Oscar B.	6m	W	D.C.	21 JUN 1860	Mt. Olivet
423	Christian, Eliza	2y	C	D.C.	21 OCT 1869	Washington Asylum
426	Christian, Elva	6m	C		01 NOV 1869	Young Mens
513	Christian, Fanny	80y	C	Va.	05 MAR 1871	Washington Asylum

Page	Name	Age	Race	Birth	Death Date	Burial Ground
535	Christian, John	1y	C	D.C.	16 SEP 1871	Young Mens
082	Christian, Marie Antoine	1y	W	Md.	06 JUL 1857	Congressional
771	Christian, Oliver	52y	C	U.S.	08 JUN 1874	Washington Asylum
270	Christine, Henry C., printer	35y	W		03 AUG 1867	Glenwood
416	Christopher, Betsy Ann	1y	C		14 SEP 1869	
140	Christopher, Mrs.	45y	W	Ire.	10 FEB 1859	Washington Asylum
113	Chromiller, E.A.	58y	W	Va.	16 MAY 1858	Washington Asylum
161	Chubb, Chas. St. John, banker	30y	W	U.S.	11 SEP 1859	Oak Hill
038	Chubb, Warrington	2y	W	D.C.	20 MAR 1856	Oak Hill
670	Chum, Elizabeth	22y	W	U.S.	14 FEB 1873	Small Pox
519	Chum, Margret	22y	C		16 MAY 1871	Potters Field
662	Chunn, Cecelia, servant	38y	C	U.S.	12 JAN 1873	
519	Chunn, Maggie, servant	22y	C	Va.	15 MAY 1871	Potters Field
203	Church, Alfred, laborer	48y	C	Md.	26 MAY 1861	Young Mens
318	Church, Ben. Franklin	5m	W	D.C.	27 JUN 1868	Congressional
110	Churchill, Elnora	2y	W		03 APR 1858	Foundry
454a	Churchill, Louis, pauper	95y	C	Va.	16 MAY 1870	Washington Asylum
537	Churchill, Wm.	21y	C		21 SEP 1871	Va.
534	Churchwell, James	7m	C	D.C.	27 AUG 1871	Young Mens
042	Cirtis, Mary	67y	W	Ire.	23 APR 1856	St. Patricks
445	Cissel, Ella	17y	W		07 MAR 1870	Oak Hill
463	Cissel, Mary Thomas		W	D.C.	20 JUL 1870	Glenwood
764	Cissell, Ann	65y	W	unk.	01 MAY 1874	Glenwood
557	Cissell, Edwin	1y	W	D.C.	01 FEB 1872	Glenwood
182	Cissell, Eliza	51y	W	D.C.*	24 JUN 1860	Oak Hill
691	Cissell, Frederick	23y	C	U.S.	07 MAY 1873	Small Pox*
330	Cissell, [blank]	3m	C	D.C.	13 JUL 1868	Young Mens
410	Claburn, George, laborer	65y	C	Va.	13 AUG 1869	Young Mens
287	Clagett, Charles		C		c.10 DEC 1867	Alms House
469	Clagett, Gertrude	7m	W	D.C.	16 AUG 1870	Mt. Olivet
391	Claggett, Addie	8y	W		09 MAY 1869	Mt. Olivet
409	Claggett, Ann Maria	7m	C		24 AUG 1869	
378	Claggett, Betty	20y	C	Md.	14 FEB 1869	Freedmen's Hospital
697	Claiburn, Adlene	9m		D.C.	08 JUN 1873	Harmony
323	Clair, Charles C.	6m	W	D.C.	14 JUL 1868	Glenwood
612	Clampine, John	15d	W	U.S.	03 JUL 1872	
746	Clampitt, W.H.	7y	W	U.S.	24 FEB 1874	Glenwood
592	Clancey, Christine I.	4m	W	D.C.	14 APR 1872	Mt. Olivet
338	Clancey, James Wm.	10m	W	D.C.	24 AUG 1868	Mt. Olivet
609	Clancy, Mary	28y	W	Ire.	15 JUN 1872	Mt. Olivet*
375	Clapp, R.W., Mrs.	42y	W	Mass.	17 FEB 1869	Mass.
207	Clare, Mr.	52y	W		21 JUL 1862	Western
457	Claridge, C.T.	8m	W	U.S.	22 JUN 1870	Congressional
528	Claridge, Willie	6m	W	D.C.	21 JUL 1871	Congressional
282	Clark, A., Mrs.	75y	W		01 NOV 1867	Congressional*
707	Clark, Alfred M., clerk	58y	W	Amer.	29 JUL 1873	Harrisburg, Pa.
603	Clark, Alfred, shoemaker	43y	C	Ire.	14 JUN 1872	Potters Field
310	Clark, Ann	79y	W		c.23 APR 1868	Mt. Olivet
779	Clark, Atkin A., merchant	62y	W	U.S.	12 JUL 1874	Boston, Mass.
307	Clark, B., Mrs.	35y	W	Ire.	12 APR 1868	Mt. Olivet
710	Clark, Bridget	43y	W	Ire.	07 AUG 1873	Mt. Olivet
410	Clark, Cappie	21d	W		10 AUG 1869	Methodist
244	Clark, Catherine	33y	W	Md.	10 NOV 1866	Congressional
606	Clark, Charles	2y	W	D.C.	11 JUN 1872	
484	Clark, Charles	1y	W	Eng.	16 OCT 1870	Congressional
015	Clark, Charles	44y	C	Md.	22 JUL 1855	Young Mens
312	Clark, Charles Albert	8m	W	D.C.	04 MAY 1868	Mt. Olivet*
537	Clark, Charles O.	13d	W	D.C.	22 SEP 1871	Congressional

District of Columbia Interments (Index to Deaths), 1855-1874

Page	Name	Age	Race	Birth	Death Date	Burial Ground
635	Clark, Charlotte	14m	W	U.S.	04 NOV 1872	Small Pox
611	Clark, Cora	10m	C	U.S.	14 JUL 1872	
429	Clark, Cornelia	40y	W	Va.	15 DEC 1869	Congressional
456	Clark, Dora	2y	W	D.C.	08 JUN 1870	Prospect Hill
024	Clark, Ellen	1m	W	D.C.	17 SEP 1855	Congressional*
357	Clark, Ellen	1y	B	D.C.	28 OCT 1868	Washington Asylum
012	Clark, Emma	1m	C		01 JUN 1855	Alms House
231	Clark, Francis	6d	W		19 AUG 1866	Holmead
764	Clark, Frank, laborer	40y	C	U.S.	13 MAY 1874	
704	Clark, Fred	18m	C	D.C.	07 JUL 1873	
026	Clark, Geo. A.D., asst. P.M.	40y	W	N.Y.	14 OCT 1855	Congressional
336	Clark, George	1y	C	Md.	06 AUG 1868	
242	Clark, George D., servant	24y	C	Md.	26 OCT 1866	Colored Methodist
060	Clark, Gloviana	30y	C	D.C.	21 OCT 1856	Young Mens
013	Clark, Goodman C.	6m	W	D.C.	15 JUL 1855	Congressional
721	Clark, H. Lee	c.3d	W	D.C.	30 SEP 1873	Congressional
385	Clark, Henry C., merchant	26y	W	R.I.	06 APR 1869	Congressional
489	Clark, Henry Porter, gentleman	79y	W	Mass.	18 NOV 1870	N.Y.
265	Clark, Ida	7m	C	D.C.	24 JUL 1867	Young Mens
622a	Clark, J.W.	1m	W	U.S.	21 AUG 1872	Congressional*
663	Clark, James	8y	C	U.S.	06 JAN 1873	Small Pox*
483	Clark, James T., clerk	46y	W	D.C.	28 OCT 1870	Congressional
451	Clark, Jane	80y	C	Va.	13 APR 1870	Washington Asylum
454	Clark, Jane	80y	C	Va.	25 MAY 1870	Washington Asylum
007	Clark, Jas. F.	c.45y		D.C.	25 APR 1855	St. Matthews
616	Clark, Jno. H.	3y	C	U.S.	31 JUL 1872	
643	Clark, Jno. T.	70y	W	U.S.	12 DEC 1872	Congressional
187	Clark, John	84y	W		01 AUG 1860	Glenwood
029	Clark, John C., clerk	58y	W	Mass.	22 NOV 1855	Congressional
011	Clark, John, painter	55y	W	Md.	21 JUN 1855	Methodist Epis.
317	Clark, John, watchman	54y	W	Ire.	12 JUN 1868	Alms House
307	Clark, Josephine Antonia	16y	W	D.C.	28 APR 1868	Western
396	Clark, Judson, laborer	50y	Y	Md.	20 JUN 1869	Union
521	Clark, Julia C.	4m	W	D.C.	09 JUN 1871	Congressional
308	Clark, Julia R., Mrs.	28y	W	Ohio	09 APR 1868	Congressional
020	Clark, Lambert	16m	W		16 AUG 1855	St. Matthews
265	Clark, Laura M.	6m	W	D.C.	01 JUL 1867	Presbyterian
765	Clark, Lilly J.	2y	W	U.S.	30 MAY 1874	Prospect Hill
360	Clark, Louisa, Mrs.	61y	W	U.S.	23 NOV 1868	Ann Arbor, Mich.
719	Clark, M. Elizabeth	50y	W	D.C.	19 SEP 1873	Oak Hill
625	Clark, M.A.	3y	C	U.S.	21 SEP 1872	
138	Clark, Maria May	2y	W		10 JAN 1859	
720	Clark, Mary A.	5m	W	D.C.	24 SEP 1873	St. Marys
711	Clark, Mary Elizabeth	1y	C	D.C.	12 AUG 1873	Ebenezer
419	Clark, Mason E.	1y	W		02 OCT 1869	Congressional
023	Clark, Mat. St.C.	17m	W	D.C.	— SEP 1855	Congressional*
269	Clark, Maurice Brady	4m	W	D.C.	22 AUG 1867	Congressional
726	Clark, Nancy	74y	W	U.S.	26 OCT 1873	Congressional
690	Clark, Rainder	15y	C	U.S.	30 MAY 1873	Small Pox
256	Clark, Robert, plasterer	60y	C	Va.	17 MAR 1867	Young Mens
658	Clark, S.C., Dr.	81y	W		01 JAN 1873	
687	Clark, Samuel H.	7d	C	D.C.	05 MAY 1873	
601	Clark, Sarah E.	13y	W	U.S.	15 MAY 1872	Va.
689	Clark, Stewart Dodge, clerk	34y	W	U.S.	30 MAY 1873	Amherst, Mass.
185	Clark, Thomas, carpenter	48y	W	U.S.	24 JUL 1860	Western
556	Clark, Willie	1y	C		31 JAN 1872	Jones Chapel
582	Clark, Wilson C., gardener	30y	W	U.S.	20 FEB 1872	Congressional
190	Clark, Wm. Thomas, granite cutter	20y	W	D.C.	21 SEP 1860	Glenwood

Page	Name	Age	Race	Birth	Death Date	Burial Ground
236	Clark, [blank]	Still	C	D.C.	24 SEP 1866	Holmead
253	Clark, [blank]		C		02 FEB 1867	Young Mens
124	Clarke, Ann	60y	C	Md.	13 AUG 1858	Young Mens
303	Clarke, Charles	Still	W	D.C.	23 MAR 1868	Glenwood
108	Clarke, Charles, soldier	63y	W	N.Y.	16 MAR 1858	Washington Asylum
103	Clarke, Eliza	40y	C	Va.	28 JAN 1858	Foundry
065	Clarke, Emily	29y	C		10 DEC 1856	Young Mens
525	Clarke, Enoch	7m	C	D.C.	30 JUN 1871	Holy Rood
311	Clarke, Frank		W		c.12 APR 1868	Alms House
447	Clarke, Frederick	2m	C	D.C.	31 MAR 1870	Washington Asylum
434	Clarke, Frederick H.	71y	W	R.I.	08 JAN 1870	Congressional
298	Clarke, Geo.	87y	C		13 FEB 1868	Va.
605	Clarke, Granville, laborer	38y	C	Md.	23 JUN 1872	Asylum
128	Clarke, Henry	1y	W	D.C.	21 SEP 1858	St. Patricks
115	Clarke, J.H., Mrs., child of	Still	W		11 JUN 1858	Foundry
435	Clarke, James, barber	39y	W		04 JAN 1870	Mt. Olivet
176	Clarke, James F., carpenter	29y	C	Md.	02 APR 1860	Harmony
134	Clarke, Jas. B.	42y	W	D.C.	30 NOV 1858	Congressional
073	Clarke, John	29y	W	Eng.	12 MAR 1857	Washington Asylum
021	Clarke, John F.	5y	W	D.C.	31 AUG 1855	Congressional
065	Clarke, John Mechlin	17d	W	D.C.	10 DEC 1856	Congressional
537	Clarke, Joseph, clerk	69y	W	N.Y.	19 SEP 1871	Glenwood
494	Clarke, Martha A.	3m	W	D.C.	28 DEC 1870	Mt. Olivet
093	Clarke, Mary I.	38y	C	Md.	04 OCT 1857	Harmony
161	Clarke, Mary M.	5y	C	D.C.	06 SEP 1859	Western
143	Clarke, Rebecca, cook	20y	C	D.C.	16 MAR 1859	Harmony
170	Clarke, Robert Jas.	18y	W	U.S.	25 JAN 1860	
408	Clarke, Robert Wesley	1y	C		14 AUG 1869	Young Mens
003	Clarke, Robt. W., machinist	29y	W	D.C.	18 FEB 1855	Washington
548	Clarke, Ruth Jane		W	D.C.	12 DEC 1871	Congressional
434	Clarke, Sophia	2m	W		22 JAN 1870	Mt. Olivet
173	Clarke, Spencer R.		W	Conn.	26 FEB 1860	Conn.
174	Clarke, Thomas, messenger	76y	W	Ire.	04 MAR 1860	Mt. Olivet
315	Clarke, William	95y	W		c.29 MAY 1868	Mt. Olivet
047	Clarke, William H., grocer	40y	W	Va.	24 JUN 1856	Oak Hill
771	Clarke, William, pointer	72y	W	Eng.	21 JUN 1874	Oak Hill
608	Clarke, Willie S.	1y	W	D.C.	24 JUN 1872	Congressional*
214	Clarke, Wm.		C		07 MAR 1866	Young Mens
210	Clarke, [blank]		C		17 JAN 1866	Western
032	Clarke, [blank]	35y	C		20 DEC 1855	Young Mens
414	Clarkson, C.	1y	W		— SEP 1869	Glenwood
645	Clarkson, James	60y	C	U.S.	24 DEC 1872	Washington Asylum
771	Clarkson, John F.	24d	W	U.S.	29 JUN 1874	Glenwood/Mt. Olivet
225	Clarkson, Martha	8m	W	D.C.	23 JUN 1866	
318	Clarvoe, Edgar	2m	W	D.C.	24 JUN 1868	Congressional
705	Clarvoe, K.H.	10m	W	D.C.	21 JUL 1873	Congressional
237	Clarvoe, Willie	1y	W	D.C.	18 SEP 1866	Congressional
440	Clary, Sarah E.	29y	W		01 FEB 1870	Glenwood
479	Claten, Betsy	24y	C	Va.	04 SEP 1870	Ebenezer
464	Clatterback, Lilly M.	1y	W	D.C.	26 JUL 1870	Glenwood
674	Clauson, Carl. F., draughtsman	39y	W	Den.	18 MAR 1873	Glenwood
308	Clauson, Geo. Robert	5y	W	U.S.	21 APR 1868	Congressional
626	Claxton, A.B.	60y	W	U.S.	25 SEP 1872	
062	Claxton, John, jeweller	20y	W	D.C.	11 NOV 1856	Oak Hill
193	Clay, Mary	70y	W	Eng.	25 NOV 1860	Congressional
383	Clay, Sarah I.	4y	C	Va.	10 MAR 1869	Washington Asylum
779	Clay, Susan, laundress	30y	C	U.S.	31 JUL 1874	
070	Clay, Timothy, clerk	73y	W	Ire.	04 FEB 1857	Alexandria, Va.

Page	Name	Age	Race	Birth	Death Date	Burial Ground
609	Clay, Wm. Henry	1y	W	U.S.	29 JUN 1872	
508	Clayborn, Charity	46y	C	Va.	24 FEB 1871	Union
600	Claybourn, Cyrus	2y	C	U.S.	21 MAY 1872	Young Mens
557	Clayton, Ada Lee	1y	W	D.C.	01 FEB 1872	Mt. Olivet
478	Clayton, Alfred, engineer	32y	C	Va.	18 SEP 1870	Young Mens
598	Clayton, Edith G.	11y	C	U.S.	12 MAY 1872	Young Mens
597	Clayton, Edith G.	11y	C	U.S.	12 MAY 1872	Young Mens
288	Clayton, Harriet J.	14y	W	D.C.	16 DEC 1867	Congressional
715	Clayton, Julianna	25y	C	U.S.	08 AUG 1873	
668	Clayton, Monroe	1y	W	U.S.	18 FEB 1873	Glenwood
373	Clayton, Samuel	1y	C		28 JAN 1869	Young Mens
313	Clayton, William, whitewasher	70y	C	Va.	10 MAY 1868	Young Mens
103	Clayton, [blank]		W	D.C.	04 JAN 1858	
053	Clayton, [blank]	1y	W	D.C.	21 AUG 1856	Oak Hill
528	Clayton, [blank]	1y	C	D.C.	15 JUL 1871	Young Mens
533	Cleary, Edw. Thomas	1y	W	U.S.	26 AUG 1871	Mt. Olivet
092	Cleary, James	5m	W	D.C.	28 SEP 1857	St. Peters
294	Cleary, John P.	3m	W	D.C.	02 FEB 1868	Mt. Olivet
636	Cleary, M.L.	8m	W	U.S.	11 NOV 1872	
779	Cleary, Michael A.	1m	W	U.S.	10 JUL 1874	Holyrood
752	Cleaveland, Edward, officer USN	64y	W	U.S.	07 MAR 1874	Congressional
213	Clements, Alexander	38y			15 FEB 1866	Mt. Olivet*
102	Clements, Alice L.	60y	W	Va.*	15 JAN 1858	Congressional
746	Clements, Aloysius, painter	83y	W	U.S.	11 FEB 1874	Mt. Olivet
506	Clements, Annie V.	4m	W	D.C.	06 FEB 1871	Congressional
340	Clements, Bertha	11m	W	D.C.	05 AUG 1868	Congressional
141	Clements, Catharin	1y	W	D.C.	18 FEB 1859	Methodist
170	Clements, Catharine	22y	W	D.C.	24 JAN 1860	
230	Clements, Charles H., butcher	45y	W	Md.	27 JUL 1866	Methodist
182	Clements, Edmund C.	5m	W	D.C.	22 JUN 1860	Mt. Olivet
599	Clements, Ellen	11d	C	U.S.	06 MAY 1872	Ebenezer
066	Clements, Frank Bennet	15d	W	D.C.	19 DEC 1856	Congressional
405	Clements, Henry	1m	C	D.C.	13 JUL 1869	Washington Asylum
354	Clements, J.W.	44y	W	D.C.	29 OCT 1868	Holyrood
636	Clements, Jno. T., clerk	63y	W	U.S.	08 NOV 1872	
127	Clements, John	58y	W	Md.	08 SEP 1858	Washington Asylum
038	Clements, Joseph	9m	W		20 MAR 1856	Methodist
118	Clements, Maria	3y	W	D.C.	04 JUN 1858	Congressional
087	Clements, Maria	15d	W	D.C.	13 AUG 1857	Congressional
133	Clements, Mary A.	48y	W	Md.	22 NOV 1858	Glenwood
281	Clements, Mary Ann E.	61y	W	Md.	15 OCT 1867	Mt. Olivet
430	Clements, Mary Emily	55y	W	D.C.	18 DEC 1869	Mt. Olivet
211	Clements, Mr., colored girl of	16y	C		31 JAN 1866	Mt. Olivet
307	Clements, Rachel, Miss	82y	W	D.C.	24 APR 1868	Mt. Olivet
508	Clements, Wash., paper hanger	35y	C	D.C.	27 FEB 1871	Union
237	Clements, William, soldier	48y	W	Md.	21 SEP 1866	Mt. Olivet*
230	Clements, [Henry], son of Mrs.	14y	W		15 JUL 1866	Mt. Olivet*
341	Clendaniel, John	53y	W	D.C.	29 AUG 1868	Congressional
725	Clendaniel, Jos. H., clerk	33y	W	U.S.	21 OCT 1873	Congressional
269	Clendening, [blank]	2d	W	D.C.	31 AUG 1867	Congressional
517	Clenson, Lovine	7d	C	D.C.	01 APR 1871	Ebenezer
297	Clephane, Lavinia A.	44y	W	D.C.	20 FEB 1868	Glenwood
589	Cleveland, Adelia	30y	W	Ohio	31 MAR 1872	Ohio
620	Clifton, Mary A.B.	22m	W	U.S.	10 AUG 1872	
620	Clifton, Mary A.C.	7m	W	U.S.	12 AUG 1872	
053	Cline, Mariah	44y		Md.	29 AUG 1856	Congressional
010	Cline, Wm. F.	11y	W	Md.	14 JUN 1855	Congressional
715	Clinket, Henry, school boy	13y	C	D.C.	07 AUG 1873	

Page	Name	Age	Race	Birth	Death Date	Burial Ground
311	Clinkett, Rose		C		c.12 APR 1868	Alms House
658	Clinkins, Jno.	18m			08 JAN 1873	
155	Clinn, [blank]	1y	W	D.C.	29 JUL 1859	Mt. Olivet
350	Clinton, Ellen, domestic	40y	W	Ire.	21 SEP 1868	Mt. Olivet
270	Clintoner, Alice	1m	W	D.C.	11 AUG 1867	Glenwood
725	Clitch, Henrietta	64y	W	Ger.	22 OCT 1873	Oak Hill
175	Clokey, John, carpenter	57y	W	U.S.	27 MAR 1860	Congressional
607	Clokey, Robt. B., carpenter	73y	W	D.C.	25 JUN 1872	Congressional
397	Clomax, Mary	6m	C	Amer.	05 JUN 1869	Ebenezer
200	Clopsey, Clarissa	3y	W		23 FEB 1861	
332	Close, Mary A.	23y	W	N.Y.	09 JUL 1868	Glenwood
680	Cloughly, Eudora	29y	W	U.S.	06 APR 1873	Glenwood
096	Clymer, Harriet	6y	W	D.C.	10 NOV 1857	Oak Hill
172	Coad, John Q.,	79y	W	U.S.	14 FEB 1860	
489	Coakley, Aaron	16y	C	D.C.	05 NOV 1870	Ebenezer
469	Coakley, Aniese, seamstress	47y	C	U.S.	12 AUG 1870	Harmony
735	Coakley, E.D.	2m	W	U.S.	12 DEC 1873	Baltimore, Md.
779	Coakley, Jno. R., hay weigher	30y	C	U.S.	16 JUL 1874	Holyrood
623	Coakley, Philip E., hay weigher	33y	C	U.S.	20 AUG 1872	Holy Rood
622	Coan, Emma	31y	W	U.S.	07 AUG 1872	
335	Coat, Martha	7m	C	D.C.	24 JUL 1868	Ebenezer
050	Coates, Dinah	65y	C	Md.	15 JUL 1856	Young Mens
335a	Coates, Eliz.				21 JUL 1868	Washington Asylum
454	Coates, Henriette	27y	C	Va.	17 MAY 1870	Washington Asylum
549	Coates, Zenia	8y	C	Md.	23 DEC 1871	
769	Coats, Ann, infant of	6d	C	U.S.	01 MAY 1874	
378	Coats, Caroline, servant	32y	C	Va.	04 FEB 1869	Freedmen's Hospital
488	Coats, Catharine, cook	60y	C	Md.	29 NOV 1870	Harmony
295	Coats, Jane	70y	C		14 FEB 1868	Ebenezer
737	Coats, Robert	2m	C	U.S.	24 DEC 1873	Mt. Olivet
329	Cobbins, Sarah	4y	C	Va.	07 JUL 1868	Alms House
669	Cobley, Margaret, housekeeper	47y	W	Ire.	28 FEB 1873	
269	Coburn, John, merchant	71y	W	Mass.	10 AUG 1867	Oak Hill
620	Cochlin, [blank]	6d	W	U.S.	30 AUG 1872	Mt. Olivet
186	Cochran, Anna	81y	C	U.S.	29 JUL 1860	Western
001	Cochran, James [N.]	24y	W	Va.	15 JAN 1855	Congressional
108	Cochran, Robert	9y	W	D.C.	24 MAR 1858	Glenwood
203	Cochran, Robert	1y	W	D.C.	10 MAY 1861	Mt. Olivet
533	Cochran, Willie	14y	W	U.S.	19 AUG 1871	Glenwood
240	Cochrane, John T., clerk	54y	W	Md.	21 OCT 1866	Mt. Olivet
668	Cocker, Mary Jane	6m	W	U.S.	20 FEB 1873	Congressional
545	Cockerell, [blank]	Still	W	D.C.	14 NOV 1871	
047	Cockley, Sarah, cook	65y	C	Md.	23 JUN 1856	St. Matthews
269	Cockran, Mrs.	70y	W		06 AUG 1867	Congressional
507	Cockran, Robert, bookkeeper	67y	W	N.C.	04 FEB 1871	Glenwood
666	Cockrell, Annie	3y	W	U.S.	07 FEB 1873	Mt. Olivet
764	Codmer, John	1d	W	U.S.	24 MAY 1874	Mt. Olivet
007	Codrich, Amelia	40y	W	Va.	02 APR 1855	Methodist
399	Codrick, Hannah Jane	1y	W		30 JUL 1869	Congressional
593	Codrick, Sarah	40y	W	Va.	22 APR 1872	Congressional
053	Codrick, [blank]	1y	W	D.C.	10 AUG 1856	Methodist, East
386	Coe, Benj. C., Sr., coach trimmer	57y	W	N.Y.	12 APR 1869	Oak Hill
281	Coe, Sarah	22y	W	Mich.	20 OCT 1867	Alms House
487	Coe, Sarah Lee	7d	W	D.C.	23 NOV 1870	Congressional
188	Coffee, Michael	8m	W	D.C.	16 AUG 1860	Mt. Olivet
049	Coffee, Michael	35y	W	Ire.	10 JUL 1856	St. Peters
329	Coffey, John	2y	W	D.C.	04 JUL 1868	Mt. Olivet
724	Coffey, Michael, laborer	56y	W	Ire.	11 OCT 1873	Mt. Olivet

District of Columbia Interments (Index to Deaths), 1855-1874

Page	Name	Age	Race	Birth	Death Date	Burial Ground
525	Coffin, Eliza, lady	73y	W	U.S.	28 JUN 1871	Oak Hill
521	Coffin, James B.	3y		D.C.	07 JUN 1871	Washington
548	Coffin, Louisa H.	56y	W	Md.	17 DEC 1871	Oak Hill
090	Coffin, Mr., servant of	2y	C	D.C.	01 SEP 1857	Western
092	Coffin, Mr., servant of	90y	C	Md.	24 SEP 1857	Western
344	Cogar, Rosa E.	2m	C	D.C.	07 AUG 1868	Georgetown
752	Cogg, Benj. H., barber	17y	C	U.S.	18 MAR 1874	Young Mens
707	Coggins, Corra	13m	W	Md.	02 JUL 1873	Congressional
403	Cohen, A.	2y	W	Eur.	11 JUL 1869	Washington Hebrew
402	Cohen, Henry	1y	W		07 JUL 1869	Hebrew
662	Cohill, John M.	10y	W	U.S.	04 JAN 1873	Congressional*
302	Coke, Beverly, cook	30y	C	D.C.	06 MAR 1868	Western
025	Coke, [blank]	22y	C		30 SEP 1855	Western
680	Colbath, Mary A.	23y	W	U.S.	04 APR 1873	Mt. Olivet
071	Colbert, H., servant	50y	C		18 FEB 1857	St. Patricks
588	Colbert, Holmes	44y	I	Miss.	24 MAR 1872	Washington
400	Colbert, Jane Elizabeth	1y	C		— JUL 1869	Harmony
276	Colbert, John, whitewasher	53y	C	Va.*	07 SEP 1867	
345	Colbert, Mathew	11m	W	D.C.	13 AUG 1868	Mt. Olivet
443	Colbert, Minty	90y	C	Md.	28 FEB 1870	Washington Asylum
447	Colbert, Teressa, servant	27y	C		18 MAR 1870	Ebenezer
600	Colbun, Jane	35y	C	U.S.	16 MAY 1872	Mt. Zion
521	Colby, Daniel C., patent atty.	51y	W	N.H.	08 JUN 1871	
030	Colclasier, Henry	4y	W	D.C.	03 NOV 1855	Foundry
184	Colclasier, Joseph	1y	W	D.C.	01 JUL 1860	Mt. Olivet
352	Cole, Abraham	20y	C	Md.	16 SEP 1868	Washington Asylum
276	Cole, Annie	10m	C	D.C.	10 SEP 1867	
596	Cole, Baret M.	1y	W	D.C.	25 APR 1872	Glenwood
472	Cole, Betsy, servant	16y	C	Va.	09 AUG 1870	Freedmen's Hospital
422	Cole, Betty	8d	C		02 OCT 1869	
299	Cole, Catherine	46y	C	Md.	01 MAR 1868	Young Mens
592	Cole, Cecelia A., dressmaker	23y	C	D.C.	03 APR 1872	Mt. Olivet
278	Cole, Charles Henry	1y	C	D.C.	29 OCT 1867	Ebenezer
154	Cole, Elizabeth	63y	C	Md.	15 JUL 1859	Harmony
116	Cole, Elizabeth	80y	C	Va.	23 JUN 1858	Washington Asylum
674	Cole, Francis	8m	W	U.S.	18 MAR 1873	Congressional*
066	Cole, G.S.	2y	W	D.C.	22 DEC 1856	Glenwood
621	Cole, Geo. H.V.	10m	C	U.S.	19 AUG 1872	Mt. Olivet
770	Cole, George	1y	C	U.S.	01 JUN 1874	Mt. Olivet
335	Cole, George Marshall	7m	C	D.C.	12 JUL 1868	
498	Cole, Georgiana, pauper	4m	B	D.C.	31 JAN 1871	Washington Asylum
005	Cole, James, laborer	24y	C	Va.*	21 MAR 1855	Methodist, East
018	Cole, Jas., child of	1y	C		21 AUG 1855	Young Mens
230	Cole, John Brandt	9m	W	D.C.	30 JUL 1866	Congressional
133	Cole, John T., shoemaker	38y	W	Va.	23 NOV 1858	Glenwood
713	Cole, Lee Emma	1y	C	D.C.	22 AUG 1873	
015	Cole, Leonora	1y	C	D.C.	02 JUL 1855	St. Patricks
707	Cole, Martha L.	2y		D.C.	19 JUL 1873	Beckett's
150	Cole, Mary	3y	W	D.C.	13 JUN 1859	Foundry
051	Cole, Mary	57y	W	Md.	20 JUL 1856	Laurel Factory
063	Cole, Mary Jane	20y	W	Md.	29 NOV 1856	New Market, Md.
212	Cole, Richard, farmer	45y	W	Md.	16 FEB 1866	Congressional
341	Cole, Robert M.	1y	W	D.C.	28 AUG 1868	Congressional
399	Cole, Rosetta	8m	W	D.C.	04 JUL 1869	Congressional
077	Cole, Sarah E.	32y	W	Va.	13 MAY 1857	Oak Hill
212	Cole, Thomas, 2nd cl. foreman USN	25y	W	Ire.	03 FEB 1866	Mt. Olivet
743	Cole, Viola	80y	C	U.S.	24 JAN 1874	
361	Cole, William	26y	C	Va.	25 NOV 1868	

Page	Name	Age	Race	Birth	Death Date	Burial Ground
508	Cole, William		C	Va.	15 FEB 1871	Young Mens
752	Cole, William H.	26y	C	U.S.	25 MAR 1874	Young Mens
210	Cole, [blank]	2y			16 JAN 1866	
548	Cole, [blank]	2m	W	D.C.	15 DEC 1871	Congressional
223	Cole, [blank]	1y	C		03 JUN 1866	Ebenezer
052	Colegate, James L.	9y	W	D.C.	30 JUL 1856	Congressional
104	Coleman (Myers), [blank]	Still	C		12 FEB 1858	Washington Asylum
583	Coleman, Abbott	5y	C	D.C.	29 FEB 1872	
464	Coleman, Ada E.	27y	W	Amer.	31 JUL 1870	N.Y.
449	Coleman, Ann	8m	W		30 APR 1870	Mt. Olivet
343	Coleman, Barbery, laundress	55y	C	Va.	21 AUG 1868	Congressional
659	Coleman, Dan	45y	C	U.S.	10 JAN 1873	Washington Asylum
284	Coleman, Frank	1m	W		03 NOV 1867	Mt. Olivet
613	Coleman, Henry	2y	C	U.S.	15 JUL 1872	
090	Coleman, Isabella	4m	C	D.C.	01 SEP 1857	Young Mens
389	Coleman, Jane	27y	C	U.S.	27 APR 1869	Washington Asylum
678	Coleman, Jas.	50y	C	U.S.	28 MAR 1873	Small Pox
538	Coleman, Laura H.	55y	W	U.S.	29 SEP 1871	N.Y.
591	Coleman, Lawson, laborer	19y	C	Va.	19 APR 1872	
302	Coleman, Lizzie, child of	Still	C	D.C.	20 MAR 1868	
684	Coleman, Martha	8y	C	U.S.	11 APR 1873	Small Pox*
472	Coleman, Martha	13y	C	Va.	02 AUG 1870	Union
730	Coleman, Mary	30y	C	U.S.	17 NOV 1873	Washington Asylum
070	Coleman, Mary E., lady	23y	W	D.C.	02 FEB 1857	St. Patricks
540	Coleman, Matthew	12y	W		02 OCT 1871	Mt. Olivet
472	Coleman, Morris, laborer	25y	C		19 AUG 1870	Freedmen's Hospital
518	Coleman, Peter, laborer	26y	C	Va.	09 MAY 1871	Potters Field
589	Coleman, Robert E.	3m	W	U.S.	28 MAR 1872	Mt. Olivet
388	Coleman, Sarah	2y	C	D.C.	02 APR 1869	
582	Coleman, Toney	1y	C	D.C.	22 FEB 1872	Young Mens
770	Coleman, [blank]	7m	C	U.S.	03 JUN 1874	
389	Coleman, [blank], Mr.	80y	C	U.S.	30 APR 1869	Washington Asylum
007	Coles, Emily J.	10m	C	D.C.	24 APR 1855	
321	Coles, John Storm	11m	W	Md.	29 JUN 1868	Baltimore, Md.
225	Colison, William G.	1y	W	D.C.	24 JUN 1866	Congressional
292a	Collam, Amanda	28y	W		21 JAN 1868	Oak Hill
736	Collier, Jas. S., school boy	10y	W	U.S.	21 DEC 1873	Glenwood
248	Collier, Robert Jackson	8y	W	D.C.	21 DEC 1866	Glenwood
324	Collin, James	37y	W	Ire.	17 JUL 1868	Mt. Olivet
028	Collings, [blank]	10m	W		06 OCT 1855	St. Matthews
143	Collingsmith, Rebecca	9y	W	Va.	01 MAR 1859	Alexandria, Va.
719	Collingsworth, Laura	20y	W	Va.	16 SEP 1873	Congressional
646	Collins, Abram, stone mason	66y	W	Ire.	20 DEC 1872	Congressional
522	Collins, Adam	10m	C	D.C.	12 JUN 1871	Holmead
191	Collins, Albert	1y	W	D.C.	03 OCT 1860	Congressional
752	Collins, Ann	5d	W	U.S.	17 MAR 1874	Mt. Olivet
737	Collins, Catharine, servant	50y	W	Ire.	25 DEC 1873	
247	Collins, Catherine	2y	W	D.C.	07 DEC 1866	Mt. Olivet
305	Collins, Catherine	32y	W		c.29 MAR 1868	Mt. Olivet
409	Collins, Cordelia	4d	C		10 AUG 1869	Young Mens
428	Collins, Cornelius, laborer	54y	W	Ire.	02 NOV 1869	Mt. Olivet
332	Collins, D.W., child of	1m	W	D.C.	01 JUL 1868	Glenwood
414	Collins, Ellen	76y	W	Ire.	09 SEP 1869	Congressional
524	Collins, Eve	11d	C	D.C.	20 JUN 1871	Western
021	Collins, James	22y	W	Ire.	02 AUG 1855	St. Peters
157	Collins, James	2m	W	D.C.	13 AUG 1859	Western
292	Collins, James	22d	C	D.C.	01 JAN 1868	Young Mens
114	Collins, James H., carpenter	33y	W		17 MAY 1858	Rock Creek

District of Columbia Interments (Index to Deaths), 1855-1874

Page	Name	Age	Race	Birth	Death Date	Burial Ground
118	Collins, Jane	2y	W	D.C.	08 JUN 1858	St. Matthews
609	Collins, Jas. R.	7y	W	U.S.	11 JUN 1872	
014	Collins, Jenny	8m	W	D.C.	22 JUL 1855	Rock Creek
421	Collins, Johanna	60y	W	Ire.	22 OCT 1869	Mt. Olivet
423	Collins, John	54y	C	Ire.	27 OCT 1869	Washington Asylum
771	Collins, John, bricklayer	32y	W	U.S.	19 JUN 1874	Congressional
609	Collins, John G.	5y	W	U.S.	12 JUN 1872	
610	Collins, John J., butcher	22y	W	U.S.	13 JUL 1872	
718	Collins, John, laborer	60y	W	Ire.	13 SEP 1873	Mt. Olivet
146	Collins, John, laborer	67y	W	Md.	20 APR 1859	Rock Creek
603	Collins, Joseph	6y	C	Va.	15 JUN 1872	Small Pox
411	Collins, Josephine R.	20y	W	U.S.	31 AUG 1869	Rock Creek
415	Collins, Kate, domestic	40y	W	Ire.	17 SEP 1869	Mt. Olivet
335b	Collins, Laura				07 JUL 1868	Washington Asylum
377	Collins, Lena	30y	C	Md.	25 FEB 1869	Union
593	Collins, Louise	24y	W	D.C.	11 APR 1872	Glenwood
140	Collins, Maria, wife	20y	W	Va.	08 FEB 1859	Congressional
689	Collins, Martha M.	48y	W	U.S.	31 MAY 1873	Glenwood
305	Collins, Mary	8m	W		c.11 MAR 1868	Mt. Olivet
452	Collins, Mary	2m	C	D.C.	07 APR 1870	Washington Asylum
137	Collins, Mary	19y	W	D.C.	06 JAN 1859	Washington Asylum
758	Collins, Mary, merchant	40y	W	Ire.	12 APR 1874	
746	Collins, Mary, servant	30y	W	Ire.	01 FEB 1874	Mt. Olivet
153	Collins, Michael	8d	W	D.C.	02 JUL 1859	Mt. Olivet
323	Collins, Michael	8m	W	D.C.	06 JUL 1868	Mt. Olivet
023	Collins, Michael	4y	W	D.C.	10 SEP 1855	St. Patricks
779	Collins, Nannie	5y	W	U.S.	23 JUL 1874	St. Josephs
149	Collins, Owen, carpenter	38y	W	Md.	18 MAY 1859	Rock Creek
752	Collins, Patrick, grocer	37y	W	Ire.	30 MAR 1874	Mt. Olivet
779	Collins, Patrick J.	4m	W	U.S.	08 JUL 1874	Mt. Olivet
074	Collins, Robert, mason	59y	W	Ire.	02 MAR 1857	Congressional
609	Collins, Saml. H.	9y	W	U.S.	11 JUN 1872	
082	Collins, Sarah	78y	W		08 JUL 1857	Western
143	Collins, Sarah M.	1½d	W	D.C.	04 MAR 1859	Glenwood
010	Collins, Sarah, washerwoman	36y	C	D.C.*	18 JUN 1855	Catholic
551	Collins, Shedrac, carpenter	45y	C	Va.	— DEC 1871	
530	Collins, Susan	1y	C	Va.	31 JUL 1871	Young Mens
112	Collins, Thomas J.	13y	W	D.C.	23 APR 1858	St. Patricks
018	Collins, Van	2y	W	Ire.	16 AUG 1855	Rock Creek
271	Collins, William	9m	W	D.C.	30 AUG 1867	Rock Creek
637	Collins, Wm.	1y	C	U.S.	08 NOV 1872	
469	Collins, [blank]	25y	W	Ire.	30 AUG 1870	Mt. Olivet
154	Collins, [blank]	18d	W	D.C.	17 JUL 1859	Western
382	Collins, [blank]	7d	C		05 MAR 1869	Young Mens
313	Collisan, Ruth A.	20y	C	Md.	25 MAY 1868	Freedmen's Hospital
002	Collison, Catharine	58y	W	Md.	31 JAN 1855	St. Peters
287	Collison, [blank]		C		c.16 DEC 1867	Alms House
195	Collman, Charles L., miller	59y	W	D.C.	15 DEC 1860	Congressional
332	Colly, Martha M.	10m	W	Mich.	02 JUL 1868	Glenwood
746	Colman, Martha	4m	C	U.S.	03 FEB 1874	
453	Colman, Mary	87y	W		16 MAY 1870	Congressional
404	Colman, Polly	1m	C	D.C.	08 JUL 1869	Washington Asylum
680	Colne, Ann, Mrs.	64y	W	Fra.	02 APR 1873	Holyrood
104	Coloman, Lewis	2y	C		04 FEB 1858	Young Mens
345	Colter, Margaret	11m	W	D.C.	18 AUG 1868	Mt. Olivet
507	Coltman, Sophia E.	71y	W	Ger.	12 FEB 1871	Glenwood
214	Coltman, [blank], supt. Treas. bldg.	54y	W	Ger.	10 MAR 1866	Glenwood
305	Colton, John	21d	W		c.09 MAR 1868	Mt. Olivet

District of Columbia Interments (Index to Deaths), 1855-1874

Page	Name	Age	Race	Birth	Death Date	Burial Ground
737	Colton, Mary	4m	W	U.S.	26 DEC 1873	Congressional*
356	Columbus, Andrew J.	1y	W	D.C.	13 OCT 1868	Mt. Olivet
523	Columbus, Carver C.	5m	W	D.C.	15 JUN 1871	Glenwood
395	Columbus, Cora B.	5m	W	D.C.	13 JUN 1869	Glenwood
020	Columbus, E.S.Y.	1y	W	D.C.	05 AUG 1855	Foundry
309	Columbus, Eliza	64y	W	Va.*	06 APR 1868	Mt. Olivet
779	Columbus, Grace J.	11m	W	U.S.	18 JUL 1874	Glenwood
304	Columbus, Joanah D.	10m	W	D.C.	c.10 MAR 1868	Glenwood
054	Columbus, Mary Eliza	3m	W	D.C.	05 AUG 1856	Foundry
065	Columbus, Sarah C.	1y	W	D.C.	01 DEC 1856	Glenwood
172	Colvin, Adeline		W	U.S.	14 FEB 1860	Congressional
398	Comb, Philip R., seaman	62y	W	Md.	22 JUN 1869	Baltimore, Md.
134	Combs, Alex. F.	8y	W	D.C.	30 NOV 1858	Congressional
134	Combs, Alexander	8y	W	D.C.	30 NOV 1858	Congressional
675	Combs, Catherine	48y	W	U.S.	20 MAR 1873	Mt. Olivet
638	Combs, Vincent	64y	C	U.S.	05 NOV 1872	
518	Combs, William	10y	C	Va.	07 MAY 1871	Young Mens
613	Combs, Wm. H.	1y	C	U.S.	18 JUL 1872	
019	Combs, [blank]	6h	W		23 AUG 1855	St. Marys
461	Comerford, Mahala	66y	W	Amer.	30 JUL 1870	Congressional
713	Comerford, Mike	63y	W	Ire.	21 AUG 1873	Congressional*
311	Commodore, Maria		C		c.19 APR 1868	Alms House
389	Commodore, Millie	4m	C	D.C.	06 APR 1869	Washington Asylum
373	Commonore, Louisa, servant	68y	C	Md.	07 JAN 1869	Harmony
132	Compton, Elizabeth	45y	W	Va.	07 NOV 1858	Alexandria, Va.
149	Compton, James, soldier	32y	W	Va.	21 MAY 1859	Marine
313	Compton, Rebecca	2y	C	D.C.	14 MAY 1868	Young Mens
409	Compton, Webster	8m	C		14 AUG 1869	Harmony
245	Conally, John, private marines	35y	W	Ire.	21 NOV 1866	Congressional*
231	Conard, Reuben J.	4y	W	D.C.	06 AUG 1866	Congressional
697	Conaway, Adison	4y	C	U.S.	06 JUN 1873	Washington Asylum
675	Conaway, Laura V.	29y	C	U.S.	22 MAR 1873	Harmony
197	Conaway, Wesley	16y	C		26 JAN 1861	Georgetown
252	Condon, Philip, laborer	58y	W	Ire.	07 FEB 1867	Mt. Olivet*
313	Conelly, Alice	22y	W	Ire.	01 MAY 1868	Mt. Olivet
313	Conelly, Alice, child of	Still	W	D.C.	01 MAY 1868	Mt. Olivet
160	Coner, [blank]	3m	W	D.C.	03 AUG 1859	Mt. Olivet
042	Conklin, Mary	8m	W	D.C.	14 APR 1856	Congressional
309	Conlan, Eleanor	67y	W	Ire.	10 APR 1868	Mt. Olivet
462	Conlan, William	4y	W	Ire.	16 JUL 1870	Mt. Olivet
238	Conly, Michael, laborer	35y	W	Ire.	26 SEP 1866	Mt. Olivet
318	Conn, Lucy	5m	W	U.S.	29 JUN 1868	Congressional
285	Conna, John, steel contractor	33y	W	Ire.	26 DEC 1867	Mt. Olivet
099	Connally, Ellen, seamstress	25y	W	N.Y.	23 DEC 1857	Washington Asylum
285	Connas, Margaret	5m	W	D.C.	31 DEC 1867	Mt. Olivet
496	Connealy, William, clerk	24y	W	N.H.	05 DEC 1870	Mt. Olivet
682	Connell, Ellen, housekeeper	35y	W	Ire.	29 APR 1873	Mt. Olivet
238	Connell, Estella Cecelia	4y	W		25 SEP 1866	
501	Connell, Honora L.	21y	W	Ire.	30 JAN 1871	Mt. Olivet
035	Connell, Infant				26 FEB 1856	St. Patricks
249	Connell, J.W., child of	1h	W	D.C.	19 JAN 1867	Mt. Olivet
729	Connell, John E., stonecutter	17y	W	U.S.	05 NOV 1873	Glenwood
218	Connell, Mary	1m	W	D.C.	12 APR 1866	Mt. Olivet
477	Connell, Mary A.	7y	W	D.C.	12 SEP 1870	Mt. Olivet
255	Connell, Mary C.C.	33y	W	Ire.	30 MAR 1867	Mt. Olivet
661	Connell, Mary O.	18y	W	Ire.	23 JAN 1873	Mt. Olivet
304	Connell, Michael	40y	W		c.05 MAR 1868	Mt. Olivet
088	Connell, Michael	7m	W	D.C.	19 AUG 1857	St. Patricks

District of Columbia Interments (Index to Deaths), 1855-1874

Page	Name	Age	Race	Birth	Death Date	Burial Ground
417	Connell, Nancy	78y	W	Ire.	05 SEP 1869	Washington Asylum
605	Connell, [blank]	8d	W	D.C.	06 JUN 1872	Mt. Olivet
711	Connelly, Katie	6m	W	D.C.	12 AUG 1873	Mt. Olivet
771	Connelly, Mary, housekeeper	25y	W	U.S.	10 JUN 1874	Mt. Olivet
118	Connelly, Mary M.	15d	W	D.C.	06 JUN 1858	St. Patricks
170	Conner, Catharine	26y	W	Ire.	29 JAN 1860	Trinity
084	Conner, Charles A.	5y	W	D.C.	26 JUL 1857	Ebenezer
746	Conner, E.	5m	W	U.S.	16 FEB 1874	Mt. Olivet
182	Conner, E., machinist	35y	W	Ire.	20 JUN 1860	
295	Conner, F.	5m	C	D.C.	24 FEB 1868	Alms House
229	Conner, Jemina	61y	W		18 JUL 1866	Glenwood
057	Conner, John	1y	W	D.C.	01 SEP 1856	Congressional
723	Conner, John	2y	W	D.C.	08 OCT 1873	Mt. Olivet
357	Conner, John	38y	B	Va.	16 OCT 1868	Washington Asylum
669	Conner, John, harness maker	32y	W	Ire.	26 FEB 1873	New Haven, Conn.
346	Conner, Laura Emily	10m	W	D.C.	28 AUG 1868	
544	Conner, Maria	34y	W	Eng.	03 NOV 1871	N.J.
041	Conner, Martin, driver	36y	W	Md.	13 APR 1856	St. Matthews
169	Conner, Mary	11y	W	D.C.	14 JAN 1860	Ebenezer
110	Conner, Mary		W		01 APR 1858	Potters Field
041	Conner, Mary	60y	W	Ire.	11 APR 1856	St. Peters
220	Conner, Michael, clerk	23y	W	Ire.	06 MAY 1866	Philadelphia, Pa.
478	Conner, Michael, laborer	45y	W	Ire.	02 SEP 1870	Methodist
149	Conner, Michael, tailor	69y	W	Ire.	31 MAY 1859	Georgetown, Catholic
593	Conner, Paul C.	2m	W	D.C.	03 APR 1872	
191	Conner, Rebecca	32y	W	Md.	14 OCT 1860	Ebenezer
116	Conner, Sofen	5m	W	D.C.	23 JUN 1858	St. Patricks
190	Conner, Thomas	1y	W	D.C.	21 SEP 1860	Mt. Olivet
087	Conner, Thomas	29y	W	Ire.	14 AUG 1857	St. Patricks
155	Conner, William	1y	W	D.C.	27 JUL 1859	Congressional
271	Conners, Ellen	1y	W	D.C.	25 AUG 1867	Mt. Olivet
538	Conney, Bridget	75y	W	Ire.	24 SEP 1871	Mt. Olivet
030	Connington, Jas.	7y	W	D.C.	04 NOV 1855	St. Patricks
140	Connolly, Jeremiah, laborer	50y	W	Ire.	09 FEB 1859	Washington Asylum
174	Connolly, John	3d	W	D.C.	04 MAR 1860	St. Patricks
161	Connolly, John, undertaker	40y	W	Md.	01 SEP 1859	St. Patricks
003	Connoly, Owen, grocer	51y	W	Ire.	08 FEB 1855	
063	Connor, Ann	42y	W	Ire.	28 NOV 1856	St. Patricks
299	Connor, Cassandra L., Miss	75y	W	Md.	03 MAR 1868	Alexandria, Va.
199	Connor, Catharine	2y	W	D.C.	13 FEB 1861	Mt. Olivet
182	Connor, Christopher, machinist	27y	W		27 JUN 1860	Mt. Olivet
771	Connor, Danl. Joseph	1m	W	U.S.	20 JUN 1874	Mt. Olivet
399	Connor, Elmyra	1y	W		11 JUL 1869	Congressional
020	Connor, Hannorah	2m	W	Ire.	07 AUG 1855	St. Peters
752	Connor, Harriet, laundress	30y	C	U.S.	15 MAR 1874	
472	Connor, Hattie	1y	W	D.C.	02 AUG 1870	Methodist
074	Connor, Honora	28y	W	Ire.	21 MAR 1857	Washington Asylum
103	Connor, James, laborer	40y	W	Ire.	30 JAN 1858	St. Patricks
114	Connor, James, laborer	40y	W	Ire.	26 MAY 1858	St. Patricks
752	Connor, John	4m	C	U.S.	02 MAR 1874	
735	Connor, John C., Ex-M.C.	31y	W	U.S.	10 DEC 1873	Indianapolis, Ind.
150	Connor, John, storekeeper	69y	W	Ire.	01 JUN 1859	Trinity
297	Connor, Juda		C		c.27 FEB 1868	Alms House
680	Connor, M., Mrs.				03 APR 1873	
734	Connor, Margaret	8y	W	U.S.	01 DEC 1873	Mt. Olivet
430	Connor, Mary		W	D.C.	02 DEC 1869	Culpeper, Va.
292a	Connor, Mary E.	4m	W	D.C.*	08 JAN 1868	Mt. Olivet
687	Connor, Maurice J.	5m	W	D.C.	09 MAY 1873	Mt. Olivet

Page	Name	Age	Race	Birth	Death Date	Burial Ground
110	Connor, Samuel	2y	W	D.C.	03 APR 1858	Methodist
306	Connor, Susan, cook	100y	C	Va.	17 APR 1868	Young Mens
087	Connor, William	5y	W	D.C.	11 AUG 1857	Ebenezer
764	Connors, Margaret	33y	W	Ire.	25 MAY 1874	Mt. Olivet
771	Connors, Sarah, housekeeper	56y	W	Ire.	08 JUN 1874	Holyrood
128	Connoway, Mary	5y	C	D.C.	18 SEP 1858	Foundry
061	Connuighton, John	19y	W	D.C.	04 OCT 1856	St. Patricks
045	Conolly, John	7d	W	D.C.	26 MAY 1856	St. Patricks
391	Conor, Julia	54y	W	Ire.	23 MAY 1869	Mt. Olivet
638	Conore, Harriet	2y	C	U.S.	10 NOV 1872	
280	Conoroy, Resin, laborer	75y	C	Md.	14 OCT 1867	Young Mens
677	Conoroy, Roberta	1y	C	U.S.	15 MAR 1873	Ebenezer
425	Conors, Mary, domestic	40y	W	Ire.	19 NOV 1869	Mt. Olivet
662	Conover, Jno., laborer	60y	C	U.S.	18 JAN 1873	
335a	Conoway, Eddie				27 JUL 1868	Washington Asylum
413	Conoway, Mary, servant	20y	C	Va.	30 AUG 1869	Washington Asylum
175	Conroy, Dominic, messenger	78y	W	Ire.	20 MAR 1860	Mt. Olivet
015	Conroy, James	1y	W	D.C.	03 JUL 1855	St. Peters
248	Conroy, Margaret	26y	W	Ire.	31 DEC 1866	Trinity
370	Conroy, Mrs., domestic	60y	W	Ire.	03 JAN 1869	Mt. Olivet
371	Conroy, Patrick Henry	11y	W	Ire.	20 JAN 1869	Mt. Olivet
636	Conrway, Edward	1y	W	U.S.	08 NOV 1872	
382	Constable, W.M.		W		17 MAR 1869	
427	Contee, Cornelius	10y	C	Md.	30 NOV 1869	Washington Asylum
121	Contee, Getty	10m	C	D.C.	11 JUL 1858	Young Mens
373	Contee, John H.	4d	C		12 JAN 1869	Western
331	Contee, John W.	11y	C	D.C.	14 JUL 1868	Freedmen's Hospital
621	Contee, Rose E.	10m	C	U.S.	15 AUG 1872	
306	Contee, Saml.	4y	C	D.C.	23 APR 1868	Alms House
771	Contee, Susan	3y	C	U.S.	16 JUN 1874	
746	Contie, James H.	1y	C	U.S.	23 FEB 1874	Beckett's
352	Contree, George	2y	C	D.C.	01 SEP 1868	Washington Asylum
333	Conway, Eddie	7m	C	D.C.	27 JUL 1868	Alms House
029	Conway, Eliza	19y		Ire.	27 NOV 1855	Congressional
587	Conway, Francis	77y	W	Md.	22 MAR 1872	Md.
385	Conway, Kate	2d	W	U.S.	11 APR 1869	Congressional
752	Conway, Mary A.	38y	W	U.S.	15 MAR 1874	Mt. Olivet
779	Conway, Mattie C.	15m	W	U.S.	03 JUL 1874	Mt. Olivet
371	Conway, Michael	24y	W	D.C.	22 JAN 1869	Mt. Olivet
328	Conway, Mrs., soldier's wife	40y	W	N.Y.	13 JUL 1868	Western
327	Conway, Patrick	10m	W	D.C.	15 JUL 1868	Mt. Olivet
587	Conway, Sallie	75y	C	Va.	19 MAR 1872	Asylum
279	Conway, Sarah P.	50y	W	Md.	10 OCT 1867	Harford Co., Md.
602	Conway, Thomas	2m	W	U.S.	17 MAY 1872	Mt. Olivet
770	Conway, Walter Scott	5m	W	U.S.	08 JUN 1874	Baltimore, Md.
029	Conwell, Geo.	1y	W	D.C.	02 NOV 1855	Congressional
441	Cony, Joseph S.	1m	W		21 FEB 1870	Boston, Mass.
099	Cook, Alfred, waiter	51y	C	D.C.	29 DEC 1857	Harmony
481	Cook, Alice	35y	C	Va.	15 OCT 1870	Holmead
537	Cook, Allen C.	1y	W	D.C.	20 SEP 1871	Methodist
425	Cook, Allen, soldier	45y	W	N.Y.	10 NOV 1869	Congressional
225	Cook, Anna	2y	W	D.C.	23 JUN 1866	Ebenezer
308	Cook, Anna F.	21y	W	Mass.	28 APR 1868	Congressional
084	Cook, Arthur	1m	W	D.C.	27 JUL 1857	Methodist
135	Cook, C.W.F., bar keeper	23y	W	Ger.	17 DEC 1858	Congressional
465	Cook, Charles L.	1m	W	D.C.	16 JUL 1870	Methodist
103	Cook, Charles W.	8m			28 JAN 1858	St. Patricks
256	Cook, D., child of	4m	W	D.C.	23 MAR 1867	Baltimore, Md.

District of Columbia Interments (Index to Deaths), 1855-1874

Page	Name	Age	Race	Birth	Death Date	Burial Ground
644	Cook, Elizabeth	19y	W	U.S.	21 DEC 1872	German Catholic
492	Cook, Fanny F.	69y	W	Pa.	04 DEC 1870	Congressional
608	Cook, Fred.	1y	W	D.C.	14 JUN 1872	Mt. Olivet*
586	Cook, G.A.	2y	C	D.C.	13 MAR 1872	Holmead
467	Cook, Geo. Lewis	5m	W	D.C.	04 JUL 1870	Glenwood
710	Cook, Geo. W.	45y	W	Va.	08 AUG 1873	Congressional
408	Cook, George A., asst. engineer	28y	W	U.S.	20 AUG 1869	Baltimore, Md.
345	Cook, Harry	10m	W	D.C.	02 AUG 1868	Glenwood
632	Cook, Hattie M.	11y	W	U.S.	25 OCT 1872	
415	Cook, Henry, cabinet maker	53y	W	Md.	14 SEP 1869	Baltimore, Md.
631	Cook, Herbert C.	19y	W	U.S.	25 OCT 1872	
226	Cook, Isabella A.	40y	W	D.C.	26 JUN 1866	Oak Hill
091	Cook, James, tavern keeper	28y	W	Ire.	16 SEP 1857	St. Patricks
307	Cook, John B.	5y	W	D.C.	06 APR 1868	Prospect Hill
005	Cook, John F., Rev.	45y	C	D.C.	22 MAR 1855	Harmony
590	Cook, John, laborer	23y	C	Ohio	18 APR 1872	Asylum
388	Cook, Lilly A.	2y	W	D.C.	01 APR 1869	Glenwood
519	Cook, Littleton T., pressman	22y	W	D.C.	16 MAY 1871	Oak Hill
352	Cook, Lizzie	1y			01 SEP 1868	
306	Cook, Lizzie	12y	W	Md.	13 APR 1868	Young Mens
549	Cook, Margret A.	58y		D.C.	21 DEC 1871	Congressional
752	Cook, Maria L.	14y	C	U.S.	11 MAR 1874	
289	Cook, Martha	20y	W	Md.	03 JAN 1868	Glenwood
289	Cook, Martha E.	20y	W		02 JAN 1868	Glenwood
630	Cook, Mary	30y	C	U.S.	17 OCT 1872	Small Pox
401	Cook, Mary	30y	C		29 JUL 1869	Young Mens
630	Cook, Mary A.	9m	C	U.S.	25 OCT 1872	Small Pox
107	Cook, Mary Ida	10m	C	D.C.	03 MAR 1858	Harmony
189	Cook, Mathias, laborer	38y	W	Ger.	01 SEP 1860	St. Marys
036	Cook, Mrs.	70y		Ger.	10 FEB 1856	German
639	Cook, Mrs.	60y	W	U.S.	10 DEC 1872	Small Pox*
674	Cook, Nancy	70y	C	U.S.	13 MAR 1873	Washington Asylum
396	Cook, O.	3m	W	D.C.	23 JUN 1869	Western
393	Cook, O.	3m	C		24 MAY 1869	Western
117	Cook, P.J., shoemaker	31y	W	Ger.	27 JUN 1858	German Lutheran
636	Cook, Priscilla	8y	W	U.S.	25 NOV 1872	
462	Cook, Richard J., moulder	29y	W	Amer.	09 JUL 1870	Congressional
071	Cook, Robert, servant	35y	C	D.C.	14 FEB 1857	Washington Asylum
762	Cook, Sallie	90y	C	U.S.	30 APR 1874	Washington Asylum
151	Cook, Sarah A.	52y	W	D.C.	16 JUN 1859	Congressional
507	Cook, Sarah C.	18y	W	D.C.	10 FEB 1871	Glenwood
601	Cook, Selina	19d	W	U.S.	21 MAY 1872	Asylum
157	Cook, Sophy	66y	W	Md.	04 AUG 1859	Harmony
325	Cook, Thomas, machinist	60y	W	Md.	20 JUL 1868	Washington
292a	Cook, Truman	1y	C	D.C.	04 FEB 1868	Mt. Zion
172	Cook, W.B., painter	65y	W	Va.	08 FEB 1860	Congressional
530	Cook, William	4m	W	D.C.	31 JUL 1871	Congressional
185	Cook, Wm.	8m	W	D.C.	14 JUL 1860	Congressional
132	Cooke, Catharine	61y	W		09 NOV 1858	Congressional
244	Cooke, Ida Regina	11y	W	Md.	14 NOV 1866	Baltimore, Md.
421	Cooke, Thomas, porter	60y	C	D.C.	30 OCT 1869	Harmony
397	Cooke, [blank]		W		15 JUN 1869	Harmony
233	Cookendorfer, Jane	71y	W		31 AUG 1866	Oak Hill
499	Cooksey, Joshua, child of	Still	W	D.C.	14 JAN 1871	Congressional
355	Cooksey, Mary I.	26y	W	Md.	29 OCT 1868	Congressional
359	Cooksey, Sarah S.	4m	W		04 NOV 1868	Congressional
725	Cooksey, Thos. E., laborer	28y	W	U.S.	23 OCT 1873	Congressional
144	Cooksie, Nathan W.	2m	W	D.C.	18 MAR 1859	Congressional

Page	Name	Age	Race	Birth	Death Date	Burial Ground
239	Cooksie, [Kidwell], infant of	2d	W	D.C.	09 OCT 1866	Congressional*
027	Coolage, Lucy	85y	C	Md.	09 OCT 1855	Young Mens
286	Cooledge, Catherine Alice	22y	W	I.T.	19 DEC 1867	Congressional*
285	Cooley, Azariah	69y	W	Mass.	23 DEC 1867	Glenwood
771	Cooley, J.W. & Kate, child of	1d	W	U.S.	22 JUN 1874	Glenwood
596	Cooley, Susana	73y	W	U.S.	22 APR 1872	Glenwood
066	Coombe, [Mary]	83y	W	Del.	20 DEC 1856	Congressional*
706	Coombs, Alice S.	5m	W	D.C.	25 JUL 1873	Oak Hill
022	Coombs, Ethelbert	1y	W	D.C.	16 AUG 1855	Congressional
395	Coombs, Henry P.	12y	W	U.S.	02 JUN 1869	Glenwood
218	Coombs, J.J., Mrs.	40y	W	D.C.	18 APR 1866	Oak Hill
190	Coombs, James W., merchant	33y	W	Va.	02 SEP 1860	Mt. Olivet
523	Coombs, L.A.	75y	W	Md.	18 JUN 1871	Congressional
204	Coombs, Mary	70y	C		10 JUN 1861	Mt. Olivet
459	Coombs, Robert M., merchant	56y	W	Md.	30 JUN 1870	Congressional
270	Coombsa, Cecelia	100y	C	Md.	19 AUG 1867	Mt. Olivet
461	Coomes, Cecelia N.	7y	W	D.C.	10 JUL 1870	Congressional
212	Coomes, Geo. W.	6m	W	D.C.	17 FEB 1866	Congressional
087	Coomes, Margaret	8m	W	D.C.	16 AUG 1857	Congressional
580	Coomes, Sam. W., painter	40y	W	Md.	10 FEB 1872	Congressional
587	Coon, Elisabeth	43y	W	N.Y.	21 MAR 1872	N.Y.
318	Coon, Mary Eliza	8m	W	S.C.	02 JUN 1868	Congressional
771	Coon, Nelson	27y	C	U.S.	12 JUN 1874	Washington Asylum
099	Cooney, Michael	10m	W	D.C.	24 DEC 1857	St. Patricks
708	Cooper, Ben	61y	C	Md.	29 JUL 1873	Washington Asylum
437	Cooper, Bessie Almira	2y	W		25 JAN 1870	Baltimore, Md.
475	Cooper, Bishop, auctioneer	31y	W	Md.	02 SEP 1870	Baltimore, Md.
736	Cooper, Elizabeth	32y	C	U.S.	16 DEC 1873	Harmony
377	Cooper, Elizabeth Ann	45y	C	Md.	10 FEB 1869	Harmony
746	Cooper, Frances	3m	W	U.S.	06 FEB 1874	Mt. Olivet
779	Cooper, George	4m	C	U.S.	10 JUL 1874	Mt. Pleasant
717	Cooper, Harry DeCamp	10m	W	D.C.	04 SEP 1873	Congressional
426	Cooper, Isabel	22y	W	Md.	20 NOV 1869	Baltimore, Md.
074	Cooper, James, waiter	21y	C	Va.	27 MAR 1857	Colored
224	Cooper, Janie S.	7m	W	D.C.	13 JUN 1866	Congressional
492	Cooper, Jas. E., child of	1d	C	D.C.	05 DEC 1870	Ebenezer
437	Cooper, Jennie	2y	C	D.C.	26 JAN 1870	Washington Asylum
546	Cooper, Jessie, laborer	25y	C	Va.	26 NOV 1871	Washington
383	Cooper, Letitia	2d			23 MAR 1869	
287	Cooper, Mary		C		c.27 DEC 1867	Alms House
338	Cooper, Mary Ann	3m	C		30 AUG 1868	Washington Asylum
735	Cooper, Mary E.H.	3m	W	U.S.	11 DEC 1873	Congressional*
096	Cooper, Mary Jane	25y	C	D.C.	15 NOV 1857	Harmony
605	Cooper, Mary, servant	25y	C	U.S.	16 JUN 1872	
629	Cooper, Matilda	20y	C	U.S.	16 OCT 1872	
531	Cooper, Minnie F.	5m	W	D.C.	08 AUG 1871	Washington
670	Cooper, Richard	21y	C	U.S.	16 FEB 1873	Small Pox
527	Cooper, Samuel, huckster	49y	C	U.S.	12 JUL 1871	Washington
520	Cooper, Sarah Jane	3m	W	D.C.	30 MAY 1871	Md.
659	Cooper, Sophia	17y	C	U.S.	11 JAN 1873	Ebenezer
391	Cooper, Susan, Mrs.	60y	W	Va.*	10 MAY 1869	Glenwood
329	Cooper, Thomas	2m	W	D.C.	15 JUL 1868	Glenwood
397	Cooper, William, plasterer	49y	B	D.C.	22 JUN 1869	Harmony
681	Cooper, [blank]	Still	W	U.S.	19 APR 1873	Glenwood
514	Coot, Margaret	14y	C	Md.	21 MAR 1871	Ebenezer
172	Cope, Samuel, farmer	50y	W	Ohio	08 FEB 1860	Ohio
349	Copeland, Albert H.	1y	W	D.C.	04 SEP 1868	Glenwood/Rock Creek
308	Copeland, Jane Bates, Mrs.	81y	W	Pa.	28 APR 1868	Congressional

District of Columbia Interments (Index to Deaths), 1855-1874

Page	Name	Age	Race	Birth	Death Date	Burial Ground
758	Copeland, Mary Jane	28y	W	U.S.	12 APR 1874	Glenwood/Rock Creek
362	Copeland, Wm.	2y	C	D.C.	09 NOV 1868	Washington Asylum
403	Copelli, John	21y	W	Italy	20 JUL 1869	German Catholic
019	Copland, Hugh	2y			11 AUG 1855	
138	Copp, Catharine	11m	W	D.C.	29 JAN 1859	German Catholic
216	Coppinger, Morris Hodgkin	1y			22 MAR 1866	
062	Copps, Mrs., child of	Still	W		02 NOV 1856	St. Patricks
291	Corban, Delsey		W		06 JAN 1868	Alms House
398	Corbin, Ann	14y	C	Va.	18 JUN 1869	
695	Corbin, Bird, laborer	40y	C	Md.	08 JUN 1873	Washington Asylum
509	Corbin, Lillie	2y	C	D.C.	22 FEB 1871	Washington Asylum
631	Corbin, Mary	2y	C	U.S.	09 OCT 1872	
746	Corbitt, John M., law clerk	19y	W	U.S.	26 FEB 1874	Lockport, N.Y.
591	Corbitt, Martha	1y	C	D.C.	13 APR 1872	Asylum
038	Corcoran, Child of Jno.		W		12 MAR 1856	Methodist
144	Corcoran, Hannah, slave	90y	C	Md.	17 MAR 1859	Young Mens
725	Corcoran, James	60y	W	Ire.	17 OCT 1873	Mt. Olivet
327	Corcoran, James Linden	10m	W	D.C.	27 JUL 1868	Mt. Olivet*
494	Corcoran, Maggie Beck, lady	21y	W	Ky.	27 DEC 1870	Oak Hill
327	Corcoran, Margaret	9m	W	D.C.	07 JUL 1868	Mt. Olivet*
099	Corcoran, Thomas, school boy	16y	W	D.C.	25 DEC 1857	Oak Hill
343	Corcoran, Timothy, laborer	45y	W	Ire.	16 AUG 1868	Mt. Olivet*
661	Corkhill, Olivia M.	28y	W	U.S.	22 JAN 1873	Mt. Pleasant
318	Cornelius, Catherine	39y	W	D.C.	07 JUN 1868	Congressional
333	Cornelius, Harry	2y	W	D.C.	02 JUL 1868	Methodist
122	Cornelius, Isaiah	1y	W	Md.	19 JUL 1858	Congressional
260	Cornelius, Samuel	1m	W	D.C.	10 MAY 1867	Holmead
035	Cornelius, William	5m	C	D.C.	07 FEB 1856	Alms House
014	Cornell, Ellen	11m	W	D.C.	22 JUL 1855	St. Patricks
636	Corner, Cath., storekeeper	30y	W	U.S.	02 NOV 1872	
263	Cornick, Charley R.	5m	W	Va.	27 JUN 1867	Glenwood
109	Cornish, Amelia, laundress	28y	C	Md.	30 MAR 1858	Washington Asylum
532	Cornwall, Josephine	30y	W	Va.	10 AUG 1871	Congressional
226	Cornwall, Katy A.	3m	W	D.C.	29 JUN 1866	N.Y. City
172	Cornwall, Martha E.	17y	W	U.S.	09 FEB 1860	Congressional*
273	Cornwell, Michael	9m	W	D.C.	27 SEP 1867	Mt. Olivet
354	Cornwell, [blank]	Still	W		16 OCT 1868	Congressional
447	Corridon, Nellie L.	5y	W		25 MAR 1870	Mt. Olivet
308	Corrigan, James	12y	W	D.C.	21 APR 1868	Mt. Olivet
041	Corrigan, James	27y	W	Ire.	01 APR 1856	St. Patricks
619	Corrox, J.	1y	C	U.S.	27 AUG 1872	
668	Corsin, Andrew	14d	W	U.S.	18 FEB 1873	Mt. Olivet
080	Corson, Emile Joseph	4m	W	D.C.	25 JUN 1857	Glenwood
258	Corson, William S., satler	27y	W	N.J.	22 APR 1867	Wilmington, Del.
238	Cort, Icon John	1y	W	D.C.	10 SEP 1866	
026	Cortells, Johanna	3m	W	D.C.	06 OCT 1855	St. Peters
310	Cory, C.W., clerk	31y	W	Ver.	03 APR 1868	Ver.
300	Cosbey, William	5m	C	U.S.	14 MAR 1868	Alms House
764	Coseloe, John	5m	W	U.S.	07 MAY 1874	Mt. Olivet
521	Cosgrode, Ellen M.	8m	W	D.C.	06 JUN 1871	Methodist
490	Cosgrode, Mary E.	18y	W	D.C.	19 NOV 1870	Methodist
172	Cosgrove, John, gardener	65y	W	Ire.	15 FEB 1860	Mt. Olivet
742	Cosgrove, Mary J.	3y	W	U.S.	20 JAN 1874	Mt. Olivet
111	Cosgrove, Mathias	2y	W	D.C.	18 APR 1858	St. Patricks
349	Costello, Hannah	1y	W		27 SEP 1868	Mt. Olivet
605	Costello, James	8m	W	D.C.	24 JUN 1872	Mt. Olivet
323	Costello, Jeremiah	1y	W	D.C.	18 JUL 1868	Mt. Olivet
531	Costello, Johana	1y	W	D.C.	01 AUG 1871	Mt. Olivet

Page	Name	Age	Race	Birth	Death Date	Burial Ground
402	Costello, John	4m	W	D.C.	20 JUL 1869	Mt. Olivet
209	Costello, William	65y	W	Ire.	— JAN 1866	[torn]
681	Costello, [blank]	Still	W	U.S.	15 APR 1873	Mt. Olivet
069	Costen, George, laborer	48y	C	D.C.	20 JAN 1857	Washington Asylum
022	Costen, Wm., daughter of	2m	C	D.C.	28 AUG 1855	Harmony
113	Coster, Mary	2y	W	D.C.	08 MAY 1858	Congressional
044	Costigan, Maria, teacher	22y	W	Ohio	09 MAY 1856	St. Peters
163	Costin, Mary A.	28y	C	Ohio	17 OCT 1859	Harmony
153	Cotter, Jas. Henry	6m	W	U.S.	09 JUL 1859	Baltimore, Md.
348	Cotter, John, laborer	58y	W	Ire.	05 SEP 1868	Mt. Olivet
123	Cotter, Nicholas	1y	W	Md.	28 JUL 1858	Baltimore, Md.
135	Cottman, Charles C., brick maker	33y	W	D.C.	07 DEC 1858	Congressional
779	Cotton, Benj. F.	1y	W	U.S.	16 JUL 1874	
030	Cotton, Hannah	1m	W	D.C.	05 NOV 1855	St. Peters
614	Cottrell, Geo. T.	32y	W	U.S.	09 JUL 1872	
758	Cottrell, Parmelee N.	48y	W	U.S.	18 APR 1874	N.Y. City
335b	Cough, Rosannah				01 JUL 1868	Washington Asylum
746	Coughlin, Martha	11y	W	U.S.	21 FEB 1874	Alexandria, Va.
224	Coulson, James	50y		Md.	13 JUN 1866	Baltimore Co., Md.
734	Coulson, John, lime manuf.	76y	W	Ire.	01 DEC 1873	Congressional*
475	Coumbe, Irene Smith	3y	W	D.C.	04 SEP 1870	Congressional
150	Countee, Mary	60y	C	Md.	02 JUN 1859	Young Mens
232	Couradis, Anna	1y	W	D.C.	27 AUG 1866	
214	Couris, J., child of	Still	W	D.C.	12 MAR 1866	Mt. Olivet
286	Courtain, Mary Colly	30y	W	Ire.	08 DEC 1867	Mt. Olivet
286	Courtain, Mrs., child of	Still	W	D.C.	06 DEC 1867	Mt. Olivet
429	Courtenay, Florence	2y	W		16 DEC 1869	Congressional
487	Courtney, Geo., Jr.	1y	W	D.C.	25 NOV 1870	Mt. Olivet
432	Courtney, Lizzie G.	2y	C	Va.	02 DEC 1869	Washington Asylum
489	Courtney, Mary L.	6m	W	D.C.	20 NOV 1870	Mt. Olivet
467	Coventry, Margaret	19y	C		19 JUL 1870	
248	Covert, Edward L., clerk	34y	W	N.Y.	22 DEC 1866	N.J.
637	Covington, Eliza	52y	W	U.S.	23 NOV 1872	Mt. Olivet
606	Covington, Jemima	18y	C	Md.	27 JUN 1872	Asylum
644	Covington, Julia, Mrs., servant	33y	C	U.S.	15 DEC 1872	Mt. Pleasant
526	Covington, Robert, laborer	50y	C	D.C.	03 JUL 1871	Washington
308	Cowan, Frank C.	11m	W	D.C.	10 APR 1868	Congressional
116	Cowan, Jane	3m	W	D.C.	15 JUN 1858	Western
284	Cowan, William, sailor	29y	W	Pa.	27 NOV 1867	Western
003	Cowan, [blank]	2y	W	D.C.	03 FEB 1855	Western
507	Cowing, William, clerk	71y	W	Eng.	21 FEB 1871	Glenwood
555	Cowling, Edw.	73y	W	Eng.	30 JAN 1872	Glenwood
349	Cowling, Edward, hackman	39y	W	Eng.	19 SEP 1868	Glenwood
628	Cowling, Thos., livery	37y	W	U.S.	10 SEP 1872	
188	Cowling, Thos. Reed	11m	W	D.C.	27 AUG 1860	Glenwood
682	Cowperthwait, H.	71y	W	U.S.	28 APR 1873	
288	Cox, Alexander S., claim agent	38y	W	N.Y.	16 DEC 1867	Glenwood
281	Cox, Andrew	1m	W		30 OCT 1867	Mt. Olivet
070	Cox, Ann	25y	W	D.C.	10 FEB 1857	
666	Cox, Ann	61y	C	U.S.	02 FEB 1873	
169	Cox, Elizabeth	1y	W	D.C.	06 JAN 1860	Methodist
339	Cox, Ida May	4m	W	D.C.	30 AUG 1868	Methodist, East
135	Cox, Jno. Florentius, gentleman	76y	W	N.Y.	11 DEC 1858	Rock Creek
771	Cox, Joseph W., clerk Treas.	54y	W	U.S.	30 JUN 1874	
619	Cox, Julia	14m	C	U.S.	04 AUG 1872	
215	Cox, Lewis D.	4m	C	D.C.	14 MAR 1866	Young Mens
673	Cox, Mason	3y	W	U.S.	08 MAR 1873	Va.
662	Cox, Richard C., laborer	27y	W	U.S.	14 JAN 1873	

District of Columbia Interments (Index to Deaths), 1855-1874

Page	Name	Age	Race	Birth	Death Date	Burial Ground
691	Cox, Sarah, Mrs.	33y	W	U.S.	06 MAY 1873	Small Pox*
104	Cox, William, constable	47y	W	Va.	12 FEB 1858	Congressional
111	Cox, [blank]		W	D.C.	19 APR 1858	Congressional
306	Coxen, Elizabeth	30y	W	D.C.	09 APR 1868	Methodist
115	Coxen, James, laborer	35y	C	Md.	06 JUN 1858	Harmony
306	Coxen, James T.	4d	W	D.C.	03 APR 1868	Methodist
028	Coxen, Wm.	11y	W	Va.*	01 OCT 1855	Methodist
431	Coxson, Josephine	2m	C		05 DEC 1869	Washington Asylum
044	Coxton, May	1y	C	D.C.	02 MAY 1856	Harmony
031	Coy, George	40y	W	D.C.	17 DEC 1855	Congressional
454	Coyle, A.	52y	W	Ire.	27 MAY 1870	Mt. Olivet
027	Coyle, Andrew, Sr.	73y	W	Pa.	30 OCT 1855	Congressional
274	Coyle, Catherine	32y	W	Ire.	13 SEP 1867	Mt. Olivet
261	Coyle, Emma F.		W	D.C.	05 MAY 1867	Congressional
170	Coyle, John, laborer	28y	C	Ire.	30 JAN 1860	St. Patricks (vault)
325	Coyle, Leonidas, retired	59y	W	D.C.	31 JUL 1868	Oak Hill
726	Coyle, Margaret	33y	W	Ire.	26 OCT 1873	Mt. Olivet
370	Coyle, Mary A.	2y	W		23 JAN 1869	Mt. Olivet
354	Coyle, Matilda	78y	W	Md.	09 OCT 1868	Mt. Olivet*
160	Coyle, [blank]	30y	W	Ire.	05 AUG 1859	St. Patricks
715	Cozine, Sarah	36y	W	Md.	08 AUG 1873	
623	Cozzens, A.J.	1m	W	U.S.	07 JUL 1872	Methodist, Georgetown
688	Crachfield, L., Mrs.	35y	C	U.S.	14 MAY 1873	Beckett's
611	Cracy, Wm.	2y	W	U.S.	12 JUL 1872	
604	Crafford, Ellen	35y	C	D.C.	07 JUN 1872	Ebenezer
241	Craft, A.	6y	W	Md.	29 OCT 1866	Holmead
248	Craggin, George H.	3y	W	D.C.	08 DEC 1866	Congressional
627	Craggon, Richd. C., Dr.	33y	W	U.S.	22 SEP 1872	Congressional*
436	Craig, Edwin	6m	C		12 JAN 1870	
014	Craig, Ella	8m	W		07 JUL 1855	Alexandria, Va.
432	Craig, Henry Knox, U.S.A.	76y	W	Pa.	07 DEC 1869	Oak Hill
122	Craig, Jeannette	1y	W	D.C.	26 JUL 1858	Congressional
758	Craig, John	1y	C	U.S.	10 APR 1874	
170	Craig, Julia	5y	W	D.C.	18 JAN 1860	Congressional
595	Craig, Maria	76y	W	Pa.	17 APR 1872	Washington
404	Craig, Nellie	1m	C	D.C.	07 JUL 1869	Washington Asylum
264	Craige, John W., printer	38y	W	Pa.	05 JUL 1867	Philadelphia, Pa
446	Craigly, George	1y	C		04 MAR 1870	
053	Crampsey, Naomi	10m	W	D.C.	29 AUG 1856	Congressional
718	Crampton, Charles	80y	C	Md.	09 SEP 1873	Washington Asylum
734	Crampton, Josephine	20y	W	U.S.	06 DEC 1873	Congressional*
200	Crampton, Sarah	67y	W	Eng.	26 FEB 1861	Congressional
661	Crampton, Serena, cook	63y	C	U.S.	23 JAN 1873	Young Mens
631	Crampton, [blank]	2y	C	U.S.	— OCT 1872	
152	Crampton, [blank]	2y	C	D.C.	10 JUN 1859	Eastern
147	Crampton, [blank]	9m	C	D.C.	13 APR 1859	Colored, Eastern
555	Cranch, Wm. G., clerk	76y	W	D.C.	25 JAN 1872	Congressional
023	Cranch, Wm., Hon., chief justice	86y	W	Mass.	01 SEP 1855	Congressional
097	Crandell, George, carpenter	79y	W	Md.	21 NOV 1857	Foundry
500	Crane, Matthew	37y	W	D.C.	— JAN 1871	Mt. Olivet
707	Cranford, Jane	115y	C	Md.	22 JUL 1873	Beckett's
149	Cranford, Robert I., hackman	32y	W		25 MAY 1859	Glenwood
149	Cranford, S.C.	5m	W	Va.	18 MAY 1859	
620	Crangle, Mary F.	19m	W	U.S.	18 AUG 1872	Glenwood
427	Crans, Albert	25y	C		28 NOV 1869	Young Mens
005	Cratly, Michael	26y	W	Ire.	14 MAR 1855	St. Peters
707	Crats, Arthur	8m	C	D.C.	23 JUL 1873	Beckett's
752	Cratty, A.C.	2y	W	U.S.	17 MAR 1874	Mt. Olivet

Page	Name	Age	Race	Birth	Death Date	Burial Ground
746	Cratty, Wm. P., printer	27y	W	U.S.	12 FEB 1874	Mt. Olivet
475	Craven, Anna J.	53y	W	Va.	20 SEP 1870	Congressional
300	Craven, Elizabeth H.	35y	W	U.S.	09 MAR 1868	Oak Hill
111	Craver, Philip, mechanic	77y	W	Pa.	19 APR 1858	Methodist
299	Crawford, Archd., carpenter	67y	W	Md.	25 MAR 1868	Pr. Geo. Co., Md.
764	Crawford, Eliza	15y	C	U.S.	06 MAY 1874	Graceland
312	Crawford, Eliza, washerwoman	27y	C	Md.	31 MAY 1868	Mt. Olivet
127	Crawford, Frances	1y	W	D.C.	06 SEP 1858	Congressional
184	Crawford, Frederick	8m	W	D.C.	10 JUL 1860	Congressional
389	Crawford, H.	90y	C	U.S.	29 APR 1869	Washington Asylum
254	Crawford, J.P.R.		W	Va.	02 FEB 1867	
147	Crawford, John	46y	C	Va.	27 APR 1859	Washington Asylum
543	Crawford, John, blacksmith	69y	W	Eur.	29 OCT 1871	Glenwood
588	Crawford, John, laborer	63y	C	Va.	24 MAR 1872	Washington
354	Crawford, Lydia May	8m	W	N.J.	11 OCT 1868	Newark, N.J.
098	Crawford, Mary A.	4m	C	D.C.	14 DEC 1857	St. Matthews
717	Crawford, Mary E.	2y	W	D.C.	03 SEP 1873	Congressional
498	Crawford, Mary I., pauper	4w	B	D.C.	27 JAN 1871	Washington Asylum
201	Crawford, Sarah C.	74y	W	Md.	27 MAR 1861	Congressional
375	Crawford, Susan, Miss	28y	W	D.C.	21 FEB 1869	Mt. Olivet
321	Crawford, William Henry	3m	C	D.C.	15 JUN 1868	Mt. Olivet
221	Crawford, Zacharia T.	11m	W	D.C.	23 MAY 1866	Montgomery Co., Md.
214	Crean, Jeremiah H., military ofcr.		W		05 MAR 1866	Mt. Olivet
621	Creaser, Thos., clerk	63y	W	Eng.	16 AUG 1872	Congressional*
367	Credit, Adelia	Still	B	D.C.	28 DEC 1868	Washington Asylum
603	Credit, Adol, servant	25y	C	Va.	01 JUN 1872	Small Pox
353	Credit, Margaret	31y	C	Va.	19 SEP 1868	
603	Credit, Thomas	3y	C	D.C.	08 JUN 1872	Small Pox
604	Credit, Wm.	5y	C	D.C.	24 JUN 1872	Small Pox
022	Credlon, Geo. C.	5y	W	Va.	31 AUG 1855	Methodist, East
022	Crees, Joseph G.	14d	W	D.C.	28 AUG 1855	St. Peters
091	Crehan, Patrick, laborer	60y	W	Ire.	13 SEP 1857	St. Matthews
018	Crehen, Thos., laborer	22y	W	Ire.	14 AUG 1855	St. Matthews
353	Creig, Delley	1y	C	D.C.	10 SEP 1868	Western
289	Creighton, Ann	77y	W	Md.	18 JAN 1868	Congressional
231	Creighton, Anna L., student	15y	W	Va.*	17 AUG 1866	Alexandria, Va., St. Paul's
549	Creighton, M.W., clerk	35y	W	D.C.	23 DEC 1871	Congressional
474	Cresswell, Arthur	24y	C		28 AUG 1870	Washington Asylum
422	Creswell, Eva	29y	C	Va.	27 OCT 1869	Ebenezer
279	Crider, James W., bookbinder	30y	W	D.C.	14 OCT 1867	Mt. Olivet
214	Cridland, Isabella		W	Va.	01 MAR 1866	Congressional
554	Crioler, Jonathan B.	1y	W	D.C.	15 JAN 1872	Prospect Hill
297	Crippen, Causen B., clerk	63y	W	N.Y.	26 FEB 1868	Glenwood
439	Cripps, Geo. S.	41y	W		28 FEB 1870	Congressional
454	Crismer, William, huckster	58y	W	Ger.	23 MAY 1870	German Catholic
307	Criswell, Thomas, manufacturer	54y	W	Ire.	25 APR 1868	Western
314	Crittenden, Harvey	79y	W	Conn.	05 MAY 1868	Congressional*
419	Crittenden, Mary M.	90y	W		09 OCT 1869	Congressional*
107	Crocker, Calvin J.	35y	W	Me.	07 MAR 1858	Me.
663	Crockson, Minnie	6y	C	U.S.	06 JAN 1873	Small Pox*
641	Crockson, Spotson	58y	C	U.S.	27 DEC 1872	Small Pox*
742	Croffman, G.E. & L., infant of	2d	W	U.S.	16 JAN 1874	Prospect Hill
215	Croft, M.M., Col.	50y	W	N.Y.	18 MAR 1866	N.Y.
756	Crogan, Patrick, Dr.		W	Ire.	27 MAR 1874	
746	Crogan, Sarah, clerk Treas.	29y	W	Ire.	11 FEB 1874	Mt. Olivet
712	Croggan, James	11m	W	D.C.	14 AUG 1873	Congressional*
314	Croggin, LeRoy A.	16y	W	D.C.	06 MAY 1868	Glenwood
527	Croggon, Christopher	5m	W	U.S.	11 JUL 1871	Congressional

District of Columbia Interments (Index to Deaths), 1855-1874

Page	Name	Age	Race	Birth	Death Date	Burial Ground
593	Croggon, Saml., painter	35y	W	U.S.	07 APR 1872	Glenwood
360	Croghan, Catharine	45y	W	Ire.	28 NOV 1868	Mt. Olivet
469	Croghan, Catharine	5y	W	D.C.	29 AUG 1870	Mt. Olivet*
645	Croghan, John, bar tender	32y	W	Ire.	25 DEC 1872	Mt. Olivet
391	Croley, Bernard, clerk Treas.	51y	W	Ire.	12 MAY 1869	Mt. Olivet
450	Crolly, Mary	19y	W	N.Y.	21 APR 1870	Mt. Olivet
729	Crolly, Wm. J., carpenter	25y	W	U.S.	09 NOV 1873	Mt. Olivet
207	Cromell, D.		C		23 JUL 1862	Western
736	Cromwell, Arthur	7m	C	U.S.	19 DEC 1873	
177	Cromwell, Ella	2y	W	Mo.	21 APR 1860	Mt. Olivet
044	Cromwell, Nimrod	78y	W	Md.	19 MAY 1856	Baltimore, Md.
322	Cromwell, Richd., farmer	66y	W	Md.	16 JUN 1868	Montgomery Co., Md.
031	Cronan, Mary	1y	W	Md.	04 DEC 1855	St. Patricks
375	Crone, Ann	6m	W	D.C.	08 FEB 1869	Mt. Olivet
437	Cronin, Elizabeth	75y	W	Ire.	30 JAN 1870	Mt. Olivet
270	Cronin, Lissabeth	10m	W	D.C.	05 AUG 1867	Mt. Olivet
380	Cronin, Michael, laborer	34y	W	Ire.	22 MAR 1869	Mt. Olivet
666	Cronwell, Sarah B.	77y	W	U.S.	05 FEB 1873	Newburg, N.Y.
008	Crook, Agness V.	11m	W	D.C.	01 MAY 1855	Congressional
273	Crook, Charles H.	1m	W	D.C.	28 SEP 1867	Glenwood
105	Crook, Elizabeth	25y	W	D.C.	25 FEB 1858	Congressional
729	Crook, Sinah Ann, dressmaker	54y	C	U.S.	04 NOV 1873	Congressional
419	Crooks, Melissa	27y	W		01 OCT 1869	Congressional
524	Croon, Estille	1m	W	D.C.	21 JUN 1871	Congressional*
138	Cropley, Edward S., printer	55y	W	Eng.	10 JAN 1859	Congressional
412	Crops, Harvy	2y	C	D.C.	18 AUG 1869	Washington Asylum
019	Cropsy, Susan	24y	W	Md.	14 AUG 1855	Foundry
612	Crosby, Florence	1m	W	U.S.	17 JUL 1872	
398	Crosby, Mary E.	4m	B	U.S.	26 JUN 1869	Washington Asylum
107	Crosdale, William		W		12 MAR 1858	Glenwood
356	Crosland, Mary E.	5y	W	D.C.	09 OCT 1868	Mt. Olivet*
141	Cross, Alexander, brass finisher	43y	W	D.C.	16 FEB 1859	Congressional
291	Cross, Alexander H.	45y	W	Va.	17 JAN 1868	Congressional
155	Cross, Alice M.	10y	C	D.C.	27 JUL 1859	Young Mens
581	Cross, Amos, laborer	32y	C	Va.	15 FEB 1872	
758	Cross, Brooks	2y	W	U.S.	15 APR 1874	
107	Cross, Charles	1y	W	D.C.	10 MAR 1858	Congressional
522	Cross, Charles	6m	W	Amer.	13 JUN 1871	Methodist
317	Cross, Charlotte	1y	W	D.C.	24 JUN 1868	Congressional
688	Cross, Chas. A.	36y	W	U.S.	14 MAY 1873	Mt. Olivet
003	Cross, D.G.C., machinist	23y	W	D.C.	29 FEB 1855	
531	Cross, Eliza Jane		W		06 AUG 1871	Congressional*
593	Cross, Ella	19y	C	D.C.	28 APR 1872	Harmony
594	Cross, Ellen	18y	C	Va.	11 APR 1872	Washington
630	Cross, Frances A.	2y	W	U.S.	31 OCT 1872	Small Pox
002	Cross, Franklin	7m	W	D.C.	— JAN 1855	
630	Cross, Geo. W.	34y	W	U.S.	09 OCT 1872	Small Pox
729	Cross, Henry L.	63y	W	U.S.	08 NOV 1873	Congressional
159	Cross, James F.	2y	W	D.C.	30 AUG 1859	Congressional
263	Cross, James, mute student	18y	W	Pa.	01 JUN 1867	Glenwood
484	Cross, John F., mechanic	28y	W	U.S.	05 OCT 1870	Congressional
228	Cross, John F.	6m	W	D.C.	13 JUL 1866	Prospect Hill
604	Cross, John H.	1m	C	D.C.	09 JUN 1872	Ebenezer
557	Cross, John W.	29y		D.C.	01 FEB 1872	Congressional
086	Cross, Kate	2y	W	D.C.	09 AUG 1857	Congressional
442	Cross, Lucy	20y	C		13 FEB 1870	Washington Asylum
013	Cross, M.A.	43y	W	D.C.	20 JUL 1855	St. Peters
161	Cross, Martha	18y	C	U.S.	09 SEP 1859	Western

Page	Name	Age	Race	Birth	Death Date	Burial Ground
583	Cross, Mary E.	11y	C	D.C.	28 FEB 1872	
674	Cross, Mary J.	29y	W	U.S.	16 MAR 1873	Congressional
347	Cross, Milton I.	2y	W	D.C.	20 SEP 1868	Congressional
293	Cross, Richard E.	9m	C	D.C.*	24 FEB 1868	Methodist
380	Cross, Robie Mason	1y	W	Md.	18 MAR 1869	Pr. Geo. Co., Md.
065	Cross, Thomas	6m	C	D.C.	11 DEC 1856	Young Mens
546	Cross, Thomas B., blacksmith	63y	W	D.C.	26 NOV 1871	Congressional
591	Cross, Tishiana	2y	C	U.S.	16 APR 1872	
734	Cross, Wm. S.	2m	C	U.S.	03 DEC 1873	
450	Crossen, Aloysia, teacher	37y	W	Ohio	08 APR 1870	Mt. Olivet
068	Crossfield, Charles J.	24y	W	D.C.*	12 JAN 1857	Glenwood
489	Crossland, William	12y	W	Md.	20 NOV 1870	Mt. Olivet
396	Croton, Elizabeth	5m	C	D.C.	12 JUN 1869	Young Mens
336	Croton, Jacob	1y	C	D.C.	02 AUG 1868	Young Mens
237	Crouch, Catherine	22y	C	D.C.	21 SEP 1866	Harmony
237	Crouch, Catherine, child of		C		21 SEP 1866	Harmony
364	Crouch, John W.	2y	W	Md.	28 DEC 1868	Congressional*
199	Crouner, [blank]	7y	C	D.C.	06 FEB 1861	Colored
666	Crounlien, Rowland, merchant	69y	W	Eng.	02 FEB 1873	Mt. Olivet
548	Crow, Frances	1y	W	D.C.	13 DEC 1871	Mt. Olivet*
149	Crow, Joseph B.	3y	W	Md.	19 MAY 1859	Mt. Olivet
593	Crow, Joseph L., printer	48y	W	Md.	21 APR 1872	Holy Rood*
591	Crow, Joseph, printer	48y	W	Md.	22 APR 1872	
449	Crow, Mildred	74y	W	Md.	09 APR 1870	Catholic
240	Crowley, John, driver	15y	W	D.C.	11 OCT 1866	Mt. Olivet
309	Crowley, Julia H.	48y	W	Ire.	21 APR 1868	Mt. Olivet*
689	Crowley, Wm. M.	1y	W	U.S.	26 MAY 1873	Catholic
177	Crowly, Mrs., child of	Still	W	D.C.	30 APR 1860	St. Patricks
234	Crown, Charles Edward	1y	W	D.C.	01 SEP 1866	Mt. Olivet
235	Crown, Clara Regina	3y	W	D.C.	16 SEP 1866	Mt. Olivet
536	Crown, Edw.	9d	W	D.C.	18 SEP 1871	Congressional*
153	Crown, Florence	1y	W	D.C.	12 JUL 1859	Glenwood
082	Crown, George F.	8m	W	D.C.	08 JUL 1857	Glenwood
542	Crown, Maggie A.	5y	W	D.C.	25 OCT 1871	Congressional
343	Crown, Martha A.	28y	W	Md.	12 AUG 1868	Mt. Olivet
476	Crown, Sarah	4y	C	D.C.	19 SEP 1870	
259	Crown, Thomas, builder	78y	W	D.C.	12 APR 1867	Congressional
536	Crown, Thomas, builder	78y	W	D.C.	17 SEP 1871	Congressional
232	Crown, W.J.F., child of	Still			22 AUG 1866	Mt. Olivet*
200	Crown, [blank]	Still	W		26 FEB 1861	Glenwood
540	Crowne, Frank	3y		D.C.	01 OCT 1871	Glenwood
158	Crowner, Jane	10y	C	D.C.	14 AUG 1859	Colored, Eastern
222	Crowner, Mary, servant	45y	C	Md.	30 MAY 1866	Harmony
334	Crowse, Ann	66y	W	Md.	23 JUL 1868	Glenwood
691	Crowther, Thos. W.	26y	W	U.S.	09 MAY 1873	
771	Cruikshank, Richd., clerk Treas.	72y	W	U.S.	18 JUN 1874	Oak Hill
069	Cruit, Ella Mina	11m	W	D.C.	20 JAN 1857	Baltimore, Md.
195	Cruit, John, jeweller	36y	W	D.C.	02 DEC 1860	Glenwood
069	Cruit, Sally, servant	30y	C	Md.	20 JAN 1857	Washington Co.
146	Crumble, Daniel	4m	C	D.C.	02 APR 1859	Western
009	Crumell, John	3m	C		25 MAY 1855	Western
494	Crumin, Mary	54y	W	Ire.	14 DEC 1870	Mt. Olivet
015	Crummey, M.C.	9m	C	D.C.	20 JUL 1855	Eastern
289	Crump, Dallas, banjo picker	30y	C	Va.	05 JAN 1868	Alms House
399	Crump, Hattie V.	4y	W		31 JUL 1869	Congressional
283	Crump, Joseph	18y	C		03 NOV 1867	Freedmen's Hospital
292	Crump, Lucy, child of		C		13 JAN 1868	Alms House
746	Crump, Sarah	30y	C	U.S.	16 FEB 1874	Washington Asylum

District of Columbia Interments (Index to Deaths), 1855-1874

Page	Name	Age	Race	Birth	Death Date	Burial Ground
352	Crump, Thomas	14y	C	D.C.	07 SEP 1868	Washington Asylum
667	Crump, William	22y	C	U.S.	10 FEB 1873	Washington Asylum
495	Crump, William, laborer	45y	C	Md.	16 DEC 1870	Potters Field
719	Crumpt, Mary, laborer	85y	C	Va.	15 SEP 1873	Beckett's
422	Crupp, Erdrige, laborer	26y	W	Va.	26 OCT 1869	
201	Crussell, Harriet	40y	W		11 MAR 1861	Congressional
367	Crutches, [blank]	Still	B	D.C.	04 DEC 1868	Washington Asylum
312	Crutchet, Jennie	3y	W	D.C.	18 MAY 1868	Mt. Olivet
272	Crutchfield, Mitchel	59y	C		27 AUG 1867	Freedmen's Bureau
476	Crutchly, Granville M.	2y	W	D.C.	22 SEP 1870	Congressional
258	Crutchly, John W., locksmith	52y	W	Va.	26 APR 1867	Congressional
346	Cry, Annie	3y	W	Md.	31 AUG 1868	Prospect Hill
549	Cryer, Camelia M.	65y	W	Md.	19 DEC 1871	Congressional
001	Cryer, [James]	41y		Md.	23 JAN 1855	Congressional
252	Cudliff, George	25y	W	D.C.	17 FEB 1867	Glenwood
658	Cudlip, Edward D., telegrapher	28y	W	U.S.	09 JAN 1873	Congressional
304	Cudlipp, Francis Oscar	17y	W	D.C.*	05 MAR 1868	Congressional
323	Cudmar, Patrick	6m	W	D.C.	17 JUL 1868	Mt. Olivet
527	Cue, Mary G.	6d	W		07 JUL 1871	Congressional
752	Cuelmor, James	4y	W	U.S.	20 MAR 1874	Mt. Olivet
060	Culher, Michael	6m	W	D.C.	27 OCT 1856	St. Peters
530	Cull, James, J.P.	65y	W	Eng.	31 JUL 1871	Congressional*
697	Cull, Michael	3m	C	U.S.	10 JUN 1873	
604	Cull, Priscilla	65y	C	Md.	24 JUN 1872	Small Pox
697	Cull, Sarah	12m	W	D.C.	28 JUN 1873	Washington Asylum
005	Cullan, Mary	1y	W	D.C.	10 MAR 1855	St. Patricks
046	Cullen, Benj. D.	3m	W	D.C.	13 JUN 1856	St. Patricks
038	Cullen, Sarah R.	26y	W	Md.	19 MAR 1856	St. Patricks
613	Cullinan, Elizabeth	6y	W	U.S.	05 JUL 1872	
698	Cullinan, Francis	14d	W	D.C.	19 JUN 1873	Mt. Olivet
240	Cullinan, M.	35y	W	Ire.	17 OCT 1866	Mt. Olivet
514	Cullom, Eliabeth	1y	W	Ill.	08 MAR 1871	Springfield, Ill.
244	Cullum, John, engraver	70y	W		04 NOV 1866	Congressional
102	Culney, James, seaman	30y	W	Va.	18 JAN 1858	Washington Asylum
292	Culver, Barney		C		13 JAN 1868	Alms House
218	Culverwill, Samuel			D.C.	21 APR 1866	Mt. Olivet
533	Cumberland, Charles	66y	W	D.C.	22 AUG 1871	Mt. Olivet
078	Cumberland, James	16y	W	D.C.	28 MAY 1857	Holmead
116	Cumberland, Mary	3y	W	D.C.	23 JUN 1858	Holmead
673	Cumberland, Susan	1y	W	U.S.	04 MAR 1873	Mt. Olivet
061	Cummings, Josephine	28y	W	Pa.	21 OCT 1856	Congressional
370	Cummiskey, H.A., housekeeper	49y	W	N.J.	31 JAN 1869	Camden, N.J.
466	Cumpton, Ann	2m	C	D.C.	03 JUL 1870	Harmony
103	Cunigham, Catharine	70y	W	Ire.	28 JAN 1858	St. Patricks
425	Cunningham, Alice	61y	W	D.C.	26 NOV 1869	Congressional
426	Cunningham, Ann	1y	W		01 NOV 1869	Mt. Olivet
523	Cunningham, Augustus, painter	71y	W	N.Y.	15 JUN 1871	Congressional*
270	Cunningham, Bridget	10m	W	D.C.	17 AUG 1867	Glenwood
541	Cunningham, Henry W.	65y	W	Me.	08 OCT 1871	Glenwood
414	Cunningham, Jane	16y	W	Ire.	27 SEP 1869	Congressional
582	Cunningham, Jessie	1m	W	U.S.	23 FEB 1872	
252	Cunningham, Joseph	6y	W	D.C.	03 FEB 1867	
710	Cunningham, Josephine	7m	W	D.C.	01 AUG 1873	Glenwood
217	Cunningham, Louisa R.	11m	W	D.C.	03 APR 1866	Congressional
141	Cunningham, Lucy	60y	W		18 FEB 1859	
053	Cunningham, Samuel, carpenter	16y	W	Pa.	01 AUG 1856	Washington
616	Cunningham, Samuel G., laborer	29y	W	U.S.	16 JUL 1872	
399	Cunningham, Sarah J.	15y	W		11 JUL 1869	Congressional

Page	Name	Age	Race	Birth	Death Date	Burial Ground
414	Cunningham, Solome D.	69y	W	Conn.	01 SEP 1869	Congressional
500	Cunningham, W.H., coachman	70y	W	Ire.	25 JAN 1871	Mt. Olivet
407	Cunningham, William	1y	W		14 AUG 1869	Congressional
221	Cunningham, William	6y	W	Pa.	15 MAY 1866	Mt. Olivet*
431	Cupp, George	9m	W		28 DEC 1869	Mt. Olivet
660	Cuptal, Sarah	11m	W		17 JAN 1873	
746	Curl, Joseph, carpenter	52y	W	U.S.	21 FEB 1874	Congressional
439	Curl, Sarah V.	19y	W	Va.	17 FEB 1870	Congressional
425	Curl, William M.	3m	W	D.C.	16 NOV 1869	Congressional
325	Curn, John	Still	W	D.C.	20 JUL 1868	Congressional
440	Curran, Charles	3y	W		18 FEB 1870	Mt. Olivet
317	Curran, John	5m	W	D.C.	24 JUN 1868	Congressional
246	Curran, William A., claim agent	30y	W	Ind.	02 DEC 1866	Ind.
050	Curran, William W., printer	44y	W	Md.	18 JUL 1856	Congressional
247	Curray, Edwd.	30y	W	R.I.	09 DEC 1866	Alms House
711	Curren, M.E.	17y	W	D.C.	11 AUG 1873	
428	Curry, Charles	21d	C		02 NOV 1869	
217	Curry, Charles	2y	C	D.C.	09 APR 1866	Harmony
336	Curry, Francis	1y	C	D.C.	19 AUG 1868	Ebenezer
006	Curry, Judith	80y	C	Va.	07 APR 1855	Union
335	Curry, Maria, house curry	32y	C	Va.	22 JUL 1868	
351	Curry, Mary Ida	2y	C	D.C.	26 SEP 1868	
398	Curry, Zachariah	40y	B	D.C.	11 JUN 1869	Washington Asylum
421	Curtain, Charles	1y	W	W.Va.	31 OCT 1869	Mt. Olivet
719	Curtain, Chas.	1y	W	D.C.	19 SEP 1873	Congressional
135	Curtain, Florinda	3m	W	D.C.	01 DEC 1858	Congressional
184	Curtain, James	6m	W	D.C.	09 JUL 1860	Congressional
074	Curtain, Mary	9d	W	D.C.	26 MAR 1857	Congressional
135	Curtain, Mary	5y	W	D.C.	10 DEC 1858	Congressional
758	Curtain, Mary	40y	W	Ire.	11 APR 1874	Mt. Olivet
116	Curtain, Thomas	1y	W	D.C.	23 JUN 1858	St. Patricks
612	Curtin, Cath.	3m	W	U.S.	03 JUL 1872	
770	Curtin, Charles A.	3y	W	U.S.	07 JUN 1874	Mt. Olivet
426	Curtin, Daniel		W		27 NOV 1869	Mt. Olivet
758	Curtin, James R.W., laborer	51y	W	U.S.	26 APR 1874	Congressional
236	Curtin, Johanna	1y	W	D.C.	16 SEP 1866	Congressional
538	Curtin, Nora	1y	W	D.C.	25 SEP 1871	Mt. Olivet
463	Curtin, Patrick	6m	W	D.C.	18 JUL 1870	Mt. Olivet
153	Curtis, Bridget	30y	W	Ire.	03 JUL 1859	Washington Asylum
493	Curtis, Elizabeth, laborer	80y	C	Va.	19 DEC 1870	Ebenezer
423	Curtis, George	46y	C		18 OCT 1869	Washington Asylum
146	Curtis, J.	2m	C		16 APR 1859	Western
158	Curtis, James	2y	C	D.C.	15 AUG 1859	Western
147	Curtis, John Albert	3y	C	D.C.	08 APR 1859	Methodist
275	Curtis, Lucius		W		02 SEP 1867	New Haven, Conn.
087	Curtis, Margaret	40y	W	Ire.	15 AUG 1857	St. Patricks
213	Curtis, Mary	77y	W	Va.	22 FEB 1866	Glenwood
598	Curtis, Mary Ann	2y	W	U.S.	29 MAY 1872	Mt. Olivet
660	Curtis, Mrs.	32y	W	U.S.	19 JAN 1873	Prospect Hill
234	Curtis, Mrs., housekeeper	56y	W	N.Y.	03 SEP 1866	Congressional
096	Curtis, Patrick	70y	W	Ire.	01 NOV 1857	St. Patricks
210	Curtis, [blank]	9m			24 JAN 1866	
187	Curtz, C.	58y	W	Md.	12 AUG 1860	
709	Cushing, J.H., clerk	67y	W	U.S.	03 JUL 1873	
401	Cusic, Margaret, servant	26y	W	Ire.	15 JUL 1869	Mt. Olivet
315	Cusick, Catherine	4y	W		c.27 MAY 1868	Mt. Olivet
010	Cusir, Daniel	12m	W	D.C.	28 JUN 1855	St. Patricks
632	Custar, John	72y	W	U.S.	19 OCT 1872	

Page	Name	Age	Race	Birth	Death Date	Burial Ground
384	Custis, Henry	2y	C	Va.	20 MAR 1869	Washington Asylum
447	Custis, Samuel	15y	C		22 MAR 1870	Potters Field
197	Custly, [blank]	4m	C	D.C.	07 JAN 1861	Harmony
764	Cuthbert, James H., student	21y	W	U.S.	28 MAY 1874	Oak Hill
519	Cuthbert, Mary A.	65y	W	Eng.	23 MAY 1871	Congressional*
707	Cuthing, Rachael T.	62y	W	Ver.	12 JUL 1873	Great Falls, N.H.
680	Cutler, Clarence H., clerk	43y	W	U.S.	03 APR 1873	Glenwood/Arlington
274	Cutler, John	1y	C	D.C.	03 SEP 1867	Harmony
724	Cutler, Lena	1y	B	D.C.	13 OCT 1873	Young Mens
637	Cutter, Carrie	2y	W	U.S.	21 NOV 1872	Young Mens
276	Cutting, Chauncey L., clerk	45y	W	N.Y.	01 SEP 1867	Wisc.
771	Cutts, Douglas A.	7m	W	U.S.	10 JUN 1874	Mt. Olivet
104	Cuvelier, William	1m	W	D.C.	06 FEB 1858	Congressional
527	Cuvillier, Harry	7y	W	D.C.	07 JUL 1871	Congressional
522	Cuvillier, Jos.	2y	W	U.S.	13 JUN 1871	Congressional*
049	Cyrus, Eliza	4m	C	D.C.	03 JUL 1856	Western

Page	Name	Age	Race	Birth	Death Date	Burial Ground
D						
606	Dabb, Isaac, laborer	58y	C	Va.	26 JUN 1872	Young Mens
725	Dabney, Clara, housekeeper	50y	B	Va.	18 OCT 1873	Piney Branch
478	Dabney, Henrietta	11m	C	D.C.	13 SEP 1870	Young Mens
377	Dabney, Mary	3m	C		01 FEB 1869	Young Mens
042	Dabny, [blank]		W	D.C.	23 APR 1856	Alms House
212	Dacey, Margaret, domestic	40y	W	Ire.	06 FEB 1866	Mt. Olivet
249	Dade, E.C., barber	23y	C	Va.	28 JAN 1867	Beckett's
715	Dade, Jane	21d	C	D.C.	06 AUG 1873	
366	Dade, Oliver		B	R.I.	03 DEC 1868	
297	Dade, Washington, driver	24y	C	Md.	24 FEB 1868	Smith's
157	Dade, [blank]	1y	C	D.C.	10 AUG 1859	Western
099	Dagenhart, Mary A.	35y	W	Md.	28 DEC 1857	Congressional
416	Daggs, Lucy	65y	C		30 SEP 1869	Ebenezer
107	Daggs, Mary E.	2y	C	D.C.	10 MAR 1858	Foundry
752	Dahle, John W., tailor	62y	W	Han.	04 MAR 1874	Prospect Hill
507	Dahler, Gustave, cigar maker	42y	W	Ger.	— FEB 1871	Prospect Hill
111	Dahlgreen, Lizzie	17y	W		17 APR 1858	Philadelphia, Pa.
535	Dahlgren, Hildreth		W	D.C.	16 SEP 1871	Oak Hill
012	Dahlgren, Mary	35y	W	Pa.	06 JUN 1855	Philadelphia, Pa.
660	Dailey, Anna	26y	W	U.S.	19 JAN 1873	Mt. Olivet
639	Dailey, Jno., book agent	30y	W		04 NOV 1872	
380	Dailey, John M.	10d	W		18 MAR 1869	Mt. Olivet
015	Dailey, Mary	20y	W	Ire.	01 JUL 1855	St. Patricks
001	Dailey, Michael	46y			15 JAN 1855	St. Patricks
050	Dailey, Robert E.	18y	W	Ala.	19 JUL 1856	St. Matthews
005	Dailey, Thomas	7m	W	D.C.	04 MAR 1855	St. Patricks
463	Daily, Catherine	80y	W	Ire.	05 JUL 1870	Mt. Olivet
154	Daily, Frances	10m	C	D.C.	16 JUL 1859	Harmony
155	Daily, Honora	32y	W	Ire.	26 JUL 1859	Mt. Olivet
533	Daily, John	10m	W	D.C.	20 AUG 1871	Mt. Olivet
689	Daily, Mary	1m	W	U.S.	23 MAY 1873	Washington Asylum
620	Dainon, G.	2y	W	U.S.	08 AUG 1872	Glenwood
259	Dakin, [blank]	2m	W	D.C.	22 APR 1867	Congressional*
637	Dalaver, David	42y	C	U.S.	19 NOV 1872	
451	Dale, Charles, laborer	62y	C	Md.	13 APR 1870	Washington Asylum
263	Dale, Ellen L.	33y	W	D.C.	07 JUN 1867	Glenwood
115	Dale, John M.	7y	W	D.C.	11 JUN 1858	Oak Hill
132	Dale, Mary	1y	W	D.C.	06 NOV 1858	Georgetown
214	Daley, Mary Ann	40y	W	D.C.	02 MAR 1866	Mt. Olivet*
717	Daley, Mary Jane	3y	W	U.S.	01 SEP 1873	Mt. Olivet
189	Daley, Sarah C.	16y	W	D.C.	20 SEP 1860	Mt. Olivet
629	Dallas, B.	8y	W	U.S.	03 OCT 1872	Congressional*
066	Dallas, James L.	7y	W	D.C.	17 DEC 1856	Congressional
462	Dallas, Napoleon B.	5m	W	D.C.	04 JUL 1870	Congressional
153	Dallas, Olympia M.	6m	W	D.C.	01 JUL 1859	Congressional
079	Dalrymple, Archibald, brakeman	28y	W	Md.	01 JUN 1857	Baltimore, Md.
061	Dalton, Amy Amelia	7m	W	D.C.	10 OCT 1856	Congressional
265	Dalton, Gertrude H.	17y	W	D.C.	29 JUL 1867	Glenwood
332	Dalton, Lucie Eloise	1m	W	D.C.	10 JUL 1868	Congressional
075	Dalton, Wm., carpenter	21y	W	D.C.	01 APR 1857	St. Patricks
746	Daly, Hanson	70y	W	Ire.	13 FEB 1874	Fairfax Station, Va.
494	Daly, James	49y	W	Va.	02 DEC 1870	Mt. Olivet*
616	Daly, Jer., laborer	35y	W	U.S.	09 JUL 1872	
315	Daly, Mary C.	17y	W		c.01 MAY 1868	Mt. Olivet*
371	Daly, Michael, fruit store		W	Ire.	24 JAN 1869	Mt. Olivet
735	Dandridge, Eliza	75y	C	U.S.	10 DEC 1873	Washington Asylum
581	Dandridge, Frank	75y	W	Va.	15 FEB 1872	Washington

District of Columbia Interments (Index to Deaths), 1855-1874

Page	Name	Age	Race	Birth	Death Date	Burial Ground
367	Dandridge, James	6y	B	D.C.	31 DEC 1868	Washington Asylum
531	Dandridge, Maria E.	65y	C		07 AUG 1871	Young Mens
478	Danelett, J.B., infant of	Still			08 SEP 1870	Holmead
413	Danfont, Mabel	21d	W		30 AUG 1869	Glenwood
166	Danford, Mary	24y	W	U.S.	06 NOV 1859	Mt. Olivet
450	Dangerfield, Wm.	3y	C		25 APR 1870	Young Mens
068	Daniel, H. Elizabeth	33y	W	Pa.	04 JAN 1857	Oak Hill
296	Daniel, Lizzie	45y	W		21 FEB 1868	Alms House
111	Daniel, Mary L.	27y	W	Va.*	20 APR 1858	Methodist
300	Daniels, B.G., infant of	1m	W	U.S.	14 MAR 1868	Oak Hill
167	Daniels, Francis, painter	58y	W		09 DEC 1859	Washington Asylum
244	Daniels, Henry E., clerk	45y	W		16 NOV 1866	N.Y.
718	Daniels, Hester	7m	C	D.C.	10 SEP 1873	
614	Daniels, Jas. H.	61y	W	U.S.	15 JUL 1872	
550	Daniels, Mary	4y	W	U.S.	29 DEC 1871	Methodist
130	Daniels, Susanna	11y	W	Va.	01 OCT 1858	Congressional
146	Dankworth, Frederick, engraver	62y	W	Pa.	19 APR 1859	Alexandria, Va.
713	Danning, Maggie	2y	C	D.C.	26 AUG 1873	
684	Dannport, Bertha	26y	C	U.S.	10 APR 1873	Small Pox*
664	Dant, Clarence W.	6m	W	U.S.	21 JAN 1873	Small Pox*
093	Dant, Edward, servant	13y	C	D.C.	12 OCT 1857	Harmony
267	Dant, Elizabeth A. Dull	4y	W	D.C.	15 JUL 1867	Baltimore, Md.
338	Dant, Hattie May	7m	W	D.C.	25 AUG 1868	Mt. Olivet
073	Dant, Jeremiah, laborer	55y	C	D.C.	15 MAR 1857	St. Patricks
149	Dant, Jerry	14y	C	D.C.	24 MAY 1859	Mt. Olivet
285	Dant, Martha B., Mrs.	73y	W	Eng.	11 DEC 1867	Mt. Olivet
237	Dant, Martha E.	8d			29 SEP 1866	Western
663	Dant, Mary	35y	W	U.S.	02 JAN 1873	Small Pox*
064	Dant, Mary Ann	35y	C	D.C.	13 NOV 1856	Washington Asylum
224	Dant, Rachel	7m			17 JUN 1866	Baltimore Md.
536	Dant, Richd. B.	4y	W		17 SEP 1871	Congressional*
279	Dant, Susan	72y	W	D.C.	10 OCT 1867	Mt. Olivet
011	Dant, William	64y	W	Md.	08 JUN 1855	St. Patricks
663	Dant, Wm. T.	44y	W	U.S.	11 JAN 1873	Small Pox
516a	Daran, John, pauper	46y	W	Fra.	31 MAR 1871	Washington Asylum
167	Darathy, James, tailor	42y	W	Md.	05 DEC 1859	Congressional
741	Darby, Ellen	40y	W	U.S.	07 JAN 1874	Mt. Olivet
735	Darby, Wales	11d	C	U.S.	09 DEC 1873	
292	Dare, Ellen	5m	C		25 JAN 1868	Alms House
736	Dare, Fred F.	17y	W	U.S.	19 DEC 1873	Mt. Olivet
380	Darley, Chloe	85y	W	Va.	31 MAR 1869	Glenwood
046	Darley, Thomas	69y	W	Md.	13 JUN 1856	Glenwood
513	Darling, Lucy	65y	C	Va.	21 MAR 1871	Washington Asylum
333	Darling, Sidney	5m	W		18 JUL 1868	Methodist
111	Darling, [blank]	Still	W	D.C.	11 APR 1858	Congressional
298	Darnall, W.	14y	W		07 FEB 1868	Glenwood
438	Darnel, Israel, laborer	15y	C	Va.	04 JAN 1870	
666	Darnell, Martin V.	13m	W	U.S.	05 FEB 1873	Glenwood
112	Darnes, Mrs.	28y	W		29 APR 1858	St. Matthews
080	Darnes, [blank]	6m	W		29 JUN 1857	St. Matthews
124	Darr, Sarah Elizabeth	1y	W		04 AUG 1858	St. Peters
411	Darrell, Child	Still	W		31 AUG 1869	Oak Hill
221	Darrell, J., Mrs., child of	Still	W		15 MAY 1866	Congressional
495	Dashick, James, laborer	78y	C	Md.	11 DEC 1870	Beckett's
592	Dasler, Jane, storekeeper	37y	W	Scot.	18 APR 1872	
283	Dassenbute, Bernard	3y	W	D.C.	24 NOV 1867	German Catholic
427	Datcher, Henry	65y	C	Md.	04 NOV 1869	Washington Asylum
765	Datcher, Josephine	17y	C	U.S.	23 MAY 1874	

Page	Name	Age	Race	Birth	Death Date	Burial Ground
044	Datcher, Julia	45y	C	Md.	16 MAY 1856	Young Mens
630	Datcher, Sarah C.	13y	C	U.S.	13 OCT 1872	
594	Datler, Jane	37y	W	Scot.	15 APR 1872	Congressional
105	Dauerty, Ann	35y	W	Ire.	15 FEB 1858	St. Patricks
166	Daughaday, Henry, tailor	50y	W	Md.	26 NOV 1859	Congressional
107	Daugherty, John, blacksmith	49y	W	Pa.	09 MAR 1858	Glenwood
226	Daulton, Wm., child of	Still			29 JUN 1866	Congressional
348	Dausch, Nicholas, music prof.	44y	W	Bav.	19 SEP 1868	Congressional
041	Davenport, Child of Lt. H.K.		W	D.C.	05 APR 1856	Congressional*
410	Davenport, Edward	10m	C	D.C.	05 AUG 1869	Young Mens
369	Davenport, Margaret	61y	W	Va.	24 JAN 1869	Congressional
554	Davenport, Sophia D.	76y	W	Eng.	20 JAN 1872	Congressional*
097	Davenport, [blank]	4y	W		28 NOV 1857	Georgetown/Arlington
410	Davenport, [blank], laborer	10y	C	Va.	— AUG 1869	Young Mens
367	Daver, Amelia	75y	B	D.C.	30 DEC 1868	Washington Asylum
450	David, Isidor	8m	W		12 APR 1870	Washington Hebrew
410	David, Sophia	35y	W	Ger.	22 AUG 1869	Washington Hebrew
440	Davidge, T.B.F., infant of	14d	W		25 FEB 1870	Oak Hill
585	Davids, Julia A.	72y	W	U.S.	10 MAR 1872	Congressional
451	Davidson, Betty	27y	C	Va.	23 APR 1870	Washington Asylum
616a	Davidson, Dolly	14d	W	U.S.	18 JUL 1872	Congressional
235	Davidson, Eliza	71y	W	D.C.	19 SEP 1866	Oak Hill
507	Davidson, John	72y	W	Eng.	17 FEB 1871	Dranesville, Va.
373	Davidson, John H., carpenter	68y	W	Amer.	31 JAN 1869	Mt. Olivet
345	Davidson, Samuel L.	1m	W	D.C.	17 AUG 1868	Glenwood
542	Davidson, Thos. H., policeman	29y	W		18 OCT 1871	Glenwood
753	Davis, Albata	2m	W	U.S.	29 MAR 1874	Glenwood
438	Davis, Albert, clerk, Surv. Gen.	38y	W	Pa.	28 JAN 1870	Glenwood
771	Davis, Alice	10m	W	U.S.	09 JUN 1874	Mt. Olivet
006	Davis, Allen, laborer	50y	C	Va.	08 APR 1855	Young Mens
527	Davis, Amelia	39y	C	D.C.	07 JUL 1871	Young Mens
780	Davis, Amos, laborer	25y	C	U.S.	29 JUL 1874	Potters Field
275	Davis, Ann	50y	W	D.C.	22 SEP 1867	Ebenezer
536	Davis, Ann	49y	W	Va.	18 SEP 1871	Glenwood
243	Davis, Anna	1m	C	D.C.	13 NOV 1866	Harmony
552	Davis, Anna B.	6m	W	D.C.	05 JAN 1872	Congressional*
482	Davis, Aurilia	60y	C	Va.	28 OCT 1870	Harmony
475	Davis, Benedict	80y	C	Va.	17 SEP 1870	Freedmen's Hospital
292a	Davis, Beverly	5m	C	D.C.*	30 JAN 1868	Brooke's
664	Davis, Charles	5y	C	U.S.	10 JAN 1873	Small Pox*
174	Davis, Charles E., clerk	35y	W	U.S.	11 MAR 1860	Western
051	Davis, Charles H.	4y	W	D.C.	21 JUL 1856	Glenwood
454	Davis, Charles, laborer	35y	C	Va.	14 MAY 1870	Washington Asylum
088	Davis, Charlotte	58y	C		21 AUG 1857	Western
611	Davis, Chas.	1y	C	U.S.	04 JUL 1872	
611	Davis, Chas.	1y	W	U.S.	24 JUL 1872	
487	Davis, Chas. W., Dr.	64y	W	D.C.	14 NOV 1870	Congressional
581	Davis, Cyrus, laborer	23y	C	Md.	18 FEB 1872	Glenwood
508	Davis, Daniel	4y	C	D.C.	14 FEB 1871	Ebenezer
253	Davis, Daniel F.	1y	W	D.C.	20 FEB 1867	Congressional
485	Davis, Edward	53y	W	Va.	28 OCT 1870	Potters Field
448	Davis, Edward, laborer	22y	C	Va.	14 MAR 1870	Washington Asylum
448	Davis, Eliza	22y	C	Md.	21 MAR 1870	Washington Asylum
005	Davis, Elizabeth	70y	W	Va.	03 MAR 1855	
189	Davis, Elizabeth	8y	C	D.C.	14 SEP 1860	Ebenezer
324	Davis, Elizabeth	62y	W	Md.	03 JUL 1868	Mt. Olivet
712	Davis, Ellen	30y	W	D.C.	17 AUG 1873	Washington Asylum
608	Davis, Ellen E.	7y	W	D.C.	21 JUN 1872	Glenwood

Page	Name	Age	Race	Birth	Death Date	Burial Ground
091	Davis, Emily R.	1y	W	D.C.	17 SEP 1857	Methodist
225	Davis, Emma	3m			24 JUN 1866	Alms House
704	Davis, Evans	6m	W	D.C.	07 JUL 1873	Glenwood
163	Davis, Exey M.	31y	W	Md.	16 OCT 1859	Methodist
516a	Davis, Fielder, pauper	12m	C	Md.	15 MAR 1871	Washington Asylum
658	Davis, Florance May	1y	W		02 JAN 1873	Congressional
329	Davis, Florence	3m	C	D.C.	08 JUL 1868	
112	Davis, Geo. Washington	5y	W		26 APR 1858	Baltimore, Md.
508	Davis, George	1y	C	D.C.	13 FEB 1871	Ebenezer
523	Davis, George A.	6m	W	Md.	15 JUN 1871	Young Mens
245	Davis, Hanson, child of	1m	C	D.C.	04 NOV 1866	Beckett's
011	Davis, Harriet	39y	W	Md.	16 JAN 1855	Harford Co., Md.
382	Davis, Harry, laborer	65y	C	Va.	09 MAR 1869	Young Mens
771	Davis, Henry, laborer	80y	C	U.S.	26 JUN 1874	Washington Asylum
765	Davis, Hunter	12d	W	U.S.	22 MAY 1874	Congressional
308	Davis, Ida	10m	W	D.C.	05 APR 1868	Congressional
581	Davis, Ida M.	1y	W	D.C.	15 FEB 1872	Congressional
161	Davis, James	18y	W	U.S.	05 SEP 1859	Baltimore, Md.
443	Davis, James, laborer	70y	C	Va.	19 FEB 1870	Washington Asylum
621	Davis, Jane	20y	C	U.S.	03 AUG 1872	
619	Davis, Jane	29y	C	U.S.	07 AUG 1872	Small Pox
106	Davis, Jane, servant	45y	C	Va.	15 FEB 1858	Alexandria, Va.
449	Davis, Jemima, Mrs.	78y	W	Md.	03 APR 1870	Congressional
101	Davis, Jeremiah	5m	C	D.C.	13 JAN 1858	Foundry
295	Davis, John	67y	W	Wales	18 FEB 1868	Congressional
481	Davis, John	1y	C	D.C.	23 OCT 1870	Ebenezer
177	Davis, John, land dealer	36y	W	U.S.	30 APR 1860	Va.
615	Davis, John W.	3y	C	U.S.	14 JUL 1872	
304	Davis, John W.	2m	W	D.C.	c.11 MAR 1868	Glenwood
328	Davis, Joseph	2y	C	D.C.	24 JUL 1868	Young Mens
116	Davis, Joseph F.	1y	W	D.C.	24 JUN 1858	Georgetown
199	Davis, Josephine	20y	W	D.C.	01 FEB 1861	Mt. Olivet
330	Davis, Judson, laborer	70y	C	Md.	19 JUL 1868	Mt. Olivet
319	Davis, Julia A.	28y	W	Ver.	19 JUN 1868	Conn.
399	Davis, Laura M.	7m	W	D.C.	05 JUL 1869	Congressional
052	Davis, Letitia	2y	C		30 JUL 1856	Western
190	Davis, Lewis, laborer	33y	W	Va.	25 SEP 1860	Glenwood
450	Davis, Lewis M.	7m	C		22 APR 1870	Young Mens
398	Davis, Lizzie	80y	B	U.S.	19 JUN 1869	Washington Asylum
470	Davis, Louise, servant	17y	C	Md.	22 AUG 1870	Bennings Bridge, near
417	Davis, Lucy	5d	C		06 SEP 1869	Young Mens
235	Davis, M.	11m	W	D.C.	18 SEP 1866	Glenwood
057	Davis, Margaret	86y	W	Va.	04 SEP 1856	Va.
459	Davis, Marietta	7m	C	D.C.	30 JUN 1870	Potters Field
627	Davis, Martha	85y	C	U.S.	02 SEP 1872	
011	Davis, Martha E.	18y	W	Va.	01 JUN 1855	Glenwood
582	Davis, Mary	45y	C	D.C.	24 FEB 1872	Asylum
162	Davis, Mary	1m	W	D.C.	22 SEP 1859	Congressional
029	Davis, Mary	59y			08 NOV 1855	Ebenezer
765	Davis, Mary	80y	W	U.S.	— MAY 1874	Oak Hill
436	Davis, Mary	2d	C	D.C.	03 JAN 1870	Washington Asylum
447	Davis, Mary	4m	C	D.C.	19 MAR 1870	Washington Asylum
608	Davis, Mary A.	2y	W	D.C.	24 JUN 1872	Glenwood
646	Davis, Mary Eliza	49y	W	U.S.	13 DEC 1872	Congressional
534	Davis, Mary, housekeeper	27y	W	Md.	27 AUG 1871	Methodist
725	Davis, Mary L.	8y	B	Ga.	17 OCT 1873	
473	Davis, Matilda	22y	C	D.C.	28 AUG 1870	Ebenezer
465	Davis, Melinda, laborer	c.80y	C	Va.	17 JUL 1870	Ebenezer

Page	Name	Age	Race	Birth	Death Date	Burial Ground
472	Davis, Moses, laborer	50y	C	Md.	04 AUG 1870	Freedmen's Hospital
016	Davis, Mr.	65y	C		14 JUL 1855	Catholic, Georgetown
304	Davis, Mrs., child of	7y	W	Md.	20 MAR 1868	Congressional
549	Davis, Nancy	75y	C	D.C.	22 DEC 1871	Mt. Olivet
758	Davis, Peter	28y	C	U.S.	20 APR 1874	Washington Asylum
723	Davis, Peter, laborer	85y	M	Md.	04 OCT 1873	
292	Davis, Philip		C		16 JAN 1868	Alms House
435	Davis, Rachael	16y	C		14 JAN 1870	Ebenezer
195	Davis, Rebecca		W	D.C.	08 DEC 1860	
615	Davis, Sandy	24y	C	U.S.	28 JUL 1872	
620	Davis, Sarah	16y	W	U.S.	21 AUG 1872	Philadelphia, Pa.
362	Davis, Sarah Elizabeth	24d	C	D.C.	07 NOV 1868	Ebenezer
658	Davis, Sidney, laborer	29y	C	U.S.	09 JAN 1873	Washington Asylum
413	Davis, Spencer, laborer	70y	C	Md.	13 AUG 1869	Washington Asylum
753	Davis, Susanah E.	45y	W	U.S.	17 MAR 1874	Congressional*
364	Davis, Susie V.	9m	W	D.C.	18 DEC 1868	Congressional
197	Davis, T., child of	Still	W	D.C.	04 JAN 1861	Western
187	Davis, Thomas	10m	W	D.C.	08 AUG 1860	Congressional
354	Davis, Thomas J., tailor	57y	W	D.C.	12 OCT 1868	Mt. Olivet
592	Davis, Thornton, laborer	82y	C	Va.	07 APR 1872	
540	Davis, Virginia	35y	W	Va.	05 OCT 1871	Washington
016	Davis, Wm.	1m	W		14 JUL 1855	Methodist
360	Davis, Wm. A.	28y	W		03 NOV 1868	Glenwood
669	Davis, Wm. B., barber	38y	C	U.S.	05 FEB 1873	
624	Davis, Wm. R., shoemaker	38y	C	U.S.	28 SEP 1872	
217	Davis, Wm. W.	68y	W	Va.	06 APR 1866	Pohick, Va.
108	Davis, [blank]	1y	C	D.C.	16 MAR 1858	Young Mens
241	Davis, [blank], child of	6m	C		20 OCT 1866	Young Mens
044	Davison, John	4m	W	D.C.	05 MAY 1856	Glenwood
024	Davison, Joseph	1y	W	D.C.	08 SEP 1855	Congressional
120	Davison, Mary	45y	W	Md.	08 JUL 1858	St. Peters
217	Davison, William	3y	W	D.C.	04 APR 1866	
166	Dawes, Rufus, agent	57y	W	U.S.	30 NOV 1859	Congressional
488	Dawnes, Hester, servant	27y	C	Md.	07 NOV 1870	Washington Asylum
237	Dawsey, [blank]	1y	C		23 SEP 1866	Western
336	Dawson, Laura Louisa	12y	C		02 AUG 1868	Glenwood
642	Dawson, Rose, servant	29y	C	U.S.	31 DEC 1872	Small Pox
167	Dawson, Thomas J., blacksmith	29y	W	D.C.	19 DEC 1859	
026	Dawson, Wm. W.	7d	W		07 OCT 1855	Ebenezer
233	Dawson, [blank], infant of				07 AUG 1866	Western
640	Day, Anna	2y	C	U.S.	26 DEC 1872	Small Pox*
487	Day, Charles	34y	W	D.C.	11 NOV 1870	Congressional
758	Day, Elizabeth, nurse	75y	C	U.S.	10 APR 1874	Ebenezer
320	Day, Elizabeth O.	1y	W	D.C.	15 JUN 1868	Mt. Olivet
337	Day, Francis	1y	C	U.S.	14 AUG 1868	Washington Asylum
044	Day, George	2y	C		19 MAY 1856	Young Mens
167	Day, George, laborer	45y	C	D.C.	20 DEC 1859	Washington Asylum
354	Day, Harry	1y	W	D.C.	16 OCT 1868	Congressional
151	Day, James Henry	12y	C	D.C.	24 JUN 1859	Young Mens
405	Day, John	3m	C		02 JUL 1869	Ebenezer
397	Day, John	3m	B	Amer.	01 JUN 1869	Ebenezer
752	Day, John F.	6m	C	U.S.	06 MAR 1874	
501	Day, John F., bricklayer	43y	W	D.C.	31 JAN 1871	Alexandria, Va., Meth.
228	Day, John O.	9m	W	D.C.	13 JUL 1866	Mt. Olivet
330	Day, Joseph	60y	C	Va.	23 JUL 1868	Young Mens
242	Day, Josephine	1m	C	D.C.	29 OCT 1866	Young Mens
396	Day, Mary	6m	C	D.C.	18 JUN 1869	Young Mens
715	Day, Matilda		C	U.S.	08 AUG 1873	

Page	Name	Age	Race	Birth	Death Date	Burial Ground
400	Day, Oprin, restaurant keeper	46y	W	Amer.	31 JUL 1869	Glenwood
117	Day, Osceola	9m	W	D.C.	26 JUN 1858	Methodist, East
454	Day, Rachel	25y	C	Va.	25 MAY 1870	Washington Asylum
513	Day, Saml. E.	4y	W	D.C.	08 MAR 1871	Glenwood
426	Day, Sarah A.	48y	W	Md.	14 NOV 1869	Methodist
641	Day, Sarah A.	24y	C	U.S.	20 DEC 1872	Small Pox
638	Day, Smith, laborer	24y	C	U.S.	21 NOV 1872	Washington Asylum
518	Day, Thomas, boatman	50y	W	D.C.	02 MAY 1871	Methodist
706	Day, William	50y	C	U.S.	02 JUL 1873	
453	Day, Willie	1y	W		05 MAY 1870	Congressional
613	Day, Wm.	6m	C	U.S.	05 JUL 1872	
584	Day, Wm., laborer	40y	C	Va.	05 MAR 1872	Asylum
132	Day, [blank]	38y	W		16 NOV 1858	Young Mens
006	Day, [blank]		C		18 APR 1855	Young Mens
006	Day, [blank]		C		17 APR 1855	Young Mens
330	Daya, James A.	2½m	C	D.C.	11 JUL 1868	Young Mens
023	Days, G.	2d	C		02 SEP 1855	
015	Days, [blank]		C		06 JUL 1855	Young Mens
493	Deakins, Agnes M.	1y	W	D.C.	25 DEC 1870	Mt. Olivet
779	Deakins, Caroline	58y	W	U.S.	16 JUL 1874	Glenwood
188	Deamott, Anne R.	61y	W	D.C.	20 AUG 1860	Congressional
079	Deams, Francis M., clerk	39y	W	Md.	01 JUN 1857	Cumberland, Md.
094	Dean, Ann	8m	W	D.C.	20 OCT 1857	
634	Dean, Anna, prostitute	30y	W	U.S.	24 OCT 1872	
595	Dean, George A., laborer	25y	W	D.C.	15 APR 1872	Washington
717	Dean, Jessie	3m	W	Pa.	07 SEP 1873	Oak Hill
054	Dean, John H.	2y	W	D.C.	14 AUG 1856	German
585	Dean, Joseph J.	2y		D.C.	08 MAR 1872	
518	Dean, Margret	2y	C	Va.	12 MAY 1871	
113	Dean, Samuel	1y	W		09 MAY 1858	German Catholic
167	Dean, William, servant	13y	C	D.C.	09 DEC 1859	Congressional
462	Deane, William W., officer USA	37y	W	Me.	22 JUL 1870	Portland, Me.
520	Dearing, Elisabeth	4y	W	D.C.	26 MAY 1871	Glenwood
291	Dearing, Geo.		W	D.C.	30 JAN 1868	Glenwood
291	Dearing, John		W	D.C.	30 JAN 1868	Glenwood
085	Dearing, Louisa S.	4m	W	D.C.	31 JUL 1857	Glenwood
087	Dearing, May E.	2y	W	D.C.	15 AUG 1857	Glenwood
062	Deas, Joanna	35y	W	Md.	07 NOV 1856	Oak Hill
522	DeAthma, Carl August	11m	W	Bav.	10 JUN 1871	Congressional*
682	DeAtley, Rose	4y	W	U.S.	28 APR 1873	Congressional
384	DeBaas, Albert	68y	W	Belg.	06 MAR 1869	Washington Asylum
241	DeBow, Mary		W		06 OCT 1866	Poor House
068	DeCamp, Adelaide H.	5y	W	D.C.	18 JAN 1857	Foundry
089	DeCamp, Sidney	4m	W	D.C.	02 AUG 1857	Glenwood
246	Deckard, Edwd.	11m	W	D.C.	24 DEC 1866	Congressional
527	Decker, Anna	4m	W		07 JUL 1871	Congressional
369	Decker, Jno., infant of	6d	W	D.C.	06 JAN 1869	Congressional
287	Decker, Mary		C		c.06 DEC 1867	Alms House
673	Deckor, Eva	73y	W	Bav.	07 MAR 1873	St. Marys
209	DeCoursey, Thomas	35y	W	Ire.	08 JAN 1866	Mt. Olivet
719	Decover, Martha Ellen	28y	W	D.C.	20 SEP 1873	Congressional
347	DeCover, Francis M., clerk	29y	W		18 SEP 1868	Congressional
419	Dee, Michael, fireman	28y	W	Ire.	27 OCT 1869	Congressional
386	Deeble, Edward	77y	W	Eng.	16 APR 1869	Oak Hill
093	Deeble, Ida	4m	W	D.C.	03 OCT 1857	Oak Hill
307	Deeble, Margaret	82y	W	Va.	16 APR 1868	Oak Hill
278	Deely, Mary	78y	W	Ire.	04 OCT 1867	Mt. Olivet
137	Deely, Michael, laborer	81y	W	Ire.	01 JAN 1859	Catholic

District of Columbia Interments (Index to Deaths), 1855-1874

Page	Name	Age	Race	Birth	Death Date	Burial Ground
682	Deeter, Joseph, contractor	34y	W	U.S.	29 APR 1873	Dauphin Co., Pa.
548	Deeton, Geo. E.	2y	W	D.C.	09 DEC 1871	Union
246	Deevers, Eliza	52y	W		25 DEC 1866	Congressional
394	Deevy, [blank]	Still	W	D.C.	16 JUN 1869	Mt. Olivet
057	DeFalco, Pasquale, musician	54y	W	Italy	12 SEP 1856	Congressional
229	deFiondal, [blank]	21d	W	D.C.	23 JUL 1866	St. Patricks (vault)
644	Degan, Henry	6y	W	U.S.	23 DEC 1872	St. Marys
055	Degee, Celia, nurse	66y	C	Va.	06 AUG 1856	St. Matthews
752	Degere, Wm.	7d	W	U.S.	11 MAR 1874	
765	Degges, Ailcy, servant	70y	C	U.S.	10 MAY 1874	Mt. Olivet
099	Deggs, Wm. B. Magruder	4y	W		29 DEC 1857	Western
350	Dehan, Arnold W.	9m	W	D.C.	11 SEP 1868	German Catholic
720	Dehn, Chas.	61y	W		27 SEP 1873	
591	Deigs, Frank	8m	C	U.S.	06 APR 1872	
758	Deitz, William	55y	C	U.S.	01 APR 1874	Albany, N.Y.
084	DelaCamp, John, Mrs., child	6d	W	D.C.	21 JUL 1857	German
400	DeLaCamp, John Henry	2y	W		— JUL 1869	Prospect Hill
301	DeLacey, Annie	3y	W	D.C.	13 MAR 1868	Mt. Olivet
729	Delafield, Richard, Gen., USA	75y	W	U.S.	05 NOV 1873	Greenwood, N.Y.
752	Deland, Alma A.	3y	W	U.S.	15 MAR 1874	Graceland/Rock Creek
725	Deland, Flora Bell	6y	W	U.S.	22 OCT 1873	Graceland
724	Deland, Margaret J., housekeeper	37y	W	Pa.	16 OCT 1873	Graceland/Rock Creek
256	Delaney, Anna	4m	C	D.C.	01 MAR 1867	Holmead
601	Delaney, Henry	5d	W	U.S.	27 MAY 1872	Mt. Olivet
482	Delaney, Morris W.	7d	C	D.C.	04 OCT 1870	Harmony
546	Delaney, Thomas	54y	C	Md.	26 NOV 1871	Mt. Olivet
016	Delaney, Timothy	4m	W	D.C.	11 JUL 1855	St. Patricks
388	Delany, Caroline	7d	C	D.C.	12 APR 1869	
163	Delany, Charles	2m	C	U.S.	28 OCT 1859	Harmony
191	Delany, Robert, waiter	38y	C	U.S.	10 OCT 1860	Mt. Olivet
465	Delavergne, Henry	2m	W	D.C.	02 JUL 1870	Mt. Olivet
235	Delehanty, Patrick	60y	W	Ire.	15 SEP 1866	Mt. Olivet
294	DeLeon, R.L., Mrs.	71y	W	S.C.	06 FEB 1868	Columbia, S.C.
355	Deleplaine, Robert	8m	W	D.C.	08 OCT 1868	Glenwood
134	Dellaway, I.W.	72y	W		30 NOV 1858	Glenwood
067	Dellett, Chistiana Ida	2y	W	Nebr.	30 DEC 1856	Pa.
096	Dellis, George H.	6d	W	D.C.	06 NOV 1857	Congressional
404	Delmer, Willie	1y	C	D.C.	07 JUL 1869	Washington Asylum
103	Delphy, Rebecca	40y	W	Md.	27 JAN 1858	Glenwood
301	Delter, Charles, cook	37y	C	D.C.	24 MAR 1868	Mt. Olivet
521	Demain, Sarah	64y	W	Va.	01 JUN 1871	Congressional
270	DeMain, Martha	29y	W	D.C.	15 AUG 1867	Mt. Olivet
273	DeMaine, John William	15d	W	D.C.	01 SEP 1867	Congressional
227	Demeaux, Charles A., messenger		W	Fra.	03 JUL 1866	Holmead
268	Dement, Charles E.	4m	W	D.C.	28 AUG 1867	Congressional
156	Dement, Mary E.	63y	W	Md.	08 JUL 1859	Congressional
643	Dement, Mary J.	41y	W	U.S.	13 DEC 1872	Congressional
003	Dement, Richd., clerk	67y	W	Md.	12 FEB 1855	Congressional
233	Demm, A.F.	21y	W		09 AUG 1866	
450	DeMoll, Adam J., clerk	58y	W	Ger.	18 APR 1870	Prospect Hill
309	Demonet, Charles, confectioner	58y	W	Fra.	17 APR 1868	Mt. Olivet*
618	Demott, Chas. E.	5m	W	U.S.	10 AUG 1872	Baltimore, Md.
601	Dempsey, Francis	3y	W	U.S.	c.21 MAY 1872	Mt. Olivet*
321	Dempsey, J.P.	1y	W	D.C.	30 JUN 1868	Mt. Olivet
758	Dempsey, Margaret E.	1m	W	U.S.	27 APR 1874	Mt. Olivet
601	Dempsey, Moses	10y	W	U.S.	c.21 MAY 1872	Mt. Olivet*
746	Dempsey, Moses, laborer		W	Ire.	08 FEB 1874	Mt. Olivet*
263	Dempsy, Margaret	26y	W	D.C.	28 JUN 1867	Glenwood

District of Columbia Interments (Index to Deaths), 1855-1874

Page	Name	Age	Race	Birth	Death Date	Burial Ground
719	Dene, Thomas	27y	C	Va.	21 SEP 1873	Washington Asylum
108	Deneal, [blank]	Still	W	D.C.	14 MAR 1858	Md.
364	Deneale, Emma J.	4y	W	D.C.	21 DEC 1868	Congressional*
439	DeNeale, Hattie Earlene	12d	W		18 FEB 1870	Congressional
550	DeNeale, Sarah A.	50y	W	N.C.	28 DEC 1871	Congressional
265	Denelman, Gertrude	1y	W	D.C.	26 JUL 1867	German Catholic
150	Deneuf, Sophia	37y	W	Ger.	02 JUN 1859	Prospect Hill
124	DeNeuf, William	1y	W	N.Y.	03 AUG 1858	German
415	Dengel, Henry, baker	28y	W	Md.	22 SEP 1869	Mt. Olivet
487	Dengel, John H.	2y	W	D.C.	03 NOV 1870	Mt. Olivet
294	Denham, L.J., child of	3d	W	D.C.	01 FEB 1868	Congressional
268	Denham, Milton Kimball	2m	W	D.C.	14 AUG 1867	Congressional
379	Denham, Oliver B., messenger	56y	W		12 MAR 1869	Congressional
453	Denham, Willie	6y	W		07 MAY 1870	Congressional
031	Denham, Wm. E.	3y	W	D.C.	04 DEC 1855	Congressional
414	Deniae, M.T.	21d	W		09 SEP 1869	Congressional
387	Denison, Egar R.	2y	W	Amer.	21 APR 1869	Glenwood
464	Denison, Ernest	4d	W	D.C.	21 JUL 1870	Glenwood
137	Denison, Mary	6d	C		17 JAN 1859	Western
371	Denman, Hampton W.	1m	W		16 JAN 1869	Mt. Olivet
322	Denman, Jennie L.	11m	W	D.C.	20 JUN 1868	Glenwood
282	Denman, Mary	1m	W	D.C.	01 NOV 1867	Mt. Olivet
055	Denna, Martha	12y	C		30 AUG 1856	St. Matthews
735	Denning, A.S.	4m	W	U.S.	09 DEC 1873	Glenwood
546	Denning, Wm. H.	7m	W		26 NOV 1871	Glenwood/Rock Creek
549	Dennis, James T.	31y	W	Mass.	22 DEC 1871	Congressional
348	Dennis, John Bennet	7y	W	D.C.	28 SEP 1868	Congressional
153	Dennis, Manuel B.	1y	W	D.C.	01 JUL 1859	Congressional
122	Dennison, Cornelia	8m	W	D.C.	26 JUL 1858	Congressional
634	Dennison, John J., printer	53y	W	U.S.	13 OCT 1872	Congressional
135	Dennison, Mary	5y	W	D.C.	13 DEC 1858	Congressional
154	Dennison, Mary	32y	W	D.C.	18 JUL 1859	Methodist
136	Dennison, Wm. H.	3y	W	D.C.	23 DEC 1858	Congressional
765	Dennoon, Dennis	65y	C	U.S.	23 MAY 1874	
321	Denny, John	34y	W		c.27 JUN 1868	Alms House
082	Dennys, James M., farmer	38y	C	Md.	04 JUL 1857	Oak Hill
057	Denoon, Elizabeth	80y	C		01 SEP 1856	Congressional
779	Denrick, Mary C.	7m	W	U.S.	12 JUL 1874	Mt. Olivet
209	Densby, John	65y	W		04 JAN 1866	
404	Dent, Ann R.J.	8m	C		01 JUL 1869	
687	Dent, Caroline		C	D.C.	04 MAY 1873	Ebenezer
417	Dent, Daisy	2m	W		23 SEP 1869	Mt. Olivet
343	Dent, Harry	1m	W	D.C.	07 AUG 1868	Mt. Olivet
711	Dent, Robt.	3m	C	U.S.	09 AUG 1873	Washington Asylum
262	Dent, Rose	8d	W	D.C.	18 JUN 1867	Mt. Olivet
209	Dent, Sarah G.	16y	C	D.C.	06 JAN 1866	Harmony
401	Dent, Thomas Neal, farm laborer	72y	C	Md.	16 JUL 1869	Young Mens
603	Dent, W.F.	3y	C	Va.	15 JUN 1872	Small Pox
554	Denton, Mary, washerwoman	23y	C	Md.	18 JAN 1872	Harmony
746	Derby, Flora	39y	W	U.S.	03 FEB 1874	
601	Derby, J.W.		W	U.S.	16 MAY 1872	Ill.
706	Dereher, Maria Sophia	1y	W	D.C.	29 JUL 1873	Prospect Hill
245	DeRemer, Isaac	41y	W		21 NOV 1866	Oak Hill
284	Derfoss, Fredk., gardener	60y	W	Fra.	01 NOV 1867	Holmead
096	Dermy, Anna E.	4y	W		02 NOV 1857	St. Matthews
746	DeRuisile, Thos. W.	25y	W	U.S.	22 FEB 1874	Rock Creek
152	DeSales, [blank]	2y	W	D.C.	27 JUN 1859	Mt. Olivet
082	DeSaules, Peter A., tavern keeper	56y	W	Switz.	05 JUL 1857	Congressional

District of Columbia Interments (Index to Deaths), 1855-1874

Page	Name	Age	Race	Birth	Death Date	Burial Ground
142	DeSelding, Julia		W	D.C.	24 FEB 1859	Congressional*
376	Deshill, Rachel	95y	C		17 FEB 1869	Young Mens
307	Desly, Patrick, grocer	37y	W	Ire.	26 APR 1868	Mt. Olivet
409	Desmond, Andrew	1y	W	D.C.	08 AUG 1869	Mt. Olivet
097	Desmond, Dennis	60y	W	Ire.	02 NOV 1857	St. Patricks
338	Desmond, Michael	1y	W	D.C.	27 AUG 1868	Mt. Olivet
431	Dessan, Andreas, piano maker	48y	W		09 DEC 1869	Glenwood
141	Dessen, Alexander	2m	W	D.C.	19 FEB 1859	Washington Co.
469	DeThoware, Rudolph, clerk	25y	W	Fra.	06 AUG 1870	Glenwood
184	Detweiler, Ela	1y	W	D.C.	12 JUL 1860	Glenwood
343	Detweiler, Helen	5m	W	D.C.	07 AUG 1868	Glenwood
128	Devaner, Charles	25y	C		24 SEP 1858	Baltimore, Md.
265	Devaughn, Saml.	68y	W	Va.	05 JUL 1867	Congressional
216	Devaughn, Thomas L.	18d	W	D.C.	22 MAR 1866	Congressional
444	Devaughn, Walter	62y	W	Md.	27 MAR 1870	Congressional
530	DeVaughn, Virginia	2y	W	D.C.	31 JUL 1871	Washington
090	Develin, John S., gentleman	59y	W	Ire.	05 SEP 1857	St. Peters
050	Dever, Mary	80y		Md.	14 JUL 1856	
033	Devereux, Jno.	18y	W		22 JAN 1856	Catholic
096	Devers, Alex., child of		W	D.C.	17 NOV 1857	Congressional
149	Devers, Ellen	7m	W	D.C.	27 MAY 1859	Congressional
289	Devers, James Joshua	22h	W	D.C.	28 JAN 1868	Glenwood
127	Devers, John Wm.	1y	W	D.C.	05 SEP 1858	Glenwood
101	Devers, Mary	1y	W	D.C.	11 JAN 1858	Congressional
157	Devers, Sarah A.	25y	W	U.S.	10 AUG 1859	Congressional
046	Devilly, Isaac, painter	59y	W	Va.	20 JUN 1856	Foundry
045	Devine, Bernard, grocer	23y	W	Ire.	24 MAY 1856	St. Peters
038	Devlin, John, clerk	58y	W	Ire.	21 MAR 1856	St. Patricks
330	Devote, Anthony L.	9m	W	D.C.	12 JUL 1868	Mt. Olivet
345	Dewantier, Augusta Helene	1y	W	D.C.	24 AUG 1868	Mt. Olivet
758	Dewdeny, Catherine E.	38y	W	U.S.	19 APR 1874	Oak Hill
481	Dewdney, Hannah	66y	W	Eng.	11 OCT 1870	Oak Hill
435	Dewdney, Ida May	3y	W		03 JAN 1870	Oak Hill
478	Dewdney, John, collector	69y	W	Eng.	08 SEP 1870	Oak Hill
662	Dewees, George, collector	50y	W	U.S.	03 JAN 1873	Congressional*
450	Dewey, John	9y	W	Md.	18 APR 1870	Baltimore, Md.
501	Dewey, Matild, housekeeper	34y	W	Va.	18 JAN 1871	Fairfax, Va.
585	DeWolf, Henrietta	17y	W	Md.	06 MAR 1872	
482	Dexter, Minnie	8d	W	D.C.	06 OCT 1870	Mt. Olivet
008	Dey, Matilda, servant	34y	C	D.C.	26 MAY 1855	St. Peters
236	DeYoung, Lizzie F.	1y	W	D.C.	10 SEP 1866	Philadelphia, Pa.
334	Dianna, Tilly	1m	C		29 JUL 1868	
143	Dice, Christina	53y	W	Ger.	13 MAR 1859	Prospect Hill
614	Dice, Clara	8m	C	U.S.	24 JUL 1872	
058	Dicerson, Canelious	17d	W		27 SEP 1856	St. Patricks
168	Dick, Ellie	2y	W	D.C.	21 DEC 1859	Glenwood
217	Dick, Ida E.	13y	W	D.C.	05 APR 1866	Glenwood
708	Dick, Jas. H.	2m	C	D.C.	15 JUL 1873	
747	Dick, John W.	2y	W	U.S.	26 FEB 1874	Glenwood
273	Dick, Josephus, laborer		C	Md.	18 SEP 1867	Harmony
553	Dick, Margret, servant	25y	C	Va.	08 JAN 1872	Washington
147	Dickens, Lilias Arnot		W		10 APR 1859	Congressional
332	Dickens, Mary	1y	W	D.C.	22 JUL 1868	Mt. Olivet
625	Dickerson, Ellen	4y	W	U.S.	22 SEP 1872	
466	Dickerson, Henry	2y	C	D.C.	21 JUL 1870	Western
125	Dickey, Williams	1y	W	D.C.	04 AUG 1858	
526	Dickins, Edw. A., farmer	52y	W	D.C.	02 JUL 1871	Congressional
695	Dickinson, Eliza	5m	C	U.S.	26 JUN 1873	Ebenezer

District of Columbia Interments (Index to Deaths), 1855-1874

Page	Name	Age	Race	Birth	Death Date	Burial Ground
413	Dickinson, John	4m	C	D.C.	26 AUG 1869	Washington Asylum
054	Dickinson, Samuel E.	6m	W	D.C.	05 AUG 1856	Glenwood
409	Dickinson, William	7m	C	D.C.	02 AUG 1869	
538	Dickson, A.		C	Va.	29 SEP 1871	
502	Dickson, Chas. H.	2d	W	D.C.	13 JAN 1871	Glenwood
315	Dickson, Eliza	22y	C	Va.	25 MAY 1868	Young Mens
428	Dickson, Fanny	2y	C	Va.	29 NOV 1869	Western
348	Dickson, Francis L.	2y	W	D.C.	01 SEP 1868	Congressional
336	Dickson, John Edwin	2m	C	D.C.	01 AUG 1868	
617	Dickson, Johnson	11m	C	U.S.	08 AUG 1872	
629	Dickson, Mary N.	60y	W	U.S.	22 OCT 1872	
779	Diebitsch, Alice L.	2y	W	unk.	13 JUL 1874	Congressional*
133	Diebitsche, M.	35y	W	Ger.	25 NOV 1858	Congressional
409	Diedrich, Theodore	8d	W		10 AUG 1869	Prospect Hill
112	Diefenbach, Philip, shoemaker	29y	W	Ger.	28 APR 1858	Glenwood
499	Diemar, [blank]	20h	W	D.C.	29 JAN 1871	Congressional
612	Diemer, John	12y	W	U.S.	27 JUL 1872	
415	Dieste, Amelia	13y	W		21 SEP 1869	Glenwood
488	Diet, John W.S.	3m	C	D.C.	26 NOV 1870	Harmony
231	Dieterich, Gustavus	8m	W	D.C.	03 AUG 1866	Prospect Hill
544	Dieterich, Henry, tailor	36y	W	Ger.	09 NOV 1871	St. Marys
703	Dieterick, Conrad, tailor	73y	W	Ger.	23 JUL 1873	Prospect Hill
528	Dietrich, J.	11m	W	D.C.	14 JUL 1871	Prospect Hill
058	Dietrich, John	1y	W	D.C.	20 SEP 1856	
611	Dietrich, Thos.	1y	W	U.S.	18 JUL 1872	
018	Diggens, Agnes	55y	W	Ire.	17 AUG 1855	St. Patricks
251	Diggins, Mary E.	2m	W	D.C.	19 JAN 1867	Mt. Olivet
214	Diggins, [blank]		W		09 MAR 1866	Alms House
275	Diggle, James, carpenter	67y	W	Eng.	15 SEP 1867	Congressional
619	Diggs, Anna	16y	C	U.S.	08 AUG 1872	
368	Diggs, Charles	100y	C	Va.	22 DEC 1868	Freedmen's Hospital
378	Diggs, Daniel, laborer	80y	C	Va.	11 FEB 1869	Freedmen's Hospital
241	Diggs, Harriet	68y	C		14 OCT 1866	Harmony
373	Diggs, Henrietta	5m	C	U.S.	08 JAN 1869	Harmony
432	Diggs, James	21y	C		21 DEC 1869	Washington Asylum
201	Diggs, Lizzie	4y	W	D.C.	13 MAR 1861	Glenwood
146	Diggs, Louisa	59y	C	Va.	19 APR 1859	Young Mens
646	Diggs, M., infant child of		C	D.C.	13 DEC 1872	
317	Diggs, Mary Catherine Jane	1y	C	D.C.	22 JUN 1868	Queen's
373	Diggs, Sandy, servant		C		27 JAN 1869	Harmony
223	Diggs, Wm. Dudley	8y	W	D.C.	03 JUN 1866	Rock Creek
360	Diggs, Wm. E.	3y	W	D.C.	17 NOV 1868	Mt. Olivet
019	Digion, Anna	22y	W	Ire.	17 AUG 1855	St. Patricks
368	Digney, [blank]	2d	W	D.C.	03 DEC 1868	Mt. Olivet
779	Dikerman, Wm. R.	77y	W	U.S.	18 JUL 1874	
691	Diliod, Thomas	3y	C	U.S.	08 MAY 1873	Small Pox*
523	Dill, Fred.	4m	W	D.C.	15 JUN 1871	Prospect Hill
508	Dill, Mary	30y	W	Ger.	26 FEB 1871	Glenwood
741	Dille, Israel, clerk	71y	W	U.S.	11 JAN 1874	Ohio
309	Diller, Francis	75y	W	Ger.	20 APR 1868	Glenwood
588	Dilli, George, bar keeper	73y	W	Ger.	26 MAR 1872	Prospect Hill
331	Dillion, Edward	60y	C		22 JUL 1868	Freedmen's Hospital
304	Dillon, Mabel	10m	W		d.31 MAR 1868	Glenwood
582	Dillon, Mary	32y	W	Ire.	21 FEB 1872	Mt. Olivet
532	Dillon, Thomas	8m	W	D.C.	15 AUG 1871	Mt. Olivet
780	Dillon, [blank]	2d	W	unk.	26 JUL 1874	
372	Dillwer, Bettie	7d	C	D.C.	26 JAN 1869	Washington Asylum
328	Dines, Charles, laborer	28y	C	D.C.	31 JUL 1868	Mt. Olivet

Page	Name	Age	Race	Birth	Death Date	Burial Ground
115	Dingfelder, Alfred		W	D.C.	13 JUN 1858	German
524	Dinnis, Alfred J.	60y	W		22 JUN 1871	Congressional*
049	Dioz, Sarah	4d	W		05 JUL 1856	Western
168	Dippel, Elizabeth, servant	15y	W	Ger.	28 DEC 1859	Prospect Hill
598	Diserou, Catharine	88y	W	U.S.	29 MAY 1872	Mt. Olivet
637	Dishman, A.E.	30y	W	U.S.	18 NOV 1872	
553	Dishman, H.E.	1y	W	D.C.	12 JAN 1872	Methodist
779	Dismer, Mary A.	42y	W	Ger.	20 JUL 1874	Mt. Olivet
073	Disney, David T., lawyer	54y	W		14 MAR 1857	Removed from City
291	Disney, Geo., engineer	23y	W	Ire.	11 JAN 1868	N.Y.
262	Dittall, Lewis	12d	W	D.C.	26 JUN 1867	Prospect Hill
420	Divine, John A.	26y	W	Va.	06 OCT 1869	Leesburg, Va.
771	Dix, Aleatha	89y	W	U.S.	03 JUN 1874	Glenwood
394	Dixon, Gilmore	14d	W	D.C.	15 JUN 1869	Congressional
334	Dixon, H.J.	3y	C	D.C.	08 JUL 1868	Beckett's
028	Dixon, James	4y	W	Md.	29 OCT 1855	
603	Dixon, James, laborer	49y	C	Va.	02 JUN 1872	
104	Dixon, Margaret Jane, seamstress	30y	W	Ire.	11 FEB 1858	St. Patricks (vault)
771	Dixon, Mary, child of	7d	C	U.S.	26 JUN 1874	Mt. Olivet
494	Dixon, Ruth	84y	W	D.C.	15 DEC 1870	Glenwood
452	Dixon, Ruth Ann	3y	C	D.C.	30 APR 1870	Washington Asylum
452	Dixon, Sicelia	20y	C	Va.	30 APR 1870	Washington Asylum
042	Dixon, Solomon, laborer	95y	C	Va.	25 APR 1856	Harmony
006	Dixon, Thos.	70y	C	Va.	12 APR 1855	Asylum
474	Dixon, Wm.	31y	C		19 AUG 1870	Washington Asylum
472	Dixon, Zachariah	5m	C		02 AUG 1870	Young Mens
234	Dixson, Charity	68y	C	Va.	03 SEP 1866	Harmony
051	Dlankey, Mary	1y	W	D.C.	22 JUL 1856	St. Peters
449	Dobbins, Eddie L.	11m	W		01 APR 1870	Congressional
676	Dobbins, Sallie	12y	C	U.S.	06 MAR 1873	Small Pox
500	Dobbyn, Matilda	86y	W	Md.	24 JAN 1871	Mt. Olivet
557	Dobson, Emma V.	5m	C	D.C.	02 FEB 1872	Young Mens
603	Dobson, M.E.	40y	W	D.C.	07 JUN 1872	Congressional
439	Dodd, Mary, Mrs.	61y	W	Va.	23 FEB 1870	Congressional
193	Dodds, James	84y	W	Scot.	11 NOV 1860	Congressional
375	Dodge, Custis L.	2y	W	Md.	09 FEB 1869	Baltimore, Md.
284	Dodge, Emily Pomeroy	55y	W	Mass.	09 NOV 1867	Oak Hill
375	Dodge, Flora E.	3y	W	D.C.	05 FEB 1869	Glenwood
159	Dodge, Kate, cyprian	22y	W	N.Y.	25 AUG 1859	
499	Dodge, M.M.	53y	W	Me.	12 JAN 1871	Congressional
712	Dodge, Mary S.	4m	W	D.C.	19 AUG 1873	Glenwood
295	Dodge, Sherburne F., merchant	58y	W	Mass.	09 FEB 1868	Congressional
457	Dodrich, Elizabeth	35y	W	Ire.	28 JUN 1870	Mt. Olivet
235	Dodson, A.	62y	C	Md.	20 SEP 1866	Harmony
718	Dodson, Alexr.	3y	C	D.C.	11 SEP 1873	Beckett's
633	Dodson, D.S.	3m	C	U.S.	15 OCT 1872	Small Pox*
128	Dodson, Eliza	50y	C		26 SEP 1858	Foundry
447	Dodson, Elizabeth	92y	C	Va.	13 MAR 1870	Mt. Olivet
329	Dodson, George	1y	C	D.C.	08 JUL 1868	Moore's
334	Dodson, George W.	2y	C	D.C.	09 JUL 1868	Mt. Olivet
133	Dodson, Harriet	5y	C	D.C.	21 NOV 1858	Ebenezer
514	Dodson, John	7m	C	U.S.	02 MAR 1871	
611	Dodson, John	1y	C	U.S.	28 JUL 1872	
455	Dodson, John Henry	9m	C		10 MAY 1870	
553	Dodson, Jonathan, laborer	74y	C	Va.	08 JAN 1872	Washington
060	Dodson, Lucinda	40y	C	D.C.	14 OCT 1856	St. Matthews
710	Dodson, Margaret	7m	W	D.C.	04 AUG 1873	Harmony
079	Dodson, Mary	5m	C	D.C.	13 JUN 1857	St. Matthews

Page	Name	Age	Race	Birth	Death Date	Burial Ground
080	Dodson, Mary Jane	28y	C	D.C.*	21 JUN 1857	St. Matthews
187	Dodson, Robt. Whitely	4m	W	D.C.	09 AUG 1860	Congressional
332	Dodson, Susan Ann	10m	C	D.C.	09 JUL 1868	Mt. Olivet
412	Dodson, William, messenger	42y	C	D.C.	06 AUG 1869	Harmony
137	Dodson, [blank]		W		01 JAN 1859	Congressional
053	Dodson, [blank]	11m	W	D.C.	17 AUG 1856	Congressional
169	Dogan, James	42y	C	Md.	12 JAN 1860	Harmony
473	Dogans, Andrew	42y	C		02 AUG 1870	
490	Dogens, Susan, Mrs.	26y	C	D.C.	08 NOV 1870	Ebenezer
601	Doherty, Susan	4y	W	U.S.	04 MAY 1872	Mt. Olivet
765	Dohrearty, Julia	33y	W	Ire.	15 MAY 1874	
689	Dolan, Annie	24y	W	Ire.	22 MAY 1873	Mt. Olivet
779	Dolan, Emma Rose	7m	W	U.S.	07 JUL 1874	Holyrood
632	Dolan, Jas. P.	1y	W	U.S.	06 OCT 1872	
462	Dolan, Rebecca	22y	W	D.C.	21 JUL 1870	Glenwood
253	Doleman, James H., laborer	36y	W	Va.	17 FEB 1867	Ebenezer
645	Dolen, Susanna	43y	W		26 DEC 1872	Baltimore, Md.
454	Dolser, Mary	1y	W		28 MAY 1870	Mt. Olivet
118	Domminick, Bernard	3m	W		30 JUN 1858	Country
273	Donahu, James, laborer	80y	W	Ire.	24 SEP 1867	Mt. Olivet
425	Donahue, Bridget	45y	W	Ire.	12 NOV 1869	Mt. Olivet
765	Donahue, Patrick	77y	W	Ire.	14 MAY 1874	Mt. Olivet
536	Donald, John M., shoemaker	29y	W	Ire.	18 SEP 1871	Unknown
148	Donald, [blank]	Still	W	D.C.	14 MAY 1859	Congressional
273	Donaldson, Anna Mary	5m	W	D.C.	13 SEP 1867	Philadelphia, Pa.
297	Donaldson, Charles J.	10y	W	Pa.	27 FEB 1868	Philadelphia, Pa.
780	Donaldson, F.C.	49y	W	U.S.	29 JUL 1874	Oak Hill
035	Donaldson, G.H.	9m	W	D.C.	21 FEB 1856	Congressional
310	Donaldson, Geo., child of	2y	W		c.14 APR 1868	Mt. Olivet
735	Donaldson, George	37y	W	Ger.	10 DEC 1873	
612	Donaldson, Jas. E.	1y	W	U.S.	02 JUL 1872	
388	Donaldson, Katie	9y	W	D.C.	16 APR 1869	
224	Donaldson, Kendall	1y	C	D.C.	13 JUN 1866	Pr. Geo. Co., Md.
622a	Donaldson, Marg. A.	55y	W	U.S.	11 AUG 1872	
643	Donaldson, Mary	13y	W	U.S.	11 DEC 1872	Congressional
278	Donaldson, Mary, Mrs.	31y	W		05 OCT 1867	Glenwood
736	Donaldson, Willie E.	1m	W	U.S.	19 DEC 1873	Glenwood
771	Donders, Mary T.	7d	W	U.S.	13 JUN 1874	St. Marys
151	Donef, Frederick A.	15d	W	D.C.	17 JUN 1859	Prospect Hill
112	Donelly, Peter	55y	W	Ky.	30 APR 1858	Washington Asylum
216	Donelly, Thomas	40y	W	Ire.	24 MAR 1866	Mt. Olivet*
440	Donelly, William	2y	W		03 FEB 1870	Mt. Olivet
041	Donelson, Frances E.	9m	W	D.C.	07 APR 1856	Methodist, East
274	Donelson, George Benjamin	5m	W	D.C.	09 SEP 1867	Glenwood
765	Donigan, Patrick, civil engineer	43y	W	Ire.	08 MAY 1874	
016	Donlin, C.W.	1y	W	D.C.	24 JUL 1855	St. Peters
172	Donn, Gabriel T.	15y	W	D.C.	04 FEB 1860	
138	Donn, John C.	3y	W	D.C.	25 JAN 1859	Glenwood
240	Donn, Margaret S.	31y	W	Md.	01 OCT 1866	Glenwood
492	Donn, Orlanda H., painter	42y	W	D.C.	16 DEC 1870	Congressional
640	Donn, Thos. C.	6y	W	U.S.	26 DEC 1872	Small Pox*
690	Donnard, Nelly	8y	C	U.S.	18 MAY 1873	Small Pox
612	Donnelly, Cornelius	1y	W	U.S.	20 JUL 1872	
159	Donnelly, Easteranna	4m	W	D.C.	26 AUG 1859	Mt. Olivet
621	Donnelly, Elizabeth	3y	W	U.S.	13 AUG 1872	Mt. Olivet
123	Donnelly, James	7y	W	D.C.	03 JUL 1858	St. Patricks
360	Donnelly, Samuel J., Rev.	38y	W	Pa.	16 NOV 1868	Havre de Grace, Md.
044	Donogan, James	18y	W	Ire.	10 MAY 1856	St. Patricks

District of Columbia Interments (Index to Deaths), 1855-1874

Page	Name	Age	Race	Birth	Death Date	Burial Ground
432	Donogher, P.A.	10m	C	D.C.	31 DEC 1869	Washington Asylum
019	Donoghue, Michael, laborer	29y	W	Ire.	09 AUG 1855	St. Marys, Geo.
131	Donoghue, Teresa	29y	W		01 OCT 1858	Mt. Olivet
131	Donoho, Ann E.	6m	W		31 OCT 1858	St. Patricks
614	Donohoe, Ellen	7y	W	U.S.	30 JUL 1872	
541	Donohoe, Fannie	60y	W	Ire.	13 OCT 1871	Mt. Olivet
695	Donohoe, Harriet T.	17y	W	D.C.	06 JUN 1873	Glenwood
557	Donohoe, Michael, grocer	39y	W	Ire.	04 FEB 1872	Ebenezer
069	Donohue, Mary	5m	W	D.C.	21 JAN 1857	St. Patricks
332	Donohue, [blank]	1y	W	D.C.	23 JUL 1868	Mt. Olivet
354	Donovan, Agnes	24y	W	Pa.	23 OCT 1868	N.Y.
381	Donovan, Bridget, domestic	25y	W	Ire.	22 MAR 1869	Mt. Olivet
154	Donovan, Catharine, washerwoman	30y	W	Ire.	14 JUL 1859	
315	Donovan, D., infant of	1d	W		c.26 MAY 1868	Mt. Olivet
502	Donovan, Dennis, laborer	63y	W	Ire.	08 JAN 1871	Mt. Olivet*
021	Donovan, Johanna	7m	W	D.C.	07 AUG 1855	St. Patricks
221	Donovan, Margaret	11m	W	D.C.	23 MAY 1866	Mt. Olivet
502	Donovan, Nancy	48y	W	Ire.	12 JAN 1871	Mt. Olivet
345	Donovan, Patrick	7m	W	D.C.	14 AUG 1868	Mt. Olivet
016	Donovan, Timothy, laborer	50y	W	Ire.	30 JUL 1855	St. Patricks
381	Donoyhue, Dennis, laborer	60y	W	Ire.	22 MAR 1869	Mt. Olivet
779	Doody, Margaret	55y	W	Ire.	21 JUL 1874	Mt. Olivet
483	Dooley, Julia	1y	W	D.C.	22 OCT 1870	Mt. Olivet
341	Doon, James T.	9y	W	D.C.	16 AUG 1868	Congressional
664	Dooney, Jas. T.	unk.	W	U.S.	08 JAN 1873	Small Pox*
123	Dooyd, Ellen	8m	W	D.C.	22 JUL 1858	St. Peters
602	Dorain, Julia	79y	W	Eng.	01 MAY 1872	St. Patricks
252	Doran, Francis W.	7d	W	D.C.	23 FEB 1867	Mt. Olivet
707	Doran, [blank]	14m	W	D.C.	15 JUL 1873	Mt. Olivet
713	Dorcey, Wm.	8m	W	D.C.	23 AUG 1873	Md.
753	Dorian, Thomas H.	43y	C	U.S.	16 MAR 1874	Glenwood
114	Dorian, William	1y	W	D.C.	31 MAY 1858	Congressional
593	Dority, James	2d	W	D.C.	10 APR 1872	
175	Dorman, Albert, Dr.	89y	W	Fra.	19 MAR 1860	
274	Dorman, Anthony, carpenter	56y	W	N.Y.	04 SEP 1867	Oak Hill
119	Dorr, Frank	2y	W	D.C.	14 JUN 1858	Congressional*
214	Dorrant, John, piano tuner	45y	W	Ger.	03 MAR 1866	Mt. Olivet
771	Dorsch, Michael	7d	W	U.S.	22 JUN 1874	
692	Dorsett, Fielder	79y	W	Md.	30 MAY 1873	Congressional
667	Dorsett, Fielder Russell, printer	43y	W	U.S.	13 FEB 1873	Congressional
340	Dorsett, Ida L.	2y	W	D.C.	23 AUG 1868	Congressional
302	Dorsett, James H.	9d	C	D.C.	06 MAR 1868	Western
068	Dorsett, James M., clerk	38y	W	Va.	08 JAN 1857	Congressional
090	Dorsett, [James]	1y	W	D.C.	08 SEP 1857	Congressional*
489	Dorsey, Ann	61y	W	Md.	16 NOV 1870	Lisbon, Hwd. Co., Md.
443	Dorsey, Ann	26y	C	Md.	20 FEB 1870	Washington Asylum
250	Dorsey, Ann	99y	C		10 JAN 1867	Young Mens
018	Dorsey, Ann, paper waiter	25y	C	Va.	11 AUG 1855	Young Mens
316	Dorsey, Anna	10y	C	Md.	09 MAY 1868	Harmony
509	Dorsey, Anne R.	10m	C	D.C.	27 FEB 1871	Washington Asylum
041	Dorsey, Child of Mary		W	D.C.	04 APR 1856	Foundry
708	Dorsey, Daniel	48y	C	Va.	30 JUL 1873	Washington Asylum
195	Dorsey, Harriet	30y	C		20 DEC 1860	Young Mens
625	Dorsey, Ida	2y	C	U.S.	02 OCT 1872	
090	Dorsey, Ida Louisa	11m	W	D.C.*	10 SEP 1857	Congressional
681	Dorsey, James	57y	C	U.S.	20 APR 1873	Harmony
117	Dorsey, James	9m	C		26 JUN 1858	Young Mens
745	Dorsey, John	45y	C	U.S.	03 JAN 1874	

Page	Name	Age	Race	Birth	Death Date	Burial Ground
590	Dorsey, John	42y	C	Md.	01 APR 1872	Young Mens
105	Dorsey, John B., clerk	54y	W	Md.	16 FEB 1858	Oak Hill
489	Dorsey, John E., waiter	21y	C	Md.	05 NOV 1870	Ebenezer
223	Dorsey, John T.	14d	C	D.C.	09 JUN 1866	Beckett's
336	Dorsey, M.H.	10m	C	D.C.	20 AUG 1868	Ebenezer
625	Dorsey, Mary	1y	C	U.S.	12 SEP 1872	
687	Dorsey, Mary	40y	C	U.S.	05 MAY 1873	Washington Asylum
403	Dorsey, Mary Ann E., Mrs.?	9m	C	D.C.	17 JUL 1869	Harmony
028	Dorsey, Mary F.	5y	W	Md.	03 OCT 1855	Baltimore, Md.
264	Dorsey, Mary Jane	7d			04 JUL 1867	Beckett's
513	Dorsey, Presley W.	58y	W	U.S.	28 MAR 1871	Oak Hill
753	Dorsey, Richard, infant of	1y	C	U.S.	18 MAR 1874	
404	Dorsey, Sarah Jane	8m	C	D.C.	17 JUL 1869	
765	Dorsey, Soffa	5m	W	U.S.	03 MAY 1874	Oberlin, Ohio
708	Dorsey, Susan F.	7m	W	Va.	10 JUL 1873	
334	Dorsey, Tacy Frances, Mrs.	29y	C		25 JUL 1868	
485	Dorsey, Tilman, infant of	2d	C	D.C.	18 OCT 1870	Beckett's
703	Dorsey, Warren	22y	C		19 JUL 1873	Beckett's
545	Dorsey, [blank]	20y	C	D.C.	14 NOV 1871	Ebenezer
120	Dorsey, [blank]	Still	W		01 JUL 1858	Glenwood
605	Dorum, Richd., druggist	37y	W	Va.	07 JUN 1872	Va.
340	Doubleday, Charlotte	83y	W	Eng.	17 AUG 1868	Congressional
116	Doudall, James F.	9m	W	D.C.	17 JUN 1858	Alabama
333	Dougherty, Charles H.	2m	W	D.C.	10 JUL 1868	Congressional
263	Dougherty, Edward C.	1y	W		04 JUN 1867	Glenwood
318	Dougherty, Edwd. J., marine	22y	W	Ire.	03 JUN 1868	Congressional
221	Dougherty, Elizabeth	41y	W	Md.	24 MAY 1866	Baltimore, Md.
158	Dougherty, Elizabeth	10m	W	D.C.	22 AUG 1859	Glenwood
351	Dougherty, Elizabeth F.	1y	W	D.C.	16 SEP 1868	Methodist
176	Dougherty, Ellen	30y	W	Ire.	14 APR 1860	Mt. Olivet
014	Dougherty, Hugh	3m	W	D.C.	29 JUL 1855	German, E.K.
369	Dougherty, John, clerk	37y	W	N.Y.	26 JAN 1869	Congressional
314	Dougherty, Mary A.	39y	W	Md.	15 MAY 1868	Congressional
039	Dougherty, Mary J.	19y	W	D.C.	05 MAR 1856	Glenwood
371	Dougherty, William C., gov. clerk	25y	W	Md.	11 JAN 1869	Glenwood
142	Dougherty, [blank]	81y	W	Ire.	08 FEB 1859	Mt. Olivet
031	Doughery, Alfred S., clerk 5th aud.	43y	W	Pa.	06 DEC 1855	Glenwood
463	Doughtery, [blank]		W		13 JUL 1870	Mt. Olivet
557	Doughty, Eunice	77y	W	U.S.	01 FEB 1872	Congressional
241	Douglas, Ann	65y	W	D.C.	27 OCT 1866	Congressional
285	Douglas, Annie V.	3m	W	D.C.	26 DEC 1867	Oak Hill
258	Douglas, Florence M.	2m	W	D.C.	01 APR 1867	Glenwood
427	Douglas, Henry	1m	C	D.C.	12 NOV 1869	Washington Asylum
718	Douglas, Jane, laundress	40y	C	D.C.	13 SEP 1873	Beckett's
703	Douglas, Maria	52y	C	D.C.	30 JUL 1873	Beckett's
627	Douglas, Wm.	16y	C	U.S.	29 SEP 1872	
125	Douglas, Wm. Kirby	6y	W	D.C.	26 AUG 1858	Congressional
746	Douglass, Charles	1m	W	U.S.	08 FEB 1874	Mt. Olivet*
202	Douglass, Daniel, clerk	36y	W	D.C.	23 APR 1861	Congressional
181	Douglass, Ellen	8m	W	D.C.	04 JUN 1860	Mt. Olivet
584	Douglass, George	6y	C	D.C.	05 MAR 1872	Harmony
362	Douglass, George N.	7m	W	D.C.	24 NOV 1868	Glenwood
137	Douglass, Henry, laborer	40y	C		08 JAN 1859	St. Patricks
335	Douglass, Mathew	3y	C	D.C.	26 JUL 1868	
199	Douglass, Mrs., colored boy of	14y	C		10 FEB 1861	Western
449	Douglass, Priscilla I.	67y	W		21 APR 1870	Congressional
603	Douglass, R.E.	8m	W	D.C.	27 JUN 1872	Congressional
746	Douglass, Sarah	30y	W	Ire.	02 FEB 1874	Washington Asylum

Page	Name	Age	Race	Birth	Death Date	Burial Ground
535	Douglass, Wm.	1y	C	D.C.	05 SEP 1871	
157	Douglass, [blank]	6m	C	D.C.	11 AUG 1859	Western
124	Dounay, Mary Ann	7m	W	D.C.	11 AUG 1858	St. Patricks
212	Douty, W.	1y	W	D.C.	08 FEB 1866	Mt. Olivet
339	Dove, Elenora	9m	W	D.C.	05 AUG 1868	Glenwood
609	Dove, Elizabeth	6m	C	U.S.	10 JUN 1872	
080	Dove, Elizabeth	88y	W	Md.	18 JUN 1857	Congressional
403	Dove, Frank W.	1y	W	D.C.	01 JUL 1869	Methodist
522	Dove, George Clemm	6m	W	D.C.	10 JUN 1871	Methodist
744	Dove, George McCauley, Dr.	56y	W	U.S.	30 JAN 1874	Congressional
151	Dove, Jilson, blacksmith	39y	W	Va.	15 JUN 1859	Congressional
024	Dove, John F.	2m	W	D.C.	07 SEP 1855	Potters Field
082	Dove, John G.	70y	W	Md.	05 JUL 1857	St. Patricks
227	Dove, Joseph	1y			07 JUL 1866	Young Mens
113	Dove, Margaret	72y	W	Conn.	06 MAY 1858	Congressional
189	Dove, Mary Ann	1d	W	D.C.	18 SEP 1860	Congressional
667	Dove, Mrs.	70y	W	U.S.	14 FEB 1873	Holmead
623	Dove, R.	25y	W	U.S.	07 JUL 1872	Presbyterian
058	Dove, Robert	2y	W	D.C.	15 SEP 1856	Glenwood
283	Dove, William Francis	6m	W	D.C.	05 NOV 1867	Methodist
070	Dover, Lucinda	65y	C	Va.*	06 FEB 1857	Harmony
067	Dover, Mary M.	3d	C	D.C.	29 DEC 1856	St. Matthews
001	Dovilliers, [Eugene]	7m		D.C.	10 JAN 1855	Congressional
640	Dow, Helen	3m	C	U.S.	26 DEC 1872	Small Pox*
425	Dowd, Daniel, farmer	57y	W	Ire.	24 NOV 1869	Mt. Olivet
621	Dowden, John	8m	W	U.S.	30 AUG 1872	St. Marys
519	Dowdy, John	4y	C	U.S.	16 MAY 1871	
467	Dowell, David	6m	W	D.C.	01 JUL 1870	Congressional
385	Dowell, Estelle	2y	W	D.C.	19 APR 1869	Congressional
379	Dowell, Frank Carlisle	4y	W		01 MAR 1869	Congressional
323	Dowell, Mary E.	1y	W	D.C.	31 JUL 1868	Mt. Olivet
643	Dowell, Viola	18m	W	U.S.	12 DEC 1872	Congressional
092	Dower, Mary	25y	W	Ire.	27 SEP 1857	St. Peters
421	Dowling, Catharine West	53y	W	Va.	07 OCT 1869	Mt. Olivet
780	Dowling, Loretta J.	3y	W	U.S.	25 JUL 1874	Oak Hill
214	Dowling, Mary	36y	W	Ire.	05 MAR 1866	Philadelphia, Pa.
779	Dowling, Mary F.	29y	W	U.S.	17 JUL 1874	Oak Hill
327	Dowling, Thomas	6m	W	D.C.	04 JUL 1868	Mt. Olivet
101	Downer, Joel, carpenter	74y	W		12 JAN 1858	Glenwood/Rock Creek
691	Downes, John	6y	W	U.S.	10 MAY 1873	Small Pox*
338	Downey, Bridget	8m	W		31 AUG 1868	Mt. Olivet
441	Downey, Catharina	2y	W		07 FEB 1870	Mt. Olivet
219	Downey, Catherine, housekeeper	55y	W	Ire.	22 APR 1866	Mt. Olivet
141	Downey, Charles	12d	W	D.C.	19 FEB 1859	Methodist
142	Downey, Edward	3y	W	Md.	13 FEB 1859	St. Patricks (vault)
476	Downey, Elizabeth	74y	W	Md.	25 SEP 1870	Congressional
462	Downey, Estella	5m	W	D.C.	08 JUL 1870	Congressional
680	Downey, Hiram Lee	1m	W	U.S.	08 APR 1873	Congressional*
044	Downey, John, blacksmith	21y	W	Va.	20 MAY 1856	Congressional
734	Downey, Mary H.	1y	W	U.S.	01 DEC 1873	Congressional
341	Downey, Thomas W.	9d	W	D.C.	10 AUG 1868	Congressional
315	Downey, Timothy	45y	W		c.13 MAY 1868	Mt. Olivet
324	Downey, Timothy, Mrs.	49y	W	Ire.	12 JUL 1868	Mt. Olivet
053	Downey, William, child of				05 AUG 1856	Methodist
180	Downey, Wm.	3m	W	D.C.	28 MAY 1860	Methodist
470	Downey, [blank]	Still	W	D.C.	10 AUG 1870	Congressional
103	Downing, Clay	3y	W	D.C.	29 JAN 1858	St. Matthews
378	Downing, Cora Estelle	6y	W	D.C.	12 FEB 1869	Glenwood

District of Columbia Interments (Index to Deaths), 1855-1874

Page	Name	Age	Race	Birth	Death Date	Burial Ground
272	Downing, Eda	11m	C		30 AUG 1867	Freedmen's Bureau
758	Downing, Emma J.	2y	W	U.S.	07 APR 1874	Glenwood
518	Downing, Geo. W., blacksmith	28y	W	D.C.	02 MAY 1871	Methodist
169	Downing, Georgiana	3y	W	D.C.	10 JAN 1860	
380	Downing, Henry Sipes	10m	W		22 MAR 1869	
507	Downing, Jas. P.	4y	W	D.C.	24 FEB 1871	Glenwood
378	Downing, John Thomas	1m	W	D.C.	20 FEB 1869	Mt. Olivet
368	Downing, Joseph M.	46y	W	D.C.	24 DEC 1868	Glenwood
310	Downing, Margaret	12y	W		c.27 APR 1868	Mt. Olivet
612	Downing, Mary A.	9m	W	U.S.	22 JUL 1872	
136	Downing, Mrs.	65y	W	Ire.	08 DEC 1858	Mt. Olivet
323	Downing, Stephen B.	5m	W	D.C.	13 JUL 1868	Mt. Olivet*
159	Downing, Thos. Foster	5m	W	D.C.	25 AUG 1859	Glenwood
138	Downing, William	2y	W	D.C.	08 JAN 1859	Mt. Olivet
545	Downs, Ann	66y	W	U.S.	16 NOV 1871	Glenwood
187	Downs, Benjamin J.	24y	W	Md.	04 AUG 1860	Glenwood
407	Downs, George	1y	W		10 AUG 1869	Congressional
658	Downs, George, collector	50y	W	U.S.	03 JAN 1873	
105	Downs, Jane	1y	W	D.C.	22 FEB 1858	Congressional
163	Downs, Joseph I., carpenter	24y	W	Va.	11 OCT 1859	Wheeling, Va.
148	Downs, Julia	7m	W	D.C.	05 MAY 1859	Methodist
153	Downs, Timothy, laborer	30y	W	Ire.	03 JUL 1859	Mt. Olivet
322	Doxan, Cath. Rosalia	3m	W	D.C.	21 JUN 1868	Mt. Olivet
714	Doyle, Agnes	6m	W	D.C.	31 AUG 1873	Mt. Olivet
471	Doyle, Andrew	1y	W	D.C.	04 AUG 1870	Congressional
220	Doyle, Bridget	20y	W	Ire.	01 MAY 1866	Mt. Olivet
122	Doyle, Bridget	5y	W	D.C.	25 JUL 1858	St. Patricks
550	Doyle, Francis M., policeman	38y	W	Ire.	29 DEC 1871	Congressional
410	Doyle, Joseph P.	9m	W		20 AUG 1869	Mt. Olivet*
592	Doyle, Kate	1m	W	U.S.	26 APR 1872	Mt. Olivet
752	Doyle, Mary	70y	C	U.S.	02 MAR 1874	
620	Doyle, Mary	58y	W	Ire.	12 AUG 1872	Mt. Olivet
463	Doyle, Michael, driver	48y	W	Ire.	18 JUL 1870	Baltimore, Md.
325	Doyle, Michael H.	30d	W	D.C.	10 JUL 1868	Congressional
294	Doyle, Michael, soldier USA	39y	W	Ire.	25 FEB 1868	Mt. Olivet*
165	Dozier, Mary, servant	27y	C	U.S.	19 NOV 1859	Harmony
614	Draeger, Elise L.	4y	W	U.S.	09 JUL 1872	
613	Draeger, Frank M.	1y	W	U.S.	06 JUL 1872	
322	Draine, Mary	18y	W	D.C.	13 JUN 1868	Mt. Olivet
074	Drake, John B.	25d	W	D.C.	23 MAR 1857	St. Patricks
140	Draly, Josephine	11m	W	D.C.	03 FEB 1859	German
759	Drane, Mary C.S.	7m	W	U.S.	27 APR 1874	Mt. Olivet
201	Drane, Tho.	6m	W	D.C.	16 MAR 1861	Mt. Olivet
097	Dranes, Julia Ann	40y	W		19 NOV 1857	Foundry
075	Draper, William B., merchant	27y	W	N.Y.	01 APR 1857	
506	Drennan, Thos., clerk	49y	W		14 FEB 1871	Congressional
779	Drew, Harry	10m	W	U.S.	16 JUL 1874	Glenwood
771	Drew, John F.	3m	C	U.S.	25 JUN 1874	Young Mens
172	Drew, Michael	41y	W	Ire.	04 FEB 1860	Mt. Holly
255	Drew, Michael, laborer	73y	W	Ire.	11 MAR 1867	Mt. Olivet
383	Drew, Rebecca	2y	C		27 MAR 1869	Harmony
680	Drexler, Constantine, taxidermist	44y	W	Ger.	03 APR 1873	
492	Dreyer, Dorethia	45y	W	Ger.	25 DEC 1870	Prospect Hill
336	Dreyfuss, Harry	6m	W	D.C.*	04 AUG 1868	Washington Hebrew
220	Drinkard, Samuel G.	17y	W	D.C.	10 MAY 1866	Oak Hill
356	Driscol, Mary	35y	W	Va.	06 OCT 1868	Glenwood
395	Driscole, Jeremiah, gardener	27y	W	Ire.	08 JUN 1869	Mt. Olivet
478	Driscoll, Catharine, school girl	11y		Ire.	07 SEP 1870	Mt. Olivet

Page	Name	Age	Race	Birth	Death Date	Burial Ground
718	Driscoll, James	66y	W	Ire.	08 SEP 1873	Mt. Olivet
645	Driscoll, Jane	15y	W	U.S.	30 DEC 1872	Mt. Olivet
077	Driscoll, Julia	19y	W		03 MAY 1857	St. Patricks
320	Driscoll, Mary	61y	W	Ire.	01 JUN 1868	Mt. Olivet
401	Driscoll, Mary	20y	W	Ire.	18 JUL 1869	Mt. Olivet
376	Driscoll, Michael	3y	W		14 FEB 1869	Mt. Olivet
064	Driskins, [blank]	2y	W	D.C.	19 NOV 1856	St. Peters
694	Driver, Ann, Mrs.	73y	W	Eng.	14 JUN 1873	Mt. Moriah, Phila.
765	Driver, C.R., dress maker	38y	W	U.S.	12 MAY 1874	Congressional
631	Driver, F.	48y	C	U.S.	14 OCT 1872	
343	Driver, George	2m	W	D.C.	24 AUG 1868	Glenwood
230	Driver, H.E.	18y			25 JUL 1866	Western
325	Driver, John W.	7y	W	Va.	20 JUL 1868	Congressional
557	Driver, Polly	97y	C	Va.	02 FEB 1872	Ebenezer
362	Driver, Robert	25y	C	Va.	23 NOV 1868	
465	Driver, Stacey	2y	C	Md.	23 JUL 1870	Mt. Olivet
765	Driver, William L.	6y	W	U.S.	29 MAY 1874	Congressional
400	Droney, Thomas	1y	W	U.S.	17 JUL 1869	Mt. Olivet
411	Drowns, Louisa Marion	7m	W		23 AUG 1869	Glenwood
080	Drudge, George	38y	W		22 JUN 1857	St. Peters
017	Druge, George	11m	W	D.C.	24 JUL 1855	Holmead
779	Drummond, Nellie	5m	W	U.S.	01 JUL 1874	Oak Hill
218	Drunning, Mary, Mrs.	73y	W	Md.	24 APR 1866	Glenwood
540	Drury, James	4d	W	D.C.	02 OCT 1871	Mt. Olivet
212	Drury, Louisa	38y	W	D.C.	09 FEB 1866	Mt. Olivet*
256	Drury, Mary	72y	W	Eng.	28 MAR 1867	Mt. Olivet*
267	Drury, [blank]	1y	W	D.C.	31 JUL 1867	Congressional
431	Dryer, Henry, tinner	17y	W		06 DEC 1869	Prospect Hill
553	Duantier, G.C.	13d	W	D.C.	09 JAN 1872	Prospect Hill
469	Dubant, Geo. G., eating saloon kpr.	33y	W	D.C.	09 AUG 1870	Mt. Olivet
581	Dubant, Henry, bookbinder	34y	W	D.C.	15 FEB 1872	Mt. Olivet
411	Dubant, Henry, child of	Still	W		13 AUG 1869	Mt. Olivet
727	Dubary, Isaac, laborer	66y	B	U.S.	11 OCT 1873	
067	Dubois, John Robbins	1y	W	Pa.	29 DEC 1856	Congressional
426	Ducheux, Clesimus	43y	W	Fra.	10 NOV 1869	Mt. Olivet
431	Ducket, Daniel	80y	C	Md.	19 DEC 1869	Western
454	Ducket, Georgiana	16y	C	Md.	16 MAY 1870	Washington Asylum
544	Ducket, Willie	10y	C	D.C.	01 NOV 1871	
771	Duckett, Harriet, house servant	85y	C	U.S.	12 JUN 1874	Young Mens
583	Duckett, Judson, laborer	65y	C	Va.	28 FEB 1872	Washington
152	Duckett, Mary	1y	W	D.C.	28 JUN 1859	Congressional
446	Duckett, Oleria	Still	C	D.C.	03 MAR 1870	Washington Asylum
300	Dudley, Ann	18y	C	Va.	15 MAR 1868	Alms House
238	Dudley, Elzey	3d	W	D.C.	29 SEP 1866	Congressional
155	Dudley, Irene	12d	W	D.C.	25 JUL 1859	Foundry
661	Dudley, Joseph, clerk	55y	W	U.S.	24 JAN 1873	Yarmouth, Mass.
471	Dudley, Mary C.	3m	W	D.C.	23 AUG 1870	Congressional
462	Dudley, Matilda A.	26y	W	D.C.	07 JUL 1870	Congressional
765	Dudley, Stephen A.	38y	W	U.S.	31 MAY 1874	Mt. Olivet
747	Dudly, Joseph T., carpenter	42y	W	U.S.	27 FEB 1874	Congressional*
752	Dudman, Ellen A.	32y	W	U.S.	12 MAR 1874	Oak Hill
266	Duehay, Harrie S.	1y	W	D.C.	09 JUL 1867	Oak Hill
104	Duerocks, Henry	3y	W	D.C.	12 FEB 1858	German
502	Duff, Eliza	37y	W	Pa.	31 JAN 1871	Congressional
623	Duffin, J.	3y	C	U.S.	09 AUG 1872	Va.
088	Duffy, Edmund F.	5y	W	D.C.	26 AUG 1857	Glenwood
310	Duffy, Ellen, Mrs.	37y	W		c.16 APR 1868	Mt. Olivet
538	Duffy, Fannie C.	4y	W	D.C.	26 SEP 1871	Glenwood

District of Columbia Interments (Index to Deaths), 1855-1874

Page	Name	Age	Race	Birth	Death Date	Burial Ground
246	Duffy, Patrick				26 DEC 1866	Mt. Olivet
143	Duffy, Patrick, laborer	33y	W	Ire.	10 MAR 1859	Mt. Olivet
087	Duffy, Rebecca Jane	32y	W	Md.	10 AUG 1857	Carroll Chapel
437	Duffy, T.A., infant of	Still	W		06 JAN 1870	Mt. Olivet
091	Duglis, Sophia E.	3y	W	D.C.	16 SEP 1857	Glenwood
030	Dulaney, Adam, huckster	48y	C		30 NOV 1855	Harmony
157	Dulaney, Alfred	1m	C	D.C.	04 AUG 1859	Foundry
066	Dulaney, Bladen, com. USN	63y	W	Va.	26 DEC 1856	Rock Creek
350	Dulaney, Caleb, coachman	23y	C	D.C.	28 SEP 1868	Harmony
101	Dulaney, Margaret	70y	W	Ire.	12 JAN 1858	St. Patricks
425	Dulaney, Mary Eliza	3m	W		12 NOV 1869	Congressional
176	DuLaney, Wm. H., porter	26y	C	D.C.	15 APR 1860	Harmony
596	Dulany, E.A.	66y	W	U.S.	15 APR 1872	
158	Dulany, John	1m	C	D.C.	13 AUG 1859	Foundry
668	Dulany, William	32y	C	U.S.	16 FEB 1873	Young Mens
161	Duley, Robert, tailor	32y	W		16 SEP 1859	Western
771	Duley, Wesley, farmer	79y	W	U.S.	10 JUN 1874	Oak Hill
133	Dulin, Emma	6y	W	D.C.	26 NOV 1858	Congressional
134	Dulin, Emma I.	6y	W	D.C.	28 NOV 1858	Congressional
517	Dulin, John, laborer	38y	W	Ire.	09 APR 1871	Holly Wood
102	Dulin, Mary	69y	W	Va.	19 JAN 1858	Congressional
400	Dulmare, John William	5m	W		— JUL 1869	Prospect Hill
624	Duly, Michael, plumber	17y	W	U.S.	25 SEP 1872	
084	Dumfrey, Julia		W	Ire.	25 JUL 1857	St. Patricks
223	Dummick, Elizabeth J.	6m	W	D.C.	06 JUN 1866	Mt. Olivet
181	Dumminski, Alexander, laborer	55y	W	Pol.	03 JUN 1860	St. Marys
616a	Dun, Anna	55y	W	D.C.	05 JUL 1872	Congressional
266	Dunan, Charles W.	1y	W	D.C.	29 JUL 1867	Glenwood
097	Dunawin, Mary E.	4y	W	D.C.	22 NOV 1857	St. Patricks
247	Dunbar, Saml., laborer	46y	C	D.C.	07 DEC 1866	Alms House
177	Duncan, Elizabeth	3m	W	D.C.	27 APR 1860	Congressional
660	Duncan, George	100y	C	U.S.	20 JAN 1873	Washington Asylum
241	Duncan, Nelson				14 OCT 1866	
177	Duncan, Stephen, clerk	73y	W	N.J.	17 APR 1860	Oak Hill
519	Duncanson, Ida	32y	W	D.C.	15 MAY 1871	Congressional*
711	Duncanson, J.M.	18m	W	D.C.	10 AUG 1873	Congressional*
111	Duncanson, John A.M., miller	54y	W	D.C.	15 APR 1858	Congressional
197	Dundas, William H., 2nd apt. port	68y	W	Va.	24 JAN 1861	Congressional
589	Dundee, Hester V.	5y	W	D.C.	23 MAR 1872	
063	Dungan, James, iron worker	41y	W	N.Y.	22 NOV 1856	N.Y.
239	Dunigan, Ellen				— OCT 1866	Mt. Olivet
321	Dunigan, Ellen	28y	W	Ire.	05 JUN 1868	Mt. Olivet
268	Dunington, Henry W.	7m	W	D.C.	04 AUG 1867	Congressional
779	Dunjie, Jno. W.	4m	C	U.S.	09 JUL 1874	Winchester, Va.
555	Dunkins, Wm.	10y	W	D.C.	25 JAN 1872	Mt. Olivet
035	Dunkinson, Infant	Still	W		25 FEB 1856	Congressional
756	Dunlap, Carl, laborer	26y	C	P.R.	16 MAR 1874	
328	Dunlap, Edward	1y	C	D.C.	12 JUL 1868	Western
637	Dunlap, Geo. W.	11m	C	U.S.	17 NOV 1872	Holmead
033	Dunlap, William, laborer	40y	W	Ire.	14 JAN 1856	Foundry
779	Dunlass, Jas. & Eliz., infant of	5d	C	U.S.	22 JUL 1874	Young Mens
125	Dunlop, Geo. W.	62y	C	Va.	20 AUG 1858	Harmony
066	Dunlop, James H.M., barber	25y	C	D.C.	18 DEC 1856	Harmony
600	Dunlop, James, lawyer	79y	W	U.S.	06 MAY 1872	Oak Hill
067	Dunlop, Maria Ann	17y	C		30 DEC 1856	Ebenezer
633	Dunlop, W.	41y	C	U.S.	31 OCT 1872	Small Pox*
664	Dunmore, John	45y	C	U.S.	15 JAN 1873	Small Pox*
494	Dunmore, P., child of	1d	C	D.C.	27 DEC 1870	Ebenezer

Page	Name	Age	Race	Birth	Death Date	Burial Ground
664	Dunmore, Walter	45y	C	U.S.	09 JAN 1873	Small Pox*
304	Dunn, Catherine	45y	W	Ire.	23 MAR 1868	Congressional
305	Dunn, Daniel	45y	W		c.17 MAR 1868	Mt. Olivet
347	Dunn, Edith V.	2y	W	D.C.	11 SEP 1868	Congressional
191	Dunn, Edwd., child of	Still	W	D.C.	02 OCT 1860	Methodist
419	Dunn, James	4y	W		14 OCT 1869	Congressional
193	Dunn, James, laborer	40y	W	Ire.	20 NOV 1860	
726	Dunn, Margaret	57y	W	Ire.	25 OCT 1873	
046	Dunn, Mary	72y	W		08 JUN 1856	Congressional
536	Dunn, Robt. A.L.	1y	W	D.C.	17 SEP 1871	Congressional
614	Dunn, Wm. E.	26y	W	U.S.	03 JUL 1872	
086	Dunnawin, William, carpenter	67y	W	Md.	03 AUG 1857	St. Patricks
150	Dunne, Lizzie	6y	W	D.C.	11 JUN 1859	Mt. Olivet
054	Dunne, Michael	27y	W	Ire.	19 AUG 1856	Washington Asylum
373	Dunwood, Anna	22y	C		22 JAN 1869	Union
705	Duran, Lewis, clerk	47y	W	Md.	24 JUL 1873	
142	Durand, Mary E.F.	7y	C	D.C.	22 FEB 1859	Colored
703	Durch, Harriet, chambermaid	25y	C	D.C.	11 JUL 1873	Mt. Pleasant
519	Durfer, Anna	24y	W	D.C.*	14 MAY 1871	Oak Hill
601	Durity, Alice B.	12y	W	U.S.	23 MAY 1872	Glenwood
601	Durity, Anna	86y	W	U.S.	16 MAY 1872	Glenwood
426	Durity, Rebecca M.	38y	W		02 NOV 1869	Glenwood
401	Durkin, Kate	10m	W		31 JUL 1869	Mt. Olivet
488	Dury, Cate	4m	W		18 NOV 1870	Mt. Olivet
771	Dury, Ellen	30y	W	U.S.	16 JUN 1874	Mt. Olivet
475	Duskins, Celia	50y	C	Md.	05 SEP 1870	Freedmen's Hospital
451	Dutch, Catharine	95y	C	Md.	28 APR 1870	Carroll's Church
703	Dutch, Harriet E., chambermaid	25½y	C	D.C.	11 JUL 1873	Mt. Pleasant
172	Dutch, Henry	12y	C	D.C.	04 FEB 1860	Western
431	Dutch, Hillary, waiter		C		06 DEC 1869	
723	Dutch, Lottie	9d	B	D.C.	04 OCT 1873	Mt. Pleasant
454	Dutch, Lucy, laundress	55y	C	Md.	01 MAY 1870	Union
055	Dutch, [blank]	1y	C	D.C.	08 AUG 1856	Western
292a	Duval, Christiana E.		W	Va.*	10 FEB 1868	Catholic
326	Duval, James	8m	W	D.C.	07 JUL 1868	Congressional
675	Duval, Jno. W., blacksmith	35y	W	U.S.	22 MAR 1873	Glenwood
498	Duval, Mary, pauper	1d	B	D.C.	13 JAN 1871	Washington Asylum
724	Duvall, Alice Rose	5y	W	D.C.	15 OCT 1873	Glenwood
372	Duvall, Bettie Hays	10y	C	D.C.	24 JAN 1869	
309	Duvall, Enoch, duvall	64y	W	Md.	06 APR 1868	Pr. Geo. Co., Md.
086	Duvall, George	3y	W		07 AUG 1857	Congressional
453	Duvall, Helen	10m	W		10 MAY 1870	Congressional
780	Duvall, John	16m	C	U.S.	30 JUL 1874	
215	Duvall, John	7m	W		13 MAR 1866	Western
006	Duvall, John P., sexton Luth. Ch.	64y	W	Va.*	03 APR 1855	Foundry
391	Duvall, Laura V.	1y	W		13 MAY 1869	Glenwood
114	Duvall, Mary	42y	W	Md.	23 MAY 1858	Congressional
133	Duvall, Mary A.	1y	W	Va.*	23 NOV 1858	Alexandria, Va.
262	Duvall, Mary A.	53y	W	Md.	27 JUN 1867	Congressional
600	Duvall, Mary E.	3y	W	U.S.	12 MAY 1872	Glenwood
216	Duvall, Mr.		W		21 MAR 1866	Western
493	Duvall, Rosa	21y	W	D.C.	27 DEC 1870	Congressional
201	Duvall, Sarah	83y	W	Md.	31 MAR 1861	Pr. Geo. Co., Md.
487	Duvall, Washington, block maker	76y	W	Md.	29 NOV 1870	Congressional
461	Duvall, Will. A.	4m	W	D.C.	10 JUL 1870	Congressional
488	Duvall, Zach	49y	W		25 NOV 1870	Annapolis, Md.
439	Duvall, [blank]	2y	W		07 FEB 1870	Congressional
215	Duvant, Henry, child of	6m	W	D.C.	19 MAR 1866	Congressional

District of Columbia Interments (Index to Deaths), 1855-1874

Page	Name	Age	Race	Birth	Death Date	Burial Ground
274	Duvaul, Mrs. [Eliza]		W		28 SEP 1867	Congressional*
054	Duys, Mary		C		14 AUG 1856	Harmony
462	Dwyer, Frank	19d	W		22 JUL 1870	Mt. Olivet
238	Dwyer, [blank]	5m	W	D.C.	30 SEP 1866	
580	Dyar, Mary, cook	28y	W	D.C.	09 FEB 1872	Young Mens
385	Dye, John, grocer	28y	W	Va.	11 APR 1869	Congressional
765	Dyer, A.B., Gen. USA	59y	W	U.S.	20 APR 1874	Oak Hill/Arlington
341	Dyer, Albert P.	11y	W	D.C.	09 AUG 1868	Congressional
250	Dyer, Edward, merchant		W	Md.	27 JAN 1867	Mt. Olivet
241	Dyer, Henry	23y	W	Va.	18 OCT 1866	Va.
262	Dyer, Henson, laborer	64y	C	Va.	19 JUN 1867	Alexandria, Va.
470	Dyer, Joseph T.	9m	W	D.C.	16 AUG 1870	Congressional
555	Dyer, Maria F.	47y	W		28 JAN 1872	Congressional
535	Dyer, Mary E.	1y	C		07 SEP 1871	Mt. Olivet
120	Dyer, Mary Martha	1y	W	D.C.	05 JUL 1858	St. Patricks
409	Dyer, Mrs.	80y	C	Va.	03 AUG 1869	Young Mens
234	Dyer, Robert	10m	C	D.C.	08 SEP 1866	Mt. Olivet
769	Dyer, Sandy	17y	C	U.S.	02 MAY 1874	
457	Dyer, Thos. Dexter	4d	W	D.C.	30 JUN 1870	Congressional
705	Dyer, Wm. B., exchange ofcr.	53y	W	D.C.	27 JUL 1873	Congressional
421	Dyer, [blank]	7d	C		09 OCT 1869	Mt. Olivet
106	Dyker, Franklin	3m	W	D.C.	26 FEB 1858	German
153	Dykes, George Edgar	2m	W	D.C.	09 JUL 1859	Congressional
431	Dyle, Caroline, seamstress	24y	C		01 DEC 1869	
254	Dyly, Mary Josephine				27 FEB 1867	
273	Dymond, Henry	42y	W		01 SEP 1867	Holmead
228	Dyre, Anna S.	1m	W	D.C.	16 JUL 1866	Congressional
616a	Dyre, Frank	3m	W	D.C.	05 JUL 1872	Congressional
221	Dyre, James W., clerk	44y	W	Mass.	18 MAY 1866	Congressional*
630	Dyser, Henry	3y	W	U.S.	10 OCT 1872	Small Pox
630	Dyser, Jacob	40y	W	U.S.	11 OCT 1872	Small Pox
628	Dyser, Viola	4y	C	U.S.	26 SEP 1872	Small Pox
630	Dyson, Celia M.	5m	W	U.S.	10 OCT 1872	Small Pox
779	Dyson, Chas.	76y	C	U.S.	23 JUL 1874	
670	Dyson, George	7y	C	U.S.	01 FEB 1873	Small Pox*
353	Dyson, Glem	60y	C	Md.	24 SEP 1868	Freedmen's Hospital
660	Dyson, Henry, laborer	72y	C	U.S.	21 JAN 1873	Washington Asylum
531	Dyson, Lucinda		C	D.C.	03 AUG 1871	Unknown
475	Dyson, Mary	75y	C	Va.	17 SEP 1870	Freedmen's Hospital
107	Dyson, Owen, farmer	60y	W	Md.	09 MAR 1858	Congressional
664	Dyson, Wm. I.	3y	C	U.S.	17 JAN 1873	Small Pox*
723	Dywer, O.	3m	W	D.C.	08 OCT 1873	Mt. Olivet

Page	Name	Age	Race	Birth	Death Date	Burial Ground

E

Page	Name	Age	Race	Birth	Death Date	Burial Ground
115	Eagan, Mary	9m	W	D.C.	09 JUN 1858	Congressional
224	Eaggelston, Francis E.	8y	W	D.C.	16 JUN 1866	Glenwood
263	Eagleston, Harrie	Still	W		26 JUN 1867	Glenwood
255	Eames, Charles, attorney	55y	W	Mass.	16 MAR 1867	Congressional
365	Earkard, Wm., laborer	30y	C	Va.	04 DEC 1868	Young Mens
381	Earl, Martha	52y	W	N.J.	05 MAR 1869	Glenwood
740	Earl, Robert, gentleman	74y	W	Eng.	06 JAN 1874	Glenwood
125	Early, D. William	2m	W	D.C.	26 AUG 1858	Glenwood
169	Early, Lawrence, hack driver	23y	W	Ire.	13 JAN 1860	Mt. Olivet
663	Early, Robert	48y	W	Ire.	03 JAN 1873	Small Pox*
276	Earp, Charles	12y	W	D.C.	09 SEP 1867	Congressional
747	Earp, J.W., painter	46y	W	U.S.	06 FEB 1874	Congressional*
036	Earrett, Maria	4y	C	D.C.	10 FEB 1856	Harmony
401	Ease, Setta	6m	C		13 JUL 1869	Young Mens
260	Easten, Melinda	40y	W	D.C.*	26 MAY 1867	Ebenezer
623	Eastern, Mary	2y	C	U.S.	29 JUL 1872	
501	Eastern, Mary	80y	C		16 JAN 1871	Mt. Olivet
673	Easterud, Carrie	13y	W	U.S.	11 MAR 1873	Glenwood
215	Eastman, N., child of	Still	W	D.C.	13 MAR 1866	Congressional
215	Eastman, N., chlid of	Still	W	D.C.	13 MAR 1866	Congressional
329	Eastman, Robt. M.	6m	W	D.C.	09 JUL 1868	Oak Hill
189	Easton, Cordelia	22y	C	D.C.	18 SEP 1860	Foundry
255	Easton, Julia		C		28 MAR 1867	Young Mens
720	Easton, Thomas	13d	C	D.C.	23 SEP 1873	Young Mens
447	Eatman, Richard F.	4m	C	D.C.	20 MAR 1870	Washington Asylum
314	Eaton, Elizabeth Selden, Mrs.	72y	W	Conn.	08 MAY 1868	New Haven, Conn.
062	Eaton, John H., former Sec'y./War	70y	W	Tenn.	17 NOV 1856	Oak Hill, Lot #79
269	Eaton, Lota M.	4y	W	D.C.	14 AUG 1867	Congressional
508	Eaton, Mary	26d	W	D.C.	18 FEB 1871	Holmead
269	Eaton, Mary Alice	7m	W		26 AUG 1867	Mt. Olivet
340	Eaton, P. Howard, child of	Still	W	D.C.	21 AUG 1868	Congressional
021	Eaton, Rachael	unk.	C	unk.	20 AUG 1855	Foundry
532	Eaton, Wm. H.	36y	W	D.C.	14 AUG 1871	
747	Ebbet, Rotha	64y	W	U.S.	22 FEB 1874	Glenwood
276	Ebeling, Mary	20y	W	D.C.	05 SEP 1867	Mt. Olivet
632	Ebener, Ferdinand	70y	W	Ger.	22 OCT 1872	
327	Eber, Conrad	2y	W	D.C.	30 JUL 1868	Prospect Hill
387	Eber, Henry C.	14m	W	D.C.	27 APR 1869	Prospect Hill
049	Eberhart, Marsellena C.	4y	W	Va.	02 JUL 1856	St. Matthews
387	Eberly, Anna M.	4y	W	D.C.	02 APR 1869	Glenwood
497	Echard, J.	1m	W	D.C.	04 DEC 1870	Mt. Olivet
621	Echler, Wm., watchmaker	56y	W	Ger.	07 AUG 1872	Prospect Hill
462	Eck, Ellen M.	22y	W	Mo.	30 JUL 1870	Mt. Olivet*
318	Eckert, Adam	6y	W	D.C.	15 JUN 1868	Congressional
340	Eckert, Catharine	8m	W		08 AUG 1868	Congressional
554	Eckert, Charles	1m	W	D.C.	14 JAN 1872	Prospect Hill
687	Eckert, Elwood D.	12y	W	U.S.	01 MAY 1873	N.Y. City
780	Eckhardt, Chas. H., dept. clerk	32y	W	U.S.	25 JUL 1874	Philadelphia, Pa.
072	Eckhardt, Mary	62y	W	D.C.	15 FEB 1857	Rock Creek
321	Eckloff, Bernadine M.A.	3m	W	D.C.	30 JUN 1868	Mt. Olivet
364	Eckloff, Caroline F.	86y	W	Ger.	01 DEC 1868	Congressional*
497	Eckloff, Elizabeth	39y	W		11 DEC 1870	St. Patricks
304	Eckloff, Godfrey F., tailor	85y	W	Prus.	20 MAR 1868	Congressional
310	Eckloff, Mary Anastatia	22y	W	D.C.	15 APR 1868	Mt. Olivet
464	Eckloff, Wm. G.	14y	W	D.C.	10 JUL 1870	St. Patricks
735	Eddee, Emeline M., clerk	62y	W	U.S.	12 DEC 1873	Oak Hill
455	Eddin, Judith T.	66y	W	D.C.	03 MAY 1870	Broad Creek, Md.

District of Columbia Interments (Index to Deaths), 1855-1874

Page	Name	Age	Race	Birth	Death Date	Burial Ground
753	Eddington, Gilbert, sail maker	64y	W	U.S.	23 MAR 1874	Potters Field
291	Eddins, Wm. H., mail agent	27y	W	N.C.	03 JAN 1868	N.C.
233	Eddleman, Emma J.	1m	W	D.C.	30 AUG 1866	Glenwood
333	Edel, Mr., child of	6m	W		15 JUL 1868	Prospect Hill
742	Edel, [blank]	6m	W	U.S.	21 JAN 1874	Prospect Hill
780	Edelen, William, farmer	57y	W	U.S.	05 JUL 1874	Congressional
383	Edelin, A.	Still	C	D.C.	09 MAR 1869	Washington Asylum
663	Edelin, Catherine	52y	C	U.S.	03 JAN 1873	Small Pox*
582	Edelin, Chas. R.	2y	W	D.C.	19 FEB 1872	Congressional*
771	Edelin, Mary E.	1m	C	U.S.	16 JUN 1874	
355	Edelin, Sidney, Mrs.	65y	W	Md.	23 OCT 1868	Congressional
419	Edeling, Alfred R., collector	49y	W	Md.	22 OCT 1869	Congressional
399	Edeling, Caroline R.	17y	W		21 JUL 1869	Congressional
120	Edgar, Elizabeth	2y	W		09 JUL 1858	Philadelphia, Pa.
252	Edmoindson, Elijah, shoe dealer	57y	W	Md.	14 FEB 1867	Glenwood
406	Edmonds, Charlotte	2m	C	D.C.	04 JUL 1869	
049	Edmonds, Grayson H.	3m	W	D.C.	09 JUL 1856	Oak Hill
645	Edmonds, Ida Ann	4m	C	U.S.	29 DEC 1872	
402	Edmonds, James Wm.	7y	W	D.C.	28 JUL 1869	Rock Creek
707	Edmonds, Martha	17y	C	Va.	21 JUL 1873	Beckett's
442	Edmondson, Betsy	70y	W	Va.	05 FEB 1870	Washington Asylum
172	Edmons, G.H., grocer	52y	W	N.Y.	10 FEB 1860	Congressional
017	Edmonson, Cath. V.	8m	W	D.C.	26 JUL 1855	Glenwood
780	Edmonson, Joseph	1y	C	U.S.	04 JUL 1874	
155	Edmonson, [blank]	Still	W	D.C.	23 JUL 1859	
014	Edmonston, Elbert	1y	W	D.C.	25 JUL 1855	Glenwood
001	Edmonston, Elizabeth V.	23y			16 JAN 1855	
051	Edmonston, Franklin, printer	77y	W		24 JUL 1856	Congressional
614	Edmonston, Jackson	54y	W	U.S.	01 JUL 1872	
667	Edmonston, Jane E.	53y	W	U.S.	13 FEB 1873	Glenwood
001	Edmonston, Mary	78y		Md.	04 JAN 1855	Glenwood
437	Edmonston, Mary E.	48y	C	D.C.	16 JAN 1870	Harmony
415	Edmonston, Mary Virginia	9m	W	Md.	18 SEP 1869	
614	Edmonston, Nathan	73y	W	U.S.	03 JUL 1872	
289	Edmonston, Rebecca	63y	W	Va.	24 JAN 1868	Glenwood
734	Edmunds, Geo. N., clerk	23y	W	U.S.	05 DEC 1873	Glenwood
372	Edmunds, L.	Still	C		25 JAN 1869	Washington Asylum
552	Edmunds, Lucinda	1y	C	D.C.	03 JAN 1872	Union
298	Edmundson, S.H., child of	1½d	W	D.C.	02 FEB 1868	Glenwood
310	Edmunson, Enoch	19y	W	U.S.	01 APR 1868	Glenwood
046	Edwards, Ann, seamstress	43y	W	D.C.	06 JUN 1856	St. Matthews
731	Edwards, Charles	1y	C	U.S.	19 NOV 1873	Mt. Pleasant
227	Edwards, Frances	22y	W	D.C.*	08 JUL 1866	Mt. Olivet
110	Edwards, Francis W.	3y	W	D.C.	09 APR 1858	Oak Hill
780	Edwards, Ida E.	2m	W	U.S.	09 JUL 1874	Methodist
017	Edwards, J.H., carpenter	24y	W	D.C.*	20 JUL 1855	St. Matthews
021	Edwards, J.W.B.	8m	W	D.C.	07 AUG 1855	Methodist, East
595	Edwards, James	35y	W	U.S.	17 APR 1872	Congressional*
275	Edwards, James L.	81y	W	Va.	18 SEP 1867	Congressional
342	Edwards, James L.	2y	C	D.C.	22 AUG 1868	Union
532	Edwards, Jane	13d	W	D.C.	10 AUG 1871	Congressional*
075	Edwards, Jane	93y	W		10 APR 1857	Western
351	Edwards, John H.	10d	C	D.C.	18 SEP 1868	Young Mens
118	Edwards, John Tayler, wood sawyer	81y	C	Va.	30 JUN 1858	Holmead
542	Edwards, Joseph, bricklayer	76y	W	Eng.	17 OCT 1871	Glenwood
765	Edwards, Joseph H., boilermaker	48y	W	U.S.	15 MAY 1874	Congressional*
322	Edwards, Lena Ashford	6m	W	D.C.	19 JUN 1868	Glenwood
287	Edwards, Lewis		C		c.23 DEC 1867	Alms House

Page	Name	Age	Race	Birth	Death Date	Burial Ground
287	Edwards, Lucinda		C		c.23 DEC 1867	Alms House
301	Edwards, Martin	4y	C	Va.	23 MAR 1868	Young Mens
115	Edwards, Mary	6y	W	D.C.	03 JUN 1858	Congressional
098	Edwards, Mary E.	3y	W	D.C.	16 DEC 1857	Congressional
759	Edwards, Nathan	40y	C	U.S.	29 APR 1874	Washington Asylum
743	Edwards, R.	25y	C	U.S.	25 JAN 1874	
299	Edwards, Richard Madison	9y	W	D.C.	16 MAR 1868	Glenwood
718	Edwards, Richd.	45y	C	D.C.	14 SEP 1873	Washington Asylum
466	Edwards, Samuel	11m	C	D.C.	14 JUL 1870	Young Mens
075	Edwards, Thomas	50y	W	Md.	13 APR 1857	Holmead
232	Edwards, Thomas C.	27y	W	D.C.	27 AUG 1866	Glenwood
071	Edwards, Thompson B., engineer	24y	W	D.C.*	20 FEB 1857	Congressional
452	Edwards, William	6d	C	D.C.	21 APR 1870	Washington Asylum
405	Edwards, Wm.	6m	C	D.C.	30 JUL 1869	Washington Asylum
093	Edwards, [blank]		W		15 OCT 1857	Foundry
626	Edwins, Mary L.	26y	W	U.S.	25 SEP 1872	
597	Egan, Maggie M.	3y	W	U.S.	05 MAY 1872	Congressional
339	Egan, Mary Lovell	1m	W	D.C.	20 AUG 1868	Glenwood
137	Egan, Mrs., domestic	45y	W	Ire.	22 JAN 1859	Rockville
176	Eggleston, Virginia	23d	W	D.C.	15 APR 1860	Glenwood
216	Ehern, Michael	3y	W	D.C.	27 MAR 1866	Mt. Olivet
359	Ehle, Robert G.	2d	W		12 NOV 1868	Congressional
007	Ehwey, Mary	62y	W	S.C.	07 MAY 1855	Congressional
608	Eibel, John H.	2y	W	D.C.	16 JUN 1872	
675	Eichelberger, Edgar	21d	W	U.S.	27 MAR 1873	Mt. Olivet
626	Eichelberger, H.L.	17m	W	U.S.	30 SEP 1872	
390	Eichelberger, John	1m	W	D.C.	10 MAY 1869	Mt. Olivet
391	Eichmann, Mrs.	38y	W	Ger.	07 MAY 1869	4th St. Church
528	Eicholz, Dora	28y	W	Ger.	21 JUL 1871	Glenwood
303	Eichorn, Joseph	2y	W	D.C.	06 MAR 1868	German Catholic
136	Eichorne, James G.	72y	W	Ger.	30 DEC 1858	St. Marys
157	Eichorne, John G.	11m	W	D.C.	08 AUG 1859	St. Marys
112	Einloff, Augustus	7y	W	D.C.	22 APR 1858	Congressional
019	Ekhard, Mary E.	2y	W	D.C.	14 AUG 1855	Glenwood
692	Elbert, John, tailor	68y	W	Ger.	23 MAY 1873	Mt. Olivet
269	Elbert, Mary	5m	C		10 AUG 1867	Georgetown
265	Elderkin, Wm. A.	4d	W	D.C.	14 JUL 1867	Congressional
487	Eldredge, James M., surg./dentist	24y	W	N.Y.	16 NOV 1870	Glenwood
500	Eldridge, Dewitt F., clerk	26y	W	Amer.	05 JAN 1871	Glenwood
439	Eldridge, Emma Irene	1y	W		28 FEB 1870	Congressional
622	Eliason, Elias A., leather dlr.	68y	W	U.S.	01 AUG 1872	
127	Eliot, Mary	73y	W	Md.	15 SEP 1858	Congressional
075	Eliot, Mary L.	1y	W	D.C.	15 APR 1857	St. Peters
080	Eliot, Wallace	8m	W	D.C.	28 JUN 1857	Glenwood
214	Elkin, [blank]	3m			06 MAR 1866	Glenwood
080	Elkins, Lucinda	56y	C	Va.	26 JUN 1857	Young Mens
678	Elkins, Wm.	23y	C	U.S.	31 MAR 1873	Small Pox
008	Ellen, Benjn., gardener	41y	W	Eng.	14 MAY 1855	Oak Hill
269	Eller, Leonard, laborer	52y	W	Ger.	13 AUG 1867	Prospect Hill
166	Ellicott, Philip, agent		W	U.S.	25 NOV 1859	Ellicott's Mills
426	Elliot, Eliza	8y	C		13 NOV 1869	Ebenezer
473	Elliot, Emma	1y	C	D.C.	19 AUG 1870	
639	Elliot, Emmi	70y	W	U.S.	02 NOV 1872	
398	Elliot, James B.	49y	W		04 JUN 1869	Baltimore, Md.
487	Elliot, Robert L.	2y	W	D.C.	21 NOV 1870	Oak Hill
674	Elliot, Seth A., clerk	71y	W	U.S.	19 MAR 1873	Congressional*
035	Elliot, Walter	2y	W	Pa.	03 FEB 1856	Holmead
446	Elliott, Ailey	109y	C	Va.	14 MAR 1870	Washington Asylum

District of Columbia Interments (Index to Deaths), 1855-1874

Page	Name	Age	Race	Birth	Death Date	Burial Ground
594	Elliott, Alfred, Navy officer	24y	W	D.C.	11 APR 1872	Congressional
422	Elliott, Annie	40y	C		25 OCT 1869	Ebenezer
266	Elliott, Charles E.	6m	W	D.C.	01 JUL 1867	Glenwood
529	Elliott, Charles E.	1y	W	D.C.	24 JUL 1871	Potters Field
051	Elliott, E.P.	29y	W	D.C.	26 JUL 1856	Congressional
435	Elliott, Elijah	7m	C		10 JAN 1870	Ebenezer
529	Elliott, Elisabeth	83y	W	N.C.	27 JUL 1871	Congressional*
771	Elliott, Fanne Norman	9m	W	U.S.	10 JUN 1874	Mt. Olivet
294	Elliott, Geo., child of	1h	C		04 FEB 1868	
521	Elliott, Grace	7m	W	D.C.	07 JUN 1871	
304	Elliott, John W., chaplain USA	43y	W	Pa.	12 MAR 1868	Congressional
401	Elliott, Mary	32y	W	Md.	21 JUL 1869	Mt. Olivet
717	Elliott, Mary E.	30y	W	Va.	01 SEP 1873	Mt. Olivet
112	Elliott, Mary Eliza	1m	W	D.C.	21 APR 1858	Congressional
588	Elliott, Rezin, wagoner	60y	C	Va.	25 MAR 1872	
765	Ellis, Augustus	1y	C	U.S.	01 MAY 1874	Graceland
137	Ellis, Charles	4y	W	D.C.	17 JAN 1859	Mt. Olivet
372	Ellis, D.	2y	C	Md.	22 JAN 1869	Washington Asylum
619	Ellis, Eddie	2y	C	U.S.	08 AUG 1872	
658	Ellis, Edmund I., carpenter	59y	W	U.S.	06 JAN 1873	Glenwood
697	Ellis, George	8m	W	D.C.	10 JUN 1873	Mt. Olivet
590	Ellis, George	6y	C	D.C.	10 APR 1872	Small Pox
687	Ellis, George J., clerk	19y	W	D.C.	06 MAY 1873	Glenwood
381	Ellis, George W.	1y	W		04 MAR 1869	Congressional
451	Ellis, Gracie	90y	C	Md.	15 APR 1870	Young Mens
601	Ellis, Henry C., marble cutter	43y	W	U.S.	24 MAY 1872	Glenwood
030	Ellis, Henry, grocer	49y	W	Ire.	24 NOV 1855	Glenwood
452	Ellis, James	4m	C	D.C.	20 APR 1870	Washington Asylum
557	Ellis, James G., carpenter	51y	W	D.C.	02 FEB 1872	Glenwood
263	Ellis, James William	4m	W	D.C.	30 JUN 1867	Congressional
012	Ellis, John, watchman at USPO	72y	W	Md.	23 JUN 1855	Foundry
590	Ellis, Lucy	50y	C	U.S.	07 APR 1872	Small Pox
377	Ellis, Martha	8m	C	D.C.	04 FEB 1869	Washington Asylum
385	Ellis, Mary Ann	63y	W	Amer.	20 APR 1869	Congressional
339	Ellis, Mary Rebecca	16d	W	D.C.	15 AUG 1868	Mt. Olivet
667	Ellis, Mollie	2y	W	U.S.	14 FEB 1873	Mt. Olivet
516	Ellis, Sarah	21y	W	Pa.	28 MAR 1871	Congressional
680	Ellis, Susan K.	48y	W	U.S.	09 APR 1873	Glenwood
713	Ellis, Teressa	5m	W	D.C.	26 AUG 1873	Mt. Olivet
598	Ellis, Thomas	4y	C	U.S.	05 MAY 1872	Small Pox
143	Ellis, Vespasian, lawyer	59y	W	Va.	14 MAR 1859	Congressional*
247	Ellis, William	33y	C		30 DEC 1866	Harmony
765	Ellis, William, barkeeper	45y	W	U.S.	09 MAY 1874	Holyrood
304	Ellis, William M., machinist	61y	W	Pa.	16 MAR 1868	Congressional
187	Elliss, Celestial A.A.	1y	C	D.C.	10 AUG 1860	Ebenezer
437	Ellsworth, Abba Anna	2y	W		07 JAN 1870	Glenwood
226	Ellsworth, Charles	1y	W	D.C.	29 JUN 1866	Glenwood
533	Ellsworth, Chas. H.	2m	W	U.S.	21 AUG 1871	
455	Ellsworth, George L., clerk	37y	W		24 MAY 1870	Glenwood
058	Ellsworth, James H., printer	45y	W	D.C.	27 SEP 1856	St. Patricks
668	Ellwell, Isadora	27y	W	U.S.	22 FEB 1873	
237	Ellwood, Ella E.	3y	W	D.C.	02 SEP 1866	Glenwood
265	Elmes, Kate	2m	W	D.C.	10 JUL 1867	Congressional
691	Elms, Mary G.	25y	W	U.S.	02 MAY 1873	Congressional
212	Elting, Mary A.	29y	W	N.Y.	07 FEB 1866	Congressional
278	Elvans, Frank	52y	W	Eng.	17 OCT 1867	Oak Hill
249	Elwood, Helenor M.				— JAN 1867	Oak Hill
635	Elwood, J.H.	6y	C	U.S.	11 NOV 1872	Small Pox

District of Columbia Interments (Index to Deaths), 1855-1874

Page	Name	Age	Race	Birth	Death Date	Burial Ground
635	Elwood, Mary	1½y	C	U.S.	25 NOV 1872	Small Pox
335a	Emerson, Cathr.	2y	B	Va.	22 JUL 1868	Washington Asylum
173	Emerson, Isaiah, printer	29y	W	U.S.	26 FEB 1860	
396	Emerstine, Frank	50y	W	Ger.	16 JUN 1869	Hebrew
351	Emery, Susan	2y	C	Va.	07 SEP 1868	Young Mens
707	Emlong, Nancy	20y	W	Pa.	16 JUL 1873	Washington Asylum
243	Emmerson, Geo. W., clerk	27y	W		27 NOV 1866	N.Y.
530	Emmerson, Sally	80y	C	Ky.	31 JUL 1871	Washington
260	Emmert, Henry	48y	W		23 MAY 1867	Glenwood
106	Emmert, Louisa	37y	W	Ger.	14 FEB 1858	Glenwood
545	Emmett, Annie	21d	W	D.C.	16 NOV 1871	Prospect Hill
550	Emmett, Leonard			D.C.	30 DEC 1871	
278	Emmons, Frank	2y	W	D.C.	— OCT 1867	Congressional
246	Emmons, H.E., seamstress	35y	W	Md.	31 DEC 1866	Congressional
731	Emmons, Mary Ann	69y	W	U.S.	18 NOV 1873	Oak Hill
046	Emons, Hester L.	25y	C	D.C.	18 JUN 1856	Methodist, East
016	Emory, Matilda	11m	W	D.C.	01 JUL 1855	Washington
256	Emrich, Peter, restaurant keeper	42y	W	Ger.	09 MAR 1867	Oak Hill
688	Ender, Robert	3y	C	U.S.	11 MAY 1873	Beckett's
050	Enders, Margaretta	50y	W	Ger.	17 JUL 1856	German Catholic
140	Endirs, Josephine E.	3y	W	D.C.	02 FEB 1859	German
553	Engel, Henry, shoemaker	65y	W	Ger.	09 JAN 1872	Prospect Hill
395	Engel, Maria	1y	W		30 JUN 1869	Prospect Hill
680	Engelhard, Kathrina	72y	W	Ger.	02 APR 1873	St. Marys
588	Engels, Ewald, bar keeper	39y	W	Ger.	25 MAR 1872	Prospect Hill
666	England, Chas. E., salesman	32y	W	U.S.	01 FEB 1873	Glenwood
235	England, George	20y	C		18 SEP 1866	Mt. Olivet
720	England, Robt. C.	2y	W	D.C.	28 SEP 1873	Glenwood
450	England, Sandford P., clerk	33y	W	Ire.	26 APR 1870	Mt. Olivet
496	England, Susan E.	3m	W		31 DEC 1870	Mt. Olivet
632	Engle, Henrietta	2y	W	U.S.	20 OCT 1872	
016	Engle, Tilman			Ger.	— JUL 1855	German Evangelic
552	Englehart, Catharine	11m	W	D.C.	07 JAN 1872	German
476	Englehart, John G.	1y	W	D.C.	14 SEP 1870	St. Marys
371	English, Patrick, grocer	27y	W	Ire.	16 JAN 1869	Mt. Olivet
172	English, William, laborer	47y	W	Eng.	02 FEB 1860	Washington Asylum
310	English, Wm.	1y	W		c.01 APR 1868	Mt. Olivet
599	Enliaih, Louis	10y	W	U.S.	26 MAY 1872	German
088	Ennis, Catharine Ann	1y		D.C.	25 AUG 1857	St. Patricks
027	Ennis, John	40y	W		09 OCT 1855	St. Patricks
140	Ennis, John, plasterer	22y	W	D.C.	09 FEB 1859	Glenwood
524	Ennis, Jos. H.	8m		D.C.	25 JUN 1871	Young Mens
105	Ennis, Mary	10m	W	D.C.	18 FEB 1858	St. Patricks
753	Ennis, Richard	36y	C	U.S.	06 MAR 1874	
177	Enright, Edward	9m	W	D.C.	27 APR 1860	St. Patricks
150	Ensalow, Martha	65y	W	Md.	11 JUN 1859	Washington Asylum
069	Entwisle, Ada	4y	W	D.C.	25 JAN 1857	St. Patricks
164	Entwisle, Isaac	8y	W	D.C.	07 OCT 1859	Congressional
222	Entz, Conrad, mason	49y	W		25 MAY 1866	Holmead
414	Enwright, Priscilla	57y	W	Va.	c.07 SEP 1869	Congressional*
583	Eopoluce, Josephine	1y	W	D.C.	29 FEB 1872	Congressional*
695	Epps, Arthur, laborer	108y	C	Va.	07 JUN 1873	Washington Asylum
383	Epps, Mary E.	2m	C	D.C.	07 MAR 1869	Washington Asylum
641	Eps, Moses	22y	C	U.S.	08 DEC 1872	Small Pox
303	Erb, Margaretta	62y	W	Ger.	03 MAR 1868	Prospect Hill
279	Erickson, Julius E., Capt., clerk	65y	W		27 OCT 1867	Brooklyn, N.Y.
697	Ernest, James	7m	W	D.C.	19 JUN 1873	Mt. Olivet
759	Ernshaw, C.L.	27y	W	U.S.	23 APR 1874	Congressional

District of Columbia Interments (Index to Deaths), 1855-1874

Page	Name	Age	Race	Birth	Death Date	Burial Ground
370	Errington, Lizzie, seamstress	20y	W	Ire.	18 JAN 1869	Mt. Olivet
262	Erving, Elizabeth, washerwoman	27y	W	D.C.	13 JUN 1867	Union
207	Erwin, Elizabeth	24y	W		19 JUL 1862	Mt. Olivet
313	Esanger, Elizabeth	18y	C		06 MAY 1868	
240	Esch, Annie	8m	W	D.C.	26 OCT 1866	German
771	Esch, Gustave	13y	W	U.S.	13 JUN 1874	Glenwood
032	Escloth, Sarah	54y	W	Va.	27 DEC 1855	Alms House
376	Esher, George, child of	21d	W		21 FEB 1869	Prospect Hill
250	Eshleman, Mary	17y	W	Pa.	17 JAN 1867	Congressional
118	Eslin, Ann	59y	W	Md.	30 JUN 1858	Holmead
733	Eslin, William, brickmaker	78y	W	U.S.	20 NOV 1873	
244	Esperta, Francisco, musician	71y	W	Spain	15 NOV 1866	Mt. Olivet
736	Espey, John, bookbinder	58y	W	U.S.	15 DEC 1873	Oak Hill
395	Espey, Sarah C.E.	7m	W	D.C.	29 JUN 1869	Glenwood
158	Espy, Eliza, lady	20y	W	D.C.	22 AUG 1859	Oak Hill
138	Espy, Margaret Jane	18y	W	D.C.	27 JAN 1859	Oak Hill
035	Esselbruegge, Anna H.	28y	W	Ger.	18 FEB 1856	12th St.
167	Essellsbrugge, Charlotte	17y	W	D.C.	14 DEC 1859	Prospect Hill
266	Essex, Josiah, Mrs., child of	Still	W	D.C.	11 JUL 1867	Glenwood
493	Essher, Frangott	10d	W	D.C.	28 DEC 1870	Prospect Hill
456	Essig, H.J.	7m	W	D.C.	20 JUN 1870	Prospect Hill
001	Estep, Rezin	60y			03 JAN 1855	Glenwood
780	Estmart, Wm.	11d	W	U.S.	08 JUL 1874	Prospect Hill
210	Etchinson, Rudolph, clerk	23y	W	D.C.	24 JAN 1866	Glenwood
090	Etchmen, John	6m	W	D.C.	04 SEP 1857	German Catholic
485	Etter, Eva	4y	W	D.C.	01 OCT 1870	Congressional
117	Eurich, Melinda M.	7m	W	D.C.	24 JUN 1858	German Lutheran
605	Evanitt, Andrew	20d	W	D.C.	06 JUN 1872	Md.
216	Evans, A.E.	1y	C		31 MAR 1866	Young Mens
244	Evans, Alice	16y	C	Md.	03 NOV 1866	Harmony
476	Evans, Charlotte	1y	C		20 SEP 1870	Baptist, colored
780	Evans, Edith G.	6d	W	U.S.	29 JUL 1874	Holyrood
239	Evans, Edwin T., printer	61y	W	Eng.	15 OCT 1866	N.Y.
537	Evans, Elisabeth	25y	C	Va.	19 SEP 1871	
151	Evans, Elizabeth H., lady	28y	W	D.C.	26 JUN 1859	Congressional
488	Evans, Georgeana, seamstress	23y	W	D.C.	24 NOV 1870	Mt. Olivet
184	Evans, Georgiana	3y	W	D.C.	10 JUL 1860	Holmead
379	Evans, Harry E.	2y	W	D.C.	30 MAR 1869	Congressional
488	Evans, Henry, laborer	22y	C	Md.	18 NOV 1870	Washington Asylum
583	Evans, James, hostler	45y	W	unk.	29 FEB 1872	Glenwood
113	Evans, James L.	1y	W	D.C.	07 MAY 1858	Congressional
379	Evans, Jane E.	60y	W		09 MAR 1869	Congressional
199	Evans, Jas.	2y	W	D.C.	15 FEB 1861	Congressional
176	Evans, John	26d	C	D.C.	04 APR 1860	Harmony
202	Evans, John, geologist	48y	W	N.H.	13 APR 1861	Congressional
001	Evans, John H.	6y			15 JAN 1855	Congressional
710	Evans, Louisa Annette	11d	W	D.C.	07 AUG 1873	Congressional
231	Evans, M.E.	19y	W	Pa.	22 AUG 1866	Ill.
690	Evans, Margaret, cook	35y	W	Ire.	04 MAY 1873	
633	Evans, Maria J.	15m	W	U.S.	31 OCT 1872	Glenwood
319	Evans, Marian	2y	W	D.C.	10 JUN 1868	Holmead
587	Evans, Mary A.	47y	W	Ger.	23 MAR 1872	St. Marys
595	Evans, Matilda	45y	W	U.S.	22 APR 1872	Washington
461	Evans, Maud Gertude	7m	W	D.C.	29 JUL 1870	Congressional
275	Evans, Nancy, domestic	78y	W	Md.	21 SEP 1867	Congressional
769	Evans, Nonnan	21y	W	U.S.	03 MAY 1874	
429	Evans, Rachel	76y	W	Ger.	19 DEC 1869	Congressional
431	Evans, Richard S.	1m	W		19 DEC 1869	Mt. Olivet

Page	Name	Age	Race	Birth	Death Date	Burial Ground
742	Evans, Sinclare	72y	W	U.S.	18 JAN 1874	
555	Evans, Susan, Mrs.	72y	W	Va.	27 JAN 1872	Congressional
771	Evans, Walter	1y	W	U.S.	14 JUN 1874	Mt. Olivet
710	Evans, William	4m	W	D.C.	05 AUG 1873	Beckett's
044	Evans, William E.	1y	W	D.C.	02 MAY 1856	Methodist
380	Evans, William Elbert	52y	W		08 MAR 1869	Philadelphia, Pa.
747	Evans, Wm. D., clerk	26y	W	U.S.	15 FEB 1874	Congressional*
557	Evans, Wm. J.	31y	W	D.C.	04 FEB 1872	Mt. Olivet
765	Evans, Wm. W.	16y	W	U.S.	25 MAY 1874	Glenwood
434	Evans, [blank]	6m	W		11 JAN 1870	Congressional
668	Eveans, Isabella W.	50y	W	Scot.	20 FEB 1873	Oak Hill
673	Eveans, Willie	1m	C	U.S.	03 MAR 1873	Mt. Olivet
248	Eveleth, Mary W.	66y	W	Va.*	28 DEC 1866	Oak Hill*
032	Eveleth, [blank]	6y	C		27 DEC 1855	Western
058	Evelett, Mary E.	8y	C	D.C.	28 SEP 1856	Holmead
623	Evening, Anza	2y	C	U.S.	05 JUL 1872	Mt. Zion
629	Evens, A.M.	38y	W	Scot.	15 OCT 1872	
113	Evens, J.J., U.S. senator	72y	W	S.C.	06 MAY 1858	Congressional
155	Evens, Susan	82y	W	Md.	07 JUL 1859	Md.
771	Everett, Ann Rebecca	38y	W	U.S.	02 JUN 1874	Glenwood
717	Everett, Thos. T., attorney	62y	W	U.S.	06 SEP 1873	Congressional
613	Everette, Wm.	4m	C	U.S.	11 JUL 1872	
618	Ewald, John	40y	W	Ger.	07 AUG 1872	
372	Ewel, James	60y	C	Va.	20 JAN 1869	Washington Asylum
011	Ewell, Alberta	29y	W	Va.	09 JUN 1855	Va.
307	Ewell, Fanny, domestic	32y	C	Va.	14 APR 1868	Alms House
066	Exline, James S.	13y	W	Va.	26 DEC 1856	Methodist, East
434	Eyermann, Annie	4m	W		13 JAN 1870	Prospect Hill
264	Eyrmann, Margaretta	4m	W	D.C.	10 JUL 1867	German
144	Eytinge, Samuel D., actor	29y	W	Pa.	24 MAR 1859	N.Y. City

District of Columbia Interments (Index to Deaths), 1855-1874

Page	Name	Age	Race	Birth	Death Date	Burial Ground
F						
305	Fabus, Christian	40y	W		c.17 MAR 1868	Mt. Olivet
321	Faddin, Michael		W		c.24 JUN 1868	Alms House
324	Fagan, Frank L.	5m	W	D.C.	19 JUL 1868	Washington
496	Fagan, M.A.	84y	W	Md.	28 DEC 1870	Mt. Olivet
456	Fagan, Owen Albert	2m	W	D.C.	20 JUN 1870	Mt. Olivet
750	Fagan, Walter, laborer	54y	W	Ire.	12 FEB 1874	
108	Fahnstein, John, tinner	20y	W	Ger.	21 MAR 1858	German Catholic
108	Fahnstein, Margaret	5y	W	D.C.	18 MAR 1858	German Catholic
535	Fahrenbruela, Augustus	43y	W	Ger.	07 SEP 1871	Prospect Hill
645	Fairall, Eugene	16y	W	U.S.	26 DEC 1872	Alexandria, Va.
249	Fairall, Jason	3m	W	D.C.	12 JAN 1867	Congressional
499	Fairall, Joseph, carpenter	48y	W	Md.	03 JAN 1871	Congressional
347	Fairall, Julia C.	1y	W		26 SEP 1868	Congressional
121	Fairbanks, Joel D., clerk	35y	W	Ver.	12 JUL 1858	Congressional
032	Fairee, [blank]	30y	W	Md.	21 DEC 1855	Holmead
740	Fairfax, John	3y	C	U.S.	02 JAN 1874	
725	Fairfax, Laura	65y	B	U.S.	21 OCT 1873	Beckett's
302	Fairfax, Sarah	14d	C		20 MAR 1868	Ebenezer
350	Fairfax, Sarah	38y	C	Md.	08 SEP 1868	Young Mens
465	Fairfax, [blank]	1y	C	D.C.	17 JUL 1870	Ebenezer
270	Fait, Anna, child of	8m	W	D.C.	17 AUG 1867	German Catholic
301	Faiter, John, child of	Still			06 MAR 1868	Mt. Olivet
352	Falconer, Albert B., clerk	18y	W	Md.	07 SEP 1868	Glenwood
628	Falconer, Chas. E.	20y	W	U.S.	09 SEP 1872	
299	Falconer, Geo. E., grocer	27y	W	D.C.	23 MAR 1868	Glenwood
348	Falconer, John Bennett	1y	W		26 SEP 1868	Glenwood
469	Falconer, Mahlon, carpenter	63y	W	Md.	25 AUG 1870	Glenwood
131	Falconer, Wm. B.	11m	W	D.C.	22 OCT 1858	Glenwood
359	Fales, Almira L.	59y	W	N.Y.	10 NOV 1868	Glenwood
532	Fales, John George	1y	C	Va.	12 AUG 1871	Potters Field
532	Falk, Frederick E.	11m	W	U.S.	16 AUG 1871	Congressional
484	Falkner, Fannie	70y	C	Eng.	07 OCT 1870	Potters Field
551	Fall, Louza	6m	C	D.C.	— DEC 1871	Western
325	Fallon, Chas. M.	9m	W	D.C.	03 JUL 1868	Congressional
378	Fallon, Mary A.	24y	W		— FEB 1869	Washington Asylum
614	Fallon, Schuyler C.	4y	W	U.S.	08 JUL 1872	
133	Falon, James, laborer	32y	W	Ire.	21 NOV 1858	Washington Asylum
624	Falts, P.P.	6y	C	U.S.	26 SEP 1872	
019	Falty, Mary	63y	W	Ire.	13 AUG 1855	St. Patricks
445	Falvey, Hannah	65y	W	Ire.	13 MAR 1870	Mt. Olivet
162	Falvey, Margaret	47y	W	Md.	26 SEP 1859	
442	Fanleroy, Patrick H.	37y	C	Va.	23 FEB 1870	Young Mens
118	Fanning, Wm. H.	9y	W	D.C.	10 JUN 1858	Congressional
492	Fantelroy, Lucinda	20y	C	Va.	26 DEC 1870	Young Mens
306	Fanteroy, Lettie	60y	C	S.C.	19 APR 1868	Alms House
517	Fantroy, Charlotte	43y	C	Va.	02 APR 1871	
677	Fantroy, Lucy	54y	C	U.S.	11 MAR 1873	Small Pox
743	Fantroy, M.	18y	C	U.S.	26 JAN 1874	Mt. Pleasant
624	Faren, Thos., clerk	72y	W	U.S.	01 SEP 1872	
042	Farguerson, James	3y	C	D.C.	24 APR 1856	Foundry
780	Farless, Isadore A.	30y	W	U.S.	07 JUL 1874	Oak Hill
307	Farley, Edwd. W., teacher	43y	W	Va.	23 APR 1868	Glenwood
456	Farley, Kate, housekeeper	25y	W	Ire.	24 JUN 1870	Mt. Olivet
517	Farley, Peter, grocer	31y	W	Ire.	26 APR 1871	Holy Rood
116	Farmeir, Caroline	7m	W	D.C.	22 JUN 1858	German Catholic
080	Farmington, [blank]		W		20 JUN 1857	Foundry
267	Farnham, Alice	3m			20 JUL 1867	

Page	Name	Age	Race	Birth	Death Date	Burial Ground
031	Farnham, Elizabeth S.	8y	W	D.C.	12 DEC 1855	Glenwood
765	Farnum, Abigail A.	56y	W	U.S.	04 MAY 1874	Port Jarvis, N.Y.
399	Faron, Roberta	4m	W	D.C.	25 JUL 1869	Congressional
735	Farqauar, Eliza E.	2y	W	U.S.	11 DEC 1873	Glenwood
697	Farquha, Sarah B.	36y	W	Va.	03 JUN 1873	Glenwood
519	Farr, Charity L.	43y	W	Md.	21 MAY 1871	Glenwood
355	Farr, Flora	1y	W	D.C.	16 OCT 1868	Glenwood
445	Farr, Wm. Walter	8m	W		28 MAR 1870	Glenwood
731	Farra, Wm. H., lawyer	46y	W	U.S.	21 NOV 1873	Mt. Olivet
149	Farrall, John, laborer	32y	W	Ire.	31 MAY 1859	Mt. Olivet
493	Farrel, Minty	8m	C	D.C.	20 DEC 1870	Mt. Olivet
675	Farrell, Bridget	70y	W	Ire.	28 MAR 1873	Mt. Olivet
306	Farrell, Cato, blacksmith	36y	W	Ire.	07 APR 1868	Mt. Olivet
662	Farrell, Edward, soldier	53y	W	Ire.	09 JAN 1873	
228	Farrell, Edwd., laborer	79y	W	Ire.	12 JUL 1866	Alms House
209	Farrell, Edwin F.	3m	W	D.C.	07 JAN 1866	Mt. Olivet
747	Farrell, John, sexton	27y	W	Ire.	20 FEB 1874	Holyrood
301	Farrell, John T.	3y	W	D.C.	05 MAR 1868	Mt. Olivet
153	Farren, Elizabeth	8m	W	D.C.	04 JUL 1859	Mt. Olivet
430	Farrill, Bridget	54y	W	Ire.	31 DEC 1869	Mt. Olivet
747	Farrington, James, laborer	19y	W	Ire.	01 FEB 1874	
514	Farrington, Rosa	44y	W	N.Y.	30 MAR 1871	Glenwood
780	Farris, Peter	27y	W	U.S.	31 JUL 1874	Mt. Olivet
735	Farrish, French	8y	W	U.S.	13 DEC 1873	Congressional
299	Farwell, Frances A., Mrs.	37y	W	U.S.	15 MAR 1868	Glenwood
209	Fastnaught, Mary Ellen	6y	W	D.C.	10 JAN 1866	Prospect Hill
371	Fauler, John	52y	W	Ger.	20 JAN 1869	German Catholic
318	Faulkner, John H., carpenter	35y	W	D.C.	03 JUN 1868	Congressional
029	Faulkner, Oliver	24d	W	D.C.	09 NOV 1855	Congressional
694	Faunce, George I.	9m	W	D.C.	03 JUN 1873	Mt. Olivet
463	Faunce, George W.		W		19 JUL 1870	Mt. Olivet
488	Faunce, Mary E.	4y	W	D.C.	04 NOV 1870	Congressional
280	Faunt, Catherine	15y	C	Md.	30 OCT 1867	Young Mens
544	Fauntelroy, John	3y	W	D.C.	11 NOV 1871	
430	Faust, John, horse drover	41y	W	Ire.	24 DEC 1869	Mt. Olivet
496	Faust, Leonora	70y	W	Amer.	03 DEC 1870	Rock Creek
496	Faust, Vaughan Lewis	2y	W	D.C.	22 DEC 1870	Rock Creek
345	Faust, William	3y	W	Ger.	28 AUG 1868	Mt. Olivet
594	Fawcet, Robert	12y	W	D.C.	05 APR 1872	
247	Fawcett, [blank]	Still	W	D.C.	07 DEC 1866	Congressional
535	Faxen, Charles, clerk	52y	W	N.Y.	07 SEP 1871	Hartford, Conn.
586	Faxon, Charles W.	40y	W	D.C.	12 MAR 1872	Conn.
308	Fay, Charles M., lawyer	22y	W	N.J.	25 APR 1868	Oak Hill
659	Fay, Edward L., ice dealer	34y	W	U.S.	14 JAN 1873	Boston, Mass.
674	Fay, Mary Augusta	22y	W	U.S.	19 MAR 1873	Prospect Hill
593	Fay, Minnie L.	7m	W	D.C.	26 APR 1872	Glenwood
747	Fay, Thomas, laborer	43y	W	Ire.	04 FEB 1874	Mt. Olivet
441	Fayman, James William	2y	W	N.Y.	16 FEB 1870	Cypress
521	Fazelaman, Kate	6m	W	D.C.	07 JUN 1871	Prospect Hill
292a	Fearson, Samuel S., wood mercht.	74y	W	Va.	14 JAN 1868	Vault
092	Fearson, [blank]		W	D.C.	27 SEP 1857	Georgetown
324	Feby, Margaret	10m	W	D.C.	21 JUL 1868	Mt. Olivet
153	Feeney, William, watchman	54y	W	Ire.	07 JUL 1859	St. Patricks
629	Feete, Louisa M.	2y	W	U.S.	04 OCT 1872	
397	Feete, M.	9m	W	D.C.	25 JUN 1869	Middletown, Md.
401	Fegan, Isabella	39y	W	Ire.	18 JUL 1869	Mt. Olivet
459	Fegundis, Cath.	70y	W	D.C.	29 JUN 1870	Potters Field
210	Fehenback, C.	1y	W		15 JAN 1866	Western

District of Columbia Interments (Index to Deaths), 1855-1874

Page	Name	Age	Race	Birth	Death Date	Burial Ground
270	Feldglass, Louisa	9m	W	D.C.	16 AUG 1867	Prospect Hill
784	Feldross, Wilhelmina	16d	W	U.S.	27 JUL 1874	Prospect Hill
057	Felger, Emma	26d	W	D.C.	13 SEP 1856	Congressional
421	Felix, John	5m	C		13 OCT 1869	Mt. Olivet
290	Fellar, William	11y	W	D.C.	04 JAN 1868	German Catholic
144	Feller, Mary	4y	W	D.C.	17 MAR 1859	German
546	Fellows, Chas. C.	5y	W	Mo.	23 NOV 1871	N.Y.
252	Felt, Mary Lillian	1y		D.C.	23 FEB 1867	Oak Hill
396	Felt, Nelson	4m	W	D.C.	30 JUN 1869	Oak Hill
276	Felton, Henderson	16y	C		11 SEP 1867	Freedmen's Hospital
402	Fely, William	7d	W	D.C.	07 JUL 1869	Mt. Olivet
111	Fencht, F.	5d	W	D.C.	11 APR 1858	German
349	Fendall, Clarence, coast survey	34y	W	D.C.	20 SEP 1868	Glenwood
163	Fendall, Elizabeth M.	55y	W	U.S.	07 OCT 1859	Alexandria, Va.
297	Fendall, Philip Richard, counsellor	73y	W	Va.*	16 FEB 1868	Glenwood
356	Fennell, Ella	2y	W	N.Y.	17 OCT 1868	Mt. Olivet
086	Fennell, John	14y	W	Ire.	05 AUG 1857	St. Patricks
554	Fennell, John F., clerk	26y	W	D.C.	13 JAN 1872	Mt. Olivet
383	Fenny, Lucy	1y	C	D.C.	07 MAR 1869	Washington Asylum
311	Fenst, Charles		C		c.30 APR 1868	Alms House
210	Fenton, Elizabeth L.	3m	W	D.C.	28 JAN 1866	Congressional
308	Fenton, Martha Holmes	1m	W	D.C.	08 APR 1868	Congressional
582	Fentress, Harriet	56y	W	Va.	22 FEB 1872	Va.
704	Fentroy, Ann	25y	W	Va.	09 JUL 1873	Small Pox
780	Fentroy, Mary S.	3y	C	unk.	30 JUL 1874	
420	Fentz, Ida	8m	W		16 OCT 1869	Prospect Hill
408	Fenwick, Emily	3m	W		10 AUG 1869	Mt. Olivet
765	Fenwick, Louisa S.	39y	W	U.S.	10 MAY 1874	Mt. Olivet
348	Fenwick, Robt. W.	7d	W	D.C.	12 SEP 1868	Congressional
360	Fenwick, William H., farmer	29y	W	D.C.	26 NOV 1868	Mt. Olivet
592	Fenwick, Wm. A.	1y	W	D.C.	19 APR 1872	Mt. Olivet
093	Fergueson, Wm. A.	11m	C	D.C.	12 OCT 1857	Harmony
158	Fergurson, James, laborer	48y	W	Ire.	19 AUG 1859	Mt. Olivet
380	Ferguson, Albert B.	64y	W	N.Y.	16 MAR 1869	Methodist
542	Ferguson, Ann	76y	C	Va.	22 OCT 1871	Washington
664	Ferguson, Catherine	40y	W	U.S.	15 JAN 1873	Small Pox*
592	Ferguson, Chas. F.	4m	W	D.C.	09 APR 1872	Methodist Epis.
458	Ferguson, E.	14d	C	D.C.	16 JUN 1870	Potters Field
643	Ferguson, Edward	10d	W	U.S.	07 DEC 1872	Glenwood
330	Ferguson, Eliza	2y	C	D.C.	06 JUL 1868	Young Mens
371	Ferguson, Elizabeth	80y	C	D.C.	01 JAN 1869	Washington Asylum
355	Ferguson, Emma	17y	W	Va.	24 OCT 1868	Congressional
583	Ferguson, Francis	89y	W	U.S.	25 FEB 1872	Methodist
348	Ferguson, George	6m	W	D.C.	01 SEP 1868	Congressional
132	Ferguson, John H.	21y	C	D.C.	15 NOV 1858	Young Mens
334	Ferguson, Louisa	1y	W	D.C.	11 JUL 1868	Glenwood
130	Ferguson, Mary		W		13 OCT 1858	Baltimore, Md.
226	Ferguson, Susan	43y	C	Va.	28 JUN 1866	Young Mens
588	Ferguson, Wm. H.	8m	C	D.C.	25 MAR 1872	Harmony
221	Ferguson, [blank]	Still			19 MAY 1866	Georgetown
296	Fernaught, William Henry	3m	W	D.C.	15 FEB 1868	Prospect Hill
710	Ferrara, Mary	9m	W	D.C.	03 AUG 1873	Mt. Olivet
093	Ferris, Margaret	63y	W	Md.	09 OCT 1857	St. Patricks
049	Fertner, Charles E.	1y	W	D.C.	01 JUL 1856	Holmead
351	Fessel, Margaret	67y	W	Ger.	04 SEP 1868	Prospect Hll
221	Field, Julia	2y	C	D.C.	24 MAY 1866	Holmead
166	Field, L.W.	38y	W	N.Y.	27 NOV 1859	Washington Asylum
669	Field, Richard, Indian agent	70y	W	U.S.	26 FEB 1873	Congressional*

Page	Name	Age	Race	Birth	Death Date	Burial Ground
729	Field, Samuel, furniture dealer	41y	W	Ger.	02 NOV 1873	Baltimore, Md.
154	Fielder, Chas. R., seaman	21y	W	N.J.	15 JUL 1859	Washington Asylum
472	Fields, Albert, child of	Still	C		17 AUG 1870	Young Mens
451	Fields, Anna	5m	C		26 APR 1870	Union
405	Fields, Anne	6m	C	D.C.	28 JUL 1869	Washington Asylum
389	Fields, Lucy	21y	C	Va.	04 APR 1869	Washington Asylum
741	Fields, Reuben	26y	C	U.S.	07 JAN 1874	Mt. Pleasant
737	Fields, Roy, laborer	17y	C	U.S.	24 DEC 1873	
536	Fields, Sarah	2y	C	D.C.	17 SEP 1871	Ebenezer
191	Fields, [blank]		W	D.C.	10 OCT 1860	Methodist
310	Figara, Sarah	65y	W		c.27 APR 1868	Mt. Olivet
483	Filbert, Catherine	2y	W	D.C.	21 OCT 1870	Mt. Olivet
637	Filbrown, Mary S.	77y	W	U.S.	04 NOV 1872	Oak Hill
251	Fili, John, laborer	34y	W	Ger.	16 JAN 1867	Alms House
356	Filley, Elizabeth, Mrs.	25y	C	Ger.	29 OCT 1868	Prospect Hill
434	Fillian, J., Mr., dentist	38y		Ger.	03 JAN 1870	Congressional
185	Fillins, Virginia, child of	Still	W	D.C.	14 JUL 1860	Congressional
659	Fillman, Betsey	65y	C	U.S.	12 JAN 1873	Ebenezer
013	Filton, J.R.	7m	W	D.C.	30 JUL 1855	Methodist, East
013	Filton, W.W.	5y	W	D.C.	18 JUL 1855	Methodist, East
624	Finagan, Geo. A.	2y	W	U.S.	07 SEP 1872	
097	Finagan, Michael, soldier	23y	W	Ire.	22 NOV 1857	Congressional
349	Finan, John Joseph	1y	W	Ire.	02 SEP 1868	Mt. Olivet
532	Finch, Lewis	70y	W	N.Y.	12 AUG 1871	Congressional
607	Finch, Maggie	19y	W	D.C.	29 JUN 1872	
622a	Finch, Maggie	9m	W	U.S.	29 AUG 1872	
259	Finckle, George, child of	6m	W		03 APR 1867	Glenwood
189	Finegan, Elizabeth	33y	W	D.C.	02 SEP 1860	
689	Finigan, Edward	4m	W	U.S.	14 MAY 1873	Mt. Olivet
147	Fink, John B.	4y	W	D.C.	26 APR 1859	Oak Hill
743	Fink, Louisa B.	2y	W	U.S.	23 JAN 1874	Oak Hill
063	Fink, Maria	21y	W	D.C.*	26 NOV 1856	Catholic
375	Fink, Mrs.				13 FEB 1869	
188	Finkman, Edward	4m	W	D.C.	17 AUG 1860	
361	Finlan, T.I., Mr., infant of	Still	W		28 NOV 1868	
344	Finn, Eliza	2y	W	Ire.	19 AUG 1868	
268	Finn, Elizabeth	75y	W	Ire.	15 AUG 1867	Mt. Olivet
772	Finn, Margaret	24y	W	U.S.	09 JUN 1874	Mt. Olivet
417	Finney, Josh.	1y	C	D.C.	01 SEP 1869	Washington Asylum
338	Finshay, Mary E.	1y	W		28 AUG 1868	Mt. Olivet
258	Finster, John, laborer	25y	W	Md.	20 APR 1867	Georgetown, Catholic
033	Fipps, N., Mrs., child of	Still	W		19 JAN 1856	Foundry
062	Firor, Ephram A., carpenter	28y	W	Md.	12 NOV 1856	Glenwood
257	Firt, William Ellwin, clerk	21y	W	N.J.	10 MAR 1867	Glenwood
430	Fischer, Andrew	4m			06 DEC 1869	Prospect Hill
148	Fischer, Harriet		W		16 MAY 1859	Congressional
083	Fischer, Henry	1y	C		14 JUL 1857	Harmony
636	Fischer, Josephine	22y	W	U.S.	10 NOV 1872	
537	Fish, Ellen Virginia	1y	W	D.C.	22 SEP 1871	Greenmount, Balto.
583	Fish, Morgan				26 FEB 1872	
645	Fish, Valentine S.	35y	W	U.S.	28 DEC 1872	
258	Fisher, Ann	39y	W	D.C.	19 APR 1867	Congressional
697	Fisher, Annie	2m	B	D.C.	10 JUN 1873	Holmead
114	Fisher, Charlott	30y	C	D.C.	25 MAY 1858	Harmony
619	Fisher, Chas.	3w	C	U.S.	18 AUG 1872	
666	Fisher, Christiana	66y	W	Ger.	02 FEB 1873	Washington Asylum
176	Fisher, Elizabeth	76y	W	Va.	11 APR 1860	Oak Hill
297	Fisher, Geo.		C		c.26 FEB 1868	Alms House

District of Columbia Interments (Index to Deaths), 1855-1874

Page	Name	Age	Race	Birth	Death Date	Burial Ground
635	Fisher, George	19y	W	U.S.	27 NOV 1872	Small Pox
780	Fisher, Hattie	1d	C	U.S.	12 JUL 1874	Harmony
399	Fisher, Hiram L., clerk	32y	W	N.Y.	18 JUL 1869	Congressional
426	Fisher, Jacob	8y	W	Md.	10 NOV 1869	Washington Hebrew
164	Fisher, Jacob, laborer	71y	W	Ger.	14 OCT 1859	German Lutheran
368	Fisher, Jesica	40y	W	Eng.	24 DEC 1868	Glenwood
527	Fisher, John	60y	W	Ala.	12 JUL 1871	Congressional
137	Fisher, John	35y	W		16 JAN 1859	Washington Asylum
694	Fisher, Joseph	3m	W	D.C.	14 JUN 1873	St. Marys
635	Fisher, Josephine	22y	W	U.S.	11 NOV 1872	Small Pox
772	Fisher, Kate	22y	C	U.S.	05 JUN 1874	Mt. Olivet
780	Fisher, Leonard	8m	W	U.S.	17 JUL 1874	Congressional
105	Fisher, Lilly	9y	W	D.C.	21 FEB 1858	Oak Hill
593	Fisher, Louis H.	1y	W	Mass.	18 APR 1872	Mt. Olivet*
395	Fisher, Margaret	70y	W	Md.	17 JUN 1869	Glenwood
124	Fisher, Marvin H.	8y	W	D.C.	10 AUG 1858	Congressional
694	Fisher, Mary	10y	C	Va.	03 JUN 1873	Beckett's
254	Fisher, Mary Jane	42y	W	D.C.	08 FEB 1867	Baltimore, Md.
307	Fisher, Mr., child of	2m	W	D.C.	20 APR 1868	Prospect Hill
376	Fisher, Mr., infant of	16d	W		04 FEB 1869	Prospect Hill
311	Fisher, Nelson		C		c.15 APR 1868	Alms House
266	Fisher, Paul, cooper	66y	W	Ger.	26 JUL 1867	German Catholic
102	Fisher, Rachael, cook	59y	C	D.C.	20 JAN 1858	Foundry
513	Fisher, William	8m	W	D.C.	27 MAR 1871	German Catholic
103	Fisher, [blank]	11m	C	D.C.	30 JAN 1858	Holmead
057	Fitch, Mary A.	67y	W	Va.	09 SEP 1856	Alexandria, Va.
513	Fitch, Sarah B.	34y	W	N.Y.	27 MAR 1871	Oak Hill
472	Fitchugh, [blank], carpenter	59y	C	Va.	10 AUG 1870	Young Mens
697	Fitler, Ida Mary	4½m	W	D.C.	16 JUN 1873	Prospect Hill
172	Fitnam, Eliza	20h	W	D.C.	04 FEB 1860	Glenwood
667	Fitz, Hannah	70y	W	U.S.	11 FEB 1873	Glenwood
155	Fitzgerald, Ann Eliza	20y	C	Va.*	28 JUL 1859	Harmony
123	Fitzgerald, Bridget	30y	W	Ire.	01 JUL 1858	St. Patricks
266	Fitzgerald, Catherine	7m	W	D.C.	27 JUL 1867	Mt. Olivet
354	Fitzgerald, David, farmer	52y	W	Ire.	26 OCT 1868	Mt. Olivet
111	Fitzgerald, Edmond	2y	W	Md.	14 APR 1858	St. Peters
092	Fitzgerald, Edmund, laborer		W	Ire.	22 SEP 1857	St. Patricks
724	Fitzgerald, Ellen	5y	W	D.C.	14 OCT 1873	Mt. Olivet
621	Fitzgerald, Ellen	25y	C	U.S.	16 AUG 1872	Mt. Olivet
007	Fitzgerald, Ellen	40y	W	Ire.	06 MAY 1855	St. Patricks
269	Fitzgerald, James	4y	W		01 AUG 1867	Mt. Olivet
058	Fitzgerald, James, hotel keeper	65y	W	Ire.	20 SEP 1856	St. Matthews
151	Fitzgerald, John	21d	W	D.C.	19 JUN 1859	Mt. Olivet
288	Fitzgerald, John		W	D.C.	21 DEC 1867	Mt. Olivet
102	Fitzgerald, John	2y	W	D.C.	25 JAN 1858	St. Patricks
096	Fitzgerald, John	12y	W	D.C.	07 NOV 1857	St. Peters
094	Fitzgerald, John, laborer	66y	W	Ire.	30 OCT 1857	St. Patricks
772	Fitzgerald, Julia	16y	W	Ire.	20 JUN 1874	Holyrood
394	Fitzgerald, Kate	40y	W	Ire.	20 JUN 1869	Mt. Olivet
696	Fitzgerald, M.	4m	W	D.C.	16 JUN 1873	
223	Fitzgerald, Margaret		W	D.C.	02 JUN 1866	Mt. Olivet
621	Fitzgerald, Margaret	38y	W	Ire.	21 AUG 1872	Mt. Olivet
073	Fitzgerald, Margaret	22y	W	Ire.	09 MAR 1857	St. Matthews
644	Fitzgerald, Margt.	66y	W	U.S.	23 DEC 1872	Mt. Olivet
620	Fitzgerald, Mary	8m	W	U.S.	25 AUG 1872	
163	Fitzgerald, Mary	6m	C	D.C.	10 OCT 1859	Harmony
582	Fitzgerald, Mary	1y	W	D.C.	20 FEB 1872	Mt. Olivet
084	Fitzgerald, Mary	9m	W	D.C.	21 JUL 1857	St. Matthews

Page	Name	Age	Race	Birth	Death Date	Burial Ground
111	Fitzgerald, Mary	1y	W		19 APR 1858	St. Patricks
189	Fitzgerald, Mary A.	91y	W	Mass.	18 SEP 1860	Mt. Olivet
069	Fitzgerald, Mary Ann	2y	W		30 JAN 1857	St. Matthews
128	Fitzgerald, Michael, laborer	52y	W	Ire.	24 SEP 1858	St. Peters
176	Fitzgerald, Mrs.	40y	W	Ire.	— APR 1860	
331	Fitzgerald, Patrick	1y	W	D.C.	23 JUL 1868	Mt. Olivet
398	Fitzgerald, Patrick	35y	W		— JUN 1869	Washington Asylum
229	Fitzgerald, Patrick, child of				19 JUL 1866	Mt. Olivet
322	Fitzgerald, Patrick, laborer	58y	W	Ire.	18 JUN 1868	St. Patricks
436	Fitzgerald, R.B., Mrs.	46y	W	Va.	03 JAN 1870	Oak Hill
123	Fitzgerald, William	21d	W	D.C.	06 JUL 1858	St. Patricks
780	Fitzgerald, Willie D.	2y	W	U.S.	21 JUL 1874	Mt. Olivet
360	Fitzgerald, Wm. A., printer	59y	W	Md.	21 NOV 1868	Glenwood
021	Fitzgerrald, Hanorah	7m	W	D.C.	25 AUG 1855	
004	Fitzgerrel, C.W.	4y	W	D.C.	29 MAR 1855	St. Peters
759	Fitzgibbins, Joseph	1y	W	U.S.	16 APR 1874	Mt. Olivet
278	Fitzgibbons, Bridget	37y	W	Ire.	03 OCT 1867	Mt. Olivet
289	Fitzgibbons, Mary	75y	W	Ire.	31 JAN 1868	Mt. Olivet
030	Fitzgivens, [blank], laborer	44y	W	Ire.	18 NOV 1855	St. Matthews
459	Fitzhew, Daniel, laborer	30y	C	Va.	22 JUN 1870	
638	Fitzhugh, A.	62y	C	U.S.	23 NOV 1872	
408	Fitzhugh, Charles	1y	W		20 AUG 1869	Mt. Olivet
493	Fitzhugh, Ed.	5m	C	D.C.	19 DEC 1870	Ebenezer
553	Fitzhugh, Elisabeth	20y	C	Md.	08 JAN 1872	Washington
614	Fitzhugh, Ellen	78y	W	U.S.	12 JUL 1872	
520	Fitzhugh, Ernest	11m	W	D.C.	25 MAY 1871	Glenwood
087	Fitzhugh, George		W	D.C.	13 AUG 1857	Glenwood
673	Fitzhugh, John W., carpenter	48y	W	U.S.	11 MAR 1873	
005	Fitzhugh, Joshua	80y	C	Va.	06 APR 1855	Foundry
014	Fitzhugh, Linah, slave	72y	C	Va.	14 JUL 1855	Foundry
163	Fitzhugh, Rosalie A.	11m	W	D.C.	01 OCT 1859	Congressional
042	Fitzpatrick, Cath. Ann	3m	W	D.C.	19 APR 1856	St. Patricks
622a	Fitzpatrick, Chas. F.	10m	W	U.S.	16 AUG 1872	
310	Fitzpatrick, James	3m	W		c.03 APR 1868	Mt. Olivet*
202	Fitzpatrick, Jno. C., clerk	19y	W	D.C.	08 APR 1861	St. Peters
164	Fitzpatrick, Jno. M.	25y	W		28 OCT 1859	Baltimore, Md.
164	Fitzpatrick, John, stone cutter	26y	W	Md.	29 OCT 1859	Baltimore, Md.
028	Fitzpatrick, Mary	23y	W	Ire.	21 OCT 1855	St. Patricks
026	Fitzpatrick, McHue, laborer	45y	W	Ire.	19 OCT 1855	St. Patricks
059	Fitzpatrick, Patrick, butcher	75y	W	Ire.	29 SEP 1856	St. Peters
239	Fitzpatrick, Patrick, laborer	25y	W	Ire.	27 OCT 1866	Mt. Olivet
087	Fitzpatrick, William, clerk	29y	W	D.C.	14 AUG 1857	St. Peters
381	Fitzsimmons, Hugh, liquor dealer	41y	W	Ire.	05 MAR 1869	Mt. Olivet
240	Fitzsimmons, Mary	1m	W		13 OCT 1866	Mt. Olivet
365	Fitzsimmons, Thos., clerk	35y	W	Ire.	25 DEC 1868	Mt. Olivet
780	Fitzwilliam, Thos. F., printer	30y	W	Unk.	07 JUL 1874	Glenwood
632	Fix, Christina	28d	W	U.S.	14 OCT 1872	
712	Fix, Corolic	10d	W	D.C.	21 AUG 1873	Prospect Hill
293a	Flagg, Harriet, Mrs.	75y	W	Me.	24 JAN 1868	Glenwood
140	Flagg, Sarah	31y	W		02 FEB 1859	Glenwood
065	Flaggs, [blank]	1m	W		05 DEC 1856	St. Matthews
731	Flaharty, Thomas	70y	W	Ire.	23 NOV 1873	Mt. Olivet
091	Flahaty, Mary I.	6m	W	D.C.	11 SEP 1857	St. Peters
714	Flaherty, Agnes	1y	W	D.C.	31 AUG 1873	Mt. Olivet
339	Flaherty, Andrew	9m	W	D.C.	09 AUG 1868	Mt. Olivet
361	Flaherty, Catharine	4y	W		08 NOV 1868	Mt. Olivet
077	Flaherty, James, laborer	30y	W	Ire.	03 MAY 1857	St. Matthews
008	Flaherty, Jas. H.	3y	W	Md.	12 MAY 1855	St. Patricks

District of Columbia Interments (Index to Deaths), 1855-1874

Page	Name	Age	Race	Birth	Death Date	Burial Ground
229	Flaherty, John	50y	W	Ire.	17 JUL 1866	Mt. Olivet
077	Flaherty, Julia E.	27y	W	Ire.	17 MAY 1857	St. Patricks
273	Flaherty, Michael, laborer		W	Ire.	22 SEP 1867	Mt. Olivet
181	Flaherty, William, watchman	46y	W	Ire.	11 JUN 1860	Mt. Olivet
308	Flanagan, Bev., infant of	Still	W		10 APR 1868	Mt. Olivet
001	Flanagan, Cordelia M.	56y		Md.	17 JAN 1855	
643	Flanagan, John	42y	W	Ire.	07 DEC 1872	Bordentown, N.J.
097	Flanagan, Patrick	75y	W	Ire.	20 NOV 1857	St. Peters
046	Flanery, Thomas, stone cutter	35y	W	Ire.	01 JUN 1856	St. Patricks
315	Flanigan, Ann	34y	W		c.23 MAY 1868	Mt. Olivet
018	Flannery, Lott	1y	W	D.C.	03 AUG 1855	St. Patricks
312	Flannigan, Bernard, laborer	35y	W	Ire.	08 MAY 1868	Mt. Olivet
463	Flannigan, Fanny	5m	W	D.C.	12 JUL 1870	
517	Flannigan, Mary	35y	W	Ger.	01 APR 1871	Holly Wood
659	Flaring, Henry, shoemaker	43y	W	Ger.	15 JAN 1873	St. Marys
626	Flasher, Amy L.	1y	W	U.S.	24 SEP 1872	
124	Flathiry, Timothy	2y	W	Va.	04 AUG 1858	St. Peters
046	Flavety, Mathew	22y	W		19 JUN 1856	Georgetown, Catholic
069	Flax, Louisa	3y	W	D.C.	30 JAN 1857	St. Matthews
772	Fleet, Julia	96y	C		20 JUN 1874	Washington Asylum
706	Fleet, Mary E.	14y	C	D.C.	15 JUL 1873	
715	Fleet, Rebecca	2y	C	U.S.	08 AUG 1873	
780	Fleischman, Louis	8m	W	U.S.	12 JUL 1874	Mt. Olivet
213	Fleming, Ellen	5d	W		28 FEB 1866	Mt. Olivet
233	Fleming, Eugene	31y			04 AUG 1866	Congressional
373	Fleming, Joseph	5m	C		11 JAN 1869	Young Mens
408	Fleming, Mary	2y	W		14 AUG 1869	Mt. Olivet
639	Fleming, Mary J.	1y	C	U.S.	11 DEC 1872	Small Pox*
772	Fleming, Wm. A.	9m	W	U.S.	09 JUN 1874	Mt. Olivet
249	Flemings, Jesse	22y	W	Va.	04 JAN 1867	Congressional
016	Flemings, Wm. H.	8m			02 JUL 1855	Foundry
377	Flemmens, Priscilla	30y	C	Va.	15 FEB 1869	Washington Asylum
414	Flemming, Harriet Matilda	23y	W	Va.	21 SEP 1869	Congressional
607	Flemming, Thos.	2m	W	D.C.	25 JUN 1872	Mt. Olivet
437	Fletcher, Addie	8y	W		15 JAN 1870	Mt. Olivet
759	Fletcher, Arthur W., clerk	60y	W	U.S.	14 APR 1874	Congressional
278	Fletcher, Basil	65y			05 OCT 1867	Mt. Olivet
732	Fletcher, Burley	27y	C	U.S.	29 NOV 1873	Mt. Pleasant
204	Fletcher, Charles, waiter	17y	C	D.C.	27 JUN 1861	Harmony
772	Fletcher, Edward	2m	C	U.S.	16 JUN 1874	Young Mens
765	Fletcher, Harriet A.	1y	W	U.S.	21 MAY 1874	Mt. Olivet
780	Fletcher, Ida G.	2m	W	U.S.	09 JUL 1874	Chester, Pa.
538	Fletcher, James	21y	C	Va.	30 SEP 1871	Washington
142	Fletcher, James H.	7m	C	D.C.	27 FEB 1859	Harmony
228	Fletcher, Jessie Eliza	47y	W	Eng.	15 JUL 1866	Congressional
250	Fletcher, John A.	21y	W		15 JAN 1867	
753	Fletcher, John, foreman	30y	W	Ire.	06 MAR 1874	Mt. Olivet
622	Fletcher, Marcia F.	13m	W	U.S.	15 AUG 1872	
086	Fletcher, Mary	21y	C	Md.	08 AUG 1857	County
451	Fletcher, Mary	85y	C		07 APR 1870	Mt. Olivet
634	Fletcher, Mary Ann	65y			10 OCT 1872	
780	Fletcher, Mary E.	80y	W	U.S.	03 JUL 1874	Mt. Olivet
074	Fletcher, Noah	71y	W	Mass.	23 MAR 1857	Congressional
062	Fletcher, Oscar William	6m	C	D.C.	12 NOV 1856	Young Mens
376	Fletcher, Robert B.	6m	C		21 FEB 1869	
335b	Fletcher, Robt.	2m	B		07 JUL 1868	Washington Asylum
350	Fletcher, Sarah	70y	C	Md.	30 SEP 1868	Young Mens
386	Fletcher, Sarah M.	67y	W	Md.	19 APR 1869	Congressional

Page	Name	Age	Race	Birth	Death Date	Burial Ground
174	Fletcher, Sophia	6y	C	D.C.	04 MAR 1860	
165	Fletcher, William, contractor	69y	W	U.S.	11 NOV 1859	Mt. Olivet
759	Fletcher, Wm. A., ship carpenter	55y	W	U.S.	08 APR 1874	Congressional*
481	Fletcher, [blank], servant	82y	C		07 OCT 1870	Holmead
414	Fleury, Wm. Warren	1y	W		20 SEP 1869	Congressional
255	Flinn, Catherine	36y	W	Ire.	18 MAR 1867	Alms House
181	Flinn, Mary	14d	W	D.C.	03 JUN 1860	St. Patricks
250	Flint, [blank]		W		— JAN 1867	Glenwood
093	Flood, Ann	50y	W	Ire.	05 OCT 1857	Washington Asylum
517	Flood, Francis Eva	1y	W	D.C.	05 APR 1871	Presbyterian
759	Flood, James	15y	W	U.S.	07 APR 1874	Mt. Olivet
330	Flood, Samuel M.	4y	W	Md.	21 JUL 1868	Md.
077	Flood, Sidney	1m	W	D.C.	12 MAY 1857	Rock Creek
077	Flood, William M.	2y	W	D.C.	18 MAY 1857	Rock Creek
723	Florence, Eleanor L., clerk	48y	W	Pa.	07 OCT 1873	Philadelphia, Pa.
063	Florence, Joseph R., clerk	38y	W	Pa.	19 NOV 1856	Philadelphia, Pa.
221	Florence, Lucy Ellen Norman	42y	W	Pa.	20 MAY 1866	Philadelphia, Pa.
477	Flority, Ella	4y	W	D.C.	21 SEP 1870	Mt. Olivet
001	Flowers, Margaret	44y			08 JAN 1855	
302	Flowers, Mary Ann	2m	W	D.C.	02 MAR 1868	Western
172	Floyd, B. Rush, lawyer	50y	W	Va.	16 FEB 1860	Va.
070	Floyd, John B., clerk	37y	W	N.Y.	05 FEB 1857	Congressional
398	Floyd, Richd.	6m	B	U.S.	20 JUN 1869	Washington Asylum
044	Flurry, James R.	2y	W	Va.	02 MAY 1856	Methodist, East
307	Fly, Thomas	65y	C	Va.	09 APR 1868	Freedmen's Hospital
155	Flyn, Thomas	2m	W	D.C.	25 JUL 1859	St. Patricks
463	Flynn, Brien, laborer	40y	W	Ire.	17 JUL 1870	Mt. Olivet
698	Flynn, Chronas, laborer	58y	W	Ire.	16 JUN 1873	Mt. Olivet
305	Flynn, Dennis	1d			c.16 MAR 1868	Mt. Olivet
323	Flynn, John	11m	W	D.C.	12 JUL 1868	Mt. Olivet
099	Flynn, John I.	2y	W	D.C.	15 DEC 1857	St. Patricks
496	Flynn, John, laborer	41y	W	Ire.	20 DEC 1870	Glenwood
395	Flynn, Julia	13m	W	D.C.	20 JUN 1869	Mt. Olivet
202	Flynn, Margarette	5m	W	D.C.	26 APR 1861	Mt. Olivet
060	Flynn, Mary	2y	W	D.C.	20 OCT 1856	St. Patricks
500	Flynn, Mary, servant	37y	W	Ire.	15 JAN 1871	Mt. Olivet
400	Flynn, Michael	9m	W		15 JUL 1869	Mt. Olivet
283	Flynn, Patrick, fruit dealer	40y	W	Ire.	23 NOV 1867	Mt. Olivet
375	Flynn, Peter	72y	W	Ire.	28 FEB 1869	Mt. Olivet*
610	Flynn, S.	47y	W		04 JUN 1867	Mt. Olivet
402	Flynt, Horatio, collector Int. Rev.	47y	W		29 JUL 1869	Mt. Olivet
613	Fogarty, Mary A.	2y	W	U.S.	20 JUL 1872	
314	Fogle, Mary	30y	W	Ire.	15 MAY 1868	Alms House
161	Foiley, James, laborer	35y	W	Ire.	03 SEP 1859	Mt. Olivet
189	Foitey, John	1m	W	D.C.	15 SEP 1860	Mt. Olivet
614	Foley, Bridget	7y	W	U.S.	30 JUL 1872	
199	Foley, Daniel, laborer	35y	W	Ire.	11 FEB 1861	St. Patricks
747	Foley, Ella	17y	W	U.S.	11 FEB 1874	Mt. Olivet
401	Foley, Ellen	1y	W		24 JUL 1869	Mt. Olivet
079	Foley, Ellen	26y	W	Ire.	08 JUN 1857	St. Patricks
019	Foley, Honora	24y	W	Ire.	21 AUG 1855	St. Patricks
629	Foley, Mary	11m	W	U.S.	09 OCT 1872	
092	Foley, Michael, laborer	33y	W	Ire.	23 SEP 1857	St. Peters
096	Foley, Thomas, laborer	50y	W	Ire.	03 NOV 1857	Washington Asylum
123	Foley, Wm.	9m	W	D.C.	07 JUL 1858	St. Peters
152	Folk, Henry A.	4m	W	D.C.	22 JUN 1859	Catholic
182	Folk, Mary E.	5y	W		21 JUN 1860	Western
677	Folke, Wm. H.	28y	W	U.S.	c.27 MAR 1873	Congressional

Page	Name	Age	Race	Birth	Death Date	Burial Ground
684	Folkes, Chandler	6y	W	U.S.	18 APR 1873	Small Pox*
684	Folkes, Saml.	50y	W	U.S.	16 APR 1873	Small Pox*
234	Follansbee, Ellen Webster	9m	W	Tex.	01 SEP 1866	Ebenezer
248	Follansbee, Joseph, carpenter	73y	W	Mass.	12 DEC 1866	Glenwood
122	Foller, Thomas	39y	W	Ger.	24 JUL 1858	German Protestant
394	Folson, Chas.	11m	C	D.C.	19 JUN 1869	Mt. Olivet
212	Folson, Elizabeth B.	1m	W	D.C.	02 FEB 1866	Rock Creek
487	Foltz, George, clerk	65y	W	N.Y.	24 NOV 1870	Congressional
697	Foly, Jno.	1y	W	D.C.	18 JUN 1873	Mt. Olivet
645	Foly, Thomas	6y	W	U.S.	24 DEC 1872	Mt. Olivet
310	Foneslett, Bridget, nurse	65y	W	Ire.	28 APR 1868	Baltimore, Md.
285	Foos, Francis	7m	W	D.C.	17 DEC 1867	Congressional
734	Foos, Susie	25y	W	U.S.	03 DEC 1873	Congressional
082	Foot, Andrew, hackman	65y	C		08 JUL 1857	Harmony
047	Foot, James	8m	C	D.C.	25 JUN 1856	Harmony
216	Foot, Solomon, U.S. senator	63y	W	Ver.	28 MAR 1866	Ver.
093	Forbes, Harry D.	3y	W		16 OCT 1857	Methodist
121	Forbes, James	11m	W	D.C.	13 JUL 1858	St. Peters
634	Forbes, Jane	1m	W	U.S.	07 SEP 1872	
322	Force, Georgiana L.	24y	W	D.C.	14 JUN 1868	Glenwood
074	Force, Hannah E.	58y	W	Del.	26 MAR 1857	Congressional
197	Force, Marion Evans, clerk	22y	W	D.C.	30 JAN 1861	Congressional
289	Force, Peter, historian	77y	W	N.J.	22 JAN 1868	Glenwood
039	Force, Saml. S.	20y	W	D.C.	07 MAR 1856	Congressional
107	Ford, A.	8d	C		04 MAR 1858	Georgetown
414	Ford, Alice	53y	W	Eng.	01 SEP 1869	Congressional
706	Ford, Charlotte	36y	W	Va.	08 JUL 1873	
235	Ford, Clara E.L.	8m	C	D.C.	18 SEP 1866	Ebenezer
441	Ford, Columbus	30y	C		02 FEB 1870	Harmony
476	Ford, D.S.M., clerk Treas.	29y	W	Amer.	13 SEP 1870	Oswego, N.Y.
534	Ford, Daniel	3y	C	D.C.	27 AUG 1871	Young Mens
638	Ford, Easter	40y	C	U.S.	14 NOV 1872	
165	Ford, Elizabeth	64y	W	U.S.	19 NOV 1859	Western
753	Ford, Gabriel S., lawyer	30y	W	W.I.	07 MAR 1874	Young Mens
090	Ford, James, stone mason	38y	W	Ire.	01 SEP 1857	St. Patricks
110	Ford, Jas. Edward	2y	W	Mass.	04 APR 1858	St. Matthews
107	Ford, John	43h	W	D.C.	09 MAR 1858	Catholic
270	Ford, John N.	66y	W		11 AUG 1867	Glenwood
020	Ford, Josiah		W		08 AUG 1855	St. Patricks
420	Ford, Kate	25y	W	Ire.	12 OCT 1869	Mt. Olivet
356	Ford, Lewis, waiter in hotel	14y	C	Va.	08 OCT 1868	Young Mens
022	Ford, Marcus	4m			15 AUG 1855	
108	Ford, Mark	2y	W		17 MAR 1858	St. Patricks
352	Ford, Mary J.	1y	C	D.C.	02 SEP 1868	Washington Asylum
244	Ford, Patty	65y	C		24 NOV 1866	Young Mens
018	Ford, Philomena	1y	W	D.C.	23 AUG 1855	
663	Ford, Robert	43y	C	U.S.	01 JAN 1873	Small Pox*
531	Ford, Rose		C	Va.	05 AUG 1871	Unknown
600	Ford, Sally	26y	C	U.S.	06 MAY 1872	Young Mens
315	Ford, Saml.		C		c.02 MAY 1868	Alms House
228	Ford, Sophia	80y	C	Md.	14 JUL 1866	Ebenezer
177	Ford, Susa, cook	48y	C	D.C.	30 APR 1860	Mt. Olivet
298	Ford, Thomas H., lawyer	56y	W	Va.	29 FEB 1868	Congressional
167	Ford, Willie T.	8y	W	D.C.	13 DEC 1859	Congressional
521	Foreman, Amelia	68y	C	Md.	01 JUN 1871	Young Mens
392	Foreman, Eliza E.	25y	C	Md.	22 MAY 1869	Young Mens
127	Foreman, Georgianna	18y	C	D.C.	14 SEP 1858	
531	Foristic, Chas. F.	21d		U.S.	06 AUG 1871	Prospect Hill

Page	Name	Age	Race	Birth	Death Date	Burial Ground
031	Forman, Cathn.	73y	W	N.Y.	05 DEC 1855	Glenwood
324	Forman, R.H., child of	Still	W	D.C.	06 JUL 1868	Glenwood
244	Forney, Helen	2m	W	D.C.	03 NOV 1866	York, Pa.
643	Forney, Jacob D., engineer	36y	W	U.S.	14 DEC 1872	York Co., Pa.
765	Forrest, Annie M.S.	75y	W	U.S.	— MAY 1874	
217	Forrest, E.L.	1y	C	D.C.	08 APR 1866	Ebenezer
104	Forrest, George W.	2y	W	D.C.	06 FEB 1858	Methodist, East
726	Forrest, Gustav	8m	W	U.S.	27 OCT 1873	Mt. Olivet
736	Forrest, Jean G.	82y	W	Scot.	16 DEC 1873	Glenwood
245	Forrest, John, grocer	45y	W	D.C.	20 NOV 1866	
735	Forrest, L.M.	20y	C	U.S.	08 DEC 1873	Congressional
645	Forrest, Malinda	73y	W	U.S.	27 DEC 1872	Oak Hill
669	Forrest, Mary C.	14y	W	U.S.	27 FEB 1873	Glenwood
088	Forrest, Miss, servant of	16y	C		16 AUG 1857	Young Mens
028	Forrest, Miss, servant of	24y	C		06 OCT 1855	Young Mens
029	Forrest, Miss, servant of	42y	C		29 NOV 1855	Young Mens
017	Forrest, Richd. H., waiter	28y	C	D.C.	20 JUL 1855	Young Mens
027	Forrest, Stephney	95y	C	Md.	13 OCT 1855	Young Mens
675	Forrester, Nelly, cook	70y	C	U.S.	23 MAR 1873	Richmond, Va.
097	Forshee, Moses, cart man	80y	C	Va.	30 NOV 1857	Western
015	Forshee, Mrs.	60y	C		28 JUL 1855	West
772	Forshing, [blank]	5m	W	U.S.	30 JUN 1874	Mt. Olivet
340	Forsyth, Ada S.	1y	W	D.C.	07 AUG 1868	Congressional
044	Fort, Georgianna	14y	C	Va.*	17 MAY 1856	Foundry
218	Fort, Richard W., student	17y	W	N.J.	13 APR 1866	Glenwood
261	Fort, Wilbur, clerk	28y	W		01 MAY 1867	Glenwood
725	Fortenay, Edwin W., clerk	56y	W	Va.	19 OCT 1873	Oak Hill
414	Fortune, Peter, private marine	32y	W	Eng.	18 SEP 1869	Congressional
231	Fosdick, Harrison, clerk	31y	W	N.Y.	02 AUG 1866	Carlisle, Pa.
422	Foster, Ben, laborer	30y	C	Md.	26 OCT 1869	
747	Foster, Benj. F., ship carpenter	32y	W	U.S.	17 FEB 1874	Congressional*
295	Foster, Benjamin G.	35y	W	Mass.	01 FEB 1868	Congressional
626	Foster, Chas.	1y	W	U.S.	21 SEP 1872	
736	Foster, Edward, draughtsman	79y	W	U.S.	16 DEC 1873	Congressional
126	Foster, Elizabeth	9m	W	D.C.	09 AUG 1858	
266	Foster, Elizabeth	61y	W	Md.	13 JUL 1867	Glenwood
101	Foster, Emeline	2y	W	Ill.	11 JAN 1858	N.Y.
315	Foster, Francis		C		c.06 MAY 1868	Alms House
396	Foster, Franz	14d	W	D.C.	27 JUN 1869	Prospect Hill
608	Foster, Gottlieb, messenger	42y	W	Ger.	04 JUN 1872	Prospect Hill
102	Foster, Harriet	32y	W	N.Y.	19 JAN 1858	N.Y.
335	Foster, Harry Sidney	8m	W	D.C.	04 JUL 1868	Presbyterian
414	Foster, Harty Elizabeth	1y	W	D.C.	26 SEP 1869	Conn.
283	Foster, Jane Beary	23y	W	D.C.	13 NOV 1867	Congressional
591	Foster, Joseph R.	8y	C	D.C.	23 APR 1872	Small Pox
591	Foster, Joseph R.	8y	C	U.S.	24 APR 1872	Small Pox
695	Foster, Laura	15m	C	Va.	20 JUN 1873	
555	Foster, Laura M.	56y	W		25 JAN 1872	Congressional
231	Foster, Lottie W.	5m	W	D.C.	06 AUG 1866	Congressional
210	Foster, Mary	62y	W	Md.	15 JAN 1866	Congressional
318	Foster, Mary Maria Isabel	1y	W	Md.	23 JUN 1868	Congressional
289	Foster, Mary, Miss, clerk Treas.	32y	W	Me.	06 JAN 1868	Waterford, Me.
299	Foster, Reuben, laborer	65y	C	Va.	02 MAR 1868	Young Mens
009	Foster, Robt. P.	10y	W	Miss.	25 MAY 1855	Congressional
315	Foster, Saml.		C		c.05 MAY 1868	Alms House
085	Foster, Theodore A.	42y	W		12 JUL 1857	Congressional
299	Foster, Thomas, printer	26y	W	Pa.	29 MAR 1868	Harrisburg, Pa.
374	Foster, Willie James	3m	W		13 FEB 1869	Congressional

Page	Name	Age	Race	Birth	Death Date	Burial Ground
229	Foster, [child of]	Still	W		18 JUL 1866	Holmead
780	Foulk, Albert E.	8m	W	U.S.	28 JUL 1874	Glenwood
175	Foulkes, John E., clerk	67y	W	S.Wa.	27 MAR 1860	Congressional
311	Foundling		W		c.09 APR 1868	Alms House
423	Foundling	1d	W	D.C.	14 OCT 1869	Washington Asylum
423	Foundling	Still	W	D.C.	11 OCT 1869	Washington Asylum
747	Foundling, John	2m	C	U.S.	07 FEB 1874	Mt. Olivet
734	Foundling, Mary	1m	C	U.S.	02 DEC 1873	Mt. Olivet
771	Foundling, Mary	1m	C	U.S.	02 JUN 1874	Mt. Olivet
731	Foundling, Michael	1m	C	U.S.	23 NOV 1873	Mt. Olivet
025	Fountain, Addison	35y	W	Va.	20 SEP 1855	Holmead
292	Fountain, Joshua		C		14 JAN 1868	Alms House
001	Foust, George	62y			1_ JAN 1855	Glenwood
125	Fouvenal, Minna	5m	W	D.C.	17 AUG 1858	German
681	Fowke, Samuel	50y	W	U.S.	15 APR 1873	Congressional
099	Fowler, Benj. F., soldier	60y	W	Md.	23 DEC 1857	Marine
001	Fowler, C.H.	1m			16 JAN 1855	Congressional
618	Fowler, Chas. H.	1y	W	U.S.	07 AUG 1872	
366	Fowler, E.M., Mrs.	83y	W	Pa.	13 DEC 1868	Congressional*
499	Fowler, Henderson	11y	W	D.C.	02 JAN 1871	Congressional
266	Fowler, Isaac	7m	W	D.C.	02 JUL 1867	Oak Hill
711	Fowler, James I., real estate	53y	W	D.C.	11 AUG 1873	Rock Creek
522	Fowler, Jessie Florence	6m	W	D.C.	11 JUN 1871	Glenwood
529	Fowler, John W.	4m	W	D.C.	27 JUL 1871	
434	Fowler, Joseph, bricklayer	54y	W		04 JAN 1870	Congressional
364	Fowler, Margaret A.	6m	W		06 DEC 1868	Congressional
107	Fowler, Margaret L.	9d	W	D.C.	13 MAR 1858	Glenwood
688	Fowler, Maria		W	U.S.	12 MAY 1873	Oak Hill
246	Fowler, Maria Louisa	39y	W	Ky.	15 DEC 1866	
263	Fowler, Martha E.	5m	W	D.C.	30 JUN 1867	Congressional
041	Fowler, Mary	40y	W	D.C.	06 APR 1856	Congressional
186	Fowler, Mary A.	70y	W	Eng.	29 JUL 1860	Congressional
288	Fowler, Mrs.	70y	W		31 DEC 1867	Tenley Town
225	Fowler, Rebecca	64y	W		20 JUN 1866	Oak Hill
286	Fowler, Robert B., gentleman	67y	W	Md.	21 DEC 1867	Oak Hill
383	Fowler, Robt.	37y	W	D.C.	08 MAR 1869	Washington Asylum
715	Fowler, Washington, laborer	35y	C	Md.	05 AUG 1873	
533	Fowler, Wm. B.	1y	W	D.C.	20 AUG 1871	Congressional*
197	Fowler, Wm., child of	Still	W	D.C.	01 JAN 1861	Congressional
010	Fowler, [blank]	1m	W	D.C.	14 JUN 1855	Congressional
669	Fox, Beutie	1y	W	U.S.	25 FEB 1873	Prospect Hill
372	Fox, Charlotte	3y	C		08 JAN 1869	Freedmen's Hospital
407	Fox, Elizabeth	93y	W	Amer.	21 AUG 1869	Congressional
317	Fox, Geo.	1y	W	D.C.	01 JUN 1868	Congressional
536	Fox, George	1y	C	D.C.	18 SEP 1871	Ebenezer
274	Fox, George P.	28y	W	Md.	15 SEP 1867	
335a	Fox, Harriet				25 JUL 1868	Washington Asylum
148	Fox, Hugh, clerk	63y	W	Ire.	12 MAY 1859	Mt. Olivet
463	Fox, John Henry	6m	C		21 JUL 1870	Beckett's
513	Fox, Letty	71y	C	Ky.	28 MAR 1871	Washington Asylum
535	Fox, Lorenzo	47y	C	Va.	06 SEP 1871	
726	Fox, Margaret	80y	W	Ire.	25 OCT 1873	
492	Fox, Maria, servant	18y	C	Va.	11 DEC 1870	Young Mens
735	Fox, Mary, storekeeper	75y	W	U.S.	12 DEC 1873	Congressional
597	Fox, Philip B.	5y	W	U.S.	01 MAY 1872	Congressional*
314	Fox, Willie	1y	W	D.C.	27 MAY 1868	Congressional
515	Fox, [blank]	11m	C	D.C.	24 MAR 1871	Union
213	Fox, [blank]		C		19 FEB 1866	Western

Page	Name	Age	Race	Birth	Death Date	Burial Ground
027	Foy, John, tavern keeper	64y	W	Ire.	14 OCT 1855	St. Patricks
161	Frailer, Caroline	7y	W	D.C.	05 SEP 1859	
090	Frailer, Charles, merchant	60y	W	Ger.	11 SEP 1857	German Catholic
078	Frailey, Charles S., clerk	53y	C	Md.	24 MAY 1857	Congressional
690	Fraily, Thomas	37y	C	U.S.	05 MAY 1873	Small Pox
723	Frain, John V.	4y	W	Calif.	02 OCT 1873	
522	France, Clinton	2y	W	D.C.	10 JUN 1871	Glenwood
720	Francico, Idia	1m	C	D.C.	26 SEP 1873	Mt. Pleasant
269	Francis, John	2m	W		05 AUG 1867	Mt. Olivet
412	Francis, John	11m	C	D.C.	19 AUG 1869	Washington Asylum
314	Francis, Mary	3m	W		25 MAY 1868	Mt. Olivet
546	Francis, Sarah	42y	W	U.S.	29 NOV 1871	Congressional
103	Francis, Thomas	2m	W	D.C.	30 JAN 1858	St. Peters
017	Francis, Wm., slave	1y	C		29 JUL 1855	St. Patricks
354	Frank, Mary	82y	W	Ger.	06 OCT 1868	Mt. Olivet*
086	Frankenberger, Charles, hotel kpr.	32y	W	Bav.	02 AUG 1857	St. Patricks
724	Franklin, Ann	78y	W	Md.	14 OCT 1873	Christ Church
318	Franklin, J.W., child of	11m	W	D.C.	18 JUN 1868	Congressional
400	Franklin, Jane	9d			08 JUL 1869	Congressional
726	Franklin, Jos. W., policeman	38y	W	U.S.	24 OCT 1873	Glenwood
592	Franklin, Robert	12m		D.C.	16 APR 1872	
309	Franklin, William Asbury, clerk	37y	W	U.S.	04 APR 1868	Glenwood
759	Franklin, William, proofreader	72y	W	Eng.	03 APR 1874	Glenwood
402	Franklin, Wm.	11m	W	D.C.	07 JUL 1869	Mt. Olivet
015	Franklinberger, Mary K.	1y	W	D.C.	27 JUL 1855	St. Patricks
315	Frantwein, George		W		c.02 MAY 1868	Alms House
079	Franze, Louisa	6y	W	N.Y.	01 JUN 1857	Congressional
546	Franzoni, Jane	75y	W	Italy	29 NOV 1871	Congressional
298	Frase, Patsy	70y	C		14 FEB 1868	
519	Fraser, Emma J.	21y	W	D.C.	20 MAY 1871	Glenwood
061	Fraser, Mary	43y	C		09 OCT 1856	St. Patricks
731	Frash, Nellie		W	U.S.	22 NOV 1873	
124	Frasier, Franklin A.	2m	W		16 AUG 1858	Congressional
439	Frasier, Mary Elizabeth	43y	W		19 FEB 1870	Congressional
306	Frautwein, Geo., laborer		W		30 APR 1868	Alms House
772	Frawley, Jno. & Johanna, child of	1d	W	U.S.	18 JUN 1874	Mt. Olivet
516a	Frazer, Martha, pauper	30y	C	Va.	08 MAR 1871	Washington Asylum
704	Frazer, Robt.	24y	W	Va.	01 JUL 1873	Small Pox
074	Frazier, Benjamin, coachman	33y	C	Md.	26 MAR 1857	St. Matthews
012	Frazier, Charles	14y	W	Md.	07 JUN 1855	Glenwood
466	Frazier, Cornelius	13d	C		22 JUL 1870	Union
150	Frazier, Frances M.	40y	W	Md.	09 JUN 1859	Glenwood
631	Frazier, Frank, stone cutter	52y	W	Ire.	13 OCT 1872	Glenwood
501	Frazier, Geo. H.	10y	C	Va.	15 JAN 1871	White Haven
747	Frazier, Geo. Wm., policeman	58y	W	U.S.	01 FEB 1874	Glenwood
780	Frazier, George	1y	C	U.S.	04 JUL 1874	Young Mens
713	Frazier, Harry	1y	W	D.C.	22 AUG 1873	Congressional
516	Frazier, Isabella	34y	W	Va.	17 MAR 1871	Congressional
113	Frazier, Lucy	60y	C	Md.	13 MAY 1858	St. Matthews
293	Frazier, Martha, cook	41y	C	D.C.*	14 MAR 1868	Holmead
177	Frazier, Mary	85y	W	Md.	21 APR 1860	
488	Frazier, Sam., laborer	24y	C	Va.	18 NOV 1870	Washington Asylum
529	Frazier, Saml. J.			D.C.	25 JUL 1871	
530	Frazier, Saml. J., clerk	24y	W	U.S.	29 JUL 1871	Glenwood
633	Frazier, Wm.	25y	C	U.S.	17 OCT 1872	Small Pox*
144	Frazier, Wm. Robert, boatman	16y	W	Va.	27 MAR 1859	Prospect Hill
502	Frechter, Alice Smith	5y	W	W.I.	29 JAN 1871	Glenwood
545	Frederich, Joseph	8y	W	D.C.	19 NOV 1871	Congressional*

District of Columbia Interments (Index to Deaths), 1855-1874

Page	Name	Age	Race	Birth	Death Date	Burial Ground
014	Frederick, J.E.	1y	W		19 JUL 1855	German
193	Frederick, Magdaline	55y	W	Ger.	25 NOV 1860	Prospect Hill
341	Free, Wm. Henry	7m	W	D.C.	17 AUG 1868	Congressional
104	Freeberger, Margaret	9y	W	Md.	07 FEB 1858	Baltimore, Md.
705	Freeland, Anna E.	16m	W	Md.	13 JUL 1873	
283	Freeland, Charles P., clerk	30y	W	N.Y.	17 NOV 1867	Brooklyn, N.Y.
091	Freeland, [blank], servant	14y	C	D.C.	13 SEP 1857	Holmead
212	Freely, Hugh W., private marines	18y	W	Eng.	13 FEB 1866	Marine
740	Freeman, A. & E.A., infant of	7d	W	U.S.	01 JAN 1874	Washington Asylum
223	Freeman, B.	54y	C		02 JUN 1866	Western
217	Freeman, Edwin W.	7y	C	D.C.	08 APR 1866	Holmead
667	Freeman, Eliza C.	4y	C	U.S.	08 FEB 1873	Harmony
338	Freeman, Elizabeth C.	1y	W	D.C.	31 AUG 1868	Harmony
417	Freeman, Francis A.	2y	C	D.C.	23 SEP 1869	Washington Asylum
175	Freeman, George	5y	C	D.C.	29 MAR 1860	Harmony
713	Freeman, J. Thos.	1y	C	D.C.	21 AUG 1873	Washington Asylum
604	Freeman, James	5d	C	D.C.	25 JUN 1872	Ebenezer
070	Freeman, John	3y	C	D.C.	02 FEB 1857	Ebenezer
035	Freeman, John	1y	W	D.C.	15 FEB 1856	Not Reported
130	Freeman, John, freeman	50y	C	Md.	19 OCT 1858	Ebenezer
703	Freeman, John W.	14y	C	U.S.	21 JUL 1873	Harmony
269	Freeman, Lizza	2m	C	D.C.	26 AUG 1867	Young Mens
712	Freeman, Louisa	4y	C	Md.	19 AUG 1873	Mt. Olivet
488	Freeman, Lucinda	3m	C	D.C.	20 NOV 1870	Harmony
161	Freeman, Malinda	72y	W	U.S.	04 SEP 1859	
181	Freeman, Margaret, teacher		W	D.C.	16 JUN 1860	Congressional
006	Freeman, Mr., child of	4m	C		18 APR 1855	Western
297	Freeman, Nelson H.	12y	C	D.C.	14 FEB 1868	Harmony
384	Freeman, Pauley	75y	C		01 MAR 1869	
403	Freeman, Richard	1d	C		19 JUL 1869	Holmead
694	Freeman, Robt. T., dentist	30y	C	D.C.	06 JUN 1873	Harmony
371	Freeman, Sophia A.	56y	W	Md.	12 JAN 1869	Chestertown, Md.
354	Freeman, Walter F., carpenter	68y	C	N.C.	26 OCT 1868	Harmony
359	Freer, Richard	6y	W	D.C.	29 NOV 1868	Congressional
123	Freiman, M.A.	3y	W	D.C.	30 JUL 1858	German Catholic
356	Freitag, Susannah	42y	W	Ger.	02 OCT 1868	
639	Freland, Delia B.	29y	W	U.S.	15 NOV 1872	Philadelphia, Pa.
538	Frelling, Dorothea	35y	W	Ger.	25 SEP 1871	Prospect Hill
151	Freman, Matilda I.		C	U.S.	17 JUN 1859	Ebenezer
696	Fremont, Nelly	1h	C	D.C.	11 JUN 1873	
415	French, Amanda Jane	43y	W	D.C.	16 SEP 1869	Mt. Olivet
181	French, Anna	13d	W	D.C.	05 JUN 1860	Glenwood
471	French, Benj. B.	70y	W	N.H.	20 AUG 1870	Congressional
001	French, Chas. Thos.	10y			05 JAN 1855	Glenwood
368	French, Edwin, clerk	47y	W	Mass.	27 DEC 1868	Glenwood
765	French, Elizabeth	84y	W	U.S.	17 MAY 1874	Mt. Olivet
013	French, F.J.	1y	W	D.C.	03 JUL 1855	Congressional*
024	French, Frances E.	10m	W	D.C.	13 SEP 1855	St. Patricks
229	French, Harry B.	11m	W	D.C.	24 JUL 1866	Glenwood
549	French, James A.	1m		D.C.	23 DEC 1871	Congressional*
545	French, James G.	5y	W	D.C.	21 NOV 1871	
057	French, Jane	40y	W	D.C.	09 SEP 1856	Congressional
517	French, L.M., Mrs.	64y	W	Mass.	05 APR 1871	Glenwood
395	French, Othniel, marble worker	33y	W	Amer.	13 JUN 1869	Glenwood
102	French, Sarah	77y	W	Md.	23 JAN 1858	Glenwood
599	French, Sarah	60y	W	U.S.	28 MAY 1872	Va.
058	French, Winifred A.	2y	W	D.C.	16 SEP 1856	Glenwood
354	French, Wm. T., painter	32y	W	D.C.	16 OCT 1868	Glenwood

Page	Name	Age	Race	Birth	Death Date	Burial Ground
023	French, [blank]	4y	W		18 SEP 1855	St. Matthews
132	Frere, Thomas	1y	W	D.C.	15 NOV 1858	Mt. Olivet
366	Frere, Thompson A.	4m	W	N.C.	05 DEC 1868	
002	Frerley, Chas. W.	14y	W	D.C.	_5 JAN 1855	Methodist
450	Frerntsein, Annie	55y	W	Ger.	20 APR 1870	German Catholic
675	Freund, Less P., clerk	20y	W	U.S.	29 MAR 1873	Chicago, Ill.
426	Freund, Rosa	32y	W	Ger.	25 NOV 1869	Baltimore, Md.
445	Freund, [blank]	62y	W	Ger.	17 MAR 1870	Glenwood
374	Frey, Leonora V.	26y	W	Va.	18 FEB 1869	Congressional
326	Fribby, Minnie	10m	W	D.C.	11 JUL 1868	Congressional
366	Friday, Lewis	4m	W	Va.	19 DEC 1868	Prospect Hill
581	Fridley, Benj. F.	6y	W	D.C.	17 FEB 1872	Glenwood
426	Fridley, Mary A.	23y	W		02 NOV 1869	Glenwood
390	Fridley, Rosa A.B.	6y	W		28 MAY 1869	Glenwood
370	Fridley, Sarah Ann	59y	W		26 JAN 1869	Glenwood
550	Friedman, Sarah	1y	W	Md.	31 DEC 1871	
187	Friel, John	1m	W	D.C.	01 AUG 1860	Mt. Olivet
593	Frielocke, Natalie	36y	W	Ger.	08 APR 1872	
282	Fries, Christopher, undertaker	46y	W	Ger.	21 NOV 1867	Prospect Hill
120	Fries, John	37y	W	Ger.	01 JUL 1858	Congressional
303	Fries, John William	1y	W	D.C.	25 MAR 1868	Prospect Hill
691	Friman, John	26y	C	U.S.	16 MAY 1873	Small Pox*
703	Frisbee, Wm., laborer	53y	C	D.C.	05 JUL 1873	Harmony
068	Frisbey, William H.	2y	W	N.Y.	05 JAN 1857	Congressional
582	Frisby, Ann M.	56y	W	Md.	20 FEB 1872	Md.
528	Frisby, Annie	1m	W	U.S.	17 JUL 1871	Glenwood
547	Fritz, John Joseph	4y	W	D.C.	04 DEC 1871	Mt. Olivet
044	Fritzzell, John, carpenter	28y	W	Ire.	10 MAY 1856	Alexandria, Va.
103	Frizzell, John, messenger	58y	W	Ire.	09 JAN 1858	Alexandria, Va., Cath.
753	Frost, Chas. H., tobacco dealer	48y	W	U.S.	20 MAR 1874	Congressional
589	Frugel, Martha	7y	W	D.C.	08 MAR 1872	Presbyterian
002	Fruland, [blank]	3y	C	D.C.	— JAN 1855	Western
397	Frustner, Freeddy	1y	W	D.C.	29 JUN 1869	Hebrew
030	Fry, Ann M.	70y	W	Ger.	18 NOV 1855	Foundry
706	Fry, John	3m	W	D.C.	22 JUL 1873	Prospect Hill
595	Fry, John J., builder	65y	W	Md.	27 APR 1872	Oak Hill
094	Fry, John, laborer	50y	W		23 OCT 1857	Foundry
030	Fry, Joseph	72y	W	Ger.	09 NOV 1855	Foundry
697	Fry, Mary Louisa	3m	W	D.C.	27 JUN 1873	Prospect Hill
347	Fry, S. Viola	3y	W		07 SEP 1868	Congressional
088	Frye, Louisa	40y	W		19 AUG 1857	Foundry
032	Frye, Nathaniel, paymaster gen.	77y	W	Me.	31 DEC 1855	Rock Creek
597	Frye, Wesley	50y	C	U.S.	24 MAY 1872	Washington
601	Fryer, Wesley	38y	W	U.S.	23 MAY 1872	Congressional
744	Fuge, Sallie	75y	C	U.S.	29 JAN 1874	Young Mens
557	Fugett, Phobe	72y	W		05 FEB 1872	Congressional*
025	Fugitt, Benjn.	1y	W	D.C.	09 SEP 1855	
444	Fugitt, Joseph	62y	W	Md.	07 MAR 1870	Congressional
488	Fugitt, Laura	20y	W	Va.	12 NOV 1870	Alexandria, Va.
295	Fugitt, Mary F.	1y	W	D.C.	24 FEB 1868	Congressional
077	Fugitt, Melissa	6m			15 MAY 1857	Methodist, East
587	Fugitt, Saml. W.	4m	W	D.C.	23 MAR 1872	Congressional*
410	Fuld, Carrie	8m	W	Ger.	03 AUG 1869	Washington Hebrew
765	Fuler, Margaret, seamstress	23y	C	U.S.	05 MAY 1874	Harmony
407	Fullalove, Clara	6m	W		08 AUG 1869	Congressional
494	Fullalove, Wm., carpenter	36y	W	D.C.	17 DEC 1870	Oak Hill
537	Fullar, Wilson	7m	W	D.C.	22 SEP 1871	
144	Fuller, Azariah Chas.	6y	W	D.C.	29 MAR 1859	Congressional*

District of Columbia Interments (Index to Deaths), 1855-1874

Page	Name	Age	Race	Birth	Death Date	Burial Ground
210	Fuller, Edwd. N., merchant	48y	W	N.Y.	29 JAN 1866	Washington
114	Fuller, Emily	7m	W	D.C.	19 MAY 1858	Congressional
608	Fuller, Emma L.	4y	W	D.C.	11 JUN 1872	Glenwood
610	Fuller, Lavinia	76y	C	U.S.	07 JUL 1872	
710	Fuller, Mary E.	2y	W	D.C.	03 AUG 1873	Holmead
499	Fuller, Perry, gentleman	45y	W	U.S.	11 JAN 1871	Congressional
411	Fuller, William Sprague	1y	W		16 AUG 1869	Glenwood
251	Fullmore, John A., laborer	55y	W	Va.	11 JAN 1867	Alms House
157	Fulmer, George H.	56y	W	Eng.	12 AUG 1859	Mt. Olivet
132	Fulmer, Mary S.	60y	W	Va.	08 NOV 1858	St. Peters
271	Fultin, Mary Ellen	20y	W	N.H.	04 AUG 1867	N.H.
371	Funk, Barbara, Mrs.	56y	W	Ger.	18 JAN 1869	Holmead
149	Furgerson, Hannah A.	6y	C	D.C.	26 MAY 1859	Harmony
004	Furgerson, Jos., porter	63y	C	Md.	18 MAR 1855	Harmony
534	Furgerson, Wm. E., blacksmith	26y	W	D.C.	27 AUG 1871	Congressional*
425	Furgison, Oliver, C.	1y	W		14 NOV 1869	Congressional
271	Furguson, Clara	1y	W	D.C.	25 AUG 1867	Congressional
247	Furlough, James, laborer	70y	W	Ire.	03 DEC 1866	Mt. Olivet*
547	Furse, John	67y	W	Eng.	08 DEC 1871	Congressional
049	Furtener, Virginia	2y	W	D.C.	02 JUL 1856	Glenwood
241	Furtner, Elizabeth	65y	W	Va.	11 OCT 1866	Glenwood
089	Furtner, Richard, sexton	54y	W	Va.	19 AUG 1857	Glenwood
632	Fuss, Henrietta	48y	W	U.S.	14 OCT 1872	
780	Fuss, Susie	6m		U.S.	02 JUL 1874	Glenwood
060	Fuss, [blank]	2m	W	D.C.	18 OCT 1856	German Lutheran
772	Fussell, Leonard, coachman	75y	C	U.S.	09 JUN 1874	

Page	Name	Age	Race	Birth	Death Date	Burial Ground
G						
265	Gaddis, Adam	76y	W		21 JUL 1867	Congressional
225	Gaddis, Harry Milton	2y	W	D.C.	20 JUN 1866	Congressional
106	Gadsby, Provy	74y	W		09 FEB 1858	Congressional
008	Gadsby, Robt., Mrs., servant of	100y	C	Va.	12 MAY 1855	Holmead
780	Gae, Rose	67y	W	U.S.	22 JUL 1874	Rock Creek
645	Gage, Amelia [cor. from Guys]	25y	W	U.S.	24 DEC 1872	Oak Hill
617	Gage, Frank A.	6m	W	U.S.	17 AUG 1872	
610	Gage, Harry S.	1m	W	U.S.	23 JUL 1872	
666	Gagle, Joseph	2m	W	U.S.	05 FEB 1873	St. Marys
260	Gainer, George, porter	14y	C	Md.	11 MAY 1867	Young Mens
189	Gaines, Geo. Washington	26y	C	D.C.	18 SEP 1860	
508	Gaines, Lavinia	2y	C	D.C.	21 FEB 1871	Ebenezer
344	Gaines, Mary V.	6m	C	D.C.	21 AUG 1868	Harmony
598	Gaines, Mary V.	1m	C	U.S.	01 MAY 1872	Mt. Pleasant
342	Gaines, Nancy	7m	C	D.C.	18 AUG 1868	Union
264	Gaines, Robert	80y	C	Md.	17 JUL 1867	Ebenezer
291	Gaineway, Rosta	35y	C		28 JAN 1868	Alms House
286	Gainey, Julia, laundress	23y	W	Ire.	21 DEC 1867	Mt. Olivet
079	Gainor, John, messenger	69y	W	Ire.	07 JUN 1857	St. Patricks
247	Gainor, Robert, laborer	21y	C	Md.	04 DEC 1866	Young Mens
469	Gaio, Antonio, machinist	58y	W	Italy	14 AUG 1870	German
141	Gaither, James, carpenter	73y	W	Md.	19 FEB 1859	Methodist
765	Gaither, Sarah A.	55y	W	U.S.	17 MAY 1874	Glenwood
667	Galacar, E.A.H.	62y	W	U.S.	13 FEB 1873	Gloucester, Mass.
224	Galbrath, Arana J.	54y	W	Md.	12 JUN 1866	Montgomery Co., Md.
369	Gale, Anson, carpenter		W	N.Y.	10 JAN 1869	Congressional
545	Gales, Joseph, laborer	75y	C	Va.	12 NOV 1871	Washington
546	Gallagan, Mary	1y	W	D.C.	30 NOV 1871	Mt. Olivet
017	Gallager, Thos.	27y	W	D.C.	14 JUL 1855	St. Patricks
551	Gallaghan, Patrick	3y	W	D.C.	— DEC 1871	Mt. Olivet
584	Gallagher, Alice	30y	W	Ire.	01 MAR 1872	
738	Gallagher, Ann, infant of	3m	W	U.S.	01 DEC 1873	
766	Gallagher, Catherine	73y	W	U.S.	27 MAY 1874	Mt. Olivet
060	Gallagher, Daniel	60y	W	Ire.	27 OCT 1856	St. Patricks
102	Gallagher, Dennis E., printer	24y	W	D.C.	20 JAN 1858	St. Patricks
339	Gallagher, Mary Margaret	1y	W	D.C.	13 AUG 1868	Mt. Olivet
236	Gallagher, Patrick, laborer	40y	W	Ire.	30 SEP 1866	Alms House
273	Gallagher, Sarah	68y	W	D.C.	21 SEP 1867	Mt. Olivet
073	Gallagher, Sarah C.	20y	W	D.C.	05 MAR 1857	St. Patricks
339	Gallagher, Thomas Henry	4y	W		15 AUG 1868	Mt. Olivet
437	Gallagher, Thomas, printer	77y	W	Ire.	20 JAN 1870	Mt. Olivet
144	Gallahan, Elizabeth	3y	W	D.C.	30 MAR 1859	Glenwood
583	Gallahan, Gracie	5m	W	D.C.	28 FEB 1872	Congressional
435	Gallaway, Elizabeth	15y	C	Md.	23 JAN 1870	Harmony
406	Galleger, M.A.	11m	W		24 JUL 1869	Holyrood
419	Galliher, Sula May	2y	W	Md.	03 OCT 1869	Md.
513	Galloway, Ben	80y	C	Va.	30 MAR 1871	Washington Asylum
667	Galloway, William	60y	C	U.S.	10 FEB 1873	Washington Asylum
265	Galloway, Wm. A.	1y	C	D.C.	23 JUL 1867	Mt. Olivet
094	Galpin, John, clerk	41y	W	Conn.	19 OCT 1857	Newbears, Conn.
249	Galrett, [blank]	21d	W		17 JAN 1867	Glenwood
148	Galt, Albert H.	5y	W	D.C.	16 MAY 1859	Congressional
038	Galt, Mary Jane	35d	W		03 MAR 1856	Oak Hill
743	Galvin, B. Clifford, lawyer	40y	W	Ire.	24 JAN 1874	Congressional
765	Galvin, Joseph	4m	W	U.S.	06 MAY 1874	Mt. Olivet
015	Galvin, Thos., laborer	25y	W	Ire.	29 JUL 1855	St. Patricks
397	Galzniger, Francis	1y	W		20 JUN 1869	German Catholic

District of Columbia Interments (Index to Deaths), 1855-1874

Page	Name	Age	Race	Birth	Death Date	Burial Ground
583	Gambell, Benjamin	1y			25 FEB 1872	
599	Gambell, Joseph	25y	C	U.S.	11 MAY 1872	Unknown
664	Gamerick, Andrew	8y	C	U.S.	11 JAN 1873	Small Pox*
689	Gamet, Marion	15m	W	U.S.	11 MAY 1873	Mt. Olivet
294	Gannan, Margt.	69y	W	Ire.	11 FEB 1868	Mt. Olivet*
730	Gannon, John T.	3y	W	U.S.	11 NOV 1873	
479	Ganrans, Child				20 SEP 1870	Prospect Hill
431	Gans, Selig, merchant	55y	W	Ger.	05 DEC 1869	Hebrew
727	Gant, Agnes		B		31 OCT 1873	Beckett's
780	Gant, Ann E.	3m	C	unk.	23 JUL 1874	
383	Gant, Anna	70y	C	Md.	16 MAR 1869	Harmony
465	Gant, Annie		C		19 JUL 1870	Union
479	Gant, Catharine A.	1y	C		08 SEP 1870	Ebenezer
188	Gant, Ellen	11m	C	D.C.	29 AUG 1860	Foundry
264	Gant, Francis	9m	C	D.C.	02 JUL 1867	Union
549	Gant, George, waiter	36y	C	Md.	24 DEC 1871	Mt. Olivet
459	Gant, Jno. Thos.	1y	C	D.C.	30 JUN 1870	Potters Field
011	Gant, John Allen	22m	C	D.C.	25 JUN 1855	Methodist, East
674	Gant, Mary Ann	68y	C	U.S.	12 MAR 1873	
315	Gant, Matilda	6d	C		10 MAY 1868	
389	Gant, Rachel	25y	C		16 APR 1869	Washington Asylum
011	Gant, Saml.	2m	C		08 JUN 1855	Methodist, East
234	Gant, Thomas	2y	C	D.C.	06 SEP 1866	Beckett's
501	Gant, W. Joseph	21d	C		10 JAN 1871	Mt. Olivet
273	Gant, William	6m	C	D.C.	13 SEP 1867	Union
362	Gant, Wm. Henry	6m	C	D.C.	28 NOV 1868	Young Mens
336	Gant, Wm. M.	11m	C	D.C.	15 AUG 1868	
275	Gant, [blank]		C		03 SEP 1867	Young Mens
287	Gantt, Charles		C		c.17 DEC 1867	Alms House
287	Gantt, Mary		C		c.23 DEC 1867	Alms House
482	Gantt, Sarah G.	2y	C	D.C.	15 OCT 1870	Young Mens
123	Gantt, Thos. H.	1y	C		29 JUL 1858	Colored, East
197	Gantt, Wm. Henry	9m	C	D.C.	17 JAN 1861	Foundry
105	Gantt, [blank]	38y	W		24 FEB 1858	Pr. Geo. Co., Md.
033	Garden, Catharine		W	Md.	07 JAN 1856	Methodist Epis.
147	Gardener, Jno. C.	9y	W	D.C.	20 APR 1859	Congressional*
405	Gardener, Levi	65y	C	Va.	17 JUL 1869	Washington Asylum
023	Gardener, Louisa	11m	W		04 SEP 1855	Western
120	Garder, Jane	14y	W	Scot.	09 JUL 1858	Congressional
143	Gardiner, Cath.	7y	W	D.C.	12 MAR 1859	Congressional
765	Gardiner, Margaret	28d	W	U.S.	08 MAY 1874	Congressional
161	Gardner, Amelia	45y	W	U.S.	08 SEP 1859	Western
297	Gardner, Anne E.J., Mrs.	32y	W	U.S.	23 FEB 1868	Glenwood
425	Gardner, C.R., Col.	82y	W	N.J.	01 NOV 1869	Congressional
639	Gardner, Charity	50y	C	U.S.	09 DEC 1872	Small Pox*
524	Gardner, Charles, laborer	52y	C	N.C.	21 JUN 1871	
635	Gardner, J.H.	20y	C	U.S.	28 NOV 1872	Small Pox
471	Gardner, John J.	3y	W	D.C.	05 AUG 1870	Congressional
137	Gardner, Julia Ann	68y	W	N.J.	17 JAN 1859	Congressional
135	Gardner, Julia Ann	9m	W	D.C.	09 DEC 1858	Congressional
601	Gardner, Laura A.	13y	W	U.S.	21 MAY 1872	Congressional
237	Gardner, Margaret	60y	W		27 SEP 1866	Mt. Olivet
364	Gardner, Mrs.	35y	W	Md.	01 DEC 1868	Congressional*
747	Gardner, Richard	24y	C	U.S.	28 FEB 1874	Washington Asylum
420	Gardner, Richard, soldier	46y	W	Ire.	22 OCT 1869	Mt. Olivet
417	Gardner, Robt.	16d	W	D.C.	24 SEP 1869	Washington Asylum
306	Gardner, Willie	8m	C	D.C.	28 APR 1868	Alms House
296	Gardner, Wm.	56y	C	W.Va.	22 FEB 1868	Young Mens

Page	Name	Age	Race	Birth	Death Date	Burial Ground
548	Gardoff, Samuel	5y		D.C.	12 DEC 1871	Washington
134	Garesche, Edgar	4m	W	D.C.	26 NOV 1858	Mt. Olivet
200	Garesche, Lauscille	3y	W	D.C.	27 FEB 1861	Mt. Olivet
035	Garey, Sarah Ann	64y	W		21 FEB 1856	Oak Hill
706	Garnely, John	36y	C	Md.	25 JUL 1873	Washington Asylum
086	Garner, Catharine F.	56y	W	Va.	10 AUG 1857	Glenwood
163	Garner, Charles, blacksmith	36y	W	D.C.	28 OCT 1859	Congressional
240	Garner, Charles H.	33y	W		28 OCT 1866	Congressional
392	Garner, Floyd	3d	C		29 MAY 1869	
720	Garner, Fred., carpenter	37y	W	Md.	28 SEP 1873	Glenwood
421	Garner, Fred., infant of	Still	W		20 OCT 1869	Glenwood
202	Garner, Geo. W.	67y	W	Md.	12 APR 1861	Glenwood
600	Garner, Grandle, laborer	60y	C	U.S.	24 MAY 1872	Unknown
228	Garner, Hida	9m	W	D.C.	14 JUL 1866	Glenwood
711	Garner, Julia, servant	43y	C	Va.	10 AUG 1873	
706	Garner, Manuel, laborer	70y	C	D.C.	01 JUL 1873	
694	Garner, Martha A.	31y	W	Md.	03 JUN 1873	Glenwood
007	Garner, Mary E.	10y	C	D.C.	02 APR 1855	Foundry
427	Garner, Philip	2m	C	D.C.	30 NOV 1869	Washington Asylum
023	Garner, Sarah	2y	C	D.C.	06 SEP 1855	St. Patricks
053	Garner, Thomas J.	7d	W		05 AUG 1856	Congressional
548	Garner, Thomas, merchant	49y	W	Va.	15 DEC 1871	Congressional*
618	Garner, Walter	21m	W	U.S.	03 AUG 1872	Glenwood
772	Garner, Walter	2y	C	U.S.	22 JUN 1874	Mt. Pleasant
176	Garner, William, blacksmith	35y	W	Md.	01 APR 1860	Congressional
083	Garner, Wm. H. Thos.				12 JUL 1857	Congressional
091	Garner, [blank]	3y	W	D.C.	15 SEP 1857	Congressional
328	Garner, [blank]	1y	C	D.C.	31 JUL 1868	Ebenezer
514	Garnet, Frank, laborer	29y	C	Va.	30 MAR 1871	Ebenezer
591	Garnet, James	Still	C	D.C.	19 APR 1872	
550	Garnett, Amanda, servant	35y	C		27 DEC 1871	
431	Garnett, Churchill	35y	C		06 DEC 1869	Ebenezer
473	Garnett, Gideon	1y	C		23 AUG 1870	Ebenezer
342	Garnett, Harlan	3y	C	D.C.	18 AUG 1868	Young Mens
481	Garnett, Robert	50y	C	D.C.	— OCT 1870	Ebenezer
397	Garney, Michae, laborerl	26y	W	Ire.	25 JUN 1869	
034	Garretson, Jno. G., soldier	55y	W	N.J.	23 JAN 1856	Congressional
331	Garretson, Julia A.	58y	W	Pa.	27 JUL 1868	York, Pa.
644	Garretson, William, clerk	71y	W	U.S.	21 DEC 1872	Tioga P.
338	Garrett, George Lawson	1y	C		24 AUG 1868	Harmony
374	Garrett, Henry A., police officer	49y	W		17 FEB 1869	Congressional
461	Garrett, John M.	1y	C	D.C.	03 JUL 1870	Congressional
380	Garrett, Rebecca	73y	W	Md.	10 MAR 1869	Glenwood
060	Garrett, Richard, laboer	43y	C	Va.*	15 OCT 1856	Harmony
390	Garrett, Wilton, farmer	56y	W	Va.	21 MAY 1869	Congressional
253	Garrett, [blank]	3d	C	D.C.	22 FEB 1867	Harmony
162	Garrettson, Chas. W.	15y	C	D.C.	25 SEP 1859	Harmony
687	Garrettson, Harriet	65y	W	Md.	07 MAY 1873	Glenwood
623	Garrigan, Ellen	14m	W	U.S.	21 AUG 1872	Holy Rood
149	Garrison, Alice	2y	C	D.C.	28 MAY 1859	Harmony
323	Garrison, Catherine	22d	B		29 JUL 1868	Harmony
461	Garrison, Sianna G.	2y	W	D.C.	06 JUL 1870	Congressional
162	Garrison, Wesley H.	14y	C	D.C.	24 SEP 1859	Harmony
135	Garrott, Mr., servant of	4y	C		19 DEC 1858	Western
765	Garter, Ann	73y	C	U.S.	04 MAY 1874	Mt. Pleasant
580	Garthguet, Anna	2y	W	U.S.	09 FEB 1872	
714	Gartland, Wm. Thos.	5m	W	N.Y.	29 AUG 1873	Congressional
675	Garton, John	72y	W	U.S.	28 MAR 1873	Congressional

District of Columbia Interments (Index to Deaths), 1855-1874

Page	Name	Age	Race	Birth	Death Date	Burial Ground
055	Gasaway, James	5m	C	D.C.	17 AUG 1856	Harmony
027	Gasch, Emilie	11m	W	D.C.	27 OCT 1855	German
248	Gasch, Katie Augusta	7m	W	D.C.	22 DEC 1866	Glenwood
481	Gaskill, Charles, machinist	49y	W	Pa.	08 OCT 1870	Mt. Olivet
695	Gaskin, A.	20m	C	D.C.	08 JUN 1873	
780	Gasking, John H.	1y	C	U.S.	18 JUL 1874	Mt. Pleasant
609	Gaskins, Anna L.	6m	W	U.S.	25 JUN 1872	
759	Gaskins, Lota	7d	W	U.S.	14 APR 1874	Congressional
765	Gaskins, Phoebe	71y	C	U.S.	10 MAY 1874	Washington Asylum
366	Gaskins, Wm.	43y	B		30 DEC 1868	Union
500	Gass, Fredk. Park	2y	W	D.C.	23 JAN 1871	Glenwood
078	Gass, John G., watchman	50y	W	Ger.	23 MAY 1857	German
766	Gass, Laura M.	4y	W	U.S.	27 MAY 1874	Congressional
593	Gassaway, A.F.	19y	C	D.C.	26 APR 1872	
689	Gassaway, Amelia	17y	C	U.S.	14 MAY 1873	Harmony
705	Gassaway, E.M.	5m	W	D.C.	12 JUL 1873	Congressional*
023	Gassaway, Geo. W.	7y	C	D.C.	19 SEP 1855	Harmony
373	Gassaway, George, cartman	35y	C	Md.	16 JAN 1869	Western
431	Gassaway, J. Madison, boot maker	58y	W	Md.	17 DEC 1869	Glenwood
353	Gassaway, Mary V.	1y	C	D.C.	12 SEP 1868	Western
272	Gassaway, William Henry	25y	C	D.C.	02 AUG 1867	Harmony
673	Gassaway, Willie H.	3y	W	U.S.	05 MAR 1873	Congressional
141	Gassaway, [blank]	6m	C		20 FEB 1859	Young Mens
336	Gassenheimer, Emma	1y	W	D.C.	19 AUG 1868	Washington Hebrew
729	Gastoner, Ella	10y	C	U.S.	11 NOV 1873	Beckett's
494	Gatchell, Joshua L., contractor	31y	W	Pa.	19 DEC 1870	Elkton, Md.
658	Gately, Jno. A., merchant	28y	W	Ire.	03 JAN 1873	Mt. Olivet
493	Gately, John F.	3y	W	D.C.	07 DEC 1870	Mt. Olivet
190	Gates, Anna	20y	W	Md.	23 SEP 1860	
734	Gates, Chas. A.	4m	W	U.S.	07 DEC 1873	Congressional*
053	Gates, Franklin	8m	W	D.C.	01 AUG 1856	Congressional
475	Gates, Harry	5y	W	D.C.	20 SEP 1870	Congressional
259	Gates, James F.	3y	W	D.C.	16 APR 1867	Congressional*
024	Gates, John S.	1y	W	D.C.	22 SEP 1855	Congressional
308	Gates, Julius	1y	W	D.C.	25 APR 1868	Congressional
404	Gates, Lewis	1y	W		31 JUL 1869	Mt. Olivet
606	Gates, Mary	96y	W	Md.	23 JUN 1872	Congressional
184	Gates, Mary	1y	C	D.C.	03 JUL 1860	Washington Asylum
287	Gates, Nelson, foundry man	58y	W	N.Y.	24 DEC 1867	Glenwood
150	Gates, Richard	1y	W	D.C.	14 JUN 1859	Congressional
246	Gates, Sarah	65y	W	Md.	18 DEC 1866	Congressional
310	Gates, Sylvester	39y	W		c.03 APR 1868	Mt. Olivet
135	Gates, Thomas, bricklayer	37y	W	Md.	03 DEC 1858	Congressional
265	Gates, Thomas, Son of	5m	W	D.C.	18 JUL 1867	Congressional
483	Gates, Wm.	35y	W	N.Y.	22 OCT 1870	Congressional
130	Gates, [blank], Mr., laborer	67y	W	Md.	14 OCT 1858	St. Peters
644	Gatewood, Eliza, nurse	52y	C	U.S.	17 DEC 1872	Ebenezer
472	Gatewood, Samuel H.	1y	C	Pa.	03 AUG 1870	Beckett's
090	Gatewood, William	91y	W	Va.	11 SEP 1857	Congressional
734	Gatis, Peter, laborer	30y	W	U.S.	05 DEC 1873	
494	Gatley, Arthur W.	2y	W	D.C.	24 DEC 1870	Glenwood
169	Gatrell, James	6d	W	D.C.	14 JAN 1860	Ebenezer
050	Gattan, Lewis, laborer	71y	W	Md.	11 JUL 1856	St. Peters
446	Gaunt, Cathrine	60y	C	Md.	09 MAR 1870	Washington Asylum
431	Gaunt, John, laborer	30y	C		09 DEC 1869	
147	Gawler, John C.W.	1y	W	D.C.	26 APR 1859	Congressional*
522	Gawler, Steuart	1m	W		13 JUN 1871	Oak Hill
152	Gawler, Willie B.	1y	W	D.C.	22 JUN 1859	Oak Hill

Page	Name	Age	Race	Birth	Death Date	Burial Ground
488	Gayer, Mary	P.B.	W		16 NOV 1870	Mt. Olivet
370	Gayer, Mary E.	4y	W		31 JAN 1869	Mt. Olivet
400	Gayer, Morris	14d	W		12 JUL 1869	Mt. Olivet
268	Gazasa, Rosy	8m	W	D.C.	09 AUG 1867	Mt. Olivet
026	Gear, Patrick, laborer	38y	W	Ire.	09 OCT 1855	St. Patricks
015	Gear, William	2y	W	D.C.	10 JUL 1855	Glenwood
188	Gebhardt, Louis	4m	W	D.C.	27 AUG 1860	Prospect Hill
091	Geddis, Jessie	1y	W	D.C.	12 SEP 1857	Ebenezer
390	Gedins, Andrew J.	12y	W	Ger.	14 MAY 1869	Congressional
218	Gee, Matthew, clerk	27y	W	Conn.	16 APR 1866	Glenwood
772	Geery, James	14d	W	U.S.	27 JUN 1874	Mt. Olivet
620	Geier, Ann T.	2y	W	U.S.	21 AUG 1872	St. Marys
255	Geier, Catherine	43y	W	Ger.	28 MAR 1867	German Catholic
266	Geier, George	4m	W	D.C.	18 JUL 1867	German Catholic
269	Geiger, Cathrine J., dressmaker	42y	W	Ger.	12 AUG 1867	Prospect Hill
488	Geiger, Fredericka	71y	W		29 NOV 1870	Prospect Hill
527	Geiger, I.I., carpenter	42y	W	D.C.	11 JUL 1871	Prospect Hill
169	Geiger, Jas. G. Berret	5m	W	D.C.	17 JAN 1860	Prospect Hill
659	Geiger, Jno. E., jeweler	20y	W	U.S.	11 JAN 1873	Mt. Olivet
122	Geiger, Wm. H.	10m	W	D.C.	18 JUL 1858	German
204	Geir, Catharine	3y	W		26 JUN 1861	German Catholic
697	Geisler, Otto		W	U.S.	— JUN 1873	Prospect Hill
536	Geist, Wm., shoemaker	46y	W	Ger.	17 SEP 1871	Prospect Hill
585	Genan, George		W	U.S.	07 MAR 1872	Catholic
585	Genan, John		W	U.S.	09 MAR 1872	German
034	Gencke, Jno. F.	3m	W	D.C.	20 JAN 1856	German
415	Gender, William	1y	W		30 SEP 1869	German Catholic
024	Gennon, Vincent	65y			08 SEP 1855	Glenwood
011	Gent, Joseph	3m	W	D.C.	28 JUN 1855	Father Mathieus
118	Gentle, Alice	5y	W	D.C.	05 JUN 1858	
742	Gentner, Ann M.	38y	W	U.S.	18 JAN 1874	St. Marys
342	George, Spencer	14d	C	D.C.	11 AUG 1868	Young Mens
321	George, Virginia	1y	C	U.S.	30 JUN 1868	Alms House
266	George, William H.	5d	C		27 JUL 1867	Harmony
705	Gerard, Oliver	1y	W	D.C.	06 JUL 1873	Congressional
531	Gerhardt, Henry	10m	W	D.C.	03 AUG 1871	Prospect Hill
403	Gerhardt, Maria	33y	W	Ger.	21 JUL 1869	Prospect Hill
343	Gerhardt, William	1y	W	D.C.	17 AUG 1868	Prospect Hill
071	Gerhart, Roberta	3m	W	D.C.	25 FEB 1857	German
296	Gerlach, Charles, child of	2d	W	D.C.	20 FEB 1868	Prospect Hill
500	Gerlach, Mary	1y	W	D.C.	12 JAN 1871	Prospect Hill
023	Germon, Ida	11m	W	D.C.	24 SEP 1855	Western
301	Gersenheimer, Ann	15y	W	Ger.	30 MAR 1868	Western
188	Gesecke, John F., merchant	58y	W	Ger.	17 AUG 1860	Congressional
116	Gesir, Margaret	9m	W	D.C.	22 JUN 1858	German Catholic
772	Gessford, Edward	1y	W	U.S.	16 JUN 1874	Congressional*
364	Gessford, Robert E.	22m	W	U.S.	19 DEC 1868	Congressional
324	Getz, Caroline	7m	W	D.C.	03 JUL 1868	Mt. Olivet
199	Getzendemer, Jane		W	Md.	01 FEB 1861	Congressional
434	Getzsinger, Mary	4y	W		02 JAN 1870	German Catholic
305	Geyson, Albert	2m	W	D.C.	12 MAR 1868	Glenwood
669	Ghant, Andrew, laborer	73y	C		28 FEB 1873	Washington Asylum
173	Ghiselen, Elizabeth	25y	W	Ger.	22 FEB 1860	Lutheran
117	Ghoeer, [blank]	Still			26 JUN 1858	Glenwood
035	Gianpaoli, D. Adele	23y	W	Italy	10 FEB 1856	Congressional
093	Gibbins, Mathew, soldier	50y	W	Md.	02 OCT 1857	Congressional
185	Gibbons, James, collector	27y	W	Md.	25 JUL 1860	Glenwood
766	Gibbons, Joseph	3m	W	U.S.	18 MAY 1874	Mt. Olivet

Page	Name	Age	Race	Birth	Death Date	Burial Ground
061	Gibbons, [blank]		W	D.C.	05 OCT 1856	Congressional
513	Gibbs, Andrew, laborer	41y	C	N.C.	28 MAR 1871	Washington Asylum
715	Gibbs, George, deck hand	30y	C	U.S.	08 AUG 1873	
045	Gibbs, Lucretia	28y	C	Va.	09 MAY 1856	Washington Asylum
106	Gibbs, Mary Ann	68y	W	Md.	04 FEB 1858	
645	Gibbs, Peter	31y	C	U.S.	25 DEC 1872	Washington Asylum
362	Gibbs, William alias Weir	72y	C	Va.	14 NOV 1868	Harmony
402	Giberson, Gilbert L., lawyer	72y	W		12 JUL 1869	Mt. Olivet
589	Gibs, Catharine	1y	W	D.C.	28 MAR 1872	
118	Gibsen, Sarah Jane	25y	W	D.C.	16 JUN 1858	Congressional
555	Gibson, Alfred, laborer	16y	C	D.C.	25 JAN 1872	Washington
403	Gibson, Augustus, coachman	36y	C	Va.*	20 JUL 1869	Harmony
017	Gibson, B. Jos.	1m	W	D.C.	01 JUL 1855	Ebenezer
133	Gibson, Carrie	10m	W	D.C.	21 NOV 1858	Congressional
339	Gibson, Carrie Adele	11m	W	D.C.	05 AUG 1868	Glenwood
585	Gibson, Carter	35y	C	Va.	11 MAR 1872	Young Mens
133	Gibson, Catharine	58y	W	Md.	26 NOV 1858	Congressional*
483	Gibson, Clara W.	2y	W	D.C.	12 OCT 1870	Congressional
617	Gibson, Eliza	15y	C	U.S.	12 AUG 1872	
112	Gibson, Elizabeth	5y	W	Scot.	21 APR 1858	Oak Hill
306	Gibson, Emma	35y	C	Va.	25 APR 1868	Young Mens
615	Gibson, Florence	5y	C	U.S.	08 JUL 1872	
552	Gibson, Frances J., bookbinder	42y	W	Pa.	04 JAN 1872	Congressional*
484	Gibson, Francis H.	3y	W	D.C.	29 OCT 1870	Congressional
555	Gibson, Frank	40y	W	U.S.	22 JAN 1872	
554	Gibson, Frank, bookbinder	40y	W	U.S.	17 JAN 1872	
379	Gibson, George	1d	W		27 MAR 1869	Congressional
074	Gibson, George H.	3d			24 MAR 1857	Ebenezer
111	Gibson, George W.	9m	W	D.C.	11 APR 1858	Oak Hill
216	Gibson, Grace	3m	W	D.C.	30 MAR 1866	Congressional
638	Gibson, H.	16y	C	U.S.	11 NOV 1872	Washington Asylum
527	Gibson, Hannah	76y	W	U.S.	12 JUL 1871	German Catholic
165	Gibson, Henry H., laborer	39y	C	Va.*	12 NOV 1859	Alexandria, Va.
658	Gibson, Ida	10m	C	U.S.	08 JAN 1873	Ebenezer
113	Gibson, James H.	3y	W	Scot.	01 MAY 1858	Oak Hill
021	Gibson, Jas. G.	11m	W	D.C.	19 AUG 1855	Congressional
396	Gibson, John	19m	W	D.C.	28 JUN 1869	Oak Hill
182	Gibson, John H.	3m	W	D.C.	27 JUN 1860	Congressional
759	Gibson, John H., druggist	68y	W	U.S.	02 APR 1874	Mt. Olivet
304	Gibson, Josephine	1y	W	D.C.	04 MAR 1868	Congressional
444	Gibson, Joshua, calker	61y	W	D.C.	17 MAR 1870	Congressional
668	Gibson, Kate		W	U.S.	23 FEB 1873	
694	Gibson, Louisa	45y	C	Va.	16 JUN 1873	Beckett's
431	Gibson, Louisa	35y	C		27 DEC 1869	Young Mens
369	Gibson, Margaret A.	2y	W	D.C.	11 JAN 1869	Congressional
753	Gibson, Margaret A.	58y	W	U.S.	14 MAR 1874	Congressional*
633	Gibson, Martha, housewife	30y	C	U.S.	31 OCT 1872	
420	Gibson, Mary	28y	W	Va.	04 OCT 1869	Mt. Olivet
352	Gibson, Mary	7m	C		17 SEP 1868	Washington Asylum
420	Gibson, Mary Ann	Still	W		02 OCT 1869	German
532	Gibson, Mary L.	10m	W	D.C.	12 AUG 1871	Methodist
645	Gibson, Obediah, sadler	45y	W	U.S.	23 DEC 1872	Congressional
725	Gibson, Rachel	14y	B	Va.	18 OCT 1873	Young Mens
641	Gibson, Richard	45y	C	U.S.	08 DEC 1872	Small Pox
046	Gibson, Richard, artist	64y	W		19 JUN 1856	Georgetown, Trinity
435	Gibson, Rosa	1m	W		12 JAN 1870	Mt. Olivet
646	Gibson, Thomas, laborer	37y	C	Va.	18 DEC 1872	
176	Gibson, Walter U., bricklayer	29y	W	D.C.	15 APR 1860	Ebenezer

Page	Name	Age	Race	Birth	Death Date	Burial Ground
374	Gibson, William, policeman	43y	W		08 FEB 1869	Congressional
599	Gibson, Wm.	10y	W	U.S.	23 MAY 1872	Oak Hill
118	Gibson, Wm. E., clerk	26y	W	Md.	29 JUN 1858	Congressional
631	Gibson, [blank] [lined out]	Still	W	U.S.	23 OCT 1872	Glenwood
387	Gidding, Mary E.	52y	W		21 APR 1869	Glenwood
395	Giddings, Maria V.	4m	W	D.C.	11 JUN 1869	Glenwood
339	Giddings, Thomas	2y	W	D.C.	14 AUG 1868	Glenwood
004	Giddings, [blank]	Still	W	D.C.	31 MAR 1855	Washington Asylum
714	Gideon, Walter	16m	C	U.S.	31 AUG 1873	Young Mens
404	Gielbellet, Stephen	1m	W	D.C.	21 JUL 1869	
053	Gieseke, Henry, laborer	31y	W	Ger.	20 AUG 1856	Washington Asylum
667	Gieseking, Dorathea	80y	W	Ger.	10 FEB 1873	Oak Hill
050	Gigon, Peter Charles	10m	W	D.C.	19 JUL 1856	St. Matthews
320	Gilbert, Chas. W.	2m	C	D.C.	29 JUN 1868	Young Mens
291	Gilbert, Dorcas, washerwoman	92y	C	Md.	12 JAN 1868	Colored Women's
283	Gilbert, Geo. D.	6y	W	D.C.	03 NOV 1867	Glenwood/Oak Hill
283	Gilbert, Helen W.	10m	W	D.C.	17 NOV 1867	Glenwood/Oak Hill
419	Gilbert, Julia Ann	21y	W		03 OCT 1869	Congressional
589	Gilbert, Mary	19y	W	Ill.	30 MAR 1872	St. Marys
033	Gilbert, Saml. S.	22y	W	Mass.	06 JAN 1856	Boston, Mass.
128	Gilbert, [blank], barber		C	Md.	25 SEP 1858	Baltimore, Md.
719	Gilbot, Horatio, real estate	73y	W	N.Y.	21 SEP 1873	Glenwood
216	Gild[ner], Mary E., infant of	3m	W	D.C.	31 MAR 1866	Mt. Olivet
272	Giles, Saml. M., Rev.		W		— AUG 1867	
637	Giles, Wm. H.	5m	C	U.S.	13 NOV 1872	
101	Gilham, John	5y	W	D.C.	13 JAN 1858	Rock Creek
044	Gilham, Lucinda	30y	W	Va.	04 MAY 1856	Alms House
476	Gill, Annie	2y	W	D.C.	23 SEP 1870	Congressional
089	Gill, Elizabeth	65y	W	Va.	28 AUG 1857	Foundry
292	Gill, James E., armorer	45y	W	D.C.	26 JAN 1868	Congressional
536	Gill, Jane	40y	W	Va.	17 SEP 1871	Washington
485	Gill, Joseph L.	5m	W		03 OCT 1870	Congressional
614	Gill, Margaret A.	38y	W	U.S.	20 JUL 1872	
478	Gill, Maria	54y	W	Ire.	03 SEP 1870	Mt. Olivet*
058	Gill, P.E.	36y	W		15 SEP 1856	Congressional
526	Gill, Sarah Jane	10m	W	Mass.	06 JUL 1871	Mass.
042	Gillan, [blank]		W		26 APR 1856	Alms House
127	Gillchrist, Mary	1y	W	N.Y.	14 SEP 1858	Congressional
780	Gillen, Joseph F.	4m	W	U.S.	10 JUL 1874	Mt. Olivet
035	Gillet, Augustus C., clerk	34y	W	N.Y.	17 FEB 1856	Congressional
498	Gillin, Thomas, pauper	2y	B	D.C.	21 JAN 1871	Washington Asylum
597	Gillis, Henry, stone cutter	43y	C	Eng.	25 MAY 1872	Washington
500	Gillis, Maria T.	75y	W	N.Y.	09 JAN 1871	Glenwood
007	Gillison, Frank	60y	C	Va.	07 APR 1855	Harmony
177	Gilliss, Levin J., Rev.	64y	W	U.S.	30 APR 1860	Glenwood
772	Gillman, Laura Ann		W	U.S.	14 JUN 1874	Congressional*
062	Gilman, Caroline	30y	W	N.C.	10 NOV 1856	Congressional
668	Gilman, Edwin C.	2y	W	U.S.	17 FEB 1873	Meredith Village, N.H.
498	Gilman, Hester, pauper	21y	B	Md.	05 JAN 1871	Washington Asylum
118	Gilman, John, clerk	38y	W	Mass.	30 JUN 1858	Congressional
209	Gilman, Mr., servant child	10m	C		04 JAN 1866	Harmony
020	Gilman, Percy	1y	W	D.C.	03 AUG 1855	Congressional
320	Gilmar, Orville J., lawyer	35y	W	Ver.	06 JUN 1868	Salem, N.Y.
528	Gilmore, Preston	25y	C	Md.	13 JUL 1871	Potters Field
658	Gilroy, Edward, printer	38y	W	N.Y.	02 JAN 1873	Philadelphia, Pa.
249	Gilroy, Julia	24y	W	Ire.	14 JAN 1867	Mt. Olivet
262	Gilroy, Mary A.	5m	W	D.C.	27 JUN 1867	Mt. Olivet
612	Giltor, Mary W.	8m	W	U.S.	26 JUL 1872	

District of Columbia Interments (Index to Deaths), 1855-1874

Page	Name	Age	Race	Birth	Death Date	Burial Ground
002	Ginapher, Rachael	85y	C	Md.	— JAN 1855	Methodist
199	Giney, Jos., laborer	64y	W	Ire.	17 FEB 1861	
189	Ginity, Kate	1y	W	D.C.	15 SEP 1860	Mt. Olivet
046	Ginnaly, Thos. W.	7m	W	D.C.	12 JUN 1856	St. Patricks
501	Ginnatty, Jas., grocer	41y	W	Ire.	11 JAN 1871	Mt. Olivet
125	Ginnaty, Mary E.	8m	W	D.C.	17 AUG 1858	St. Patricks
323	Ginnity, Jane	8m	W	D.C.	04 JUL 1868	Mt. Olivet*
766	Ginster, Mary	78y	W	Eng.	28 MAY 1874	Oak Hill
337	Gipson, M.E.	7m	C	U.S.	06 AUG 1868	Washington Asylum
765	Girard, Infant	28d	W	U.S.	08 MAY 1874	Congressional*
479	Girard, M.	45y	W	Fra.	11 SEP 1870	Washington Asylum
170	Gittings, Ella	13y	C	Md.	30 JAN 1860	Glenwood
448	Given, Eddie E.	6y	W		26 MAR 1870	Oak Hill
231	Given, Emily S., Mrs.				01 AUG 1866	Glenwood
675	Givens, Alex Douglass	2m	C	U.S.	22 MAR 1873	
162	Givens, Caroline	18y	W	U.S.	18 SEP 1859	Western
605	Givens, Margret	60y	C	Ky.	24 JUN 1872	Small Pox
603	Givens, Washington, laborer	65y	C	Va.	12 JUN 1872	Small Pox
108	Gladden, Jane Eliza, mantua maker	32y	W	Va.	16 MAR 1858	Congressional
411	Gladmore, Effie	1y	W		26 AUG 1869	Oak Hill
152	Glaney, John, laborer	30y	W	Ire.	06 JUN 1859	Mt. Olivet
624	Glardon, Thos., laborer	29y	C	U.S.	17 SEP 1872	
540	Glargar, Ulricke L.	4m	W	D.C.	05 OCT 1871	
547	Glascock, Cornelia	25y	W	D.C.	02 DEC 1871	Congressional
435	Glascon, Darcus, laundress	33y	C	Va.	04 JAN 1870	Ebenezer
477	Glaser, Selma Elizabeth	5m	W	D.C.	07 SEP 1870	Prospect Hill
447	Glasgoe, Mary	19y	C	Va.	16 MAR 1870	Washington Asylum
014	Glasgow, Elizabeth	3m	W	D.C.	12 JUL 1855	Methodist, East
545	Glasgow, Jane E.	10m	W	D.C.	16 NOV 1871	Methodist
681	Glasgow, Rachael	25y	C	U.S.	20 APR 1873	Washington Asylum
622a	Glasgow, Sintha O.	3m	W	U.S.	17 AUG 1872	
756	Glass, Robert, carpenter	25y	W	Scot.	14 MAR 1874	
036	Glassco, [blank]	1m	C		22 FEB 1856	Not Reported
594	Glater, Oscar	85y	C	Md.	13 APR 1872	Washington
295	Glaze, Eva Catherine	1y	W	D.C.	24 FEB 1868	Congressional
780	Glaze, Henrietta A.	4m	W	U.S.	12 JUL 1874	Glenwood
780	Glaze, Maggie A.	4m	W	U.S.	15 JUL 1874	Glenwood
753	Glaze, Margaret A.	32y	W	U.S.	05 MAR 1874	Glenwood
234	Gleason, Daniel	2y	W	D.C.	01 SEP 1866	St. Patricks
713	Gleason, Ellen	8m	W	D.C.	22 AUG 1873	Mt. Olivet
781	Gleason, Grace	5m	W	U.S.	29 JUL 1874	Congressional
345	Gleason, Margaret	3m	W	D.C.	13 AUG 1868	Mt. Olivet
713	Gleason, Margaret	63y	W	Ire.	22 AUG 1873	Mt. Olivet
024	Gleason, Margaret	24d	W	D.C.	18 SEP 1855	St. Patricks
019	Gleason, Mary	32y	W	Ire.	26 AUG 1855	St. Peters
104	Gleason, Mary	10y	W	D.C.	14 FEB 1858	St. Peters
270	Gleason, Thomas	6m	W	D.C.	17 AUG 1867	Mt. Olivet
608	Gleeson, Bridget	80y	W	Ire.	15 JUN 1872	
605	Gleeson, Bridget	80y	W	Ire.	16 JUN 1872	
210	Gleeson, Mary	10y	C		27 JAN 1866	
351	Gleim, Henry, saddler	27y	W	Ger.	23 SEP 1868	Baltimore, Md.
756	Glen, Elizabeth, infant of	1h	W	U.S.	13 MAR 1874	
400	Glenn, Evans Rea	1m	W		12 JUL 1869	Oak Hill
759	Glover, John	32y	W	U.S.	23 APR 1874	Alexandria, Va.
106	Glover, John	9m	W	D.C.	26 FEB 1858	Congressional
547	Glover, Maria	1m	W	U.S.	07 DEC 1871	Methodist
193	Glover, Mary	65y	W	D.C.*	26 NOV 1860	Glenwood
222	Glover, Mary	43y			31 MAY 1866	Moore's

District of Columbia Interments (Index to Deaths), 1855-1874

Page	Name	Age	Race	Birth	Death Date	Burial Ground
410	Glover, Mary	7d	W		05 AUG 1869	Methodist
108	Glover, Molly B.		W	D.C.	17 MAR 1858	Congressional
417	Glover, Samuel, barber	55y	C	S.C.	01 SEP 1869	
525	Gloyd, James C., printer	23y	W	D.C.	26 JUN 1871	Congressional
738	Gluh, Catharine	58y	W	Ger.	30 DEC 1873	Prospect Hill
765	Glynn, John F.	10y	W	U.S.	12 MAY 1874	Mt. Olivet
494	Gmailes, George, cigar maker	36y	W	Ger.	14 DEC 1870	Mt. Olivet
104	Gnasser, A., tailor	40y	W	Ger.	06 FEB 1858	Holmead
189	Gneiss, Henry	8m	W	D.C.	08 SEP 1860	German Lutheran
052	Gnowder, Gracy	1y	C	D.C.	30 JUL 1856	Harmony
729	Goabasy, Chas. E., laborer	17y	C	U.S.	07 NOV 1873	Harmony
246	Goarman, Margaret, domestic	35y	W	Ire.	30 DEC 1866	Mt. Olivet*
098	Gockeler, Rosina	25y	W	Ger.	11 DEC 1857	German
620	Gockler, B.	36y	W	Ger.	12 AUG 1872	Prospect Hill
130	Godard, Thomas B.	43y	W	Md.	17 OCT 1858	Congressional
482	Goddard, Benj., laborer	84y	W	Md.	17 OCT 1870	Methodist
170	Goddard, Emma A.C.	71y	W	U.S.	12 JAN 1860	Congressional*
611	Goddard, Geo. E.S.	2y	W	U.S.	21 JUL 1872	
528	Goddard, George	4m	W	D.C.	16 JUL 1871	Glenwood
045	Goddard, Isaac, grocer	43y	W	Md.	20 MAY 1856	St. Patricks
747	Goddard, John	74y	C	Eng.	16 FEB 1874	Boston, Mass.
221	Goddard, Julian A.	2y	W	D.C.	22 MAY 1866	Congressional
502	Goddard, Maggie	2y	W	Va.	16 JAN 1871	Mt. Olivet
249	Goddard, Solomon	42y	W	D.C.	04 JAN 1867	Congressional
329	Godding, Thomas	1y	C		03 JUL 1868	Ebenezer
616	Godey, W.H., lime burner	56y	W	U.S.	13 JUL 1872	
532	Godfrey, Mary I.	8m	W	Miss.	10 AUG 1871	Congressional
213	Godfrey, Mrs.		W		23 FEB 1866	Western
167	Godfrey, [blank]	4m	C	D.C.	10 DEC 1859	Young Mens
187	Godle, Jas. Hamilton	9m	W	D.C.	10 AUG 1860	Western
493	Godman, John R.	1m	W	D.C.	10 DEC 1870	Congressional
732	Godron, W.H., sadler	62y	W	U.S.	30 NOV 1873	Prospect Hill
407	Godron, [blank]	Still	W		09 AUG 1869	Congressional
668	Goell, Goerge F.	37y	W	U.S.	16 FEB 1873	Glenwood
706	Goerner, Max E.	17d	W	D.C.	18 JUL 1873	Prospect Hill
482	Goerner, Rob.	18d	W	D.C.	10 OCT 1870	Prospect Hill
462	Goettel, Henry W., clerk PO	67y	W	Pa.	11 JUL 1870	Congressional
329	Goff, Rose	10m	C	D.C.	01 JUL 1868	Alms House
110	Goggin, Ida H.	3y	W	D.C.	03 APR 1858	Glenwood
118	Goggin, Julia A., boading hse. kpr.	58y	W	Va.	29 JUN 1858	Glenwood
300	Goggin, Sarah Ellen	36y	W	D.C.	12 MAR 1868	Glenwood
109	Going, Robert W.	7y	W	D.C.	30 MAR 1858	Glenwood
296	Goham, Lena	1y	C	D.C.	18 FEB 1868	Young Mens
422	Goheen, Cornelia	11y	C	Va.	03 OCT 1869	Harmony
089	Gohen, Margrette F.	21d	W		30 AUG 1857	Glenwood
055	Gohens, Mary	6m	W	D.C.	24 AUG 1856	Glenwood
290	Going, Charlotte	70y	C	Va.	11 JAN 1868	Freedmen's Hospital
152	Gold, Charles	13y	W	D.C.	27 JUN 1859	Congressional
718	Goldburg, Willie	7m	W		08 SEP 1873	
753	Golden, Cordelia	43y	W	U.S.	20 MAR 1874	Glenwood
094	Golden, John, tavern keeper	46y	W	Ire.	28 OCT 1857	St. Peters
324	Golden, Margaret	54y	W	Ire.	28 JUL 1868	Mt. Olivet
333	Golden, Mary, Mrs.		W	Va.	10 JUL 1868	Prospect Hill
280	Golden, Sarah A.	21y	C		11 OCT 1867	Freedmen's Hospital
099	Goldin, John, shoemaker	70y	W	Md.	29 DEC 1857	Oak Hill
017	Golding, Ann	31y	C	D.C.	23 JUL 1855	St. Patricks
220	Goldsborough, Lizzie W.	23y	W	D.C.	10 MAY 1866	Congressional
032	Goldsborough, Lucy	25y	W	Eng.	29 DEC 1855	Holmead

District of Columbia Interments (Index to Deaths), 1855-1874

Page	Name	Age	Race	Birth	Death Date	Burial Ground
301	Goldschmidt, Catharina	47y	W	Ger.	31 MAR 1868	St. Marys
444	Goldschmidt, William	28y	W		24 MAR 1870	Congressional
075	Goldsmith, Catharine	31y	W	Md.	05 APR 1857	St. Peters
312	Goldsmith, Henry Clarence	1y	W		02 MAY 1868	Broad Creek, Md.
014	Goldsmith, J.W.	6m	W	D.C.	12 JUL 1855	St. Peters
457	Goldsmith, Lucretia, Mrs.	55y	W		18 JUN 1870	Congressional
169	Goldsmith, Oliver	24y	W	D.C.	13 JAN 1860	St. Peters
780	Goldsmith, Robert	1m	W	U.S.	01 JUL 1874	Mt. Olivet
083	Goldsmith, Samuel	6m	W	D.C.	19 JUL 1857	St. Peters
234	Goldsmith, Susan	19y	W	D.C.*	11 SEP 1866	
483	Goldsmith, Willie	2y	W		03 OCT 1870	Congressional
555	Goldsmith, [blank]	1y	W	D.C.	26 JAN 1872	Congressional
304	Golley, Catherine	60y	W	Md.	21 MAR 1868	Congressional
765	Golthheart, Geo. F.	1y	W	U.S.	10 MAY 1874	Prospect Hill
105	Gomer, Daniel	3y	W	D.C.	17 FEB 1858	Congressional
704	Gonnel, Jane	7m	C	D.C.	04 JUL 1873	
259	Gonsalves, Estelle Charlotte		W	Sto.	24 APR 1867	Oak Hill
065	Gonter, Adam Eugene	4y	W	D.C.	12 DEC 1856	Congressional
772	Goodal, Jacob	2y	C	U.S.	19 JUN 1874	Mt. Pleasant
394	Goodall, Alice	4m	W	U.S.	12 JUN 1869	Mt. Olivet
520	Goodall, Florence	9m	W	D.C.	27 MAY 1871	N.H.
520	Goodall, Florence	9m	W	D.C.	27 MAY 1871	N.H.
613	Goodall, Jessie	6y	W	U.S.	03 JUL 1872	
348	Goodall, Willie Garnet	1y	W	D.C.	13 SEP 1868	Congressional
236	Goodchild, Francis R.	2y	W	D.C.	21 SEP 1866	Oak Hill
610	Gooding, E.		C		16 JUN 1867	Young Mens
076	Goodman, Barney	7m	W	D.C.	27 APR 1857	Georgetown, Catholic
082	Goodman, Ella	2m	W		01 JUL 1857	Congressional
023	Goodrich, H.W., watch maker	24y	W	Ver.	07 SEP 1855	Congressional
743	Goodrich, Josiah, clerk	58y	W	U.S.	24 JAN 1874	Oak Hill
710	Goodrich, Margth.	7m	C	D.C.	02 AUG 1873	
325	Goodrich, Rebecca	91y	W	Mass.	13 JUL 1868	Congressional
587	Goodrich, [blank], clerk	75y	W	Va.	21 MAR 1872	Congressional
394	Goods, Ella	4m	W	D.C.	17 JUN 1869	Congressional
228	Goods, Wm. H.	10m	W	D.C.	10 JUL 1866	Congressional
014	Goods, Wm. Thos.	3m	W	D.C.	16 JUL 1855	Holmead
212	Goodsman, Henry W.	5y	W	D.C.	14 FEB 1866	Prospect Hill
631	Goodwin, Emily	41y	W	U.S.	14 OCT 1872	Congressional*
159	Goodwin, Henry	77y	W	Md.	27 AUG 1859	Washington Asylum
040	Goodyear, Aleathea	38y	W	Md.	16 MAR 1856	Congressional
328	Goodyear, Ida	13y	W	D.C.	30 JUL 1868	Holmead
042	Goodyear, Mrs., fortune teller		W	D.C.	20 APR 1856	West
169	Goodyear, Peter, watchman	32y	W	D.C.	06 JAN 1860	Western
192	Goodyear, William	17y	W	D.C.	28 OCT 1860	Western
172	Goodyear, Wm. H.	6m	W	D.C.	06 FEB 1860	Western
103	Goran, Michael, laborer	30y	W	Ire.	30 JAN 1858	St. Patricks
015	Gorbutt, M.R.	24y	W	D.C.	27 JUL 1855	Congressional
243	Gorden, Willie N.	6y	W	Me.	27 NOV 1866	Glenwood
759	Gordon, Agnes	1m	W	U.S.	02 APR 1874	Mt. Olivet
481	Gordon, Alice	2m	C	Md.	16 OCT 1870	Holmead
587	Gordon, Angelina	6m	C	D.C.	20 MAR 1872	
516a	Gordon, Ann, pauper	2m	C	D.C.	11 MAR 1871	Washington Asylum
393	Gordon, Basil	2y	C		23 MAY 1869	
393	Gordon, Basil	2y	C		24 MAY 1869	
236	Gordon, Charles R.	1m	W	D.C.	19 SEP 1866	Mt. Olivet
383	Gordon, Chas. E.	2y	C	D.C.	10 MAR 1869	Washington Asylum
181	Gordon, Chas. H., clerk	57y	W	Ohio	12 JUN 1860	Congressional
777a	Gordon, Edgar	2m	C	U.S.	21 JUN 1874	

District of Columbia Interments (Index to Deaths), 1855-1874

Page	Name	Age	Race	Birth	Death Date	Burial Ground
035	Gordon, Elizabeth E.	2m	W	D.C.	21 FEB 1856	Congressional
086	Gordon, Elizabeth E.	34y	W		03 AUG 1857	Congressional
439	Gordon, Elizabeth Manley	69y	W	Md.	24 FEB 1870	Congressional
499	Gordon, Ellen	23y	W	D.C.	23 JAN 1871	Congressional
404	Gordon, Fannie Josephine	2y	W		21 JUL 1869	
399	Gordon, Hames H., policeman	32y	W	D.C.	15 JUL 1869	Congressional
162	Gordon, James A.	8m	C	D.C.	03 SEP 1859	German Lutheran
359	Gordon, James M.	Still	W		09 NOV 1868	Congressional
513	Gordon, Jerry	80y	C	Va.	22 MAR 1871	Washington Asylum
412	Gordon, Joseph	11m	C	D.C.	10 AUG 1869	Washington Asylum
772	Gordon, Josephine	29y	C	U.S.	04 JUN 1874	Washington Asylum
384	Gordon, Kitty	6d	C	D.C.	27 MAR 1869	Washington Asylum
251	Gordon, Laura	2m	W	D.C.	30 JAN 1867	Alms House
096	Gordon, Laurence	76y	C	D.C.	03 NOV 1857	Holmead
395	Gordon, Malcom	11m	W		23 JUN 1869	Glenwood
259	Gordon, Maria	55y	W	D.C.	26 APR 1867	Congressional*
078	Gordon, Martha Ann	2y	W	D.C.	27 MAY 1857	Congressional
278	Gordon, Molly, cook	70y	C	Va.	30 OCT 1867	Holmead
359	Gordon, Mrs., child of	Still		D.C.	09 NOV 1868	Congressional
495	Gordon, N., child of	7d	C	D.C.	08 DEC 1870	Potters Field
492	Gordon, Nettie	2y	W	D.C.	08 DEC 1870	Congressional
766	Gordon, Olin	11m	C	U.S.	25 MAY 1874	
120	Gordon, Samuel B., clerk	19y	W	Va.	02 JUL 1858	Baltimore, Md.
772	Gordon, Thos. Ross	14d	C	U.S.	28 JUN 1874	Mt. Pleasant
032	Gordon, W.H.	15y	W	D.C.	25 DEC 1855	Congressional
522	Gordon, William	8m	C	D.C.	10 JUN 1871	Ebenezer
483	Gordon, Wm., laborer	28y	C	Md.	07 OCT 1870	Freedmen's Hospital
734	Gorham, James, stone cutter	40y	W	U.S.	07 DEC 1873	
310	Gorlinski, Kate	3y	W	D.C.	29 APR 1868	St. Marys
455	Gorman, Andrew, blacksmith	80y	C		07 MAY 1870	Young Mens
430	Gorman, Annie, housekeeper	26y	W	Ire.	25 DEC 1869	Mt. Olivet
681	Gorman, B.	7m	W	U.S.	16 APR 1873	Mt. Olivet
350	Gorman, Bartholomew F.	6m	W	D.C.	28 SEP 1868	Mt. Olivet
618	Gorman, David	6m	W	U.S.	14 AUG 1872	
714	Gorman, J.B.	6m	W	D.C.	27 AUG 1873	Mt. Olivet*
306	Gorman, Mary	1y	W	D.C.	15 APR 1868	Mt. Olivet
011	Gorman, Michael, laborer	38y	W	Ire.	30 JUN 1855	St. Patricks
007	Gorman, Patrick				— APR 1855	
003	Gorman, Patrick	1y	W	Va.	03 FEB 1855	
151	Gorman, Stephen, painter	31y	W	D.C.	17 JUN 1859	Georgetown, Catholic
772	Gormley, Henry Pierce	3m	W	U.S.	29 JUN 1874	Holyrood
765	Gormley, Mary	78y	W	Ire.	07 MAY 1874	
155	Gormly, Amanda I.	1y	W	D.C.	22 JUL 1859	Glenwood
408	Gormly, Richard, tailor	40y	W	N.Y.	01 AUG 1869	Mt. Olivet
551	Gornum, Edw., watchman	40y	W	Ire.	— DEC 1871	Mt. Olivet
690	Gorum, Alfred	30y	C	U.S.	02 MAY 1873	Small Pox
440	Gosling, Mary, domestic	16y	W		03 FEB 1870	Mt. Olivet
292a	Gosnell, [Infant]	2h	W	D.C.*	23 JAN 1868	Protestant
132	Goss, Jno. A.	3y	W	Md.	16 NOV 1858	Congressional
228	Goss, Robert E.	1y	W	D.C.	14 JUL 1866	Congressional
223	Gossman, Herman	34y	W	Ger.	09 JUN 1866	Alms House
184	Gothe, John, laborer	45y	W	Ger.	01 JUL 1860	
557	Gottenking, Mary L.	3m	W	D.C.	01 FEB 1872	St. Marys
629	Gottliff, A.	30y	W	Ger.	01 OCT 1872	
231	Gotz, Louise	11m	W	D.C.	18 AUG 1866	Prospect Hill
469	Gotz, M.	40y	W	Ger.	— AUG 1870	Prospect Hill
636	Gough, Sylvestor	48y	C	U.S.	24 NOV 1872	Small Pox
624	Gould, A.E., clerk	26y	W	U.S.	17 SEP 1872	

District of Columbia Interments (Index to Deaths), 1855-1874

Page	Name	Age	Race	Birth	Death Date	Burial Ground
552	Gould, Frank	1y	W	D.C.	05 JAN 1872	Congressional*
718	Gould, Laura V.	5y	W	D.C.	12 SEP 1873	Congressional
742	Gould, Stephen, carpenter	52y	W	U.S.	15 JAN 1874	Congressional
225	Goulding, [blank]	14d	W	D.C.	21 JUN 1866	Glenwood
175	Goune, Henrietta	51y	W	Ger.	23 MAR 1860	Prospect Hill
278	Gourson, Franck	1y	W		04 OCT 1867	Congressional
237	Goushiet, Rudolph, baker	30y	W	Ger.	21 SEP 1866	Prospect Hill
028	Governando, Francisco	23y	W	Ger.	01 OCT 1855	Catholic, Georgetown
052	Gowand, Mary M.	8m	W	Pa.	28 JUL 1856	Philadelphia, Pa.
478	Grace, Ann	77y	W	Amer.	21 SEP 1870	Philadelphia, Pa.
332	Grace, Julia A.	2y	W	D.C.	09 JUL 1868	Mt. Olivet
506	Grace, Susan	35y	W	Va.	20 FEB 1871	Washington Asylum
069	Grace, [blank]	1d	C		20 JAN 1857	Western
555	Grady, E.	8d	W	D.C.	27 JAN 1872	Mt. Olivet
339	Grady, Francis Joseph		W	D.C.	15 AUG 1868	Mt. Olivet
532	Grady, Hannah	59y	W	Ire.	15 AUG 1871	Mt. Olivet*
704	Grady, John Francis	13m	W	D.C.	11 JUL 1873	Mt. Olivet
469	Grady, Katie	3y	W	D.C.	24 AUG 1870	Mt. Olivet
467	Grady, Maurice, stone cutter	21y	W	Ire.	15 JUL 1870	Mt. Olivet
780	Grady, Thomas	2m	W	U.S.	09 JUL 1874	
546	Grady, Thomas, gardener	69y	W	Ire.	24 NOV 1871	Mt. Olivet*
628	Grady, Thos.	62y	W	Ire.	28 SEP 1872	Mt. Olivet
226	Graff, Car.	6m	C		29 JUN 1866	Young Mens
721	Graff, Henry J.	6d	W	D.C.	29 SEP 1873	Congressional*
721	Graff, Mary Ann, Mrs.	43y	W	Lanc.	29 SEP 1873	Congressional
201	Graff, Mary Jane	34y	W	Pa.	11 MAR 1861	Prospect Hill
608	Graff, S.A.	11m	W	Va.	27 JUN 1872	Rock Creek
592	Graham, Alice	10y	C	D.C.	09 APR 1872	
518	Graham, Elises	11m	C	D.C.*	02 MAY 1871	Mt. Zion
210	Graham, Eliza	64y	C		13 JAN 1866	
487	Graham, Elizabeth	3y	W	D.C.	22 NOV 1870	Congressional
336	Graham, Hanibal	67y	C	Md.	19 AUG 1868	
159	Graham, Harriet	83y	C	Md.	22 AUG 1859	Young Mens
546	Graham, Henry A.	8m	W	Va.	29 NOV 1871	Mt. Olivet
319	Graham, James Duncan, Lt. Cav.	25y	W	U.S.	18 JUN 1868	Baltimore, Md.
429	Graham, Jane L., Mrs.	70y	W	Va.	20 DEC 1869	Congressional/Arl., Va.
427	Graham, Jos. R.	10m	C	D.C.	30 NOV 1869	Washington Asylum
681	Graham, Lewellyn	15m	C	U.S.	16 APR 1873	Mt. Olivet
343	Graham, Lincoln	1m	C	D.C.	17 AUG 1868	
047	Graham, M.V.	2m	W		25 JUN 1856	Glenwood
502	Graham, Mary	4m	W		31 JAN 1871	Mt. Olivet
068	Graham, Mary	1y	W	D.C.	14 JAN 1857	St. Patricks
642	Graham, Mary E.	74y	W	U.S.	01 DEC 1872	Glenwood
429	Graham, Mrs., infant of	7m	W		26 DEC 1869	Congressional
445	Graham, Nelly	5y	W		17 MAR 1870	Mt. Olivet
710	Graham, Thalbin	10m	W	U.S.	07 AUG 1873	Prospect Hill
427	Graham, Thomas, laborer	71y	C	Md.	24 NOV 1869	Ebenezer
227	Graham, Thos. B., clerk	40y	W	Ind.	02 JUL 1866	Glenwood
323	Graham, Walter Jordan	9m	W	D.C.	01 JUL 1868	Glenwood
282	Grahame, John, printer	45y	W	Ire.	13 NOV 1867	Glenwood
298	Grahame, Mary	71y	W	Ky.	26 FEB 1868	Glenwood
309	Grahame, [blank], tailor	40y	W	Ire.	20 APR 1868	Glenwood
730	Grahan, B.A.	4y	W	U.S.	14 NOV 1873	
283	Grainer, John	13d	W	D.C.	24 NOV 1867	German Catholic
147	Grainger, William, carpenter	74y	W		29 APR 1859	Congressional
663	Gramly, Jacob	40y	C	U.S.	30 JAN 1873	Small Pox
179	Grammar, Alfred P.	2y	W	D.C.	20 MAY 1860	Glenwood
121	Grammar, Fred.	21y	W	D.C.	11 JUL 1858	Congressional

Page	Name	Age	Race	Birth	Death Date	Burial Ground
068	Grammar, G.C., banker	69y	W	Ger.	14 JAN 1857	Congressional
051	Grammar, Mary	1d		D.C.	28 JUL 1856	German Catholic
513	Grammer, Louis M.	29y	W	D.C.	25 MAR 1871	Congressional
631	Granaster, Ann E.	1y	C	U.S.	27 OCT 1872	
163	Granberry, Jennie M.	25y	W	D.C.	17 OCT 1859	Glenwood
627	Grandison, Chas.	3y	C	U.S.	17 SEP 1872	Small Pox
630	Grandison, Sarah	1y	C	U.S.	08 OCT 1872	Small Pox
352	Grandison, Sarah	55y	C	Md.	15 SEP 1868	Washington Asylum
032	Grandville, [blank], Mr.	80y	W	Va.	20 DEC 1855	Not Reported
073	Graney, Mary	1y	W	D.C.	05 MAR 1857	St. Patricks
741	Grangle, Nicholas B., watchman	41y	W	Eng.	13 JAN 1874	
345	Grant, Anna A.	2y	C	D.C.	06 AUG 1868	Western
772	Grant, Bessie	22y	W	Scot.	19 JUN 1874	Congressional
593	Grant, Bridget	5m	W	D.C.	21 APR 1872	Mt. Olivet*
237	Grant, Charlotte	65y	C		26 SEP 1866	Young Mens
060	Grant, Elisha, musician	37y	C	D.C.	03 OCT 1856	Harmony
338	Grant, Eliza	1y	C		19 AUG 1868	Washington Asylum
367	Grant, Francis	10m	B	D.C.	01 DEC 1868	Washington Asylum
721	Grant, Henry P., school boy	6y	W	D.C.	12 SEP 1873	Congressional*
454a	Grant, Isaac, pauper	56y	C	U.S.	30 MAY 1870	Washington Asylum
004	Grant, Jo. H.	2y	C	D.C.	19 MAR 1855	Harmony
137	Grant, Lewis E., clerk	30y	W	La.	04 JAN 1859	
715	Grant, Lucinda B.	39y	W	U.S.	08 AUG 1873	
288	Grant, Martin	17d	C		19 DEC 1867	Freedmen's Hospital
026	Grant, Mary	4y	W	D.C.	10 OCT 1855	
175	Grant, Mary	22y	W	Ire.	16 MAR 1860	Mt. Olivet
780	Grant, Mary	50y	C	U.S.	01 JUL 1874	Mt. Pleasant
167	Grant, Mary, washerwoman	25y	C	D.C.	06 DEC 1859	Harmony
715	Grant, Mollie	11y	W	U.S.	08 AUG 1873	
494	Grant, Oscar K., clerk	46y	W	Me.	08 DEC 1870	Me.
759	Grant, Rebecca, domestic	38y	C	U.S.	20 APR 1874	Young Mens
343	Grant, William	4m	C	D.C.	21 AUG 1868	Alms House
436	Grant, William H., baker [sic]	1m	C		28 JAN 1870	
500	Grantham, Patsy	85y	C	Md.	04 JAN 1871	Harmony
068	Granton, George A.	1y	C	D.C.	05 JAN 1857	Ebenezer
465	Grantum, Michael, cook	49y	C	D.C.	19 JUL 1870	Holmead
057	Graser, Adam	1y	W	D.C.	02 SEP 1856	Holmead
260	Grasty, Fanny	23y	C	Va.	25 MAY 1867	Beckett's
246	Gratiot, G.H., clerk		W	Wisc.	18 DEC 1866	Ill.
428	Graves, Albert, laborer	28y	C	Va.	26 NOV 1869	Washington Asylum
234	Graves, Ann	1y	W	D.C.	01 SEP 1866	Georgetown, Catholic
254	Graves, Cecilia Annette	25y	W	N.Y.	05 FEB 1867	Glenwood
420	Graves, E.O. & C.A., infant of	Still	W		15 OCT 1869	Oak Hill
075	Graves, Elizabeth	32y	W	Md.	01 APR 1857	Congressional
456	Graves, John	8m	C	Va.	24 JUN 1870	Young Mens
548	Graves, Robert S.	5y	C	D.C.	11 DEC 1871	Mt. Olivet
437	Graves, [blank]	2d	W	D.C.	15 JAN 1870	Washington Asylum
122	Graw, James, laborer	50y	W	Ire.	21 JUL 1858	St. Patricks
311	Gray, Anna		C		c.08 APR 1868	Alms House
626	Gray, Annie H.	14m	W	U.S.	18 SEP 1872	
780	Gray, Aston	4m	W	U.S.	20 JUL 1874	Mt. Olivet
465	Gray, Barbary	70y	W	D.C.	23 JUL 1870	Methodist
131	Gray, Basil		C		29 OCT 1858	Harmony
447	Gray, Betty, housekeeper	26y	C	Va.	17 MAR 1870	
317	Gray, Charles Henry	5m	C	D.C.	15 JUN 1868	
707	Gray, Chas., baker	50y	C	Md.	04 JUL 1873	Beckett's
466	Gray, Daniel	10m	C	D.C.	07 JUL 1870	
447	Gray, Daniel, coachman	55y	C		17 MAR 1870	

Page	Name	Age	Race	Birth	Death Date	Burial Ground
629	Gray, E.A.	29y	W	U.S.	05 OCT 1872	
356	Gray, Edward	2y	C	D.C.	24 OCT 1868	
603	Gray, Eliza	27y	C	Va.	16 JUN 1872	Small Pox
506	Gray, George	16y	C	Va.	19 FEB 1871	Washington Asylum
476	Gray, George, wood sawyer	45y	C	D.C.	15 SEP 1870	Ebenezer
381	Gray, Harry Leslie	7m	W		21 MAR 1869	Glenwood
625	Gray, Hattie	14m	C	U.S.	02 SEP 1872	
675	Gray, James	53y	C	U.S.	19 MAR 1873	Ebenezer
396	Gray, Jamie		C	D.C.	14 JUN 1869	Ebenezer
605	Gray, John, laborer	25y	C	U.S.	02 JUN 1872	Asylum
592	Gray, John W.	30y	W	U.S.	20 APR 1872	
595	Gray, John W., storekeeper	30y	W	U.S.	20 APR 1872	Oak Hill
222	Gray, John, waiter	32y	C	D.C.	25 MAY 1866	Freedmen's
470	Gray, Kate C.	3y	W	D.C.	21 AUG 1870	Glenwood
412	Gray, Louisa	3y	C		02 AUG 1869	
132	Gray, Louisa	1y	W	Md.	16 NOV 1858	Catholic
004	Gray, Martha Ann	28y	C	Md.	21 MAR 1855	Young Mens
007	Gray, Mary	56y	W	Md.	05 APR 1855	
372	Gray, Mary	3y	C		20 JAN 1869	Freedmen's Hospital
391	Gray, Mary Ella	23y	W	Mass.	09 MAY 1869	Oak Hill
780	Gray, Mary H.	4y	W	U.S.	04 JUL 1874	Glenwood
667	Gray, Milley	80y	C	U.S.	08 FEB 1873	Washington Asylum
659	Gray, Mrs.	72y	C	U.S.	12 JAN 1873	
243	Gray, Mrs.				12 NOV 1866	Va.
175	Gray, Nelly	68y	C	U.S.	24 MAR 1860	
519	Gray, Reuben, laborer	70y	C	Va.	21 MAY 1871	Potters Field
386	Gray, Richard, laborer	51y	D		14 APR 1869	Mt. Olivet
132	Gray, Richardson, barber	36y	C	D.C.	16 NOV 1858	Young Mens
610	Gray, Robt.	1y	W	U.S.	18 JUL 1872	
258	Gray, Sarah	32y	C		26 APR 1867	Young Mens
396	Gray, Sarah C.	20y	D	D.C.	07 JUN 1869	Ebenezer
320	Gray, William, Dr.	56y	W	Mass.	18 JUN 1868	Glenwood
643	Gray, Willie E.	4y	W	U.S.	05 DEC 1872	Glenwood
540	Gray, Wm.	1y	C		05 OCT 1871	Ebenezer
506	Gray, [blank]	Still	W	D.C.	14 FEB 1871	Congressional
160	Gray, [blank]	1y	W	D.C.	05 AUG 1859	Mt. Olivet
029	Gray, [blank]	35y	C		20 NOV 1855	Van Ness'
147	Grayson, Kitty C.	6y	W	D.C.	22 APR 1859	Glenwood
423	Grayson, Mary	30y	C	Va.	30 OCT 1869	Washington Asylum
684	Grayson, Wm.	17y	C	U.S.	30 APR 1873	Small Pox*
077	Grayson, [blank], laborer	45y	C	Md.	04 MAY 1857	
170	Greaser, John Baptist	1y	W	D.C.	25 JAN 1860	German Catholic
663	Greason, Jos.	16y	C	U.S.	05 JAN 1873	Small Pox*
261	Greaves, Cecelia L.	44y	W	D.C.	17 MAY 1867	
116	Green, Alice	2y	W	D.C.	20 JUN 1858	Glenwood
759	Green, Amanda	14y	C	U.S.	04 APR 1874	Mt. Pleasant
753	Green, Ammon, auctioneer	73y	W	U.S.	01 MAR 1874	Glenwood
377	Green, Betty	7d	C	D.C.	04 FEB 1869	Washington Asylum
765	Green, Bridget	27y	W	Ire.	01 MAY 1874	Mt. Olivet
112	Green, Charles	2m	C	D.C.	28 APR 1858	Catholic
309	Green, Charles Edwin, merchant	26y	W	D.C.	26 APR 1868	Oak Hill
421	Green, Chas. P.	1y	C		30 OCT 1869	
377	Green, Clara	70y	C	Va.	19 FEB 1869	Young Mens
305	Green, Clara S.	2y	W	D.C.	02 MAR 1868	Oak Hill
742	Green, Cora Ellen	3y	W	U.S.	21 JAN 1874	Hillsdale
281	Green, Cora, school girl	13y	C	Md.	18 OCT 1867	
619	Green, D.	3m	C	U.S.	20 AUG 1872	
392	Green, Eddie	17m	C		04 MAY 1869	Young Mens

Page	Name	Age	Race	Birth	Death Date	Burial Ground
605	Green, Edw., collector	27y	C	U.S.	12 JUN 1872	
604	Green, Edw., garbage man	47y	C	Va.	10 JUN 1872	Ebenezer
660	Green, Edward S.	2y	W	U.S.	21 JAN 1873	Oak Hill
411	Green, Edwin	1y	C		18 AUG 1869	Beckett's
026	Green, Eliza	10m	C		04 OCT 1855	Young Mens
282	Green, Elizabeth	70y	W	Va.	24 NOV 1867	Congressional
540	Green, Elizabeth	5d	C	D.C.	05 OCT 1871	Ebenezer
053	Green, Elizabeth	2m			02 AUG 1856	German
422	Green, Elizabeth	4y	C		20 OCT 1869	Harmony
292a	Green, Elizabeth W.	2y	C	D.C.*	03 JAN 1868	Catholic
378	Green, Ellen	47y	W		— FEB 1869	Washington Asylum
021	Green, Emma	11m	C	D.C.	26 AUG 1855	Young Mens
633	Green, Ester	60y	C	U.S.	11 OCT 1872	
617	Green, Fanny	26y	C	U.S.	20 AUG 1872	
625	Green, Flora	100y	C	U.S.	12 SEP 1872	Mt. Olivet
287	Green, Francis		C		c.08 DEC 1867	Alms House
328	Green, Frank L.	21d	W	D.C.	28 JUL 1868	Oak Hill
263	Green, Geo. C., Mr., child of	Still			01 JUN 1867	Glenwood
388	Green, George P.	3m	W		27 APR 1869	
617	Green, Hattie	11m	C	U.S.	24 AUG 1872	
549	Green, Henrietta L.	36y	W	Unk.	21 DEC 1871	Oak Hill
677	Green, Henry	23y	C	U.S.	10 MAR 1873	Small Pox
638	Green, Hester	3m	C	U.S.	07 NOV 1872	
335a	Green, Hy., laborer	70y	C	U.S.	17 JUL 1868	Washington Asylum
306	Green, Ida	2y	C	D.C.	11 APR 1868	Alms House
160	Green, Isabella	26y	W	D.C.	09 AUG 1859	Glenwood
409	Green, James	26y	C		26 AUG 1869	Harmony
089	Green, James C.	4y	W		29 AUG 1857	St. Patricks
483	Green, James, laborer	27y	W		27 OCT 1870	Congressional
435	Green, Jane Linton, Mrs.	79y	W	Va.	19 JAN 1870	Middleburg, Va.
622	Green, Jas. A., laborer	35y	C	U.S.	27 AUG 1872	
673	Green, John	18y	C	U.S.	08 MAR 1873	Ebenezer
352	Green, John	11y	C		08 SEP 1868	Washington Asylum
537	Green, John	22y	C	Md.	19 SEP 1871	Washington
047	Green, John Edward	5m	W		22 JUN 1856	St. Patricks
741	Green, John, laborer	73y	C	U.S.	08 JAN 1874	Mt. Olivet
676	Green, Joseph	50y	C	U.S.	05 MAR 1873	Small Pox
724	Green, Joseph H.	16y	B	D.C.	12 OCT 1873	Young Mens
753	Green, Julia	41y	W	U.S.	29 MAR 1874	Holyrood
743	Green, Julia J.	28y	C	U.S.	26 JAN 1874	
372	Green, Laura	16y	C	Va.	07 JAN 1869	Washington Asylum
474	Green, Liddy	21d	C		08 AUG 1870	Washington Asylum
431	Green, Lilly	1y	C		18 DEC 1869	Harmony
523	Green, Lina Emilia	2y	C		19 JUN 1871	
313	Green, Louisa	3y	C	D.C.	24 MAY 1868	Young Mens
606	Green, Lucy	25y	C	Md.	03 JUN 1872	Asylum
527	Green, Mama	1y	C	D.C.	11 JUL 1871	Ebenezer
619	Green, Marg.	4m	C	U.S.	15 AUG 1872	Asylum
509	Green, Margt.	3m	C	D.C.	15 FEB 1871	Washington Asylum
630	Green, Maria	25y	C	U.S.	06 OCT 1872	Small Pox
759	Green, Mary	70y	C	U.S.	24 APR 1874	
482	Green, Mary	8m	C		04 OCT 1870	Ebenezer
365	Green, Mary	16y	B	Md.	19 DEC 1868	Mt. Olivet
703	Green, Mary	2w	W	D.C.	06 JUL 1873	Mt. Olivet
029	Green, Mary	50y	W	Ire.	10 NOV 1855	St. Patricks
417	Green, Mary	1y	C	D.C.	20 SEP 1869	Washington Asylum
110	Green, Mary	12y	C	D.C.	04 APR 1858	Young Mens
191	Green, Mary	11m	C	D.C.	17 OCT 1860	Young Mens

Page	Name	Age	Race	Birth	Death Date	Burial Ground
128	Green, Mary A.	35y	W		29 SEP 1858	St. Peters
050	Green, Mary C.	10m	W		11 JUL 1856	Congressional
301	Green, Mary E.	1m	C	D.C.	29 MAR 1868	Alms House
753	Green, Mary Jane	1y	C	U.S.	16 MAR 1874	Ebenezer
469	Green, Mary M.V., huckster	24y	C	D.C.	14 AUG 1870	Harmony
502	Green, Nancy		C		02 JAN 1871	
766	Green, Nellie	17y	C	U.S.	17 MAY 1874	Ebenezer
019	Green, Noah	31y	W	N.Y.	07 AUG 1855	Washington Asylum
116	Green, Owen, grocer	40y	W	Ire.	21 JUN 1858	St. Matthews
400	Green, Patrick	80y	W	Ire.	18 JUL 1869	Mt. Olivet
780	Green, Perry W.	8d	W	U.S.	25 JUL 1874	Mt. Olivet
349	Green, Prater Hut	1y	C	D.C.	06 SEP 1868	Harmony
466	Green, Rebecca	4m	C	D.C.	19 JUL 1870	Young Mens
217	Green, Rebecca, Mrs.				07 APR 1866	Elmyra, N.Y.
019	Green, Richd.	2y	C	D.C.	23 AUG 1855	Young Mens
011	Green, Saml.	24y	C	Md.	30 JUN 1855	Harmony
225	Green, Sarah, seamstress	80y	W	D.C.	20 JUN 1866	Congressional
595	Green, Saulsbury	85y	C	Md.	10 APR 1872	
720	Green, Stephen, laborer	77y	C	Va.	26 SEP 1873	Washington Asylum
370	Green, Susan	30y	W		09 JAN 1869	John J. McQuille's
500	Green, Susan	25y	C	Va.	20 JAN 1871	Young Mens
312	Green, Susan, domestic	30y	C	Va.	13 MAY 1868	Alms House
282	Green, Thomas	7y	W	D.C.	02 NOV 1867	Congressional
320	Green, Thomas	5m	C	D.C.	19 JUN 1868	Ebenezer
766	Green, Thomas, laborer	88y	C	U.S.	23 MAY 1874	Mt. Olivet
423	Green, Thomas, [infant of]	Still	C	D.C.	21 OCT 1869	Washington Asylum
020	Green, Vincent	100y	C	Va.	30 AUG 1855	Young Mens
742	Green, Virginia	24y	C	U.S.	21 JAN 1874	Harmony
501	Green, Virginia	34y	W	D.C.	28 JAN 1871	Potters Field
002	Green, Washington, domestic	19y	C	Md.	— JAN 1855	Harmony
199	Green, William, printer	76y	W	Va.	14 FEB 1861	Congressional
741	Green, Willie	1y	C	U.S.	12 JAN 1874	Beckett's
514	Green, Wm.	2y	C	U.S.	17 MAR 1871	Beckett's
594	Green, Wm. W.	4d	W	D.C.	06 APR 1872	Congressional*
051	Green, Zachariah N., sailor	24y	W	D.C.	22 JUL 1856	Washington Asylum
008	Green, [blank]	3y	W		15 MAY 1855	St. Matthews
023	Green, [blank]		W	D.C.	27 SEP 1855	St. Matthews
111	Green, [blank]		C	D.C.	15 APR 1858	Young Mens
508	Green, [male]	1y	C		— FEB 1871	Ebenezer
169	Greene, Charlotte T.	34y	C	D.C.	17 JAN 1860	Harmony
149	Greene, EdwD. Thos., stonecutter	22y	W	D.C.	22 MAY 1859	Glenwood
158	Greene, John Frederick	2m	C	D.C.	22 AUG 1859	
451	Greene, Joseph Clifton	2y	C		28 APR 1870	
158	Greene, M.A.	23y	W	Va.	16 AUG 1859	Glenwood
279	Greene, Rebecca Ann	15y	C	D.C.	12 OCT 1867	Mt. Olivet
009	Greenfield, E. Ellen	4y	W	D.C.	02 MAY 1855	Congressional
113	Greenfield, George	9y	W		09 MAY 1858	Congressional
444	Greenfield, Mary E.	49y	W		25 MAR 1870	Congressional
201	Greenhow, Gertrude L.	18y	W	D.C.	17 MAR 1861	Mt. Olivet
487	Greenleaf, Alexander	8y	C	D.C.	17 NOV 1870	Young Mens
110	Greenleaf, Nannie S.	8y	W	D.C.	08 APR 1858	Holmead
343	Greenleaf, William C., treasurer	67y	W	Mass.	21 AUG 1868	Boston, Mass.
141	Greenlief, [blank]		W	Md.	21 FEB 1859	Glenwood
665	Greenly, John	1y	C	U.S.	30 JAN 1873	Small Pox*
294	Greenwell, A.E., Mrs.	26y	W	Md.	27 FEB 1868	Congressional
326	Greenwell, Caroline	5m	W	D.C.	06 JUL 1868	Congressional
552	Greenwell, James	8d	W	D.C.	01 JAN 1872	Congressional
013	Greenwell, Mary E.	7y	W	D.C.	01 JUL 1855	St. Peters

District of Columbia Interments (Index to Deaths), 1855-1874

Page	Name	Age	Race	Birth	Death Date	Burial Ground
002	Greenwell, Philip, carpenter	54y	W	D.C.	25 JAN 1855	Harmony
191	Greenwell, [blank]	2m	W	D.C.	03 OCT 1860	Congressional
463	Greenwood, Frantz E.	5m	W	D.C.	26 JUL 1870	
697	Greenwood, R.L.	6y	W	U.S.	29 JUN 1873	Congressional*
665	Greer, Joseph Henry, carpenter	24y	W	U.S.	01 JAN 1873	Glenwood
428	Greer, Lula Florence	5m	W		02 NOV 1869	
327	Greer, R.	6m	W	D.C.	09 JUL 1868	Western
596	Greer, Richd. T.	3y	W	D.C.	28 APR 1872	
730	Greer, Susan J., lady	88y	W	U.S.	14 NOV 1873	Baltimore, Md.
694	Greer, T.J., carpenter	43y	W	U.S.	14 JUN 1873	Glenwood
163	Gregg, Mary Jane	3m	W	D.C.	11 OCT 1859	Baltimore, Md.
229	Gregory, Charles Jefferson	15y	W	D.C.	18 JUL 1866	Congressional
187	Gregory, Esther Emanuel	3d	W	D.C.	05 AUG 1860	Glenwood
519	Gregory, Hannah A.	43y	W	Pa.	17 MAY 1871	Congressional*
470	Gregory, Kate	9½m	W	D.C.	14 AUG 1870	Congressional
312	Gregory, Mrs.	30y	W	N.Y.	01 MAY 1868	Hebrew
586	Gregory, P., lady	84y	W	U.S.	11 MAR 1872	Mich.
772	Gregory, [blank]	1m	W	U.S.	14 JUN 1874	Mt. Olivet
009	Grenadar, Mathew	7m	W	D.C.	15 MAY 1855	German
295	Grenwell, Adalade	21d	W	U.S.	21 FEB 1868	Mt. Olivet
393	Grey, Ann		C	D.C.	24 MAY 1869	Washington Asylum
684	Grey, Annie L.	7y	C	U.S.	06 APR 1873	Small Pox*
753	Grey, Basil, laborer	34y	C	U.S.	21 MAR 1874	
032	Grey, F.B., child of	Still			30 DEC 1855	Ebenezer
392	Grey, George, laborer	45y	C	Md.	27 MAY 1869	Holmead
102	Grey, Isabella	1y	C	D.C.	17 JAN 1858	Young Mens
032	Grey, J.W.	3y	C	D.C.	26 DEC 1855	Foundry
045	Grey, John, hotel keeper	71y	W	Md.	22 MAY 1856	Baltimore, Md.
087	Grey, Julia, servant	102y	C	Va.	11 AUG 1857	Methodist
446	Grey, Mary	3m	C	D.C.	02 MAR 1870	Washington Asylum
157	Grey, Mary E.	3m	W	D.C.	09 AUG 1859	Glenwood
099	Grey, Mary Francis	2m	C	D.C.	30 DEC 1857	Foundry
336	Grey, Minnie	30y	C	Va.	05 AUG 1868	Young Mens
138	Grffin, [blank]	2y	W	D.C.	28 JAN 1859	Mt. Olivet
233	Grice, Willie N.L.	11m	W	D.C.	29 AUG 1866	Congressional
688	Grier, Emily Annie	1y	W	U.S.	17 MAY 1873	
462	Grieve, Jane	35y	W	Scot.	12 JUL 1870	Prospect Hill
364	Grifenshultz, Ann	62y	W	D.C.	08 DEC 1868	Congressional*
027	Griffen, [blank]	72y	W	Md.	11 OCT 1855	Catholic, Georgetown
055	Griffen, [blank]	30y	W	Ire.	22 AUG 1856	St. Patricks
184	Griffin, Agnes	3m	W	D.C.	10 JUL 1860	Mt. Olivet
467	Griffin, Allen	5y	C	D.C.	31 JUL 1870	Union
627	Griffin, Chas. E.	18m	W	U.S.	28 SEP 1872	
229	Griffin, Cornelia M.	37y	W	D.C.	20 JUL 1866	Congressional
197	Griffin, Daniel	9m	C	D.C.	19 JAN 1861	Young Mens
458	Griffin, E.	10m	C	D.C.	26 JUN 1870	Potters Field
415	Griffin, Elizabeth A.	43y	W		28 SEP 1869	Oak Hill
381	Griffin, Ellen	1y	W		13 MAR 1869	Mt. Olivet
006	Griffin, Geo. Thos.	8m	C		07 APR 1855	
742	Griffin, George	1y	C	U.S.	16 JAN 1874	
163	Griffin, James, farmer	43y	W	Md.	18 OCT 1859	
094	Griffin, Johana	83y	W	Ire.	28 OCT 1857	St. Patricks
075	Griffin, Johanna	69y	W	Md.	20 APR 1857	Congressional
332	Griffin, John	3m	W	D.C.	11 JUL 1868	Georgetown, Catholic
264	Griffin, John H.	5m			04 JUL 1867	
715	Griffin, John, laborer	45y	C	U.S.	30 AUG 1873	
436	Griffin, John, laborer	88y	C	Md.	05 JAN 1870	Young Mens
696	Griffin, Jos.	3m	C	D.C.	05 JUN 1873	Washington Asylum

District of Columbia Interments (Index to Deaths), 1855-1874

Page	Name	Age	Race	Birth	Death Date	Burial Ground
581	Griffin, Josephine	56y	W	Conn.	18 FEB 1872	Congressional
458	Griffin, M.	7d	C	D.C.	23 JUN 1870	Potters Field
051	Griffin, Mary	9m	W		24 JUL 1856	Glenwood
667	Griffin, Mary	1m	W	U.S.	12 FEB 1873	Mt. Olivet
772	Griffin, Mary	7m	C	U.S.	10 JUN 1874	Mt. Olivet
031	Griffin, Mary	2m	W		13 DEC 1855	St. Patricks
038	Griffin, Mary	6d	W	D.C.	24 MAR 1856	Trinity
454	Griffin, Mary, servant	37y	C	Va.	22 MAY 1870	Union
665	Griffin, Mrs.	41y	W	U.S.	26 JAN 1873	Small Pox*
064	Griffin, Mrs.	30y	W		09 NOV 1856	St. Patricks
582	Griffin, Richd.	1y	C	Md.	20 FEB 1872	
337	Griffin, Thomas	1y	C	U.S.	07 AUG 1868	Washington Asylum
253	Griffin, Thomas	70y	C		10 FEB 1867	Young Mens
753	Griffin, Willie	12y	C	U.S.	06 MAR 1874	Washington Asylum
454a	Griffin, Wilson, pauper	23y	C	Md.	02 MAY 1870	Washington Asylum
094	Griffin, [blank]		W		31 OCT 1857	St. Patricks
359	Griffith, Edward, machinist	42y	W	Va.*	29 NOV 1868	Congressional
483	Griffith, John H., machinist	52y	W	Va.*	24 OCT 1870	Congressional
026	Griffith, Laura M.	1y	W	D.C.	01 OCT 1855	Congressional
639	Griffith, Lily	1y	C	U.S.	01 DEC 1872	Small Pox*
340	Griffith, Mary S.	32y	W	D.C.	14 AUG 1868	Congressional
518	Griffith, Matilda	33y	W	D.C.	03 MAY 1871	Glenwood
066	Griffith, Richard, gardener	78y	W	Md.	26 DEC 1856	Congressional
554	Griffith, Signet	26y	W	Va.	17 JAN 1872	Congressional
331	Griffith, William Joshua	6m	C	D.C.	10 JUL 1868	
439	Griffith, Willie E.	5y	W	Pa.	24 FEB 1870	Congressional
463	Griffiths, Ida	9y	W	D.C.	11 JUL 1870	Oak Hill
537	Griffiths, Peray	3y	W	Md.	22 SEP 1871	Congressional
638	Griggs, Anthony	71y	C	U.S.	12 NOV 1872	Washington Asylum
707	Griggs, Eliza	2y	W	D.C.	28 JUL 1873	
197	Griggs, Samuel	3m	W	D.C.	24 JAN 1861	Methodist
557	Grigsby, Bushrod	3y	W	D.C.	02 FEB 1872	Washington
741	Grigsby, Mary L.	29y	W	U.S.	13 JAN 1874	Congressional*
065	Grigsby, Phena		C		10 DEC 1856	
453	Grigsby, Robert, huckster	55y	W	Va.	08 MAY 1870	Congressional
266	Grimes, Catherine	76y	W	Va.	10 JUL 1867	Methodist
395	Grimes, Emily T.	34y	D	D.C.	11 JUN 1869	Mt. Olivet
164	Grimes, Emma	6y	W	D.C.*	19 OCT 1859	Georgetown
609	Grimes, George Anna	7m	C	U.S.	20 JUN 1872	
454	Grimes, Isaac, laborer	25y	C	Va.	01 MAY 1870	Washington Asylum
600	Grimes, Jessie	7m	W	U.S.	10 MAY 1872	Unknown
124	Grimes, John	Still	W		11 AUG 1858	Congressional
750	Grimes, John P., carpenter	62y	W	U.S.	10 FEB 1874	
080	Grimes, Juliet H.P.	24y	W	Md.	19 JUN 1857	Md.
527	Grimes, Lucinda	27y	C	Va.	11 JUL 1871	Ebenezer
360	Grimes, Margaret, Miss	20y	W		26 NOV 1868	Broad Creek, Md.
149	Grimes, Mary	4m	W	D.C.	26 MAY 1859	Mt. Olivet
753	Grimes, Mary A.	73y	W	U.S.	16 MAR 1874	Congressional*
292a	Grimes, Melinda, cook	64y	C	D.C.*	06 FEB 1868	Holy Rood
521	Grimes, Midrad H., shoemaker	59y	W	D.C.	07 JUN 1871	Washington
122	Grimes, [blank]	6y	W	D.C.	20 JUL 1858	Western
314	Grimley, James, barber	18y	W	Eng.	26 MAY 1868	Congressional
696	Grimm, Anthony, Rev.	45y	W	Fra.	12 JUN 1873	
698	Grimm, Anthony, Rev.	45y	W	Fra.	12 JUN 1873	St. Joseph Church
540	Grinage, Nellie	80y	C	Va.	04 OCT 1871	
374	Grindall, George, tinner		W	Amer.	11 FEB 1869	Congressional
731	Grinder, Adam, brickmaker	57y	W	U.S.	24 NOV 1873	Congressional*
325	Grinder, Ed. M.	14d	W	D.C.	14 JUL 1868	Congressional

Page	Name	Age	Race	Birth	Death Date	Burial Ground
099	Grinder, Isabella	7y	W	D.C.	30 DEC 1857	Congressional
049	Grinder, Melissa	9m	W	D.C.	09 JUL 1856	Congressional
023	Grinder, [blank], Mr.	67y	W	Ger.	10 SEP 1855	Congressional
687	Grindlay, Letitia M.	29y	W	U.S.	01 MAY 1873	Albany, N.Y.
643	Grinnell, Laura	3y	W	U.S.	11 DEC 1872	Congressional
243	Grinnell, Mary L.	92y	W	Can.	01 NOV 1866	Mt. Olivet
412	Grinnell, Stephen	19y	C	Mo.	10 AUG 1869	Washington Asylum
112	Grinning, Bay	3y	W	D.C.	27 APR 1858	Washington Asylum
417	Griswold, Cecelia C.D.	5m	W		12 SEP 1869	Mt. Olivet
402	Griswold, Julia S.	70y	W	Pa.	16 JUL 1869	Glenwood
450	Groff, Eliza Matilda	1m	W		26 APR 1870	Mt. Olivet
747	Grogan, Mary	13y	W	U.S.	22 FEB 1874	Mt. Olivet
594	Groggin, Edward	42y	W	Va.	27 APR 1872	Washington
403	Groggins, Milly, housekeeper	24y	C	Va.	20 JUL 1869	Va.
228	Groh, Frederick, driver	32y	W	Ger.	16 JUL 1866	Prospect Hill
740	Grohirt, Nellie	50y	W	Ger.	03 JAN 1874	Washington Asylum
268	Groom, Bridget	68y	W	Ire.	09 AUG 1867	Congressional
607	Groomes, Jane	45y	C	D.C.	12 JUN 1872	Harmony
333	Grosner, Ann Mary	6m	W	D.C.	27 JUL 1868	Prospect Hill
405	Gross, Fannie	7m	C	Va.	17 JUL 1869	Washington Asylum
519	Gross, Francis, butcher	76y	W	D.C.	18 MAY 1871	Receiving Vault
621	Gross, Geo. L.	3m	W	U.S.	13 AUG 1872	Prospect Hill
542	Gross, Hannah	76y	W	Ger.	22 OCT 1871	St. Marys
409	Gross, Jenny	1y	C		16 AUG 1869	
419	Gross, Margaret	95y	W	Ger.	17 OCT 1869	Congressional
545	Gross, Mary	45y	C		17 NOV 1871	Union
457	Gross, Mary I.	24y	W	Md.	02 JUN 1870	Congressional
777a	Gross, Rosa, housekeeper	64y	W	Ire.	24 JUN 1874	10th St. Wharf
073	Grossfield, Ann Eliza	50y	W	Eng.	05 MAR 1857	Glenwood
420	Grossmans, Mrs., child of	12h	W		20 OCT 1869	Prospect Hill
084	Grouard, George M., printer	68y	W	N.H.	25 JUL 1857	Congressional
243	Grovanan, Mary	5m	W	D.C.	17 NOV 1866	Alms House
111	Grove, John Case	10m	W		14 APR 1858	St. Patricks
554	Grover, John, marine	27y	W	Eng.	19 JAN 1872	Congressional
621	Groverman, Harry	5m	W	U.S.	06 AUG 1872	Mt. Olivet
698	Groves, Henry F.	5m	W		24 JUN 1873	Tennallytown
230	Grovier, [blank]	1y	W	D.C.	28 JUL 1866	Methodist
116	Gruard, Mary E.	9y	W	D.C.	24 JUN 1858	Congressional
766	Grubb, Caroline F.	50y	W	U.S.	22 MAY 1874	Mt. Olivet*
514	Grubb, Susan	47y	W	U.S.	05 MAR 1871	Philadelphia, Pa.
294	Gruber, Mary, Mrs.	29y	W	Ire.	17 FEB 1868	Glenwood
519	Gruds, Henrietta	15y	W	Pa.	23 MAY 1871	Congressional*
165	Grymes, Mary E.P.	22y	W	Md.	09 NOV 1859	Congressional
244	Gude, Wm. F., clerk	23y	W	Ger.	24 NOV 1866	Baltimore, Md.
120	Gudger, [blank]	8m	W	D.C.	09 JUL 1858	St. Matthews
221	Gudgin, Richard, surgeon	53y	W	Eng.	14 MAY 1866	Rock Creek
772	Guecca, A., cook	26y	W	Italy	03 JUN 1874	Mt. Olivet
096	Guecke, Augustus	3m	W	D.C.	02 NOV 1857	German Lutheran
349	Guerin, Elizabeth	42y	W	Ire.	21 SEP 1868	Mt. Olivet
417	Guggins, Louisa	13y	C	Va.	18 SEP 1869	Washington Asylum
333	Guidise, Willie	2y	W	D.C.	12 JUL 1868	Prospect Hill
330	Guiest, Edward G., clerk	44y	W	Md.	28 JUL 1868	Oak Hill
477	Guinand, Minnie	12d	W	D.C.	04 SEP 1870	Congressional
130	Guinard, Charles	1y	W	D.C.	10 OCT 1858	Congressional
759	Guinn, Mrs.	56y	C	U.S.	21 APR 1874	Mt. Pleasant
541	Guirard, Nellie	2m	W	D.C.	10 OCT 1871	Congressional
614	Guista, Michael A.	87y	W	Italy	31 JUL 1872	
098	Gulian, Margaret I.	3y	W	D.C.	09 DEC 1857	St. Patricks

Page	Name	Age	Race	Birth	Death Date	Burial Ground
117	Gulic, Mary	11m	W	D.C.	26 JUN 1858	Oak Hill
714	Gulick, Maggie E.G.	39y	W	Pa.	28 AUG 1873	Congressional
622	Gunison, J.P.	70y	W	U.S.	16 AUG 1872	
113	Gunnell, Lucia	15y	W	Va.	02 MAY 1858	Va.
475	Gunnell, Mary A.	49y	W	D.C.	27 SEP 1870	Congressional
621	Gunnison, Jno. P., sailor	70y	W	Ger.	16 AUG 1872	
523	Gunther, Daniel P.	3y	W	D.C.	18 JUN 1871	Congressional
115	Gunton, Betsy	70y	W	Eng.	02 JUN 1858	Congressional
718	Gurdy, Marietta	4y	W	D.C.	14 SEP 1873	Holmead
606	Gurley, Grace G.	7m	W	D.C.	02 JUN 1872	Congressional
602	Gurley, Helen P.	28y	W	U.S.	18 MAY 1872	Congressional
353	Gurley, Phineas D., Rev.	52y	W		30 SEP 1868	Glenwood
614	Gurley, Ralph R.	75y	W	U.S.	30 JUL 1872	
405	Gurley, Sarah	1y	C	D.C.	29 JUL 1869	Washington Asylum
011	Gurley, Thos. W.	9m		D.C.	24 JUN 1855	
220	Gurowski, Count Adam, author	62y	W	Pol.	04 MAY 1866	Oak Hill
272	Gurton, Charles	1y	W	D.C.	14 AUG 1867	Holmead
364	Gusman, Isaac	12y	W	Amer.	03 DEC 1868	Congressional
772	Gustin, Alfred F.	3m	W	U.S.	24 JUN 1874	Mt. Olivet
387	Gutherage, William	92y	C		03 APR 1869	Harmony
634	Guthridge, Ann R., housekeeper	35y	W	U.S.	01 OCT 1872	
659	Guthrie, Abelard, farmer	52y	W	U.S.	13 JAN 1873	Congressional
404	Guthrie, Paul C.	2y	W	D.C.	14 JUL 1869	Philadelphia, Pa.
705	Gutman, Rosa	14m	W	U.S.	07 JUL 1873	Congressional*
312	Gutrick, Julia	1y	C	U.S.	22 MAY 1868	Mt. Olivet
008	Gutridge, Laura Jane	20y	W	Va.	16 MAY 1855	Methodist, East
241	Gutridge, Margaret	72y	C		21 OCT 1866	Young Mens
695	Guttride, Frederick	9m	C	D.C.	20 JUN 1873	
036	Guvenator, Louisa	1y	W	D.C.	26 FEB 1856	German
318	Guy, Elizabeth Ellen	3y	W	D.C.	01 JUN 1868	Congressional
447	Guy, Kate	2m	C		25 MAR 1870	
285	Guy, William, Capt.	60y	W		22 DEC 1867	Baltimore, Md.
086	Gwin, Lucy	10y	C	Va.	08 AUG 1857	Western
162	Gwinard, Wm.		W	D.C.	27 SEP 1859	Congressional
162	Gwinard, [blank]	Still	W	D.C.	27 SEP 1859	Congressional
007	Gypson, Wm., waterman	56y	W	Md.	16 APR 1855	Congressional
519	G[illegible]k, Dora	7d	W	D.C.	14 MAY 1871	Prospect Hill

Page	Name	Age	Race	Birth	Death Date	Burial Ground
H						
334	Haag, Bertha	4m	W	D.C.	29 JUL 1868	Prospect Hill
445	Haag, Henry, Weiss beer brewer	35y	W	Ger.	25 MAR 1870	Prospect Hill
370	Haase, Francisca Adolphina	2m	W		12 JAN 1869	Prospect Hill
333	Haase, Louisa Cha.	3y	W		25 JUL 1868	Prospect Hill
226	Habbert, Mary	1m	W	D.C.	25 JUN 1866	Mt. Olivet
478	Haberman, Helen	14y	W	Md.	27 SEP 1870	Prospect Hill
263	Habit, John R.	6m	C	D.C.	05 JUN 1867	Young Mens
669	Habremehl, Geo., shoemaker	52y	W	Ger.	16 FEB 1873	
407	Hack, William, private marine	25y	W	Ger.	18 AUG 1869	Congressional
313	Hackeney, Ezekiel, waiter		C	N.Y.	06 MAY 1868	Young Mens
098	Hackett, Emma Gurley	8m	W	D.C.	17 DEC 1857	Glenwood
482	Hackett, Polly, laundress	85y	C	Md.	11 OCT 1870	Mt. Olivet
668	Hackley, Emily	80y	C	U.S.	17 FEB 1873	Ebenezer
167	Hackley, Harriet	76y	W	Va.	01 DEC 1859	Richmond, Va.
541	Hackley, Henry	15y	C	Va.	09 OCT 1871	
687	Hackley, Lucy Ann	5y	C	U.S.	01 MAY 1873	
684	Hackley, Mary A.	13y	C	U.S.	16 APR 1873	Small Pox*
607	Hackman, A.	3m	W	D.C.	25 JUN 1872	Congressional
644	Hadaway, Chas. Francis	2y	W	U.S.	18 DEC 1872	Congressional
507	Haden, Mary	62y	W	Va.	17 FEB 1871	Glenwood
040	Hading, John	3m	W	D.C.	12 MAR 1856	German Catholic
058	Hadley, Ann E.	2y	C	N.Y.	21 SEP 1856	Methodist
759	Hadley, Attilka, farmer	21y	W	U.S.	30 APR 1874	
772	Hadley, John Hays	1y	W	U.S.	27 JUN 1874	Glenwood
285	Hadley, Manning, carpenter	57y	W	Conn.	31 DEC 1867	Congressional
360	Haegel, Fred.	3y	W	Ger.	17 NOV 1868	Prospect Hill
329	Hafelfinger, Ida	1y	W	Md.	16 JUL 1868	Prospect Hill
329	Hafelfinger, Verlinda	2m	W	D.C.	16 JUL 1868	Prospect Hill
632	Haffner, Frank J.	3y	W	U.S.	24 OCT 1872	
287	Hagan, Catherine O.	6y	W	D.C.	30 DEC 1867	Mt. Olivet
140	Hagan, Elizabeth	76y	W		10 FEB 1859	St. Peters
234	Hagan, Lieut., U.S.A., child of	2y	W		07 SEP 1866	Rutland, Me.
280	Hagan, Mary V.	3m	W	D.C.	15 OCT 1867	Holmead
664	Hagar, Elizabeth	14y	C	U.S.	10 JAN 1873	Small Pox*
175	Hagen, Mary Anne	18y	W	U.S.	21 MAR 1860	Methodist
163	Hager, Catharine C.	14y	W	D.C.	15 OCT 1859	
357	Hager, Francis C.	1y	W	Amer.	11 OCT 1868	
152	Hager, Mary, housekeeper	35y	W	Va.*	07 JUN 1859	Alexandria, Va.
482	Hager, Wm. B.	2y	C	Md.	20 OCT 1870	Young Mens
069	Hager, [blank]	67y	W		28 JAN 1857	Western
114	Hagerty, Elizabeth	6y	W	D.C.	28 MAY 1858	St. Patricks
391	Hagerty, Frank E.	4y	W	D.C.	13 MAY 1869	Glenwood
024	Hagerty, John	2m	W	D.C.	17 SEP 1855	St. Matthews
118	Hagerty, Mary	7y	W	D.C.	08 JUN 1858	St. Patricks
494	Hagerty, Rose Ella	19y	W	D.C.	10 DEC 1870	Glenwood
250	Hagerty, Solomon W., pr. marines	24y	W	N.J.	29 JAN 1867	Pa.
550	Hagerty, Thomas, clerk	32y	W		25 DEC 1871	Glenwood
057	Haggerty, Anna DeLacy	3y	W	N.Y.	02 SEP 1856	Oak Hill
552	Hagner, Chas. E.	2m	W	D.C.	05 JAN 1872	Oak Hill
410	Hahl, Nicholas	40y	W	Ger.	20 AUG 1869	Prospect Hill
023	Hahn, Caroline W.C.	16y	W	Ger.	14 SEP 1855	
676	Hahn, Frank, drover	23y	W		31 MAR 1873	
240	Hahn, Mary E.	1m	W	D.C.	11 OCT 1866	Congressional
094	Haight, Anna	21y	W	N.Y.	28 OCT 1857	Fairfax Co., Va.
019	Haight, Frank	6m	W		13 AUG 1855	Congressional
274	Haight, Lillie	4m	W	D.C.	12 SEP 1867	Glenwood
319	Haight, Rose, servant	22y	C		25 JUN 1868	Mt. Olivet

District of Columbia Interments (Index to Deaths), 1855-1874

Page	Name	Age	Race	Birth	Death Date	Burial Ground
048	Haik, Robert	26y	W	Ire.	30 JUN 1856	Western
740	Hailer, Frederick	2y	W	U.S.	04 JAN 1874	Prospect Hill
453	Hainard, Charles	53y	W	Den.	23 MAY 1870	Prospect Hill
611	Haines, Mary E.	1y	C	U.S.	30 JUL 1872	
753	Haines, William, Jr., bookkeeper	22y	W	U.S.	06 MAR 1874	Glenwood
472	Hais, John	11m	W	D.C.	01 AUG 1870	Prospect Hill
092	Haislip, Jas. Edward	5y	W	D.C.	26 SEP 1857	Foundry
209	Haislup, Mary	60y	W	Md.	08 JAN 1866	Holmead
440	Haislup, William Bernard	1y	W		01 FEB 1870	
243	Haiti, Addie	19y	W	D.C.	22 NOV 1866	Mt. Olivet
397	Haland, Catharine	30y	W	Eng.	21 JUN 1869	Philadelphia, Pa.
110	Halany, David	4y	W	Ire.	06 APR 1858	St. Patricks
280	Hale, E.	8m	W	D.C.	10 OCT 1867	Oak Hill
218	Hale, Mary D.	21y	W	N.Y.	26 APR 1866	Glenwood
130	Haley, Catharine	50y	W	Ire.	01 OCT 1858	Washington Asylum
627	Hall, Ann	45y	C	U.S.	23 SEP 1872	
735	Hall, Annie	26y	C	U.S.	09 DEC 1873	Washington Asylum
012	Hall, Benjn. Bright	3m	W	D.C.	29 JUN 1855	Glenwood
262	Hall, Catherine A.	45y	W	D.C.	18 JUN 1867	Congressional
553	Hall, Charles	80y	C	Va.	08 JAN 1872	Washington
302	Hall, Charles	60y	C	Md.	06 MAR 1868	Western
450	Hall, Charles W.	13y	W		27 APR 1870	Oak Hill
012	Hall, Clarence Edgar	3m	W	D.C.	28 JUN 1855	Glenwood
124	Hall, Clarissa	72y	W	Mass.	04 AUG 1858	Baltimore, Md.
195	Hall, D.W., merchant	75y	W	Ver.	04 DEC 1860	Baltimore, Md.
493	Hall, David A., lawyer	75y	W	Ver.	24 DEC 1870	Congressional
154	Hall, E.	30y	W	U.S.	19 JUL 1859	Washington Asylum
607	Hall, Edw. C.	1y	W	D.C.	15 JUN 1872	Congressional
310	Hall, Edward	55y	C		c.22 APR 1868	Mt. Olivet
235	Hall, Edward, grocer	53y	W	Md.	21 SEP 1866	Oak Hill
347	Hall, Edward William, reporter	23y	W	Ver.	08 SEP 1868	Congressional
271	Hall, Eliza	60y	C	D.C.	22 AUG 1867	Harmony
609	Hall, Elizabeth	2y	C	U.S.	18 JUN 1872	
441	Hall, Emeline	30y	C	Va.	— FEB 1870	Ebenezer
264	Hall, Emeline, Mrs.	50y	W	N.Y.	08 JUL 1867	Congressional
296	Hall, Emma	2y	C	D.C.	23 FEB 1868	Alms House
661	Hall, Emma J.	8y	W	U.S.	27 JAN 1873	Congressional
621	Hall, Geo. W.	24y	W	U.S.	16 AUG 1872	
514	Hall, George W.	74y	W	Me.	31 MAR 1871	Congressional
601	Hall, Harry A.	1y	W	U.S.	16 MAY 1872	Congressional
766	Hall, Hattie	4m	C	U.S.	22 MAY 1874	Ebenezer
071	Hall, Henry, servant	32y	C	Md.	15 FEB 1857	St. Patricks
063	Hall, Henry, waiter	50y	C	D.C.	26 NOV 1856	St. Matthews
003	Hall, Ida Virginia	16m	W	D.C.	20 FEB 1855	Congressional
241	Hall, Isabella M.	26y	W	D.C.	24 OCT 1866	Congressional
308	Hall, Jane Ann	9y	C	Md.	21 APR 1868	Mt. Olivet
535	Hall, Jane, midwife	69y	W	Md.	07 SEP 1871	Ebenezer
020	Hall, Jas. F.	1y	W	Va.	16 AUG 1855	Pr. Geo. Co., Md.
024	Hall, John	55y	W	Md.	12 SEP 1855	Congressional
357	Hall, John	49y	B	Md.	23 OCT 1868	Freedmen's Hospital
501	Hall, John C., supposed to be	30y	W		26 JAN 1871	N.Y.
727	Hall, John, laborer	66y	B	U.S.	11 OCT 1873	
339	Hall, John R.	1y	W	D.C.	03 AUG 1868	Mt. Olivet
094	Hall, Josephus, laborer	27y	C	Md.	18 OCT 1857	Foundry
346	Hall, Maria	70y	C		10 AUG 1868	Freedmen's Hospital
094	Hall, Mary	4y	W	D.C.	21 OCT 1857	Congressional
199	Hall, Mary	28y	W	Md.	17 FEB 1861	Congressional
616	Hall, Mary E.	16m	W	U.S.	11 JUL 1872	

Page	Name	Age	Race	Birth	Death Date	Burial Ground
478	Hall, Mary E.	40y	C	D.C.	23 SEP 1870	Harmony
226	Hall, Mary, seamstress	44y	W	Eng.	29 JUN 1866	Glenwood
733	Hall, Matilda		C	U.S.	25 NOV 1873	
717	Hall, Milly	80y	C	Md.	07 SEP 1873	Holmead
361	Hall, Olive Morton	2y	W		26 NOV 1868	Glenwood
383	Hall, Polly	100y	C	U.S.	08 MAR 1869	Washington Asylum
309	Hall, Susan	1y	C		07 APR 1868	Mt. Olivet
747	Hall, Susan G.	44y	W	U.S.	12 FEB 1874	Congressional
488	Hall, Thomas, shoemaker	66y	W	U.S.	16 NOV 1870	Congressional
726	Hall, Thomas, waiter	30y	B	U.S.	26 OCT 1873	Harmony
036	Hall, William	3y	W	Md.	02 FEB 1856	Baltimore, Md.
411	Hall, Wm.	6m	C		21 AUG 1869	
597	Hall, Wm. H.	5y	W	U.S.	28 MAY 1872	Small Pox
359	Hall, Wm. R.	2y	W	D.C.	12 NOV 1868	Congressional
353	Hallahan, Anna	35y	W	Ire.	27 SEP 1868	Washington Asylum
235	Hallener, Thomas, laborer	45y	W	Ire.	15 SEP 1866	Mt. Olivet
703	Hallener, [blank]	1d	W	D.C.	16 JUL 1873	Holmead
390	Hallet, William Paxton, clerk	39y	W	N.Y.	13 MAY 1869	Congressional
706	Halley, Margaret	50y	W	Ire.	23 JUL 1873	Washington Asylum
313	Halliman, William Ross	3y	W	U.S.	14 MAY 1868	Glenwood
738	Halls, Jane M., infant of	1d	C	U.S.	14 DEC 1873	
590	Halpin, John E.		W	D.C.	18 APR 1872	Mt. Olivet
555	Halstead, Mary	80y	W	N.J.	29 JAN 1872	Laurel Hill
675	Halsted, Fannie	47y	W	U.S.	25 MAR 1873	Philadelphia, Pa.
063	Halton, Judah, cook	84y	C	Va.	30 NOV 1856	Young Mens
515	Haly, Mrs., lady	39y	W	Eng.	19 MAR 1871	Congressional
737	Ham, William, shoemaker	46y	C	U.S.	26 DEC 1873	Mt. Pleasant
772	Haman, George	6m	W	U.S.	10 JUN 1874	Congressional*
766	Hamann, Walter A.	12d	W	U.S.	09 MAY 1874	Glenwood
098	Hamback, Frederick, baker	50y	W	Ger.	09 DEC 1857	German
614	Hambleton, J.W.B.	6y	W	U.S.	03 JUL 1872	
132	Hamer, Wm.	4m	W	D.C.	16 NOV 1858	Congressional
027	Hames, John	2y	C	D.C.	02 OCT 1855	Harmony
494	Hamill, Jane	83y	W	Ire.	01 DEC 1870	Glenwood
054	Hamill, Robert S., cabinet maker	40y	W	Md.	06 AUG 1856	Glenwood
225	Hamill, Wm. F.	1y	W	D.C.	24 JUN 1866	Glenwood
187	Hamilton, Alexander, farmer	40y	W	Md.	14 AUG 1860	Md.
357	Hamilton, Anna	25y	B	Md.	19 OCT 1868	Freedmen's Hospital
534	Hamilton, Bertha L.	2y	W	D.C.	27 AUG 1871	Congressional*
606	Hamilton, Carrie	23y	C	Va.	29 JUN 1872	
121	Hamilton, Charles	14m	W	D.C.	13 JUL 1858	Congressional
462	Hamilton, Claude, actor	39y	W	Eng.	12 JUL 1870	Glenwood
383	Hamilton, Daniel	2y	C	Md.	10 MAR 1869	Washington Asylum
200	Hamilton, Edward	32y	W	Md.	20 FEB 1861	Mt. Olivet
201	Hamilton, Eliza	27y	W	D.C.	10 MAR 1861	Mt. Olivet
024	Hamilton, Elizabeth	15m	W		11 SEP 1855	Congressional
191	Hamilton, Elizabeth	50y	W	D.C.	16 OCT 1860	Methodist
584	Hamilton, Francis S.	7d	W	D.C.	02 MAR 1872	
054	Hamilton, Frank	10m	W	D.C.	12 AUG 1856	Holmead
354	Hamilton, Jacob M.	2y	W	D.C.	20 OCT 1868	Congressional
379	Hamilton, James, child of	Still			14 MAR 1869	Congressional
624	Hamilton, James, laborer	65y	C	U.S.	17 SEP 1872	
382	Hamilton, John	85y	C	Va.	23 MAR 1869	Harmony
138	Hamilton, Liney J.	23y	W		08 JAN 1859	Congressional*
533	Hamilton, Maria F.	10y	W	Md.	23 AUG 1871	
585	Hamilton, Mary	9m	C		10 MAR 1872	
086	Hamilton, Mary A.	2m	W	D.C.	05 AUG 1857	Congressional
772	Hamilton, Mary D.	20y	C	U.S.	22 JUN 1874	Mt. Olivet

Page	Name	Age	Race	Birth	Death Date	Burial Ground
439	Hamilton, Mary J.	69y	W	Va.	05 FEB 1870	Oak Hill
176	Hamilton, Samuel, merchant	32y	W	D.C.	02 APR 1860	Mt. Olivet
519	Hamilton, Sarah	70y	W	D.C.	13 MAY 1871	Congressional*
314	Hamilton, Thomas	4m	W	D.C.	13 MAY 1868	Congressional
766	Hamilton, Vockos, domestic	85y	C	U.S.	02 MAY 1874	Ebenezer
306	Hamilton, William	55y	C	D.C.	14 APR 1868	Young Mens
557	Hamilton, Wm., Rev.	73y	W	Pa.	03 FEB 1872	Oak Hill
304	Hamilton, Zolina Gertrude	1m	W	D.C.	27 MAR 1868	Congressional
114	Hamilton, [blank]	1y	W	D.C.	30 MAY 1858	Methodist
612	Haminen, Alex. A.	3m	W	U.S.	02 JUL 1872	
614	Hamiot, Victer	45y	W	Ger.	27 JUL 1872	
698	Hamlet, William, Dr.	49y	W	Mass.	27 JUN 1873	Manchester, N.H.
694	Hamlet, Wm., Dr.	49y	W	U.S.	27 JUN 1873	
668	Hamlin, Joseph E.	16m	W	U.S.	15 FEB 1873	Baltimore, Md.
032	Hamlin, Mary P.	3y	W	Pa.	26 DEC 1855	Baltimore, Md.
371	Hamlink, Thomas Allen	2y	W		09 JAN 1869	Oak Hill
258	Hammack, John D., restaurant	39y	W	Va.	09 APR 1867	Congressional
544	Hammack, Winifred S.	75y	W	Va.	03 NOV 1871	Congressional
033	Hammel, Barbara	36y	W	Ger.	27 JAN 1856	Alms House
753	Hammer, Michael, laborer	54y	W	Ger.	07 MAR 1874	Mt. Olivet
759	Hammersley, Catherine	56y	W	Ger.	14 APR 1874	Congressional*
148	Hammersly, Lewis	40y	W		12 MAY 1859	Congressional*
598	Hammon, Thomas	9m	C	U.S.	06 MAY 1872	Unknown
238	Hammond, Edward, whitewasher	48y	C	Md.	15 SEP 1866	Ebenezer
707	Hammond, Elizabeth	33y	W	Md.	05 JUL 1873	Congressional
772	Hammond, Ernest Theo.	7m	W	U.S.	13 JUN 1874	Glenwood/Rockv., Md.
407	Hammond, George W.	14d	W		02 AUG 1869	Congressional
435	Hammond, Georgiana	7m	C	D.C.	14 JAN 1870	Ebenezer
622a	Hammond, Henry	30y	C	U.S.	14 AUG 1872	
376	Hammond, Homer	4m	C		16 FEB 1869	Harmony
420	Hammond, I.T., infant of	Still	W		02 OCT 1869	Glenwood
698	Hammond, James	4m	W	D.C.	21 JUN 1873	Congressional
473	Hammond, John E.	1y	C	Va.	11 AUG 1870	Holmead
599	Hammond, Philip	6y	W	U.S.	14 MAY 1872	Cemetery
492	Hammond, Solomon, huckster	23y	W	Md.	18 DEC 1870	Glenwood
335	Hammond, Wm. DeCraft	11m	C	D.C.	13 JUL 1868	
160	Hammond, [blank]	1y	C	D.C.	08 AUG 1859	Eastern
349	Hamna, Willis	10m	W	Va.	07 SEP 1868	Oak Hill
216	Hamond, Charles H.	4m	C	D.C.	23 MAR 1866	Ebenezer
080	Hamond, Walter	24y	W	Md.	27 JUN 1857	Foundry
244	Hampton, Maggie J.	2y	W	D.C.	23 NOV 1866	Chester Co.
244	Hampton, Robert H.	4y	W	D.C.	27 NOV 1866	Chester Co.
029	Hamy, Mrs.		W		05 NOV 1855	St. Matthews
140	Hanagan, Garret, plasterer	50y	W	Ire.	09 FEB 1859	St. Patricks
710	Hancey, Matilda		C	U.S.	08 AUG 1873	Poor House
291	Hancock, Maud	2y	W	D.C.	24 JAN 1868	Oak Hill
127	Handley, Christina	52y	W	Md.	15 SEP 1858	Glenwood
110	Handly, James, painter	56y	W	Ire.	07 APR 1858	Glenwood
028	Handly, John, stone cutter	45y	W	Ire.	02 OCT 1855	St. Patricks
525	Handy, Edw. G., J.P.	49y	W	U.S.	28 JUN 1871	Congressional
038	Handy, Edward G.	11y	W	D.C.	23 MAR 1856	Congressional
609	Handy, Ham	6d	C	U.S.	10 JUN 1872	
108	Handy, Mary	6y	W	D.C.	14 MAR 1858	Catholic
347	Handy, Mary Ann	1y	W		02 SEP 1868	Congressional
128	Handy, Mary G.	75y	W	Md.	26 SEP 1858	Congressional
146	Handy, Robert S.	32y	W	D.C.	11 APR 1859	Congressional
168	Handy, S.W.	14d	W	D.C.	30 DEC 1859	Congressional
066	Handy, Saml. W., merchant	65y	W	Md.	23 DEC 1856	Holmead

Page	Name	Age	Race	Birth	Death Date	Burial Ground
526	Handy, Virginia	41y	W	D.C.	02 JUL 1871	Glenwood
058	Hanes, John, soap boiler	60y	C		24 SEP 1856	Washington Asylum
021	Haney, A.R.	10m	C		06 AUG 1855	Holmead
269	Haney, Hiram H.	1y	W		22 AUG 1867	Congressional
250	Haney, M. Mc.	26y	W	N.Y.	27 JAN 1867	Mt. Olivet
593	Hanks, Freeman	11y	W	Ohio	06 APR 1872	Prospect Hill
664	Hanley, Annie	9y	C	U.S.	13 JAN 1873	Small Pox*
584	Hanley, Clara	21y	W	Md.	04 MAR 1872	Washington
738	Hanley, Guy	4m	W	U.S.	30 DEC 1873	Oak Hill
478	Hanley, Judith	69y	W	Ire.	15 SEP 1870	Me.
713	Hanlon, Jon	34y	W	Ire.	25 AUG 1873	Washington Asylum
370	Hanna, Rosa	3m	W		04 JAN 1869	Mt. Olivet
001	Hannah, Charles	11m			19 JAN 1855	St. Peters
753	Hannan, Owen, laborer	73y	W	Ire.	23 MAR 1874	Baltimore, Md.
275	Hannegan, Anna J.	1y	W	D.C.	12 SEP 1867	Congressional
066	Hanrahan, Patrick, laborer	61y	W	Ire.	25 DEC 1856	St. Matthews
483	Hansell, Elizabeth A.	52y	W	Amer.	08 OCT 1870	Congressional
047	Hanson, Amelia	6m	C	D.C.	29 JUN 1856	Harmony
632	Hanson, Ann, spinster	80y	W	U.S.	08 OCT 1872	Congressional*
159	Hanson, Grafton D.	76y	W		24 AUG 1859	Congressional
772	Hanson, Hattie	28y	W	U.S.	22 JUN 1874	Washington Asylum
174	Hanson, Isaac, clerk	68y	W		04 MAR 1860	Congressional*
033	Hanson, James F.	8y	C		21 JAN 1856	Harmony
738	Hanson, John M., clerk	42y	W	U.S.	05 DEC 1873	
044	Hanson, Luke	100y	C		13 MAY 1856	St. Peters
293	Hanson, Peter	60y	W		06 MAR 1868	Catholic
224	Hanson, Samuel, clerk	40y	W	D.C.	14 JUN 1866	Congressional
638	Hanson, Sarah	28y	C	U.S.	11 NOV 1872	
547	Happ, Charles A.	4m	W	D.C.	07 DEC 1871	St. Marys
388	Happ, George I.	13y	W	D.C.	05 APR 1869	Mt. Olivet
537	Harbaugh, Danl., carpenter	81y	W	Md.	19 SEP 1871	Congressional
411	Harbaugh, Ellen	52y	W	D.C.	13 AUG 1869	Glenwood
195	Harbaugh, Jno. Randolph, clerk	51y	W	D.C.	06 DEC 1860	Glenwood
085	Harbaugh, Joseph F.	3m	W	D.C.	31 JUL 1857	St. Patricks
781	Harbaugh, Maria	68y	W	U.S.	17 JUL 1874	Holyrood
459	Harbinson, Lizzie A.M.	11m	W	D.C.	23 JUN 1870	Methodist
451	Harbonson, Annie M.	23y	C		06 APR 1870	Washington
026	Harbough, Mary A.	4y	W	D.C.	19 OCT 1855	St. Patricks
781	Harbour, Jos. A.G.	1y	W	U.S.	14 JUL 1874	Glenwood
591	Harcomb, Winnie Ann, laundress	32y	C	Va.	22 APR 1872	
060	Harcourt, Jane, seamstress	28y	W	Md.	16 OCT 1856	Washington Asylum
369	Hardee, Rose	23y	W	D.C.	12 JAN 1869	Congressional
414	Hardee, Sarah E.	20y	W	D.C.	13 SEP 1869	Congressional
108	Harden, [blank], Mr., clerk	57y	W		25 MAR 1858	Alexandria, Va.
159	Hardenfeller, William	10m	W	Md.	24 AUG 1859	German Reformed
279	Hardesty, William	6d	W		04 OCT 1867	Congressional
659	Hardie, Alford	1y	C	U.S.	16 JAN 1873	Holy Rood
644	Hardie, Hester, servant	22y	C	U.S.	19 DEC 1872	
667	Hardie, Susan	1y	C	U.S.	09 FEB 1873	
136	Harding, Frederick	1y	W	D.C.	25 DEC 1858	Holmead
710	Harding, Josiah, clerk	29y	W	Me.	03 AUG 1873	Glenwood
710	Harding, Robertiena	6m	W	Va.	07 AUG 1873	Glenwood
349	Harding, Thomas, gardener	61y	W	Eng.	03 SEP 1868	Glenwood
437	Harding, Thos. J.	38y	W	Eng.	08 JAN 1870	Glenwood
712	Harding, William	2m	W	D.C.	13 AUG 1873	Congressional*
179	Hardy, Walter, child of	Still	W	D.C.	01 MAY 1860	Congressional
229	Hardy, William	8m	W	D.C.	22 JUL 1866	Mt. Olivet
053	Hare, John N.F.	1y	W	D.C.	04 AUG 1856	Congressional

District of Columbia Interments (Index to Deaths), 1855-1874

Page	Name	Age	Race	Birth	Death Date	Burial Ground
087	Harey, Mary, servant	78y	C	Va.	12 AUG 1857	Holmead
666	Hargrove, Henry K., merchant	56y	W	U.S.	05 FEB 1873	Congressional*
130	Harkbascht, Margerett	8m	W	D.C.	05 OCT 1858	Catholic
659	Harkel, Leonidas, merchant	50y	W	U.S.	15 JAN 1873	
319	Harkins, Anna Louisa	2y	W	U.S.	16 JUN 1868	Mt. Olivet
069	Harkness, Daniel	4y	W	D.C.	24 JAN 1857	Methodist
138	Harkness, Martha Eleanor	39y	W	D.C.	28 JAN 1859	Glenwood
212	Harkness, Saml., clerk	63y	W	D.C.	08 FEB 1866	Congressional
525	Harkum, Annie	14y	C	Va.	26 JUN 1871	
541	Harlan, Nelson	4y	W	D.C.	09 OCT 1871	Glenwood
506	Harlow, James E.	2y	W	W.Va.	10 FEB 1871	Congressional
265	Harlow, Ricard	6m	W	Va.	18 JUL 1867	Mt. Olivet
369	Harman, Henry M.	14d	W	D.C.	02 JAN 1869	Congressional
348	Harman, John	11m	W	D.C.	03 SEP 1868	Congressional
781	Harmon, John	1d	W	U.S.	01 JUL 1874	Glenwood
081	Harmon, Mary	36y	W	Md.	30 JUN 1857	Glenwood
340	Harnden, [blank]	6m	W	D.C.	17 AUG 1868	Congressional
602	Harne, Mary W.	1y	W	U.S.	21 MAY 1872	Congressional
048	Harner, William	35y	C	D.C.	22 JUN 1856	
689	Harper, Edward, laborer	60y	W	U.S.	23 MAY 1873	Washington Asylum
537	Harper, Emma A.	10m	C	D.C.	19 SEP 1871	
227	Harper, Henry Wilson	10m	W	D.C.	01 JUL 1866	Congressional
676	Harper, Jno. M., merchant	32y	W	U.S.	29 MAR 1873	Centreville, Md.
708	Harper, John W., laborer	28y	W	D.C.	26 JUL 1873	
473	Harper, John Walter	3m			26 AUG 1870	
459	Harper, L.E.	64y	W	Eng.	20 JUN 1870	Montgomery Co., Md.
028	Harper, Mary	8y	W	D.C.	21 OCT 1855	St. Matthews
484	Harrian, Mic	1y	W		21 OCT 1870	Congressional
435	Harrigan, John, tailor	56y	W	Ire.	22 JAN 1870	Mt. Olivet
213	Harrington, A.S., painter	62y	W	D.C.	22 FEB 1866	
122	Harrington, Douglass, painter	21y	W	D.C.	18 JUL 1858	Ebenezer
110	Harrington, John, laborer	30y	W	Ire.	03 APR 1858	St. Patricks
313	Harrington, Maria	48y	W	Ire.	25 MAY 1868	Mt. Olivet
252	Harrington, Mary	60y	W		13 FEB 1867	Congressional
018	Harrington, Mary	26y	W	Ire.	10 AUG 1855	St. Patricks
694	Harrington, Virginia Ridgly	20m	W	D.C.	21 JUN 1873	Dover, Del.
412	Harris, Alex.	2m	C	D.C.	11 AUG 1869	Washington Asylum
456	Harris, Alice		W	D.C.	20 JUN 1870	Glenwood
274	Harris, Alverta Anderson	4m	C	D.C.	12 SEP 1867	Harmony
547	Harris, Andrew F.	2m	W	D.C.	05 DEC 1871	Congressional
329	Harris, Anna K., Mrs.	86y	W	N.J.	18 JUL 1868	Camden, N.J.
120	Harris, Arnold	11m	W	D.C.	05 JUL 1858	Oak Hill
404	Harris, Benjamin	1y	C		17 JUL 1869	
590	Harris, Cara V.	9m	C	D.C.	18 APR 1872	Asylum
420	Harris, Catharine	1y	W	D.C.	14 OCT 1869	Methodist
075	Harris, Catharine, slave	60y	C	Md.	15 APR 1857	Methodist, East
305	Harris, Charles, laborer	80y	C	Md.	17 MAR 1868	Harmony
384	Harris, Chas. E.	1y	C	U.S.	22 MAR 1869	Washington Asylum
118	Harris, Chas. Edmund	5m	W	D.C.	30 JUN 1858	Foundry
463	Harris, Chas., seaman	31y	W	Md.	08 JUL 1870	Mt. Olivet
381	Harris, Clara	Still	W		17 MAR 1869	Oak Hill
262	Harris, Cornelius	9m	C	D.C.	29 JUN 1867	Union
384	Harris, E.	Still	C	D.C.	17 MAR 1869	Washington Asylum
608	Harris, George, barber	60y	C	D.C.	10 JUN 1872	
781	Harris, George, laborer	56y	C	U.S.	16 JUL 1874	Holyrood
299	Harris, George W.	1d	C	D.C.	03 MAR 1868	Young Mens
340	Harris, Gertrude	10m	W	D.C.	18 AUG 1868	Congressional
703	Harris, Helen	50y	C	Va.	04 JUL 1873	Beckett's

Page	Name	Age	Race	Birth	Death Date	Burial Ground
554	Harris, Henrietta	24y	C	D.C.	17 JAN 1872	
618	Harris, Henry	60y	C	U.S.	12 AUG 1872	Washington Asylum
675	Harris, Henry	50y	C	U.S.	23 MAR 1873	Washington Asylum
547	Harris, Hetty	2y		D.C.	01 DEC 1871	
604	Harris, Ida L.	1y	C	D.C.	15 JUN 1872	Ebenezer
416	Harris, James	21y	C		19 SEP 1869	Western
079	Harris, James C., laborer	22y	C	D.C.	07 JUN 1857	Young Mens
638	Harris, Jane S.	3y	C	U.S.	08 NOV 1872	
619	Harris, Jas. E.	1y	C	U.S.	24 AUG 1872	Mt. Pleasant Plains
638	Harris, Jennie	4y	C	U.S.	22 NOV 1872	
615	Harris, John	45y	C	U.S.	03 JUL 1872	
155	Harris, John	4m	W	U.S.	28 JUL 1859	Western
554	Harris, John E.	50y	C	D.C.	19 JAN 1872	
294	Harris, John T., barber	27h	C	D.C.	03 FEB 1868	Holmead
166	Harris, Joseph	8d	C	D.C.	27 NOV 1859	Western
091	Harris, Lee	2y	C	D.C.	16 SEP 1857	
019	Harris, Louisa	32y	C		15 AUG 1855	Young Mens
704	Harris, M. Abbie	11d	W	D.C.	28 JUL 1873	Glenwood
534	Harris, M.E.	2y	C	D.C.	31 AUG 1871	Young Mens
638	Harris, M.H.	3m	C	U.S.	16 NOV 1872	
772	Harris, M.R.	1y	W	U.S.	10 JUN 1874	Congressional*
642	Harris, Mabel	2y	W	U.S.	04 DEC 1872	Congressional*
359	Harris, Martha	1y	W	D.C.	21 NOV 1868	Glenwood
244	Harris, Mary	71y	W	Md.	05 NOV 1866	Congressional
479	Harris, Mary	2y	C	D.C.	14 SEP 1870	Washington Asylum
150	Harris, Mary	35y	C	D.C.	02 JUN 1859	Washington Asylum
426	Harris, Mary A.	1m	W	D.C.	12 NOV 1869	Methodist
582	Harris, Mary E.	10y	C	D.C.	19 FEB 1872	
264	Harris, Mary E.	1y	W	D.C.	13 JUL 1867	Mt. Olivet
619	Harris, Mary J.	4y	C	U.S.	11 AUG 1872	
617	Harris, Mary J.	4y	C	U.S.	11 AUG 1872	Mt. Olivet
328	Harris, Mary O.	65y	C	Md.	22 JUL 1868	Mt. Olivet
094	Harris, Mary R.	1y	W	D.C.	19 OCT 1857	Methodist
422	Harris, Mary, servant	25y	C	Md.	10 OCT 1869	
630	Harris, Moses	22y	C	U.S.	28 OCT 1872	Small Pox
199	Harris, Mrs.	25y	C	D.C.	16 FEB 1861	Methodist
241	Harris, Mrs.	48y			06 OCT 1866	Mt. Olivet
255	Harris, Naw Doman	12y	C	D.C.	30 MAR 1867	Beckett's
664	Harris, Peter	25y	C	U.S.	13 JAN 1873	Small Pox*
093	Harris, Rachael	70y	W	Md.	04 OCT 1857	Congressional
077	Harris, Sampson W.	42y		Ala.	02 MAY 1857	
544	Harris, T.H.	30y	W	Mich.	02 NOV 1871	Mich.
599	Harris, Tallie	3d	W	U.S.	19 MAY 1872	Unknown
033	Harris, Thomas H.	2y	C		10 JAN 1856	Alms House
302	Harris, William		C		06 MAR 1868	Alms House
696	Harris, William, barber	22y	C	Va.	09 JUN 1873	
529	Harris, Wm.	7m	C	D.C.	25 JUL 1871	Young Mens
611	Harris, Wm. H.	9m	C	U.S.	16 JUL 1872	
047	Harris, Wm. H.	45y	W	Md.	29 JUN 1856	Foundry
124	Harris, [blank]	16y	C		11 AUG 1858	
695	Harris, [blank]	11m	C	D.C.	13 JUN 1873	Ebenezer
120	Harris, [blank]	68y	C		01 JUL 1858	Western
141	Harris, [blank]		C		24 FEB 1859	Western
410	Harris, [blank]	6m	C		17 AUG 1869	Young Mens
152	Harris, [blank], Mr., servant	35y	C	D.C.	23 JUN 1859	Harmony
349	Harrison, Ann Eliza	5y	W		20 SEP 1868	Glenwood
452	Harrison, Caroline	7d	C	D.C.	18 APR 1870	Washington Asylum
285	Harrison, Charles H.	1y	W	D.C.	21 DEC 1867	Congressional

District of Columbia Interments (Index to Deaths), 1855-1874

Page	Name	Age	Race	Birth	Death Date	Burial Ground
583	Harrison, Cynthia	22y	W	Va.	26 FEB 1872	Congressional
367	Harrison, D.	Still	B	D.C.	08 DEC 1868	Washington Asylum
449	Harrison, Edwin Eugene	2m	W		03 APR 1870	Congressional
528	Harrison, Elisabeth	74y	W	Va.	14 JUL 1871	Washington
446	Harrison, Elizabeth		C	Md.	29 MAR 1870	
681	Harrison, Elizabeth	18m	C	U.S.	17 APR 1873	Young Mens
632	Harrison, Emily	33y	C	U.S.	14 OCT 1872	
130	Harrison, Emma	7m	W	D.C.	14 OCT 1858	Congressional
237	Harrison, Emma	1y			28 SEP 1866	Western
146	Harrison, Fannie	28y	W	Md.	04 APR 1859	Congressional
308	Harrison, Francis E., carpenter	38y	W	Eng.	15 APR 1868	Congressional
642	Harrison, Frank	12y	C	U.S.	26 DEC 1872	Small Pox
386	Harrison, Frenklin U., doorkeeper	36y	W	Md.	08 APR 1869	Mt. Olivet
431	Harrison, George	12y	C	Md.	25 DEC 1869	Western
627	Harrison, Henry	25y	C	U.S.	19 SEP 1872	Small Pox
241	Harrison, Henry	58y			23 OCT 1866	Western
141	Harrison, Henry L.		W		24 FEB 1859	
201	Harrison, Horace W.		W		29 MAR 1861	Oak Hill
284	Harrison, James E., Col. USA	38y	W	D.C.	04 NOV 1867	Congressional*
020	Harrison, John	8m	C	D.C.	05 AUG 1855	Union
473	Harrison, John W.	6d	C	D.C.	28 AUG 1870	Western
097	Harrison, Joseph, billiard saloon	48y	W	Md.	24 NOV 1857	Baltimore, Md.
154	Harrison, Kate	4m	W	D.C.	13 JUL 1859	Baltimore, Md.
543	Harrison, Lucy A.	67y	W	U.S.	30 OCT 1871	Methodist
547	Harrison, Maggie	3y	W	D.C.	01 DEC 1871	Congressional
221	Harrison, Margaret A.	54y	W	Va.	23 MAY 1866	Congressional
075	Harrison, Mary	76y	W	Md.	01 APR 1857	Congressional
091	Harrison, Mary	20y	W	D.C.	12 SEP 1857	Methodist
345	Harrison, Mary	1y	C	Va.	22 AUG 1868	Western
337	Harrison, Mary Louisa				04 AUG 1868	Washington Asylum
628	Harrison, Nancy	78y	C	U.S.	17 SEP 1872	Small Pox
062	Harrison, Rachael	76y	W	Md.	09 NOV 1856	St. Matthews
272	Harrison, Richard	76y	W	Eng.	01 AUG 1867	Methodist
530	Harrison, Rosa	2y	C	D.C.	31 JUL 1871	
710	Harrison, Rosa	10m	W	U.S.	06 AUG 1873	Washington Asylum
541	Harrison, Rose	1y	C	Va.	09 OCT 1871	
535	Harrison, Rose	1y	C		07 SEP 1871	
337	Harrison, Samuel	1y	C	U.S.	07 AUG 1868	Washington Asylum
403	Harrison, Sarah F.	6m	C		09 JUL 1869	Western
432	Harrison, Sophia	10m	C	D.C.	09 DEC 1869	Washington Asylum
146	Harrison, Susan A.	55y	W		05 APR 1859	Oak Hill
300	Harrison, William	13d	C	D.C.	08 MAR 1868	Alms House
475	Harrison, Wm.	95y	C	Va.	18 SEP 1870	Freedmen's Hospital
531	Harrison, Wm.	8m	W	D.C.	02 AUG 1871	Glenwood
675	Harrison, Wm.	26y	C	U.S.	21 MAR 1873	Washington Asylum
294	Harrison, Wm. H., machinist	38y	W	D.C.	21 FEB 1868	Congressional
010	Harrison, Wm., laborer	35y	C	D.C.	18 JUN 1855	Harmony
113	Harrod, Jane	28y	C	D.C.	13 MAY 1858	Young Mens
122	Harrod, Polly	56y		N.Y.	27 JUL 1858	Washington Asylum
403	Harrod, Rachel	9m	C	D.C.	27 JUL 1869	Union
295	Harron, Columbus	48y	W	Md.	08 FEB 1868	Congressional
115	Harrover, John	12y	W	D.C.	02 JUN 1858	Congressional
515	Harrover, [blank]	Still	W		04 MAR 1871	Congressional
327	Harry, George W., dentist	39y	W	Va.	14 JUL 1868	Glenwood
713	Hars, E.W.W.	2y	C	U.S.	24 AUG 1873	
759	Hart, Hugh		W	U.S.	30 APR 1874	Mt. Olivet
753	Hart, John	1m	C	U.S.	31 MAR 1874	
137	Hart, John W.	20y	W	D.C.	21 JAN 1859	Western

Page	Name	Age	Race	Birth	Death Date	Burial Ground
458	Hart, Joseph	38y	C	S.C.	11 JUN 1870	Potters Field
695	Hart, Letta, child of	12m	C	D.C.	18 JUN 1873	Ebenezer
704	Hart, M.	11d	W	D.C.	24 JUL 1873	German
252	Hart, Mary L.	36y	W	D.C.	23 FEB 1867	Glenwood
073	Hart, Moses, segar maker	36y	W	Ger.	02 MAR 1857	Washington Asylum
389	Hart, Robt.	5y	C	U.S.	15 APR 1869	Washington Asylum
384	Hart, Thomas	3y	C	Va.	11 MAR 1869	Washington Asylum
500	Hart, Thos., tailor	51y	W	Ire.	07 JAN 1871	Mt. Olivet
429	Hart, Willie	21d	W		30 DEC 1869	Congressional
181	Hart, [boy]	11d	W	D.C.	05 JUN 1860	Washington Asylum
392	Hart, [illegible]	1y	C		22 MAY 1869	Washington Asylum
321	Hartbrecht, Emma	1y	W	D.C.	05 JUN 1868	German Catholic
321	Hartbrecht, Otto	4y	W	D.C.	15 JUN 1868	German Catholic
317	Harte, William C., clerk	19y	W	D.C.	25 JUN 1868	Congressional
394	Hartenstein, Margaret N.	32y	W	Md.	04 JUN 1869	Congressional
449	Hartley, David	1y	W		14 APR 1870	Congressional
759	Hartley, Marion P.	4m	W	U.S.	30 APR 1874	Congressional*
410	Hartman, Charles, restaurant kpr.	54y	W	Prus.	23 AUG 1869	Prospect Hill
018	Hartman, [blank]	9m	C	D.C.	02 AUG 1855	Congressional
454	Hartmans, John, tailor	44y	W	Ger.	08 MAY 1870	Prospect Hill
118	Hartmell, Rosa May	1m	W	D.C.	30 JUN 1858	Glenwood
623	Hartneck, Thos.	43y	W	U.S.	08 JUL 1872	Holy Rood
533	Hartnekt, Johana, housekeeper	56y	W	Ire.	22 AUG 1871	Mt. Olivet
229	Hartnell, Mrs., infant at	Still	W	D.C.	18 JUL 1866	Mt. Olivet
781	Hartnett, John, laborer	47y	W	Ire.	21 JUL 1874	Mt. Olivet
473	Hartnett, Mary E.	1y	W	D.C.	30 AUG 1870	Mt. Olivet
155	Hartnett, Patrick, stone cutter	68y	W	Ire.	27 JUL 1859	St. Patricks
078	Hartwim, Char[l]es	1y	W	D.C.	30 MAY 1857	German
289	Harvey, Francis Walter	1y	W	D.C.	25 JAN 1868	Mt. Olivet
047	Harvey, Henry J.	11m	W	Va.	30 JUN 1856	St. Matthews
041	Harvey, James F., undertaker	40y	W	D.C.*	13 APR 1856	Oak Hill
270	Harvey, James S., gentleman	73y	W	Md.	11 AUG 1867	Mt. Olivet
154	Harvey, John S.	5m	W	D.C.	14 JUL 1859	Country
514	Harvey, Joseh W., printer	26y	W	N.Y.	08 MAR 1871	Glenwood
457	Harvey, Maria Theresa	9m	W	D.C.	26 JUN 1870	Mt. Olivet
414	Harvey, Mary, Miss	76y	W	D.C.	21 SEP 1869	Mt. Olivet
645	Harvey, Mollie A.	33y	W	U.S.	29 DEC 1872	Oak Hill
388	Harvey, R.	2m	W	D.C.	27 APR 1869	Mt. Olivet
225	Harvey, Sophia	41y	C		20 JUN 1866	Harmony
747	Harveycutter, [blank]	5d	W	U.S.	15 FEB 1874	Glenwood
487	Harvy, Annie C.	36y	W	Va.	15 NOV 1870	Congressional
766	Harvy, James	P.B.	W	U.S.	27 MAY 1874	Glenwood
177	Harvy, Mary A.	54y	W	D.C.	25 APR 1860	Congressional
270	Harvy, Ruth Ann	71y	W	Md.	16 AUG 1867	Pr. Geo. Co., Md.
410	Harzehn, John, shoemaker	40y	W		08 AUG 1869	Prospect Hill
488	Hashboyle, James	17y	W	Amer.	09 NOV 1870	Congressional
329	Hasis, Harry	30y			04 JUL 1868	Young Mens
105	Haskell, Florence E.	11m	W	D.C.	20 FEB 1858	Mass.
028	Haskell, Margaret	11m	W		23 OCT 1855	Glenwood
331	Haskins, Frank	7m	C	D.C.	03 JUL 1868	Freedmen's Hospital
388	Haskins, Jane		C		12 APR 1869	
759	Haskins, Wm. H.	1y	W	U.S.	23 APR 1874	Mt. Olivet
526	Haskum, Lola	12y	C	Va.	04 JUL 1871	
360	Haslett, Thomas	1m	W		09 NOV 1868	Glenwood
455	Hasset, Ann	70y	W	Ire.	16 MAY 1870	Mt. Olivet
297	Haswell, David B.	59y	W	N.Y.	14 FEB 1868	Mt. Olivet
271	Hatcher, Mary Estelle	9m	W	D.C.	30 AUG 1867	Rock Creek
704	Hatchfeld, A.B.	17d	W	D.C.	11 JUL 1873	

District of Columbia Interments (Index to Deaths), 1855-1874

Page	Name	Age	Race	Birth	Death Date	Burial Ground
698	Hatton, Lydia H.	1y	C		02 JUN 1873	Harmony
614	Hatton, Wm.	65y	W	U.S.	19 JUL 1872	
625	Hauck, Florence	2m	W	U.S.	01 SEP 1872	
262	Haufman, Anton	10m	W	D.C.	27 JUN 1867	German Catholic
632	Haufman, Mary	3y	W	U.S.	10 OCT 1872	
356	Haukins, Mary Jane	32y	C	Md.	31 OCT 1868	Mt. Olivet
604	Haulstork, Annice	6y	C	D.C.	18 JUN 1872	Ebenezer
295	Haun, [Catherine], Mrs.	36y	W	Md.	12 FEB 1868	Congressional
723	Hauptman, Danl., tinsmith	82y	W	Md.	09 OCT 1873	Oak Hill
723	Hause, Louise, servant	20y	W	Ger.	03 OCT 1873	Prospect Hill
753	Hauser, [blank]	51y	W	Ger.	04 MAR 1874	Prospect Hill
390	Havener, Thomas Harvey	20y	W	D.C.	25 MAY 1869	Congressional
536	Havenner, Thomas, baker	84y	W		18 SEP 1871	Congressional
069	Haw, John S.	24y	W	D.C.	30 JAN 1857	Congressional
125	Haw, Wm. Henry	2y	C	D.C.	18 AUG 1858	Young Mens
210	Hawes, Charles	5y	W		17 JAN 1866	Glenwood
262	Hawes, Edith	7d	W	D.C.	13 JUN 1867	Congressional
366	Hawes, Geo. F.	16y	W	D.C.	22 DEC 1868	Congressional*
210	Hawes, William B.	1y	W		15 JAN 1866	Glenwood
125	Hawke, Anna Jane	17y	W	D.C.	30 AUG 1858	St. Patricks
439	Hawke, Mary J.	2y	W		25 FEB 1870	Congressional
258	Hawkin, C.	13y	C		14 APR 1867	Young Mens
665	Hawkins, Adaline	33y	C	U.S.	27 JAN 1873	Small Pox*
680	Hawkins, Agusta A.	78y	W	U.S.	11 APR 1873	Glenwood
590	Hawkins, Anna	1y	C	D.C.	05 APR 1872	Small Pox
437	Hawkins, Caroline	21d	C	D.C.	08 JAN 1870	Washington Asylum
533	Hawkins, Catharine J.	26y	C	D.C.	26 AUG 1871	Union
688	Hawkins, Cornelia	22y	C	U.S.	15 MAY 1873	
585	Hawkins, Dennis	7d	C	D.C.	10 MAR 1872	Mt. Zion
676	Hawkins, Dennis, laborer	30y	C	U.S.	18 MAR 1873	
393	Hawkins, Elenora	2y	C		18 MAY 1869	
513	Hawkins, Eliza	36y	C	Md.	19 MAR 1871	Washington Asylum
630	Hawkins, Elizabeth	25y	C	U.S.	28 OCT 1872	Small Pox
292	Hawkins, Emma		C		23 JAN 1868	Alms House
633	Hawkins, Flora	13y	C	U.S.	10 OCT 1872	Small Pox*
759	Hawkins, Frank, laborer	76y	W	U.S.	30 APR 1874	Mt. Olivet
448	Hawkins, George, laborer	72y	C	Va.	23 MAR 1870	Washington Asylum
753	Hawkins, George W.	2m	C	U.S.	23 MAR 1874	Ebenezer
492	Hawkins, Georgiana	9y	C	D.C.	15 DEC 1870	Ebenezer
361	Hawkins, Hannah, laundress	65y	C	Md.	06 NOV 1868	Harmony
615	Hawkins, Henry	30y	C	U.S.	14 JUL 1872	
469	Hawkins, Ignatius, laborer	40y	C	Md.	19 AUG 1870	Mt. Olivet
362	Hawkins, Infant	2d	C		17 NOV 1868	Ebenezer
484	Hawkins, James E.	3y	C	D.C.	10 OCT 1870	Potters Field
125	Hawkins, James, laborer	40y	C	D.C.	23 AUG 1858	St. Matthews
289	Hawkins, Jane	5y	C	Va.	22 JAN 1868	Alms House
663	Hawkins, Jeremiah	23y	C	U.S.	27 JAN 1873	Small Pox
690	Hawkins, John	28y	C	U.S.	04 MAY 1873	Small Pox
330	Hawkins, Johnny	11m	C		30 JUL 1868	Young Mens
278	Hawkins, Joseph P.	2y	C		03 OCT 1867	
509	Hawkins, Margaret	49y	C		14 FEB 1871	Ebenezer
055	Hawkins, Marian	9m	C	D.C.	20 AUG 1856	Harmony
122	Hawkins, Mary	1y	C	D.C.	24 JUL 1858	Young Mens
484	Hawkins, Mary A.	21d	C	D.C.	04 OCT 1870	Potters Field
472	Hawkins, Oliver W.	5½m	C	D.C.	03 AUG 1870	Union
473	Hawkins, R.H.	1y	C	D.C.	01 AUG 1870	Holmead
018	Hawkins, Robt. Alex.	8m	W	D.C.	18 AUG 1855	Methodist
542	Hawkins, Rosa A.	1y	C		20 OCT 1871	Mt. Olivet

Page	Name	Age	Race	Birth	Death Date	Burial Ground
311	Hawkins, Susan, infant of	Still	C		c.29 APR 1868	Mt. Olivet
392	Hawkins, Susan, Mrs.	84y	C		27 MAY 1869	Mt. Olivet
554	Hawkins, Thomas, laborer	75y	C	Va.	14 JAN 1872	Washington
446	Hawkins, Thomas R., messenger	29y	C	Pa.	02 MAR 1870	Harmony
590	Hawkins, Wm.	5y	C	D.C.	04 APR 1872	Small Pox
054	Hawkins, Wm. H.	10m	C	D.C.	08 AUG 1856	Foundry
479	Hawkins, Wm. H.	1d	C	D.C.	13 SEP 1870	Washington Asylum
378	Hawkins, Wm., laborer	70y	C	Md.	14 FEB 1869	Freedmen's Hospital
520	Hawkins, Wm. R.	9m	C	D.C.	23 MAY 1871	Harmony
476	Hawkins, Wm. T.	1y	C	Amer.	29 SEP 1870	Ebenezer
029	Hawkins, [blank]	60y			03 NOV 1855	Georgetown
730	Hawley, Nancy, dressmaker	45y	W	U.S.	16 NOV 1873	Congressional*
187	Hawley, Samuel, coach painter	33y	W	Md.	05 AUG 1860	Washington Asylum
014	Hawley, [blank]	10m	C		22 JUL 1855	Western
759	Hawlig, Kate	13y	W	U.S.	25 APR 1874	Prospect Hill
255	Hayden, Charles F.		W		23 MAR 1867	Mt. Olivet
694	Hayes, Ella Virginia	43y	W	D.C.	04 JUN 1873	Congressional
547	Hayes, Henry	1m	W	D.C.	04 DEC 1871	Congressional*
608	Hayes, Joseph, Dr.	46y	W	N.Y.	08 JUN 1872	Glenwood
215	Hayes, Michael	10m	W	D.C.	14 MAR 1866	Mt. Olivet
629	Hayes, T.	83y	W	U.S.	21 OCT 1872	
753	Hayes, William, farmer	19y	W	U.S.	12 MAR 1874	Congressional
283	Hayghe, John L.	2y	W	D.C.	22 NOV 1867	Congressional
285	Hayghe, Laura V.	1y	W	D.C.	20 DEC 1867	Congressional
255	Hayley, Henry	26y	C	Md.	08 MAR 1867	
298	Haymour, Sarah	96y	W	Eng.	29 FEB 1868	Congressional
430	Hayne, Charlotte	65y	W	N.Y.	07 DEC 1869	N.Y.
351	Haynes, Eustis	9m	C	D.C.	12 SEP 1868	Young Mens
153	Haynes, Jane	40y	W	U.S.	11 JUL 1859	Congressional
506	Haynie, E. Estelle	1y	W	D.C.	22 FEB 1871	Congressional
314	Haynie, Ella	1y	W	D.C.	31 MAY 1868	Congressional
667	Haynie, Harriet M.	3y	W	U.S.	07 FEB 1873	Congressional
676	Haynie, Henry B.	1m	W	U.S.	31 MAR 1873	Congressional
401	Hays, Annie	11m	W		28 JUL 1869	Mt. Olivet
696	Hays, D. Perry, school teacher	29y	C	N.C.	05 JUN 1873	Young Mens
151	Hays, Honora	50y	W	Ire.	23 JUN 1859	Mt. Olivet
474	Hays, John	22y	C		20 AUG 1870	Washington Asylum
135	Hays, John H., barber	22y	C	D.C.	13 DEC 1858	Young Mens
457	Hays, John T.	1m	W	D.C.	12 JUN 1870	Congressional
157	Hays, Margaret	17y	W	D.C.	06 AUG 1859	Mt. Olivet
425	Hays, Margaret R.	49y	W		29 NOV 1869	Congressional
280	Hays, Mary	36y	W	Ire.	14 OCT 1867	Mt. Olivet
435	Hays, Mary A.	1y	W		07 JAN 1870	
142	Hays, Mary Florinda	4m	W	D.C.	26 FEB 1859	Congressional
064	Hays, Timothy	10m	W	D.C.	30 NOV 1856	St. Patricks
077	Hays, [blank]	2y	W		02 MAY 1857	Western
167	Hayse, Francis G., clerk	37y	W	D.C.	12 DEC 1859	Congressional
687	Hayson, Henry, carpenter	68y	C	D.C.	07 MAY 1873	Ebenezer
308	Haythorpe, John E.	2m	W	D.C.	21 APR 1868	Congressional
747	Hayward, Joshua, laudryman	48y	W	Eng.	02 FEB 1874	Rock Creek
638	Haywood, Geo., laborer	37y	C	U.S.	07 NOV 1872	Washington Asylum
096	Hazard, Elizabeth	40y	W	Md.	11 NOV 1857	Holmead
006	Hazard, Jno. Duncan	8m	W	Pa.	17 APR 1855	Congressional
659	Hazard, Robt. P., pump maker	58y	W	U.S.	12 JAN 1873	Congressional
390	Hazel, Minnie	7m	W	D.C.	26 MAY 1869	Oak Hill
227	Hazeltine, Margaret W.	50y	W		05 JUL 1866	Mt. Olivet
390	Hazelton, Kate, Mrs.	35y	W	N.Y.	05 MAY 1869	Congressional
021	Hazelton, [blank]	38y	W		28 AUG 1855	

District of Columbia Interments (Index to Deaths), 1855-1874

Page	Name	Age	Race	Birth	Death Date	Burial Ground
399	Hazen, Ervin	8m	W		25 JUL 1869	Congressional
668	Hazlet, Cunningham, clerk	38y	W	U.S.	25 FEB 1873	Union Town, Ohio
462	Head, Samuel, gentleman	74y	W	Eng.	19 JUL 1870	Dranesville, Va.
753	Headley, Mary V.	26y	W	U.S.	01 MAR 1874	Congressional
108	Headley, May A.	36y	W	Va.*	20 MAR 1858	Alexandria, Va., Meth.
116	Heaight, Mary	1y	W	D.C.	19 JUN 1858	
781	Healdenback, A.J.	6m	W	U.S.	04 JUL 1874	Methodist
759	Healey, Julia	2y	W	U.S.	16 APR 1874	Mt. Olivet
737	Healey, Mary	77y	W	Ire.	21 DEC 1873	
500	Healley, L.G.	4y	W	D.C.	19 JAN 1871	Holmead
323	Healy, James P.	6m	W	D.C.	23 JUL 1868	Mt. Olivet
103	Hearbert, [blank], whitewasher	59y	C	D.C.	09 JAN 1858	Washington Asylum
140	Hearld, [blank]	6m	W		08 FEB 1859	Western
190	Hearld, [blank]	6m	W		10 SEP 1860	Western
500	Hearns, Wm.	Child	C	D.C.	10 JAN 1871	Western
213	Heart, Mr., son of	8y	W		11 FEB 1866	Congressional
078	Heartman, Mrs.	40y	W	Ger.	30 MAY 1857	Methodist
738	Hease, Allie	21d	W	U.S.	30 DEC 1873	Congressional
088	Heasly, John	1y	W	D.C.	25 AUG 1857	Holmead
232	Heath, Anna	22y	W	N.Y.	24 AUG 1866	Congressional
221	Heath, J. Harrie, clerk	34y	W	N.Y.	21 MAY 1866	Glenwood
062	Heath, Richard, agent	30y	W	Va.	07 NOV 1856	Richmond, Va.
396	Heath, [blank]	6y	W		23 JUN 1869	Prospect Hill
440	Heatley, Mary	6m	W		01 FEB 1870	
665	Hebb, Clement W.	22m	W	U.S.	01 JAN 1873	Congressional
520	Hebb, Sarah	78y	W	Amer.	28 MAY 1871	Congressional
665	Hebb, Wm. Vernon	4y	W	U.S.	01 JAN 1873	Congressional
738	Hebbern, Wm.	6d	W	U.S.	29 DEC 1873	
307	Hebrons, Prissey	50y	C	Md.	25 APR 1868	Western
401	Heck, E.M.	10m	W		25 JUL 1869	Mt. Olivet
341	Heck, G.H.	1y	W	D.C.	16 AUG 1868	Congressional
667	Heck, Lilly May	3y	W	U.S.	08 FEB 1873	Prospect Hill
611	Heck, Tennie	1y	W	U.S.	04 JUL 1872	
458	Hedgeman, Amanda	21y	C	Va.	10 JUN 1870	Potters Feld
086	Hedges, Fanny	62y	C	D.C.	03 AUG 1857	Washington Asylum
343	Hedinger, Anna M.	2y	W	D.C.	27 AUG 1868	Congressional
356	Hedner, John	7m	W	D.C.	03 OCT 1868	Prospect Hill
698	Heeney, Nancy, governess	81y	W	Mass.	12 JUN 1873	Not Stated
222	Heffernan, [child of]	Still	W	D.C.	27 MAY 1866	Mt. Olivet
222	Heffley, Hessie L.	1y	W	D.C.	26 MAY 1866	Holmead
058	Heffley, Mary R.	7y	W	Va.	22 SEP 1856	Oak Hill
471	Heiberger, Mary B.	7m	W	D.C.	28 AUG 1870	Congressional
344	Heide, Anna Rouder	32y	W	Ger.	04 AUG 1868	Prospect Hill
324	Heider, Charles E.	2y	W	D.C.	24 JUL 1868	Prospect Hill
471	Heidermiller, Clinton	1y	W		29 AUG 1870	Prospect Hill
463	Heidhart, Margarett	1m	W	D.C.	06 JUL 1870	Glenwood
327	Heiges, Cora	16h	W	D.C.	20 JUL 1868	Oak Hill
410	Heil, Henry, gardener	42y	W	Ger.	08 AUG 1869	Prospect Hill
738	Heil, Katerina	45y	W	Ger.	29 DEC 1873	
740	Heilbrun, Adela	32y	W	Ger.	02 JAN 1874	Jewish
075	Heileman, Julia	22y	W	Ger.	17 APR 1857	German Catholic
313	Heinecke, Susan Amelia	20y	W	Ohio	27 MAY 1868	Glenwood
318	Heinline, Elizabeth	12y	W	D.C.	25 JUN 1868	Congressional
039	Heinline, Rachel A.	2y	W	D.C.	28 MAR 1856	Congressional
355	Heinline, Susan	25y	W	D.C.	19 OCT 1868	Congressional
747	Heinline, Wm. H.	24d	W	U.S.	01 FEB 1874	Congressional
682	Heinrich, Charlotte	66y	W	Ger.	27 APR 1873	Prospect Hill
627	Heins, Geo. P.	22m	W	U.S.	17 SEP 1872	

District of Columbia Interments (Index to Deaths), 1855-1874

Page	Name	Age	Race	Birth	Death Date	Burial Ground
627	Heins, Gustave	35y	W	Rus.	05 SEP 1872	Washington Asylum
390	Heiper, Georgiana	3y	W	D.C.	13 MAY 1869	Congressional
444	Heishley, Conrad, blacksmith	42y	W	Ger.	16 MAR 1870	Glenwood
018	Heiskell, Henry Lee, surgeon USA	53y	W	Va.	12 AUG 1855	Congressional
115	Heislen, Antan	7m	W	D.C.	09 JUN 1858	German Catholic
417	Heisler, Lavania S.	6d	C	D.C.	11 SEP 1869	Washington Asylum
077	Heisler, Peter, huckster	22y	W	Ger.	14 MAY 1857	German
246	Heitling, Mary	11m	C		25 DEC 1866	
117	Heitmiller, Carl H.	26d	W	D.C.	25 JUN 1858	Glenwood
130	Heitmiller, Mary	40y	W	Ger.	10 OCT 1858	Glenwood
115	Heitmiller, Mary	21y	W	D.C.	05 JUN 1858	Glenwood
781	Heitmishe, W.H.	3m	W	U.S.	08 JUL 1874	
224	Heitmuller, Fritz, bar keeper	28y	W	Ger.	16 JUN 1866	Prospect Hill
759	Helbling, Dorethea	1y	W	U.S.	26 APR 1874	Prospect Hill
246	Helfish, Mary	11m	W	D.C.	14 DEC 1866	
355	Helfrich, John	90y	W	Ger.	14 OCT 1868	Mt. Olivet
500	Hellen, Eugene Leland	4d	W	D.C.	29 JAN 1871	Oak Hill
250	Hellen, Johnson, lawyer	67y	W	D.C.	21 JAN 1867	Mt. Olivet
113	Heller, George I., farmer	52y	W	Ger.	10 MAY 1858	Washington Asylum
464	Heller, Wilda	48y	W	Ger.	08 JUL 1870	Prospect Hill
146	Hellinger, Sophia	4y	W	Ger.	04 APR 1859	Prospect Hill
781	Hellyer, Wm. S., lawyer	44y	W	U.S.	12 JUL 1874	Glenwood/Newark, N.J.
415	Helmick, George R., clerk	35y	W	U.S.	14 SEP 1869	Glenwood
295	Helmler, Maximillian	3m	W	D.C.	04 FEB 1868	Congressional
269	Hemert, Augusta	37y	W	Ger.	15 AUG 1867	Prospect Hill
411	Hemneally, John Joseph	6m	W		14 AUG 1869	Mt. Olivet
087	Hempler, Rebecca	2y	W	D.C.	12 AUG 1857	Congressional*
680	Hempsley, Ann	4y	W	U.S.	02 APR 1873	Holmead
466	Hempstead, Louis, cook	35y	C	Va.	29 JUL 1870	Union
688	Henderson, Andrew, laborer	28y	C	U.S.	10 MAY 1873	Washington Asylum
336	Henderson, Ann Amelia	11m	C	D.C.	03 AUG 1868	Young Mens
137	Henderson, Anne M.C.	56y	W		20 JAN 1859	Congressional
137	Henderson, Archibald, Gen.	76y	W	Va.	06 JAN 1859	Congressional
416	Henderson, Charles	2y	C		17 SEP 1869	Western
406	Henderson, Eliza	9m	C		27 JUL 1869	Beckett's
730	Henderson, Elizabeth	38y	C	U.S.	17 NOV 1873	Mt. Olivet
115	Henderson, J. Pinkney, senator	49y	W	N.C.	04 JUN 1858	Congressional
729	Henderson, James M.	5m	W	U.S.	09 NOV 1873	Congressional*
006	Henderson, Jno. E.	1m	W	D.C.	29 APR 1855	Baltimore, Md.
329	Henderson, Laura, domestic	65y	C	Va.	09 JUL 1868	Mt. Olivet
180	Henderson, Lemuel M.	11m	W	D.C.	30 MAY 1860	Oak Hill
357	Henderson, Mary	30y	M	Va.	13 OCT 1868	
712	Henderson, Mary	2m	C	unk.	14 AUG 1873	
330	Henderson, Mary	12d	W	D.C.	21 JUL 1868	Holyrood
204	Henderson, Mary	8m	C	D.C.	21 JUN 1861	Young Mens
687	Henderson, Mildred	40y	C	Va.	02 MAY 1873	Young Mens
077	Henderson, Milly	80y	C	Va.	11 MAY 1857	Washington Asylum
302	Henderson, Nancy	60y	C	Va.	01 MAR 1868	Western
720	Henderson, Sarah	21m	W	U.S.	25 SEP 1873	Culpeper, Va.
766	Henderson, Talton T., mason	83y	W	U.S.	08 MAY 1874	Oak Hill
182	Henderson, Thomas, waiter	63y	C	Va.	26 JUN 1860	Harmony
642	Henderson, Thornton	18y	C	U.S.	26 DEC 1872	Small Pox
042	Hendley, Eliza D., lady	62y	W	Ga.	18 APR 1856	Congressional
266	Hendley, Henry W.	1y	W	D.C.	27 JUL 1867	Congressional
001	Hendley, Marian M.	1m			20 JAN 1855	
340	Hendley, Mary Virginia	10m	W	D.C.	12 AUG 1868	Congressional
402	Hendricks, Edmund C.	2y	W		02 JUL 1869	Glenwood
610	Hening, Joseph Sidney	4y	W		30 JUN 1867	Congressional

District of Columbia Interments (Index to Deaths), 1855-1874

Page	Name	Age	Race	Birth	Death Date	Burial Ground
475	Hening, Laura D.	32y	W	Md.	06 SEP 1870	Glenwood
735	Hening, Mary I.	37y	W	U.S.	09 DEC 1873	Glenwood
641	Henion, Chas. E.	5y	W	U.S.	31 DEC 1872	Small Pox*
193	Hennan, George	4y	C	D.C.	27 NOV 1860	Young Mens
641	Hennesey, Thomas	20y	C	U.S.	19 DEC 1872	Small Pox
684	Henneson, Milly	8y	C	U.S.	28 APR 1873	Small Pox
724	Henning, Bennett, carpenter	56y	W	Md.	11 OCT 1873	Oak Hill
185	Henning, Cecelia	1y	W	D.C.	23 JUL 1860	Congressional
436	Henning, Ellen	80y	C	Va.	20 JAN 1870	Washington Asylum
123	Henning, Henrietta	11m	W	D.C.	28 JUL 1858	Congressional
426	Henning, Horace Wilson, clerk	24y	W	Md.	13 NOV 1869	Glenwood
610	Henning, Katie L.	6m	W	U.S.	12 JUL 1872	
753	Henning, Stephen	77y	W	U.S.	31 MAR 1874	Congressional
524	Henning, Thomas	1y			22 JUN 1871	Glenwood
483	Henning, William F.	7m	W	D.C.	25 OCT 1870	Mt. Olivet
632	Hennsch, R.	23m	W	U.S.	29 OCT 1872	
636	Henrich, Julia	7d	W	U.S.	22 NOV 1872	
781	Henricks, Albert O.	8m	W	U.S.	23 JUL 1874	Graceland
731	Henry, Agnes	20d	C	U.S.	21 NOV 1873	Ebenezer
117	Henry, Ann W.	54y	W	Md.	28 JUN 1858	Glenwood
163	Henry, Capt., child of	4m	C	D.C.	06 OCT 1859	Young Mens
204	Henry, Charles E.	2m	W	D.C.	27 JUN 1861	Congressional
410	Henry, George	1y	C		04 AUG 1869	
444	Henry, George Francis, printer	21y	W		07 MAR 1870	N.Y.
721	Henry, James	1y	C	D.C.	12 SEP 1873	
397	Henry, James E.S.	14d	C	U.S.	13 JUN 1869	Ebenezer
643	Henry, James, marine	23y	W	U.S.	10 DEC 1872	Congressional
302	Henry, John		C		10 MAR 1868	Alms House
526	Henry, John	9m	W	Md.	02 JUL 1871	Prospect Hill
589	Henry, John, blacksmith		W		29 MAR 1872	Prospect Hill
084	Henry, Mary	10m	W	D.C.	24 JUL 1857	
452	Henry, Mary	Still	C	D.C.	14 APR 1870	Washington Asylum
005	Henry, Mrs.	42y	W	Ger.	28 MAR 1855	Western
432	Henry, Patrick	7d	C	D.C.	21 DEC 1869	Washington Asylum
690	Henry, Samuel	24y	C	U.S.	14 MAY 1873	Small Pox
342	Henry, William D.	3y	W		21 AUG 1868	Congressional
300	Henry, William, laborer	45y	C	U.S.	05 MAR 1868	Alms House
203	Henry, William S.	21d	W		13 MAY 1861	Congressional
448	Henry, Wm.		W		13 MAR 1870	
188	Henry, [blank], laborer	20y	W	Ger.	27 AUG 1860	
467	Hensain, Wm., laborer	25y	C		26 JUL 1870	
148	Henshaw, Foster	2m	W	D.C.	05 MAY 1859	Congressional
235	Henshaw, Joshua L., clerk	67y	W	Mass.	14 SEP 1866	Congressional
429	Henshaw, Susannah G., Mrs.	72y	W	Md.	10 DEC 1869	Congressional
595	Hensley, Samuel, carpenter	40y	W	Va.	12 APR 1872	Congressional*
422	Henson, Arline	8m	C		26 OCT 1869	
628	Henson, David, sailor	30y	C	U.S.	03 SEP 1872	
718	Henson, Ellen, Mrs.	25y	C	Md.	10 SEP 1873	Beckett's
683	Henson, Emma	2y	C	U.S.	09 APR 1873	
432	Henson, Frederick, laborer	21y	C	Md.	24 DEC 1869	
615	Henson, Harriett	60y	C	U.S.	01 JUL 1872	
262	Henson, Hoky Ann	6m	C	D.C.	26 JUN 1867	Union
455	Henson, James Ed.	9m	C	U.S.	26 MAY 1870	Beckett's
665	Henson, John	8y	C	U.S.	30 JAN 1873	Small Pox*
490	Henson, Joseph, laborer	55y	C	Md.	02 NOV 1870	Ebenezer
363	Henson, Latesia	Still	C	D.C.	16 NOV 1868	Washington Asylum
514	Henson, Lizzie, child of	4m	C	D.C.	19 MAR 1871	Ebenezer
007	Henson, Lucinda, house servant	35y	C	D.C.	01 APR 1855	Harmony

District of Columbia Interments (Index to Deaths), 1855-1874

Page	Name	Age	Race	Birth	Death Date	Burial Ground
138	Henson, Mary	45y	C	D.C.	06 JAN 1859	Ebenezer
411	Henson, Mary A., cook	34y	C	Md.	05 AUG 1869	Uniontown
493	Henson, Matthew, laborer	42y	C	D.C.	16 DEC 1870	Ebenezer
441	Henson, Mrs.	28y	C		01 FEB 1870	Ebenezer
630	Henson, Susan, chamber maid	20y	C	U.S.	20 OCT 1872	
537	Henson, Thomas	1y	C	D.C.	23 SEP 1871	
598	Henson, Thomas	4y	C	U.S.	13 MAY 1872	Small Pox
524	Henwood, Wm., clerk	47y	W	Eng.	20 JUN 1871	Washington
148	Hepburn, Ann		W		09 MAY 1859	Congressional*
444	Hepburn, Annie	8y	W		28 MAR 1870	Congressional
610	Hepburn, Frank M.	5m	W	U.S.	12 JUL 1872	
740	Hepburn, Jeremiah, clerk	72y	W	U.S.	02 JAN 1874	Congressional
367	Hepburn, Jeresa	Still	B	D.C.	15 DEC 1868	Washington Asylum
271	Hepburn, Olive	8m	W	D.C.	25 AUG 1867	Congressional
112	Hepburn, Peter, carpenter	66y	W	D.C.	29 APR 1858	Congressional
688	Herbaugh, Leonard P.	9m	W	U.S.	18 MAY 1873	
753	Herbel, Elizabeth	57y	W	Ger.	08 MAR 1874	Prospect Hill
207	Herberger, George Walter	8y	W	D.C.	15 JUL 1862	Congressional
464	Herbert, Charles	1y	W	D.C.	30 JUL 1870	Prospect Hill
436	Herbert, Charles H.	7d	C		18 JAN 1870	Young Mens
089	Herbert, Charlotte	78y	C	Md.	28 AUG 1857	Young Mens
726	Herbert, Clara, housewife	40y	W	U.S.	25 OCT 1873	Congressional*
733	Herbert, Fred W.	9m	W	U.S.	29 NOV 1873	
732	Herbert, Fred W.	9m	W	U.S.	29 NOV 1873	Prospect Hill
452	Herbert, Frederick		C		09 APR 1870	Washington Asylum
348	Herbert, James	2y	W	D.C.	03 SEP 1868	Mt. Olivet
334	Herbert, Jessie	11m	C		30 JUL 1868	Harmony
339	Herbert, Julia	9m	W	D.C.	02 AUG 1868	Mt. Olivet
682	Herbert, Laura	1y	C	U.S.	21 APR 1873	Harmony
718	Herbert, Leonard F., carpenter	47y	W	Md.	13 SEP 1873	Mt. Olivet
237	Herbert, Matthew	28y	C		25 SEP 1866	Western
015	Herbert, Milley, slave	64y	C	Md.	01 JUL 1855	Harmony
607	Herbert, Robt.	71y	C	Va.	26 JUN 1872	Mt. Olivet
261	Herbert, Saml. M., tailor	42y	W	D.C.	13 MAY 1867	Glenwood
222	Herbert, T.F., Mrs., child of	Still			29 MAY 1866	Glenwood
286	Herbert, Thomas S.	5y	W	D.C.	05 DEC 1867	Oak Hill
710	Herbert, William	9m	W	D.C.	06 AUG 1873	Mt. Olivet
600	Herbert, Wm. E.	10y	C	U.S.	21 MAY 1872	Unknown
360	Hereby, Catharine	1y	W	D.C.	23 NOV 1868	Mt. Olivet
533	Herforth, [blank], Mr.	79y	W	Ger.	19 AUG 1871	Prospect Hill
395	Herfurth, Annia	1y	W	D.C.	29 JUN 1869	Prospect Hill
400	Herfurth, Emelia	34y	W	Ger.	04 JUL 1869	Prospect Hill
237	Herfurth, Frank		W		20 SEP 1866	Prospect Hill
307	Hergesheimer, Sarah	59y	W	Md.	03 APR 1868	Baltimore, Md.
074	Herlbright, Anthony	2m	W	D.C.	25 MAR 1857	
747	Herlihy, Alice L.	8m	W	U.S.	18 FEB 1874	Mt. Olivet
586	Herlihy, Catharine	3y	W	D.C.	14 MAR 1872	Mt. Olivet
557	Herlihy, Catharine E.	9m	W	D.C.	02 FEB 1872	Mt. Olivet
121	Herlihy, Dennis	9m	W	D.C.	14 JUL 1858	St. Patricks
586	Herlihy, Francis P.	11m	W	D.C.	16 MAR 1872	Mt. Olivet
228	Herlihy, John	67y	W	Ire.	13 JUL 1866	Mt. Olivet
232	Herlihy, Mary Ellen	1y	W	D.C.	23 AUG 1866	Mt. Olivet
235	Herlihy, Patrick, laborer	23y	W	Ire.	18 SEP 1866	Mt. Olivet
355	Herlihy, Timothy	2y	W	D.C.	16 OCT 1868	Mt. Olivet
626	Herman, Hannah	39y	W	Ger.	19 SEP 1872	
402	Herman, Nanny	2y	W		27 JUL 1869	Hebrew
182	Hermit, Jem.	68y	W	Md.	26 JUN 1860	Washington Asylum
772	Hermond, Annie May	3m	W	U.S.	28 JUN 1874	Oak Hill

District of Columbia Interments (Index to Deaths), 1855-1874

Page	Name	Age	Race	Birth	Death Date	Burial Ground
252	Hernden, Mary F.	11m	C	D.C.	15 FEB 1867	Young Mens
513	Herndon, Albert, laborer	36y	C	Va.	30 MAR 1871	Washington Asylum
399	Herold, James, officer US Navy	37y	W	U.S.	11 JUL 1869	Congressional
222	Heron, Annie R.	10m	W	D.C.	25 MAY 1866	Oak Hill
121	Heron, Mary Ellen	1y	W	D.C.	15 JUL 1858	St. Peters
340	Heron, Mary Etta	6m	W	D.C.	28 AUG 1868	Congressional
409	Herpel, Thomas Friedrich	5y	W		04 AUG 1869	Prospect Hill
453	Herrell, Edward E.	1y	W		31 MAY 1870	Congressional
470	Herrell, Geo. M.	10m	W	D.C.	18 AUG 1870	Congressional*
434	Herrell, George N., grocer	42y	W	Va.	11 JAN 1870	Congressional
020	Herrell, Infant	1y	W		15 AUG 1855	West
737	Herrell, Sarah E.	8y	W	U.S.	26 DEC 1873	Congressional*
005	Herrell, [blank]	7m	W	D.C.	19 MAR 1855	Western
740	Herrinch, Auguste	1m	W	U.S.	03 JAN 1874	Prospect Hill
411	Herring, Edith	1y	W		12 AUG 1869	Glenwood
736	Hersemar, Mary, housewife	54y	W	U.S.	15 DEC 1873	St. Marys
529	Herstkamp, John H.	1y	W	D.C.	26 JUL 1871	German Catholic
753	Hertinger, Michael, laborer	63y	W	Ger.	20 MAR 1874	Prospect Hill
032	Hertle, Herman	2y	W	D.C.	27 DEC 1855	German
344	Herzog, Carolina A.	1y	W	D.C.	17 AUG 1868	Prospect Hill
094	Heshley, Sarah	4y	W	D.C.	18 OCT 1857	Glenwood
753	Hesler, Arnold	1m	W	U.S.	06 MAR 1874	Prospect Hill
753	Hesler, Elisa	38y	W	Wurt.	24 MAR 1874	Prospect Hill
355	Hess, Bertha	1y	W	D.C.	19 OCT 1868	Congressional
462	Hess, Eda L.	1m	W	D.C.	25 JUL 1870	Congressional
376	Hess, Frederick	10d	W		06 FEB 1869	Prospect Hill
618	Hess, Jno. G.	60d	W	U.S.	30 AUG 1872	Prospect Hill
734	Hess, Lucinda, housewife	57y	W	U.S.	06 DEC 1873	Congressional
307	Hess, Luther	3y	C	Va.	06 APR 1868	Alms House
349	Hess, Rachel	82y	W	Pa.	18 SEP 1868	Glenwood
334	Hess, William	7m	W	D.C.	12 JUL 1868	Prospect Hill
611	Hesse, Frank	1y	W	U.S.	27 JUL 1872	
434	Hesse, Louisa	4y	W		25 JAN 1870	German Catholic
216	Hesse, Louise Maria	8m	W	D.C.	30 MAR 1866	Congressional
545	Hessler, John	3y	W	U.S.	14 NOV 1871	Prospect Hill
747	Hetcher, Rachael	50y	C	U.S.	28 FEB 1874	
521	Heues, Alexander	80y	C	Va.	08 JUN 1871	Potters Field
322	Heus, Amelia		C		15 JUN 1868	Freedmen's Hospital
339	Heuston, Lucy	33y	W	D.C.	12 AUG 1868	Mt. Olivet
552	Hevelke, Louis, clerk	35y	W	Ger.	01 JAN 1872	Prospect Hill
279	Hewes, Mary E.	4y	W	D.C.	29 OCT 1867	Mt. Olivet
615	Hewett, Isaac	19y	C	U.S.	17 JUL 1872	
621	Hewett, L.	8m	W	U.S.	25 AUG 1872	Glenwood
626	Hewitt, A.R.	47y	W	U.S.	20 SEP 1872	Congressional*
400	Hewitt, Alexander	5m	C		— JUL 1869	Holmead
781	Hewitt, Henry, laborer	23y	C	U.S.	14 JUL 1874	Potters Field
665	Hewlett, John	24y	C	U.S.	26 JAN 1873	Small Pox*
695	Hewlett, Mary C.	4m	C	D.C.	26 JUN 1873	Ebenezer
383	Hexter, David, trader	73y	W	Ger.	18 MAR 1869	Washington Hebrew
396	Hexter, Simon, merchant	25y	W	Amer.	06 JUN 1869	Hebrew
028	Heydes, B., Mrs.	23y	W		25 OCT 1855	
099	Heyerman, Wm. J., gardener	45y	W	Ger.	27 DEC 1857	Washington Asylum
705	Heyman, Blanch	23m	C	D.C.	14 JUL 1873	
345	Heys, William Henry	1y	C		25 AUG 1868	Ebenezer
256	Heyward, Decima C., Mrs.	70y	W	S.C.	03 MAR 1867	Wilmington, Del.
020	Heywood, Bridget	36y	W	Pa.	26 AUG 1855	Glenwood
426	Hibben, Vanderbilt T.	2m	W	Va.	18 NOV 1869	Glenwood
624	Hice, Geo. T.	1y	C	U.S.	09 SEP 1872	

Page	Name	Age	Race	Birth	Death Date	Burial Ground
209	Hichheim, [Chri]stina	3y	W	Eng.	— JAN 1866	[torn]
013	Hick, Virginia	1y	C		04 JUL 1855	
144	Hickerman, William, overseer	42y	W		20 MAR 1859	Congressional*
348	Hickey, Andrew	8m	W	D.C.	06 SEP 1868	Mt. Olivet
018	Hickey, Ann F.	36y	W	D.C.	17 AUG 1855	St. Peters
187	Hickey, Anna	5m	W	D.C.	02 AUG 1860	Mt. Olivet
271	Hickey, Catherine	30y	W	Ire.	23 AUG 1867	Mt. Olivet
546	Hickey, Elisabeth	3y	W	N.Y.	23 NOV 1871	Congressional
548	Hickey, Eliza	69y	W	D.C.	14 DEC 1871	Mt. Olivet
016	Hickey, Ellen	2y	W	Ver.	10 JUL 1855	
225	Hickey, Ellen	Still	W	D.C.	22 JUN 1866	Mt. Olivet
725	Hickey, Emily C.	4y	W	D.C.	18 OCT 1873	Mt. Olivet
738	Hickey, Harry	6y	W	U.S.	30 DEC 1873	Mt. Olivet
464	Hickey, Johanna	5m	W	D.C.	25 JUL 1870	Mt. Olivet
151	Hickey, Mary	20y	W	D.C.	22 JUN 1859	Mt. Olivet
046	Hickey, Sarah Jane	2m	W	D.C.	03 JUN 1856	St. Peters
076	Hickman, Charles	3m	C	D.C.	29 APR 1857	Harmony
660	Hickman, Danl.	Still	C	U.S.	17 JAN 1873	Ebenezer
781	Hickman, Lizzie	3y	C	U.S.	24 JUL 1874	
492	Hickman, Mary, servant	80y	C	Md.	13 DEC 1870	Ebenezer
717	Hickman, Robt. L.	60y	W	Va.	03 SEP 1873	Washington Asylum
271	Hickman, Sibby Ann	17y	C	D.C.	25 AUG 1867	Harmony
302	Hicks, Alice		C		18 MAR 1868	Alms House
078	Hicks, Columbus	5y	C	D.C.	26 MAY 1857	Foundry
602	Hicks, Eleck, laborer	85y	C	Va.	14 MAY 1872	Asylum
279	Hicks, Eliza	4d	C	D.C.	06 OCT 1867	Union
292	Hicks, Emma	7m	C		25 JAN 1868	Alms House
363	Hicks, Jeremiah	36y	C	Md.	24 NOV 1868	Washington Asylum
110	Hicks, Josiah W., clerk	39y	W	Md.	02 APR 1858	Congressional
396	Hicks, Margaret J.	2m	C		01 JUN 1869	Young Mens
385	Hicks, Oliver T.	1y	W	Va.	23 APR 1869	Congressional
623	Hicks, Racy E.	5m	W	U.S.	01 JUL 1872	Presbyterian
373	Hicks, Rebeca, servant	21y	C	Md.	17 JAN 1869	Harmony
595	Hicks, Thomas, watchman	44y	W	N.Y.	12 APR 1872	Congressional*
612	Hicks, Willie A.	8m	C	U.S.	12 JUL 1872	
110	Hicks, Wm. Henry	2m	C		03 APR 1858	Colored, Methodist
329	Hickson, Murky	23y	C	Md.	08 JUL 1868	
316	Hiese, John C., laborer	53y	W	D.C.	26 MAY 1868	Glenwood
018	Higdon, John C.	1y	W	D.C.	05 AUG 1855	Foundry
187	Higgins, Benjamin N.	7m	W	D.C.	09 AUG 1860	Western
469	Higgins, Chas. C.	18y	W	D.C.	05 AUG 1870	Glenwood
508	Higgins, Deffner E.	2y	C	D.C.	24 FEB 1871	Holmead
127	Higgins, Letitia	70y	C	Md.	10 SEP 1858	Washington Asylum
084	Higgins, Mathew G.	2m	W	D.C.	24 JUL 1857	Oak Hill
312	Higgins, William	43y	W	Eng.	20 MAY 1868	Glenwood
398	Higginson, Mary	4m	W	Amer.	28 JUN 1869	Holmead
410	Higginson, Mrs.	23y	W	Eng.	16 AUG 1869	Holmead
135	Highfield, Willie	4y	W		08 DEC 1858	Western
734	Higley, Mary A.	5d	W	U.S.	05 DEC 1873	Congressional
115	Higson, Mary	8m	W	D.C.	12 JUN 1858	St. Patricks
729	Hilbrun, Mary Ann, nurse	30y	W	U.S.	08 NOV 1873	Congressional*
534	Hilbus, Francis P., carpenter	66y	W	Md.	31 AUG 1871	Mt. Olivet
025	Hilbus, W.A.	1y	W	D.C.	10 SEP 1855	
319	Hilbush, Ann, Mrs.	73y	W	Md.	15 JUN 1868	Mt. Olivet*
226	Hilgard, Catherine S.	8m	W	D.C.	26 JUN 1866	Oak Hill
209	Hilgard, Christina	c.60	W		05 JAN 1866	Mt. Olivet
116	Hilgard, Julius E.		W		20 JUN 1858	Congressional
188	Hill, Ada	2y	W	D.C.	17 AUG 1860	Ebenezer

District of Columbia Interments (Index to Deaths), 1855-1874

Page	Name	Age	Race	Birth	Death Date	Burial Ground
439	Hill, Alice	7m	W		24 FEB 1870	Mt. Olivet
720	Hill, Annie	34y	W	Va.	26 SEP 1873	
096	Hill, Augustus H., printer	22y	W	D.C.	07 NOV 1857	St. Patricks
255	Hill, C. Ernest, messenger	28y	W	Va.	06 MAR 1867	Congressional
726	Hill, Charles	51y	B	U.S.	25 OCT 1873	Washington Asylum
393	Hill, Chas. H.	1m	C		04 MAY 1869	
362	Hill, Cora Francis	1y	C	D.C.	16 NOV 1868	Young Mens
598	Hill, Daniel	5m	C	U.S.	14 MAY 1872	Small Pox
756	Hill, Edgar, laborer	25y	C	U.S.	28 MAR 1874	
515	Hill, Edward	1m	C	D.C.	26 MAR 1871	Mt. Olivet
404	Hill, Edward	1y	C	D.C.	07 JUL 1869	Washington Asylum
155	Hill, Eliza	46y	W	Eng.	31 JUL 1859	Congressional
508	Hill, Eliza	2y	C	D.C.	13 FEB 1871	Ebenezer
122	Hill, Eliza	20d	C		26 JUL 1858	Young Mens
719	Hill, Elizabeth	3d	W		18 SEP 1873	Congressional*
191	Hill, Elizabeth	26y	C	Md.	24 OCT 1860	Mt. Olivet
677	Hill, Elizabeth	40y	C	U.S.	12 MAR 1873	Small Pox
732	Hill, Elizabeth S.	4m	W	U.S.	30 NOV 1873	
107	Hill, Ellen	75y	W	Md.	02 MAR 1858	St. Peters
698	Hill, Elmer	2m	W	D.C.	28 JUN 1873	Congressional
443	Hill, Eveline	46y	W		03 FEB 1870	Washington Asylum
744	Hill, Francis C.	1y	W	U.S.	22 JAN 1874	Mt. Olivet
534	Hill, Helen, cook	40y	C	Va.	30 AUG 1871	Young Mens
190	Hill, Henry	1y	C	D.C.	24 SEP 1860	Foundry
772	Hill, Henry	3m	W	U.S.	14 JUN 1874	Graceland
362	Hill, Henry	1y	C		05 NOV 1868	Washington Asylum
608	Hill, Ida	7m	W		14 JUN 1872	
733	Hill, James	30y	C	U.S.	02 NOV 1873	
191	Hill, James, laborer	50y	C	Md.	05 OCT 1860	
101	Hill, John	2y	C		12 JAN 1858	
343	Hill, John	4m	C	D.C.	21 AUG 1868	
544	Hill, John	55y	C	Md.	04 NOV 1871	
669	Hill, John	28y	C	U.S.	01 FEB 1873	Small Pox
148	Hill, John C.C.	3y	W	D.C.	14 MAY 1859	Mt. Olivet
435	Hill, John Henry	3y	W		01 JAN 1870	German Catholic
501	Hill, John J., sailor	26y	W	Can.	06 JAN 1871	Mt. Olivet
766	Hill, John, watchman	32y	W	U.S.	07 MAY 1874	Congressional
593	Hill, Joseph	6y	W	D.C.	07 APR 1872	German
597	Hill, Joseph	14y	C	U.S.	13 MAY 1872	Washington
384	Hill, Joshua, farmer	54y	W	Can.	01 MAR 1869	Plainwell, Mich.
376	Hill, Joshua, farmer	54y	W	Can.	28 FEB 1869	Plainwell, Mich.
766	Hill, Lilian, May	5m	W	U.S.	15 MAY 1874	Glenwood
392	Hill, Louisa, infant of	1m	C		25 MAY 1869	
759	Hill, Malvina	8m	C	U.S.	27 APR 1874	Washington Asylum
135	Hill, Margaret	19y	C		09 DEC 1858	Georgetown
038	Hill, Margaret, laundress	45y	C		09 MAR 1856	Georgetown
386	Hill, Margarett	19y	C	Md.	16 APR 1869	Mt. Olivet
744	Hill, Maria	70y	C	U.S.	29 JAN 1874	Washington Asylum
065	Hill, Mary	1m	C	D.C.	06 DEC 1856	
619	Hill, Mary	2m	C	U.S.	17 AUG 1872	Asylum
096	Hill, Mary	20y	W	D.C.	17 NOV 1857	St. Matthews
120	Hill, Mary	5m	W	D.C.	10 JUL 1858	St. Patricks
137	Hill, Mary V.	47y	W	D.C.	04 JAN 1859	Congressional
114	Hill, Mr., servant of	14y	C		16 MAY 1858	Pr. Geo. Co., Md.
023	Hill, Mrs.	62y	W		07 SEP 1855	Western
153	Hill, Polly, nurse	76y	C	Md.	11 JUL 1859	Georgetown
150	Hill, Richard	4m	C	D.C.	01 JUN 1859	Georgetown
042	Hill, Richard	1y	C	D.C.	22 APR 1856	Georgetown

District of Columbia Interments (Index to Deaths), 1855-1874

Page	Name	Age	Race	Birth	Death Date	Burial Ground
642	Hill, Robert	76y	C	U.S.	04 DEC 1872	
337	Hill, Robert	39y	C	U.S.	17 AUG 1868	Washington Asylum
448	Hill, Samuel	14y	C	Va.	21 MAR 1870	Washington Asylum
635	Hill, Sarah	8y	C	U.S.	02 NOV 1872	Small Pox
507	Hill, Sarah Anne	50y	W	D.C.	25 FEB 1871	Congressional
487	Hill, Sarah Ellen	2m	C	D.C.	20 NOV 1870	Young Mens
031	Hill, Serena	7y	C	D.C.	20 DEC 1855	Asbury
191	Hill, Silas H., attorney	52y	W	N.H.	13 OCT 1860	Congressional
377	Hill, Stephen	4d	C		07 FEB 1869	Washington Asylum
738	Hill, Susan M.J.	39y	W	U.S.	31 DEC 1873	Mt. Olivet
608	Hill, Tashnia	4m	C	Va.	20 JUN 1872	
066	Hill, Theodore	59y	W	Md.	21 DEC 1856	St. Peters
271	Hill, Theresa	70y	W	Md.	25 AUG 1867	Mt. Olivet
094	Hill, Thomas	11m	W		24 OCT 1857	St. Peters
526	Hill, Tobias	1m	C	D.C.	05 JUL 1871	Eastern Branch
055	Hill, Walter S.	1y	W		27 AUG 1856	Pr. Geo. Co., Md.
588	Hill, Wilhemina	2y	W	D.C.	25 MAR 1872	Prospect Hill
351	Hill, William	1y	C	D.C.	21 SEP 1868	
301	Hill, William	34y	C	D.C.	17 MAR 1868	Freedmen's Hospital
106	Hill, William, coach maker	44y	W	Va.	02 FEB 1858	Congressional
138	Hill, Willie	5m	C	D.C.	25 JAN 1859	Foundry
660	Hill, Willie	5y	C	U.S.	20 JAN 1873	Washington Asylum
600	Hill, Wm., laborer	55y	C	U.S.	20 MAY 1872	Unknown
150	Hill, [blank]	6m	W	D.C.	05 JUN 1859	Alexandria, Va.
632	Hillar, Jonas	52y	W	Ger.	20 OCT 1872	
300	Hillard, James	1d	W	D.C.	05 MAR 1868	Mt. Olivet
049	Hilleary, James	4y	C	Md.	04 JUL 1856	Pr. Geo. Co., Md.
090	Hilleary, Mary	13y	C		08 SEP 1857	Country
227	Hillegeist, Walter	10m	W	Md.	03 JUL 1866	Glenwood
723	Hiller, John, market gardener	54y	W	Ger.	05 OCT 1873	
042	Hillery, Jno.	7y	C	Md.	27 APR 1856	Country
041	Hills, George T., ship master	44y	W	Mass.	20 APR 1856	Congressional
446	Hills, Jno. Sargeant	4y	W		27 MAR 1870	Oak Hill
759	Hills, Mary A.	77y	W	U.S.	18 APR 1874	Lowell, Mass.
161	Hills, Russell	1y	W	D.C.	11 SEP 1859	Congressional
781	Hilman, Agnes	8m	C	U.S.	21 JUL 1874	Mt. Olivet
691	Hilmer, Fredk., cutter	25y	W	Prus.	01 MAY 1873	Congressional*
639	Hilmer, Wm. D.	1m	C	U.S.	06 DEC 1872	Small Pox*
069	Hilton, A.K.	2m	W	D.C.	28 JAN 1857	Glenwood
374	Hilton, Elizabeth	43y	W	Scot.	09 FEB 1869	Congressional
120	Hilton, G.	4y	W	D.C.	08 JUL 1858	Holmead
309	Hilton, George	4y	W	U.S.	04 APR 1868	Glenwood
063	Hilton, John	10d	W	D.C.	26 NOV 1856	Glenwood
050	Hilton, John	69y		Md.	18 JUL 1856	Holmead
299	Hilton, Julien A., boarding house	64y	W	Md.	10 MAR 1868	Oak Hill
339	Hilton, Norvelle Eugene	1y	W	D.C.	05 AUG 1868	Methodist, Prot.
385	Hilton, Soloma	29y	W	Iowa	01 APR 1869	Congressional
023	Hilton, Susan	6m	W		03 SEP 1855	Holmead
122	Hilton, William	46y	W	Md.	20 JUL 1858	Frederick City
161	Hilton, [blank]	Still	W	D.C.	03 SEP 1859	Congressional
588	Himmerlich, Fred., laborer	33y	W	Ger.	25 MAR 1872	Prospect Hill
456	Hinchcock, George	10m	W	D.C.	16 JUN 1870	Mt. Olivet
280	Hinchess, George H.	10y	W	N.H.	30 OCT 1867	N.H.
185	Hinds, Mrs. [Hannah M.]	53y	W		23 JUL 1860	Congressional*
553	Hine, David, clerk	50y	W	Ohio	11 JAN 1872	Ohio
759	Hineline, Inez	5d	W	U.S.	04 APR 1874	Congressional*
072	Hines, A.M.	26y	W	D.C.*	26 FEB 1857	Oak Hill
365	Hines, Bridget, servant	40y	W	Ire.	12 DEC 1868	Mt. Olivet

Page	Name	Age	Race	Birth	Death Date	Burial Ground
067	Hines, Buchanan	6m	W	D.C.	30 DEC 1856	Congressional
712	Hines, Christianna	47y	W	D.C.	17 AUG 1873	Congressional
478	Hines, Edward	2y	W	D.C.	29 SEP 1870	Mt. Olivet
107	Hines, Eliza Jane	35y	W	D.C.	03 MAR 1858	Rock Creek
115	Hines, Ella	5y	W		03 JUN 1858	Congressional
015	Hines, Henry		W		29 JUL 1855	Congressional
116	Hines, L.F.	1y	W	D.C.	22 JUN 1858	Foundry
098	Hines, Maria	65y	C	Va.*	15 DEC 1857	Ebenezer
237	Hines, Mrs.	32y	W		17 SEP 1866	Georgetown
170	Hines, Philip, messenger	80y	W	U.S.	28 JAN 1860	Glenwood
029	Hines, [Abraham]	64y	W		25 NOV 1855	Congressional*
398	Hingle, Anna		W	D.C.	— JUN 1869	Washington Asylum
659	Hinkel, Frederick A.	3y	W	U.S.	15 JAN 1873	Prospect Hill
449	Hinman, C.M.C., gov. clerk	22y	W	Ill.	16 APR 1870	Mo.
088	Hinning, Charles	2y	W	D.C.	23 AUG 1857	Congressional
400	Hinsch, Edward	1y	W		— JUL 1869	Prospect Hill
058	Hinton, Jas. M.	1y	W	D.C.	15 SEP 1856	Congressional
040	Hinton, Marion	17y	W	D.C.	31 MAR 1856	Congressional
753	Hinton, Mary F.	20y	C	U.S.	16 MAR 1874	Washington Asylum
476	Hinton, Mildred K.C.	10y		N.Y.	25 SEP 1870	
452	Hinton, [blank]	14d	C	D.C.	15 APR 1870	Washington Asylum
236	Hipkins, Richard	2m	W	D.C.	23 SEP 1866	Glenwood
354	Hippkins, George F.	2m	W	D.C.	29 OCT 1868	Glenwood
078	Hird, Francis	33y	W	Ger.	22 MAY 1857	German
155	Hitchcock, Alfred, blacksmith	24y	W	Md.	29 JUL 1859	Glenwood
586	Hitchcock, Mary E., seamstress	24y	W	D.C.	16 MAR 1872	Glenwood
233	Hitchcock, Robert J., mattress mkr.	70y	W	Md.	08 AUG 1866	Congressional*
484	Hitman, Joseph	7m	W	D.C.	05 OCT 1870	Congressional
332	Hittner, E.M.	1m	W	D.C.	14 JUL 1868	Congressional
552	Hoag, Agnes	79y	W	N.Y.	07 JAN 1872	Glenwood
536	Hoag, Moses	72y	W	Ire.	17 SEP 1871	Glenwood
441	Hoag, Norman, congressman	54y	W	Ohio	05 FEB 1870	Toldeo, Ohio
546	Hoard, Francis, clerk	42y	W	N.S.	28 NOV 1871	Glenwood
759	Hoax, John W.	39y	W	U.S.	08 APR 1874	Glenwood
050	Hobbs, Ann	65y	W	unk.	13 JUL 1856	Congressional
267	Hobbs, [blank]	7m	W	D.C.	17 JUL 1867	Congressional
174	Hobens, Lewis	4m	C	D.C.	01 MAR 1860	Mt. Olivet
581	Hockens, Burnett	2y	C		15 FEB 1872	
645	Hockings, L., Mrs.	60y	C	U.S.	24 DEC 1872	
586	Hockman, Florence	14d	W	D.C.	15 MAR 1872	Congressional
524	Hodge, Briscoe, laborer	21y	C		22 JUN 1871	Young Mens
130	Hodge, Mary	55y	W	Eng.	11 OCT 1858	Congressional
315	Hodge, [blank]	45y	W		c.23 MAY 1868	Mt. Olivet
516a	Hodges, Cath. A., pauper	48y	W	D.C.	08 MAR 1871	Washington Asylum
266	Hodges, Fannie E.	10m	W	D.C.	16 JUL 1867	Congressional
049	Hodges, Mary	2d	W		09 JUL 1856	Holmead
376	Hodges, Wm. H., whitewasher	64y	C	Md.	20 FEB 1869	Harmony
772	Hodgkin, Robbie D.	2m	W	U.S.	21 JUN 1874	Glenwood
535	Hodgson, Alice M.	1y	W	D.C.	06 SEP 1871	Congressional*
399	Hodgson, Elizabeth	4m	W		14 JUL 1869	Congressional
143	Hodgson, Jas. Edmund	2m	W	D.C.	06 MAR 1859	Congressional
342	Hodgson, John W., gun/locksmith	52y	W	D.C.	09 AUG 1868	Congressional
078	Hodgson, M.F.	68y	W	Del.	28 MAY 1857	St. Patricks
257	Hodgson, Mary Isabella	36y	W	D.C.	01 MAR 1867	Mt. Olivet
273	Hoe, Ager	100y	C		10 SEP 1867	Freedmen's Bureau
220	Hoe, Allie	1m	C	D.C.	04 MAY 1866	Harmony
591	Hoe, Thomas	1y	C	D.C.	17 APR 1872	
463	Hoester, Augusta	10y	W	D.C.	08 JUL 1870	Prospect Hill

Page	Name	Age	Race	Birth	Death Date	Burial Ground
450	Hofer, Silas, cooper	45y	W	Ger.	22 APR 1870	German Catholic
417	Hoff, Augustus	Still	W		05 SEP 1869	Glenwood
759	Hoff, Lousia, housewife	52y	C	U.S.	10 APR 1874	Potters Field
738	Hoff, Mary Ann, housewife	40y	W	Eng.	30 DEC 1873	Mt. Olivet
315	Hoffleman, Adolph		W		c.02 MAY 1868	Alms House
307	Hoffman, Adolph, laborer		W		29 APR 1868	Alms House
538	Hoffman, Amelia	3y	W	D.C.	29 SEP 1871	Congressional
627	Hoffman, Ann	65y	W	Ger.	04 SEP 1872	German
395	Hoffman, Annie	11m	W		09 JUN 1869	Prospect Hill
696	Hoffman, Charlotte	73y	W		20 JUN 1873	
013	Hoffman, Emily T.	7m	W		11 JUL 1855	German
030	Hoffman, George	26y	W	Ger.	17 NOV 1855	German
530	Hoffman, L.H.H.	1y	W	N.Y.	30 JUL 1871	Glenwood
456	Hoffman, Madelina	23y	W	Ger.	08 JUN 1870	German Catholic
542	Hoffman, Wm.	17y	W	D.C.	22 OCT 1871	Congressional*
147	Hoffman, [blank]	9m	W	D.C.	25 APR 1859	Glenwood
586	Hoffman, [blank], grocer	49y	W	D.C.	14 MAR 1872	St. Patricks
464	Hofman, Peter, carpet weaver	60y	W	Ger.	24 JUL 1870	German Catholic
048	Hofmeister, Mary	2m	W	D.C.	02 JUN 1856	German Lutheran
214	Hogan, Daniel	17y	W	Ire.	02 MAR 1866	Alexandria, Va., Cath.
170	Hogan, Daniel	18d	W	D.C.	28 JAN 1860	St. Patricks
232	Hogan, Dennis, bar keeper	30y	W	Ire.	30 AUG 1866	Mt. Olivet
256	Hogan, Ellen	23y	W	D.C.	10 MAR 1867	Congressional
360	Hogan, Ellen	54y	W	Ire.	08 NOV 1868	Mt. Olivet
329	Hogan, Frances	73y	W	Eng.	05 JUL 1868	N.Y. City
587	Hogan, Johannah	31y	W	Ire.	21 MAR 1872	Mt. Olivet
181	Hogan, Kate	7y	W	D.C.	13 JUN 1860	St. Patricks
032	Hogan, Mary Ann	4y	W		25 DEC 1855	St. Peters
623	Hogan, Nora	3y	W	U.S.	17 JUL 1872	Presbyterian
308	Hogan, Sarah	75y	W	N.Y.	28 APR 1868	N.Y.
187	Hogan, Thomas, carpenter	55y	W	Ire.	05 AUG 1860	Mt. Olivet
312	Hogan, Thomas H., clerk	23y	W	Ire.	13 MAY 1868	Mt. Olivet
484	Hogg, Ann	49y	W	D.C.	12 OCT 1870	Congressional
136	Hohman, John M., teacher	23y	W	Ger.	27 DEC 1858	
188	Hohmann, Cath. Elizabeth	1y	W	D.C.	17 AUG 1860	German Catholic
018	Holand, Mary	1d	C		11 AUG 1855	Young Mens
125	Holbrook, Susan	32y	W	Va.	23 AUG 1858	St. Peters
263	Holcomb, Malachi, mute student	25y	W	Mich.	01 JUN 1867	Glenwood
462	Holden, Bernard	1y	W	D.C.	19 JUL 1870	Mt. Olivet
324	Holden, Catherine Geneva	11m	W	D.C.	12 JUL 1868	Mt. Olivet
772	Holden, Ellen C.	2y	W	U.S.	28 JUN 1874	Mellville, Mass.
161	Holden, Francis	54y	W	Mass.	15 SEP 1859	Congressional
214	Holden, Garrett	1y	W	D.C.	08 MAR 1866	Mt. Olivet
028	Holden, Mary	1m	W		27 OCT 1855	St. Patricks
085	Holden, Mary Ann	8m	W	D.C.	29 JUL 1857	St. Patricks
726	Holden, Nellie May	3m	W	U.S.	28 OCT 1873	Congressional
276	Holden, Randall, accountant	75y	W	R.I.	10 SEP 1867	Sent Away
535	Holderby, Jane	36y	W	Scot.	16 SEP 1871	Glenwood
084	Holdon, James	40y	W	Mich.	28 JUL 1857	Congressional
098	Holdren, Jacob, sailor	77y	W		02 DEC 1857	Washington Asylum
267	Holf, Joseph Edward	3m	W		01 JUL 1867	Mt. Olivet
374	Holford, Mary Ellen	36y	W	Va.	05 FEB 1869	Congressional
285	Holiday, James F., real estate	59y	W	D.C.	05 DEC 1867	Congressional
049	Holihan, James	3d	W		03 JUL 1856	St. Patricks
112	Holland, Ann E.	12y	W	D.C.	24 APR 1858	Glenwood
268	Holland, Anna	14y	C		11 AUG 1867	Methodist
357	Holland, Cath.	4y	B	D.C.	18 OCT 1868	Washington Asylum
014	Holland, E.J.	41y	W	D.C.	26 JUL 1855	Glenwood

District of Columbia Interments (Index to Deaths), 1855-1874

Page	Name	Age	Race	Birth	Death Date	Burial Ground
753	Holland, George H., laborer	30y	C	U.S.	29 MAR 1874	Mt. Pleasant
483	Holland, Henry, laborer	50y	C	Md.	14 OCT 1870	Freedmen's Hospital
132	Holland, Isaac, clerk	60y	W	Md.	01 NOV 1858	Georgetown
422	Holland, John, laborer	39y	C	Md.	04 OCT 1869	
017	Holland, Ovid V.		W	D.C.	16 JUL 1855	Glenwood
660	Holland, Patrick	58y	W	Ire.	20 JAN 1873	Washington Asylum
215	Holland, Thomas	39y	W	N.Y.	13 MAR 1866	Congressional
114	Holland, Wm.	32y	C	Md.	30 MAY 1858	Young Mens
455	Holle, Lewis	1y	W		17 MAY 1870	Leesburg, Va.
711	Hollehan, Robt., bar tender	34y	W	Ire.	09 AUG 1873	Mt. Olivet
005	Hollend, Cornelia, servant	38y	C	N.J.	12 MAR 1855	Foundry
506	Hollens, Joseph E.	8m	W	D.C.	12 FEB 1871	Congressional
740	Holley, Mary	1y	C	U.S.	01 JAN 1874	Beckett's
374	Holley, Mrs.	30y	W	D.C.	02 FEB 1869	Congressional
220	Holley, Mrs.	60y	C		06 MAY 1866	Harmony
195	Hollidge, Elizabeth	77y	W	Eng.	30 DEC 1860	Congressional*
612	Hollidge, Robt. C.	8m	W	U.S.	09 JUL 1872	
274	Hollidge, William E.	6m	W	D.C.	05 SEP 1867	Glenwood
152	Hollingshead, Washington	1y	W	D.C.	29 JUN 1859	Presbyterian
326	Hollins, Edwin C.	3m	W	D.C.	08 JUL 1868	Congressional
053	Hollis, Lavinia	2y	W	D.C.	08 AUG 1856	Glenwood
590	Holloran, Willie	2y	W	D.C.	02 APR 1872	Mt. Olivet
732	Holly, Dennis	60y	C	U.S.	28 NOV 1873	Washington Asylum
163	Holly, Eliza H., lady	60y	W	N.Y.	17 OCT 1859	N.Y.
256	Holly, Nelson	15y	W	Md.	30 MAR 1867	Glenwood
599	Holly, Sarah, servant	17y	C	U.S.	11 MAY 1872	Beckett's
662	Hollyand, Benjamin	17y	C	U.S.	11 JAN 1873	Small Pox
605	Holman, Annie	20y	W	Pa.	18 JUN 1872	Mt. Olivet
388	Holman, James Perry	Still	C	D.C.	26 APR 1869	
635	Holman, Sarah	19y	C	U.S.	18 NOV 1872	Small Pox
027	Holmead, Anthony	32y	W	Md.	29 OCT 1855	Congressional
256	Holmead, Matilda	60y	W	D.C.	09 MAR 1867	Rock Creek
072	Holmead, Sarah	82y	W		28 FEB 1857	Rock Creek
454	Holmes, Catharine, housekeeper	20y	C		30 MAY 1870	Young Mens
549	Holmes, Charles	1y	C	D.C.	24 DEC 1871	
413	Holmes, Chas.	1y	C	D.C.	22 AUG 1869	Washington Asylum
641	Holmes, Ella	6m	C	U.S.	03 DEC 1872	Small Pox
781	Holmes, Emiary	6m	C	U.S.	08 JUL 1874	
620	Holmes, Emily E.	11m	W	U.S.	07 AUG 1872	
781	Holmes, Emma	5m	C	U.S.	01 JUL 1874	
487	Holmes, F.D.	1y	W	D.C.	18 NOV 1870	Congressional
427	Holmes, Fanny	1y	C	D.C.	08 NOV 1869	Washington Asylum
442	Holmes, James	37y	C	Va.	13 FEB 1870	Washington Asylum
022	Holmes, John	11m	W	D.C.	30 AUG 1855	Congressional
311	Holmes, John, child of		C		c.26 APR 1868	Alms House
350	Holmes, Leanora	1y	C		13 SEP 1868	Young Mens
714	Holmes, Lizzie	1y	C	U.S.	31 AUG 1873	
628	Holmes, Mary V.	10m	W	U.S.	17 SEP 1872	Congressional*
313	Holmes, Mary, washerwoman	24y	C	Va.	18 MAY 1868	Young Mens
446	Holmes, Roy	1m	C	D.C.	16 MAR 1870	Washington Asylum
454	Holmes, Sarah	6m	C		07 MAY 1870	Young Mens
732	Holmes, Sarah Ann	4y	W	U.S.	29 NOV 1873	Congressional
604	Holmes, W.	1y	C	D.C.	01 JUN 1872	Ebenezer
594	Holmes, Wm.	14y	C	D.C.	11 APR 1872	Washington
246	Holms, Regina, domestic	30y	C	D.C.	21 DEC 1866	Young Mens
070	Holms, Richard G., clerk	43y	W	N.Y.	11 FEB 1857	Congressional
084	Holohan, John	80y	W	Ire.	28 JUL 1857	St. Patricks
475	Holohan, Kate, domestic	24y	W	N.Y.	10 SEP 1870	Congressional

Page	Name	Age	Race	Birth	Death Date	Burial Ground
030	Holohon, Christofer	7y	W	Md.	10 NOV 1855	St. Patricks
021	Holohon, Mary	10m	W	D.C.	02 AUG 1855	St. Patricks
626	Holoran, Deborah	64y	W	U.S.	19 SEP 1872	
264	Holroyd, Isabella G.	5m	W	D.C.	14 JUL 1867	Congressional
253	Holroyd, Mary J.	23y	W	D.C.	03 FEB 1867	Congressional
210	Holroyd, [Julia F.]	20y	W	D.C.	— JAN 1866	Congressional
706	Holsten, Anna	9d	W	D.C.	25 JUL 1873	Prospect Hill
766	Holston, John G.F., Dr.	63y	W	Hamb.	01 MAY 1874	Zanesville, Ohio
369	Holt, Agnes A.	2m	W	D.C.	06 JAN 1869	Congressional
773	Holt, Joshua Howard	1y	W	U.S.	29 JUN 1874	Glenwood
049	Holt, Laura V.	10m	W		05 JUL 1856	Congressional
359	Holt, Mary A.	2y	W	D.C.	01 NOV 1868	Congressional
502	Holt, Wm. O., undertaker	38y	W		29 JAN 1871	Glenwood
753	Holtz, Benj. C.	32y	W	U.S.	02 MAR 1874	Congressional*
261	Holtzclaw, Martha	8m	W	D.C.	02 MAY 1867	Glenwood
334	Holtzkneckt, John George	1y	W	D.C.	15 JUL 1868	German Catholic
370	Holtzlan, Irene	10m	W		08 JAN 1869	Glenwood
190	Holtzlane, Mary	4d	W	D.C.	28 SEP 1860	Glenwood
747	Holtzman, Chas., taylor	40y	W	Ger.	04 FEB 1874	German
232	Holtzman, Francis N., painter	29y	W	D.C.	25 AUG 1866	Mt. Olivet*
544	Holzach, Susan L.	59y	W	Me.	03 NOV 1871	
623	Holzman, Mary Fannie	6m	W	U.S.	09 AUG 1872	Presbyterian
202	Homan, Thomas		W		12 APR 1861	Washington Asylum
113	Homans, Maria Teresa	9m	W	D.C.	05 MAY 1858	German Catholic
489	Home, Margaret	35y	W		06 NOV 1870	Mt. Olivet
697	Homer, Charles	21y	C	U.S.	14 JUN 1873	
311	Homer, Charles Everett	21y	W	D.C.	30 APR 1868	Congressional
379	Homer, Charles H., child of	13h	W		12 MAR 1869	Congressional
309	Homes, Washington, infant of				24 APR 1868	Harmony
028	Homsbury, [blank]	8m	C		02 OCT 1855	Western
133	Honesty, John, laborer	62y	C	Va.	25 NOV 1858	Washington Asylum
637	Honoretty, M.C.	27y	W	U.S.	12 NOV 1872	Baltimore, Md.
332	Hood, Alfred	4m	C	D.C.	06 JUL 1868	Alms House
448	Hood, Jane A.	1y	C		25 MAR 1870	Holmead
262	Hood, John, clerk	60y	W	Pa.	04 JUN 1867	Glenwood
759	Hood, Martha	4m	C	U.S.	09 APR 1874	
058	Hood, Statton	14y	W	D.C.	25 SEP 1856	Congressional
729	Hood, W.G., carpenter	35y	W	U.S.	08 NOV 1873	Mt. Olivet
376	Hooe, Berna[rd], Esq., lawyer	19y	W	Va.	22 FEB 1869	Alexandria, Va.
668	Hooe, Kate, Miss	18y	W	U.S.	18 FEB 1873	Manassas, Va.
153	Hoofnagle, Jane	6m	W	D.C.	12 JUL 1859	Congressional
105	Hook, Blanch May	8m	W	D.C.	25 FEB 1858	Baltimore, Md.
414	Hook, Elizabeth Ann	45y	W	Md.	27 SEP 1869	Baltimore, Md.
317	Hook, W., Rev.	81y	W	Pa.	09 JUN 1868	Philadelphia, Pa.
249	Hooker, Lelola M.	36y	W		03 JAN 1867	Oak Hill
524	Hooper, Dora Ellis	1y	W	U.S.	23 JUN 1871	Congressional*
451	Hooper, Elizabeth	40y	C	Va.	27 APR 1870	Washington Asylum
260	Hooper, Joseph		W		16 MAY 1867	Mt. Olivet
213	Hooper, Mrs.	48y	W		24 FEB 1866	
539	Hooper, Rudolph	Still	W	D.C.	30 SEP 1871	Congressional*
544	Hooper, Susan E.	17y	W	D.C.	04 NOV 1871	Washington
614	Hooper, T.	60y	W	U.S.	20 JUL 1872	
024	Hoostercoup, Henry	40y	W	Ger.	30 SEP 1855	
113	Hooton, Joseph, carpenter	69y	W	N.J.	05 MAY 1858	Washington Asylum
128	Hoove, James, laborer	60y	W	Ire.	19 SEP 1858	St. Patricks
130	Hoove, Virginia S.	7m	W		13 OCT 1858	Western
076	Hoover, Andrew	56y	W		21 APR 1857	Oak Hill
772	Hoover, Carrie	3m	W	U.S.	27 JUN 1874	Congressional

Page	Name	Age	Race	Birth	Death Date	Burial Ground
319	Hoover, Charles	5y	W	D.C.	17 JUN 1868	Western
225	Hoover, Elberta	1y	W	D.C.	21 JUN 1866	Glenwood
522	Hoover, Ellen S.	1y	W	D.C.	12 JUN 1871	Oak Hill
045	Hoover, Eva, huckstress	42y	W	Ger.	29 MAY 1856	German Catholic
445	Hoover, Jane McElvie	1y	W		23 MAR 1870	Glenwood
458	Hoover, Jonah D., gentleman	44y	W	U.S.	24 JUN 1870	Oak Hill
018	Hoover, Lydia Ann	5m	W	D.C.	06 AUG 1855	Congressional
020	Hoover, Sarah	51y	W		30 AUG 1855	Oak Hill
394	Hoover, Thos. G.	3m	W	D.C.	21 JUN 1869	Congressional
230	Hoover, Wiolette	1h	W		29 JUL 1866	Glenwood
713	Hoover, Wm. Seitz	1y	W	D.C.	23 AUG 1873	Glenwood
668	Hoover, [blank]	6d	W	U.S.	21 FEB 1873	Congressional
473	Hopewell, James H.	1y	C	D.C.	31 AUG 1870	
482	Hopewill, Rachel	24y	C	Md.	10 OCT 1870	
529	Hopkings, Wm. F.	5m	W	D.C.	22 JUL 1871	Md.
376	Hopkins, Brook	6y	W		22 FEB 1869	Oak Hill
064	Hopkins, Eliza	39y	W	D.C.*	24 NOV 1856	Oak Hill
540	Hopkins, Emma K.	7y	W	D.C.	07 OCT 1871	Congressional
469	Hopkins, Eugene R.	9m	W	D.C.	20 AUG 1870	Mt. Olivet
457	Hopkins, Harry V.	9m	W	D.C.	28 JUN 1870	Glenwood
227	Hopkins, J.G.	7d	W	N.Y.	02 JUL 1866	N.Y.
717	Hopkins, Keziah S., housewife	61y	W	Ohio	03 SEP 1873	Nonesuch (private)
261	Hopkins, Lewis R., coach trimmer	26y	W	D.C.	20 MAY 1867	Glenwood
626	Hopkins, M.B.	11m	W	U.S.	12 SEP 1872	
103	Hopkins, Mary A.	2y	W	D.C.	31 JAN 1858	Oak Hill
703	Hopkins, Mary E.	11m	W	D.C.	04 JUL 1873	Glenwood
169	Hopkins, Minnie H.	2m	W	D.C.	06 JAN 1860	
245	Hopkins, Mrs., child of		C		07 NOV 1866	Western
372	Hopkins, Ned, laborer	29y	C	Md.	15 JAN 1869	Freedmen's Hospital
014	Hopkins, Phil., taylor	40y	W		17 JUL 1855	Glenwood
026	Hopkins, W.H.	1y	W	D.C.	05 OCT 1855	
450	Hopkins, William	9y	C		27 APR 1870	Harmony
513	Hopkins, Wm. M.	1y	W	D.C.	15 MAR 1871	Glenwood
721	Hopp, Henry, watchman	65y	C	D.C.	09 SEP 1873	
165	Hopp, Margaret	83y	W	Ger.	06 NOV 1859	St. Marys
046	Hopps, William, brickmaker	62y	C	Md.	01 JUN 1856	Young Mens
598	Hopson, Randolph	7d	W	U.S.	05 MAY 1872	Unknown
781	Horan, Ellen, housekeeper	68y	W	Ire.	19 JUL 1874	Mt. Olivet
781	Horan, Michael	4m	Unk.	U.S.	18 JUL 1874	Mt. Olivet
106	Horan, Timothy, laborer	19y	W	Ire.	26 FEB 1858	St. Patricks
013	Horback, Eddy	2y	W	Pa.	02 JUL 1855	Congressional
197	Horfnagle, Chas.	5y	W	Md.	24 JAN 1861	Congressional
530	Horn, Joseph		W	Eng.	31 JUL 1871	Prospect Hill
158	Hornig, Anna	1m	W	D.C.	15 AUG 1859	German
082	Hornig, Henry W.	3m	W		04 JUL 1857	
380	Hornig, John	11d	W		04 MAR 1869	Glenwood
605	Horning, George D., baker	64y	W	Ger.	14 JUN 1872	Glenwood
472	Horning, Henry, baker	28y	W	D.C.	11 AUG 1870	Glenwood
661	Hornleck, E., coppersmith	50y	W	Pol.	23 JAN 1873	Prospect Hill
018	Hornsberry, Theresa	1y	C	D.C.	20 AUG 1855	St. Patricks
766	Horrigan, Jane	46y	W	U.S.	16 MAY 1874	Holyrood
315	Horsey, J.E.	1y	C		c.26 MAY 1868	Mt. Olivet
120	Horsman, Jas. B.	37y	W	Md.	05 JUL 1858	Washington Asylum
173	Horst, Henry	3y	W	D.C.	24 FEB 1860	
071	Horsthamp, Mary S.T.	5y	W	D.C.	25 FEB 1857	German Catholic
673	Horstkamn, Marion G.	9m	W	U.S.	08 MAR 1873	St. Marys
629	Hort, John	45y	W	U.S.	11 OCT 1872	
628a	Hort, Josiah George, clerk	45y	W	Eng.	11 OCT 1872	Glenwood

District of Columbia Interments (Index to Deaths), 1855-1874

Page	Name	Age	Race	Birth	Death Date	Burial Ground
195	Hort, Kate	26y	W	La.	17 DEC 1860	N.Y.
303	Hortogenses, E.S., child of	10d	W	D.C.	27 MAR 1868	Hebrew
740	Horton, L.R., lady	23y	W	U.S.	01 JAN 1874	Congressional*
207	Horwitz, Dr., child of	1y	W		01 JUL 1862	Congressional
184	Horwitz, [blank]	10d	W	D.C.	07 JUL 1860	Oak Hill
527	Hosch, Julia	1y	W	D.C.	08 JUL 1871	Prospect Hill
687	Hoskey, Mary E.	18y	C	U.S.	01 MAY 1873	Young Mens
781	Hotchkiss, W.T. & L., infant of	2m	W	U.S.	10 JUL 1874	
437	Hott, Charles M.	2y	W		31 JAN 1870	Glenwood
142	Hotton, John F.	4m	W	D.C.	28 FEB 1859	German
251	Hough, Bettie	55y	W	D.C.	19 JAN 1867	Alms House
252	Hough, Charles Lovejoy	1y	W	D.C.	17 FEB 1867	Glenwood
212	Hough, H.R., Mrs.	61y	W	Va.*	21 FEB 1866	Congressional*
747	Hough, Oscar R., clerk	35y	W	U.S.	19 FEB 1874	Congressional*
470	Hough, Peyton, gentleman	73y		U.S.	19 AUG 1870	Congressional
176	Hough, Virginia	3y	W	D.C.	04 APR 1860	
062	Houghton, Elizabeth	4y	W	D.C.	18 NOV 1856	Congressional
609	Houghton, Emma	1y	W	U.S.	27 JUN 1872	
515	Houghton, John A., machinist	22y	W	Amer.	13 MAR 1871	Congressional
609	Houghton, Leonard C.	7m	W	U.S.	29 JUN 1872	
409	Houghton, Maria Louise	10m	W	D.C.	30 AUG 1869	N.Y.
031	Houlahan, Michl., laborer	37y	W	Ire.	05 DEC 1855	St. Peters
117	Houseman, Fred	1y	W	D.C.	27 JUN 1858	Congressional
042	Houstin, Wife of G.S.	37y	W		20 APR 1856	Alabama
440	Houston, John H., clerk	74y	W		18 FEB 1870	Oak Hill
340	Houston, Olivia Maude	1y	W	D.C.	26 AUG 1868	Congressional
554	Houston, Wm., clerk	72y	W	Tenn.	17 JAN 1872	Oak Hill
745	Houx, Elizabeth	2m	W	U.S.	26 JAN 1874	
596	Houx, Susie R.	2y	W	D.C.	08 APR 1872	
624	Howard, Aby, laborer	50y	C	U.S.	04 SEP 1872	
079	Howard, B.F., child of		W	D.C.	09 JUN 1857	Methodist, Georgetown
169	Howard, Catharine	56y	W		08 JAN 1860	St. Patricks (vault)
599	Howard, Catharine	90y	C	U.S.	18 MAY 1872	Unknown
613	Howard, Christine	2m	C	U.S.	12 JUL 1872	
284	Howard, Edward E.	10m	W	N.H.	29 NOV 1867	Glenwood
084	Howard, Eliza	67y	C		26 JUL 1857	Foundry
301	Howard, Elizabeth	96y	W	Va.	14 MAR 1868	Mt. Olivet
049	Howard, Ella	6m	W	D.C.	10 JUL 1856	Ebenezer
772	Howard, Emaline	62y	W	U.S.	14 JUN 1874	Mt. Olivet
011	Howard, Emma	10m	W	N.Y.	17 JUN 1855	St. Peters
607	Howard, F.	6y	W	D.C.	01 JUN 1872	Congressional
602	Howard, Hall	28y	W	U.S.	11 MAY 1872	Congressional
521	Howard, J.B., lawyer/farmer	54y	W	Md.	09 JUN 1871	Congressional*
522	Howard, J.B., lawyer	54y	W	Md.	09 JUN 1871	Congressional*
405	Howard, James	5m	C	D.C.	19 JUL 1869	Washington Asylum
181	Howard, James B.	4m	W	D.C.	07 JUN 1860	Ebenezer
532	Howard, James, laborer	75y	C	Md.	17 AUG 1871	Washington
509	Howard, Jane	17y	W	D.C.	25 FEB 1871	Methodist
159	Howard, John	11m	C	D.C.	22 AUG 1859	Ebenezer
766	Howard, John C., mail contractor	47y	W	U.S.	22 MAY 1874	Oak Hill
391	Howard, John, driver	19y	W	D.C.	09 MAY 1869	
203	Howard, John R., carpenter	22y	W	D.C.	08 MAY 1861	St. Patricks
759	Howard, John W., merchant	28y	W	U.S.	22 APR 1874	Fredericksburg, Va.
038	Howard, Joseph, lawyer	56y	W	Ohio	31 MAR 1856	Congressional
113	Howard, Laura	14y	W	D.C.	15 MAY 1858	St. Peters
374	Howard, Lewis	6m	W		28 FEB 1869	Congressional
307	Howard, Lloyd D.	3y	W	D.C.	18 APR 1868	Glenwood
603	Howard, Louisa	90y	C	D.C.	15 JUN 1872	

Page	Name	Age	Race	Birth	Death Date	Burial Ground
606	Howard, Louise	80y	C	Md.	14 JUN 1872	Asylum
239	Howard, Luke, clerk	44y	W	Eng.	02 OCT 1866	Ann Arbor, Mich.
637	Howard, Marg. A.	3y	W	U.S.	02 NOV 1872	Glenwood
481	Howard, Mary	4m	C	D.C.	31 OCT 1870	Ebenezer
677	Howard, Mary	19y	C	U.S.	11 MAR 1873	Small Pox
474	Howard, Mary	44y	W		01 AUG 1870	Washington Asylum
405	Howard, Mary	Still	C	D.C.	29 JUL 1869	Washington Asylum
631	Howard, Mary, domestic	24y	W	U.S.	24 OCT 1872	Mt. Olivet
543	Howard, Moses, farmer	35y		Md.	30 OCT 1871	Unknown
292	Howard, Peter	3y			16 JAN 1868	
454	Howard, Pleasant, laborer	50y	C	Va.	23 MAY 1870	Washington Asylum
202	Howard, Richard, painter	27y	W	D.C.	13 APR 1861	Ebenezer
398	Howard, Richd.	21d	B	D.C.	25 JUN 1869	Washington Asylum
346	Howard, Robert Francis	5m	W	D.C.	12 AUG 1868	Congressional*
115	Howard, Rose	2y	W	D.C.	15 JUN 1858	Congressional
042	Howard, Sarah E.	1m	W	D.C.	17 APR 1856	Georgetown
546	Howard, Sophia	80y	C	Md.	28 NOV 1871	
766	Howard, Susan R.	18y	W	U.S.	02 MAY 1874	Congressional
537	Howard, Theresa	80y	C	Va.	22 SEP 1871	Washington
528	Howard, Thomas, laborer	64y	W	U.S.	18 JUL 1871	Congressional*
725	Howard, U.S. Grant	23m	W	D.C.	19 OCT 1873	Baltimore, Md.
435	Howard, Virginia, servant	19y	C	Va.	12 JAN 1870	
753	Howard, William, sailor	27y	C	U.S.	07 MAR 1874	Washington Asylum
747	Howard, Willie	4y	W	U.S.	06 FEB 1874	Baltimore, Md.
188	Howard, [blank]	5m	C	D.C.	14 AUG 1860	Ebenezer
174	Howard, [blank]		W	D.C.	04 MAR 1860	Methodist
641	Howardtown, Louisa	3y	C	U.S.	06 DEC 1872	Small Pox
286	Howe, Albion Parris	1m	W	D.C.	30 DEC 1867	Oak Hill
766	Howe, Annie V.	5y	W	U.S.	17 MAY 1874	Congressional*
352	Howe, Joseph, watchman	35y	W	Ire.	10 SEP 1868	Mt. Olivet
538	Howell, Daniel	64y	W	U.S.	26 SEP 1871	Pa.
429	Howell, Gustavus	33y	W	Md.	12 DEC 1869	Congressional
430	Howell, John Augustus, hotel kpr.	37y	W	Md.	11 DEC 1869	Congressional
151	Howell, Lemuel, laborer	27y	W	D.C.	18 JUN 1859	Congressional
552	Howell, Louisa	10y	W	D.C.	02 JAN 1872	Prospect Hill
292a	Howell, Mrs., nurse	68y	W	N.H.	24 JAN 1868	Presbyterian
181	Howell, Thomas	48y	W	Ire.	14 JUN 1860	Washington Asylum
096	Howell, William, laborer		W	Md.	04 NOV 1857	Congressional
362	Howes, John, driver on city r.r.	54y	W	Md.	08 NOV 1868	Petit's vault, G'tn.
636	Howison, M.E.	32y	W		28 NOV 1872	Congressional*
083	Howle, Parke G., marine officer	69y	W	Va.	16 JUL 1857	St. Patricks
616b	Howlett, H.M., carpenter	34y	W	U.S.	13 JUL 1872	Glenwood
387	Howlett, John B.	3m	W	D.C.	16 APR 1869	Brooklyn, N.Y.
093	Hoy, Margaret	77y	W	Ire.	07 OCT 1857	St. Patricks
074	Hubbard, E. Stiles	3m	W	D.C.	21 MAR 1857	Oak Hill
781	Hubbard, John	50y	W	U.S.	15 JUL 1874	Cambridge, N.Y.
618	Hubbell, Augustus	16m	W	U.S.	30 AUG 1872	
691	Hubner, Adam, tailor	48y	W	Bav.	13 MAY 1873	
479	Huddleston, John, child of	2y	W	D.C.	19 SEP 1870	Congressional*
744	Huddleston, John E., slater	63y	W	Eng.	28 JAN 1874	Congressional*
703	Hudnall, Howard	5m	C	D.C.	18 JUL 1873	Harmony
445	Hudson, Albert J.	3y	W		01 MAR 1870	Glenwood
725	Hudson, Elnora K.	30y	W	U.S.	23 OCT 1873	Methodist
582	Hudson, George, waiter	49y	C	U.S.	19 FEB 1872	Young Mens
589	Hudson, James	20y	W	D.C.	23 MAR 1872	Presbyterian
472	Hudson, Madison, laborer	45y	C	Va.	03 AUG 1870	Freedmen's Hospital
116	Hudson, William, laborer	40y	W	Ire.	20 JUN 1858	St. Matthews
306	Hues, Georgeanna	2m	C	D.C.	08 APR 1868	Alms House

Page	Name	Age	Race	Birth	Death Date	Burial Ground
443	Hues, Wesley, laborer	60y	C	Va.	05 FEB 1870	Washington Asylum
665	Huff, Florence	15y	C	U.S.	31 JAN 1873	Small Pox*
364	Huffman, Wm., tailor	45y	W	Eng.	22 DEC 1868	Congressional
549	Hufty, Chas. L.	2y	W	D.C.	22 DEC 1871	Oak Hill
482	Huges, Lillie Lee	1y	C		10 OCT 1870	Ebenezer
369	Hughes, Amanda M.	45y	W	Tenn.	03 JAN 1869	Congressional
193	Hughes, Annetta H.	7m	W	D.C.	05 NOV 1860	Glenwood
645	Hughes, Catherine, housewife	64y	W	U.S.	31 DEC 1872	St. Matthews
620	Hughes, Elizabeth	42y	W	U.S.	18 AUG 1872	Holy Rood
220	Hughes, Ellen, child of	1m	W	D.C.	07 MAY 1866	Mt. Olivet*
291	Hughes, F., child of	2y	W	D.C.	29 JAN 1868	Mt. Olivet
740	Hughes, F.T.	3m	W	U.S.	03 JAN 1874	Glenwood
509	Hughes, Henry	30y	W	Va.	12 FEB 1871	Washington Asylum
639	Hughes, James	6y	C	U.S.	12 DEC 1872	Small Pox*
721	Hughes, Jas.	1y	C	D.C.	04 SEP 1873	
452	Hughes, Lilly	1y	C		15 APR 1870	
108	Hughes, Lucilla	15y	W		14 MAR 1858	Glenwood
097	Hughes, M.	1y	W	D.C.	24 NOV 1857	Congressional
684	Hughes, Maria J.			U.S.	03 APR 1873	Small Pox*
422	Hughes, Maria M.	20y	C	Va.	27 OCT 1869	
592	Hughes, Mary	50y	W	Ire.	18 APR 1872	
227	Hughes, Mary A.	21y	W	N.Y.	02 JUL 1866	Cold Spring, N.Y.
136	Hughes, Patrick, stone mason	32y	W	Ire.	12 DEC 1858	
708	Hughes, Sed, laborer	21y	C	Va.	04 JUL 1873	
413	Hughes, Thornton	26y	C	U.S.	27 AUG 1869	Washington Asylum
443	Hughes, Victoria	Still	W		27 FEB 1870	Washington Asylum
082	Hughes, W., carpenter		W		02 JUL 1857	Methodist
613	Hughes, Wm.	2m	C	U.S.	18 JUL 1872	
680	Hughes, Wm. C.	8m	W	U.S.	02 APR 1873	Congressional
162	Hughs, James		W	U.S.	30 SEP 1859	Washington Asylum
481	Hughs, James Joseph	11m	W	D.C.	06 OCT 1870	Mt. Olivet
626	Huhn, Cath.	21y	W	U.S.	29 SEP 1872	St. Marys
730	Huhn, Frank J.	3m	W	U.S.	16 NOV 1873	Prospect Hill
659	Huhn, Henry	4m	W	U.S.	15 JAN 1873	St. Marys
001	Huhn, J.H.B.	3y			1_ JAN 1855	
680	Huhn, Joseph, butcher	33y	W	Ger.	03 APR 1873	St. Marys
324	Hull, Francis P.	2y	W	D.C.	23 JUL 1868	Mt. Olivet
077	Hull, Mary Elizabeth	1y	W	D.C.	04 MAY 1857	Congressional
142	Hull, Rebecca, washerwoman	80y	C		18 FEB 1859	
772	Hulse, Ned Davenport	8m	W	U.S.	16 JUN 1874	Oak Hill
621	Humbert, Robt., barber	33y	C	U.S.	18 AUG 1872	
072	Hume, David, merchant	45y	W	Va.	28 FEB 1857	Orange Co., Va.
179	Humes, Andrew J., printer	27y	W	D.C.	02 MAY 1860	Congressional
525	Humes, Jane	82y	W	Ire.	27 JUN 1871	Congressional
732	Humes, John, real estate broker	45y	W	U.S.	26 NOV 1873	Congressional
007	Humpheries, Kate	4y	W	D.C.	25 MAY 1855	Congressional
139	Humphrey, Letitia A.	73y	W		24 JAN 1859	
401	Humphrey, Mary Corine	16d	W	D.C.	12 JUL 1869	Mt. Olivet
639	Humphreys, Sarah G.	50y	W	U.S.	05 DEC 1872	Small Pox*
253	Humphreys, William, clerk	35y	W	Ire.	26 FEB 1867	
429	Humphreyville, Frances	56y		Va.	22 DEC 1869	Congressional
352	Humphries, Thomas Henry	1y	C		07 SEP 1868	Ebenezer
636	Humphry, Robt., clerk	34y	W	U.S.	01 NOV 1872	Congressional*
076	Humphrys, Margaret	20y	C	D.C.	22 APR 1857	Washington Asylum
409	Hungerford, Baby	5m	C		21 AUG 1869	Congressional
698	Hungerford, Carrie B.	7m	W	U.S.	17 JUN 1873	Oak Hill
551	Hungerford, Fenton	1y	C	U.S.	— DEC 1871	
498	Hungerford, Francis, pauper	6m	B	D.C.	02 JAN 1871	Washington Asylum

District of Columbia Interments (Index to Deaths), 1855-1874

Page	Name	Age	Race	Birth	Death Date	Burial Ground
102	Hungerford, Helen	70y	W	Va.	16 JAN 1858	St. Peters
391	Huniger, Ann E.	38y	W	Pa.	19 MAY 1869	
599	Hunt, Barton	38y	W	Ger.	21 MAY 1872	German
221	Hunt, Charles, child of				20 MAY 1866	Young Mens
518	Hunt, Charles E., clerk	31y	W	N.Y.	12 MAY 1871	N.Y.
304	Hunt, child, at 358 L St.	Still	W		c.21 MAR 1868	Glenwood
677	Hunt, Dora	2y	W	U.S.	01 MAR 1873	Congressional
341	Hunt, Edward C.	3y	W		01 AUG 1868	Congressional
596	Hunt, George	4y	W	U.S.	11 APR 1872	
367	Hunt, Honora	32y	W	Pa.	30 DEC 1868	Washington Asylum
088	Hunt, Jas. B.	59y	W		16 AUG 1857	Congressional
223	Hunt, Louisa	23y	C	Va.	06 JUN 1866	Young Mens
349	Hunt, Minnie	4m	W	D.C.	10 SEP 1868	Glenwood
781	Hunt, Perca V.	9d	W	U.S.	06 JUL 1874	Oak Hill
670	Hunt, Samuel	5y	W	U.S.	10 FEB 1873	Small Pox*
365	Hunt, Samuel H.	3y	B	D.C.	17 DEC 1868	Mt. Olivet
091	Hunt, William, claim aget	46y	W	Eng.	15 SEP 1857	Congressional
233	Hunt, [blank]		C		19 AUG 1866	Western
584	Hunter, Alfred	60y	W	N.Y.	02 MAR 1872	Mt. Olivet
781	Hunter, Anna	60y	C	U.S.	01 JUL 1874	Mt. Pleasant
275	Hunter, Appelina	5m	C	D.C.	28 SEP 1867	
715	Hunter, Daniel	4m	C	D.C.	19 AUG 1873	
399	Hunter, Edward	1y	W	D.C.	15 JUL 1869	Congressional
707	Hunter, Elizabeth	24y	W	Ire.	06 JUL 1873	Congressional
706	Hunter, Elizabeth	24y	W	Ire.	06 JUL 1873	Washington Asylum
747	Hunter, Fannie	28y	C	U.S.	24 FEB 1874	Beckett's
163	Hunter, George, laborer	40y	C	Md.	18 OCT 1859	Young Mens
434	Hunter, J.R. & Julia, infant of	Still	W	D.C.*	11 JAN 1870	Congressional
303	Hunter, James Cowan	11d	W		02 MAR 1868	Congressional
353	Hunter, Joseph	11m	C	D.C.	22 SEP 1868	Western
688	Hunter, Mary, clerk	60y	C	U.S.	18 MAY 1873	Mt. Olivet
610	Hunter, Mary E.	9m	C	U.S.	27 JUL 1872	
388	Hunter, Mrs., cook		C	Va.	14 APR 1869	Western
259	Hunter, Robert F.	5y	W	D.C.	02 APR 1867	Congressional
674	Hunter, Sarah, Mrs.	74y	W	U.S.	19 MAR 1873	Congressional
306	Hunter, W.J.H.	3m	C	D.C.	08 APR 1868	Harmony
380	Hunter, [blank]	6d	W		14 MAR 1869	Congressional
250	Hunter, [blank]	1y	C		02 JAN 1867	Young Mens
499	Huntingdon, Geo. R.	3y	W	D.C.	10 JAN 1871	Congressional
589	Huntington, Wm. S.	32y	W	D.C.	20 MAR 1872	Oak Hill
390	Huntress, Charles Albert, ltr. car.	30y	W	N.H.	02 MAY 1869	Congressional
625	Hurbert, Laura	1m	C	U.S.	04 SEP 1872	
207	Hurbett, George	21y	C		23 JUL 1862	Western
138	Hurbright, Frank	4y	W	Ger.	25 JAN 1859	German Catholic
629	Hurd, Geo. W.	6m	C		11 OCT 1872	
602	Hurdle, Margret	45y	W	U.S.	01 MAY 1872	Va.
005	Hurdle, Mary M.	31y	W	Md.	09 MAR 1855	Alexandria, Va., Meth.
185	Hurdle, Mrs.	48y	W		26 JUL 1860	Presbyterian
550	Hurdley, Mary	65y		Ire.	25 DEC 1871	Mt. Olivet
548	Hurdoch, Henry M., clerk	35y	W	Scot.	14 DEC 1871	Mt. Olivet
015	Hurlbans, M.	10m	W	D.C.	28 JUL 1855	German Lutheran
158	Hurle, [blank]	2m	W	D.C.	21 AUG 1859	St. Patricks
612	Hurley, Alfred M.	10m	W	U.S.	07 JUL 1872	
545	Hurley, Catharine	66y	W	Ire.	17 NOV 1871	Mt. Olivet
531	Hurley, Charles, laborer	19y	W	U.S.	06 AUG 1871	Congressional*
531	Hurley, Charles, laborer	19y	W	U.S.	06 AUG 1871	Unknown
544	Hurley, Cornelius	54y	W	Ire.	01 NOV 1871	
309	Hurley, Daniel, clerk	43y	W	Ire.	24 APR 1868	Mt. Olivet

District of Columbia Interments (Index to Deaths), 1855-1874

Page	Name	Age	Race	Birth	Death Date	Burial Ground
781	Hurley, John S., laborer	40y	W	U.S.	25 JUL 1874	Congressional
542	Hurley, John W.	4y	W	U.S.	25 OCT 1871	Georgetown
112	Hurley, Joseph	1m	W	D.C.	21 APR 1858	Congressional
659	Hurley, Josephine	3y	W	U.S.	17 JAN 1873	Congressional*
781	Hurley, Mary	5m	W	U.S.	21 JUL 1874	Holyrood
356	Hurley, Richard		W	D.C.	16 OCT 1868	Methodist
550	Hurley, Sarah	55y	W	Md.	30 DEC 1871	Methodist
669	Hurley, Theodore	50y	W	U.S.	13 FEB 1873	Small Pox
086	Hurley, William	8y	W	D.C.	05 AUG 1857	Congressional
015	Hurley, [blank]	1y	W		26 JUL 1855	West
435	Hurran, Annie	19y	W		16 JAN 1870	Laurel, Md.
772	Hurse, J.H.	1m	W	U.S.	23 JUN 1874	Mt. Olivet
304	Hurst, Ann Elizabeth	1h	W		22 MAR 1868	Congressional
298	Hurst, Henry T., photographist	21y	W	D.C.	09 FEB 1868	Glenwood
071	Hurtz, Henry, servant		C	unk.	24 FEB 1857	Potters Field
330	Huse, Joseph L.	2m	C	D.C.	11 JUL 1868	Mt. Olivet
159	Husemann, Louisa	34y	W	Ger.	27 AUG 1859	Congressional*
729	Huses, Theo.	3m	C	U.S.	10 NOV 1873	Holmead
715	Hussey, Michael	30y	W		08 AUG 1873	
270	Hussman, Henrietta	1y	W	D.C.	16 AUG 1867	Prospect Hill
174	Hutchens, Peter, painter	44y	W	Md.	02 MAR 1860	St. Mary's Co., Md.
279	Hutchenson, William, foreman	49y	W	Ire.	16 OCT 1867	Congressional
382	Hutcherson, A.	60y	C	Va.	11 MAR 1869	
304	Hutcheson, Martha J.	43y	W	U.S.	22 MAR 1868	Congressional
220	Hutchin, S.S., child of	Still	W	D.C.	08 MAY 1866	Congressional
582	Hutchings, Ignatius H., mason	72y	W	D.C.	19 FEB 1872	Glenwood
500	Hutchingson, Albert E.	2y	W	D.C.	01 JAN 1871	Mt. Olivet
626	Hutchins, Benedict	47y	W	U.S.	11 SEP 1872	
375	Hutchins, Charles	65y	W	Md.	22 FEB 1869	Baltimore, Md.
274	Hutchins, Francis, bricklayer	66y	C	Md.	09 SEP 1867	Trinity, Georgetown
142	Hutchins, Matilda	56y	W	D.C.*	26 FEB 1859	St. Patricks
475	Hutchinson, Abraham, laborer	62y	C	Md.	13 SEP 1870	Freedmen's Hospital
157	Hutchinson, Benjamin, waterman	23y	W	Md.	08 AUG 1859	Annapolis, Md.
390	Hutchinson, Bettie	18y	W	D.C.	28 MAY 1869	Congressional
500	Hutchinson, Ellen, laundress	45y	C	Va.	22 JAN 1871	Young Mens
147	Hutchinson, Fillmore B.	7m	W	D.C.	22 APR 1859	Congressional
659	Hutchinson, Frank	15m	C	U.S.	15 JAN 1873	Harmony
365	Hutchinson, Harriet G.	9m	W	D.C.	06 DEC 1868	Congressional*
729	Hutchinson, Mary Ann	67y	W	U.S.	06 NOV 1873	Glenwood
113	Hutchinson, Sarah	76y	W	N.Y.	12 MAY 1858	Congressional
633	Hutchinson, Susan, cook	51y	C	U.S.	20 OCT 1872	
235	Hutchinson, [blank], child of	Still			14 SEP 1866	Congressional
020	Hutchison, [blank]	40y	C	Md.	09 AUG 1855	Foundry
354	Hutherford, John, stone cutter	57y	W	Eng.	11 OCT 1868	Congressional
326	Hutten, Francis	7m	W	D.C.	21 JUL 1868	Congressional
083	Hutton, Mary C.	9m	W	D.C.	15 JUL 1857	Glenwood
228	Hutton, Perry McDonald	3m			09 JUL 1866	Congressional
199	Hutton, Willie R.	1y	W	D.C.	12 FEB 1861	Montgomery Co., Md.
484	Hyatt, Elizabeth	46y	W		18 OCT 1870	Congressional
110	Hyatt, Richard G., merchant	35y	W	Md.	05 APR 1858	Congressional
151	Hyatt, Richard G.	1y	W	D.C.	17 JUN 1859	Congressional
756	Hyde, Catherine	28y	W	U.S.	16 MAR 1874	
036	Hyde, Elizabeth A.	28y	W	D.C.	05 FEB 1856	Glenwood
099	Hyde, Mary	65y	W	Ire.	25 DEC 1857	Alexandria, Va.
393	Hyde, Mary A.H.	48y	W		27 MAY 1869	Md.
596	Hyde, Richd.	10m	W	D.C.	20 APR 1872	Glenwood
035	Hyde, Samuel A.	7m	W	D.C.	27 FEB 1856	Glenwood
732	Hyer, M.C.	34y	W	U.S.	30 NOV 1873	Glenwood

District of Columbia Interments (Index to Deaths), 1855-1874

Page	Name	Age	Race	Birth	Death Date	Burial Ground
718	Hyman, Saml. Roger	4m	W	D.C.	10 SEP 1873	Glenwood
723	Hyrus, Elizabeth	74y	W	Ger.	06 OCT 1873	Prospect Hill
242	Hyson, Catherine E.	9m	C	D.C.	10 OCT 1866	Harmony

District of Columbia Interments (Index to Deaths), 1855-1874

Page	Name	Age	Race	Birth	Death Date	Burial Ground
I						
083	Iardella, Frank	4y	W	D.C.	18 JUL 1857	Glenwood
209	Iglehart, Isaac B.	55y	W	Md.	06 JAN 1866	Laurel Factory
256	Ihrig, John P., clerk	25y	W	Ger.	09 MAR 1867	Oak Hill
441	Imhof, Caroline, Mrs.	34y	W	Ger.	15 FEB 1870	Prospect Hill
464	Imhof, Frederick	5m	W	D.C.	06 JUL 1870	Prospect Hill
781	Imlay, Eugene F.	10m	W	U.S.	15 JUL 1874	Graceland
645	Imlay, Mary, tailoress	81y	W	U.S.	30 DEC 1872	Holmead
371	Indermaner, Jeremiah, machinist	84y	W	Switz.	24 JAN 1869	Prospect Hill
719	Inderson, Ann	61y	W	Switz.	22 SEP 1873	Prospect Hill
305	India, Casandra	49y	C	D.C.	c.30 MAR 1868	Mt. Olivet
493	Infant	4d	C	D.C.	29 DEC 1870	Ebenezer
209	Infant		W		04 JAN 1866	
007	Infant	8d	C		11 APR 1855	
003	Infant	Still	W		29 FEB 1855	
274	Infant	6m	C	D.C.	15 SEP 1867	
422	Infant		C		02 OCT 1869	
609	Infant	1d	C	U.S.	01 JUN 1872	
005	Infant		W		09 MAR 1855	Alms House
014	Infant		W		14 JUL 1855	Alms House
287	Infant		C		c.27 DEC 1867	Alms House
286	Infant				— DEC 1867	Alms House
151	Infant	Still	W	D.C.	25 JUN 1859	Baltimore, Md.
302	Infant		C		19 MAR 1868	Alms House
086	Infant		W		09 AUG 1857	Congressional
098	Infant		W	D.C.	07 DEC 1857	Congressional
102	Infant		W		26 JAN 1858	Congressional
150	Infant	Still	W	D.C.	03 JUN 1859	Congressional
101	Infant		W	D.C.	01 JAN 1858	Congressional
169	Infant	Still	W	D.C.	11 JAN 1860	Congressional
165	Infant	Still	W	D.C.	03 NOV 1859	Congressional
326	Infant	1d	W	D.C.	06 JUL 1868	Congressional
385	Infant	Still	W	D.C.	12 APR 1869	Congressional
429	Infant	Still			26 DEC 1869	Congressional
385	Infant	1d	W		17 APR 1869	Congressional
369	Infant	Still	W		04 JAN 1869	Congressional
473	Infant	Still	C		10 AUG 1870	Ebenezer
174	Infant	Still	W	D.C.	01 MAR 1860	Ebenezer
157	Infant	Still	W	D.C.	12 AUG 1859	Foundry
158	Infant	Still	W	Va.	19 AUG 1859	Foundry
131	Infant	1h	W	D.C.	25 OCT 1858	Foundry
067	Infant	Still	W	D.C.	28 DEC 1856	Foundry
062	Infant	Still	W		04 NOV 1856	Foundry
187	Infant		W	D.C.	11 AUG 1860	Foundry
080	Infant	5m	W		27 JUN 1857	German
079	Infant		W		07 JUN 1857	Glenwood
082	Infant		W		06 JUL 1857	Glenwood
411	Infant	Still	W		27 AUG 1869	Glenwood
057	Infant	1m	W	D.C.	06 SEP 1856	Glenwood
166	Infant	Still	W	D.C.	29 NOV 1859	Glenwood
165	Infant		W	D.C.	07 NOV 1859	Glenwood
110	Infant	Still	W	D.C.	03 APR 1858	Glenwood
453	Infant	Still	W	D.C.	04 MAY 1870	Glenwood
065	Infant	2d	C	D.C.	12 DEC 1856	Harmony
074	Infant		C		25 MAR 1857	Harmony
412	Infant	4m	C		29 AUG 1869	Harmony
327	Infant	Still			10 JUL 1868	Holmead
153	Infant	Still	W	D.C.	01 JUL 1859	Holmead

District of Columbia Interments (Index to Deaths), 1855-1874

Page	Name	Age	Race	Birth	Death Date	Burial Ground
165	Infant	Still	W	D.C.	07 NOV 1859	Holmead
158	Infant	Still	W	D.C.	17 AUG 1859	Mt. Olivet
293	Infant	1m	C		20 MAR 1868	Methodist
293	Infant	1y	C		26 MAR 1868	Methodist
293	Infant	18m	C		18 MAR 1868	Methodist
292a	Infant	Still	W	D.C.*	17 JAN 1868	Methodist
215	Infant		W		19 MAR 1866	Mt. Olivet
212	Infant	Still	W	D.C.	17 FEB 1866	Mt. Olivet
216	Infant		W		20 MAR 1866	Mt. Olivet
210	Infant		W		14 JAN 1866	Mt. Olivet
210	Infant				24 JAN 1866	Mt. Olivet
215	Infant		W		15 MAR 1866	Mt. Olivet
209	Infant		W		02 JAN 1866	Mt. Olivet
217	Infant		W		02 APR 1866	Mt. Olivet
209	Infant		W		07 JAN 1866	Mt. Olivet
365	Infant	6d	W	D.C.	27 DEC 1868	Mt. Olivet
283	Infant	Still	W	D.C.	22 NOV 1867	Mt. Olivet
150	Infant	Still	W	D.C.	09 JUN 1859	Oak Hill
292a	Infant	Still	W	D.C.*	17 JAN 1868	Oak Hill
292a	Infant	4d	W	D.C.*	02 JAN 1868	Oak Hill
012	Infant				11 JUN 1855	Poor House
307	Infant	1m	W	D.C.	09 APR 1868	Prospect Hill
074	Infant		W		19 MAR 1857	Potters Field
381	Infant	1m	W		16 MAR 1869	Prospect Hill
098	Infant		W	D.C.	18 DEC 1857	St. Matthews
070	Infant		W		01 FEB 1857	St. Patricks
084	Infant		W		24 JUL 1857	St. Patricks
090	Infant		W		11 SEP 1857	St. Patricks
169	Infant	Still	W	D.C.	04 JAN 1860	St. Patricks
084	Infant		W		24 JUL 1857	St. Patricks
070	Infant		W		06 FEB 1857	St. Patricks
062	Infant	Still	W		02 NOV 1856	St. Patricks
032	Infant	Still	C	D.C.	27 DEC 1855	St. Patricks
392	Infant	7d	C		19 MAY 1869	Union
364	Infant	12h	W	D.C.	12 DEC 1868	Washington
050	Infant		W		20 JUL 1856	Washington Asylum
051	Infant	5m	C	D.C.	22 JUL 1856	Washington Asylum
190	Infant		W	D.C.	18 SEP 1860	Washington Asylum
377	Infant	Still	C	D.C.	04 FEB 1869	Washington Asylum
371	Infant	Still	C	D.C.	02 JAN 1869	Washington Asylum
377	Infant	Still	C	D.C.	11 FEB 1869	Washington Asylum
371	Infant	Still	C	D.C.	01 JAN 1869	Washington Asylum
377	Infant	Still	C	D.C.	11 FEB 1869	Washington Asylum
061	Infant	Still	C		15 OCT 1856	Western
336	Infant	6d	W		09 AUG 1868	Washington Hebrew
371	Infant	Still	W	D.C.	18 JAN 1869	Washington Hebrew
068	Infant	2y	C		04 JAN 1857	Western
328	Infant	Still	W	D.C.	08 JUL 1868	Western
302	Infant	14d	W	D.C.	08 MAR 1868	Western
328	Infant	Still	C		18 JUL 1868	Young Mens
101	Infant		C	D.C.	06 JAN 1858	Young Mens
330	Infant	5d	C	D.C.	24 JUL 1868	Young Mens
330	Infant	9d	C		17 JUL 1868	Young Mens
096	Infant		C		03 NOV 1857	Young Mens
301	Infant	3d	C		10 MAR 1868	Young Mens
005	Infant	12d	C		12 MAR 1855	Young Mens
247	Infant, at asylum				10 DEC 1866	
220	Infant, at asylum				05 MAY 1866	Mt. Olivet

District of Columbia Interments (Index to Deaths), 1855-1874

Page	Name	Age	Race	Birth	Death Date	Burial Ground
224	Infant, at asylum	8w			15 JUN 1866	Mt. Olivet*
233	Infant, at asylum				29 AUG 1866	Mt. Olivet*
220	Infant, at asylum				10 MAY 1866	Mt. Olivet
223	Infant, at asylum				04 JUN 1866	Mt. Olivet
223	Infant, at asylum				01 JUN 1866	Mt. Olivet
222	Infant, at asylum				29 MAY 1866	Mt. Olivet*
220	Infant, at asylum	6m			02 MAY 1866	Mt. Olivet*
226	Infant, at asylum	6w			29 JUN 1866	Mt. Olivet*
219	Infant, at asylum				29 APR 1866	Mt. Olivet
219	Infant, at asylum				29 APR 1866	Mt. Olivet
237	Infant, at asylum				05 SEP 1866	Mt. Olivet
221	Infant, at asylum				25 MAY 1866	Mt. Olivet*
253	Infant, at asylum				25 FEB 1867	Mt. Olivet
241	Infant, at asylum				12 OCT 1866	Mt. Olivet
256	Infant, at asylum		W		29 MAR 1867	Mt. Olivet
217	Infant, at asylum	1m	W		04 APR 1866	Mt. Olivet*
241	Infant, at asylum				22 OCT 1866	Mt. Olivet
237	Infant, at asylum				10 SEP 1866	Mt. Olivet
237	Infant, at asylum				05 SEP 1866	Mt. Olivet
237	Infant, at asylum				02 SEP 1866	Mt. Olivet
245	Infant, at asylum		W		25 NOV 1866	Mt. Olivet
218	Infant, at asylum				18 APR 1866	Mt. Olivet
230	Infant, at asylum	2d	W		05 JUL 1866	Mt. Olivet
237	Infant, at asylum				28 SEP 1866	Mt. Olivet
610	Infant, at Asylum				23 JUN 1867	Mt. Olivet
263	Infant, at Columbia Hospital	2m	W	D.C.	25 JUN 1867	Holmead
214	Infant, at Infant Asylum		W		09 MAR 1866	Mt. Olivet
189	Infant of J.C.	4d	W	D.C.	15 SEP 1860	Congressional
463	Ingalls, Carrie B.	1y	W	Ill.	17 JUL 1870	Glenwood
243	Ingersoll, Freddie	3y	W	Me.	17 NOV 1866	Glenwood
366	Ingiman, Julia A.	66y	W	D.C.*	29 DEC 1868	Glenwood
461	Ingle, Alfred E.	6m	W	D.C.	05 JUL 1870	Congressional
292a	Ingle, Grace	18d	W	D.C.*	18 FEB 1868	Congressional
385	Ingle, James A.				05 APR 1869	Congressional
166	Ingle, Mary Ann, seamstress	50y	W	Va.*	25 NOV 1859	Congressional
325	Ingle, Mary P.	19y	W	D.C.	15 JUL 1868	Congressional
023	Ingle, Susan	39y	W		14 SEP 1855	Congressional
021	Ingman, Wallace W., printer	23y	W	D.C.	13 AUG 1855	St. Patricks
402	Ingolds, Frank D., infant of	Still	W		25 JUL 1869	Congressional
062	Ingraham, Maria	16y	C	D.C.	13 NOV 1856	Young Mens
696	Ingraham, Mary, servant	56y	C	Va.	02 JUN 1873	
096	Ingraham, [blank]	14d	C	D.C.	17 NOV 1857	Young Mens
520	Ingram, Alexander, photographer	21y	W	Scot.	25 MAY 1871	Congressional*
529	Ingram, Edward	1y	C	D.C.	24 JUL 1871	Young Mens
052	Ingram, John	71y	C		28 JUL 1856	Young Mens
010	Ingram, Peter, laborer	82y	C		23 JUN 1855	West
103	Ingram, [blank]	21y	C		09 JAN 1858	Young Mens
104	Ingram, [blank]	30y	C		09 FEB 1858	Young Mens
160	Ioden, [blank]	Still	W	D.C.	08 AUG 1859	Mt. Olivet
405	Ireland, Richard	13d	C	D.C.	30 JUL 1869	Washington Asylum
386	Ireland, Susan	80y	W		09 APR 1869	Oak Hill
366	Irick, Mrs., domestic	60y	W	Ind.	11 DEC 1868	
149	Ironside, Edward LeRoy	5y	W	D.C.	23 MAY 1859	Glenwood
290	Irvine, Gertrude	3m	W	D.C.	17 JAN 1868	Glenwood
546	Irving, David E., merchant	63y	W	D.C.	28 NOV 1871	Glenwood
148	Irving, George H., child of	Still	W	D.C.	17 MAY 1859	Glenwood
553	Irving, Mary	1y	W	U.S.	09 JAN 1872	Glenwood
356	Irvings, Martha	7d	B	D.C.	05 OCT 1868	Young Mens

Page	Name	Age	Race	Birth	Death Date	Burial Ground
395	Irwin, Thomas G.	7m	W	Amer.	24 JUN 1869	Glenwood
378	Isaacks, Rachel A.	2m	C	D.C.	21 FEB 1869	Washington Asylum
027	Isaacs, M.L.B.	29y	W	D.C.	11 OCT 1855	Pr. Geo. Co., Md.
398	Isaacs, Mary	1d	B	D.C.	22 JUN 1869	Washington Asylum
311	Isaacs, Richard		C		c.22 APR 1868	Alms House
014	Isaacs, Richd., farmer	63y	W	Md.	21 JUL 1855	Pr. Geo. Co., Md.
449	Iseman, Catherine	1y	W		12 APR 1870	Congressional
374	Isherwood, R., Mrs.	64y	W	Md.	17 FEB 1869	Congressional
279	Israel, Anna Lee	2y	W	D.C.	09 OCT 1867	Glenwood
612	Israel, O. Lecta	6m	W	U.S.	07 JUL 1872	
368	Israel, Robert, merchant	44y	W		10 DEC 1868	Glenwood
597	Itearnear, Polly	99y	C	U.S.	26 MAY 1872	Washington
021	Ivis, Mrs.	43y	W	D.C.	08 AUG 1855	Foundry

Page	Name	Age	Race	Birth	Death Date	Burial Ground
J						
246	Jabo, Wilson	32y	W	Fra.	10 DEC 1866	Mt. Olivet
356	Jack, Alexander	21y	B	Md.	14 OCT 1868	Freedmen's Hospital
039	Jack, Mary Ann		W	D.C.	02 MAR 1856	St. Peters
231	Jack, Sarah W.	45y	W	Va.*	05 AUG 1866	Glenwood
345	Jackson, A.P.	28y	C	Va.	17 AUG 1868	Western
152	Jackson, Ada	9m	W	D.C.	30 JUN 1859	Congressional
336	Jackson, Adaline	4m	C	D.C.	04 AUG 1868	
398	Jackson, Alex	2d	B	D.C.	03 JUN 1869	Washington Asylum
663	Jackson, Alexander	19y	C	U.S.	23 JAN 1873	Small Pox
427	Jackson, Alonzo	22y	C		16 NOV 1869	Ebenezer
632	Jackson, Andrew	35y	C	U.S.	31 OCT 1872	
477	Jackson, Andrew	25y	C	Iowa	15 SEP 1870	Holmead/Mt. Zion
731	Jackson, Andrew	35y	C	U.S.	20 NOV 1873	Washington Asylum
401	Jackson, Andrew, butcher	22y	C		05 JUL 1869	Holmead
313	Jackson, Ann	21y	C	Va.	20 MAY 1868	Freedmen's Hospital
047	Jackson, Ann E.	25y	C	D.C.*	29 JUN 1856	Georgetown
734	Jackson, Anna	7m	C	U.S.	04 DEC 1873	
335	Jackson, Anna	45y	C	D.C.	18 JUL 1868	Ebenezer
705	Jackson, Anna	8m	C	D.C.	29 JUL 1873	Ebenezer
280	Jackson, Anna	3d	C		26 OCT 1867	Freedmen's Hospital
485	Jackson, Anna E.	3m	C	D.C.	15 OCT 1870	Western
481	Jackson, Anna E.	3m	C	D.C.	17 OCT 1870	Western
466	Jackson, Benjamin	5y	C	D.C.	26 JUL 1870	
467	Jackson, Benjamin	5y	C	D.C.	26 JUL 1870	Beckett's
718	Jackson, Bessie	1y	C	D.C.	09 SEP 1873	Harmony
479	Jackson, Betty		C		23 SEP 1870	Western
377	Jackson, Blanny	2y	C	D.C.	02 FEB 1869	
688	Jackson, Caroline	55y	C	U.S.	18 MAY 1873	Washington Asylum
187	Jackson, Catharine V.	6d	C	D.C.	05 AUG 1860	Foundry
451	Jackson, Catherine	72y	C	Md.	16 APR 1870	Mt. Olivet
642	Jackson, Cecelia	1m	C	U.S.	28 DEC 1872	Small Pox
170	Jackson, Charles, servant	21y	C	Va.	19 JAN 1860	Foundry
472	Jackson, Chas.	3m	C	D.C.	16 AUG 1870	Young Mens
082	Jackson, Cora	3m	W	Va.	06 JUL 1857	Foundry
025	Jackson, David M.	3y	W		23 SEP 1855	Oak Hill
316	Jackson, Earthy	8m	C	D.C.	01 MAY 1868	Union
392	Jackson, Edmonia	23y	C	Va.	17 MAY 1869	Union
127	Jackson, Edward		C		12 SEP 1858	
365	Jackson, Edward	6m	B	D.C.	26 DEC 1868	Young Mens
141	Jackson, Elizabeth	45y	C	Md.	18 FEB 1859	Mt. Olivet
498	Jackson, Elizth., pauper	37y	B	U.S.	— JAN 1871	Washington Asylum
372	Jackson, Ella K.	8m	C	D.C.	17 JAN 1869	Young Mens
256	Jackson, Ellen, house servant	18y	C	Va.	10 MAR 1867	Young Mens
508	Jackson, Ellsworth	1y	C	D.C.	23 FEB 1871	Holmead/Mt. Zion
514	Jackson, Emma	2y	C	Va.	22 MAR 1871	Ebenezer
662	Jackson, Florra	20y	C	U.S.	11 JAN 1873	Small Pox
781	Jackson, Frank	18y	C	U.S.	13 JUL 1874	Potters Field
359	Jackson, Franklin, shoemaker	22y	W	Pa.	06 NOV 1868	Congressional
113	Jackson, George	10m	C	D.C.	13 MAY 1858	St. Patricks
337	Jackson, George	9y	C	U.S.	11 AUG 1868	Washington Asylum
732	Jackson, George, gardener	36y	C	U.S.	29 NOV 1873	Beckett's
554	Jackson, George, laborer	48y	C	Md.	22 JAN 1872	
247	Jackson, Georgiana	1y	C		15 DEC 1866	Ebenezer
673	Jackson, Getitia	37y	C	U.S.	07 MAR 1873	Washington Asylum
373	Jackson, Grace	83y	W		20 JAN 1869	Glenwood
426	Jackson, Hanna	4m	C		24 NOV 1869	Ebenezer
290	Jackson, Harriet	50y	C	Va.	25 JAN 1868	Freedmen's Hospital

Page	Name	Age	Race	Birth	Death Date	Burial Ground
705	Jackson, Henry	5y		D.C.	19 JUL 1873	
603	Jackson, Henry, laborer	90y	C	D.C.	02 JUN 1872	Small Pox
173	Jackson, Henry, Rev.	48y	C	Va.	26 FEB 1860	Young Mens
680	Jackson, Ida	14y	C	U.S.	03 APR 1873	Ebenezer
541	Jackson, Isabella	23y	W		09 OCT 1871	Congressional*
230	Jackson, J.N., child of	2m			12 JUL 1866	Young Mens
526	Jackson, James	5y	C	U.S.	06 JUL 1871	
115	Jackson, James	1y	C	D.C.	01 JUN 1858	Methodist
466	Jackson, James	10m	C	D.C.	25 JUL 1870	Union
383	Jackson, James	3y	C		09 MAR 1869	Washington Asylum
580	Jackson, James, laborer	21y	C	Va.	09 FEB 1872	Washington
514	Jackson, Jane	29y	C	Md.	20 MAR 1871	Ebenezer
637	Jackson, Jas.	17y	C	U.S.	15 NOV 1872	
518	Jackson, Jefferson, laborer	30y	C	Va.	06 MAY 1871	Potters Field
638	Jackson, Jerry	55y	C	U.S.	19 NOV 1872	
538	Jackson, Jerry	75y	C	Va.	30 SEP 1871	Washington
675	Jackson, Jno., laborer	35y	C	U.S.	28 MAR 1873	
747	Jackson, John	2m	W	U.S.	20 FEB 1874	Mt. Olivet
466	Jackson, John	10m	C	D.C.	21 JUL 1870	Union
051	Jackson, John	56y	W	Md.	24 JUL 1856	Washington Asylum
392	Jackson, John, child of	Still	C		10 MAY 1869	Young Mens
403	Jackson, John H.F.	6m	C		19 JUL 1869	Harmony
327	Jackson, Joseph	2y	C	D.C.	29 JUL 1868	Ebenezer
458	Jackson, Lavania	5m	C	D.C.	23 JUN 1870	Potters Field
336	Jackson, Lemuel	1y	C	D.C.	11 AUG 1868	Beckett's
125	Jackson, Letty, servant	70y	C	Va.	24 AUG 1858	Young Mens
712	Jackson, Louis	53y	C	D.C.	16 AUG 1873	Washington Asylum
249	Jackson, Lucy	53y	C	Md.	03 JAN 1867	Mt. Olivet
452	Jackson, Lucy	Still	C	D.C.	19 APR 1870	Washington Asylum
131	Jackson, Lucy		C		26 OCT 1858	Washington Asylum
223	Jackson, M.	34y			08 JUN 1866	Young Mens
437	Jackson, M.E.	21y	C		09 JAN 1870	Washington Asylum
759	Jackson, M.P.	1y	C	U.S.	13 APR 1874	Mt. Pleasant
460	Jackson, Madison, laborer	30y	C	Va.	21 JUN 1870	Ebenezer
382	Jackson, Manuel, laborer	50y	C	Va.	19 MAR 1869	Bethel
328	Jackson, Margaret Gray	14y	C	Va.	31 JUL 1868	Harmony
674	Jackson, Margaret, servant	25y	C	U.S.	15 MAR 1873	
295	Jackson, Maria	74y	C	Md.	16 FEB 1868	Alms House
297	Jackson, Maria		C		c.17 FEB 1868	Alms House
762	Jackson, Martha	1y	C	U.S.	28 APR 1874	Ebenezer
427	Jackson, Mary	21y	C	Md.	13 NOV 1869	
287	Jackson, Mary		C		c.28 DEC 1867	Alms House
162	Jackson, Mary	40y	C	U.S.	29 SEP 1859	Harmony
659	Jackson, Mary	3m	W	U.S.	13 JAN 1873	Mt. Olivet
515	Jackson, Mary C.	9m	C	D.C.	06 MAR 1871	Ebenezer
645	Jackson, Mary E.	3y	W	U.S.	26 DEC 1872	Congressional
275	Jackson, Mary E.	1y	C		19 SEP 1867	Freedmen's Hospital
633	Jackson, Mary E.	25y	W	U.S.	04 OCT 1872	Small Pox*
372	Jackson, Mary E.	2m	C	D.C.	28 JAN 1869	Washington Asylum
435	Jackson, Mary Ellen	3y	W		03 JAN 1870	
725	Jackson, Mary Ellen	3m	B	U.S.	23 OCT 1873	Poor House
633	Jackson, Mary F.	5y	C	U.S.	12 OCT 1872	Small Pox*
253	Jackson, Mary J.	43y	W	D.C.	07 FEB 1867	Congressonal
179	Jackson, Mary Jane	2y	C	D.C.	08 MAY 1860	Foundry
473	Jackson, Mary L.	1y	C	D.C.	06 AUG 1870	Holmead
353	Jackson, Mary P.	92y	W	Md.	26 SEP 1868	Md.
133	Jackson, Mary, slave	11y	C	D.C.	23 NOV 1858	Colored
423	Jackson, Matilda	21d	C	D.C.	07 OCT 1869	Washington Asylum

Page	Name	Age	Race	Birth	Death Date	Burial Ground
756	Jackson, Maud P.	1y	C	U.S.	13 MAR 1874	
432	Jackson, May	50y	C	D.C.	14 DEC 1869	Washington Asylum
316	Jackson, Melevian	8y	C	Md.	01 MAY 1868	
313	Jackson, Melvina		C		01 MAY 1868	Freedmen's Hospital
717	Jackson, Moses	24y	C	Va.	04 SEP 1873	Washington Asylum
378	Jackson, Mrs.	22y	C		— FEB 1869	Washington Asylum
354	Jackson, Mrs., child of	6d	C	D.C.	19 OCT 1868	Mt. Olivet
301	Jackson, Nancy	1y	C	Va.	30 MAR 1868	Young Mens
687	Jackson, Nora	6m	C	D.C.	03 MAY 1873	Washington Asylum
684	Jackson, Norton	7y	C	U.S.	06 APR 1873	Small Pox*
311	Jackson, P.	12y	C		c.27 APR 1868	Mt. Olivet
012	Jackson, Polly	55y			09 JUN 1855	Young Mens
516a	Jackson, Polly, pauper	15y	C	Va.	24 MAR 1871	Washington Asylum
742	Jackson, Richard	65y	C	U.S.	20 JAN 1874	Beckett's
396	Jackson, Robert, laborer	35y	B	Va.	25 JUN 1869	
670	Jackson, Rose	20y	C	U.S.	15 FEB 1873	Small Pox
692	Jackson, Saml.	6y	C	Amer.	26 MAY 1873	Washington Asylum
615	Jackson, Sarah	25y	C	U.S.	10 JUL 1872	
773	Jackson, Sarah	26y	C	U.S.	04 JUN 1874	Washington Asylum
436	Jackson, Sarah	25y			16 JAN 1870	Washington Asylum
495	Jackson, Sarah, servant	28y	C	Va.	26 DEC 1870	Potters Field
301	Jackson, Shadrach	48y	C		22 MAR 1868	Dover, Morris Co., N.J.
054	Jackson, Simon	85y	C	Md.	07 AUG 1856	Harmony
071	Jackson, Sopyhia	1y	C	D.C.	23 FEB 1857	St. Patricks
691	Jackson, Stephen	12y	C	U.S.	20 MAY 1873	Small Pox*
309	Jackson, Susan, cook	30y	C	Md.	30 APR 1868	Methodist, Georgetown
781	Jackson, Susan, nurse	75y	C	U.S.	07 JUL 1874	Holyrood
730	Jackson, Thomas	1y	C	U.S.	14 NOV 1873	Congressional
353	Jackson, Thomas	1y	C	D.C.	14 SEP 1868	Holmead
718	Jackson, Thos.	28y	C	Md.	12 SEP 1873	Beckett's
721	Jackson, Thos., school boy	7y	C	D.C.	11 SEP 1873	
450	Jackson, Wesley, laborer	1y	C		05 APR 1870	Ebenezer
170	Jackson, William	4m	C	D.C.	30 JAN 1860	Washington Asylum
367	Jackson, William B.	88y	W	Md.	04 DEC 1868	Rock Creek
078	Jackson, William, laborer	45y	C	Va.	24 MAY 1857	St. Matthews
478	Jackson, William, waiter	44y	C	Md.	03 SEP 1870	
695	Jackson, Willie	2y	C	D.C.	22 JUN 1873	
333	Jackson, Willie	6m	C	D.C.	13 JUL 1868	Alms House
335b	Jackson, Willie				14 JUL 1868	Washington Asylum
251	Jackson, Wm. & Mary, infant of	3d	C	D.C.	23 JAN 1867	Beckett's
759	Jackson, Wm., infant of	10d	C	U.S.	11 APR 1874	
616	Jackson, [blank]	3y	C	U.S.	20 JUL 1872	
151	Jackson, [blank]	2y	C	D.C.	24 JUN 1859	Colored
121	Jackson, [blank]	62y	W		14 JUL 1858	Oak Hill
148	Jackson, [blank]	60y	W		03 MAY 1859	Va.
082	Jackson, [Dyele]	80y	C	Va.	06 JUL 1857	Holmead
398	Jacob, Clementine	33y	W	Belg.	24 JUN 1869	Mt. Olivet
298	Jacob, Geo. Henry, waiter	37y	C	D.C.	07 FEB 1868	Mt. Olivet
212	Jacob, Willis	56y	W	Fra.	15 FEB 1866	
103	Jacobi, Adolphus, tailor	49y	W	Ger.	28 JAN 1858	Glenwood
128	Jacobi, Susan	44y	W	Pa.	20 SEP 1858	Congressional
427	Jacobs, Chas.	70y	C	Va.	28 NOV 1869	Young Mens
627	Jacobs, Country	14m	C	U.S.	26 SEP 1872	
662	Jacobs, Edward N., clerk	30y	W	U.S.	19 JAN 1873	Congressional*
240	Jacobs, Eugene, boatman	14y	C	D.C.	08 OCT 1866	Harmony
002	Jacobs, Fanny	1m	C	D.C.	— JAN 1855	Young Mens
595	Jacobs, Jacobus	5y	W	Han.	06 APR 1872	
548	Jacobs, Julia, housewife	53y	W	D.C.	12 DEC 1871	Congressional

District of Columbia Interments (Index to Deaths), 1855-1874

Page	Name	Age	Race	Birth	Death Date	Burial Ground
557	Jacobs, Lizzie A.		W	D.C.	03 FEB 1872	Congressional*
240	Jacobs, Mary Louisa	11m	W	Pa.	30 OCT 1866	Congressional
374	Jacobs, Mrs.	23y	W	Pa.	14 FEB 1869	Congressional
130	Jacobs, Sallie A.	36y	W	Va.	17 OCT 1858	Congressional
461	Jacobs, Simpsonia M.	1m	W		16 JUL 1870	Congressional
606	Jacobs, Thos., tailor	62y	W	D.C.	17 JUN 1872	Congressional*
303	Jacobs, Willie	4m	W	D.C.	10 MAR 1868	Congressional
086	Jacobs, [blank]		W	D.C.	08 AUG 1857	Congressional
351	Jacobson, Amelia E.	28y	W		21 SEP 1868	Washington Hebrew
380	Jaine, John	4m	W		20 MAR 1869	Mt. Olivet
479	James, Alex. E.	Still	C	D.C.	05 SEP 1870	Washington Asylum
459	James, Ann	6m	C		06 JUN 1870	Ebenezer
224	James, C., infant of	2d	W		13 JUN 1866	Mt. Olivet
207	James, Charles H.	52y	W		03 JUL 1862	Congressional
066	James, Eliza	82y	W	Pa.	23 DEC 1856	Congressional
015	James, Ella, seamstress	3m	W	Ire.	08 JUL 1855	Catholic
115	James, Emily	22y	W		01 JUN 1858	Rock Creek
698	James, Henrietta	1y	W	D.C.	20 JUN 1873	
513	James, Herbert	60y	C	Va.	20 MAR 1871	Washington Asylum
689	James, John	8m	C	U.S.	31 MAY 1873	Young Mens
325	James, John, private US marines	51y	W	Eng.	14 JUL 1868	Congressional*
507	James, Joseph, saloon keeper	29y	W		22 FEB 1871	Baltimore, Md.
422	James, Lottie, servant	25y	C	Va.	03 OCT 1869	
036	James, Mary	65y	C	Md.	07 FEB 1856	Young Mens
029	James, Mary Ann	1y	W		08 NOV 1855	St. Matthews
735	James, Mattie	6m	W	U.S.	09 DEC 1873	Congressional*
239	James, Robert	3y			28 OCT 1866	Congressional
717	James, Robt. Henry	6y	C	D.C.	07 SEP 1873	Young Mens
199	James, Samuel, Dr.	72y	W		12 FEB 1861	Congressional
436	James, Samuel Grant	2m	C		17 JAN 1870	Young Mens
781	James, Susan	2m	C	U.S.	22 JUL 1874	Mt. Olivet
551	James, Susan	6m	C	D.C.	— DEC 1871	Young Mens
246	James, W.W., dentist	32y	W	Ohio	28 DEC 1866	Philadelphia, Pa.
269	James, William	7m	C	D.C.	19 AUG 1867	Young Mens
121	James, [blank]	2m	C		11 JUL 1858	St. Matthews
781	Jameson, Mary	77y	W	Eng.	07 JUL 1874	Congressional*
227	Janey, Edwin	3m	C	D.C.	07 JUL 1866	Young Mens
383	Janifer, Harriet, housekeeper	31y	C	Md.	27 MAR 1869	Harmony
691	Jannifer, Abraham	1y	C	U.S.	01 MAY 1873	Small Pox*
139	Jantus, Elizabeth	47y	W	D.C.	15 JAN 1859	Congressional
243	January, Desdemona				09 NOV 1866	Harmony
166	Jarboe, C.C.	48y	W	Md.	27 NOV 1859	Congressional
419	Jarboe, George W., farmer	73y	W	Md.	12 OCT 1869	Congressional
199	Jarboe, John W.	10m	W	D.C.	09 FEB 1861	Congressional
326	Jarboe, Martha	2y	W	U.S.	01 JUL 1868	Congressional
225	Jarboe, Thomas	26y	W	D.C.	22 JUN 1866	Glenwood
048	Jarboe, William	22y	W	Va.	23 JUN 1856	
101	Jardeer, [blank]		W	D.C.	10 JAN 1858	Catholic
218	Jardella, A.M.	26y	W	D.C.	16 APR 1866	Congressional
207	Jardella, Annette	1y	W	D.C.	26 JUL 1862	Congressional
079	Jarres, Margaret	7d		D.C.	11 JUN 1857	St. Matthews
520	Jarvis, George A.	8y	W		27 MAY 1871	Glenwood
225	Jarvis, H.				24 JUN 1866	Mt. Olivet
427	Jasper, Martha	22y	C	N.C.	13 NOV 1869	
113	Jasper, [blank]	2d	C	D.C.	02 MAY 1858	Young Mens
296	Jauberschmidt, E.M.	69y	W	Ger.	18 FEB 1868	Prospect Hill
117	Jay, John Henry	7y	W	D.C.	27 JUN 1858	Glenwood
493	Jay, Susan	55y	W	Md.	22 DEC 1870	Congressional

District of Columbia Interments (Index to Deaths), 1855-1874

Page	Name	Age	Race	Birth	Death Date	Burial Ground
417	Jeems, Wm.	25y	C	Mass.	16 SEP 1869	Washington Asylum
681	Jeffers, Columbus, clerk	35y	W	U.S.	19 APR 1873	Congressional
552	Jeffers, George, fireman	24y	W	D.C.	07 JAN 1872	
328	Jeffers, L.	Still	C	D.C.	31 JUL 1868	Ebenezer
591	Jefferson, Alice	25y	C	Va.	02 APR 1872	
455	Jefferson, Caroline	4m	C	U.S.	29 MAY 1870	Ebenezer
297	Jefferson, Charles		C		03 FEB 1868	Alms House
225	Jefferson, Charles A.	10m	W	D.C.	24 JUN 1866	Glenwood
624	Jefferson, Ed	5y	C	U.S.	10 SEP 1872	
027	Jefferson, Elizabeth	51y	W		16 OCT 1855	Holmead
718	Jefferson, Jemmie	21y	C	Va.	13 SEP 1873	Beckett's
517	Jefferson, Lizzie	38y	W	Amer.	21 APR 1871	Glenwood
635	Jefferson, Lucy	22y	C	U.S.	07 NOV 1872	Small Pox
321	Jefferson, Peggy		C		c.21 JUN 1868	Alms House
508	Jefferson, Peter, porter	60y	C	U.S.	09 FEB 1871	Ebenezer
054	Jefries, Thomas	4y	W	Va.	14 AUG 1856	Foundry
603	Jemesson, Henrietta, servant	35y	C	D.C.	09 JUN 1872	Small Pox
257	Jenifer, Ellen	45y	C	Md.	09 MAR 1867	Young Mens
293	Jenifer, Henry, day laborer	56y	C	Md.	24 FEB 1868	Mt. Zion
442	Jenifer, Lucy	30y	C	Md.	18 FEB 1870	Washington Asylum
214	Jenkins, A.		C		12 MAR 1866	Young Mens
460	Jenkins, Andrew	17m	W	D.C.	25 JUN 1870	Mt. Olivet
215	Jenkins, B., child of	Still	C	D.C.	19 MAR 1866	Young Mens
057	Jenkins, Catharine	65y	W	Md.	03 SEP 1856	Howard Co., Md.
537	Jenkins, Chas. W., printer	22y	W	D.C.	22 SEP 1871	Glenwood
613	Jenkins, Claiborne G.	7m	C	U.S.	23 JUL 1872	
437	Jenkins, Clyde	2y	W		20 JAN 1870	Glenwood
357	Jenkins, Ella	5y	B	U.S.	15 OCT 1868	Washington Asylum
125	Jenkins, Frank, slave	23y	C	Md.	23 AUG 1858	Md.
766	Jenkins, George W.	16m	W	U.S.	12 MAY 1874	Congressional
314	Jenkins, Henrietta, seamstress	32y	W	Md.	12 MAY 1868	Congressional
403	Jenkins, Hestell	9m	C	Pa.	12 JUL 1869	Union
737	Jenkins, Isdore	1d	W	U.S.	23 DEC 1873	Methodist Epis.
703	Jenkins, Jas. A., clerk	58y	W	Ill.	24 JUL 1873	
091	Jenkins, Jessey, painter	52y	W	Md.	18 SEP 1857	Glenwood
630	Jenkins, John	40y	C	U.S.	15 OCT 1872	
260	Jenkins, John H.B., merchant	27y	W	D.C.	29 MAY 1867	Congressional
176	Jenkins, John, laborer	45y	C	Md.	12 APR 1860	Foundry
403	Jenkins, Joseph	6m	C	D.C.	12 JUL 1869	Union
214	Jenkins, Laura	5m	C		12 MAR 1866	
597	Jenkins, Lavinia	24y	C	U.S.	14 MAY 1872	Not Known
602	Jenkins, Lavinia, seamstress	21y	W	U.S.	15 MAY 1872	Harmony
410	Jenkins, Lelia T.	11m	C		28 AUG 1869	Mt. Olivet
451	Jenkins, Lizzie, nurse	25y	C		28 APR 1870	Union
595	Jenkins, Mary	6y	W	Md.	04 APR 1872	
386	Jenkins, Mrs.	37y	W	U.S.	27 APR 1869	Glenwood
108	Jenkins, Patsy	54y	C	Md.	17 MAR 1858	Washington Asylum
689	Jenkins, Susan A.	54y	W	U.S.	31 MAY 1873	Glenwood
482	Jenkins, Thomas	8m	C	D.C.	26 OCT 1870	Union
390	Jenkins, Wiley A.	9y	W		04 MAY 1869	Congressional
781	Jenkins, Wm.	13m	C	U.S.	31 JUL 1874	Mt. Olivet
008	Jenkins, Wm., servant of	2y	C	D.C.	20 MAY 1855	Harmony
356	Jenkins, Zola	14y	M	D.C.	07 OCT 1868	Freedmen's Hospital
180	Jenks, [blank], Mr., clerk	56y	W	Pa.	31 MAY 1860	
675	Jenner, Melvina	8m	C	U.S.	29 MAR 1873	Harmony
217	Jenner, Sarah	2y	W	D.C.	10 APR 1866	Congressional
557	Jenness, Job R., hotelkeeper	33y	W	N.H.	03 FEB 1872	N.H.
670	Jennifer, Cornelius	13y	C	U.S.	02 FEB 1873	Small Pox*

District of Columbia Interments (Index to Deaths), 1855-1874

Page	Name	Age	Race	Birth	Death Date	Burial Ground
454	Jennifer, Louisa, servant	16y	C	D.C.	16 MAY 1870	Washington Asylum
773	Jennifer, Sam, laborer	35y	C	U.S.	19 JUN 1874	Washington Asylum
331	Jennings, Amanda	24y	C	Va.	12 JUL 1868	Freedmen's Hospital
410	Jennings, Charles	14d	C		20 AUG 1869	Young Mens
499	Jennings, Edward, baker	19y	W	Va.	01 JAN 1871	Congressional
670	Jennings, Henry	2y	C	U.S.	01 FEB 1873	Small Pox*
093	Jennings, James, shoemaker	65y	W	Ire.	05 OCT 1857	St. Patricks
414	Jennings, Jas., infant of	Still	W		17 SEP 1869	Congressional
705	Jennings, Jno. Thos.	1½m	W	D.C.	14 JUL 1873	Congressional
323	Jennings, John	8m	W	D.C.	20 JUL 1868	Mt. Olivet
393	Jennings, Maria Louisa	10m	C	Md.	13 MAY 1869	Holmead
705	Jennings, Mary Jane	45y	W	D.C.	12 JUL 1873	Congressional
441	Jennings, Nancy	70y	C		25 FEB 1870	Union
664	Jennings, Rose	13y	C	U.S.	11 JAN 1873	Small Pox*
732	Jennings, [blank]	4m	W	U.S.	30 NOV 1873	Graceland
720	Jensins, Robt. A.	21y	W	Va.	26 SEP 1873	Glenwood
553	Jessenofsky, Louis, wheelwright	74y	W	Prus.	13 JAN 1872	Congressional*
173	Jessie, Emma	3y	W	D.C.	24 FEB 1860	Glenwood
191	Jesunofsky, Thomas	4y	W	D.C.	04 OCT 1860	Congressional
181	Jesup, Thomas S., officer U.S.A.	71y	W	Va.	10 JUN 1860	Oak Hill*
607	Jesuworsky, Jacob, moulder	50y	W	Ger.	27 JUN 1872	Congressional*
346	Jet, Melinda	30y	C		19 AUG 1868	Freedmen's Hospital
754	Jet, William	48y	C	U.S.	25 MAR 1874	Washington Asylum
397	Jeter, Fanny, teacher		W	Va.	12 JUN 1869	Pr. Wm. Co., Va.
624	Jett, H., laborer	38y	C	U.S.	23 SEP 1872	
295	Jett, Jane, Mrs., washer	30y	C	Va.	20 FEB 1868	
168	Jewell, David	68y	W	U.S.	29 DEC 1859	Congressional
463	Jewell, John A.	4m	W	D.C.	03 JUL 1870	Mt. Olivet
004	Jewelle, Reginald H., auctioneer	26y	W	N.Y.	23 MAR 1855	Glenwood
698	Jewett, Mary A.	8m	W	D.C.	20 JUN 1873	Mt. Olivet
423	Jewson, Dabrey	Still	C	D.C.	04 OCT 1869	Washington Asylum
082	Jillard, John B.	9y	W		08 JUL 1857	Baltimore, Md.
055	Jillard, Mary	81y	W	Va.	30 AUG 1856	Glenwood
049	Jillson, Emma			D.C.	— JUL 1856	Foundry
115	Jirdensten, Mary E.	23y	W	D.C.	08 JUN 1858	Trinity
754	Joachim, Jacob F.	11d	W	U.S.	27 MAR 1874	St. Marys
724	Jochum, Jacob, grocer	44y	W		14 OCT 1873	Prospect Hill
723	Johansen, Mary F.	4d	W	D.C.	09 OCT 1873	Glenwood
314	John, Mary	15d	W		22 MAY 1868	Mt. Olivet
403	Johns, Charles	9m	W		17 JUL 1869	Western
273	Johns, Joseph P., hosp. steward	33y	W	Pa.	17 SEP 1867	Philadelphia, Pa.
634	Johns, Martha H.	25y	W	U.S.	01 OCT 1872	Glenwood
375	Johns, William Jesse, sail maker	28y	W	U.S.	02 FEB 1869	Baltimore, Md.
264	Johns, Wilson B.	6y	C	D.C.	20 JUL 1867	Union
328	Johns, Wm.	1y	C	D.C.	21 JUL 1868	Alms House
309	Johnson, A.	7d	W	D.C.	15 APR 1868	
607	Johnson, A.W.	3m	W	D.C.	25 JUN 1872	Congressional
384	Johnson, Abbey	Still	C	D.C.	21 MAR 1869	Washington Asylum
665	Johnson, Abby	3y	C	U.S.	29 JAN 1873	Small Pox*
676	Johnson, Abraham	4y	C	U.S.	08 MAR 1873	Small Pox
781	Johnson, Agnes	38y	C	U.S.	06 JUL 1874	Mt. Pleasant
712	Johnson, Albert T.	2y	C	D.C.	19 AUG 1873	Alms House
613	Johnson, Alex	1y	C	U.S.	29 JUL 1872	
684	Johnson, Alice	4y	W	U.S.	02 APR 1873	Small Pox*
514	Johnson, Alice C.	2m	C	D.C.	24 MAR 1871	Ebenezer
588	Johnson, Alsey	65y	C	Va.	25 MAR 1872	Western
615	Johnson, Amanda	50y	C	U.S.	11 JUL 1872	
520	Johnson, Amanda	22y	W	Va.	30 MAY 1871	Glenwood

District of Columbia Interments (Index to Deaths), 1855-1874

Page	Name	Age	Race	Birth	Death Date	Burial Ground
359	Johnson, Andw. Benton, pressman	22y	W	D.C.	28 NOV 1868	Congressional
492	Johnson, Angelina	8y	C	Va.	18 DEC 1870	Young Mens
070	Johnson, Ann	2y	C	D.C.	06 FEB 1857	Colored
524	Johnson, Ann	50y	C	Va.	21 JUN 1871	Prospect Hill
080	Johnson, Ann Eliza	32y	C		23 JUN 1857	St. Patricks
454	Johnson, Anna	5m	C		08 MAY 1870	
394	Johnson, Anna	62y	W	Va.	23 JUN 1869	Mt. Olivet
658	Johnson, Anna	3y	W	U.S.	05 JAN 1873	Mt. Olivet
102	Johnson, Anna	72y	W		17 JAN 1858	St. Patricks
437	Johnson, Anne	4d	C	D.C.	12 JAN 1870	Washington Asylum
447	Johnson, Annie	78y	C	Md.	27 MAR 1870	
766	Johnson, Annie V.	5m	W	U.S.	29 MAY 1874	
331	Johnson, Archy	22y	C		06 JUL 1868	Freedmen's Hospital
466	Johnson, Arthur	8m	C	D.C.	12 JUL 1870	
357	Johnson, Auther	3y	B	U.S.	02 OCT 1868	Washington Asylum
295	Johnson, B., infant of		C	D.C.	23 FEB 1868	
594	Johnson, Belinda	101y	C	Va.	28 APR 1872	Washington
584	Johnson, Bernard, laborer	48y	W	Pa.	03 MAR 1872	Mt. Olivet
706	Johnson, Bertha S.	4y	W	D.C.	06 JUL 1873	
687	Johnson, Bertie	12y	C	D.C.	01 MAY 1873	
275	Johnson, Betty	10m	C		23 SEP 1867	Freedmen's Hospital
622	Johnson, Britain	45y	C	U.S.	15 AUG 1872	
207	Johnson, C.	2m	C		22 JUL 1862	Western
038	Johnson, C.R., messenger	70y	W	Mass.	27 MAR 1856	Glenwood
298	Johnson, Caroline		W		08 FEB 1868	
698	Johnson, Caroline	30y	W	Amer.	16 JUN 1873	Congressional
633	Johnson, Castor	10y	C	U.S.	19 OCT 1872	Small Pox*
697	Johnson, Catherine	1m	W	D.C.	26 JUN 1873	Mt. Olivet
781	Johnson, Catherine	75y	W	U.S.	20 JUL 1874	Mt. Olivet
239	Johnson, Catherine		C		24 OCT 1866	Young Mens
429	Johnson, Catherine, MRs.	85y	W	Va.*	25 DEC 1869	Congressional
676	Johnson, Celia	2m	C	U.S.	07 MAR 1873	Small Pox
600	Johnson, Celia	80y	C	U.S.	10 MAY 1872	Unknown
533	Johnson, Charles	24y	C		19 AUG 1871	
395	Johnson, Charles	9m	W	D.C.	29 JUN 1869	Glenwood
402	Johnson, Charles	10m	W	D.C.	08 JUL 1869	Mt. Olivet
323	Johnson, Charlie		W	D.C.	19 JUL 1868	Glenwood
351	Johnson, Charlie	9d	C	D.C.	14 SEP 1868	Young Mens
372	Johnson, Charlotte	12y	C		09 JAN 1869	Freedmen's Hospital
629	Johnson, Chas.	1y	C	U.S.	28 OCT 1872	
708	Johnson, Chas.	7m	C	D.C.	03 JUL 1873	Beckett's
477	Johnson, Chas.	19d	W	D.C.	16 SEP 1870	Holmead
643	Johnson, Chas. H., clerk	35y	W	U.S.	14 DEC 1872	Glenwood
276	Johnson, child	21d	C	D.C.	23 SEP 1867	Beckett's
276	Johnson, child	23d	C	D.C.	24 SEP 1867	Beckett's
303	Johnson, Claiborne		C		26 MAR 1868	Alms House
629	Johnson, Clara	17y	C	U.S.	02 OCT 1872	
695	Johnson, Clary	26y	C	D.C.	09 JUN 1873	Ebenezer
673	Johnson, Clifton	11y	C	U.S.	08 MAR 1873	
160	Johnson, Cornelius	5d	C	D.C.	05 AUG 1859	Harmony
508	Johnson, David	2y	C	D.C.	18 FEB 1871	Ebenezer
275	Johnson, Dennis	33y	C		18 SEP 1867	Freedmen's Hospital
338	Johnson, Dora	3y	C		30 AUG 1868	Washington Asylum
268	Johnson, Dorcas Ann				22 AUG 1867	Ebenezer
459	Johnson, Dumas, laborer	68y	C	Va.	03 JUN 1870	
422	Johnson, E.T.	3y	C	Md.	11 OCT 1869	
624	Johnson, Ed	7m	C	U.S.	01 SEP 1872	
357	Johnson, Edward	60y	B	Va.	05 OCT 1868	Washington Asylum

District of Columbia Interments (Index to Deaths), 1855-1874

Page	Name	Age	Race	Birth	Death Date	Burial Ground
314	Johnson, Edwd.	9m	W	D.C.	28 MAY 1868	Congressional
470	Johnson, Edwin E.	3m	W	D.C.	04 AUG 1870	Congressional
729	Johnson, Eleanor C.	22y	W	U.S.	04 NOV 1873	Glenwood
315	Johnson, Eliza		C		c.03 MAY 1868	Alms House
743	Johnson, Eliza	45y	C	U.S.	23 JAN 1874	Mt. Pleasant
436	Johnson, Eliza	21y	C		07 JAN 1870	Washington Asylum
381	Johnson, Eliza, housekeeper	68y	W	Va.	18 MAR 1869	Oak Hill
014	Johnson, Elizabeth	10m	W	D.C.	— JUL 1855	
289	Johnson, Emanuel John	1y	W	Eng.	12 JAN 1868	Congressional
082	Johnson, Emeline	6d	W		08 JUL 1857	Congressional*
707	Johnson, Emiline	9m	C	D.C.	03 JUL 1873	Beckett's
295	Johnson, Emma F.	21d	W	D.C.	04 FEB 1868	Congressional
583	Johnson, Eva	70y	C	Va.	28 FEB 1872	Washington
538	Johnson, Eveline	16y	C	Va.	25 SEP 1871	
515	Johnson, Fanny	40y	C	Va.	19 MAR 1871	Union
411	Johnson, Frances	1y			17 AUG 1869	
389	Johnson, Frank	19y	C	Va.	03 APR 1869	Washington Asylum
425	Johnson, Fred.	1y	W	D.C.	09 NOV 1869	Congressional
249	Johnson, Garner	4m	C		18 JAN 1867	Harmony
588	Johnson, Garrison, farm hand	60y	C	D.C.	26 MAR 1872	Holmead
766	Johnson, George	3m	W	U.S.	05 MAY 1874	
514	Johnson, George	3y	C		18 MAR 1871	Beckett's
781	Johnson, George	4d	C	U.S.	09 JUL 1874	Potters Field
330	Johnson, George	9m	C	D.C.	28 JUL 1868	Young Mens
337	Johnson, George Hy.	1y	C	U.S.	17 AUG 1868	Washington Asylum
436	Johnson, George, servant	21y	C		04 JAN 1870	Washington Asylum
252	Johnson, George, shoemaker	40y	C	Va.	05 FEB 1867	Alms House
335	Johnson, George Thomas	6m			20 JUL 1868	
210	Johnson, H.	70y	C		— JAN 1866	Young Mens
630	Johnson, Hannah	1y	C	U.S.	14 OCT 1872	
267	Johnson, Harriet	9m	C	D.C.	25 JUL 1867	Colored, Methodist
665	Johnson, Harriet A.	1y	C	U.S.	27 JAN 1873	Small Pox*
415	Johnson, Harry	6m	W		05 SEP 1869	Glenwood
507	Johnson, Harry C.	6y	W		17 FEB 1871	Glenwood
450	Johnson, Harry W.	3m	C		24 APR 1870	Harmony
526	Johnson, Henry, laborer	25y	C	Md.	04 JUL 1871	Washington
665	Johnson, Henry [Wash. Simpson]	23y	C	U.S.	31 JAN 1873	Small Pox*
362	Johnson, Hermetta		C	D.C.	22 NOV 1868	
616b	Johnson, Ida S.	1y	W	U.S.	22 JUL 1872	Mt. Olivet
138	Johnson, Indiana Belle	3y	W		06 JAN 1859	Congressional
216	Johnson, Isaac	19y	C		29 MAR 1866	
707	Johnson, J.H., attorney at law	51y	W	D.C.	24 JUL 1873	
640	Johnson, J.W.	3y	C	U.S.	18 DEC 1872	Small Pox*
545	Johnson, James	3y	C	D.C.	17 NOV 1871	
080	Johnson, James	4m	C		26 JUN 1857	Foundry
743	Johnson, James	2y	C	U.S.	23 JAN 1874	Mt. Olivet
026	Johnson, James	17y	C		08 OCT 1855	St. Matthews
431	Johnson, James	7y	C	Va.	24 DEC 1869	Union
659	Johnson, James	30y	C	U.S.	13 JAN 1873	Washington Asylum
492	Johnson, James, laborer	35y	C	Md.	09 DEC 1870	Young Mens
455	Johnson, James, servant	15y	C	Md.	18 MAY 1870	Beckett's
342	Johnson, James, waiter	32y	C	Md.	27 AUG 1868	Young Mens
307	Johnson, Jane	20y	C	D.C.	11 APR 1868	Freedmen's Hospital
330	Johnson, Jane	1y	C	D.C.	17 JUL 1868	Harmony
628	Johnson, Jane E., housekeeper	28y	C	U.S.	28 SEP 1872	
518	Johnson, Jefferson, laborer	30y	C		06 MAY 1871	Potters Field
357	Johnson, Jno.	Still	B	D.C.	23 OCT 1868	Washington Asylum
458	Johnson, Jno. W.	5m	C	D.C.	15 JUN 1870	Potters Field

District of Columbia Interments (Index to Deaths), 1855-1874

Page	Name	Age	Race	Birth	Death Date	Burial Ground
246	Johnson, John	10m	C	Md.	20 DEC 1866	
754	Johnson, John	3m	C	U.S.	19 MAR 1874	
185	Johnson, John	15y	W	D.C.	27 JUL 1860	Congressional
333	Johnson, John	1y	W	D.C.	10 JUL 1868	Mt. Olivet
781	Johnson, John	9d	W	U.S.	14 JUL 1874	Mt. Olivet
683	Johnson, John	26y	C	U.S.	12 APR 1873	Small Pox
599	Johnson, John	3y	C	U.S.	07 MAY 1872	Unknown
292	Johnson, John	38y	C	D.C.	18 JAN 1868	Young Mens
073	Johnson, John, carpenter	56y	W		02 MAR 1857	
293	Johnson, John, farm hand	35y	C	Va.	20 MAR 1868	Methodist
450	Johnson, John L.	3y	W	D.C.	05 APR 1870	Mt. Olivet
667	Johnson, John, laborer	65y	C	U.S.	10 FEB 1873	
152	Johnson, John, laborer	25y	C	D.C.	16 JUN 1859	Eastern
611	Johnson, Joseph	1y	C	U.S.	06 JUL 1872	
065	Johnson, Joseph	50y	C		09 DEC 1856	St. Patricks
740	Johnson, Joseph J.	11m	C	U.S.	05 JAN 1874	
518	Johnson, Josephine, seamstress	40y	C	Md.	06 MAY 1871	Baltimore, Md.
642	Johnson, Joshua	70y	C	U.S.	20 DEC 1872	Small Pox
621	Johnson, Juliet	37y	C	U.S.	26 AUG 1872	
387	Johnson, Julius Cesar, Rev.	49y	C	Md.	26 APR 1869	Annapolis, Md.
389	Johnson, L.	Still			29 APR 1869	Washington Asylum
302	Johnson, Laura		C		23 MAR 1868	Alms House
676	Johnson, Lavinia	19y	C	U.S.	07 MAR 1873	Small Pox
707	Johnson, Leddie	50y	C	Va.	14 JUL 1873	Beckett's
514	Johnson, Lena	1y	C		23 MAR 1871	Ebenezer
524	Johnson, Lewis	1y	C	U.S.	21 JUN 1871	
039	Johnson, Lilley R.	1y	W	D.C.	19 MAR 1856	Methodist
506	Johnson, Lizzie, servant	21y	C	Md.	13 FEB 1871	Washington Asylum
343	Johnson, Louisa				16 AUG 1868	
604	Johnson, Louisa	80y	C	Va.	24 JUN 1872	Ebenezer
176	Johnson, Lucy	44y	C	D.C.	06 APR 1860	Harmony
338	Johnson, Lucy	2y	C		09 AUG 1868	Harmony
392	Johnson, Lucy	4d	C		04 MAY 1869	Washington Asylum
756	Johnson, Lulu	5y	C	U.S.	03 MAR 1874	
224	Johnson, M.				15 JUN 1866	Western
737	Johnson, Maggie	9y	C	U.S.	23 DEC 1873	
220	Johnson, Mahaly	40y	C	Va.	08 MAY 1866	Young Mens
591	Johnson, Malida	110y	C	Va.	27 APR 1872	
676	Johnson, Maline	1y	C	U.S.	04 MAR 1873	Small Pox
337	Johnson, Margaret	1y	C	D.C.	11 AUG 1868	
353	Johnson, Margaret	36y	W	Pa.	28 SEP 1868	Glenwood
773	Johnson, Margaret Ann	90y	C	U.S.	09 JUN 1874	Holyrood
242	Johnson, Margaret G.		C	Md.	21 OCT 1866	Young Mens
521	Johnson, Maria	23y	C	Va.	07 JUN 1871	Young Mens
094	Johnson, Maria, wife	25y	C	Md.	28 OCT 1857	
039	Johnson, Martha	12y	C	D.C.	22 MAR 1856	Alms House
676	Johnson, Martha, servant	60y	C	U.S.	13 MAR 1873	
002	Johnson, Martin, laborer	65y	C	Va.	— JAN 1855	Western
062	Johnson, Mary	66y	W	Md.	12 NOV 1856	
535	Johnson, Mary	40y	C	Md.	06 SEP 1871	
712	Johnson, Mary	4m	C	D.C.	18 AUG 1873	Beckett's
087	Johnson, Mary	60y	W	Va.	13 AUG 1857	Congressional
508	Johnson, Mary	2y	C	Va.	11 FEB 1871	Ebenezer
246	Johnson, Mary		C		11 DEC 1866	Harmony (new)
221	Johnson, Mary	35y	W	Md.	20 MAY 1866	Harmony
106	Johnson, Mary	69y	W	D.C.	04 FEB 1858	Holmead
075	Johnson, Mary	23y	W	D.C.	04 APR 1857	Methodist
535	Johnson, Mary	40y	C	Md.	05 SEP 1871	Potters Field

District of Columbia Interments (Index to Deaths), 1855-1874

Page	Name	Age	Race	Birth	Death Date	Burial Ground
459	Johnson, Mary	5y	C	D.C.	02 JUN 1870	Union
442	Johnson, Mary	2m	C		15 FEB 1870	Washington Asylum
225	Johnson, Mary				23 JUN 1866	Western
296	Johnson, Mary	50y	C	Va.	03 FEB 1868	Young Mens
760	Johnson, Mary A.	9y	W	U.S.	24 APR 1874	Mt. Olivet
179	Johnson, Mary Ann V.	4y	W	U.S.	22 MAY 1860	Glenwood
124	Johnson, Mary Ann	3y	C	D.C.	09 AUG 1858	Harmony
069	Johnson, Mary Cath.	22d	C	D.C.	27 JAN 1857	Young Mens
705	Johnson, Mary E.	11m	C	D.C.	09 JUL 1873	
781	Johnson, Mary E.	1y	C	U.S.	30 JUL 1874	Beckett's
024	Johnson, Mary E.	58y	W	N.H.	06 SEP 1855	Glenwood
330	Johnson, Mary E.	3y	C	D.C.	22 JUL 1868	Harmony
580	Johnson, Mary E.	3m	C	D.C.	08 FEB 1872	Holmead
623	Johnson, Mary E.	1y	C	U.S.	27 AUG 1872	Mt. Zion
423	Johnson, Mary Eliza	3y	C	D.C.	22 OCT 1869	Washington Asylum
439	Johnson, Mary Ellen	1y	W		23 FEB 1870	Mt. Olivet
773	Johnson, Mary F.	1m	C	U.S.	25 JUN 1874	
376	Johnson, Mary J.	4y	C		16 FEB 1869	
340	Johnson, Mary Jane	2y	W	Pa.	10 AUG 1868	Congressional
411	Johnson, Mary M.	34y	W	Md.	23 AUG 1869	Glenwood
454a	Johnson, Mary, pauper	3m	C	D.C.	03 MAY 1870	Washington Asylum
747	Johnson, Mary, servant	22y	C	U.S.	20 FEB 1874	
523	Johnson, Mary W.	1y	C	D.C.	17 JUN 1871	
396	Johnson, Mary W.	67y	W	Va.	12 JUN 1869	Oak Hill
436	Johnson, Matilda	25y	C	Va.	03 JAN 1870	
759	Johnson, Matilda L., nurse	55y	W	U.S.	24 APR 1874	Mt. Olivet
443	Johnson, Matilda, servant	25y	C	Va.	03 FEB 1870	Washington Asylum
300	Johnson, Matthew, laborer	40y	C	Va.	12 MAR 1868	Alms House
724	Johnson, Maud Annie	5m	B	N.Y.	12 OCT 1873	
406	Johnson, Middleton	4m			22 JUL 1869	Ebenezer
488	Johnson, Miles, laborer	30y	C	Md.	14 NOV 1870	Washington Asylum
769	Johnson, Millie, infant of	8d	C	U.S.	10 MAY 1874	
472	Johnson, Milly	60y	C		07 AUG 1870	Freedmen's Hospital
619	Johnson, Minnie	7y	C	U.S.	07 AUG 1872	
674	Johnson, Moses	20y	C	U.S.	14 MAR 1873	
296	Johnson, Nancy	60y	C		23 FEB 1868	Freedmen's Hospital
668	Johnson, Oda	4y	C	U.S.	17 FEB 1873	Washington Asylum
137	Johnson, Peter	54y	C		12 JAN 1859	Georgetown
670	Johnson, Peter	60y	C	U.S.	24 FEB 1873	Small Pox
611	Johnson, Philip	26d	C	U.S.	01 JUL 1872	
157	Johnson, Philip C., clerk	64y	W	U.S.	10 AUG 1859	Glenwood
251	Johnson, Philip, congressman	49y	W	N.J.	31 JAN 1867	Easton, Pa.
640	Johnson, Pocohontas	10y	C	U.S.	21 DEC 1872	Small Pox*
461	Johnson, Priscilla	36y	W	D.C.	19 JUL 1870	Congressional
427	Johnson, Rachel	60y	C	Va.	23 NOV 1869	Washington Asylum
086	Johnson, Rebecca	68y	C		01 AUG 1857	Young Mens
747	Johnson, Rena	50y	C	U.S.	26 FEB 1874	Washington Asylum
687	Johnson, Richard	7m	C	D.C.	02 MAY 1873	
431	Johnson, Richard	4m	C		26 DEC 1869	Young Mens
306	Johnson, Richard, messenger	22y	C	D.C.	28 APR 1868	Young Mens
595	Johnson, Richd.	5m	W	D.C.	25 APR 1872	Mt. Zion
753	Johnson, Richmond, Dr.	83y	W	U.S.	12 MAR 1874	Congressional
084	Johnson, Richmond, Jr.	9m	W	D.C.	21 JUL 1857	Congressional
303	Johnson, Robert		C		24 MAR 1868	Alms House
413	Johnson, Robert	1y	C		04 AUG 1869	Holmead
315	Johnson, Robert	22y	C		c.09 MAY 1868	Mt. Olivet
641	Johnson, Robert	10y	C	U.S.	10 DEC 1872	Small Pox
681	Johnson, Robert	5m	C	U.S.	14 APR 1873	Washington Asylum

District of Columbia Interments (Index to Deaths), 1855-1874

Page	Name	Age	Race	Birth	Death Date	Burial Ground
461	Johnson, Robert H.	1y	W	D.C.	22 JUL 1870	Congressional
619	Johnson, Robt.	6d	C	U.S.	21 AUG 1872	
608	Johnson, Robt., laborer	63y	W	Va.	07 JUN 1872	Holmead
303	Johnson, Roland		C		25 MAR 1868	Alms House
327	Johnson, Rose Etta	1y	W		20 JUL 1868	Mt. Olivet
428	Johnson, Sabra, domestic	60y	C	Va.	01 NOV 1869	Holmead
398	Johnson, Sallie	25y	B	U.S.	24 JUN 1869	Washington Asylum
674	Johnson, Sallie, child of			U.S.	17 MAR 1873	
745	Johnson, Sallie, infant of	9d	C	U.S.	23 JAN 1874	
225	Johnson, Sallie M.	2y	W	D.C.	21 JUN 1866	Glenwood
234	Johnson, Sally	80y	C	Md.	05 SEP 1866	Ebenezer
362	Johnson, Sally	1m	C	D.C.	11 NOV 1868	Washington Asylum
552	Johnson, Sam. B., laborer	35y	C	D.C.	08 JAN 1872	Washington
773	Johnson, Saml. H.	1y	W	U.S.	07 JUN 1874	Glenwood
394	Johnson, Samuel	5m	W	Amer.	30 JUN 1869	Congressional
676	Johnson, Samuel	22y	C	U.S.	30 MAR 1873	Washington Asylum
689	Johnson, Samuel	23y	C	U.S.	27 MAY 1873	Washington Asylum
676	Johnson, Samuel, laborer	68y	C	U.S.	04 MAR 1873	
060	Johnson, Samuel S.	3y	W	D.C.	09 OCT 1856	Congressional
553	Johnson, Sanford	21y		Va.	12 JAN 1872	Young Mens
530	Johnson, Sarah	10m	C	D.C.	31 JUL 1871	
253	Johnson, Sarah		C		10 FEB 1867	Baltimore, Md.
112	Johnson, Sarah	1y	W		28 APR 1858	Congressional
266	Johnson, Sarah	25y	C		26 JUL 1867	Ebenezer
401	Johnson, Sarah	4m	C	U.S.	19 JUL 1869	Young Mens
743	Johnson, Sarah A.	35y	C	U.S.	26 JAN 1874	
028	Johnson, Sarah B.	3y	W	D.C.	18 OCT 1855	Foundry
422	Johnson, Sarah, servant	23y	C	Va.	15 OCT 1869	
265	Johnson, Sarah V.	4m	W	D.C.	10 JUL 1867	Mt. Olivet
296	Johnson, Scipio	18y	C	Va.	06 FEB 1868	Freedmen's Hospital
409	Johnson, Seryna	1y	C		16 AUG 1869	
584	Johnson, Simion M., lawyer	56y	W	U.S.	01 MAR 1872	
421	Johnson, Solomon	1y	C		21 OCT 1869	Harmony
005	Johnson, Sophia	62y	W	Md.	04 MAR 1855	Baltimore, Md.
492	Johnson, Spencer	30y	C	Va.	12 DEC 1870	Young Mens
005	Johnson, Susan	45y	C	D.C.*	31 MAR 1855	Catholic, Georgetown
479	Johnson, Thomas	16y	C	D.C.	23 SEP 1870	Washington Asylum
550	Johnson, Thomas	4y	C	D.C.	27 DEC 1871	Young Mens
031	Johnson, Thomas J., clerk	34y	W	Ky.	17 DEC 1855	Glenwood
249	Johnson, Thomas, laborer	55y	W	Ire.	01 JAN 1867	Mt. Olivet
705	Johnson, Tiresa	2y	C	D.C.	05 JUL 1873	
441	Johnson, Townley	80y	C		11 FEB 1870	Ebenezer
367	Johnson, Undora	17y	B	Va.	12 DEC 1868	Washington Asylum
627	Johnson, Walter C.	2y	W	U.S.	24 SEP 1872	
410	Johnson, Washington, laborer	30y	C	Md.	09 AUG 1869	
459	Johnson, Washington, laborer	30y	C	Md.	19 JUN 1870	
624	Johnson, Wellington	2y	C	U.S.	17 SEP 1872	
331	Johnson, William	6m	C	D.C.	12 JUL 1868	
167	Johnson, William	88y	W	Eng.	18 DEC 1859	
101	Johnson, William	2y	C	D.C.	08 JAN 1858	
723	Johnson, William	70y	B	Va.	09 OCT 1873	
290	Johnson, William	50y	C		13 JAN 1868	Freedmen's Hospital
363	Johnson, William	2y	C		17 NOV 1868	Holmead
675	Johnson, William	50y	C	U.S.	20 MAR 1873	Washington Asylum
335a	Johnson, William				31 JUL 1868	Washington Asylum
387	Johnson, William, cook	6m	C	Md.	14 APR 1869	Young Mens
138	Johnson, William J.	5y	W	D.C.	14 JAN 1859	Georgetown
600	Johnson, William, ship carpenter	38y	W	U.S.	07 MAY 1872	Congressional*

Page	Name	Age	Race	Birth	Death Date	Burial Ground
272	Johnson, Willie	1m	W	D.C.	28 AUG 1867	Alms House
292a	Johnson, Wilson	3d	C	D.C.*	06 JAN 1868	Mt. Zion
670	Johnson, Wm.	5m	C	U.S.	01 FEB 1873	Small Pox*
335a	Johnson, Wm.				21 JUL 1868	Washington Asylum
176	Johnson, Wm. C.[N.], lawyer	54y	W	Md.	15 APR 1860	Frederick Co., Md.
646	Johnson, Wm. E.	4m	C	D.C.	25 DEC 1872	
460	Johnson, Wm. H.	5m	C	D.C.	28 JUN 1870	Mt. Olivet
395	Johnson, Wm. S.	10y	W	Ohio	28 JUN 1869	Glenwood
589	Johnson, Wyatt F., merchant	24y	W		29 MAR 1872	Glenwood
176	Johnson, [blank]	1y	C	D.C.	— APR 1860	
617	Johnson, [blank]	11m	C	U.S.	14 AUG 1872	
169	Johnson, [blank]	3y	W	D.C.	12 JAN 1860	Congressional
293	Johnson, [blank]	26y	C		02 MAR 1868	Methodist
005	Johnson, [blank]	40d	C	D.C.	17 MAR 1855	Scott Farm
451	Johnson, [blank]	P.B.	C	D.C.	04 APR 1870	Washington Asylum
026	Johnson, [blank]	9m	C		07 OCT 1855	Western
213	Johnson, [blank]		C		13 FEB 1866	Young Mens
154	Johnson, [blank]	6m	C	D.C.	20 JUL 1859	Young Mens
215	Johnson, [Henry C.]		W		14 MAR 1866	Congressional*
216	Johnson, [James]				25 MAR 1866	Congressional*
032	Johnson, [Joseph L.]	22y	W		06 DEC 1855	Congressional
273	Johnston, Addie	9m	W	D.C.	18 SEP 1867	Glenwood
278	Johnston, Albert P.	3m			22 OCT 1867	Oak Hill
402	Johnston, Arthur T., stone cutter	43y	W		18 JUL 1869	Glenwood
026	Johnston, Chas.	20y	C		17 OCT 1855	St. Patricks
062	Johnston, Clement, shoemaker	90y	W	Md.	07 NOV 1856	St. Patricks
259	Johnston, Frederick, clerk	32y	W	N.Y.	07 APR 1867	Oak Hill
444	Johnston, Harriet	13y	W	Md.	09 MAR 1870	Congressional
014	Johnston, Jas.	3y	C	D.C.	18 JUL 1855	Harmony
199	Johnston, John, gentleman	86y	W	Pa.	18 FEB 1861	Ohio
163	Johnston, John, laborer	35y	C	D.C.	26 OCT 1859	Ebenezer
104	Johnston, Louisa D.	2y	W	D.C.	08 FEB 1858	Glenwood
435	Johnston, Lucy A.	39y	W		08 JAN 1870	Young Mens
781	Johnston, Madora	1m	W	U.S.	13 JUL 1874	Congressional
133	Johnston, Marion	28y	W	D.C.	24 NOV 1858	Ebenezer
008	Johnston, Sarah Ann	15y	W	Ind.	17 MAY 1855	Congressional
330	Johnston, Solomon	1y			15 JUL 1868	Young Mens
009	Johnston, Susan, house servant	46y	C	Md.	21 MAY 1855	St. Patricks
060	Johnston, Thomas, butcher	47y	C	Md.	30 OCT 1856	Ebenezer
483	Johnston, Wm. B.	26y	W	Ohio	07 OCT 1870	Congressional
226	Johnstone, M.T., Mr., lawyer	63y	W	Eng.	30 JUN 1866	Congressional
305	Joliffe, John, lawyer	63y	W	Va.	28 MAR 1868	Frederick Co., Va.
265	Jolly, James G.	1m	W	D.C.	21 JUL 1867	Congressional
292	Jones, A.		C		28 JAN 1868	Alms House
082	Jones, Adalade V.	1y	W	D.C.	10 JUL 1857	Glenwood
038	Jones, Agnes	60y	C	Va.	12 MAR 1856	West
076	Jones, Alexius	66y	W	Ire.	22 APR 1857	Washington Asylum
227	Jones, Alfred, fireman	24y	W	D.C.	01 JUL 1866	Glenwood
061	Jones, Ann	1m			19 OCT 1856	
291	Jones, Ann	16y	C	Va.	28 JAN 1868	Potters Field
248	Jones, Annie	36y	W	N.J.	29 DEC 1866	Congressional
331	Jones, Archibald	30y	C		10 JUL 1868	Freedmen's Hospital
090	Jones, Ben.		C		11 SEP 1857	Western
197	Jones, Benjamin	4d	C		16 JAN 1861	Harmony
586	Jones, C.	43y	C	U.S.	16 MAR 1872	Asylum
253	Jones, C.	4m	C		17 FEB 1867	Young Mens
542	Jones, Carrie	1y	W	D.C.	18 OCT 1871	
017	Jones, Catherine	8m	C	D.C.	02 JUL 1855	

Page	Name	Age	Race	Birth	Death Date	Burial Ground
586	Jones, Charles	15y	C	Va.	17 MAR 1872	Ebenezer
177	Jones, Charles	9m	C	D.C.	20 APR 1860	Harmony
742	Jones, Charles	99y	W	U.S.	21 JAN 1874	Mt. Pleasant
301	Jones, Charles H.	6y	C	D.C.	11 MAR 1868	Western
554	Jones, Charles, laborer	25y	C	Va.	24 JAN 1872	Washington
160	Jones, Charles W.H.	15y	C	D.C.	13 AUG 1859	Harmony
090	Jones, Charlotte	26y	W	D.C.	09 SEP 1857	Washington Asylum
172	Jones, Chas. Fremont	10y	W	D.C.	15 FEB 1860	Mt. Olivet
012	Jones, Christopher, soldier	23y	W	Ire.	22 JUN 1855	Marine
012	Jones, Cicilia	9m	C	D.C.	26 JUN 1855	Harmony
591	Jones, Cornelius	5m	C	D.C.	05 APR 1872	
604	Jones, David	37y	C	D.C.	08 JUN 1872	Ebenezer
367	Jones, David	3y	B	U.S.	17 DEC 1868	Washington Asylum
442	Jones, Delia	5m	C		08 FEB 1870	Washington Asylum
055	Jones, Dennis	2m	C	D.C.	03 AUG 1856	Harmony
078	Jones, E.	43y	C	Va.	20 MAY 1857	Holmead
427	Jones, E.	Still	C	D.C.	21 NOV 1869	Washington Asylum
721	Jones, Edward	3m	B	U.S.	30 SEP 1873	Beckett's
641	Jones, Edward	2y	C	U.S.	17 DEC 1872	Small Pox
545	Jones, Edward B.	4m	C	D.C.	14 NOV 1871	Union
380	Jones, Eliza	65y	W	D.C.	08 MAR 1869	Glenwood
362	Jones, Elizabeth, house servant	28y	W	Va.	05 NOV 1868	Young Mens
711	Jones, Elizabeth, Mrs.	29y	C	D.C.	11 AUG 1873	Beckett's
362	Jones, Elizabety	28y	C		03 NOV 1868	Washington Asylum
713	Jones, Ellan A.	14y	W	U.S.	21 AUG 1873	Waverly Station, Va.
524	Jones, Emily T.	36y	W	D.C.	20 JUN 1871	Glenwood
136	Jones, Emma	36y	W	Pa.	13 DEC 1858	Mt. Olivet
260	Jones, Ernest W.	7m	W	D.C.	09 MAY 1867	Congressional
684	Jones, Fannie	6y	C	U.S.	13 APR 1873	Small Pox*
759	Jones, Fannie, Infant of	1d	C	U.S.	06 APR 1874	
396	Jones, Flora	3m	M	D.C.	01 JUN 1869	
321	Jones, Florence Virginia	9y	C		24 JUN 1868	Harmony
339	Jones, Frances Catherine	1y	W	D.C.	21 AUG 1868	Glenwood
098	Jones, George H.	50y	W	Va.	04 DEC 1857	Richmond, Va.
501	Jones, George, laborer	35y	C	Va.	16 JAN 1871	Potters Field
696	Jones, Grace Ann	3m	C	D.C.	20 JUN 1873	
417	Jones, Harriet	2m	C	D.C.	25 SEP 1869	Washington Asylum
720	Jones, Harvey W., merchant	30y	W	Pa.	25 SEP 1873	Stevensville, Pa.
766	Jones, Henrietta	2m	W	U.S.	08 MAY 1874	Mt. Olivet
404	Jones, Henrietta	11m	C		— JUL 1869	Young Mens
490	Jones, Henry	21d	C	D.C.	18 NOV 1870	Ebenezer
016	Jones, Henry, hostler	35y	C	Md.	14 JUL 1855	Harmony
299	Jones, Hester	18y	C	D.C.	01 MAR 1868	Young Mens
629	Jones, Ida	7m	C	U.S.	02 OCT 1872	
061	Jones, Jaccob P., laborer	21y	W	Md.	19 OCT 1856	Congressional
642	Jones, James	14y	C	U.S.	23 DEC 1872	Small Pox
295	Jones, James, coach driver	43y	W	Va.	14 FEB 1868	Congressional
741	Jones, James H.	1d	C	U.S.	09 JAN 1874	
168	Jones, James, storekeeper	37y	W	D.C.	22 DEC 1859	Congressional
670	Jones, Jno. Henry	2y	C	U.S.	20 FEB 1873	Small Pox
613	Jones, John A.	10m	C	U.S.	21 JUL 1872	
050	Jones, John, huckster	23y	W	D.C.	19 JUL 1856	Addison's Chapel
611	Jones, John J.	2y	C	U.S.	13 JUL 1872	
245	Jones, John, laborer	38y	C	Ill.	09 NOV 1866	Ebenezer
531	Jones, John W.	11m	W	Ohio	02 AUG 1871	Glenwood
584	Jones, Joseph	28y	C	Md.	03 MAR 1872	Potters Field
590	Jones, Joseph	3y	C	D.C.	07 APR 1872	Small Pox
317	Jones, Joseph, huckster	63y	C	Va.	12 JUN 1868	

District of Columbia Interments (Index to Deaths), 1855-1874

Page	Name	Age	Race	Birth	Death Date	Burial Ground
331	Jones, Langston	35y	C	D.C.*	01 JUL 1868	Freedmen's Hospital
552	Jones, Laura M.	1y	W	D.C.	05 JAN 1872	Congressional*
373	Jones, Lee	5y	C	D.C.	27 JAN 1869	Union
165	Jones, Lewis, clerk	19y	W	D.C.	03 NOV 1859	Rock Creek
644	Jones, Lizzie	39y	C	U.S.	19 DEC 1872	Washington Asylum
640	Jones, Louisa	15y	C	U.S.	25 DEC 1872	Small Pox*
024	Jones, Lucy	28d	C		18 SEP 1855	Harmony
498	Jones, Lucy, pauper	40y	B	U.S.	27 JAN 1871	Washington Asylum
049	Jones, M., child of		C		03 JUL 1856	Foundry
111	Jones, M. Dowell	1y	W	D.C.	11 APR 1858	Removed from City
027	Jones, Mable, clerk	22y	W	Md.	11 OCT 1855	St. Patricks
521	Jones, Maggie, lady	22y	W	D.C.	05 JUN 1871	Congressional*
403	Jones, Margaret	79y	W	Md.	12 JUL 1869	Methodist
354	Jones, Margaret, Mrs.	33y	W	Va.	13 OCT 1868	Congressional
602	Jones, Margret, washwoman	41y	C	U.S.	18 MAY 1872	Harmony
742	Jones, Maria		C	U.S.	18 JAN 1874	Beckett's
506	Jones, Maria	46y	W	Md.	03 FEB 1871	Congressional
265	Jones, Maria	1y	C	D.C.	01 JUL 1867	Harmony
422	Jones, Martha	50y	C	Md.	13 OCT 1869	Mt. Olivet
262	Jones, Mary	42y	C	Md.	03 JUN 1867	Ebenezer
447	Jones, Mary	4m	C		11 MAR 1870	Ebenezer
472	Jones, Mary	30y	C	Md.	08 AUG 1870	Freedmen's Hospital
153	Jones, Mary	1m	C	D.C.	03 JUL 1859	St. Patricks
258	Jones, Mary	22y	C		10 APR 1867	Young Mens
644	Jones, Mary A.M.	72y	W	U.S.	21 DEC 1872	Congressional
711	Jones, Mary Ann, Mrs.	56y	W	N.Y.	09 AUG 1873	Glenwood
262	Jones, Mary B.	47y	W	W.I.	05 JUN 1867	Pa.
060	Jones, Mary, cook	35y	C	Md.	12 OCT 1856	Young Mens
458	Jones, Mary E.	7d	C	D.C.	02 JUN 1870	Potters Field
338	Jones, Mary E.	4y	C		23 AUG 1868	Washington Asylum
536	Jones, Mary E.	3y	C	D.C.	17 SEP 1871	Young Mens
738	Jones, Mary, housekeeper	40y	C	U.S.	08 DEC 1873	
135	Jones, Mary, servant	19y	C	D.C.	09 DEC 1858	Young Mens
718	Jones, Matilda E.	14m	C	U.S.	13 SEP 1873	Harmony
471	Jones, Melvina	10m	W	D.C.	24 AUG 1870	Congressional
323	Jones, Michael	9m	W	D.C.	07 JUL 1868	Mt. Olivet
234	Jones, Mr., child of	2y	C	D.C.	04 SEP 1866	Young Mens
028	Jones, Mrs.	50y	W		17 OCT 1855	St. Matthews
140	Jones, Nancy	89y	C	Va.	02 FEB 1859	St. Patricks
106	Jones, Nancy, servant	98y	C	Md.	07 FEB 1858	Young Mens
408	Jones, Nicholas, laborer	37y	C	U.S.	28 AUG 1869	Mt. Olivet
181	Jones, Paul		C	D.C.	07 JUN 1860	Foundry
290	Jones, Philander	28y	C		17 JAN 1868	Freedmen's Hospital
346	Jones, Phinny	2m	C		13 AUG 1868	Freedmen's Hospital
063	Jones, Rachel	55y	W	D.C.	02 NOV 1856	Washington Asylum
272	Jones, Robert	30y	C		19 AUG 1867	Freedmen's Bureau
542	Jones, Robt. Glenn	7y	W	D.C.	22 OCT 1871	Oak Hill
177	Jones, Roxana	5m	C	D.C.	20 APR 1860	Young Mens
482	Jones, S.A.	2y	W	D.C.	25 OCT 1870	Oak Hill
412	Jones, Sam. A.	33y	W	Wales	12 AUG 1869	Washington Asylum
724	Jones, Samuel	25y	B	S.C.	16 OCT 1873	
215	Jones, Sarah	78y		Md.	16 MAR 1866	Congressional
285	Jones, Sarah	9d	C	D.C.	16 DEC 1867	Union
153	Jones, Sarah, cook	58y	C	Va.	04 JUL 1859	Foundry
747	Jones, Sarah, cook	23y	C	U.S.	17 FEB 1874	Mt. Pleasant
696	Jones, Sarah Jane	5m	C	D.C.	01 JUN 1873	
584	Jones, Sarah V.	24y	W	Va.	04 MAR 1872	Congressional
331	Jones, Smachen	35y	C	Va.	02 JUL 1868	Freedmen's Hospital

District of Columbia Interments (Index to Deaths), 1855-1874

Page	Name	Age	Race	Birth	Death Date	Burial Ground
039	Jones, Sophia	36y	W	D.C.	20 MAR 1856	Congressional
124	Jones, Sophia	21y	W		06 AUG 1858	Glenwood
260	Jones, Sophia, housekeeper	33y	C	D.C.	01 MAY 1867	Beckett's
383	Jones, Stewart	30y	C	N.C.	06 MAR 1869	Washington Asylum
090	Jones, Tabitha	80y	W	Md.	09 SEP 1857	Congressional
501	Jones, Theodore	14y	C	Md.	21 JAN 1871	Young Mens
747	Jones, Thomas B.	5m	W	U.S.	26 FEB 1874	Mt. Olivet*
224	Jones, Thomas J., barber	26y	C	D.C.	16 JUN 1866	Harmony
149	Jones, Thomas W., wood merhant	42y	W	D.C.	23 MAY 1859	Congressional
041	Jones, Virginia J.	35y	W	Va.	03 APR 1856	Rock Creek
361	Jones, William	6m	C	D.C.	27 NOV 1868	
690	Jones, William	22y	C	U.S.	12 MAY 1873	Small Pox
263	Jones, William, Dr.	77y	W	Md.	25 JUN 1867	Oak Hill
187	Jones, William, laborer	45y	C	D.C.	05 AUG 1860	Harmony
093	Jones, William, painter	57y	W	Eng.	02 OCT 1857	Washington Asylum
416	Jones, Willie	1y	C		28 SEP 1869	
055	Jones, Willie Columbus	5m	C	D.C.	11 AUG 1856	Holmead
612	Jones, Willie O.	2m	W	U.S.	20 JUL 1872	
005	Jones, Wm.	80y	C	Va.	04 APR 1855	
622	Jones, Wm. C.	13m	W	U.S.	13 AUG 1872	
090	Jones, Wm., child of	1y	W	D.C.	10 SEP 1857	Congressional
628	Jones, Wm. H., soldier	30y	C	U.S.	22 SEP 1872	
029	Jones, Wm., machinist	29y	W	Md.	01 NOV 1855	Congressional
179	Jones, [blank]	2d	W	D.C.	— MAY 1860	
015	Jones, [blank]	10m	C		15 JUL 1855	Navy Yard (Col'd)
014	Jones, [blank]	16h	W	D.C.	11 JUL 1855	Trinity, Geo.
367	Jones, [blank]	Still	B	D.C.	26 DEC 1868	Washington Asylum
032	Jones, [blank]	7m	C		10 DEC 1855	Western
234	Jones, [blank], child of	1y	C	D.C.	06 SEP 1866	Young Mens
411	Jones, [blank], laborer	45y	C		28 AUG 1869	Ebenezer
003	Jones, [blank], laborer	25y	C	Va.*	22 FEB 1855	Freedmen's
034	Jones, [blank], Mr.	64y	C		02 JAN 1856	St. Matthews
357	Jones. [blank]	1m	B	D.C.	13 OCT 1868	Washington Asylum
523	Jonson, Henry, laborer	45y	C	Md.	19 JUN 1871	
454a	Jonson, Mary	40y	W		31 MAY 1870	Washington Asylum
030	Jonter, F.E.	25y	W	Md.	24 NOV 1855	
228	Jordan, Alice	4y	W	D.C.	12 JUL 1866	Mt. Olivet
441	Jordan, Alice Sophia	4y	C		13 FEB 1870	
292	Jordan, Harris		C		30 JAN 1868	Alms House
291	Jordan, Henry, wood sawyer	45y	C	Va.	28 JAN 1868	Potters Field
555	Jordan, Jacob, cigar maker	57y	W		26 JAN 1872	Prospect Hill
377	Jordan, Julia	55y	C	Va.	18 FEB 1869	Harmony
415	Jordan, Marcellina	10d			03 SEP 1869	
082	Jordan, Mary A.	49y	W	Va.	06 JUL 1857	Oak Hill
349	Jordan, Robert A.	12d	W	D.C.	08 SEP 1868	Glenwood
166	Jordan, Virginia	4y	W	Va.	22 NOV 1859	Foundry
158	Jordan, William	1m	W	D.C.	17 AUG 1859	German Lutheran
703	Jordan, [blank]	3m	W	D.C.	26 JUL 1873	
711	Jorden, Lilley Maud	3y	W	D.C.	09 AUG 1873	Congressional
369	Jordi, Caspar, peddler	55y	W	Switz.	07 JAN 1869	Congressional
022	Jordin, Mary D.	2y	W	Ire.	12 AUG 1855	Congressional
610	Jordon, Clementine	8y	W		28 JUN 1867	Mt. Olivet
642	Jordon, James	30y	C	U.S.	04 DEC 1872	Washington Asylum
124	Jordon, Robert	2y	W	D.C.	04 AUG 1858	Congressional
362	Jordon, Tamaha	Still	C	D.C.	07 NOV 1868	
773	Jordon, Walter W.	9m	W	U.S.	28 JUN 1874	Wilmington, Del.
724	Joseph, Richard C., clerk	65y	W	Mass.	15 OCT 1873	Oak Hill
737	Josh, John	65y	C	U.S.	25 DEC 1873	Washington Asylum

District of Columbia Interments (Index to Deaths), 1855-1874

Page	Name	Age	Race	Birth	Death Date	Burial Ground
098	Joshua, R.	54y	W	Ger.	02 DEC 1857	Washington Asylum
047	Joullesby, Mornus, bricklayer	25y	W	Eng.	27 JUN 1856	Holmead/Oak Hill
479	Jouvenal, Peter		W	Ger.	02 SEP 1870	
247	Jox, J.	55y	C		25 DEC 1866	Young Mens
023	Joy, Ada	4y	W	D.C.	09 SEP 1855	Methodist
386	Joy, Artta R.	28m	W		26 APR 1869	Mt. Olivet
360	Joy, Bartary E.	3y	W	D.C.	27 NOV 1868	Mt. Olivet
015	Joy, Elizabeth	1m	W	D.C.	30 JUL 1855	St. Matthews
017	Joy, Elizabeth	1m	W		31 JUL 1855	St. Patricks
668	Joy, Linus C.	22m	C	U.S.	24 FEB 1873	Young Mens
149	Joy, Mary	62y	W		24 MAY 1859	Foundry
534	Joy, Tilley	2y	W	D.C.	27 AUG 1871	Mt. Olivet
071	Joy, Wm., tailor	45y	W	Md.	25 FEB 1857	Congressional
643	Joyce, Archer, laborer	33y	C	U.S.	13 DEC 1872	Ebenezer
118	Joyce, F., cook	27y	C		12 JUN 1858	
637	Joyce, Fannie	2y	W	U.S.	02 NOV 1872	Mt. Olivet
448	Joyce, Frank, laborer				01 MAR 1870	Mt. Olivet
663	Joyce, James	12y	C	U.S.	25 JAN 1873	Small Pox
723	Joyce, John Lewis, clerk	29y	W	D.C.	10 OCT 1873	Mt. Olivet
087	Joyce, Mary	57y	W	Ire.	15 AUG 1857	St. Patricks
122	Joyce, Mary	14d	C	D.C.	23 JUL 1858	Washington
719	Joyce, Thomas	7y	W	D.C.	22 SEP 1873	Holywood
637	Joyce, Wm.	24y	C	U.S.	27 NOV 1872	
781	Joyce, Wm. H.	7m	W	U.S.	16 JUL 1874	Glenwood
380	Joyse, Jas. W., child of	Still	W		13 MAR 1869	Glenwood
155	Judah, Sarah S., house servant	34y	C	Va.	29 JUL 1859	Holmead
461	Judefind, John	8m	W	D.C.	19 JUL 1870	Congressional
587	Judge, Frank	3y	W	U.S.	19 MAR 1872	Glenwood
585	Judge, John, carpenter	17y	W	Ire.	07 MAR 1872	Mt. Olivet
098	Judge, Mary	25y	W	Md.	14 DEC 1857	Baltimore, Md.
631	Judy, Emma A.	2y	W	U.S.	13 OCT 1872	
163	Jueremann, Mary C.	24y	W	Ger.	25 OCT 1859	German Catholic
400	Juger, Frederick A.	3y	W		— JUL 1869	Prospect Hill
177	Julian, Martha	11d	W	D.C.	24 APR 1860	St. Patricks
526	Julian, Mary	31y		D.C.	06 JUL 1871	
387	Jullien, Adelaide, school teacher	62y	W	D.C.	19 APR 1869	St. Patricks
659	Jupeter, Valinda	20y	C	U.S.	10 JAN 1873	Ebenezer
695	Jupiter, William	10m	C	U.S.	18 JUN 1873	
060	Jurich, [blank]	Still	W		26 OCT 1856	
112	Juridan, Kate	1y	W	D.C.	24 APR 1858	St. Patricks
165	Juruper, [blank]		C	D.C.	15 NOV 1859	Washington Asylum
077	Just, Charles	1y	W	D.C.	11 MAY 1857	German
697	Just, Godferid, miller	71y	W	Ger.	24 JUN 1873	Glenwood
687	Jutten, George W.	4y	W	D.C.	06 MAY 1873	Freehold, N.J.
084	Juvenal, Gustaf	11m	W	D.C.	24 JUL 1857	German
090	Juvenal, Mina	6m	W	D.C.	09 SEP 1857	German
104	Juvenal, Wm.		W	Ger.	04 FEB 1858	German

Page	Name	Age	Race	Birth	Death Date	Burial Ground
K						
614	Kader, Joseph	70y	W	U.S.	30 JUL 1872	
670	Kadruck, Arthur	4y	C	U.S.	23 FEB 1873	Small Pox
708	Kafe, James	35y	W	Ire.	24 JUL 1873	
266	Kagelr, Isador	3m	W	D.C.	07 JUL 1867	German Catholic
283	Kahis, Mari Willimane	14d	W	D.C.	25 NOV 1867	German Catholic
744	Kahl, Johanna	65y	W	Ger.	31 JAN 1874	Prospect Hill
025	Kahl, John F.	53y	W		13 SEP 1855	German
694	Kahler, Jacob, stone cutter	82y	W	Ger.	06 JUN 1873	Glenwood
325	Kahler, Lizzie	9h	W	D.C.	15 JUL 1868	Congressional
338	Kahoe, Wm.	1d	W	D.C.	28 AUG 1868	Mt. Olivet
079	Kaibel, John B., carpenter	28y	W	Ger.	14 JUN 1857	Glenwood
773	Kaighn, Walter H.	8m	W	U.S.	12 JUN 1874	Graceland
410	Kaiser, Annie C.	8m	W		18 AUG 1869	Prospect Hill
410	Kaiser, Charles	2y	W		27 AUG 1869	Prospect Hill
680	Kaiser, Edward	7m	W	U.S.	02 APR 1873	Prospect Hill
283	Kaiser, John	1y	W	D.C.	01 NOV 1867	German Catholic
734	Kaiser, John Henry, clerk	21y	W	U.S.	06 DEC 1873	Prospect Hill
593	Kaiser, John, pump maker	55y	W	Ger.	18 APR 1872	Prospect Hill
546	Kaiser. [blank]	1y	W	D.C.	22 NOV 1871	Prospect Hill
640	Kaldenbach, Richd.	5y	W	U.S.	21 DEC 1872	Small Pox*
629	Kaldenbach, W.H.	2m	W	U.S.	05 OCT 1872	
580	Kallean, C.	8d	W	U.S.	10 FEB 1872	
596	Kallfus, Danl.	4m	W	U.S.	12 APR 1872	Oak Hill
187	Kamerer, Christian G., agent	53y	W	Prus.	03 AUG 1860	Prospect Hill
690	Kammel, Rudy	19y	C	U.S.	28 MAY 1873	Small Pox
386	Kamp, Robert, laborer	21y	W	Amer.	19 APR 1869	Mt. Olivet
319	Kane, Ceclia	53y	W	Ire.	26 JUN 1868	Mt. Olivet*
680	Kane, John	21y	W	U.S.	05 APR 1873	Mt. Olivet
016	Kane, John	1m	W	N.Y.	14 JUL 1855	St. Patricks
683	Kane, John, butcher	21y	W	U.S.	05 APR 1873	
236	Kane, John, laborer	45y	W	Ire.	30 SEP 1866	Mt. Olivet
446	Kane, Laura	19y	C		02 MAR 1870	
224	Kane, Mary	8y	W	D.C.	13 JUN 1866	Mt. Olivet
747	Kane, Mary Ann	54y	W	U.S.	15 FEB 1874	Queens Chapel, Md.
055	Kane, Sylvester	1m	W	D.C.	18 AUG 1856	Foundry
602	Kaph, [blank]		W	U.S.	16 MAY 1872	St. Marys
682	Kapplee, Fred	16m	W	U.S.	24 APR 1873	St. Marys
018	Kappler, Edwd.	9m	W	D.C.	02 AUG 1855	St. Marys
526	Kappler, Elisabeth	17m	W	D.C.	01 JUL 1871	German Catholic
550	Kappler, N.	42y	W	Ger.	31 DEC 1871	
441	Karcher, Charles	9y	W		08 FEB 1870	Prospect Hill
334	Karff, Catherine E.	1y	W		26 JUL 1868	German Catholic
207	Karie, Maria Ann, house servant	34y	C	Va.	27 JUL 1862	Holmead
046	Karl, Mary	48y	W	Ger.	16 JUN 1856	Congressional
117	Karll, Henry, laborer	52y	W	Ger.	28 JUN 1858	Congressional
004	Karn, Edwin Sylvestus	1m	W	D.C.	30 MAR 1855	Foundry
631	Karney, Jas. A.	3y	W	U.S.	29 OCT 1872	
782	Karo, Mary	80y	W	U.S.	22 JUL 1874	Glenwood
440	Karpeles, Sara	25y	W		12 FEB 1870	Washington Hebrew
101	Karrick, Rebecca Ord	83y	W	Pa.	12 JAN 1858	Rock Creek
620	Kass, Mary L.	19m	W	U.S.	08 AUG 1872	Glenwood
281	Kassen, Eugene	1y	W		01 OCT 1867	Mt. Olivet
407	Kathman, Henry, child of	7m	W		16 AUG 1869	Congressional
723	Kauf, Matilda, domestic	23y	W	Ger.	02 OCT 1873	Washington Asylum
233	Kaufman, A.	32y	W	Ger.	10 AUG 1866	
265	Kaufman, Frederick G.	5y	W	D.C.	10 JUL 1867	Zanesville, Ohio
507	Kaufman, George, gardener	69y	W	Ger.	27 FEB 1871	Glenwood

District of Columbia Interments (Index to Deaths), 1855-1874

Page	Name	Age	Race	Birth	Death Date	Burial Ground
414	Kaufman, Infant	Still	W		17 SEP 1869	Washington Hebrew
336	Kaufman, Isaac	1m	W		11 AUG 1868	Washington Hebrew
706	Kaufman, John	9d	W	D.C.	22 JUL 1873	Prospect Hill
773	Kaufman, Jos. A., shoemaker	59y	W	Ger.	22 JUN 1874	
405	Kaufmann, Ernst	11m			17 JUL 1869	Prospect Hill
782	Kaughe, Michael, laborer	38y	W	Ire.	17 JUL 1874	
004	Kavanagh, Annie	21y	W	D.C.	22 MAR 1855	St. Patricks
075	Kavanah, Charles	11d	W	D.C.	09 APR 1857	St. Matthews
075	Kavanah, Mary	36y	W	Ire.	09 APR 1857	St. Matthews
594	Kavanauff, Kate	29y	W	Ire.	16 APR 1872	Mt. Olivet
058	Kavanaugh, Emma	2y	W	D.C.	18 SEP 1856	St. Patricks
022	Kaw, Lucy		C		05 AUG 1855	Congressional
707	Kay, Ed T., druggist	20y	W	Mass.	09 JUL 1873	Westmore, Mass.
720	Kayre, James	5m	W		28 SEP 1873	Congressional
093	Kealty, Dennis Thomas	1m	W	D.C.	05 OCT 1857	St. Patricks
325	Keanan, Pat., laborer	40y	W	Ire.	06 JUL 1868	Congressional
199	Keans, Elizabeth	18y	W		19 FEB 1861	Glenwood
464	Kearn, Willie	7m	W	D.C.	03 JUL 1870	Prospect Hill
101	Kearney, [blank]	40y	W	Md.	10 JAN 1858	
587	Kearns, Danl.	2y	W	D.C.	23 MAR 1872	Holy Grove
130	Kearns, Sarah	35y	W	N.J.	19 OCT 1858	Glenwood
093	Kearon, Mary Jane	6y	W	D.C.	01 OCT 1857	St. Patricks
754	Keating, Catharine	65y	W	Ire.	12 MAR 1874	Mt. Olivet
046	Keating, Catharine	23y	W	Me.	01 JUN 1856	St. Patricks
694	Keating, George W.	29m	W	Va.	07 JUN 1873	Weaverton, Ind.
001	Keating, John E.	15y			13 JAN 1855	St. Patricks
694	Keating, John M.	6m		D.C.	10 JUN 1873	Weaverton, Ind.
047	Keating, Margarette A.	3m	C	D.C.	23 JUN 1856	St. Patricks
044	Keating, Thomas, waiter	30y	W	Ire.	08 MAY 1856	St. Patricks/Mt. Olivet
782	Keating, [blank]	17y	W	Ire.	11 JUL 1874	
307	Kebener, John	3m	W	D.C.	26 APR 1868	Western
309	Keck, Anthony J., student	20y	W	Wisc.	16 APR 1868	Bloomfield, Walw. Co.
484	Keck, Nettie V.	1y	W	D.C.	18 OCT 1870	Congressional
019	Kedre, Thos.	8h	W	D.C.	18 AUG 1855	St. Patricks
670	Kedrick, Richard	16y	C	U.S.	27 FEB 1873	Small Pox
179	Keech, John C., clerk	24y	W	Md.	20 MAY 1860	Congressional*
016	Keef, A.J.	1y	W	D.C.	06 JUL 1855	
213	Keef, Ellen	40y	W	Ire.	23 FEB 1866	Mt. Olivet
034	Keefe, Arthur, carpenter	60y	W	Ire.	01 JAN 1856	St. Peters
289	Keefe, Francis J.	3m	W	D.C.	24 JAN 1868	Holyrood
364	Keefer, David H.	7d	W	D.C.	16 DEC 1868	Congressional
629	Keefer, E.L.	45y	W	U.S.	20 OCT 1872	
489	Keefer, Susan C.	33y	W	Md.	01 NOV 1870	Oak Hill
616	Keegan, Jno., actor	24y	W	U.S.	25 JUL 1872	
616b	Keegan, John, actor	24y	W	U.S.	23 JUL 1872	
364	Keek, Nellie	4y	W	D.C.	03 DEC 1868	Congressional*
667	Keelan, Wm. S., reporter	50y	W	Scot.	08 FEB 1873	Mt. Olivet
642	Keeler, E.S., messenger	39y	C	U.S.	01 DEC 1872	Mt. Olivet
644	Keeler, Wm. F.	14m	W	U.S.	22 DEC 1872	Mt. Olivet
631	Keen, Irena	6y	W	U.S.	24 OCT 1872	
631	Keen, Nelly	2y	W	U.S.	16 OCT 1872	
266	Keena, Winnie Dallas	4m	W	D.C.	04 JUL 1867	Baltimore, Md.
044	Keenan, Alice	1y	W	D.C.	14 MAY 1856	St. Matthews
393	Keenan, Elizabeth, Mrs.	83y	W	Md.	31 MAY 1869	Baltimore, Md.
391	Keenan, Elizabeth, Mrs.	83y	W	Md.	31 MAY 1869	Baltimore, Md.
058	Keenan, James, paver	65y	W	Ire.	19 SEP 1856	Holmead
517	Keenan, Lillie E.	6m	W	Amer.	13 APR 1871	Glenwood
439	Keene, Clarence T.	2y	W		02 FEB 1870	Congressional

District of Columbia Interments (Index to Deaths), 1855-1874

Page	Name	Age	Race	Birth	Death Date	Burial Ground
367	Keener, Biddy	100y	B	U.S.	12 DEC 1868	Washington Asylum
174	Keener, Mary W.	4m	W	D.C.	13 MAR 1860	Washington Asylum
594	Keenon, Bridget	76y	W	Ire.	09 APR 1872	Mt. Olivet
075	Keepler, Sees	21d	W	D.C.	11 APR 1857	German Catholic
053	Kees, Daniel	2y	W	D.C.	10 AUG 1856	
104	Keese, Caroline	15h	W	D.C.	06 FEB 1858	German
324	Keffer, Abraham, tailor	62y	W		25 JUL 1868	Mt. Olivet
151	Kehan, John S.	7d	W	D.C.	20 JUN 1859	St. Peters
121	Kehun, Mary C.S.	3m	W	D.C.	14 JUL 1858	St. Patricks
305	Keigan, Catherine	4d	W		c.24 MAR 1868	Mt. Olivet
531	Keightley, Charles H.	2y	W	D.C.	04 AUG 1871	Methodist
112	Keil, Henry	3y	W	D.C.	22 APR 1858	German Catholic
091	Keiler, Hannah	1y	W	D.C.	15 SEP 1857	Glenwood
507	Kein, Mary L., housekeeper	55y	W	Prus.	26 FEB 1871	Prospect Hill
331	Keisecker, Caroline	2y	W	D.C.	23 JUL 1868	Glenwood
596	Keisle, John, carpenter	48y	W	Bad.	27 APR 1872	Oak Hill
670	Keitch, Emma	35y	C	U.S.	20 FEB 1873	Small Pox
677	Keitch, Geo. A.	8y	C	U.S.	21 MAR 1873	Small Pox
670	Keitch, Jno. H.	17y	C	U.S.	22 FEB 1873	Small Pox
670	Keitch, Mary	4y	C	U.S.	22 FEB 1873	Small Pox
105	Keith, Jno. B.	9y	C	D.C.	25 FEB 1858	Ebenezer
669	Keith, William	30y	C	U.S.	10 FEB 1873	Small Pox
581	Keithley, Wm.	1y	W	D.C.	18 FEB 1872	Congressional*
199	Keithley, [blank]		W		19 FEB 1861	Congressional
684	Keitz, Henrick	54y	W	Ger.	25 APR 1873	Small Pox
673	Kelaher, Ann	44y	W	Ire.	10 MAR 1873	Mt. Olivet
464	Kellegan, Mary	79y	W	Ire.	15 JUL 1870	Mt. Olivet
234	Kelleher, Mary M.	1y	W	D.C.	11 SEP 1866	Mt. Olivet
322	Kelleher, Thomas, book binder	35y	W	U.S.	03 JUN 1868	Glenwood
347	Keller, B. Margaret	74y	W	Pa.	25 SEP 1868	Congressional
532	Keller, Barbara C.	76y	W	Ger.	10 AUG 1871	Congressional
084	Keller, Hardee R.	7m	W	Calif.	25 JUL 1857	Methodist
320	Keller, Margaret	28y	W	Scot.	25 JUN 1868	Glenwood
469	Keller, William	6y	W	D.C.	18 AUG 1870	Glenwood
355	Kelley, Andrew W., child of	Still	W		26 OCT 1868	Congressional
160	Kelley, J.W.	11m	W	Md.	07 AUG 1859	Methodist
704	Kelley, James	28y	W	Md.	01 JUL 1873	Small Pox
355	Kelley, John	3y	W	D.C.	31 OCT 1868	Mt. Olivet*
209	Kelley, John C.	36y	W		02 JAN 1866	Congressional
782	Kelley, M.R.	7y	W	U.S.	31 JUL 1874	Congressional
533	Kellia, Chris.	1m	W	D.C.	25 AUG 1871	Prospect Hill
235	Kelliher, M., dairyman	43y	W	Ire.	21 SEP 1866	Georgetown, Catholic
271	Kellogg, George E.	1y	W	D.C.	24 AUG 1867	Congressional
320	Kelly, Alice	1y	W	D.C.	19 JUN 1868	Mt. Olivet*
302	Kelly, Ann Elizabeth	1m	W	D.C.	17 MAR 1868	Holmead
131	Kelly, Benjamin, slave	50y	C	Md.	21 OCT 1858	Washington Asylum
323	Kelly, Daniel	11m	W	D.C.	25 JUL 1868	Mt. Olivet
035	Kelly, David W.	1y	W	D.C.	22 FEB 1856	Glenwood
234	Kelly, Edwd., laborer	46y	W	Ire.	02 SEP 1866	Mt. Olivet
506	Kelly, Eliza	24y	W	N.Y.	11 FEB 1871	Congressional
238	Kelly, Elizabeth	56y	W	Pa.	30 SEP 1866	Congressional
360	Kelly, Elizabeth A.	27y	W	Md.	08 NOV 1868	Mt. Olivet
324	Kelly, Ellen P.	25y	W	Ire.	09 JUL 1868	Mt. Olivet*
535	Kelly, Emma	1y	W	D.C.	16 SEP 1871	Congressional
425	Kelly, George D., gardener	22y	W	Ver.	15 NOV 1869	Congressional
292	Kelly, Gertrude Elizabeth	3m	W	U.S.	22 JAN 1868	Congressional
408	Kelly, Ida	2m	W	D.C.	31 AUG 1869	Western
674	Kelly, Johannah	3y	W	U.S.	17 MAR 1873	Mt. Olivet

District of Columbia Interments (Index to Deaths), 1855-1874

Page	Name	Age	Race	Birth	Death Date	Burial Ground
662	Kelly, John	32y	C	U.S.	03 JAN 1873	Small Pox
436	Kelly, John D., blacksmith	39y	W		20 JAN 1870	Congressional
760	Kelly, John S., clerk	27y	W	U.S.	04 APR 1874	Glenwood
645	Kelly, Julia	47y	W	Ire.	29 DEC 1872	Mt. Olivet
250	Kelly, Martha K.	21y	W	D.C.	11 JAN 1867	Glenwood
272	Kelly, Mary Ann	3m	C		06 AUG 1867	Freedmen's Bureau
675	Kelly, Mary Ellen	6m	W	U.S.	23 MAR 1873	Mt. Olivet
683	Kelly, Michael	25y	C	U.S.	15 APR 1873	Small Pox
322	Kelly, Michael, carpenter	25y	W	Ire.	15 JUN 1868	Mt. Olivet
484	Kelly, Nettie E.	5m	W		14 OCT 1870	Congressional
365	Kelly, Norra [Hanorah]	3y	W	D.C.	04 DEC 1868	Mt. Olivet*
487	Kelly, Patk. J., clerk	46y	W	Ire.	08 NOV 1870	Mt. Olivet
006	Kelly, Patrick	40y	W	Ire.	04 APR 1855	St. Peters
087	Kelly, Patrick, laborer	45y	W	Ire.	14 AUG 1857	St. Patricks
589	Kelly, Peter, watchman	37y	W	Ire.	29 MAR 1872	Mt. Olivet
243	Kelly, Robert	4m	W	D.C.	21 NOV 1866	Mt. Olivet
469	Kelly, Thomas J.	19y	W	D.C.	09 AUG 1870	Mt. Olivet
111	Kelly, Thos. Johnston	3y	W	D.C.	14 APR 1858	Glenwood
153	Kelly, William	2m	W	D.C.	08 JUL 1859	Glenwood
290	Kelly, William M., detective	31y	W	D.C.	18 JAN 1868	Glenwood
210	Kelly, [blank]				24 JAN 1866	Congressional
152	Kelly, [blank]	1y	W	D.C.	15 JUN 1859	Mt. Olivet
668	Kelpy, Bernard	1m	W	U.S.	23 FEB 1873	Congressional
165	Kelsy, James, blacksmith	55y	W	Ire.	15 NOV 1859	
395	Kemdry, Mary	29y	W	Ire.	13 JUN 1869	Mt. Olivet
669	Kemp, Aug., laborer	20y	C	U.S.	08 FEB 1873	
242	Kemp, Charles	1y	W	N.C.	28 OCT 1866	Methodist
554	Kemp, Lizzie	7y	W	D.C.	20 JAN 1872	Mt. Olivet
290	Kemp, [torn]	2y	C	D.C.	— JAN 1868	Mt. Olivet
747	Kemper, Elizabeth	70y	W	U.S.	12 FEB 1874	Va.
428	Kendall, Amos, Hon.	80y	W	Mass.	12 NOV 1869	Glenwood
754	Kendall, George M., clerk	87y	W	U.S.	08 MAR 1874	Congressional
420	Kendall, Ida	22y	W		07 OCT 1869	Olk Hill
377	Kendall, Mary Ellen	2y	C	D.C.	02 FEB 1869	Harmony
423	Kendrick, Catharine	35y	W	N.Y.	12 OCT 1869	Washington Asylum
747	Kene, Mary	46y	W	Ire.	12 FEB 1874	Mt. Olivet
301	Kene, Sarah	110y	C	Va.	17 MAR 1868	Young Mens
727	Kenedy, Ann, infant of	P.B.	W	D.C.	24 OCT 1873	
155	Kenedy, Eleanor	28y	W	Ire.	29 JUL 1859	Washington Asylum
395	Kenedy, Francis E.	1m	W		11 JUN 1869	Glenwood
397	Kenedy, Henry C.	7m	W	D.C.	26 JUN 1869	Clemot?
662	Kenedy, Maggie	20y	W	U.S.	03 JAN 1873	Small Pox
188	Kenedy, Mary I.	11y	W	Ire.	02 AUG 1860	Washington Asylum
185	Kenedy, Thomas	4y	W	D.C.	21 JUL 1860	Washington Asylum
020	Kenedy, [blank]	14m	W	D.C.	05 AUG 1855	St. Patricks
725	Kenn, Charles H., messenger	40y	W	U.S.	23 OCT 1873	Glenwood
031	Kenna, Caroline, servant	28y	C	Va.	07 DEC 1855	Young Mens
467	Kennaugh, Sarah, lady	74y	W	D.C.	13 JUL 1870	Congressional
111	Kennedy, Henry, laborer	45y	W	Eng.	10 APR 1858	St. Patricks
675	Kennedy, Jas. C.	49y	W	U.S.	25 MAR 1873	Albany, N.Y.
243	Kennedy, John	12d	W	D.C.	29 NOV 1866	Mt. Olivet
193	Kennedy, John, laborer	40y	W	Ire.	18 NOV 1860	Mt. Olivet
019	Kennedy, Julia	11m	W	D.C.	29 AUG 1855	St. Patricks
476	Kennedy, Mary E.	4y	W	D.C.	05 SEP 1870	Mt. Olivet
400	Kennedy, Mary, infant of	Still	W		04 JUL 1869	Congressional
613	Kennedy, Mary J.	1y	W	U.S.	26 JUL 1872	
249	Kennedy, Thomas	21y	W	D.C.	05 JAN 1867	Mt. Olivet
138	Kennedy, William, laborer	35y	W	Ire.	28 JAN 1859	Mt. Olivet

District of Columbia Interments (Index to Deaths), 1855-1874

Page	Name	Age	Race	Birth	Death Date	Burial Ground
334	Kennedy, Winfield E.	5m	W	D.C.	16 JUL 1868	Glenwood
285	Kennedy, Wm. H.	1y	W	D.C.	10 DEC 1867	Glenwood
287	Kenner, Clarissa		C		c.24 DEC 1867	Alms House
524	Kenney, Anna M.		W	D.C.	26 JUN 1871	Glenwood
592	Kenney, Julius F.	5m	W	D.C.	21 APR 1872	
259	Kenney, Mary	7m	W		01 APR 1867	Ft. Hamilton, N.Y.
127	Kenney, Mathew, laborer	60y	W	Ire.	11 SEP 1858	
525	Kennon, J.C.W., Dr.	37y	W	U.S.	28 JUN 1871	Ohio
713	Kenny, Chas. S., cigar maker	46y	W	N.J.	26 AUG 1873	Congressional
645	Kenny, Peter	60y	W	Ire.	26 DEC 1872	Mt. Olivet
598	Kensy, Lucy	54y	C	U.S.	06 MAY 1872	Unknown
335b	Kent, Henry	4m	B		04 JUL 1868	Washington Asylum
404	Kent, Martha	3m	C		31 JUL 1869	Potters Field
689	Kent, Simon	21y	C	U.S.	27 MAY 1873	Washington Asylum
691	Kentler, Florence	2y	W	U.S.	09 MAY 1873	Small Pox*
286	Keoble, Geo.	3y	W	D.C.	22 DEC 1867	German Catholic
766	Keogh, Thomas, bookbinder	40y	W	Ire.	11 MAY 1874	Congressional
661	Keohler, George, bricklayer	31y	W	Ger.	23 JAN 1873	
213	Keough, Charles	2d	W		03 FEB 1866	Mt. Olivet
188	Kepler, John George	10m	W	D.C.	25 AUG 1860	German Catholic
077	Keppler, Caroline	36y	W	Ger.	03 MAY 1857	St. Marys
464	Keppler, Margaret	80y	W	Ger.	21 JUL 1870	Mt. Olivet
435	Keppler, Marion Tyler	10m	W		17 JAN 1870	Congressional
234	Ker, A.A. [died at Marietta]				06 SEP 1866	Glenwood
534	Ker, Mary C., lady	25y	W	D.C.	28 AUG 1871	Glenwood
008	Ker, Wm. W.S., hatter	28y	W		06 MAY 1855	Congressional
022	Keramer, C.H.	1y	W	D.C.*	01 AUG 1855	German Evangelic
010	Kerby, Cornelia Rosiline	1y		D.C.	24 JUN 1855	Congressional
083	Kerby, [blank]	1m	W		17 JUL 1857	Western
441	Kercher, Cora	4d	W		16 FEB 1870	Prospect Hill
457	Kercheval, Willis A., gentleman	64y	W	Va.	08 JUN 1870	Glenwood
673	Kericher, Annie V.	2y	W	U.S.	11 MAR 1873	Glenwood
220	Keridan, Cornelius	8m	W	D.C.	03 MAY 1866	Mt. Olivet
209	Kermon, Mary C.H.	22y	W	Md.	04 JAN 1866	Congressional
020	Kern, Frank	10m	W		31 AUG 1855	Glenwood
228	Kern, George, clerk	48y	W	Scot.	16 JUL 1866	Glenwood
731	Kern, Margaret E.	71y	W	U.S.	19 NOV 1873	Philadelphia, Pa.
210	Kern, William, restaurant	36y	W	Fra.	27 JAN 1866	Prospect Hill
014	Kernelly, Mary	9m	W	D.C.	25 JUL 1855	St. Patricks
529	Kerner, Nellie	1y	W	D.C.	27 JUL 1871	
740	Kernes, Adolph L., policeman	42y	W	Ger.	03 JAN 1874	
258	Kerney, Mary	7m	W	D.C.	01 APR 1867	Ft. Hamilton, N.Y.
434	Kerper, Anetta G.	4y	W		16 JAN 1870	Congressional
434	Kerper, Emma Vida	8m	W		09 JAN 1870	Congressional
304	Kerr, Chas. H. & Alice, child of	Still	W	D.C.	05 MAR 1868	Congressional
248	Kerr, Elizabeth	6y	W	D.C.	03 DEC 1866	Mt. Olivet
163	Kerr, James D., clerk	65y	W	Va.*	10 OCT 1859	Alexandria, Va.
349	Kerr, John	67y	W	Va.	21 SEP 1868	Mt. Olivet
310	Kerr, John, child of	Still	W		c.14 APR 1868	Mt. Olivet
773	Kerr, Julia A.	74y	W	N.S.	28 JUN 1874	Alexandria, Va.
400	Kerr, Peter, carpenter	43y	W	Ire.	05 JUL 1869	Mt. Olivet
718	Kerr, Thos. Peter	5y	W	D.C.	14 SEP 1873	Mt. Olivet
425	Kerr, Virginia Ellen	1y	W	D.C.	11 NOV 1869	Congressional
313	Kerregan, Bernard	3m	W		03 MAY 1868	Mt. Olivet
323	Kerrigan, Bridget	1y	W	D.C.	28 JUL 1868	Mt. Olivet
528	Kersey, Mary Jane	42y	W	U.S.	19 JUL 1871	Congressional*
127	Kershaw, Newton	1y	W	D.C.	14 SEP 1858	Congressional
385	Kershaw, [blank]	6d	W	D.C.	04 APR 1869	Congressional

District of Columbia Interments (Index to Deaths), 1855-1874

Page	Name	Age	Race	Birth	Death Date	Burial Ground
581	Kerthly, Eva	4y	W	D.C.	16 FEB 1872	Beckett's
249	Kertis, Charles		C	Va.	22 JAN 1867	Ebenezer
422	Keslar, Mary Elizabeth, servant	18y	C		04 OCT 1869	Mt. Olivet
252	Kesler, Mary Margaret	2m	W	D.C.	18 FEB 1867	
231	Kessler, George, laborer	16y	W	D.C.*	14 AUG 1866	Alms House
209	Kessler, Hattie	25y	W	Ger.	08 JAN 1866	
453	Ketchum, Eleanor J., clerk Treas.	23y		Berm.	22 MAY 1870	Harmony
231	Ketchum, Rebecca Ord		W		03 AUG 1866	Rock Creek
488	Kettler, Henry F.	1y	W		10 NOV 1870	Prospect Hill
675	Keuber, Geo. H.	4m	W	U.S.	25 MAR 1873	
092	Keuran, Ellen	58y	W		23 SEP 1857	St. Patricks
275	Key, Caroline	56y	C	D.C.	16 SEP 1867	Mt. Olivet
003	Key, Ellen	33y	W	D.C.	20 FEB 1855	Baltimore, Md.
167	Key, G.	Still	W	D.C.	12 DEC 1859	St. Peters
727	Key, Mary A.	33y	B	U.S.	31 OCT 1873	Congressional
142	Key, Philip Barton, lawyer	39y	W	D.C.	27 FEB 1859	Baltimore, Md.
327	Keyes, Juliette C., Mrs.	28y	W	Me.	27 JUL 1868	Franklin Co., Me.
482	Keyley, Morris	1y	W	D.C.	12 OCT 1870	Mt. Olivet
088	Keynedy, [blank]	6y	C		22 AUG 1857	St. Patricks
387	Keys, Bradley, laborer	18y	C	Va.	23 APR 1869	Beckett's
766	Keys, Fannie	unk.	C	U.S.	18 MAY 1874	Young Mens
331	Keys, Fanny	50y	C	Md.	17 JUL 1868	Freedmen's Hospital
320	Keys, Frank	5m	C	D.C.	20 JUN 1868	Young Mens
773	Keys, John	5m	C	U.S.	03 JUN 1874	Young Mens
082	Keys, Kate E.	4m	W	D.C.	08 JUL 1857	Glenwood
041	Keys, Michael, laborer	65y	W	Ire.	04 APR 1856	St. Patricks
665	Keys, Stephen	27y	C	U.S.	26 JAN 1873	Small Pox*
621	Keys, [blank]	8h	W	U.S.	28 AUG 1872	
366	Keyser, Benjamin F., watchmaker	26y	W	Pa.	19 DEC 1868	Glenwood
445	Keyser, Charles M., clerk	29y	W	Pa.	20 MAR 1870	Glenwood
694	Keyser, Harry Nelson	12h	W		11 JUN 1873	Martinsburg, W.Va.
353	Keyser, Peter	85y	C		02 SEP 1868	Freedmen's Hospital
035	Keyworth, Robert, jeweller	61y	W	Eng.	18 FEB 1856	Congressional
285	Kibbey, Isabella	20y	W	D.C.	16 DEC 1867	Congressional*
754	Kibby, Charles	1d	W	U.S.	15 MAR 1874	Congressional*
144	Kiddie, A.J., stone cutter	41y	W	Mass.	18 MAR 1859	Congressional
320	Kidney, Harriet	1y	W	Wales	14 JUN 1868	Mt. Olivet
441	Kidrick, Ida	2y	C		10 FEB 1870	
008	Kidwell, Allison	50y	W	Md.	12 MAY 1855	Congressional
323	Kidwell, Charles	5m	W	Amer.	22 JUL 1868	Oak Hill
118	Kidwell, Elijah, laborer	63y	W	Md.	22 JUN 1858	Congressional
011	Kidwell, Elizabeth	31y	W	Md.	15 JUN 1855	Ebenezer
683	Kidwell, Frank	23y	W	U.S.	15 APR 1873	Small Pox
523	Kidwell, Guy	11m	W	Md.	19 JUN 1871	Methodist
625	Kidwell, Ira	6m	W	U.S.	12 SEP 1872	
670	Kidwell, John	58y	C	U.S.	07 FEB 1873	Small Pox*
326	Kidwell, John F.	2y	W	D.C.	29 JUL 1868	Congressional
639	Kidwell, Maria	6m	C	U.S.	12 DEC 1872	Small Pox*
101	Kidwell, Martha	24y	W	D.C.	02 JAN 1858	Congressional
139	Kidwell, Mary F.	43y	W		29 JAN 1859	Oak Hill*
726	Kidwell, Maud	21d	W	U.S.	25 OCT 1873	Methodist
332	Kidwell, Thomas	45y	W	D.C.	17 JUL 1868	Alms House
335a	Kidwell, Thomas				17 JUL 1868	Washington Asylum
332	Kiedly, Harriet	59y	C	Va.	17 JUL 1868	Young Mens
469	Kief, Johanna M.	45y	W	Ire.	09 AUG 1870	Mt. Olivet
168	Kiegne, Connell	7m	W	D.C.	31 DEC 1859	German Catholic
365	Kiernan, Charles	66y	W	Ire.	25 DEC 1868	Mt. Olivet
288	Kietzer, John	3y	W	Md.	19 DEC 1867	Glenwood

Page	Name	Age	Race	Birth	Death Date	Burial Ground
494	Kilafoyle, Mary	20y	W	D.C.*	20 DEC 1870	Mt. Olivet
607	Kilby, Thomas	9y	W	D.C.	27 JUN 1872	Congressional*
289	Kile, Thomas, driver	23y	C	Va.	07 JAN 1868	Young Mens
371	Killay, Morris, soldier	40y	W	Ire.	22 JAN 1869	Mt. Olivet
743	Killen, Susan, clerk Treas.	22y	W	Ire.	26 JAN 1874	Mt. Olivet
760	Killian, John	60y	W	Ger.	03 APR 1874	
159	Killian, Marianna	49y	W	Switz.	31 AUG 1859	Prospect Hill
766	Killigan, Catharine	32y	W	Ire.	28 MAY 1874	Mt. Olivet
526	Killman, Josephine	7m	W	D.C.	06 JUL 1871	Congressional
676	Killoss, Ham	28y	C	U.S.	01 MAR 1873	Small Pox
260	Kilmartin, Bridget	26y	W	Ire.	31 MAY 1867	Mt. Olivet
551	Kilroy, Edw.	2y	W	D.C.	— DEC 1871	Mt. Olivet
329	Kilroy, Peter	5m	W	D.C.	06 JUL 1868	Mt. Olivet
540	Kilroy, Thomas	6y	W	D.C.	04 OCT 1871	Mt. Olivet
548	Kilsinger, Andrew, shoemaker	23y	W	Ger.	12 DEC 1871	German
434	Kilsinger, Barbara	62y	W	Ger.	02 JAN 1870	German Catholic
718	Kimball, John	51y	W	N.H.	09 SEP 1873	Washington Asylum
263	Kimball, Mary Hope	3m	W	D.C.	16 JUN 1867	Me.
773	Kimberly, Mrs., dress maker	54y	W	U.S.	26 JUN 1874	Potters Field
660	Kimbro, Elizabeth V.	60y	W	U.S.	18 JAN 1873	Nashville, Tenn.
547	Kimerly, Maggie	1y	W	D.C.	08 DEC 1871	Mt. Olivet
689	Kimmel, Edgar M.	9m	W	U.S.	28 MAY 1873	Congressional
325	Kimmell, Abraham F., hotel kpr.	55y	W	Pa.	17 JUL 1868	Congressional
782	Kimmell, Laura E.	50y	W	U.S.	14 JUL 1874	Glenwood
532	Kimmell, Rosa		W	D.C.	c.17 AUG 1871	Glenwood
330	Kinaly, W.H.	6m	W	D.C.	10 JUL 1868	Mt. Olivet
712	Kindrick, Daniel	4y	W	Va.	18 AUG 1873	Congressional*
668	King, Agnes	2y	W	U.S.	18 FEB 1873	Mt. Olivet
225	King, Albert F.	2y	C	D.C.	23 JUN 1866	Harmony
721	King, Andrew	1y	C	D.C.	30 SEP 1873	
366	King, Anna	45y	C	Md.	03 DEC 1868	
383	King, Belle	1m	W	D.C.	01 MAR 1869	Washington Asylum
096	King, Catharine	70y	W	Va.	11 NOV 1857	Congressional
063	King, Catharine W.	74y	W	Md.	24 NOV 1856	Oak Hill
214	King, Catherine	2m	W		11 MAR 1866	Mt. Olivet
013	King, Charles	12d	W	D.C.	05 JUL 1855	Congressional
295	King, Charles A., child of	Still	W		10 FEB 1868	Congressional
112	King, Charles, servant	23y	C	Md.	22 APR 1858	Washington Asylum
736	King, Chas. F.	23d	W	U.S.	18 DEC 1873	
153	King, Clarence	4y	W	D.C.	10 JUL 1859	Oak Hill
458	King, E.	59y	W	Eng.	20 JUN 1870	Potters Field
618	King, Edwd.	75y	C	U.S.	26 AUG 1872	Washington Asylum
241	King, Eliza	55y	C	D.C.	29 OCT 1866	Holmead
138	King, Elizabeth	20y	W	D.C.	29 JAN 1859	Methodist, East
760	King, Emma M.	6m	W	U.S.	29 APR 1874	Rock Creek
197	King, Enoch	34y	W		20 JAN 1861	Western
687	King, Henry	54y	W	Me.	07 MAY 1873	Saco, Me.
317	King, Henry Clinton	10m	W		18 JUN 1868	Glenwood
090	King, Ida	4m	W	D.C.	11 SEP 1857	St. Patricks
594	King, Ida Moffitt	1y	W	D.C.	28 APR 1872	Congressional
027	King, Ignatius	28y	W		04 OCT 1855	St. Matthews
742	King, J. & L., infant of	1d	C	U.S.	20 JAN 1874	
725	King, Jacob, laborer	19y	W	Md.	19 OCT 1873	Prospect Hill
596	King, James	33y	W	D.C.	06 APR 1872	Glenwood
326	King, James K.	21d	W	D.C.	13 JUL 1868	Congressional
646	King, James L.	12m	W	U.S.	21 DEC 1872	Glenwood
782	King, Jas. B., printer	26y	W	U.S.	08 JUL 1874	Mt. Olivet
048	King, John	76y	W	Ire.	04 JUN 1856	

District of Columbia Interments (Index to Deaths), 1855-1874

Page	Name	Age	Race	Birth	Death Date	Burial Ground
260	King, John	4m	C		24 MAY 1867	Young Mens
589	King, John, architect	84y	W	Va.	27 MAR 1872	Oak Hill
309	King, John Bernadine	6m	W	D.C.	20 APR 1868	Baltimore, Md.
385	King, John, carpenter	56y	W	Md.	13 APR 1869	Congressional
302	King, Joseph		C		14 MAR 1868	Alms House
191	King, Julia		C		16 OCT 1860	Mt. Olivet
429	King, Julia V.	34y	W		10 DEC 1869	Congressional
039	King, Landon	11m	W	D.C.	01 MAR 1856	Congressional
713	King, Lewis B.	30y	W	D.C.	23 AUG 1873	Mt. Olivet
434	King, Lilly	½d	W		17 JAN 1870	Methodist
253	King, Margaret, storekeeper	52y	W	Ire.	11 FEB 1867	Alms House
324	King, Martin, clerk	64y	W	Md.	07 JUL 1868	Mt. Olivet
110	King, Mary	32y	W	D.C.	08 APR 1858	Oak Hill
589	King, Mary	14y	W	D.C.	27 MAR 1872	Rock Creek
066	King, Mary Ann, lady	61y	W	Del.	17 DEC 1856	Western
369	King, Mary E.	76y	W	Amer.	30 JAN 1869	Congressional
740	King, Mary E.	30y	W	U.S.	05 JAN 1874	Congressional*
360	King, Mary Elizabeth	74y	W	U.S.	07 NOV 1868	Oak Hill
294	King, Mary Virginia	13d	W	D.C.	21 FEB 1868	Congressional
782	King, Nancy C.	45y	C	U.S.	17 JUL 1874	
071	King, Nancy, child of		W	D.C.	21 FEB 1857	Congressional
634	King, Pat. H.	52y	W	U.S.	15 OCT 1872	
201	King, Priscilla, washerwoman	50y	C	D.C.	10 MAR 1861	Foundry
295	King, Rachael, Mrs.		W		10 FEB 1868	Congressional
624	King, Raechal	35y	C	U.S.	24 SEP 1872	
454a	King, Robert	39y	W	D.C.	03 MAY 1870	Washington Asylum
516	King, Saml. J.	1m	W		12 MAR 1871	Congressional
499	King, Saml. L.	5y	W	D.C.	09 JAN 1871	Congressional
754	King, Sarah	25y	C	U.S.	13 MAR 1874	
199	King, Sarah	30y	W	D.C.	08 FEB 1861	Congressional
228	King, Sarah	18d	C	D.C.	11 JUL 1866	Mt. Olivet
128	King, Sarah E.	1y	W	D.C.	18 SEP 1858	Md.
022	King, Sarah R. [of John]	6m	W	D.C.	27 AUG 1855	Congressional
725	King, Susan, twin of	P.B.	M	D.C.	16 OCT 1873	Washington
725	King, Susan, twin of	P.B.	M	D.C.	16 OCT 1873	Washington
293	King, W.C. O'Neal	6y	W	D.C.*	04 MAR 1868	Vault
731	King, Webster E.	3m	W	U.S.	20 NOV 1873	Salem, Md.
025	King, William	16y	W	D.C.	06 SEP 1855	St. Patricks
093	King, Wm., child of		W	D.C.	06 OCT 1857	Rock Creek
275	King, Wm. H., farmer	1y	W	D.C.	20 SEP 1867	Congressional
354	King, Wm. T., tinner	23y	W	Md.	25 OCT 1868	Congressional
215	King, Wm. Whetcroft, clerk	70y	W	Md.	18 MAR 1866	Oak Hill
005	King, [blank]	4m	W	D.C.	12 MAR 1855	Catholic, Georgetown
029	King, [blank]		W		10 NOV 1855	St. Patricks
090	King, [blank]	10d	C		09 SEP 1857	Western
034	King, [blank]	45y	C		07 JAN 1856	Western
047	Kingsbury, J.J.B., gentleman	57y	W	Conn.	26 JUN 1856	Congressional
155	Kingsford, Edward, Rev.	71y	W	Eng.	27 JUL 1859	Glenwood
736	Kinner, John, laborer	40y	C	U.S.	19 DEC 1873	Washington Asylum
350	Kinner, Patty, servant	70y	C	Va.	01 SEP 1868	Young Mens
662	Kinney, Andrew H., clerk	29y	W		25 JAN 1873	
639	Kinney, Johnson	3y	C	U.S.	12 DEC 1872	Small Pox*
636	Kinney, [blank]	8d	W	U.S.	18 NOV 1872	
210	Kinsey, Benj. S., Hon.	58y	W	Va.*	— JAN 1866	Alexandria, Va.
310	Kinsley, William, bricklayer	40y	W	Ire.	04 APR 1868	Mt. Olivet
622a	Kinslow, Chas.	2y	W	U.S.	04 AUG 1872	Congressional*
101	Kinslow, Mary M.	3m	W	D.C.	02 JAN 1858	St. Peters
017	Kinsy, Saml., officer USA	20y	W	Pa.	14 JUL 1855	Philadelphia, Pa.

Page	Name	Age	Race	Birth	Death Date	Burial Ground
275	Kipp, Caleb	29y	W	N.Y.	15 SEP 1867	Western
481	Kipp, Ezra, wheelwright	63y	W	N.Y.	09 OCT 1870	N.Y. City
533	Kirby, Eliza May	2m	W	D.C.	19 AUG 1871	Glenwood
457	Kirby, Ernest Albert	4m	W	D.C.	24 JUN 1870	Glenwood
400	Kirby, Fayette F., notary public	58y	W	Amer.	15 JUL 1869	Glenwood
555	Kirby, George	2y	W	D.C.	26 JAN 1872	Glenwood
535	Kirby, George H.	1y	W	Md.	01 SEP 1871	Glenwood
312	Kirby, Harry B.	4m	W	Pa.	22 MAY 1868	Glenwood
401	Kirby, Kate	1y	W		10 JUL 1869	Mt. Olivet
706	Kirby, Thomas, laborer	60y	W	Ire.	14 JUL 1873	
555	Kirby, Willie	2y	W	D.C.	29 JAN 1872	Glenwood
109	Kirk, Anna P.J.	5y	W	D.C.	20 MAR 1858	Congressional
727	Kirk, James, paver	60y	W	Scot.	20 OCT 1873	
729	Kirk, Mary	62y	W	Eng.	08 NOV 1873	Mt. Olivet
019	Kirk, Mary E.	13y	W	D.C.	19 AUG 1855	Congressional
642	Kirk, Mary E.	22y	W	U.S.	04 DEC 1872	Congressional
020	Kirk, Sidney L.	4m	W	D.C.	17 AUG 1855	Congressional
506	Kirker, James M., clerk	20y	W	Ohio	25 FEB 1871	Congressional
019	Kirkhon, Watson, stone cutter	49y	W	Scot.	11 AUG 1855	Congressional
513	Kirkland, Caroline	74y	W	Conn.	11 MAR 1871	Conn.
749	Kirkman, Lavinia	1y	C	U.S.	27 FEB 1874	Glenwood
308	Kirkpatrick, John A., stone cutter	52y	W	Ire.	19 APR 1868	Mt. Olivet
703	Kirkwood, Ellen	72y	W	Md.	15 JUL 1873	
290	Kirsch, Caroline	34y	W	Ger.	09 JAN 1868	Mt. Olivet
454a	Kirtley, Peggy, pauper	45y	C	Va.	04 MAY 1870	Washington Asylum
625	Kitly, Milly	45y	C	U.S.	02 SEP 1872	
420	Klakring, Arthur	3y	W		19 OCT 1869	Glenwood
141	Kleiber, Erskine	8y	W	D.C.	23 FEB 1859	Congressional
140	Kleiber, Francis H., painter	34y	W	D.C.	08 FEB 1859	Congressional
419	Kleiber, Mary Ann	54y	W		16 OCT 1869	Congressional
673	Kleindiensey, Jos. W., grocer	26y	W	U.S.	11 MAR 1873	St. Marys
080	Kleindienst, John A.	10m	W	Va.*	24 JUN 1857	St. Peters
074	Kleinhause, Wm.	8y	W	D.C.	30 MAR 1857	Methodist
122	Kleiss, Daniel	55y	W	Ger.	21 JUL 1858	St. Peters
712	Klenk, Leonard, butcher	23y	W	Ger.	20 AUG 1873	Prospect Hill
229	Kline, Sarah M.	2m	W	D.C.	25 JUL 1866	Congressional
246	Klinediest, Aloysius	17y	W	D.C.	20 DEC 1866	St. Marys
632	Klinkett, Wm.	9y	C	U.S.	11 OCT 1872	
161	Kloeppinger, C., baker	34y	W	Ger.	09 SEP 1859	Prospect Hill
135	Kloeppinger, Frederick C.	3m	W	D.C.	02 DEC 1858	German
088	Klopfer, Florence A.	1m	W	D.C.	24 AUG 1857	Congressional
113	Klopfer, Martha I.	10m	W	Md.	06 MAY 1858	Glenwood
174	Klopfer, Rachael	69y	W	Md.	10 MAR 1860	Glenwood
111	Klopper, Chas. Hansin	4y	W	D.C.	20 APR 1858	Glenwood
112	Klopper, Saml. Aug.	8y	W	D.C.	26 APR 1858	Glenwood
062	Klotz, A. Rebecca	20y	W	D.C.	07 NOV 1856	Glenwood
411	Klotz, August L.	9m	W	D.C.	10 AUG 1869	Glenwood
013	Klotz, Charles	8m	W	Eng.	01 JUL 1855	German Evangelic
102	Klotz, Frederick		W		25 JAN 1858	Glenwood
607	Klotzbach, Annie	3m	W	D.C.	30 JUN 1872	St. Marys
229	Klug, John	5d	W	D.C.	18 JUL 1866	Mt. Olivet
587	Klug, Peter	8y	W	U.S.	23 MAR 1872	
532	Klug, Wm.	4y	W	D.C.	08 AUG 1871	German
471	Knall, Gertrude	1y	W	D.C.	06 AUG 1870	German Catholic
092	Knapp, Gabriel	36y	W	Ger.	28 SEP 1857	St. Patricks
747	Kneese, C.	3d	W	U.S.	15 FEB 1874	Prospect Hill
092	Knight, Eliza	7m	W	D.C.	26 SEP 1857	St. Patricks
476	Knight, Howard M.	11y	W	Md.	07 SEP 1870	Glenwood

Page	Name	Age	Race	Birth	Death Date	Burial Ground
499	Knight, Jas. T., engraver	30y	W	N.J.	24 JAN 1871	Congressional
259	Knight, Jennie C.	4y	W	D.C.	25 APR 1867	Oak Hill
782	Knight, Lilly	2m	W	U.S.	09 JUL 1874	
079	Knight, William	17y	W	Md.	07 JUN 1857	Glenwood
063	Knight, Wm. F., carpenter	47y	W	Md.	27 NOV 1856	Glenwood
341	Knight, Wm. Henry	1m	W	D.C.	12 AUG 1868	Congressional
010	Knight, [blank]	30y	W	Ire.	16 JUN 1855	Poor House
532	Knoles, Mr.		W	D.C.	10 AUG 1871	Oak Hill
007	Knoll, F., musician	51y	W	Ger.	01 MAY 1855	German
482	Knoll, Gotthrod, butcher	22y	W	Ger.	11 OCT 1870	Prospect Hill
366	Knoll, John	3y	W	Ger.	12 DEC 1868	German Catholic
773	Knoors, Henry, child of	1d	W	U.S.	01 JUN 1874	Prospect Hill
687	Knorr, Charles	9m	W	U.S.	01 MAY 1873	Glenwood
257	Knott, Louis J., senate page	15y	W	D.C.	07 MAR 1867	Mt. Olivet
093	Knott, Mary	43y	W	Md.	12 OCT 1857	St. Peters
600	Knott, W.R.	1y	W	U.S.	06 MAY 1872	Cemetery
595	Knoules, Jos. R.	12y	W	D.C.	10 APR 1872	
727	Knowblock, H.	2m	W	U.S.	31 OCT 1873	Prospect Hill
452	Knowlden, Jno. F.	4m	W	D.C.	23 APR 1870	Washington Asylum
273	Knowles, Anna, housekeeper	40y	W	Ire.	16 SEP 1867	Mt. Olivet
782	Knowles, Janett	77y	W	U.S.	01 JUL 1874	Oak Hill
472	Knowles, Josephine	10m	W	D.C.	19 AUG 1870	Mt. Olivet
760	Knowles, Robt. M.	54y	W	Eng.	20 APR 1874	Baltimore, Md.
616	Knowles, Wm., carpenter	86y	W	U.S.	02 JUL 1872	Oak Hill*
730	Knowlton, James W., corresp.	30y	W	U.S.	12 NOV 1873	Oak Hill
437	Knox, Anna S.	6m	W		15 JAN 1870	Glenwood
690	Knox, George A.	11m	C	U.S.	28 MAY 1873	Small Pox
666	Knox, Mary	3y	C	U.S.	04 FEB 1873	Washington Asylum
533	Knox, Mary Ann	36y	W	Ire.	26 AUG 1871	Mt. Olivet
582	Knox, Patrick	1y	W	D.C.	24 FEB 1872	Mt. Olivet
024	Knox, Simon B.	35y	W	Va.	19 SEP 1855	Congressional
135	Koch, Begina M.	2y	W	D.C.	16 DEC 1858	Glenwood
697	Koch, Caroline, seamstress	65y	W	Ger.	27 JUN 1873	Prospect Hill
720	Koch, George, conductor	23y	W	Ger.	25 SEP 1873	St. Marys
645	Koch, Johanna L.	6y	W		26 DEC 1872	Congressional
046	Kock, Mary E.	6y	W	D.C.	12 JUN 1856	Ebenezer
754	Koechling, Amelia T.	28y	W	U.S.	08 MAR 1874	Glenwood
469	Koechling, Hy. C.A.W.	19d	W	D.C.	05 AUG 1870	Glenwood
041	Koehler, Cathe. C.	6m	W	D.C.	03 APR 1856	Congressional
297	Koehler, Emma	21y	W	Pa.	17 FEB 1868	Glenwood
766	Koeiver, Kattie	1y	W	U.S.	24 MAY 1874	Glenwood
543	Koenig, John M.	2m	W	D.C.	29 OCT 1871	Congressional
024	Koestner, Rosa E.	21d	W	D.C.	09 SEP 1855	
347	Koffman, C.M.O.	1y	W		05 SEP 1868	Congressional
501	Kohand, Johanna, chambermaid		W	Ire.	23 JAN 1871	Mt. Olivet
049	Kohrman, Casper	37y	W	Ger.	04 JUL 1856	German
419	Kolb, Adolphine	19y	W	Prus.	31 OCT 1869	Prospect Hill
513	Kolb, Jacob, farmer	41y	W	Ger.	09 MAR 1871	Glenwood
144	Kolb, William	7y	W	Va.	17 MAR 1859	Congressional
381	Kolb, William	10m	W	D.C.	28 MAR 1869	German Catholic
045	Kolgate, Harvey, farmer	53y	W		22 MAY 1856	Congressional
279	Kolipenski, Mrs.	45y	W		12 OCT 1867	German Catholic
545	Koltman, [blank]	Still	W	D.C.	21 NOV 1871	Prospect Hill
274	Kondrup, George Alexander	11m	W	D.C.	09 SEP 1867	Congressional
112	Konns, Catharine A.	9m	W		26 APR 1858	St. Patricks
403	Kons, Henry George Lewis	9m	W	D.C.	21 JUL 1869	German Catholic
310	Koockogg, Frank	1m	W	D.C.	29 APR 1868	Glenwood
216	Koogen, Mrs., infant of	Still	W	D.C.	27 MAR 1866	Mt. Olivet

Page	Name	Age	Race	Birth	Death Date	Burial Ground
216	Koogen, Mrs., infant of	Still	W	D.C.	27 MAR 1866	Mt. Olivet
283	Ko_o_h, Elizabeth	73y	W	Prus.	20 NOV 1867	Prospect Hill
332	Kook, Millie Leonore	7m	W	D.C.	17 JUL 1868	Mt. Pleasant
067	Koones, David, clerk	72y	W	Md.	30 DEC 1856	Congressional
174	Koones, Rebecca W.	60y	W	Va.	01 MAR 1860	Alexandria, Va.
425	Koons, Cecilia C.	45y	W	D.C.	13 NOV 1869	Congressional
669	Koppleman, Henry	28y	W	U.S.	02 FEB 1873	
274	Korff, Mary Louisa	20y	W	D.C.	01 SEP 1867	Congressional
632	Korhammer, Carl	13d	W	U.S.	28 OCT 1872	
290	Korts, Jefferson B., merchant	43y	W	N.Y.	05 JAN 1868	Congressional
687	Kosack, Frederick W.	3y	W	D.C.	02 MAY 1873	
149	Koscialowski, Napoleon, draughtsman	43y	W	Pol.	29 MAY 1859	Glenwood
152	Kossuth, Mary A.	4m	W	D.C.	26 JUN 1859	Washington Asylum
704	Kotzman, Frederick	11m	W	D.C.	10 JUL 1873	Prospect Hill
172	Kough, Jane	72y	W	Ire.	10 FEB 1860	Mt. Olivet
029	Kowles, John	54y	W	N.J.	03 NOV 1855	Methodist, Georgetown
233	Kraft, John	48y	W		31 AUG 1866	
598	Kraft, Mary L.	2m	W	U.S.	14 MAY 1872	Glenwood
553	Kraft, Philip, blacksmith	44y	W	Ger.	10 JAN 1872	Prospect Hill
414	Kramer, Barbara	36y	W	Ger.	28 SEP 1869	Washington Hebrew
612	Kramer, John	3m	W	U.S.	27 JUL 1872	
240	Krantze, Mary	21y	W	Ire.	15 OCT 1866	Mt. Olivet
411	Krauch, Louis Chas., wine merchant	48y	W	Ger.	24 AUG 1869	Prospect Hill
529	Kraus, Elisabeth H.	22y	W	Ger.	24 JUL 1871	Prospect Hill
623	Krause, Chris.	2y	W	U.S.	03 JUL 1872	Holy Rood
147	Kreamer, Chas. Henry	8y	W	D.C.	29 APR 1859	Holmead
296	Kreater, Marie	3m	W	D.C.	29 FEB 1868	Glenwood
351	Kredter, Katharina	4y	W	D.C.	13 SEP 1868	Glenwood
128	Kres, Barbry	9y	W		19 SEP 1858	German Catholic
658	Krey, Charles, tailor	44y	W	Ger.	08 JAN 1873	Prospect Hill
098	Krey, Lotta	25y	W	Ger.	04 DEC 1857	German
478	Krey, Wm. C.	11m	W	D.C.	10 SEP 1870	Prospect Hill
329	Krichelt, Helen Cecilia	9m	W	D.C.	09 JUL 1868	Mt. Olivet*
688	Krielecke, Anna E.G.	9y	W	U.S.	20 MAY 1873	Glenwood
365	Krock, Caroline	14y	C	Va.	21 DEC 1868	Young Mens
140	Krofft, Christopher, messenger	65y	W	Ger.	07 FEB 1859	Glenwood
425	Kroft, [blank]	1y	W	D.C.	12 NOV 1869	Congressional
773	Krohr, Aloysius	4m	W	U.S.	19 JUN 1874	Mt. Olivet
747	Krohr, Elizabeth A.	25d	W	U.S.	19 FEB 1874	Mt. Olivet
602	Krohr, Wm. A.	2y	W	U.S.	14 MAY 1872	Mt. Olivet
266	Krouse, Henry	1y	W	D.C.	12 JUL 1867	
364	Krowheimer, Carrie	2m	W	Amer.	21 DEC 1868	Congressional
522	Kruff, Caroline, fruit dealer	70y	W	Ger.	12 JUN 1871	Congressional
350	Krug, Mary	7y	W	D.C.	05 SEP 1868	German Catholic
471	Krull, Henreich	1y	W	Amer.	10 AUG 1870	Prospect Hill
333	Krull, Lovie	8m	W	D.C.	23 JUL 1868	Prospect Hill
434	Kuester, Johanna	40y	W	Ger.	05 JAN 1870	Prospect Hill
473	Kuhn, Rosina	1y	W	D.C.	21 AUG 1870	German Catholic
471	Kuhn, Rosina		W	D.C.	21 AUG 1870	German Catholic
773	Kuhner, Augustus	9m	W	U.S.	14 JUN 1874	Prospect Hill
506	Kuhniot, John, rigger		W	Eur.	18 FEB 1871	Congressional
634	Kuhns, John, laborer	24y	W	U.S.	23 OCT 1872	
660	Kuhns, Michael, butcher	37y	W	U.S.	17 JAN 1873	Catholic
593	Kulass, Margret	2y	W	U.S.	18 APR 1872	Holmead
721	Kunert, Hedwig	46y	W	Sax.	24 SEP 1873	
720	Kuonn, Nat	1d	W	D.C.	24 SEP 1873	Washington Asylum
526	Kurtz, Annie	1y	W	D.C.	03 JUL 1871	Glenwood
229	Kurtz, Catherine	8m	W	D.C.	18 JUL 1866	Glenwood

District of Columbia Interments (Index to Deaths), 1855-1874

Page	Name	Age	Race	Birth	Death Date	Burial Ground
673	Kurtz, Mary Ann	3y	W	U.S.	06 MAR 1873	Mt. Olivet*
309	Kurtz, Sarah	43y	W		04 APR 1868	Rock Creek
138	Kurtze, Elizabeth	63y	W	Md.	28 JAN 1859	Rock Creek
214	Kyle, Mary F.	12m	W	Va.	01 MAR 1866	Congressional
005	Kyles, Sarah	70y	W	Md.	30 MAR 1855	Methodist, East

Page	Name	Age	Race	Birth	Death Date	Burial Ground
L						
066	LaBille, Ann C.	20y	W	Pa.	19 DEC 1856	St. Patricks
052	Lacey, Margarette, servant	17y	W	Ire.	29 JUL 1856	St. Patricks
617	Lacey, Solomon	9m	C	U.S.	15 AUG 1872	
471	Lacey, Willie B.	1y		Amer.	03 AUG 1870	Congressional
409	Lachner, John M., hotel keeper	35y	W	Ger.	27 AUG 1869	Prospect Hill
184	Lackey, Andrew	1y	W	D.C.	08 JUL 1860	Mt. Olivet
038	Lackey, Hannah	60y	W	Ire.	16 MAR 1856	St. Patricks
004	Lackey, Joanna Leigh	33y	W	Va.*	19 MAR 1855	Glenwood
039	Lackie, Robert B., printer	21y	W	D.C.	07 MAR 1856	St. Patricks
415	Lackner, Regina	26y	W	Eur.	18 SEP 1869	Prospect Hill
690	Lacy, Fanny	38y	C	U.S.	14 MAY 1873	Small Pox
118	Lacy, John	6y	C	D.C.	02 JUN 1858	Potters Field
641	Lacy, John	12y	C	U.S.	19 DEC 1872	Small Pox
426	Lacy, Julia E.	5y	C		20 NOV 1869	Ebenezer
477	Lacy, Kate	1y	W	D.C.	15 SEP 1870	Congressional
169	Lacy, Maria, washerwoman	60y	C	Md.	15 JAN 1860	
408	Lacy, Thos. James	7m	W	D.C.	03 AUG 1869	Mt. Olivet
617	Lacy, Wm.	6m	C	U.S.	01 AUG 1872	
782	Ladson, Anna M.	1m	W	U.S.	24 JUL 1874	Graceland
782	Ladson, Mary C.	46y	W	Eng.	14 JUL 1874	Graceland
643	Laha, Mary	31y	W	Ire.	09 DEC 1872	Mt. Olivet
150	Lahagne, Auguste H.	1y	W	D.C.	10 JUN 1859	Prospect Hill
170	Lahanna, Otto, painter	29y	W	Ger.	31 JAN 1860	Prospect Hill
482	Lainharendt, John, sexton	61y	W	Md.	01 OCT 1870	Methodist
499	Lake, H.H.	23y	W	Eng.	11 JAN 1871	Congressional
705	Lake, Mary	1½m	W	D.C.	01 JUL 1873	Congressional
215	Lakeman, John D., tailor		W	Va.	18 MAR 1866	Glenwood
144	Lakemeyer, Elizabeth	36y	W		22 MAR 1859	Glenwood
766	Lalor, Frank M., clerk	37y	W	Ire.	07 MAY 1874	Mt. Olivet
332	Laman, Elizabeth	1m	C	D.C.	16 JUL 1868	Alms House
466	Lamar, Ellen, housekeeper	30y	C	Va.	04 JUL 1870	
542	Lamb, Ann E.	21d	W	D.C.	20 OCT 1871	Congressional
359	Lamb, David	1y	W	D.C.	13 NOV 1868	Congressional
237	Lamb, Eliza, housekeeper	67y	W	D.C.	10 SEP 1866	Congressional
060	Lamb, Elizabeth	31y	W	D.C.	11 OCT 1856	Congressional
605	Lamb, Francis Henry	39d	W	D.C.	20 JUN 1872	Oak Hill*
698	Lamb, George	14d	W	D.C.	28 JUN 1873	Congressional
033	Lamb, George, saddle maker	66y	W	Md.	03 JAN 1856	Foundry
782	Lamb, John M., clerk	45y	W	unk.	09 JUL 1874	Potters Field
054	Lamb, Theodore L.	1m	W	D.C.	06 AUG 1856	Congressional
105	Lamb, Thomas, cutler	73y	W	Eng.	21 FEB 1858	Glenwood
313	Lambell, Ketchum H., brick maker	53y	W	D.C.	31 MAY 1868	Congressional
494	Lambert, Alpheus H., clerk	23y	C	Md.	10 DEC 1870	Pr. Geo. Co., Md.
616a	Lambord, Vergie M.	11m	W	U.S.	15 JUL 1872	Congressional*
707	Lamborn, Edith	8m	W	D.C.	02 JUL 1873	Graceland/Glenwood
375	Lamkin, Anna Josephine	3y	W	D.C.	14 FEB 1869	German Catholic
265	Lamkin, B. Smith	32y			01 JUL 1867	N.Y.
380	Lamkin, John	5y	W	D.C.	22 MAR 1869	German Catholic
191	Lammond, A., Jr., clerk	25y	W	Va.*	23 OCT 1860	Alexandria, Va.
546	Lammond, Chas. M., clerk	34y	W	U.S.	22 NOV 1871	Congressional
396	Lammond, Gertrude G.	2y	W	D.C.	02 JUN 1869	Oak Hill
664	Lammond, Henry	19y	C	U.S.	24 JAN 1873	Small Pox*
179	Lammond, Mary C.	39y	W	Md.	23 MAY 1860	Rock Creek
590	Lammond, PEter	6y	W	N.Y.	09 APR 1872	Ebenezer
730	Lamnz, [blank]	7d	W	U.S.	13 NOV 1873	Beckett's
361	Lanahan, Michael, wagon driver	45y	W	Ire.	20 NOV 1868	Mt. Olivet
132	Lanahan, [blank]	6m	W		03 NOV 1858	Methodist

District of Columbia Interments (Index to Deaths), 1855-1874

Page	Name	Age	Race	Birth	Death Date	Burial Ground
096	Lancaster, Basil, porter	60y	C		08 NOV 1857	Georgetown
383	Lancaster, Charity	82y	C	Md.	11 MAR 1869	Mt. Olivet
181	Lancaster, Chas. Walter	9m	C	D.C.	16 JUN 1860	Mt. Olivet
331	Lancaster, Colin	40y	C	Va.	23 JUL 1868	Freedmen's Hospital
319	Lancaster, Ellen, domestic	25y	C	Md.	16 JUN 1868	Mt. Olivet
297	Lancaster, Harry		C		c.07 FEB 1868	Alms House
076	Lancaster, M.	65y	C		26 APR 1857	Young Mens
098	Lancaster, Mary	70y	C	Va.	18 DEC 1857	Young Mens
073	Lancaster, Mary F.	1y	C	D.C.	15 MAR 1857	St. Matthews
224	Lancaster, Rachel	18y	C	D.C.	17 JUN 1866	Harmony (new)
408	Lancaster, Richard	8m		D.C.	24 AUG 1869	Mt. Olivet
352	Lancaster, Rose	4m	C		10 SEP 1868	Washington Asylum
154	Lancell, Charles	7y	C	D.C.	19 JUL 1859	Foundry
465	Lancutch, Chas. Ed.	3y	W		13 JUL 1870	Mt. Olivet
401	Lander, Chas. W.	1m	C	D.C.	04 JUL 1869	Young Mens
298	Landers, Ann Maria	57y	W	Md.	11 FEB 1868	Rock Creek
337	Landon, Harriet	12y	C	U.S.	06 AUG 1868	Washington Asylum
683	Landon, Henry	22y	C	U.S.	21 APR 1873	Small Pox
450	Landon, James, servant	15y	C		24 APR 1870	Union
677	Landon, Jas.	41y	C	U.S.	07 MAR 1873	Small Pox
711	Landy, Patsey		W	Va.	08 AUG 1873	Alexandria, Va.
328	Lane, Charles	7m	C	D.C.	29 JUL 1868	Western
454	Lane, Charles M.	2y	W		19 MAY 1870	Glenwood
754	Lane, Charles M., clerk	33y	W	U.S.	19 MAR 1874	Glenwood
470	Lane, E.E.	26y	W	D.C.	15 AUG 1870	Congressional*
527	Lane, Eliza	35y	C	Md.	08 JUL 1871	Young Mens
290	Lane, Fannie	22y	C	Md.	27 JAN 1868	Freedmen's Hospital
320	Lane, Geo. Henry	9m	W	D.C.	20 JUN 1868	Glenwood
782	Lane, Hannah L.	50y	C	U.S.	11 JUL 1874	Pa.
754	Lane, Harriet, messenger Treas.	39y	C	U.S.	26 MAR 1874	Mt. Olivet
432	Lane, Jane	105y	C	D.C.	31 DEC 1869	Washington Asylum
152	Lane, Jane H.	49y	W	Ire.	29 JUN 1859	Mt. Olivet
289	Lane, John [S.], laborer	25y	W	Ire.	24 JAN 1868	Mt. Olivet
199	Lane, Maggie	1y	W		20 FEB 1861	Mt. Olivet
373	Lane, Mrs.	24y	C	D.C.	17 JAN 1869	Harmony
601	Lane, N. Henry	2y	W	U.S.	29 MAY 1872	Glenwood
305	Lane, P.H.	30y	C	Md.	c.16 MAR 1868	Mt. Olivet
127	Lane, Richard Fendly	2m	W	D.C.	17 SEP 1858	Congressional
203	Lane, Sally Belt	2m	W	D.C.	02 MAY 1861	Congressional
444	Lane, Sue D.	7m	W		18 MAR 1870	Congressional
368	Lane, Timothy J., laborer	54y	W	Ire.	08 DEC 1868	Mt. Olivet
385	Lane, Willie D.	9m	W	D.C.	20 APR 1869	Congressional
001	Lanehan, Patrick	18y			02 JAN 1855	St. Patricks
339	Lang, Annie	17y	W	D.C.	26 AUG 1868	Methodist, East
229	Lang, Christian, musician	57y	W	Ger.	22 JUL 1866	Prospect Hill
754	Lang, Clara L.	2y	W	U.S.	05 MAR 1874	Glenwood
708	Lang, Cora		C	D.C.	05 JUL 1873	Washington Asylum
003	Lang, Ed.	19y	W	Md.	02 FEB 1855	
609	Lang, Emily	68y	W	U.S.	16 JUN 1872	
594	Lang, Henry	63y	C	N.C.	11 APR 1872	Washington
426	Lang, John, gardener	59y	W	Ger.	12 NOV 1869	Prospect Hill
295	Lang, John, laborer	52y	W	Fra.	12 FEB 1868	Congressional
188	Lang, Robt., child of	Still	W	D.C.	26 AUG 1860	Methodist
395	Lang, Walter E.	10m	W	D.C.	12 JUN 1869	Glenwood
743	Langcaster, G.C.	10y	C	U.S.	23 JAN 1874	
033	Langdon, Harriet C.	52y	W	N.Y.	11 JAN 1856	Glenwood
436	Langdon, Nancy, infant of	7m	C		27 JAN 1870	
634	Lange, C., laborer	45y	W	Ger.	13 OCT 1872	

Page	Name	Age	Race	Birth	Death Date	Burial Ground
204	Lange, John, jeweller	46y	W	Prus.	02 JUN 1861	Glenwood
557	Langford, Saml., carpenter	34y	W	U.S.	05 FEB 1872	Congressional
011	Langley, Agnes S.	2y	W	D.C.	10 JUN 1855	Congressional*
471	Langley, Aly	2y	W	D.C.	28 AUG 1870	Congressional
063	Langley, Ann	58y	W	Md.	28 NOV 1856	St. Peters
537	Langley, Ann E.F.	50y	W	D.C.	22 SEP 1871	Congressional
535	Langley, Ann E.F.	50y		D.C.	01 SEP 1871	Congressional
121	Langley, Caroline	6m	W	D.C.	10 JUL 1858	Congressional
102	Langley, Caroline	24y	W	D.C.	24 JAN 1858	Congressional
773	Langley, Eva	2y	W	U.S.	17 JUN 1874	Congressional*
326	Langley, Francis	1y	W	D.C.	03 JUL 1868	Congressional
782	Langley, Francis B.	11m	W	U.S.	18 JUL 1874	Congressional
530	Langley, Francis H.	3y	W	Md.	31 JUL 1871	Washington
128	Langley, Francis, laborer	40y	W	Md.	18 SEP 1858	Congressional
122	Langley, Gabriel, huckster	35y	W	Md.	25 JUL 1858	
529	Langley, Geo. H.	2y	W	D.C.	22 JUL 1871	Congressional*
550	Langley, Geo. S., mechanic	35y	W	U.S.	29 DEC 1871	Congressional*
182	Langley, George	5m	W	D.C.	23 JUN 1860	Congressional
681	Langley, George H., carpenter	61y	W	U.S.	17 APR 1873	Baltimore, Md.
348	Langley, George H.	2y	W		06 SEP 1868	Congressional
529	Langley, George S.	1y	W	D.C.	27 JUL 1871	Congressional*
773	Langley, Lillie Mary	6m	W	U.S.	26 JUN 1874	Oak Hill
138	Langley, Mary	11m	W	D.C.	28 JAN 1859	Congressional
034	Langley, Mary	3m	W		13 JAN 1856	Western
582	Langley, Mary Ann	22y	W	D.C.	20 FEB 1872	Congressional
250	Langley, Mary E.	45y	W	Md.	25 JAN 1867	Glenwood
132	Langley, Mary E.	9y	W	D.C.	03 NOV 1858	Glenwood
407	Langley, Mary Emma	1y	W		27 AUG 1869	Congressional
431	Langley, Nancy	25y	C	Va.	30 DEC 1869	
387	Langley, S.G., Col., hotel keeper	43y	W	N.H.	29 APR 1869	N.H.
374	Langley, Samie T.	2y	W		13 FEB 1869	Congressional
390	Langley, Sarah	33y	W	Md.	16 MAY 1869	Congressional
664	Langley, W.H.	50y	W	U.S.	09 JAN 1873	Small Pox*
077	Langley, William	48y	W	Md.	16 MAY 1857	St. Peters
308	Langley, Wm. R.	3m	W	D.C.	02 APR 1868	Congressional
101	Langly, Elizabeth	91y	W	Md.	10 JAN 1858	Congressional
449	Langly, Ellen	P.B.	W		20 APR 1870	Congressional
519	Langran, Wm., engraver	36y	W	Ire.	13 MAY 1871	Oak Hill
426	Langrass, John August	3y	W	D.C.	30 NOV 1869	Prospect Hill
363	Langster, Emma	1y	C	D.C.	27 NOV 1868	Washington Asylum
357	Langston, Marsellus	25y	B	Md.	08 OCT 1868	Freedmen's Hospital
602	Langston, [blank]		W	U.S.	11 MAY 1872	Congressional
461	Langtree, Chas. M.	8m	W	D.C.	15 JUL 1870	Congressional
334	Languinard, Henric, cook	40y	W	Fra.	18 JUL 1868	Glenwood
388	Lanhady, John, laborer	28y	W	Ire.	21 APR 1869	Mt. Olivet
638	Lanham, Henry	45y	C	U.S.	02 NOV 1872	
367	Lanham, James	40y	W	Ire.	28 DEC 1868	Washington Asylum
082	Lanham, Thomas	9y	W	D.C.	03 JUL 1857	Ebenezer
315	Lanigan, Ann	4y	W		c.16 MAY 1868	Mt. Olivet
157	Lankan, Catharine	29y	W	Ger.	05 AUG 1859	Prospect Hill
158	Lankan, Leopoldine Ida	4m	W	D.C.	21 AUG 1859	Prospect Hill
063	Lankaster, [blank]	12d	C		21 NOV 1856	Young Mens
216	Lannahan, Margaret	10m	W	D.C.	27 MAR 1866	Mt. Olivet
134	Lannin, Thomas, laborer	40y	W	Ire.	21 NOV 1858	
078	Lannum, John	45y	C		29 MAY 1857	Young Mens
352	Lannum, Maria	60y	C		05 SEP 1868	Washington Asylum
237	Lansing, Wm. N.	35y	W	N.Y.	18 SEP 1866	Congressional
533	Lantell, Wm. B.	1y	W	D.C.	23 AUG 1871	Prospect Hill

District of Columbia Interments (Index to Deaths), 1855-1874

Page	Name	Age	Race	Birth	Death Date	Burial Ground
223	Laporte, John	2y	W	D.C.	06 JUN 1866	Glenwood
266	Laporte, Saml. N.	5m	W	D.C.	05 JUL 1867	Glenwood
527	Lararoni, Teresa	61y	W	Italy	11 JUL 1871	St. Marys
643	Larchman, Mary B., housewife	28y	W	U.S.	06 DEC 1872	Prospect Hill
107	Larcomb, [blank]	11m	W		10 MAR 1858	Oak Hill
782	Larcombe, John	85y	W	U.S.	01 JUL 1874	Glenwood
626	Lardheuer, Josephine	4y	W	U.S.	20 SEP 1872	
737	Lare, Mrs.	53y	W	U.S.	22 DEC 1873	Mt. Olivet
639	Large, James	50y	C	U.S.	11 DEC 1872	Small Pox*
414	Larinam, Gertrue	10m	W		19 SEP 1869	Congressional
696	Larkin, Elizabeth A.	9m	W	D.C.	17 JUN 1873	
355	Larmon, (child)		W		23 OCT 1868	Congressional
075	Larner, Harry Day	3m	W		14 APR 1857	Congressional
291	Larner, N.D., child of	Still	W	D.C.	10 JAN 1868	Congressional
262	Larnstaen, Mary	4d	W		21 JUN 1867	Mt. Olivet
312	Larnum, Mintie, domestic	17y	C	Md.	25 MAY 1868	Alms House
621	Larry, Jas., clerk	75y	W	U.S.	27 AUG 1872	Glenwood
586	LaRue, Jennie	4y	W		14 MAR 1872	Oak Hill
364	Lascullette, Helen	2m	W	D.C.	17 DEC 1868	Congressional*
484	Laskey, Harriet		W		25 OCT 1870	Congressional
110	Laskey, Mary H.	30y	W	D.C.	07 APR 1858	Glenwood
088	Lasy, John	6m	W	D.C.	26 AUG 1857	Potters Field
595	Latham, Ann	65y	W	Md.	15 APR 1872	Congressional
458	Lathrop, Henry A.	1y	W	D.C.	09 JUN 1870	Rochester, N.Y.
520	Latimer, Mary E.	4m	W	D.C.	30 MAY 1871	Glenwood
343	Latimer, Susie May	9m	W	D.C.	03 AUG 1868	Glenwood
402	Latimer, Walter D.	7m	W		22 JUL 1869	Mt. Olivet
553	Lattimer, Rebecca R.	40y	W	Md.	12 JAN 1872	Oak Hill
666	Lattimore, Sarah E.	32y	W	U.S.	04 FEB 1873	Glenwood
629	Lattin, Mary J.	73y	W	U.S.	31 OCT 1872	
115	Laubcher, Louisa	4y	W	D.C.	01 JUN 1858	German Lutheran
464	Laubsher, Chas.	9y	W	D.C.	20 JUL 1870	Glenwood
464	Laubsher, Wm. Chas.	11y	W	D.C.	22 JUL 1870	Glenwood
380	Lauck, Henry C., clerk pens. bur.	40y	W	Va.	19 MAR 1869	Congressional
097	Lauck, Joseph M., dentist	23y	W	D.C.	23 NOV 1857	Congressional
493	Lauer, Louisa	8d	W		15 DEC 1870	Mt. Olivet
464	Laughlin, Geo. Alexander	1y	W	D.C.	22 JUL 1870	Glenwood
754	Laughlin, James T.	7m	W	U.S.	09 MAR 1874	Glenwood
696	Laurance, William, laborer	16y	W	Md.	24 JUN 1873	
471	Laurence, Valentine T., brickmaker	68y	W	Md.	05 AUG 1870	Congressional
748	Laurie, Margaret C.	5m	W	U.S.	02 FEB 1874	Congressional
083	Lavan, Charles, laborer	45y	W	Ire.	13 JUL 1857	Potters Field
189	Lavazzi, Frank M.	1y	W	D.C.	15 SEP 1860	Congressional
499	Lavezze, Antonia E.	9d	W	D.C.	17 JAN 1871	Congressional
278	Lavezzi, John B.	8m	W	D.C.	04 OCT 1867	Congressional
184	Law, John George, clerk	66y	W	Eng.	05 JUL 1860	Mt. Olivet
536	Lawler, Early	3d	C	D.C.	17 SEP 1871	Glenwood
331	Lawlor, M.D.	35y	W	Ire.	17 JUL 1868	Glenwood
073	Lawrence, Alex. H., lawyer	46y	W	N.H.	16 MAR 1857	Oak Hill
175	Lawrence, Babe	6d	W	D.C.	24 MAR 1860	Washington Asylum
063	Lawrence, Cath., child of	Still	W		23 NOV 1856	Washington Asylum
063	Lawrence, Cath., child of	Still	W		23 NOV 1856	Washington Asylum
155	Lawrence, Julia	3m	W	D.C.	22 JUL 1859	Congressional
170	Lawrence, Julia I.	20y	W	D.C.	28 JAN 1860	Congressional
467	Lawrence, Mary	75y	C	Va.	26 JUL 1870	
020	Lawrence, [blank]	21y	W		13 AUG 1855	West
085	Lawrenson, Ann E.	1y	W	D.C.	30 JUL 1857	Glenwood
336	Laws, Eliza	1y	C	D.C.	03 AUG 1868	Young Mens

Page	Name	Age	Race	Birth	Death Date	Burial Ground
331	Laws, Johanna A.	7m	W	D.C.	30 JUL 1868	Mt. Olivet
367	Lawson, Agnes	Still	B	D.C.	04 DEC 1868	Washington Asylum
425	Lawson, Cecilia		W		29 NOV 1869	Congressional
782	Lawson, E.L.C.	1m	W	U.S.	27 JUL 1874	Graceland
619	Lawson, Ellen	20y	C	U.S.	01 AUG 1872	
496	Lawson, Emma, housekeeper	20y	C	Md.	07 DEC 1870	Beckett's
369	Lawson, John	14y	W	D.C.	27 JAN 1869	Congressional
357	Lawson, Lewis	35y	B	U.S.	26 OCT 1868	Washington Asylum
296	Lawson, Maria	6m	C	D.C.	18 FEB 1868	Alms House
286	Lawson, Mary E.	1y	C		18 DEC 1867	Freedmen's Hospital
283	Lawson, Mary E.	1y	C		18 NOV 1867	Freedmen's Hospital
372	Lawson, Mary Jane	6m	C	D.C.	21 JAN 1869	Washington Asylum
760	Lawson, Samuel	60y	C	U.S.	02 APR 1874	Washington Asylum
715	Lawson, Talefrin	35y	C	U.S.	10 AUG 1873	
695	Lawson, Thos. Henry	10m	C	D.C.	21 JUN 1873	Ebenezer
460	Lawson, Willie	8m	C	D.C.	05 JUN 1870	
664	Lawson, Wm.	35y	C	U.S.	17 JAN 1873	Small Pox*
391	Lay, Lucy Morton	5y	W	L.I.	22 MAY 1869	Mt. Olivet
766	Lay, Thomas W.	1m	W	U.S.	26 MAY 1874	Mt. Olivet
290	Lazenby, B.C.	8m	W	D.C.	17 JAN 1868	Glenwood
447	Lazenby, Isabella S.	39y	W		06 MAR 1870	Glenwood
382	Lea, Celia, nurse	65y	C	Md.	15 MAR 1869	Harmony
456	Leach, Benj. F.	1y	W	U.S.	18 JUN 1870	Glenwood
385	Leach, Elizabeth	32y	W	Mass.	07 APR 1869	Congressional
580	Leach, Emma C.	25y	W	Pa.	12 FEB 1872	Congressional*
246	Leach, Georgeanna	1y	W	D.C.	01 DEC 1866	Mt. Olivet
324	Leacy, Edward	75y	W	Va.*	29 JUL 1868	Oak Hill
045	Leahey, Michael, carpenter	45y	W	Ire.	05 MAY 1856	Baltimore, Md.
090	Leahy, Bridget	3y	W	D.C.	03 SEP 1857	St. Patricks
038	Leahy, Edmund, blacksmith	17y	W	Ire.	28 MAR 1856	St. Patricks
065	Lear, Frances D., gentlewoman	77y	W	Va.	02 DEC 1856	Congressional
197	Learned, Charles	45y	W		18 JAN 1861	Congressional
348	Leary, Dennis	10m	W	D.C.	04 SEP 1868	Mt. Olivet
643	Leary, John, clerk	42y	W	U.S.	08 DEC 1872	Mt. Olivet
327	Leary, Thomas V.	11m	W	D.C.	30 JUL 1868	Western
666	Lease, Emma	16y	W	U.S.	05 FEB 1873	Glenwood
213	Leatherberg, Augusta E.	54y	M	Md.	23 FEB 1866	Young Mens
665	Leatherberry, James	2y	C	U.S.	30 JAN 1873	Small Pox*
077	Leay, Mary	3y	W	D.C.	11 MAY 1857	Congressional
131	Leazer, E.D., clerk	32y	W	N.J.	28 OCT 1858	N.J.
741	Lebron, Simon	24y	C	U.S.	14 JAN 1874	
463	Leckron, Eliza	59y	W	Md.	23 JUL 1870	Oak Hill
012	Leckron, John M.	15y	W	Md.	07 JUN 1855	Holmead
376	Lecoe, Wm., shoemaker	60y	C	Va.	28 FEB 1869	Union
379	Ledden, Mary C., Mrs.	23y	W	D.C.	06 MAR 1869	Congressional
169	Leddy, Malinda	36y	W	Va.*	17 JAN 1860	Mt. Olivet
712	Lederer, Mary L.	3y	W	D.C.	18 AUG 1873	Holly Woods
026	Ledon, Cathn. E.	48y	W	Md.	13 OCT 1855	Congressional
441	Lee, A.T., Lieut., army officer	24y	W	Mass.	18 FEB 1870	Boston, Mass.
168	Lee, Alexander, broker	52y	W	Va.	28 DEC 1859	Congressional
347	Lee, Alice, seamstress	19y	C	D.C.	06 SEP 1868	Congressional
427	Lee, Alpheus	1y	C	D.C.	17 NOV 1869	Washington Asylum
696	Lee, Anna	72y	C	Md.	01 JUN 1873	Washington Asylum
662	Lee, Anna, child of	1m	C	U.S.	01 JAN 1873	
584	Lee, Augustus, lamp lighter	18y	C	U.S.	01 MAR 1872	
661	Lee, Bertie	4y	C	U.S.	24 JAN 1873	Washington Asylum
594	Lee, Billy, laborer	21y	C	Md.	03 APR 1872	Washington
253	Lee, Carrie, housekeeper	73y	C	Md.	02 FEB 1867	Ebenezer

District of Columbia Interments (Index to Deaths), 1855-1874

Page	Name	Age	Race	Birth	Death Date	Burial Ground
042	Lee, Catharine	40y	W	Va.	23 APR 1856	Congressional
041	Lee, Charles	9m	C	D.C.	11 APR 1856	Ebenezer
513	Lee, Charles, laborer	70y	C	Va.	18 MAR 1871	Washington Asylum
351	Lee, Charlotte	1y	C	D.C.	20 SEP 1868	Mt. Olivet
490	Lee, Charlotte, laborer	85y	C	Va.	28 NOV 1870	Ebenezer
782	Lee, Cora	1m	C	unk.	25 JUL 1874	Mt. Olivet
417	Lee, Cordelia, seamstress	28y	C		24 SEP 1869	Harmony
622a	Lee, Daisy	3m	W	U.S.	29 AUG 1872	
087	Lee, Daniel S., lawyer	35y	W	Va.	15 AUG 1857	Strasburg, Va.
363	Lee, Edward	14d	C	D.C.	30 NOV 1868	Washington Asylum
637	Lee, Elisha, laborer	65y	C	U.S.	14 NOV 1872	
075	Lee, Elisha Smith, clerk	63y	W	N.Y.	12 APR 1857	Congressional
117	Lee, Elizabeth	92y	W	Pa.	24 JUN 1858	Congressional
137	Lee, Elizabeth	64y	C		12 JAN 1859	Young Mens
534	Lee, Ella V.C.	2y	C	D.C.	27 AUG 1871	Union
252	Lee, Ellen	2y	C	Md.	14 FEB 1867	Mt. Olivet
447	Lee, Emily				20 MAR 1870	Ebenezer
327	Lee, Emmeline	1y	C		08 JUL 1868	Holmead
773	Lee, Estelle	4m	C	U.S.	09 JUN 1874	Young Mens
496	Lee, Eva	2y	W	D.C.	11 DEC 1870	
631	Lee, Florence	8y	C	U.S.	14 OCT 1872	
627	Lee, Geo.	10y	C	U.S.	10 SEP 1872	Small Pox
526	Lee, George	21y	C	D.C.	02 JUL 1871	
402	Lee, George	2y	C	D.C.	10 JUL 1869	Mt. Olivet
455	Lee, George W., shoemaker	42y	C		29 MAY 1870	
540	Lee, George W.	7m	W	U.S.	05 OCT 1871	Congressional
316	Lee, Hanson		C		c.29 MAY 1868	Alms House
442	Lee, Harriet	11m	C		17 FEB 1870	
412	Lee, Henry	7d	C	D.C.	17 AUG 1869	Washington Asylum
079	Lee, Henry, cart man		C	Va.	05 JUN 1857	Union
399	Lee, Herminia, infant of	7m			01 JUL 1869	Congressional
691	Lee, Hewn	72y	C	U.S.	11 MAY 1873	Small Pox*
509	Lee, James	1m	C	D.C.	23 FEB 1871	Washington Asylum
382	Lee, James N., feed dealer	28y	C		25 MAR 1869	Harmony
630	Lee, Jas.	2y	C	U.S.	19 OCT 1872	
669	Lee, Jerry	18y	C	U.S.	07 FEB 1873	Small Pox
782	Lee, Jno. & Mary, infant of	8h	C	U.S.	22 JUL 1874	Holyrood
695	Lee, John, laborer		C	U.S.	18 JUN 1873	Ebenezer
188	Lee, John, waiter	22y	C	D.C.	29 AUG 1860	Mt. Olivet
319	Lee, Julia	5d	C	D.C.	— JUN 1868	
487	Lee, Julia A.E.	1y	C	D.C.	15 NOV 1870	Young Mens
090	Lee, L. Frances	1y	C	D.C.	04 SEP 1857	
478	Lee, Laura	2y	C	D.C.	24 SEP 1870	Harmony
275	Lee, Laura Gertrude	20y	W	D.C.	24 SEP 1867	Congressional
677	Lee, Leonard	17y	C	U.S.	10 MAR 1873	Small Pox
658	Lee, Lucy	64y	C	U.S.	05 JAN 1873	Washington Asylum
748	Lee, Mabel N.	11m	W	U.S.	16 FEB 1874	Congressional
731	Lee, Margaret	72y	C	U.S.	19 NOV 1873	
239	Lee, Margaret	7m	W	D.C.	15 OCT 1866	Catholic
740	Lee, Marion W.	38y	W	U.S.	03 JAN 1874	Baltimore, Md.
442	Lee, Mary	1m			21 FEB 1870	
227	Lee, Mary	42y	C	D.C.	08 JUL 1866	Alms House
402	Lee, Mary	2m	C		31 JUL 1869	St. Patricks
443	Lee, Mary	40y	C	Va.	15 FEB 1870	Washington Asylum
777a	Lee, Mary Ann, housekeeper	23y	C	U.S.	14 JUN 1874	
598	Lee, Mary Ann	1d	C	U.S.	13 MAY 1872	Unknown
381	Lee, Mary D., Mrs.	63y	W	Mass.	18 MAR 1869	Madison, Ind.
034	Lee, Mary Ellen	14y	C	Va.	27 JAN 1856	St. Peters

Page	Name	Age	Race	Birth	Death Date	Burial Ground
506	Lee, Mary, servant	18y	C	Va.	03 FEB 1871	Washington Asylum
131	Lee, Mathew	1y	W	D.C.	20 OCT 1858	Catholic
426	Lee, Matilda	34y	C	Md.	29 NOV 1869	Young Mens
457	Lee, Nathaniel	4m	W	D.C.	28 JUN 1870	Congressional
280	Lee, Perry	30y	C		22 OCT 1867	Freedmen's Hospital
598	Lee, Roberta	1d	C	U.S.	13 MAY 1872	Unknown
446	Lee, Romaine	17y	C	Va.	20 MAR 1870	Young Mens
351	Lee, Sallie E., Mrs.	22y	W		22 SEP 1868	Methodist
532	Lee, Thomas	45y	W	Ire.	10 AUG 1871	Mt. Olivet
581	Lee, Thomas, soldier	30y	W	Ire.	16 FEB 1872	Congressional*
303	Lee, W.E.		C		24 MAR 1868	Alms House
782	Lee, William	11m	C	U.S.	21 JUL 1874	Graceland
551	Lee, Wm. E.	7m	C	D.C.	— DEC 1871	Ebenezer
316	Lee, Wm. Henry	1m	C		20 MAY 1868	Ebenezer
239	Lee, Wm. Henry	2y	C	D.C.	17 OCT 1866	Young Mens
346	Lee, [blank]	7m	C		— AUG 1868	Freedmen's Hospital
159	Lee, [blank]	24y	C	Md.	02 AUG 1859	Md.
055	Lee, [blank]	10y	C	D.C.	19 AUG 1856	Western
319	Leech, Emily	25y	W	D.C.	30 JUN 1868	Glenwood
252	Leech, Martha A.	50y	W	Va.*	15 FEB 1867	Glenwood
298	Leech, [blank]		W		02 FEB 1868	Glenwood
339	Leech, [blank]	1y	W	D.C.	13 AUG 1868	Glenwood
374	Leefe, George Eubank	56y	W	Eng.	10 FEB 1869	Congressional
397	Leens, Jerimah	5y	C		04 JUN 1869	Ebenezer
760	Leescallett, Sarah	20y	W	U.S.	02 APR 1874	Congressional
727	Leesnitzer, James W.	1y	W	U.S.	04 OCT 1873	Congressional
687	Lefrie, Lucinda	76y	C	Va.	01 MAY 1873	Ebenezer
226	Leftwich, J.W., Hon., child of	16d	W	D.C.	27 JUN 1866	Congressional
217	Leftwich, Laura L.	1y	W	Tenn.	02 APR 1866	Congressional
506	Legge, Juliana L.	74y	W	Md.	10 FEB 1871	Congressional
209	Leghorne, John	36y	W	Ger.	08 JAN 1866	Alms House
080	Lehayn, Otto, child of	1y	W	D.C.	28 JUN 1857	German
199	Lehey, Margaret	33y	W	Ire.	01 FEB 1861	Mt. Olivet
068	Lehman, Charles H., boot maker	52y	W	Ger.	18 JAN 1857	Holmead
400	Lehoy, James	9y	W	Ire.	23 JUL 1869	Mt. Olivet
167	Leib, John, draughtsman	47y	W	Ger.	20 DEC 1859	Norfolk, Va.
303	Leibold, Clara	1y	W	D.C.	14 MAR 1868	Prospect Hill
305	Leighy, Catherine	30y	W		c.28 MAR 1868	Mt. Olivet
533	Leinbach, John V., saddler	46y	W	Ger.	20 AUG 1871	Prospect Hill
422	Leiper, Ida	4m	C		02 OCT 1869	
587	Leisman, Julia D.	1y	W	Md.	21 MAR 1872	Prospect Hill
005	Leitch, Chas. B.	2y	W	D.C.	07 APR 1855	[N.]Y. City
104	Leman, H., waiter	55y	C	Md.	14 FEB 1858	Washington Asylum
354	LeMerle, Augustus S.	2m	W	D.C.	06 OCT 1868	Mt. Olivet
441	Lemmer, George	2y	W		02 FEB 1870	Prospect Hill
547	Lemmer, Wilhelm	8y			05 DEC 1871	Prospect Hill
105	Lemmon, Frances	2y	W	D.C.	19 FEB 1858	Foundry
592	Lemmon, Lottie	23y	W	U.S.	01 APR 1872	
113	Lemmons, Hillary, laborer	24y	C	D.C.	05 MAY 1858	Washington Asylum
312	Lemon, P., cook	70y	C	D.C.	10 MAY 1868	Mt. Olivet
028	Lemon, Virginia	1y	W	D.C.	15 OCT 1855	St. Peters
542	Lemons, Caroline	22y	C	D.C.	25 OCT 1871	Washington
342	Lenam, Eliza	22y	C	D.C.	28 AUG 1868	Union
370	Lenan, Mary	3y	W		12 JAN 1869	Glenwood
050	Lenehan, Margarette	59y	W	Ire.	12 JUL 1856	St. Patricks
191	Lenman, George B., lumber mcht.	36y	W	D.C.	02 OCT 1860	Mt. Olivet
697	Lenny, Willie	7m	W	D.C.	18 JUN 1873	Mt. Olivet
434	LeNoir, Martha A.	85y	W	S.C.	18 JAN 1870	Prospect Hill

District of Columbia Interments (Index to Deaths), 1855-1874

Page	Name	Age	Race	Birth	Death Date	Burial Ground
073	Lenox, Margaret	77y	W	Md.	18 MAR 1857	Congressional
453	Lenz, Henry, clerk	31y	W	Fra.	03 MAY 1870	Congressional
265	Leon, C.	1d	C		17 JUL 1867	
241	Leonard, Emma	45y	W		15 OCT 1866	Congressional*
122	Leonard, Frank B.	1m	W	D.C.	25 JUL 1858	Congressional
748	Leonard, John	65y	W	Spain	18 FEB 1874	Mt. Olivet
502	Leonard, Margaret	35y	W		30 JAN 1871	Glenwood
370	Leonard, Mary E., Mrs.	20y	W	Del.	08 JAN 1869	Wilmington, Del.
327	Leonard, Thomas	2m	W	D.C.	27 JUL 1868	Mt. Olivet
387	Leonard, Thomas J., clerk Treas.	50y	W	N.Y.	25 APR 1869	N.Y.
278	Leonard, [blank]	7y	W	D.C.	09 OCT 1867	Mt. Olivet
748	Leonberger, C.M.	42y	W	Ger.	11 FEB 1874	German
682	Leonburger, Christiana	35y	W	Ger.	23 APR 1873	Prospect Hill
475	Leonhardt, Mary V.	8m	W	U.S.	08 SEP 1870	Prospect Hill
381	Lepley, Frank A.	7m	W	D.C.	21 MAR 1869	Mt. Olivet
518	Lepper, Mr., child of		W	D.C.	03 MAY 1871	Congressional*
262	Lepreux, Jane	69y	W	Scot.	23 JUN 1867	Oak Hill
191	Leslie, James, artist	34y	W	Eng.	16 OCT 1860	Congressional
199	Leslie, John	1y	W	D.C.	12 FEB 1861	Trinity
396	Leslie, John	1y			29 JUN 1869	Union
554	Leslie, Robert, merchant	79y	W	Scot.	16 JAN 1872	Md.
744	Lester, Alice Clifton	23y	W	U.S.	28 JAN 1874	Mt. Olivet
340	Letournace, Mary M.	7m	W	D.C.	19 AUG 1868	Congressional
475	Letournan, Hattie R.	5m	W	D.C.	03 SEP 1870	Congressional
473	LeTournan, F.W.W., clerk	37y	W	Md.	31 AUG 1870	Congressional
283	Letsinger, Marie	10m	W	D.C.	18 NOV 1867	Congressional
536	Lett, Marcellus	25y	W	Md.	18 SEP 1871	Glenwood
439	Leutner, Lili	8m	W		11 FEB 1870	Congressional*
324	Leutze, Emanuel, artist	52y	W	Ger.	18 JUL 1868	Glenwood
421	Levi, Toney, laborer	75y	W	Md.	08 OCT 1869	Ebenezer
735	Lewis, Agnes E.	2m	W	U.S.	12 DEC 1873	Oak Hill
281	Lewis, Alexander	40y	C		08 OCT 1867	Young Mens
731	Lewis, Alfred	9m	C	U.S.	21 NOV 1873	
426	Lewis, Alice	4y	C		13 NOV 1869	Young Mens
515	Lewis, Andrew	5y	C	Va.*	02 MAR 1871	Union
101	Lewis, Ann	35y	W	Va.	13 JAN 1858	Catholic, Georgetown
313	Lewis, Betsy	24y	C	D.C.	02 MAY 1868	Young Mens
249	Lewis, Bridget	60y	W	Ire.	29 JAN 1867	Mt. Olivet
629	Lewis, C., laborer	60y	C	U.S.	12 OCT 1872	
246	Lewis, Catherine				23 DEC 1866	Young Mens
237	Lewis, Clara	40y	W		24 SEP 1866	Mt. Olivet
734	Lewis, Clara A., clerk	42y	W	U.S.	07 DEC 1873	
236	Lewis, Dallas May	2y	W	Pa.	26 SEP 1866	Congressional
342	Lewis, Edward	10m	C	Va.	08 AUG 1868	Young Mens
323	Lewis, Edward Francis	8m	W	Amer.	15 JUL 1868	Oak Hill
052	Lewis, Edward P.	1y	W	D.C.	30 JUL 1856	Oak Hill
363	Lewis, Eliza	1y	C	D.C.	28 NOV 1868	Washington Asylum
735	Lewis, Elizabeth	49y	C	U.S.	08 DEC 1873	Mt. Olivet
541	Lewis, Ella	18y	C	Va.	13 OCT 1871	Va.
393	Lewis, Emma	4y	C		23 MAY 1869	Beckett's
532	Lewis, Fielding, laborer	40y	C		15 AUG 1871	Washington
347	Lewis, Florence May	1y	W	D.C.	11 SEP 1868	Congressional
782	Lewis, George, laborer	38y	C	U.S.	25 JUL 1874	Potters Field
431	Lewis, George, laborer	20y	C	Va.	08 DEC 1869	Union
118	Lewis, Georgiana, teacher	14y	W		19 JUN 1858	Congressional
443	Lewis, Hanston, laborer	26y	C	Md.	04 FEB 1870	Washington Asylum
022	Lewis, Harriet	65y	C	Va.	29 AUG 1855	
766	Lewis, Harriet	1y	C	U.S.	07 MAY 1874	

Page	Name	Age	Race	Birth	Death Date	Burial Ground
335b	Lewis, Harvey				13 JUL 1868	Washington Asylum
333	Lewis, Harvey, wheelwright	30y	C	Va.	13 JUL 1868	Alms House
272	Lewis, Henry	2y	C		24 AUG 1867	Freedmen's Bureau
663	Lewis, Henry	25y	C	U.S.	17 JAN 1873	Small Pox
554	Lewis, Henry W.	4y	W		18 JAN 1872	
522	Lewis, Isaac	3m	C	D.C.	11 JUN 1871	Young Mens
595	Lewis, Isabella	9m	W	D.C.	27 APR 1872	Congressional
269	Lewis, James	4m	C		13 AUG 1867	Young Mens
181	Lewis, James H., watchman	27y	W	D.C.	12 JUN 1860	Glenwood
292	Lewis, James, oyster shucker	22y	C	Va.	21 JAN 1868	Young Mens
662	Lewis, Jane K.	13d	W	U.S.	31 JAN 1873	N.Y.
618	Lewis, John	45y	W	U.S.	21 AUG 1872	
540	Lewis, John	79y	W	N.Y.	02 OCT 1871	N.Y.
369	Lewis, John E., chirographer	25y	W	Conn.	11 JAN 1869	Congressional
540	Lewis, John T.	1y	W	Pa.	03 OCT 1871	Methodist
349	Lewis, John Vaughan	1y	W		22 SEP 1868	Rock Creek
674	Lewis, Jos. Henry	12y	W	U.S.	17 MAR 1873	Mt. Olivet
714	Lewis, Jos., laborer	100y	C	Va.	31 AUG 1873	
711	Lewis, Josephine	6m	C	D.C.	11 AUG 1873	
080	Lewis, Josephine	17y	C	D.C.	22 JUN 1857	Western
121	Lewis, L.	8m	C		15 JUL 1858	Young Mens
495	Lewis, L., child of	Still	C	D.C.	12 DEC 1870	Potters Field
697	Lewis, Letitia	15y	C	Va.	12 JUN 1873	Arlington Heights
529	Lewis, Maggie E.	5m	W	U.S.	28 JUL 1871	Congressional*
005	Lewis, Maj., slave of	20y	C		17 MAR 1855	Young Mens
220	Lewis, Margaret	23y	W	Ohio	10 MAY 1866	Ohio
187	Lewis, Margaret, nurse	60y	C	Va.	04 AUG 1860	Foundry
357	Lewis, Maria E.	4y	B	D.C.	08 OCT 1868	Washington Asylum
687	Lewis, Marshal	3y	W	D.C.	08 MAY 1873	Congressional
184	Lewis, Martha	6m	C	D.C.	03 JUL 1860	Ebenezer
782	Lewis, Martina	2m	C	U.S.	08 JUL 1874	Potters Field
272	Lewis, Mary	25y	C		21 AUG 1867	Freedmen's Bureau
367	Lewis, Mary	4m	W	D.C.	04 DEC 1868	Washington Asylum
389	Lewis, Mary	8m	C	D.C.	07 APR 1869	Washington Asylum
478	Lewis, Mary	1y	C	Va.	10 SEP 1870	Young Mens
719	Lewis, Mary Agnes	3y	W	D.C.	22 SEP 1873	Mt. Olivet
523	Lewis, Mary Ann	55y	W	Va.	17 JUN 1871	Congressional
080	Lewis, Mary Ann	11m	C	D.C.	29 JUN 1857	Young Mens
397	Lewis, Mary E.	2y	B		14 JUN 1869	Holmead
343	Lewis, Matilda, house servant	17y	C	Va.	14 AUG 1868	
342	Lewis, Matilda, washerwoman	22y	C	Va.	15 AUG 1868	Young Mens
449	Lewis, Mr., infant of	Still			03 APR 1870	Congressional
133	Lewis, Mrs.	48y	W		20 NOV 1858	Western
606	Lewis, Nathan	55y	W	D.C.	15 JUN 1872	
254	Lewis, Payne	23d			17 FEB 1867	Mt. Olivet
639	Lewis, Peyton	20y	C	U.S.	15 NOV 1872	
470	Lewis, R.J.	3y	W	D.C.	06 AUG 1870	Oak Hill
478	Lewis, Rebecca, domestic	20y	C	Va.	13 SEP 1870	Rappahannock, Va.
397	Lewis, Rebeck	3y	B	U.S.	01 JUN 1869	Holmead
118	Lewis, Reeve, machinist	46y	W		25 JUN 1858	Congressional
592	Lewis, Richard	10m	C	D.C.	15 APR 1872	
644	Lewis, S.	3m	W	U.S.	24 DEC 1872	Mt. Olivet
524	Lewis, S.D.		W	D.C.	22 JUN 1871	Congressional*
201	Lewis, Saloma	85y	W	Va.	29 MAR 1861	Alexandria, Va.
734	Lewis, Samuel D., bricklayer	43y	W	U.S.	07 DEC 1873	Glenwood
003	Lewis, Sara Ann	37y	W	D.C.	05 FEB 1855	
457	Lewis, Sarah	8m	W	D.C.	27 JUN 1870	Philadelphia, Pa.
754	Lewis, Simond	9d	C	U.S.	26 MAR 1874	Young Mens

Page	Name	Age	Race	Birth	Death Date	Burial Ground
423	Lewis, Spotsy	8m	C	D.C.	12 OCT 1869	Washington Asylum
252	Lewis, Susan, washerwoman	22y	C	D.C.	20 FEB 1867	Harmony
587	Lewis, Theodore	28d	W	D.C.	23 MAR 1872	Methodist
253	Lewis, W.	21y	C		12 FEB 1867	Harmony
152	Lewis, Washington, watchman	62y	W	U.S.	28 JUN 1859	Glenwood
383	Lewis, William	7d	C	D.C.	03 MAR 1869	Washington Asylum
227	Lewis, Wilson, conductor st. car		W		01 JUL 1866	Congressional
528	Lewis, Wm. Henry	11y	C		18 JUL 1871	Young Mens
436	Lewis, Wm. I., carpenter	39y	W		07 JAN 1870	Oak Hill
394	Lewis, [blank]		W		13 JUN 1869	Congressional
508	Lewis, [blank]	45y	C	U.S.	13 FEB 1871	Union
481	Lewis, [blank]	30y	C	Va.	13 OCT 1870	Western
111	Lewis, [Mrs. Reeve]	35y	W		15 APR 1858	Congressional*
466	Lewiser, Martha	6m	C	D.C.	19 JUL 1870	Harmony
669	Lews, Elizabeth	60y	C	U.S.	03 FEB 1873	Small Pox
155	Ley, George Karl	8m	W	D.C.	30 JUL 1859	Prospect Hill
303	Ley, Gosiphina	4m	W	D.C.	16 MAR 1868	German Catholic
609	Libbey, Charlotte M.	7m	W	U.S.	20 JUN 1872	
605	Libbey, [blank]	6m	W	D.C.	03 JUN 1872	Me.
268	Libeck, John, tailor	35y	W	Belg.	28 AUG 1867	Mt. Olivet
451	Libenth, Edmon	2d	C	D.C.	04 APR 1870	Washington Asylum
641	Liber, Minnie	16y	C	U.S.	08 DEC 1872	Small Pox
298	Librey, Daphne, servant	30y	C	Va.	09 FEB 1868	Young Mens
479	Lichtenmeyer, Mich.	71y	W	Ger.	29 SEP 1870	Washington Asylum
193	Lieberman, Louisa C.	36y	W	Va.*	14 NOV 1860	Rock Creek
594	Lietch, Elizabeth E.	64y	W	D.C.	06 APR 1872	Mt. Olivet
088	Liggin, Ida	3m	C	D.C.	22 AUG 1857	St. Matthews
041	Lightell, George	6m	W	Va.	07 APR 1856	Methodist
027	Lighter, Ann E.M.	1y	W	D.C.	23 OCT 1855	Methodist
092	Lighter, [blank]		W	D.C.	25 SEP 1857	Methodist
754	Lightfoot, Willie	8m	C	U.S.	23 MAR 1874	Mt. Pleasant
380	Lightner, Hopkins	57y	W	Pa.	11 MAR 1869	Baltimore, Md.
045	Lijah, Child of Jas. M.E.		W		23 MAY 1856	Methodist
717	Liles, Rebecca A.	1y	C	D.C.	07 SEP 1873	Mt. Olivet
535	Lillian, Eva	2y		D.C.	16 SEP 1871	Prospect Hill
303	Lilp, Godfred, butcher	32y	W	Ger.	08 MAR 1868	Prospect Hill
286	Lily, Benj.	7y	C		07 DEC 1867	Western
395	Limberger, Waldin, painter	44y	W	Ger.	28 JUN 1869	Prospect Hill
782	Limerick, Dollie	58y	W	unk.	02 JUL 1874	Glenwood
121	Limerwell, Jno. H., clerk	40y	W	Md.	16 JUL 1858	Pr. Geo. Co., Md.
642	Lin, Wm.	30y	C	U.S.	20 DEC 1872	Small Pox
603	Lina, W.B.	6m	W	D.C.	05 JUN 1872	Prospect Hill
619	Linch, Noel	15y	C	U.S.	07 AUG 1872	
622a	Lincoln, E.L.	59y	W	U.S.	20 AUG 1872	
359	Lincoln, Egbert, clerk	29y	W	N.Y.	23 NOV 1868	Congressional
398	Lincoln, Nannie M.	36y	W	Md.	10 JUN 1869	Oak Hill
212	Linden, Henry, tinner		W	Ger.	15 FEB 1866	
079	Lindig, Christian, appr. tinner	16y	W	Sax.	01 JUN 1857	German
748	Lindley, John M.	42y	W	U.S.	12 FEB 1874	
698	Lindquist, Fredk.	8m	W	D.C.	20 JUN 1873	Congressional
555	Lindsay, Alfred, clerk	65y	W	Va.	30 JAN 1872	Congressional
092	Lindsay, Geo. F., officer USMC	54y	W	Va.	27 SEP 1857	Congressional
061	Lindsay, Thos. Oliver	4y	W	Ala.	31 OCT 1856	Oak Hill*
421	Lindsey, Kate	2m	W		28 OCT 1869	Glenwood
658	Lindsey, Samuel	50y	C	U.S.	09 JAN 1873	Washington Asylum
754	Lindsley, Benjamin	8y	W	U.S.	29 MAR 1874	Baltimore, Md.
419	Lindsley, Howard	38y	W	D.C.	19 OCT 1869	Congressional
529	Lindsley, Mary F.	11m	C	D.C.	27 JUL 1871	Young Mens

Page	Name	Age	Race	Birth	Death Date	Burial Ground
231	Lindsly, Webster, surgeon USA	30y	W	D.C.	08 AUG 1866	Oak Hill
718	Liner, Peter B., sailor	65y	W	N.Y.	14 SEP 1873	Congressional
346	Lines, David	60y	C		27 AUG 1868	Freedmen's Hospital
612	Lingar, Geo. E.	1m	W	U.S.	12 JUL 1872	
228	Linikin, Wm. H., boatman		W	Me.	08 JUL 1866	Alms House
782	Linkins, C.H.	2y	W	U.S.	26 JUL 1874	Holyrood
288	Linkins, Helen C.	26y	W	D.C.	31 DEC 1867	Congressional*
363a	Linkins, Helen C.	26y	W	D.C.	31 DEC 1867	Congressional*
066	Linkins, John, shoemaker	67y	W		23 DEC 1856	Western
072	Linkins, Joseph	10y	W		26 FEB 1857	Western
632	Linkins, Lewis	44y	W	U.S.	28 OCT 1872	
742	Linkins, Mary	45y	W	U.S.	20 JAN 1874	Congressional
158	Linkins, Mary Ellen	19y	W	D.C.	18 AUG 1859	Western
061	Linkins, [blank]	2m	W	D.C.	18 OCT 1856	Western
019	Linkins, [blank]	1y	W		23 AUG 1855	West
221	Linn, Franka, Mrs.	80y	C	Va.	18 MAY 1866	Holmead
218	Linnett, Amelia, Mrs.	66y	W	Md.	21 APR 1866	Oak Hill
268	Linnett, James, painter	38y	W	D.C.	28 AUG 1867	Oak Hill
708	Linsay, Jane	3d	C	D.C.	05 JUL 1873	Washington Asylum
619	Linsay, Jno.	8m	C	U.S.	11 AUG 1872	
309	Linsey, Jane	6y	W	D.C.	02 APR 1868	Mt. Olivet*
708	Linsey, Willie	8d	C	D.C.	05 JUL 1873	Washington Asylum
247	Linthicum[87], Sarah	48y	W		14 DEC 1866	Congressional*
271	Linton, Arthur W.	9m	W	D.C.	22 AUG 1867	Congressional
220	Linton, Edw. Hall		W	D.C.	05 MAY 1866	Oak Hill
143	Linton, Elmira P.	5m	W	D.C.	09 MAR 1859	Methodist
500	Linton, Jeannette H.	37y	W	D.C.	20 JAN 1871	Glenwood
276	Linton, William A.	76y	W	Va.	24 SEP 1867	Congressional
396	Lintz, Abraham	1m	W		13 JUN 1869	Hebrew
381	Linville, James, carpenter	82y	W	Pa.	25 MAR 1869	Pa.
538	Lions, Laura	4y	C	U.S.	28 SEP 1871	
185	Lipinger, Mary, domestic	25y	W	Ger.	16 JUL 1860	
773	Lippard, Jno. A.	7d	W		01 JUN 1874	Congressional*
743	Lipphard, John	20y	W	U.S.	22 JAN 1874	Congressional*
153	Lipscomb, Alice	10y	W	U.S.	12 JUL 1859	Congressional
412	Lipscomb, Maria	34y	C	Va.	06 AUG 1869	Washington Asylum
116	Lipscomb, Robert C.	8m	W	D.C.	24 JUN 1858	Congressional
533	Lipscourt, Annie M.	25y	W	Va.	19 AUG 1871	
727	Lisibolt, M.		B	U.S.	31 OCT 1873	
223	Liston, James	11m	W	D.C.	07 JUN 1866	Mt. Olivet
448	Liston, James	2m	W		05 MAR 1870	Mt. Olivet
024	Liston, Mary	25y		Ire.	08 SEP 1855	St. Patricks
359	Litchfield, S.M., Mrs.	60y	W	U.S.	03 NOV 1868	Congressional
629	Little, Emma	4m	C	U.S.	07 OCT 1872	
116	Little, Henrietta, washerwoman	40y	C	Md.	20 JUN 1858	Young Mens
176	Little, James, laborer	68y	W	Ire.	09 APR 1860	Congressional
402	Little, Jas., tailor	59y	W	Md.	15 JUL 1869	Mt. Olivet
215	Little, Lewis W., clerk	36y	W	Ohio	18 MAR 1866	Elmira, N.Y.
632	Little, Marg. F.	6y	W	U.S.	10 OCT 1872	Congressional*
120	Little, Mary	4m	W		08 JUL 1858	Congressional
217	Little, Mary	1y	C		03 APR 1866	Young Mens
439	Little, Mary E.	22y	W	Va.	27 FEB 1870	Congressional
057	Little, Peter	80y	W		01 SEP 1856	Congressional
008	Little, Robt. Barry	3y	W	D.C.	26 MAY 1855	Congressional
012	Little, Saml., butcher	43y	W	D.C.	28 JUN 1855	Congressional

---

[87] Corrected from the Register's "Lithagum."

District of Columbia Interments (Index to Deaths), 1855-1874

Page	Name	Age	Race	Birth	Death Date	Burial Ground
295	Littlefield, N.H., child of	17d	W	U.S.	23 FEB 1868	Congressional
732	Littlejohn, A.E.	39y	W	U.S.	05 NOV 1873	
014	Littlejone, Mr., blacksmith	35y	W	Ger.	26 JUL 1855	German, North
631	Littleton, E.E., painter	20y	W	U.S.	24 OCT 1872	
218	Littleton, Lawson	3y	W	D.C.	25 APR 1866	Glenwood
514	Littleton, Sarah	58y	W	Va.	13 MAR 1871	Glenwood
083	Littleton, Sarah F.	7m	W	D.C.	16 JUL 1857	Glenwood
365	Livan, Sarah	21y	W		10 DEC 1868	Congressional*
465	Liverpool, J.	1y	C		26 JUL 1870	Ebenezer
543	Liverpool, M.E.	4y	C		30 OCT 1871	Unknown
143	Liverpool, Patsy	76y	C	Md.	05 MAR 1859	Colored, Eastern
732	Livingsgood, Owen, carpenter	60y	W	U.S.	29 NOV 1873	Congressional*
605	Livingston, Moses, soldier	57y	W	Eng.	19 JUN 1872	
515	Livingstone, Angeline	59y	W	Md.	18 MAR 1871	Congressional
026	Lloyd, John	29y	W	D.C.	16 OCT 1855	Congressional
304	Lloyd, Owen	6y	W	D.C.	01 MAR 1868	Congressional
440	Lloyd, Richard Bennett	58y	W	Va.	19 FEB 1870	Glenwood
683	Lloyd, Samuel	23y	C	U.S.	20 APR 1873	Small Pox
639	Lloyd, Sarah E.	85y	W		28 NOV 1872	Congressional
782	Lloyd, Willie	4m	C	U.S.	08 JUL 1874	Potters Field
740	Loane, Hannah R.M.		C	U.S.	03 JAN 1874	
243	Lobe, Mary Ann	11m	W	D.C.	22 NOV 1866	Baltimore, Md.
120	Lobsher, Mary	11m	W	D.C.	05 JUL 1858	Glenwood
425	Loch, Selma	5y	W	D.C.	29 NOV 1869	Congressional
334	Lochbeoler, Barbara	2y	W	D.C.	13 JUL 1868	German Catholic
773	Lochbisler, Elizabeth	6m	W	U.S.	17 JUN 1874	
493	Lochbochler, Rosa	1d	W	D.C.	24 DEC 1870	German Catholic
147	Lochery, Hugh, stone cutter	45y	W	Ire.	20 APR 1859	Mt. Olivet
636	Lochler, George	10m	W	U.S.	12 NOV 1872	
120	Lochrey, H.	35y	W	Ire.	02 JUL 1858	St. Patricks
012	Lochrey, Margaret		W		28 JUN 1855	St. Patricks
643	Lochs, Chas. F.	40y	W	Ger.	10 DEC 1872	Washington Asylum
001	Locke, Andrew R.	49y			16 JAN 1855	St. Patricks
068	Locke, Andrew R.	24y	W	D.C.	19 JAN 1857	St. Patricks
536	Locke, Darcus	68y	W	N.C.	17 SEP 1871	Congressional*
411	Locker, Esther	69y	W	Md.	14 AUG 1869	Pr. Geo. Co., Md.
748	Lockey, Fannie	5m	W	U.S.	19 FEB 1874	Congressional
461	Lockwood, Jesse B.	1y	W	D.C.	29 JUL 1870	Congressional
462	Locraft, Margaret	1y	W	N.Y.	16 JUL 1870	N.Y.
462	Locraft, Mary	5m	W	D.C.	23 JUL 1870	N.Y.
525	Loeb, Mary E.	1y	C		28 JUN 1871	Prospect Hill
464	Loeffler, Anna M.	5m	W	D.C.	10 JUL 1870	Prospect Hill
167	Loeffler, Elizabeth	26y	W	Ger.	15 DEC 1859	Glenwood
375	Loeffler, Mary	7m	W		15 FEB 1869	Prospect Hill
612	Loeffler, Walter	3m	W	U.S.	15 JUL 1872	
216	Loelner, John, lieut.		W		28 MAR 1866	Congressional
241	Loewenthal, Jacob, claim agent	30y	W	Ger.	29 OCT 1866	Congressional
748	Lofter, Philip, laborer	76y	W	Ger.	01 FEB 1874	Prospect Hill
704	Logan, Danl. L.	1m	W	Amer.	04 JUL 1873	Glenwood
365	Logan, David C.	18m	W	Pa.	12 DEC 1868	Mt. Olivet
688	Logan, James	60y	C	U.S.	16 MAY 1873	Washington Asylum
238	Logan, John	15y	C	Md.	19 SEP 1866	
165	Logan, Mary	6m	C	D.C.	17 NOV 1859	Harmony
640	Logan, Mary E.	11y	C	U.S.	24 DEC 1872	Small Pox*
189	Logan, Mrs.		W		04 SEP 1860	Baltimore, Md.
696	Logan, Sarah, servant	19y	C	D.C.	29 JUN 1873	
760	Logan, Susan, infant of	28d	C	U.S.	20 APR 1874	
255	Logbiller, Mary A.	1y	W	D.C.	20 MAR 1867	German Catholic

Page	Name	Age	Race	Birth	Death Date	Burial Ground
524	Loir, Charlie	3m	C	D.C.	22 JUN 1871	Young Mens
513	Lokey, James B., Mrs.	57y	W	N.J.	07 MAR 1871	Methodist
015	Lolmes, Margarette	80y	W	D.C.	29 JUL 1855	
683	Lomax, David	24y	C	U.S.	03 APR 1873	Small Pox
635	Lomax, John	68y	C	U.S.	24 NOV 1872	Small Pox
509	Lomax, John	4m	C	D.C.	10 FEB 1871	Washington Asylum
291	Lomax, Malinda	65y	C	Va.	30 JAN 1868	Colored
454	Lomax, Martha	78y	W	Md.	16 MAY 1870	Mt. Olivet
388	Lomax, Martha	47y	C	Va.	15 APR 1869	Western
713	Lomax, Mary	1y	C	Md.	24 AUG 1873	
392	Lomax, Robt. J.	7m	C		20 MAY 1869	Holmead
141	Lonberger, Sophia F.	4m	W	D.C.	22 FEB 1859	German
029	London, M.J.	27y	W	Va.	23 NOV 1855	Portsmouth, Va.
313	London, Mary Eliza Arnold	10y	C	D.C.	19 MAY 1868	Mt. Olivet
263	Long, A.R., Col., child of	Still	W		17 JUN 1867	Greensboro, Pa.
355	Long, David	1y	W	D.C.	07 OCT 1868	Mt. Olivet
670	Long, J.D.	11y	W	U.S.	04 FEB 1873	Small Pox*
766	Long, Jesse	1y	C	U.S.	03 MAY 1874	
676	Long, Mary	21d	W	D.C.*	22 MAR 1873	
091	Long, Mrs.	50y	W	Ire.	17 SEP 1857	St. Patricks
400	Long, Nathalie	1y	W	Pa.	— JUL 1869	Md.
622a	Long, Nellie	6m	W	U.S.	01 AUG 1872	
545	Long, Pags	22y	C	Md.	16 NOV 1871	Washington
310	Long, Pearl B.	2m	W	D.C.	03 APR 1868	Conn.
430	Long, Sallie P.R.	21y	W	Mass.	26 DEC 1869	New Haven, Conn.
420	Long, Theodore C.	1y	W		14 OCT 1869	Alexandria, Va.
514	Long, Thos. H., printer	24y	W		11 MAR 1871	Saratoga Springs
189	Long, Virginia	25y	W	D.C.	14 SEP 1860	Congressional
042	Long, William	1y	C	D.C.	15 APR 1856	Methodist
274	Long, Willie	1y	W	D.C.	13 SEP 1867	Congressional
760	Long, Wm. B.	44y	W	Scot.	27 APR 1874	Washington Asylum
610	Long, Wm. F.	34y	C		08 JUN 1867	Young Mens
643	Longden, Elizabeth	80y	W	U.S.	11 DEC 1872	Oak Hill
607	Longfellow, Wm. E., farmer	52y	W	Md.	13 JUN 1872	Methodist
405	Longhran, Robert J.	3m	W		30 JUL 1869	Mt. Olivet
130	Longland, Josephine	24y	W	Ire.	18 OCT 1858	Washington Asylum
766	Lono, Michael	70y	C	U.S.	09 MAY 1874	Washington Asylum
153	Lony, Margaret	8m	W	U.S.	12 JUL 1859	Mt. Olivet
645	Lookie, Maggie	13d	W	U.S.	29 DEC 1872	
737	Loomes, Frank L.	1y	W	U.S.	26 DEC 1873	
628	Loomis, Olando C.	54y	W	U.S.	04 SEP 1872	
535	Loomis, Stephen, clerk	60y	W	Ohio	01 SEP 1871	Ohio
401	Looney, Catharine	70y	W	Ire.	16 JUL 1869	Mt. Olivet
149	Looney, James, storekeeper	23y	W	Ire.	19 MAY 1859	Mt. Olivet
739	Looney, L.	51y	C	U.S.	02 DEC 1873	
008	Looney, Mary	28y	W	Ire.	27 MAY 1855	St. Patricks
060	Looney, Mrs., child of	Still	W		11 OCT 1856	St. Patricks
143	Looney, William	2y	W	D.C.	12 MAR 1859	Mt. Olivet
012	Looney, Wm.	21d	W	D.C.	14 JUN 1855	St. Patricks
149	Loonie, Cornelius, storekeeper	30y	W	Ire.	18 MAY 1859	Mt. Olivet
320	Lopp, Lizzie	3m	W	D.C.	25 JUN 1868	Prospect Hill
014	Lord, A.H.	9m	W	D.C.	24 JUL 1855	Glenwood
605	Lord, Ebenezer, clerk	42y	W	D.C.	18 JUN 1872	Glenwood
004	Lord, Francis B.	20m	W	D.C.	27 MAR 1855	Glenwood
004	Lord, Marian W.	3y	W	D.C.	23 MAR 1855	Glenwood
760	Lord, Sarah J.	44y	W	U.S.	25 APR 1874	Glenwood
226	Lord, Wm. C., lawyer	53y	W	N.H.	29 JUN 1866	Congressional
020	Lording, Cornelius	11m	W	D.C.	29 AUG 1855	St. Patricks

District of Columbia Interments (Index to Deaths), 1855-1874

Page	Name	Age	Race	Birth	Death Date	Burial Ground
680	Loring, Chas. G., clerk	36y	W	U.S.	04 APR 1873	Bridgewater, Mass.
351	Lorvere, John	1y	C		19 SEP 1868	Mt. Olivet
247	Losano, Frances	28d	W	D.C.	23 DEC 1866	Mt. Olivet
307	Lotz, Henry	1m	W	D.C.	22 APR 1868	German Catholic
226	Louden, James		C	D.C.	25 JUN 1866	Harmony
217	Louden, [blank]	40y	C		10 APR 1866	Young Mens
188	Louder, John Q., blacksmith	54y	W	Ger.	27 AUG 1860	German Catholic
284	Louderbach, Caroline E.	2y	W	D.C.	19 NOV 1867	Glenwood
632	Loudin, John	20y	C	U.S.	24 OCT 1872	
516a	Loudon, Judy, pauper	1d	B	D.C.	08 MAR 1871	Washington Asylum
521	Loudon, Mary	2y	C	Va.	06 JUN 1871	
521	Loudon Mary	2y	C	Va.	08 JUN 1871	
219	Loudon, Rebecca	25y	C	D.C.	28 APR 1866	Young Mens
489	Loughran, Fannie M.	3m	W	D.C.	13 NOV 1870	Mt. Olivet
690	Louis, Anna	20y	C	U.S.	28 MAY 1873	Small Pox
690	Louis, Maggie	28d	C	U.S.	25 MAY 1873	Small Pox
166	Louis, Mary, servant	35y	W	Ire.	27 NOV 1859	
727	Louiz, Willie	13m	B	U.S.	05 OCT 1873	
591	Loumax, Frank	2y	C	D.C.	27 APR 1872	
158	Lounds, Cecelia C.	23y	W	D.C.	22 AUG 1859	Oak Hill
587	Lounds, Isaac	50y	C	D.C.	22 MAR 1872	Ebenezer
162	Lounds, John Calvin	1m	W	D.C.	25 SEP 1859	Oak Hill
158	Lounds, Mary	1y	C	D.C.	18 AUG 1859	Young Mens
036	Lounds, Noah, brick maker	46y	C		28 FEB 1856	Holmead
179	Lounds, Richard W., painter	63y	W	D.C.*	14 MAY 1860	Ebenezer
471	Loupster, Gofea	5y	W	D.C.	08 AUG 1870	Glenwood
534	Louse, Richard, baker	53y	C	D.C.	28 AUG 1871	Mt. Zion
608	Louxmes, Catharine	67y	W	Ger.	17 JUN 1872	
489	Love, Leon, cook	76y	W	Rus.	31 NOV 1870	Mt. Olivet
582	Lovedell, Ann O.	78y	W	Md.	21 FEB 1872	Congressional*
243	Lovejoy, Maria L.	28y	W	N.Y.	01 NOV 1866	Glenwood
493	Lovejoy, Wm. S.	1y	W	Md.	29 DEC 1870	Oak Hill
360	Lovelace, Alice E.	14d	W	D.C.	14 NOV 1868	Methodist
773	Lovelace, Mary Blanch	11m	W	U.S.	21 JUN 1874	
630	Loveless, L.	6y	W	U.S.	31 OCT 1872	Small Pox
013	Loveless, Wm. R.	60y	W	Md.	25 JUL 1855	Congressional
090	Loveless, [blank]	1m	W	D.C.	01 SEP 1857	
367	Lovell, Josh.	Still	B	D.C.	23 DEC 1868	Washington Asylum
292a	Lovett, Maheila, servant	45y	C	Va.	04 FEB 1868	Mt. Zion
471	Loving, Clara	1y	W	Amer.	21 AUG 1870	German Catholic
756	Loving, Lizzi, infant of	2m	W	U.S.	22 MAR 1874	
050	Lovney, Jane, child of	1d	W		20 JUL 1856	St. Patricks
526	Low, Berthnal	1y	W	U.S.	05 JUL 1871	Congressional
197	Low, Jerry	113y	C	Md.	13 JAN 1861	Mt. Olivet
476	Lowber, John, gentleman	93y	W	Amer.	31 SEP 1870	N.Y.
390	Lowe, Charles	3y	W		03 MAY 1869	Congressional
598	Lowe, Chas. W.	1y	W	U.S.	17 MAY 1872	Glenwood
041	Lowe, Elizabeth	38y	W		10 APR 1856	Congressional
131	Lowe, Geo. W.	10m	W	D.C.	22 OCT 1858	Congressional
343	Lowe, Helen E.	2y	W	D.C.	25 AUG 1868	Glenwood
773	Lowe, John Malachi, clerk	25y	W	U.S.	16 JUN 1874	Glenwood
190	Lowe, Mary	16y	C	D.C.	29 SEP 1860	Mt. Olivet
140	Lowe, Millard F.	3y	W	D.C.	03 FEB 1859	Glenwood
111	Lowe, Nicholas	62y	W	Md.	20 APR 1858	Holmead
408	Lowe, Warren, farmer	69y	W	Md.	17 AUG 1869	Glenwood
286	Lowe, William, musician 12th Inf.	29y	W	N.Y.	16 DEC 1867	Arlington Heights
782	Lowe, Wm. J., clerk	32y	W	U.S.	18 JUL 1874	Glenwood
598	Lowe, [blank]	4y	W	U.S.	18 MAY 1872	Glenwood

Page	Name	Age	Race	Birth	Death Date	Burial Ground
457	Lowell, Chas. Russell, librarian	63y	W	Mass.	23 JUN 1870	Boston, Mass.
754	Lowery, Ann M.	61y	W	U.S.	17 MAR 1874	Glenwood
329	Lownes, Harriet, housekeeper	27y	C	D.C.	06 JUL 1868	Ebenezer
367	Lowrie, Rosa E.	21y	W	Mo.	05 DEC 1868	Rock Creek
007	Lowry, Elmey	62y	W	S.C.	07 MAY 1855	Congressional*
250	Lowry, Margaret, servant	23y	W		07 JAN 1867	N.Y.
668	Lowry, Wm. H., land agent	62y	W	U.S.	21 FEB 1873	Oak Hill
184	Loyd, William, manufactuer	52y	W	Pa.	07 JUL 1860	
380	Lubbe, Lewis	38y	W	Prus.	05 MAR 1869	Prospect Hill
386	Luby, John S.	53y	W	D.C.	18 APR 1869	Oak Hill
151	Luby, Margaret	11y	W		15 JUN 1859	Mt. Olivet
677	Lucas, Albert	22y	C	U.S.	14 MAR 1873	Small Pox
441	Lucas, Baby	10d	C		11 FEB 1870	Union
637	Lucas, Beverly, carpenter	74y	C	U.S.	17 NOV 1872	
226	Lucas, Charles H.	10m	C	D.C.	26 JUN 1866	Harmony
190	Lucas, Charles H.	5d	C	D.C.	23 SEP 1860	Harmony
598	Lucas, Chas. W.	1y	C	U.S.	21 MAY 1872	Mt. Olivet
040	Lucas, Ellen	73y	W	Md.	25 MAR 1856	Congressional
456	Lucas, Eugene J.	8m	W	U.S.	10 JUN 1870	Congressional
367	Lucas, Francis	3y	B	U.S.	28 DEC 1868	Washington Asylum
588	Lucas, George	3y	W	D.C.	26 MAR 1872	Mt. Olivet
706	Lucas, Ignatius, messenger	75y	W	D.C.	19 JUL 1873	Mt. Olivet
782	Lucas, James	50y	C	U.S.	02 JUL 1874	Potters Field
403	Lucas, John E.	4y	C	D.C.	04 JUL 1869	Harmony
132	Lucas, Louisa F., seamstress	18y	C	D.C.	03 NOV 1858	Harmony
239	Lucas, Lucy	26y	C	D.C.	26 OCT 1866	Harmony
133	Lucas, Mary	9m	W	D.C.	26 NOV 1858	Laurel Factory
782	Lucas, Matilda, housekeeper	80y	C	U.S.	07 JUL 1874	
062	Lucas, Mrs., child of	Still			09 NOV 1856	Methodist
103	Lucas, Phillis		C		28 JAN 1858	Young Mens
330	Lucas, Solomon	1y	C	D.C.	20 JUL 1868	Washington
473	Lucas, Walter	1y	C	D.C.	05 AUG 1870	Young Mens
454a	Lucas, William, pauper	2½y	C	D.C.	24 MAY 1870	Washington Asylum
184	Lucas, [blank], Mr., wood sawyer	50y	C	U.S.	06 JUL 1860	Harmony
062	Lucasey, A., painter	25y	W	D.C.	01 NOV 1856	St. Matthews
135	Luce, Charlotte	69y	W	N.Y.	05 DEC 1858	Oak Hill
668	Luce, Cora E.	1y	W	U.S.	15 FEB 1873	Congressional
061	Luce, Vial, clerk	74y	W		15 OCT 1856	Oak Hill
538	Luck, Austena G.	34y	W		27 SEP 1871	German Catholic
626	Lucke, Maria	45y	W	U.S.	01 SEP 1872	
766	Lucke, Wm. H., Dr.	55y	W	U.S.	25 MAY 1874	
268	Lucket, Mary Jane	3m	W	D.C.	10 AUG 1867	Congressional
246	Lucket, Wm. W.	3m	C	D.C.	29 DEC 1866	Ebenezer
212	Lucket, [Jere]miah W.	24y	W	D.C.	21 FEB 1866	Glenwood
109	Luckett, Ashman, bookbinder	20y	W	D.C.	29 MAR 1858	Glenwood
734	Luckett, Ellsworth	7d	W	U.S.	04 DEC 1873	Congressional*
769	Luckett, Francis, laborer	56y	W	U.S.	12 MAY 1874	
220	Luckett, Jacob, house servant	58y	C	Md.	09 MAY 1866	Mt. Olivet*
528	Luckett, Joseph	6m	C		13 JUL 1871	
476	Luckett, Mary	1d	W	D.C.	22 SEP 1870	Mt. Olivet
447	Luckett, Minerva T.	60y	W		06 MAR 1870	Glenwood
766	Luckett, Murray D.	5m	W	U.S.	16 MAY 1874	Glenwood
125	Luckett, [blank]	1y	W	D.C.	27 AUG 1858	Washington Asylum
385	Lucketts, Alex.	13d	W		17 APR 1869	Congressional
255	Lucus, Jane, infant of	14d	C	D.C.	09 MAR 1867	Beckett's
260	Lucus, [blank]	18y	C		05 MAY 1867	Western
024	Lucy, Martin	7d	W	D.C.	03 SEP 1855	St. Patricks
116	Ludman, Carl	5m	W	D.C.	19 JUN 1858	German Lutheran

District of Columbia Interments (Index to Deaths), 1855-1874

Page	Name	Age	Race	Birth	Death Date	Burial Ground
773	Luff, Garrett, clerk	70y	W	U.S.	12 JUN 1874	Oak Hill
546	Luigenbach, Emma M.	24y	W	Md.	22 NOV 1871	Prospect Hill
052	Luke, Ann M.	25y	W		30 JUL 1856	Glenwood
115	Luke, George, laborer	40y	W	Eng.	09 JUN 1858	Washington Asylum
108	Luke, Mrs.	62y	W		24 MAR 1858	Glenwood
706	Lumacs, James	42y	C	D.C.	05 JUL 1873	Brightwood
454	Lumax, Elias, laborer	44y	C	Md.	01 MAY 1870	Washington Asylum
782	Lumber, Frank	1y	W	U.S.	15 JUL 1874	Mt. Olivet
342	Lumpkins, Lydia, cook	70y	C	Va.	21 AUG 1868	Harmony
016	Lumsford, Anna E.	7m	W	D.C.*	21 JUL 1855	Oak Hill
058	Lunay, Jeremiah	1m	W	D.C.	17 SEP 1856	St. Patricks
756	Lundy, Bubbie	2y	C	U.S.	30 MAR 1874	
193	Lunin, Mary	18y	C	U.S.	01 NOV 1860	Mt. Olivet
041	Lunt, Arthur, clerk	32y	W	Va.*	10 APR 1856	Alexandria, Va., Meth.
687	Lurdy, Thomas, carpenter	84y	W	Eng.	02 MAY 1873	Glenwood
340	Lusby, Hattie	1y	W	D.C.	28 AUG 1868	Congressional
473	Lusby, James H.	1y	W	D.C.	17 AUG 1870	Rock Creek
039	Lusby, James J.	4y	W	D.C.	19 MAR 1856	Congressional
717	Lusby, James O.	41y	W	D.C.	07 SEP 1873	Congressional
470	Lusby, Jas. H.	1y	W	D.C.	17 AUG 1870	Rock Creek
176	Lusby, John, child of	Still	W	D.C.	14 APR 1860	Congressional
039	Lusby, Thomas	27y	W	D.C.	17 MAR 1856	Congressional
741	Lusby, Thomas, watchman	79y	W	U.S.	08 JAN 1874	Congressional
275	Lusby, William A.	1y	W	D.C.	30 SEP 1867	Congressional
595	Luskey, Effie B.	3y	W	D.C.	10 APR 1872	Congressional
229	Lusley, James, brick maker	63y	W	Md.	22 JUL 1866	Glenwood
726	Luther, Almon C., watchman	33y	W	U.S.	24 OCT 1873	Congressional
150	Luther, Stephen	4m	W	D.C.	13 JUN 1859	German Catholic
495	Lutz, Conrad, soldier	65y	W	Ger.	12 DEC 1870	Potters Field
435	Lutz, John	1y	W		17 JAN 1870	German Catholic
550	Lutz, Thomas				31 DEC 1871	
456	Luzy, Mary	1y	C	D.C.	22 JUN 1870	
138	Lybelt, Edward	35y	W	Ire.	07 JAN 1859	Mt. Olivet
773	Lyburn, Jerry, laborer	80y	C	U.S.	16 JUN 1874	
385	Lycett, Edward, bookbinder	76y	W	Eng.	03 APR 1869	Baltimore, Md.
088	Lycett, Patrick	5y	W	D.C.	17 AUG 1857	St. Peters
101	Lyddan, James	1y	W	D.C.	08 JAN 1858	St. Patricks
632	Lyden, Kate	36y	W	Ire.	09 OCT 1872	
388	Lyle, Harlan G.	5y	W	D.C.	11 APR 1869	Mt. Olivet
124	Lyles, Aaron, cart man	45y	C	Va.	07 AUG 1858	Ebenezer
411	Lyles, James	9m	C		16 AUG 1869	Mt. Olivet
068	Lyles, Margaret	26y	C	D.C.	10 JAN 1857	Ebenezer
482	Lyles, Semars, ladies nurse	93y	C	D.C.	31 OCT 1870	Harmony
444	Lyman, Julia, Mrs.	46y	W	Md.	02 MAR 1870	Baltimore, Md.
248	Lymerson, Peter, clerk	25y	W		03 DEC 1866	N.Y.
681	Lynch, Annie, Mrs.	46y	W	U.S.	20 APR 1873	Mt. Olivet
706	Lynch, Catharine	1m	W	D.C.	23 JUL 1873	
053	Lynch, Charles	5m	W	D.C.	01 AUG 1856	Ebenezer
084	Lynch, Daniel	7d	W	D.C.	28 JUL 1857	St. Peters
177	Lynch, David, lawyer	67y	W	Pa.	24 APR 1860	Mt. Olivet
234	Lynch, Dennis, carpenter	37y	W	Ire.	01 SEP 1866	Mt. Olivet
542	Lynch, Elisabeth E.	21y	W	D.C.	21 OCT 1871	Congressional*
429	Lynch, Eliza V.	1y	W		27 DEC 1869	Congressional
236	Lynch, Ellen	75y	W	Ire.	23 SEP 1866	Mt. Olivet
725	Lynch, Emma C.	17y	W	Md.	19 OCT 1873	Mt. Olivet
773	Lynch, Ida	16d	W	U.S.	23 JUN 1874	Mt. Olivet
151	Lynch, James	36y	W	Ire.	24 JUN 1859	Washington Asylum
195	Lynch, Jannetta A.	10y	W	D.C.	20 DEC 1860	Congressional

Page	Name	Age	Race	Birth	Death Date	Burial Ground
462	Lynch, John	46y	W	Ire.	19 JUL 1870	Mt. Olivet
252	Lynch, John, laborer	55y	W	Ire.	11 FEB 1867	Mt. Olivet
315	Lynch, John M.	6d	W		c.23 MAY 1868	Mt. Olivet
766	Lynch, Levi	50y	C	U.S.	26 MAY 1874	Mt. Pleasant
407	Lynch, Mary	17y	W		02 AUG 1869	Congressional
015	Lynch, Mary	29y	W	Ire.	12 JUL 1855	St. Patricks
062	Lynch, Mary	1y	W	D.C.	12 NOV 1856	St. Patricks
147	Lynch, Mary	13y	W	D.C.	04 APR 1859	Va.
093	Lynch, Mary	32y	W	Ire.	03 OCT 1857	St. Peters
636	Lynch, Rebecca	18y	W	U.S.	15 NOV 1872	
478	Lynch, Sarah	2y	W	D.C.	24 SEP 1870	Mt. Olivet
292a	Lynch, Truman	86y	C		07 JAN 1868	Holmead
356	Lynch, Ulisius S.G.	25d	W	D.C.	02 OCT 1868	Mt. Olivet
268	Lynch, William	2y	W	D.C.	01 AUG 1867	Congressional
197	Lynch, [blank]	1y	W	D.C.	02 JAN 1861	Congressional
395	Lynch, [blank]	Still	W	D.C.	08 JUN 1869	Mt. Olivet
477	Lynde, Alex C., clerk	27y	W	Ill.	13 SEP 1870	Elgin, Ill.
244	Lyntch, George, laborer	29y	W	Md.	05 NOV 1866	Congressional*
244	Lyntch, Mrs.	30y	W	Md.	08 NOV 1866	Congressional*
453	Lyon, Clara, Mrs.	34y	W		05 MAY 1870	Congressional
624	Lyon, John	13m	W	U.S.	12 SEP 1872	Mt. Olivet
760	Lyon, John L.	46y	W	U.S.	14 APR 1874	Congressional*
462	Lyon, Katie	3m	W		04 JUL 1870	Congressional
165	Lyons, Catharine, servant	50y	W	Md.	13 NOV 1859	
645	Lyons, Fanny	2y	C	U.S.	25 DEC 1872	
289	Lyons, Hannalene	7m	W		21 JAN 1868	Mt. Olivet
288	Lyons, Joseph, gentleman	63y	W	Ire.	04 DEC 1867	Glenwood
457	Lyons, Mary	Still	W	D.C.	03 JUN 1870	Congressional
611	Lyons, Patrick	1y	W	U.S.	— JUL 1872	
434	Lyons, Weillamena P.	2y	W		04 JAN 1870	Prospect Hill
292	Lytle, Ann Eliza	4y	W	Ohio	28 JAN 1868	Glenwood

District of Columbia Interments (Index to Deaths), 1855-1874

Page	Name	Age	Race	Birth	Death Date	Burial Ground
M						
157	Maack, Anna	9m	W	D.C.	09 AUG 1859	Mt. Olivet
154	Maack, Mary	50y	W	Ire.	19 JUL 1859	Mt. Olivet
345	Maahenheimer, G.L., Rev.	68y	W	Md.	01 AUG 1868	Alexandria, Va.
666	Maber, Kate	8m	W	U.S.	06 FEB 1873	Prospect Hill
492	Mac, Edward	8m	C	U.S.	14 DEC 1870	Ebenezer
298	Mac, Ewdw.	3m	W		02 FEB 1868	Mt. Olivet
261	Macauley, [blank]	2d	W	D.C.	24 MAY 1867	Congressional
261	Macauley, [blank]	1d	W	D.C.	23 MAY 1867	Congressional
379	Mace, Frances, Mrs.	60y	W		21 MAR 1869	Congressional
229	Mace, James, horse doctor	35y	W	Eng.	18 JUL 1866	Alms House
632	Machear, Jane	49y	W	U.S.	15 OCT 1872	
331	Machen, Joseph Benjamin	6m	C	D.C.	12 JUL 1868	Mt. Olivet
449	Mack, Ellen, Mrs.		W		06 APR 1870	Mt. Olivet*
519	Mack, James, laborer	40y	C	Md.	18 MAY 1871	Ebenezer
047	Mack, Margaret	5m	W	D.C.	29 JUN 1856	Georgetown, Catholic
026	Mack, Margaret	11m	W	Md.	05 OCT 1855	St. Peters
033	Mack, Martin, laborer	54y	W	Ire.	20 JAN 1856	St. Peters
016	Mack, Mary	2y	W		22 JUL 1855	
278	Mack, Owen, laborer	80y	W	Ire.	15 OCT 1867	Holyrood
014	Mack, Peter	7m	W	D.C.	02 JUL 1855	
556	Mack, Willie	7d	C	D.C.	31 JAN 1872	Ebenezer
379	Mackay, William, brick maker	58y	W	D.C.	09 MAR 1869	Congressional
499	Mackeboy, James, laborer	84y	W	Va.	02 JAN 1871	Congressional
719	Mackey, Annie M.	34y	W		22 SEP 1873	Congressional*
216	Mackey, Henrietta A.	46y	W	Md.	23 MAR 1866	Mt. Olivet
344	Mackey, James	1y	W	D.C.	17 AUG 1868	St. Aloysius
099	Mackey, John, shoemaker	55y	W	Ire.	04 DEC 1857	St. Patricks
007	Mackey, Mary	8y	W	D.C.	07 MAY 1855	Congressional
077	Mackey, Thos.	18d			01 MAY 1857	St. Peters
612	Mackle, Sarah	2y	C	U.S.	27 JUL 1872	
612	MacNahaney, Wm.	1y	W	U.S.	30 JUL 1872	
390	Macomb, Harriet B.	87y	W	D.C.*	22 MAY 1869	Oak Hill
687	Macon, Marion, servant	24y	C	Va.	07 MAY 1873	
397	Madden, Mrs. [,child of?]	4m	Y	Amer.	22 JUN 1869	Ebenezer
610	Maddigan, Pat.	1y	W	U.S.	24 JUL 1872	
754	Maddix, Mary	16y	C	U.S.	09 MAR 1874	Mt. Pleasant
743	Maddox, Bevley	1y	C	U.S.	25 JAN 1874	Mt. Pleasant
387	Maddox, Eola	9m	W	Md.	14 APR 1869	Baltimore, Md.
128	Maddox, Laura C.	5m	W	D.C.	27 SEP 1858	Congressional
600	Maddox, Mrs.	74y	W	U.S.	12 MAY 1872	Mt. Zion
230	Maddox, T.	14y	C		16 JUL 1866	Young Mens
542	Maddox, Wilhelmina	6y	W	U.S.	21 OCT 1871	Congressional*
760	Maddox, Wm., infant of	1y	C	U.S.	26 APR 1874	Mt. Pleasant
279	Madegan, Mary	28y	W	Ire.	17 OCT 1867	Mt. Olivet
279	Madegan, Mrs., child of	Still	W		14 OCT 1867	Mt. Olivet
024	Madigan, Bridget	56y	W	Ire.	27 SEP 1855	St. Patricks
079	Madigan, Bridget	65y	W	Ire.	10 JUN 1857	St. Peters
121	Madigan, Catharine	9m	W		13 JUL 1858	St. Peters
236	Madigan, Mary	14y	W	D.C.	29 SEP 1866	Mt. Olivet
348	Madigan, Patrick, laborer	42y	W	Ire.	05 SEP 1868	Mt. Olivet
773	Madigan, Winefred	2y	W	U.S.	10 JUN 1874	
401	Madison, Alice	3y	C	D.C.	31 JUL 1869	Young Mens
684	Madison, Cordelia	4y	C	U.S.	07 APR 1873	Small Pox*
058	Madison, Luke	1y	C	D.C.	28 SEP 1856	Ebenezer
677	Madison, Wm. H.	9y	C	U.S.	24 MAR 1873	Small Pox
769	Madney, Alice	1y	C	U.S.	05 MAY 1874	
275	Madraid, Mary	30y	C	N.C.	16 SEP 1867	Young Mens

District of Columbia Interments (Index to Deaths), 1855-1874

Page	Name	Age	Race	Birth	Death Date	Burial Ground
626	Madrain, Maria	53y	W	Eng.	17 SEP 1872	
346	Madulla, Eliza	60y	C		29 AUG 1868	Freedmen's Hospital
601	Maeche, Caroline	63y	W	Sax.	18 MAY 1872	Prospect Hill
073	Maerkt, Anna Barbara, servant	30y	W	Ger.	11 MAR 1857	German
345	Maester, Annie	6m	W	D.C.	15 AUG 1868	German Catholic
243	Maffitt, James	55y	W		07 NOV 1866	Pa.
640	Mafus, Mary E.	8y	W	U.S.	24 DEC 1872	Small Pox*
023	Magallon, Infant	11m	W		23 SEP 1855	St. Matthews
042	Magan, B.A.	3y	W	D.C.	14 APR 1856	Congressional
325	Magan, T.J., clerk	51y	W	N.Y.	16 JUL 1868	Congressional
601	Magar, Beneta S.	22y	W	U.S.	02 MAY 1872	Congressional
172	Magar, John, shoemaker	60y	W	Pa.	12 FEB 1860	Congressional
125	Magee, Catharine		W		27 AUG 1858	St. Matthews
484	Magee, John	10m	W	D.C.	26 OCT 1870	Congressional
108	Magee, Owen, grocer	47y	W	Ire.	13 MAR 1858	St. Peters
038	Magee, Patrick, grocer	30y	W	Ire.	15 MAR 1856	St. Matthews
463	Magee, Susan	8m	W		29 JUL 1870	Mt. Olivet
248	Magie, Constant, cook	40y	W	Fra.	21 DEC 1866	Congressional
535	Magill, Katie Imogene	1y	W	D.C.	07 SEP 1871	Glenwood
032	Magill, Thos., MD. & farmer	30y	W	Md.	28 DEC 1855	Pr. Geo. Co., Md.
022	Magill, Wm. B.	11m	W	D.C.	18 AUG 1855	St. Peters
402	Magitt, James	7m	W	D.C.	11 JUL 1869	Mt. Olivet
003	Magle, Jacob	60y	W		21 FEB 1855	
041	Magnes, Mary E.	17y	W	Md.	08 APR 1856	Catholic
210	Magnet, [blank], merchant		W	Ger.	21 JAN 1866	Mt. Olivet
760	Magor, John	41y	C	U.S.	01 APR 1874	Washington Asylum
001	Magran, Theodore	1y			— JAN 1855	Glenwood
243	Magraw, John Thomas	5d	W	D.C.	14 NOV 1866	Mt. Olivet
589	Magruder, Calvin	7m	W	D.C.	15 MAR 1872	Mt. Zion
741	Magruder, Chas. T.	2m	C	U.S.	11 JAN 1874	
275	Magruder, Dennis	95y	C		17 SEP 1867	Young Mens
508	Magruder, E.	26y	C	Md.	06 FEB 1871	Union
496	Magruder, Elizabeth, housekeeper	66y	W	Md.	10 DEC 1870	Rock Creek
760	Magruder, H.	48y	C	U.S.	28 APR 1874	
783	Magruder, Hezekiah, Dr.	70y	W	U.S.	20 JUL 1874	Oak Hill
521	Magruder, Ida	1y	W	D.C.	09 JUN 1871	
767	Magruder, J.E.M.	22y	W	U.S.	17 MAY 1874	
580	Magruder, Jane, servant	72y	C	Md.	11 FEB 1872	Congressional
245	Magruder, John, brick burner	57y	C	Md.	03 NOV 1866	Harmony
320	Magruder, Maria	38y	C	Md.	22 JUN 1868	
748	Magruder, Mariah	50y	C	U.S.	28 FEB 1874	Harmony
125	Magruder, Mary	8y	C	D.C.	17 AUG 1858	
617	Magruder, Mary	5y	C	U.S.	01 AUG 1872	Mt. Olivet
041	Magruder, Mary T.	9m	W	D.C.	05 APR 1856	Glenwood
310	Magruder, Octavia	4y	C	D.C.	05 APR 1868	Young Mens
392	Magruder, Reson, messenger	65y	C	Md.	23 MAY 1869	Mt. Zion
170	Magruder, Virginia	8m	W	D.C.	21 JAN 1860	Glenwood
390	Magruder, William Beane, Dr.	59y	W	Md.	30 MAY 1869	Oak Hill
400	Maguerlos, Louise Hortense	9m	W	N.Y.	17 JUL 1869	Prospect Hill
496	Maguerlot, Alfred, clerk	30y	W	Fra.	09 DEC 1870	German Catholic
474	Maguire, Fanny	3y	C		19 AUG 1870	Washington Asylum
148	Maguire, John	19y	W	D.C.	14 MAY 1859	Mt. Olivet
420	Maguire, Mary	24y	W	Ire.	14 OCT 1869	Mt. Olivet
011	Mahan, Margaret	60y	W	Ire.	17 JUN 1855	St. Patricks
682	Mahaney, John, contractor	31y	W	Ire.	30 APR 1873	Mt. [blank]
131	Maher, Bridget	65y	W	Ire.	17 OCT 1858	Mt. Olivet
146	Maher, James, public gardener	67y	W	Ire.	15 APR 1859	Mt. Olivet
618	Maher, Jas. H.	1m	W	U.S.	11 AUG 1872	

Page	Name	Age	Race	Birth	Death Date	Burial Ground
730	Maher, John H.	9d	W	U.S.	12 NOV 1873	Mt. Olivet
226	Maher, John M., school boy	8y	W	N.Y.	25 JUN 1866	Mt. Olivet*
107	Maher, John, soldier	69y	W	Ire.	10 MAR 1858	Washington Asylum
348	Maher, William James	1y	W	D.C.	06 SEP 1868	Mt. Olivet
432	Mahew, Cecelia	69y	C		09 DEC 1869	Washington Asylum
077	Mahon, Vandorah	61y	W	Italy	02 MAY 1857	St. Peters
603	Mahoney, Annie, servant	25y	C	Va.	15 JUN 1872	Small Pox
754	Mahoney, Benj. C.	5m	W	U.S.	23 MAR 1874	Congressional
026	Mahoney, Danl.	30y	W	Ire.	20 OCT 1855	St. Peters
715	Mahoney, Danl. F., bookbinder	35y	W	Ire.	03 AUG 1873	
471	Mahoney, Emily	60y	W	D.C.	07 AUG 1870	Congressional
640	Mahoney, Emily	3y	W	U.S.	14 DEC 1872	Small Pox*
767	Mahoney, Francis E.	9m	W	U.S.	22 MAY 1874	Oak Hill
290	Mahoney, Francis R.	24y	W	Ire.	16 JAN 1868	Mt. Olivet
731	Mahoney, Henrietta	65y	C	U.S.	24 NOV 1873	Mt. Olivet
003	Mahoney, Henry M.	4y	W	Va.	14 FEB 1855	
412	Mahoney, Jos. A.	4m	C	D.C.	02 AUG 1869	Washington Asylum
615	Mahoney, Lewis	34y	C	U.S.	02 JUL 1872	
269	Mahoney, Mary E.	2y	C		11 AUG 1867	Young Mens
472	Mahoney, Silva Ann	1y	C		08 AUG 1870	Young Mens
187	Mahony, Benj. Franklin	1y	C	D.C.	09 AUG 1860	Young Mens
590	Mahorney, John	1y	W	D.C.	06 APR 1872	Mt. Olivet
496	Mahorney, [blank]	Still	W		01 DEC 1870	Mt. Olivet
682	Mahr, Henry	11m	W	U.S.	25 APR 1873	Prospect Hill
760	Mahr, Michael	2m	W	U.S.	15 APR 1874	
545	Mahrer, Annie	3y	W	D.C.	21 NOV 1871	
581	Mahrer, Henry	8m	W		15 FEB 1872	
550	Mahrer, John	5y	C	D.C.	25 DEC 1871	German
404	Maier, John	4y	W	D.C.	05 JUL 1869	Prospect Hill
176	Maier, Martha W.	1y	W	D.C.	04 APR 1860	Prospect Hill
028	Maily, Jane	25y	W	Ire.	01 OCT 1855	St. Patricks
063	Maison, Mary, servant	18y	C		29 NOV 1856	Young Mens
456	Major, Edward	6m	W	D.C.	26 JUN 1870	Congressional
467	Major, Edward	6m	W	D.C.	26 JUL 1870	Congressional
537	Maken, Ann R.	53y	W	D.C.	22 SEP 1871	Congressional
436	Maker, James	3m	C		19 JAN 1870	Union
308	Makle, Eliza	80y	C		04 APR 1868	Alms House
515	Malay, Patrick, sailor	26y	W	Md.	13 MAR 1871	Congressional
170	Malihan, Alice	48y	W	Ire.	22 JAN 1860	St. Patricks (vault)
444	Maling, James H., painter	23y	W		25 MAR 1870	Congressional
058	Mallard, Frederick W.A.	19y	W	N.H.	14 SEP 1856	Glenwood
231	Mallern, Anna	9m	W	D.C.	15 AUG 1866	Prospect Hill
203	Malley, John	40y	W	Ire.	18 MAY 1861	Mt. Clivet
380	Malloney, Gillam Harvey	2y	W		11 MAR 1869	Congressional
020	Mallony, Edward	34y	W	Ire.	21 AUG 1855	St. Patricks
107	Mallory, Frank M.	11y	W	Fla.	12 MAR 1858	Congressional
724	Malone, Daniel	47y	W	Ire.	15 OCT 1873	Mt. Olivet
520	Malone, John	78y	W	Ire.	31 MAY 1871	Mt. Olivet
107	Malone, Lawrence	6y	W	D.C.	09 MAR 1858	Trinity
324	Malone, Margaret	2y	W	D.C.	24 JUL 1868	Mt. Olivet
008	Malone, Mary	6y	W	D.C.	17 MAY 1855	Trinity, Georgetown
213	Malone, Mrs., infant of	Still	W	D.C.	25 FEB 1866	Mt. Olivet
338	Malone, Timothy, laborer	30y	W	Ire.	20 AUG 1868	Mt. Olivet
231	Maloney, B.	32y	W	Ire.	04 AUG 1866	Mt. Olivet
058	Maloney, Catharine	4m	W		24 SEP 1856	St. Patricks
316	Maloney, James		C		c.15 MAY 1868	Alms House
394	Maloney, James	60y	W	Ire.	01 JUN 1869	Mt. Olivet
078	Maloney, James, laborer	27y	W	Ire.	19 MAY 1857	St. Matthews

Page	Name	Age	Race	Birth	Death Date	Burial Ground
024	Maloney, John	1y	W	D.C.	01 SEP 1855	St. Patricks
039	Maloney, Lot	5y	W	Ire.	30 MAR 1856	St. Peters
231	Maloney, M. Thomas	5m	W	D.C.	15 AUG 1866	Mt. Olivet
274	Maloney, Mary	35y	W	Ire.	03 SEP 1867	Mt. Olivet
300	Maloney, Mary	35y	W	Ire.	04 MAR 1868	Mt. Olivet
338	Maloney, Mary	60y	W	Ire.	30 AUG 1868	Mt. Olivet
080	Maloney, Mary	1y			29 JUN 1857	St. Patricks
253	Maloney, Patrick, gardener	27y	W	Ire.	22 FEB 1867	Mt. Olivet
697	Maloney, Thomas	8m	W	D.C.	05 JUN 1873	Mt. Olivet
097	Maloney, [blank]	4y	W		24 NOV 1857	Western
079	Malony, Margaret	26y	C	D.C.	04 JUN 1857	Young Mens
097	Malony, Patrick	68y	W	Ire.	12 NOV 1857	Washington Asylum
783	Malster, William, dentist	64y	W	U.S.	12 JUL 1874	Glenwood
754	Manahan, [blank]	37y	W	Ire.	15 MAR 1874	Mt. Olivet
299	Manders, Annie E.	20y	W	Md.	04 MAR 1868	Baltimore, Md.
308	Manders, Francis L.	1m	W	D.C.	21 APR 1868	Congressional
396	Manfield, Mary	9m	C	D.C.	— JUN 1869	Young Mens
629	Manford, Laura	13m	C	U.S.	20 OCT 1872	
310	Mangan, Ann	20y	W		c.01 APR 1868	Mt. Olivet
370	Mangen, Anna	2y	W		23 JAN 1869	Mt. Olivet
201	Mangett, Mary Annie	74y	W	Fra.	12 MAR 1861	German Catholic
614	Manguara, Mary	35y	W	Ire.	16 JUL 1872	
760	Manguin, Mary	22y	W	U.S.	26 APR 1874	Congressional
499	Mangum, Wm. B.	7d	W	D.C.	20 JAN 1871	Congressional
282	Maning, Margaret Barrett	1m	W	D.C.	17 NOV 1867	Mt. Olivet
207	Mankins, E.	35y	W		28 JUL 1862	[torn]
032	Mankins, Kate	1y	W		26 DEC 1855	St. Patricks
748	Manley, Mary J.	11d	W	U.S.	11 FEB 1874	Alexandria, Va.
622	Manman, Anna	10m	W	U.S.	05 AUG 1872	
460	Mann, Eddie	8m	W	D.C.	19 JUN 1870	Mt. Olivet
094	Mann, George	2y	W	D.C.	29 OCT 1857	Congressional
518	Mann, Henry	45y	W	D.C.	06 MAY 1871	Washington
600	Mann, Jane	9d	C	U.S.	01 MAY 1872	Unknown
724	Mann, John	2y	W	D.C.	14 OCT 1873	Mt. Olivet
174	Mann, William, messenger	69y	W	Pa.	16 MAR 1860	Glenwood
620	Manning, Cath.	28y	W	Ire.	10 AUG 1872	
074	Manning, Lewis, house servant	64y	C	Va.	16 MAR 1857	Holmead
212	Manning, Mary	22y	W	Ire.	07 FEB 1866	
305	Manning, Michael	1d	W		c.09 MAR 1868	Mt. Olivet
773	Manning, R.G.	5m	W	U.S.	20 JUN 1874	
042	Manning, Rachael, cook	60y	C	Va.	26 APR 1856	Harmony
279	Manning, Sallie L., lady	58y	W	Va.	13 OCT 1867	Mt. Olivet
345	Mansell, Anthony	3y	W	Can.	30 AUG 1868	
229	Mansell, Peter, hotel porter	32y	W	Ire.	18 JUL 1866	Mt. Olivet
013	Mansfield, A.F.	11m	W	D.C.	11 JUL 1855	Methodist, East
459	Mansfield, Ida V.	3y	W	D.C.	27 JUN 1870	Methodist
091	Mansfield, Isabella	1y	W	D.C.	15 SEP 1857	Methodist
118	Mansfield, John	11m	W	D.C.	17 JUN 1858	Methodist
247	Mansfield, Joseph S.		W		06 DEC 1866	Methodist
783	Mansfield, Laura V.	10m	W	U.S.	23 JUL 1874	Methodist
184	Mansfield, Thomas	5m	W	D.C.	08 JUL 1860	
050	Mansfield, [blank], Mr., farmer	50y	W	Ire.	15 JUL 1856	Washington Asylum
246	Manship, Ann	72y	W	Md.	27 DEC 1866	Congressional
540	Manson, Thomas	2y	C	D.C.	05 OCT 1871	
075	Mantz, George, clerk	38y	W	Md.	03 APR 1857	Congressional
179	Mantz, Sarah A.	42y	W	D.C.	14 MAY 1860	Congressional
610	Manul, Joseph P.	4m	C	U.S.	31 JUL 1872	
152	Marada, Ellen	10m	W	D.C.	27 JUN 1859	Mt. Olivet

District of Columbia Interments (Index to Deaths), 1855-1874

Page	Name	Age	Race	Birth	Death Date	Burial Ground
731	Maraen, Frank H.	3y	W	U.S.	22 NOV 1873	Oak Hill
454	Maran, Mary	60y	C	Va.	28 MAY 1870	Washington Asylum
028	Marble, Chs.	60y	C		27 OCT 1855	Harmony
466	Marble, Mary	8m	C	D.C.	03 JUL 1870	Young Mens
382	Marbray, Harriet	3y	C		23 MAR 1869	Young Mens
634	Marbury, Leonard, farmer	81y	W	U.S.	30 OCT 1872	
748	Marbury, William, merchant	31y	W	U.S.	27 FEB 1874	Oak Hill
028	Marcelet, John B.C.	35d	W		07 OCT 1855	Glenwood
035	Marcellas, Ann E.	40y	W	Md.	12 FEB 1856	Greenmount, Balto.
150	Marcellus, Aaron L.	2y	W	N.Y.	11 JUN 1859	
688	Marceron, Elizabeth	40y	W	U.S.	17 MAY 1873	Mt. Olivet
042	Marceron, Jno. L., merchant	28y	W	D.C.	14 APR 1856	Washington
319	March, Mary	75y	W	Md.	13 JUN 1868	Oak Hill
159	Marche, Clotilda	4m	W	D.C.	25 AUG 1859	Mt. Olivet
429	Marders, James E.	23y	W		10 DEC 1869	Congressional
399	Mardes, John H., seaman	28y	W	Amer.	16 JUL 1869	Congressional
422	Margain, Samuel, laborer	23y	C	Md.	10 OCT 1869	Washington Asylum
186	Marggraf, Catharine	58y	W	Ger.	30 JUL 1860	Congressional
782	Marggrass, Chas.	7m	W	U.S.	01 JUL 1874	Prospect Hill
583	Marggrof, Francis	7y	W	D.C.	26 FEB 1872	Prospect Hill
069	Mari, Francis, gentleman	86y	W	Italy	21 JAN 1857	St. Patricks
782	Marix, Henry, clerk State Dept.	65y	W	Ger.	08 JUL 1874	Jewish
513	Marke, Valinda	53y	W	Va.	16 MAR 1871	Methodist
374	Marke, William	1y	W		02 FEB 1869	Congressional
342	Marker, Earnest	11m	W	S.C.	23 AUG 1868	Congressional
240	Markriter, John, infant of	Still			06 OCT 1866	Mt. Olivet
291	Marks, Andrew		C		07 JAN 1868	Alms House
061	Marks, Andrew		W		14 OCT 1856	Methodist, East
477	Marks, Ann H.	56y	W	Eng.	11 SEP 1870	Congressional
127	Marks, Charles	1y	W	D.C.	11 SEP 1858	Congressional
084	Marks, Estelle C.	2m	W	D.C.	27 JUL 1857	Methodist
264	Marks, James M., laborer	42y	W	Md.	05 JUL 1867	Mt. Olivet
588	Marks, Joseph C., bricklayer	29y	W	Pa.	28 MAR 1872	Pa.
232	Marks, M.M.	1y	W	N.Y.	29 AUG 1866	Mt. Olivet
516a	Marks, Valinda, pauper	53y	C	Va.	16 MAR 1871	Washington Asylum
191	Marks, [blank]	75y	W	Md.	22 OCT 1860	Methodist
295	Markwalder, Jacob, hatter	66y	W	Switz.	16 FEB 1868	Congressional
584	Markwood, Manda	1y	W	U.S.	02 MAR 1872	Congressional
545	Marledoy, Cornelia	35y		D.C.	12 NOV 1871	
349	Marll, Rosa Isabel	5m	W		09 SEP 1868	Oak Hill
364	Marlow, Frank M.	8y	W	Amer.	23 DEC 1868	Congressional*
079	Marlow, Jas.	1y	W	D.C.	09 JUN 1857	Foundry
465	Marlow, Joseph	3y	C	D.C.	15 JUL 1870	Good Hope
625	Marlow, Sophy	80y	C	U.S.	21 SEP 1872	
382	Marlow, Wm.	7m	C	D.C.	11 MAR 1869	Mt. Olivet
698	Marmaduke, Sarah B.	74y	W	Va.	13 JUN 1873	Congressional
091	Maroney, John	74y	W	Ire.	17 SEP 1857	Washington Asylum
033	Maroney, Mary	3y	W		03 JAN 1856	St. Patricks
027	Maroney, Michael	68y	W	Ire.	12 OCT 1855	St. Peters
548	Maroney, Wm. Andrew	10m	W	D.C.	11 DEC 1871	St. Marys
370	Marooney, Ellen	75y	W	Ire.	20 JAN 1869	Mt. Olivet
137	Marr, J.H.	2m	W		19 JAN 1859	Glenwood
135	Marr, Mrs.	25y	W	D.C.	07 DEC 1858	Glenwood
161	Marriett, Catharine		W	D.C.	15 SEP 1859	Congressional
165	Marriett, John	3y	W	D.C.	19 NOV 1859	Congressional
022	Marriett, Magdaline R.	2y	W	D.C.	01 AUG 1855	Congressional
005	Marriner, Joanna	5y	W	D.C.	15 MAR 1855	Congressional
274	Marriott, Lucy	26y	W	Md.	13 SEP 1867	Glenwood

Page	Name	Age	Race	Birth	Death Date	Burial Ground
202	Marrk, Margaret	25y	W	Va.	26 APR 1861	Washington Asylum
143	Marron, John, asst. to post master	56y	W	Ky.	04 MAR 1859	Mt. Olivet
380	Marsden, William L., clerk	57y	W	Eng.	16 MAR 1869	Mt. Olivet
003	Marsh, Emma L.	27y	W	Conn.	22 FEB 1855	
050	Marsh, Harriet	1y	W	D.C.	14 JUL 1856	Congressional
242	Marsh, Kate W.	1y	W	D.C.	27 OCT 1866	Mt. Olivet
597	Marsh, L. Agnes	38y	W	Ire.	02 MAY 1872	Mt. Olivet
388	Marsh, Rachel M.	2y	W		30 APR 1869	Ohio
003	Marshal, John	4y	W	D.C.	28 FEB 1855	
719	Marshal, Richd. H.	11m	C	D.C.	19 SEP 1873	Beckett's
278	Marshal, Wm. Henry, waiter	14y	C	Md.	16 OCT 1867	Potters Field
580	Marshall, Ada	1m	W	D.C.	06 FEB 1872	Congressional*
442	Marshall, Amelia	13y	C		24 FEB 1870	Washington Asylum
760	Marshall, Amy J.	10m	W	U.S.	08 APR 1874	Congressional*
078	Marshall, Ann, servant	32y	C	D.C.	24 MAY 1857	Foundry
340	Marshall, Betty, Mrs.	72y	W	U.S.	29 AUG 1868	Congressional
420	Marshall, Charles, clerk	18y	W		25 OCT 1869	Poughkeepsie, N.Y.
521	Marshall, Chas. B.	3m	W	La.	07 JUN 1871	Congressional
448	Marshall, Flora, servant	19y	C		01 MAR 1870	Washington Asylum
670	Marshall, Granston	35y	C	U.S.	05 FEB 1873	Small Pox*
405	Marshall, Ida	4m	C		05 JUL 1869	Mt. Olivet
542	Marshall, James	80y	C	Va.	18 OCT 1871	Washington
674	Marshall, Jno. A.	33y	C	U.S.	16 MAR 1873	Harmony
666	Marshall, John		C	U.S.	04 FEB 1873	Harmony
422	Marshall, Julia	30y	C	Va.	25 OCT 1869	Ebenezer
420	Marshall, Maggie	9y	W	Md.	06 OCT 1869	Mt. Olivet
286	Marshall, Margaret	59y	C		13 DEC 1867	Young Mens
415	Marshall, Maud	5m	W		22 SEP 1869	Poughkeepsie, N.Y.
447	Marshall, Miriah	6y	C	Md.	29 MAR 1870	Washington Asylum
392	Marshall, Priscilla	49y	C	Md.	16 MAY 1869	Mt. Olivet
607	Marshall, T., housewife	72y	W	D.C.	30 JUN 1872	
688	Marshall, Thomas H., sea capt.	76y	W	U.S.	16 MAY 1873	Congressional*
617	Marshall, Wash., laborer	56y	C	U.S.	14 AUG 1872	
371	Marshall, William H.	11m	W	Md.	01 JAN 1869	Oak Hill
583	Marsland, M.H.	50y	W	Eng.	27 FEB 1872	
557	Marston, Isaiah, blacksmith	48y	W	Md.	03 FEB 1872	Congressional*
199	Marten, Charles	1y	W	D.C.	01 FEB 1861	Congressional
179	Martens, [boy]	1m	W	D.C.	01 MAY 1860	Washington Asylum
537	Martin, A.M.	44y	W	U.S.	23 SEP 1871	Methodist
600	Martin, A.S.	21d	W	U.S.	20 MAY 1872	Georgetown
581	Martin, Ada E.	4y	W	D.C.	15 FEB 1872	Congressional*
021	Martin, Albertina	1y	W	D.C.	27 AUG 1855	Alexandria, Va.
587	Martin, Andrew	9m	W	D.C.	23 MAR 1872	Mt. Olivet
071	Martin, Ann	95y	W	Md.	25 FEB 1857	Md.
729	Martin, Annie, servant	19y	C	U.S.	10 NOV 1873	
782	Martin, August I.O.	1y	W	U.S.	07 JUL 1874	Prospect Hill
536	Martin, Barbara	51y	W	Md.	17 SEP 1871	Methodist
744	Martin, C., Mrs.	37y	W	U.S.	28 JAN 1874	
585	Martin, Clara R.	2y	W	D.C.	09 MAR 1872	Congressional*
754	Martin, Clara, servant	28y	C	U.S.	23 MAR 1874	
429	Martin, Clarence Perrie	3m	W		24 DEC 1869	Congressional
267	Martin, Cornelia	43y	W	Va.*	29 JUL 1867	Glenwood
016	Martin, E.P.	70y	W	Md.	27 JUL 1855	St. Patricks
026	Martin, Elizabeth	63y	W		10 OCT 1855	Methodist
172	Martin, Elizabeth	Still	W	D.C.	17 FEB 1860	Prospect Hill
230	Martin, Ellen N.	3y	C		31 JUL 1866	Beckett's
372	Martin, Frances	26y	C	D.C.	22 JAN 1869	Harmony
371	Martin, George, boot/shoemaker	28y	W	Ger.	06 JAN 1869	Prospect Hill

District of Columbia Interments (Index to Deaths), 1855-1874

Page	Name	Age	Race	Birth	Death Date	Burial Ground
278	Martin, George, laborer	105y	C	Md.	31 OCT 1867	Harmony
332	Martin, Harry Winfield	1y	W		23 JUL 1868	Methodist
223	Martin, Helen M.	2y	W	D.C.	02 JUN 1866	Oak Hill
231	Martin, Howard	9m	W	D.C.	21 AUG 1866	Congressional
375	Martin, Howard	1y	W	Md.	04 FEB 1869	Oak Hill
303	Martin, J.L., child of	1m	W	D.C.	14 MAR 1868	Congressional
170	Martin, James, blacksmith	24y	W	Pa.	23 JAN 1860	Alms House
238	Martin, James F., blacksmith	34y	W	D.C.	30 SEP 1866	
041	Martin, James J., messenger	45y	W	Md.	14 APR 1856	St. Patricks
214	Martin, Joanna	30y	W	Md.	12 MAR 1866	Congressional
525	Martin, John	2m	W	D.C.	27 JUN 1871	Congressional
783	Martin, John D.	11m	W	U.S.	23 JUL 1874	Baltimore, Md.
231	Martin, Joseph	5m	W	D.C.	11 AUG 1866	Congressional
553	Martin, Joseph, fireman [sic]	2m	W	D.C.	10 JAN 1872	Methodist
379	Martin, Leo	2h	W		19 MAR 1869	Congressional
053	Martin, Lewis, farmer	63y	W	N.Y.	19 AUG 1856	Congressional
228	Martin, Lillie Jane	9m	W	D.C.	14 JUL 1866	Mt. Olivet
475	Martin, Lizzie, servant	20y	C	Va.	04 SEP 1870	Freedmen's Hospital
013	Martin, Margaret	22y	W	Md.	04 JUL 1855	
454	Martin, Maria	35y	C	Va.	14 MAY 1870	Washington Asylum
522	Martin, Maria E.	6m	W	D.C.	10 JUN 1871	Prospect Hill
407	Martin, Mary	68y	W	Va.	05 AUG 1869	Congressional
334	Martin, Mary E.	2y	W	D.C.	19 JUL 1868	Mt. Olivet
534	Martin, Mary Jane	3y	W	D.C.	27 AUG 1871	
380	Martin, Mrs.	46y	W		13 MAR 1869	Mt. Olivet
055	Martin, Nancy, servant	38y	W	Ire.	27 AUG 1856	Congressional
131	Martin, Nelly	52y	C		29 OCT 1858	Western
610	Martin, Philip		W		15 JUN 1867	Mt. Olivet
343	Martin, Rachel	80y	C	Md.	26 AUG 1868	
029	Martin, Saml., laborer	55y	W	Md.	16 NOV 1855	Methodist, East
071	Martin, Sarah	16y	C	Md.	21 FEB 1857	Rockville, Md.
429	Martin, Sarah Ann, Mrs.	54y	W	Va.*	04 DEC 1869	Congressional
179	Martin, Sarah C.	29y	W	D.C.	05 MAY 1860	Glenwood
625	Martin, Terasa	4y	W	U.S.	24 SEP 1872	Mt. Olivet
110	Martin, Thomas L., carpenter	36y	W	Va.*	01 APR 1858	Alexandria, Va.
063	Martin, Tobias, clerk	45y	W	Eng.	17 NOV 1856	Congressional
266	Martin, Walter	1y	C		29 JUL 1867	Poor House
386	Martin, William B.	9y	W	Md.	19 APR 1869	Oak Hill
408	Martin, William, bar keeper	22y	W	Va.	23 AUG 1869	Prospect Hill
394	Martin, William T.	8m	C	D.C.	27 JUN 1869	Mt. Olivet
611	Martin, Wm.	1y	W	U.S.	12 JUL 1872	Congressional*
074	Martin, [blank]	1y	W	D.C.	25 MAR 1857	German
507	Martin. [blank]	3m	W		02 FEB 1871	Mt. Olivet
261	Martinet, George	3y	W	D.C.	18 MAY 1867	Baltimore, Md.
548	Martinet, Slalie	4y	W	D.C.	18 DEC 1871	Md.
241	Martinez, Anna C.	43y	W	N.J.	21 OCT 1866	Oak Hill
128	Marting, Octavia		C		25 SEP 1858	Washington Asylum
304	Martise, Isaac A.	60y	W		c.06 MAR 1868	Glenwood
258	Martz, Joseph, watchman at capl.	38y	W		11 APR 1867	Congressional
449	Maryman, Ella	32y	W		24 APR 1870	Mt. Olivet
501	Maryman, Martha, dressmaker	49y	C	Va.	13 JAN 1871	Mt. Olivet
015	Masi, Charles	16y	W	D.C.	14 JUL 1855	St. Patricks
165	Masi, Vincent, gentleman	52y	W	Italy	08 NOV 1859	St. Patricks
104	Masin, Mr., servant of	72y	C		12 FEB 1858	Young Mens
251	Maskell, Jane, infant of	1m	C	D.C.	14 JAN 1867	Beckett's
676	Mason, Alice Virgilia	2y	W	U.S.	30 MAR 1873	Va. H.W.M.
055	Mason, Anna E.	8m	C	D.C.	04 AUG 1856	Young Mens
386	Mason, Annie E.	9m	M		14 APR 1869	Mt. Olivet

Page	Name	Age	Race	Birth	Death Date	Burial Ground
680	Mason, Clementine A.	17y	C	U.S.	07 APR 1873	Baltimore, Md.
529	Mason, Elisabeth	6m	C	D.C.	26 JUL 1871	Harmony
123	Mason, Emily	18y	C	D.C.	28 JUL 1858	Washington Asylum
099	Mason, G.	4d	C	D.C.	26 DEC 1857	Young Mens
483	Mason, George	1m	C	D.C.	16 OCT 1870	Mt. Olivet
083	Mason, George	10m	C	D.C.	15 JUL 1857	Young Mens
223	Mason, George H.	9m	W		07 JUN 1866	Congressional
402	Mason, James	32y	W	Ire.	08 JUL 1869	Mt. Olivet
371	Mason, James	8y	C	D.C.	03 JAN 1869	Washington Asylum
554	Mason, James, cook	30y	W	Eng.	17 JAN 1872	
555	Mason, James, cook	50y	W	Eng.	29 JAN 1872	Congressional
097	Mason, Jen., Mrs.	76y	W		29 NOV 1857	Alexandria, Va.
276	Mason, John	8m	W	D.C.	13 SEP 1867	Mt. Olivet
633	Mason, John, laborer	48y	W	Ire.	03 OCT 1872	
063	Mason, John W., waiter	41y	C	D.C.	19 NOV 1856	Young Mens
309	Mason, Julia	3m	W	D.C.	23 APR 1868	Mt. Olivet
411	Mason, Julia	37y	W	Ire.	24 AUG 1869	Mt. Olivet
711	Mason, Lizzie	9m	C	D.C.	10 AUG 1873	Mt. Olivet
518	Mason, M.H.	30y	W	Ohio	12 MAY 1871	Oak Hill
740	Mason, Mary	84y	C	U.S.	01 JAN 1874	Mt. Pleasant
024	Mason, Mary	2d	W	D.C.	20 SEP 1855	St. Peters
038	Mason, Mary E.	15y	C	D.C.	20 MAR 1856	Young Mens
704	Mason, Melvina, housekeeper	35y	C	Ark.	12 JUL 1873	Ebenezer
093	Mason, Michael, laborer	35y	W	Ire.	06 OCT 1857	St. Peters
232	Mason, Milton	11y	W	D.C.	23 AUG 1866	Congressional*
109	Mason, Mr., servant of	22y	C		29 MAR 1858	Young Mens
387	Mason, Rhacel	19m	C	D.C.	05 APR 1869	Harmony
336	Mason, Robert, farmer	32y	C	Va.	01 AUG 1868	
500	Mason, Robt.	7y	C	D.C.	27 JAN 1871	Harmony
202	Mason, Sarah E.	1y	C	D.C.	18 APR 1861	Young Mens
501	Mason, Thomas, laborer	30y	C	Conn.	27 JAN 1871	Union
470	Mason, V.L.T.	8m	W	Amer.	07 AUG 1870	Congressional
589	Mason, Wilson N.	22y	C	Md.	15 MAR 1872	
460	Massey, Geo. Henry	6m	C	D.C.	21 JUN 1870	Ebenezer
124	Massey, John H.	38y	C	D.C.	13 AUG 1858	Harmony
694	Massey, Mary C.	53y	W	Md.	22 JUN 1873	Baltimore, Md.
398	Massey, Wm.	2m	B	D.C.	28 JUN 1869	Washington Asylum
447	Massy, Lucy R., servant	20y	C		30 MAR 1870	
633	Massy, Sarah H., lady	84y	W	U.S.	04 OCT 1872	Oak Hill
710	Mastbrook, H. Henry	19m	W	D.C.	06 AUG 1873	Prospect Hill/Rock Cr.
748	Masters, Amelia	50y	W	U.S.	07 FEB 1874	Congressional*
060	Masterson, Mary	64y	W	Ire.	17 OCT 1856	St. Peters
405	Mathews, Elizabeth	2m	C	D.C.	19 JUL 1869	Washington Asylum
161	Mathews, Francis, porter	45y	C	D.C.	14 SEP 1859	Harmony
705	Mathews, G.T.	3m	W	U.S.	18 JUL 1873	
669	Mathews, George	18y	C	U.S.	10 FEB 1873	Small Pox
170	Mathews, George L.		W	Va.	25 JAN 1860	Washington Asylum
643	Mathews, Hannah	85y	C	U.S.	08 DEC 1872	Ebenezer
023	Mathews, Infant	1y	W		03 SEP 1855	Glenwood
508	Mathews, John, draughtsman	35y	W	Switz.	21 FEB 1871	Prospect Hill
355	Mathews, Maggie, domestic	26y	W	Ire.	13 OCT 1868	Mt. Olivet
691	Mathews, Mary	19y	W	U.S.	09 MAY 1873	Congressional*
738	Mathews, Nillen	10y	C	U.S.	31 DEC 1873	
409	Mathews, Susan	72y	C	Md.	18 AUG 1869	Young Mens
190	Mathews, Susan, servant	26y	C	D.C.	21 SEP 1860	Young Mens
335	Mathews, William	2y	C	D.C.	25 JUL 1868	
455	Mathews, William	75y	C	Md.	19 MAY 1870	
182	Mathews, Willie C.	7m	W	D.C.	29 JUN 1860	Presbyterian

District of Columbia Interments (Index to Deaths), 1855-1874

Page	Name	Age	Race	Birth	Death Date	Burial Ground
335a	Mathews, Wm. H.	4m	B	D.C.	29 JUL 1868	Washington Asylum
714	Mathews, [blank]		W	D.C.	31 AUG 1873	
057	Mathieson, John	3y	W	D.C.	11 SEP 1856	Methodist
095	Mathiot, Adelaide D.	7y	W	D.C.	08 OCT 1857	Glenwood
026	Mathiot, Selena B.	1y	W	D.C.	05 OCT 1855	Glenwood
313	Mathue, Jesse	11m	C	D.C.	21 MAY 1868	Harmony
003	Matingly, Ann	73y	W	Md.	09 FEB 1855	St. Patricks
016	Matingly, Francis V.	19m	W	D.C.	13 JUL 1855	Catholic, Georgetown
158	Matlock, Margaret	32y	W	D.C.	18 AUG 1859	Glenwood
026	Matlock, Wm., taylor	41y	W	D.C.	24 OCT 1855	Foundry
097	Matmarow, Patrick	2y	W	D.C.	24 NOV 1857	St. Patricks
300	Matten, Isaac	4y	C	D.C.	25 MAR 1868	Alms House
581	Mattfield, Gustave, grocer	38y	W	Ger.	15 FEB 1872	Prospect Hill
708	Mattheny, Daniel	76y	C	Va.	01 JUL 1873	Washington Asylum
537	Matthews, blank]	6m	C	D.C.	19 SEP 1871	Ebenezer
783	Matthews, Chas. P.	12d	W	U.S.	09 JUL 1874	Mt. Olivet
292a	Matthews, Edward	2y	C	Md.	11 FEB 1868	Mt. Zion
232	Matthews, Elizabeth	61y	C	Md.	27 AUG 1866	Ebenezer
590	Matthews, Gertrude	10m	W	U.S.	09 APR 1872	
485	Matthews, James, laborer	25y	W	Ire.	02 OCT 1870	Catholic, Georgetown
251	Matthews, Jane R.	3y			19 JAN 1867	Mt. Olivet
459	Matthews, Margtt., servant	25y	C	Va.	26 JUN 1870	
472	Matthews, Maria	60y	C	Md.	17 AUG 1870	Freedmen's Hopsital
239	Matthews, Mary		C		05 OCT 1866	Young Mens
523	Matthews, Mary Ann	3m	W	D.C.	17 JUN 1871	Methodist
255	Matthews, Richard	10y	C		18 MAR 1867	Harmony
214	Matthews, Sarah, laborer	38y	C	D.C.	09 MAR 1866	Harmony
153	Mattingley, Joseph	4y	W	D.C.	08 JUL 1859	Glenwood
115	Mattingley, Walter, tinner	33y	W	Md.	11 JUN 1858	Georgetown
062	Mattingly, Ann	73y	W	Mass.	09 NOV 1856	St. Peters
242	Mattingly, Henrietta	57y	W	Md.	03 OCT 1866	Congressional
213	Mattingly, Mary	63y	W		28 FEB 1866	Mt. Olivet
481	Mattingly, Rose Anna	8m	W	D.C.*	22 OCT 1870	Holmead
259	Mattingly, W., Mrs., child of	Still	W		06 APR 1867	Glenwood
696	Mattiot, George, clerk	50y	W	U.S.	02 JUN 1873	
233	Mattlin, [blank]	55y	W		10 AUG 1866	N.Y.
162	Mattock, Wm. G.	1y	W	D.C.	19 SEP 1859	Glenwood
408	Mattox, Wm. H.	2y	C	D.C.	13 AUG 1869	Western
462	Maud, Frances	10m	W	Md.	09 JUL 1870	Congressional
676	Maury, Chas. F., clerk	31y	W	U.S.	31 MAR 1873	Congressional
538	Maury, Thomas J., Dr.	36y	W	D.C.	25 SEP 1871	Congressional*
091	Maus, David	1y	W	D.C.	18 SEP 1857	German
364	Maxwell, Joseph	4m		D.C.	11 DEC 1868	Congressional*
588	Maxwell, Margret	1y	W	D.C.	26 MAR 1872	Mt. Olivet
088	Maxwell, Sarah W.	4y	W	D.C.	24 AUG 1857	Methodist
590	May, Catharine	1d	W	D.C.	12 APR 1872	
322	May, Hannah	70y	C	Va.	29 JUN 1868	Freedmen's Hospital
159	May, James R., clerk	25y	W	D.C.*	31 AUG 1859	Mt. Olivet
319	May, John	11m	C	D.C.	25 JUN 1868	Western
120	May, John P.	2d	W	D.C.	03 JUL 1858	German Catholic
382	May, William, waiter		C		23 MAR 1869	Western
034	Maydelina, Mary	1y	W	D.C.	10 JAN 1856	German
453	Mayer, C.	69y	W	Ger.	23 MAY 1870	Prospect Hill
723	Mayer, Henry I., produce dealer	32y	W	Pa.	03 OCT 1873	Glenwood
689	Mayers, Mary E.	23y	W	U.S.	22 MAY 1873	Prospect Hill
635	Mayhew, Edward	14y	W	U.S.	10 NOV 1872	Small Pox
029	Mayhew, Mary Ann	45y	W	Md.	03 NOV 1855	Methodist
710	Mayhew, Sabarah	64y	W	Amer.	02 AUG 1873	Glenwood

Page	Name	Age	Race	Birth	Death Date	Burial Ground
404	Mayill, Heenan B.	1y	W	D.C.	09 JUL 1869	Baltimore, Md.
397	Maylin, Mary E.		C		25 JUN 1869	Holmead
526	Maynadier, Wm., officer U.S.A.	64y	W	Md.	03 JUL 1871	Oak Hill
635	Maynard, Albert	6y	W	U.S.	27 NOV 1872	Small Pox
745	Maynard, Phillis	80y	C	U.S.	18 JAN 1874	
224	Maynard, William	6m	W	Md.	15 JUN 1866	Baltimore, Md.
584	Mayne, J.G., clerk	28y	W	Pa.	04 MAR 1872	
782	Mayo, E.	74y	W	Scot.	06 JUL 1874	Congressional
744	Mazzullo, George W.	1y	W	U.S.	30 JAN 1874	Congressional
195	Mazzullo, Philip Francis	8d	W	D.C.	15 DEC 1860	Congressional
227	McAleer, Philip	11m	W	D.C.	06 JUL 1866	Mt. Olivet
105	McAlister, Amelia S.	4m	W	D.C.	25 FEB 1858	Congressional
531	McAlister, James F., clerk	20y		D.C.	06 AUG 1871	Congressional*
112	McAlister, James R., clerk	33y	W	Mo.	29 APR 1858	Congressional
008	McAlister, Lizzie Beall	6m	W		01 MAY 1855	Congressional
165	McAlister, [blank]	7y	W	D.C.	03 NOV 1859	Congressional*
143	McAlligate, Thomas	1y	W	D.C.	13 MAR 1859	St. Patricks
661	McAllister, Francis A.	1m	W	U.S.	23 JAN 1873	Mt. Olivet
597	McArdle, Eliza M.	80y	W	U.S.	11 MAY 1872	Congressional
470	McArdle, W.O.	1y	W	D.C.	08 AUG 1870	Philadelphia, Pa.
359	McAuley, Hanson C.	3y	W	D.C.	29 NOV 1868	Congressional
703	McAuliffe, Denis P.	8m	W	D.C.	23 JUL 1873	Mt. Olivet
349	McAuliffe, Mary	5m	W		25 SEP 1868	Mt. Olivet
411	McAuliffe, Patrick	8d	W		24 AUG 1869	Mt. Olivet
165	McAvoy, George, gilder & carver	37y	W	Scot.	11 NOV 1859	Mt. Olivet
403	McBeth, Nancy S.E.	1m	C	D.C.	21 JUL 1869	Harmony
055	McBoye, Kate	22y	W	Va.*	26 AUG 1856	Alexandria, Va., Cath.
690	McBride, Anna, housekeeper	44y	W	Ire.	28 MAY 1873	
051	McBride, Catharine	23y	W	Ire.	21 JUL 1856	St. Peters
485	McBride, Martha E.	1m	W	D.C.	06 OCT 1870	Glenwood
132	McBride, Mary A.	3y	W	D.C.	09 NOV 1858	St. Patricks
078	McBride, Theophilus, soldier	31y	W	Pa.	28 MAY 1857	Philadelphia, Pa.
688	McBride, William, stone cutter	22y	W	Ire.	11 MAY 1873	Glenwood
228	McCabe, Hubert	1y	W	D.C.	15 JUL 1866	Mt. Olivet
172	McCadden, George	4y	W	D.C.	06 FEB 1860	St. Patricks
131	McCadden, Thomas	9m	W	D.C.	28 OCT 1858	St. Patricks
060	McCafferty, C.	28y	W	Md.	20 OCT 1856	Glenwood
021	McCafferty, Elizabeth	80y	W	Ire.	13 AUG 1855	St. Patricks
168	McCaffey, Ann, domestic	50y	W	Ire.	13 DEC 1859	
166	McCaffrey, Jane Frances	4y	W	D.C.	20 NOV 1859	Congressional*
263	McCalla, Allen	8m	W	D.C.	28 JUN 1867	Congressional
261	McCalla, Andrew J., clerk	50y	W		24 MAY 1867	Congressional
341	McCalla, Kenneth Bruce	20d	W	D.C.	18 AUG 1868	Congressional
213	McCann, Daniel	11m	W		22 FEB 1866	
426	McCann, Mary Martha, housekpr.	30y	W	D.C.	07 NOV 1869	Oak Hill
292a	McCann, Rosanna	4m	W	D.C.*	16 JAN 1868	Catholic
421	McCanna, Margaret, domestic	42y	W	Ire.	16 OCT 1869	Mt. Olivet
014	McCardy, Wm.	55y	W	D.C.	30 JUL 1855	Congressional
038	McCarren, Jno., r.r. conductor	35y	W		06 MAR 1856	Glenwood
760	McCartee, Louisa, domestic	1y	C	U.S.	28 APR 1874	
597	McCarter, Blanche E.	1y	W	D.C.	01 MAY 1872	Congressional
457	McCarter, Geo. B., infant of	Still	W		21 JUN 1870	Congressional
386	McCarter, Mrs., seamstress	36y	W	Amer.	18 APR 1869	Congressional
704	McCarthey, Michael, laborer	47y	W	Ire.	08 JUL 1873	Mt. Olivet
689	McCarthy, Ann M., Mrs.	32y	W	U.S.	24 MAY 1873	Frederick, Md.
408	McCarthy, Ann, Mrs., housekpr.	45y	W	Ire.	23 AUG 1869	Mt. Olivet
150	McCarthy, Annie T.	1y	W	N.J.	10 JUN 1859	N.Y.

District of Columbia Interments (Index to Deaths), 1855-1874

Page	Name	Age	Race	Birth	Death Date	Burial Ground
380	McCarthy, B., laborer	38y	W	Ire.	17 MAR 1869	Mt. Olivet
469	McCarthy, Chas., laborer	40y	W	Ire.	25 AUG 1870	Mt. Olivet
116	McCarthy, Dennis	1y	W	D.C.	22 JUN 1858	
274	McCarthy, Dennis	1y	W	D.C.	14 SEP 1867	Mt. Olivet
667	McCarthy, James	7m	W	U.S.	08 FEB 1873	Mt. Olivet
774	McCarthy, John	36y	W	Ire.	30 JUN 1874	Mt. Olivet
401	McCarthy, Mary	8m	W		24 JUL 1869	Mt. Olivet
149	McCarthy, Mary	7m	W	D.C.	22 MAY 1859	St. Patricks
774	McCarthy, May, Mrs.	40y	W	Ire.	30 JUN 1874	Mt. Olivet
151	McCarthy, [blank]	Still	W	D.C.	23 JUN 1859	
528	McCartney, Francis A.	43y	W		19 JUL 1871	Congressional*
262	McCarty, Alfred B., waiter	24y	C	D.C.	08 JUN 1867	Mt. Olivet
023	McCarty, Cate	11m	W	Va.	03 SEP 1855	St. Patricks
783	McCarty, Catherine	1y	W	U.S.	27 JUL 1874	Mt. Olivet
093	McCarty, Florence, laborer	35y	W	Ire.	14 OCT 1857	St. Patricks
338	McCarty, J.	1y	W		13 AUG 1868	Mt. Olivet
059	McCarty, John	1y	W	D.C.	22 SEP 1856	St. Patricks
488	McCarty, Louisa, nurse	25y	C	D.C.	07 NOV 1870	Mt. Olivet
627	McCarty, M.	96y	C	U.S.	21 SEP 1872	
634	McCarty, M., housekeeper	70y	W	Ire.	30 OCT 1872	
645	McCarty, Maggie	5y	W	U.S.	27 DEC 1872	Frederick City, Md.
121	McCarty, Mary A.	6y	W	D.C.	14 JUL 1858	St. Matthews
010	McCarty, Mary Ann	8m	W	D.C.	28 JUN 1855	St. Patricks
356	McCarty, Michael, laborer	56y	W	Ire.	20 OCT 1868	Mt. Olivet
767	McCarty, Thomas, grocer	45y	W	Ire.	13 MAY 1874	Mt. Olivet
142	McCaskie, Peter, upholsterer	55y	W	Scot.	14 FEB 1859	Congressional*
221	McCatheran, Mary A.	41y	W		15 MAY 1866	Glenwood
773	McCatherine, Joseph	2m	W	U.S.	26 JUN 1874	Mt. Olivet
499	McCathran, Donald	9y	W	Md.	25 JAN 1871	Congressional
088	McCathran, Ella V.	2y	C	D.C.	21 AUG 1857	Methodist
188	McCathran, Eva E.	1y	W	D.C.	23 AUG 1860	Congressional
262	McCathran, Harry Ford	1y	W	D.C.	25 JUN 1867	Congressional
268	McCathran, W.W., teacher	38y	W	D.C.	31 AUG 1867	Congressional
519	McCathran, Wm. T., clerk	21y	W	U.S.	21 MAY 1871	Congressional*
390	McCauley, Chas. Stewart, USN	75y	W	Pa.	23 MAY 1869	Oak Hill
715	McCauley, Cornelius	8m	W	D.C.	02 AUG 1873	
606	McCauley, Jas.	29y	W	Pa.	22 JUN 1872	Congressional
117	McCauley, John, tinner	53y	W		27 JUN 1858	Congressional
018	McCauley, Mary Jane	1y	W	D.C.	02 AUG 1855	Glenwood
141	McCauley, William, tinner	64y	W		13 FEB 1859	Congressional*
581	McCauley, Wm.	4y	C	D.C.	16 FEB 1872	
471	McCaully, [blank]	Still	W		28 AUG 1870	Congressional
528	McChesney, Robert, farmer	69y	W	D.C.	15 JUL 1871	Rock Creek
071	McChesney, [blank], shoemaker	50y	W	D.C.	18 FEB 1857	Washington Asylum
289	McClain, Charles	3y	C	Va.	05 JAN 1868	Union
723	McClay, Eliza	45y	B	D.C.	02 OCT 1873	Washington Asylum
527	McClear, Fechn	32y	W	Pa.	12 JUL 1871	Congressional
449	McCleary, Hugh, private marine	37y	W	Ire.	24 APR 1870	Congressional
133	McCleland, Biddy	35y	W	Ire.	26 NOV 1858	St. Peters
434	McClellan, A.R.	25y	W		01 JAN 1870	Congressional
594	McClellan, Gurley Eliza	60y	W	Me.	27 APR 1872	Oak Hill
007	McClellan, Jane J.	30y	W	Md.	07 APR 1855	Congressional
439	McClellan, Thomas R.	3y	W	D.C.	12 FEB 1870	Congressional
476	McClellan, Walter	1m	W	D.C.	02 SEP 1870	Mt. Olivet
666	McClelland, Jno.	16m	W	U.S.	04 FEB 1873	
127	McClelland, Rosina	2y	W	D.C.	13 SEP 1858	Holmead
324	McClelland, Rosina	8m	W	D.C.	22 JUL 1868	Mt. Olivet
021	McClellen, Mary E.	18m	W		30 AUG 1855	Holmead

District of Columbia Interments (Index to Deaths), 1855-1874

Page	Name	Age	Race	Birth	Death Date	Burial Ground
783	McClenlan, John	14d	W	U.S.	20 JUL 1874	
034	McClery, Edwin J., clerk	31y	W	D.C.	28 JAN 1856	Not Reported
457	McClery, Eva	19y	W	D.C.	02 JUN 1870	Congressional
169	McClery, James, clerk	84y	W	Ire.	15 JAN 1860	Washington
506	McClery, Jas. F.I., Dr.	51y	W	D.C.	15 FEB 1871	Congressional
239	McClery, Morven J., clerk	44y	W	D.C.	24 OCT 1866	Congressional
666	McClintock, Mary E.	15m	C	U.S.	04 FEB 1873	Mt. Pleasant
625	McClomic, Anna	2y	W	U.S.	16 SEP 1872	
271	McCloskey, Ellen J.	66y	W	D.C.	25 AUG 1867	Holmead
228	McCloskey, James, soldier		W	Ire.	17 JUL 1866	Mt. Olivet
550	McCloskey, Lizzie	5y	W	D.C.	29 DEC 1871	
018	McCloskey, Mary H.	1y	W	Va.	10 AUG 1855	St. Matthews
400	McClosky, Charles H.S.	10m	W		15 JUL 1869	Glenwood
364	McCloud, Alexander	2y	W	D.C.	22 DEC 1868	Congressional*
410	McCloud, Eliz. G.	12y	W		02 AUG 1869	Methodist
712	McClune, Jane	3y	W	D.C.	21 AUG 1873	Congressional
012	McCoakley, [blank]	21d	W	D.C.	16 JUN 1855	Foundry
079	McColley, Ellen, servant	20y	W	Ire.	01 JUN 1857	St. Peters
407	McCollin, Arthur J., private marine	25y	W	Del.	28 AUG 1869	Congressional
067	McCollum, John	8d	W		30 DEC 1856	St. Patricks
261	McCologan, James	23y	W	D.C.	01 MAY 1867	Baltimore, Md.
025	McComb, Mary	69y	W	Ire.	17 SEP 1855	Congressional
471	McCommonds, Maria	53y	W	N.J.	21 AUG 1870	Congressional
229	McConany, Bridget	42y	W	Ire.	22 JUL 1866	Mt. Olivet
112	McConchie, John T.S., gardener	65y	W		27 APR 1858	
624	McConnel, Isaac	16m	W	U.S.	17 SEP 1872	
166	McConnell, Annie E.	15y	W	D.C.	09 NOV 1859	Washington
368	McConnell, Ella	1y	W	D.C.	05 DEC 1868	Mt. Olivet
643	McConnell, Hannah G.	19y	W	U.S.	08 DEC 1872	Glenwood
528	McConnell, Wm., dentist	73y	W	Pa.	18 JUL 1871	Glenwood
667	McConvey, Mary A.	4y	W	U.S.	14 FEB 1873	
783	McCook, James	17y	W	U.S.	28 JUL 1874	Mt. Olivet
767	McCook, Mary T.	27y	W	U.S.	12 MAY 1874	Oak Hill
086	McCook, Patrick	7y	W	D.C.	03 AUG 1857	St. Patricks
735	McCormac, Hugh, clerk	72y	W	U.S.	10 DEC 1873	Congressional
732	McCormack, Catherine	20y	W	U.S.	25 NOV 1873	Mt. Olivet
239	McCormick, Catherine	35y	W	Ire.	01 OCT 1866	Mt. Olivet
720	McCormick, Geo. P.	5m	W	Md.	27 SEP 1873	Congressional*
549	McCormick, H.P.	87y	W	U.S.	19 DEC 1871	Congressional
201	McCormick, John		W		14 MAR 1861	Washington Asylum
137	McCormick, John, laborer	54y	W	Pa.	14 JAN 1859	Methodist
388	McCormick, John Thomas	6m	W		13 APR 1869	Baltimore, Md.
711	McCormick, L. Francis	11m	W	D.C.	12 AUG 1873	Mt. Olivet
705	McCormick, Maggie	13m	W	Pa.	06 JUL 1873	Mt. Olivet*
297	McCormick, Mary Jane	2m	W	D.C.	01 FEB 1868	Mt. Olivet*
132	McCormick, Pat., laborer	45y	W	Ire.	01 NOV 1858	Washington Asylum
718	McCormick, Thos., groceryman	35y	W	Ire.	13 SEP 1873	Mt. Olivet*
094	McCormick, Wm. J., clerk	62y	W	D.C.	29 OCT 1857	St. Peters
229	McCormick, Wm. P.	8m	W	Md.	21 JUL 1866	Baltimore, Md.
325	McCornell, Mary L.	25y	W	D.C.	14 JUL 1868	Congressional
719	McCorpin, Joshua	14m	C	D.C.	15 SEP 1873	Young Mens
125	McCoy, Ann	51y	W	Scot.	23 AUG 1858	Congressional
273	McCoy, Benjamin	1y	C	D.C.	18 SEP 1867	Harmony
493	McCoy, Fredk. T.	4y	W	D.C.	24 DEC 1870	Congressional
619	McCoy, Harriet E.	70y	C	U.S.	23 AUG 1872	
754	McCoy, James H.		C	U.S.	24 MAR 1874	Harmony
783	McCoy, James, infant of	13d	C	U.S.	20 JUL 1874	Mt. Pleasant
132	McCoy, Jane	69y	C	Va.	15 NOV 1858	Harmony

District of Columbia Interments (Index to Deaths), 1855-1874

Page	Name	Age	Race	Birth	Death Date	Burial Ground
227	McCoy, Jasper, blacksmith		W		06 JUL 1866	Congressional*
188	McCoy, Kate	2y	W	D.C.	20 AUG 1860	Congressional
054	McCoy, M. Samuel	1y	W	D.C.	07 AUG 1856	Congressional
518	McCoy, Mary M.	38y	C	Va.	04 MAY 1871	Potters Field
024	McCoy, Robt.	3y	W	D.C.	20 SEP 1855	Congressional
518	McCoyle, Rachel	3m	C	D.C.	04 MAY 1871	Potters Field
537	McCraffrey, Thomas, supt.	58y	W		19 SEP 1871	Mt. Olivet
429	McCreary, William G., clerk Int.	38y	W	Pa.	12 DEC 1869	Congressional
131	McCrete, Margaret	43y	W	Ire.	30 OCT 1858	St. Patricks
720	McCuin, Elizabeth	55y	W	Va.	26 SEP 1873	Mt. Olivet
053	McCuin, Levi, farmer	49y	W	Va.	20 AUG 1856	Va.
425	McCulbin, Priscilla	9m	W	D.C.	26 NOV 1869	Congressional
001	McCullogh, Edwd.	27y			28 JAN 1855	Congressional
605	McCunn, Mary Jane	4m	W	D.C.	18 JUN 1872	Md.
445	McCurry, William, farmer	85y	W	Ire.	05 MAR 1870	Mt. Olivet
440	McCutchen, Ann	64y	W	D.C.	— FEB 1870	Glenwood
214	McDaley, William				01 MAR 1866	Mt. Olivet
767	McDane, Mary E.	1y	W	U.S.	17 MAY 1874	Oak Hll
135	McDaniel, Enoch, child of	Still	W	D.C.	18 DEC 1858	Congressional
294	McDaniel, James, Capt.	45y	I	I.C.	01 FEB 1868	Congressional
003	McDaniel, Rebecca Alice	5m	W	Md.	08 FEB 1855	
387	McDaniels, Lucy Ellen, servant	12y	C	U.S.	25 APR 1869	
632	McDavitt, [blank]	7m	W	U.S.	25 OCT 1872	
688	McDennott, Patk. H.	2y	W	U.S.	12 MAY 1873	
253	McDermott, Ann Agnes	38y	W		10 FEB 1867	Mt. Olivet
159	McDermott, Anna C.	18y	W	Md.	25 AUG 1859	Baltimore, Md.
593	McDermott, Mary	45y	W	D.C.	08 APR 1872	Mt. Olivet
742	McDermott, Phillip, boat builder	23y	W	U.S.	15 JAN 1874	Mt. Olivet
767	McDermott, Sarah, housekeeper	45y	W	Ire.	11 MAY 1874	Holyrood
267	McDermott, William Joseph	2y	W	D.C.	11 JUL 1867	Mt. Olivet*
070	McDevitt, Bella M.	6m	W	D.C.	04 FEB 1857	Philadelphia, Pa.
687	McDevitt, Cecelia Estelle	8m	W	D.C.	03 MAY 1873	Mt. Olivet
507	McDevitt, Chas. F., stone cutter	38y	W	D.C.	26 FEB 1871	Baltimore, Md.
333	McDevitt, James	7m	W		12 JUL 1868	Mt. Olivet
240	McDevitt, John	75y	W	Ire.	01 OCT 1866	Baltimore, Md.
175	McDewell, J., clerk	30y	W	Ohio	26 MAR 1860	Ohio
348	McDonald, A., Mrs., child of	Still	W		29 SEP 1868	Mt. Olivet
170	McDonald, Ann	25y	W	Ire.	20 JAN 1860	Mt. Olivet
105	McDonald, Anna	24y	W	D.C.	21 FEB 1858	Country
694	McDonald, Daisy	6m	W	D.C.	14 JUN 1873	Glenwood
011	McDonald, Eugene	56y	W	Ire.	25 JUN 1855	St. Peters
549	McDonald, Harry L.	1y	W	D.C.	23 DEC 1871	Glenwood
748	McDonald, James A., printer	19y	W	U.S.	20 FEB 1874	Baltimore, Md.
668	McDonald, James B.	65y	W	U.S.	15 FEB 1873	Congressional
199	McDonald, James, shoemaker	29y	W		14 FEB 1861	Rock Creek
011	McDonald, John, laborer	c.35	W	Scot.	29 JUN 1855	Poor House
633	McDonald, Joseph	26y	W	U.S.	28 OCT 1872	Small Pox*
299	McDonald, Joseph, bar tender	18y	W	Ire.	15 MAR 1868	Mt. Olivet
232	McDonald, R., infant of	2d	W	D.C.	29 AUG 1866	Mt. Olivet
415	McDonald, [blank]	67y	W	Ire.	17 SEP 1869	Mt. Olivet
362	McDonalds, Cath.	24y	C		16 NOV 1868	Ebenezer
636	McDonnel, Patrick, laborer	53y	W	Ire.	25 NOV 1872	
601	McDonough, Hugh	10m	W	U.S.	22 MAY 1872	Unknown
774	McDonough, M.	13d	W	U.S.	29 JUN 1874	Holyrood
742	McDonough, Margaret	2m	W	U.S.	20 JAN 1874	Holyrood
212	McDonough, Peter	40y	W	Ire.	02 FEB 1866	Mt. Olivet
599	McDougal, George	56y	W	U.S.	15 MAY 1872	Ind.
581	McDowell, Chas.	1m	W	D.C.	15 FEB 1872	Mt. Olivet

Page	Name	Age	Race	Birth	Death Date	Burial Ground
680	McDowney, Elizth.	6y	C	U.S.	04 APR 1873	
554	McDowney, Hugh, laborer	30y	C	U.S.	17 JAN 1872	
241	McDuel, John	74y	W		01 OCT 1866	Glenwood
620	McDuell, Cora	2y	W	U.S.	09 AUG 1872	Glenwood
674	McDuell, Frank R.	13m	W	U.S.	18 MAR 1873	Glenwood
680	McDuell, [blank]	12y	W	U.S.	05 APR 1873	Glenwood
449	McDuffy, Louisa	62y	W		24 APR 1870	Ohio
437	McDunott, C.V., infant of	Still	W		14 JAN 1870	Mt. Olivet
204	McElfresh, Agnes	10m	W		08 JUN 1861	Glenwood
203	McElfresh, Emma V.	4y	W	D.C.	20 MAY 1861	Glenwood
339	McElfresh, Frances Cecelia	1y	W	D.C.	06 AUG 1868	Glenwood
554	McElfresh, Guy H.	6m	W	D.C.	16 JAN 1872	
696	McElfresh, Oliver S.	6m	W	D.C.	06 JUN 1873	Congressional*
235	McElfresh, Zachariah, child of	3h	W		17 SEP 1866	Glenwood
394	McElory, J. Edward	5m	W	D.C.	27 JUN 1869	Congressional
534	McElroy, Ann E.	24y	W	Va.	27 AUG 1871	Washington
587	McElroy, George	23y	W	Md.	23 MAR 1872	Congressional*
456	McElroy, James A.	7m	W	D.C.	23 JUN 1870	Congressional
698	McElroy, Robert J., fireman	26y	W	Md.	27 JUN 1873	Congressional
602	McElroy, Wm.	1y	W	U.S.	14 MAY 1872	Congressional
159	McElvoy, Elizabeth	29y	W	Ire.	29 AUG 1859	Mt. Olivet
066	McEnnis, Philip, tailor	50y	W	Ire.	26 DEC 1856	Baltimore, Md.
593	McEntee, Bridget	2y	W	Va.	13 APR 1872	Mt. Olivet
151	McEvann, James	5y	W	D.C.	16 JUN 1859	St. Peters
024	McFadden, [Wm.], magazine keeper	40y	W	Ire.	15 SEP 1855	Congressional
283	McFalls, Louise B.	5m	W	D.C.	04 NOV 1867	Glenwood
689	McFalls, Thadeus B., Rev., USA	39y	W	U.S.	22 MAY 1873	Glenwood
523	McFarlan, Bertha	2m	W	D.C.	19 JUN 1871	Glenwood
101	McFarlan, Josephine	52y	W	Italy	06 JAN 1858	Glenwood
521	McFarlan, Mary E.	19y	W	D.C.	01 JUN 1871	Congressional*
013	McFarland, J.H.S.	9m	W	D.C.	19 JUL 1855	Methodist, East
182	McFarland, Michael	85y	W	Ire.	26 JUN 1860	Mt. Olivet
453	McFarland, R.W.	24y	W		07 MAY 1870	Congressional
057	McFarlin, Chas. L.	1y	W	D.C.	11 SEP 1856	Congressional
697	McGarry, Jos.	7m	W	D.C.	14 JUN 1873	Mt. Olivet
698	McGaw, Phobe M.	5m	W		20 JUN 1873	Glenwood
262	McGee, Ellen	4m	W	D.C.	25 JUN 1867	Mt. Olivet
255	McGee, Mary	60y	W	Md.	15 MAR 1867	Rock Creek
144	McGee, Virginia F.	26y	W	Va.	27 MAR 1859	Congressional
782	McGee, William	3m	W	U.S.	08 JUL 1874	Mt. Olivet
586	McGill, Francis J.	9m	W	D.C.	16 MAR 1872	Holy Rood
327	McGill, James, messenger	50y	W	Ire.	18 JUL 1868	Philadelphia, Pa.
249	McGill, W.W., child of	Still	W	D.C.	29 JAN 1867	Congressional
095	McGill, William	4m			29 OCT 1857	St. Peters
010	McGill, Wm.	6d	W	D.C.	20 JUN 1855	Glenwood
034	McGill, [blank]	2m	W		07 JAN 1856	St. Matthews
741	McGinley, Winnie	47y	W	Ire.	09 JAN 1874	Mt. Olivet
010	McGinn, Chs. L.	60y	W	Ire.	07 JUN 1855	St. Patricks
149	McGinnis, James M., blacksmith	51y	W	Pa.	20 MAY 1859	Congressional
049	McGirkin, Edward	10m	W		01 JUL 1856	Congressional
193	McGiven, Daniel	3y	W	N.Y.	07 NOV 1860	Mt. Olivet
715	McGiven, Daniel H., school boy	14y	W	D.C.	23 AUG 1873	
323	McGiven, Ferdinand	1y	W	D.C.	17 JUL 1868	Mt. Olivet
006	McGlen, John	39y	W	D.C.	10 APR 1855	Asylum
143	McGlue, Mary A.	14y	W	D.C.	15 MAR 1859	Western
079	McGlue, [blank]	10m	W	D.C.	17 JUN 1857	Western
275	McGowan, Mary	1m	W	Pa.	18 SEP 1867	Mt. Olivet
769	McGowan, William	3y	C	U.S.	13 MAY 1874	

District of Columbia Interments (Index to Deaths), 1855-1874

Page	Name	Age	Race	Birth	Death Date	Burial Ground
007	McGowan, [blank]	79y	W	Ire.	01 APR 1855	St. Patricks
176	McGrann, Francis	4y	W	D.C.	15 APR 1860	St. Patricks
254	McGrasan, Harry S., farmer		W	Md.	01 FEB 1867	Cecil Co., Md.
110	McGrath, Francis J.	9m	W	D.C.	06 APR 1858	St. Patricks
318	McGravey, James & A., twin of	P.B.	W	D.C.	02 JUN 1868	Congressional
318	McGravey, James & A., twin of	P.B.	W	D.C.	02 JUN 1868	Congressional
554	McGraw, Edw.	5y	W	D.C.	17 JAN 1872	Mt. Olivet
617	McGraw, Jas. F.	9m	W	U.S.	16 AUG 1872	
582	McGraw, John	4y	W		21 FEB 1872	Mt. Olivet
754	McGraw, John V., bookbinder	24y	W	U.S.	07 MAR 1874	Mt. Olivet
115	McGrea, Mary E.	1y	W	D.C.	07 JUN 1858	St. Peters
520	McGrew, Grace A.	16h	W	D.C.	27 MAY 1871	Congressional*
278	McGruder, Hattie	6m	C	D.C.	11 OCT 1867	Colored Methodist
209	McGuggan, [Ar]thur	5m	W	D.C.	— JAN 1866	[torn]
550	McGuinn, John E., cooper	38y	C	Va.	28 DEC 1871	Union
406	McGuinn, Owen, gardener	27y	W	Ire.	01 JUL 1869	Methodist
111	McGuire, Hannah	3m	W	D.C.	16 APR 1858	St. Peters
294	McGuire, Nellie	4m	W		04 FEB 1868	Glenwood
642	McGuire, Patrick, grocer	21y	W	Ire.	01 DEC 1872	
644	McGuire, Susan, servant	80y	C	U.S.	14 DEC 1872	
316	McGuire, Walter		C		c.16 MAY 1868	Alms House
143	McGuire, William	2m	W	D.C.	06 MAR 1859	St. Patricks
017	McGurrey, Mary J.	4y	W	D.C.	23 JUL 1855	St. Matthews
386	McGwin, Virginia	5m	W	Amer.	07 APR 1869	Mt. Olivet
130	McHard, Mary Ann	5y	W	Md.	01 OCT 1858	
167	McHenry, Elizabeth	35y	W	U.S.	08 DEC 1859	Mt. Olivet
189	McHenry, Mary Hellen	4y	W	Md.	12 SEP 1860	Baltimore, Md.
001	McHenry, Mary Jane	34y			11 JAN 1855	
450	McHugh, Ellen	19d	W		30 APR 1870	Mt. Olvet
239	McHugh, Mary	1y	W	D.C.	01 OCT 1866	Mt. Olivet
645	McHugh, Mary	1m	W	U.S.	28 DEC 1872	Mt. Olivet
449	McIlvaine, John, gov. messenger	37y	W	Ire.	27 APR 1870	Congressional
170	McIntine, Alexander, clerk	68y	W	Del.	24 JAN 1860	Glenwood
637	McIntire, Ann Pope	33y	W	U.S.	16 NOV 1872	Congressional
457	McIntosh, Charlotte V.	8m	W	D.C.	14 JUN 1870	Congressional
018	McIntosh, Clara	5y	W		27 AUG 1855	Holmead
419	McIntosh, Columbus	1y	W		04 OCT 1869	Congressional
589	McIntosh, Ebenezer, clerk	34y	W		05 MAR 1872	
155	McIntosh, Eleanor A.	26y	W	U.S.	02 JUL 1859	
609	McIntosh, J.M.	2y	W	U.S.	15 JUN 1872	
352	McIntyre, Bernard, laborer	35y	W	Ire.	07 SEP 1868	Mt. Clivet
557	McIntyre, Mabel	1m	W	D.C.	02 FEB 1872	Oak Hill
193	McIntyre, Sarah E.	34y	W	Md.	18 NOV 1860	Glenwood
319	McJevernay, James	1y	W	D.C.	23 JUN 1868	Mt. Olivet
059	McKary, Rosy	4d	W	D.C.	22 SEP 1856	St. Patricks
741	McKay, Edward A.	58y	W	U.S.	11 JAN 1874	Warsaw, N.Y.
161	McKay, George, soldier	55y	W	Scot.	03 SEP 1859	Congressional
367	McKea, James, journalist	68y	W	Va.	25 DEC 1868	Alexandria, Va.
294	McKean, Samuel Wiley, clerk	78y	W	Pa.	08 FEB 1868	Oak Hill
185	McKean, Sarah	32y	W	Va.	19 JUL 1860	Washington Asylum
151	McKee, Charles C.	19d	W	D.C.	16 JUN 1859	Congressional
447	McKee, Harry E.	5y	W		11 MAR 1870	Glenwood
015	McKeeser, [blank]	4h	W		01 JUL 1855	St. Matthews
377	McKeever, Henry	6m	C		24 FEB 1869	Washington Asylum
593	McKeiser, Margret	4y	W	D.C.	03 APR 1872	Md.
101	McKelden, Alice	2y	W	D.C.	06 JAN 1858	Glenwood
027	McKelden, Cara E.	21m	W	D.C.	29 OCT 1855	Glenwood
324	McKelden, Clara A.	3m	W	D.C.	04 JUL 1868	Oak Hill

Page	Name	Age	Race	Birth	Death Date	Burial Ground
179	McKelden, Mary	16y	W	D.C.	12 MAY 1860	Glenwood
376	McKenna, Andrew	3m	W		10 FEB 1869	Glenwood
773	McKenna, Ellen	16m	W	U.S.	17 JUN 1874	Mt. Olivet
355	McKenna, Francis		W		31 OCT 1868	Baltimore, Md.
425	McKenna, John, stone cutter	45y	W	Ire.	02 NOV 1869	Congressional
125	McKenna, Patrick, laborer	18y	W	Ire.	05 AUG 1858	
773	McKenney, Albert	10h	W	U.S.	15 JUN 1874	Congressional
439	McKenney, Elizabeth S., Mrs.	34y	W		04 FEB 1870	Congressional
444	McKenney, George W.	3y	W		31 MAR 1870	Congressional
371	McKenney, John J.	2y	W		08 JAN 1869	Mt. Olivet
444	McKenney, Mary V.	11m	W		19 MAR 1870	Congressional
292a	McKenney, Samuel, gentleman	77y	W	Md.	21 FEB 1868	Oak Hill
024	McKenney, Wm.	12y	W	Ire.	22 SEP 1855	St. Patricks
077	McKenney, William, chaplain USN	66y	W	Md.	04 MAY 1857	Foundry
167	McKenny, Ellen	26y	W	Ire.	16 DEC 1859	Mt. Olivet
516	McKenny, John F.	1m	W	D.C.	06 MAR 1871	Congressional
218	McKenny, John Newton	3y	W	D.C.	15 APR 1866	Glenwood
128	McKenny, William	5y	W	D.C.	17 SEP 1858	St. Patricks
170	McKenny, [blank]	6y	W	D.C.	21 JAN 1860	Congressional
479	McKenzie, Margaret	25y	W	Ire.	30 SEP 1870	Mt. Olivet
117	McKenzie, Mary E.	56y	C	Va.	27 JUN 1858	Foundry
379	McKenzie, William	1m	W		04 MAR 1869	Congressional
049	McKeown, James	1d	W		03 JUL 1856	Foundry
460	McKever, Alice	1d	C	D.C.	07 JUN 1870	Holmead
470	McKie, Arthur	21d	W		11 AUG 1870	Alexandria, Va.
221	McKim, Augusta E.M.	70y	W	Md.	15 MAY 1866	Congressional
394	McKim, Caroline L. Gibbs	41y	W	N.Y.	07 JUN 1869	Congressional
219	McKim, James	12m	W	D.C.	30 APR 1866	Congressional
783	McKim, W.B.	4m	W	U.S.	11 JUL 1874	Congressional
197	McKing, M.J. Bennett	5m			08 JAN 1861	Baltimore, Md.
623	McKinley, Joseph	8m	W	U.S.	23 JUL 1872	Holy Rood
231	McKir, Williamson	1y	W	D.C.	21 AUG 1866	Alexandria, Va.
783	McKnew, Annie C.	10y	W	U.S.	25 JUL 1874	Oak Hill
175	McKnew, Jeremiah, clerk	29y	W	Md.	27 MAR 1860	Glenwood
437	McKnew, Laura	25y	W	Va.	05 JAN 1870	Glenwood
384	McKnew, N.C., merchant	37y	W		24 MAR 1869	Oak Hill
077	McKnight, Geo. B., Dr.	65y	W	N.Y.	14 MAY 1857	Congressional
035	McKnight, James M., clerk	35y	W	Va.	28 FEB 1856	Congressional
659	McKnight, Martha H.	66y	W	U.S.	12 JAN 1873	Congressional
439	McKnight, Orlando, clerk	60y	W	N.Y.	07 FEB 1870	Congressional
767	McKnight, Rebecca H.	64y	W	Ire.	24 MAY 1874	Oak Hill
185	McKnight, Sheldon, mail contractor	52y	W	Mich.	21 JUL 1860	Congressional
031	McKoy, Elizabeth	11m	W	D.C.*	08 DEC 1855	Foundry
294	McLain, Addison	9m	C	D.C.	05 FEB 1868	
213	McLain, Robert T.	9y	W	D.C.	23 FEB 1866	Glenwood
667	McLain, William, Rev.	66y	W	U.S.	13 FEB 1873	Oak Hill
444	McLane, William G., machinist	29y	W		02 MAR 1870	Congressional
360	McLarme, Lawrence	2y	W	D.C.	19 NOV 1868	Mt. Olivet
385	McLaud, [blank]	Still	W	D.C.	11 APR 1869	Congressional
599	McLaughlin, Catharine	19y	W	U.S.	24 MAY 1872	Mt. Olivet
760	McLaughlin, Mary	10m	W	U.S.	17 APR 1874	
285	McLaughlin, Patrick, stone cutter	48y	W	Ire.	25 DEC 1867	Mt. Olivet*
268	McLaughlin, Wm., laborer	15y	W	D.C.	04 AUG 1867	Mt. Olivet
547	McLean, Caroline, lady	39y	W	Md.	02 DEC 1871	Oak Hill
477	McLean, Edward	44y	W		19 SEP 1870	Congressional
748	McLean, John	5y	W	U.S.	06 FEB 1874	Congressional
243	McLean, Joseph	45y	W	N.Y.	09 NOV 1866	Alms House
370	McLean, Mary Ann	47y	W	Pa.	30 JAN 1869	Mt. Olivet

District of Columbia Interments (Index to Deaths), 1855-1874

Page	Name	Age	Race	Birth	Death Date	Burial Ground
310	McLean, Thaddeus M.	2y	W	D.C.	06 APR 1868	Glenwood
241	McLean, Wm. D., clerk	28y	W	N.Y.	25 OCT 1866	Oswego, N.Y.
783	McLear, Wm. J., printer	18y	W	U.S.	16 JUL 1874	Glenwood
411	McLeod, Donald	60y	W	Va.	29 AUG 1869	Rock Creek
668	McLeod, Helen T.	17y	W	U.S.	22 FEB 1873	Congressional
767	McLeod, Isabella, domestic	32y	W	N.S.	15 MAY 1874	Rock Creek
203	McLeod, Jan	49y	W	Scot.	08 MAY 1861	Glenwood
273	McLeod, Jean, Miss	30y	W	D.C.	30 SEP 1867	Glenwood
083	McLeod, John R., carpenter	27y	W	Md.	20 JUL 1857	Glenwood
767	McLeod, Martha E.	21y	W	U.S.	17 MAY 1874	Oak Hill
133	McLeod, Rebecca	84y	W	Md.	18 NOV 1858	St. Patricks
228	McLevan, Helen Mary	5m	W	D.C.	17 JUL 1866	Mt. Olivet
391	McLinder, Joanna Tyler	4y	W		23 MAY 1869	Mt. Olivet
289	McLochran, Mollie	21y	W	D.C.	07 JAN 1868	Glenwood
208	McLure, Charles S.	9m	W	N.M.	28 JUL 1862	Oak Hill
535	McMahen, John, laborer	30y	W	Ire.	16 SEP 1871	
154	McMahon, Alice	29y	W	Ire.	14 JUL 1859	Mt. Olivet
660	McMahon, Mary	9m	W	U.S.	19 JAN 1873	Mt. Olivet
010	McMahon, Michael	9m	W	D.C.	13 JUN 1855	St. Patricks
011	McMahon, Thos.	12m	W	D.C.	18 JUN 1855	St. Patricks
256	McMan, [blank]	7d			17 MAR 1867	Mt. Olivet
447	McMann, Edward	42y	W	Ire.	28 MAR 1870	Washington Asylum
244	McMann, Mary A.	1y	W	D.C.	27 NOV 1866	Mt. Olivet
367	McManna, Francis G., clerk	32y	W	Unk.	17 DEC 1868	Congressional*
179	McManus, Thomas	4y	W	D.C.	07 MAY 1860	Mt. Olivet
247	McManus, Thos.	2y	W	D.C.	19 DEC 1866	Mt. Olivet
748	McMarrow, Mary A.	1y	W	U.S.	11 FEB 1874	Mt. Olivet
111	McMechen, Ann	35y	W	Md.	18 APR 1858	Congressional
062	McMechen, Sarah A.	41y	W		06 NOV 1856	Alexandria, Va.
698	McMenamin, W. Louis	6m	W	D.C.	15 JUN 1873	Glenwood
047	McMillen, Hugh, soldier	56y	W	Ire.	29 JUN 1856	Marine
484	McMim, Abbie	80y	W		13 OCT 1870	Congressional
645	McMinters, Wm. B., clerk	57y	W	U.S.	30 DEC 1872	Philadelphia, Pa.
320	McMorrow, James D.	8m	W	U.S.	17 JUN 1868	Mt. Olivet
057	McMullen, Wm. C.	25y	W	N.Y.	01 SEP 1856	Congressional
255	McMullin, Timothy, laborer	56y	W	Ire.	29 MAR 1867	Alms House
729	McMurray, E., printer	40y	W	U.S.	02 NOV 1873	Mt. Olivet
711	McMurray, Lizzie	2m	W	D.C.	12 AUG 1873	Mt. Olivet
361	McMurry, Mrs., infant of	Still	W		06 NOV 1868	Glenwood
324	McNair, Libbie	7m	W	N.Y.	02 JUL 1868	Oak Hill
592	McNair, Mary	4y	W	D.C.	23 APR 1872	
044	McNair, Wm. S., M.G.	25y	W	Pa.	03 MAY 1856	Congressional
158	McNalley, Kate	2y	W	D.C.	20 AUG 1859	Congressional
687	McNally, Francis J., clerk	37y	W	Ire.	09 MAY 1873	Mt. Olivet
252	McNally, Mary	40y	W	Ire.	13 FEB 1867	Mt. Olivet
268	McNally, Nettie O.	1y	W	D.C.	18 AUG 1867	Congressional
582	McNally, Norval	1m	W	D.C.	21 FEB 1872	Congressional*
326	McNally, Stephen S.	11m	W	D.C.	20 JUL 1868	Congressional
310	McNalty, Ellen	19y	W		c.23 APR 1868	Mt. Olivet
035	McNaly, Bridget	44y	W	Ire.	12 FEB 1856	St. Peters
327	McNamara, Dennis	2y	W	D.C.	30 JUL 1868	Mt. Olivet
315	McNamara, Dennis, laborer	64y	W	Ire.	09 MAY 1868	Mt. Olivet
621	McNamara, Jas., clerk	29y	W	Ire.	04 AUG 1872	
756	McNamara, John, laborer	62y	W	Ire.	13 MAR 1874	
008	McNamara, Margt.	55y	W	Ire.	23 MAY 1855	St. Peters
324	McNamara, Mary	43y	W	Ire.	02 JUL 1868	Mt. Olivet
783	McNamara, Matthew M., confect.	16y	W	Ire.	31 JUL 1874	
726	McNamara, [blank]	14d	W	U.S.	24 OCT 1873	Mt. Olivet

Page	Name	Age	Race	Birth	Death Date	Burial Ground
783	McNamard, Ellen, servant	46y	W	Ire.	16 JUL 1874	
177	McNamee, Catharine	70y	W	Ire.	21 APR 1860	Mt. Olivet
609	McNamee, Chas., Jr.	26y	W	U.S.	04 JUN 1872	
534	McNamee, Henry	1y	W	D.C.	29 AUG 1871	Mt. Olivet
535	McNamee, Jane	70y	W	Ire.	05 SEP 1871	Mt. Olivet
361	McNamee, P., Mr., infant of	Still	W		26 NOV 1868	Mt. Olivet
254	McNancey, Catherine	15y	W	D.C.	21 FEB 1867	Mt. Olivet
294	McNanna, Patrick, dairyman	50y	W	Ire.	01 FEB 1868	Mt. Olivet
375	McNeal, Clive, Mrs.	41y	W	N.Y.	02 FEB 1869	Oak Hill
369	McNeal, Mrs.				31 JAN 1869	
773	McNeary, Bartholomew	60y	W		23 JUN 1874	Mt. Olivet
499	McNeill, Joseph, soldier	58y	W	N.J.	18 JAN 1871	Congressional
682	McNeir, Annie J.	22y	C	U.S.	26 APR 1873	Glenwood
382	McNeir, Emily R.	50y	W	Md.	31 MAR 1869	Glenwood
079	McNeir, George, claim agent	63y	W	Md.	12 JUN 1857	Glenwood
061	McNeir, James B., printer	30y	W	Md.	27 OCT 1856	Congressional
445	McNeir, James Henry	15d	W		04 MAR 1870	Mt. Olivet
060	McNeir, L.S.		W		20 OCT 1856	Foundry
527	McNeir, Sarah A.	35y	W	D.C.	07 JUL 1871	St. Patricks
229	McNeir, Sarah L.	7y	W		19 JUL 1866	Glenwood
010	McNelly, Sarah Jane	1y		Md.	20 JUN 1855	Elk Ridge Landing
717	McNerhany, Blanch	1m	W	D.C.	01 SEP 1873	Mt. Olivet
415	McNerhany, Philip Henry	8m	W		11 SEP 1869	Mt. Olivet
025	McNerhenny, Patrick	27y	W	Ire.	14 SEP 1855	St. Patricks
102	McNew, Anne J.	1m	W	D.C.	15 JAN 1858	Glenwood
279	McNier, Elizabeth	73y	W	Md.	01 OCT 1867	Glenwood
278	McPherson, Ann	40y	W	Ire.	18 OCT 1867	Mt. Olivet
044	McPherson, Danl., constable	69y	W	Scot.	07 MAY 1856	Methodist
312	McPherson, Edwd., Jr.	2m	W	U.S.	06 MAY 1868	Gettysburgh, Pa.
385	McPherson, Edwin T.	8m	W	Amer.	23 APR 1869	Congressional
002	McPherson, Elizabeth W.	30y	W	Md.	24 JAN 1855	Oak Hill
283	McPherson, Henry M.B., grocer	31y	W	Md.	23 NOV 1867	Glenwood
444	McPherson, John S.	3y	W		31 MAR 1870	Congressional
522	McPherson, Martha W.	3m	W	D.C.	11 JUN 1871	Congressional*
773	McPherson, Matilda	8y	C	U.S.	26 JUN 1874	Washington Asylum
760	McPherson, Percella, domestic	80y	C	U.S.	12 APR 1874	Mt. Olivet
304	McPherson, R.A., child of	6d	W		06 MAR 1868	Congressional
380	McPherson, [Angus]	52y	W	N.Y.	25 MAR 1869	Congressional*
465	McPherson, [blank]	81y	C		12 JUL 1870	Ebenezer
080	McPhesson, M.E.S.	4m	W	D.C.	22 JUN 1857	Glenwood
666	McQuay, Emily	47y	W	U.S.	02 FEB 1873	Congressional
713	McQuay, Henry, clerk	23y	W	D.C.	22 AUG 1873	Congressional*
065	McQueen, John	1m	W	D.C.	09 DEC 1856	St. Peters
102	McQueen, Mary	30y	W	Ire.	16 JAN 1858	St. Peters
127	McQuillan, John	9y	W	D.C.	02 SEP 1858	St. Patricks
421	McQuillan, Mary Ann	23y	W	Ire.	21 OCT 1869	Mt. Olivet
133	McQullan, Mary	3y	W	D.C.	24 NOV 1858	St. Patricks
500	McRae, Margaret L.	38y	W	Ire.	21 JAN 1871	Mt. Olivet
104	McRea, Minnie	23y	W	D.C.	15 FEB 1858	St. Patricks
318	McRoberts, Mary M.	1m	W		24 JUN 1868	Congressional
455	McRoberts, Maury	3y	W		01 MAY 1870	Congressional*
708	McRoberts, Thos., lawyer	30y	W	Va.	11 JUL 1873	Congressional*
250	McSheehy, Annie	30y	W	D.C.	06 JAN 1867	Mt. Olivet
360	McSweeney, Margaret	1y	W	D.C.	17 NOV 1868	Mt. Olivet
187	McSweeney, Thos., child of	Still	W	D.C.	03 AUG 1860	Mt. Olivet
459	McSweeny, Randolph	1m	C	D.C.	30 JUN 1870	Holmead
489	McSweney, Emma T.	7m	W	D.C.	20 NOV 1870	Mt. Olivet
329	McSwiney, Kate	3m	W	D.C.	07 JUL 1868	Mt. Olivet

District of Columbia Interments (Index to Deaths), 1855-1874

Page	Name	Age	Race	Birth	Death Date	Burial Ground
244	McTally, Mary F., milliner	45y	W	Va.	12 NOV 1866	Holmead
361	McVerhany, John F., apothecary	22y	W	N.Y.	07 NOV 1868	Mt. Olivet
034	McVerry, [blank]	33y	W	Ire.	19 JAN 1856	St. Peters
494	McVery, Peter J.	3m	W	U.S.	06 DEC 1870	Mt. Olivet
669	McWilliams, Isabella	29y	W	U.S.	25 FEB 1873	Mt. Olivet
286	McWilliams, James, stone cutter	53y	W	Scot.	31 DEC 1867	Congressional
217	McWilliams, Margaret	22y	W	Eng.	09 APR 1866	Congressional
258	Meacham, Fordyce, printer	44y	W	Pa.	26 APR 1867	Congressional
705	Mead, Albert	3y	W	D.C.	18 JUL 1873	Congressional*
355	Mead, Bertha	1y	W	D.C.	12 OCT 1868	Congressional
087	Mead, Daniel	2y	W	D.C.	10 AUG 1857	Methodist
371	Mead, Delilah M.	4y	W	D.C.	05 JAN 1869	Methodist
041	Mead, James, blacksmith	74y	W	Md.	20 APR 1856	Congressional
272	Mead, Wm. H.	4m	C		21 AUG 1867	Freedmen's Bureau
430	Meade, Fanny	93y	W	Md.	10 DEC 1869	Methodist
669	Meade, Rosa	33y	C	U.S.	07 FEB 1873	Small Pox
444	Meade, Susan	45y	W		25 MAR 1870	Congressional
419	Meader, Henry, watchman	63y	W	Md.	19 OCT 1869	Congressional
343	Meads, Mary Priseter	6m	C	D.C.	13 AUG 1868	
736	Meafuss, Francis	3y	W	U.S.	14 DEC 1873	Glenwood
420	Meagher, Maria, Mrs.	41y	W	Ire.	11 OCT 1869	Mt. Olivet
371	Meaher, James, storekeeper	35y	W	Ire.	20 JAN 1869	Mt. Olivet
603	Mealy, Hanibal	18y	C	Va.	14 JUN 1872	Small Pox
294	Meany, John	Still	W	D.C.	11 FEB 1868	Mt. Olivet*
416	Measdag, Rosala, domestic	26y	W	Ger.	22 SEP 1869	Prospect Hill
148	Mechan, Frederick	59y	W	Ger.	10 MAY 1859	Congressional
268	Mechs, John	1y	C		02 AUG 1867	Ebenezer
529	Meckall, Lizzie	11m	C	D.C.	22 JUL 1871	Young Mens
324	Medara, Joseph, clerk	30y	W	N.J.	31 JUL 1868	Oak Hill
361	Medford, Chas. Franklin	7y	W	D.C.	12 NOV 1868	Glenwood
361	Medford, Grant L.	5y	W	D.C.	15 NOV 1868	Glenwood
361	Medford, James Fred.	2y	W	D.C.	12 NOV 1868	Glenwood
354	Medford, Mary T.	10y	W	D.C.	08 OCT 1868	Glenwood
280	Meding, Elizabeth Estelle	1y	W	D.C.	27 OCT 1867	Glenwood
412	Medley, William	1y	C	D.C.	12 AUG 1869	Washington Asylum
235	Medman, Joseph A.	2y	W	D.C.	19 SEP 1866	Mt. Olivet
078	Meeabe, Daniel, porter	28y	W	Ire.	20 MAY 1857	St. Peters
620	Meedroon, Mary S.	20m	W	U.S.	07 AUG 1872	
296	Meeds, Ida	19y	C	Md.	12 FEB 1868	Alms House
767	Meeds, Juliana	79y	W	U.S.	02 MAY 1874	Mt. Olivet
471	Meeds, [blank]	9m	W	D.C.	16 AUG 1870	Congressional
616b	Meehan, C.H.W.	54y	W	U.S.	05 JUL 1872	Congressional*
360	Meek, Rev. John B., clerk	71y	W	Pa.	28 NOV 1868	Pa.
252	Meek, Sophia	27y	C	Md.	15 FEB 1867	Ebenezer
754	Meeker, Charles, clerk	45y	W	U.S.	15 MAR 1874	Mt. Olivet
691	Meekins, Joseph, seaman	62y	W	U.S.	03 MAY 1873	Congressional
609	Meem, Elizabeth	34y	W	U.S.	22 JUN 1872	
320	Meeny, Henry, child of	Still	W	D.C.	05 JUN 1868	Methodist, East
617	Meggs, Emma	51y	C	U.S.	20 AUG 1872	
289	Meguire, Frances	11d	W	D.C.	04 JAN 1868	Camden, N.J.
621	Mehlery, John	1y	W	U.S.	17 AUG 1872	St. Marys
420	Mehrling, Annie Laura	2y	W		10 OCT 1869	Glenwood
456	Mehrling, H. Susan	32y	W	Md.	14 JUN 1870	Glenwood
184	Meier, Margaret	4m	W	Md.	04 JUL 1860	German Catholic
065	Meigs, [blank]	Still	W	D.C.	12 DEC 1856	Oak Hill
232	Meimer, Sarah	1y	C	D.C.	28 AUG 1866	Ebenezer
783	Meiners, Ludwig A., paper hanger	54y	W	Ger.	28 JUL 1874	Prospect Hill

Page	Name	Age	Race	Birth	Death Date	Burial Ground
148	Meiners, Paul	3y	W	D.C.	06 MAY 1859	Prospect Hill
445	Meiners, William, cigar maker	21y	W	Ger.	07 MAR 1870	Prospect Hill
163	Meisel, Louisa	24y	W	D.C.	09 OCT 1859	Georgetown
147	Mela, Bartold	12y	W		13 APR 1859	
293	Melby, John, laborer	30y	C		07 MAR 1868	Methodist
300	Melcher, Charles A., clerk	33y	W	Md.	02 MAR 1868	Mt. Olivet
476	Melcher, Mary J.	56y	W	Md.	23 SEP 1870	Mt. Olivet
257	Meldoon, John A., clerk war dept.	22y	W	Ohio	15 MAR 1867	Glenwood
199	Meldoon, Rosa	14y	W		01 FEB 1861	Congressional
481	Melhorn, Emily	58y	W	Amer.	22 OCT 1870	Glenwood
767	Mellish, David B., congressman	43y	W	U.S.	23 MAY 1874	Auburn, Mass.
429	Mellson, Eva	3m	W		28 DEC 1869	Congressional
673	Melson, Clara L.	18y	W	U.S.	08 MAR 1873	Congressional
549	Melson, Harry	5y	W	D.C.	21 DEC 1871	Congressional
696	Melson, Jno. Edgar, student	12y	W	D.C.	28 JUN 1873	
698	Melson, John Edgar	12y	W	D.C.	28 JUN 1873	
368	Melson, Martha Ann, Mrs.	60y	W	Md.	23 DEC 1868	Mt. Olivet
335a	Melton, Jos.	6m	B	U.S.	28 JUL 1868	Washington Asylum
714	Melton, Joseph, laborer	45y	C	Md.	31 AUG 1873	Holmead
187	Melvin, Ellen M.	52y	W	Eng.	11 AUG 1860	Congressional
282	Melvin, Josiah, printer	63y	W	U.S.	26 NOV 1867	Glenwood
289	Melvin, Laban T.	9y	W	D.C.	08 JAN 1868	Glenwood
773	Melvin, Martha A.	42y	W	U.S.	15 JUN 1874	Congressional
160	Melvin, Sarah M.	1y	W	D.C.	07 AUG 1859	Congressional*
338	Mendenhall, Wm. Henry	8m	W		15 AUG 1868	Glenwood
410	Mendinghall, Margragy, housekpr.	27y	W		29 AUG 1869	Glenwood
236	Meniklein, Margaret	1y	W	D.C.	14 SEP 1866	Congressional
416	Menkling, Margaret Jane	5y	W		12 SEP 1869	Prospect Hill
730	Menmor, Mary	4y	C	U.S.	13 NOV 1873	
162	Mensel, Anna	20y	W	Ger.	22 SEP 1859	Prospect Hill
217	Mensrel, George	56y	W		04 APR 1866	Oak Hill
247	Menzer, Herman, musician	56y	W	Ger.	19 DEC 1866	Alms House
289	Mequire, Elizabeth Martin	10d	W	D.C.	04 JAN 1868	Camden, N.J.
658	Mercer, Elizabeth, seamstress	36y	W	U.S.	05 JAN 1873	Harmony
619	Mercer, Nellie	4y	C	U.S.	01 AUG 1872	Small Pox
618	Mercer, Saml.	6y	C	U.S.	01 AUG 1872	
487	Mercer, Sarah Ann	1y	C	D.C.	02 NOV 1870	Young Mens
319	Mercer, William H.	3m	W	D.C.	23 JUN 1868	N.Y.
344	Merdian, Mary, milliner	24y	W	Ger.	28 AUG 1868	Prospect Hill
707	Meredith, Jas. M., tailor	55y	W		22 JUL 1873	Congressional
587	Meredith, Maria	70y	C	Va.	19 MAR 1872	
233	Meredith, Mary, child of	Still			13 AUG 1866	Alms House
697	Meredith, William	45y	C	Va.	27 JUN 1873	Washington Asylum
419	Meredith, William W.	1y	W	Va.	17 OCT 1869	Congressional
587	Merge, Juliet	8m	W	D.C.	22 MAR 1872	Oak Hill
760	Merian, Helen F.	3y	W	U.S.	13 APR 1874	Congressional*
708	Meriford, Josephine	1y	C	D.C.	01 JUL 1873	Beckett's
340	Merker, Angelica	4y	W	S.C.	23 AUG 1868	Congressional
252	Merkins, Emily	8d	C	D.C.	13 FEB 1867	Good Hope
663	Merret, Robert	21y	C	U.S.	21 JAN 1873	Small Pox
447	Merrewith, Fanny		C	D.C.	31 MAR 1870	Washington Asylum
720	Merrick, D.C., Dr.	81y	W	Me.	26 SEP 1873	Congressional
340	Merrick, Florence R.	3y	W	Ohio	08 AUG 1868	Congressional
595	Merrick, Francis W.	15y	W	Ohio	15 APR 1872	Congressional*
070	Merrick, Wm. D., farmer	63y	W	Md.	05 FEB 1857	Catholic vault
615	Merriday, Lewis	28y	C	U.S.	11 JUL 1872	
376	Merrill, Fred. H.	1m	W		24 FEB 1869	Glenwood
267	Merriman, Annie	3m	W	D.C.	30 JUL 1867	Mt. Olivet

Page	Name	Age	Race	Birth	Death Date	Burial Ground
263	Merritt, A.E., Mrs., child of	Still	W		01 JUN 1867	Mt. Olivet
197	Merritt, Anna	21y	W	Pa.	27 JAN 1861	York, Pa.
105	Merritt, George, printer	26y	W	Pa.	16 FEB 1858	Congressional
641	Merryman, Florance	2y	W	U.S.	29 DEC 1872	Small Pox*
783	Merryweather, Thomas	10m	C	U.S.	29 JUL 1874	Mt. Olivet
767	Merrywether, Albert H., clerk	64y	W	Eng.	13 MAY 1874	Oak Hill
601	Merton, Nye Ralph	5y	W	U.S.	11 MAY 1872	Glenwood
262	Merwin, Marion				05 JUN 1867	
237	Merz, Wm. Joseph Louis	3m	W	Va.	19 SEP 1866	Prospect Hill
614	Mesa, C.A. dela	45y	W	Spain	04 JUL 1872	
365	Mesmer, Annie M.	2y	W		12 DEC 1868	Mt. Olivet
620	Messee, Ann	1y	W	U.S.	05 AUG 1872	Congressional*
329	Messenger, George	11m	W	N.Y.	18 JUL 1868	N.Y. City
214	Messer, Harriet	25y	W	Ire.	01 MAR 1866	Congressional
439	Messer, Jennie	4y	W	D.C.	12 FEB 1870	Congressional
488	Messer, Mary	1y	W		12 NOV 1870	Congressional
148	Metcalf, John, soldier	35y	W	R.I.	01 MAY 1859	Marine
307	Metler, Julia, Miss	18y	W	Ger.	01 APR 1868	German Catholic
767	Metteldorfs, Frederick	2d	W	U.S.	11 MAY 1874	Prospect Hill
244	Mettle, Henry, bricklayer	30y	W	D.C.	14 NOV 1866	Glenwood
711	Metz, John P.	14m	W	D.C.	11 AUG 1873	Prospect Hill
117	Metzerott, Marie	62y	W	Ger.	24 JUN 1858	Glenwood
344	Meuden, Frederick G.	1y	W	D.C.	14 AUG 1868	Prospect Hill
297	Meyer, John Thomas	1y	W	D.C.	25 FEB 1868	Mt. Olivet
760	Meyers, Charles, laborer	23y	C	U.S.	05 APR 1874	Ebenezer
070	Meyers, John	6m	W	D.C.	05 FEB 1857	German
239	Meyers, John, laborer	50y	W	Ire.	13 OCT 1866	Mt. Olivet
375	Meyers, Mary, laundress	40y	W	Ire.	12 FEB 1869	Mt. Olivet
344	Michael, George, child of	1y	W	D.C.	08 AUG 1868	St. Aloysius
483	Michels, Barbara	19y	W	Ger.	21 OCT 1870	Hebrew
157	Micholls, Louis	12d	C	D.C.	07 AUG 1859	Harmony
477	Mickenberger, Paul, clerk	29y	W	Prus.	08 SEP 1870	Prospect Hill
541	Mickins, Wm.	96y	C	Va.	08 OCT 1871	
487	Mickle, Alex. Smyth	1y	W	D.C.	18 NOV 1870	Congressional
487	Middleton, Agnes	1y	W	D.C.	29 NOV 1870	Congressional
413	Middleton, Blossy	2y	C		04 AUG 1869	Holmead
783	Middleton, Clara	4m	C	U.S.	16 JUL 1874	
329	Middleton, Daniel	6m	C	D.C.	02 JUL 1868	
427	Middleton, David	2m	C		14 NOV 1869	
548	Middleton, Edw. C.	3m			14 DEC 1871	Congressional*
634	Middleton, Henrietta	41y	W	U.S.	29 SEP 1872	Congressional
280	Middleton, Horace P., Dr.	28y	W	D.C.	27 OCT 1867	Congressional
602	Middleton, Isaac, laborer	73y	C	Va.	01 MAY 1872	Asylum
689	Middleton, Jessie	27y	W	U.S.	26 MAY 1873	Oak Hill
466	Middleton, John R.	1y	C	D.C.	19 JUL 1870	Western
075	Middleton, Jonas, stone cutter	51y	W	Eng.	02 APR 1857	Congressional
783	Middleton, Lettia	104y	C	U.S.	26 JUL 1874	Beckett's
412	Middleton, Louisa	4y	C	D.C.	20 AUG 1869	Washington Asylum
461	Middleton, Mariana M.	1y	W	D.C.	16 JUL 1870	Congressional
602	Middleton, Marshall	65y	C	Md.	07 MAY 1872	Asylum
154	Middleton, Mary Jane	2m	W	D.C.	18 JUL 1859	Congressional
256	Middleton, Robert S., printer	32y	W	Pa.	05 MAR 1867	Oak Hill
669	Middleton, Robert W., clerk	68y	W	U.S.	25 FEB 1873	Oak Hill
291	Middleton, Susannah	8m	C	D.C.	23 JAN 1868	Mt. Olivet
207	Middleton, William	6m	C		06 JUL 1862	Western
111	Mighty, Mary V.	1y	W	D.C.	17 APR 1858	German
188	Milburn, Benedict	1y	W	D.C.	17 AUG 1860	Congressional
622a	Milburn, Geo. A.	6m	W	U.S.	11 AUG 1872	

Page	Name	Age	Race	Birth	Death Date	Burial Ground
754	Milburn, Jos. P., druggist	38y	W	U.S.	01 MAR 1874	Glenwood
355	Milburn, Martha	5m	C	Md.	22 OCT 1868	Mt. Olivet
619	Milburn, Mattie	3y	C	U.S.	09 AUG 1872	Young Mens
031	Milburn, W.M.	8y	W	D.C.	21 DEC 1855	Ebenezer
420	Milds, Mary Adell	5m	W		08 OCT 1869	
446	Miles, Albert	7m	C		26 MAR 1870	Western
063	Miles, Andrew, musician	73y	C	Va.	27 NOV 1856	St. Matthews
594	Miles, Chas.	75y	C	Va.	28 APR 1872	Washington
431	Miles, Ellen	28y	C		04 DEC 1869	
586	Miles, Ellen, laundress	25y	C	Va.	15 MAR 1872	Arlington, Va.
592	Miles, Hattie B.	3m	W	D.C.	15 APR 1872	Methodist
128	Miles, Jane	7d	C	D.C.	29 SEP 1858	St. Matthews
094	Miles, Jane O.	3y	W	Md.	19 OCT 1857	St. Patricks
446	Miles, Joseph, laborer	60y	C	Va.	12 MAR 1870	Western
318	Miles, Louise Elizabeth	5m	W	U.S.	25 JUN 1868	Congressional
308	Miles, Lucy A., dress maker	32y	W	Eng.	08 APR 1868	Congressional
659	Miles, Mary	68y	W	U.S.	16 JAN 1873	Baltimore, Md.
446	Miles, Mary L.	1y	C		05 MAR 1870	Western
584	Miles, Mary V.	4m	C	U.S.	01 MAR 1872	
552	Miles, Owen, laborer	21y	C	Md.	04 JAN 1872	Washington
372	Miles, Polly	70y	C	Va.	15 JAN 1869	Freedmen's Hospital
436	Miles, Sarah	22y	C		01 JAN 1870	Washington Asylum
476	Miles, Virginia	8m	C	D.C.	17 SEP 1870	
271	Miles, William	49y	C		28 AUG 1867	Mt. Olivet
232	Miles, William, soldier	54y	W	Ire.	25 AUG 1866	Mt. Olivet
613	Miles, Wm.	1m	C	U.S.	22 JUL 1872	
240	Milford, Josephine	1y	C	D.C.	23 OCT 1866	Harmony
443	Milldust, John, laborer	28y	C		03 FEB 1870	Washington Asylum
743	Millen, Ellen	33y	W	Ire.	25 JAN 1874	Baltimore, Md.
606	Miller, Amelia	58y	W	Eur.	07 JUN 1872	Congressional*
659	Miller, Amelia	1d	W	U.S.	16 JAN 1873	Mt. Olivet
255	Miller, Appollon	54y	W	Ger.	24 MAR 1867	Mt. Olivet
713	Miller, Armelia	22y	W	D.C.	25 AUG 1873	Congressional
444	Miller, August	27y	W	Ger.	27 MAR 1870	Congressional
319	Miller, Bettie	30y	W	U.S.	30 JUN 1868	Western
031	Miller, C., Mrs., child of				08 DEC 1855	
405	Miller, C.M.	1m	W		04 JUL 1869	Holmead
267	Miller, Calra	7m	W		13 JUL 1867	Mt. Olivet
301	Miller, Caroline, alias Towers	1y	C	D.C.	19 MAR 1868	Young Mens
094	Miller, Catharine	32y	W	Ger.	22 OCT 1857	Congressional
445	Miller, Charles J.	2y	W		07 MAR 1870	Prospect Hill
449	Miller, Charles Marshal	13y	W		24 APR 1870	Congressional
500	Miller, Chas. L., clerk	60y	W		04 JAN 1871	Mich.
148	Miller, Conrad	21y	W	Ire.	07 MAY 1859	Washington Asylum
621	Miller, Danl. B.	11m	W	U.S.	01 AUG 1872	Philadelphia, Pa.
618	Miller, David	16m	W	U.S.	14 AUG 1872	Baltimore, Md.
010	Miller, David P.	7m	W	D.C.	28 JUN 1855	Foundry
114	Miller, Edward	4y	W		29 MAY 1858	German Catholic
039	Miller, Eliza A.	56y	W	Va.	05 MAR 1856	St. Patricks
280	Miller, Ellen	72y	W	D.C.	21 OCT 1867	Congressional
268	Miller, Ellen, Mrs.		W		24 AUG 1867	Mt. Olivet
408	Miller, Emma A.	17y	W		13 AUG 1869	Glenwood
074	Miller, Fanny, cook	67y	C	Va.	20 MAR 1857	Young Mens
108	Miller, Florence R.	2y	W	D.C.	26 MAR 1858	Foundry
430	Miller, Frances May	4y	W	Pa.	16 DEC 1869	Philadelphia, Pa.
028	Miller, Geo. F.	21d	W	D.C.	25 OCT 1855	Congressional
453	Miller, George	11m	W		08 MAY 1870	Congressional
557	Miller, George	15d	W	D.C.	04 FEB 1872	Mt. Olivet

District of Columbia Interments (Index to Deaths), 1855-1874

Page	Name	Age	Race	Birth	Death Date	Burial Ground
282	Miller, George, laborer	32y	C	Va.	12 NOV 1867	Mt. Olivet
267	Miller, H. Theodore	9m	W		10 JUL 1867	Mt. Olivet
168	Miller, Hannah [L.]	32y	W	D.C.	26 DEC 1859	Rock Creek
547	Miller, Harriett	71y	W	Va.	08 DEC 1871	Mt. Olivet*
773	Miller, Harry Elmer	8m	W	U.S.	06 JUN 1874	Frederick City
243	Miller, Henry	1m	W	D.C.	04 NOV 1866	Glenwood
272	Miller, Hester	10m	W	D.C.	10 AUG 1867	Glenwood
580	Miller, Ida E.	7y	W	U.S.	06 FEB 1872	Congressional
058	Miller, Isaiah	2y	W	D.C.	17 SEP 1856	Foundry
439	Miller, J.I., infant son of	2y	W		13 FEB 1870	Congressional
538	Miller, J.S.	1y	W	D.C.	27 SEP 1871	Mt. Olivet
329	Miller, Jacob	3½m	C		02 JUL 1868	Ebenezer
293	Miller, James, collector	83y	W	Pa.	17 MAR 1868	Oak Hill
275	Miller, James, painter	56y	W	D.C.*	29 SEP 1867	Glenwood
434	Miller, Jane I., Mrs.	69y	W		06 JAN 1870	Congressional
616a	Miller, Jno. T.	12y	W	U.S.	08 JUL 1872	Congressional
163	Miller, John	47y	W	Ger.	11 OCT 1859	
626	Miller, John	8m	W	U.S.	13 SEP 1872	
065	Miller, John	4m	W	D.C.	10 DEC 1856	Congressional
736	Miller, John	9d	W	U.S.	21 DEC 1873	Mt. Olivet
264	Miller, John Aug.	8m	W	D.C.	26 JUL 1867	Mt. Olivet
550	Miller, John C., bar tender	24y	W	Ger.	31 DEC 1871	German
428	Miller, John, Mrs., infant of	Still	W	D.C.	06 NOV 1869	Mt. Olivet
279	Miller, John P.	65y	W	Md.	12 OCT 1867	Glenwood
025	Miller, John, stone cutter	28y	W	Fra.	18 SEP 1855	St. Peters
051	Miller, John W.A.	15d	W		24 JUL 1856	St. Matthews
270	Miller, Joseph	1y	W	D.C.	15 AUG 1867	St. Marys
043	Miller, Julia	21y	W	Md.	30 APR 1856	St. Peters
270	Miller, Julia A.	31y	W	D.C.*	30 AUG 1867	Mt. Olivet
069	Miller, Julius	3y	W	D.C.	23 JAN 1857	Holmead
414	Miller, Kate, infant of	Still	W		10 SEP 1869	Congressional
280	Miller, Kate, Miss	29y	W		16 OCT 1867	Mt. Olivet
364	Miller, Kate, Mrs.	23y	W	Amer.	20 DEC 1868	Congressional
397	Miller, Laura M.	1m	C	Amer.	05 JUN 1869	Ebenezer
337	Miller, Lewis, laborer	Old	C	D.C.	12 AUG 1868	Ebenezer
411	Miller, Lizzie H.	7m	W	D.C.	22 AUG 1869	Philadelphia, Pa.
283	Miller, Lucy R.	70y	W	Va.	22 NOV 1867	Glenwood
717	Miller, Margaretta	8m	W	D.C.	02 SEP 1873	Congressional*
518	Miller, Margret Louise	1y	W	D.C.	09 MAY 1871	Glenwood
283	Miller, Maria	60y	W	Va.	16 NOV 1867	Mt. Olivet
117	Miller, Mary	3m	W	D.C.	26 JUN 1858	Foundry
156	Miller, Mary	3m	W	D.C.	09 JUL 1859	Foundry
093	Miller, Mary	48y	W	D.C.	10 OCT 1857	Glenwood
080	Miller, Mary	38y	W	Scot.	18 JUN 1857	Glenwood
598	Miller, Mary	8m	W	U.S.	06 MAY 1872	Glenwood
465	Miller, Mary	80y	C	Md.	18 JUL 1870	Mt. Olivet
547	Miller, Mary D.	66y	W	Md.	02 DEC 1871	Mt. Olivet*
519	Miller, Mary E.	9m	W	D.C.	18 MAY 1871	Congressional*
736	Miller, Mary E.	3m	W	U.S.	15 DEC 1873	Congressional
593	Miller, Mary E.	1y	C	D.C.	22 APR 1872	Young Mens
671	Miller, Melvina	1m	C	U.S.	15 FEB 1873	Small Pox*
598	Miller, Nannie	26y	C	U.S.	14 MAY 1872	Unknown
350	Miller, Peter, butcher	23y	W	D.C.	04 SEP 1868	German Catholic
114	Miller, Robert	4y	W	D.C.	28 MAY 1858	
475	Miller, Sarah	31y	W	Eng.	20 SEP 1870	Prospect Hill
681	Miller, Sarah Francis	68y	W	U.S.	14 APR 1873	Glenwood
580	Miller, Susan E.	8m	W	D.C.	07 FEB 1872	Congressional
677	Miller, Susie Mary	1y	W	U.S.	20 MAR 1873	Glenwood

Page	Name	Age	Race	Birth	Death Date	Burial Ground
114	Miller, Teresa	4y	W	D.C.	12 MAY 1858	Catholic
719	Miller, Thos., Dr.	67y	W	Va.	20 SEP 1873	Rock Creek
475	Miller, Warwick W., clerk Treas.	27y	W	Mich.	20 SEP 1870	Congressional
136	Miller, William	4y	W	D.C.	16 DEC 1858	Congressional
029	Miller, Wm.	11y	W	Ire.	29 NOV 1855	Methodist, East
754	Miller, Wm. E.	3y	C	U.S.	11 MAR 1874	Mt. Olivet
018	Miller, Wm. H.	16m	W	D.C.	07 AUG 1855	German Lutheran
719	Miller, Wm., laborer	35y	C	Va.	21 SEP 1873	
481	Miller, [blank]	50y	W		12 OCT 1870	Mt. Olivet
189	Miller, [blank]	40y	W	Ger.	14 SEP 1860	Prospect Hill
760	Milligan, Samuel, Hon. USCC	59y	W	U.S.	20 APR 1874	Tenn.
106	Milligan, [blank]	1m	W	D.C.	26 FEB 1858	St. Matthews
390	Mills, Ada M.	9y	W	D.C.	10 MAY 1869	Congressional
043	Mills, Ann	38y	W	Md.	29 APR 1856	Alms House
276	Mills, Anna	23y	C		27 SEP 1867	Freedmen's Hospital
586	Mills, Charles	2y	W	D.C.	16 MAR 1872	Methodist
089	Mills, Clara A.	11y	W	D.C.	07 AUG 1857	Congressional
363	Mills, Henry	Still	C	D.C.	16 NOV 1868	Washington Asylum
742	Mills, Henry J.	1y	C	U.S.	18 JAN 1874	Ebenezer
727	Mills, John, farmer	82y	W	U.S.	08 OCT 1873	
334	Mills, Josephine	8m	W	D.C.	06 JUL 1868	Methodist
635	Mills, Mary	26y	C	U.S.	03 NOV 1872	Small Pox
240	Mills, Mary Ann	8d	W	D.C.	20 OCT 1866	Congressional
025	Mills, Mary F.	15y	C	Va.	25 SEP 1855	
352	Mills, Matilda	2y	C	D.C.	04 SEP 1868	Washington Asylum
419	Mills, Rena I.	7y	W		22 OCT 1869	Congressional
526	Mills, Robert	4y	C	D.C.	04 JUL 1871	Harmony
409	Mills, Robert	3d	W	D.C.	03 AUG 1869	Mt. Olivet
004	Mills, Robt., architect	62y	W	N.C.	03 MAR 1855	Congressional
725	Mills, Saml. Clarence	3y	W	U.S.	22 OCT 1873	Congressional*
201	Mills, Susan	100y	C	Md.	13 MAR 1861	Washington Asylum
008	Milson, Henry Waller	5y	C	D.C.	24 MAY 1855	Young Mens
488	Milson, Jane C.	1y	W	Amer.	10 NOV 1870	Congressional
141	Milstead, Catharine	10y	W	D.C.	18 FEB 1859	Congressional
410	Milstead, Eliza		W		10 AUG 1869	Methodist
003	Milstead, Sarah Maria	11y	W	D.C.	11 FEB 1855	
737	Milstead, Wm. A.	1m	W	U.S.	28 DEC 1873	Congressional*
347	Milstrad, Laura	4y	W		21 SEP 1868	Congressional
241	Milton, Emma	1y	W		01 OCT 1866	Western
222	Milton, George N.	8m	W	D.C.	28 MAY 1866	Congressional
311	Milton, Thomas		C		c.17 APR 1868	Alms House
617	Milton, Wm.	2y	C	U.S.	18 AUG 1872	
098	Minder, Jacob	9d	W	D.C.	22 DEC 1857	German
333	Minder, Mrs., child of	6m	W	D.C.	15 JUL 1868	Prospect Hill
586	Miner, Mary	23y	C	Va.	17 MAR 1872	
592	Miner, Thurston	1y	C	D.C.	04 APR 1872	
148	Miners, C.W.	3y	W	D.C.	01 MAY 1859	Prospect Hill
057	Ming, Sally	93y	W	Va.	05 SEP 1856	
160	Mingraw, [blank]	10y	C	D.C.	05 AUG 1859	Balls X Roads, Va.
534	Minite, Thomas	42y	W	Ire.	27 AUG 1871	
165	Miniter, Mary	28y	W	Ire.	18 NOV 1859	Mt. Olivet
019	Minitor, Johanna	9m	W		18 AUG 1855	St. Patricks
296	Minnis, D.A., Mrs.	50y	W	Va.	07 FEB 1868	Norfolk, Va.
580	Minnix, J.P.	2m	W	U.S.	06 FEB 1872	Methodist
146	Minnix, Wm. H.	2y	W	D.C.	17 APR 1859	
319	Minor, Benjamin	50y	C	D.C.	16 JUN 1868	Young Mens
588	Minor, Bettie	2y	C	D.C.	26 MAR 1872	Western
118	Minor, Ida	11m	W		25 JUN 1858	Congressional

District of Columbia Interments (Index to Deaths), 1855-1874

Page	Name	Age	Race	Birth	Death Date	Burial Ground
627	Minor, James, laborer	84y	C	U.S.	09 SEP 1872	Mt. Olivet
280	Minor, Lindsy	52y	C		22 OCT 1867	Freedmen's Hospital
493	Minor, Lucy A.	12y	C	Va.	20 DEC 1870	Ebenezer
404	Minor, Matilda	Still	C	D.C.	02 JUL 1869	Washington Asylum
413	Minor, Samuel	1y	C		22 AUG 1869	
304	Minor, Silah R.	5m	W	D.C.	c.18 MAR 1868	Glenwood
589	Minor, Thomas	8m	C	D.C.	28 MAR 1872	Western
157	Minor, Thos. Edw. Frank	5m	C	D.C.	02 AUG 1859	Young Mens
332	Minor, Timothy	27y	W	D.C.	03 JUL 1868	Mt. Olivet
026	Minor, Yaba	55y	C		07 OCT 1855	Young Mens
007	Minor, [blank]		C	D.C.	13 APR 1855	
311	Minson, Lizzie		C		c.24 APR 1868	Alms House
312	Minster, Michael	4y	W	U.S.	08 MAY 1868	Hebrew
332	Minster, Mrs., housekeeper	31y	W	Ger.	02 JUL 1868	German Catholic
333	Mintagh, Mary C.	68y	W	Md.	15 JUL 1868	Glenwood
541	Mirroratty, J.W.	5y	C	D.C.	14 OCT 1871	Mt. Olivet
225	Mister, Arthur D.	10m	W		24 JUN 1866	Congressional
246	Mister, Louisa	6m	W	D.C.	19 DEC 1866	German
293a	Mitchel, Charles W.	39y	W		30 JAN 1868	Congressional
311	Mitchel, E.		C		c.08 APR 1868	Alms House
280	Mitchel, Elizabeth	20y	C		05 OCT 1867	Freedmen's Hospital
321	Mitchel, Evaline	4m	C		c.29 JUN 1868	Alms House
409	Mitchel, John, bricklayer	52y	C	D.C.	30 AUG 1869	Beckett's
210	Mitchel, Mary R.	1y	W	D.C.	— JAN 1866	Congressional
291	Mitchel, Mary R.	50y	W	U.S.	28 JAN 1868	Mt. Olivet
222	Mitchel, Mrs.				27 MAY 1866	Georgetown
582	Mitchel, Violet	1y	C	D.C.	22 FEB 1872	Holy Rood
233	Mitchel, William Henry	9m	C	D.C.	03 AUG 1866	Alms House
018	Mitchel, [blank]	2d	W	Md.	01 AUG 1855	West
335a	Mitchell, Alice	3y	B	D.C.	31 JUL 1868	Washington Asylum
621	Mitchell, Allen	1y	W	U.S.	15 AUG 1872	
017	Mitchell, Bridgett	48y	W	Ire.	25 JUL 1855	
368	Mitchell, Briscoe S., student	18y	W	D.C.	23 DEC 1868	Oak Hill
502	Mitchell, Charles	18y	W	U.S.	18 JAN 1871	Oak Hill
047	Mitchell, Child of Mary		C	D.C.	24 JUN 1856	Ebenezer
028	Mitchell, Chs.	8y	W		19 OCT 1855	Glenwood
412	Mitchell, David	1y	C	D.C.	02 AUG 1869	Washington Asylum
073	Mitchell, Dennis R., gardener	50y	W		16 MAR 1857	St. Peters
518	Mitchell, Edith	17m	W	D.C.	13 MAY 1871	Congressional*
723	Mitchell, Edmund, cart driver	17y	B	Md.	05 OCT 1873	Mt. Olivet
666	Mitchell, Eliza	25y	C	U.S.	03 FEB 1873	Washington Asylum
737	Mitchell, Emma	4y	W	U.S.	25 DEC 1873	Alexandria, Va.
416	Mitchell, Francis	6m	C		12 SEP 1869	
348	Mitchell, Francis W.	21d	W	D.C.	07 SEP 1868	Congressional
368	Mitchell, George C.B., lawyer	34y	W		28 DEC 1868	Oak Hill
522	Mitchell, Harriet M.	63y	W	Md.	12 JUN 1871	Glenwood
483	Mitchell, Henrietta	75y	W	Md.	04 OCT 1870	Congressional
338	Mitchell, Henry	8y	W	N.Y.	10 AUG 1868	Mt. Olivet
364	Mitchell, Henry C., huckster	50y		Va.	25 DEC 1868	Congressional
756	Mitchell, James E.	27y	C	U.S.	09 MAR 1874	
066	Mitchell, John	83y	W	Md.	24 DEC 1856	Congressional
061	Mitchell, John	28y	W	Md.	28 OCT 1856	Congressional
697	Mitchell, John	1y	W	D.C.	20 JUN 1873	Mt. Olivet
345	Mitchell, John H.	3y	W	Md.	05 AUG 1868	Congressional
643	Mitchell, John R., merchant	54y	W	U.S.	06 DEC 1872	Oak Hill
462	Mitchell, Joseph H.	14d	W	D.C.	06 JUL 1870	Congressional
531	Mitchell, Julia S.	1m	C	D.C.	08 AUG 1871	Ebenezer
531	Mitchell, Julia S.	1m	C	D.C.	09 AUG 1871	Ebenezer

Page	Name	Age	Race	Birth	Death Date	Burial Ground
695	Mitchell, L.Y.	Still	W	D.C.	12 JUN 1873	
436	Mitchell, Leah	18y	C		23 JAN 1870	
393	Mitchell, Livinia, housekeeper	60y	C	Va.	27 MAY 1869	Holmead
585	Mitchell, Martha L.	36y	C	D.C.	08 MAR 1872	Holy Rood
684	Mitchell, Mary	6m	C	U.S.	25 APR 1873	Small Pox
039	Mitchell, Mary E.	11y	C	D.C.	11 MAR 1856	Ebenezer
032	Mitchell, Mary E.	28y	W	Md.	30 DEC 1855	Methodist, East
041	Mitchell, Mary F.	27y	W	Va.	08 APR 1856	Congressional
381	Mitchell, Mary Rebecca	7m	W		02 MAR 1869	Mt. Olivet
331	Mitchell, Molly	9m	C	D.C.	16 JUL 1868	
411	Mitchell, Robt., dau. of	17h	W		17 AUG 1869	Mt. Olivet
730	Mitchell, S.L., dressmaker	28y	C	U.S.	15 NOV 1873	Harmony
436	Mitchell, Serena	3m	C		12 JAN 1870	
453	Mitchell, Thomas Wierman	1y	W	Pa.	15 MAY 1870	Oak Hill
175	Mitchell, William, child of	Still	W	D.C.	26 MAR 1860	Congressional
052	Mitchell, William K.	4m	W	D.C.	29 JUL 1856	Methodist
382	Mitchell, Wm.	1y	C		15 MAR 1869	Young Mens
242	Mitchner, Annie	5y	W	Pa.	21 OCT 1866	Pa.
705	Mitten, Earnest		W	D.C.	26 JUL 1873	
348	Mitten, James	1m	W		27 SEP 1868	Congressional
754	Moan, Mary, servant	28y	W	Ire.	26 MAR 1874	Mt. Olivet
782	Mobley, Martha C.	72y	W	U.S.	02 JUL 1874	Dubuque, Iowa
009	Mocbee, Margaret E.	36y	W	Md.	08 MAY 1855	Glenwood
083	Moccobee, J.M.	3m	W		20 JUL 1857	Congressional
234	Mockabee, Alice		W	D.C.	06 SEP 1866	Congressional
347	Mockabee, Emma V.	1y	W		05 SEP 1868	Congressional
044	Mockabee, Infant		W		07 MAY 1856	Congressional
453	Mockabee, Julia A.	25y	W		14 MAY 1870	Congressional
550	Mockabee, R. Jessie	2y	M	D.C.	29 DEC 1871	Glenwood
318	Mockabee, Sarah Frances	5m	W	D.C.	26 JUN 1868	Congressional
584	Mockabee, Thomas	1d	W	U.S.	01 MAR 1872	Congressional
484	Mockabee, Thos. L.	3y	W	D.C.	13 OCT 1870	Congressional
033	Mockbee, Eliza	60y	W	Md.	18 JAN 1856	Rock Creek
320	Moe, F.S.	2m	W	D.C.	29 JUN 1868	Chattanooga, Tenn.
594	Moe, Wm.	21y	C	Md.	03 APR 1872	Washington
743	Moffat, Mary E.	14d	W	U.S.	21 JAN 1874	Congressional*
369	Moffat, Noah	13d	W	D.C.	12 JAN 1869	Congressional
541	Moffett, Henry Martin	1y	W	D.C.	10 OCT 1871	Congressional
276	Mogan, Thomas, laborer	52y	W	Ire.	29 SEP 1867	Glenwood
637	Mohler, Sally M.	5y	W	U.S.	02 NOV 1872	Mt. Olivet*
754	Mohler, Wm. H.	26d	W	U.S.	29 MAR 1874	Glenwood
615	Mohoney, Louisa	25y	C	U.S.	09 JUL 1872	
357	Mohoney, Louisa	Still	B	D.C.	07 OCT 1868	Washington Asylum
282	Mohun, Catherine	87y	W	Ire.	16 NOV 1867	Mt. Olivet
092	Mohun, Catherine	1y	W	D.C.	24 SEP 1857	St. Patricks
469	Mohun, Frank	20y	W	D.C.	11 AUG 1870	Mt. Olivet
174	Mohun, Laura Rose	12y	W	D.C.	05 MAR 1860	St. Patricks
035	Mohun, Philip, paver	74y	W	Ire.	20 FEB 1856	St. Patricks
767	Mohun, Susannah E.	60y	W	Ire.	28 MAY 1874	Mt. Olivet
324	Moiraty, Mary	80y	W	Ire.	14 JUL 1868	Mt. Olivet
429	Mokell, John, shoemaker	49y		Fra.	07 DEC 1869	Congressional
231	Molan, Elizabeth	29d	W	D.C.	19 AUG 1866	Mt. Olivet
223	Moland, Annie	27y	W	Ire.	02 JUN 1866	Mt. Olivet
315	Molholland, P.	52y	W		c.29 MAY 1868	Mt. Olivet
188	Moline, John	9m	W	D.C.	22 AUG 1860	Mt. Olivet
369	Moling, Dorodo J.	52y	W	Amer.	25 JAN 1869	Congressional
555	Moling, E.A.	47y	W	U.S.	25 JAN 1872	Congressional*
312	Molista, Georgeanna	10m	W	D.C.	24 MAY 1868	St. Marys

District of Columbia Interments (Index to Deaths), 1855-1874

Page	Name	Age	Race	Birth	Death Date	Burial Ground
243	Molley, Mary Jane	1y	W	D.C.	20 NOV 1866	Mt. Olivet
345	Molony, Thomas	2y	W	D.C.	25 AUG 1868	Mt. Olivet
736	Molton, Samuel	1y	C	U.S.	18 DEC 1873	
704	Monaghan, Kate, Mrs.	34y	W	Ire.	21 JUL 1873	Mt. Olivet
227	Monaghan, Mary E.	7m	W	D.C.	06 JUL 1866	Mt. Olivet
315	Monahan, M., infant of	1d	W		c.26 MAY 1868	Mt. Olivet
454a	Monapan, [blank], pauper	1w	C	D.C.	01 MAY 1870	Washington Asylum
683	Monday, Filmore	15y	C	U.S.	10 APR 1873	Small Pox
695	Monroe, Daphne	79y	C	Va.	18 JUN 1873	Washington Asylum
783	Monroe, Jefferson, laborer	75y	C	U.S.	11 JUL 1874	
634	Montague, R., servant	13y	C	U.S.	30 OCT 1872	
344	Montberger, Mary	6m	W	D.C.	21 AUG 1868	Prospect Hill
228	Monteiro, Edward H., gentleman	43y	W	Port.	11 JUL 1866	Richmond, Va.
207	Montgomery A.	123y	C		22 JUL 1862	Young Mens
348	Montgomery, B.D., painter	38y	W	Va.	01 SEP 1868	Congressional
529	Montgomery, Dr.		W	U.S.	28 JUL 1871	Congressional
229	Montgomery, Emily	1y	W	D.C.	18 JUL 1866	Congressional
063	Montgomery, Francis		W		08 NOV 1856	Congressional
551	Montgomery, James, laborer	72y	C	Va.	— DEC 1871	Washington
252	Montgomery, Mary	1y	W	N.Y.	04 FEB 1867	Mt. Olivet
429	Montgomery, Paul C., carpenter	45y	W	Va.	07 DEC 1869	Congressional
481	Montgomery, Richd. M., pl. printer	50y	W	Pa.	03 OCT 1870	Philadelphia, Pa.
073	Montgomery S.S.M.	20y	W		18 MAR 1857	Oak Hill
413	Montgomery, William S.	67y	W	Ire.	03 AUG 1869	
482	Montgriffo, Angeline	1m	W	D.C.	22 OCT 1870	St. Marys
783	Montigue, Lewis E.	2m	C	U.S.	24 JUL 1874	Beckett's
080	Moodie, Sarah	80y	C	Va.	29 JUN 1857	Western
524	Moody, Ellis	19y	C	Md.	23 JUN 1871	Potters Field
202	Moody, Frank W.	1y	W	D.C.	18 APR 1861	Glenwood
432	Moody, Robt.	1d	C	D.C.	05 DEC 1869	Washington Asylum
522	Moog, John	1y	W	D.C.	12 JUN 1871	Prospect Hill
161	Mooney, Mrs.	34y	W	Ire.	13 SEP 1859	Mt. Olivet
600	Moor, Ida S.	1y	W	U.S.	29 MAY 1872	Presbyterian
466	Moore, Aaron	9m	C	D.C.	10 JUL 1870	Young Mens
260	Moore, Ada Dougherty	6m			31 MAY 1867	Ebenezer
385	Moore, Albert W., clerk	22y	W	Amer.	19 APR 1869	Congressional
544	Moore, Ann, housekeeper	73y	W	D.C.	09 NOV 1871	
142	Moore, Annie	13y	W	Eng.	26 FEB 1859	Washington Asylum
474	Moore, Cath.	45y	W		07 AUG 1870	Mt. Olivet
051	Moore, Catharine	1y	W		23 JUL 1856	St. Patricks
221	Moore, Cator, laborer	70y	C	Va.	23 MAY 1866	Holmead
748	Moore, Charles	2y	W	U.S.	18 FEB 1874	Glenwood/Rock Creek
783	Moore, Charles	9m	C	U.S.	26 JUL 1874	Potters Field
022	Moore, Chas. H.	9m	W	D.C.	26 AUG 1855	
434	Moore, D.D., painter	35y	W	N.Y.	01 JAN 1870	Congressional
596	Moore, E.T.	66y	W	D.C.	26 APR 1872	Congressional
239	Moore, Ebenezer, clerk	58y	W	Me.	04 OCT 1866	Congressional
349	Moore, Fanny E.	3y	W		29 SEP 1868	Glenwood
544	Moore, Festus H.	51y	W	U.S.	11 NOV 1871	Glenwood
488	Moore, Francis W., seaman	53y	W	Md.	30 NOV 1870	Mt. Olivet
375	Moore, Frank W.	1y	W	D.C.	16 FEB 1869	Oak Hill
448	Moore, George, laborer	26y	C	Md.	27 MAR 1870	Washington Asylum
150	Moore, Hamilton W.	3y	W	D.C.	11 JUN 1859	Washington
108	Moore, Hannah	34y	W	Ire.	18 MAR 1858	St. Patricks
684	Moore, Harriett	7y	C	U.S.	06 APR 1873	Small Pox*
343	Moore, harry W.	10m	W	D.C.	12 AUG 1868	Glenwood
007	Moore, Henry J.	5y	C	D.C.	11 APR 1855	St. Patricks
465	Moore, Henry W.	1m	W		07 JUL 1870	Methodist

Page	Name	Age	Race	Birth	Death Date	Burial Ground
632	Moore, Ida	6y	W	U.S.	18 OCT 1872	Congressional*
151	Moore, James	1y	W	D.C.	24 JUN 1859	Mt. Olivet
214	Moore, James	40y	W	Ire.	02 MAR 1866	Mt. Olivet
218	Moore, James H., grocer	25y	W	D.C.	28 APR 1866	Rock Creek
309	Moore, James, merchant	74y	W	Va.	11 APR 1868	Baltimore, Md.
202	Moore, James T., carpenter	37y	W	D.C.	20 APR 1861	Congressional
118	Moore, Jane, cook	22y	C	D.C.	12 JUN 1858	
297	Moore, Jane, Mrs.	38y	W	Ire.	20 FEB 1868	Mt. Olivet
290	Moore, John	28y	C	Va.	17 JAN 1868	Freedmen's Hospital
586	Moore, John	55y	W	D.C.	16 MAR 1872	Mt. Olivet
670	Moore, John	50y	C	U.S.	13 FEB 1873	Small Pox
374	Moore, John F., clerk Int. Dept.	31y	W	D.C.	01 FEB 1869	Congressional
202	Moore, John M., clerk	65y	W	D.C.	21 APR 1861	Oak Hill
029	Moore, John W.	2m	W	D.C.	01 NOV 1855	Methodist, East
729	Moore, Julia Ann, clerk	23y	W	U.S.	03 NOV 1873	Alexandria, Va.
305	Moore, Julia Ann	23y	C	D.C.	30 MAR 1868	Mt. Zion
611	Moore, Katie	1y	W	U.S.	— JUL 1872	
636	Moore, Lewis	2y	W	U.S.	18 NOV 1872	
326	Moore, Lilly	2m	W	D.C.	10 JUL 1868	Congressional
661	Moore, Lizzie	19y	C	U.S.	26 JAN 1873	Washington Asylum
748	Moore, Marian	45y	W	Ire.	19 FEB 1874	Washington Asylum
294	Moore, Martin/Ella, child of	8d	C	D.C.	09 FEB 1868	
338	Moore, Mary	6m	W		03 AUG 1868	Baltimore, Md.
687	Moore, Mary	53y	W	Ger.	04 MAY 1873	Mt. Olivet
065	Moore, Mary	36y	W	Va.	11 DEC 1856	Washington Asylum
101	Moore, Mary Eliza	1m	W	D.C.	08 JAN 1858	Glenwood
368	Moore, Mary Ellen	2y	W	D.C.	22 DEC 1868	Mt. Olivet
124	Moore, Mary Jane	5m	W	D.C.	02 AUG 1858	St. Patricks
032	Moore, Mrs., child of	Still	W		29 DEC 1855	Glenwood
475	Moore, Olivia E.	22y	W	D.C.	03 SEP 1870	Congressional
059	Moore, Patrick	1y	W	D.C.	21 SEP 1856	St. Patricks
413	Moore, Paul, laborer	80y	C	Va.	18 AUG 1869	Washington Asylum
224	Moore, Robert	11m	W	D.C.	13 JUN 1866	Mt. Olivet
131	Moore, Robt. Greenhow	1y	W		31 OCT 1858	Congressional*
232	Moore, Rolla	1y	C	Va.	28 AUG 1866	Harmony
272	Moore, Sarah	40y	C		20 AUG 1867	Freedmen's Bureau
421	Moore, Sarah, Mrs.	94y	W	Md.	13 OCT 1869	Mt. Olivet
335a	Moore, Thomas				16 JUL 1868	Washington Asylum
068	Moore, Thos. P.	6m	W	D.C.	09 JAN 1857	St. Patricks
677	Moore, Virginia	6y	C	U.S.	15 MAR 1873	Small Pox
428	Moore, W.E., infant of	Still	W		25 NOV 1869	Glenwood
708	Moore, Walter	11m	W	D.C.	15 JUL 1873	
305	Moore, William	25y	W		c.25 MAR 1868	Mt. Olivet
335a	Moore, Wm. H.				27 JUL 1868	Washington Asylum
050	Moran, Alexander, ship carpenter	31y	W	Md.	15 JUL 1856	Foundry
375	Moran, Ann L.	44y	W	Md.	15 FEB 1869	Mt. Olivet
774	Moran, Arthur Beverly	4m	W	U.S.	27 JUN 1874	Oak Hill
625	Moran, D.H.	6y	W	U.S.	19 SEP 1872	
098	Moran, Dison	66y	W	Md.	02 DEC 1857	Holmead
167	Moran, Eleary	75y	W	Md.	02 DEC 1859	Charles Co., Md.
445	Moran, Elidia H.	13y	W	Md.	05 MAR 1870	Glenwood
582	Moran, Eliza	18y	W	U.S.	24 FEB 1872	Mt. Olivet
031	Moran, Isabella	25y	W		13 DEC 1855	St. Patricks
520	Moran, John, store keeper	27y	W	D.C.	29 MAY 1871	
065	Moran, Margrette A.	35y	W	Ire.	01 DEC 1856	St. Patricks
118	Moran, Martha I.	1y	W	D.C.	22 JUN 1858	Congressional
633	Moran, Michael F., tobacconist	31y	W	U.S.	06 OCT 1872	Holy Rood
782	Moran, Michael, laborer	60y	W	Ire.	03 JUL 1874	Mt. Olivet

Page	Name	Age	Race	Birth	Death Date	Burial Ground
269	Moran, Mrs.	30y	W	Ire.	30 AUG 1867	Mt. Olivet
608	Moran, O.A., clerk	23y	W	Md.	29 JUN 1872	
152	Moran, Pat., coachman	27y	W	Ire.	29 JUN 1859	Washington Asylum
001	Moran, Patrick	40y			_ JAN 1855	St. Matthews
326	Moran, Samuel E.	1y	W	D.C.	23 JUL 1868	Congressional
611	Moran, Solena	1y	W	U.S.	31 JUL 1872	
306	Moran, Thomas	1d	W	D.C.	16 APR 1868	Mt. Olivet
087	Moran, [blank]	3y	W	D.C.	12 AUG 1857	Glenwood
303	Morand, James, clerk	35y	W		03 MAR 1868	Prospect Hill
209	Morcoe, Theresa [Culverwell]	35y	W	D.C.	05 JAN 1866	Glenwood
629	Mordoth, Sarah	4m	C	U.S.	05 OCT 1872	
041	Moreland, John	1m	W	D.C.	08 APR 1856	Md.
545	Moreland, John H.	5m	W	D.C.	17 NOV 1871	Congressional*
400	Morell, Ernst Albert	3m	W		— JUL 1869	Prospect Hill
542	Moretus, Robert	1y	C	D.C.	22 OCT 1871	
262	Morgan, Albert L.	6m	W	D.C.	26 JUN 1867	Glenwood
041	Morgan, Ann E.	64y	W	D.C.	01 APR 1856	St. Peters
616a	Morgan, Chas. F.	6m	W	U.S.	16 JUL 1872	Congressional
462	Morgan, Clarence	3m	W	D.C.	01 JUL 1870	Congressional
307	Morgan, Eliza	68y	W	Eng.	12 APR 1868	Mt. Olivet
189	Morgan, Elizabeth B.	59y	W		04 SEP 1860	Congressional*
494	Morgan, Elizabeth, lady clerk	21y	W	Amer.	29 DEC 1870	Richmond, Va.
607	Morgan, J.T.	3m	W	D.C.	12 JUN 1872	Mt. Olivet
232	Morgan, James	1y	W	D.C.	24 AUG 1866	Congressional
783	Morgan, James A., lawyer	40y	W	U.S.	18 JUL 1874	Glenwood
528	Morgan, John	7m	W	D.C.	17 JUL 1871	Congressional*
546	Morgan, John B., printer	60y	W	N.Y.	24 NOV 1871	Congressional
333	Morgan, John, clerk	40y	W	N.Y.	17 JUL 1868	Congressional
028	Morgan, John W.	15m	W	D.C.	16 OCT 1855	Philadelphia, Pa.
265	Morgan, Joseph D.	8m	W	D.C.	11 JUL 1867	Mt. Olivet
555	Morgan, Julia	59y	W	D.C.	30 JAN 1872	Glenwood
404	Morgan, M.M.	33y	C		26 JUL 1869	
493	Morgan, Martha	22y	W	D.C.	23 DEC 1870	Congressional
625	Morgan, Mary	4y	W	U.S.	17 SEP 1872	
449	Morgan, Mary	30y	W	Ire.	24 APR 1870	Catholic
140	Morgan, Mary	11y	W	D.C.	01 FEB 1859	Congressional
114	Morgan, Mary I.	26y	W	Va.	18 MAY 1858	Congressional
385	Morgan, Monica	75y	W	Ire.	05 APR 1869	Mt. Olivet
583	Morgan, Nora	2m	W	D.C.	26 FEB 1872	Md.
093	Morgan, Richard B.	1m	W	D.C.	04 OCT 1857	Congressional
522	Morgan, Robert, teamster	35y	W		10 JUN 1871	Mt. Olivet
264	Morgan, William E.	8m	W	D.C.	04 JUL 1867	Congressional
078	Morgan, William, tanner	50y	W	Md.	28 MAY 1857	Methodist
272	Morgan, Willie	10m	C		04 AUG 1867	Freedmen's Bureau
748	Morgan, Wm. H.	2m	W	U.S.	10 FEB 1874	Congressional
330	Morganthal, [blank]		W	D.C.	21 JUL 1868	Washington Hebrew
420	Morgenthal, Mrs., infant of	Still	W		02 OCT 1869	Washington Hebrew
367	Moriarty, Ann, laundress	50y	W	Eng.	29 DEC 1868	Mt. Olivet
345	Moriarty, John, clerk	28y	W	Ire.	10 AUG 1868	Mt. Olivet
430	Morley, Ellen J.A.	16y	W	Ire.	28 DEC 1869	Mt. Olivet
116	Moroe, Susan E.	9m	W	D.C.	16 JUN 1858	St. Matthews
549	Morran, Mary	45y	W	Ire.	21 DEC 1871	Mt. Olivet
388	Morrell, Cyrus D., clerk	60y	W	Amer.	10 APR 1869	Me.
446	Morrice, Anna	19y	C		04 MAR 1870	Western
471	Morris, Augustus T.	5m	W	D.C.	20 AUG 1870	Congressional
033	Morris, Charles, Cmdr. USN	71y	W		27 JAN 1856	Oak Hill
697	Morris, Chas.	11d	W	D.C.	11 JUN 1873	Prospect Hill
467	Morris, Cynthia	75y	C	Va.	08 JUL 1870	

Page	Name	Age	Race	Birth	Death Date	Burial Ground
392	Morris, Harriet	19y	C	Va.	20 MAY 1869	Young Mens
432	Morris, Henry	9d	C	D.C.	30 DEC 1869	Washington Asylum
522	Morris, James	30y	C	Md.	10 JUN 1871	Potters Field
732	Morris, John M., editor	36y	W	U.S.	27 NOV 1873	
364	Morris, John, printer	30y	W	U.S.	15 DEC 1868	Congressional
741	Morris, John W., waiter	24y	C	U.S.	11 JAN 1874	Beckett's
047	Morris, John W.	3m	W		23 JUN 1856	Glenwood
343	Morris, Jordon, laborer	29y	C	Ga.	31 AUG 1868	
783	Morris, Josephine, housewife	31y	C	U.S.	27 JUL 1874	Mt. Olivet
627	Morris, Madison	30y	C	U.S.	27 SEP 1872	Small Pox
742	Morris, Margaret	1y	W	U.S.	17 JAN 1874	Mt. Olivet
182	Morris, Mina Jeanet	5m	W	D.C.	29 JUN 1860	Glenwood
607	Morris, Sallie	110y	C	D.C.	30 JUN 1872	Mt. Olivet
335a	Morris, Sarah	1m	B	D.C.	23 JUL 1868	Washington Asylum
047	Morris, Sarah E.	21y		D.C.	21 JUN 1856	Glenwood
231	Morris, Sarah F.	11m	W	D.C.	11 AUG 1866	Glenwood
737	Morris, Susan M.	26y	W	U.S.	25 DEC 1873	N.Y.
275	Morris, William H., smith	37y	W	D.C.	30 SEP 1867	Congressional
477	Morris, Wm. H. Boyd	1y	W	D.C.	11 SEP 1870	Glenwood
622a	Morrisette, Josephine	2y	W	U.S.	12 AUG 1872	
515	Morrisey, Jane, chambermaid	35y	C	Pa.	15 MAR 1871	Union
741	Morrisey, Margret, servant	43y	W	U.S.	14 JAN 1874	Mt. Olivet
336	Morrison, Andrew	79y	W	U.S.	25 AUG 1868	Washington Asylum
380	Morrison, Carrie	2y	W	N.Y.	31 MAR 1869	Glenwood
463	Morrison, Edward	14d	W	D.C.	24 JUL 1870	Glenwood
482	Morrison, George	3y	C	D.C.	14 OCT 1870	Harmony
499	Morrison, Katie, servant	45y	W	U.S.	25 JAN 1871	Congressional
492	Morrison, Laura	31y	W		21 DEC 1870	Congressional
434	Morrison, Martha H.	1y	W		21 JAN 1870	Glenwood
110	Morrison, Will.	2d	W	D.C.	03 APR 1858	Glenwood
463	Morrison, Wm. Henry	14d	W	D.C.	24 JUL 1870	Glenwood
743	Morrissey, Margaret, servant	20y	W	Ire.	25 JAN 1874	Mt. Olivet
385	Morrow, James F.	5m	W	Amer.	23 APR 1869	Congressional
420	Morrow, Robert, clerk	64y	W	Va.	15 OCT 1869	Glenwood
102	Morrow, William	64y	W	Md.	23 JAN 1858	Congressional
418	Morse, Afton, laborer	18y	C	Va.	24 SEP 1869	
025	Morse, C.E.	1m	W	D.C.	04 SEP 1855	Congressional
051	Morse, Elizabeth, seamstress	40y	W	D.C.	24 JUL 1856	St. Peters
122	Morse, Jane	22y	W	Va.	19 JUL 1858	Washington Asylum
632	Morse, John O.	4y	W	U.S.	24 OCT 1872	
197	Morse, Maria H.	1y	W	D.C.	28 JAN 1861	Congressional
513	Morsell, Eleanor W.	74y	W	Md.	29 MAR 1871	Oak Hill
507	Morsell, Jno. C.	88y	W	Md.	20 FEB 1871	Pr. Geo. Co., Md.
318	Mortimer, Caroline Willett Stevenson	57y	W	U.S.	26 JUN 1868	Congressional
180	Mortimer, Emeline	22y	W	D.C.	28 MAY 1860	Mt. Olivet
236	Mortimer, J.	13y	C	D.C.	22 SEP 1866	Glenwood
513	Mortimer, John T., farmer	49y	W	D.C.	24 MAR 1871	Glenwood
033	Mortimer, Sarah A.	29y	W	Va.	07 JAN 1856	Methodist
268	Mortimore, B., seaman	30y	W	Md.	28 AUG 1867	Mt. Olivet
690	Mortin, Horace M., schoolboy	6y	W	D.C.	13 MAY 1873	Congressional*
683	Morton, C.	4m	C	U.S.	08 APR 1873	
104	Morton, Jackson	8y	W	D.C.	10 FEB 1858	Va.
128	Morton, Jas. F., clerk	63y	W		26 SEP 1858	Ebenezer
591	Morton, Sarah J.	49y	C	D.C.	12 APR 1872	Asylum
007	Mosely, Manuel T.	17d	W	D.C.	05 APR 1855	Holmead
635	Moser, Neal	24y	C	U.S.	20 NOV 1872	Small Pox
594	Moses, Amos, laborer	20y	C	Md.	13 APR 1872	Washington
259	Moses, Louis B., clerk	21y	W	N.Y.	12 APR 1867	Glenwood

District of Columbia Interments (Index to Deaths), 1855-1874

Page	Name	Age	Race	Birth	Death Date	Burial Ground
249	Moses, Sophia	7y	W	D.C.	04 JAN 1867	Congressional
141	Moss, Elizabeth	32y	W		25 FEB 1859	Congressional
144	Moss, Emma V.	3y	W	D.C.	06 MAR 1859	Congressional
201	Moss, J.T., clerk	29y	W	Va.	16 MAR 1861	Glenwood
031	Moss, W.E.	3m	W	D.C.	08 DEC 1855	Glenwood
371	Moss, William, soldier	27y	W		11 JAN 1869	Mt. Olivet
105	Moss, [blank]	60y	C		25 FEB 1858	Holmead
014	Mothershead, Jeannetta	17m	W		02 JUL 1855	Congressional
097	Mothershead, Sarah	45y	W	Va.	23 NOV 1857	Congressional
500	Motley, Silas, laborer	45y	C	Va.	03 JAN 1871	Ebenezer
754	Mott, Jane	68y	W	U.S.	16 MAR 1874	N.Y.
729	Moulden, Chas. B.	9y	W	U.S.	01 NOV 1873	
070	Moulder, John W., printer	40y	W	D.C.	06 FEB 1857	Holmead
623	Moulding, Geo.	11m	W	U.S.	27 JUL 1872	Old Catholic
467	Moulton, Georgia M.	1m	W	D.C.	05 JUL 1870	Holmead
756	Moulton, Jesse	65y	C	U.S.	30 MAR 1874	
492	Mounding, Josephine	10d	C	U.S.	02 DEC 1870	Ebenezer
592	Mountz, James	3y	W	D.C.	03 APR 1872	Methodist Eps.
153	Moury, Alfred	6m	W	Pa.	10 JUL 1859	Holmead
068	Mowbray, Ezekiel	20y	W	Md.	17 JAN 1857	Congressional
087	Mowton, Mary	1y	C	D.C.	14 AUG 1857	Foundry
224	Moxly, John W.	5m	W	D.C.	11 JUN 1866	Oak Hill
634	Moyers, Anthoney, gardener	45y	W	Ger.	08 OCT 1872	
247	Mozine, Moses, hack driver	45y	W	D.C.	11 DEC 1866	Mt. Olivet
174	Mozingley, [girl]	22d	W	D.C.	10 MAR 1860	Washington Asylum
608	Mudd, Benja., waiter	30y	C	Va.	08 JUN 1872	
475	Mudd, Carrie V.	3y	W	U.S.	30 SEP 1870	Prospect Hill
091	Mudd, Edw., child of		W	D.C.	16 SEP 1857	Methodist
640	Mudd, Edward, Jr.	2y	W	U.S.	17 DEC 1872	Small Pox*
640	Mudd, Edwin B.	25y	W	U.S.	17 DEC 1872	Small Pox*
046	Mudd, Joanna	20y	W	D.C.	10 JUN 1856	Congressional
058	Mudd, Joanna	3m	W	D.C.	14 SEP 1856	Congressional
515	Mudd, John A.	4y	C	Md.	21 MAR 1871	Ebenezer
214	Mudd, John H.C.	45y	W	D.C.	04 MAR 1866	St. Patricks
668	Mudd, Joseph	4m	C	U.S.	24 FEB 1873	
598	Mudd, Lemuel	8y	C	U.S.	01 MAY 1872	Unknown
616a	Mudd, Mary V.	15m	W	U.S.	13 JUL 1872	Congressional*
013	Mudd, [blank]		W	D.C.	19 JUL 1855	Congressional
125	Muddiman, Jacob	1y	W	D.C.	28 AUG 1858	Congressional
748	Muds, Lillian	8d	W	U.S.	15 FEB 1874	Graceland
464	Mueden, Theodore	11m	W	D.C.	25 JUL 1870	Prospect Hill
620	Mueller, Augusta	16y	W	Ger.	18 AUG 1872	Brooklyn, N.Y.
274	Mueller, Geo. M.	14y	W		19 SEP 1867	
104	Muir, John	3y	W	Can.	14 FEB 1858	Ebenezer
538	Muir, Mary Ann	30y	W	D.C.	24 SEP 1871	Glenwood
236	Mulcahy, Mary N.	1y	W	D.C.	30 SEP 1866	Mt. Olivet
668	Mulcare, Joseph	1m	W	U.S.	21 FEB 1873	Laurel, Md.
478	Mulcarr, Michael J.	1y	W	D.C.	13 SEP 1870	Laurel, Md.
375	Muldrick, Mary	2y	W	D.C.	15 FEB 1869	Mt. Olivet
268	Muleare, John P.	2y	W		04 AUG 1867	Country
323	Mulens, Mary	3y	W	D.C.	16 JUL 1868	Mt. Olivet
371	Mullan, Jonathan, sexton	73y	W	Md.	20 JAN 1869	Baltimore, Md.
674	Mullaney, Ellen	5y	W	U.S.	18 MAR 1873	Mt. Olivet
016	Mullar, M.J.	1y		D.C.	19 JUL 1855	German Evangelic
011	Mullen, Elizabeth, washwoman	65y	C	Md.	05 JUN 1855	
538	Mullen, Eva	1y	W	D.C.	28 SEP 1871	Congressional
641	Mullen, George	35y	C	U.S.	18 DEC 1872	Small Pox
767	Mullen, Martha	2y	W	U.S.	25 MAY 1874	Mt. Olivet

Page	Name	Age	Race	Birth	Death Date	Burial Ground
031	Mullen, Pat.	2d	W		07 DEC 1855	St. Patricks
323	Mullens, John	14m	W	D.C.	17 JUL 1868	Mt. Olivet
622a	Muller, John	37y	W	Ire.	21 AUG 1872	
122	Muller, Millins	11m	W	D.C.	18 JUL 1858	German Catholic
113	Mullican, Elizabeth, housekeeper	50y	W		14 MAY 1858	Oak Hill
610	Mullican, John A.	3y	C		26 JUN 1867	Georgetown
235	Mulligan, John	3m	W	D.C.	17 SEP 1866	Mt. Olivet
608	Mulligan, P.M.	3y	W	D.C.	19 JUN 1872	
437	Mulligan, Patrick	67y	W	Ire.	20 JAN 1870	Washington Asylum
608	Mulligan, Peter	1y	W	D.C.	23 JUN 1872	
313	Mullikin, Mary	83y	W	U.S.	15 MAY 1868	Rock Creek
066	Mullikin, Mary	10d	W	D.C.	18 DEC 1856	St. Patricks
099	Mullikins, James, stone cutter	45y	W	Ire.	23 DEC 1857	St. Peters
552	Mullins, Porter	3y	C	D.C.	03 JAN 1872	
143	Mullowny, I.F.	7d	W	D.C.	11 MAR 1859	Congressional
135	Mulloy, F.S.	4y	W	D.C.	05 DEC 1858	Congressional
167	Mulloy, Mary G.	40y	W	D.C.	18 DEC 1859	Congressional
222	Mulloy, Richard H.	9y	W	N.Y.	29 MAY 1866	N.Y.
738	Mulloy, Thos. J.	21y	W	U.S.	29 DEC 1873	
036	Mulloy, Wm. S.	13y	W		11 FEB 1856	Congressional
304	Mulquan, Patrick	2y	W		c.05 MAR 1868	Mt. Olivet
092	Mulvaney, Thomas, store keeper	67y	W	Ire.	25 SEP 1857	St. Patricks
088	Muma, Alfred H.	10m	C		24 AUG 1857	Western
641	Mumberger, Catherine	7y	W	U.S.	29 DEC 1872	Small Pox*
518	Mumberry, Annie	4y	W	D.C.	09 MAY 1871	Prospect Hill
244	Munch, Christian H., gun/locksmith	51y	W	Ger.	14 NOV 1866	Glenwood
350	Munday, Wm. Henry	2m	C	D.C.	29 SEP 1868	Washington Asylum
401	Munday, [blank]	10m	C	D.C.	08 JUL 1869	Young Mens
231	Mundell, Joseph, Jr., letter carrier	30y	W	D.C.	18 AUG 1866	Congressional
231	Mundell, Martha M.	1y	W	D.C.	19 AUG 1866	Congressional
594	Mundell, Mary Jane, clerk	30y	W	D.C.	07 APR 1872	Congressional*
731	Munder, Wm. A., butcher	41y	W	Ger.	25 NOV 1873	Prospect Hill
250	Mundine, Saml.	21y	C		03 JAN 1867	Harmony
615	Mundy, Lewis	28y	C	U.S.	11 JUL 1872	
601	Mundy, Louise F.	6y	W		18 MAY 1872	Unknown
469	Mungen, Kate A.	20y	W	N.Y.	16 AUG 1870	Glenwood
762	Mungman, Catherine	35y	W	Ire.	30 APR 1874	Mt. Olivet
714	Munn, William	1y	W	D.C.	30 AUG 1873	Mt. Olivet
260	Munro, George	45y	W		09 MAY 1867	
127	Munroe, Fanny	84y	W	D.C.	16 SEP 1858	Oak Hill
311	Munroe, Harriet		C		c.08 APR 1868	Alms House
461	Munroe, Hector H., professor	50y	W	Scot.	23 JUL 1870	Congressional
451	Munroe, Mary	1y	C		02 APR 1870	Mt. Olivet
305	Munroe, Patrick	45y	W		c.16 MAR 1868	Mt. Olivet
325	Munson, Cornelia Pryor	58y	W	N.Y.	23 JUL 1868	Congressional
314	Munson, Owen, Dr.	60y	W	Ver.	19 MAY 1868	Congressional
635	Murdock, A.M.	1½y	W	U.S.	27 NOV 1872	Small Pox
385	Murdock, Elizabeth		W		05 APR 1869	
020	Murldon, Wm.	37y	C		19 AUG 1855	St. Patricks
288	Murphey, Mary	1y	W	D.C.	19 DEC 1867	Mt. Olivet
712	Murphey, Mary	70y	W	Ire.	19 AUG 1873	Mt. Olivet
703	Murphey, Mary	55y	W	Ire.	23 JUL 1873	Rock Creek
710	Murphey, Thomas, farmer	61y	W	Ire.	02 AUG 1873	Rock Creek
092	Murphey, [blank]	12d	W		23 SEP 1857	St. Matthews
157	Murphy, Alexander, carpenter	67y	W	Md.	05 AUG 1859	Tennallytown
470	Murphy, Angela D.	11m	W	D.C.	06 AUG 1870	Congressional
660	Murphy, Arthur S.	3y	W	U.S.	18 JAN 1873	Glenwood
542	Murphy, Bartholomew	1y	W	D.C.	20 OCT 1871	Mt. Olivet

District of Columbia Interments (Index to Deaths), 1855-1874

Page	Name	Age	Race	Birth	Death Date	Burial Ground
782	Murphy, Bridget	40y	W	Ire.	06 JUL 1874	Mt. Olivet
127	Murphy, Bridget	10y	W	D.C.	17 SEP 1858	St. Patricks
236	Murphy, Catherine	4y	W	D.C.*	25 SEP 1866	Mt. Olivet
535	Murphy, Charles	1y	W	U.S.	16 SEP 1871	Washington
513	Murphy, Charles M., printer	33y	W	D.C.	26 MAR 1871	Oak Hill
017	Murphy, Denis	10m	W	D.C.	20 JUL 1855	St. Patricks
054	Murphy, Dennis	5y	W	D.C.	05 AUG 1856	St. Patricks
298	Murphy, Edwd. W.	2m	W		27 FEB 1868	Mt. Olivet
490	Murphy, Ellen	40y	W	Ire.	07 NOV 1870	Mt. Olivet
590	Murphy, Ellen	1y	W	Ire.	07 APR 1872	Mt. Olivet
634	Murphy, Ellen, Mrs.	49y	W	Ire.	26 OCT 1872	Mt. Olivet
726	Murphy, H., infant of	10d	B		25 OCT 1873	Beckett's
361	Murphy, Harriet A.	63y	W	Va.	06 NOV 1868	St. Patricks
007	Murphy, Honora	27y	W	Ire.	09 APR 1855	St. Patricks
270	Murphy, Ida L.	1y	W	Va.	12 AUG 1867	Glenwood
445	Murphy, James, laborer	40y	W	Ire.	24 MAR 1870	Mt. Olivet
118	Murphy, Jane	27y	W	Ire.	12 JUN 1858	
241	Murphy, Jane Eliza	44y	W	D.C.	27 OCT 1866	Mt. Olivet*
445	Murphy, Jeremiah, sailor	28y	W	Ire.	13 MAR 1870	Mt. Olivet*
773	Murphy, Jno. A.	49y	W	U.S.	01 JUN 1874	Congressional
019	Murphy, John (twins)		W		10 AUG 1855	St. Patricks
390	Murphy, John, former grocer	55y	W	Ire.	31 MAY 1869	Rock Creek
184	Murphy, John, laborer	43y	W	Ire.	07 JUL 1860	
270	Murphy, John, Mrs.	35y	W	Ire.	17 AUG 1867	Mt. Olivet
307	Murphy, Laurence Frances	2m	W	D.C.	09 APR 1868	Mt. Olivet
547	Murphy, Lawrence	60y	W	Ire.	05 DEC 1871	Mt. Olivet*
602	Murphy, Lewis, laborer	45y	C	Md.	13 MAY 1872	Asylum
602	Murphy, M.J.C.	20y	W	U.S.	25 MAY 1872	
622a	Murphy, Mary	1y	W	U.S.	29 AUG 1872	
767	Murphy, Mary	13y	W	U.S.	18 MAY 1874	
063	Murphy, Mary	19y	W	D.C.	19 NOV 1856	Glenwood
324	Murphy, Mary	7y	W	D.C.	07 JUL 1868	Mt. Clivet
726	Murphy, Mary	88y	W	Ire.	29 OCT 1873	Mt. Clivet
594	Murphy, Mary	3y	W	D.C.	10 APR 1872	Mt. Clivet
783	Murphy, Mary	40y	W	Ire.	12 JUL 1874	Mt. Olivet
378	Murphy, Mary	80y	C	U.S.	28 FEB 1869	Washington Asylum
276	Murphy, Mary	25y	W	Ohio	05 SEP 1867	Youngstown, Ohio
025	Murphy, Mary E.	17m	W	D.C.	01 SEP 1855	Rock Creek
767	Murphy, Mary Ellen	6d	W	U.S.	29 MAY 1874	Mt. Olivet*
082	Murphy, Mary, pauper	1y	W	Pa.	06 JUL 1857	Washington Asylum
233	Murphy, Matthew	2m	W	D.C.	29 AUG 1866	Mt. Olivet
730	Murphy, Michael, grocer	60y	W	Ire.	12 NOV 1873	Mt. Olivet*
234	Murphy, Michael, money engraver	37y	W	N.Y.	11 SEP 1866	
097	Murphy, Michael, stone cutter	36y	W	Ire.	21 NOV 1857	St. Patricks
673	Murphy, Moses	85y	C	U.S.	02 MAR 1873	Washington Asylum
227	Murphy, Nicholas	10m	W	D.C.	06 JUL 1866	Mt. Olivet
015	Murphy, Pat.	8m	W	D.C.	20 JUL 1855	St. Patricks
283	Murphy, William, seaman	29y	W	Ire.	18 NOV 1867	Congressional
586	Murphy, [blank]	3m	W	D.C.	13 MAR 1872	
627	Murray, Austin	48y	C	U.S.	16 SEP 1872	Small Pox
053	Murray, Catharine	2m	W	D.C.	23 AUG 1856	St. Peters
590	Murray, Charles	7y	C	D.C.	02 APR 1872	Holmead
524	Murray, Chas. H.	1m	W	U.S.	25 JUN 1871	Congressional*
705	Murray, Chas. H.	58y	W	Pa.	02 JUL 1873	Philadelphia, Pa.
229	Murray, D.L., late col. USA	45y	W	Pa.	19 JUL 1866	Carlisle, Pa.
680	Murray, Daniel Ashford	9m	W	U.S.	05 APR 1873	Mt. Olivet*
380	Murray, Edwin B.	11m	W	D.C.	01 MAR 1869	N.Y.
381	Murray, Elizabeth	58y	W	Va.	04 MAR 1869	

Page	Name	Age	Race	Birth	Death Date	Burial Ground
498	Murray, Hanson, pauper	40y	B	Va.	11 JAN 1871	Washington Asylum
783	Murray, James	3y	W	U.S.	24 JUL 1874	Mt. Olivet
181	Murray, John E.	1m	W	D.C.	02 JUN 1860	Mt. Olivet
498	Murray, Lucy, pauper	8m	B	D.C.	04 JAN 1871	Washington Asylum
425	Murray, Margaret Ann	5m	W	D.C.	12 NOV 1869	Congressional
378	Murray, Mary	80y	C	Md.	14 FEB 1869	Holmead
046	Murray, Mary F.	36y	W	Va.	04 JUN 1856	Congressional
541	Murray, Mary L.	30y	W	N.Y.	17 OCT 1871	
153	Murray, Matilda B.	1y	W	D.C.	03 JUL 1859	Mt. Olivet
046	Murray, Patrick	13y	W	Ire.	20 JUN 1856	St. Patricks
724	Murray, Rebecca, nurse	52y	M	Md.	16 OCT 1873	Beckett's
723	Murray, Rebecca, servant	22y	M	Va.	04 OCT 1873	Washington Asylum
715	Murray, Richard		W		08 AUG 1873	
325	Murray, S.S., govt. clerk	33y	W	Pa.	14 JUL 1868	Congressional
487	Murray, Sarah	75y	W	Ire.	25 NOV 1870	Mt. Olivet
034	Murray, [blank]	2m	W		01 JAN 1856	Western
366	Murry, Alexander	17m	L	D.C.	03 DEC 1868	Harmony
187	Murry, Catherine	4m	C	D.C.	01 AUG 1860	Young Mens
104	Murry, Ellen	32y	W	Ire.	07 FEB 1858	St. Patricks
641	Murry, George	22y	C	U.S.	16 DEC 1872	Small Pox
314	Murry, John H.	14d	W	D.C.	25 MAY 1868	Congressional
330	Murry, Mary Susan	8m	C	D.C.	20 JUL 1868	Young Mens
748	Murx, Bermard [sic], Rev.	28y	W	U.S.	23 FEB 1874	Baltimore, Md.
684	Muse, Joseph	7y	C	U.S.	05 APR 1873	Small Pox*
684	Muse, Maria	4y	C	U.S.	07 APR 1873	Small Pox*
711	Muse, Sarah F., Mrs.	30y	W	Va.	08 AUG 1873	Congressional
711	Muse, Willie P.	10y	W	Va.	08 AUG 1873	Congressional
435	Mussey, Lucina S.B., Mrs.		W	Me.	13 JAN 1870	Oak Hill
552	Muth, Teresa	40y	W	Ger.	01 JAN 1872	Glenwood
732	Muth, [blank]	7d	W	U.S.	28 NOV 1873	St. Marys
688	Myer, Gracie			U.S.	17 MAY 1873	
233	Myer, James	32y	W	Ger.	16 AUG 1866	
225	Myers, Andrew C.	10y	W	D.C.	23 JUN 1866	Mt. Olivet*
470	Myers, Annie E.	1y	W		24 AUG 1870	Congressional
254	Myers, Charles A., tailor	35y	C	Md.	04 FEB 1867	Mt. Olivet
783	Myers, Charles F.	58y	W	Ger.	29 JUL 1874	Potters Field
249	Myers, Charles, waiter	44y	C	D.C.	25 JAN 1867	Young Mens
073	Myers, E.	40y	W		09 MAR 1857	Montgomery Co., Md.
023	Myers, Eliza C.	11m	W		03 SEP 1855	Catholic, Georgetown
292a	Myers, Elizabeth A.	1y	W	D.C.*	03 FEB 1868	Presbyterian
667	Myers, Elvina	43y	W	U.S.	10 FEB 1873	Glenwood
666	Myers, Frank C.	Still	W	U.S.	01 FEB 1873	Glenwood
549	Myers, Frank D.	2y	W	U.S.	23 DEC 1871	Glenwood
344	Myers, Greenberry, farmer	62y	C		06 AUG 1868	Harmony
101	Myers, Harriet W.	2y	W	N.J.	04 JAN 1858	Glenwood
415	Myers, Harry F.	11m	W	Ohio	26 SEP 1869	Ohio
099	Myers, Infant		W	D.C.	30 DEC 1857	Foundry
258	Myers, James	32y	C		03 APR 1867	Western
446	Myers, Jane		C	D.C.	14 MAR 1870	Washington Asylum
710	Myers, Jeremiah W.	15m	C	D.C.	01 AUG 1873	Congressional
624	Myers, John F.	21m	W	U.S.	18 SEP 1872	
207	Myers, Joseph B.	6m	W	D.C.	12 JUL 1862	Holmead
250	Myers, Joseph L.	4m	C	D.C.	05 JAN 1867	Harmony
408	Myers, Laura Rebecca	7m	C		18 AUG 1869	Holmead
352	Myers, M.	22d	C		09 SEP 1868	Washington Asylum
264	Myers, Martha, dress maker	27y	C	S.C.	17 JUL 1867	Harmony
600	Myers, Mary	9d	W	U.S.	25 MAY 1872	Presbyterian
378	Myers, Mary	41y	W	Md.	— FEB 1869	Washington Asylum

Page	Name	Age	Race	Birth	Death Date	Burial Ground
169	Myers, Patrick	2m	W	D.C.	16 JAN 1860	
530	Myers, Samuel	1y	C	D.C.	28 JUL 1871	Young Mens
253	Myers, Sarah	60y	C	Va.	09 FEB 1867	Ebenezer
103	Myers, William, blacksmith	15y	W	D.C.	05 JAN 1858	Holmead
065	Myers, [blank], Mr.	37y	W	Ger.	15 DEC 1856	German Lutheran
456	Mygatt, Julia C.	59y	W	Conn.	29 JUN 1870	Glenwood
609	Myles, J.J., police officer	38y	W	Ire.	24 JUN 1872	
024	Myles, Sarah	55y	W	Md.	09 SEP 1855	Congressional
229	Myrick, Mr., infant of	2m			23 JUL 1866	Congressional

Page	Name	Age	Race	Birth	Death Date	Burial Ground
N						
622	Nagle, Carl A., carpenter	42y	W	Ger.	29 AUG 1872	
581	Nailer, [blank]	3y	C	D.C.	15 FEB 1872	
319	Nailor, A.	1y	C	D.C.	18 JUN 1868	Young Mens
224	Nailor, Harriet Elizabeth	77y	W	Va.	13 JUN 1866	Rock Creek
619	Nailor, Jno. R.	11m	C	U.S.	09 AUG 1872	
112	Nailor, Mary	10y	W	D.C.	21 APR 1858	Holmead
118	Nailor, Sarah Jane	1m	W	D.C.	30 JUN 1858	Rock Creek
136	Nailor, Thompson, servant of	18y	C	Md.	31 DEC 1858	Foundry
119	Nailor, William	6y	W	D.C.	17 JUN 1858	Methodist
073	Nairn, Joseph	6m	W	D.C.	14 MAR 1857	Glenwood
636	Nairn, R.B.	1y	W	U.S.	29 NOV 1872	
359	Nalley, Caroline	50y	W	D.C.	12 NOV 1868	Glenwood
258	Nalley, Emma W.	1y	W	D.C.	03 APR 1867	Glenwood
515	Nalley, James	49y	W	Md.	30 MAR 1871	Congressional
121	Nalley, Jane	1y	W		15 JUL 1858	Congressional
308	Nalley, John Francis, laborer	35y	W	Md.	30 APR 1868	Mt. Olivet
187	Nalley, Mary	7y	W	D.C.	13 AUG 1860	Congressional
073	Nalley, Mary Ann	42y	W	Md.	14 MAR 1857	St. Patricks
723	Nalley, Mary Catharine	3y	W	D.C.	08 OCT 1873	Congressional
731	Nally, Annie R.	28y	W	U.S.	22 NOV 1873	Mt. Olivet
295	Nally, Christine C.	54y	W	Md.	13 FEB 1868	Congressional
783	Nally, Ellen	73y	W	U.S.	28 JUL 1874	Congressional*
315	Nally, John F.	35y	W		c.01 MAY 1868	Mt. Olivet
176	Nally, Mary P.	17y	W	D.C.	12 APR 1860	St. Patricks
691	Nally, Wm. J., scholar	13y	W		29 MAY 1873	Congressional
617	Nandain, [blank]	7m	W	U.S.	21 AUG 1872	
225	Nares, Fanny	5m	W	N.Y.	19 JUN 1866	Congressional
028	Nash, Anna M.				25 OCT 1855	St. Peters
694	Nash, Elizabeth	45y	W	D.C.	01 JUN 1873	Glenwood
724	Nash, Emma, authoress & poet	34y	W	La.	13 OCT 1873	
412	Nash, Fanny	19y	C	Va.	13 AUG 1869	Washington Asylum
004	Nash, Geo. W.R.	6m	W	D.C.	28 MAR 1855	Foundry
094	Nash, Jane	79y	W	Eng.	26 OCT 1857	Alexandria, Va.
544	Nash, Jane E.	37y	W	D.C.	04 NOV 1871	Congressional
243	Nash, Jarrett J.	7y	W	D.C.	11 NOV 1866	Congressional
337	Nash, Jno.	2m	C	U.S.	10 AUG 1868	Washington Asylum
266	Nash, Martha E.	4m	W	D.C.	06 JUL 1867	Glenwood
317	Nash, Mary	11m	C	D.C.	29 JUN 1868	
256	Nash, Mary, servant	23y	C	Va.	13 MAR 1867	Moore's
697	Nash, Robert, Mrs.	45y	W	U.S.	01 JUN 1873	
161	Nash, Sarah Catharine	2y	W	D.C.	02 SEP 1859	Congressional
006	Nash, [blank]		W		02 APR 1855	Western
400	Nass, George	3m	W	D.C.	04 JUL 1869	Prospect Hill
620	Nater, S.E.	23y	W	U.S.	17 AUG 1872	Allentown, Pa.
697	Nauck, Effie	24d	W	D.C.	30 JUN 1873	Prospect Hill
091	Nauman, Ann	10m	W	D.C.	16 SEP 1857	German Lutheran
703	Nayler, Lillie G.	5y	C	U.S.	10 JUL 1873	Harmony
540	Naylor, Ann E.	2m	W	D.C.	01 OCT 1871	Mt. Olivet*
493	Naylor, Charlotte	65y	C	Md.	15 DEC 1870	Harmony
514	Naylor, E.E.A.L., housewife	59y	W	Md.	25 MAR 1871	Rock Creek
045	Naylor, Elizabeth	38y	W	D.C.	30 MAY 1856	Methodist
085	Naylor, Harry	5m	W	D.C.	30 JUL 1857	Rock Creek
502	Naylor, Henry, gentleman	71y	W	D.C.	24 JAN 1871	Congressional
583	Naylor, James		C	D.C.	28 FEB 1872	
442	Naylor, Mary E.	35y	C		08 FEB 1870	Young Mens
083	Naylor, Rachael L.	5m	W	D.C.	19 JUL 1857	Rock Creek
541	Naylor, Sarah	65y	W	D.C.	09 OCT 1871	Congressional*

District of Columbia Interments (Index to Deaths), 1855-1874

Page	Name	Age	Race	Birth	Death Date	Burial Ground
532	Naylor, Susan E.	47y	W	Va.	11 AUG 1871	Pr. Geo. Co., Md.
329	Neacey, Edward	1y	W	D.C.	07 JUL 1868	Mt. Olivet
586	Neaff, Mary E.	21y	W	D.C.	17 MAR 1872	St. Marys
290	Neal, Henrietta	25y	C	Va.	25 JAN 1868	Freedmen's Hospital
476	Neal, Henrietta, cook	80y	C	Md.	26 SEP 1870	Ebenezer
472	Neal, Hester, servant	22y	C	Va.	19 AUG 1870	Freedmen's Hospital
033	Neal, Jno. T., merchant	30y	W	N.H.	10 JAN 1856	Congressional
182	Neal, Mrs.		C		28 JUN 1860	Ebenezer
637	Neal, Robt.	7y	C	U.S.	15 NOV 1872	
549	Neal, Sarah, nurse	36y	C	D.C.	24 DEC 1871	Mt. Olivet
104	Neal, William, servant	75y	C	Md.	09 FEB 1858	Colored, Methodist
407	Neale, Charles, gardener	73y	W	Eng.	12 AUG 1869	Congressional
116	Neale, George M.	10m	C	D.C.	19 JUN 1858	St. Matthews
754	Neale, Henrietta	35y	C	U.S.	20 MAR 1874	
079	Neale, Ramsy, wood sawyer	50y	C	Md.	01 JUN 1857	Young Mens
164	Neale, William C.	1y	C	D.C.	28 OCT 1859	Ebenezer
736	Nealey, thomas, tinner	33y	W	Ire.	15 DEC 1873	Mt. Olivet
502	Neaston, J.	Still	W		02 JAN 1871	Glenwood
397	Neat, Fanny J.	25y	W	Md.	16 JUN 1869	Va.
387	Neat, Mellie	11d	W	D.C.	21 APR 1869	
313	Nebbs, Philip	81y	W	Ger.	20 MAY 1868	Va.
376	Neckly, Mary	1y	C		20 FEB 1869	
530	Neely, Alice H.	8m	W	D.C.	31 JUL 1871	Congressional*
407	Neely, John Thomas	14d	W		20 AUG 1869	Congressional
401	Neenan, Ann, Mrs.	29y	W	Ire.	25 JUL 1869	Mt. Olivet
582	Neff, Amelia	3y	W	D.C.	22 FEB 1872	St. Marys
334	Neff, Ida Seraphina	1y	W		05 JUL 1868	German Catholic
582	Neffe, Andrew F.	2y	W	U.S.	20 FEB 1872	St. Marys
073	Neffin, Israael	63y	W	N.Y.	07 MAR 1857	Washington Asylum
774	Neidfeldt, Fannie	25y	W	Ger.	05 JUN 1874	Prospect Hill
774	Neidfull, Willie	8m	W	U.S.	25 JUN 1874	Mt. Olivet
411	Neidhardt, John Mathews	1m	W	Pa.	07 AUG 1869	Glenwood
458	Neigle, George	48y	W	Md.	14 JUN 1870	Potters Field
158	Neil, Ellen	62y	C	Md.	20 AUG 1859	Harmony
447	Neil, John H.	1m	C		25 MAR 1870	Ebenezer
160	Neios, George S.	6y	W	D.C.	11 AUG 1859	German
754	Neitz, Jane L.	40y	W	U.S.	10 MAR 1874	Prospect Hill
085	Neitz, Joseph	1y	W	D.C.	03 JUL 1857	German
550	Neitze, Alice	15y	W	D.C.	31 DEC 1871	German
774	Neitze, Alice Jane	4m	W	U.S.	28 JUN 1874	Prospect Hill
384	Nelligan, E.	1y	W		16 MAR 1869	Mt. Olivet
330	Nelms, Lycene Y.	4m	C	D.C.	31 JUL 1868	Mt. Olivet
760	Nelson, Alice, domestic	17y	C	U.S.	25 APR 1874	Beckett's
676	Nelson, Baker	60y	C	Md.	04 MAR 1873	
541	Nelson, Benjamin	60y	C	D.C.	09 OCT 1871	Washington
529	Nelson, Daniel, gardener	75y	C	Md.	27 JUL 1871	
544	Nelson, Edward	1m	W		02 NOV 1871	Congressional
509	Nelson, Ellen, child of	14d	C	D.C.	23 FEB 1871	Washington Asylum
614	Nelson, Emma	30y	W	U.S.	14 JUL 1872	
409	Nelson, Fanny	12y	C		09 AUG 1869	Young Mens
166	Nelson, George, teamster	30y	W	N.C.	27 NOV 1859	Washington Asylum
451	Nelson, Harriet	27y	C	Md.	24 APR 1870	Young Mens
124	Nelson, Jane	52y	W	Md.	05 AUG 1858	Washington Asylum
750	Nelson, Jennie	10m	C	U.S.	09 FEB 1874	
358	Nelson, John	2y	C		09 OCT 1868	Holmead
621	Nelson, Laura	5y	C	U.S.	31 AUG 1872	
284	Nelson, Martha	25y	C		— NOV 1867	
673	Nelson, Mary	40y	C	U.S.	05 MAR 1873	Washington Asylum

Page	Name	Age	Race	Birth	Death Date	Burial Ground
338	Nelson, Mary Ann	5m	C		25 AUG 1868	Washington Asylum
541	Nelson, Mary E.	21y	W	D.C.	13 OCT 1871	Congressional
430	Nelson, Mary, housekeeper	55y	W	Ire.	08 DEC 1869	Mt. Olivet
748	Nelson, Matilda	63y	W	U.S.	05 FEB 1874	Congressional*
300	Nelson, Randal, laborer	40y	C	Va.	09 MAR 1868	Alms House
760	Nelson, Richard	1y	C	U.S.	25 APR 1874	Washington Asylum
312	Nelson, William	8m	C	D.C.	26 MAY 1868	Alms House
598	Nelson, Wm.	1y	C	U.S.	11 MAY 1872	
598	Nelson, Wm.	1y	C	U.S.	11 MAY 1872	Unknown
597	Nelson, Wm.	1y	C	U.S.	12 MAY 1872	Washington
432	Nelson, [blank]	1d	C	D.C.	15 DEC 1869	Washington Asylum
140	Nenah, [blank]	1y	W	D.C.	01 FEB 1859	Mt. Olivet
767	Neolon, Thomas, laborer	38y	W	Ire.	26 MAY 1874	Mt. Olivet
282	Nephew, Elizabeth	4y	W		— NOV 1867	Mt. Olivet
594	Neser, Florence	6y	W	D.C.	18 APR 1872	Mt. Olivet
720	Neslein, Mary R.	1m	W	D.C.	24 SEP 1873	
710	Neslin, Catherine	43y	W	Ger.	08 AUG 1873	
340	Nesmith, Ann	84y	W	Eng.	03 AUG 1868	Congressional
143	Nessensohn, Conrad R.F.	1y	W	D.C.	01 MAR 1859	Washington
070	Nessensohn, Margaret	8m	W	D.C.	06 FEB 1857	Congressional*
707	Nessinson, Jos., machinist	53y	W	Ger.	06 JUL 1873	Congressional
228	Nester, Ann Hays	46y	W	Ire.	16 JUL 1866	Mt. Olivet
221	Netter, Laura	18y	C	D.C.	23 MAY 1866	Beckett's
631	Netter, Sampson, messenger	60y	C	U.S.	26 OCT 1872	
234	Netter, [blank]	5d	C	D.C.	04 SEP 1866	Harmony
588	Neufali, Mary	2y	W	D.C.	27 MAR 1872	Holy Rood
664	Neuman, Jos.	16m	C	U.S.	14 JAN 1873	Small Pox*
706	Neuman, L.	1y	W		09 JUL 1873	Prospect Hill
344	Neumann, Maria Rosina	9m	W	D.C.	16 AUG 1868	Prospect Hill
748	Neumeyer, Vinsent P.	9d	W	U.S.	09 FEB 1874	Mt. Olivet
546	Neumyer, Laura V.	19y	W	D.C.	23 NOV 1871	Mt. Olivet
688	Neunaier, Henry, huckster	32y	W	U.S.	21 MAY 1873	Mt. Olivet
244	Nevill, Sarah E.	42y	C	D.C.	19 NOV 1866	Glenwood
105	Nevins, John C., clerk	30y	W	D.C.*	15 FEB 1858	St. Patricks
445	Nevins, Margaret E.	69y	W		27 MAR 1870	Congressional
637	Nevis, Henry	42y	C	U.S.	24 NOV 1872	
165	Nevitt, Charlotte LeC.	37y	W	D.C.	08 NOV 1859	Congressional
605	New, Henry G., clerk	50y	W	Eng.	07 JUN 1872	Asylum
729	Newcomer, Laura	12y	W	U.S.	04 NOV 1873	Glenwood
547	Newell, Geo. W., tinner	24y	W	D.C.	04 DEC 1871	Harmony
059	Newell, John, tailor	32y	W	Eng.	02 SEP 1856	Congressional*
235	Newgent, Mary E.V.	2y	C	D.C.	19 SEP 1866	Harmony
549	Newhall, Mabel A.	1y	W	U.S.	21 DEC 1871	Mt. Olivet
708	Newkirk, A.V.	1m	W		02 JUL 1873	Congressional*
613	Newkirk, Josephine	7m	W	U.S.	03 JUL 1872	
515	Newlands, John B., clerk	31y	W	U.S.	29 MAR 1871	Congressional
391	Newmaiar, Annie	1y	W		05 MAY 1869	Mt. Olivet
666	Newman, Adlay	1y	C	U.S.	01 FEB 1873	
544	Newman, Ann J.	48y	W		08 NOV 1871	Washington
382	Newman, Charles	2y	C		12 MAR 1869	Young Mens
290	Newman, Cornelius	28y	C	Va.	12 JAN 1868	Harmony
002	Newman, Elizabeth H.	60+	W	R.I.	26 JAN 1855	St. Patricks
065	Newman, Francis	1m	W	D.C.	11 DEC 1856	Congressional
351	Newman, James	1y	W		01 SEP 1868	Methodist
732	Newman, Margaret	15y	C	U.S.	30 NOV 1873	Harmony
351	Newman, Maria	1y	C	D.C.	27 SEP 1868	Ebenezer
783	Newman, Minnie	2y	W	U.S.	17 JUL 1874	Prospect Hill
033	Newman, Mrs., child of	Still	W		24 JAN 1856	Foundry

District of Columbia Interments (Index to Deaths), 1855-1874

Page	Name	Age	Race	Birth	Death Date	Burial Ground
663	Newman, Richard	4y	C	U.S.	03 JAN 1873	Small Pox*
635	Newman, Robt.	22y	C	U.S.	12 NOV 1872	Small Pox
740	Newman, Willie	11m	W	U.S.	04 JAN 1874	
476	Newmey, Rosa Ella	1y	W	Amer.	27 SEP 1870	St. Marys
420	Newmiller, Catharine	64y	W	Ger.	25 OCT 1869	Mt. Olivet
061	Newton, Alfred, soldier		W		02 OCT 1856	Marine
381	Newton, Ann E.	68y	W	Md.	12 MAR 1869	Mt. Olivet
326	Newton, Ann S.	78y	W		27 JUL 1868	Alexandria, Va.
548	Newton, Elisabeth	68y	W	Md.	11 DEC 1871	Glenwood
298	Newton, Emily T.	31y	W	N.H.	06 FEB 1868	Glenwood
263	Newton, Isaac, comr. agriculture	67y	W	N.J.	19 JUN 1867	N.J.
084	Newton, John Thos., naval officer	64y	W	Va.*	28 JUL 1857	Congressional*
256	Newton, Polly	50y	C	Va.	18 MAR 1867	Moore's
082	Newton, [blank]	3m	W	D.C.	04 JUL 1857	St. Patricks
502	Nibbo, Catharine	83y	W	Md.	10 JAN 1871	Mt. Olivet
485	Nicholas, Albert, prisoner US jail	40y	C		25 OCT 1870	Washington Asylum
386	Nicholas, Alice G.	5y	W		04 APR 1869	Congressional
527	Nicholas, Charlotte	2y	C	D.C.	12 JUL 1871	
316	Nicholas, James		C		c.17 MAY 1868	Alms House
286	Nicholas. [blank]	1m	W		14 DEC 1867	Mt. Olivet
489	Nichols, A.W.	32y	W	Amer.	08 NOV 1870	N.Y.
350	Nichols, Anna E.	1y	C	D.C.	13 SEP 1868	Harmony
237	Nichols, Aquilla, driver	60y	W	Md.	22 SEP 1866	Congressional
507	Nichols, Clara V., seamstress	30y	C	Md.	07 FEB 1871	Union
783	Nichols, Elizabeth	71y	W	U.S.	30 JUL 1874	Presbyterian
760	Nichols, Esther, housewife	75y	C	U.S.	02 APR 1874	
237	Nichols, George	12y	W	Md.	22 SEP 1866	Mt. Olivet*
454a	Nichols, Henry, pauper	10m	C	D.C.	02 MAY 1870	Washington Asylum
286	Nichols, Jasper, Sr., butcher	61y	W	N.Y.	31 DEC 1867	Holmead
646	Nichols, Lewis, fireman	35y	C	S.C.	19 DEC 1872	
525	Nichols, Martha A.	1y	C		26 JUN 1871	Union
332	Nichols, Rebecca	5m	C	D.C.	20 JUL 1868	
392	Nichols, Sarah	2y	C		10 MAY 1869	Washington Asylum
253	Nichols, William A., furniture dlr.	36y	C	D.C.	19 FEB 1867	Harmony
618	Nichols, Wm. D.	21m	W	U.S.	11 AUG 1872	Prospect Hill
407	Nichols, Wm. T.	51y	W	Md.	21 AUG 1869	Congressional
013	Nicholson, A[gustus] A., Q.M.	53y	W	S.C.	18 JUL 1855	Congressional
413	Nicholson, Jane	11m	W		31 AUG 1869	Glenwood
269	Nicholson, Thomas W., watchman	30y	W	D.C.	31 AUG 1867	Congressional
664	Nickens, Ida	4m	C	U.S.	23 JAN 1873	Small Pox*
306	Nicklas, Henry	6y	C	D.C.	23 APR 1868	Young Mens
554	Nicklaus, Carrie	1y	W	D.C.	22 JAN 1872	Methodist
544	Nicklaus, Jacob, baker	48y	W	Ger.	08 NOV 1871	Methodist
347	Nickle, John, child of	10m	W		01 SEP 1868	Congressional
010	Nickleson, Laura	10m	W		28 JUN 1855	Foundry
608	Niedlfeldt, J.F., tailor	57y	W	Ger.	23 JUN 1872	
738	Night, Florance	81y	C	U.S.	28 DEC 1873	
231	Night, Margaret D.	8m	W	D.C.	18 AUG 1866	Prospect Hill
617	Nightengale, Edwd.	15m	C	U.S.	18 AUG 1872	
552	Nightingale, J., Mrs.	65y	W	Va.	01 JAN 1872	
144	Nileas, Elizabeth	61y	W	Ger.	17 MAR 1859	German
618	Nilson, Stephen	24y	C	U.S.	14 AUG 1872	
275	Nimmo, James D., USN	17y	W	Md.	17 SEP 1867	Glenwood
445	Nisbet, Jane	70y	W	Pa.	21 MAR 1870	Oak Hill
177	Nitzee, Isabella	5y	W	D.C.	22 APR 1860	Prospect Hill
176	Nitzee, William	8y	W	D.C.	15 APR 1860	Prospect Hill
456	Nix, Moses, laborer	40y	C	Va.	22 JUN 1870	Young Mens
326	Nixon, Jane P.	57y	W	Va.	06 JUL 1868	Alexandria, Va.

Page	Name	Age	Race	Birth	Death Date	Burial Ground
489	Nixon, Richard, jeweller	76y	W	Del.	26 NOV 1870	
264	Nixon, William N.	3m	C	D.C.	30 JUL 1867	Harmony
447	No Name	Still	C		23 MAR 1870	
422	No Name	Still	C		02 OCT 1869	
434	No Name	Still	W		21 JAN 1870	Congressional
399	No Name		W		30 JUL 1869	Congressional
425	No Name	Still	W	D.C.	16 NOV 1869	Congressional
446	No Name	Still	C		28 MAR 1870	Harmony
460	No Name	16h	W	D.C.	06 JUN 1870	Hebrew
485	No Name	Still	C	D.C.	24 OCT 1870	Potters Field
484	No Name	3d	C	D.C.	03 OCT 1870	Potters Field
484	No Name	Still	C	D.C.	17 OCT 1870	Potters Field
458	No Name	Still	C	D.C.	26 JUN 1870	Potters Field
484	No Name	Still	C	D.C.	15 OCT 1870	Potters Field
495	No Name	Still	C	D.C.	25 DEC 1870	Potters Field
484	No Name	3d	C	D.C.	10 OCT 1870	Potters Field
495	No Name		W	D.C.	20 DEC 1870	Potters Field
495	No Name	7h	C	D.C.	31 DEC 1870	Potters Field
495	No Name		C	D.C.	17 DEC 1870	Potters Field
495	No Name	Still	C	D.C.	02 DEC 1870	Potters Field
459	No Name		C	D.C.	29 JUN 1870	Potters Field
459	No Name	Still	C	D.C.	30 JUN 1870	Potters Field
495	No Name		W		09 DEC 1870	Potters Field
458	No Name	Still	C	D.C.	16 JUN 1870	Potters Field
484	No Name	Still	C	D.C.	14 OCT 1870	Potters Field
458	No Name		C	D.C.	28 JUN 1870	Potters Field
495	No Name	Still	C	D.C.	31 DEC 1870	Potters Field
484	No Name	Still	C	D.C.	09 OCT 1870	Potters Field
365	No Name	Still	W		11 DEC 1868	Washington
363	No Name	60y	C	U.S.	27 NOV 1868	Washington Asylum
363	No Name	Still	C	D.C.	11 NOV 1868	Washington Asylum
363	No Name	7d	C	D.C.	14 NOV 1868	Washington Asylum
363	No Name	7d	C	D.C.	27 NOV 1868	Washington Asylum
357	No Name	Still			13 OCT 1868	Washington Asylum
363	No Name	28y	C		21 NOV 1868	Washington Asylum
335a	No Name	Still			31 JUL 1868	Washington Asylum
352	No Name	2m			13 SEP 1868	Washington Asylum
352	No Name	Still			03 SEP 1868	Washington Asylum
367	No Name		C	D.C.	24 DEC 1868	Washington Asylum
398	No Name		W	D.C.	— JUN 1869	Washington Asylum
432	No Name	Still	C	D.C.	12 DEC 1869	Washington Asylum
417	No Name	Still	C	D.C.	22 SEP 1869	Washington Asylum
427	No Name	Still	C	D.C.	30 NOV 1869	Washington Asylum
405	No Name	Still	C	D.C.	28 JUL 1869	Washington Asylum
427	No Name	Still	B	D.C.	26 NOV 1869	Washington Asylum
423	No Name	Still	W	D.C.	28 OCT 1869	Washington Asylum
432	No Name	Still	W	D.C.	22 DEC 1869	Washington Asylum
427	No Name	Still	W	D.C.	23 NOV 1869	Washington Asylum
427	No Name		C	D.C.	16 NOV 1869	Washington Asylum
427	No Name	Still	C	D.C.	23 NOV 1869	Washington Asylum
432	No Name	Still	C	D.C.	08 DEC 1869	Washington Asylum
405	No Name	Still	W	D.C.	29 JUL 1869	Washington Asylum
427	No Name	Still	C		05 NOV 1869	Washington Asylum
412	No Name	Still	W	D.C.	13 AUG 1869	Washington Asylum
427	No Name	Still	C	D.C.	20 NOV 1869	Washington Asylum
417	No Name	Still	C		11 SEP 1869	Washington Asylum
427	No Name		C	D.C.	11 NOV 1869	Washington Asylum

District of Columbia Interments (Index to Deaths), 1855-1874

Page	Name	Age	Race	Birth	Death Date	Burial Ground
413	No Name	Still	C	D.C.	25 AUG 1869	Washington Asylum
405	No Name	20d	C	D.C.	29 JUL 1869	Washington Asylum
417	No Name	Still	C	D.C.	25 SEP 1869	Washington Asylum
432	No Name	Still	C	D.C.	23 DEC 1869	Washington Asylum
405	No Name	Still	C	D.C.	30 JUL 1869	Washington Asylum
398	No Name		B	D.C.	09 JUN 1869	Washington Asylum
423	No Name	Still	C	D.C.	30 OCT 1869	Washington Asylum
398	No Name	Still	B	D.C.	27 JUN 1869	Washington Asylum
479	No Name	Still	C	D.C.	17 SEP 1870	Washington Asylum
452	No Name		C	D.C.	20 APR 1870	Washington Asylum
479	No Name	Still	C	D.C.	29 SEP 1870	Washington Asylum
452	No Name		C	D.C.	20 APR 1870	Washington Asylum
474	No Name	Still	C		11 AUG 1870	Washington Asylum
446	No Name	Still	W	D.C.	11 MAR 1870	Washington Asylum
474	No Name	Still	C		09 AUG 1870	Washington Asylum
442	No Name	Still	C		26 FEB 1870	Washington Asylum
437	No Name	Still	C	D.C.	05 JAN 1870	Washington Asylum
442	No Name	Still	C		03 FEB 1870	Washington Asylum
442	No Name		C		28 FEB 1870	Washington Asylum
479	No Name	Still	C	D.C.	17 SEP 1870	Washington Asylum
474	No Name	2h	C		20 AUG 1870	Washington Asylum
446	No Name	Still	W	D.C.	13 MAR 1870	Washington Asylum
437	No Name	Still	C	D.C.	13 JAN 1870	Washington Asylum
479	No Name	Still	C	D.C.	19 SEP 1870	Washington Asylum
479	No Name	Still	W	D.C.	19 SEP 1870	Washington Asylum
447	No Name	Still	C	D.C.	25 MAR 1870	Washington Asylum
447	No Name	Still	C	D.C.	24 MAR 1870	Washington Asylum
473	No Name	2y	C	Va.	04 AUG 1870	Washington Asylum
447	No Name	Still	C	D.C.	23 MAR 1870	Washington Asylum
474	No Name	Still	C		09 AUG 1870	Washington Asylum
437	No Name	Still	C	D.C.	26 JAN 1870	Washington Asylum
474	No Name	Still	C		10 AUG 1870	Washington Asylum
436	No Name		C	D.C.	03 JAN 1870	Washington Asylum
446	No Name	Still	C	D.C.	07 MAR 1870	Washington Asylum
452	No Name		C	D.C.	12 APR 1870	Washington Asylum
437	No Name	Still	C	D.C.	06 JAN 1870	Washington Asylum
474	No Name	1d	W		24 AUG 1870	Washington Asylum
479	No Name	Still	W	D.C.	19 SEP 1870	Washington Asylum
509	No Name	Still	C	D.C.	06 FEB 1871	Washington Asylum
509	No Name	21d	C	D.C.	07 FEB 1871	Washington Asylum
509	No Name	Still	C	D.C.	27 FEB 1871	Washington Asylum
509	No Name	Still	C	D.C.	19 FEB 1871	Washington Asylum
474	No Name	Still	W		19 AUG 1870	Washington Asylum
452	No Name (twin)	Still	C	D.C.	27 APR 1870	Washington Asylum
452	No Name (twin)	Still	C	D.C.	26 APR 1870	Washington Asylum
352	No Name, foundling				21 SEP 1868	Washington Asylum
352	No Name, foundling				24 SEP 1868	Washington Asylum
352	No Name, infant				25 SEP 1868	Washington Asylum
454a	No Name, pauper			D.C.	20 MAY 1870	Washington Asylum
454a	No Name, pauper		C	D.C.	06 MAY 1870	Washington Asylum
454a	No Name, pauper	Still	C	D.C.	16 MAY 1870	Washington Asylum
498	No Name, pauper	Still	B	D.C.	10 JAN 1871	Washington Asylum
498	No Name, pauper	Still	B	D.C.	25 JAN 1871	Washington Asylum
498	No Name, pauper	Still	B		04 JAN 1871	Washington Asylum
498	No Name, pauper		B	D.C.	19 JAN 1871	Washington Asylum
357	Nobbs, Eliza	18y	B	U.S.	03 OCT 1868	Washington Asylum
125	Noble, Theodore, cart driver	12y	C	D.C.	19 AUG 1858	Harmony

District of Columbia Interments (Index to Deaths), 1855-1874

Page	Name	Age	Race	Birth	Death Date	Burial Ground
027	Noivia, Mary	11m	W	D.C.*	01 OCT 1855	St. Patricks
317	Noke, Mary Regina	1y	W	D.C.	17 JUN 1868	Congressional
200	Nokes, Ellen	14d	W	D.C.	28 FEB 1861	Congressional
606	Nokes, James	1y	W	D.C.	19 JUN 1872	Congressional*
347	Nokes, Jane Adelaide	20y	W	D.C.	14 SEP 1868	Congressional
274	Nokes, John	21d	W	D.C.	25 SEP 1867	Congressional*
595	Nokes, Nellie	8m	W	D.C.	23 APR 1872	Washington
154	Nokes, William	26y	W	D.C.	14 JUL 1859	Congressional
370	Nolan, Anna	23y	W	Ire.	22 JAN 1869	Mt. Olivet
323	Nolan, Ellen	2y	W	D.C.	30 JUL 1868	Mt. Olivet
366	Nolan, Geo. W.	11m	C		24 DEC 1868	
581	Nolan, George R.	2y	C	D.C.	15 FEB 1872	Ebenezer
704	Nolan, Ida	4m	C	D.C.	11 JUL 1873	
172	Nolan, James A., seaman	27y	W	Md.	06 FEB 1860	Congressional
015	Nolan, Jane	27y	W	Ire.	25 JUL 1855	Father Donnely
322	Nolan, Laurence, bricklayer	36y	W	Ire.	28 JUN 1868	Mt. Olivet
258	Nolan, Lizzie	22y	W		08 APR 1867	Mt. Olivet
730	Nolan, Mary Ann, housekeeper	22y	W	U.S.	12 NOV 1873	Mt. Olivet
356	Nolan, Patrick, coachman	45y	W	Ire.	18 OCT 1868	Mt. Olivet
376	Nolan, Thomas	1m	W		04 FEB 1869	Mt. Olivet
007	Noland, Mary	22y	W	Ire.	03 APR 1855	St. Patricks
313	Noland, Robert, laborer	27y	C	Md.	13 MAY 1868	Young Mens
345	Nolcott, Lola	12y	W		17 AUG 1868	N.Y.
760	Nolen, John H.	1d	C	U.S.	08 APR 1874	Mt. Zion
027	Nolen, Mary	10m	W	D.C.	05 OCT 1855	St. Patricks
270	Noll, Charles K.	1y	W	D.C.	30 AUG 1867	German Catholic
336	Noll, Fannie	21y	C	Va.	02 AUG 1868	Harmony
485	Nolty, Mary	2d	W	D.C.	04 OCT 1870	German Catholic
623	Noonan, Annie	17d	W	U.S.	11 AUG 1872	Holy Rood
250	Noonan, C., Mrs.	30y	W	Ire.	04 JAN 1867	Mt. Olivet
435	Noonan, Michael, laborer	23y	W	Ire.	07 JAN 1870	Red Hill
020	Noone, Sarah	18m	W	D.C.	20 AUG 1855	Catholic
340	Norbeck, Ellen Frances	12h	W		08 AUG 1868	Congressional
633	Norbeck, Wm.	63y	W	U.S.	14 OCT 1872	
631	Norbush, Geo.	6y	W	U.S.	28 OCT 1872	
268	Norman, Catherine	70y	W	Pa.	01 AUG 1867	Philadelphia, Pa.
451	Norman, Christopher, laborer	60y	C	Va.	20 APR 1870	Washington Asylum
383	Norman, Mary	9d	C	D.C.	05 MAR 1869	Washington Asylum
394	Norman, Mrs.	87y	W	Va.	16 JUN 1869	Congressional
630	Norman, Samuel	12y	C	U.S.	11 OCT 1872	Small Pox
030	Normant, Ada B.	7y	W	D.C.	07 NOV 1855	Glenwood
388	Norment, Mary E., lady	43y	W	D.C.	15 APR 1869	Glenwood
783	Norment, Nellie	1m	W	U.S.	16 JUL 1874	Congressional/Rock Cr.
038	Norment, Robert	14d	C		11 MAR 1856	West
721	Norment, Wm., hack driver	35y	C	Md.	01 SEP 1873	
007	Normyle, Michael, laborer	62y	W	Ire.	21 APR 1855	St. Peters
349	Norris, A.R., Mrs.	46y	W	Md.	28 SEP 1868	Frederick, Md.
630	Norris, Amelia	10m	C	U.S.	05 OCT 1872	Small Pox
494	Norris, Bazil G.	1m	W	D.C.	14 DEC 1870	Gettysburg, Md.
620	Norris, C.S.	4m	W	U.S.	19 AUG 1872	
036	Norris, Catharine	70y	W	Md.	08 FEB 1856	
553	Norris, Chas. A.	43y	W	Va.	11 JAN 1872	Congressional*
446	Norris, Dickenson Sergeant	1y	W	Pa.	29 MAR 1870	Philadelphia, Pa.
742	Norris, Elizabeth	78y	W	U.S.	18 JAN 1874	Congressional*
398	Norris, Ella M.	11m	W		28 JUN 1869	Gatesbury
347	Norris, Emma I.	1y	W		25 SEP 1868	Congressional
167	Norris, George	8m	C	D.C.	02 DEC 1859	Young Mens
639	Norris, Jno. H.	6m	C	U.S.	03 DEC 1872	Small Pox*

District of Columbia Interments (Index to Deaths), 1855-1874

Page	Name	Age	Race	Birth	Death Date	Burial Ground
035	Norris, John	1y	W	D.C.	25 FEB 1856	St. Peters
293	Norris, John, Mrs.		W		07 MAR 1868	Vault
140	Norris, Lois Martha	4m	W	D.C.	11 FEB 1859	Ebenezer
176	Norris, Maria	30y	C	Md.	14 APR 1860	Harmony
774	Norris, Maria R.G.	10m	W	U.S.	10 JUN 1874	Rock Creek
304	Norris, Mary	1y	W	D.C.	27 MAR 1868	Congressional
105	Norris, Mattie T.	24y	W	Va.	18 FEB 1858	Oak Hill
001	Norris, Moses	53y			11 JAN 1855	
743	Norris, Nancy, laborer	26y	C	U.S.	26 JAN 1874	Holmead
710	Norris, Pinkey	1m	C	D.C.	08 AUG 1873	
324	Norris, Rev. E.S., surveyor	59y	W	Me.	05 JUL 1868	Dubuque, Iowa
688	Norris, Willis G.	4m	W	U.S.	12 MAY 1873	Littlestown, Pa.
596	Norris, [blank]	3d	W	D.C.	12 APR 1872	Congressional*
435	Norrisage, Soffa	1y	C		03 JAN 1870	
502	North, Minnie F.	17y	W	Ala.	18 JAN 1871	Glenwood
314	Northedge, William, clerk	62y	W	Can.	11 MAY 1868	Congressional
001	Northrup, Henry [Capt.]	77y			19 JAN 1855	Congressional
601	Northrup, M.J.	6y	W	U.S.	25 MAY 1872	N.J.
774	Norton, A. Amelia, Mrs.	75y	W	U.S.	10 JUN 1874	Orange, N.J.
707	Norton, A.B., clerk	50y	W	Mass.	05 JUL 1873	Congressional
326	Norton, Andrew M.	1y	W	D.C.	12 JUL 1868	Congressional
713	Norton, Chas. A.	1y	W	D.C.	25 AUG 1873	Congressional
767	Norton, Clara E.	17y	W	U.S.	05 MAY 1874	Mt. Olivet
462	Norton, Danl. S., U.S. senator	42y	W	Amer.	14 JUL 1870	Baltimore, Md.
774	Norton, Hannah	5m	W	U.S.	10 JUN 1874	Congressional*
726	Norton, Mary E.	7m	W	U.S.	29 OCT 1873	Mt. Olivet
536	Norton, Robert	1y	C		19 SEP 1871	
411	Norton, William J., machinist	26y	W		19 AUG 1869	Mt. Olivet
027	Norwood, Chas., clerk	35y	W	Mass.	22 OCT 1855	Boston, Mass.
146	Norwood, [blank]	Still	W	D.C.	08 APR 1859	Congressional
783	Notley, John	10m	W	U.S.	04 JUL 1874	Mt. Olivet
215	Nott, Charles	6m	W		14 MAR 1866	Glenwood
549	Nott, J.R.	73y	W	D.C.	25 DEC 1871	Glenwood
714	Nott, Jennie E.	29y	W	Pa.	12 AUG 1873	Glenwood
580	Nottingham, Ida R.	3y	W	D.C.	11 FEB 1872	Washington
717	Nottingham, Lizie M.	11m	W	U.S.	02 SEP 1873	Congressional
040	Notts, Wm. Edwin	1y	W	D.C.	30 MAR 1856	Glenwood
187	Nourse, Ada C.	17y	W	D.C.	09 AUG 1860	Glenwood
188	Nourse, Alice	7m	W	D.C.	27 AUG 1860	Glenwood
053	Nourse, Charlotte C.	37y	W	N.Y.	06 AUG 1856	Private Ground
254	Nourse, Mary R.	87y	W	Pa.	17 FEB 1867	Congressional
053	Nourse, Selden	1m	W	D.C.	20 AUG 1856	
293	Nowlan, Louisa, nurse	70y	W		27 FEB 1868	Presbyterian
783	Nowlin, Florence	11m	C	U.S.	23 JUL 1874	Mt. Clivet
548	Noyes, Benjamin, gunsmith	84y	W	N.H.	15 DEC 1871	Glenwood
131	Noyes, Chas. H.	2y	W	D.C.	29 OCT 1858	Holmead
114	Noyes, Emma S.	18y	W	D.C.	17 MAY 1858	St. Patricks
449	Noyes, Ida M.	15y	W		02 APR 1870	Holmead
774	Noyes, Jeanette	75y	W	U.S.	12 JUN 1874	Presbyterian
071	Noyes, Sarah M.	21d	W	D.C.	15 FEB 1857	Congressional
312	Noyes, William H., clerk War dept.	25y	W	N.C.	08 MAY 1868	Mass.
123	Nsyhim, Mary	4m	W	D.C.	27 JUL 1858	St. Patricks
542	Nugent, A.C.S.	3y	W	U.S.	20 OCT 1871	Congressional
580	Nugent, Dorcas J.	55y	W	N.Y.	07 FEB 1872	Mo.
305	Nugent, Edward A.	1y	C	D.C.	12 MAR 1868	Young Mens
200	Nugent, Eli, teacher	71y	C	Md.	23 FEB 1861	Foundry
322	Nugent, Emma		C		26 JUN 1868	Freedmen's Hospital
301	Nugent, Geo. H.	1y	C	D.C.	23 MAR 1868	Young Mens

Page	Name	Age	Race	Birth	Death Date	Burial Ground
273	Nugent, James, laborer	60y	W	Ire.	27 SEP 1867	Mt. Olivet
380	Nugent, Janie	76y	W	Ire.	11 MAR 1869	Mt. Olivet
404	Nugent, John Francis, barber	30y	C		28 JUL 1869	
615	Nugent, Nellie	3y	C	U.S.	— JUL 1872	
410	Nugent, Thadia	1y	C	D.C.	21 AUG 1869	Young Mens
073	Nugent, [blank]	4y	C	D.C.	03 MAR 1857	Holmead
325	Nuggins, Thomas, druggist	42y	W	D.C.	14 JUL 1868	Congressional
225	Nurnberg, John B.	5m	W	D.C.	23 JUN 1866	Glenwood
002	Nutrell, Sally Ann	58y	W	Va.	06 JAN 1855	St. Matthews
584	Nutter, Royal E., confectioner	40y	W	U.S.	01 MAR 1872	
496	Nutzey, Elizabeth	18d	W	D.C.	24 DEC 1870	German
526	Nye, John, gentleman	58y	W	N.Y.	07 JUL 1871	Congressional*
754	Nye, Mary Ann	65y	W	U.S.	23 MAR 1874	Glenwood
406	Nye, Mary Isabella	11m	W		19 JUL 1869	Glenwood
370	Nye, Mary, Mrs.	63y	W	Ver.	25 JAN 1869	Glenwood

District of Columbia Interments (Index to Deaths), 1855-1874

Page	Name	Age	Race	Birth	Death Date	Burial Ground

O

Page	Name	Age	Race	Birth	Death Date	Burial Ground
379	Oakley, Catharine A.	67y	W	Md.	12 MAR 1869	Congressional
640	Oakley, Lily M.	2y	W	U.S.	18 DEC 1872	Small Pox*
013	Oakley, Thos.	1y		D.C.	05 JUL 1855	Congressional
428	Oates, Francis	48y	W	Eng.	27 NOV 1869	Washington Asylum
365	Oates, Thos., carpenter	35y	W		15 DEC 1868	Mt. Olivet
195	Ober, Francis, child of	Still	W	D.C.	18 DEC 1860	Congressional
462	Ober, Harry Francis	1y	W	D.C.	02 JUL 1870	Congressional
607	Ober, Henry N., clerk	44y	W	D.C.	14 JUN 1872	Congressional*
237	Oberheim, Elise	2y	W	D.C.	18 SEP 1866	Prospect Hill
360	Oberheim, Juliana	1y	W	D.C.	18 NOV 1868	Prospect Hill
608	Oberheim, Matilda B.K.C.	1y	W	D.C.	15 JUN 1872	
187	Oberheim, [blank]	11m	W	D.C.	12 AUG 1860	Prospect Hill
760	Oberst, John, farmer	29y	W	Switz.	17 APR 1874	Glenwood
014	Obrin, [blank]	3m	W	D.C.	14 JUL 1855	St. Patricks
711	Ocarney, W.H.	1y	W	D.C.	11 AUG 1873	Mt. Olivet
593	Ochsenreiter, Rosina	1y	W	D.C.	30 APR 1872	St. Marys
182	Ock, Barbara	9m	W	D.C.	[3?] JUN 1860	Prospect Hill
341	Ockhardt, Frederick	1y	W	D.C.	09 AUG 1868	Congressional
661	Odens, T.E.	1m	C	U.S.	27 JAN 1873	
343	Oentrich, Henry, restaurant kpr.	37y	W	Han.	19 AUG 1868	Glenwood
021	Oettley, F.	78y	W	Ger.	28 AUG 1855	German
784	Ofensten, Margaret	22y	W	U.S.	22 JUL 1874	Mt. Olivet
313	Offenstein, John, gardener	71y	W	Ger.	08 MAY 1868	German Catholic
643	Offman, Ernie	2y	W	U.S.	10 DEC 1872	N.Y.
084	Offuit, William J.	1m	W	D.C.	27 JUL 1857	Ebenezer
182	Offutt, Emily	22y	W	U.S.	23 JUN 1860	Ebenezer
072	Offutt, J.B.	4m	W	D.C.	26 FEB 1857	Baltimore, Md.
054	Offutt, John	2y	W	D.C.	31 AUG 1856	Baltimore, Md.
066	Offutt, Mahala A.	31y	W	Md.	26 DEC 1856	Baltimore, Md.
005	Offutt, Margaret F.	28y	W	Md.	12 MAR 1855	Georgetown
151	Offutt, Wm. R.M., painter	29y	W	U.S.	16 JUN 1859	Ebenezer
083	Offutt, Z.K., painter	56y	W		16 JUL 1857	Congressional*
698	Ogden, L.L.	1y	W	D.C.	24 JUN 1873	Mt. Olivet
660	Ogilvie, Walter, photographer	40y	W	Scot.	17 JAN 1873	Congressional
017	Oland, Susan	9m	W	D.C.	26 JUL 1855	St. Patricks
754	Olden, Algey	1m	C	U.S.	28 MAR 1874	
348	Olds, Mark L., Rev.	40y	W	Ohio	19 SEP 1868	Congressional
320	Olin, Henry, laborer	30y	W	Va.	25 JUN 1868	Ebenezer
090	Oliphant, Richard	1y	W	Mass.	08 SEP 1857	Glenwood
233	Oliphant, [blank]		W		21 AUG 1866	Alms House
297	Olive, Susan J.	49y	W	Md.	07 FEB 1868	Glenwood
232	Oliver, Henry L.	3m	W	D.C.	22 AUG 1866	Congressional
589	Oliver, John M., lawyer	47y	W	N.Y.	30 MAR 1872	N.Y.
457	Oliver, Louis, infant of	Still	W	D.C.	22 JUN 1870	Congressional
658	Oliver, Nicholes	55y	C	U.S.	09 JAN 1873	Young Mens
322	Oliver, Rosetta	30y	C	Md.	06 JUN 1868	Freedmen's Hospital
249	Oliver, Sarah	35y	W	Va.	23 JAN 1867	Mt. Olivet
139	Oliver, William	75y	C	Md.	04 JAN 1859	Washington Asylum
257	Ollans, John, seaman	25y	W	Eng.	18 MAR 1867	Congressional*
521	Olmstead, John, clerk	20y	C	Va.	06 JUN 1871	Georgetown
767	Olmstead, Moses	80y	W	U.S.	09 MAY 1874	Madison, Ohio
394	Olmsted, Addie	6m	W	D.C.	08 JUN 1869	Congressional
001	Olves, [blank]	1y			— JAN 1855	St. Peters
176	Oneal, Rodia	89y	W		04 APR 1860	Oak Hill
073	Oneal, Singleton	32y	W	Md.	06 MAR 1857	Md.
410	Oppenheimer, Max	21d	W		17 AUG 1869	Washington Hebrew
402	Oppenheimer, Moses	6m	W		05 JUL 1869	Hebrew

Page	Name	Age	Race	Birth	Death Date	Burial Ground
467	Orange, George, laborer	25y	C	Va.	27 JUL 1870	Union
011	Orm, Frank Pierce	9m	W	D.C.	04 JUN 1855	Congressional
508	Orme, D., messenger	50y	C	Md.	23 FEB 1871	Union
754	Orme, W.D.M.	86y	W	U.S.	15 MAR 1874	Gracewood
481	Orr, Phoebe, housekeeper	45y	C	D.C.	08 OCT 1870	Holmead
006	Orr, Sarah Jane	30y	W	N.Y.	20 APR 1855	Congressional
014	Orr, Susan Jane	2m	W	D.C.	10 JUL 1855	Pr. Geo. Co., Md.
707	Orth, Fredk.	5m	W	D.C.	10 JUL 1873	Prospect Hill
584	Orth, John P.	5m	W	D.C.	04 MAR 1872	German/Rock Creek
707	Orth, Wm.	5m	W	D.C.	09 JUL 1873	Prospect Hill
117	Osbodby, Thomas, carpenter	33y	W	D.C.	24 JUN 1858	Glenwood
669	Osborn, Ada	10y	W	U.S.	27 FEB 1873	
076	Osborn, Cath.	75y	W	Md.	27 APR 1857	Methodist
030	Osborn, Chs.	17d	C	D.C.	30 NOV 1855	Harmony
597	Osborn, Clara	4m	W	U.S.	08 MAY 1872	Unknown
039	Osborn, Francis A., laborer	38y	W	Md.	16 MAR 1856	Congressional
184	Osborn, Jane	6m	W	D.C.	02 JUL 1860	Congressional
625	Osborn, Jennie S.	41y	W	U.S.	17 SEP 1872	N.Y.
616a	Osborn, Joseph, laborer	71y	W	U.S.	14 JUL 1872	Congressional*
760	Osborn, Joseph, butcher	33y	W	U.S.	08 APR 1874	Mt. Olivet
402	Osborn, Margaret	67y	W	Md.	10 JUL 1869	Glenwood
039	Osborn, Maria A.	16y	W	Md.	16 MAR 1856	Congressional
411	Osborn, Sarah Catharine		W	D.C.	06 AUG 1869	Glenwood
521	Osborn, Sarah	2y	W		03 JUN 1871	Congressional*
519	Osborne, Henry S.		W	U.S.	20 MAY 1871	Congressional*
339	Osborne, William	1y	W	D.C.	15 AUG 1868	Glenwood
461	Osburn, [blank]	11m	W	D.C.	06 JUL 1870	Congressional
711	Oschman, Henry, marine U.S.	21y	W	Ger.	09 AUG 1873	Congressional
182	Osgood, John, laborer	45y	W	Del.	27 JUN 1860	
774	Ossinger, Margaret R.	24y	W	U.S.	17 JUN 1874	Glenwood
724	Ossinger, Wm. John	9m	W	D.C.	12 OCT 1873	Prospect Hill
148	Ostass, Edward, bricklayer	64y	W	Ger.	16 MAY 1859	Washington Asylum
506	Oswell, [blank]	3m	W	D.C.	05 FEB 1871	Congressional
783	Oswill, Martha J.	23y	W	U.S.	16 JUL 1874	Congressional
471	Oswill, William, brickmaker	49y	W	Pa.	24 AUG 1870	Congressional
079	Ott, Henry	6m	C	D.C.	03 JUN 1857	German
506	Otterback, Cordelia	32y	W	D.C.	24 FEB 1871	Congressional
060	Otterback, Mary Rosetta	20y	W	D.C.	16 OCT 1856	Congressional
104	Otterback, Philip, butcher	71y	W	Wurt.	04 FEB 1858	Congressional
712	Otto, Anna E.	11m	W	D.C.	21 AUG 1873	Prospect Hill
529	Otto, Anna W.M.	1y	W	D.C.	28 JUL 1871	German Catholic
396	Otto, Barbarbara [sic]	13m	W	D.C.	05 JUN 1869	Prospect Hill
334	Otto, George Albert	1y	W	D.C.	14 JUL 1868	Prospect Hill
025	Oublovan, Patrick	6m	W		22 SEP 1855	St. Peters
547	Oulenger, Jack, wheelwright	57y	W	Fra.	04 DEC 1871	Mt. Olivet
430	Ouragar, Dominick	2y	W	D.C.	22 DEC 1869	St. Marys
320	Ourand, Elmer Burrows	7m	W	D.C.	13 JUN 1868	Methodist, East
500	Ourand, J.H.	10y	W	D.C.	24 JAN 1871	Congressional
068	Ousley, John, gardener	72y	W	Ire.	13 JAN 1857	St. Patricks
471	Out, A., butcher	24y	W	Ger.	18 AUG 1870	German Catholic
217	Over, Edwd.	1m	C	D.C.	06 APR 1866	Methodist
690	Overton, Elizabeth	2y	C	D.C.	23 MAY 1873	
642	Overton, Sylvester	33y	C	U.S.	29 DEC 1872	Small Pox
332	Owen, Elizabeth	8m	W	D.C.	10 JUL 1868	Mt. Olivet
263	Owen, Jane	16y	W		08 JUN 1867	Holmead
292a	Owen, Robert H., produce dealer	55y	W	Ire.	07 JAN 1868	Presbyterian
740	Owen, Samuel W., hotel keeper	47y	W	Eng.	02 JAN 1874	Oak Hill
593	Owen, Wm. Howard	6y	W	D.C.	18 APR 1872	Oak Hill

District of Columbia Interments (Index to Deaths), 1855-1874

Page	Name	Age	Race	Birth	Death Date	Burial Ground
087	Owens, Eliza A.	48y	W	D.C.	15 AUG 1857	St. Patricks
399	Owens, James E.	9d	W	D.C.	31 JUL 1869	Congressional
622	Owens, Jno.	3y	C	U.S.	24 AUG 1872	
109	Owens, John, laborer	57y	W	D.C.	28 MAR 1858	Congressional
176	Owens, Joseph	67y	W	Md.	08 APR 1860	Md.
409	Owens, Margaret Ann	1y	W		25 AUG 1869	Mt. Olivet
181	Owens, Mary Frances	19y	W	D.C.	03 JUN 1860	St. Peters
738	Owens, Mary	39y	W	Ire.	26 DEC 1873	
234	Owens, Nancy	61y	W	Md.	01 SEP 1866	Addison's Chapel
107	Owens, Richard W.	1m	W	D.C.	03 MAR 1858	Congressional
136	Owens, Rosena	50y	W	Md.	30 DEC 1858	Mt. Olivet
784	Owens, Winefried M.	3y	W	U.S.	23 JUL 1874	Mt. Olivet
094	Owens, Winnifred	47y	W		17 OCT 1857	St. Patricks
093	Owings, Thos. F., farmer	42y	W	Va.	08 OCT 1857	Washington Asylum
348	Owner, William	75y	W	Pa.	20 SEP 1868	Congressional
668	Oxley, Drucilla V.	4y	W	U.S.	22 FEB 1873	Glenwood
682	Oxley, Everett J.	74y	W	U.S.	26 APR 1873	Glenwood
673	Oxley, Susia	15m	W	U.S.	10 MAR 1873	Glenwood
464	Oye, William, sailor	43y	W	Ger.	23 JUL 1870	Prospect Hill
313	O'Brian, Edward, carpenter	47y	W	Md.	29 MAY 1868	Congressional
232	O'Brian, Harriet	1y	W		28 AUG 1866	Mt. Olivet
112	O'Brian, Joseph H., musician	41y	W	Ire.	21 APR 1858	Congressional
230	O'Brian, Margaret	3m	W		31 JUL 1866	Mt. Olivet
151	O'Brian, Margarett	32y	W	Ire.	23 JUN 1859	Mt. Olivet
062	O'Brian, Mary A.	16y	C	D.C.	12 NOV 1856	St. Patricks
320	O'Brian, Mary	5m	W	D.C.	08 JUN 1868	Mt. Olivet
620	O'Brian, Mary	40y	W	Ire.	26 AUG 1872	
664	O'Brian, Mary C.	1y	W	U.S.	19 JAN 1873	Small Pox*
224	O'Brian, Patrick		W	D.C.	12 JUN 1866	Mt. Olivet
058	O'Brian, Timothy	2y	W	D.C.	13 SEP 1856	St. Patricks
003	O'Brian, Wm.	8m	W	D.C.	13 FEB 1855	
202	O'Brian, [blank]	Still	W	D.C.	14 APR 1861	Glenwood
748	O'Brien, Ann, storekeeper	65y	W	Ire.	19 FEB 1874	Mt. Olivet
444	O'Brien, Catherine	70y	W	Ire.	06 MAR 1870	N.Y. City
322	O'Brien, Charles N.	7m	W	U.S.	27 JUN 1868	Glenwood
322	O'Brien, Charles	8m	W	D.C.	28 JUN 1868	Mt. Olivet
248	O'Brien, Ethie Rives	6m	W	D.C.	12 DEC 1866	Glenwood
298	O'Brien, Hanorah	6m	W	D.C.	12 FEB 1868	Mt. Olivet
502	O'Brien, Ida May	1y	W	D.C.	26 JAN 1871	Glenwood
290	O'Brien, James H., waterman	44y	W	Md.	04 JAN 1868	Congressional
331	O'Brien, James	2y	W	D.C.	25 JUL 1868	Glenwood
274	O'Brien, James	1m	W	D.C.	16 SEP 1867	Mt. Olivet
114	O'Brien, Jeremiah	20y	W		20 MAY 1858	Baltimore, Md.
291	O'Brien, John, school boy	6y	W	Ire.	28 JAN 1868	Mt. Olivet
341	O'Brien, John, hospital steward		W		02 AUG 1868	Congressional
282	O'Brien, John, house carpenter	49y	W	Md.	20 NOV 1867	Congressional
435	O'Brien, John, stone cutter	30y	W		17 JAN 1870	Mt. Olivet
292	O'Brien, Laurence	12d	W	D.C.	28 JAN 1868	Glenwood
430	O'Brien, Mary	17y	W	Ire.	07 DEC 1869	Mt. Olivet
445	O'Brien, Mary	31y	W	Pa.	03 MAR 1870	Philadelphia, Pa.
582	O'Brien, Michael, watchman	32y	W	Ire.	19 FEB 1872	Congressional
429	O'Brien, Owen Hugh	1y	W		13 DEC 1869	Congressional
636	O'Brien, Patrick, grocer	54y	W	Ire.	27 NOV 1872	
243	O'Brien, Patrick	8y	W	D.C.	17 NOV 1866	Alms House
181	O'Brien, Samuel, clerk	20y	W	N.J.	03 JUN 1860	Glenwood
641	O'Brien, Thos.	7y	W	U.S.	30 DEC 1872	Small Pox*
431	O'Brien, William H.	10m	W		28 DEC 1869	Berryville, Va.

District of Columbia Interments (Index to Deaths), 1855-1874

Page	Name	Age	Race	Birth	Death Date	Burial Ground
440	O'Brien, Wm., printer	26y	W	Md.	06 FEB 1870	Baltimore, Md.
338	O'Brien, Wm.	10m	W		21 AUG 1868	Mt. Olivet
304	O'Brien, Wm., cigar maker	42y	W	Md.	06 MAR 1868	Congressional
783	O'Bryan, Ernest	8m	W	U.S.	13 JUL 1874	Glenwood
507	O'Bryan, James, painter	65y	W	Md.	18 FEB 1871	Glenwood
705	O'Connell, Mary Ellen	3m	W	D.C.	21 JUL 1873	Mt. Olivet
323	O'Connell, Mary Eva	1m	W	Amer.	03 JUL 1868	Mt. Olivet
458	O'Connell, Robert Emmet	7m	W	U.S.	05 JUN 1870	Mt. Olivet
217	O'Connell, T.I., agent	38y	W	Ire.	01 APR 1866	Mt. Olivet
216	O'Connell, Timothy I., clerk	28y	W	Ire.	31 MAR 1866	Mt. Olivet
636	O'Conner, A.P.	2m	W	U.S.	28 NOV 1872	
107	O'Conner, Brian	2y	W	D.C.	11 MAR 1858	St. Peters
218	O'Conner, Dennis, laborer	35y	W	Ire.	18 APR 1866	Mt. Olivet
065	O'Conner, John, laborer	65y	W	Ire.	15 DEC 1856	St. Peters
593	O'Conner, Mary		W	D.C.	20 APR 1872	Mt. Olivet
080	O'Conner, Mary	6y	W	D.C.	18 JUN 1857	St. Patricks
234	O'Conner, Patrick, farmer	16y	W	Va.	01 SEP 1866	Mt. Olivet
138	O'Connolly, E.	25y	W	Ire.	27 JAN 1859	
470	O'Connor, Andrew	2m	W	D.C.	16 AUG 1870	Mt. Olivet
334	O'Connor, Andrew	14d	W		17 JUL 1868	Mt. Olivet
046	O'Connor, Catherine	2y	W	D.C.	09 JUN 1856	St. Peters
682	O'Connor, Elizabeth	45y	W	Ire.	28 APR 1873	
301	O'Connor, Ellen	40y	W	Ire.	25 MAR 1868	Mt. Olivet
020	O'Connor, Jas.	3y	W		22 AUG 1855	St. Patricks
015	O'Connor, M. Ann	5m	W	D.C.	01 JUL 1855	St. Peters
447	O'Connor, Mary	47y	W	Ire.	30 MAR 1870	Mt. Olivet
320	O'Connor, Mary	6y	W	D.C.	09 JUN 1868	Mt. Olivet
732	O'Connor, Mary C.	29y	W	U.S.	29 NOV 1873	Mt. Olivet
726	O'Connor, Patrick	43y	W	Ire.	30 OCT 1873	Mt. Olivet
706	O'Connor, Thos.	21m	W	D.C.	05 JUL 1873	Mt. Olivet
729	O'Conor, Julia	8d	W	U.S.	03 NOV 1873	
628	O'Corner, Mich., laborer	35y	W	Ire.	10 SEP 1872	
174	O'Day, Andrew	6m	W	D.C.	06 MAR 1860	Georgetown, Catholic
721	O'Day, John, stone cutter	22y	W	Ire.	06 SEP 1873	
132	O'Day, Pat.	1y	W	D.C.	06 NOV 1858	Georgetown
162	O'Dea, Luke	1m	W	D.C.	26 SEP 1859	Trinity
244	O'Donnell, John, laborer	29y	W	Ire.	13 NOV 1866	Mt. Olivet
376	O'Donnell, Patrick	7y	W		13 FEB 1869	Mt. Olivet
185	O'Donohue, James, chandler	33y	W	D.C.*	17 JUL 1860	
756	O'Donour, John	30y	W	Ire.	14 MAR 1874	
234	O'Donovan, James, laborer	23y	W	Ire.	02 SEP 1866	Mt. Olivet
477	O'Dwyer, Agnes M.	13y	W	D.C.	17 SEP 1870	Mt. Olivet
381	O'Dwyer, May A.	28y	W	Ire.	23 MAR 1869	Mt. Olivet
371	O'Farrol, Michael, laborer	45y	W	Ire.	30 JAN 1869	Mt. Olivet
248	O'Hagan, John C.	16d	W	D.C.	21 DEC 1866	Mt. Olivet
783	O'Hagan, Maggie G.	6m	W	U.S.	02 JUL 1874	
541	O'Hagan, Susanna	71y	W	Ire.	17 OCT 1871	Mt. Olivet*
305	O'Halburten, Mary Helena	7m	W	D.C.	31 MAR 1868	Mt. Olivet
735	O'Hallaron, James, clerk	56y	W	Ire.	10 DEC 1873	Mt. Olivet
459	O'Hallohan, Margt.	4y	W	D.C.	05 JUN 1870	Potters Field
743	O'Halloran, Eddie	1y	W	U.S.	21 JAN 1874	Mt. Olivet
378	O'Hara, Catharine, printing office	30y	W		05 FEB 1869	Mt. Olivet
784	O'Hara, Joseph	11m	W	U.S.	25 JUL 1874	Mt. Olivet
411	O'Hara, Mary Cecilia	9m	W		31 AUG 1869	Mt. Olivet
179	O'Hare, Dennis, engraver	49y	W		18 MAY 1860	Rock Creek
113	O'Hare, Elizabeth	15y	W	D.C.	12 MAY 1858	St. Patricks
540	O'Hare, Ellen	38y	W	Ire.	05 OCT 1871	Mt. Olivet
201	O'Hare, Richard A., printer	42y	W	D.C.	10 MAR 1861	Trinity

District of Columbia Interments (Index to Deaths), 1855-1874

Page	Name	Age	Race	Birth	Death Date	Burial Ground
160	O'Heren, David	2m	W	D.C.	05 AUG 1859	St. Patricks
540	O'Hern, Peter	70y	W	Del.	04 OCT 1871	Mt. Olivet
718	O'Leary, Dennis, stone mason	46y	W	Ire.	13 SEP 1873	Mt. Olivet
173	O'Leary, Kate, domestic	25y	W	Ire.	23 FEB 1860	
527	O'Leary, Mary	1y	W	D.C.	07 JUL 1871	Mt. Olivet
077	O'Maney, May C.	3m	W		04 MAY 1857	St. Patricks
005	O'Meahn, Lucy Ann	4m	W	D.C.	10 MAR 1855	
260	O'Neal, Dennis	70y	W		02 MAY 1867	Mt. Olivet
004	O'Neal, James	17m	W	D.C.	18 MAR 1855	St. Patricks
226	O'Neal, Joseph	2m	W	D.C.	27 JUN 1866	Mt. Olivet
774	O'Neal, Matilda	80y	W	U.S.	10 JUN 1874	Trinity, Old
625	O'Neal, Sarah	7m	W	U.S.	01 SEP 1872	
227	O'Neal, Timothy, laborer	27y	W	Ire.	08 JUL 1866	Mt. Olivet
193	O'Neale, J., child of	7d	W	D.C.	19 NOV 1860	Congressional
193	O'Neale, John, child of	Still	W	D.C.	18 NOV 1860	Congressional
008	O'Neil, Michael, plasterer	22y	W	Eng.	28 MAY 1855	Poor House
487	O'Neil, Thomas, watchman	30y	W	Ire.	26 NOV 1870	Mt. Olivet
527	O'Neil, Thomas J.	1y	W	D.C.	12 JUL 1871	Glenwood
309	O'Neill, Annie E.	22y	W	Pa.	20 APR 1868	Lancaster, Pa.
318	O'Neill, Chas.	14d	W	D.C.	06 JUN 1868	Congressional
172	O'Neill, James, bookbinder	39y	W	D.C.	01 FEB 1860	Glenwood
361	O'Neill, Mary, domestic	20y	W	Ire.	30 NOV 1868	Mt. Olivet
784	O'Rear, Harry, banker	40y	W	U.S.	20 JUL 1874	Oak Hill
428	O'Reilly, Sister Loretto, sis. charity	36y	W	Ire.	02 NOV 1869	Mt. Olivet
188	O'Riley, Margaret	36y	W	D.C.	14 AUG 1860	Mt. Olivet
054	O'Riley, Philip, shoemaker	77y	W	Ire.	06 AUG 1856	St. Peters
380	O'Rourke, Bridget, Mrs.	63y	W	Ire.	24 MAR 1869	Mt. Olivet
760	O'Rourke, Maggie, domestic	24y	W	U.S.	17 APR 1874	Mt. Olivet
102	O'Toole, Owen	75y	W	Ire.	25 JAN 1858	St. Patricks
585	O'Will, Sarah	44y	W	D.C.	08 MAR 1872	Congressional

Page	Name	Age	Race	Birth	Death Date	Burial Ground
P						
344	Pabet, William	9m	W	D.C.	21 AUG 1868	Prospect Hill
774	Pabst, Adolpf, engineer	23y	W	Ger.	09 JUN 1874	Prospect Hill
658	Pabst, Catherine	45y	W	Ger.	03 JAN 1873	Prospect Hill
057	Paca, Theophilus, seaman	22y	W	D.C.*	06 SEP 1856	Georgetown
289	Padd, Kitty		C		12 JAN 1868	Alms House
329	Paddon, Agnes L.	7m	W	D.C.	07 JUL 1868	Mt. Olivet
513	Paddon, Henrietta, seamstress	24y	W		20 MAR 1871	Glenwood
267	Paddon, Mary E.	10m	W	D.C.	31 JUL 1867	Mt. Olivet
526	Padget, Blanche	4m	W	D.C.	04 JUL 1871	Congressional*
026	Padget, J.	25y	W	Md.	25 OCT 1855	Congressional
580	Padgett, Arthur	14y	W	U.S.	06 FEB 1872	
476	Padgett, Elizabeth	63y	W	Md.	05 SEP 1870	Congressional
094	Padgett, Emily	43y	W	Md.	22 OCT 1857	Methodist
366	Padgett, George	1m	W	D.C.	24 DEC 1868	Methodist
419	Padgett, Jane Louisa	22y	W	Md.	10 OCT 1869	Congressional
126	Padgett, John	1y	W	D.C.	31 AUG 1858	Congressional
231	Padgett, Joseph E.	1y	W	D.C.	15 AUG 1866	Congressional
774	Padgett, Mara	12y	W	U.S.	05 JUN 1874	Congressional*
774	Padgett, Martha B.	5m	W	U.S.	18 JUN 1874	Congressional*
507	Padgett, Sarah	65y	W	Md.	17 FEB 1871	Glenwood
743	Padgett, Thos. & A., infant of	4d	W	U.S.	22 JAN 1874	Congressional
606	Padgett, Wm. B.	11m	W	D.C.	07 JUN 1872	Congressional*
087	Padgett, [blank]	6d	W	D.C.	15 AUG 1857	Methodist
204	Padgitt, Mary	6m	W	D.C.	21 JUN 1861	Mt. Olivet
287	Paeder, Lizzie		C		c.18 DEC 1867	Alms House
593	Pagan, Mary	40y	C	D.C.	16 APR 1872	Beckett's
451	Page, Amanda	14y	C	Va.	24 APR 1870	Union
666	Page, Ann	23y	W	U.S.	03 FEB 1873	Augusta, Me.
452	Page, Ann	1m	C	D.C.	20 APR 1870	Washington Asylum
125	Page, Ann, lady	84y	W	Va.	31 AUG 1858	Alexandria, Va.
091	Page, Annie Gass	5y	W	D.C.	21 SEP 1857	Congressional
312	Page, Charles G., patent exam.	56y	W	Mass.	05 MAY 1868	Oak Hill
388	Page, D.D.	79y	W	Me.	28 APR 1869	St. Louis, Mo.
658	Page, Eliza J.	44y	W	U.S.	03 JAN 1873	Oak Hill
530	Page, Lucien, plasterer	20y	W	D.C.	29 JUL 1871	Congressional
367	Page, Lucy	Still	B	D.C.	24 DEC 1868	Washington Asylum
307	Page, Maria	5d	C	D.C.	16 APR 1868	Freedmen's Hospital
365	Page, Martha	32y	C	Va.	23 DEC 1868	Young Mens
442	Page, Mary	1m	C		06 FEB 1870	Washington Asylum
516	Page, N., child of	Still	W	D.C.	07 MAR 1871	Congressional
270	Page, Peter	8m	C	D.C.	12 AUG 1867	Young Mens
073	Page, Sarah	22y	C	D.C.	16 MAR 1857	Harmony
217	Page, Thomas Taylor, Jr.	11m	W	D.C.	10 APR 1866	Oak Hill
052	Page, Thos. Miller	1y	W	D.C.	30 JUL 1856	Congressional
755	Page, Warner	45y	C	U.S.	26 MAR 1874	Washington Asylum
703	Pagestons, W.T.	5m	W	D.C.	16 JUL 1873	
124	Pagett, James	7m	W	D.C.	12 AUG 1858	
525	Pagle, Edward	8m	W	D.C.	26 JUN 1871	Oak Hill
524	Pagles, Edward	8m	W	D.C.	25 JUN 1871	Oak Hill
357	Paine, Anna	6m	M	D.C.	16 OCT 1868	
254	Paine, George Hay, topographer	31y	W	D.C.	19 FEB 1867	Oak Hill
165	Paine, Thomas, naval officer	73y	W	R.I.	09 NOV 1859	Congressional
688	Painter, Catherine	68y	W	U.S.	15 MAY 1873	Roxbury, Conn.
729	Pairall, Horace	3y	W	U.S.	10 NOV 1873	Congressional
060	Pallant, Sarah	52y	W	Eng.	04 OCT 1856	Glenwood
429	Pally, Elizabeth	42y	W	Va.	06 DEC 1869	Congressional
414	Palmer, Annie L.	1y	W	D.C.	13 SEP 1869	Congressional

District of Columbia Interments (Index to Deaths), 1855-1874

Page	Name	Age	Race	Birth	Death Date	Burial Ground
062	Palmer, Chas. William	1m	C	D.C.	12 NOV 1856	Georgetown
150	Palmer, F., Mrs.	90y	W	Va.	14 JUN 1859	Loudon Co., Va.
399	Palmer, Fannie, Mrs.	52y	W		20 JUL 1869	Congressional
548	Palmer, Isaac	38y	W	N.C.	13 DEC 1871	
038	Palmer, John	40y	W	Va.	04 MAR 1856	Va.
738	Palmer, Maud A.	1y	W	U.S.	31 DEC 1873	Congressional*
630	Palmer, Theresa, servant	70y	C	U.S.	13 OCT 1872	
048	Palmer, William, music teacher	42y	W	Eng.	30 JUN 1856	Congressional
382	Palmer, [blank]	1d	C		09 MAR 1869	Western
723	Panney, Benjamin	28y	B	Md.	05 OCT 1873	Washington Asylum
366	Panwart, Geo. L., Dr.	30y	W	N.J.	15 DEC 1868	Glenwood
050	Papst, Mathias	1m	W	D.C.	12 JUL 1856	German
463	Paradol, Lucien Anatole Prevost	41y		Fra.	20 JUL 1870	Paris, via N.Y.
104	Parish, Levi H., clerk	64y	W	N.Y.	14 FEB 1858	Glenwood
006	Parkam, Mary	2y	W	D.C.	25 APR 1855	Congressional
069	Parke, J.M.	2y	C	D.C.	23 JAN 1857	Harmony
552	Parke, Sidney	6d	C	D.C.	01 JAN 1872	Young Mens
121	Parker, Alice	1y	C	D.C.	16 JUL 1858	Foundry
458	Parker, Alice	Still	C	D.C.	20 JUN 1870	Potters Field
473	Parker, Alice	3y	C	Md.	04 AUG 1870	Washington Asylum
094	Parker, Andrew J., painter	29y	W	D.C.	17 OCT 1857	Oak Hill
260	Parker, Anna B.	8m	W		07 MAY 1867	Oak Hill
179	Parker Annie	12y	C	D.C.	04 MAY 1860	Harmony
415	Parker, Blanch Murdock	2y			20 SEP 1869	Philadelphia, Pa.
332	Parker, Caroline	11m	W	D.C.	20 JUL 1868	Young Mens
661	Parker, Catherine	47y	W	U.S.	29 JAN 1873	Carroll Chapel
263	Parker, Catherine	57y	W		07 JUN 1867	Congressional
729	Parker, Catherine, servant	30y	W	U.S.	05 NOV 1873	Washington Asylum
394	Parker, Charles	14m	W	Amer.	28 JUN 1869	Congressional
582	Parker, Chas. R., clerk	39y	C		23 FEB 1872	Ebenezer
662	Parker, David	30y	C	U.S.	09 JAN 1873	Small Pox
695	Parker, Ed. Jno.	5m	W	D.C.	03 JUN 1873	
249	Parker, Eddie	2y	C	D.C.	23 JAN 1867	Young Mens
463	Parker, Edward J.	8m	W	D.C.	10 JUL 1870	Mt. Olivet*
548	Parker, Edwin H.	8m	W	D.C.	12 DEC 1871	Glenwood
467	Parker, Elijah, laborer	26y	C	Va.	26 JUL 1870	
459	Parker, Elijah, laborer	55y	C	Va.	22 JUN 1870	
734	Parker, F.M., actress	26y	W	U.S.	01 DEC 1873	
478	Parker, Fannie, nurse	74y	C		02 SEP 1870	Young Mens
314	Parker, Flora Agusta	6y	W	D.C.	08 MAY 1868	Oak Hill
011	Parker, Florence	3m	W	D.C.	20 JUN 1855	Congressional
127	Parker, Frank Pearce		W	D.C.	09 SEP 1858	Oak Hill
726	Parker, Geo. Stanley, lawyer	56y	W	U.S.	26 OCT 1873	Oak Hill
690	Parker, George	23y	C	U.S.	12 MAY 1873	Small Pox
668	Parker, George	45y	C	U.S.	16 FEB 1873	Washington Asylum
082	Parker, George, servant	39y	C		03 JUL 1857	Washington Asylum
036	Parker, Giles	78y	C		02 FEB 1856	Not Reported
581	Parker, Henry M.	13y	C	Md.	15 FEB 1872	Mt. Olivet
266	Parker, James E.	9m	W	D.C.	05 JUL 1867	Glenwood
328	Parker, John	4m	C		30 JUL 1868	Alms House
132	Parker, John	9m	W	D.C.	08 NOV 1858	Congressional
460	Parker, John	33y	C	Va.	09 JUN 1870	Ebenezer
641	Parker, John	4y	W	U.S.	27 DEC 1872	Small Pox*
760	Parker, John, laborer	50y	C	U.S.	15 APR 1874	Beckett's
684	Parker, Joseph	10y	C	U.S.	27 APR 1873	Small Pox*
642	Parker, Joseph	34y	C	U.S.	20 DEC 1872	Small Pox
533	Parker, Judy	20y	C	Va.	25 AUG 1871	Washington
683	Parker, Julia	30y	C	U.S.	22 APR 1873	Small Pox

Page	Name	Age	Race	Birth	Death Date	Burial Ground
641	Parker, Kate	28y	W	U.S.	30 DEC 1872	Small Pox*
729	Parker, Lincoln	4m	C	U.S.	11 NOV 1873	
734	Parker, Lottie	11m	C	U.S.	03 DEC 1873	Holmead
437	Parker, Louisa	2m	C	La.	29 JAN 1870	Washington Asylum
404	Parker, Louisa A.	2y	C	D.C.	10 JUL 1869	Washington Asylum
727	Parker, Lucy Ann	1y	B	U.S.	30 OCT 1873	
224	Parker, M.				14 JUN 1866	Western
718	Parker, Maria L.	29y	C	Va.	10 SEP 1873	Mt. Pleasant
063	Parker, Martha W.	11y	W	D.C.*	30 NOV 1856	Foundry
414	Parker, Mary	48h	W		30 SEP 1869	Glenwood
635	Parker, Mary	25y	C	U.S.	20 NOV 1872	Small Pox
669	Parker, Mary, child of			U.S.	04 FEB 1873	
508	Parker, Mary E.	5y	C	D.C.	23 FEB 1871	Union
323	Parker, Meda	2m	W	D.C.	14 JUL 1868	Beltsville, Md.
290	Parker, Milly	25y	C	Va.	26 JAN 1868	Freedmen's Hospital
241	Parker, P., child of	4m	C		19 OCT 1866	Mt. Olivet
629	Parker, Richd.	112y	C	U.S.	07 OCT 1872	
151	Parker, Rumina	36y	W	U.S.	19 JUN 1859	Oak Hill
588	Parker, Saml.	34y	C	Md.	24 MAR 1872	Small Pox
248	Parker, Sarah A.	55y	W	Va.*	29 DEC 1866	Glenwood
432	Parker, Thomas	30y	C	N.J.	16 DEC 1869	Washington Asylum
611	Parker, W.	2y	C	U.S.	10 JUL 1872	
141	Parker, W.H., gentleman	42y	W	N.Y.	23 FEB 1859	Congressional
241	Parker, William H.	11m	W	D.C.	26 OCT 1866	Mt. Olivet
443	Parker, William, laborer	20y	C	Va.	11 FEB 1870	Washington Asylum
708	Parker, Wm.	8m	C	D.C.	14 JUL 1873	
601	Parker, Wm. A.	40y	W	U.S.	09 MAY 1872	Congressional
658	Parker, Wm. T., clerk	42y	W	U.S.	01 JAN 1873	Congressional
001	Parker, [blank]	1d			30 JAN 1855	Foundry
292a	Parker, [blank]		C		03 FEB 1868	Methodist
034	Parker, [blank]	54y	C		12 JAN 1856	Western
532	Parkes, Wm.	75y	C	Md.	10 AUG 1871	Potters Field
755	Parkhurst, Chas. B., Dr.	31y	W	U.S.	06 MAR 1874	Wallingsford, Conn.
342	Parkhurst, Geo.	11m	W	D.C.	27 AUG 1868	Congressional
379	Parkhurst, George F.	6m			15 MAR 1869	Congressional
595	Parkhurst, Harry R.	1m	W	U.S.	13 APR 1872	
004	Parkhurst, M.B.	25y	W	Mass.	01 MAR 1855	
240	Parkhurst, William G., clerk	46y	W		10 OCT 1866	Glenwood
622a	Parkinson, Carrie	7m	W	U.S.	01 AUG 1872	Congressional*
340	Parkinson, Louisa I.	30y	W	Eng.	24 AUG 1868	Congressional
428	Parks, Emeline A.	42y	W	Ohio	01 NOV 1869	Ohio
720	Parks, Geo.	21m	C	D.C.	23 SEP 1873	Young Mens
478	Parks, Mary	2y	C	D.C.	05 SEP 1870	Mt. Olivet
774	Parks, Robt. Elsworth	3m	W	U.S.	10 JUN 1874	Graceland
421	Parm, Joseph Alonzo	11d	W		27 OCT 1869	Glenwood
391	Parrale, Mrs.	67y	W	Ire.	12 MAY 1869	Mt. Olivet
398	Parry, Alfred	7m	B	D.C.	30 JUN 1869	Washington Asylum
535	Parsch, Elenor, servant	40y	W	Eng.	04 SEP 1871	Congressional
310	Parson, Eliza, child of		C		c.03 APR 1868	Mt. Olivet
527	Parsons, Dereca	1y	W	D.C.	07 JUL 1871	Congressional
425	Parsons, Luther, laborer	54y	W		18 NOV 1869	Congressional
532	Parsons, Maria	1m	W	D.C.	10 AUG 1871	Congressional
165	Parsons, Mary	81y	W	Va.	09 NOV 1859	Mt. Olivet
054	Parsons, Thomas H.	2y	W	D.C.	28 AUG 1856	Baltimore, Md.
103	Parsons, [blank]		W	D.C.	28 JAN 1858	Washington Asylum
735	Part, John F.	21d	W	U.S.	10 DEC 1873	St. Marys
705	Parten, Wm.	10m	C	Va.	16 JUL 1873	Ebenezer
325	Partridge, Albert J., clerk	53y	W	N.Y.	16 JUL 1868	Congressional*

Page	Name	Age	Race	Birth	Death Date	Burial Ground
727	Partridge, James, soldier	65y	W	Eng.	29 OCT 1873	
687	Partridge, John H.	73y	W	D.C.	10 MAY 1873	Congressional
663	Partridge, Susan	74y	W	U.S.	08 JAN 1873	Small Pox*
019	Pasey, Richd.	2m	C	D.C.	13 AUG 1855	Young Mens
403	Pasper, Mary	10m	W		21 JUL 1869	German Catholic
055	Pastin, Jane	55y	W		16 AUG 1856	Congressional
263	Patch, James	2y	C	D.C.	13 JUN 1867	Congressional
185	Patch, John	3m	W	D.C.	24 JUL 1860	Congressional
303	Patch, Joseph	1y	W	D.C.	15 MAR 1868	Congressional
541	Patch, Mary E.	2m	W	D.C.	14 OCT 1871	Congressional*
625	Pate, Ann C.	1y	W	U.S.	09 SEP 1872	Congressional
529	Pate, Fannie Evans	1y	W	D.C.	24 JUL 1871	Glenwood
724	Pate, Susanna	25y	W	Va.	14 OCT 1873	Congressional
303	Paterson, Blanche	1m	W	D.C.	08 MAR 1868	Congressional
767	Paterson, Infant	11d	C	U.S.	27 MAY 1874	Mt. Olivet
364	Paterson, Louisa	5h	W	D.C.	11 DEC 1868	Congressional*
007	Paterson, Margaret	68y	W	Ire.	09 APR 1855	Methodist, 14th St.
703	Paterson, Walter E.	5m		D.C.	25 JUL 1873	Congressional*
340	Patie, Mary	Still	W	D.C.	03 AUG 1868	Congressional
218	Paton, Uris	1m	C	D.C.	19 APR 1866	Holmead
533	Patrick, James	1y	W	D.C.	22 AUG 1871	Mt. Olivet
304	Patrie, W.J. & J., infant of	1d	W		21 MAR 1868	Congressional
596	Patten, Vernon, Jr.	34y	W	U.S.	27 APR 1872	Congressional
703	Patter, Wm. L.	9y	W	D.C.	01 JUL 1873	Glenwood
585	Patterson, Albert, laborer	23y	C	Md.	09 MAR 1872	Asylum
213	Patterson, Basil				24 FEB 1866	
537	Patterson, Bridget	50y	W	Md.	20 SEP 1871	Congressional
487	Patterson, Edgar	63y	W	D.C.*	05 NOV 1870	Oak Hill
169	Patterson, Elizabeth	49y	W	D.C.	07 JAN 1860	Congressional
169	Patterson, George W.	1y	W	D.C.	05 JAN 1860	Glenwood
731	Patterson, Helen	5d	W	U.S.	24 NOV 1873	Congressional
162	Patterson, James, merchant	38y	W	Ire.	24 SEP 1859	Trinity
389	Patterson, Lucy Ann	3y	C	D.C.	29 APR 1869	Washington Asylum
244	Patterson, Mary J., lady	28y	W	N.H.	28 NOV 1866	Oak Hill
341	Patterson, Robt.	1y	W	D.C.	17 AUG 1868	Congressional
608	Patterson, Sadie E.	4m	W	N.Y.	26 JUN 1872	Congressional*
513	Patterson, Virginia A.	19y	W	Mex.	14 MAR 1871	Glenwood
703	Patterson, W.E.	5m	W	U.S.	22 JUL 1873	Congressional*
349	Patterson, William P., watchman	49y	W	La.	25 SEP 1868	Mt. Olivet
132	Patterson, [blank]	7d	C	D.C.	07 NOV 1858	Foundry
237	Patterson, [blank]	6m	C		26 SEP 1866	Young Mens
350	Patton, Beverly	28y	C	Va.	21 SEP 1868	Beckett's
291	Pauper		C		08 JAN 1868	Alms House
540	Payne, Absalom	20y	C	Va.	04 OCT 1871	Young Mens
280	Payne, Alice	4y	C	Va.	23 OCT 1867	Holmead
774	Payne, Anna L.	7m	W	U.S.	07 JUN 1874	Oak Hill
316	Payne, Belford		C		c.22 MAY 1868	Alms House
413	Payne, Bellford, laborer	42y	C		10 AUG 1869	Washington Asylum
454	Payne, Charity	10m	C		13 MAY 1870	
440	Payne, Charles	1y	C		18 FEB 1870	Holmead
402	Payne, Flora E.	3y	W		31 JUL 1869	Glenwood
322	Payne, George	22y	C	Va.	20 JUN 1868	Freedmen's Hospital
442	Payne, Henry	25y	C	Md.	23 FEB 1870	Washington Asylum
739	Payne, Howard T., clerk	28y	W	U.S.	21 DEC 1873	
251	Payne, Hugh, laborer	27y	C	Va.	20 JAN 1867	Ebenezer
537	Payne, Jane	27y	C		21 SEP 1871	Va.
604	Payne, Joseph	2m	C	D.C.	20 JUN 1872	Ebenezer
440	Payne, Kate Weed	22y	W	N.Y.	24 FEB 1870	N.Y. City

District of Columbia Interments (Index to Deaths), 1855-1874

Page	Name	Age	Race	Birth	Death Date	Burial Ground
265	Payne, Lucinda	49y	C	Va.	16 JUL 1867	Young Mens
335	Payne, Lucius	9m	C	D.C.	14 JUL 1868	Ebenezer
343	Payne, Lylie E.	6m	W	D.C.	03 AUG 1868	Glenwood
594	Payne, Mary		C	D.C.	16 APR 1872	Beckett's
598	Payne, Mr., laborer	65y	C	U.S.	05 MAY 1872	Small Pox
616	Payne, Penrose, carpenter	26y	C	U.S.	23 JUL 1872	
750	Payne, Robert, laborer	30y	C	U.S.	13 FEB 1874	
384	Payne, William	18y	W	D.C.	27 MAR 1869	Washington Asylum
613	Payne, Wm. A.	1y	C	U.S.	10 JUL 1872	
372	Paynes, Martha	7d	C	D.C.	19 JAN 1869	Washington Asylum
031	Payntor, Levia S.	27y	W	N.H.	13 DEC 1855	Congressional
344	Payton, Henry W.	7m	C	D.C.	07 AUG 1868	Western
715	Payton, [blank]		C	U.S.	08 AUG 1873	
087	Peabody, Joseph L., clerk	50y	W	Mass.	12 AUG 1857	St. Patricks
622a	Peabody, Julia D.	9m	W	U.S.	15 AUG 1872	Baltimore, Md.[88]
439	Peabody, [blank]	Still	W		13 FEB 1870	Congressional
535	Pead, Ann	37y	C	Va.	03 SEP 1871	Young Mens
584	Peak, Eda	1y	W	D.C.	01 MAR 1872	Methodist
467	Peak, John A., grocery merchant	39y	W	Ire.	17 JUL 1870	Mt. Olivet
462	Peak, John A., grocery merchant	39y	W	Ire.	17 JUL 1870	Mt. Olivet
044	Peake, Julia Ann	45y	W	Md.	10 MAY 1856	Methodist, East
218	Peake, Lucretia	41y	W	D.C.	21 APR 1866	Congressional
557	Peal, Sopha, laborer	60y	W		01 FEB 1872	
177	Peale, Samuel, waiter	40y	C	Md.	19 APR 1860	Young Mens
777a	Pearce, Chas. G., umbrella mkr.	47y	C	U.S.	10 JUN 1874	
665	Pearce, Mary	48y	W	U.S.	30 JAN 1873	Small Pox*
517	Pearce, Mary S.	47y	W	Md.	30 APR 1871	Cumberland, Md.
086	Pearce, Mrs.	48y	W	Md.	07 AUG 1857	
029	Pearce, Sarah J.	11y	W		01 NOV 1855	Methodist, West
120	Pearce, [blank]	1y	W		10 JUL 1858	Western
414	Pearse, Mary M.	60y	W	R.I.	01 SEP 1869	Bristol, R.I.
774	Pearsen, Nettie V.	10m	W	U.S.	25 JUN 1874	Oak Hill
341	Pearson, Fish H.	1y	W		18 AUG 1868	Congressional
381	Pearson, Jennie I.	10m	W		15 MAR 1869	Glenwood
485	Pearson, John	52y	W	Md.	11 OCT 1870	Potters Field
259	Peck, David	40y	C	Md.	14 APR 1867	Ebenezer
660	Peck, Earline	1m	C	U.S.	18 JAN 1873	
714	Peck, Elyzan	47y	W	D.C.	27 AUG 1873	Congressional
774	Peck, Henry	40y	W	U.S.	09 JUN 1874	Glenwood
144	Peck, John	2y	C	D.C.	30 MAR 1859	
604	Peck, John, laborer	19y	C	Md.	25 JUN 1872	Ebenezer
613	Peck, Jos. A.	1y	C	U.S.	07 JUL 1872	
090	Peck, Joseph C.	25y	W	D.C.	01 SEP 1857	Glenwood
270	Peck, Joseph, Col., clerk	58y	W	D.C.*	07 AUG 1867	Glenwood
330	Peck, Maggie	7m	C	D.C.	09 JUL 1868	Young Mens
593	Peck, Margaret	63y	W	D.C.	28 APR 1872	Glenwood
660	Peck, Mary T.	60y	W	U.S.	19 JAN 1873	Ohio
658	Peck, Oden, laborer	17y	C	Md.	01 JAN 1873	
603	Peck, Thos.	5y	C	D.C.	18 JUN 1872	Small Pox
784	Peck, William, laborer	45y	C	U.S.	07 JUL 1874	Mt. Olivet
399	Pedigru, William, sea captain	67y	W	Eng.	30 JUL 1869	Congressional
091	Pedrick, Henry D.	8m	W	D.C.	14 SEP 1857	Rock Creek
507	Pedrick, James C.	66y	W	Mass.	18 FEB 1871	Oak Hill
683	Peebles, Hatty	2y	C	U.S.	16 APR 1873	Small Pox
592	Peebles, Nannie	1y	C	D.C.	08 APR 1872	

---

[88] Interment record from St. Matthew's Cathedral, Rhode Island Avenue, N.W., Washington, D.C.

District of Columbia Interments (Index to Deaths), 1855-1874

Page	Name	Age	Race	Birth	Death Date	Burial Ground
683	Peebles, Sarah	5m	C	U.S.	07 APR 1873	Small Pox
141	Peebles, [blank]		W		18 FEB 1859	Glenwood
413	Peel, Lucy	23y	C	Md.	23 AUG 1869	Washington Asylum
470	Pegg, Annie	1y	W	D.C.	09 AUG 1870	Congressional
218	Pegg, Thomas, farmer & judge	65y	I	Ala.	22 APR 1866	Congressional
444	Pegg, William A., painter	28y	W		04 MAR 1870	Congressional
493	Pegg, Wm., blacksmith	66y	W	Va.	06 DEC 1870	Congressional
299	Pekin, Charles	5m	C	D.C.	07 MAR 1868	Young Mens
506	Pelham, Edward, laborer	70y	C	Va.	03 FEB 1871	Washington Asylum
784	Pelham, Malinda	38y	C	U.S.	27 JUL 1874	Mt. Pleasant/Rock Cr.
294	Pelham, Silas	8m	C	D.C.	04 FEB 1868	Western
189	Peltier, Henrietta	20y	W	Mich.	01 SEP 1860	Mich.
298	Pelz, Henriette, Mrs.	67y	W	Ger.	12 FEB 1868	Glenwood
743	Penchy, Peter	43y	C	U.S.	22 JAN 1874	Washington Asylum
489	Pendegrass, Johanna, lady	31y	W	Ire.	29 NOV 1870	Mt. Olivet
376	Pendel, Thos. & Sarah, infant of		W		22 FEB 1869	Glenwood
784	Pendle, Blanch	2y	W	U.S.	09 JUL 1874	Glenwood
661	Pendleton, James	2y	W	U.S.	26 JAN 1873	Mt. Olivet
146	Pendleton, Jaqueline S., lady	38y	W	D.C.	17 APR 1859	Congressional
546	Penicks, Thos. B.	2y	W	U.S.	28 NOV 1871	Glenwood
390	Penman, Robert, printer	55y	W	N.Y.	30 MAY 1869	Glenwood
220	Penn, Alexander G., ex congress.	67y	W	La.	07 MAY 1866	Glenwood
337	Penn, Amelia	40y	C	U.S.	10 AUG 1868	Washington Asylum
712	Penn, Chas., soldier	23y	W	Eng.	18 AUG 1873	Congressional
253	Penn, Mrs.	28y	C		06 FEB 1867	Alexandria, Va.
404	Penner, May, infant of	4m	C		13 JUL 1869	Mt. Olivet
349	Pennibacker, Foster Thomas	6y	W	Ky.	13 SEP 1868	Ky.
674	Penniman, Harriett	70y	W	U.S.	18 MAR 1873	Greenmount, Balto.
128	Pennington, Alfred, copper refiner	25y	W	Md.	22 SEP 1858	Congressional
386	Pennington, Lillie M.	7y	W	D.C.	25 APR 1869	Congressional
025	Penny, Henry	57y	C	Md.	26 SEP 1855	St. Matthews
317	Penny, Mary E.	30y	C		05 JUN 1868	Mt. Olivet
143	Penny, Mary Jane	25y	C	D.C.	16 MAR 1859	Washington Asylum
361	Pennybacker, Fred. Jarvis	1y	W		03 NOV 1868	Ky.
213	Pepper, Jennie	3y	W		23 FEB 1866	Mt. Olivet
632	Pepper, John	4d	W	U.S.	28 OCT 1872	
252	Pepper, John Patterson	71y	W	Pa.	24 FEB 1867	Congressional
550	Pepper, Mary E.	5m	W		27 DEC 1871	Mt. Olivet
590	Pepper, Nellie	2y	W	D.C.	07 APR 1872	Mt. Olivet
719	Pepper, Thomas	74y	W	Ire.	17 SEP 1873	Mt. Olivet
246	Pepper, Thomas, grandchild of	6m	W	D.C.	26 DEC 1866	Congressional
069	Perce, Martha Ann	15y	W	Va.	28 JAN 1857	Glenwood
414	Perkins, Bine L., Mrs.	37y	W	Mich.	03 SEP 1869	Glenwood
581	Perkins, Catharine	1y	W	D.C.	15 FEB 1872	Mt. Olivet
256	Perkins, Debbie J.	32y	W		19 MAR 1867	Baltimore, Md.
481	Perkins, Emma E.	36y	W	Conn.	17 OCT 1870	N.Y. City
688	Perkins, F. Henry, storekeeper	26y	W	U.S.	13 MAY 1873	Baltimore, Md.
713	Perkins, Henry	40y	C	Md.	23 AUG 1873	Beckett's
338	Perkins, Henry		C		19 AUG 1868	Washington Asylum
168	Perkins, John	5y	W	D.C.	21 DEC 1859	Washington
760	Perkins, Louis G.	23y	W	U.S.	27 APR 1874	Congressional
469	Perkins, Mary R.	11m	W	D.C.	23 AUG 1870	Mt. Olivet
784	Perkins, Sarah E.	5m	W	U.S.	08 JUL 1874	
379	Perkins, Susan, Mrs.	60y	W	Md.	02 MAR 1869	Congressional
518	Perkins, Thomas, laborer	22y	C	Md.	12 MAY 1871	Potters Field
371	Perkins, Wash. D., photographer	26y	W	Md.	27 JAN 1869	Baltimore, Md.
359	Perley, Gale W.	6m	W	D.C.	14 NOV 1868	Congressional
466	Pernell, Wm., steward	39y	C	Md.	24 JUL 1870	Western

281

Page	Name	Age	Race	Birth	Death Date	Burial Ground
033	Perrie, C.F. & M., son of	Still	W		08 JAN 1856	Congressional
082	Perrie, Edward D.	6y	W	D.C.	01 JUL 1857	Glenwood
181	Perrie, Elizabeth E.	4m	W	D.C.	06 JUN 1860	Congressional
534	Perrie, Helen M.	35y	W	Md.	30 AUG 1871	Glenwood
114	Perrin, [blank]	Still			21 MAY 1858	Holmead
396	Perry, Albert	39y	C	Va.	17 JUN 1869	Young Mens
684	Perry, Alonza	21y	C	U.S.	14 APR 1873	Small Pox*
143	Perry, Annie R.	2y	W	D.C.	05 MAR 1859	
223	Perry, Eliza	2y	C	D.C.	02 JUN 1866	Colored
101	Perry, Elizabeth	11m	W		09 JAN 1858	Rock Creek
689	Perry, Ella L.	12y	W	U.S.	31 MAY 1873	Oak Hill
181	Perry, Frank	1y	W	D.C.	01 JUN 1860	Rock Creek
397	Perry, Henry D., lawyer	83y	W	Conn.	23 JUN 1869	Macomb Co., Mich.
135	Perry, Janie A.M. Pierce	2y	W	D.C.	09 DEC 1858	Congressional
302	Perry, Josephine	7y	C	D.C.	23 MAR 1868	Ebenezer
307	Perry, Josephine		C		28 APR 1868	Freedmen's Hospital
321	Perry, Margaret	6y	W	D.C.	23 JUN 1868	German Catholic
615	Perry, Oliver	30y	C	U.S.	11 JUL 1872	
383	Perry, R.H., child of	Still	C		10 MAR 1869	Young Mens
710	Perry, Thomas Edward	16m	W	D.C.	06 AUG 1873	
731	Perry, W.D., clerk	55y	W	U.S.	20 NOV 1873	Front Royal, Ga.
238	Perry, Waman	7m	C	D.C.	16 SEP 1866	
630	Perry, Wm.	2y	C	U.S.	29 OCT 1872	Small Pox
597	Perry, [blank]	1y	W	D.C.	01 MAY 1872	Oak Hill
230	Peter, [Mr.], child of	4m			30 JUL 1866	Young Mens
589	Peters, Elisabeth	56y	C	D.C.	04 MAR 1872	Mt. Zion
285	Peters, Eugene	32y	C		06 DEC 1867	Young Mens
467	Peters, Franz Jacobus	17d	W	D.C.	31 JUL 1870	Congressional
706	Peters, Fredk.	6m	W	D.C.	11 JUL 1873	
500	Peters, Johanne L.	7y	W	Amer.	06 JAN 1871	Prospect Hill
660	Peters, John	5y	C	U.S.	19 JAN 1873	Harmony
580	Peters, Mary A.	62y	W	Switz.	08 FEB 1872	Oak Hill
029	Peters, Mary F.	2d	C	D.C.	15 NOV 1855	St. Matthews
376	Peters, Miss, laundress	22y	C	Va.	17 FEB 1869	Young Mens
035	Peters, Onslow, judge in Ill.	51y	W	Mass.	28 FEB 1856	Not Reported
675	Peters, Salena	35y	C	U.S.	25 MAR 1873	Harmony
086	Peters, [blank]	1m	C		04 AUG 1857	Western
431	Petersen, Nathaniel	8y	W		14 DEC 1869	Oak Hill
377	Peterson, Emma	31y	C		16 FEB 1869	
767	Peterson, James	3m	C	U.S.	04 MAY 1874	
683	Peterson, James	23y	C	U.S.	12 APR 1873	Small Pox
708	Peterson, Nels Jno.	28y	W	Swe.	25 JUL 1873	
523	Peterson, Wm., tailor	58y	W	Ger.	18 JUN 1871	Prospect Hill
031	Peticord, Augts. H., cabinet maker	27y	W	Md.	06 DEC 1855	Washington
415	Petignat, Joseph, infant of	Still	W		12 SEP 1869	Glenwood
038	Petit, Charles, messenger	39y	W	Pa.	12 MAR 1856	Congressional
400	Petrie, Arnold, clerk	39y	W	N.Y.	08 JUL 1869	Little Falls, N.Y.
338	Petteys, Clara	16y	W	N.Y.	30 AUG 1868	Glenwood
051	Pettibone, Willie	1y	W	D.C.	21 JUL 1856	Oak Hill
073	Pettigru, Thomas, naval officer	60y	W	S.C.	06 MAR 1857	Congressional
131	Pettit, Jas. Seneca, engraver	28y	W	D.C.	25 OCT 1858	Congressional
131	Pettit, Mary Alice	6y	W	D.C.	22 OCT 1858	Glenwood
754	Pettit, Walter C.	6m	W	U.S.	06 MAR 1874	Congressional
112	Pettit, Wm. Newton	7y	W	D.C.	21 APR 1858	Glenwood
411	Pettitt, Lydia	2y	W	D.C.	22 AUG 1869	Glenwood
345	Petty, James DeShields	7d	W	D.C.	17 AUG 1868	Glenwood
625	Petty, Robt. A.	6y	W	U.S.	04 OCT 1872	
713	Petty, Thomas S.	4m	W	D.C.	23 AUG 1873	Glenwood

District of Columbia Interments (Index to Deaths), 1855-1874

Page	Name	Age	Race	Birth	Death Date	Burial Ground
726	Pettys, Carrie J.	24y	W	U.S.	28 OCT 1873	Glenwood
784	Pettys, Martin D., clerk	60y	W	U.S.	10 JUL 1874	Glenwood
472	Peugh, Elizabeth	24y	C	Va.	20 AUG 1870	Young Mens
710	Pevrell, Samuel	6m	W	D.C.	07 AUG 1873	Mt. Olivet
661	Peyton, Bettie B.	22y	W	U.S.	23 JAN 1873	Congressional
032	Peyton, Edward	14d	W	D.C.	24 DEC 1855	Congressional
253	Peyton, Fannie	10y	W	Md.	03 FEB 1867	Congressional
353	Peyton, Hugh	75y	C	Va.	06 SEP 1868	Freedmen's Hospital
412	Peyton, Jenny	14d	C		01 AUG 1869	
703	Peyton, John	8m	C	D.C.	03 JUL 1873	
581	Peyton, John B., clerk	54y	W	Conn.	18 FEB 1872	Congressional
337	Peyton, Mary	1y	C	D.C.	04 AUG 1868	Washington Asylum
060	Peyton, Rosa	3y	W	Va.*	22 OCT 1856	Alexandria, Va., Ivy Hill
149	Pfeil, Louis	4y	W	D.C.	24 MAY 1859	Prospect Hill
464	Pfister, Henry	4y	W	D.C.	09 JUL 1870	Prospect Hill
371	Pflaeger, George, baker	38y	W	Ger.	25 JAN 1869	Prospect Hill
054	Pflieger, [blank]	11m	W	Md.	06 AUG 1856	German
784	Pfling, Henry C.	1m	W	U.S.	22 JUL 1874	Prospect Hill
344	Pflueger, Anna K.	9m	W	D.C.	26 AUG 1868	Glenwood
366	Pflueger, Ricker	6y	W	D.C.	03 DEC 1868	Glenwood
477	Pfluger, Christian	1y	W		14 SEP 1870	Prospect Hill
723	Pfluger, John, laborer	52y	W	Ger.	08 OCT 1873	Prospect Hill
241	Pfoile, Daniel	3y	W	D.C.	08 OCT 1866	Prospect Hill
241	Pfoile, Mrs.				21 OCT 1866	Prospect Hill
019	Phalen, Agnes P.	18m	W		11 AUG 1855	St. Patricks
774	Pheeney, Patrick	2m	W	U.S.	15 JUN 1874	Holyrood
058	Pheiffer, Jno. F.	18d	W	D.C.	27 SEP 1856	German
299	Phelan, John, bricklayer	40y	W	Ire.	01 MAR 1868	Mt. Olivet
435	Phelan, Nicholas, merchant	49y	W	Ire.	10 JAN 1870	Mt. Olivet
074	Phelph, George H.	1y		D.C.	24 MAR 1857	St. Patricks
261	Phelps, Daniel, clerk	37y	W	N.Y.	28 MAY 1867	N.Y.
239	Phelps, Emma Agnes	2y	W	D.C.	30 OCT 1866	Mt. Olivet
169	Phelps, Ezra, carpenter	72y	W	U.S.	10 JAN 1860	St. Patricks (vault)
008	Phelps, Geo.		W		05 MAY 1855	St. Matthews
190	Phelps, John	19d	W	D.C.	21 SEP 1860	Congressional
091	Phelps, [blank]		W	D.C.	17 SEP 1857	Congressional
106	Phigge, Minna	8d	W	D.C.	22 FEB 1858	Glenwood
527	Philip, Cate	2y	C	D.C.	07 JUL 1871	Young Mens
175	Philipp, Henry August	2y	W	D.C.	24 MAR 1860	Prospect Hill
395	Philips, Catherine	21y	W	N.C.	02 JUN 1869	Mt. Olivet
240	Philips, Kate Lee	13d	W	D.C.	10 OCT 1866	Glenwood
113	Philips, Mary Louisa	1y	W	D.C.	06 MAY 1858	St. Patricks
020	Philips, [blank]	9d	W	D.C.	29 AUG 1855	Congressional
202	Philips, [blank]	Still	W	D.C.	06 APR 1861	Washington Asylum
674	Phillips, Benjamin	72y	W	U.S.	15 MAR 1873	Lynn, Mass.
522	Phillips, Clara	1y	W	Amer.	13 JUN 1871	Mt. Olivet
662	Phillips, Claracy	72y	W	U.S.	31 JAN 1873	Glenwood
774	Phillips, Cora Estelle	8m	W	U.S.	16 JUN 1874	Glenwood
760	Phillips, James, coach maker	45y	W	U.S.	07 APR 1874	Oak Hill
697	Phillips, Jane	3y	C	D.C.	28 JUN 1873	Washington Asylum
289	Phillips, John Thomas	1m	W	D.C.	27 JAN 1868	Mt. Olivet
354	Philp, John, clerk Freedmen's B.	27y	W	Eng.	15 OCT 1868	Congressional
784	Philpot, [?] E.	2y	W	U.S.	31 JUL 1874	Holyrood
013	Phipps, Elizabeth	2m	W	D.C.	23 JUL 1855	St. Peters
057	Phipps, Ernest	3y	W	D.C.	01 SEP 1856	St. Matthews
523	Phlilips, Mary M.	7m			15 JUN 1871	Glenwood
431	Phoenix, Ann, domestic	10y	C	D.C.	08 DEC 1869	Mt. Olivet
453	Picard, Julius	1y	W		26 MAY 1870	Washington Hebrew

District of Columbia Interments (Index to Deaths), 1855-1874

Page	Name	Age	Race	Birth	Death Date	Burial Ground
444	Picken, Thomas, watchman	61y	W	Scot.	21 MAR 1870	Congressional
094	Pickerell, [blank]	28y	W	Va.	29 OCT 1857	Washington Asylum
616a	Pickett, James C., lawyer	81y	W	U.S.	10 JUL 1872	Congressional*
731	Picklin, Thomas	1m	W	U.S.	19 NOV 1873	Congressional
298	Pickney, Martha	1y	W		28 FEB 1868	Congressional
250	Pickrell, Benjamin, carpenter	84y	W	Md.	30 JAN 1867	Congressional*
032	Pickrell, [blank]	54y	W	Md.	23 DEC 1855	St. Patricks
022	Pierce, Franklin	6m	W	D.C.	01 AUG 1855	Methodist, East
514	Pierce, Georgiana	8m	C	D.C.	28 MAR 1871	Ebenezer
282	Pierce, James				— NOV 1867	Congressional
368	Pierce, John	23y	C	Va.	28 DEC 1868	Freedmen's Hospital
698	Pierce, John H.	2m	W	D.C.	22 JUN 1873	Harmony
347	Pierce, Minnie	3y	W	D.C.	02 SEP 1868	Congressional
661	Pierce, Mrs. [John]	48y	W	U.S.	30 JAN 1873	Congressional*
540	Pierre, Florence	6m	W	U.S.	05 OCT 1871	
690	Pierson, Ann Maria	4m	C	U.S.	15 MAY 1873	Small Pox
348	Pierson, Clarence R.	10m	W	D.C.	27 SEP 1868	Congressional
404	Pierson, Eliza Jane	10y	C	Va.	08 JUL 1869	Washington Asylum
784	Pierson, Emma J.	24y	W	U.S.	20 JUL 1874	Congressional
690	Pierson, Henretta	20y	C	U.S.	05 MAY 1873	Small Pox
350	Pierson, J., Mrs., servant	24y	C		08 SEP 1868	Young Mens
035	Pierson, Madeline	16y	W	Va.	17 FEB 1856	Foundry
784	Pierson, W.T. & E.J., infant of	12h	W	U.S.	16 JUL 1874	Congressional
689	Pierson, [blank]	Still	W	U.S.	30 MAY 1873	Congressional
184	Pigg, Wm.	11d	W	D.C.	02 JUL 1860	Congressional
054	Piggott, William E.	1m	W	D.C.	03 AUG 1856	Congressional
237	Piggott, Wm. C., soldier	38y	W	D.C.	16 SEP 1866	Congressional
584	Pignot, Charles, fireman	32y	W	Ger.	01 MAR 1872	
102	Pigott, Charlotte	26y	W	N.C.	21 JAN 1858	Congressional
493	Pilkington, Wm. M.	17y	W		05 DEC 1870	Mt. Olivet
127	Pilkinton, Patrick	3m	W	D.C.	01 SEP 1858	St. Peters
593	Pilson, Bettie	20y	W	D.C.	04 APR 1872	Glenwood
590	Pilson, Elisabeth	19y	W	D.C.	07 APR 1872	Glenwood
270	Pin, Ellen	54y	C	Va.	13 AUG 1867	Harmony
451	Pin, Hannah	80y	C		05 APR 1870	Ebenezer
080	Pinckney, Richard		C		23 JUN 1857	Washington Asylum
026	Pindon, Catherine	50y	W		22 OCT 1855	St. Matthews
726	Piniion, Geo.	44y	B	U.S.	30 OCT 1873	Mt. Pleasant/Yg. Mens
387	Pinkard, Caroline	5m	C		08 APR 1869	Young Mens
215	Pinkard, Sraah	77y	W	Va.	17 MAR 1866	Ebenezer
331	Pinkney, Betty	20y	C	Md.	06 JUL 1868	Freedmen's Hospital
443	Pinkney, Charles, laborer	80y	C	Va.	04 FEB 1870	Washington Asylum
502	Pinkney, Ellen E.	1m	W	D.C.	26 JAN 1871	Methodist
499	Pinkney, Ellen W.	1m	W	D.C.	25 JAN 1871	Methodist
434	Pinkney, George, laborer	23y	W		02 JAN 1870	Congressional
555	Pinkney, Jane	5y	C	D.C.	28 JAN 1872	Holmead
526	Pinkney, Thomas	3y	C	D.C.	05 JUL 1871	Holmead
606	Pinkney, Wm. H.	14y	W	D.C.	27 JUN 1872	Congressional
784	Pinn, John, laborer	80y	C	U.S.	06 JUL 1874	Mt. Pleasant
431	Pinn, Mary	21y	C	Va.	02 DEC 1869	
454	Pinn, Nettie	10m	C		24 MAY 1870	Alexandria, Va.
049	Pio, Jose, officer's steward	39y	W	Port.	03 JUL 1856	St. Peters
593	Piper, Gerald	40y	W	Ire.	07 APR 1872	Mt. Olivet
181	Piper, Jno. Alexander	1y	C	D.C.	11 JUN 1860	Harmony
062	Piper, John				18 NOV 1856	Washington Asylum
515	Piper, John R., Dr.	60y	W	Md.	16 MAR 1871	Congressional
021	Piper, Mrs., child of		W		01 AUG 1855	Glenwood
748	Piper, Sarah	45y	C	U.S.	09 FEB 1874	Alexandria, Va.

District of Columbia Interments (Index to Deaths), 1855-1874

Page	Name	Age	Race	Birth	Death Date	Burial Ground
127	Pipher, Sarah A.	27y	W	Va.	10 SEP 1858	Glenwood
725	Pippart, Martha E.	68y	W	Rots.	16 OCT 1873	Congressional
135	Pipsico, M.S.	19y	C	Md.	05 DEC 1858	Ebenezer
374	Pitchlynn, Edward Everett	9y	W	D.C.	21 FEB 1869	Congressional
754	Pitney, Helen J.	28y	W	U.S.	02 MAR 1874	Oak Hill
616b	Pitsbury, E.V.	2m	W	U.S.	22 JUL 1872	
630	Pitts, Wm.	1y	C	U.S.	15 OCT 1872	
416	Pitts, Wm. L.	14d	W		03 SEP 1869	Western
302	Pivion, Armedia	1y	C	D.C.	21 MAR 1868	Western
108	Piwell, A.L.	6m	W	D.C.	23 MAR 1858	Rock Creek
461	Pixton, Gertrude	5m	W	D.C.	27 JUL 1870	Congressional
710	Planon, Joseph, laborer	33y	C	D.C.	03 AUG 1873	
599	Plant, George	3y	W	U.S.	07 MAY 1872	Mt. Olivet
471	Plant, J.W. & Alice M., child of	Still	W	D.C.	01 AUG 1870	Congressional
748	Plant, James K.	72y	W	Eng.	26 FEB 1874	Congressional
374	Plant, Rose D.	20y	W	Amer.	13 FEB 1869	Congressional
247	Plater, Alexander	3m			23 DEC 1866	Young Mens
454a	Plater, George, pauper	75y	C	Md.	14 MAY 1870	Washington Asylum
138	Plater, Gertrude	1y	C	D.C.	07 JAN 1859	Methodist
727	Plater, Maria L.	31y	W	U.S.	15 OCT 1873	
740	Plater, Mary Jane	8y	C	U.S.	04 JAN 1874	
767	Plater, Virgil, servant	22y	C	U.S.	06 MAY 1874	
002	Platt, Anna Elizabeth	3m	W	Md.	24 JAN 1855	Holmead
516	Platt, Mary J.	1y	W	D.C.	10 MAR 1871	Congressional
526	Platt, Saml. H., lawyer	68y	W	N.Y.	03 JUL 1871	Congressional
346	Pleasant, Celia	30y	C		08 AUG 1868	Freedmen's Hospital
500	Pleasant, Joseph, laborer	50y	C	Va.	04 JAN 1871	Harmony
001	Pleasanton, Stephen	79y			31 JAN 1855	Congressional
416	Pleasants, Arthur, ice carrier	13y	C	Va.*	07 SEP 1869	
186	Pleasants, Henry, porter	45y	C	Va.	31 JUL 1860	Mt. Olivet
276	Pleasants, Matthew	2y	W	D.C.	24 SEP 1867	Oak Hill/Winchester
638	Plentz, Treasa	60y	W	U.S.	13 NOV 1872	
616	Ploman, Henry	2y	C	U.S.	30 JUL 1872	
135	Plowden, Verlinda	70y	C		06 DEC 1858	Mt. Olivet
462	Plowman, Joseph W.	1y	W	D.C.	08 JUL 1870	Congressional
153	Plowman, Kate	2y	W	D.C.	09 JUL 1859	Congressional
607	Plugge, Wm.	19d	W	D.C.	23 JUN 1872	Glenwood
479	Plumer, Wm.	6d	C	D.C.	15 SEP 1870	Western
458	Plummer, C.W.	4d	C	D.C.	26 JUN 1870	Potters Field
615	Plummer, Eliza	40y	C	U.S.	02 JUL 1872	
144	Plummer, Fielder B., carpenter	43y	W	Md.	25 MAR 1859	Mt. Olivet
058	Plummer, Fielder M.	1y	W	D.C.	18 SEP 1856	St. Matthews
339	Plummer, John W.	1y	W	D.C.	15 AUG 1868	Mt. Olivet
743	Plummer, Maria, housewife	50y	C	U.S.	25 JAN 1874	Ebenezer
113	Plummer, Mary	44y	C	Md.	05 MAY 1858	Ebenezer
740	Plummer, Mary	4m	C	U.S.	04 JAN 1874	Mt. Pleasant
662	Plummer, Mary	80y	C	U.S.	31 JAN 1873	Washington Asylum
666	Plummer, Mary	80y	C	U.S.	02 FEB 1873	Washington Asylum
150	Plummer, Mary L.	38y	W	D.C.	11 JUN 1859	Mt. Olivet
638	Plummer, Nancey	13m	C	U.S.	18 NOV 1872	
076	Plummer, Richard	45y	C	Md.	25 APR 1857	
122	Plummer, Susan, washerwoman	30y	C	D.C.	24 JUL 1858	St. Peters
141	Plummer, Thos. H.	9y	C	D.C.	21 FEB 1859	Ebenezer
150	Plummer, [blank]	Still	W	D.C.	10 JUN 1859	Mt. Olivet
748	Plumseill, Eliza	70y	W	U.S.	22 FEB 1874	Congressional
089	Pochellon, Mary C.	23y	W		29 AUG 1857	Congressional
516	Pocock, Thos., bricklayer	42y	W	Md.	11 MAR 1871	Congressional
524	Pohlers, Anna	1y	W		25 JUN 1871	Glenwood

District of Columbia Interments (Index to Deaths), 1855-1874

Page	Name	Age	Race	Birth	Death Date	Burial Ground
696	Poindexter, Cicely, servant	65y	C	Va.	13 JUN 1873	
732	Poland, Geo. W.	14y	W	U.S.	05 NOV 1873	
774	Pole, Richard Charles	7m	W	U.S.	17 JUN 1874	
204	Poletti, Joseph, soldier	78y	W	Italy	12 JUN 1861	Mt. Olivet
345	Polglase, Lily Estelle	1y	W		19 AUG 1868	Glenwood
184	Polish, Martha	67y	W	Fra.	01 JUL 1860	Mt. Olivet
414	Polish, Peter	93y	W		28 SEP 1869	Congressional
317	Polk, Catherine W.	78y	W	Md.	17 JUN 1868	Congressional
189	Polk, Josiah F., clerk	68y	W	Md.	09 SEP 1860	Congressional
161	Polk, Sarah Cochrane, lady	71y	W	Md.	16 SEP 1859	Congressional
013	Polkinhorn, Edwin	16d	W	D.C.	05 JUL 1855	Methodist
138	Polkinhorn, Jno. Thompson	2y	W	D.C.	14 JAN 1859	Methodist
080	Polkinhorn, Marianna	38y	W	Eng.	22 JUN 1857	Oak Hill
732	Polkinhorn, R.W., gentleman	78y	W	U.S.	28 NOV 1873	Glenwood
146	Polkinhorn, Sarah	54y	W	Md.	17 APR 1859	Glenwood
726	Pollard, Benj.	15m	B	U.S.	29 OCT 1873	
529	Pollard, Eddy	1y	C	D.C.	25 JUL 1871	Union
631	Pollard, Ellen E.	1y	W	U.S.	16 OCT 1872	Congressional*
720	Pollard, Elliza	2m	C	D.C.	23 SEP 1873	
737	Pollard, John	4m	C	U.S.	25 DEC 1873	Young Mens
515	Pollard, Lucy Ann	1y	C	D.C.	03 MAR 1871	Union
309	Pollard, Margaret	12d	W	D.C.	23 APR 1868	Mt. Olivet
733	Pollard, Moses, laborer	30y	C	U.S.	21 NOV 1873	
331	Pollard, Richard	2y	C	D.C.	19 JUL 1868	
189	Pollard, Richard	5y	W	D.C.	04 SEP 1860	Oak Hill
328	Pollard, Richard	2y	C	D.C.	18 JUL 1868	Young Mens
047	Pollock, William B.	1y	W	D.C.	25 JUN 1856	Glenwood
075	Pollock, William, blacksmith	40y	W	N.Y.	11 APR 1857	Congressional
674	Polly, Maranda	73y	W	U.S.	17 MAR 1873	N.Y.
784	Poney, Josephine, washerwoman	21y	C	U.S.	09 JUL 1874	Potters Field
054	Pool, Elizabeth Kate	6m	W	D.C.	16 AUG 1856	St. Peters
403	Pool, James A.	1y	C	D.C.	23 JUL 1869	Union
675	Pool, Jno. W.	45y	W	U.S.	25 MAR 1873	Glenwood
163	Pool, Lewis, painter	37y	W	D.C.	04 OCT 1859	Mt. Olivet
724	Pool, Mary Elizabeth	37y	W	N.C.	16 OCT 1873	Oak Hill
039	Pool, William C.	3y	W	D.C.	09 MAR 1856	St. Peters
181	Poole, Howard Grafton	4m	W	Md.	12 JUN 1860	Rock Creek
603	Poole, Martha	5y	C	D.C.	17 JUN 1872	Small Pox
628	Poole, Mary G.	5y	W	U.S.	26 SEP 1872	Rock Creek
767	Poor, Amelia	58y	W	U.S.	02 MAY 1874	Congressional
245	Poor, P.G.	56y	W	Pa.	03 NOV 1866	Philadelphia, Pa.
199	Pope, C.S., clerk	45y	W	Me.	19 FEB 1861	Mt. Olivet
507	Pope, Edgar C., clerk	28y	W	D.C.	22 FEB 1871	Glenwood
310	Pope, Effie Hamline	1y	W	D.C.	28 APR 1868	Glenwood
202	Pope, Emily H.	9y	W	D.C.	20 APR 1861	Glenwood
013	Pope, John F.	5y	W	D.C.	31 JUL 1855	Congressional
369	Popkins, Henry Winter	9y	W	U.S.	18 JAN 1869	Congressional
401	Porning, Margaret	1d			08 JUL 1869	Young Mens
225	Pornum, Mrs., child of	7m			19 JUN 1866	
620	Port, Bertha	34y	W	Ger.	04 AUG 1872	Glenwood
464	Port, John	7m	W	D.C.	06 JUL 1870	Glenwood
108	Portch, Precious	68y	W	Va.	26 MAR 1858	Congressional
526	Porter, Ann	75y	C	Md.	04 JUL 1871	Washington
014	Porter, Danl. P., clerk	67y	W	Va.	17 JUL 1855	Congressional
142	Porter, Denton S., painter	41y	W	D.C.	11 FEB 1859	Washington Asylum
117	Porter, Elizabeth R.	67y	W	Va.	25 JUN 1858	Congressional
362	Porter, Geo.	2y	C	D.C.	08 NOV 1868	Washington Asylum
015	Porter, Mary Roberta	9m	W	D.C.	29 JUL 1855	Methodist, 14th St.

Page	Name	Age	Race	Birth	Death Date	Burial Ground
029	Porter, Priscilla C.	28y	W	Va.*	04 NOV 1855	Alexandria, Va.
585	Porter, Robt.	1y	W	D.C.	10 MAR 1872	
053	Porter, Rufena Ithella	1y	W	Mass.	27 AUG 1856	Methodist
102	Porter, Thomas W.	8m	W	D.C.	20 JAN 1858	Foundry
019	Porter, Wm. T., painter	42y	W	Md.	19 AUG 1855	Methodist, 14th St.
132	Porter, [blank]	Still	W	D.C.	06 NOV 1858	Congressional
132	Porter, [blank]	Still	W	D.C.	06 NOV 1858	Congressional
774	Porterigg, Lottie O.	8d	W	U.S.	24 JUN 1874	Congressional
154	Ports, Adam S.C.	1y	W	D.C.	15 JUL 1859	Congressional
632	Posey, Catharine	56y	W	U.S.	20 OCT 1872	Congressional*
381	Posey, Catharine Moore	3y	W	Md.	27 MAR 1869	Md.
373	Posey, Charles, body servant	19y	C		27 JAN 1869	Mt. Olivet
213	Posey, Charles F.	1y	C	D.C.	27 FEB 1866	Harmony
450	Posey, Charles, laborer	25y	W	D.C.	07 APR 1870	Mt. Olivet
332	Posey, Clara Emily	2m	W	D.C.	12 JUL 1868	Md.
043	Posey, Ellen	53y	C	Md.	28 APR 1856	Foundry
342	Posey, Emma I.	1y	C	D.C.	26 AUG 1868	Harmony
431	Posey, Emma Jane	1y	C		30 DEC 1869	Harmony
028	Posey, Francis	60y	C	D.C.	26 OCT 1855	St. Patricks
071	Posey, Henry	5m	C		17 FEB 1857	Harmony
054	Posey, James	1y	C	D.C.	06 AUG 1856	Young Mens
767	Posey, John H.	1y	W	U.S.	30 MAY 1874	Congressional
392	Posey, Julia	1y	C		11 MAY 1869	Mt. Olivet
083	Posey, Mary	1y	C		20 JUL 1857	Foundry
060	Posey, Rebecca, child of	Still	W		08 OCT 1856	Foundry
226	Posey, Richard, child of	1y	C		27 JUN 1866	Harmony (new)
617	Post, Grove, farmer	89y	W	U.S.	09 AUG 1872	Oneida, N.Y.
507	Post, Wm. L., clerk	63y	W	Pa.	26 FEB 1871	Montrose, Pa.
760	Posy, Molly	21y	C	U.S.	15 APR 1874	
202	Posy, Richmond	63y	C	D.C.	22 APR 1861	Mt. Olivet
735	Pote, Bella Irene	1y	W	U.S.	11 DEC 1873	Congressional*
266	Pote, Mary	50y	W	Va.	26 JUL 1867	Congressional
499	Pote, Phil	3y	W	D.C.	05 JAN 1871	Congressional
680	Poter, Thos., infant child of		W	U.S.	10 APR 1873	Congressional*
024	Potergal, John	15d	W	D.C.	10 SEP 1855	
658	Potsler, Kate	18m	W		04 JAN 1873	Prospect Hill
461	Potter, Albert I.	6m	W	D.C.	29 JUL 1870	Congressional
103	Potter, Henrietta R.	72y	W	Md.	29 JAN 1858	Baltimore, Md.
542	Potter, Jessie W.	21y	W	D.C.	25 OCT 1871	Congressional
614	Potts, John	54y	W	U.S.	24 JUL 1872	
095	Potts, John	70y	W		29 OCT 1857	Georgetown
170	Potts, Mary A.	64y	W	U.S.	20 JAN 1860	Presbyterian
659	Potzler, Johanna	3y	W	U.S.	15 JAN 1873	Prospect Hill
307	Potzler, Mr., child of	Still	W	D.C.	21 APR 1868	Prospect Hill
784	Poulton, William, cooper	73y	W	Eng.	21 JUL 1874	Glenwood
379	Pous, Julia	55y	W	Mrca.	26 MAR 1869	Congressional
367	Powell, Ada	3y	B	D.C.	30 DEC 1868	Washington Asylum
640	Powell, Catherine	66y	C	U.S.	14 DEC 1872	Small Pox*
553	Powell, Charles, laborer	42y	C	D.C.	08 JAN 1872	Washington
586	Powell, J.H.	76y	W	D.C.	17 MAR 1872	Congressional
247	Powell, John	70y	C		24 DEC 1866	Western
080	Powell, Mary	5m	W	D.C.	18 JUN 1857	Glenwood
587	Powell, Virginia	28y	C	U.S.	20 MAR 1872	
613	Powell, W.A.	2y	C	U.S.	26 JUL 1872	
346	Powell, William	34y	C	Va.	24 AUG 1868	Freedmen's Hospital
227	Powell, Willie	4m	W	D.C.	04 JUL 1866	Congressional
639	Powell, Wm.	26y	C	U.S.	05 DEC 1872	Small Pox*
589	Powell, Wm. A.	3y	C	D.C.	29 MAR 1872	

Page	Name	Age	Race	Birth	Death Date	Burial Ground
544	Powell, Wm. A.	11m	W	D.C.	04 NOV 1871	Congressional
167	Powell, [blank]	6m	C	D.C.	11 DEC 1859	Western
074	Powell, [blank]	12y	C		28 MAR 1857	Western
762	Powels, Josephine	31y	C	U.S.	29 APR 1874	Mt. Olivet
521	Power, Annie	1y	W	D.C.	03 JUN 1871	Mt. Olivet
117	Power, James, bar keeper	19y	W	Md.	26 JUN 1858	Baltimore, Md.
182	Power, Mary E.	5d	W	D.C.	24 JUN 1860	Mt. Olivet
098	Powers, Ann	65y	W	Md.	15 DEC 1857	Congressional
292	Powers, Ann, Mrs.	73y	W	D.C.	16 JAN 1868	Congressional
784	Powers, Anna P.	35y	W	Unk.	18 JUL 1874	
604	Powers, Eleanor	3y	C	D.C.	14 JUN 1872	Ebenezer
530	Powers, Eugene	2y	C	Conn.	31 JUL 1871	Ebenezer
300	Powers, James	10d	C	D.C.	16 MAR 1868	Alms House
663	Powers, Louisa	27y	C	U.S.	21 JAN 1873	Small Pox
338	Powers, Nancy	3y	C		23 AUG 1868	Washington Asylum
599	Powers, Saml.	55y	C	U.S.	21 MAY 1872	Unknown
519	Powers, W.	41y	W	D.C.	16 MAY 1871	Receiving Vault
292a	Powls, [Infant]	1y	C	D.C.*	19 JAN 1868	Mt. Zion
253	Praten, Elizabeth	26y	C	Md.	25 FEB 1867	Baltimore, Md.
120	Prater, Isabella	4y	C	D.C.	08 JUL 1858	Washington Asylum
528	Prater, Norris	4m	W	D.C.	13 JUL 1871	Methodist
324	Prather, A.	1y	W	D.C.	14 JUL 1868	Ebenezer
311	Prather, Alethia	73y	W	Md.	30 APR 1868	Congressional
038	Prather, Benjamin A.	1m	W	D.C.	16 MAR 1856	Ebenezer
038	Prather, Elizabeth A.	18y	W	Md.	13 MAR 1856	Baltimore, Md.
132	Prather, Ellen	73y	W	Md.	12 NOV 1858	Glenwood
212	Prather, H.D., contractor	59y	W	Md.	20 FEB 1866	Glenwood
167	Prather, Mary	15y	W	D.C.	17 DEC 1859	Ebenezer
606	Prather, Sarah J.	2m	W	D.C.	16 JUN 1872	Congressional*
554	Prather, Thomas [sic]	55y	W	U.S.	18 JAN 1872	Glenwood
784	Prather, William G.	4m	W	U.S.	30 JUL 1874	Congressional*
585	Prather, York, laborer	70y	C	Md.	09 MAR 1872	Asylum
551	Prather, [blank]	70y	W	D.C.	— DEC 1871	
292	Pratt, Bernard H.	71y	W	Prus.	09 JAN 1868	German Catholic
760	Pratt, Delia Ann	3y	C	U.S.	05 APR 1874	
357	Pratt, Ellen	Still	B	D.C.	18 OCT 1868	Washington Asylum
696	Pratt, Ida	8y	C	D.C.	09 JUN 1873	Washington Asylum
280	Pratt, Josephine	19y	C	D.C.	03 OCT 1867	Harmony
455	Pratt, Lucy	7y	C	Va.	19 MAY 1870	Beckett's
617	Pratt, Mary	14m	C	U.S.	03 AUG 1872	
416	Pratt, Mary J.	1y	C		13 SEP 1869	
646	Pratt, Thomas, seaman	65y	W	U.S.	30 DEC 1872	Congressional*
754	Pratt, William	4m	W	U.S.	02 MAR 1874	Mt. Olivet
445	Prender, Sarah Anne	26y	W	Ire.	03 MAR 1870	Glenwood
317	Prenskest, Philip	1y	W	D.C.	18 JUN 1868	Prospect Hill
706	Prentiss, Chas. E., children	3h	W	D.C.	16 JUL 1873	Washington
545	Prentiss, Sarah Ann	64y	W	D.C.	19 NOV 1871	Glenwood
660	Preroan, Wm.	28y	W	U.S.	18 JAN 1873	Glenwood
494	Prescott, Frances A.	7y	W	N.H.	16 DEC 1870	Glenwood
074	Preston, John T., gentleman	31y	W	D.C.	22 MAR 1857	Congressional
546	Price, Addie	6m	W	Fla.	29 NOV 1871	
238	Price, Ann		C	Md.	27 SEP 1866	Harmony
374	Price, Ann J., housewife	61y	W	D.C.	18 FEB 1869	Congressional
524	Price, Elisabeth	6m			23 JUN 1871	
147	Price, Elizabeth	64y	W	Pa.	22 APR 1859	Philadelphia, Pa.
346	Price, Emeline	2y	C		08 AUG 1868	Freedmen's Hospital
643	Price, Emma	2y	C	U.S.	11 DEC 1872	Ebenezer
093	Price, Ephy, wife		W	Md.	14 OCT 1857	Congressional*

District of Columbia Interments (Index to Deaths), 1855-1874

Page	Name	Age	Race	Birth	Death Date	Burial Ground
514	Price, Etta	3y	C	U.S.	25 MAR 1871	Ebenezer
611	Price, Geo.	1y	C	U.S.	23 JUL 1872	
661	Price, George, laborer	25y	C	U.S.	29 JAN 1873	
525	Price, Harry	8y	W		26 JUN 1871	Va.
292	Price, Ida Jane	2m		D.C.	16 JAN 1868	Young Mens
705	Price, Jas. H.	7m	C	D.C.	19 JUL 1873	
413	Price, John	21y	C	Md.	23 AUG 1869	Washington Asylum
155	Price, John	33y	W	Pa.	29 JUL 1859	Washington Asylum
404	Price, John H.	9m	C	D.C.	05 JUL 1869	Washington Asylum
740	Price, Joseph, laborer	69y	C	U.S.	05 JAN 1874	
268	Price, Leila B.	11y	W	D.C.	01 AUG 1867	Congressional
473	Price, Lillie	5m	C	D.C.	19 AUG 1870	Ebenezer
343	Price, Mary	1y	C	D.C.	14 AUG 1868	Washington Asylum
714	Price, Mary	27y	C	Md.	30 AUG 1873	Washington Asylum
342	Price, Mary	1y	C	D.C.	14 AUG 1868	Young Mens
484	Price, Mary J.	2y	W	D.C.	21 OCT 1870	Congressional
714	Price, Mary, servant	20y	C	U.S.	31 AUG 1873	
095	Price, Mrs.	39y	W	Va.	24 OCT 1857	Holmead
366	Price, Sophia	3y	B	D.C.	31 DEC 1868	Union
636	Price, Thomas, policeman		W	U.S.	09 NOV 1872	
586	Price, W.J.	1y	W	U.S.	15 MAR 1872	Congressional*
659	Price, Walter	11d	C	U.S.	11 JAN 1873	Mt. Olivet
464	Price, William	2y	W	D.C.	29 JUL 1870	Alexandria, Va.
645	Price, Willie	3y	C	U.S.	26 DEC 1872	
718	Price, Willie	23m	C	D.C.	13 SEP 1873	Young Mens
638	Price, Wm.	17y	C	U.S.	06 NOV 1872	Washington Asylum
170	Price, [blank]	2y	W	D.C.	23 JAN 1860	Congressional
537	Primis, Catharine E.	4y	C	D.C.	22 SEP 1871	Mt. Olivet
280	Prince, Ada	3y	W	Md.	12 OCT 1867	Baltimore, Md.
232	Prince, Granville James	7m	W	D.C.	22 AUG 1866	Glenwood
582	Princehorn, Maryann	2y	W	D.C.	22 FEB 1872	Glenwood
784	Prindle, Annie E.	30y	W	U.S.	25 JUL 1874	Glenwood
619	Prindle, Thos.	40y	C	U.S.	23 AUG 1872	
233	Pringle, Ann		C		21 AUG 1866	Harmony
784	Prinzhorn, Lizzie	38y	C	U.S.	27 JUL 1874	Glenwood/Rock Creek
694	Prior, Mary B.	39y	W	Conn.	02 JUN 1873	
391	Prior, Thomas O., carpenter	45y	W	N.Y.	08 MAY 1869	Mt. Olivet
052	Prior, [blank]	4m	W	D.C.	30 JUL 1856	Oak Hill
107	Pristy, George E.	4y	W	Pa.	10 MAR 1858	
034	Pritchard, Chas. Wm.	4m	W	D.C.	20 JAN 1856	Not Reported
688	Pritchard, Jas. H.	14m	C	U.S.	14 MAY 1873	
710	Pritchard, Margaret, Miss	53y	W	D.C.	01 AUG 1873	Congressional
427	Pritchard, Mary	2y	C		11 NOV 1869	
499	Pritchard, Sarah, housewife	95y	W	Va.	14 JAN 1871	Congressional
527	Pritchett, Elisabeth	81y	W	D.C.	07 JUL 1871	Congressional*
292a	Probey, Mary E.	57y	W	D.C.*	08 JAN 1868	Vault
628	Probey, Mary, housekeeper	34y	W	U.S.	16 SEP 1872	
425	Procise, Frank C.	2y	W	D.C.	22 NOV 1869	Congressional
594	Procise, Virginia F.	7y	W	D.C.	29 APR 1872	Congressional
165	Procter, Henrietta	66y	C	Md.	20 NOV 1859	Mt. Olivet
437	Proctor, Catharine S.	50y	W		28 JAN 1870	Glenwood
500	Proctor, Chas. S.	5y	C	D.C.	02 JAN 1871	Harmony
712	Proctor, Cordelia Ann	6m	C	D.C.	17 AUG 1873	Harmony
463	Proctor, Francis G.	3m	W	D.C.	05 JUL 1870	Mt. Olivet
058	Proctor, James A.	2y	C	D.C.	24 SEP 1856	Young Mens
638	Proctor, Mary	73y	C	U.S.	09 NOV 1872	
784	Proctor, Nellie C.	3m	W	U.S.	09 JUL 1874	Glenwood
383	Proctor, Sarah	7m	C	D.C.	06 MAR 1869	Washington Asylum

District of Columbia Interments (Index to Deaths), 1855-1874

Page	Name	Age	Race	Birth	Death Date	Burial Ground
232	Prof, Thomas, editor	55y	W	Va.	26 AUG 1866	Mt. Olivet
294	Prosise, Samuel O.	3m	W	D.C.	26 FEB 1868	Congressional
624	Prosneham, John, laborer	55y	W	Ire.	20 SEP 1872	
130	Prosperi, Frances E.	5m	W	D.C.	— OCT 1858	Congressional
003	Prosperi, John T.	5m	W	D.C.	28 FEB 1855	
071	Prosperi, Josephine	9m	W	D.C.	13 FEB 1857	Congressional
743	Proud, Mary	70y	W	Ire.	27 JAN 1874	Mt. Olivet
238	Provost, Sarah M.	11y	W	N.J.	26 SEP 1866	Trenton, N.J.
708	Pruce, Mary L.	15m	C	D.C.	28 JUL 1873	Washington Asylum
682	Pruden, Winthrop	6m	W	U.S.	23 APR 1873	Congressional*
354	Pruett, Frankie	8m	W		03 OCT 1868	Congressional
467	Pruett, May	21d	W		27 JUL 1870	Congressional
303	Pruett, William, carpenter	39y	W	Va.	04 MAR 1868	Congressional
688	Pruett, Woodson, Mr., laborer	32y	W	U.S.	18 MAY 1873	
675	Pruit, Woodson M.	12m	W	U.S.	23 MAR 1873	Congressional
740	Prusell, Elizabeth	41y	W	U.S.	05 JAN 1874	Congressional
552	Pryer, Sally	65y	C	Va.	03 JAN 1872	Washington
247	Pryor, Virginia	13y	C		04 DEC 1866	Harmony
144	Pugh, Alice Mary		W	Ohio	21 MAR 1859	Cincinnati, Ohio
203	Pugh, Julia	29y	W		30 MAY 1861	Congressional
585	Pulaski, Alonzo F.	5y	W	D.C.	11 MAR 1872	Mt. Olivet
430	Puley, Euphemia, Mrs.	71y	W	Conn.	02 DEC 1869	
726	Puliski, Edward	1y	W	U.S.	28 OCT 1873	Glenwood
499	Pullen, Anne	29y	W	D.C.	27 JAN 1871	Congressional
461	Pullen, John	1m	W	D.C.	15 JUL 1870	Congressional
407	Pullin, Mr., child of		W		18 AUG 1869	Congressional
449	Pullin, William L., tinner	25y	W	Scot.	08 APR 1870	Congressional*
104	Pullison, Mary, servant	16y	C	D.C.	07 FEB 1858	St. Patricks
727	Pully, Eliza Ann	50y	W	U.S.	02 OCT 1873	Congressional*
618	Pulson, Arazona	2y	W	U.S.	05 AUG 1872	Holmead
553	Pumphrey, Alfred M.	3y	W	D.C.	10 JAN 1872	Congressional*
193	Pumphrey, Ann	1y	W	D.C.	12 NOV 1860	Congressional
477	Pumphrey, Blanch	9m	W	D.C.	26 SEP 1870	Congressional
590	Pumphrey, Dennis	75y	W	Md.	02 APR 1872	Congressional
386	Pumphrey, Emma [Gates]	33y	W	D.C.	08 APR 1869	Congressional*
249	Pumphrey, Fredk. L.	9m	W	D.C.	01 JAN 1867	Congressional
395	Pumphrey, Geo. M.	5m	W	D.C.	27 JUN 1869	Glenwood
349	Pumphrey, Hattie Connelly	5m	W	D.C.	11 SEP 1868	Oak Hill
549	Pumphrey, Jas. W.	5y	W	D.C.	19 DEC 1871	Congressional
376	Pumphrey, Judson E., farmer	69y	W	Md.	14 FEB 1869	Longold Fields, Md.
128	Pumphrey, Levi, livery stable kpr.	68y	W	Md.	25 SEP 1858	Congressional
172	Pumphrey, Mary Ann	48y	W	Md.	04 FEB 1860	County
224	Pumphrey, Mary J.	30y	W	D.C.	15 JUN 1866	Methodist Epis.
316	Pumphrey, Robt.		C		c.15 MAY 1868	Alms House
326	Pumphrey, Willie	1y	W	D.C.	04 JUL 1868	Congressional
590	Pumphrey, Wm.	6d	W	D.C.	06 APR 1872	Congressional
385	Pumphrey. [blank]	12d	W	D.C.	05 APR 1869	Congressional
024	Pumphry, Mary E.	1y	W	D.C.	28 SEP 1855	Congressional
708	Puper, Henry, baker	27y	W	Ger.	17 JUL 1873	
429	Purcell, H.R.	21y	W		17 DEC 1869	Congressional
151	Purcell, James B.	2y	W	D.C.	20 JUN 1859	Congressional*
053	Purcell, James K.	6y	W		18 AUG 1856	Congressional
321	Purcell, John, laborer	28y	W	Ire.	22 JUN 1868	Mt. Olivet*
741	Purcell, Josephine	6m	W	U.S.	10 JAN 1874	Mt. Olivet
723	Purcell, Martin, foreman	38y	W	Ire.	01 OCT 1873	Chicago, Ill.
110	Purcell, Mary	1y	W	D.C.	05 APR 1858	St. Patricks
157	Purcell, Mary	2y	W	D.C.	10 AUG 1859	Western
549	Purcell, Wm. F., lawyer	60y	W	Va.	23 DEC 1871	Congressional

District of Columbia Interments (Index to Deaths), 1855-1874

Page	Name	Age	Race	Birth	Death Date	Burial Ground
249	Purcell, [blank]	Still	W	D.C.	03 JAN 1867	Mt. Olivet
634	Purdon, Joseph S., painter	28y	W	U.S.	29 OCT 1872	St. Patricks
369	Purdy, Henry C., merchant	37y	W	D.C.	09 JAN 1869	Congressional
429	Purdy, Jno., Jr., infant of	Still	W		20 DEC 1869	Congressional
476	Purdy, Mary	35y	W	Amer.	11 SEP 1870	Glenwood
476	Purdy, Mary	1m	W	Amer.	30 SEP 1870	Glenwood
041	Purdy, Richd. G., boot maker	38y	W	Md.	03 APR 1856	Glenwood
525	Purle, Emma	11d	C	D.C.	27 JUN 1871	
725	Purman, Mattie L.	20min	W	D.C.	20 OCT 1873	Mt. Olivet
275	Purnell, A.E.	2y	C		07 SEP 1867	Philadelphia, Pa.
529	Purnell, JOhn	42y	C	Md.	28 JUL 1871	Harmony
710	Purnette, Madison, laborer	29y	C	Va.	01 AUG 1873	
506	Pursell, Thos., merchant	70y	W	Eng.	26 FEB 1871	Congressional
312	Putnam, William F.	45y	W	N.H.	01 MAY 1868	N.H.
307	Putnam, Wm. F.	48y	W	N.H.	30 APR 1868	N.H.
661	Putney, Hester A.	58y	W	U.S.	28 JAN 1873	Baltimore, Md.
603	Pye, John, laborer	23y	C	Md.	13 JUN 1872	Small Pox
349	Pyfer, William Henry	1y	W	Md.	03 SEP 1868	Baltimore, Md.
318	Pyle, Adolphus Newton	10m	W	U.S.	27 JUN 1868	Congressional
285	Pyles, Thomas E., storekeeper	45y	W	Md.	08 DEC 1867	Congressional
154	Pyne, Ann E.	9m	W	D.C.	19 JUL 1859	Mt. Olivet
203	Pywell, Wallace E.	2y	W	D.C.	13 MAY 1861	Holmead
428	Pywell, Wm. R., infant of	Still	W		25 NOV 1869	Glenwood

Page	Name	Age	Race	Birth	Death Date	Burial Ground
	Q					
168	Quackenbush, Nicholas	4m	W	D.C.	28 DEC 1859	Oak Hill
668	Quah-quah-luppe-quah	56y	I	U.S.	22 FEB 1873	Congressional
068	Quaile, Daniel, gardener	45y	W	Ger.	01 JAN 1857	Holmead
744	Qualls, Henry, laborer	19y	C	U.S.	31 JAN 1874	
682	Quals, Mary	23y	C	U.S.	27 APR 1873	Holmead
055	Quantille, Alwina	4m	W	D.C.	16 AUG 1856	
405	Queen, Anne	14d	C	D.C.	27 JUL 1869	Washington Asylum
458	Queen, Chas. J.	48y	W	D.C.	27 JUN 1870	Queen's Chapel
143	Queen, Chas. R., Dr.	34y	W	D.C.	04 MAR 1859	Catholic
626	Queen, Louisa M.	38y	W	U.S.	14 SEP 1872	
494	Queen, Maria, washwoman	80y	C	Md.	19 DEC 1870	Mt. Olivet
279	Queen, Martha	6d	C	D.C.	24 OCT 1867	Beckett's
502	Queen, Rebecca	8m	C	D.C.	30 JAN 1871	Mt. Olivet
172	Queen, Roger, barber	28y	C	Md.	19 FEB 1860	Harmony
117	Queen, Thomas, clothes dyer	33y	C	Md.	28 JUN 1858	St. Patricks
133	Queen, [blank]	80y			18 NOV 1858	St. Matthews
414	Queen, [illegible], clerk [sic]	2y	W	Eng.	19 SEP 1869	Congressional
703	Quid, Mary M.	7m	W	D.C.	19 JUL 1873	Mt. Olivet
392	Quiet, Archie	2m	C		04 MAY 1869	Young Mens
720	Quiet, Elizabeth, servant	40y	C	Va.	26 SEP 1873	
489	Quigg, Mary	Still	W		01 NOV 1870	Glenwood
151	Quigley, Anna	10y	W	D.C.	22 JUN 1859	Mt. Olivet
065	Quigley, Edward, butcher	47y	W	D.C.	08 DEC 1856	St. Peters
583	Quigley, Hattie	1y	W	D.C.	27 FEB 1872	Mt. Olivet
393	Quigley, J.	50y	W	Pa.	22 MAY 1869	Washington Asylum
252	Quigley, Mary	Still	W	D.C.	02 FEB 1867	Mt. Olivet
038	Quigley, Michael, bar keeper	46y	W	Ire.	25 MAR 1856	St. Patricks
046	Quigley, Owen		W	Ire.	03 JUN 1856	St. Patricks
525	Quigley, Sarah E.	22y	W	Va.	26 JUN 1871	Congressional*
605	Quill, Bridget	2y	W	U.S.	09 JUN 1872	Asylum
592	Quill, Dahl, farmer	89y	W	Ire.	14 APR 1872	
762	Quill, Ellen, domestic	31y	W	Ire.	29 APR 1874	Mt. Olivet
240	Quill, Patrick	61y	W	Ire.	01 OCT 1866	Mt. Olivet
521	Quilla, James	1y	C	D.C.	08 JUN 1871	
098	Quin, Edmond, laborer	34y	W	Ire.	02 DEC 1857	St. Peters
444	Quincey, Susan, Miss	50y	W	D.C.	22 MAR 1870	Congressional
359	Quincy, Nancy S.	60y	W	Mass.	20 NOV 1868	Congressional
204	Quinlan, Biddy	28y	W	Ire.	16 JUN 1861	Mt. Olivet
288	Quinlan, Edward	25y	W	Ire.	11 DEC 1867	Mt. Olivet
204	Quinlan, Mary	1y	W	D.C.	16 JUN 1861	Mt. Olivet
183	Quinlan, Robert, soldier	23y	W	N.Y.	17 JUN 1860	Congressional
158	Quinn, Charles	8y	W	U.S.	16 AUG 1859	Mt. Olivet
405	Quinn, Charles	45y	W	Ire.	12 JUL 1869	Mt. Olivet
614	Quinn, Emmett	54y	W	U.S.	26 JUL 1872	
121	Quinn, Jno. Morris	1y	W	Md.	14 JUL 1858	St. Peters
629	Quinn, Maggie	1y	W	U.S.	11 OCT 1872	
130	Quinn, Mary	1y	W	D.C.	17 OCT 1858	St. Peters
213	Quinn, Mr., child at		W		05 FEB 1866	Mt. Olivet
076	Quinn, Patrick	1y	W	D.C.	30 APR 1857	St. Peters
481	Quinn, [blank]	1m	W	D.C.	05 OCT 1870	Mt. Olivet
666	Quivers, John	16m	C	U.S.	05 FEB 1873	

District of Columbia Interments (Index to Deaths), 1855-1874

Page	Name	Age	Race	Birth	Death Date	Burial Ground
R						
113	Raab, Catharine	3y	W	D.C.	11 MAY 1858	German Catholic
464	Raba, Lou	6m	W	D.C.	23 JUL 1870	Prospect Hill
676	Rabbes, John, shoemaker	39y	W	Ire.	30 MAR 1873	Glenwood
470	Rabbit, Eugene D.	1y	W		03 AUG 1870	Congressional
021	Rabbit, [blank]	14m	W	D.C.	14 AUG 1855	St. Patricks
247	Rabbitt, John, blacksmith	21y	W	D.C.	10 DEC 1866	Congressional
591	Rabbitt, Wm. A.	2y	W	U.S.	27 APR 1872	Small Pox
457	Raber, C.C.	5m	W		11 JUN 1870	Congressional
236	Rabi, John, butcher	52y	W	Ger.	23 SEP 1866	Mt. Olivet
667	Rabillard, Clementine	42y	W	Fra.	10 FEB 1873	Mt. Olivet
168	Raborg, C.W., merchant	38y	W	Pa.	23 DEC 1859	
038	Racks, Matilda	49y	C	Va.	24 MAR 1856	Harmony
033	Radan, James, butcher	38y	W	Md.	09 JAN 1856	Foundry
014	Radcliff, Chas., tollman	63y	W	Md.	21 JUL 1855	St. Peters
425	Raddish, [blank]	1y	W		24 NOV 1869	Congressional
005	Rady, Bartholomew	30y	W	Ire.	16 MAR 1855	St. Matthews
644	Rady, Daniel, laborer	37y	W	Ire.	16 DEC 1872	Mt. Olivet
149	Rady, M.	55y	W	Ire.	29 MAY 1859	Mt. Olivet
016	Rady, Mary	16m	W	D.C.	09 JUL 1855	St. Patricks
004	Rady, Mary Ann	3y		D.C.	21 MAR 1855	St. Patricks
777	Raeder, George	8m	W	U.S.	30 JUN 1874	Prospect Hill
141	Raedy, Jeremiah	6y	W	D.C.	17 FEB 1859	Mt. Olivet
089	Raedy, Michael, shoemaker	60y	W	Ire.	28 AUG 1857	St. Patricks
601	Rafser, Wm., clerk	56y	W	U.S.	29 MAY 1872	Ohio
585	Ragan, Annie	32y	W	D.C.	09 MAR 1872	Congressional
055	Ragan, Dennis	2m	W		24 AUG 1856	St. Patricks
403	Ragan, Dennis	70y	W	Ire.	07 JUL 1869	St. Patricks
671	Ragan, Elizabeth	3y	W	U.S.	10 FEB 1873	Small Pox.*
046	Ragan, Ellen	2y	W		08 JUN 1856	St. Patricks
588	Ragan, J.R.	15y	W	D.C.	25 MAR 1872	Congressional*
308	Ragan, Jennie	2y	W	U.S.	06 APR 1868	Glenwood
357	Ragan, Jno.	54y	W	Va.	03 OCT 1868	Congressional
223	Ragan, Joanna	4m	W	D.C.	05 JUN 1866	Mt. Olivet
718	Ragan, Jose. H.	33y	W		14 SEP 1873	Congressional
209	Ragan, Louisa	21y	W	Md.	03 JAN 1866	Congressional
055	Ragan, Mary	1y	W	D.C.	25 AUG 1856	St. Patricks
191	Ragan, Mary A.	26y	W	Ire.	07 OCT 1860	Mt. Olivet
316	Ragan, Mr., child of	Still	W	D.C.	19 MAY 1868	Holyrood
624	Ragan, [blank]		W	U.S.	18 SEP 1872	Congressional
112	Ragen, Anne	5y	W	D.C.	21 APR 1858	St. Patricks
332	Raglan, James G.	21d	W	D.C.	28 JUL 1868	Western
518	Rahlert, Edwin F.	2y	W	D.C.	05 MAY 1871	Washington
040	Railey, Benedict	65y	W	Md.	22 MAR 1856	St. Peters
274	Rainer, John, restaurant keeper	32y	W	Pa.	10 SEP 1867	Philadelphia, Pa.
408	Rainey, George Jerome	4m	W	Md.	30 AUG 1869	Mt. Olivet
748	Rainey, Jane	4m	W	U.S.	14 FEB 1874	
135	Rainey, Robert, book binder	20y	W	D.C.*	02 DEC 1858	Georgetown
430	Rainy, John, clerk	25y	W	D.C.	10 DEC 1869	Red Hill
610	Raley, Martha	20y	W	D.C.	10 JUN 1867	
552	Ralls, George	27y	C	Va.	08 JAN 1872	Washington
488	Ramphff, Sophia	72y	W	Md.	27 NOV 1870	Methodist
761	Ramsdell, Hayward	3y	W	U.S.	19 APR 1874	Oak Hill
294	Ramsdell, W.C.	1m	W	U.S.	26 FEB 1868	Oak Hill
104	Ramsey, James	37y	W		06 FEB 1858	Frederick, Md.
068	Ramsey, [blank]	4m	W		16 JAN 1857	Frederick, Md.
644	Rand, Edward	1m	W	U.S.	20 DEC 1872	Glenwood
767	Rand, Louisa	29y	W	U.S.	09 MAY 1874	Glenwood

Page	Name	Age	Race	Birth	Death Date	Burial Ground
089	Rand, Samuel F., clerk	37y	W	Me.	14 AUG 1857	Congressional
243	Randall, A.F., infant of	9m	W	D.C.	25 NOV 1866	Congressional
362	Randall, Alice	7d	C	D.C.	02 NOV 1868	Washington Asylum
520	Randall, Beverly, laborer	70y	C	Md.	25 MAY 1871	Potters Field
487	Randall, Jessie	3m	W	D.C.	21 NOV 1870	Congressional
293	Randall, Josiah	2m	W	D.C.*	26 MAR 1868	Philadelphia, Pa.
528	Randall, Mary Ann	28y	W	D.C.	21 JUL 1871	Glenwood
629	Randall, Nancy	67y	W	Ire.	04 OCT 1872	Congressional*
116	Randall, Nich. A., clerk	48y	W		21 JUN 1858	Congressional
258	Randall, Richd.	69y	W	Va.	03 APR 1867	Glenwood
597	Randall, Sarah, servant	40y	C	U.S.	25 MAY 1872	Washington
605	Randall, Wm. W.	72y	W	Va.	22 JUN 1872	Glenwood
674	Randell, Sarah W.	10y	W	U.S.	13 MAR 1873	Glenwood
602	Randle, Wm., bricklayer	50y	W	U.S.	26 MAY 1872	Congressional
382	Randolph, Charles	7m	C	D.C.	02 MAR 1869	Young Mens
377	Randolph, Clara	1y	C	D.C.	11 FEB 1869	Washington Asylum
734	Randolph, Henry A.	1y	W	U.S.	06 DEC 1873	Boston, Mass.
005	Randolph, Margaret E.	23y	W	D.C.	23 MAR 1855	Oak Hill
378	Randolph, Nathaniel, laborer	80y	C	Md.	25 FEB 1869	Freedmen's Hospital
312	Randolph, William B., clerk	78y	W	Va.	15 MAY 1868	Oak Hill
015	Randolph, [blank]	3m	W	D.C.	08 JUL 1855	Oak Hill
393	Raney, J.C.	50y	C		29 MAY 1869	Washington Asylum
619	Rankin, Edwd.	4y	C	U.S.	10 AUG 1872	
316	Rankin, Fanny, cook	55y	C	Va.	02 MAY 1868	Young Mens
689	Raper, Pauline	4m	W	U.S.	26 MAY 1873	Glenwood
557	Rapp, Henry	1y	W	U.S.	05 FEB 1872	Prospect Hill
614	Rapp, John	56y	W	Ger.	09 JUL 1872	
236	Rarden, Cath.	35y	W	Ire.	11 SEP 1866	Mt. Olivet
394	Rarden, Rebecca	7y	W	D.C.	22 JUN 1869	Congressional
291	Rasse, Rose	2y	W	D.C.	02 JAN 1868	Mt. Olivet
344	Ratcliff, Albert	6m	C		10 AUG 1868	Holmead
358	Ratcliff, Maraa	91y	C	Va.	19 OCT 1868	Holmead
290	Ratcliff, Miss	55y	W		07 JAN 1868	Carroll Chapel
477	Ratlif, John T.	1y	C	D.C.	12 SEP 1870	Holmead
449	Ratliff, [blank]	2y	W		19 APR 1870	Congressional
295	Ratrie, Rhoda	33y	W	Md.	13 FEB 1868	Congressional
419	Ratrie, Robert, cabinet maker	67y	W		10 OCT 1869	Congressional
507	Ratti, Mary	85y	W	Italy	12 FEB 1871	St. Marys
047	Raub, G.B.	5m	W		29 JUN 1856	Congressional*
681	Rauh, George H., shoemaker	68y	W	Ger.	17 APR 1873	Congressional*
529	Raulings, Martha	27y	C	Md.	27 JUL 1871	
637	Rault, Grace		W	U.S.	— NOV 1872	
374	Rawlett, Charles	2y	W		21 FEB 1869	Congressional
419	Rawlings, David	58y	W		24 OCT 1869	Congressional
165	Rawlings, David, laborer	42y	C	Va.	11 NOV 1859	Washington Asylum
002	Rawlings, Edwd.	57d	W	D.C.	2_ JAN 1855	Methodist, East
432	Rawlings, H.	40y	C	D.C.	31 DEC 1869	Washington Asylum
013	Rawlings, Isaac	9y	W	D.C.	14 JUL 1855	Methodist, East
018	Rawlins, Edwd., clerk in PO	60y	W	Va.	02 AUG 1855	Glenwood
735	Rawlins, Fannie K.	43y	W	U.S.	10 DEC 1873	Congressional
461	Rawlins, James, laborer	76y	W	Va.	22 JUL 1870	Congressional
027	Rawlins, Jane E.	6y	W	Md.	18 OCT 1855	Pr. Geo. Co., Md.
415	Rawlins, John A., Sec. of War	39y	W		10 SEP 1869	Congressional
610	Ray, Albert E.	1y	C	U.S.	24 JUL 1872	
228	Ray, Bell	1y	W	D.C.	11 JUL 1866	Congressional
050	Ray, Benjamin, wood sawyer	75y	C	Md.	14 JUL 1856	Young Mens
294	Ray, Bridget	40y	W	Ire.	12 FEB 1868	Holyrood
397	Ray, Clarance	6m	W	D.C.	12 JUN 1869	Baltimore, Md.

District of Columbia Interments (Index to Deaths), 1855-1874

Page	Name	Age	Race	Birth	Death Date	Burial Ground
347	Ray, Ellen	60y	W		21 SEP 1868	Congressional
419	Ray, Isabell	6y	W	D.C.	26 OCT 1869	Congressional
431	Ray, Josiah, bricklayer	72y	W	U.S.	23 DEC 1869	Congressional
344	Ray, Margaret	8m	W	D.C.	14 AUG 1868	Mt. Olivet
286	Ray, Mary		C		— DEC 1867	Alms House
272	Ray, Mary, child of	1d	C		28 AUG 1867	Freedmen's Bureau
500	Ray, Mary H.	26y	W		25 JAN 1871	Bloomington, Ill.
226	Ray, Nicholas	3y	W	D.C.	30 JUN 1866	Congressional
359	Ray, Nicholas B., policeman	36y	W	Pa.	12 NOV 1868	Congressional
698	Ray, Oliver	3½m	C	D.C.	10 JUN 1873	Mt. Olivet
139	Ray, Sarah Emily	3y	W	D.C.	28 JAN 1859	Baltimore, Md.
538	Ray, Susan E.	1y		D.C.	25 SEP 1871	Glenwood
774	Ray, Wm.	7m	C	U.S.	10 JUN 1874	
300	Raybold, S. Harrington, clerk	29y	W	Del.	08 MAR 1868	Oak Hill
158	Raymer, Charles	2m	W	D.C.	13 AUG 1859	Glenwood
482	Raymond, Elmira	1m	C	D.C.	18 OCT 1870	Union
784	Raymond, James	3m	C	U.S.	21 JUL 1874	Potters Field
027	Raymond, John T., coach painter	66y	W		23 OCT 1855	Foundry
378	Raymond, [blank]	14d	W		11 FEB 1869	Mt. Olivet
538	Rayne, Nettie	5m	C	D.C.	26 SEP 1871	Va.
774	Read, Robt., child of	6m	W	U.S.	01 JUN 1874	N.Y.
250	Read, Wm.	4m	C		04 JAN 1867	Young Mens
725	Reade, Ellen, housewife	70y	W	U.S.	22 OCT 1873	Mt. Clivet
124	Reade, Thomas	50y	W	Ire.	17 AUG 1858	Congressional
725	Reading, Frank Russell, clerk	57y	W	Eng.	20 OCT 1873	Oak Hill
761	Reading, Kitty	16y	C	U.S.	19 APR 1874	
033	Readly, Ellen	10m	C	D.C.	11 JAN 1856	Harmony
367	Readman, Henry	60y	B	Va.	02 DEC 1868	Washington Asylum
375	Ready, Catharine	68y	W	Ire.	09 FEB 1869	
703	Ready, Daniel	16m	W	D.C.	08 JUL 1873	Mt. Olivet
326	Ready, Daniel, paver	37y	W	Ire.	24 JUL 1868	Mt. Olivet
601	Ready, James, coachman	36y	W	Ire.	01 MAY 1872	Mt. Olivet
386	Ready, John	21y	W	Amer.	19 APR 1869	Mt. Olivet
015	Ready, Mary	33y	W	Ire.	20 JUL 1855	St. Patricks
226	Ready, Morris	4m	W	D.C.	30 JUN 1866	Mt. Olivet
213	Ready, Morris, laborer	49y	W	Ire.	28 FEB 1866	
234	Ready, [blank]		W		05 SEP 1866	Congressional
643	Reamey, Jane L.	69y	W	Ire.	08 DEC 1872	Glenwood
637	Rearden, M.J.	70y	W	U.S.	05 NOV 1872	Glenwood
087	Reardon, Daniel	18d	W		13 AUG 1857	St. Patricks
463	Reardon, Johanna	1y	W		26 JUL 1870	Mt. Olivet
777	Reardon, Johannah	36y	W	Ire.	30 JUN 1874	Mt. Olivet
256	Reardon, William, laborer	45y	W	Ire.	30 MAR 1867	Mt. Olivet
154	Reardon, [blank]	3m	W	D.C.	16 JUL 1859	Mt. Olivet
549	Reaves, [blank]	Still		D.C.	19 DEC 1871	Congressional
677	Redding, Aron	22y	C	U.S.	20 MAR 1873	Small Pox
624	Reddon, Frank, steward	12y	C	U.S.	07 SEP 1872	
420	Reddy, Martin	1y	W		15 OCT 1869	Mt. Olivet
444	Redfern, Elizabeth	65y	W	Eng.	19 MAR 1870	Rock Creek
110	Redgate, B.C., clerk		W	Md.	05 APR 1858	Oak Hill
444	Redgrave, Helen R.	11m	W		01 MAR 1870	Baltimore, Md.
263	Redgrave, John B.	2y	W	D.C.	02 JUN 1867	Glenwood
082	Redin, Mary, house servant	29y	C	D.C.	10 JUL 1857	St. Matthews
620	Redinger, Edmond	7y	W	U.S.	15 AUG 1872	Glenwood
529	Redman, Eliza Ann	25y	C	Va.	24 JUL 1871	
529	Redman, James H.	6m	C	D.C.	23 JUL 1871	
704	Redman, Laura V.	11m	W	D.C.	26 JUL 1873	Westmoreland Co., Va.
625	Redman, M.A.	6d	W	U.S.	04 SEP 1872	

District of Columbia Interments (Index to Deaths), 1855-1874

Page	Name	Age	Race	Birth	Death Date	Burial Ground
068	Redman, [blank]	39y		Ire.	11 JAN 1857	St. Patricks
660	Redmond, Catherine, servant	76y	W	Ire.	18 JAN 1873	Mt. Olivet
664	Redmond, Celest	20y	W	U.S.	24 JAN 1873	Small Pox*
476	Redmond, John L.	1y	C		04 SEP 1870	
306	Redmond, Juliette	1m	C	D.C.	04 APR 1868	Alms House
138	Redmond, Michael, hostler	22y	W	Ire.	26 JAN 1859	
671	Redmond, Rose	16y	W	U.S.	12 FEB 1873	Small Pox*
664	Redmond, Rosetta	56y	C	U.S.	22 JAN 1873	Small Pox*
096	Redney, Ann M.V.	1y	C	D.C.	06 NOV 1857	Foundry
466	Redwood, S.A.	9m	C	D.C.	20 JUL 1870	Union
580	Reed, A.W.	67y	W	Mass.	10 FEB 1872	
235	Reed, Andrew	58y			18 SEP 1866	Congressional
049	Reed, Charles Howard	19d	W	D.C.	09 JUL 1856	Foundry
020	Reed, Chs. H.	11m	W		13 AUG 1855	Foundry
202	Reed, David Wm.	37y	W	Md.	21 APR 1861	Foundry
662	Reed, Delphia A.	56y	W	U.S.	31 JAN 1873	Congressional
364	Reed, Edmund H.	19m	W	Kan.	23 DEC 1868	Congressional
429	Reed, Elmer		W		27 DEC 1869	Congressional
609	Reed, Geo. A.	11m	W	U.S.	20 JUN 1872	
017	Reed, Geo. H.	1y	C	D.C.	26 JUL 1855	Poor House
714	Reed, George	9m	C		27 AUG 1873	
662	Reed, George Henry	14d	C	U.S.	30 JAN 1873	
102	Reed, Henrietta	20y	C	D.C.*	19 JAN 1858	Young Mens
335a	Reed, Henry, laborer	30y	B	Va.	24 JUL 1868	Washington Asylum
305	Reed, Isaac, painter	62y	W	D.C.	31 MAR 1868	Glenwood
369	Reed, John, infant of		W	D.C.	14 JAN 1869	Congressional
051	Reed, Margarette	38y	W		26 JUL 1856	Congressional
087	Reed, Mary	50y	C	D.C.	10 AUG 1857	
620	Reed, Mary	72y	W	U.S.	06 AUG 1872	Mt. Olivet
637	Reed, Mary	72y	W	U.S.	18 NOV 1872	Peoria, Ill.
074	Reed, Mary	32y	W	Ire.	29 MAR 1857	Western
381	Reed, Mollie	2y	W	D.C.	06 MAR 1869	German Catholic
534	Reed, Mr., laborer	36y	C		31 AUG 1871	
089	Reed, Nancy Patten	70y	W		12 AUG 1857	Foundry
549	Reed, Noah, machinist	47y	W	Va.	23 DEC 1871	Congressional
538	Reed, Rosalie P.	27y	W	U.S.	27 SEP 1871	Congressional
634	Reed, Sarah Ann, nurse	46y	C	U.S.	31 OCT 1872	Young Mens
442	Reed, Sophy	1y	C		02 FEB 1870	Young Mens
755	Reed, Susan	60y	C	U.S.	02 MAR 1874	
509	Reed, Thomas	17y	W	N.Y.	24 FEB 1871	Washington Asylum
330	Reed, Victoria	1y	C	D.C.	22 JUL 1868	Young Mens
666	Reed, William	5y	C	U.S.	03 FEB 1873	
341	Reed, William, baker		W	Scot.	12 AUG 1868	Congressional
218	Reed, [blank]	87y	C		27 APR 1866	Harmony
616a	Reeder, Anna A.	11m	W	U.S.	24 JUL 1872	Congressional
612	Reeder, Grace L.	6m	W	U.S.	23 JUL 1872	
335a	Reeder, Willie				17 JUL 1868	Washington Asylum
279	Reedy, Katy	4m	W	D.C.	19 OCT 1867	Mt. Olivet
286	Reedy, Sarah E.	10m	C	D.C.	18 DEC 1867	
476	Reel, William	2y	W	D.C.	30 SEP 1870	Congressional
496	Reeler, Samuel	80y	C		04 DEC 1870	Beckett's
450	Reesch, Charles	8y	W	Ger.	13 APR 1870	Prospect Hill
731	Reese, Elberta	22y	W	U.S.	23 NOV 1873	Congressional*
174	Reese, John, water purveyor	37y	W	Ger.	06 MAR 1860	Glenwood
469	Reeside, Lucinda	23y	W	D.C.	26 AUG 1870	Glenwood
414	Reeve, John F., clerk	68y	W	N.Y.	30 SEP 1869	Congressional
348	Reeves, Charles L.	9m	W	D.C.	26 SEP 1868	Congressional
113	Reeves, Ellen	56y	W	Md.	13 MAY 1858	Glenwood

District of Columbia Interments (Index to Deaths), 1855-1874

Page	Name	Age	Race	Birth	Death Date	Burial Ground
502	Reeves, John, laborer	48y	C	Va.	16 JAN 1871	Beckett's
644	Reeves, Mark, clerk	40y	W	U.S.	18 DEC 1872	Mt. Holly
191	Reeves, Robert, messenger	77y	W	Eng.	01 OCT 1860	Congressional
748	Regan, Thompson, huxter	36y	W	U.S.	14 FEB 1874	Congressional
111	Regen, Mary	8m	W		18 APR 1858	St. Patricks
243	Reghan, J.	6m	W	D.C.	26 NOV 1866	Mt. Olivet
637	Regholds, A.M.	5m	W	U.S.	08 NOV 1872	Mt. Olivet
001	Reichenback, Oscar	1y			30 JAN 1855	Congressional
001	Reichenback, Twins	2d			09 JAN 1855	Congressional
360	Reichert, Louesa Barbara	5y	W	U.S.	30 NOV 1868	
600	Reid, Eliza	65y	W	U.S.	04 MAY 1872	Presbyterian
115	Reid, Elizabeth B.	28y	W	Scot.	13 JUN 1858	Glenwood
082	Reid, Joseph		W	D.C.	04 JUL 1857	Congressional
147	Reid, Margaret	20y	W		08 APR 1859	
286	Reid, Sarah Ann	4y	C		13 DEC 1867	Ebenezer
774	Reider, Jane	80y	C	U.S.	04 JUN 1874	Mt. Olivet
411	Reidy, Daniel C.	1y	W		07 AUG 1869	Mt. Olivet
494	Reidy, Mary	2y	W	D.C.	27 DEC 1870	Mt. Olivet
621	Reiff, Chas., butcher	28y	W		13 AUG 1872	
019	Reigle, John	1y	W	D.C.	08 AUG 1855	German
409	Reihls, William, printer	31y	W	Pa.	07 AUG 1869	Pa.
231	Reil, [Sarah]		W	Pa.	09 AUG 1866	Congressional*
748	Reiley, Catherine	1m	W	U.S.	28 FEB 1874	Mt. Olivet
529	Reiley, Harry Andrew	1y	W	U.S.	23 JUL 1871	Mt. Olivet
393	Reiley, Mary Ann	1m	W		12 MAY 1869	Mt. Olivet
554	Reiley, Rebecca Key	17y	W		18 JAN 1872	
303	Reiley, S.S., child of		W	D.C.	12 MAR 1868	Congressional
102	Reilly, Boyd	77y	W	Ire.	18 JAN 1858	Congressional
454	Reilly, Fanny		C		15 MAY 1870	Young Mens
368	Reilly, Francis, clerk	57y	W	Ire.	21 DEC 1868	Mt. Olivet
419	Reilly, Gertrude Ulrica	11m	W		17 OCT 1869	Congressional
191	Reily, Peter, gas worker	36y	W	Ire.	01 OCT 1860	Mt. Olivet
742	Reily, Philip	50y	W	Ire.	19 JAN 1874	Mt. Olivet
154	Reily, Philip	1y	W	Kan.	12 JUL 1859	St. Patricks
761	Reily, Susan W.	74y	W	U.S.	03 APR 1874	Congressional
666	Reily, [Benj. A.], draughtsman		W	U.S.	06 FEB 1873	Congressional*
041	Reimbler, Daniel, laborer	43y	W	Ger.	07 APR 1856	German
140	Reinberg, John		W	D.C.	02 FEB 1859	Congressional
140	Reinberg, [blank]		W	D.C.	01 FEB 1859	Congressional
303	Reinhard, Elizabeth	6y	W	D.C.	17 MAR 1868	Prospect Hill
110	Reinhart, Sophia	1y	W	D.C.	08 APR 1858	German
356	Reinolile, Willie	26y	W	Amer.	08 OCT 1868	Oak Hill
333	Reiser, George C.	1y	W	D.C.	07 JUL 1868	Prospect Hill
465	Reisinger, Anna D.		W	Ger.	29 JUL 1870	Prospect Hill
774	Reisinger, Annie	14m	W	U.S.	18 JUN 1874	German
784	Reisinger, Henry	12h	W	U.S.	23 JUL 1874	Prospect Hill
111	Reiss, John, painter	52y	W	Ger.	13 APR 1858	Glenwood
124	Reiss, Martha	7m	W	D.C.	05 AUG 1858	Glenwood
445	Reister, William, soldier	28y	W		07 MAR 1870	Wilkes Barre, Pa.
138	Reiter, John	6d	W		26 JAN 1859	
334	Reiter, Mary	3y	W		08 JUL 1868	German Catholic
333	Reitz, Caroline M.	8m	W	D.C.	08 JUL 1868	Prospect Hill
743	Remington, A.E.	23y	W	U.S.	25 JAN 1874	Canandagna, N.Y.
251	Remington, George R., printer	47y	W	Mass.	11 JAN 1867	
264	Renard, J.E.	1y	W	D.C.	05 JUL 1867	Congressional
582	Renenbran, Margret	48y	W	Ire.	23 FEB 1872	Mt. Olivet
645	Rengold, Benj., laborer	40y		U.S.	30 DEC 1872	Ebenezer
659	Rennady, Michael, stone mason	63y	W	Ire.	11 JAN 1873	Mt. Olivet

297

Page	Name	Age	Race	Birth	Death Date	Burial Ground
767	Renner, Mary B.	70y	W	U.S.	19 MAY 1874	Oak Hill
148	Reno, [blank]	1y	W		17 MAY 1859	Congressional*
204	Renshaw, John, hatter	42y	W	Md.	13 JUN 1861	Baltimore, Md.
626	Repp, Cath.	75y	W	Ger.	14 SEP 1872	
637	Repper, Mary	36y	W	U.S.	01 NOV 1872	Mt. Olivet
784	Reppetti, Charles	14d	W	U.S.	31 JUL 1874	Congressional*
588	Ressell, Willie	3y	W	D.C.	28 MAR 1872	
681	Rest, Bertha	1y	W	U.S.	18 APR 1873	St. Marys
397	Rest, Frederick	3m	W	D.C.	12 JUN 1869	German Catholic
784	Ret, William	4m	W	U.S.	24 JUL 1874	Prospect Hill
740	Retheford, [blank]	7m	W	U.S.	05 JAN 1874	
403	Reuter, Phil	1y	W	D.C.	11 JUL 1869	Prospect Hill
270	Reuter, [blank]	1y	W	D.C.	01 AUG 1867	Propsect Hill
713	Reyburn, Elizabeth	11m	C	Va.	23 AUG 1873	
396	Reymond, F.S.	1y	B	D.C.	29 JUN 1869	Union
467	Reynolds, Bernard	5y	W	D.C.	04 JUL 1870	Mt. Olivet
523	Reynolds, Charles	2y	W	D.C.	18 JUN 1871	Congressional
235	Reynolds, Geo. W.	10y	W	Va.	16 SEP 1866	Congressional
740	Reynolds, Ida B.	21y	W	U.S.	03 JAN 1874	Congressional*
626	Reynolds, Jane	52y	W	U.S.	13 SEP 1872	
669	Reynolds, Jas. A., clerk	40y	W	U.S.	27 FEB 1873	Mt. Olivet
131	Reynolds, Margaret	18y	W	Va.	20 OCT 1858	Washington Asylum
589	Reynolds, Mary	8m	C	D.C.	31 MAR 1872	Mt. Zion
390	Reynolds, Mary E.	2y	W	D.C.	19 MAY 1869	Congressional
478	Reynolds, May	10m	W	N.Y.	09 SEP 1870	Glenwood
725	Reynolds, Michael, laborer	56y	W	Ire.	22 OCT 1873	Mt. Olivet
632	Reynolds, Rebecca	24y	W	U.S.	22 OCT 1872	
086	Reynolds, Silas	1y	W	D.C.	— AUG 1857	
530	Reynolds, Thomas, messenger	44y	W	Md.	31 JUL 1871	Congressional
003	Reynolds, [blank]	2y	C	D.C.	01 FEB 1855	Western
530	Rheinhardt, Frank, blacksmith	74y	W	Ger.	30 JUL 1871	
176	Rhinehart, Michael, laborer	62y	W	Ger.	04 APR 1860	Washington Asylum
542	Rhoabe, Georgienne	70y	W	Ger.	23 OCT 1871	Prospect Hill
536	Rhoades, Walter W.	1y	W	D.C.	17 SEP 1871	Congressional
190	Rhoads, Elizabeth	56y	C		24 SEP 1860	Georgetown
777	Rhodes, Chas. John	2m	W	U.S.	29 JUN 1874	Mt. Olivet
661	Rhodes, George	3y	W	U.S.	23 JAN 1873	Mt. Olivet
260	Rhodes, Harriet	65y	C		28 MAY 1867	
552	Rhodes, Imogene I.	11m	W	U.S.	05 JAN 1872	Congressional*
662	Rhodes, J.L.	37y	W	U.S.	09 JAN 1873	Small Pox
399	Rhodes, James A.	7m	W	D.C.	09 JUL 1869	Congressional
348	Rhodes, Joseph Edward	3y	W		03 SEP 1868	Congressional
342	Rhodes, Robert Franklin	1y	W		02 AUG 1868	Congressional
628	Rholader, Fred., cigar maker	28y	W	U.S.	07 SEP 1872	Congressional*
110	Rhue, Elizabeth	4y	W	D.C.	07 APR 1858	St. Patricks
269	Rhule, Charles	3m	W		02 AUG 1867	Mt. Olivet
334	Rhyneheart, A.	10m	W	D.C.	28 JUL 1868	German Catholic
355	Rials, Mary Ann	50y	W	Va.	07 OCT 1868	Congressional
360	Ribbeck, Rudolph, Dr.	50y	W	Ger.	23 NOV 1868	Prospect Hill
761	Ribber, Peter, harness maker	72y	W	Ger.	18 APR 1874	Prospect Hill
213	Ribnizky, Lillie	10m	W	D.C.	26 FEB 1866	Glenwood
043	Ricard, Mr., gardener	54y	W		30 APR 1856	Western
032	Ricard, Mrs.	40y	W		19 DEC 1855	Western
004	Rice, Edwin V., grocer	32y	W	Ire.	11 MAR 1855	St. Patricks
557	Rice, Joseph	4y	W	Va.	01 FEB 1872	
255	Rice, Lewis F., Mrs.	22y	W		16 MAR 1867	Detroit, Mich.
723	Rice, Mary	2y	W	D.C.	05 OCT 1873	Mt. Olivet
172	Rice, Thos. Alexander	1d	W	D.C.	11 FEB 1860	Congressional

District of Columbia Interments (Index to Deaths), 1855-1874

Page	Name	Age	Race	Birth	Death Date	Burial Ground
466	Rich, Anna M.	1y	C	D.C.	26 JUL 1870	Young Mens
502	Rich, Gilbert, laborer	38y	C	Va.	24 JAN 1871	Harmony
508	Rich, Wm.	2y	C	D.C.	06 FEB 1871	Ebenezer
365	Richards, Annie B.	3y	W	D.C.	05 DEC 1868	Congressional*
376	Richards, Channing, clerk Treas.	64y	W	Ohio	26 FEB 1869	Ohio
364	Richards, Francis E.	1y	W	D.C.	17 DEC 1868	Congressional
625	Richards, Geneva	1y	C	U.S.	04 OCT 1872	
341	Richards, John W.	2m	W	D.C.	09 AUG 1868	Congressional
479	Richards, Joseph	1d	C	D.C.	19 SEP 1870	Washington Asylum
487	Richards, Joseph, laborer	60y	C	D.C.	30 NOV 1870	Beckett's
006	Richards, Joseph, soldier	56y	W	Ire.	09 APR 1855	Asylum
318	Richards, Mary	1d	W	D.C.	04 JUN 1868	Congressional
256	Richards, Mary	21y	C	Tenn.	18 MAR 1867	Moore's
294	Richards, Mary Margaret	4m	C		06 FEB 1868	
489	Richards, Mary V.	21y	W	D.C.	13 NOV 1870	Oak Hill
703	Richards, Minnerva, teacher	61y	W	Mass.	15 JUL 1873	Oak Hill
042	Richards, Peter D., cordwinding	75y	W	Eng.	22 APR 1856	Foundry
551	Richards, Sallie	18y	W	Fla.	— DEC 1871	
537	Richards, Sallie, lady	19y	W	Fla.	21 SEP 1871	Fla.
280	Richards, W., child of	Still	C	D.C.	09 OCT 1867	Congressional*
583	Richards, Wm.	3y	C	D.C.	25 FEB 1872	Beckett's
784	Richardson, Alice	8d	C	U.S.	30 JUL 1874	
103	Richardson, C.F.E.	1y	W	D.C.	30 JAN 1858	Congressional
691	Richardson, Carrie	2y	C	U.S.	13 MAY 1873	Small Pox*
630	Richardson, Cera, laborer	35y	C	U.S.	05 OCT 1872	
676	Richardson, Fanny	8y	C	U.S.	06 MAR 1873	Small Pox
287	Richardson, Geo.		C		c.09 DEC 1867	Alms House
691	Richardson, Harriet		C	U.S.	13 MAY 1873	Small Pox*
761	Richardson, Harry	5m	W	U.S.	22 APR 1874	Mt. Olivet
721	Richardson, Hattie A.	1y	C	U.S.	26 SEP 1873	
546	Richardson, Henry M.	1y	W	D.C.	30 NOV 1871	Congressional
256	Richardson, Ida R.	2y	W	D.C.	08 MAR 1867	Baltimore, Md.
533	Richardson, Ira, stone cutter	60y		D.C.	19 AUG 1871	Glenwood
114	Richardson, Jas. H., carpenter	33y	W	Md.	28 MAY 1858	Glenwood
161	Richardson, Jas. Henry	1m	C	D.C.	12 SEP 1859	Young Mens
017	Richardson, Josephine	15m		D.C.	04 JUL 1855	Foundry
737	Richardson, Julia		C	U.S.	26 DEC 1873	
454	Richardson, Kezia	77y	W	Eng.	12 MAY 1870	Glenwood
042	Richardson, Luke, carpenter	72y	W	Eng.	23 APR 1856	Glenwood
153	Richardson, Mary A.	28y	W	Md.	05 JUL 1859	Glenwood
115	Richardson, Simon, brickmaker	28y	C	Md.	13 JUN 1858	Baltimore, Md.
465	Richardson, Susan	7m	C	D.C.	06 JUL 1870	Ebenezer
666	Richardson, Susan	50y	W	U.S.	07 FEB 1873	Washington Asylum
405	Richardson, Thos.	1y	C	D.C.	23 JUL 1869	Washington Asylum
691	Richardson, Wm.	5y	C	U.S.	13 MAY 1873	Small Pox*
479	Richardson, Wm.	43y	W	S.C.	30 SEP 1870	Washington Asylum
084	Richardson, Wm. E.		W		21 JUL 1857	Congressional
613	Richert, Louis S.	1y		U.S.	02 JUL 1872	
033	Richey, Ann W.	46y	W	Va.	01 JAN 1856	Glenwood
044	Richey, Harriet E.	36y	W	D.C.*	05 MAY 1856	St. Patricks
105	Richey, [blank]	3y	W	D.C.	15 FEB 1858	Glenwood
707	Richmond, Chas. S.	2m	W	U.S.	20 JUL 1873	
755	Richold, Sophia	65y	W	Ger.	18 MAR 1874	Hebrew
695	Richter, Anna Isabella	6m	W	D.C.	08 JUN 1873	Mt. Olivet*
049	Richter, G.	3m	W	D.C.	01 JUL 1856	St. Peters
748	Richter, Herman, machinist	51y	W	Prus.	02 FEB 1874	Congressional*
052	Richter, Louisa	30y	W	Ger.	30 JUL 1856	German
308	Richter, Rudolph	40y	W	Ger.	01 APR 1868	Congressional

Page	Name	Age	Race	Birth	Death Date	Burial Ground
624	Richton, Thos., clerk	35y	W	Eng.	21 SEP 1872	Bloomsburg, Pa.
626	Richtor, Thos.	26y	W	Eng.	21 SEP 1872	
407	Ricker, [blank]	5m	W		06 AUG 1869	Congressional
176	Ricketts, Florida B.	20y	W	D.C.	09 APR 1860	
255	Ricketts, Mrs.	c.50y	W		10 MAR 1867	
185	Rickey, Geo. Washington	1y	W	D.C.	21 JUL 1860	Glenwood
274	Rickey, Mary C.	1y	W	D.C.	06 SEP 1867	Glenwood
391	Ricks, H.A., gardener	75y	W	Ger.	14 MAY 1869	Prospect Hill
416	Ricks, Mary	75y	C	Va.	29 SEP 1869	Ebenezer
767	Ricksey, Eliza	13y	W	U.S.	— MAY 1874	Young Mens
280	Riddell, Mary, teacher	82y	W	Ire.	22 OCT 1867	N.H.
708	Ridden, Herbert, hack driver	30y	C	Va.	27 JUL 1873	
405	Riddick, Jesse	28y	C	Va.	16 JUL 1869	Washington Asylum
036	Riddle, Ellen	44y	W		22 FEB 1856	Alms House
257	Riddle, George R., Hon., senator	60y	W	Del.	29 MAR 1867	Wilmington, Del.
374	Riddle, Ida	2y	W	D.C.	02 FEB 1869	Congressional
784	Riddle, James A., carpenter	54y	W	U.S.	26 JUL 1874	
097	Riddlemo[sn], John V.	5y	W	Md.	29 NOV 1857	Presbyterian
392	Riddles, Henry	5y	C	Va.	29 MAY 1869	Mt. Zion
107	Rider, Clark, clerk	25y	W		06 MAR 1858	St. Patricks
051	Ridgate, Edmund H.	4m	W	D.C.	26 JUL 1856	Oak Hill
139	Ridgaway, Henrietta	83y	W		28 JAN 1859	
140	Ridgeley, Charles H.	3m	C	D.C.	09 FEB 1859	Harmony
375	Ridgeley, David G., druggist	41y	W	Md.	07 FEB 1869	Oak Hill
036	Ridgely, Alfred G.	33y	W	Md.	18 FEB 1856	Oak Hill
074	Ridgely, David, clerk	64y	W	Md.	25 MAR 1857	Oak Hill
623	Ridgely, Jas., butcher	39y	C	U.S.	30 JUL 1872	Holy Rood
631	Ridgely, L., trader	77y	W	U.S.	25 OCT 1872	
774	Ridgely, Sophia	80y	W	U.S.	13 JUN 1874	Oak Hill
292a	Ridgely, Sophia M.	37y	W	D.C.*	08 FEB 1868	Woodley
385	Ridgeway, Mordacia, hatter	32y	W	Md.	30 APR 1869	Congressional
279	Ridgley, Fannie	70y	C	Md.	26 OCT 1867	Harmony
310	Ridgley, Jane, domestic	25y	C	Md.	02 APR 1868	Harmony
744	Ridgley, Mary F.	6m	C	U.S.	04 JAN 1874	
213	Ridgley, [blank]		C		20 FEB 1866	Western
014	Ridgly, Ann, cook	40y	C	Md.	20 JUL 1855	Foundry
191	Ridgly, Fanny	4y	C		22 OCT 1860	Young Mens
717	Ridgway, Jas. E., bookbinder	34y	W	D.C.	03 SEP 1873	Holy Rood*
774	Ridgway, William, merchant	49y	W	U.S.	27 JUN 1874	Congressional*
179	Ridley, George A.	1y	C	D.C.	18 MAY 1860	Young Mens
207	Ridney, M.A.		C		03 JUL 1862	Western
339	Riell, Mary Roberta	8m	W	Va.	05 AUG 1868	Oak Hill
453	Ries, Clara	62y	W	Ger.	20 MAY 1870	Washington Hebrew
426	Riethmiller, Louisa	64y	W	Ger.	13 NOV 1869	German Catholic
477	Rietz, Johanne M.E.	11m	W	Ger.	— SEP 1870	Prospect Hill
488	Rietz, John H.J.E.	2y	W	Ger.	13 NOV 1870	Prospect Hill
375	Rigdon, Anna A.	24y	W	Va.	20 FEB 1869	Va.
052	Riggles, Cornelia L.	9m	W	D.C.	29 JUL 1856	Oak Hill
626	Riggles, Ellenor H.	1y	W	U.S.	30 SEP 1872	
070	Riggles, Mary Ann M.	5m	W	D.C.	05 FEB 1857	Oak Hill
044	Riggs, Geo. Shedden	6y	W	D.C.	20 MAY 1856	Rock Creek
642	Riggs, Hagar, servant	24y	C	U.S.	30 DEC 1872	Small Pox
374	Riggs, John, printer	49y	W	Va.	09 FEB 1869	Congressional
004	Riggs, Lucretia	40y	C	D.C.	03 MAR 1855	Washington Asylum
218	Riggs, Remus G., bank clerk	31y	W	Md.	19 APR 1866	Montgomery Co., Md.
241	Riggs, Sophia	36y	W	D.C.	31 OCT 1866	Congressional*
076	Rightmuller, Mary	2y	W	D.C.	21 APR 1857	German Catholic
226	Rightstein, Nannie E.	2m	W	D.C.	25 JUN 1866	Glenwood

District of Columbia Interments (Index to Deaths), 1855-1874

Page	Name	Age	Race	Birth	Death Date	Burial Ground
009	Rightstine, Cath. Rebecca		W	D.C.	27 MAY 1855	Glenwood
083	Rightstine, Chas. T.	3½m	W	D.C.	14 JUL 1857	Glenwood
043	Rightstine, Infant		W		28 APR 1856	Glenwood
342	Rigny, Mary Ellen	26y	C	Md.	27 AUG 1868	Young Mens
011	Rigsby, Benjn.	21d	W	D.C.	18 JUN 1855	Methodist, East
184	Rigsby, Thomas, blacksmith	52y	W	D.C.	06 JUL 1860	Methodist
182	Rigsby, Thos.	5m	W	D.C.	29 JUN 1860	Congressional
066	Riks, Sophia, housekeeper	28y	W	Ger.	26 DEC 1856	German Lutheran
748	Rile, Charles	4m	W	U.S.	24 FEB 1874	Mt. Olivet
540	Riley, Bridget	33y	W	D.C.	01 OCT 1871	Congressional*
540	Riley, Bridget	3d	W	D.C.	05 OCT 1871	Washington
030	Riley, C.B.	5d	W	D.C.	04 NOV 1855	Holmead
482	Riley, Elizabeth	19y	W	D.C.	24 OCT 1870	Mt. Olivet
419	Riley, Infant	Still	W		21 OCT 1869	Congressional
717	Riley, James	4m	W	D.C.	06 SEP 1873	Mt. Olivet
622a	Riley, Jane E.	1y	W	U.S.	02 AUG 1872	
470	Riley, Jas., machinist	45y	W	Ire.	08 AUG 1870	Mt. Olivet
031	Riley, Jas. Thomas	2y	W	D.C.	02 DEC 1855	St. Patricks
055	Riley, Joseph	2y	W	D.C.	19 AUG 1856	St. Patricks
067	Riley, Margaretta H.	1y	W	Tex.	30 DEC 1856	Congressional
586	Riley, Mary W.	25y	W	D.C.	14 MAR 1872	Mt. Olivet
396	Riley, Nancy	2y	Y		27 JUN 1869	Young Mens
189	Riley, Peter	50y	W	Ire.	12 SEP 1860	Baltimore, Md.
694	Riley, Rachael, infant of	Still			20 JUN 1873	Beckett's
027	Riley, Sophia	47y	W	N.Y.	08 OCT 1855	Albany, N.Y.
408	Riley, Willie	1y	W		08 AUG 1869	Congressional
199	Ring, Michael, laborer	50y	W	Ire.	05 FEB 1861	
141	Ringgold, Mary Lee	8y	W	D.C.	14 FEB 1859	Oak Hill
132	Ringgold, Susan B.	31y	W		10 NOV 1858	Oak Hill
333	Rinsley, Henry M., hack driver	55y	W	Ire.	03 JUL 1868	St. Aloysius
013	Riordan, Cath.				01 JUL 1855	
069	Riordan, James	10y	W	D.C.	19 JAN 1857	Alexandria, Va.
266	Riordan, James S., clerk	80y	W	Ire.	14 JUL 1867	Alexandria, Va.
483	Riordan, Maggie	11m	W	D.C.	05 OCT 1870	Mt. Olivet
226	Ripley, J.H., child of	2y			26 JUN 1866	Oak Hill
715	Ripley, Jno. H., clerk	30y	W	Mass.	02 AUG 1873	
218	Ripley, Mrs.		W		16 APR 1866	Oak Hill
349	Risley, Harriet C., Mrs.	52y	W	N.Y.	30 SEP 1868	Oak Hill
401	Risley, Helene W.	1y	W	D.C.	30 JUL 1869	Mt. Olivet
127	Ritch, Elizabeth	51y	W		15 SEP 1858	Western
355	Ritchie, George Harrison	37y	W	Va.	05 OCT 1868	Richmond, Va.
415	Ritchie, James W., soldier	32y	W	D.C.	28 SEP 1869	Glenwood
286	Rithmuler, A.	43y	W	Ger.	12 DEC 1867	German Catholic
097	Ritmiler, Mary	10d	W	D.C.	24 NOV 1857	
259	Ritten, Mr.	60y	W		02 APR 1867	Western
348	Ritter, Louis	2y	W		28 SEP 1868	Congressional
051	Ritter, Mary	10m	W	D.C.	26 JUL 1856	Holmead
006	Ritter, Mrs.		W		28 APR 1855	Fairfax Co., Va.
038	Ritter, Mrs.	18y	W		05 MAR 1856	St. Matthews
587	Ritter, Mrs.	34y	C	D.C.	22 MAR 1872	Western
108	Ritter, [blank]	4y	W	D.C.	15 MAR 1858	Congressional*
144	Ritter, [blank]	6m	W		19 MAR 1859	Fairfax Co., Va.
239	Rittmuller, Mary	8d	W	D.C.	22 OCT 1866	Catholic
128	Rittmüller, Henry	1y	W	D.C.	25 SEP 1858	German Catholic
704	Rives, Caroline	9m	C	U.S.	29 JUL 1873	Congressional
605	Rives, Mary H.	2y	C	U.S.	17 JUN 1872	
594	Rives, [blank]	Still	W	D.C.	08 APR 1872	Congressional*
644	Rizer, Mary, Mrs.	79y	W	U.S.	18 DEC 1872	

District of Columbia Interments (Index to Deaths), 1855-1874

Page	Name	Age	Race	Birth	Death Date	Burial Ground
527	Roabe, Fred Augustus	2y	W	D.C.	08 JUL 1871	Prospect Hill
659	Roach, David	58y	W	Ire.	13 JAN 1873	Mt. Olivet
117	Roach, Hannah	3m	W	D.C.	28 JUN 1858	St. Patricks
489	Roach, Hanora	68y	W	Ire.	05 NOV 1870	Mt. Olivet
088	Roach, James Buchanan	9m	W	D.C.	25 AUG 1857	St. Patricks
050	Roach, John	21d	W	D.C.	20 JUL 1856	St. Patricks
278	Roach, John Stevens	9m	W	D.C.	17 OCT 1867	Mt. Olivet
581	Roach, Maggie	3y	W	D.C.	15 FEB 1872	Mt. Olivet
499	Roach, Margaret	75y	W	Md.	11 JAN 1871	Congressional
121	Roach, Mary	4m	W	D.C.	16 JUL 1858	St. Patricks
264	Roach, Mary, clerk Treas.	20y	W	D.C.	29 JUL 1867	Mt. Olivet
341	Roach, Philip	1y	W	D.C.	05 AUG 1868	Congressional
496	Roach, William, laborer	45y	W	Ire.	22 DEC 1870	Mt. Olivet
010	Roach, Wm.	9m	W	D.C.	08 JUN 1855	St. Patricks
159	Roach, [blank]	1y	W	D.C.	02 AUG 1859	Mt. Olivet
199	Roach, [blank]	70y	W		01 FEB 1861	Mt. Olivet
550	Roache, Mary T.	20y	W	D.C.	30 DEC 1871	
352	Roan, Eddie	1y	C	D.C.	04 SEP 1868	Washington Asylum
446	Roan, James	9m	C		16 MAR 1870	Young Mens
422	Roan, William, laborer	32y	C	Va.	02 OCT 1869	
207	Roatch, Armin	1y	W	D.C.	19 JUL 1862	Glenwood
761	Robb, Lanson	40y	C	U.S.	21 APR 1874	Washington Asylum
161	Robb, Margaret	38y	W	D.C.	16 SEP 1859	Congressional
161	Robb, [blank]		W	D.C.	15 SEP 1859	Congressional
338	Robbins, Charles, gardener	60y	W	Eng.	17 AUG 1868	Mt. Olivet
303	Robbins, Lina	1y	W	D.C.	29 MAR 1868	Congressional
162	Robbins, Margaret	58y	W	Ire.	27 SEP 1859	Trinity
062	Robbins, Mary	10d	W		01 NOV 1856	St. Matthews
349	Robbins, Thomas	74y	W	Ire.	30 SEP 1868	Glenwood
537	Robbitt, William, tailor	65y	W		21 SEP 1871	Washington
163	Roberg, Jerome	33y	W	D.C.	20 OCT 1859	Congressional
131	Roberson, Mary Jane	2y	W	D.C.	29 OCT 1858	St. Patricks
618	Roberson, Robt.	3m	W	U.S.	11 AUG 1872	Mt. Olivet
767	Robert, James	9y	C	U.S.	08 MAY 1874	Ebenezer
246	Roberts, Ann	81y	W	Md.	10 DEC 1866	Congressional
353	Roberts, Annie	3y	W	D.C.	10 SEP 1868	
734	Roberts, Betty, infant of	19d	C	U.S.	03 DEC 1873	
326	Roberts, Charles	4m	W	D.C.	06 JUL 1868	Prospect Hill
357	Roberts, Eddie	7y	W		02 OCT 1868	
587	Roberts, James E.	1y	C	D.C.	19 MAR 1872	
698	Roberts, Jno. L., Rev.	55y	W	Ver.	24 JUN 1873	Glenwood
066	Roberts, Livy, white washer	35y	C		20 DEC 1856	Young Mens
774	Roberts, Lula	10y	W	U.S.	08 JUN 1874	Glenwood
285	Roberts, Mary Louise	1m	W	D.C.	30 DEC 1867	Holmead
607	Roberts, Matilda	6m	W	D.C.	27 JUN 1872	Congressional
267	Roberts, Mr., child of	2h			19 JUL 1867	Western
246	Roberts, Peter, coachman	44y	C	Md.	11 DEC 1866	Young Mens
104	Roberts, [blank]	Still	W	D.C.	06 FEB 1858	St. Matthews
442	Robertson, Abraham	27y	C	Va.	04 FEB 1870	Young Mens
633	Robertson, Alx.	43y	C	U.S.	31 OCT 1872	Small Pox*
453	Robertson, Charlotte I.	29y	W	Ver.	26 MAY 1870	Congressional
633	Robertson, Daniel	20y	C	U.S.	31 OCT 1872	Small Pox*
639	Robertson, Daniel B.	17m	W	U.S.	14 NOV 1872	Congressional
019	Robertson, Danl. R.	18m	W		15 AUG 1855	Congressional
446	Robertson, E.	25y	C		24 MAR 1870	Young Mens
202	Robertson, E.L.	28y	W	Md.	30 APR 1861	Congressional
528	Robertson, Ellen J.	2y	C	D.C.	19 JUL 1871	
536	Robertson, Eveline M.	6y	W	U.S.	17 SEP 1871	Congressional

District of Columbia Interments (Index to Deaths), 1855-1874

Page	Name	Age	Race	Birth	Death Date	Burial Ground
146	Robertson, Henry B., court crier	79y	W	Md.	04 APR 1859	Ebenezer
502	Robertson, James	55y	W	D.C.	14 JAN 1871	Congressional
677	Robertson, James	24y	C	U.S.	25 MAR 1873	Small Pox
658	Robertson, Jas. H.	14d	C	U.S.	06 JAN 1873	Young Mens
117	Robertson, John A., carpenter	26y	W	Md.	26 JUN 1858	Frederick, Md.
207	Robertson, M.	4m	W		28 JUL 1862	[torn]
734	Robertson, Mary C.	75y	W	U.S.	02 DEC 1873	Congressional*
217	Robertson, Mary E.	2y	W	D.C.	06 APR 1866	Congressional
214	Robertson, Mary E.	34y	W	D.C.	02 MAR 1866	Congressional
584	Robertson, Mary J., seamstress	55y	W	U.S.	01 MAR 1872	
475	Robertson, Milly	80y	C	Md.	22 SEP 1870	Congressional
270	Robertson, Sarah	few hrs.	W		04 AUG 1867	Congressional
380	Robertson, William, private marine	56y	W	N.Y.	24 MAR 1869	Congressional
132	Robertson, Wm.	6m	C	D.C.	12 NOV 1858	Foundry
623	Robertson, Wm.	1y	C	U.S.	23 JUL 1872	Mt. Zion
688	Robertson, [blank]	Still	C	U.S.	15 MAY 1873	
190	Robertson, [blank]	4m	W		13 SEP 1860	Alexandria, Va.
034	Robertson, [blank], Mr.	67y	C		05 JAN 1856	Georgetown
585	Robeson, John, laborer	35y	C	Va.	07 MAR 1872	Ebenezer
228	Robey, Andrew	10m	W	D.C.	17 JUL 1866	Uniontown
755	Robey, Charles, farmer	74y	W	U.S.	15 MAR 1874	Vienna, Va.
095	Robey, Edwd.	16y	W	D.C.	29 OCT 1857	Congressional
177	Robey, Henry	4m	W	D.C.	29 APR 1860	Congressional
550	Robey, James	57y	W	Md.	28 DEC 1871	
457	Robey, Johnn, infant of	½h	W	D.C.	20 JUN 1870	Congressional
268	Robey, Mary	77y	W	Md.	20 AUG 1867	Methodist
243	Robey, Mrs.	54y	W	Md.	17 NOV 1866	Alms House
674	Robey, T.B., farmer	61y	W	U.S.	19 MAR 1873	Congressional
333	Robey, Thomas, ship carpenter	43y	W	D.C.	09 JUL 1868	Mt. Olivet
712	Robey, Thos. G.	18d	W	D.C.	14 AUG 1873	Congressional
038	Robey, William D.	1y	W	D.C.	01 MAR 1856	St. Patricks
493	Robey, Wm. H.D.	10m	W	D.C.	22 DEC 1870	Congressional
359	Robey, Wm. T.	2y	W	D.C.	25 NOV 1868	Congressional
279	Robins, A., Miss	22y	W	D.C.	23 OCT 1867	Mt. Olivet
725	Robins, Elizabeth, domestic	55y	W	Va.	18 OCT 1873	Mt. Olivet
372	Robinson, Abraham, laborer	27y	C	Md.	09 JAN 1869	Freedmen's Hospital
412	Robinson, Alfred	1y	C		08 AUG 1869	
664	Robinson, Andrew	1y	C	U.S.	17 JAN 1873	Small Pox*
405	Robinson, Ann E.	Still	C	D.C.	24 JUL 1869	Washington Asylum
272	Robinson, Anna	15y	C		18 AUG 1867	Freedmen's Bureau
190	Robinson, Anna Eliza	2y	W	D.C.	26 SEP 1860	Glenwood
534	Robinson, Augustus	1y	C		28 AUG 1871	Washington
447	Robinson, Celia	95y	C	Va.	30 MAR 1870	Washington Asylum
774	Robinson, Charles, student	15y	I	U.S.	24 JUN 1874	Rock Creek
313	Robinson, Charles W.	10d	C	D.C.	27 MAY 1868	Young Mens
713	Robinson, Chas.	8m	C	D.C.	25 AUG 1873	Ebenezer
718	Robinson, Chas. W., printer	60y	W	Pa.	08 SEP 1873	
386	Robinson, Ebenezer, Rev.	56y	W	N.Y.	08 APR 1869	Glenwood
715	Robinson, Edward, laborer	65y	C	Va.	18 AUG 1873	
039	Robinson, Elizabeth	27y	W		19 MAR 1856	St. Peters
784	Robinson, Ellen	8d	C	U.S.	27 JUL 1874	
663	Robinson, Ellen	37y	C	U.S.	13 JAN 1873	Small Pox
367	Robinson, Ellen	2m	B		14 DEC 1868	Washington Asylum
548	Robinson, Emma	6y	W	D.C.	16 DEC 1871	Mt. Olivet
426	Robinson, Eva	2y	C		08 NOV 1869	Ebenezer
744	Robinson, Geo. A.	19d	W	U.S.	28 JAN 1874	Congressional
731	Robinson, Geo. B.	1y	W	U.S.	19 NOV 1873	Congressional
073	Robinson, Geo. W.	2y	W	D.C.	14 MAR 1857	Congressional

Page	Name	Age	Race	Birth	Death Date	Burial Ground
735	Robinson, George	1y	C	U.S.	10 DEC 1873	
613	Robinson, Gergie	6m	C	U.S.	04 JUL 1872	
526	Robinson, Harry	1y	C	D.C.	03 JUL 1871	
370	Robinson, Hattie L.	4m	W	D.C.	16 JAN 1869	Glenwood
372	Robinson, Henry, laborer	80y	C	Va.	01 JAN 1869	Freedmen's Hospital
767	Robinson, Infant	2m	C	U.S.	14 MAY 1874	
640	Robinson, J.H.	4y	W	U.S.	21 DEC 1872	Small Pox*
537	Robinson, James	1y	C	D.C.	23 SEP 1871	
353	Robinson, James		C		28 SEP 1868	Washington Asylum
734	Robinson, James M., clerk	33y	W	U.S.	06 DEC 1873	
222	Robinson, James W.	3y	W	D.C.	26 MAY 1866	Congressional
366	Robinson, Jane, seamstress	39y	B		05 DEC 1868	
378	Robinson, Jessie, laborer	65y	C	Md.	12 FEB 1869	Freedmen's Hospital
534	Robinson, Jno. Wm.	13y	W	Mass.	27 AUG 1871	Mass.
003	Robinson, John	1m	W	D.C.	28 FEB 1855	
452	Robinson, John	1y	C		28 APR 1870	Ebenezer
493	Robinson, John H., Dr.	49y	W	Md.	30 DEC 1870	Congressional
399	Robinson, John, merchant	56y	W	Va.	20 JUL 1869	Congressional
755	Robinson, John, sailor	19y	W	U.S.	01 MAR 1874	
327	Robinson, Joseph	1y	W	D.C.	18 JUL 1868	Mt. Olivet*
436	Robinson, Joseph, harness maker	40y	W	Ire.	03 JAN 1870	Mt. Olivet
644	Robinson, Julia A.	41y	C	U.S.	22 DEC 1872	
730	Robinson, Juliet	62y	C	U.S.	15 NOV 1873	Mt. Olivet
731	Robinson, Laura, lady	23y	W	U.S.	18 NOV 1873	Congressional
321	Robinson, Lizzie		C		c.09 JUN 1868	Alms House
669	Robinson, Louisa	6y	C	U.S.	07 FEB 1873	
635	Robinson, Lucy	6y	C	U.S.	01 NOV 1872	Small Pox
228	Robinson, M.A.	1y	C	D.C.	15 JUL 1866	Young Mens
382	Robinson, Mary	3d	C		13 MAR 1869	
375	Robinson, Mary	71y	W	Ire.	21 FEB 1869	Mt. Olivet
338	Robinson, Mary	5m	C		24 AUG 1868	Washington Asylum
454a	Robinson, Mary F., pauper	2½y	C	D.C.	05 MAY 1870	Washington Asylum
488	Robinson, Mary L.	2y	W	D.C.	08 NOV 1870	Congressional
475	Robinson, Mary S.	30y	W	Va.	15 SEP 1870	Congressional
595	Robinson, Mary T.D.	15y	W	D.C.	15 APR 1872	Congressional
429	Robinson, Nettie	14y	W		13 DEC 1869	Congressional
435	Robinson, Owen	10m	C		15 JAN 1870	Beckett's
735	Robinson, Persilla	45y	C	U.S.	10 DEC 1873	
287	Robinson, Philip		C		c.25 DEC 1867	Alms House
629	Robinson, R.	2y	C	U.S.	06 OCT 1872	
706	Robinson, Rebecca	68y	C	Va.	19 JUL 1873	Washington Asylum
389	Robinson, Richd.	2d	C	D.C.	20 APR 1869	Washington Asylum
744	Robinson, Rosa A.	2y	W	U.S.	28 JAN 1874	Congressional
442	Robinson, Rose	Still	C		08 FEB 1870	Washington Asylum
373	Robinson, Sandy, laborer	40y	C	D.C.	19 JAN 1869	
661	Robinson, Sol, merchant	40y	W	U.S.	23 JAN 1873	Augusta, Ga.
186	Robinson, Susan	25y	W	U.S.	31 JUL 1860	Glenwood
010	Robinson, Thos. F., farmer	68y	W	Md.	16 JUN 1855	Glenwood
473	Robinson, Walter	11m	C	D.C.	21 AUG 1870	Young Mens
474	Robinson, William	1y	C		15 AUG 1870	Washington Asylum
449	Robinson, William H., jeweller	21y	W	D.C.	07 APR 1870	Congressional
323	Robinson, Willie	5m	W	D.C.	10 JUL 1868	Glenwood
413	Robinson, Wm.	3h	C	D.C.	24 AUG 1869	Washington Asylum
385	Robinson, Wm. H.	24d	W	D.C.	12 APR 1869	Congressional
755	Robinson, Wm. J.	74y	W	Ire.	23 MAR 1874	Mt. Olivet
373	Robinson, [blank]	1d	C	D.C.	29 JAN 1869	
166	Robisham, Anna G.	5d	W	D.C.	20 NOV 1859	
755	Roby, Catherine	52y	W	U.S.	06 MAR 1874	Methodist

District of Columbia Interments (Index to Deaths), 1855-1874

Page	Name	Age	Race	Birth	Death Date	Burial Ground
232	Roby, Edward	9y	W	Va.	25 AUG 1866	Methodist, Georgetown
109	Roby, Fanny	4y	W	Md.	30 MAR 1858	Congressional
160	Roby, Susie	1y	W	D.C.	13 AUG 1859	Congressional*
208	Roby, Washington, Rev.	45y	W	Md.	31 JUL 1862	Oak Hill
612	Roby, Wm. A.	6m	W	U.S.	01 JUL 1872	
090	Rocem, Jno. G.	5m	W	D.C.	06 SEP 1857	German Catholic
767	Rochart, Mary R.	59y	W	U.S.	04 MAY 1874	Mt. Olivet
339	Roche, Catherine	60y	W	Ire.	09 AUG 1868	Mt. Olivet
123	Roche, Ellen	9m	W	D.C.	31 JUL 1858	St. Patricks
361	Roche, M.R., merchant	41y	W	Ire.	30 NOV 1868	Mt. Olivet
774	Roche, Mary	11m	W	U.S.	10 JUN 1874	Mt. Olivet
010	Roche, Mary A.	35y		Ire.	— JUN 1855	St. Patricks
616	Roche, Mary E.	1y	W		25 JUL 1872	
501	Roche, Richd., gentleman	92y	W	Ire.	27 JAN 1871	Mt. Olivet
118	Roche, Robert J., clerk	40y	W	D.C.	18 JUN 1858	Oak Hill
725	Roche, Susan E.	41y	W	U.S.	22 OCT 1873	Glenwood
475	Rochford, Joanna	30y	W	Ire.	27 SEP 1870	Mt. Olivet
380	Rochiccole, Christofano	75y	W	Italy	27 MAR 1869	German Catholic
280	Rock, Andrew J., drawkeeper	47y	W	Ver.	24 OCT 1867	Congressional
737	Rock, Delia	11y	W	U.S.	28 DEC 1873	
253	Rock, John	11m	W	D.C.	07 FEB 1867	Alms House
271	Rock, Richard, fruit seller	17y	W	Italy	18 AUG 1867	St. Marys
143	Rock, Sarah E.	1y	W	D.C.	10 MAR 1859	Congressional
521	Rocket, Charles H.	3y	W	D.C.	04 JUN 1871	Congressional*
286	Rocket, Matilda C.	68y	W	Md.	04 DEC 1867	Charles Co., Md.
212	Rocket, [blank]	5y	W	D.C.	10 FEB 1866	Congressional
182	Rodbird, Ebenezer	57y	W	Eng.	25 JUN 1860	Congressional
184	Rodbird, Geo. Ephraim	18d	W	D.C.	10 JUL 1860	Glenwood
774	Roderick, Florence G.	9m	W	U.S.	15 JUN 1874	Harpers Ferry
456	Rodgers, Augustus, composite	55y	W	N.Y.	09 JUN 1870	Catskill, N.Y.
774	Rodgers, Charles O.	4m	W	U.S.	28 JUN 1874	Congressional*
175	Rodgers, Clara M.	7m	W	D.C.	26 MAR 1860	Georgetown
148	Rodgers, George	5y	W	D.C.	06 MAY 1859	Mt. Olivet
429	Rodgers, Johnson	58y	W	Ga.	06 DEC 1869	Congressional
104	Rodgers, L.	2m	W	D.C.	05 FEB 1858	Baltimore, Md.
628	Rodgers, Lillie	1y	C	U.S.	21 SEP 1872	Small Pox
628	Rodgers, Martha E.	18y	C	U.S.	06 SEP 1872	Small Pox
077	Rodgers, Mrs.	67y	W	Md.	02 MAY 1857	St. Peters
355	Rodgers, Susie M.	7m	W		08 OCT 1868	Congressional
185	Rodgers, Thomas	1y	W	D.C.	28 JUL 1860	Washington Asylum
087	Roding, Mary, washwoman	50y	C	D.C.	15 AUG 1857	St. Matthews
252	Rodney, Martha	39y	C	Md.	24 FEB 1867	Mt. Olivet
319	Rodric, William	3y	C	D.C.	— JUN 1868	
710	Roe, Hannorah	40y	W	Ire.	07 AUG 1873	Mt. Olivet*
639	Roe, Mary, spinster	70y	W		30 NOV 1872	Catholic, Georgetown
366	Roeben, Henry W.	2y	W	D.C.	17 DEC 1868	Prospect Hill
420	Roeca, Pasquals, fruit dealer	57y	W	Italy	22 OCT 1869	St. Marys
244	Rogannie, Wm. S.	Still	W	D.C.	04 NOV 1866	Glenwood
646	Rogenski, Saml., peddler	40y	W	Pol.	23 DEC 1872	
387	Rogers, Ann	78y	W	Md.	08 APR 1869	Glenwood
075	Rogers, Jane E.	21y	W	N.H.	14 APR 1857	Congressional
361	Rogers, Janny, child of	1y	C	D.C.	15 NOV 1868	
719	Rogers, John, varnisher		W	Va.	17 SEP 1873	Glenwood
150	Rogers, Jonathan, waiter	22y	C	Va.	01 JUN 1859	Harmony
035	Rogerson, Mary Alice	4m	W	D.C.	25 FEB 1856	Methodist
737	Rohleder, Francis	57y	W	Prus.	25 DEC 1873	Congressional
344	Rohn, Conrad	37y	W	Ger.	22 AUG 1868	Prospect Hill
253	Roil, Lewis, laborer	35y	W	Ger.	16 FEB 1867	Alms House

Page	Name	Age	Race	Birth	Death Date	Burial Ground
293	Rola, R.	1y	C		29 MAR 1868	Methodist
214	Roland, Clara	1y	W	D.C.	11 MAR 1866	Congressional
536	Rolins, Leonard C.	1y	W	D.C.	18 SEP 1871	
441	Roll, Virginia L.	1y	W		21 FEB 1870	Prospect Hill
179	Rolla, John, child of	2m	W	D.C.	02 MAY 1860	Prospect Hill
580	Rollings, Geo. W., boatman	27y	W	D.C.	10 FEB 1872	Glenwood
105	Rollings, John C.	15y	W	D.C.	20 FEB 1858	Foundry
091	Rollings, Mary Ann	49y	W	Va.*	21 SEP 1857	Glenwood
233	Rollings, Walter	2y	C		23 AUG 1866	Georgetown
535	Rollings, Washington	60y	W	Md.	09 SEP 1871	Glenwood
544	Rollins, Ann	68y	W	D.C.	08 NOV 1871	Congressional*
528	Rollins, Ann W.	90y	W	Md.	13 JUL 1871	Glenwood
496	Rollins, Fanny	84y	C	Va.	04 DEC 1870	Potters Field
725	Rollins, J. & Mary, infant of	14d	B	Md.	16 OCT 1873	Mt. Pleasant
407	Rollins, J.H., infant of	6d	W		09 AUG 1869	Congressional
738	Rollins, Jane, infant of	5d	C	U.S.	08 DEC 1873	
483	Rollins, Joseph, laborer	40y	C	Va.	26 OCT 1870	Freedmen's Hospital
317	Rollins, Lizzie	2y	C	D.C.	27 JUN 1868	Ebenezer
122	Rollins, Louis A., stone cutter	25y	W	D.C.	20 JUL 1858	Glenwood
298	Rollins, Marion	10y	W	N.H.	17 FEB 1868	N.H.
025	Rollins, Mary R.	18m	W	D.C.	28 SEP 1855	Foundry
217	Rollins, William, boatman	37y	W	D.C.	09 APR 1866	Glenwood
662	Rollins, Wm. C., potter	65y	W	U.S.	29 JAN 1873	
599	Rollois, Annie W., seamstress	40y	W	Eng.	09 MAY 1872	Methodist
189	Rolls, Keziah	75y	W	Md.	07 SEP 1860	Glenwood
257	Romaine, J.W., Mrs., child of	Still	W		08 MAR 1867	Congressional
344	Roman, Elizabeth	4d	C	D.C.	12 AUG 1868	Western
361	Roman, Mary, seamstress	27y	C	D.C.	11 NOV 1868	Harmony
761	Romey, Benjamin, laborer	27y	C	U.S.	25 APR 1874	Young Mens
382	Romill, Walter	8m	C		30 MAR 1869	
382	Ronco, Lavinia	3y	C	Va.	01 MAR 1869	Holmead
413	Rone, Martha	10m	C	Va.	05 AUG 1869	Holmead
378	Rone, Susan	2y	C	Va.	01 FEB 1869	Holmead
605	Rooney, John	2y	W	D.C.	11 JUN 1872	Mt. Olivet
224	Rooney, Mrs.		W	Ire.	13 JUN 1866	Alms House
223	Roony, John	35y	W	Ire.	08 JUN 1866	Alms House
371	Roosa, John L., gov. clerk	32y	W	Pa.	10 JAN 1869	Mt. Olivet
719	Roose, Auther	21d	W	U.S.	18 SEP 1873	Glenwood
755	Roose, Eva Jane	5y	W	U.S.	26 MAR 1874	Glenwood
376	Roose, George	6y	W		27 FEB 1869	Glenwood
266	Roose, John	5m	W	D.C.	14 JUL 1867	Glenwood
421	Root, Charley	10y	C		18 OCT 1869	Young Mens
019	Root, Jas. C.	14d	W		10 AUG 1855	Glenwood
492	Roots, Jane	58y	C	Va.	28 DEC 1870	Young Mens
774	Roots, Willie	7m	W	U.S.	08 JUN 1874	Potters Field
756	Roper, Ellen, housekeeper	67y	W	Ire.	31 MAR 1874	
730	Roper, Wm. B., laborer	76y	W	U.S.	12 NOV 1873	Graceland
588	Rorre, Goldie M.L.	2y	W	D.C.	26 MAR 1872	Congressional*
634	Rosario, Virginia, servant	23y	C	Brazil	05 OCT 1872	Mt. Olivet
635	Rose, Cath.	10y	C	U.S.	30 NOV 1872	Small Pox
397	Rose, David G., Col.	50y		Va.	08 JUN 1869	LaPorte, Ind.
635	Rose, Delia	32y	C	U.S.	28 NOV 1872	Small Pox
519	Rose, Franklin	10m	C	D.C.	22 MAY 1871	Union
583	Rose, Geo. W., carpenter	37y	W	U.S.	26 FEB 1872	Glenwood
598	Rose, George F.	18y	W	U.S.	15 MAY 1872	Glenwood
254	Rose, Harriett	4m	W	D.C.	02 FEB 1867	Congressional*
371	Rose, Harry C.	3m	W		31 JAN 1869	Glenwood
084	Rose, John R., bricklayer	29y	W	Md.	25 JUL 1857	Congressional

District of Columbia Interments (Index to Deaths), 1855-1874

Page	Name	Age	Race	Birth	Death Date	Burial Ground
380	Rose, Lewis Henry	5y	W		25 MAR 1869	Congressional
635	Rose, M.M.	8y	C	U.S.	12 NOV 1872	Small Pox
545	Rose, Peggy	35y	C	Va.	12 NOV 1871	
519	Rose, Robert, lawyer	65y	W	Va.	15 MAY 1871	Congressional*
784	Rose, Susan C.	42y	W	U.S.	12 JUL 1874	Glenwood
121	Rose, Susannah	62y	W	Va.	15 JUL 1858	Foundry
743	Rose, Susie	19y	C	U.S.	21 JAN 1874	Harmony
331	Roseberry, Elizabeth	72y			21 JUL 1868	Phillipsburg, N.J.
514	Rosenbury, Francis	6y	W	D.C.	22 MAR 1871	Prospect Hill
026	Rosengold, Georgeanna	8y	W	Md.	19 OCT 1855	German
068	Rosenthal, Charles E., grocer	54y	W	Prus.	05 JAN 1857	German
526	Rosenthal, Joseph, merchant	39y	W	Ger.	02 JUL 1871	Washington
555	Rosenthal, Wilhemina	70y	W	Ger.	25 JAN 1872	Glenwood
638	Ross, A., Miss	47y	C	U.S.	04 NOV 1872	
644	Ross, Agnes	28y	C	U.S.	22 DEC 1872	Ebenezer
552	Ross, Ann	3m	C		01 JAN 1872	Ebenezer
319	Ross, Arabella L.	33y	C	D.C.	09 JUN 1868	
626	Ross, Caroline	22y	W	U.S.	18 SEP 1872	Prospect Hill
619	Ross, Cath.	65y	C	U.S.	19 AUG 1872	
690	Ross, Charles	23m	C	U.S.	25 MAY 1873	Small Pox
159	Ross, Cora	8m	C	D.C.	01 AUG 1859	Harmony
594	Ross, Danl., laborer	87y	C	D.C.	08 APR 1872	Beckett's
622	Ross, Dewitt B.	20y	W	U.S.	22 AUG 1872	
641	Ross, Eliza	17y	C	U.S.	19 DEC 1872	Small Pox
684	Ross, Fanny	1m	C	U.S.	28 APR 1873	Small Pox*
524	Ross, Franklin	10m	C	D.C.	22 JUN 1871	Union
055	Ross, Herbert	36y	C	Va.	17 AUG 1856	Harmony
597	Ross, Isaac E., laborer	65y	C	U.S.	05 MAY 1872	Harmony
214	Ross, J.	4y	C		10 MAR 1866	Young Mens
256	Ross, James	51y	C		30 MAR 1867	Harmony
500	Ross, Jenny	20y	C	Va.	17 JAN 1871	Union
233	Ross, John	78y			01 AUG 1866	Wilmington, Del.
335	Ross, John D.	5m	C	D.C.	14 JUL 1868	Ebenezer
276	Ross, Joseph	1y	C	D.C.	10 SEP 1867	Harmony
089	Ross, Josephine	18y	W	D.C.	27 AUG 1857	Congressional
523	Ross, Letitia	5m	C	D.C.	19 JUN 1871	Young Mens
207	Ross, Lilley	1y	C		05 JUL 1862	Western
332	Ross, Lillie	4m	C	D.C.	07 JUL 1868	Harmony
260	Ross, Mariah, washerwoman	30y	C	Va.	11 MAY 1867	Harmony
694	Ross, Marion	3y	C	D.C.	10 JUN 1873	Beckett's
264	Ross, Mary	45y	C	Md.	20 JUL 1867	Harmony
695	Ross, Mary E.	7m	C	D.C.	28 JUN 1873	
352	Ross, Mary E.	9m	C	D.C.	07 SEP 1868	Washington Asylum
416	Ross, Moses	2y	C	D.C.	24 SEP 1869	
320	Ross, Rosa	3y	C	D.C.	15 JUN 1868	Harmony
684	Ross, Sallie	1m	C	U.S.	28 APR 1873	Small Pox*
690	Ross, Sarah	25y	C	U.S.	08 MAY 1873	Small Pox
469	Ross, Sarah T.	75y	W	D.C.*	22 AUG 1870	Oak Hill
755	Ross, Sophia, servant	70y	C	U.S.	22 MAR 1874	
459	Ross, Susan, servant	17y	C	Va.	15 JUN 1870	
161	Ross, Thomas	12y	C	D.C.	05 SEP 1859	Foundry
784	Ross, Wesley, laborer	78y	C	U.S.	12 JUL 1874	Potters Field
313	Ross, William Henry	3m	C	D.C.	29 MAY 1868	Young Mens
582	Ross, Wm.	35y	C	Md.	24 FEB 1872	Potters Field
269	Rosseau, Charles	1y	W		28 AUG 1867	Mt. Olivet
409	Rossiter, Thomas	1y	W	D.C.	10 AUG 1869	Mt. Olivet
254	Roszells, Ennalls	73y	W	Va.	16 FEB 1867	St. George Island
028	Rotchford, Martha	30y	W	Ire.	02 OCT 1855	St. Patricks

District of Columbia Interments (Index to Deaths), 1855-1874

Page	Name	Age	Race	Birth	Death Date	Burial Ground
441	Roth, A., Mr., carpenter	36y	W	Ger.	02 FEB 1870	Prospect Hill
517	Roth, Andros, stone cutter	66y	W	Ger.	22 APR 1871	St. Marys
334	Roth, Johanna	2y	W	D.C.	15 JUL 1868	German Catholic
608	Roth, Louise	6m	W	D.C.	28 JUN 1872	
313	Roth, Margaret, Mrs.	62y	W	Ger.	10 MAY 1868	St. Marys
472	Roth, Mrs., child of	Still	W		06 AUG 1870	Prospect Hill
636	Roth, Philip, tobacconist	35y	W	Ger.	23 NOV 1872	
232	Rothery, Clara	2y	W	D.C.	23 AUG 1866	Glenwood
675	Rothmund, Philip	3m	W	U.S.	27 MAR 1873	St. Marys
464	Rothrock, Charles	1y	W	Amer.	20 JUL 1870	Mt. Olivet
376	Rothsock, George W.	2y	W	D.C.	28 FEB 1869	Mt. Olivet
003	Rothstine, Caroline	8m	W	D.C.	04 FEB 1855	
120	Rothwell, Amelia	5y	W	D.C.	04 JUL 1858	Congressional
244	Rothwell, Ann	50y	W		23 NOV 1866	Congressional
399	Rothwell, Emma Amelia	8m	W		01 JUL 1869	Congressional
692	Rothwell, G.W., pat. agent	24y	W	D.C.	22 MAY 1873	Congressional*
122	Rothwell, Richard	9d	W	D.C.	26 JUL 1858	Congressional
586	Rothwood, Manna	35y	W	U.S.	16 MAR 1872	German
372	Rotlard, Sarah	18d	C	D.C.	31 JAN 1869	Washington Asylum
006	Roules, Edwin	1y	W	D.C.	23 APR 1855	St. Matthews
440	Roument, Louis, farmer	42y	W		03 FEB 1870	Methodist
101	Rounds, Lucinda	82y	C	Va.	12 JAN 1858	Harmony
588	Roundtree, Blanche	1y	W	D.C.	28 MAR 1872	Congressional*
207	Rouple, D.	2m	W		05 JUL 1862	Western
289	Rourk, Sarah	29y	W	Ire.	16 JAN 1868	Mt. Olivet
133	Roux, Chas. F. Luis, teacher	74y	W	Switz.	22 NOV 1858	Congressional
252	Roux, George Jacob, bar keeper	48y	W		17 FEB 1867	Glenwood
310	Roux, Hypolite, cook	24y	C	Fra.	29 APR 1868	Glenwood
636	Rovane, Margaret	50y	W	Ire.	30 NOV 1872	
741	Rowell, Geo. B., clerk	39y	W	U.S.	08 JAN 1874	Oak Hill
483	Rowland, Mattie M.	23y	W	Pa.	19 OCT 1870	Pa.
420	Rowles, Edward	6y	W		04 OCT 1869	Holmead
386	Rowles, Ellen	58y	W	Md.	15 APR 1869	Mt. Olivet
033	Rowles, Jno. T.	4d	W	D.C.	01 JAN 1856	Foundry
051	Rowles, John	1m	W	D.C.	20 JUL 1856	Ebenezer
049	Rowles, Mary	30y	W	Md.	02 JUL 1856	Ebenezer
453	Rowley, Amos & Elma, infant of		W		30 MAY 1870	Congressional
318	Rowley, Mrs., infant of	21d	W	D.C.	27 JUN 1868	Congressional
394	Rowley, [blank]	12d	W	D.C.	20 JUN 1869	Congressional
426	Rowsy, Isabella	1y	C		28 NOV 1869	Young Mens
748	Roy, Adolptus	22y	W	U.S.	18 FEB 1874	Mt. Olivet
627	Roy, Ann	22y	C	U.S.	06 SEP 1872	Small Pox
611	Roy, Eddie	1y	C	U.S.	19 JUL 1872	
465	Roy, James, barber	35y	C	Md.	03 JUL 1870	Mt. Olivet
639	Royce, Eva	5y	W	U.S.	21 NOV 1872	Congressional
471	Royce, Marion V.	9d	W	Amer.	25 AUG 1870	Congressional
361	Royce, William James	1y	W		25 NOV 1868	Glenwood
365	Royes, Wm.	48y	C	Va.	11 DEC 1868	Young Mens
298	Royster, Lucy E.	39y	W	Va.	26 FEB 1868	Richmond, Va.
115	Ruchell, Henry	51y	W	Md.	07 JUN 1858	Washington Asylum
549	Rudd, Mary Alice	8y	W	Va.	21 DEC 1871	Va.
470	Rue, Wm. T.	9m	W		08 AUG 1870	Congressional
488	Rueben, Augusta	4m	W	U.S.	16 NOV 1870	Prospect Hill
357	Rueckert, L.	26y	W	Md.	19 OCT 1868	Washington Asylum
345	Ruff, Annie	10m	W		11 AUG 1868	German Catholic
351	Ruffin, Leonora	1y	C	D.C.	20 SEP 1868	Ebenezer
242	Ruffin, Margaret, domestic	65y	C	Va.	19 OCT 1866	Ebenezer
663	Ruffin, Robert	21y	C	U.S.	13 JAN 1873	Small Pox

District of Columbia Interments (Index to Deaths), 1855-1874

Page	Name	Age	Race	Birth	Death Date	Burial Ground
228	Ruger, Oliver J., gentleman	44y	W	N.Y.	13 JUL 1866	Congressional
748	Rugers, Lucy M.	5m	W	U.S.	01 FEB 1874	Mt. Olivet
179	Ruler, John	4y	C	D.C.	12 MAY 1860	Harmony
341	Rumble, John Franklin	11m	W	Pa.	11 AUG 1868	Congressional
019	Rumbler, Philip	2y	W	D.C.	10 AUG 1855	German
540	Rumney, J.W.	19y		N.Y.	01 OCT 1871	Glenwood
519	Rumph, Martha	71y	W	N.Y.	21 MAY 1871	Cemetery
421	Rumsey, Augusta Jane	53y	W	N.Y.	22 OCT 1869	N.Y.
711	Rupert, James	1y	W	D.C.	08 AUG 1873	Mt. Olivet*
190	Rupert, Mary	6m	W	D.C.	22 SEP 1860	St. Marys
456	Rupertus, John	4y	W	D.C.	18 JUN 1870	Prospect Hill
210	Rupler, Kate	30y	W	Switz.	20 JAN 1866	Prospect Hill
229	Rupley, Clara	3y	W		24 JUL 1866	German
350	Ruppee, John G.	11m	C	D.C.	20 SEP 1868	Mt. Olivet
549	Ruppert, Elisabeth	43y	W	Ger.	19 DEC 1871	St. Marys
303	Ruppert, Ernestine	2y	W	D.C.	06 MAR 1868	Prospect Hill
110	Ruppert, Frank	1y	W	D.C.	06 APR 1858	Glenwood
454	Ruppert, Henry A.	14d	C		16 MAY 1870	German Catholic
116	Ruppert, Ignatius Jos.	3y	W	D.C.	15 JUN 1858	German Catholic
626	Ruppert, John	48y	W	Ger.	25 SEP 1872	
602	Ruppert, Jos. B.	8m	W	Ger.	30 MAY 1872	St. Marys
124	Ruppert, Margaret	2y	W	D.C.	08 AUG 1858	German Catholic
218	Ruppert, Mary E.	6y	W	D.C.	24 APR 1866	
321	Ruppert, Mary E.	8m	W		04 JUN 1868	German Catholic
218	Ruppert, Mary M.	3y	W	D.C.	13 APR 1866	
344	Ruppert, Rosa	9m	W	D.C.	07 AUG 1868	Prospect Hill
114	Ruppert, Theresa K.	1y	W		25 MAY 1858	German Catholic
714	Rush, Adaline S.	12m	W	D.C.	30 AUG 1873	Mt. Olivet
611	Rush, Alphonso	9m	C	U.S.	09 JUL 1872	
629	Rushman, May J., lady	35y	W	U.S.	18 OCT 1872	
712	Russ, Jane	36y	W	D.C.	14 AUG 1873	Congressional
381	Russ, Johanna E.	30y	W	Conn.	21 MAR 1869	Hartford, Conn.
784	Russ, Otto	6d	W	U.S.	04 JUL 1874	Prospect Hill
760	Russel, J. & H., infant of	7d	C	U.S.	01 APR 1874	
502	Russel, Jeremiah	6m	W	D.C.	23 JAN 1871	Mt. Olivet
250	Russell, Alfred, clerk	62y	W	Tenn.	03 JAN 1867	Glenwood
618	Russell, Andrew, son of	12h	W	U.S.	09 AUG 1872	Mt. Olivet*
643	Russell, Anna M.	74y	W	U.S.	08 DEC 1872	Holiday
489	Russell, Chas. H.	9m	C	D.C.	05 NOV 1870	Harmony
748	Russell, Chas. P.	72y	W	U.S.	21 FEB 1874	Congressional
676	Russell, Edward	21d	C	D.C.	22 MAR 1873	
146	Russell, Harriet A.	2y	W	D.C.	01 APR 1859	Holmead
670	Russell, John	25y	C	U.S.	09 FEB 1873	Small Pox*
271	Russell, Laura	1y	W	Eng.	18 AUG 1867	Congressional
148	Russell, Mary	28y	W	Md.	12 MAY 1859	Mt. Olivet
432	Russell, Sally	32y	C	D.C.	27 DEC 1869	Washington Asylum
042	Russell, Sarah	6y	W	D.C.	16 APR 1856	Congressional
606	Russell, Thom	45y	C	Ga.	09 JUN 1872	Asylum
605	Russell, Thomas, laborer	45y	C	U.S.	11 JUN 1872	Asylum
172	Russell, Virginia F.	32y	W	Va.*	18 FEB 1860	Congressional
411	Rustin, Ann Maria, housewife	69y	C		23 AUG 1869	St. Patricks
177	Rustin, Harry	1y	C	D.C.	18 APR 1860	Harmony
270	Ruth, Enoch F., clerk	50y	W	Tenn.	03 AUG 1867	Mt. Olivet
713	Ruth, Marianna	28y	W	D.C.	25 AUG 1873	St. Marys
736	Ruth, Venie	4y	C	U.S.	14 DEC 1873	
028	Ruther, John A.	9m	W	D.C.	05 OCT 1855	
602	Rutherford, Alex, stone cutter	57y	W	Ire.	04 MAY 1872	Congressional
256	Rutherford, William, marble cutter	23y	W	D.C.	17 MAR 1867	Congressional

Page	Name	Age	Race	Birth	Death Date	Burial Ground
163	Ryan, Daniel, laborer	35y	W	Ire.	17 OCT 1859	Mt. Olivet
229	Ryan, Gertrude	2m	W	D.C.	21 JUL 1866	Mt. Olivet
333	Ryan, Henry	1y	W	Va.	03 JUL 1868	Methodist
478	Ryan, John	15y	W	Md.	14 SEP 1870	Mt. Olivet
220	Ryan, John, clerk in PO		W	Ire.	07 MAY 1866	Mt. Olivet
312	Ryan, John J., gardener	70y	W	Ire.	09 MAY 1868	Mt. Olivet
748	Ryan, Julia	28y	W	Ire.	10 FEB 1874	Mt. Olivet
066	Ryan, Mary	30y	W	Ire.	19 DEC 1856	St. Patricks
634	Ryan, Mary Alice	4y	W	U.S.	03 OCT 1872	Mt. Olivet
625	Ryan, Mary, housekeeper	53y	W	Ire.	16 SEP 1872	Mt. Olivet
231	Ryan, Mary Julia	1y	W	D.C.	16 AUG 1866	Mt. Olivet
281	Ryan, Patrick Mohen	24d	W		15 OCT 1867	Mt. Olivet
320	Ryan, Richard J., grocer	50y	W	Md.	14 JUN 1868	Glenwood
026	Ryan, Thos. S.	9m	W	D.C.	07 OCT 1855	
465	Ryan, Tomas W.	7m	W	D.C.	05 JUL 1870	Mt. Olivet
544	Ryan, Wm., clerk	53y	W	Ire.	08 NOV 1871	Mt. Olivet*
695	Ryden, Susan	74y	C	Md.	19 JUN 1873	Washington Asylum
514	Ryder, Harriet C.L.	36y	C		24 MAR 1871	Ebenezer
075	Ryon, John, laborer	73y	W	Ire.	04 APR 1857	St. Patricks

District of Columbia Interments (Index to Deaths), 1855-1874

Page	Name	Age	Race	Birth	Death Date	Burial Ground
S						
415	Saaer, John	6y	W		28 SEP 1869	Prospect Hill
464	Sacks, Anna	63y	W	Ger.	05 JUL 1870	Prospect Hill
499	Saddler, Chas.	1m	W	D.C.	11 JAN 1871	Congressional
632	Sadle, Sarah V.	22m	W	U.S.	18 OCT 1872	
416	Sadler, Margaret V.	1y	W		13 SEP 1869	Methodist
270	Saebard, John	3d	W	D.C.	26 AUG 1867	German Catholic
458	Saffell, Anna Maria	30y	W	D.C.	01 JUN 1870	Mt. Olivet
317	Safford, H.S., child of	Still	W	D.C.	12 JUN 1868	Congressional
188	Sage, Henry B., printer	31y	W	Pa.	31 AUG 1860	Congressional
631	Sage, Javin, laborer	21y	C	U.S.	11 OCT 1872	
356	Sahreon, Pauline	2y	W	Ger.	06 OCT 1868	Prospect Hill
383	Saleo, John	1d	C	D.C.	01 MAR 1869	Washington Asylum
128	Sales, Michael, waiter	20y	W	Ire.	28 SEP 1858	Washington Asylum
635	Sales, Robert	4y	C	U.S.	22 NOV 1872	Small Pox
495	Sales, [blank]	1y	C		31 DEC 1870	Beckett's
555	Salt, George Henry	1m	W	U.S.	22 JAN 1872	Oak Hill
547	Salt, Phoeba A.	32y	W	U.S.	06 DEC 1871	Oak Hill
689	Sample, Mary Defrees	7m	W	U.S.	28 MAY 1873	Glenwood
096	Sampson, Andrew, whitewasher	37y	C	Va.	15 NOV 1857	Foundry
007	Sampson, Ann	30y	W	Va.	14 APR 1855	Foundry
614	Sampson, Danl.	32y	W	U.S.	18 JUL 1872	
130	Sampson, Eliza	34y	C		14 OCT 1858	St. Matthews
166	Sampson, Henry B.	1y	W	D.C.	28 NOV 1859	Washington Asylum
063	Sampson, James, laborer	58y	W	Va.	21 NOV 1856	Methodist
207	Sampson, Jessey	45y	C		11 JUL 1862	
669	Sampson, Mary	23y	C	U.S.	25 FEB 1873	Washington Asylum
450	Sampson, Mary E.	1m	W		18 APR 1870	Mt. Olivet
473	Sampson, Reuben	9m	C	D.C.	12 AUG 1870	Holmead
618	Samstag, Isaac	2y	W	U.S.	— AUG 1872	Prospect Hill
236	Samuel, Richmond	48y	C		30 SEP 1866	Young Mens
459	Samuels, Harriet	25y	C	Va.	14 JUN 1870	Holmead
288	Sanborn, John J., clerk	69y	W	Mass.	04 DEC 1867	Oak Hill
285	Sanders, Alfred, body servant	46y	C	Md.	30 DEC 1867	Holmead
031	Sanders, Ella R.	2y	W	D.C.	23 DEC 1855	Glenwood
229	Sanders, Frederick, soldier	32y	W	Ger.	18 JUL 1866	Arlington Heights
381	Sanders, Louise Sophie	3m	W	D.C.	29 MAR 1869	Prospect Hill
290	Sanders, Mary	5m	C	D.C.	24 JAN 1868	Freedmen's Hospital
279	Sanders, Ossafrena	1m	C	D.C.	19 OCT 1867	Holmead
330	Sanders, Robert, laborer	50y	C	Va.	30 JUL 1868	Union
620	Sanders, Sally	2y	W	U.S.	08 AUG 1872	Prospect Hill
125	Sanderson, Chas. W., machinist	26y	W	D.C.	18 AUG 1858	Congressional
266	Sanderson, Mary	30y	W	D.C.	22 JUL 1867	Congressional
399	Sanderson, Sarah, Mrs.	35y	W	D.C.	07 JUL 1869	Congressional
425	Sanderson, Sarah R.	1y	W	D.C.	19 NOV 1869	Congressional
414	Sanderson, [?] May	2y	W	D.C.	16 SEP 1869	Congressional
312	Sands, Annie	15y	W	Md.	02 MAY 1868	Annapolis, Md.
341	Sands, Frank T., undertaker	34y	W	Md.	31 AUG 1868	Congressional
553	Sands, Mary, servant	24y	W	Ire.	10 JAN 1872	Mt. Olivet
585	Sands, Thaddeus E.	47y	W	U.S.	06 MAR 1872	Congressional
202	Sands, [blank]	Still	W	D.C.	30 APR 1861	Congressional
479	Sandy, [blank]		C	D.C.	09 SEP 1870	Washington Asylum
611	Sanford, Grace V.	1y	W	U.S.	03 JUL 1872	Congressional*
479	Sanford, Hy. A.	1y	C	D.C.	03 SEP 1870	Washington Asylum
499	Sanford, James R.	3y	W	D.C.	18 JAN 1871	Congressional
761	Sanford, James S., farmer	52y	W	U.S.	12 APR 1874	Perry, N.Y.
002	Sanford, Lucy	31y	W	Va.	17 JAN 1855	Congressional
390	Sanford, Lyon, laborer	46y	W		07 MAY 1869	Congressional

Page	Name	Age	Race	Birth	Death Date	Burial Ground
024	Sanford, Mary	27y	W	Va.	10 SEP 1855	Glenwood
200	Sanford, Milly	79y	W		22 FEB 1861	St. Peters
185	Sanford, Sarah	3y	W	D.C.	17 JUL 1860	Congressional
541	Sanford, Seth T., preacher	51y	C	Me.	13 OCT 1871	Me.
440	Sanford, Stephen	10m	W	N.Y.	20 FEB 1870	Amsterdam, N.Y.
225	Sanford, Wm., sailor	40y	W	Can.	24 JUN 1866	
197	Sanger, Capt., col. woman of	45y	C		26 JAN 1861	Western
390	Sanger, Solomon	3m	W		01 MAY 1869	Washington Hebrew
349	Sangston, Wm. S.	1y	W		10 SEP 1868	Baltimore, Md.
127	Sanner, [blank]	3m	W		01 SEP 1858	Western
077	Sanning, Mrs.	28y	W	Ire.	10 MAY 1857	St. Patricks
611	Santroy, Chas. H.	4m	C	U.S.	03 JUL 1872	
265	Santry, Joseph	8m	W	D.C.	26 JUL 1867	Mt. Olivet
440	Santucci, Victoria	3y	W		14 FEB 1870	Mt. Olivet
077	Saran, Charles	57y	W		02 MAY 1857	Oak Hill
743	Sardif, Cartren	72y	C	U.S.	27 JAN 1874	Mt. Pleasant
176	Sardo, Michael, musician	84y	W	Sicily	12 APR 1860	St. Patricks
735	Sargent, John, laborer	78y	C	U.S.	11 DEC 1873	Washington Asylum
744	Sarndus, W.S., messenger	58y	W	U.S.	28 JAN 1874	South Bend, Ind.
737	Sarniels, A.M.	2m	W	U.S.	26 DEC 1873	Congressional
638	Sarrer, Sarah	4y	C	U.S.	08 NOV 1872	
398	Sarsfield, B., laborer	21y	W	Ire.	20 JUN 1869	Red Hill [sic]
610	Sarvia, Gille	38y	W	Gel.	18 JUL 1872	
276	Sauer, Ossula	54y	W	Ger.	07 SEP 1867	German Catholic
587	Sauer, [blank]	1y	W	D.C.	20 MAR 1872	St. Marys
108	Saul, James A.	7m	W	D.C.	15 MAR 1858	St. Matthews
611	Saunders, Caroline	2m	C	U.S.	23 JUL 1872	
472	Saunders, Elizabeth	8m	C	D.C.	13 AUG 1870	Young Mens
599	Saunders, Hannah	22y	C	U.S.	12 MAY 1872	Unknown
085	Saunders, Harriet	30y	C		29 JUL 1857	Harmony
203	Saunders, Harriet, servant	50y	C	Md.	13 MAY 1861	Ebenezer
530	Saunders, John, laborer	70y	C		31 JUL 1871	Young Mens
259	Saunders, Louis	51y	C		03 APR 1867	Mt. Olivet
015	Saunders, Thos. F.	27y	W	Va.	07 JUL 1855	Glenwood
162	Sauner, Julia	2y	W	D.C.	16 SEP 1859	Baltimore, Md.
386	Sauntry, Michael	2y	W	D.C.	18 APR 1869	Mt. Olivet
140	Saur, Chas. Louis	3y	W	D.C.	10 FEB 1859	German
784	Sauri, Charles, merchant	73y	W	Fra.	03 JUL 1874	Albany, N.Y.
280	Saurin, George F.	30y	W	Mass.	31 OCT 1867	Boston, Mass.
133	Saurs, Milard	3m	W	D.C.	20 NOV 1858	Washington Asylum
169	Sauter, Catharine E.	2y	W	D.C.	08 JAN 1860	St. Patricks (vault)
464	Sauter, Chas. H.	4d	W	D.C.	10 JUL 1870	Mt. Olivet
338	Sauter, George Wash.	1y	W	U.S.	24 AUG 1868	Mt. Olivet
185	Sauter, Henry Albin	1y	W	D.C.	26 JUL 1860	Mt. Olivet
339	Sauter, Jacob Ambrose	15d	W	D.C.	06 AUG 1868	Mt. Olivet
223	Sauter, Mary F.	2m	W	D.C.	08 JUN 1866	Mt. Olivet
445	Sauter, Samuel S.	9m	W		08 MAR 1870	Mt. Olivet
204	Sauter, William, confectioner	55y	W	Ger.	16 JUN 1861	Mt. Olivet
083	Savabzyi, Julietta	1y	W	D.C.	17 JUL 1857	
361	Savage, Samuel F., US naval ofcr.	32y	W	D.C.	05 NOV 1868	Mt. Olivet
111	Savage, Sue	18y	W	D.C.	13 APR 1858	St. Patricks
777	Savage, William	21y	W	Ire.	04 JUN 1874	Mt. Olivet
075	Savoy, Alice A.	1y	C	D.C.	04 APR 1857	Methodist, Georgetown
223	Savoy, Catherine	60y			08 JUN 1866	Ft. Stevens, Md.
455	Savoy, Hattie Elizabeth	27y	C		05 MAY 1870	Ebenezer
588	Savoy, Jennie, servant	19y	W		24 MAR 1872	Mt. Olivet
335a	Savoy, Jno. Hy.				28 JUL 1868	Washington Asylum
328	Savoy, John Henry	4y	C	D.C.	28 JUL 1868	Alms House

Page	Name	Age	Race	Birth	Death Date	Burial Ground
377	Savoy, Lambertie Estelle	14d	C		09 FEB 1869	
386	Sawson, Ellen	24y	W	Ire.	15 APR 1869	Mt. Olivet
094	Sawyer, Betsy	65y	C	Va.	26 OCT 1857	Young Mens
375	Sawyer, Eliza Jane	11d	W		c.22 FEB 1869	Congressional
172	Sawyer, Horace B., naval officer	62y	W	Ver.	14 FEB 1860	Burlington, Vt.
521	Sawyer, J.E.	7m		Mass.	04 JUN 1871	Congressional
673	Sawyer, Louisa Annie	3y	W	U.S.	06 MAR 1873	Oak Hill
303	Sawyer, Saml. L.	1y	W	D.C.	23 MAR 1868	Congressional
229	Saxte, Miss	17y	W	Eng.	23 JUL 1866	Prospect Hill
370	Saxton, Fanny Botums	2y	W		04 JAN 1869	Glenwood
412	Saxton, Willie	7m	C	D.C.	05 AUG 1869	Washington Asylum
727	Saxton, [Joseph], weights/meas.	74y	W	U.S.	31 OCT 1873	Congressional
477	Saxty, William B.	3y	W	Conn.	25 SEP 1870	Congressional
461	Sayers, Elizabeth	65y	W	Md.	21 JUL 1870	Congressional
582	Sayles, John	3y	C	D.C.	19 FEB 1872	
389	Sayles, Maria	70y	C	Va.	10 APR 1869	Washington Asylum
785	Sayre, Lillie	22y	W	U.S.	24 JUL 1874	Congressional
394	Sazenhopen, John F.C.	1y	W	D.C.	30 JUN 1869	Mt. Olivet
307	Scafry, Thomas	70y	C	Md.	14 APR 1868	Freedmen's Hospital
008	Scaggs, Saml., slave of	70y	C	Md.	17 MAY 1855	Pr. Geo. Co., Md.
469	Scale, Sarah S.	11m	W	D.C.	07 AUG 1870	Glenwood
046	Scalenberger, Agnes	6m	W	D.C.	02 JUN 1856	German Catholic
299	Scanlan, John, laborer	28y	W	Ire.	26 MAR 1868	Mt. Olivet
080	Scanlan, Mary, dairymaid	55y	W	Ire.	30 JUN 1857	St. Patricks
721	Scanlan, Michael, laborer	42y	W	Ire.	30 SEP 1873	
361	Scanlon, Mrs., infant of	Still	W		22 NOV 1868	Mt. Olivet
768	Scannell, Cornelius, clerk	25y	W	Ire.	19 MAY 1874	Albion, N.Y.
155	Scantling, E.	9m	W	D.C.	31 JUL 1859	Mt. Olivet
247	Scarff, Charles Alexander	6y	W	D.C.	04 DEC 1866	Congressional
414	Scarra, Martha	46y	W	D.C.	03 SEP 1869	Mt. Olivet
513	Schaale, Louis, messenger	37y	W	Prus.	10 MAR 1871	Prospect Hill
062	Schad, Elizabeth	38y	W	Ger.	12 NOV 1856	Congressional
360	Schade, Juliana, housewife	70y	W	Ger.	15 NOV 1868	Prospect Hill
114	Schaefer, Henry	9m	W	D.C.	16 MAY 1858	German Catholic
292	Schaefer, Louis	3m			09 JAN 1868	
481	Schaeffer, Fredk. C., clerk	28y	W	N.Y.	01 OCT 1870	Oak Hill
007	Schafer, Christina	6d	W	D.C.	31 MAY 1855	[torn]
450	Schafer, Dorothea	37y	W	Ger.	23 APR 1870	Prospect Hill
344	Schafer, Edward	22y	W		27 AUG 1868	Prospect Hill
681	Schaffer, Annie	18y	W	U.S.	15 APR 1873	Congressional*
723	Schaffer, Ge. Christian, prof.	58y	W	Pa.	04 OCT 1873	Oak Hill
669	Schaffer, T.H., tailor	47y	W	Ger.	01 FEB 1873	
096	Schaffer, Theodore Douglass	6m	W	D.C.	12 NOV 1857	German Lutheran
584	Schaffer, Tilas, grocer	44y	W	Ger.	04 MAR 1872	Potters Field
584	Schaffer, [blank]	4y	W	U.S.	05 MAR 1872	
200	Schaffer, [blank]	Still	W	D.C.	27 FEB 1861	Congressional
682	Schaible, [blank]	2d	W	U.S.	24 APR 1873	
195	Scharff, [blank]	60y	W	Md.	25 DEC 1860	Congressional
749	Schatzig, M.	62y	W	Den.	28 FEB 1874	Congressional*
236	Scheanholtz, Harman, upholsterer	46y	W	Ger.	30 SEP 1866	Glenwood
030	Scheckels, Thos., bricklayer	45y	W	D.C.	27 NOV 1855	Ebenezer
599	Scheitzer, Peter	5y	W	U.S.	03 MAY 1872	Prospect Hill
253	Scheldoon, Henry	3m	W	D.C.	02 FEB 1867	Mt. Olivet
248	Schell, John	19y	W		19 DEC 1866	Mt. Olivet
293	Schell, William	19d	W	D.C.*	31 MAR 1868	Oak Hill
706	Schench, Elizabeth	16y	W	D.C.	09 JUL 1873	Glenwood
247	Schenig, Mrs.	64y	W		02 DEC 1866	Western
376	Scherger, Chas., infant of	Still	W		23 FEB 1869	Glenwood

Page	Name	Age	Race	Birth	Death Date	Burial Ground
547	Schickler, Mary				06 DEC 1871	Prospect Hill
159	Schidtz, Rosana Catharine	43y	W	Ger.	26 AUG 1859	Prospect Hill
366	Schlaich, Catherine	2y	W	D.C.	25 DEC 1868	Prospect Hill
317	Schlaub, William	7m	W	D.C.	05 JUN 1868	Prospect Hill
675	Schlegd, Ferdinand, grocer	55y	W	Ger.	21 MAR 1873	Glenwood
092	Schlegel, Eliza	3y	W	D.C.	27 SEP 1857	German Lutheran
547	Schlegel, Mary Ann	14y	W	D.C.	08 DEC 1871	Glenwood
598	Schlegel, Wm.	12y	W	U.S.	02 MAY 1872	Glenwood
767	Schleith, Christopher A.	1m	W	U.S.	08 MAY 1874	Prospect Hill
303	Schlimer, child of	Still	W	D.C.	12 MAR 1868	Hebrew
521	Schlorb, William, butcher	56y	W	Ger.	08 JUN 1871	Prospect Hill
632	Schlosser, Fred.	1y	W	U.S.	18 OCT 1872	
785	Schlosser, Jno. H., granite cutter	64y	W	Ger.	20 JUL 1874	Glenwood
435	Schlothersbuch, Albert	23d	W		17 JAN 1870	Prospect Hill
453	Schluter, Sophia	77y	W	Ger.	23 MAY 1870	Prospect Hill
502	Schmid, Johanna A.	1y	W	D.C.	26 JAN 1871	Glenwood
438	Schmidberger, Joseph, clerk	32y	W	Ger.	02 JAN 1870	Prospect Hill
286	Schmidt, Catherine	35y	W	Ger.	19 DEC 1867	Prospect Hill
698	Schmidt, Dorotha	100y	W	Ger.	29 JUN 1873	Mt. Olivet
107	Schmidt, J.		W	D.C.	11 MAR 1858	Holmead
509	Schmidt, John H.	1y	W	D.C.	05 FEB 1871	Methodist
636	Schmidt, John, tobacconist	29y	W	U.S.	06 NOV 1872	
456	Schmidt, Louis		W		09 JUN 1870	
440	Schmidt, Louis	3y	W		18 FEB 1870	Glenwood
396	Schmidt, Mrs.		W	Ger.	24 JUN 1869	Prospect Hill
028	Schmidt, [blank], baker		W		23 OCT 1855	German
163	Schmitt, Catharine	55y	W	Va.	26 OCT 1859	Va.
471	Schneideger, Anna M.	10m	W	Amer.	28 AUG 1870	Prospect Hill
148	Schneider, Caroline S.	1y	W	D.C.	13 MAY 1859	Congressional*
540	Schneider, Ch.	47y	W	Eur.	04 OCT 1871	Congressional
135	Schneider, Clara Mankel	22y	W	Ger.	05 DEC 1858	German
639	Schneider, Jno. H., boatman	36y	W	Ger.	09 NOV 1872	
450	Schneider, Minnie	7m	W		10 APR 1870	Prospect Hill
768	Schneider, Nettie	21y	W	U.S.	29 MAY 1874	
224	Schneider, William H.	14y	W	D.C.	15 JUN 1866	Oak Hill
785	Schneizer, Adam	73y	W	Ger.	20 JUL 1874	St. Marys
259	Schnell, Hannah	57y	W	Ger.	13 APR 1867	
097	Schnider, Julia C.	18y	W	D.C.	26 NOV 1857	Congressional
148	Schnier, John Deiterich, carpenter	38y	W	Ger.	10 MAY 1859	Prospect Hill
368	Schoales, Jane	77y	W	Ire.	03 DEC 1868	Oak Hill
761	Schober, Charles, brewer	31y	W	Ger.	07 APR 1874	Prospect Hill
146	Schoeff, Julia M.	3y	W	D.C.	11 APR 1859	German
620	Schoenberger, L.T.	1y	W	U.S.	20 AUG 1872	Glenwood
711	Schoenborn, Alice	9m	W	U.S.	11 AUG 1873	Congressional*
730	Schoenhorn, Chas. F.	8y	W	U.S.	13 NOV 1873	Congressional
382	Schofield, Wm. Andrew	1y			17 MAR 1869	
315	Scholland, Thomas	12y	W		c.15 MAY 1868	Mt. Olivet
016	Scholtz, R.B.	1y	W	D.C.	18 JUL 1855	German
334	Schonberger, Lorenz	11m	W	D.C.	15 JUL 1868	German Catholic
225	Schonborn, [blank]	2y	W	D.C.	23 JUN 1866	Congressional
533	Schondon, Adam F.	8m	W	D.C.	26 AUG 1871	Prospect Hill
299	Schott, Nancy, Mrs.	67y	W		16 MAR 1868	Glenwood
028	Schott, Wm. P.	17y	W	Pa.	04 OCT 1855	Glenwood
623	Schotts, Alx. L.	3y	W	U.S.	29 JUL 1872	
532	Schoudan, Eva Maria	41y	W	Sax.	10 AUG 1871	Prospect Hill
022	Schraum, Magt.	60y	W	Ger.	08 AUG 1855	
546	Schroder, Hugo	30y	W	Ger.	26 NOV 1871	
583	Schroder, Robt.	1y	W	U.S.	28 FEB 1872	Congressional

District of Columbia Interments (Index to Deaths), 1855-1874

Page	Name	Age	Race	Birth	Death Date	Burial Ground
279	Schroth, John	1y	W	D.C.	22 OCT 1867	Mt. Olivet
464	Schrott, Mary	23y	W	Ger.	16 JUL 1870	Prospect Hill
464	Schubert, Amy	4m	W	D.C.	26 JUL 1870	German Catholic
131	Schuby, Anna M.C.	2y	W	D.C.	29 OCT 1858	German
039	Schuby, Coelestin, schoolmaster	22y	W	Ger.	13 MAR 1856	Alms House
697	Schuch, Henry, baker	21y	W	Ger.	07 JUN 1873	Glenwood
170	Schuerman, Sallie	7y	W	D.C.	27 JAN 1860	Glenwood
589	Schul, Caroline	35y	W	D.C.	05 MAR 1872	Oak Hill
079	Schulte, Henry, bar keeper	35y	W	Prus.	12 JUN 1857	
712	Schulthis, Chollata	26y	W	Ger.	20 AUG 1873	Glenwood
481	Schultz, Charles A., wheelwright	34y	W	Prus.	26 OCT 1870	Prospect Hill
434	Schultz, Clara Elizabeth	2y	W	D.C.	01 JAN 1870	German Catholic
612	Schultz, Eda	6m	W	U.S.	08 JUL 1872	
172	Schultz, Henry, turner	37y	W	Ger.	03 FEB 1860	Prospect Hill
668	Schultz, Jno. George, merchant	27y	W	U.S.	17 FEB 1873	Prospect Hill
087	Schultz, Joseph, painter	53y	W	Ger.	14 AUG 1857	Congressional
290	Schultz, Mary	8d	W	D.C.	23 JAN 1868	German Catholic
115	Schultz, Mary E.	9m	W	Md.	12 JUN 1858	Baltimore, Md.
279	Schultz, Philomena	1y	W		06 OCT 1867	German Catholic
761	Schultze, John C., carpenter	75y	W	Ger.	24 APR 1874	
263	Schultze, William, hosp. steward		W		18 JUN 1867	Congressional*
496	Schuly, Anton A.	7m	W	D.C.	18 DEC 1870	German Catholic
777	Schulz, Albert	1m	W	U.S.	28 JUN 1874	St. Marys
369	Schulz, Charles	1y	W	D.C.	29 JAN 1869	Congressional
391	Schulze, William, carpenter	52y	W	Ger.	30 MAY 1869	Mt. Olivet
089	Schupler, Charles, tavern keeper	57y	W	Han.	27 AUG 1857	Methodist
149	Schureman, Sarah A.	54y	C	Md.	27 MAY 1859	Harmony
175	Schusller, Mary	74y	W	Ger.	24 MAR 1860	Glenwood
036	Schuster, Martin, butcher	75y	W	Ger.	23 FEB 1856	German
279	Schutter, H., child of	Still			12 OCT 1867	Glenwood
689	Schwab, Jno. Leonard	53y		Ger.	22 MAY 1873	
103	Schwalbach, Anna C.	66y	W	Ger.	30 JAN 1858	German Catholic
403	Schwartz, Anna	22d	W	D.C.	05 JUL 1869	Prospect Hill
146	Schwartze, Lorenz	5y	W	D.C.	15 APR 1859	Glenwood
016	Schwarzenback, Adalgunde	4m	W	York	28 JUL 1855	German
725	Schwiering, Henry W., appren.	17y	W	D.C.	19 OCT 1873	Prospect Hill
083	Schwiering, Mary	5y	W	D.C.	14 JUL 1857	
050	Schwinghammer, F.L.	11m	W	D.C.	19 JUL 1856	German
232	Scissel, Mary Alfred	3m	W	D.C.	22 AUG 1866	Congressional
118	Scofield, Ellen	48y	W		30 JUN 1858	St. Patricks
415	Scofield, Julia Ann	24y	W	N.Y.	20 SEP 1869	Aden, Erie Co., Pa.
011	Scofield, Rebecca	55y	W		27 JUN 1855	Foundry
583	Scott, A.R., Mrs.	41y	W	D.C.	28 FEB 1872	Congressional
382	Scott, Agnes	5y	C		27 MAR 1869	Young Mens
418	Scott, Albert, laborer	35y	C	Va.	10 SEP 1869	
492	Scott, Alberta	4m	C		29 DEC 1870	Young Mens
176	Scott, Ann	22y	W	D.C.	16 APR 1860	Congressional
755	Scott, Ann	66y	W	U.S.	30 MAR 1874	Oak Hill
531	Scott, Ann J.	63y	W		07 AUG 1871	Congressional*
660	Scott, Benja.	10m	W	U.S.	18 JAN 1873	Congressional
391	Scott, Byron	8y	W		06 MAY 1869	Glenwood
056	Scott, Charles	5y	C	D.C.	30 AUG 1856	
612	Scott, Chas. A.	10m	W	U.S.	04 JUL 1872	
583	Scott, Chas. S.	2y	W	D.C.	28 FEB 1872	Congressional*
669	Scott, Clara A.	10y	C	U.S.	06 FEB 1873	Small Pox
767	Scott, Clara G.	28y	W	U.S.	04 MAY 1874	[torn]
347	Scott, Cora Lelia	1y	W		24 SEP 1868	Congressional
255	Scott, Daniel	4y	C		14 MAR 1867	Young Mens

Page	Name	Age	Race	Birth	Death Date	Burial Ground
245	Scott, Eleanor Ann	48y	W	Md.	03 NOV 1866	Congressional
170	Scott, Eliza	5m	C	D.C.	28 JAN 1860	Young Mens
400	Scott, Eliza Ann	20y	C	Va.	20 JUL 1869	Holmead
437	Scott, Elizabeth	84y	W	Ire.	13 JAN 1870	Baltimore, Md.
761	Scott, Ellen	16y	C	U.S.	19 APR 1874	Young Mens
269	Scott, Ellen, washerwoman	54y	C	Md.	10 AUG 1867	Ebenezer
637	Scott, Ellenora	7y	W	U.S.	05 NOV 1872	Congressional*
720	Scott, Eloise H., Treasury clerk	36y	W	Md.	27 SEP 1873	
610	Scott, Emma	10y	W	U.S.	03 JUL 1872	Congressional*
518	Scott, Francis	80y	W	Va.	10 MAY 1871	Congressional
546	Scott, George				26 NOV 1871	Congressional*
482	Scott, George	8m	C	D.C.	03 OCT 1870	Harmony
542	Scott, George W., clerk	76y	W	N.Y.	25 OCT 1871	Congressional
174	Scott, George W.	5y	C	D.C.	13 MAR 1860	Young Mens
374	Scott, Georgianna	18y	W		19 FEB 1869	Congressional
336	Scott, Georgianna	2y	C	D.C.	14 AUG 1868	Ebenezer
297	Scott, Harriet, Mrs.		C	Va.	20 FEB 1868	Smith's
390	Scott, Harry S.	4y	W	S.C.	29 MAY 1869	Congressional
090	Scott, Horace	20y	W	Md.	11 SEP 1857	Upper Marlboro, Md.
174	Scott, Horatio C., farmer	68y	W	Md.	12 MAR 1860	Pr. Geo. Co., Md.
593	Scott, Howard	9m	C	D.C.	01 APR 1872	
308	Scott, Infant	Still	W	D.C.	30 APR 1868	Methodist
239	Scott, J.H.	67y	W	D.C.*	29 OCT 1866	Mt. Olivet
357	Scott, James	15y	B	Md.	01 OCT 1868	Freedmen's Hospital
666	Scott, James	40y	C	U.S.	02 FEB 1873	Washington Asylum
090	Scott, James I.	8m	W	D.C.	02 SEP 1857	Congressional
285	Scott, Jane Elizabeth	7m	C	D.C.	18 DEC 1867	Young Mens
671	Scott, Jno. A.	3y	W	U.S.	20 FEB 1873	Small Pox*
461	Scott, John	P.B.	W	D.C.	16 JUL 1870	Congressional
301	Scott, John	50y	C	Va.	29 MAR 1868	Young Mens
057	Scott, John Augustus	6m	W	D.C.	08 SEP 1856	St. Patricks
471	Scott, John W.	7m	W	D.C.	01 AUG 1870	Congressional
362	Scott, Joseph	6m	C		07 NOV 1868	Harmony
777	Scott, Katie L.	4m	C	U.S.	10 JUN 1874	Congressional*
719	Scott, Kolt	56y	C	Va.	22 SEP 1873	
442	Scott, Lizzie	7d	C		02 FEB 1870	Washington Asylum
666	Scott, Lucinda	56y	W	U.S.	07 FEB 1873	Congressional
248	Scott, Lucretia H.	25y	W	Md.	15 DEC 1866	Congressional
383	Scott, Lucy	70y	C	Md.	10 MAR 1869	Washington Asylum
704	Scott, Lula	10m	C	Md.	27 JUL 1873	Ebenezer
344	Scott, Magude R.	6y	C	Ohio	07 AUG 1868	Western
009	Scott, Major, servant of	4y	C	D.C.	08 MAY 1855	Country
714	Scott, Manuel	70y	C	Va.	28 AUG 1873	
622a	Scott, Maria	15y	C	U.S.	04 AUG 1872	
335b	Scott, Martha	1d	B	D.C.	13 JUL 1868	Washington Asylum
061	Scott, Martha Allen	1y	W	D.C.	20 OCT 1856	Congressional
617	Scott, Martha E.	27y	C	U.S.	03 AUG 1872	Ebenezer
179	Scott, Mary	30y	C	U.S.	28 MAY 1860	Methodist
045	Scott, Mary Elizh.	3y	W	Md.	27 MAY 1856	St. Patricks
711	Scott, Mary, house maid	21y	C	U.S.	10 AUG 1873	Mt. Olivet
499	Scott, Mary Jane	1y	W	D.C.	25 JAN 1871	Congressional
440	Scott, Mary Virginia, Mrs., clerk	45y	W	Va.	17 FEB 1870	Waterford, N.Y.
506	Scott, Pat	28y	C	Va.	25 FEB 1871	Washington Asylum
400	Scott, Philliza	9m	C		06 JUL 1869	Holmead
598	Scott, Pitt	75y	C	U.S.	03 MAY 1872	Asylum
619	Scott, Rachael	34y	C	U.S.	14 AUG 1872	Asylum
597	Scott, Samuel, cart driver	15y	C	U.S.	13 MAY 1872	Washington
172	Scott, Samuel E.	4m	C	D.C.	20 FEB 1860	Young Mens

District of Columbia Interments (Index to Deaths), 1855-1874

Page	Name	Age	Race	Birth	Death Date	Burial Ground
004	Scott, Sarah	19y	W	Md.	12 MAR 1855	St. Patricks
213	Scott, Susan	10d	C		25 FEB 1866	Colored
392	Scott, Victoria	39y	W		03 MAY 1869	Washington Asylum
079	Scott, W.B., Maj.	68y	W	Md.	07 JUN 1857	Oak Hill
669	Scott, William	1m	C	U.S.	26 FEB 1873	Ebenezer
185	Scott, William	39y	C	U.S.	21 JUL 1860	Methodist
371	Scott, William	5m	W	D.C.	04 JAN 1869	Washington Asylum
210	Scott, William, shoemaker	56y	W		27 JAN 1866	
724	Scott, Willie	4y	B	D.C.	13 OCT 1873	Beckett's
376	Scott, Willie	1y	C		26 FEB 1869	Young Mens
777	Scott, Wm.	3m	C	U.S.	26 JUN 1874	
581	Scott, Wm., blacksmith	36y	W	Pa.	17 FEB 1872	Young Mens
600	Scott, Wm. F.	8y	W	U.S.	15 MAY 1872	Unknown
597	Scott, Wm. F.	7y	W	U.S.	16 MAY 1872	Washington
033	Scott, Wm. H.	7m	W		07 JAN 1856	Methodist
466	Scott, Wm. H.	1y	C	D.C.	22 JUL 1870	Young Mens
375	Scott, [blank]	Still	W	D.C.	16 FEB 1869	
581	Scott, [blank]	1d	C	U.S.	15 FEB 1872	Washington
210	Scott, [blank]	40y	C		20 JAN 1866	Western
195	Scrivener, Ada	16y	W	D.C.	02 DEC 1860	Mt. Olivet
111	Scrivener, Charles	47y	W	Va.	19 APR 1858	Congressional
136	Scrivener, Mary A.	82y	W	U.S.	22 DEC 1858	Methodist
365	Scrivener, Mary Ann	53y	W	Amer.	18 DEC 1868	Mt. Olivet
141	Scrivener, Rebecca	83y	W	Md.	13 FEB 1859	Congressional
111	Scrivener, Sarah	40y	W		17 APR 1858	Western
675	Scriver, Louisa	34y	W	U.S.	27 MAR 1873	Hudson Co., N.Y.
328	Scriviner, M.	1y	C	D.C.	31 JUL 1868	Alms House
359	Scrivner, Jas. R.	1y	W	D.C.	17 NOV 1868	Congressional
088	Scrivner, Theodore	8m	W	D.C.	19 AUG 1857	St. Patricks
540	Scroggins, George	1d	W	D.C.	03 OCT 1871	Congressional*
735	Scroggins, Wm. F., laborer	32y	W	U.S.	12 DEC 1873	
357	Seabright, Jas.	60y	W	Ger.	05 OCT 1868	Washington Asylum
451	Seabrook, Rachel	3y	C		22 APR 1870	
456	Seabrook, Wm. H.	2m	C	D.C.	13 JUN 1870	Young Mens
232	Seabury, Wm. B., Q.M. dept.	26y	W	Va.	30 AUG 1866	Glenwood
364	Seach, Mary A.	27y	W	N.Y.	28 DEC 1868	Washington
476	Seal, Daisy	1m	W	D.C.	30 SEP 1870	Congressional
407	Seal, Mrs., child of		W		17 AUG 1869	Congressional
355	Seal, Susan	3m	W	D.C.	08 OCT 1868	Congressional
364	Seale, Angelo	1y	W	D.C.	29 DEC 1868	Congressional
635	Seals, Cath.	26y	C	U.S.	11 NOV 1872	Small Pox
730	Seamaker, William, laborer	30y	W	U.S.	17 NOV 1873	
494	Seaman, Aug. L., clerk	48y	W	N.Y.	21 DEC 1870	Glenwood
605	Searl, Henry, laborer	21y	C	Md.	28 JUN 1872	
453	Searles, Bradley S.	3y	W		10 MAY 1870	Congressional
065	Searles, Isaac	79y	W	N.J.	16 DEC 1856	
441	Sears, Agnes, housekeeper	25y	C	Va.	08 FEB 1870	Holmead
617	Sears, Benjamin, moulder	46y	W	U.S.	12 AUG 1872	Congressional*
053	Sears, John Richard	2m	W	D.C.	02 AUG 1856	Methodist
351	Sears, Letta A., Mrs.	37y	W	Md.	16 SEP 1868	Methodist
370	Sears, Lizzie Elwood	24y	W	D.C.	29 JAN 1869	Oak Hill
093	Sears, Otter, machinist		W	Ger.	13 OCT 1857	Congressional
557	Sears, Patsy	2y	C	D.C.	05 FEB 1872	Ebenezer
370	Sears, Sophia F.	4m	W	D.C.	26 JAN 1869	Oak Hill
419	Sears, Tomsee, Mrs.	63y	W	Md.	31 OCT 1869	Congressional
070	Seaton, J. Gales, lawyer	40y	W	D.C.	09 FEB 1857	Congressional
030	Seaton, Josephine	28y	W	Va.	06 NOV 1855	Congressional
224	Seaton, William W., editor	81y	W	Va.	16 JUN 1866	Congressional

Page	Name	Age	Race	Birth	Death Date	Burial Ground
500	Seavas, Jon S.	10y	C	Md.	08 JAN 1871	Catholic
718	Seavorn, Margaret	1y	W	D.C.	12 SEP 1873	
263	Seay, Clinton M., druggist	27y	W	D.C.	03 JUN 1867	Oak Hill
132	Sebart, B.	45y	W	Ger.	03 NOV 1858	Congressional
292	Sedges, Alfred M., wheelwright	46y	C	Va.	13 JAN 1868	
777	Sedgewick, Philip	65y	C	U.S.	22 JUN 1874	Mt. Pleasant
273	Sedgwick, Catherine	4m	C	D.C.	04 SEP 1867	Union
215	Seeders, Sarah S.	72y	W	Va.	13 MAR 1866	Glenwood
777	Seelig, Mary H.	97y	W	U.S.	10 JUN 1874	Harpers Ferry
209	Seely, John M.	61y	W	Va.	— JAN 1866	[torn]
557	Seeney, Mary	20y	C	Md.	01 FEB 1872	
607	Seeton, Albertain	10m	W	D.C.	10 JUN 1872	Union
461	Sefton, [blank]	11m	W	D.C.	28 JUL 1870	Congressional
452	Segers, Gustina	15y	C		16 APR 1870	Ebenezer
601	Seibold, Harry	7m	W	U.S.	19 MAY 1872	Congressional
777	Seidenberg, Dietrich	50y	W	Ger.	06 JUN 1874	Prospect Hill
158	Seidensprinn, Elizabeth R.	1y	W	D.C.	17 AUG 1859	German Catholic
607	Seidenspuner, E.J.	1m	W	D.C.	09 JUN 1872	German
750	Seiders, David M., clerk	55y	W	U.S.	02 FEB 1874	
275	Seiffert, Charles, child of	5m	W	D.C.	11 SEP 1867	Alms House
495	Seift, Ambros, child of	Still	C		20 DEC 1870	Beckett's
745	Seigfred, Charles, soldier	54y	W	Ger.	14 JAN 1874	
122	Seiler, Henry	10y	W	D.C.	24 JUL 1858	Congressional*
080	Seiler, John I.	4m	W		30 JUN 1857	Congressional
282	Seiler, Wm. J.E., engineer	29y	W	N.C.	04 NOV 1867	Congressional
110	Seiler, [blank]	Still	W	D.C.	03 APR 1858	Congressional
092	Seiler, [blank]	1y	W	D.C.	23 SEP 1857	Congressional
054	Seims, Margaret	74y	W	Ger.	09 AUG 1856	German
785	Seitz, Carry Belle	5m	W	U.S.	22 JUL 1874	Congressional
240	Seitz, J., Mrs., infant of	Still			27 OCT 1866	Glenwood
033	Seitz, Susannah A.	1y	W	D.C.	17 JAN 1856	St. Patricks
004	Seitz, Wm. Magruder	2y	W	D.C.	18 MAR 1855	St. Patricks
005	Seitze, [blank]		W		02 APR 1855	Western
271	Selbey, Emma	20y	W	D.C.	04 AUG 1867	Congressional
614	Selby, Chas. D.	28y	W	U.S.	24 JUL 1872	
777	Selby, Chas. Naylor	5d	W	U.S.	04 JUN 1874	Congressional*
784	Selby, Columbus, Jr.	2y	W	U.S.	02 JUL 1874	Congressional
785	Selby, Eleanora	27y	W	U.S.	17 JUL 1874	Methodist
461	Selby, George E.E.	8m	W	D.C.	26 JUL 1870	Congressional
661	Selby, James	23y	W	U.S.	22 JAN 1873	Congressional
768	Selby, Susan	88y	W	U.S.	06 MAY 1874	Congressional*
214	Selby, Washington		W		07 MAR 1866	Poor House
163	Selden, Frank, servant	56y	C	Va.	25 OCT 1859	Washington Asylum
422	Selden, Lucinda M.	9m	C		03 OCT 1869	Beckett's
313	Selden, Robert	19y	C	Va.	10 MAY 1868	Freedmen's Hospital
397	Selden, V.E.	10m	W		25 JUN 1869	Rock Creek
761	Selden, William	83y	W	U.S.	28 APR 1874	Congressional
482	Self, Bradley, laborer	55y	W	Va.	17 OCT 1870	Methodist
394	Self, Geo. W.	10y	W	U.S.	21 JUN 1869	Congressional
287	Selley, Anthony		C		c.06 DEC 1867	Alms House
041	Sellhausen, Minna	28y	W	Ger.	04 APR 1856	Glenwood
598	Selnic, Benjamin	49d	C	U.S.	09 MAY 1872	Unknown
669	Selroedler, E.	59y	W	Ger.	28 FEB 1873	St. Marys
405	Selvey, Patrick	3m	C	D.C.	12 JUL 1869	Washington Asylum
056	Selvy, Ann	2y	W	D.C.	31 AUG 1856	Congressional
167	Semmes, Addison	20y	C	D.C.	20 DEC 1859	Young Mens
166	Semmes, Mary O.	52y	W	Md.	25 NOV 1859	St. Patricks
641	Semms, Enoch	44y	C	U.S.	14 DEC 1872	Small Pox

Page	Name	Age	Race	Birth	Death Date	Burial Ground
761	Sengstack, Louis K.	33y	W	U.S.	01 APR 1874	Oak Hill
541	Sengstuck, C.P., painter	75y	W	Md.	13 OCT 1871	Oak Hill
157	Senseney, Eugene	1y	W	D.C.	05 AUG 1859	Trinity
451	Sephus, John	12y	C	La.	20 APR 1870	
286	Sephus, Joseph	25y	C	D.C.	04 DEC 1867	Congressional
076	Sergeant, George A.	19y	W	D.C.	22 APR 1857	Congressional
731	Sergeant, Mary E.	32y	W	U.S.	24 NOV 1873	Congressional*
761	Sergeant, Mary Emma	6m	W	U.S.	20 APR 1874	Congressional
260	Serrin, Daniel, carpenter	67y	W	Md.	22 MAY 1867	Oak Hill
589	Serrin, Martha A.	1y	W	U.S.	17 MAR 1872	Oak Hill
276	Servant, Alice	9m	W	D.C.	12 SEP 1867	Mt. Olivet
302	Servel, Fanny	96y	C	Md.	01 MAR 1868	Western
312	Servis, William	4y	C		28 MAY 1868	Western
221	Ser[meal], John, tinner	48y	W	Ger.	17 MAY 1866	Holmead
054	Sessford, Agnes Virginia	1y	W	D.C.	15 AUG 1856	Glenwood
533	Sessford, Chas. E.	2m	W	D.C.	21 AUG 1871	Congressional
285	Sessford, George, harness maker	45y	W	D.C.	15 DEC 1867	Congressional
374	Sessford, Isabel Luthall	5y	W		04 FEB 1869	Congressional
605	Sessford, John, printer	57y	W	D.C.	02 JUN 1872	Congressional
541	Sessford, Margret	77y	W	Eng.	08 OCT 1871	Congressional
785	Seton, John	2m	W	U.S.	27 JUL 1874	Mt. Olivet
049	Sette, [blank]	6m			— JUL 1856	German
498	Settler, June, child of	Still	B	D.C.	16 JAN 1871	Washington Asylum
473	Settles, Albert	10d	C	D.C.	14 AUG 1870	Holmead
389	Settles, J.	1d	W	D.C.	12 APR 1869	Washington Asylum
785	Setzer, Catharina	9m	W	U.S.	19 JUL 1874	
112	Seufferle, Ella C.	2y	W	D.C.	23 APR 1858	Congressional
021	Seufferle, G.J.W.	11m	W	D.C.	27 AUG 1855	Congressional
084	Seufferle, H.C., child of	3h	W	D.C.	22 JUL 1857	Congressional
170	Seufferle, John Jacob, confect.	74y	W	Ger.	18 JAN 1860	Congressional
610	Seuft, Pauline	1y	W	Ger.	08 JUL 1872	
692	Severny, Mary C.	10m	W	Amer.	30 MAY 1873	Mt. Olivet
251	Sev[ius?], William, carpenter	65y	C	Va.	10 JAN 1867	Beckett's
240	Seward, Frances A.	22y	W	N.Y.	29 OCT 1866	Auburn, N.Y.
492	Sewel, Lucy	60y	C	Md.	05 DEC 1870	Ebenezer
620	Sewell, Anna E.	31y	W	U.S.	27 AUG 1872	Glenwood
583	Sewell, Chas. F., wheelwright	43y	W	Va.	25 FEB 1872	Congressional
357	Sewell, Fannie	1y	B	D.C.	02 OCT 1868	Washington Asylum
416	Sewell, Isadora L.	1y	C		12 SEP 1869	Ebenezer
520	Sewell, Maggie E.	11m	W	Amer.	27 MAY 1871	Glenwood
340	Sewell, Martha	1y	W	D.C.	27 AUG 1868	Congressional
744	Sewell, Reuben, sailmaker	73y	W	U.S.	28 JAN 1874	Philadelphia, Pa.
077	Sexton, James N.	1y	W	N.Y.	19 MAY 1857	Congressional
082	Sexton, Joseph, laborer	28y	W	Ire.	09 JUL 1857	St. Patricks
222	Sexton, Mary A., servant	24y	W	Ire.	31 MAY 1866	Mt. Olivet
658	Sexton, Thomas	18d	W	U.S.	06 JAN 1873	Mt. Olivet
465	Seybold, Aften Denton	1m	W	D.C.	09 JUL 1870	Methodist
508	Seyin, Virginia	4m	C	D.C.	22 FEB 1871	Holmead
226	Seymour, Thomas William	3m	W	D.C.	27 JUN 1866	Holmead
624	Shack, Daniel	7y	C	U.S.	07 SEP 1872	
292a	Shackleford, Sarah F.	30y	W	Ohio	01 JAN 1868	Vault
201	Shade, Mary	35y	W	Ire.	01 MAR 1861	Mt. Olivet
294	Shaefer, Frederick	3m			— FEB 1868	
117	Shaeffer, Wm. H., soldier	19y	W		26 JUN 1858	Marine
275	Shafer, Agnes	1y	W		02 SEP 1867	Mt. Olivet
535	Shafer, Edw. T.	38y	W	Md.	06 SEP 1871	Glenwood/Baltimore
618	Shafer, Fred	17m	W	U.S.	08 AUG 1872	Prospect Hill
273	Shafer, Henry, laborer	55y	W	Ger.	08 SEP 1867	Alms House

Page	Name	Age	Race	Birth	Death Date	Burial Ground
256	Shafer, Jacob J., bricklayer	47y	W	Ger.	21 MAR 1867	Congressional
231	Shafer, Marian	1y	W	D.C.	19 AUG 1866	Mt. Olivet
025	Shaffer, A.C.N.	2y	W	D.C.	04 SEP 1855	German
585	Shaffer, Benny	4y	W	U.S.	07 MAR 1872	St. Marys
243	Shaffer, Mary	1m	W	D.C.	24 NOV 1866	German
375	Shahy, Mrs.	71y	W	Ire.	23 FEB 1869	Mt. Olivet
446	Shaighton, M.A.	3y	C	D.C.	16 MAR 1870	Washington Asylum
090	Shaley, Patrick, laborer	45y	W	Ire.	05 SEP 1857	St. Patricks
088	Shallcross, Eva Elizabeth	1y	W	D.C.	22 AUG 1857	Foundry
440	Shanahan, James	98y	W		27 FEB 1870	Mt. Olivet
308	Shanahan, Margaret		W		04 APR 1868	Alms House
154	Shanahan, Margaret	6m	W	D.C.	15 JUL 1859	Mt. Olivet
163	Shanahan, Mary	25y	W	Ire.	03 OCT 1859	Mt. Olivet
116	Shanassy, Maurice	2y	W	D.C.	17 JUN 1858	St. Peters
010	Shanathe, Jane	25y	W		— JUN 1855	St. Peters
360	Shancey, Bridget	45y	W	Ire.	17 NOV 1868	Mt. Olivet
285	Shancey, Patrick F.	7m	W	D.C.	19 DEC 1867	Mt. Olivet
360	Shancey, Wm., storekeeper	45y	W	Ire.	16 NOV 1868	Mt. Olivet
768	Shanessee, Hanora	80y	W	Ire.	24 MAY 1874	Mt. Olivet
670	Shanklin, Angelina	14y	C	U.S.	06 FEB 1873	Small Pox*
676	Shanklin, Frank	3m	C	U.S.	05 MAR 1873	Small Pox
711	Shanklin, Julia		C	Va.	09 AUG 1873	Beckett's
677	Shanklin, Mary	1y	C	U.S.	10 MAR 1873	Small Pox
671	Shanklin, Richard	21y	C	U.S.	26 FEB 1873	Small Pox*
454	Shanklin, Susan	54y	C	Va.	14 MAY 1870	
676	Shanklin, Willie	4y	C	U.S.	05 MAR 1873	Small Pox
472	Shankling, Annie, laborer	14y	C	Va.	02 AUG 1870	Ebenezer
215	Shankling, Mary	30y	C		15 MAR 1866	Young Mens
075	Shanks, Sarah	30y	W	Ire.	12 APR 1857	St. Peters
455	Shantz, [blank]	1y	C		31 MAY 1870	Young Mens
021	Sharken, Ellen	9m	W	D.C.	05 AUG 1855	St. Peters
682	Sharkey, Wm. L., lawyer	75y	W	U.S.	29 APR 1873	Glenwood
616	Sharon, Mary C.	6m	W	U.S.	10 JUL 1872	
483	Sharp, Jenny	30y	C	Md.	25 OCT 1870	Freedmen's Hospital
458	Sharp, Jesse Grant	9m	W	D.C.	24 JUN 1870	Newville, Pa.
202	Sharp, John, bricklayer	38y	W	Md.	18 APR 1861	Baltimore, Md.
631	Sharp, Mary	47y	W	Eng.	27 OCT 1872	Congressional
390	Sharpe, Wm. H.	13y	W	Md.	28 MAY 1869	Congressional
446	Sharps, Georgiana, infant of	Still	C		07 MAR 1870	
631	Sharps, Polly	80y	C	U.S.	21 OCT 1872	
689	Shattuck, Blanch L.	3y	W	U.S.	23 MAY 1873	Natick, Mass.
114	Shaw, Ann	108y	C	Md.	16 MAY 1858	Young Mens
249	Shaw, Augustus, farmer	28y	C	D.C.	21 JAN 1867	Rock Creek
053	Shaw, Benjamin, clerk	65y	W	Me.	10 AUG 1856	Glenwood
388	Shaw, Charles B., clerk	69y	W	Va.	20 APR 1869	Glenwood
429	Shaw, Ellen R., Mrs.	64y	W	Md.	04 DEC 1869	Congressional
380	Shaw, Florence C.	11m	W		10 MAR 1869	Glenwood
348	Shaw, I.L., infant of	Still	W		20 SEP 1868	Glenwood
555	Shaw, James	13y	C		25 JAN 1872	Potters Field
785	Shaw, James Robert, bricklayer	34y	W	U.S.	14 JUL 1874	Mt. Olivet
365	Shaw, John E.	2m	W	D.C.	16 DEC 1868	Congressional*
006	Shaw, Joseph	37y	W	D.C.	10 APR 1855	Glenwood
554	Shaw, Josephine R.	73y	W	U.S.	17 JAN 1872	
140	Shaw, Lemuel	89y	W		04 FEB 1859	
110	Shaw, Richard	40y	W		07 APR 1858	Glenwood
141	Shaw, Sarah	18y	C		20 FEB 1859	Foundry
093	Shaw, Tobias, servant	20y	C	D.C.	05 OCT 1857	Colored, East
083	Shaw, William H.	1m	W	D.C.	19 JUL 1857	Congressional

District of Columbia Interments (Index to Deaths), 1855-1874

Page	Name	Age	Race	Birth	Death Date	Burial Ground
089	Shay, Daniel	7m	W	D.C.	27 AUG 1857	St. Peters
074	Shay, Mary, domestic	20y	W	Ire.	25 MAR 1857	St. Peters
160	Shay, Mrs.	55y	W	Ire.	31 AUG 1859	Georgetown
115	Shea, Daniel, laborer	35y	W	Ire.	10 JUN 1858	St. Patricks
345	Shea, Dominic	1y	W	D.C.	05 AUG 1868	Mt. Olivet
019	Shea, Elizabeth	14m			11 AUG 1855	St. Patricks
697	Shea, James	24y	W	Ire.	27 JUN 1873	Washington Asylum
724	Shea, Johanna	17m	W	D.C.	10 OCT 1873	Mt. Olivet
005	Shea, John, contractor	47y	W	Ire.	08 MAR 1855	St. Patricks
012	Shea, Justin, laborer	45y	W	Ire.	21 JUN 1855	St. Patricks
262	Shea, Margaret	25y	W	Ire.	29 JUN 1867	Mt. Olivet
042	Shea, Margaret	22y	W	Ire.	26 APR 1856	St. Patricks
072	Shea, Marie S.	7d			26 FEB 1857	St. Patricks
115	Shea, Mary	1m	W	D.C.	14 JUN 1858	St. Patricks
215	Shea, Mary E.	11d	W	D.C.	13 MAR 1866	Mt. Olivet
614	Shea, Mary E.	6y	W	U.S.	03 JUL 1872	Mt. Olivet*
288	Shea, Mary M.	24y	W	Ire.	15 DEC 1867	Mt. Olivet
322	Shea, Mary, servant	40y	W	Ire.	14 JUN 1868	Mt. Olivet
213	Shea, Matthew, disc. soldier		W		16 FEB 1866	
390	Shea, Patrick	1y	W	D.C.	21 MAY 1869	Mt. Olivet
449	Shea, Timothy	9m	W		23 APR 1870	Mt. Olivet
668	Shea, Timothy	2y	W	U.S.	16 FEB 1873	Mt. Olivet
469	Sheahan, Johanna L.	10m	W	D.C.	20 AUG 1870	Mt. Olivet
734	Sheahan, Mary	3m	W	U.S.	01 DEC 1873	Mt. Olivet
445	Sheahey, Frank, harness maker	23y	W	Ire.	01 MAR 1870	Mt. Olivet
514	Shearman, Mary Jane	34y	W	D.C.	02 MAR 1871	Oak Hill
523	Shearman, Wm. P.	3m	W	D.C.	17 JUN 1871	Oak Hill
016	Sheashnan, Wm. J.	15m	W		02 JUL 1855	St. Patricks
333	Sheback, Charles	1y			04 JUL 1868	Prospect Hill
586	Shebb, Alfred	16d	C	D.C.	18 MAR 1872	Holy Rood
449	Sheck, Margaret, Mrs.	44y	W	Va.	23 APR 1870	Congressional
177	Sheckell, Jas. Lee	4y	W	D.C.	28 APR 1860	Methodist
151	Sheckells, Emma F.	2y	W	D.C.	19 JUN 1859	St. Patricks
148	Sheckels, Jane L.	34y	W		06 MAY 1859	Montgomery Co., Md.
379	Sheckels, Mary	18y	W	D.C.	30 MAR 1869	Congressional
147	Sheckels, Theodore C.	5y	W	D.C.	28 APR 1859	St. Patricks (vault)
151	Sheckels, [blank]	4m	W	D.C.	15 JUN 1859	St. Patricks
002	Sheckles, A.	5y	W	D.C.	— JAN 1855	
675	Sheckles, Harry Lee	21m	W	U.S.	29 MAR 1873	Congressional
266	Shedd, Clara	6m	W	Pa.	17 JUL 1867	Glenwood
137	Shedd, John W.	1y	W	D.C.	15 JAN 1859	Foundry
405	Shedd, Maria	2y	C	D.C.	27 JUL 1869	Washington Asylum
137	Shedd, Mary	5y	W	D.C.	10 JAN 1859	Foundry
731	Shedd, Wm. B., Dr.	51y	W	U.S.	22 NOV 1873	Glenwood
010	Shedden, M.C.	74y	W	Ire.	19 JUN 1855	Rock Creek
101	Shedy, Patrick, pressman	15y	W	Ire.	10 JAN 1858	St. Peters
218	Sheehan, Bridget	6m			28 APR 1866	Mt. Olivet
533	Sheely, Michael J.	2y	W	U.S.	20 AUG 1871	Mt. Olivet
407	Sheets, John S.	56y	W	Pa.	29 AUG 1869	Congressional
398	Sheffield, Jno. R., clerk	25y	W	N.Y.	05 JUN 1869	Waterstown, N.Y.
447	Shegrue, Mary	15y	W		06 MAR 1870	Mt. Olivet
064	Shehan, Bridget	24y	W	Ire.	30 NOV 1856	St. Patricks
117	Shehan, Catharine	35y	W	Ire.	28 JUN 1858	St. Patricks
375	Shehan, Catharine F.	60y	W	Ire.	28 FEB 1869	Mt. Olivet
219	Shehan, Elizabeth	38y	W	Ire.	30 APR 1866	Mt. Olivet
395	Shehan, Johanna	11m	W	D.C.	29 JUN 1869	Mt. Olivet
218	Shehan, John	1y	W	D.C.	27 APR 1866	Mt. Olivet
462	Shehan, John	1y	W		02 JUL 1870	Mt. Olivet

Page	Name	Age	Race	Birth	Death Date	Burial Ground
049	Shehan, John	7m	W	D.C.	01 JUL 1856	St. Patricks
309	Shehan, John, laborer	24y	W	Ire.	07 APR 1868	Mt. Olivet
282	Shehan, Margaret	40y	W	Ire.	10 NOV 1867	Mt. Olivet
159	Shehan, Mary	6m	W	D.C.	23 AUG 1859	Mt. Olivet
616	Shehan, Nick	2y	W	U.S.	29 JUL 1872	Mt. Olivet
395	Shehan, Thomas	6m	W	D.C.	30 JUN 1869	Mt. Olivet
106	Shehan, Wm.	1y	W	D.C.	26 FEB 1858	St. Patricks
315	Shehay, James	1y	W		c.25 MAY 1868	Mt. Olivet
595	Shehee, Wm. M., sailor	27y	W	Va.	19 APR 1872	Congressional*
138	Sheid, John T.W.	1y	W		10 JAN 1859	
421	Sheid, Mary A.	68y	W	D.C.	31 OCT 1869	Glenwood
493	Sheid, Thompson G., turner	84y	W	U.S.	26 DEC 1870	Glenwood
191	Sheilds, John Francis	4y	C	D.C.	20 OCT 1860	Harmony
232	Shekell, George T.	2y	W	D.C.	29 AUG 1866	Congressional
483	Shekell, James H., clerk	41y	W	D.C.	23 OCT 1870	Mt. Olivet
217	Shekra, James, merchant	42y	W	Va.	05 APR 1866	Mt. Olivet
334	Shelan, Mary Ann	2y	W	D.C.	09 JUL 1868	Alms House
476	Sheldon, Harriet, servant	33y	C	Va.	07 SEP 1870	Ebenezer
294	Shell, Sarah Ann	47y	W	D.C.	02 FEB 1868	Mt. Olivet*
335a	Shelley, Margt.	2y	B	U.S.	28 JUL 1868	Washington Asylum
176	Shelling, George	50y	W	Ger.	11 APR 1860	Wash. A.
439	Shelton, Child	2d	W		21 FEB 1870	Congressional
534	Shelton, Ella C.	1y	W	D.C.	30 AUG 1871	Congressional*
663	Shelton, James A.	1y	W	U.S.	01 JAN 1873	Small Pox*
121	Shelton, Martha M.	11m	W	D.C.	15 JUL 1858	Congressional
325	Shelton, Mary Annie	5y	W	D.C.	16 JUL 1868	Congressional
285	Shelton, Newman E., laborer	45y	W	D.C.	05 DEC 1867	Methodist
394	Shelton, Sarah	70y	W	D.C.	12 JUN 1869	Congressional
271	Shelton, Towles, porter	23y	C	Va.	20 AUG 1867	Ebenezer
704	Shely, Mary	1½m	C	D.C.	07 JUL 1873	Beckett's
414	Sheney, Ilka	29y	W	Pol.	09 SEP 1869	Washington Hebrew
549	Sheperd, Wm. S.	55y	W	Pa.	19 DEC 1871	Congressional
743	Shephard, James A.	9y	W	U.S.	24 JAN 1874	Mt. Olivet
376	Shephard, Joseph H.	19d	W		25 FEB 1869	Prospect Hill
282	Shepherd, Elizabeth	21y	W	Md.	22 NOV 1867	Laurel
481	Shepherd, Emma	8m	W	Va.	14 OCT 1870	Holmead
367	Shepherd, George	14y	B	Va.	29 DEC 1868	Washington Asylum
377	Shepherd, Israel	6d	C	D.C.	15 FEB 1869	Washington Asylum
363	Shepherd, Jack	16y	C	Va.	10 NOV 1868	Washington Asylum
295	Shepherd, James E.	3y	W	D.C.	13 FEB 1868	Congressional
074	Shepherd, Margaret	3y	W	D.C.	24 MAR 1857	Methodist
363	Shepherd, Mary Jane	29y	C	Md.	05 NOV 1868	Washington Asylum
285	Shepherd, Peter	11m	W		14 DEC 1867	Methodist
461	Shepherd, Peyton P.	1y	W	Amer.	20 JUL 1870	Congressional
304	Shepherd, William	5m	W	D.C.	09 MAR 1868	Congressional
146	Sheppard, Lodowick	77y	W		15 APR 1859	Georgetown, Methodist
108	Sheppard, Louisa, washerwoman	75y	C	Va.	15 MAR 1858	Harmony
265	Shepperd, Alexina	7m	W	D.C.	02 JUL 1867	Oak Hill
294	Shepperd, Alice	6d	W	D.C.	03 FEB 1868	Western
658	Sheridan, Frederick, clerk	37y	W	Eng.	09 JAN 1873	Congressional
310	Sheridan, Margaret	38y	W		c.08 APR 1868	Mt. Olivet
478	Sheriff, Mary C., washerwoman	58y	W	Ger.	21 SEP 1870	Mt. Olivet
102	Sherin, Maurice, laborer	21y	W	Ire.	19 JAN 1858	St. Peters
733	Sherlock, Bridget	43y	W	Ire.	30 NOV 1873	
240	Sherlock, Walter, tinner	40y	W	Ire.	12 OCT 1866	Mt. Olivet
453	Sherlock, [blank]	82y	W	Md.	28 MAY 1870	Congressional
283	Sherman, Almond P., valve tender	35y	W	N.Y.	12 NOV 1867	Congressional
703	Sherman, Grace	6m	W	D.C.	08 JUL 1873	Oak Hill

Page	Name	Age	Race	Birth	Death Date	Burial Ground
586	Sherman, John C.	2y	W	D.C.	11 MAR 1872	Rock Creek
227	Sherman, Julia	45y	W	N.Y.	05 JUL 1866	Rockport, N.Y.
170	Sherman, Margaret A., lady	54y	W	Md.	22 JAN 1860	Congressional
761	Sherman, Mariah	25y	C	U.S.	30 APR 1874	Mt. Pleasant
516	Sherry, John W.	35y	W	U.S.	20 MAR 1871	Congressional
587	Sherry, M.	70y	W	Ire.	21 MAR 1872	
422	Sherter, Louisa	15y	C		22 OCT 1869	
225	Sherwood, Eliza J.	46y	W	Md.	22 JUN 1866	Glenwood
299	Sherwood, Florence Louise	7m	W	Md.	28 MAR 1868	Glenwood
236	Sherwood, George W., sparmaker	32y	W	Md.	11 SEP 1866	Congressional
737	Sherwood, H., carpenter	43y	W	U.S.	21 DEC 1873	Congressional
691	Sherwood, Indiana	1y	W	U.S.	21 MAY 1873	Small Pox*
690	Sherwood, Jno. S.	27y	W	U.S.	01 MAY 1873	Small Pox*
538	Sherwood, Mary E.	8y	W	D.C.	25 SEP 1871	Congressional*
692	Sherwood, Rosa Bell	2y	W	Amer.	22 MAY 1873	Washington Asylum
434	Sherwood, William A., printer	20y	W		06 JAN 1870	Congressional
107	Sheton, J.B., farmer	27y	W	Ala.	02 MAR 1858	Congressional
290	Shey, Catherine, servant	80y	W	Va.	04 JAN 1868	Baltimore, Md.
271	Shick, Charles A.	2y	W	Pa.	20 AUG 1867	Congressional
381	Shield, Jane C.R.	37y	W	Va.	27 MAR 1869	Winchester, Va.
777	Shield, Thomas, stone cutter	85y	W	Ire.	16 JUN 1874	Mt. Olivet
020	Shields, Ann	1y	W	D.C.	06 AUG 1855	St. Patricks
724	Shields, Bernard, junk business	58y	W	Ire.	15 OCT 1873	Mt. Olivet
535	Shields, Charles, laborer	60y	C	Va.	05 SEP 1871	Ebenezer
659	Shields, Chas.	2m	C	U.S.	14 JAN 1873	
067	Shields, Jane	10m	W	D.C.	27 DEC 1856	St. Patricks
159	Shields, John		W	U.S.	24 AUG 1859	Mt. Olivet
115	Shields, John	5m	W	D.C.	09 JUN 1858	St. Patricks
141	Shields, Mary	23y	W	Ire.	22 FEB 1859	Mt. Olivet
554	Shields, Mary B.	1y	C	D.C.	17 JAN 1872	
058	Shields, Mary Ellen	2y	W	D.C.	28 SEP 1856	St. Patricks
725	Shields, Melvin, cart driver	17y	B	Md.	19 OCT 1873	Harmony
714	Shields, Sarah	80y	W	Va.	28 AUG 1873	Glenwood
304	Shields, Sarah, Mrs.	68y	W	Pa.	12 MAR 1868	Congressional
144	Shiess, Herman	4y	W	Md.	26 MAR 1859	
628	Shildres, Mary R.	3y	W	U.S.	27 SEP 1872	Glenwood
107	Shilley, Marianna	20d	W	D.C.	— MAR 1858	German Catholic
449	Shillington, R.T., Capt., clerk	41y	W	Scot.	14 APR 1870	Congressional
688	Shillins, Chas. Edwd.	11m	W	U.S.	16 MAY 1873	Glenwood
371	Shine, James, tailor	43y	W	Ire.	03 JAN 1869	Mt. Olivet
591	Shiner, Isaac		C	D.C.	02 APR 1872	Ebenezer
362	Shiner, Joseph, butcher	32y	C	D.C.	30 NOV 1868	Ebenezer
261	Shiner, Ridgeway	6y	C	D.C.	08 MAY 1867	
508	Shinn, E.	2m	C	U.S.	26 FEB 1871	Ebenezer
279	Shinunassy, John	7m	W	Ire.	25 OCT 1867	Mt. Olivet
133	Shio, Peter, fresco painter	32y	W	Italy	16 NOV 1858	Congressional
611	Shipley, Florence	15d	W	U.S.	03 JUL 1872	
298	Shipley, Gust. W., merchant	44y	W	Md.	26 FEB 1868	Glenwood
501	Shippon, Elizabeth	72y	W	Eng.	16 JAN 1871	Oak Hill
191	Shirens, Charles, clerk	35y	W	Va.	03 OCT 1860	
667	Shirk, James W.	41y	W	U.S.	10 FEB 1873	Erie, Pa.
587	Shirley, John, shoemaker	50y		D.C.	23 MAR 1872	Potters Field
749	Shirley, Wm. R., seaman USN	21y	W	U.S.	25 FEB 1874	Congressional
731	Shised, Abraham	60y	C	U.S.	25 NOV 1873	Washington Asylum
761	Shiver, Minnie, clerk Treas.	21y	W	U.S.	06 APR 1874	Congressional*
451	Shly, Molly	120y	C	Va.	19 APR 1870	Washington Asylum
049	Shockey, Ed. M.	3y	W	D.C.	03 JUL 1856	Western
094	Shockey, Margaret	1y	W	D.C.	31 OCT 1857	St. Peters

District of Columbia Interments (Index to Deaths), 1855-1874

Page	Name	Age	Race	Birth	Death Date	Burial Ground
637	Shoemaker, Cornelia	1m	W	U.S.	09 NOV 1872	Congressional
548	Shoemaker, H.D.	4y	W	U.S.	18 DEC 1871	Va.
589	Shoemaker, Indiana	37y	W	D.C.	14 MAR 1872	Oak Hill
188	Shoemaker, John T.	10m	W	D.C.	25 AUG 1860	Oak Hill
516	Shoemaker, Joseph W.	5m	W	D.C.	05 MAR 1871	Congressional
120	Shoemaker, Lewis	1m	W	D.C.	08 JUL 1858	Congressional
054	Shoemaker, Margaret E.	8m	W	D.C.	23 AUG 1856	Congressional
010	Shofer, Susana B.	3y	W		26 JUN 1855	Lutheran
369	Sholes, H.C., infant of	Still	W	D.C.	31 JAN 1869	Congressional
360	Sholt, Rose	58y	W	Md.	30 NOV 1868	Mt. Olivet
459	Shoops, [blank]	Still	W		11 JUN 1870	Methodist
744	Shores, Sandy	5y	C	U.S.	21 JAN 1874	
185	Shorht, Joseph	65y	W	Ire.	21 JUL 1860	Mt. Olivet
730	Short, Annie	26y	C	U.S.	13 NOV 1873	Prospect Hill
714	Short, Carrie	17m	C	Md.	27 AUG 1873	
321	Short, David		C		c.23 JUN 1868	Alms House
508	Short, Jas.	1y	C	D.C.	12 FEB 1871	Holmead
408	Short, Louisa Julia	1y			— AUG 1869	
458	Short, Mary	5m	C	D.C.	15 JUN 1870	Potters Field
665	Short, Robert	21y	C	U.S.	31 JAN 1873	Small Pox*
785	Short, Wilmot I.	10m	W	U.S.	30 JUL 1874	Glenwood
013	Short, [blank]		W	D.C.	28 JUL 1855	St. Peters
103	Shorter, Catharine	6y	C	D.C.	16 JAN 1858	St. Patricks
384	Shorter, Eliza	3m	C	D.C.	11 MAR 1869	Washington Asylum
377	Shorter, Eliza		C	D.C.	13 FEB 1869	Washington Asylum
458	Shorter, Francis	3m	C	D.C.	17 JUN 1870	Potters Field
197	Shorter, Hannah	38y	C	D.C.	09 JAN 1861	Mt. Olivet
191	Shorter, John, child of	2y	C	D.C.	20 OCT 1860	Young Mens
767	Shorter, Mary E., domestic	22y	C	U.S.	03 MAY 1874	Harmony
258	Shorter, Mr., child of	3m			09 APR 1867	
500	Shorter, Robert, blacksmith	52y	C	Md.	17 JAN 1871	Harmony
172	Shorter, Sarah	22y	C	D.C.	19 FEB 1860	Harmony
732	Shorter, Sophia	81y	B	U.S.	29 NOV 1873	
127	Shorter, Tobias	1y	C	D.C.	05 SEP 1858	Young Mens
269	Shorter, William H.	3m	C	D.C.	24 AUG 1867	St. Patricks
338	Shorts, Wm.	1y	C		20 AUG 1868	Washington Asylum
614	Shottbeneger, Benja.	19y	W	U.S.	17 JUL 1872	
555	Shoubert, Septimus	1y	W	D.C.	25 JAN 1872	Prospect Hill
130	Shoup, Daugherty	35y	W	Ger.	11 OCT 1858	Lutheran
696	Showden, Thos.	18m	C	D.C.	23 JUN 1873	Beckett's
255	Shradel, George, shoemaker	22y	W	Ger.	23 MAR 1867	German Catholic
232	Shreve, Carrie May	3m	W	D.C.	26 AUG 1866	Congressional
239	Shreve, Christopher Newton	8y	W	D.C.	07 OCT 1866	Congressional
645	Shreve, Ida	3y	W	U.S.	30 DEC 1872	Congressional*
369	Shreve, John Henry	1y	W	D.C.	08 JAN 1869	Congressional
080	Shreve, Mary Francis	7m	W	D.C.	26 JUN 1857	Congressional
732	Shriclon, Jessie	73y	C	U.S.	30 NOV 1873	Washington Asylum
150	Shriver, Mathew L.	3y	W	D.C.	09 JUN 1859	Glenwood
602	Shroth, John	3y	W	U.S.	16 MAY 1872	Prospect Hill
768	Shubrick, Wm. B., admr. USN	83y	W	U.S.	27 MAY 1874	Oak Hill
116	Shue, Henry	6m	W		24 JUN 1858	Glenwood
761	Shugurton, Mary	9y	W	U.S.	09 APR 1874	Mt. Olivet
415	Shultz, Emma	8m	W		05 SEP 1869	Prospect Hill
189	Shultze, Christian, brewer	35y	W	Ger.	19 SEP 1860	Prospect Hill
697	Shuman, Lizzie	9m	W	D.C.	13 JUN 1873	Prospect Hill
189	Shunashea, Michael, tiner	19y	W	Ire.	12 SEP 1860	Mt. Olivet
118	Shyne, Ambrose	14d	W	D.C.	30 JUN 1858	St. Peters
189	Shyne, Michael, clerk	45y	W	Ire.	02 SEP 1860	Mt. Olivet

District of Columbia Interments (Index to Deaths), 1855-1874

Page	Name	Age	Race	Birth	Death Date	Burial Ground
312	Shyner, John Michael C.	1y	C	D.C.	16 MAY 1868	Ebenezer
167	Shyner, Richmond R.	7m	C	D.C.	14 DEC 1859	Ebenezer
166	Shyner, Vincent C.		C	D.C.	16 NOV 1859	Ebenezer
195	Sias, Catharine	27y	W		17 DEC 1860	
356	Sibert, John	43y	W	Ger.	24 OCT 1868	
197	Sibley, James	38y	W		07 JAN 1861	Oak Hill
446	Sibley, James	8d	W		21 MAR 1870	Western
027	Sibley, Mrs.	68y			20 OCT 1855	Methodist
390	Siburn, Joseph, cook	22y	W	Ger.	26 MAY 1869	Congressional
209	Sickken, Charles	16y	W	D.C.	08 JAN 1866	Baltimore, Md.
755	Siebers, Burris, plater printer	64y	W	U.S.	18 MAR 1874	Philadelphia, Pa.
354	Siebold, Philip	30y	W	Md.	11 OCT 1868	Glenwood
169	Sieck, Henry	1y	W	D.C.	10 JAN 1860	Prospect Hill
705	Sieck, Kate	3y	W	D.C.	04 JUL 1873	Prospect Hill
785	Sievers, Auguste	14d	W	U.S.	16 JUL 1874	Prospect Hill
467	Sievers, Augustus	7d	W	D.C.	21 JUL 1870	Prospect Hill
420	Sievers, Mrs., infant of	Still	W		20 OCT 1869	Prospect Hill
123	Sievers, W.I.	1y	W	D.C.	24 JUL 1858	Glenwood
008	Silance, [blank]		C		13 MAY 1855	St. Matthews
160	Silby, John	10m	C	D.C.	03 AUG 1859	Methodist
755	Silcolt, B.	27y	W	U.S.	03 MAR 1874	Congressional
224	Siles, E. [or Liles]				16 JUN 1866	Young Mens
548	Sill, Samuel	6m	W	D.C.	09 DEC 1871	Glenwood
020	Sillivan, Mary	2m	W	D.C.	08 AUG 1855	St. Patricks
287	Silman, Sarah		C		c.13 DEC 1867	Alms House
416	Sim, Charles J.	11m	C		11 SEP 1869	Ebenezer
329	Sim, Georgianna	1m	C	D.C.	04 JUL 1868	
768	Simes, Charity, domestic	18y	C	U.S.	23 MAY 1874	Mt. Olivet
421	Simes, William	6m	C		08 OCT 1869	Young Mens
057	Simkins, James	1y	W	D.C.	08 SEP 1856	Holmead
704	Simmes, Eliza Jane	26y	C	Va.	18 JUL 1873	Beckett's
695	Simmes, George	21d	C	U.S.	14 JUN 1873	
555	Simmonds, Susan C.	27y	W	Md.	28 JAN 1872	Congressional
749	Simmons, A.T., Dr.	49y	W	U.S.	21 FEB 1874	Glenwood
528	Simmons, Anna, laborer	35y	C	Va.	15 JUL 1871	
163	Simmons, Cephas	70y	W	Md.	15 OCT 1859	Congressional
306	Simmons, E., infant of	2½m	W	D.C.	28 APR 1868	Mt. Olivet
599	Simmons, Edie	60y	C	U.S.	11 MAY 1872	Harmony
420	Simmons, Francis Augustus	1m	W		14 OCT 1869	Mt. Olivet
388	Simmons, George, laborer		C	Md.	31 APR 1869	Mt. Olivet
785	Simmons, George, storekeeper	59y	W	U.S.	10 JUL 1874	Mt. Olivet
713	Simmons, Henry	26y	W	D.C.	26 AUG 1873	Congressional
464	Simmons, John Spicer	7m	W	D.C.	27 JUL 1870	Alexandria, Va.
748	Simmons, Joseph L.	11m	W	U.S.	02 FEB 1874	Alexandria, Va.
586	Simmons, Margret	75y	C	Va.	17 MAR 1872	Asylum
405	Simmons, Philip, laborer	44y	W	Ire.	10 JUL 1869	Mt. Olivet
311	Simmons, Thomas		C		c.07 APR 1868	Alms House
416	Simmons, Wm. D. Kelly	Still	W		17 SEP 1869	Methodist
507	Simmons, Wm. R., bricklayer	48y	W	D.C.	08 FEB 1871	Glenwood
581	Simms, A.	37y	C	D.C.	18 FEB 1872	Holy Rood
482	Simms, Allen, messenger	83y	C	Md.	30 OCT 1870	Beckett's
777	Simms, Ann	19y	C	U.S.	06 JUN 1874	Washington Asylum
684	Simms, Annie	10y	C	U.S.	07 APR 1873	Small Pox*
131	Simms, C.M.	59y	W	Md.	29 OCT 1858	St. Patricks
216	Simms, Charles	4y	C	D.C.	31 MAR 1866	Ebenezer
408	Simms, Charles	3y	C	U.S.	17 AUG 1869	Mt. Olivet
612	Simms, Chas.	2y	C	U.S.	02 JUL 1872	
451	Simms, Edward	5m	C	D.C.	02 APR 1870	Washington Asylum

Page	Name	Age	Race	Birth	Death Date	Burial Ground
201	Simms, Elizabeth	86y	W	Va.	08 MAR 1861	Oak Hill
498	Simms, Ellen, pauper	3y	B	Va.	15 JAN 1871	Washington Asylum
641	Simms, Emma	2y	C	U.S.	02 DEC 1872	Small Pox
707	Simms, Florence	8d	C	D.C.	14 JUL 1873	Beckett's
392	Simms, Georgie	6m	C	D.C.	20 MAY 1869	Young Mens
097	Simms, Harriet	57y	W	D.C.*	21 NOV 1857	Oak Hill
683	Simms, Henry	35y	C	U.S.	11 APR 1873	Small Pox
683	Simms, Henry	8y	C	U.S.	13 APR 1873	Small Pox
149	Simms, John	53y	W	Va.	21 MAY 1859	Washington Asylum
522	Simms, John T., barber	52y	C	D.C.	12 JUN 1871	Mt. Olivet
426	Simms, Joseph Bernard	2y	W		08 NOV 1869	Mt. Olivet
687	Simms, Julia	20y	C	U.S.	08 MAY 1873	
522	Simms, Kosanna	2m	C	U.S.	13 JUN 1871	
128	Simms, Lucy	40y	C	Md.	17 SEP 1858	Ebenezer
253	Simms, M.	48y	C		02 FEB 1867	Harmony
337	Simms, Mary	5m	C	U.S.	12 AUG 1868	Washington Asylum
217	Simms, Mary	4y	C	D.C.	01 APR 1866	Young Mens
377	Simms, Mary A.	2m	C		20 FEB 1869	Washington Asylum
522	Simms, Mary E.	3m	C	D.C.	11 JUN 1871	
002	Simms, Mary V.	2y	C		1_ JAN 1855	
212	Simms, Mr., child of				18 FEB 1866	
343	Simms, Nellie May	1y	W	D.C.	10 AUG 1868	Baltimore, Md.
514	Simms, Patsy, cook	89y	C	Va.	02 MAR 1871	Harmony
590	Simms, Riley, laborer	22y	C	Va.	13 APR 1872	Small Pox
416	Simms, Robert	2y	C		15 SEP 1869	Ebenezer
502	Simms, Robt. A., trunk maker	47y	W	Va.	27 JAN 1871	Baltimore, Md.
201	Simms, Sarah E.	12y	W		20 MAR 1861	St. Peters
621	Simms, Slater	12y	C	U.S.	05 AUG 1872	
462	Simms, Thomas F.	18y	W	Amer.	03 JUL 1870	Oak Hill
785	Simms, Thomas W.	9m	W	U.S.	08 JUL 1874	Glenwood
018	Simms, Walter, clerk	20y	W	D.C.*	08 AUG 1855	Oak Hill
785	Simms, William	6y	C	U.S.	13 JUL 1874	
777	Simms, William	1m	C	U.S.	29 JUN 1874	Potters Field
641	Simms, William	17y	C	U.S.	08 DEC 1872	Small Pox
705	Simms, Wm.	17d	W	D.C.	24 JUL 1873	Congressional
070	Simonds, Daniel	78y	W	N.H.	04 FEB 1857	Methodist
713	Simonds, John, watchman	62y	W	N.Y.	21 AUG 1873	Congressional
052	Simonds, Linus, printer	35y	W	N.Y.	30 JUL 1856	Foundry
232	Simonds, Martha	44y	W	D.C.	26 AUG 1866	Congressional
755	Simonds, Nellie	9y	W	U.S.	01 MAR 1874	Congressional
068	Simonds, Susan	1m	W	D.C.	09 JAN 1857	Methodist
105	Simonds, [blank]	12d	C		22 FEB 1858	Western
680	Simons, Cook Sanderson	2y	W	U.S.	02 APR 1873	Glenwood
723	Simons, Danl. T., photographer	33y	W	D.C.	08 OCT 1873	
611	Simons, Henrietta	2m	C	U.S.	21 JUL 1872	
115	Simons, Ida	8m	W		15 JUN 1858	Holmead
698	Simons, Marietta	11m	W	D.C.	26 JUN 1873	Congressional*
626	Simons, Mary	68y	W	U.S.	10 SEP 1872	
211	Simoux, Mr.				15 JAN 1866	
515	Simpson, Carrie	1y	C	D.C.	12 MAR 1871	Union
761	Simpson, Chas. H.	10y	W	U.S.	23 APR 1874	Oak Hill
590	Simpson, Duff G.	11y	C	D.C.	03 APR 1872	Small Pox
599	Simpson, E.A.	33y	W	U.S.	09 MAY 1872	Mt. Olivet
273	Simpson, Frank, child of	Still	W	D.C.	04 SEP 1867	Prospect Hill
698	Simpson, Jane G.	53y	W	Scot.	16 JUN 1873	Congressional*
105	Simpson, John	3y	W	Md.	18 FEB 1858	Oak Hill
077	Simpson, John	8m	W		18 MAY 1857	St. Patricks
440	Simpson, Julia, Mrs.	69y	W		11 FEB 1870	N.Y.

District of Columbia Interments (Index to Deaths), 1855-1874

Page	Name	Age	Race	Birth	Death Date	Burial Ground
741	Simpson, Peter	1y	W	U.S.	15 JAN 1874	Congressional
002	Simpson, Teresa	29y	C	Md.	— JAN 1855	Washington
348	Simpson, Thomas	70y	W	Eng.	23 SEP 1868	Congressional
748	Simpson, William	4m	W	U.S.	06 FEB 1874	Mt. Olivet
218	Simpson, William	7m	C	D.C.	22 APR 1866	Young Mens
705	Simpson, Wm. H.	15m	C	U.S.	10 JUL 1873	
101	Sims, Barshaba	82y	W	Va.	01 JAN 1858	Congressional
749	Sims, C.E.	3y	C	U.S.	25 FEB 1874	Mt. Pleasant
417	Sims, Catherine	8m	C		27 SEP 1869	Mt. Olivet
158	Sims, Cecelia	59y	C	Md.	14 AUG 1859	Harmony
767	Sims, Chas. R.	2m	W	U.S.	03 MAY 1874	Washington Asylum
618	Sims, Daniel	11m	C	U.S.	07 AUG 1872	
482	Sims, Deby Ann, laundress	40y	C	Md.	06 OCT 1870	Mt. Olivet
422	Sims, Elizabeth	4y	C		22 OCT 1869	
745	Sims, Emelene, infant of	P.B.	C	U.S.	20 JAN 1874	
387	Sims, Eva	6m	D		17 APR 1869	Young Mens
269	Sims, Francis	8m	C	D.C.	10 AUG 1867	Mt. Olivet
160	Sims, Helenora	1y	C	D.C.	02 AUG 1859	St. Patricks
002	Sims, Henry, aborer	35y	C	D.C.	2_ JAN 1855	Washington Asylum
025	Sims, James	65y	C		29 SEP 1855	Harmony
159	Sims, Joseph E.	11m	C	D.C.	01 AUG 1859	Mt. Olivet
379	Sims, Joseph W.	1y	W		15 MAR 1869	Congressional
335a	Sims, Lavinia	2w	C	U.S.	22 JUL 1868	Washington Asylum
635	Sims, Martha	12y	C	U.S.	30 NOV 1872	Small Pox
296	Sims, Richard	7d	C	D.C.	18 FEB 1868	Young Mens
155	Sims, Walter	4m	C	D.C.	28 JUL 1859	Holmead
421	Sims, William	6m	C		10 OCT 1869	Mt. Olivet
252	Sims, William, porter	24y	C	D.C.	08 FEB 1867	Harmony
509	Sims, Wm., child of	Still	C	D.C.	04 fEB 1871	Washington Asylum
010	Sims, [blank]	6d	C	D.C.	— JUN 1855	Holmead
723	Sinclair, Chas. S.	2y	W	D.C.	02 OCT 1873	Mt. Olivet
457	Sinclair, Frank H.	2m	W	D.C.	15 JUN 1870	Congressional
271	Sinclair, Jesse E.	3y	W	D.C.	22 AUG 1867	Glenwood
682	Sinclair, John, stone cutter	28y	W	U.S.	23 APR 1873	Baltimore, Md.
727	Sinclair, O.H.	1y	W	U.S.	27 OCT 1873	
785	Sinclair, Rufus S.	34y	W	U.S.	25 JUL 1874	Methodist
093	Sinclare, Ida	1y	W	D.C.	05 OCT 1857	Congressional
610	Sinders, Mary Ann	11m	W	U.S.	23 JUL 1872	
523	Singleman, Henry	5m	W	Md.	17 JUN 1871	Prospect Hill
060	Singleton, Francis, clerk	22y	W	Va.	11 OCT 1856	Winchester, Va.
141	Singleton, Nicholas	3y	W		23 FEB 1859	Oak Hill
402	Singleton, Peter, laborer	32y	W	Eng.	13 JUL 1869	Mt. Olivet
461	Singleton, [blank]	5m	W	D.C.	14 JUL 1870	Congressional
063	Singlier, Ben.	100y	C	Va.	28 NOV 1856	Washington Asylum
149	Sinnott, Elizabeth A.		W	D.C.	27 MAY 1859	
065	Sintes, Hannah	4y	W	D.C.	11 DEC 1856	Congressional
782	Sioussa, Marie E.	9y	W	U.S.	05 JUL 1874	Oak Hill
073	Sipes, Rebecca	6y	W	D.C.	08 MAR 1857	Western
442	Sissell, Joseph	1m	C		21 FEB 1870	Washington Asylum
664	Sissell, Kelly	54y	C	U.S.	13 JAN 1873	Small Pox*
594	Sissleburger, Ann	70y	W	D.C.	02 APR 1872	Congressional
592	Sissleburger, Ann	70y	W	U.S.	03 APR 1872	Congressional
317	Sisson, A.F., Mrs.	68y	W	Va.	29 JUN 1868	Congressional
718	Sisson, Ernest A.	2y	W	Va.	10 SEP 1873	Va.
643	Sister Arsenia, servant	52y	W	U.S.	10 DEC 1872	Mt. Olivet
717	Sister Benedic Mary	34y	W	Ire.	07 SEP 1873	Mt. Olivet
069	Sister, Maria	48y	W	Md.	12 JAN 1857	St. Patricks
409	Sister Philomena	41y	W	Ohio	02 AUG 1869	Mt. Olivet

Page	Name	Age	Race	Birth	Death Date	Burial Ground
777	Siston, James F.	8m	W	U.S.	29 JUN 1874	
007	Sites, Mary Rosamond	6y	W	Ind.	04 APR 1855	Congressional
388	Sitgreaves, Lucy	23m	W	Amer.	17 APR 1869	Oak Hill*
084	Sitze, Frances A.	5m	W	D.C.	22 JUL 1857	St. Patricks
047	Sivas, Eliza	45y	C	U.S.	23 JUN 1856	Western
332	Skarer, Henry	73y	W	Ger.	07 JUL 1868	Prospect Hill
403	Skaub, Marianna Celesta	18d	W	D.C.	09 JUL 1869	German Catholic
216	Skaw-ba-wis, Chief	55y	I	Wisc.	22 MAR 1866	Congressional
549	Skelly, Margret E.	45y	W	Md.	19 DEC 1871	Methodist
661	Skerrett, David C., Dr.	76y	W	U.S.	26 JAN 1873	Philadelphia, Pa.
513	Skerrett, Fanny E.	73y	W	Pa.	10 MAR 1871	Philadelphia, Pa.
246	Skerrett, Percy	1y	W	D.C.	31 DEC 1866	Congressional
217	Skidmore, Cornelia	5y	W	D.C.	11 APR 1866	Congressional
104	Skidmore, Elizabeth, seamstress	29y	W	Va.	07 FEB 1858	Methodist
540	Skidmore, Florence	2y		D.C.	01 OCT 1871	
210	Skidmore, John H.	13y	W	D.C.	22 JAN 1866	Congressional
249	Skidmore, William, huckster	46y	W	Va.	11 JAN 1867	Va.
283	Skinker, John H.	54y	W	Va.	19 NOV 1867	Va.
465	Skinner, Ida	7m	C	D.C.	16 JUL 1870	Harmony
618	Skinner, Jas.	77y	C	U.S.	17 AUG 1872	
705	Skinner, Mary E.	21y	W	Md.	15 JUL 1873	Congressional*
396	Skinner, Theodore	3m	C	D.C.	25 JUN 1869	Young Mens
239	Skinner, W.A.	5d	W	D.C.	05 OCT 1866	Congressional
471	Skinner, W.F.	Still	W	D.C.	01 AUG 1870	Congressional
051	Skippon, Mary E.	14d	W	D.C.	23 JUL 1856	Congressional
041	Skirving, Addie S.	3y	W	D.C.	11 APR 1856	Congressional
144	Skirving, Ida Caroline	4y	W	D.C.	17 MAR 1859	Oak Hill*
736	Slack, Fredrick	6m	W	U.S.	21 DEC 1873	Mt. Olivet
218	Slack, James H., car driver	28y	W	Va.	17 APR 1866	Congressional
662	Slack, Theodore	21y	W	U.S.	07 JAN 1873	Small Pox
677	Slade, Edward	48y	C	U.S.	23 MAR 1873	Small Pox
299	Slade, William, steward	53y	C		16 MAR 1868	Harmony
586	Sladen, Bessie H.	5m	W	D.C.	14 MAR 1872	
708	Slagle, Laura V.	16y	W	Va.	27 JUL 1873	Glenwood
492	Slard, Maria	25y	C	Va.	07 DEC 1870	Ebenezer
367	Slater, Benj.	14m	B	U.S.	05 DEC 1868	Washington Asylum
627	Slater, Chas.	42y	C	U.S.	12 SEP 1872	Small Pox
554	Slater, Chas. H., watchman	29y	W	U.S.	17 JAN 1872	
552	Slater, Chas. H., watchman	29y	W	U.S.	01 JAN 1872	Congressional
729	Slater, Elizabeth	13d	W	U.S.	05 NOV 1873	Congressional*
785	Slater, Georgeanna	10m	C	U.S.	29 JUL 1874	Beckett's
143	Slater, James, laborer	39y	C	Md.	02 MAR 1859	Colored, Eastern
732	Slater, James Van A.	3y	W	U.S.	25 NOV 1873	Oak Hill
552	Slater, Sam. E.	2y	W	D.C.	01 JAN 1872	Oak Hill
593	Slater, Thomas	28y	C	Va.	21 APR 1872	Mt. Pleasant
761	Slater, Wm. B., Sr.	76y	W	U.S.	04 APR 1874	Philadelphia, Pa.
096	Slatford, Robert H.	6m	W	D.C.	07 NOV 1857	Glenwood
167	Slatford, Robert, plasterer	24y	W	D.C.	13 DEC 1859	Glenwood
049	Slattery, James	10m	W		06 JUL 1856	St. Peters
301	Slaughter, Elizabeth	2y	C	D.C.	30 MAR 1868	Young Mens
489	Slaughter, Frank E.	7m	C	D.C.	01 NOV 1870	
676	Slaughter, Georgiana, servant	17y	C	U.S.	31 MAR 1873	
607	Slawser, M.A.	5m	W	D.C.	20 JUN 1872	Methodist
618	Sleman, E.W.	7m	W	U.S.	02 AUG 1872	Oak Hill
163	Sletor, Sarah	73y	W	Pa.	18 OCT 1859	Easton, Pa.
553	Sletter, S.	1y	W	D.C.	09 JAN 1872	Prospect Hill
128	Slevin, Peter, watchman	45y	W	Ire.	23 SEP 1858	Mt. Olivet
266	Slick, David A., saddler	36y	W		28 JUL 1867	Glenwood

Page	Name	Age	Race	Birth	Death Date	Burial Ground
166	Slight, Jane	24y	W	N.Y.	11 NOV 1859	Holmead
265	Sloan, A.A., tinner	49y	W	N.J.	18 JUL 1867	Beltsville, Md.
252	Sloan, Ruth A.	57y	W	Md.	07 FEB 1867	Glenwood
494	Sloane, Robert, Sr., printer	60y	W	Ire.	10 DEC 1870	Fredericksburg, Va.
603	Sloots, Francis A.	15y	C	D.C.	03 JUN 1872	Ebenezer
335a	Sloter, Frank	1y	B	D.C.	25 JUL 1868	Washington Asylum
483	Sluter, Ursula	56y	W		28 OCT 1870	Congressional
713	Slye, Margaret E.	1y	W	D.C.	22 AUG 1873	Congressional*
518	Smackum, Maria	65y	C		13 MAY 1871	Holy Rood
259	Small, Andrew, booker	73y	W	Scot.	06 APR 1867	Oak Hill
730	Small, Harriet N., lady	60y	W	U.S.	17 NOV 1873	Glenwood
415	Small, Joseph	1y	W		06 SEP 1869	Mt. Olivet
368	Small, Richard	80y	C		06 DEC 1868	Holmead
785	Small, William, tailor	50y	W	Ger.	26 JUL 1874	Prospect Hill
075	Smalland, J., laborer	40y			09 APR 1857	
602	Smallwood, Celestine	6d	C	U.S.	26 MAY 1872	Georgetown
596	Smallwood, Celestine	6y	C	D.C.	26 APR 1872	Georgetown
046	Smallwood, Daniel F., carpenter	38y	W		20 JUN 1856	Foundry
392	Smallwood, David	3y	C	D.C.	19 MAY 1869	
544	Smallwood, Edw.	25y	C	Md.	04 NOV 1871	Washington
060	Smallwood, Elizabeth A.	17y	C	D.C.	07 OCT 1856	Young Mens
065	Smallwood, Fanny A.	45y	W	Va.	09 DEC 1856	Va.
488	Smallwood, Geo., laborer	27y	C	Va.	02 NOV 1870	Washington Asylum
311	Smallwood, Hannah		C		c.05 APR 1868	Alms House
704	Smallwood, Harriet	1y	C	D.C.	29 JUL 1873	
121	Smallwood, Henrietta	18y	C	D.C.	11 JUL 1858	
502	Smallwood, Henrietta, servant	24y	C	Va.	15 JAN 1871	Mt. Olivet
588	Smallwood, J.W.	21d	C	D.C.	25 MAR 1872	Harmony
152	Smallwood, Janet B.	47y	W	U.S.	28 JUN 1859	Congressional
013	Smallwood, Jas. M.	2y	W	Va.	10 JUL 1855	Va.
724	Smallwood, Lemuel, blacksmith	33y	W	D.C.	12 OCT 1873	Congressional
481	Smallwood, Lucinda, laundress	50y	C	Md.	30 OCT 1870	Holmead
094	Smallwood, Lucy A.	1y	C	D.C.	22 OCT 1857	Young Mens
268	Smallwood, Mary Rebecca	10m	W	D.C.	25 AUG 1867	Congressional
407	Smallwood, May Omia	1y	W		31 AUG 1869	Congressional
199	Smallwood, Moses, Jr., servant	14y	C	D.C.	17 FEB 1861	Young Mens
256	Smallwood, Rebecca	55y	W	Md.	14 MAR 1867	Congressional
421	Smallwood, Richard, barber	20y	C		26 OCT 1869	Young Mens
007	Smallwood, Richd. L., clerk	36y	W	Md.	24 APR 1855	Glenwood
221	Smart, Ann M.	29y	W	D.C.	24 MAY 1866	Congressional
228	Smart, Charles H.	1y	W	D.C.	10 JUL 1866	Congressional
527	Smart, Willie L.	5y	W		08 JUL 1871	
320	Smeckum, Rachel	14d	C	D.C.	30 JUN 1868	
006	Smedley, [blank]	1d	W		21 APR 1855	Congressional
146	Smidley, John	2y	W	D.C.	11 APR 1859	Congressional*
021	Smiffen, J.R.	7m	W	D.C.	08 AUG 1855	Methodist, East
749	Smile, Henry, brick maker	62y	C	U.S.	08 FEB 1874	Beckett's
644	Smiler, Johnney	2m	C	U.S.	20 DEC 1872	
258	Smiler, Mrs.	40y	C		09 APR 1867	Congressional, near
472	Smiley, Margaret Ann	1y	C	D.C.	05 AUG 1870	Beckett's
632	Smilies, Jas.	69y	W	U.S.	16 OCT 1872	
642	Smior, Emma P.	3y	W	U.S.	05 DEC 1872	Glenwood
032	Smitch, Charles	17y	W	Ger.	28 DEC 1855	Alms House
146	Smith, A.W.	45y	W		17 APR 1859	Georgetown, Catholic
214	Smith, Adam, late soldier	25y	C		05 MAR 1866	Young Mens
615	Smith, Albert	26y	C	U.S.	04 JUL 1872	
415	Smith, Albert	4h	W		27 SEP 1869	Oak Hill
380	Smith, Alex. Goodrich	1y	W		13 MAR 1869	Oak Hill

Page	Name	Age	Race	Birth	Death Date	Burial Ground
351	Smith, Alexander	3m	C	D.C.	28 SEP 1868	Ebenezer
467	Smith, Alexander, laborer	25y	W	Md.	11 JUL 1870	
417	Smith, Alice	1y	C		03 SEP 1869	
408	Smith, Alice	6m	C	D.C.	15 AUG 1869	Western
665	Smith, Allan Lowe	5m	W	U.S.	16 JAN 1873	Glenwood
300	Smith, Amanda, Mrs.	32y	W		08 MAR 1868	Mt. Olivet
027	Smith, Ann E.H.	8y	W		08 OCT 1855	Congressional
228	Smith, Ann Elizabeth	1y	C	D.C.	12 JUL 1866	Harmony
696	Smith, Ann Matilda	5y		D.C.	12 JUN 1873	Washington Asylum
051	Smith, Anna	1y	W		25 JUL 1856	St. Matthews
239	Smith, Anna V.	31y	W	Eng.	02 OCT 1866	Congressional
300	Smith, Annette, nurse	72y	C	Md.	01 MAR 1868	Harmony
137	Smith, Anthony Delano	4y	W	D.C.	16 JAN 1859	Congressional
768	Smith, Armstead	82y	C	U.S.	21 MAY 1874	
777	Smith, Arthur	2y	C	U.S.	24 JUN 1874	Beckett's
303	Smith, Becky		C		24 MAR 1868	Alms House
604	Smith, C.A.	9y	C	D.C.	01 JUN 1872	Ebenezer
517	Smith, C.B., real estate	51y	C	N.Y.	28 APR 1871	Norwich, N.Y.
023	Smith, Caleb P.	45y	W	N.H.	19 SEP 1855	Oak Hill
638	Smith, Caroline		C	U.S.	11 NOV 1872	
015	Smith, Caroline H.	3y	W	D.C.	30 JUL 1855	Rock Creek
060	Smith, Catharine	77y	W	N.Y.	17 OCT 1856	Congressional
066	Smith, Catharine	26y	W	D.C.	17 DEC 1856	St. Patricks
384	Smith, Catharine		C	D.C.	10 MAR 1869	Washington Asylum
509	Smith, Catharine	12d	C	D.C.	14 FEB 1871	Washington Asylum
691	Smith, Catherine	57y	W	U.S.	18 MAY 1873	Congressional
402	Smith, Catherine	32y	W	Md.	12 JUL 1869	Glenwood
398	Smith, Catherine M.F.	83y	W	Eng.	30 JUN 1869	Rock Creek
445	Smith, Charles	9m	W		15 MAR 1870	German Catholic
749	Smith, Charles	8y	C	U.S.	19 FEB 1874	Mt. Pleasant
018	Smith, Charles H., engraver	19y	W	D.C.	10 AUG 1855	Congressional
155	Smith, Charles, hackman	22y	C	D.C.	24 JUL 1859	Harmony
369	Smith, Charles P.	1y	W		02 JAN 1869	Congressional
105	Smith, Charlotte B.	6y	W	D.C.	22 FEB 1858	Methodist
644	Smith, Chas. A.	4y	W	U.S.	23 DEC 1872	Baltimore, Md.
742	Smith, Chas., barber	34y	C	U.S.	19 JAN 1874	Washington Asylum
457	Smith, Chas. Danl., patent agent	25y	W	D.C.	15 JUN 1870	Congressional
713	Smith, Chas. F.	10m	W	U.S.	25 AUG 1873	Congressional*
387	Smith, Chena, Mrs.		C	Va.	29 APR 1869	Young Mens
545	Smith, Christiana H.	17y	W	D.C.	16 NOV 1871	Congressional
065	Smith, Christina	14y	C	D.C.	08 DEC 1856	St. Patricks
353	Smith, Clara	3y	C	D.C.	09 SEP 1868	
717	Smith, Cora	2y	C	D.C.	06 SEP 1873	Congressional
485	Smith, Cornelius	9y	C	U.S.	31 OCT 1870	Potters Field
768	Smith, Daisy	2m	W	U.S.	15 MAY 1874	Mt. Olivet
350	Smith, Daniel	18y	C	Md.	21 SEP 1868	Young Mens
024	Smith, Danl., blacksmith		C		12 SEP 1855	Alms House
070	Smith, Darwin C.		W	Ohio	12 FEB 1857	Glenwood
467	Smith, David	10d	W	D.C.	07 JUL 1870	Glenwood
631	Smith, David, laborer	74y	C	U.S.	01 OCT 1872	
117	Smith, Dennis	40y	W	Ire.	26 JUN 1858	St. Peters
553	Smith, E. Watson, upholsterer	40y	W	Mo.	09 JAN 1872	Congressional
280	Smith, E.M.	62y	W	Eng.	31 OCT 1867	Oak Hill
181	Smith, Ed. F.	Still	W	D.C.	03 JUN 1860	Glenwood
777	Smith, Edward	4m	W	U.S.	24 JUN 1874	
143	Smith, Edward A.	7m	C	D.C.	05 MAR 1859	Harmony
742	Smith, Edward W., clerk	36y	W	U.S.	18 JAN 1874	N.Y.
027	Smith, Edwin	3m	W	D.C.	09 OCT 1855	Congressional

District of Columbia Interments (Index to Deaths), 1855-1874

Page	Name	Age	Race	Birth	Death Date	Burial Ground
530	Smith, Elender	11m	C	D.C.	31 JUL 1871	Ebenezer
337	Smith, Eliza	1y	C	U.S.	11 AUG 1868	Washington Asylum
755	Smith, Eliza	65y	C	U.S.	22 MAR 1874	Young Mens
708	Smith, Eliza, housekeeper	38y	W	Eng.	10 JUL 1873	
297	Smith, Eliza J.	1y	W	D.C.	17 FEB 1868	
714	Smith, Elizabeth	1y	C	D.C.	27 AUG 1873	20th St. B.G.
785	Smith, Elizabeth	2m	C	U.S.	30 JUL 1874	Beckett's
293	Smith, Elizabeth, cook	56y	C	Va.	27 FEB 1868	Mt. Zion
707	Smith, Elizabeth, housekeeper	38y	W	Eng.	18 JUL 1873	Holidaysburg, Pa.
295	Smith, Elizabeth J.	1y	W	U.S.	17 FEB 1868	Congressional
263	Smith, Ellen	62y	C	D.C.*	27 JUN 1867	Harmony
400	Smith, Ellis Standish	6d	W		18 JUL 1869	Glenwood
374	Smith, Emily E.	41y	W	Md.	06 FEB 1869	Congressional
777	Smith, Emma	13m	C	U.S.	23 JUN 1874	Beckett's
461	Smith, Emma	13d	W	D.C.	30 JUL 1870	Congressional
674	Smith, Emma M.	14m	W	U.S.	19 MAR 1873	Elizabeth, N.J.
062	Smith, Enoch		C	Va.	15 NOV 1856	
768	Smith, Ernest S.	18y	W	U.S.	25 MAY 1874	Glenwood
323	Smith, Eula May	8m	W	Amer.	03 JUL 1868	Oak Hill
659	Smith, Fanny	73y	W	U.S.	15 JAN 1873	Middle, Tenn.
666	Smith, Fanny	63y	C	U.S.	04 FEB 1873	Young Mens
071	Smith, Frances G.		W	N.H.	14 FEB 1857	Boston, Mass.
416	Smith, Frank	7d	C		29 SEP 1869	Ebenezer
520	Smith, Frank Bentley	1y	W		27 MAY 1871	Oak Hill
413	Smith, Frank S.	1m	C		18 AUG 1869	Methodist
557	Smith, Fred. B.	2y	W	U.S.	01 FEB 1872	
366	Smith, Frederick, laborer	40y	D	Va.	17 DEC 1868	Union
618	Smith, Geo.	40y	C	U.S.	11 AUG 1872	
308	Smith, Geo.	6m	W	D.C.	12 APR 1868	Congressional
463	Smith, Geo. Henry	4m	W	D.C.	24 JUL 1870	Glenwood
761	Smith, Geo., Infant of	9d	C	U.S.	09 APR 1874	Harmony
335a	Smith, Geo. T.	8y	B	Va.	27 JUL 1868	Washington Asylum
105	Smith, George	1y	W	D.C.	16 FEB 1858	Congressional
238	Smith, George, boatman	30y	W	Pa.	27 SEP 1866	Northumberland
342	Smith, George Elders	16d	C	D.C.	14 AUG 1868	Young Mens
416	Smith, George Francis	1y	C		29 SEP 1869	
360	Smith, George W.	27y	W	D.C.	10 NOV 1868	Glenwood
709	Smith, Guy	23d	W	D.C.	23 JUL 1873	
481	Smith, H.	3m	C	D.C.	23 OCT 1870	Western
441	Smith, H. Clay, merchant	38y	W	Va.	01 FEB 1870	Fredericksburg, Va.
691	Smith, Harriet	3y	W	U.S.	06 MAY 1873	Small Pox*
784	Smith, Harriet & S., infant of	12d	C	U.S.	c.04 JUL 1874	Mt. Olivet
399	Smith, Harry G.	2y	W	D.C.	18 JUL 1869	Congressional
777	Smith, Harry Hulse	8m	W	U.S.	20 JUN 1874	
484	Smith, Henrietta		W		14 OCT 1870	Mt. Olivet
583	Smith, Henry	2d	C		25 FEB 1872	
713	Smith, Henry	2y	C	D.C.	23 AUG 1873	
677	Smith, Henry	45y	C	U.S.	11 MAR 1873	Small Pox
479	Smith, Henry	5m	C	D.C.	14 SEP 1870	Washington Asylum
436	Smith, Henry	17y	C		04 JAN 1870	Washington Asylum
557	Smith, Henry, laborer	20y	C	Va.	04 FEB 1872	Washington
060	Smith, Henry Magruder	4m	W	D.C.	14 OCT 1856	Congressional
138	Smith, Hezzy	2m	C	D.C.	30 JAN 1859	Foundry
785	Smith, Horace L., clerk	54y	C	U.S.	31 JUL 1874	Harmony
496	Smith, Humphrey	60y	C	Va.	05 DEC 1870	White Haven
239	Smith, Ida	20y	W	Pa.	07 OCT 1866	Alms House
185	Smith, Ida	1y	W	D.C.	22 JUL 1860	Congressional
021	Smith, Infant	11m			16 AUG 1855	Western

Page	Name	Age	Race	Birth	Death Date	Burial Ground
428	Smith, Irene	2y	W	D.C.	05 NOV 1869	Glenwood
283	Smith, Isaac		C		06 NOV 1867	Freedmen's Hospital
537	Smith, Isabella	11m	C	D.C.	20 SEP 1871	
755	Smith, J.D., infant of	6d	W	U.S.	11 MAR 1874	
466	Smith, Jacob	3m	C	D.C.	27 JUL 1870	Young Mens
140	Smith, James	2½m	W	D.C.	05 FEB 1859	Methodist
602	Smith, James	45y	C	U.S.	01 MAY 1872	Mt. Olivet
599	Smith, James	20y	C	U.S.	17 MAY 1872	Unknown
442	Smith, James	2m	C		28 FEB 1870	Washington Asylum
681	Smith, James	75y	C	U.S.	21 APR 1873	Washington Asylum
291	Smith, James H.	6m	C	D.C.	26 JAN 1868	Ebenezer
143	Smith, James L.	2y	W	D.C.	05 MAR 1859	Oak Hill
585	Smith, James, laborer	28y		Va.	07 MAR 1872	
591	Smith, James, laborer	24y	C	Va.	10 APR 1872	Washington
425	Smith, James, lawyer	31y	W	Ohio	29 NOV 1869	Arlington National
552	Smith, James R., stone cutter	44y	W	Md.	03 JAN 1872	Congressional
737	Smith, Jane	70y	C	U.S.	23 DEC 1873	Mt. Pleasant
580	Smith, Jane	38y	C	Va.	07 FEB 1872	Washington
070	Smith, Jane	3m	C	D.C.	03 FEB 1857	Young Mens
182	Smith, Jas. Arthur	3y	C	D.C.	23 JUN 1860	Foundry
717	Smith, Jas. C.	22y	W	Md.	02 SEP 1873	Glenwood
489	Smith, Jas. E., child of	4m	C	D.C.	30 NOV 1870	Ebenezer
618	Smith, Jas. H.	32y	W	U.S.	21 AUG 1872	Ind.
116	Smith, Jessey, servant	88y	C	Va.	22 JUN 1858	Holmead
590	Smith, Jno.	25y	C	Md.	03 APR 1872	Small Pox
287	Smith, John		C		c.26 DEC 1867	Alms House
341	Smith, John	68y	W	Md.	11 AUG 1868	Congressional
372	Smith, John	2y	C		06 JAN 1869	Freedmen's Hospital
073	Smith, John	1y	C		08 MAR 1857	Harmony
460	Smith, John	1h	C	D.C.	11 JUN 1870	Holmead
357	Smith, John	7d	B	U.S.	02 OCT 1868	Washington Asylum
184	Smith, John	5m	W	D.C.	12 JUL 1860	Western
258	Smith, John	4y	C		11 APR 1867	Young Mens
113	Smith, John A., seaman	32y	W	N.Y.	10 MAY 1858	Congressional
325	Smith, John Addison	76y	W	Md.	09 JUL 1868	Washington
080	Smith, John, clerk	68y	W	Md.	27 JUN 1857	Rock Creek
384	Smith, John F.	1y	C	D.C.	16 MAR 1869	Washington Asylum
304	Smith, John, laborer	68y	W	Md.	18 MAR 1868	Congressional
089	Smith, John, laborer	70y	C	Va.	30 AUG 1857	Harmony
603	Smith, John, laborer	25y	C	D.C.	02 JUN 1872	Small Pox
107	Smith, John, laborer	34y	W	Ger.	10 MAR 1858	Washington Asylum
708	Smith, John W.	35y	W	D.C.	16 JUL 1873	
260	Smith, Joseph J.	19d	W	D.C.	29 MAY 1867	Congressional
252	Smith, Joseph M., bar keeper	21y	W	R.I.	13 FEB 1867	Providence, R.I.
731	Smith, Josephine	2y	W	U.S.	22 NOV 1873	Mt. Olivet
677	Smith, Julia	16y	C	U.S.	27 MAR 1873	Small Pox
546	Smith, Julia Ann	35y	C		22 NOV 1871	Union
388	Smith, Julia C.	4y	W	D.C.	08 APR 1869	Mt. Olivet
502	Smith, Kate	30y	W	Pa.	10 JAN 1871	Mt. Olivet
768	Smith, Laura V.	24y	W	U.S.	30 MAY 1874	Oak Hill
230	Smith, Lechuria	4d	W	D.C.	27 JUL 1866	Methodist Epis.
272	Smith, Lettie	75y	C		18 AUG 1867	Freedmen's Bureau
483	Smith, Lillie May	6m	W	D.C.	31 OCT 1870	Congressional
442	Smith, Lizzie, cook	87y	C		01 FEB 1870	
619	Smith, Lucinda	4y	C	U.S.	01 AUG 1872	
071	Smith, Lucinda L.	51y		Va.*	19 FEB 1857	Glenwood
639	Smith, Lucy	1y	C	U.S.	02 DEC 1872	Small Pox*
671	Smith, Lucy	35y	C	U.S.	19 FEB 1873	Small Pox*

District of Columbia Interments (Index to Deaths), 1855-1874

Page	Name	Age	Race	Birth	Death Date	Burial Ground
312	Smith, Lucy	4y	C	D.C.	27 MAY 1868	Western
272	Smith, Lucy, child of	Still	C		27 AUG 1867	Freedmen's Bureau
414	Smith, Lucy H., clerk Int. Rev.	33y	W	N.Y.	24 SEP 1869	N.Y.
684	Smith, Madison	19y	C	U.S.	26 APR 1873	Small Pox
405	Smith, Maggie	3y	C	D.C.	24 JUL 1869	Washington Asylum
318	Smith, Malinda	68y	W	Md.	28 JUN 1868	Congressional
270	Smith, Margaret	81y	W	Md.	07 AUG 1867	Mt. Olivet*
045	Smith, Margaret	20y	W	Ire.	28 MAY 1856	St. Patricks
036	Smith, Margaret	52y	C	Md.	03 FEB 1856	Young Mens
026	Smith, Margaret A.	23y	W	D.C.	23 OCT 1855	Congressional
251	Smith, Margery	84y	C	D.C.	20 JAN 1867	Alms House
593	Smith, Margret E.	40y	W	Ger.	18 APR 1872	Baltimore, Md.
247	Smith, Maria	65y	C		14 DEC 1866	
671	Smith, Maria		C	U.S.	27 FEB 1873	Small Pox*
429	Smith, Maria Elizabeth	35y	W	Md.	28 DEC 1869	Congressional
369	Smith, Marian Gertrude	1y	W	D.C.	13 JAN 1869	Congressional
445	Smith, Marshall, civil service	35y	W	Ind.	12 MAR 1870	Mt. Olivet
617	Smith, Martha	1y	C	U.S.	17 AUG 1872	
677	Smith, Martha	20y	C	U.S.	26 MAR 1873	Small Pox
021	Smith, Martha	25y	C	D.C.	24 AUG 1855	St. Patricks
615	Smith, Mary	25y	C	U.S.	08 JUL 1872	
631	Smith, Mary	3y	C	U.S.	25 OCT 1872	
674	Smith, Mary	50y	W	U.S.	18 MAR 1873	Congressional
761	Smith, Mary	2m	C	U.S.	06 APR 1874	Ebenezer
245	Smith, Mary	70y	W		24 NOV 1866	Mt. Olivet
464	Smith, Mary	9m	W	D.C.	01 JUL 1870	Mt. Olivet
703	Smith, Mary	18m	C	D.C.	26 JUL 1873	Mt. Pleasant
553	Smith, Mary	5y	W	D.C.	10 JAN 1872	St. Marys
377	Smith, Mary	2d	C	D.C.	06 FEB 1869	Washington Asylum
372	Smith, Mary	70y	W	D.C.	05 JAN 1869	Washington Asylum
158	Smith, Mary	2y	W	D.C.	14 AUG 1859	Western
058	Smith, Mary	2y	C		24 SEP 1856	Young Mens
785	Smith, Mary	1y	C	U.S.	31 JUL 1874	Young Mens
487	Smith, Mary Belle	4y	W	Md.	26 NOV 1870	Congressional
220	Smith, Mary, child of	Still	C	D.C.	12 MAY 1866	Beckett's
470	Smith, Mary, domestic	25y	C	Md.	19 AUG 1870	Mt. Olivet
718	Smith, Mary E.	63y	W	Md.	11 SEP 1873	Congressional
611	Smith, Mary E.	10m	C	U.S.	02 JUL 1872	Harmony
785	Smith, Mary E.	12y	C	U.S.	30 JUL 1874	Mt. Pleasant
640	Smith, Mary E.	48y	W	U.S.	26 DEC 1872	Small Pox*
352	Smith, Mary E.	10d	C	D.C.	07 SEP 1868	Washington Asylum
417	Smith, Mary E.	4m	C	D.C.	21 SEP 1869	Washington Asylum
250	Smith, Mary Elizabeth	16d	W	D.C.	24 DEC 1866	Congressional
007	Smith, Mary Ellen	1y	C		02 APR 1855	Harmony
181	Smith, Mary I.K.	69y	W	Md.	17 JUN 1860	Congressional
285	Smith, Mary J.	40y	W	Va.	01 DEC 1867	Congressional*
755	Smith, Mary, seamstress	21y	W	U.S.	28 MAR 1874	Mt. Olivet
334	Smith, Mary Susan	1y	C	D.C.	31 JUL 1868	
545	Smith, Matilda	69y	W	Md.	21 NOV 1871	Methodist
785	Smith, Matilda	2y	C	U.S.	31 JUL 1874	Mt. Pleasant
224	Smith, Mattie	2y	W	D.C.	10 JUN 1866	Congressional
605	Smith, Milton	2d	C	U.S.	12 JUN 1872	
488	Smith, Molly	21y	W	Md.	12 NOV 1870	Congressional
362	Smith, Moses	120y	C	Va.	05 NOV 1868	Washington Asylum
509	Smith, Mrs.	30y	W	U.S.	27 FEB 1871	Washington Asylum
213	Smith, Mrs.	110y	C		20 FEB 1866	Young Mens
614	Smith, N.	1m	C	U.S.	30 JUL 1872	
158	Smith, Nancy	70y	C	Va.	19 AUG 1859	Harmony

Page	Name	Age	Race	Birth	Death Date	Burial Ground
423	Smith, Nelson	5m	C	D.C.	15 OCT 1869	Washington Asylum
580	Smith, P.	21d	C	D.C.	07 FEB 1872	Ebenezer
533	Smith, P.P., bookkeeper	40y	W	D.C.	19 AUG 1871	
777	Smith, Patrick, agent	37y	W	Ire.	15 JUN 1874	Mt. Olivet
684	Smith, Rachael	19y	C	U.S.	07 APR 1873	Small Pox*
385	Smith, Rachel Jane, seamstress	31y	C		01 APR 1869	
668	Smith, Rebecca	75y	C	U.S.	17 FEB 1873	Washington Asylum
065	Smith, Reuben, servant	40y	C		15 DEC 1856	Young Mens
309	Smith, Richard S.	3y	C	D.C.	06 APR 1868	Harmony
662	Smith, Richard, teamster	34y	C	U.S.	29 JAN 1873	
719	Smith, Richd.	7m	W	D.C.	16 SEP 1873	Mt. Olivet
777	Smith, Richd. G.	35y	W	Ire.	22 JUN 1874	Mt. Olivet
612	Smith, Richd. H.	1y	W	U.S.	27 JUL 1872	
600	Smith, Richd., pound man	24y	C	U.S.	24 MAY 1872	Young Mens
276	Smith, Robert	60y	C		11 SEP 1867	
484	Smith, Robert	3y	C	D.C.	14 OCT 1870	Potters Field
661	Smith, Robert H., servant	43y	C	U.S.	21 JAN 1873	Ebenezer
362	Smith, Robert, shoemaker	28y	C	Va.	29 NOV 1868	
336	Smith, Robt.	8m	C		10 AUG 1868	Ebenezer
581	Smith, Rosa E.	4y	C	D.C.	15 FEB 1872	
666	Smith, Rufus S., clerk	26y	W	U.S.	05 FEB 1873	Newburyport, Mass.
601	Smith, Saml. R.	1y	W	U.S.	19 MAY 1872	Unknown
691	Smith, Samuel	1y	C	U.S.	07 MAY 1873	Small Pox*
008	Smith, Sara A.	64y	W	Md.	16 MAY 1855	Congressional
528	Smith, Sarah	4y	C	D.C.	13 JUL 1871	
735	Smith, Sarah	1m	C	U.S.	11 DEC 1873	
179	Smith, Sarah	76y	C	U.S.	— MAY 1860	Harmony
641	Smith, Sarah	12y	C	U.S.	29 DEC 1872	Small Pox*
553	Smith, Sarah	42y	C	Va.	08 JAN 1872	Washington
741	Smith, Sarah	1m	C	U.S.	12 JAN 1874	Washington Asylum
009	Smith, Sarah Ann	52y	W	Md.	16 MAY 1855	Congressional
536	Smith, Sarah M.	57y	W	N.Y.	17 SEP 1871	N.Y.
022	Smith, Sarah V.	5m	W	D.C.	10 AUG 1855	Methodist, East
373	Smith, Sarah, washer	33y	C		29 JAN 1869	
366	Smith, Schofield C.	9m	B	D.C.	10 DEC 1868	
039	Smith, Stella J.	49y	W	Ver.	03 MAR 1856	Congressional
451	Smith, Stephen, laborer	75y	C	Va.	17 APR 1870	Washington Asylum
330	Smith, Sylvia	7m	C	D.C.	30 JUL 1868	Union
453	Smith, T.	2y	W		14 MAY 1870	Congressional
602	Smith, Teresa	56y	W	Ire.	01 MAY 1872	Mt. Olivet
697	Smith, Terisa	3m	C	D.C.	28 JUN 1873	Mt. Olivet
223	Smith, Thomas	10y	C	D.C.	02 JUN 1866	Ebenezer
207	Smith, Thomas	72y	W		12 JUL 1862	Oak Hill
352	Smith, Thomas	2y	C		09 SEP 1868	Washington Asylum
547	Smith, Thomas L.	83y	W	Va.	04 DEC 1871	Oak Hill
109	Smith, Thomas O.	1y	W	D.C.	27 MAR 1858	Congressional
248	Smith, Thomas S., waiter	46y	C	D.C.	05 DEC 1866	Mt. Olivet
083	Smith, Thos. I.	49y	W	N.Y.	13 JUL 1857	
514	Smith, Tilman	1y	C	D.C.	19 MAR 1871	Ebenezer
590	Smith, W.	2d	C	D.C.	02 APR 1872	
474	Smith, W.	45y	W		12 AUG 1870	Washington Asylum
102	Smith, Waker S.	3y	C	D.C.	24 JAN 1858	Young Mens
707	Smith, Walter	7m	C	D.C.	22 JUL 1873	Beckett's
426	Smith, Walter G., hospital steward	26y	W	N.J.	20 NOV 1869	N.J.
242	Smith, Wesley	47y	W	N.Y.	07 OCT 1866	Congressional
036	Smith, William	22y	W		17 FEB 1856	Congressional
108	Smith, William	4m	W	D.C.	20 MAR 1858	Congressional
346	Smith, William	26y	C		24 AUG 1868	Freedmen's Hospital

Page	Name	Age	Race	Birth	Death Date	Burial Ground
683	Smith, William	23y	C	U.S.	06 APR 1873	Small Pox
146	Smith, William	42y	W	Va.	14 APR 1859	Washington Asylum
068	Smith, William, carpenter	29y	W	D.C.	19 JAN 1857	St. Peters
761	Smith, William, farmer	83y	W	Ire.	16 APR 1874	Mt. Olivet
264	Smith, William H.	10m	C	D.C.	12 JUL 1867	Harmony
242	Smith, William Wallace	8d	W	D.C.	28 OCT 1866	Glenwood
328	Smith, Willie	9m	C	D.C.	30 JUL 1868	Ebenezer
021	Smith, Wm.	7m	C	D.C.	13 AUG 1855	Harmony
509	Smith, Wm.	34y	W	Md.	22 FEB 1871	Washington Asylum
548	Smith, Wm. H.	37y	W	Va.	17 DEC 1871	Congressional*
332	Smith, Wm. I., clerk	85y	W	Ire.	16 JUL 1868	Mt. Olivet
157	Smith, Wm. J., bricklayer	43y	W	Md.	13 AUG 1859	Baltimore, Md.
606	Smith, Wm., laborer	55y	C	Va.	09 JUN 1872	
624	Smith, Wm., laborer	20y	C	U.S.	24 SEP 1872	
413	Smith, Wm., laborer	60y	C	Md.	23 AUG 1869	Washington Asylum
336	Smith, Wynnie A.	4m	C	D.C.	15 AUG 1868	
127	Smith, [?]	1y	W	D.C.	08 SEP 1858	
083	Smith, [blank]	7m	C	D.C.	17 JUL 1857	Colored
133	Smith, [blank]	6d	W	D.C.	20 NOV 1858	Congressional*
199	Smith, [blank]	10d	C	D.C.	16 FEB 1861	Methodist
166	Smith, [blank]	1m	W	D.C.	26 NOV 1859	Mt. Olivet
732	Smith, [blank]		C	U.S.	30 NOV 1873	Mt. Olivet
454	Smith, [blank]				10 MAY 1870	Prospect Hill
036	Smith, [blank]	4m	W		21 FEB 1856	St. Patricks
509	Smith, [blank]	½d	C	D.C.	15 FEB 1871	Washington Asylum
105	Smith, [blank]	1d	C		20 FEB 1858	Western
102	Smith, [blank]		C		26 JAN 1858	Western
197	Smith, [blank], Mr.	40y	C		12 JAN 1861	Harmony
487	Smither, Sarah, servant	75y	C	Va.	05 NOV 1870	Young Mens
544	Smithson, Annie S.	24y	W	Pol.	08 NOV 1871	Md.
729	Smithson, C.J.	20y	W	U.S.	08 NOV 1873	Congressional*
607	Smithson, Mary	1m	W	D.C.	28 JUN 1872	Methodist
540	Smithson, Virginia	26y	W	U.S.	05 OCT 1871	Methodist
137	Smithson, William, laborer	18y	C	D.C.	17 JAN 1859	Harmony
135	Smitson, Mary A.	32y	W	D.C.	05 DEC 1858	Washington
278	Smitson, Sina	76y	W		15 OCT 1867	Congressional
712	Smitts, Elijah	1y	C	D.C.	13 AUG 1873	
768	Smlay, Wilbert H. [sic], clerk	15y	W	U.S.	20 MAY 1874	Graceland
218	Smoot, Avery E., printer	63y	W	Md.	24 APR 1866	Congressional*
325	Smoot, B.M., housekeeper	71y	W	Md.	03 JUL 1868	Congressional
191	Smoot, John	6m	C	D.C.	05 OCT 1860	Western
073	Smoot, Joseph, naval officer	66y	W	Md.	13 MAR 1857	Congressional
398	Smoot, Levi	51y	B		16 JUN 1869	Washington Asylum
236	Smoot, Samuel C., Dr.	48y	W	D.C.	29 SEP 1866	Congressional*
193	Smoot, Sarah Elizabeth	4m	W	D.C.	08 NOV 1860	Glenwood
262	Smoot, Thomas	34y	W		20 JUN 1867	Alexandria, Va.
286	Smoot, William	16y	C	Md.	17 DEC 1867	Ebenezer
367	Smoot, [blank]	Still	B	D.C.	01 DEC 1868	Washington Asylum
435	Smothers, Julia	35y	C	Md.	30 JAN 1870	Mt. Olivet
421	Smothers, Melvit	3y	C		26 OCT 1869	Mt. Olivet
025	Smyth, Martha	9m	W	D.C.	25 SEP 1855	St. Peters
477	Snape, Thomas	1y	W	D.C.	11 SEP 1870	Holmead
749	Snee, Daniel D.	7y	W	U.S.	08 FEB 1874	Mt. Olivet
157	Sniffan, Theodore	6m	W	D.C.	13 AUG 1859	Methodist
400	Sniffen, Margaret	1m	W	D.C.	20 JUL 1869	Congressional
594	Sniffen, [blank]	Still	W	D.C.	07 APR 1872	Congressional*
592	Sniffer, Ada H.	27y	W	U.S.	08 APR 1872	Oak Hill
225	Sniffin, Cornelius	22d	W	D.C.	21 JUN 1866	Methodist

District of Columbia Interments (Index to Deaths), 1855-1874

Page	Name	Age	Race	Birth	Death Date	Burial Ground
225	Sniffin, Louisa	22d	W	D.C.	21 JUN 1866	Methodist
264	Sniffin, Mary C.	39y	W	D.C.	12 JUL 1867	Methodist
419	Snooks, Infant	Still	W		19 OCT 1869	Congressional
665	Snow, Abby C.	43y	W	U.S.	26 JAN 1873	Oak Hill
643	Snow, Harriet	35y	C	U.S.	07 DEC 1872	Harmony
341	Snow, Harry B.	8m	W		12 AUG 1868	Congressional
162	Snow, Louisa	60y	C	U.S.	08 SEP 1859	Holmead
483	Snowden, Amanda	6y	C	Md.	28 OCT 1870	Bennings Bridge, over
227	Snowden, Asbury, laborer	25y	C	Md.	06 JUL 1866	Alms House
306	Snowden, Catherine E.	17y	C	D.C.	05 APR 1868	Young Mens
459	Snowden, David	2y	C	D.C.	30 JUN 1870	Potters Field
065	Snowden, Elizabeth	13y	C	D.C.	16 DEC 1856	Young Mens
016	Snowden, M.E.	16m	C		01 JUL 1855	Young Mens
259	Snowden, Margaret	62y	C	Md.	06 APR 1867	Harmony
307	Snowden, William, wood sawyer	83y	C	D.C.	21 APR 1868	Western
025	Snowden, [blank]	4m			10 SEP 1855	Harmony
114	Snowden, [blank]	Still			29 MAY 1858	Va.
086	Snowden, [blank]	10m	C		09 AUG 1857	Young Mens
157	Snyder, Clara	11m	W	D.C.	07 AUG 1859	Prospect Hill
222	Snyder, Elizabeth M., teacher	26y	W	N.Y.	30 MAY 1866	N.Y.
273	Snyder, F., huckster	25y	W	Md.	17 SEP 1867	Montgomery Co., Md.
150	Snyder, George	4m	W	D.C.	03 JUN 1859	Prospect Hill
246	Snyder, Jacob, wheelwright	30y	W	D.C.	17 DEC 1866	Congressional
777	Snyder, Joseph	9y	W	U.S.	14 JUN 1874	
785	Snyder, Joseph F.	7y	W	U.S.	21 JUL 1874	Oak Hill
744	Snyder, Susan	3y	W	U.S.	23 JAN 1874	
585	Soden, John, watchman	45y	W	U.S.	08 MAR 1872	Methodist
659	Sohn, Mary	1y	W	U.S.	13 JAN 1873	
374	Sollens, John A., upholsterer	31y	W	Amer.	11 FEB 1869	Congressional
110	Sollers, William, upholsterer	40y	W	Md.	05 APR 1858	St. Patricks
274	Solms, Sarah M.	7m	W	D.C.	02 SEP 1867	Presbyterian
083	Soloman, Caroline	4m	C		20 JUL 1857	Western
088	Soloman, Henrietta	20y	C		20 AUG 1857	Western
645	Solomon, Albert	3y	W	U.S.	31 DEC 1872	Hebrew
077	Solomon, Cyana	52y	C	Va.	13 MAY 1857	Western
438	Solomon, Kenner W.	44y	C		27 JAN 1870	Harmony
732	Somax, Rachel Ann	3y	C	U.S.	27 NOV 1873	Weathersfield, Conn.
220	Somers, Alexander		W		06 MAY 1866	Congressional
550	Somers, Henry L.	1y	W	D.C.	28 DEC 1871	Congressional*
551	Somers, Jas. T.	5m	C	D.C.	— DEC 1871	
245	Somers, Mary A.	37y	W		13 NOV 1866	Mt. Olivet
637	Somerscales, M.A.	27y	W	U.S.	08 NOV 1872	Glenwood
273	Somerville, Arnold, soap maker	73y	C	Md.	19 SEP 1867	Mt. Olivet
412	Somerville, Isabella	4y	C		31 AUG 1869	Harmony
282	Somerville, Maria	37y	C	Md.	10 NOV 1867	Colored
661	Sommenschmidt, Willie	3y	W	U.S.	25 JAN 1873	Glenwood
435	Sommers, Adelaide R.	3m	C		27 JAN 1870	Ebenezer
494	Sommers, Catharine	2m	W	Amer.	11 DEC 1870	Mt. Olivet
168	Sommers, Laura V.	5y	W	D.C.	31 DEC 1859	Prospect Hill
224	Sommers, Sarah	34y	W	Ire.	17 JUN 1866	Congressional
445	Sommers, William, watchman	48y	W	Ire.	24 MAR 1870	Mt. Olivet
785	Sones, Phoebe A.	45y	W	U.S.	08 JUL 1874	Congressional
682	Sonneman, Emma	6y	W	U.S.	26 APR 1873	Prospect Hill
410	Sonnemann, Anna	4y	W	D.C.	15 AUG 1869	Prospect Hill
354	Sonness, Wm.	67y	W	Scot.	13 OCT 1868	Congressional
335a	Sonophe, Frank				27 JUL 1868	Washington Asylum
328	Sonopher, Frank, servant	18y	C		26 JUL 1868	Alms House
602	Soodemn, E.A., clerk	41y	W	U.S.	15 MAY 1872	

District of Columbia Interments (Index to Deaths), 1855-1874

Page	Name	Age	Race	Birth	Death Date	Burial Ground
054	Sooel, Elizabeth	27y	W	D.C.	11 AUG 1856	St. Patricks
256	Soper, Ann Emily	24y	W	Ire.	11 MAR 1867	Burlington, Ver.
777	Soper, Clarence M.	2m	W	U.S.	15 JUN 1874	
027	Soper, Fanny G.	1y	W	D.C.	09 OCT 1855	Methodist
750	Soper, James S., moulder	39y	W	U.S.	08 FEB 1874	
293	Soper, Laura Lucretia	20y	W	Md.	27 MAR 1868	Oak Hill
326	Soper, Lily MM.	1y	W	D.C.	08 JUL 1868	Congressional
676	Soper, Sally	70y	C	U.S.	30 MAR 1873	Washington Asylum
482	Soper, Wm. Edward, horse r.r.	28y	W		17 OCT 1870	Glenwood
322	Sopfer, Thomas	6y	W		17 JUN 1868	Mt. Olivet
627	Sorell, Edward	60y	C	U.S.	22 SEP 1872	Small Pox
614	Sorrell, Lewis A.	34y	W	U.S.	10 JUL 1872	
293	Sorrell, Virginia A..	25y	W	Va.	05 MAR 1868	Presbyterian
075	Soter, John	2y	W	D.C.	20 APR 1857	German
537	Soter, Maria L.	8y	W	U.S.	19 SEP 1871	Prospect Hill
543	Sothoron, John, carpenter	46y	W	U.S.	30 OCT 1871	Congressional*
182	Sothoron, Richard W.	2y	W		27 JUN 1860	Methodist
128	Souer, John	11y	W	D.C.	18 SEP 1858	German Catholic
469	Soule, Chas. H.	4y	W	D.C.	24 AUG 1870	Mt. Olivet
476	Soules, Alonso S.	1y	W	D.C.	15 SEP 1870	Mt. Olivet
777	Soules, Esther Jane	6m	W	U.S.	09 JUN 1874	Mt. Olivet
075	Sousa, Ferdinand M.	2m	W	D.C.	16 APR 1857	Congressional
174	Sousa, Rosina	2y	W	D.C.	02 MAR 1860	Congressional
347	Souter, Isabella	52y	W	Scot.	30 SEP 1868	Congressional
395	South, Harrey E.	13m	W	D.C.	05 JUN 1869	Glenwood
768	South, Mary A.	54y	W	Switz.	29 MAY 1874	
444	Southall, Sophia	33y	W		30 MAR 1870	Glenwood
050	Southeran, Henry	32y	W	La.	14 JUL 1856	Washington Asylum
413	Southerland, Henriette	57y	C	Ky.	09 AUG 1869	Washington Asylum
521	Southerland, Isabella	81y	W	Scot.	07 JUN 1871	Washington
408	Southgate, Eleanor	23d	W		11 AUG 1869	Oak Hill
050	Southovan, George	5m	W	D.C.	12 JUL 1856	Western
096	Southwood, Mrs., child of				17 NOV 1857	Congressional
596	Sowning, Jos. A., printer	28y	W	D.C.	28 APR 1872	Mt. Olivet
428	Sozenhofer, [blank]	Still	W		06 NOV 1869	Mt. Clivet
130	Spaeth, Frederick Fleury	9m	W	D.C.	06 OCT 1858	
258	Spaits, Mary E.	6m	W	D.C.	19 APR 1867	Congressional
294	Spalding, Harriet H.	65y	W	U.S.	04 FEB 1868	Oak Hill
257	Spalding, Hilleary C., claim agent	61y	W	Md.	06 MAR 1867	Mt. Olivet
212	Spalding, J.G., infant of		W	D.C.	02 FEB 1866	Congressional
076	Spalding, Julia E.	3y	W	D.C.	27 APR 1857	St. Peters
581	Spalding, Maria, housekeeper	43y	W	D.C.	15 FEB 1872	Oak Hill
033	Spalding, Richd. L., messenger	43y	W		11 JAN 1856	St. Patricks
547	Spalding, Saml. McL., painter	42y	W	U.S.	01 DEC 1871	Oak Hill*
350	Spark, Mary Ann	2y	C	D.C.	09 SEP 1868	Washington Asylum
487	Sparks, A.R., Dr.	50y	W	Va.	25 NOV 1870	Congressional
485	Sparks, Elizabeth	43y	W	Md.	04 OCT 1870	Potters Field
537	Sparks, George	25y	C	Va.	22 SEP 1871	
733	Sparks, Ida	3y	C	U.S.	13 NOV 1873	
744	Sparks, Jennie	P.B.	C	U.S.	31 JAN 1874	Potters Field
523	Spates, George W., house painter	29y	W	Va.	13 JUN 1871	Congressional*
232	Spaulding, James W., corp. ofcr.	34y	W		30 AUG 1866	Mt. Olivet
318	Speake, John W., child of	Still	W	D.C.	26 JUN 1868	Congressional
613	Speaks, Alberta	7m	C	U.S.	26 JUL 1872	
688	Speaks, Jane	23y	C	U.S.	18 MAY 1873	
595	Speaks, Sarah C.	38y	W	U.S.	11 APR 1872	Congressional*
407	Speaks, [blank]	Still	W		12 AUG 1869	Congressional
370	Spear, Sarah	39y	W	Mass.	11 JAN 1869	Philadelphia, Pa.

Page	Name	Age	Race	Birth	Death Date	Burial Ground
744	Spear, Susie M.W.	36y	W	U.S.	28 JAN 1874	Glenwood
726	Speare, Herbert Lee	7m	W	U.S.	27 OCT 1873	Congressional
138	Spearing, Grace A.	10y	W	D.C.	30 JAN 1859	Glenwood
245	Speed, John M., lawyer	51y	W	Va.	01 NOV 1866	Lynchburg, Va.
670	Speers, Harrison	50y	C	U.S.	25 FEB 1873	Small Pox
419	Speicer, Chas. Edwin	18d	W		23 OCT 1869	Congressional
175	Speiser, Catharine Rosa	10m	W	D.C.	31 MAR 1860	Congressional
227	Speiser, Frederick	12y	W	D.C.	04 JUL 1866	Congressional
366	Speiss, Emma W.	4m	W	D.C.	01 DEC 1868	Prospect Hill
068	Speisser, John F.	4y	W	D.C.	19 JAN 1857	Congressional
001	Spelly, Michael	27y			12 JAN 1855	St. Patricks
616	Spelman, W.T.	10m	W	U.S.	11 JUL 1872	
217	Spence, Anna P.	30y	W	Eng.	01 APR 1866	Mt. Olivet
441	Spence, Benjamin C.	2y	C		23 FEB 1870	Union
494	Spence, C.W., child of	Still	W		26 DEC 1870	Glenwood
365	Spencer, Amelia	87y	W	Conn.	29 DEC 1868	Congressional*
010	Spencer, Cathr. M.	5y		Md.	09 JUN 1855	Oak Hill
583	Spencer, Chas. S., bookbinder	32y	W	D.C.	25 FEB 1872	Glenwood
463	Spencer, Edward, bookbinder	23y	W	Amer.	08 JUL 1870	Glenwood
696	Spencer, Laura	4m	C	D.C.	30 JUN 1873	
768	Spencer, Martha	41y	C	U.S.	12 MAY 1874	Young Mens
115	Spencer, Richard	1y	W	D.C.	02 JUN 1858	Glenwood
066	Spencer, Richard D., mkt. master	42y	W		23 DEC 1856	Glenwood
721	Spencer, Richd.	80y	C	U.S.	30 SEP 1873	
496	Spencer, Samuel, laborer	30y	C	Md.	05 DEC 1870	Beckett's
165	Spencer, Theodore	3m	W	D.C.	21 NOV 1859	Glenwood
278	Spengler, Theodore	1y	W		27 OCT 1867	Congressional
283	Spenser, Mary Ellen	15y	W	D.C.	05 NOV 1867	Congressional
541	Spicer, Barbara A.	8y	W	D.C.	09 OCT 1871	Congressional*
534	Spicer, John W., stone mason	39y	W		27 AUG 1871	Congressional*
188	Spiers, Bridget	1y	W	D.C.	22 AUG 1860	Mt. Olivet
320	Spindler, Edwd.	6y	W		01 JUN 1868	Rock Creek
179	Spink, Henry, laborer	50y	C	Va.	16 MAY 1860	Mt. Olivet
221	Spooner, Jane, school teacher	63y	W		22 MAY 1866	Congressional
342	Spotser, Fanny	1y	C	D.C.	14 AUG 1868	Young Mens
452	Spotswood, Anna	95y	C	Va.	28 APR 1870	Washington Asylum
370	Sppinson, Rebecca	79y	W	N.C.	31 JAN 1869	Baltimore, Md.
496	Sprague, Andrew	2d	C		08 DEC 1870	Beckett's
284	Sprague, Lucy	40y	C	D.C.	25 NOV 1867	Alms House
768	Sprague, William R.	1y	W	U.S.	29 MAY 1874	Aouth Amboy, N.J.
340	Spransey, Mary	2m	W	D.C.	30 AUG 1868	Congressional
428	Spreser, William	5m	W		18 NOV 1869	Prospect Hill
630	Sprig, Willy	9m	C	U.S.	01 OCT 1872	
492	Sprigg, Anne G.	71y	W	Va.	18 DEC 1870	Congressional
627	Sprigg, Augustus	2y	C	U.S.	09 SEP 1872	
741	Spriggs, Emma J.	2y	C	U.S.	11 JAN 1874	
785	Spriggs, Louisa	60y	C	U.S.	25 JUL 1874	
730	Sprigs, Miss, infant of		C	U.S.	12 NOV 1873	
064	Spring, Arthur, messenger	23y	W	Pa.	26 NOV 1856	St. Matthews
369	Springman, Infant	2h	W	D.C.	02 JAN 1869	Congressional
278	Springman, Susannah	20y	W	D.C.	20 OCT 1867	Congressional
474	Springs, Geo.	1y	C		26 AUG 1870	Washington Asylum
474	Springs, John	4y	C		26 AUG 1870	Washington Asylum
402	Sproeser, Lewis	4y	W		05 JUL 1869	Prospect Hill
333	Sprohs, Katie	1y	W	D.C.	18 JUL 1868	Prospect Hill
344	Spross, John A., child of	9d	W	D.C.	14 AUG 1868	Prospect Hill
038	Sproule, Jesse B.	1y	W	D.C.	24 MAR 1856	Congressional
348	Sputh, Benj. F.	1y	W	D.C.	12 SEP 1868	Congressional

District of Columbia Interments (Index to Deaths), 1855-1874

Page	Name	Age	Race	Birth	Death Date	Burial Ground
603	Squier, George E.	5m	W	D.C.	18 JUN 1872	Oak Hill
708	Squires, G. Martin	23m	W	D.C.	04 JUL 1873	Glenwood
777	Squires, Sarah Eva	4m	W	U.S.	21 JUN 1874	Mt. Olivet
258	Squires, Selah	40y	W	N.Y.	05 APR 1867	Green, Che. Co., N.Y.
691	St. Clair, Jos. H., bookbinder	34y	W	U.S.	12 MAY 1873	
719	St. Clair, Jos.	5m	W	D.C.	18 SEP 1873	Mt. Olivet
215	St. Germain, Chief	65y	I	Wisc.	18 MAR 1866	Congressional
260	St. John, Holley, clerk	21y	W	N.J.	07 MAY 1867	N.J.
761	Stack, John	11y	W	U.S.	03 APR 1874	Mt. Olivet
002	Stack, Sarah	54y	W	Md.	16 JAN 1855	Congressional
612	Stagner, John	3y	W	U.S.	11 JUL 1872	
477	Stahl, Alma H.	2m	W	D.C.	06 SEP 1870	Congressional
327	Stahl, C.C.	6m	W	D.C.	05 JUL 1868	Western
113	Stahl, Catharine B.	5m	W	D.C.	12 MAY 1858	German Lutheran
012	Stahl, D.	1m	W	D.C.	30 JUN 1855	German
400	Stahl, George	7m	W		— JUL 1869	Prospect Hill
445	Stahl, Henrietta, Mrs.	35y	W		18 MAR 1870	
088	Stahl, Richard	2m	C	D.C.	21 AUG 1857	
003	Stancle, Tille	5m	W	D.C.	18 FEB 1855	
603	Stanford, L.B.	7m	W	U.S.	01 JUN 1872	Congressional
018	Stanford, W.H., child of	2m	W	D.C.	01 AUG 1855	Congressional
275	Stanford, Wm. M., child of	Still	W		21 SEP 1867	Congressional
149	Stanley, Bernard	7m	C		30 MAY 1859	Foundry
326	Stanley, George Alexander	9m	W	D.C.	10 JUL 1868	Congressional
314	Stanley, Mary L., Mrs.	39y	W	N.Y.	16 MAY 1868	Congressional
069	Stanley, Thos. B.	4y	W	D.C.	24 JAN 1857	Glenwood
049	Stanly, Wm. Henry	10m	W	D.C.	04 JUL 1856	Harmony
472	Stanmore, Martha, servant	16y	C	Md.	11 AUG 1870	Young Mens
299	Stansberry, William	47y	W	Md.	19 MAR 1868	Mt. Olivet
613	Stansburg, Laura V.	2y	W	U.S.	22 JUL 1872	
602	Stansbury, Ellen R.	47y	W	U.S.	20 MAY 1872	Congressional
606	Stant, John	1d	W	D.C.	15 JUN 1872	Congressional
498	Stant, Wm., pauper	2m	W	D.C.	20 JAN 1871	Washington Asylum
432	Stanton, Edwin M., Hon.	55y	W	Ohio	24 DEC 1869	Oak Hill
462	Stanton, Ella	8m	W	D.C.	28 JUL 1870	Mt. Olivet
777	Stanton, Eva Regena	10m	W	U.S.	19 JUN 1874	Holyrood
612	Stanton, Peter	10m	W	U.S.	05 JUL 1872	
671	Staples, Emily	59y	W	U.S.	28 FEB 1873	Small Pox*
525	Staples, Jno. L., gunner U.S.N.	35y	W	Va.	28 JUN 1871	Congressional
677	Staples, Mrs. [Jane]	25y	W	U.S.	17 MAR 1873	Congressional*
341	Star, Chas. Morning, 2nd bat. NY	35y+	W		15 AUG 1868	Congressional
084	Starbuck, Mary, lady	40y	W		28 JUL 1857	St. Patricks
421	Starck, Patrick, laborer	40y	W	Ire.	09 OCT 1869	Mt. Olivet
520	Starke, Ida	1m	W	D.C.*	26 MAY 1871	Holy Rood
623	Starke, Lewis	1m	W	U.S.	18 JUL 1872	Catholic
457	Starrett, Preston, messenger	79y	W	S.C.	29 JUN 1870	Oak Hill
444	Staut, Ida	8y	W		29 MAR 1870	Congressional
347	Steadman, Adelia A.	15y	W	Md.	02 SEP 1868	Congressional
485	Steadman, Rachel Ann	38y	W		22 OCT 1870	Ebenezer
622	Stebbman, Ludy, student	12y	C	U.S.	21 AUG 1872	
485	Steel, James, hotel keeper	47y	W	Del.	07 OCT 1870	Glenwood
391	Steele, Ashbel, Rev.	73y	W	Conn.	30 MAY 1869	Boston, Mass.
036	Steele, Charles, shoemaker	66y	W	Md.	11 FEB 1856	Foundry
108	Steele, Duncan S.	1y	W	Minn.	15 MAR 1858	Oak Hill
597	Steele, E., Mrs.	77y	W	Ire.	01 MAY 1872	Congressional
304	Steele, John W., painter	33y	W	Va.	20 MAR 1868	Congressional
254	Steele, Julia C.	28y	W	N.Y.	24 FEB 1867	N.Y.
155	Steele, [blank]	12y	C	D.C.	22 JUL 1859	Western

District of Columbia Interments (Index to Deaths), 1855-1874

Page	Name	Age	Race	Birth	Death Date	Burial Ground
478	Steen, U.S.G.	4m	W	D.C.	24 SEP 1870	Mt. Olivet
370	Steer, Ann Eliza	3y	W		22 JAN 1869	Mt. Olivet
768	Steever, Margaret W.	64y	W	U.S.	20 MAY 1874	Oak Hill
152	Steffer, [blank]		W	D.C.	13 JUN 1859	German
535	Steigmeier, Mary	5y	W	D.C.	07 SEP 1871	German Catholic
317	Stein, Dorette	1m	W	D.C.	13 JUN 1868	Hebrew
431	Steinbach, Robert	14y	W	Md.	07 DEC 1869	St. Marys
526	Steinberg, Joseph	1y	W	D.C.	03 JUL 1871	Washington
452	Steinecke, [blank]		W	D.C.	15 APR 1870	Washington Asylum
706	Steiner, Anna B.	76y	W	Ger.	26 JUL 1873	Prospect Hill
524	Steiner, Frederick	8m	W	D.C.	21 JUN 1871	
004	Steiner, Jannette	69y	W	N.J.	22 MAR 1855	Congressional
364	Steinle, George	13m	W		27 DEC 1868	Congressional
240	Steinle, William	1y	W		27 OCT 1866	Congressional
146	Steinough, Thos. John	5y	W	Ger.	11 APR 1859	German
777	Stello, William	9m	W	U.S.	29 JUN 1874	Prospect Hill
597	Stenger, Christina	82y	W	U.S.	06 MAY 1872	Congressional
161	Stennett, Ann Eliza	22y	W	N.Y.	06 SEP 1859	N.Y.
522	Stephens, Caroline	4m	W	D.C.	13 JUN 1871	Congressional*
605	Stephens, Chris., wharf builder	35y	W	Md.	22 JUN 1872	
050	Stephens, Eben	23y	W		15 JUL 1856	Congressional
755	Stephens, J.H.	61y	C	U.S.	27 MAR 1874	Washington Asylum
391	Stephens, Laura V., Mrs.	32y	W		24 MAY 1869	Glenwood
694	Stephens, Mary	40y	C	Va.	17 JUN 1873	Beckett's
300	Stephens, Susan, Mrs.	77y	W	Conn.	10 MAR 1868	Norwalk, Conn.
391	Stephens, Thos. A., merchant	46y	W	Md.	11 MAY 1869	Mt. Olivet
399	Stephens, Wm.	9d	W	D.C.	16 JUL 1869	Congressional
631	Stephenson, Elizabeth	20y	W	U.S.	18 OCT 1872	Congressional*
104	Stephenson, Joseph	81y	W	Eng.	08 FEB 1858	Foundry
301	Stephenson, Mary A.	57y	W	Md.	17 MAR 1868	Glenwood
749	Stepney, Emeline	8m	C	U.S.	08 FEB 1874	
431	Stepny, Lenia	3y	W		10 DEC 1869	Mt. Olivet
749	Steptoe, Willie	2y	C	U.S.	21 FEB 1874	
582	Sterling, Mary J.	7y	W	D.C.	22 FEB 1872	
188	Sterling, William	50y	W	Ire.	30 AUG 1860	Rock Creek
321	Sternden, Thomas	5y	W	D.C.	09 JUN 1868	Mt. Olivet
216	Sterns, F.B.	1y	W	Me.	27 MAR 1866	Glenwood
268	Sterns, Robert	11m	W	D.C.	11 AUG 1867	Congressional
777	Sters, Edward	60y	C	U.S.	24 JUN 1874	Mt. Pleasant
646	Stetney, Ann, servant	40y	C	Md.	25 DEC 1872	
592	Stetson, Maria A.	39y	W	U.S.	18 APR 1872	Mass.
547	Stettins, Thaddeus S.	43y	W	N.Y.	08 DEC 1871	Glenwood
599	Steuard, L.W.	5y	W	U.S.	14 MAY 1872	Prospect Hill
593	Steuart, Alexander, contractor	49y	W	Pa.	30 APR 1872	Ohio
586	Steuart, Fannie	35y	C	Md.	16 MAR 1872	Western
580	Steuart, Fred.	39y	C	Md.	12 FEB 1872	Washington
544	Steuart, George	30y	C	Va.	04 NOV 1871	
525	Steuart, Henry	35y	C	Va.	28 JUN 1871	Potters Field
029	Steuart, Wm. E.	34y	W	D.C.	07 NOV 1855	St. Peters
661	Stevens, Ann V.	24y	W	U.S.	23 JAN 1873	Congressional*
678	Stevens, Anna	33y	W	U.S.	24 MAR 1873	Small Pox
761	Stevens, C.S., printer	39y	W	N.S.	22 APR 1874	Halifax, N.S.
295	Stevens, Cecilia W., Mme.	68y	W	N.C.	25 FEB 1868	Congressional
392	Stevens, Charles	28y	W	Mass.	08 MAY 1869	Washington Asylum
514	Stevens, David W.	1m	W	D.C.	12 MAR 1871	Glenwood
120	Stevens, Elizabeth	40y	W	D.C.	06 JUL 1858	Congressional
394	Stevens, George W., seaman	46y	W	Md.	28 JUN 1869	Congressional
734	Stevens, Georgie	5m	C	U.S.	08 DEC 1873	

District of Columbia Interments (Index to Deaths), 1855-1874

Page	Name	Age	Race	Birth	Death Date	Burial Ground
549	Stevens, L.P., Mrs.	65y	W	Md.	19 DEC 1871	Congressional*
402	Stevens, Martin	11d	W	D.C.	06 JUL 1869	Mt. Olivet
439	Stevens, Mathew H., merchant	50y	W	Conn.	25 FEB 1870	Congressional
212	Stevens, Milkey, cook		C	Md.	15 FEB 1866	
147	Stevens, Paul, Hon.	68y	W	Ver.	28 APR 1859	Georgetown
130	Stevens, Samuel	4m	W	D.C.	07 OCT 1858	Congressional
345	Stevens, Thaddeus, Hon., cong.	76y	W	Ver.	11 AUG 1868	Lancaster, Pa
664	Stevens, Virginia	24y	W	U.S.	23 JAN 1873	Small Pox*
373	Stevens, Walter	2y	C		18 JAN 1869	
500	Stevens, Wm., farmer/merchant	78y	W	N.Y.	07 JAN 1871	Glenwood
203	Stevens, [blank]	Still		D.C.	29 MAY 1861	Glenwood
717	Stevenson, James	40y	C	Va.	06 SEP 1873	Washington Asylum
600	Stevenson, Jane	70y	W	U.S.	23 MAY 1872	Unknown
436	Stevenson, Jane	50y	C		03 JAN 1870	Washington Asylum
736	Stevenson, Jerry	6m	C	U.S.	14 DEC 1873	Holmead
327	Stevenson, Mary	9m	C	D.C.	21 JUL 1868	Young Mens
432	Stevenson, R.A.	1m	C	D.C.	31 DEC 1869	Washington Asylum
360	Stevenson, Thomas A., merchant	40y	W	Ohio	16 NOV 1868	Ohio
785	Steward, Benj. & S., infant of	P.B.	W	U.S.	15 JUL 1874	
004	Steward, Donald	46y	W	Scot.	19 MAR 1855	
717	Steward, Edward	16m	C	D.C.	03 SEP 1873	Mt. Olivet
088	Steward, Elizabeth	70y	W	Va.	25 AUG 1857	Glenwood
189	Steward, Henry	1y	W	D.C.	01 SEP 1860	Congressional
197	Steward, John M., gambler	55y	W	Va.	25 JAN 1861	
197	Steward, Joseph	5d	W	D.C.	14 JAN 1861	Congressional
720	Steward, Lillie	1y	W	D.C.	25 SEP 1873	
224	Steward, Margt.	1y	W		11 JUN 1866	Holmead
087	Steward, Mary E.	22y	W	Md.	10 AUG 1857	Glenwood
696	Steward, Nancy	28y	C	U.S.	01 JUN 1873	Washington Asylum
133	Stewart, Adelia		W	D.C.	16 NOV 1858	St. Patricks
761	Stewart, Albert A., bricklayer	20y	W	U.S.	19 APR 1874	Glenwood
644	Stewart, Alex	2m	C	U.S.	15 DEC 1872	Mt. Olivet
412	Stewart, Ambrose	1y	C		16 AUG 1869	Queen's Chapel
741	Stewart, Ann	70y	C	U.S.	15 JAN 1874	Washington Asylum
466	Stewart, Annie	2y	C		— JUL 1870	
662	Stewart, Betty	Still	C	U.S.	30 JAN 1873	
013	Stewart, C.E.	6m	W	D.C.	30 JUL 1855	Congressional
121	Stewart, Caleb	7m	W	D.C.	16 JUL 1858	Congressional
039	Stewart, Catharine	1y	W	D.C.	05 MAR 1856	Congressional
449	Stewart, Cather., dress maker	32y	W	Ger.	10 APR 1870	Mt. Olivet
252	Stewart, Charles, child of	Still	W	D.C.	06 FEB 1867	Oak Hill
276	Stewart, Charles J.	6y	W	D.C.	29 SEP 1867	Mt. Olivet
098	Stewart, Chas. Wm. B.	4m	W	D.C.	06 DEC 1857	Holmead
353	Stewart, Edward	25y	C	Va.	27 SEP 1868	Washington Asylum
489	Stewart, Eliza	40y	C	Va.	22 NOV 1870	Ebenezer
191	Stewart, Elizabeth	35y	W	D.C.	11 OCT 1860	Alexandria, Va.
660	Stewart, Elizabeth	60y	W	U.S.	21 JAN 1873	Holmead
065	Stewart, Elizabeth	1d	C	D.C.	13 DEC 1856	Young Mens
457	Stewart, Estelle	½d	W	D.C.	20 JUN 1870	Congressional
335b	Stewart, Fenton, laborer	40y	B	U.S.	03 JUL 1868	Washington Asylum
190	Stewart, Florence	1y	W	D.C.	01 SEP 1860	Congressional
128	Stewart, Frank	5y	C	Va.*	28 SEP 1858	Young Mens
743	Stewart, Frederic R.	12h	W	U.S.	25 JAN 1874	Glenwood
299	Stewart, Geo. Kerr	1m	W	D.C.	26 MAR 1868	Glenwood
356	Stewart, George	1y	B	D.C.	03 OCT 1868	Union
536	Stewart, Grace	P.B.	W	D.C.	18 SEP 1871	Congressional
627	Stewart, Hattie	3y	C	U.S.	11 SEP 1872	
017	Stewart, Henrietta	9m	C	D.C.	23 JUL 1855	

Page	Name	Age	Race	Birth	Death Date	Burial Ground
729	Stewart, Henry	1y	W	U.S.	09 NOV 1873	Congressional*
733	Stewart, Infant	2d	C	U.S.	12 NOV 1873	
455	Stewart, Isaac	2y	C		13 MAY 1870	
022	Stewart, Isabella	6m	W	D.C.	07 AUG 1855	Congressional
108	Stewart, James, coachman	23y	C	D.C.	14 MAR 1858	Young Mens
408	Stewart, James S.E.	1y	W		22 AUG 1869	Mt. Olivet
466	Stewart, Jane	8m	C	D.C.	27 JUL 1870	Va.
400	Stewart, Jannett A.	4m	W		— JUL 1869	Glenwood
478	Stewart, Jas. E., agent	64y	W	Md.	06 SEP 1870	Baltimore, Md.
116	Stewart, John, cart driver	14y	C	D.C.	18 JUN 1858	Young Mens
617	Stewart, John W.	20m	W	U.S.	20 AUG 1872	Congressional*
495	Stewart, Joseph	4y	C	D.C.	17 DEC 1870	Potters Field
454	Stewart, Josephine	5y	C		31 MAY 1870	Young Mens
035	Stewart, Lawson N.	4y	W	Md.	13 FEB 1856	Baltimore, Md.
446	Stewart, Lewis	8m	C	D.C.	05 MAR 1870	Washington Asylum
151	Stewart, Louisa	25y	C	D.C.	14 JUN 1859	Harmony
110	Stewart, Maria V.	8y	W	D.C.	05 APR 1858	Holmead
150	Stewart, Mary	34y	W	D.C.*	01 JUN 1859	Oak Hill
695	Stewart, Molly	3m	C	D.C.	18 JUN 1873	Washington Asylum
620	Stewart, Mrs.	82y	W	U.S.	10 AUG 1872	
526	Stewart, Nancy	1y	C	D.C.	04 JUL 1871	
338	Stewart, Nancy	11m	W	D.C.	28 AUG 1868	Holmead
257	Stewart, Nancy	38y	W	D.C.*	23 MAR 1867	Oak Hill
706	Stewart, Rich. L.	8m	W	U.S.	29 JUL 1873	Glenwood
687	Stewart, Richard	41y	C	U.S.	05 MAY 1873	Washington Asylum
311	Stewart, Richd.	58y	W	D.C.	30 APR 1868	Congressional
220	Stewart, Robert	1y	W	D.C.	13 MAY 1866	Glenwood
475	Stewart, Sarah A.	1y	W	D.C.	11 SEP 1870	Congressional
660	Stewart, Sarah G.	75y	W	Eng.	21 JAN 1873	Congressional
193	Stewart, Susie Elizabeth	2y	W	D.C.	29 NOV 1860	
730	Stewart, Thomas, soldier	28y	W	Ire.	13 NOV 1873	Congressional
278	Stewart, Ulric	4m	W	D.C.	13 OCT 1867	Congressional
135	Stewart, William, contractor	83y	W	Md.	18 DEC 1858	St. Patricks
250	Stewart, William M., banker	29y	W		13 JAN 1867	Congressional
668	Stewart, Wm. Alex	7m	C		15 FEB 1873	
149	Stewart, Wm. Edward	1m	W	D.C.	25 MAY 1859	Holmead
749	Stewart, Wm. K., farmer	74y	W	U.S.	24 FEB 1874	Va.
638	Stewart, Wm. M., lawyer	75y	W	U.S.	09 NOV 1872	Rock Creek
165	Stewart, Wm. W., Dr.	40y	W	Md.	22 NOV 1859	Congressional*
154	Stewart, [blank]	45y	W	D.C.	20 JUL 1859	Methodist
120	Stewart, [blank]	65y	C		01 JUL 1858	Young Mens
099	Stickle, Laura E.	1m	W		25 DEC 1857	Georgetown
136	Stickles, Wm.	60y	C		30 DEC 1858	Western
307	Stief, Frederick Augs., bookbinder	56y	W	Ger.	25 APR 1868	Prospect Hill
663	Stilard, Catherine	21y	C	U.S.	03 JAN 1873	Small Pox*
256	Stiles, Jennie	24d	W	D.C.	27 MAR 1867	Boston, Mass.
255	Stiles, Kate	24y	W	Pa.	02 MAR 1867	Philadelphia, Pa.
337	Still				17 AUG 1868	Washington Asylum
228	Stilliard, Margaret	38y	C	Md.	17 JUL 1866	Mt. Olivet
471	Stillings, C.W.	56y	W	Ger.	19 AUG 1870	Congressional
026	Stillings, John, undertaker	57y	W	Md.	07 OCT 1855	Ebenezer
258	Stinemetz, Saml.	42y	W		07 APR 1867	Oak Hill
289	Stinzing, Frederick	1y	W	D.C.	14 JAN 1868	Glenwood
370	Stinzing, Henriette	6y	W		19 JAN 1869	Glenwood
271	Stock, Ella	1y	W	D.C.	07 AUG 1867	Mt. Olivet
260	Stockett, Wesley A.	40y	W	Md.	18 MAY 1867	Congressional
236	Stockholm, John, merchant	32y	W	N.Y.	29 SEP 1866	N.Y.
318	Stockton, John, child of	2m	W	D.C.	10 JUN 1868	Congressional

District of Columbia Interments (Index to Deaths), 1855-1874

Page	Name	Age	Race	Birth	Death Date	Burial Ground
421	Stockton, Lucy, Mrs.	46y	W	N.Y.	12 OCT 1869	Glenwood
712	Stoddard, John H.	53y	W	D.C.	18 AUG 1873	Mt. Olivet
075	Stoddard, Margaret	70y	W	Scot.	04 APR 1857	Washington Asylum
749	Stoddard, Teresa Mary	3m	W	U.S.	20 FEB 1874	Mt. Olivet
597	Stoech, M.L.	4y	W	D.C.	01 MAY 1872	Glenwood
597	Stokes, Ada M.	2y	W	D.C.	01 MAY 1872	Glenwood
479	Stokes, Emelia	40y	C	Md.	29 SEP 1870	Washington Asylum
673	Stokley, Annie E., housekeeper	52y	W	U.S.	07 MAR 1873	Seaferd, Del.
333	Stolp, Christian G.	33y	W	Ger.	15 JUL 1868	Prospect Hill
785	Stolpe, Fredericke J.	38y	W	Ger.	12 JUL 1874	Prospect Hill
472	Stolpp, Friedrich	4y	W		09 AUG 1870	Prospect Hill
556	Stomp, Charles	3y	W		31 JAN 1872	Prospect Hill
138	Stone, Ann Catharine		W		14 JAN 1859	
071	Stone, Catharine	22y	W	Md.	17 FEB 1857	Oak Hill
245	Stone, Dora	22y	W	N.Y.	01 NOV 1866	N.Y.
419	Stone, Eliza	55y	W	Md.	21 OCT 1869	Congressional
146	Stone, Elizabeth J.L.	4y	W	D.C.	03 APR 1859	Rock Creek
157	Stone, George	1y	W	D.C.	09 AUG 1859	Glenwood
784	Stone, George C., clerk	56y	W	U.S.	02 JUL 1874	
494	Stone, James, florist	47y	W	Amer.	05 DEC 1870	Glenwood
595	Stone, Joseph H., engineer	28y	W	D.C.	14 APR 1872	Protestant
075	Stone, Josephine	22y	W	Md.	08 APR 1857	
071	Stone, Lucy Lyons	1y	W	D.C.	24 FEB 1857	Rock Creek
084	Stone, Mary R.	2m	W	D.C.	23 JUL 1857	Oak Hill
592	Stone, Robert K., Dr.	50y	W	U.S.	23 APR 1872	Rock Creek
594	Stone, W.T.	29y	W	D.C.	03 APR 1872	Congressional
110	Stoops, Walter M., messenter	20y	W	Va.	04 APR 1858	St. Matthews
587	Stootley, Wm. M.	10y	C	D.C.	23 MAR 1872	Ebenezer
598	Storch, Ferdinand	40y	W	Ger.	10 MAY 1872	Unknown
604	Stores, Nora	2y	C	D.C.	14 JUN 1872	Ebenezer
660	Storey, Mary	42y	W	U.S.	21 JAN 1873	Congressional
479	Storey, Robert, child of	Still	W	D.C.	30 SEP 1870	Congressional
616	Story, R.N., laborer	48y	W	U.S.	06 JUL 1872	
250	Stosch, George	3m	W		13 JAN 1867	Glenwood
124	Stott, Charles	24y	W	Md.	13 AUG 1858	Rock Creek
092	Stout, John	6m	W	Miss.	26 SEP 1857	
554	Stover, Chas. J.	4y	W	D.C.	20 JAN 1872	
552	Stover, Ida	2y	W	D.C.	08 JAN 1872	Congressional*
616a	Stowe, Julia	40y	W	Ire.	07 JUL 1872	Congressional
268	Stower, Susanna	1y	W	D.C.	15 AUG 1867	Holmead
436	Stowver, James	21y	C		16 JAN 1870	Union
673	Straight, Rosa M.	5y	C	U.S.	03 MAR 1873	Congressional
458	Straighton, Mary F.	1y	C	D.C.	05 JUN 1870	Potters Field
533	Straining, Elisabeth	70y	W	Ger.	19 AUG 1871	Prospect Hill
394	Strane, Joseph F.	15m	W	Amer.	23 JUN 1869	Congressional
626	Stranning, Chas.	3y	W	U.S.	02 SEP 1872	
644	Stras, Emily C., Miss	71y	W	U.S.	14 DEC 1872	Congressional
381	Strasburger, Catharine, Mrs.	76y	W	Md.	22 MAR 1869	Frederick, Md.
414	Strasburger, Julia	8m	W	D.C.	26 SEP 1869	Washington Hebrew
768	Strattan, Jacob	80y	C	U.S.	20 MAY 1874	Washington Asylum
777	Stratton, Alfred, watchman	28y	W	U.S.	13 JUN 1874	Mt. Olivet
761	Stratton, Allen, carpenter	58y	W	U.S.	15 APR 1874	Congressional
225	Stratton, George W.	4m	W	D.C.	24 JUN 1866	Congressional
457	Stratton, John T.	3m	W		19 JUN 1870	Congressional
374	Stratton, Norval Wilson, printer	18y	W	Va.	15 FEB 1869	Congressional
230	Straub, John Joseph	17d			26 JUL 1866	
347	Strauss, Lavina		W	Va.	19 SEP 1868	Congressional
150	Streaks, George O., painter	23y	W	U.S.	03 JUN 1859	

Page	Name	Age	Race	Birth	Death Date	Burial Ground
416	Streb, Katharina	15y	W		19 SEP 1869	Prospect Hill
409	Street, Susan	2y	C		10 AUG 1869	Union
392	Streets, Sarah	26y	C	Va.	27 MAY 1869	Young Mens
470	Streibly, Georgiana	11m	W		11 AUG 1870	Glenwood
394	Stremel, Godlieb, cooper	56y	W	Ger.	20 JUN 1869	Congressional
292	Stremson, Alfred		C		16 JAN 1868	Alms House
351	Strep, Henry, shoemaker	40y	W	Ger.	19 SEP 1868	Prospect Hill
749	Stretch, Edward, student	22y	W	U.S.	14 FEB 1874	Lafayette, Ind.
003	Stribling, Helen	18m	W	D.C.	13 FEB 1855	Norfolk, Va.
185	Strickhardt, Geo. E.F.	4m	W	D.C.	28 JUL 1860	Prospect Hill
429	Strickhart, Charles W.	4m	W		26 DEC 1869	Congressional
471	Strickhart, Sarah F.D.	2m	W	D.C.	28 AUG 1870	Prospect Hill
472	Strickland, Thomas	4y	C		18 AUG 1870	Union
004	Stricklin, Mary Ellen	91y	W	Md.	20 MAR 1855	Holmead
124	Strider, John H.	8m	W	D.C.	07 AUG 1858	Havre de Grace, Md.
515	Stringfield, Alfred Eugene	9m	W	D.C.	19 MAR 1871	Congressional
523	Strisby, Mary	26y	W	U.S.	17 JUN 1871	Glenwood
740	Strobel, Charles A.	21y	W	U.S.	05 JAN 1874	Prospect Hill
785	Strobel, Margaretha	1y	W	U.S.	18 JUL 1874	Congressional
767	Strohbecker, Lind	25y	W	Ger.	09 MAY 1874	Prospect Hill
345	Strong, Edward	1y	C	D.C.	31 AUG 1868	Western
268	Strong, George H.	10m	W		24 AUG 1867	Congressional
463	Strong, H.A.	2y	W	Minn.	05 JUL 1870	Philadelphia, Pa.
170	Strong, Robert, child of	Still	W	D.C.	24 JAN 1860	Congressional
545	Strong, Saml. B.	3y	W	U.S.	14 NOV 1871	Congressional
724	Strong, Sarah	23y	W	Ohio	12 OCT 1873	Congressional
537	Strong, Thomas	8m	W	D.C.	23 SEP 1871	Congressional
605	Strotha, George, laborer	70y	C	Va.	29 JUN 1872	Asylum
611	Strotha, Jas.	2y	C	U.S.	07 JUL 1872	
761	Strother, Flora	1d	C	U.S.	20 APR 1874	
454	Strother, Lizzie	1y	C	D.C.	11 MAY 1870	Washington Asylum
496	Strothers, Robert	5y	C	D.C.	05 DEC 1870	Potters Field
768	Stroud, Jane M.	53y	W	U.S.	23 MAY 1874	Oak Hill
777a	Struks, George, butcher	16y	W	U.S.	14 JUN 1874	
452	Struther, Francis	30y	C	Va.	14 APR 1870	Washington Asylum
749	Stuart, Edward D.	4m	W	U.S.	23 FEB 1874	Glenwood
580	Stuart, Frederick	75y	W	Md.	11 FEB 1872	Young Mens
761	Stuart, Julia T.	19y	W	U.S.	18 APR 1874	Mt. Olivet
597	Stuart, Lilie	1y	W	U.S.	06 MAY 1872	Congressional
247	Stubborn, John, laborer	35y	W	N.Y.	14 DEC 1866	Alms House
584	Studey, Becky	1y	C	D.C.	01 MAR 1872	
489	Study, Cattay	1y	C	D.C.	05 NOV 1870	Ebenezer
318	Stumph, Albert Clinton	9m	W	D.C.	17 JUN 1868	Rock Creek
238	Stumph, Clara E.	1y	W	D.C.	21 SEP 1866	Rock Creek
219	Stumph, Henry	1m	W	D.C.	23 APR 1866	Prospect Hill
541	Stumph, Lewis	19y	W	U.S.	10 OCT 1871	Rock Creek
369	Stumph, Mary G.	39y	W	N.C.	11 JAN 1869	Congressional/Rk. Cr.
595	Stumph, T.W., clerk	21y	W	N.C.	12 APR 1872	Rock Creek
528	Stundon, Thomas		W	Ire.	15 JUL 1871	Mt. Olivet
293	Sturgis, Welford T.	2m	W	D.C.*	27 FEB 1868	Holy Rood
013	Stutz, Geo. L.	9m	W	Va.	31 JUL 1855	Congressional
147	Stutz, Henrietta Bertha	2y	W	D.C.	29 APR 1859	German
098	Suance, Ada T.	1y	W	D.C.	04 DEC 1857	Va.
387	Suckor, George H.	7m	C		26 APR 1869	Harmony
524	Suess, Helene	35y	W	Ger.	26 JUN 1871	Prospect Hill
036	Sugart, Infant of Jos.		W		06 FEB 1856	Foundry
550	Sugert, J.B.W., silvermaker	38y	W	Bav.	29 DEC 1871	Baltimore, Md.
682	Sugru, Daniel	45y	W	U.S.	22 APR 1873	Mt. Olivet

District of Columbia Interments (Index to Deaths), 1855-1874

Page	Name	Age	Race	Birth	Death Date	Burial Ground
124	Sugrue, Honora	5m	W	D.C.	07 AUG 1858	St. Patricks
297	Suisel, Geo.	1y	W	U.S.	14 FEB 1868	Glenwood
184	Suit, Benjamin		W	D.C.	08 JUL 1860	Methodist
123	Suit, Charles	1y	W	D.C.	29 JUL 1858	St. Patricks
250	Suit, Charles W.	1y	W	D.C.	24 JAN 1867	Congressional
191	Suit, Edwd.	3y	W	D.C.	01 OCT 1860	Methodist
325	Suit, John L., shoemaker	72y	W	Md.	28 JUL 1868	Washington
668	Sulick, Fannie	31y	W	U.S.	18 FEB 1873	Washington Asylum
323	Sulivan, Annie	10m	W	D.C.	30 JUL 1868	Mt. Olivet
131	Sullivan, Abigale	69y	W	Ire.	25 OCT 1858	Mt. Olivet
323	Sullivan, Daniel	9m	W	D.C.	31 JUL 1868	Mt. Olivet
235	Sullivan, Dennis	Still	W		17 SEP 1866	Mt. Olivet
622	Sullivan, Elijah, cigar maker	37y	W	U.S.	29 AUG 1872	
060	Sullivan, Eliza	30y	W	Ire.	19 OCT 1856	St. Peters
061	Sullivan, Eliza	21d	W		31 OCT 1856	St. Peters
594	Sullivan, Eliza P.	3m	W	D.C.	17 APR 1872	Glenwood
481	Sullivan, Elizabeth	14y	W	Pa.	08 OCT 1870	Mt. Olivet*
445	Sullivan, Ella	1y	W		16 MAR 1870	Mt. Olivet
605	Sullivan, Ella	3m	W	D.C.	04 JUN 1872	Mt. Olivet
223	Sullivan, Ellen	7m	W	D.C.	09 JUN 1866	Mt. Olivet*
179	Sullivan, Ellen	1y	W	D.C.	10 MAY 1860	Mt. Olivet
148	Sullivan, Ellen	1y	W	D.C.	09 MAY 1859	Oak Hill
531	Sullivan, Ellen D.	10m	W	D.C.	01 AUG 1871	Washington
323	Sullivan, Eugene	14d	W	D.C.	18 JUL 1868	Mt. Olivet
308	Sullivan, Eugene, child of	Still	W		03 APR 1868	Mt. Olivet
588	Sullivan, George P.	14d	W		24 MAR 1872	Congressional
064	Sullivan, Honoria	2y	W	D.C.	13 NOV 1856	St. Patricks
329	Sullivan, J.P., druggist	21y	W	D.C.*	22 JUL 1868	Holyrood
321	Sullivan, James Danl.		W		— JUN 1868	Mt. Olivet
235	Sullivan, James, laborer	25y	W	Ire.	18 SEP 1866	Mt. Olivet
004	[Silliv]an, Jeremiah, stone cutter	80y	W	Ire.	[13] MAR 1855	St. Patricks
045	Sullivan, Jerry, laborer	25y	W	Ire.	21 MAY 1856	Alms House
785	Sullivan, Jno. F., plasterer	21y	W	U.S.	27 JUL 1874	Oak Hill
163	Sullivan, John	2m	W	D.C.	18 OCT 1859	Mt. Olivet
285	Sullivan, John	1d	W	D.C.	10 DEC 1867	Mt. Olivet
713	Sullivan, John	85y	W	Ire.	21 AUG 1873	Mt. Olivet
110	Sullivan, John	1y	W	Va.*	02 APR 1858	St. Patricks
116	Sullivan, John	1y	W	D.C.	22 JUN 1858	St. Peters
170	Sullivan, John	52y	W	Ire.	29 JAN 1860	St. Peters
736	Sullivan, Julia	1y	W	U.S.	17 DEC 1873	
670	Sullivan, Julia	13y	W	U.S.	03 FEB 1873	Small Pox*
768	Sullivan, Margaret	28y	W	U.S.	29 MAY 1874	Mt. Olivet
777	Sullivan, Margaret	21d	W	U.S.	13 JUN 1874	Mt. Olivet
614	Sullivan, Mary	39y	W	Ire.	20 JUL 1872	
178	Sullivan, Mary	4m	W	D.C.	30 APR 1860	Georgetown
157	Sullivan, Mary	24y	W	Ire.	07 AUG 1859	Mt. Olivet
021	Sullivan, Mary	25y	W	Ire.	01 AUG 1855	St. Patricks
285	Sullivan, Mary Ann	2y	W	D.C.	16 DEC 1867	Mt. Olivet
299	Sullivan, Mary, monthly nurse	52y	W	Ire.	29 MAR 1868	Holyrood
102	Sullivan, Michael	2y	W	D.C.	20 JAN 1858	St. Peters
755	Sullivan, Millie A.	44y	C	U.S.	10 MAR 1874	
018	Sullivan, Morris, laborer	25y	W	Ire.	11 AUG 1855	St. Patricks
227	Sullivan, Mrs.	70y	W	Ire.	01 JUL 1866	Alms House
302	Sullivan, Nancy	45y	W	Ire.	27 MAR 1868	Alms House
091	Sullivan, Patrick	2y	W	Va.	19 SEP 1857	St. Peters
415	Sullivan, Robt. J.	7y	W		26 SEP 1869	Mt. Olivet
553	Sullivan, Thos. J.	4y	W	D.C.	09 JAN 1872	Congressional
160	Sullivan, [blank]	6m	W	D.C.	02 AUG 1859	Mt. Olivet

Page	Name	Age	Race	Birth	Death Date	Burial Ground
427	Sullivan, [blank]	5d	C	D.C.	17 NOV 1869	Washington Asylum
209	Sullivan, [torn]	61y	W	Ire.	— JAN 1866	[torn]
020	Sully, Mrs.	80y	W	Ire.	21 AUG 1855	Oak Hill
042	Summers, John H.	4y	W	D.C.	18 APR 1856	German
602	Summers, Mary J.	1y	W	U.S.	01 MAY 1872	Mt. Olivet
633	Summers, Wm., laborer	60y	W	U.S.	24 OCT 1872	
458	Summerville, Howard	7d	C	D.C.	28 JUN 1870	Potters Field
234	Summerville, W.N.	9d	C	D.C.	08 SEP 1866	Beckett's
240	Summerville, Wm., wood sawyer	85y	C	Md.	06 OCT 1866	Mt. Olivet
755	Sumner, Charles	63y	W	U.S.	22 MAR 1874	Boston, Mass.
418	Sumner, Thomas, laborer	60y	C	Va.	19 SEP 1869	
531	Sumner, Wm. E.	11y	W	D.C.	06 AUG 1871	Congressional
201	Sunbery, Robert	40y	C	U.S.	02 MAR 1861	
531	Sunderland, James, reporter	31y	W	Eng.	01 AUG 1871	Congressional
615	Sunny, Jas.	65y	C	U.S.	05 JUL 1872	
644	Supmon, Ann G.	52y	W	U.S.	22 DEC 1872	Congressional*
084	Supper, Catharina	43y	W	Ger.	26 JUL 1857	Congressional
333	Supper, Catharine	3y	W	Ger.	18 JUL 1868	Prospect Hill
626	Suppes, Henriette	1y	W	U.S.	09 SEP 1872	Prospect Hill
324	Supple, Margaret, Mrs.	76y	W	Ire.	30 JUL 1868	Mt. Olivet
379	Supplee, Alfred, child of	Still	W		29 MAR 1869	Congressional
148	Sur, Rosanna	3y	W		12 MAY 1859	Mt. Olivet
785	Surall, Lillian[89]	3y	W	U.S.	23 JUL 1874	Congressional
354	Surgeon, John W.	6m	W	D.C.	31 OCT 1868	Rock Creek
459	Susay, Mary	1y	C	D.C.	21 JUN 1870	Union
341	Suskey, James A.	12d	W	D.C.	09 AUG 1868	Congressional
673	Suted, Jane E.	21y	W	U.S.	06 MAR 1873	Glenwood
286	Suteman, Daniel, bricklayer	43y	C	Md.	26 DEC 1867	Good Hope
169	Suter, George	1m	W	D.C.	11 JAN 1860	Glenwood
087	Suter, Harvilla	10m	W	D.C.	14 AUG 1857	Glenwood
459	Suter, Julia	64y	W	Md.	29 JUN 1870	Potters Field
540	Sutherland, Elizabeth	86y	W	Va.	05 OCT 1871	Rock Creek
013	Sutherland, Ella	8m	W	D.C.	13 JUL 1855	Congressional
013	Sutherland, Mary	2y	W	D.C.	12 JUL 1855	Congressional
443	Sutherland, Robert, gov. clerk	32y	W	Ire.	21 FEB 1870	Mt. Olivet
473	Suthers, Maria	26y	C	D.C.	04 AUG 1870	Holmead
264	Sutphin, Addis Carver		W	N.J.	03 JUL 1867	Glenwood
495	Suttles, E., child of	Still	C	D.C.	05 DEC 1870	Potters Field
385	Sutton, Benj. W.	2y	W	D.C.	29 APR 1869	Congressional
378	Sutton, Coleman, laborer	32y	C	Md.	09 FEB 1869	Freedmen's Hospital
284	Sutton, Eliza	3y	W	D.C.	04 NOV 1867	Western
156	Sutton, James	34y	W	U.S.	09 JUL 1859	Mt. Olivet
727	Sutton, John	P.B.	W		31 OCT 1873	Congressional*
121	Sutton, Maggie	1y	W		17 JUL 1858	Western
011	Sutton, Mary Kate	5m	W	D.C.	04 JUN 1855	St. Patricks
099	Sutton, Robert, livery stable kpr.	41y	W	Va.*	26 DEC 1857	St. Patricks
301	Sutton, Solomon	60y	C	Va.	30 MAR 1868	Freedmen's Hospital
294	Sutton, William	21d	W	D.C.	06 FEB 1868	Western
585	Sutton, Wm.	70y	W	Va.	06 MAR 1872	
133	Sutton, [blank]	60y	W	Va.	19 NOV 1858	Western
584	Swaggard, Charles, laborer	31y	W	D.C.	01 MAR 1872	
584	Swaggott, Charles, laborer	31y	W	D.C.	01 MAR 1872	Congressional*
644	Swain, C.A., tanner	72y	W	U.S.	16 DEC 1872	White Marsh, Md.
550	Swain, Geo. W., clerk	53y	W	D.C.	30 DEC 1871	Glenwood
105	Swain, Kate	3y	W	D.C.	22 FEB 1858	Congressional

---

[89] Congressional cemetery records give "Lillian Duvall."

District of Columbia Interments (Index to Deaths), 1855-1874

Page	Name	Age	Race	Birth	Death Date	Burial Ground
549	Swain, Margaret	34y	W	D.C.	19 DEC 1871	Methodist
342	Swales, Bettie	11m	C		26 AUG 1868	Young Mens
710	Swales, Rebecca	2y	C	U.S.	01 AUG 1873	Mt. Pleasant
687	Swan, Alice Mary	6y	W	D.C.	01 MAY 1873	Congressional
736	Swan, Amanda	55y	W	U.S.	18 DEC 1873	Congressional
368	Swan, Benny Rouse	2y	W		14 DEC 1868	Augusta, Me.
642	Swan, Blanche	1m	W	U.S.	01 DEC 1872	Holmead
255	Swan, Cora	27y	C	Va.	09 MAR 1867	Beckett's
008	Swan, Elizabeth	85y	W	Va.	01 MAY 1855	Glenwood
495	Swan, L., child of	Still	C	D.C.	07 DEC 1870	Potters Field
119	Swan, Leah	78y	W	Md.	30 JUN 1858	Broad Creek Church
385	Swan, Martha	64y	W		16 APR 1869	Congressional
317	Swan, Mary	1y	C	D.C.	28 JUN 1868	Ebenezer
495	Swan, Mary C.	6y	C	D.C.	28 DEC 1870	Potters Field
407	Swan, Thomas H.	72y	W		18 AUG 1869	Congressional
507	Swank, Mable E.	11y	W	D.C.	19 FEB 1871	Glenwood
420	Swann, C.A., Mrs.		W	Md.	19 OCT 1869	Md.?
687	Swann, Edward, lawyer	61y	W	U.S.	02 MAY 1873	Preston, Alex., Va.
761	Swann, Geo. L. & M., infant of	9d	C	U.S.	29 APR 1874	
098	Swann, Mary B.B.	6y	W	D.C.	22 DEC 1857	Country farm
749	Swann, Sarah V.,	30y	W	Ire.	26 FEB 1874	Mt. Olivet
153	Swann, Zach.	1y	W	D.C.	12 JUL 1859	Methodist
599	Swate, Elisabeth	9y	W	U.S.	24 MAY 1872	Prospect Hill
695	Sweatland, Euphemia	15y	C	Md.	15 JUN 1873	
712	Sweener, John	9m	W	D.C.	18 AUG 1873	Mt. Olivet
117	Sweeney, Caroline K.	3m	W	D.C.	27 JUN 1858	St. Patricks
667	Sweeney, Dennis E.	Still	W	U.S.	09 FEB 1873	Mt. Olivet
755	Sweeney, Edward	69y	W	Ire.	27 MAR 1874	Mt. Olivet
408	Sweeney, Eliza Bernard	25y	W		18 AUG 1869	Mt. Olivet
536	Sweeney, E[torn] V.	51y	W	D.C.	19 SEP 1871	Mt. Olivet
142	Sweeney, George E.	2m	W		22 FEB 1859	Glenwood
408	Sweeney, Hugh Bernard, real est.	53y	W	D.C.	18 AUG 1869	Mt. Olivet
035	Sweeney, James, clerk	25y	W	D.C.	26 FEB 1856	St. Patricks
629	Sweeney, M. [or R.]	8m	W	U.S.	02 OCT 1872	
079	Sweeney, Mary, house maid	20y	W	Ire.	14 JUN 1857	St. Peters
349	Sweeney, Mary, servant	40y	W	Ire.	15 SEP 1868	Mt. Olivet
140	Sweeney, Richard A., musician	32y	W		10 FEB 1859	Congressional*
320	Sweeny, B.C.	26y	W	Ire.	13 JUN 1868	Baltimore, Md.
179	Sweeny, H.B., child of	Still	W	D.C.	10 MAY 1860	Mt. Olivet
224	Sweeny, Harry	3y	W	D.C.	13 JUN 1866	Mt. Olivet
066	Sweeny, Honora	16y	W	D.C.	22 DEC 1856	St. Patricks
306	Sweeny, Hugh, storekeeper	55y	W	Ire.	19 APR 1868	Mt. Olivet
297	Sweeny, Magdalena	11m	W	D.C.	28 FEB 1868	Mt. Olivet
219	Sweeny, Morris, laborer	60y	W	Ire.	30 APR 1866	Mt. Olivet
051	Sweeny, Robert	1y	W	D.C.	28 JUL 1856	Glenwood
263	Sweeny, Rosetta	21y	W	D.C.	10 JUN 1867	Mt. Olivet
267	Sweeny, William	1y	W		16 JUL 1867	Mt. Olivet
472	Sweeny, Wm., laborer	78y	C	Va.	16 AUG 1870	Freedmen's Hospital
283	Sweeny, [blank]	1d	W	D.C.	01 NOV 1867	Mt. Olivet
740	Sweet, Benj. J., clerk	42y	W	U.S.	01 JAN 1874	Chicago, Ill.
261	Sweet, Edgar	4m	W	D.C.	07 MAY 1867	Glenwood
278	Sweet, Geo. F.	1y	W	D.C.	08 OCT 1867	Congressional
549	Swetland, Silas H., attorney	44y	W	N.Y.	23 DEC 1871	Md.
723	Swift, Sarah P.	73y	W	W.I.	02 OCT 1873	Pottsville, Pa.
785	Swigart, Catharina	34y	W	Ire.	16 JUL 1874	Mt. Olivet
297	Switzer, Magdelena	66y	W	Ger.	27 FEB 1868	Philadelphia, Pa.
643	Switzer, William	62y	W	Ger.	10 DEC 1872	Washington Asylum
123	Sword, George	9y	W	Md.	28 JUL 1858	Congressional

District of Columbia Interments (Index to Deaths), 1855-1874

Page	Name	Age	Race	Birth	Death Date	Burial Ground
444	Sword, James, stone cutter	57y	W	Scot.	02 MAR 1870	Congressional
369	Sword, Mary	21d	W	D.C.	13 JAN 1869	Congressional
321	Sydner, Novelor	3y	C	D.C.	12 JUN 1868	Alms House
616a	Sydnor, Wm. R., teamster	22y	W	U.S.	05 JUL 1872	Congressional
408	Syles, Wm.	1y	C	D.C.	20 AUG 1869	Potters Field
717	Sylvester, Mary Ann	72y	W	Md.	07 SEP 1873	Congressional
124	Sylvester, Mortimer	5m	W	D.C.	05 AUG 1858	Glenwood
299	Symes, Solomon, laborer	55y	C	Va.	08 MAR 1868	Young Mens
201	Symington, Henry, carpenter	33y	W		09 MAR 1861	Congressional
226	Syphax, Charles	2m	C	D.C.	25 JUN 1866	Harmony
225	Syphax, Custis	4m	C	D.C.	20 JUN 1866	Harmony
368	Syphax, Maria	40y	C	Va.	28 DEC 1868	Freedmen's Hospital
180	Syphax, Mary	7m	C	D.C.	29 MAY 1860	Harmony
201	Syphax, [blank]	Still	C	D.C.	02 MAR 1861	Harmony
354	Szegdy, M., watchman	44y	W	Hung.	02 OCT 1868	Congressional

District of Columbia Interments (Index to Deaths), 1855-1874

Page	Name	Age	Race	Birth	Death Date	Burial Ground
T						
462	Tabe, Ambrose L.	6m	W	Amer.	19 JUL 1870	Mt. Olivet
068	Tabler, John	67y	W	Md.	05 JAN 1857	Methodist
314	Tabler, Judson Gilman, folding rm.	14y	W	Bol.	15 MAY 1868	Oak Hill
376	Tabmar, Robert	4y	C		23 FEB 1869	Young Mens
718	Tachary, Robt. J., painter	43y	W	Md.	11 SEP 1873	Mt. Olivet
235	Taff, Flora E.	4m	W	D.C.	17 SEP 1866	Mt. Olivet
661	Taff, George A.	1y	W	U.S.	23 JAN 1873	Mt. Olivet
585	Taft, M.E.	55y	W	Ire.	11 MAR 1872	Mt. Olivet
494	Tait, Alexander, policeman	45y	W	D.C.	02 DEC 1870	Glenwood
417	Tait, Ida	1y	C	Va.	05 SEP 1869	Washington Asylum
011	Tait, Joseph	35y	W	Ger.	30 JUN 1855	
495	Tait, Mary E.	3d	C	Va.	06 DEC 1870	Potters Field
332	Tait, Sarah Ann	5m	C	D.C.	14 JUL 1868	Alms House
335b	Taitt, S.A.				14 JUL 1868	Washington Asylum
625	Talbert, Annie	4m	C	U.S.	08 SEP 1872	
542	Talbert, Elisabeth	30y	W	D.C.	22 OCT 1871	Congressional*
599	Talbert, Ellen	60y	W	U.S.	01 MAY 1872	Methodist
425	Talbert, Frances C.	1y	W	D.C.	19 NOV 1869	Congressional
326	Talbert, George H.	10m	W	Md.	07 JUL 1868	Congressional
631	Talbert, Margaret, servant	34y	C	U.S.	04 OCT 1872	
610	Talbert, Martha	5y			01 JUN 1867	Young Mens
551	Talbert, Mary E.	22y		D.C.	— DEC 1871	
524	Talbert, Mary Lily	9m	W	D.C.	22 JUN 1871	Glenwood
531	Talbert, Mary M.	1y	W	D.C.	04 AUG 1871	Congressional*
673	Talbert, Sarah G.	63y	C	U.S.	02 MAR 1873	Harmony
694	Talbert, W.I.	2m	W	U.S.	16 JUN 1873	Baltimore, Md.
359	Talbert, [blank]	12h	W	D.C.	05 NOV 1868	Congressional
785	Talbot, Francis	9m	C	U.S.	12 JUL 1874	
606	Talbot, Ida G.	17y	W	D.C.	07 JUN 1872	Congressional*
225	Talbot, Mary	4m	W	D.C.	24 JUN 1866	Congressional
703	Talbot, Mary	57y	C	U.S.	13 JUL 1873	Harmony
403	Talbot, Mary	36y	C	Md.	02 JUL 1869	Union
216	Talbott, Ellen	78y	W	Pa.	27 MAR 1866	Congressional
547	Talburg, Gustavus	1y	W	D.C.	08 DEC 1871	Prospect Hill
536	Talburtt, Wm. J.	41y	W	Md.	18 SEP 1871	Glenwood
108	Talbut, Frances J.	9m	W	D.C.	24 MAR 1858	Methodist
714	Talbut, Mary A.	11m	C	U.S.	31 AUG 1873	Harmony
596	Talcott, M.E.	3m	W	D.C.	27 APR 1872	Glenwood
339	Talcott, Mary, Mrs.	45y	W	Conn.	17 AUG 1868	Hartford, Conn.
276	Taler, Anne	2y	W	D.C.	03 SEP 1867	Congressional
139	Taliaferro, Priscilla, servant	100y	C		31 JAN 1859	Foundry
677	Tallison, Saml.	24y	W	U.S.	c.11 MAR 1873	Small Pox
193	Talty, Andrew, carpenter	45y	W	Va.	16 NOV 1860	
777	Talty, Kitty F.	9m	W	U.S.	05 JUN 1874	Oak Hill
157	Talty, Michael, Sr.	73y	W	Ire.	03 AUG 1859	St. Patricks
039	Tanheady, James, laborer	19y	W	Ire.	27 MAR 1856	St. Patricks
555	Tanner, John	10m	W	D.C.	29 JAN 1872	Congressional
370	Tanner, M. Wilhlemina	1y			18 JAN 1869	Prospect Hill
481	Tanner, Mary	25y	C	Va.	13 OCT 1870	Ebenezer
459	Tanner, Samuel	19y	W	D.C.	09 JUN 1870	Potters Field
233	Taper, Daniel, whitewasher	65y	C	Va.	30 AUG 1866	Young Mens
361	Taper, Walter	5m			17 NOV 1868	Young Mens
371	Tarlton, Philip	38y	C	U.S.	03 JAN 1869	Washington Asylum
422	Tascal, Thom, laborer	44y	C	Va.	18 OCT 1869	
393	Tasco, Mira	1m	C		29 MAY 1869	Western
715	Taskell, Fanny, infant child of	14d	C	D.C.	29 AUG 1873	
683	Tasker, Allice	22y	C	U.S.	21 APR 1873	Small Pox

Page	Name	Age	Race	Birth	Death Date	Burial Ground
635	Tasker, Fanny	6y	C	U.S.	12 NOV 1872	Small Pox
394	Tasker, George	3m	W	D.C.	07 JUN 1869	Congressional
711	Taskey, J.W., Mrs.	24y	W	Va.	09 AUG 1873	Va.
152	Tassco, [blank]	3m	C	D.C.	13 JUN 1859	Washington Asylum
243	Tastet, Edwin	30y	W	D.C.	18 NOV 1866	Congressional
379	Tastet, Sarah P.	74y	W	Va.	12 MAR 1869	Congressional
155	Tate, Adolphus	2y	C	D.C.	22 JUL 1859	Georgetown
269	Tate, Ann	85y	W		14 AUG 1867	Congressional
220	Tate, Elizabeth	53y	W	Va.	08 MAY 1866	Mt. Olivet
339	Tate, Harrison Park	10m	W	D.C.	14 AUG 1868	Mt. Olivet
035	Tate, Ida	2y	W	Md.	12 FEB 1856	Glenwood (vault)
107	Tate, Jos. B., clerk	40y	W	D.C.	02 MAR 1858	Congressional
365	Tate, Joseph E.	5d	W	Amer.	05 DEC 1868	Mt. Olivet
136	Tate, Josephine Burrows	6m	W	D.C.	15 DEC 1858	Congressional
600	Tate, Ludwell, laborer	26y	C	U.S.	26 MAY 1872	
137	Tate, Maggie Addison	5y	W	D.C.	18 JAN 1859	Congressional
137	Tate, Mary Ann	4y	W	D.C.	07 JAN 1859	Congressional
472	Tate, Zane, laborer	65y	C	Va.	03 AUG 1870	Freedmen's Hospital
317	Tauberschmidt, Leonhard, driver	33y	W	Ger.	17 JUN 1868	Prospect Hill
507	Tauberschmidt, Mary	29y	W	Ger.	06 FEB 1871	Prospect Hill
450	Tauberschmidt, [blank]	2y	W		25 APR 1870	Prospect Hill
193	Taulty, Andrew	37y	W	Ire.	13 NOV 1860	St. Peters
348	Taulty, John, grocer	45y	W	Ire.	11 SEP 1868	Mt. Olivet
282	Taulty, Mrs.	32y	W	Ire.	15 NOV 1867	Mt. Olivet
778	Tavenner, Chas. H., hotel keeper	54y	W	U.S.	22 JUN 1874	Congressional
607	Tayler, George E.	7m	W	D.C.	16 JUN 1872	Congressional
011	Tayloe, Ann	83y	W	Md.	13 JUN 1855	Mt. Airy, Va.
101	Tayloe, Thomas H.	6m	C	D.C.	13 JAN 1858	Young Mens
432	Taylor, Albert	1y	C	D.C.	06 DEC 1869	Washington Asylum
521	Taylor, Albert, laborer	27y	C	Md.	08 JUN 1871	Potters Field
535	Taylor, Amelia	2y		D.C.	01 SEP 1871	
243	Taylor, Andrew	5y	W	Md.	19 NOV 1866	Baltimore, Md.
742	Taylor, Ann, infant of	16d	C	U.S.	20 JAN 1874	
557	Taylor, Anna		W	D.C.	04 FEB 1872	Va.
466	Taylor, Anna L.	9m	C	D.C.	04 JUL 1870	Young Mens
383	Taylor, Anne		C	D.C.	05 MAR 1869	Washington Asylum
498	Taylor, Anne, pauper	14m	B	D.C.	27 JAN 1871	Washington Asylum
269	Taylor, Auelia	3y	C	D.C.	22 AUG 1867	Harmony
398	Taylor, Benj. O.	7y	B		26 JUN 1869	Washington Asylum
355	Taylor, Bernard	1y	C	D.C.	30 OCT 1868	Mt. Olivet
427	Taylor, Bird	25y	C		20 NOV 1869	Washington Asylum
218	Taylor, Bridget, housekeeper	75y	W	Md.	13 APR 1866	Congressional
353	Taylor, C.		W		28 SEP 1868	Washington Asylum
121	Taylor, Caroline V.	4y	W	D.C.	15 JUL 1858	Congressional
079	Taylor, Charles	2y	W	D.C.	15 JUN 1857	Foundry
777	Taylor, Chas. Henry	50y	C	U.S.	10 JUN 1874	
683	Taylor, Daniel	22y	C	U.S.	12 APR 1873	Small Pox
362	Taylor, Edward	35y	C		07 NOV 1868	Washington Asylum
616	Taylor, Edward, clerk		W		09 JUL 1872	
741	Taylor, Eliza	53y	W	Scot.	13 JAN 1874	Congressional
719	Taylor, Elizabeth	70y	W	Eng.	23 SEP 1873	
296	Taylor, Elizabeth	68y	C	D.C.	21 FEB 1868	Alms House
212	Taylor, Elizabeth	54y	C		18 FEB 1866	Ebenezer
297	Taylor, Elizabeth	39y	W	Ire.	27 FEB 1868	Rock Creek
437	Taylor, Elizabeth, Mrs.	48y	W	Md.	17 JAN 1870	Glenwood

District of Columbia Interments (Index to Deaths), 1855-1874

Page	Name	Age	Race	Birth	Death Date	Burial Ground
756	Taylor, Elmosina	1y	C	U.S.	27 MAR 1874	
484	Taylor, Elsie G.	3y	W	D.C.	13 OCT 1870	Congressional
187	Taylor, Emma G.	1m	W	D.C.	13 AUG 1860	Congressional
180	Taylor, Ernest	10y	W	D.C.	30 MAY 1860	Oak Hill
312	Taylor, Essex		C		02 MAY 1868	
343	Taylor, Estell	4m	C	D.C.	09 AUG 1868	Washington Asylum
591	Taylor, Fannie	63y	C	Md.	06 APR 1872	Mt. Pleasant
449	Taylor, Fannie Eliza	6m	W	Va.	17 APR 1870	Congressional
328	Taylor, Ferdinand	1y	C	D.C.	19 JUL 1868	Western
432	Taylor, Frances	23y	C		10 DEC 1869	Washington Asylum
742	Taylor, Frank	3m	C	U.S.	18 JAN 1874	
703	Taylor, Frank, gentleman	62y	W	Eng.	12 JUL 1873	Oak Hill
069	Taylor, Frank, servant	20y	C	D.C.*	27 JAN 1857	
352	Taylor, Geo. W.	1m	C		12 SEP 1868	Washington Asylum
321	Taylor, George	27d	C	D.C.	22 JUN 1868	Alms House
164	Taylor, George	57y	W	Md.	01 OCT 1859	Washington Asylum
437	Taylor, George	4m	C	D.C.	04 JAN 1870	Washington Asylum
179	Taylor, George W.	28y	W	Va.*	10 MAY 1860	Congressional
755	Taylor, H., infant of	6m	C	U.S.	26 MAR 1874	
271	Taylor, Hannah	35y	W	N.Y.	13 AUG 1867	Eastern Shore, Md.
523	Taylor, Harriet Louisa	17d	W	D.C.	16 JUN 1871	Congressional
215	Taylor, Harrison, contractor	69y	W	D.C.	18 MAR 1866	Glenwood
070	Taylor, Henry, clerk	42y	W	D.C.	04 FEB 1857	Glenwood
467	Taylor, Henry, laborer	50y	C	Va.	22 JUL 1870	
507	Taylor, Henry Lee	6d	W	D.C.	16 FEB 1871	Alexandria, Va.
093	Taylor, Henry, waiter	17y	C	D.C.	12 OCT 1857	Ebenezer
628	Taylor, J.W.	4y	C	U.S.	19 SEP 1872	
316	Taylor, James		C		c.07 MAY 1868	Alms House
543	Taylor, James				29 OCT 1871	Unknown
356	Taylor, James E.	4m	Y	D.C.	31 OCT 1868	
392	Taylor, Jane	60y	C		12 MAY 1869	Washington Asylum
640	Taylor, Jim	34y	C	U.S.	15 DEC 1872	Small Pox*
719	Taylor, Jno. H.	11m	W	Scot.	17 SEP 1873	
031	Taylor, Jno. T.	1y	W	Va.*	09 DEC 1855	Washington
023	Taylor, John	4d	C		07 SEP 1855	Harmony
319	Taylor, John	2y	W	D.C.	28 JUN 1868	Western
606	Taylor, John A.	10y	C	Va.	18 JUN 1872	Young Mens
522	Taylor, John E.	10m	W	D.C.	10 JUN 1871	
476	Taylor, John L., lawyer	65y	W	Ohio	06 SEP 1870	Louisa C.H., Va.
727	Taylor, Joseph	2m	C	U.S.	31 OCT 1873	
391	Taylor, Kate Augusta	3y	W	N.J.	22 MAY 1869	Newark, N.J.
258	Taylor, Lemuel, laborer	31y	C	Md.	18 APR 1867	Baltimore, Md.
373	Taylor, Lewis, servant		C		27 JAN 1869	Harmony
350	Taylor, Louisa	14y	C	Va.	07 SEP 1868	Young Mens
407	Taylor, M.E.	18y	W		29 AUG 1869	Congressional
608	Taylor, M.J.		W	N.Y.	02 JUN 1872	Congressional
437	Taylor, Maria	37y	C	Va.	18 JAN 1870	Young Mens
184	Taylor, Mary	68y	W	Scot.	06 JUL 1860	Congressional
515	Taylor, Mary	55y	C	Va.	10 MAR 1871	Ebenezer
683	Taylor, Mary	26y	C	U.S.	05 APR 1873	Small Pox
279	Taylor, Mary Ann	2y	C	D.C.	23 OCT 1867	Union
022	Taylor, Mary E.	2y	W	D.C.	15 AUG 1855	Congressional
484	Taylor, Mary Ellen	4y	W	D.C.	13 OCT 1870	Congressional
391	Taylor, Mary Emily	2y	W		19 MAY 1869	Newark, N.J.
638	Taylor, Mary Jane	42y	W	U.S.	06 NOV 1872	
538	Taylor, Mary M.	10m	C	Va.	29 SEP 1871	Ebenezer
241	Taylor, May E.	2y			01 OCT 1866	Western
329	Taylor, Minnie Irene	2m	W	D.C.	05 JUL 1868	Glenwood

District of Columbia Interments (Index to Deaths), 1855-1874

Page	Name	Age	Race	Birth	Death Date	Burial Ground
367	Taylor, Mrs.	60y	W	Iowa	11 DEC 1868	Washington Asylum
314	Taylor, Patrick	64y	C		11 MAY 1868	Mt. Olivet
294	Taylor, Reuben	1d	C	D.C.	06 FEB 1868	Ebenezer
298	Taylor, Reuben	5y	C	Va.	29 FEB 1868	Young Mens
305	Taylor, Richard, child of	Still			c.15 MAR 1868	Mt. Olivet
587	Taylor, Richd.	8m	C	D.C.	23 MAR 1872	
354	Taylor, Robert E., carpenter	31y	W	D.C.	12 OCT 1868	Congressional
413	Taylor, Robert, laborer	30y	C	Va.	09 AUG 1869	Washington Asylum
250	Taylor, S.	6m	C		21 JAN 1867	Young Mens
301	Taylor, Samuel	18y	C	Va.	14 MAR 1868	Young Mens
364	Taylor, Sarah	1y	W	D.C.	27 DEC 1868	Congressional*
740	Taylor, Sarah	54y	W	U.S.	01 JAN 1874	Washington Asylum
225	Taylor, Sarah	4m	C	D.C.	24 JUN 1866	Young Mens
321	Taylor, Stella N.	4m	W	Md.	29 JUN 1868	Va.
629	Taylor, Susie	2m	W	U.S.	03 OCT 1872	
391	Taylor, Thomas, laborer	25y	W	Va.	06 MAY 1869	Mt. Olivet
377	Taylor, Udoro	3m	C	D.C.	04 FEB 1869	Washington Asylum
592	Taylor, Virginia A.	34y	W		02 APR 1872	Glenwood
478	Taylor, Virginia S.	9y	W	D.C.	26 SEP 1870	Glenwood
611	Taylor, Walter O.	18d	W	U.S.	03 JUL 1872	Congressional*
397	Taylor, Willard G.	6m	W	D.C.	26 JUN 1869	Newark, N.J.
595	Taylor, William	6y	W	U.S.	06 APR 1872	Congressional*
670	Taylor, William	19y	W	U.S.	13 FEB 1873	Small Pox
624	Taylor, Willie	2y	C	U.S.	15 SEP 1872	
580	Taylor, Willie	16d	W	D.C.	09 FEB 1872	Congressional
520	Taylor, Willis	16d	W	N.C.	31 MAY 1871	Congressional
416	Taylor, Willis	7m	C		20 SEP 1869	Holmead
403	Taylor, Wm. F. & Eliz., child of	18d			17 JUL 1869	Methodist
016	Taylor, Wm. H.	7d	C	D.C.	24 JUL 1855	Harmony
458	Taylor, Wm. H.C., clerk Int. Dept.	27y	W	Iowa	23 JUN 1870	Glenwood
264	Taylor, Wm. Joseph	1y	C	D.C.	23 JUL 1867	Mt. Olivet
708	Taylor, Wm., laborer	65y	C	Md.	07 JUL 1873	
704	Taylor, Wm. Raigall	3m	W	D.C.	10 JUL 1873	Congressional
622	Taylor, Wm., stone cutter	47y	W	Scot.	23 AUG 1872	Congressional*
063	Taylor, [blank[	14d	C	D.C.	18 NOV 1856	Western
515	Taylor, [blank]		C	D.C.	10 MAR 1871	Ebenezer
125	Taylor, [blank]	60y	C		17 AUG 1858	Young Mens
066	Taylor, [blank]		C	Md.	25 DEC 1856	Young Mens
350	Tayor, Charley	1y	C	D.C.	11 SEP 1868	Washington Asylum
533	Tayor, Ursula	2y	C	D.C.	25 AUG 1871	Washington
016	Teast, John M.	1y	W	D.C.	19 JUL 1855	Glenwood
660	Tebbs, D.H.	42y	W		20 JAN 1873	Baltimore, Md.
622	Tegel, Jas. S., laborer	40y	W	U.S.	10 AUG 1872	
778	Telar, Elizabeth	39y	W	Ger.	01 JUN 1874	Glenwood
185	Telford, Mrs.		W		16 JUL 1860	Washington
618	Tellheimer, Saml.	28m	W	U.S.	01 AUG 1872	Prospect Hill
526	Temple, John A.	4y	C	D.C.	07 JUL 1871	
452	Temple, Margt.	10m	C		30 APR 1870	Washington Asylum
304	Templeton, Peter B., clerk	55y	W	Eng.	13 MAR 1868	Congressional
640	Tenant, Gertrude	4y	W	U.S.	22 DEC 1872	Small Pox*
274	Tenlon, Florence Cecilia	6m	W	D.C.	06 SEP 1867	Framingham, Mass.
273	Tenlon, H.H.	6m	W	D.C.	17 SEP 1867	Framingham, Mass.
325	Tenly, Jane, Mrs.	70y	W	U.S.	11 JUL 1868	Rock Creek
534	Tenly, Mary A.E.	1y	W	D.C.	30 AUG 1871	Rock Creek
324	Tenly, Matilda Jane	47y	W	D.C.	08 JUL 1868	Rock Creek
059	Tenly, William	9m	W	Md.	02 SEP 1856	Baltimore, Md.
282	Tennally, Owen, engineer	45y	W	Ire.	15 NOV 1867	Mt. Olivet
476	Tennant, D., driver	34y	W		09 SEP 1870	Congressional

District of Columbia Interments (Index to Deaths), 1855-1874

Page	Name	Age	Race	Birth	Death Date	Burial Ground
469	Tennant, Margaret C.	5m	W	D.C.	26 AUG 1870	Mt. Olivet
335b	Tennant, Matilda				13 JUL 1868	Washington Asylum
356	Tenneat, Henry A.	2y	W	Md.	19 OCT 1868	
724	Tennent, Wm.	8y	W	D.C.	15 OCT 1873	Mt. Olivet
293	Tenney, Frank	14y	W	D.C.*	06 MAR 1868	Oak Hill
245	Tenney, Henrietta, infant of	3d	C	D.C.	03 NOV 1866	Ebenezer
006	Tenney, John	34y	W	Ire.	22 APR 1855	Washington Asylum
306	Tenney, Josepha	24y	C	W.Va.	06 APR 1868	Young Mens
263	Tenney, Mary	74y	W		17 JUN 1867	Glenwood
477	Tenny, Alice	1y	C	D.C.	14 SEP 1870	Holmead
317	Tenny, Dennis	2y	C	D.C.	21 JUN 1868	Ebenezer
428	Teresa, Martina	1m	W		01 NOV 1869	Mt. Olivet
462	Terrill, Wm., laborer	32y	C	D.C.	29 JUL 1870	Mt. Olivet
391	Terry, Georgia A.	2y	W		21 MAY 1869	
536	Terry, Hugh, stone cutter	56y	W	Md.	18 SEP 1871	Glenwood
425	Terry, Mary	10m	W	D.C.	17 NOV 1869	Congressional
327	Teuber, Frank	28d	W	D.C.	05 JUL 1868	German
348	Tew, Wm.		W	D.C.	23 SEP 1868	Congressional
246	Thaahy, Mary	2y	W	D.C.	28 DEC 1866	Mt. Olivet
614	Thaine, Solomon	72y	W	Ger.	04 JUL 1872	
735	Thames, Mary, washerwoman		C	U.S.	10 DEC 1873	
690	Thayer, Annie C.	5y	C	U.S.	01 MAY 1873	Small Pox*
420	Thayer, Eathal	7d	W		15 OCT 1869	Methodist
416	Thielecher, Charles	4m	W		30 SEP 1869	Glenwood
453	Thielocke, Friedrich P.	5y	W		07 MAY 1870	Prospect Hill
366	Thies, Ida	10m	W	D.C.	29 DEC 1868	Prospect Hill
137	Thilicke, Carol	2m	W	D.C.	12 JAN 1859	Glenwood
681	Thiras, James E., merchant	54y	W	U.S.	21 APR 1873	Mt. Holly N.J.
279	Thirmlest, William, retired mercht.	81y	W	Md.	08 OCT 1867	Glenwood
532	Thislocke, Emil F.	1m	W	D.C.	15 AUG 1871	Glenwood
588	Thom, Simson B.	2y	W	D.C.	26 MAR 1872	Congressional
258	Thoma, Charles, butcher	19y	W	D.C.	07 APR 1867	Georgetown, Catholic
138	Thoma, Charles, butcher	45y	W	Ger.	25 JAN 1859	St. Patricks (vault)
122	Thoma, Rudolf	11m	W	D.C.	22 JUL 1858	German Catholic
143	Thomas, Alfred	78y	C		12 MAR 1859	Ebenezer
050	Thomas, Alfred	10d	C	D.C.	17 JUL 1856	Foundry
683	Thomas, Alfred	48y	C	U.S.	13 APR 1873	Small Pox
591	Thomas, Alfred, waiter	52y	C	Md.	19 APR 1872	Mt. Pleasant
237	Thomas, Alice	58y	C		18 SEP 1866	Harmony
707	Thomas, Anetia	11m	W	U.S.	08 JUL 1873	Mt. Olivet
778	Thomas, Benjamin	22y	C	U.S.	17 JUN 1874	Washington Asylum
519	Thomas, Bernard	12y	C	Va.	21 MAY 1871	
586	Thomas, Betrice	6m	W	D.C.	18 MAR 1872	Congressional
393	Thomas, Betsey	7d	C	D.C.	28 MAY 1869	Washington Asylum
642	Thomas, Caroline	10y	C	U.S.	27 DEC 1872	Small Pox
549	Thomas, Carrie L.	4y	W	D.C.	21 DEC 1871	Congressional
474	Thomas, Cath. A.	1d	C		05 AUG 1870	Washington Asylum
163	Thomas, Catharine	30y	W	Pa.	03 OCT 1859	Mt. Olivet
074	Thomas, Catharine	47y	C	Md.	25 MAR 1857	Young Mens
532	Thomas, Charles	10m	C	D.C.	14 AUG 1871	
232	Thomas, Charlotte, domestic	65y	C	Va.	28 AUG 1866	Young Mens
546	Thomas, Charlotte I.	4m	W	D.C.	24 NOV 1871	Congressional
457	Thomas, Chas. E.	18y	W	D.C.	21 JUN 1870	Congressional
595	Thomas, Chas. E.	24y	W	U.S.	26 APR 1872	Congressional
592	Thomas, Chas. L.	20y	W	U.S.	26 APR 1872	Congressional*
290	Thomas, Christina	72y	W	Ger.	11 JAN 1868	German Catholic
181	Thomas, Cornelius	3m	W	D.C.	05 JUN 1860	Washington Asylum
405	Thomas, David	14d	C	D.C.	12 JUL 1869	Washington Asylum

Page	Name	Age	Race	Birth	Death Date	Burial Ground
086	Thomas, Debby	90y	C	Md.	06 AUG 1857	Young Mens
749	Thomas, Eddie	6m	C	U.S.	15 FEB 1874	
615	Thomas, Eliza	30y	C	U.S.	29 JUL 1872	
377	Thomas, Eliza	5m	C	D.C.	06 FEB 1869	Ebenezer
768	Thomas, Elizabeth, domestic	60y	C	U.S.	01 MAY 1874	Mt. Olivet
586	Thomas, Ella W.	2y	W	D.C.	14 MAR 1872	Congressional
405	Thomas, Ellen	4d	C	D.C.	29 JUL 1869	Washington Asylum
039	Thomas, Ellen, laundress	82y	C	Md.	11 MAR 1856	Alms House
495	Thomas, Emeline	10m	C	D.C.	03 DEC 1870	Potters Field
485	Thomas, Emma	4m	C	D.C.	27 OCT 1870	Potters Field
223	Thomas, Emma L.	8m	C	D.C.	04 JUN 1866	Holmead
785	Thomas, Ethet	10m	W	U.S.	09 JUL 1874	Congressional*
641	Thomas, Fannie	45y	C	U.S.	15 DEC 1872	Small Pox
181	Thomas, Faring	5h	W	D.C.	16 JUN 1860	Glenwood
523	Thomas, Francis	39y	C	D.C.	14 JUN 1871	Young Mens
012	Thomas, Fredk.	3m	W	D.C.	12 JUN 1855	Foundry
694	Thomas, Fredy	11m	W	D.C.	21 JUN 1873	Frederick City, Md.
300	Thomas, Geo.	4m	C	D.C.	08 MAR 1868	Alms House
287	Thomas, Geo. B.	4m	C	D.C.	26 DEC 1867	Mt. Olivet
131	Thomas, Geo. Henry, baker	37y	W	Ger.	29 OCT 1858	Congressional
001	Thomas, George	36y			14 JAN 1855	
111	Thomas, George	10y	W	D.C.	16 APR 1858	Congressional
458	Thomas, George	45y	W	U.S.	10 JUN 1870	Potters Field
128	Thomas, George, banker	68y	W	Md.	29 SEP 1858	Congressional
422	Thomas, George, child of		C		07 OCT 1869	Harmony
274	Thomas, George, laboer	65y	C	Md.	11 SEP 1867	Harmony
422	Thomas, George, laborer	30y	C	Md.	17 OCT 1869	
514	Thomas, George, laborer	40y	C	Va.	25 MAR 1871	Ebenezer
335b	Thomas, Georgiana				14 JUL 1868	Washington Asylum
328	Thomas, Georgianna	8m	C	D.C.	13 JUL 1868	Alms House
049	Thomas, Hannah A.	41y	C	D.C.	09 JUL 1856	Foundry
226	Thomas, Harriet, domestic	40y	C	Md.	26 JUN 1866	7th St.
466	Thomas, Harriet, servant	22y	C	Va.	26 JUL 1870	Union
640	Thomas, Harriett	9m	C	U.S.	21 DEC 1872	Small Pox*
549	Thomas, Hattie N., student	21y	W	N.Y.	20 DEC 1871	N.Y.
519	Thomas, Henry	9m	C		22 MAY 1871	
646	Thomas, Henry	3y	C	D.C.	28 DEC 1872	
641	Thomas, Henry	35y	C	U.S.	27 DEC 1872	Small Pox*
011	Thomas, Henry	54y	W	D.C.	18 JUN 1855	St. Matthews
356	Thomas, Henry, shoemaker	75y	B	Md.	12 OCT 1868	Mt. Olivet
005	Thomas, Henry W.G.	1y	W	D.C.	05 MAR 1855	Oak Hill
523	Thomas, Herbert E.	11m	C	D.C.	19 JUN 1871	Young Mens
342	Thomas, Hetty	1y	C	D.C.	19 AUG 1868	Young Mens
251	Thomas, James	11m	C	D.C.	31 JAN 1867	Young Mens
096	Thomas, James, cartman	60y	C	Va.	01 NOV 1857	Methodist
768	Thomas, James H.	1y	C	U.S.	11 MAY 1874	Ebenezer
131	Thomas, James, slave	10y	C	D.C.	22 OCT 1858	Young Mens
133	Thomas, Jane	56y	C	Md.	27 NOV 1858	Pyes Landing, Md.
459	Thomas, Jane, laborer	27y	C	Va.	04 JUN 1870	
066	Thomas, Jas. Edw., brickmaker	23y	C	D.C.	25 DEC 1856	Young Mens
590	Thomas, Jefferson	2y	C	U.S.	07 APR 1872	Small Pox
602	Thomas, Jno. C.	53y	C	U.S.	18 MAY 1872	Mt. Olivet
088	Thomas, Joanna M.C.	11m	W	D.C.	19 AUG 1857	Congressional
665	Thomas, John	1m	C	U.S.	31 JAN 1873	Small Pox*
658	Thomas, John, cabinet maker	35y	C	U.S.	09 JAN 1873	
425	Thomas, John W.	3y	W	D.C.	18 NOV 1869	Congressional
540	Thomas, Joseph	1y	C	U.S.	03 OCT 1871	
271	Thomas, Joseph	11m	C	D.C.	30 AUG 1867	Young Mens

District of Columbia Interments (Index to Deaths), 1855-1874

Page	Name	Age	Race	Birth	Death Date	Burial Ground
398	Thomas, Josephine	21y	B	D.C.	08 JUN 1869	Washington Asylum
588	Thomas, Julia	26y	W	D.C.	27 MAR 1872	Congressional
482	Thomas, Katy	10y	C	D.C.	20 OCT 1870	Union
232	Thomas, Lavinia E.	10m	W	D.C.	26 AUG 1866	Congressional*
314	Thomas, Lewis, clerk	55y	W	Ohio	25 MAY 1868	Cincinnati, Ohio
298	Thomas, Lewis, wood & coal mer.	59y	W	D.C.	29 FEB 1868	Congressional
130	Thomas, Lile, slave	3y	C	D.C.	06 OCT 1858	Young Mens
553	Thomas, Lizzie	75y	C	Ky.	09 JAN 1872	Washington
340	Thomas, Lizzie Blanche	9m	W	D.C.	15 AUG 1868	Congressional
264	Thomas, Lizzie Hamilton	1m	W	D.C.	12 JUL 1867	Congressional
587	Thomas, Logins	6y	C	Md.	23 MAR 1872	Ebenezer
501	Thomas, Lusette	7y	C	D.C.	25 JAN 1871	Young Mens
013	Thomas, M.S.E. [of Henry]	8m	W	D.C.	12 JUL 1855	Congressional
251	Thomas, Margaret	53y	C	Md.	08 JAN 1867	Beckett's
292	Thomas, Martha		C		18 JAN 1868	Alms House
182	Thomas, Martha	14y	C	D.C.	26 JUN 1860	Harmony
037	Thomas, Mary		W	Va.	15 FEB 1856	Alms House
049	Thomas, Mary	7m	W		05 JUL 1856	Congressional
169	Thomas, Mary	6m	C	D.C.	03 JAN 1860	Ebenezer
184	Thomas, Mary	30y	C	Md.	10 JUL 1860	Ebenezer
403	Thomas, Mary	2d	C		28 JUL 1869	German Catholic
029	Thomas, Mary Ann	5y	W		17 NOV 1855	Foundry
116	Thomas, Mary Ann	8y	C	Md.	24 JUN 1858	Ebenezer
493	Thomas, Mary Ann	7d	C	D.C.	17 DEC 1870	Gardner's over E. Br.
419	Thomas, Mary E.	7m	W	D.C.	29 OCT 1869	Congressional
623	Thomas, Mary Jane	22y	C	U.S.	30 JUL 1872	
414	Thomas, Mary M.	36y	W		19 SEP 1869	Congressional
498	Thomas, Mary, pauper	11m	B	D.C.	10 JAN 1871	Washington Asylum
265	Thomas, Maud Macmillan	1m	W	D.C.	15 JUL 1867	Congressional
351	Thomas, May	2y	C	D.C.	21 SEP 1868	Ebenezer
335b	Thomas, Minnie				13 JUL 1868	Washington Asylum
333	Thomas, Minnie, laundress	26y	C		13 JUL 1868	Alms House
211	Thomas, Miss				24 JAN 1866	
245	Thomas, Miss [Eliza Lee]	35y	W		17 NOV 1866	Mt. Olivet*
670	Thomas, Moses	25y	C	U.S.	15 FEB 1873	Small Pox
518	Thomas, Moses W., watchman	68y	W	Md.	04 MAY 1871	Congressional*
004	Thomas, Noble, Mrs.	25y	W	Va.*	17 MAR 1855	St. Matthews
322	Thomas, Oster	80y	C	Va.	21 JUN 1868	Freedmen's Hospital
496	Thomas, Patsy	95y	C	Md.	02 DEC 1870	Young Mens
689	Thomas, Philip	13y	C	U.S.	04 MAY 1873	
777a	Thomas, Preston	1m	C	U.S.	20 JUN 1874	
338	Thomas, Rachel	4y	C		22 AUG 1868	Washington Asylum
717	Thomas, Reginald Somae	9m	W	D.C.	07 SEP 1873	Hancock, Md.
616a	Thomas, Rhoda I.	7m	W	U.S.	15 JUL 1872	Congressional
778	Thomas, Robert	22y	C	U.S.	18 JUN 1874	Washington Asylum
326	Thomas, Rosabel	10m	W	D.C.	30 JUL 1868	Congressional
130	Thomas, Samuel	1y	C		14 OCT 1858	Young Mens
373	Thomas, Samuel, teamster	70y	C	Md.	05 JAN 1869	Young Mens
749	Thomas, Sarah M.	34y	W	U.S.	24 FEB 1874	Wilmington, Del.
189	Thomas, Sarah, midwife	59y	C	Md.	03 SEP 1860	Ebenezer
683	Thomas, Sophia	6y	C	U.S.	13 APR 1873	Small Pox
272	Thomas, Susan B.	9m	C		12 AUG 1867	Freedmen's Bureau
215	Thomas, Sylvester A.	1y	C	D.C.	18 MAR 1866	Mt. Olivet
586	Thomas, Sylvia	62y	C	D.C.	12 MAR 1872	Mt. Zion
586	Thomas, Thomas	76y	W	Va.	14 MAR 1872	Congressional
683	Thomas, Thomas	4y	C	U.S.	14 APR 1873	Small Pox
335b	Thomas, Virginia				01 JUL 1868	Washington Asylum
051	Thomas, W., sailor	35y	C	Md.	21 JUL 1856	Young Mens

Page	Name	Age	Race	Birth	Death Date	Burial Ground
508	Thomas, Walter	3m	C	D.C.	17 FEB 1871	Ebenezer
382	Thomas, Walter, laborer	3d	C		31 MAR 1869	
155	Thomas, Wesley R.	12d	W	D.C.	20 JUL 1859	Glenwood
296	Thomas, William	45y	C	Md.	10 FEB 1868	Freedmen's Hospital
684	Thomas, William	10y	C	U.S.	24 APR 1873	Small Pox
272	Thomas, Willie	3m	C		14 AUG 1867	Freedmen's Bureau
599	Thomas, Willie, student	11y	C	U.S.	12 MAY 1872	Harmony
024	Thomas, Wm.	15m	C		10 SEP 1855	Young Mens
533	Thomas, Wm. B.	8y			23 AUG 1871	Prospect Hill
399	Thomas, Wm., barber	52y	W	D.C.	20 JUL 1869	Congressional
594	Thomas, Wm. Cantury	4m	W	D.C.	12 APR 1872	Congressional
362	Thomas, Wm. H.	3y	C	D.C.	22 NOV 1868	
618	Thomas, Wm. H.	5m	C	U.S.	02 AUG 1872	Mt. Olivet
691	Thomas, Wm. H.	8y	W	U.S.	04 MAY 1873	Small Pox*
343	Thomas, Wm. H.	1y	C	D.C.	15 AUG 1868	Washington Asylum
383	Thomas, Wm. Henry	1m	C	D.C.	08 MAR 1869	Washington Asylum
341	Thomas, Wm., waterman	82y	W	Va.	07 AUG 1868	Congressional
255	Thomas, [blank]	2y	C		30 MAR 1867	Mt. Olivet
528	Thomferdt, Chas. R.	7y	W	D.C.	21 JUL 1871	Prospect Hill
456	Thomferdt, H.C.C.	8m	W	D.C.	28 JUN 1870	Prospect Hill
507	Thomferdt, Otto	2m	W	D.C.	13 FEB 1871	Prospect Hill
441	Thomforth, Eden A.B.	6y	W		04 FEB 1870	Prospect Hill
202	Thomma, Laurence	3y	W	D.C.	13 APR 1861	German Catholic
202	Thomma, Tiny	6y	W	D.C.	09 APR 1861	German Catholic
313	Thompson, Agnes	29y	W	Eng.	23 MAY 1868	Congressional
720	Thompson, Alice	7y	C	D.C.	27 SEP 1873	Holmead
643	Thompson, Allice R.	2m	W	U.S.	10 DEC 1872	Mt. Olivet
531	Thompson, Andrew H.	33y	W	U.S.	05 AUG 1871	Congressional*
540	Thompson, Ann	55y	W	Md.	04 OCT 1871	Glenwood
583	Thompson, Annie	7y	C	D.C.	27 FEB 1872	
695	Thompson, Aron	35y	C	Md.	05 JUN 1873	
174	Thompson, Arthur	11m	W	D.C.	05 MAR 1860	Washington
599	Thompson, C.A.	8m	W	U.S.	17 MAY 1872	Harmony
292	Thompson, Catherine, hse. maid	60y	W	Va.	24 JAN 1868	Rock Creek
777	Thompson, Charles	5m	W	U.S.	11 JUN 1874	Congressional*
682	Thompson, Charles	8y	C	U.S.	27 APR 1873	Washington Asylum
221	Thompson, Charles H.	1y	W	Md.	22 MAY 1866	Glenwood
399	Thompson, Charles Wm.	5m	W		12 JUL 1869	Congressional
605	Thompson, Chas.	5y	C	Va.	20 JUN 1872	Small Pox
734	Thompson, E.C.B., housekeeper	89y	W	Eng.	07 DEC 1873	Congressional*
275	Thompson, E.F.	8y	W		10 SEP 1867	Mt. Olivet
353	Thompson, Edward H., carpenter	31y	W	Va.	25 SEP 1868	
584	Thompson, Eliza	1m	W	D.C.	04 MAR 1872	Congressional*
004	Thompson, Elizabeth	62y	W	D.C.*	27 MAR 1855	Oak Hill
516a	Thompson, Elizabeth	35y	W	Can.	15 MAR 1871	Washington Asylum
768	Thompson, Elizabeth	39y	C	U.S.	12 MAY 1874	Washington Asylum
778	Thompson, Evaline	19y	W	U.S.	13 JUN 1874	Glenwood
730	Thompson, Frank	3m	W	U.S.	12 NOV 1873	Glenwood
229	Thompson, Frank	2y	W	D.C.	25 JUL 1866	Mt. Olivet
361	Thompson, Frederick	20d	C	D.C.	21 NOV 1868	
744	Thompson, Geo. & A., infant of		C	U.S.	28 JAN 1874	
481	Thompson, Geo. B.	6y	W	D.C.	09 OCT 1870	Holmead
640	Thompson, Geo. E.	13y	W	U.S.	26 DEC 1872	Small Pox*
639	Thompson, George	21y	W	U.S.	11 DEC 1872	Small Pox*
369	Thompson, George, messenger	69y	W	Eng.	17 JAN 1869	Congressional
005	Thompson, H.E.J.	57y	W	D.C.*	14 APR 1855	Oak Hill
036	Thompson, Infant of A.				10 FEB 1856	St. Patricks
588	Thompson, J.G.	3y	W	D.C.	25 MAR 1872	

District of Columbia Interments (Index to Deaths), 1855-1874

Page	Name	Age	Race	Birth	Death Date	Burial Ground
321	Thompson, James	26d	C	D.C.	16 JUN 1868	Alms House
098	Thompson, James	14y	W	D.C.	15 DEC 1857	Congressional
690	Thompson, James E.	6m	C	Va.	19 MAY 1873	
276	Thompson, James T.	46y	W	Va.	09 SEP 1867	Congressional
114	Thompson, Jane Mary	22y	W	D.C.	27 MAY 1858	Congressional
617	Thompson, Jas.	3y	C	U.S.	29 AUG 1872	
073	Thompson, Jeannette	48y	W	Md.	11 MAR 1857	Congressional
321	Thompson, Jennie	2y	C		c.29 JUN 1868	Alms House
736	Thompson, Joanna	10y	W	U.S.	18 DEC 1873	Congressional*
721	Thompson, John	1y	C	D.C.	28 SEP 1873	
333	Thompson, John	1y	C		18 JUL 1868	Alms House
053	Thompson, John	3y	W	D.C.	08 AUG 1856	Congressional
286	Thompson, John	8m	W	D.C.	04 DEC 1867	Holmead
335a	Thompson, John				17 JUL 1868	Washington Asylum
069	Thompson, John F.	4m	C	D.C.	31 JAN 1857	St. Matthews
348	Thompson, John, fisherman	30y	W	Md.	14 SEP 1868	Congressional
450	Thompson, John H.	2y	C		28 APR 1870	Union
741	Thompson, John L.	2m	W	U.S.	13 JAN 1874	Congressional*
396	Thompson, Joseph	5m	C	D.C.	24 JUN 1869	Union
297	Thompson, Josephine C., Mrs.	29y	W	D.C.*	08 FEB 1868	Glenwood
265	Thompson, Josias	50y	W	Md.	21 JUL 1867	Congressional
607	Thompson, Josie	1y	W	D.C.	27 JUN 1872	Congressional*
329	Thompson, Julia	2y	C	D.C.	06 JUL 1868	Alms House
038	Thompson, Julia	3m	W	D.C.	14 MAR 1856	Oak Hill
335b	Thompson, Julia				06 JUL 1868	Washington Asylum
262	Thompson, Leanah	22y	W	D.C.	02 JUN 1867	Congressional
231	Thompson, Lillie May	3m	W	D.C.	12 AUG 1866	Congressional
110	Thompson, Lilly	2y	W	D.C.	05 APR 1858	Glenwood
335a	Thompson, Lucinda				27 JUL 1868	Washington Asylum
483	Thompson, Lydia Helen, teacher	59y	W	Mass.	13 OCT 1870	Oak Hill
337	Thompson, Margaret	1m	C	U.S.	05 AUG 1868	Washington Asylum
050	Thompson, Margaret A.	35y	W	unk.	15 JUL 1856	St. Patricks
258	Thompson, Margaret, domestic	60y	W	Ire.	05 APR 1867	Mt. Olivet
615	Thompson, Mary	32y	C	U.S.	05 JUL 1872	
509	Thompson, Mary	40y	C	Va.	06 FEB 1871	Washington Asylum
083	Thompson, Mary Ann	75y	W	Md.	11 JUL 1857	Congressional
623	Thompson, Mary T.	2y	C	U.S.	17 JUL 1872	Holy Rood
554	Thompson, Mathias F.	34y	W	Va.	15 JAN 1872	Oak Hill
440	Thompson, Matilda	40y	W	Md.	05 FEB 1870	Washington Asylum
338	Thompson, Maud Eliza	1y	W	D.C.	26 AUG 1868	Oak Hill
327	Thompson, Mensor	1y	C	Va.	27 JUL 1868	Western
031	Thompson, Michael, laborer	35y	W	Ire.	16 DEC 1855	Catholic
104	Thompson, Mrs.	55y	W	Md.	04 FEB 1858	Washington Asylum
639	Thompson, Nathaniel	25y	C	U.S.	15 NOV 1872	
508	Thompson, Peter	6m	C		20 FEB 1871	Ebenezer
744	Thompson, Richard, brickmaker		C	U.S.	01 JAN 1874	
147	Thompson, Robert E.	3m	W	D.C.	26 APR 1859	Congressional
262	Thompson, Rosa	7m	W	D.C.	20 JUN 1867	Glenwood
369	Thompson, Sarah A.	53y	W	D.C.	03 JAN 1869	Congressional
300	Thompson, Sarah Ann	5y	C	Md.	27 MAR 1868	Alms House
093	Thompson, Thomas, laborer		W	Ire.	07 OCT 1857	Washington Asylum
658	Thompson, Thomas, plumber	38y	W	U.S.	03 JAN 1873	Glenwood
474	Thompson, Thos.	6m	W		17 AUG 1870	Washington Asylum
308	Thompson, Tyler	18y	W		15 APR 1868	Congressional
419	Thompson, William	2y	W	D.C.	30 OCT 1869	Congressional
436	Thompson, William, carpenter	51y	W	Scot.	22 JAN 1870	Port Deposit, Md.
253	Thompson, William, laborer	22y	W	N.C.	07 FEB 1867	Mt. Olivet
458	Thompson, Willie	2y	C	D.C.	20 JUN 1870	Potters Field

Page	Name	Age	Race	Birth	Death Date	Burial Ground
667	Thompson, Willie M.	15y	W	U.S.	08 FEB 1873	Oak Hill
154	Thompson, Willie M.	2m	C	D.C.	20 JUL 1859	Young Mens
626	Thompson, Wm.	26y	W	U.S.	14 SEP 1872	
271	Thompson, Wm. H., cigar dealer	40y	W	D.C.	12 AUG 1867	Congressional
526	Thompson, Wm. R.	1y	W	D.C.	03 JUL 1871	Glenwood
227	Thompson, Wm. W.	5m	W	D.C.	02 JUL 1866	Congressional
065	Thompson, Zachariah	8m	W	Md.	15 DEC 1856	Montgomery Co., Md.
008	Thompson, [blank]	6m	W	D.C.	14 MAY 1855	Georgetown, Methodist
350	Thomson, Elizabeth	1y	W	D.C.	03 SEP 1868	Young Mens
070	Thomson, Mary	72y			13 FEB 1857	Western
630	Thoranfort, Mary	14y	W	U.S.	15 OCT 1872	
584	Thorn, Elisabeth	64y	W	Md.	01 MAR 1872	Oak Hill
173	Thorn, Evelyn	6m	W	D.C.	23 FEB 1860	Congressional
042	Thorn, Margrette	49y	W	D.C.	21 APR 1856	St. Patricks
625	Thorn, Mary J.	57y	W	U.S.	20 SEP 1872	Glenwood
201	Thorne, John H., printer	42y	W		21 MAR 1861	Glenwood
044	Thornley, Thomas J.	4y	W	D.C.	13 MAY 1856	Congressional
451	Thornton, Alberta	17y	C	Md.	23 APR 1870	Washington Asylum
615	Thornton, Alfred	16y	C	U.S.	01 JUL 1872	
154	Thornton, Belle	30y	W	Eng.	18 JUL 1859	Washington Asylum
478	Thornton, Frederick	40y	W		01 SEP 1870	Methodist
401	Thornton, John, laborer	26y	C	U.S.	25 JUL 1869	Holmead
517	Thornton, Maria	90y			06 APR 1871	Ebenezer
301	Thornton, Maria	1y	C	D.C.	22 MAR 1868	Young Mens
610	Thornton, Mary Ellen	3y	W		22 JUN 1867	
430	Thornton, Mary, housekeeper	32y	W	N.J.	12 DEC 1869	Mt. Olivet
615	Thornton, Patience	33y	C	U.S.	19 JUL 1872	
740	Thornton, Robert R., blacksmith	60y	W	U.S.	03 JAN 1874	Congressional*
604	Thornton, Sammyq	95y	C	Va.	25 JUN 1872	Ebenezer
463	Thornton, Sarah S.	8m	W	D.C.	24 JUL 1870	Mt. Olivet
422	Thornton, Susan	2y	C		29 OCT 1869	Ebenezer
010	Thornton, Wm., fisherman	35y	C	Va.	18 JUN 1855	
020	Thorpe, Elizabeth	9y	W	D.C.	09 AUG 1855	
379	Thorpp, Wm., clerk	50y	W	Md.	29 MAR 1869	Cong./Pikesville, Md.
343	Thrift, C.D., Mrs.	72y	W	Va.	05 AUG 1868	Montgomery Co., Md.
412	Throckmorton, Sarah	3d	C	D.C.	15 AUG 1869	Washington Asylum
778	Throop, Benj. F.	8m	W	U.S.	19 JUN 1874	Congressional*
778	Throop, Nath. Hall	8m	W	U.S.	22 JUN 1874	Congressional*
314	Throop, Susan H.	17y	W	D.C.	04 MAY 1868	Congressional
637	Thrope, Marg. B.	59y	W	U.S.	12 NOV 1872	
729	Thumbert, Ester	80y	W	Guer.	02 NOV 1873	Glenwood
248	Thurber, Mary	26y	W	Ire.	11 DEC 1866	Mt. Olivet
248	Thurbert, Mary L.	11d	W	D.C.	14 DEC 1866	Mt. Olivet
318	Thurm, Johana Augusta	2m	W	D.C.	27 JUN 1868	Congressional
521	Thurston, Betty	3m	C	D.C.	08 JUN 1871	Young Mens
519	Thurston, Catharine	23y	C	Va.	17 MAY 1871	Union
597	Thurston, Wm. H.	3y	C	U.S.	11 MAY 1872	Unknown
777	Thysen, Lilly M.	8m	W	U.S.	10 JUN 1874	Mt. Olivet
084	Thyson, Edward P.	11m	W	D.C.	26 JUL 1857	St. Matthews
425	Thyson, Mary	1m	W	D.C.	06 NOV 1869	
785	Thyson, Poulus, merchant	71y	W	Holl.	13 JUL 1874	Mt. Olivet
158	Tibbett, Elizabeth	80y	W	Md.	18 AUG 1859	St. Peters
343	Tibbs, Espy	2y	C	D.C.	15 AUG 1868	
488	Tibbs, Mary	6d	W	D.C.	25 NOV 1870	Mt. Olivet
669	Tibbs, Milton	18y	C	U.S.	08 FEB 1873	Small Pox
350	Tibbs, Nimrod, laborer	65y	C	Va.	09 SEP 1868	Young Mens
137	Tidbell, Mary H.	33y	W		15 JAN 1859	Congressional
698	Tidmarsh, Emily	3y	W	Eng.	06 JUN 1873	Congressional

District of Columbia Interments (Index to Deaths), 1855-1874

Page	Name	Age	Race	Birth	Death Date	Burial Ground
227	Tierney, Catherine Elizabeth	2m	W	D.C.	08 JUL 1866	Mt. Olivet*
242	Tierney, Henrietta, child of	Still	C		21 OCT 1866	Ebenezer
342	Tiers, Jane	3y	C		16 AUG 1868	Young Mens
279	Tilghman, Joseph	3d	C	D.C.	07 OCT 1867	Mt. Olivet
761	Tilghman, Rosetta	77y	C	U.S.	20 APR 1874	Mt. Olivet
598	Tilghman, Rosetta	6m	C	U.S.	19 MAY 1872	Young Mens
177	Tilley, Deborah	70y	W	U.S.	21 APR 1860	Congressional*
625	Tillinghast, Lottie	14y	W	U.S.	11 SEP 1872	Oak Hill
660	Tillman, Harriett	50y	C	U.S.	17 JAN 1873	Washington Asylum
501	Tillman, John Alex., whitewasher	58y	C	D.C.	— JAN 1871	Young Mens
473	Tillman, Joseph	9m	C		26 AUG 1870	Ebenezer
498	Tillman, Levi	48y	W	Ger.	25 JAN 1871	Washington Asylum
271	Tillman, Mary L.	6m	W		10 AUG 1867	Harmony
292	Tillman, Sarah	1m	C		25 JAN 1868	Alms House
267	Tilman, Lillie M.	2m	W	D.C.	03 JUL 1867	Mt. Olivet
328	Tilman, Richard, coachman	53y	C	D.C.	17 JUL 1868	Western
193	Tilman, Thomas	64y	C	U.S.	04 NOV 1860	Mt. Olivet
061	Tilman, [blank]	2m	C		04 OCT 1856	Young Mens
092	Tilman, [blank]	10m	C		29 SEP 1857	Western
075	Tilmon, Mary Ann, nurse	21y	C	D.C.	17 APR 1857	St. Matthews
777	Tilph, Paulina, housewife	41y	W	Ger.	03 JUN 1874	Prospect Hill
263	Tilston, Samuel, merchant	40y	W	Eng.	25 JUN 1867	N.Y.
274	Tilton, Dudley, student	16y	W	Mass.	04 SEP 1867	Newburyport, Mass.
595	Tilton, Elisabeth	72y	W	Md.	17 APR 1872	Conn.
253	Tilton, Ida May	2m	W	D.C.	03 FEB 1867	Congressional
285	Tilton, Zebulon	22y	W	Ind.	11 DEC 1867	Ind.
263	Tim, J.		C		26 JUN 1867	Young Mens
755	Timers, Jane	5y	C	U.S.	13 MAR 1874	
344	Timhors, Mr., child of	3m	W		11 AUG 1868	Prospect Hill
549	Timlan, Thomas	30y		N.Y.	21 DEC 1871	Washington
597	Timmons, Henry A., huckster	31y	C	U.S.	17 MAY 1872	Small Pox
207	Tinkler, Wm. Saml.	1y	W	D.C.	20 JUL 1862	Mt. Olivet
216	Tinney, Hugh, soldier	27y	W	Ire.	26 MAR 1866	Mt. Olivet
127	Tinney, Mary Ann	6m	C		03 SEP 1858	Young Mens
376	Tippen, George	3y	C		28 FEB 1869	Union
026	Tippet, Catherine	35y	W	D.C.	17 OCT 1855	Congressional
484	Tippett, Albert A.	1y	W	D.C.	17 OCT 1870	Congressional
643	Tippett, Anna, housewife	37y	W	U.S.	07 DEC 1872	Glenwood
415	Tippett, John M.	3m	W		22 SEP 1869	Pr. Geo. Co., Md.
749	Tippett, Violet C., housekeeper	29y	W	U.S.	27 FEB 1874	Congressional
533	Tippits, Willie	9y	C	D.C.	25 AUG 1871	Union
588	Tippitt, Edith	1m	W	D.C.	26 MAR 1872	Congressional*
522	Tissington, Eliza L.	45y	W	Eng.	11 JUN 1871	Congressional*
607	Tobbins, Enoch	12d	W	D.C.	28 JUN 1872	Congressional
687	Tobin, Catherine	71y	W	Ire.	02 MAY 1873	Mt. Olivet
761	Tobin, Catherine	7y	W	U.S.	11 APR 1874	Mt. Olivet
622a	Tobin, Jas., laborer	45y	W	Ire.	30 AUG 1872	
188	Tobin, John	10m	W	D.C.	30 AUG 1860	St. Patricks
580	Tobin, Michael A.	3y	W	D.C.	09 FEB 1872	Holy Rood
181	Tobin, William	1m	W		15 JUN 1860	Mt. Olivet
761	Tobin, William, laborer	50y	C	U.S.	22 APR 1874	Ebenezer
538	Todd, David M., farmer	84y	W	Mass.	24 SEP 1871	Oak Hill
755	Todd, Seth, Dr.	31y	W	U.S.	13 MAR 1874	Congressional
674	Todd, Wm. Balch, merchant	63y	W	U.S.	13 MAR 1873	Congressional
113	Todd, Wm. L., clerk	35y	W	Ky.	07 MAY 1858	Congressional
165	Todson, George P., agent	68y	W	Den.	10 NOV 1859	Oak Hill
124	Todtschinder, F., baker	41y	W	Ger.	12 AUG 1858	Congressional
013	Tofer, Thos. F.	8m			02 JUL 1855	St. Peters

Page	Name	Age	Race	Birth	Death Date	Burial Ground
345	Tohade, Augusta	1y	W	D.C.	10 AUG 1868	Prospect Hill
430	Tohl, Mr., child of				22 DEC 1869	Prospect Hill
618	Tolbert, Edwd.	1y	C	U.S.	21 AUG 1872	
670	Tolds, Anna	21y	C	U.S.	21 FEB 1873	Small Pox
302	Tolents, Louisa	28d	C		30 MAR 1868	Ebenezer
055	Toley, Anna	4m	W	D.C.	09 AUG 1856	St. Matthews
614	Toley, Timothy	3y	W	U.S.	13 JUL 1872	
398	Tolivar, Sylvester	80y	B	Va.	19 JUN 1869	Washington Asylum
372	Toliver, Elizabeth	12y	C		02 JAN 1869	Freedmen's Hospital
302	Toliver, John		C		06 MAR 1868	Alms House
400	Toliver, Julia	1y	C		16 JUL 1869	Holmead
489	Toliver, Margaret, housekeeper	40y	C	Va.	21 NOV 1870	Ebenezer
555	Toliver, Nancy	18y	C	Va.	25 JAN 1872	Glenwood
335b	Toliver, Nancy				13 JUL 1868	Washington Asylum
333	Toliver, Nancy, housekeeper	35y	C	Va.	13 JUL 1868	Alms House
726	Toliver, Willie	1y	B	U.S.	24 OCT 1873	
557	Tollaver, Susan, midwife	100y	C	Va.	04 FEB 1872	
777a	Tolliver, Andrew, laborer	20y	C	U.S.	09 JUN 1874	
523	Tolliver, Cozena	1y	C	D.C.	15 JUN 1871	
529	Tolson, Andrew C.		C	D.C.	26 JUL 1871	Ebenezer
671	Tolson, Chas.	3y	C	U.S.	12 FEB 1873	Small Pox*
630	Tolson, Jerry	14m	C	U.S.	12 OCT 1872	Small Pox
006	Tolson, John	1m	C	D.C.	— APR 1855	
303	Tolson, Lettie Ann	48y	W	D.C.	07 MAR 1868	Congressional
316	Tolson, Louisa, washerwoman	35y	C	Md.	16 MAY 1868	Alms House
625	Tolson, Lucy	51y	W	U.S.	12 SEP 1872	Congressional
737	Tolson, Lula	2y	W	U.S.	25 DEC 1873	Congressional
322	Tolson, Susan	14y	C		05 JUN 1868	Freedmen's Hospital
008	Tolson, [blank]	Still	W	D.C.	— MAY 1855	Holmead
416	Tom, Robt.	6y	C		29 SEP 1869	Western
287	Toman, John, stone cutter	25y	W	Ire.	28 DEC 1867	Mt. Olivet
694	Tomer, Anna M.	15y	W	N.J.	03 JUN 1873	Graceland
231	Tompkins, J.R.	11m	W	D.C.	09 AUG 1866	Congressional*
506	Tompkins, Richd., caterer	48y	W	D.C.	19 FEB 1871	Congressional
058	Tompson, Richard Lewis	1y	W	D.C.	17 SEP 1856	Glenwood
469	Tomson, Katharine	39y	W	Ire.	29 AUG 1870	Mt. Olivet
328	Toner, Albert	7m	W	D.C.	09 JUL 1868	Mt. Olivet
356	Toner, Everett H.	4y	W	D.C.	22 OCT 1868	Mt. Olivet
147	Toner, John	2m	W	D.C.	03 APR 1859	St. Patricks
175	Tonet, Alexander, cook	49y	W	Fra.	17 MAR 1860	Glenwood
625	Tonge, W., lady	59y	W	Eng.	02 SEP 1872	
624	Tonge, Wm.	60y	W	U.S.	02 SEP 1872	
360	Toomay, Michael, carpenter	42y	W	Ire.	02 NOV 1868	Mt. Olivet
273	Toomey, Wm. J., bookbinder	45y	W	Ire.	30 SEP 1867	Mt. Olivet
534	Toone, Emma	1y	W	D.C.	29 AUG 1871	Methodist
216	Topham, James	1y	W	D.C.	24 MAR 1866	Oak Hill
262	Topham, Rudolph	4m	W	D.C.	14 JUN 1867	Oak Hill
246	Toppam, Lincoln	1y	W	D.C.	16 DEC 1866	Oak Hill
618	Topper, Jno. G.F.	10m	W	U.S.	10 AUG 1872	
222	Topping, Mary E.	37y	W	D.C.	25 MAY 1866	Mt. Olivet
260	Toppins, Laura V.	9y	C	Md.	11 MAY 1867	Mt. Olivet
179	Torbert, Mary Elizabeth	46y	W	D.C.	25 MAY 1860	Congressional
047	Torney, Mary C.	8m		D.C.	22 JUN 1856	Baltimore, Md.
159	Torney, Mary M.	40y	W	Md.	29 AUG 1859	Mt. Olivet
172	Torre, Joseph	75y	W	Italy	17 FEB 1860	Washington Asylum
516	Torrey, Eliza S.	55y	W	Ver.	08 MAR 1871	Congressional
642	Torrey, Sarah	48y	W	U.S.	03 DEC 1872	
435	Toumey, Mary, domestic	17y	W	Md.	18 JAN 1870	Mt. Olivet

District of Columbia Interments (Index to Deaths), 1855-1874

Page	Name	Age	Race	Birth	Death Date	Burial Ground
349	Towers, Annie E.	9y	W	D.C.	23 SEP 1868	Rock Creek
537	Towers, Edw., clerk	59y	W	Va.	20 SEP 1871	Glenwood
749	Towers, Eliza	61y	W	U.S.	09 FEB 1874	Glenwood
518	Towers, John Oliver	2y	W	D.C.	09 MAY 1871	Glenwood
280	Towers, William, grocer	65y	W	Eng.	15 OCT 1867	Rock Creek
755	Towles, Blanche	1y	C	U.S.	05 MAR 1874	
472	Towles, Henry	1y	C	D.C.	01 AUG 1870	Holmead
366	Town, Edward, bookbinder	61y	W	Me.	30 DEC 1868	Glenwood
461	Towner, John Henry	7m	W	Amer.	26 JUL 1870	Congressional
522	Townley, Annette	1y	W		13 JUN 1871	Congressional
585	Townley, Columbia, laborer	34y	W	U.S.	08 MAR 1872	Congressional
163	Townley, Josephine M.	19y	W	D.C.	18 OCT 1859	Congressional
720	Townley, Sarah	75y	W	D.C.	29 SEP 1873	Mt. Olivet
581	Townsend, Chas. H.	8y	W	Pa.	15 FEB 1872	Glenwood
749	Townsend, Henry, clerk	50y	W	U.S.	07 FEB 1874	Glenwood
096	Townsend, M.	56y	W	Md.	09 NOV 1857	Methodist
291	Townshend, Ernst	1h	W	D.C.	21 JAN 1868	Congressional
745	Townshend, Isaac, laborer	35y	C	U.S.	01 JAN 1874	
674	Towsand, Ella	3m	W	U.S.	17 MAR 1873	Laurel Hill, Phila.
415	Tracey, Delia	99y	W	Can.	14 SEP 1869	
744	Tracy, Caroline	9m	W	U.S.	11 JAN 1874	Mt. Olivet
610	Trader, D.C.	5y	W	U.S.	08 JUL 1872	
300	Trader, John	53y	C	U.S.	04 MAR 1868	Glenwood
471	Traiton, Carrie, seamstress	23y	W	Va.	03 AUG 1870	Congressional
628	Tramel, Mary E.	31y	C	U.S.	28 SEP 1872	
217	Tramell, J., laborer	48y	W	Va.	10 APR 1866	Ebenezer
093	Travailier, Felix	57y	W	Pol.	02 OCT 1857	Washington Asylum
018	Travers, James E.	1y	W	D.C.	21 AUG 1855	Glenwood
007	Traverse, Nancy	58y	W	D.C.*	01 APR 1855	Foundry
632	Trazzere, E.E.	1y	W	U.S.	20 OCT 1872	
160	Treadway, John And.	1y	W	D.C.	02 AUG 1859	Glenwood
184	Tree, Louise Matilda	55y	W	D.C.	03 JUL 1860	Glenwood
696	Tregear, Charles, plumber	21y	W	N.J.	14 JUN 1873	Congressional*
777	Trelton, Laura	7m	W	U.S.	12 JUN 1874	Glenwood
002	Tretler, Norah	4m	W	D.C.	23 JAN 1855	St. Patricks
106	Tretter, John B.	7m	W	D.C.	28 FEB 1858	Glenwood
347	Triay, James E.	22y	W	D.C.	11 SEP 1868	Congressional
025	Triay, Raphael, musician	51y	W	Spain	09 SEP 1855	St. Peters
313	Trice, Catherine, washerwooman	50y	C	Va.	19 MAY 1868	Young Mens
755	Trick, Louisa	1y	C	U.S.	27 MAR 1874	
785	Trimpe, Emma, house servant	22y	W	Ger.	10 JUL 1874	Congressional
698	Trine, John G., carpenter	19y	W	U.S.	27 JUN 1873	Glenwood
167	Trinholm, Wm. V.	1y	W	D.C.	17 DEC 1859	Oak Hill
104	Triplett, Austin, servant	65y	C	Va.	01 FEB 1858	Ebenezer
099	Triplett, Eleanor Frances	23y	W	D.C.	27 DEC 1857	St. Patricks
294	Triplett, Elizabeth, servant	65y	C	Va.*	03 FEB 1868	Ebenezer
266	Triplett, Hannah	63y	W	D.C.	17 JUL 1867	Glenwood
210	Tripp, [torn], watchman			Mass.	— JAN 1866	sent [torn]
640	Tripplett, Mary E.	1y	C	U.S.	17 DEC 1872	Small Pox*
613	Triver, Francis	2y	C	U.S.	25 JUL 1872	
494	Trivett, Maude Deno	25d	W	D.C.	14 DEC 1870	St. Patricks
216	Trott, Thomas B., clerk	66y	W		29 MAR 1866	Congressional
551	Troughman, G.	16d	C		— DEC 1871	
755	Troutman, Ann	22y	C	U.S.	05 MAR 1874	
163	Troutman, Michael	65y	W	Ger.	01 OCT 1859	Prospect Hill
233	Truax, D.A., Mrs.	30y	W	Ohio	08 AUG 1866	Cincinnati, Ohio
233	Truax, D.A., Mrs., infant of	1m	W	D.C.	14 AUG 1866	Cincinnati, Ohio
036	Truman, Henry D.	2y		D.C.	02 FEB 1856	Congressional

Page	Name	Age	Race	Birth	Death Date	Burial Ground
749	Truman, Martha	44y	W	U.S.	13 FEB 1874	Glenwood
042	Truman, Martha A.	34y	W	Va.	15 APR 1856	Congressional
133	Truman, William	85y	W	Eng.	25 NOV 1858	Washington Asylum
785	Trumball, Joseph	3m	W	U.S.	25 JUL 1874	[torn]
341	Trumbo, John Roe	5m	W		11 AUG 1868	Congressional
755	Trumbull, Frederick W.	1y	W	U.S.	02 MAR 1874	Chicago, Ill.
339	Trumbull, Lyman, Mrs.	44y	W	Ill.	17 AUG 1868	Springfield, Ill.
227	Trunnell, Isaac	74y	W	Md.	08 JUL 1866	Glenwood
339	Trunnell, Nellie	3y	W	D.C.	16 AUG 1868	Glenwood
091	Tryhy, Thomas, laborer	37y	W	Ire.	21 SEP 1857	St. Patricks
174	Tryne, Mary	2y	W	D.C.	01 MAR 1860	Glenwood
032	Tscheffely, [blank], Mr.	68y	W		23 DEC 1855	Western
028	Tschiffelly, Mrs.	42y	W		04 OCT 1855	Western
642	Tuber, July	3y	C	U.S.	05 DEC 1872	
102	Tucker, A.H.	6m	W	D.C.	23 JAN 1858	Congressional
500	Tucker, Belinda	80y	W	Amer.	08 JAN 1871	Glenwood
695	Tucker, Carl	5m	C	D.C.	20 JUN 1873	
252	Tucker, Caroline M.	27y	W	Md.	08 FEB 1867	Rock Creek
420	Tucker, Chas. P.R., huckster	29y	W	Md.	05 OCT 1869	Glenwood
619	Tucker, Ed	13m	C	U.S.	23 AUG 1872	
379	Tucker, Enoch	78y	W	Md.	15 MAR 1869	Congressional
035	Tucker, Eveline	1y	W	D.C.	28 FEB 1856	St. Peters
140	Tucker, Harriet C.	1y	W	D.C.	11 FEB 1859	Glenwood
440	Tucker, Harry C.W.	4y	W	Md.	20 FEB 1870	Oak Hill
235	Tucker, Hattie E.	1y	W	D.C.	12 SEP 1866	Rock Creek
285	Tucker, Henrietta	48y	W	Md.	03 DEC 1867	Glenwood
785	Tucker, James	P.B.	W	U.S.	22 JUL 1874	Glenwood
493	Tucker, Jenifer C., housewife	82y	W	Eng.	24 DEC 1870	Congressional
690	Tucker, John A., carpenter	42y	W	D.C.	09 MAY 1873	Congressional*
595	Tucker, John W., pump maker	38y	W	D.C.	21 APR 1872	Congressional
385	Tucker, Joseph Z.	1y	W	D.C.	28 APR 1869	Congressional
002	Tucker, Marie Louise	30y	W	Ind.	23 JAN 1855	Removed from City
096	Tucker, Mary	75y	W	Md.	07 NOV 1857	Congressional
630	Tucker, Mary L.	15m	C	U.S.	08 OCT 1872	
043	Tucker, Mrs.	49y	W	D.C.	27 APR 1856	Alms House
749	Tucker, Otis	72y	W	U.S.	01 FEB 1874	Congressional*
695	Tucker, Robert, painter		C	Va.	19 JUN 1873	
102	Tucker, Samuel T.	2y	W	D.C.	19 JAN 1858	Glenwood
713	Tucker, Stephen	60y	C	Va.	25 AUG 1873	Mt. Pleasant
104	Tucker, Thomas	36y	W	Md.	13 FEB 1858	Glenwood
462	Tucker, William W., magistrate	38y	W	D.C.	07 JUL 1870	Congressional
744	Tucker, Wm. S., carpenter	40y	W	U.S.	29 JAN 1874	Congressional
397	Tuckson, D.	1y	D		27 JUN 1869	
470	Tuckson, Rachel	1y	C	D.C.	20 AUG 1870	Beckett's
489	Tucson, Eliza, chamber maid	38y	C		05 NOV 1870	Beckett's
609	Tuel, Maria W.	37y	W	U.S.	29 JUN 1872	
604	Tuell, Henry	2m	C	D.C.	23 JUN 1872	Ebenezer
054	Tuell, John H.	14y	W	D.C.	24 AUG 1856	Congressional
109	Tuk-a-lis-tah (Pawnee)	24y	I	Md.	29 MAR 1858	Congressional
712	Tumy, William	9m	C	D.C.	13 AUG 1873	Ebenezer
366	Tunchsteine, Madeline	13m	W	D.C.	17 DEC 1868	
362	Tunia, Henry, laborer	28y	C	D.C.	30 NOV 1868	Harmony
160	Tunion, Albertine	9y	C	D.C.	05 AUG 1859	Harmony
243	Tunis, Henrietta		C	Md.	12 NOV 1866	Young Mens
322	Tunnia, Jessie	1y	C	D.C.	13 JUN 1868	Harmony
151	Tunor, Mary E.	37y	W	U.S.	23 JUN 1859	Alexandria, Va.
590	Tuohy, Margret	13y	W	D.C.	02 APR 1872	Mt. Olivet
621	Tupper, Wm.	2y	W	U.S.	17 AUG 1872	

District of Columbia Interments (Index to Deaths), 1855-1874

Page	Name	Age	Race	Birth	Death Date	Burial Ground
742	Tupper, Wm. A.	1y	W	U.S.	21 JAN 1874	Congressional
305	Turley, John M., storekeeper	41y	C	Va.*	04 MAR 1868	Harmony
047	Turley, M.A.	8m	C	D.C.	29 JUN 1856	Young Mens
275	Turnbark, Mrs.	82y	W		21 SEP 1867	Mt. Olivet
289	Turnbush, James	1y	W	U.S.	26 JAN 1868	Mt. Olivet
232	Turner, Andrew	1y	C		28 AUG 1866	Ebenezer
416	Turner, Aron, huckster	22y	C	Va.	10 SEP 1869	Holmead
158	Turner, Becky	78y	C	Va.	22 AUG 1859	Foundry
404	Turner, Ben, cook	50y	C		12 JUL 1869	
267	Turner, Carrie B.	1y	W	D.C.*	09 JUL 1867	Congressional
054	Turner, Elizabeth	24y	W	Md.	29 AUG 1856	Pr. Geo. Co., Md.
643	Turner, Ellen	45y	C	U.S.	09 DEC 1872	Ebenezer
418	Turner, Eric, laborer	26y	C	Md.	09 SEP 1869	Washington Asylum
067	Turner, Gabriel, lime burner		C	Md.	28 DEC 1856	Western
105	Turner, George, butcher	35y	W	D.C.	19 FEB 1858	Glenwood
025	Turner, Iola Forenza	2y	W	Md.	21 SEP 1855	Rock Creek
492	Turner, James Henry	26y	W	Va.	17 DEC 1870	Congressional*
257	Turner, Levi C., judge advocate	60y	W	N.Y.	15 MAR 1867	Oak Hill
332	Turner, Liney M.	23y	W	Mass.	07 JUL 1868	Williamsport, Pa.
762	Turner, Lucy Ann, servant	40y	C	U.S.	08 APR 1874	
392	Turner, Margt.	Still	C		06 MAY 1869	Washington Asylum
116	Turner, Mary	52y	C	D.C.	24 JUN 1858	Foundry
633	Turner, Mary	35y	W	U.S.	09 OCT 1872	Small Pox*
299	Turner, Mary Ann	25y	W	Me.	01 MAR 1868	Glenwood
660	Turner, Mary E.	36y	W	U.S.	20 JAN 1873	Baltimore, Md.
265	Turner, Mary Ellen	76y	W		28 JUL 1867	Glenwood
441	Turner, Mary, servant	35y	C	Md.	13 FEB 1870	Harmony
331	Turner, Mrs.		W		06 JUL 1868	Glenwood
676	Turner, Paris	72y	C	U.S.	01 MAR 1873	Small Pox
128	Turner, Patrick	2y	W	D.C.	22 SEP 1858	St. Patricks
369	Turner, Q.E.	8m	W	D.C.	21 JAN 1869	Congressional
369	Turner, Samuel R., clerk	37y	W	Md.	24 JAN 1869	Congressional
057	Turner, Sarah	25y	W	Md.	02 SEP 1856	Pr. Geo. Co., Md.
552	Turner, Sarah L.	20y	W	Md.	04 JAN 1872	Congressional*
351	Turner, Victoria	8m	C		03 SEP 1868	
551	Turner, Wm.				— DEC 1871	
671	Turner, Wm.	21y	C	U.S.	19 FEB 1873	Small Pox*
166	Turner, Wm. W., librarian	45y	W	Eng.	29 NOV 1859	Congressional
144	Turner, [blank]	Still	W	D.C.	17 MAR 1859	Methodist
237	Turner, [blank]	10m	C		28 SEP 1866	Western
236	Turner, [child of]	Still	W	D.C.	25 SEP 1866	Glenwood
627	Turney, Edward S.		W	U.S.	28 SEP 1872	
121	Turshin, Wm. H.	8m	C	D.C.	11 JUL 1858	Harmony
430	Turton, Ida	1y	W		26 DEC 1869	Glenwood
687	Turton, John B., merchant	39y	W	D.C.	09 MAY 1873	Congressional*
125	Turton, Julia B.	6y	W		19 AUG 1858	Congressional
042	Turton, Wm. S., plasterer	33y	W	D.C.	28 APR 1856	Oak Hill
217	Tush, Frank	36y	W	Ire.	12 APR 1866	Mt. Olivet
427	Tuss, William	6d	C	D.C.	15 NOV 1869	Washington Asylum
116	Tustin, Balch	9m	W	D.C.	23 JUN 1858	Oak Hill
445	Tuttle, Mary A., Mrs.	57y	W	Pa.	14 MAR 1870	Wyoming, Pa.
509	Twin Babes	Still	C	D.C.	10 FEB 1871	Washington Asylum
038	Twin Children				16 MAR 1856	Holmead
121	Twin, Mary	10m	W		12 JUL 1858	St. Patricks
023	Twine, Elizabeth	1y	C		01 SEP 1855	St. Matthews
061	Twine, Patsy, cook	48y	C	D.C.	03 OCT 1856	Western
027	Twine, [blank]	21y	C		12 OCT 1855	Western
691	Twombly, Clara	30y	W	U.S.	07 MAY 1873	Congressional

District of Columbia Interments (Index to Deaths), 1855-1874

Page	Name	Age	Race	Birth	Death Date	Burial Ground
713	Tyas, Jas. T.A.	19y	C	Va.	23 AUG 1873	
319	Tyler, Anna, chambermaid	25y	C	D.C.	28 JUN 1868	Mt. Zion
336	Tyler, Annie	1y	C	D.C.	12 AUG 1868	
411	Tyler, Annie	6m	C		08 AUG 1869	Beckett's
106	Tyler, Catharine B., lady	67y	W	Md.	27 FEB 1858	Congressional
681	Tyler, Chas.	6y	W	U.S.	12 APR 1873	Congressional
436	Tyler, Elizabeth	25y	C	Va.	31 JAN 1870	Harmony
717	Tyler, Elizabeth, housekeeper	45y	C	U.S.	07 SEP 1873	
509	Tyler, Frank	1y	C	D.C.	11 FEB 1871	Washington Asylum
640	Tyler, Geo. F.	2y	W	U.S.	24 DEC 1872	Small Pox*
345	Tyler, George Alex.	11m	C	D.C.	13 AUG 1868	
317	Tyler, Georgiana	1y	C	D.C.	16 JUN 1868	Ebenezer
313	Tyler, Henry	1y	C	D.C.	25 MAY 1868	Young Mens
768	Tyler, Ida	1y	C	U.S.	19 MAY 1874	Washington Asylum
215	Tyler, James W., painter	18y	W	Va.*	13 MAR 1866	Congressional
768	Tyler, Jane	59y	W	U.S.	13 MAY 1874	Congressional
389	Tyler, Jas. Hy.	2y	C	D.C.	09 APR 1869	Washington Asylum
462	Tyler, Joseph	6m	C	D.C.	04 JUL 1870	Mt. Olivet
516a	Tyler, Kate M.	10m	B	D.C.	27 MAR 1871	Washington Asylum
625	Tyler, L.A.	63y	W	U.S.	17 SEP 1872	Congressional
474	Tyler, Lavenia	1y	C		04 AUG 1870	Washington Asylum
365	Tyler, Lizzie	23y	C	Va.	09 DEC 1868	Young Mens
296	Tyler, Mary H.	1y	C	D.C.	20 FEB 1868	Alms House
761	Tyler, N. & A., infant of	1d	C	U.S.	20 APR 1874	Potters Field
226	Tyler, Robert W.	5m	C	D.C.	28 JUN 1866	Harmony
706	Tyler, Rose	9y	C	D.C.	19 JUL 1873	Beckett's
761	Tyler, Rosetta, domestic	17y	C	U.S.	26 APR 1874	Harmony
465	Tyler, Saml.	2y	C	D.C.	24 JUL 1870	Union
640	Tyler, Sarah E.	4m	W	U.S.	26 DEC 1872	Small Pox*
308	Tyler, Thompson, mason	18y	W		15 APR 1868	Congressional
403	Tyler, William Henry	8m	C	D.C.	26 JUL 1869	Harmony
335	Tyler, Wm. A.	3m	C	D.C.	15 JUL 1868	
470	Tyler, Wm. Ed.	11m	W	Amer.	10 AUG 1870	Congressional
466	Tyler, Wm. J.	1y	C	D.C.	09 JUL 1870	Young Mens
580	Tyler, Wm., laborer	36y	C		08 FEB 1872	Washington
003	Tyler, Wm. T.	3y	W	D.C.	12 FEB 1855	
007	Tylor, Wm.	1y	W	D.C.	01 APR 1855	Holmead
041	Tylor, [blank]	41y	W	Va.	23 APR 1856	Holmead
635	Tyney, Annie	5y	C	U.S.	30 NOV 1872	Small Pox
103	Tyning, Tim		W	Ire.	31 JAN 1858	St. Matthews
075	Tyssowski, John, examiner	46y	W	Pol.	05 APR 1857	St. Matthews

District of Columbia Interments (Index to Deaths), 1855-1874

Page	Name	Age	Race	Birth	Death Date	Burial Ground
U						
333	Uber, Frederick George	1y	W	D.C.	25 JUL 1868	Prospect Hill
315	Uffelman, Louis, blacksmith	32y	W	Ger.	19 MAY 1868	German Lutheran
021	Ullennohle, G.W., taylor	79y	W	Ger.	01 AUG 1855	Glenwood
520	Ullmer, Edw. Randolph	8m	W	D.C.*	29 MAY 1871	Oak Hill
123	Ullrick Virginia	2y	W		27 JUL 1858	Glenwood
541	Ulrich, Isaac G.	2y	W	D.C.	09 OCT 1871	Congressional
515	Umfreys, Betty	1m	C	D.C.	03 MAR 1871	Union
057	Umhofer, Charles	6m	W	D.C.	02 SEP 1856	German
761	Umphreys, Chas. A.	18y	C	U.S.	21 APR 1874	
715	Uncle, Geo. B., wheelwright	28y	W	Md.	22 AUG 1873	
282	Uncles, Ferdinan	7y	C	Md.	07 NOV 1867	Harmony
755	Underwood, Chas. M.	1y	W	U.S.	18 MAR 1874	Glenwood
734	Underwood, John C., Hon.	64y	W	U.S.	07 DEC 1873	Congressional
362	Underwood, Merinda, domestic	22y	W	D.C.	18 NOV 1868	Ebenezer
515	Underwood, Robert	2y	C	D.C.	11 MAR 1871	Union
735	Underwood, Stephens	5d	C	U.S.	11 DEC 1873	
508	Underwood, Wm., laborer	26y	C	Va.	23 FEB 1871	Ebenezer
335	Unknown	6m	C	D.C.	16 JUL 1868	
331	Unknown	6m	C	D.C.	10 JUL 1868	
331	Unknown	1y	C		21 JUL 1868	
334	Unknown				25 JUL 1868	
518	Unknown	4h		D.C.	12 MAY 1871	
551	Unknown				— DEC 1871	
519	Unknown		C	D.C.	18 MAY 1871	
551	Unknown				— DEC 1871	
551	Unknown				— DEC 1871	
554	Unknown	21y	C	D.C.	17 JAN 1872	
591	Unknown	Still	C	U.S.	21 APR 1872	
592	Unknown		W	U.S.	06 APR 1872	
404	Unknown	3m			22 JUL 1869	
591	Unknown				01 APR 1872	
592	Unknown		W	U.S.	12 APR 1872	
592	Unknown		W	U.S.	30 APR 1872	
622	Unknown	2y	W	U.S.	12 AUG 1872	
608	Unknown	9m	W	D.C.	19 JUN 1872	
604	Unknown			D.C.	04 JUN 1872	
620	Unknown		W	U.S.	20 AUG 1872	
662	Unknown	2m	C	U.S.	c.03 JAN 1873	
646	Unknown	Still	C	D.C.	04 DEC 1872	
683	Unknown	Still	C	U.S.	— APR 1873	
690	Unknown		C	U.S.	13 MAY 1873	
676	Unknown	Still	C	D.C.	05 MAR 1873	
646	Unknown	Still	C	D.C.	16 DEC 1872	
646	Unknown	Still	C	D.C.	13 DEC 1872	
715	Unknown		C		08 AUG 1873	
743	Unknown	P.B.	C	U.S.	24 JAN 1874	
212	Unknown		C		04 FEB 1866	Alms House
749	Unknown	4m	W	U.S.	20 FEB 1874	
768	Unknown	13d	W	U.S.	09 MAY 1874	
036	Unknown				27 FEB 1856	Alms House
315	Unknown		W		c.02 MAY 1868	Alms House
297	Unknown		C		03 FEB 1868	Alms House
251	Unknown		W		01 JAN 1867	Alms House
603	Unknown		C	D.C.	10 JUN 1872	Asylum
315	Unknown		W		c.06 MAY 1868	Alms House
374	Unknown	1y	W		01 FEB 1869	Congressional

District of Columbia Interments (Index to Deaths), 1855-1874

Page	Name	Age	Race	Birth	Death Date	Burial Ground
595	Unknown	1d	W	D.C.	20 APR 1872	Congressional
786	Unknown	1y	W	U.S.	— JUL 1874	Congressional
778	Unknown	23y	W	U.S.	10 JUN 1874	Congressional
778	Unknown	6m	W	U.S.	16 JUN 1874	Congressional
542	Unknown	6d	C		18 OCT 1871	Ebenezer
604	Unknown	1m	C	D.C.	14 JUN 1872	Ebenezer
551	Unknown	18y	C		— DEC 1871	Ebenezer
280	Unknown	5y	C		02 OCT 1867	Freedmen's Hospital
008	Unknown	5y	C	Md.	20 MAY 1855	Harmony
518	Unknown	9m	W	D.C.	12 MAY 1871	Methodist
402	Unknown	3m	W	D.C.	23 JUL 1869	Mt. Olivet
402	Unknown	4m	W	D.C.	17 JUL 1869	Mt. Olivet
749	Unknown	1m	W	U.S.	07 FEB 1874	Mt. Olivet
255	Unknown		W		— MAR 1867	Poor House
710	Unknown		C	unk.	08 AUG 1873	Poor House
589	Unknown	2y	W	D.C.	28 MAR 1872	Prospect Hill
603	Unknown	3m	C	D.C.	13 JUN 1872	Small Pox
548	Unknown	Still	W	D.C.	19 DEC 1871	Prospect Hill
669	Unknown	7m	C	U.S.	10 FEB 1873	Small Pox
106	Unknown	1m	W	Ire.	05 FEB 1858	St. Matthews
662	Unknown	Still	W	U.S.	30 JAN 1873	St. Marys
591	Unknown	7d	C	D.C.	10 APR 1872	Unknown
599	Unknown	1y	C	U.S.	19 MAY 1872	Unknown
599	Unknown	1y	C	U.S.	27 MAY 1872	Unknown
600	Unknown	8m	W	U.S.	27 MAY 1872	Unknown
597	Unknown	14d	C	U.S.	14 MAY 1872	Unknown
600	Unknown	14d	W	U.S.	14 MAY 1872	Unknown
598	Unknown	2d	C	U.S.	28 MAY 1872	Unknown
598	Unknown	14d	W	U.S.	14 MAY 1872	Unknown
597	Unknown	1y	W	U.S.	02 MAY 1872	Washington
597	Unknown	1y	C	D.C.	02 MAY 1872	Washington
545	Unknown	3m	W	D.C.	16 NOV 1871	Washington
533	Unknown	71y	W	D.C.	20 AUG 1871	Washington
524	Unknown	1y	W	D.C.	25 JUN 1871	Washington
522	Unknown	1h	W	D.C.	10 JUN 1871	Washington
518	Unknown	5y	W	D.C.	08 MAY 1871	Washington
377	Unknown		C		18 FEB 1869	Washington Asylum
405	Unknown		C	D.C.	12 JUL 1869	Washington Asylum
392	Unknown		W		17 MAY 1869	Washington Asylum
073	Unknown		C	unk.	09 MAR 1857	Washington Asylum
335b	Unknown	1d	W		09 JUL 1868	Washington Asylum
335b	Unknown	7d	W		06 JUL 1868	Washington Asylum
335b	Unknown	1d	C		09 JUL 1868	Washington Asylum
335b	Unknown	1d	W		07 JUL 1868	Washington Asylum
393	Unknown		C		31 MAY 1869	Washington Asylum
393	Unknown		C	D.C.	25 MAY 1869	Washington Asylum
377	Unknown		C	D.C.	18 FEB 1869	Washington Asylum
393	Unknown		W	D.C.	24 MAY 1869	Washington Asylum
335a	Unknown (foundling)				17 JUL 1868	Washington Asylum
135	Unknown (male), laborer	40y	W	Ire.	17 DEC 1858	Washington Asylum
335b	Unknown Child				14 JUL 1868	Washington Asylum
025	Unknown Child found in canal				12 SEP 1855	Alms House
616	Unknown Infant		W		— JUL 1872	
708	Unknown Infant		C		08 JUL 1873	
696	Unknown Infant		W	D.C.	28 JUN 1873	
662	Unknown Infant		W		20 JAN 1873	
669	Unknown Infant			U.S.	05 FEB 1873	
727	Unknown Infant		B	U.S.	31 OCT 1873	

District of Columbia Interments (Index to Deaths), 1855-1874

Page	Name	Age	Race	Birth	Death Date	Burial Ground
683	Unknown Infant		W		— APR 1873	
726	Unknown Infant				25 OCT 1873	
676	Unknown Infant				27 MAR 1873	
683	Unknown Infant				— APR 1873	
683	Unknown Infant	P.B.	W		— APR 1873	
683	Unknown Infant		C	U.S.	30 APR 1873	
683	Unknown Infant		C	U.S.	— APR 1873	
777a	Unknown Infant		W	U.S.	— JUN 1874	
738	Unknown Infant		C	U.S.	22 DEC 1873	
756	Unknown Infant	2m	C	U.S.	25 MAR 1874	
769	Unknown Infant		C	U.S.	14 MAY 1874	
209	Unknown Infant	2m	C		10 JAN 1866	Alms House
769	Unknown Infant	P.B.	C	U.S.	08 MAY 1874	
745	Unknown Infant	P.B.	C	U.S.	29 JAN 1874	
750	Unknown Infant			U.S.	14 FEB 1874	
769	Unknown Infant	P.B.	C	U.S.	06 MAY 1874	
769	Unknown Infant		W	U.S.	16 MAY 1874	
769	Unknown Infant		W	U.S.	11 MAY 1874	
732	Unknown Infant	P.B.	W	U.S.	30 NOV 1873	
755	Unknown Infant		C	U.S.	21 MAR 1874	Ebenezer
755	Unknown Infant	1m	C	U.S.	21 MAR 1874	Washington Asylum
025	Unknown Infant found in canal		C		22 SEP 1855	Alms House
374	Unknown Laborer	35y	W	Ire.	11 FEB 1869	Congressional
518	Unknown Laborer	55y	C	Va.	12 MAY 1871	Ebenezer
713	Unknown Male	5d	C	Md.	23 AUG 1873	
033	Unknown Male Child				06 JAN 1856	
735	Unknown Male, laborer		C	U.S.	10 DEC 1873	Glenwood
708	Unknown Man	20y	C	Md.	31 JUL 1873	
769	Unknown Man	30y	W	U.S.	15 MAY 1874	
661	Unsworth, Jno. B., bar tender	40y	W	U.S.	30 JAN 1873	Washington Asylum
694	Upperman, Jennie J.	8m	W	D.C.	13 JUN 1873	Rock Creek
293	Upperman, [blank]	8m	W	D.C.*	06 MAR 1868	Oak Hill
057	Upshur, Augustin	1y	C	D.C.	05 SEP 1856	Foundry
311	Upshur, Caroline		C		c.12 APR 1868	Alms House
084	Upshur, Mr., servant of	84y	C		24 JUL 1857	Young Mens
430	Upson, Elbridge, clerk Treas.	53y	W	Conn.	25 DEC 1869	Conn.
174	Upsure, William, laborer	75y	C	Md.	12 MAR 1860	Harmony
086	Upton, Helen Augusta	16y	W	Va.	06 AUG 1857	Congressional
022	Upton, Mary	18y	W	Va.	28 AUG 1855	Congressional
227	Uray, Clara	30y	W	Pa.	02 JUL 1866	Mt. Olivet
636	Urell, T.E., clerk	32y	W	Ire.	24 NOV 1872	
670	Usher, Wm.	2y	C	U.S.	01 FEB 1873	Small Pox*
445	Usherman, Henry, r.r. conductor	37y	W	Md.	19 MAR 1870	Mt. Olivet
314	Ute-sin-male-cum, Chief	75y	I		25 MAY 1868	Congressional
083	Utenmhule, [blank]	3m	W	D.C.	11 JUL 1857	Congressional

Page	Name	Age	Race	Birth	Death Date	Burial Ground
V						
535	Vagle, Michael, laborer	69y	W	Ire.	07 SEP 1871	Mt. Olivet
003	Valentine, Danl.	60y	W	Ire.	25 FEB 1855	
169	Valentine, William, hackman	35y	C	U.S.	15 JAN 1860	Harmony
734	Valk, Ada	2d	W	U.S.	08 DEC 1873	
544	Valle, Margret	89y			10 NOV 1871	St. Marys
300	Van Arsdale, Isaac F.	20y	W	D.C.	07 MAR 1868	Glenwood
605	Van Arsdale, John, pressman	26y	W	U.S.	08 JUN 1872	Asylum
606	Van Arsdale, John, printer	26y	W	N.J.	06 JUN 1872	Congressional
246	Van Beek, Margaret	31y	W	N.J.	07 DEC 1866	N.J.
471	Van Burghen, M.C.	65y	W	Belg.	13 AUG 1870	German Catholic
597	Van Buskirk, Andrew, waterman	72y	W	U.S.	18 MAY 1872	Congressional*
270	Van Camp, Kate L.	1y	W	D.C.	14 AUG 1867	Glenwood
270	Van Camp, M. Amanda	21y	W	N.Y.	16 AUG 1867	Glenwood
542	Van Hake, Wm., signal officer	29y	W	Ger.	22 OCT 1871	
003	Van Hyppel, [blank]	2m	W	D.C.	01 FEB 1855	Oak Hill
236	Van Leer, George	1m	W	D.C.	23 SEP 1866	Mt. Olivet
476	Van Ness, Saml., gentleman	64y	W	Amer.	14 SEP 1870	N.J.
264	Van Reswick, Bertie	7d	W	D.C.	08 JUL 1867	Congressional
212	Van Reswick, Joseph, engineer	45y	W	Va.	19 FEB 1866	
325	Van Riswick, John	1y	W	D.C.	20 JUL 1868	Congressional
534	Van Riswick, Ruth	71y	W	N.Y.	29 AUG 1871	Congressional*
590	Van Scriver, John	11d	W	D.C.	05 APR 1872	Congressional
177	Van Slyke, Helen I.	4y	W		16 APR 1860	Foundry
477	Van Tassel, Horace Y., music tea.	20y	W	N.Y.	25 SEP 1870	Congressional
506	Van Valkenburgh, Albert A.	29y	W	N.Y.	25 FEB 1871	N.Y.
742	Van Vleck, Mary C.	8d	W	U.S.	17 JAN 1874	Glenwood
741	Van Vlick, Emily C.	36y	W	U.S.	14 JAN 1874	Glenwood
778	Van Wyck, Alfred	6m	W	U.S.	24 JUN 1874	
768	Vanaman, Ana	64y	W	U.S.	11 MAY 1874	Holyrood
743	Vanarnum, Jacob B.	85y	W	U.S.	23 JAN 1874	Petersburg, Va.
191	Vanarsdale, Philip H., huckster	40y	W	N.J.	14 OCT 1860	Glenwood
602	Vanbuskirk, Andrew, watchman	72y	W	U.S.	— MAY 1872	Congressional
625	Vance, Carrie	2y	W	U.S.	21 SEP 1872	
553	Vance, Robert, clerk	35y	W	Ire.	10 JAN 1872	Congressional*
258	Vanderford, Joseph	3m	W	D.C.	15 APR 1867	Mt. Olivet
586	Vanderhold, [blank]		W	U.S.	14 MAR 1872	
740	Vanderlock, Ernest, civil engr.	37y	W	Ger.	03 JAN 1874	Congressional*
470	Vanderpool, Alice	1y	W		19 AUG 1870	Mt. Olivet
197	Vandever, [blank]		W		02 JAN 1861	Philadelphia, Pa.
712	Vanhorn, M.C.	13m	W	D.C.	18 AUG 1873	Glenwood
327	Vanlindenburg, William H.	7m	W	D.C.	15 JUL 1868	Baltimore Co., Md.
554	Vanzandt, Wm. C., student	17y	W	D.C.	14 JAN 1872	Oak Hill
130	Vanzant, [blank]	6m	W	D.C.	02 OCT 1858	Oak Hill
154	Varden, Richard, clerk	52y	W	Va.	16 JUL 1859	Congressional
526	Vardory, John	4m	C	D.C.	04 JUL 1871	Ebenezer
122	Varnell, Naomi E.	2y	W	D.C.	19 JUL 1858	Glenwood
019	Varnell, Sarah G.	1y	W	D.C.	07 AUG 1855	Glenwood
451	Vashon, Olive Howard	1y	C		19 APR 1870	Harmony
515	Vast, Fred.	1m	W	D.C.	05 MAR 1871	Union
626	Vaughn, Jas.	27y	W	U.S.	19 SEP 1872	
681	Veihmeyer, Elizabeth	3y	W	U.S.	18 APR 1873	Glenwood
267	Veihmyer, Albert	17d	W	D.C.	18 JUL 1867	
383	Veikmeyer, Mary Ann	30y	W	Md.	06 MAR 1869	Glenwood
317	Veill, Mr., child of	7m	W		23 JUN 1868	St. Aloysius
442	Veing, Hattie	21d	C		23 FEB 1870	Washington Asylum
333	Veit, Mr., child of	7m	W		14 JUL 1868	St. Aloysius
548	Velams, Laura	3y	W	D.C.	15 DEC 1871	Methodist

District of Columbia Interments (Index to Deaths), 1855-1874

Page	Name	Age	Race	Birth	Death Date	Burial Ground
681	Vella, John, soldier	71y	W	Fra.	18 APR 1873	Prospect Hill
140	Venable, Cordelia	4y	W	D.C.	05 FEB 1859	Methodist
163	Venable, George, clerk	58y	W	D.C.	23 OCT 1859	Congressional
731	Venable, Wm. S., tinner	56y	W	U.S.	19 NOV 1873	Congressional*
342	Vergas, Letty	1y	C	D.C.	10 AUG 1868	Young Mens
143	Vermilion, Mary	61y	W	Md.	12 MAR 1859	Congressional
718	Vermillion, Annie M.	41y	W	Md.	14 SEP 1873	Congressional*
465	Vermillion, Chas. A.	1y	W		23 JUL 1870	Congressional
121	Vermillion, Rosena	22y	W	Md.	17 JUL 1858	Congressional
097	Vermillion, [blank]	5y	W	D.C.	25 NOV 1857	Holmead
597	Vernatic, Henrietta	66y	C	U.S.	23 MAY 1872	Washington
506	Vernon, Elizabeth H.	59y	W		24 FEB 1871	Congressional
439	Vernon, Franklin Pierce	16y	W		27 FEB 1870	Congressional
053	Vernon, John B.	1m	W	Va.	28 AUG 1856	Washington Asylum
463	Vernon, Maria C.	78y	W		04 JUL 1870	Oak Hill
444	Vernon, Ralph		W		15 MAR 1870	Congressional
023	Vessey, Margaret	25y	W	Eng.	16 SEP 1855	Oak Hill
666	Vessey, Ruth Gertrude	19m	W	U.S.	02 FEB 1873	Oak Hill
761	Vette, George L., printer	69y	W	Ger.	15 APR 1874	
356	Vibking, Willie	1y	W	D.C.	11 OCT 1868	Prospect Hill
284	Vickers, D., child of	Still			25 NOV 1867	Mt. Olivet
306	Viehmeyer, Daniel	78y	W	Eur.	22 APR 1868	Glenwood
121	Vierbucken, Christian	7m	W	D.C.	14 JUL 1858	Washington
306	Vigel, Emily	54y	C	Va.	09 APR 1868	Young Mens
079	Vigel, George	4y	C		— JUN 1857	Western
186	Vigel, John	2y	C	D.C.	29 JUL 1860	Foundry
079	Vigel, Mariah	28y	C	Va.*	02 JUN 1857	Foundry
404	Vigl, Susan Anne	2y	C		23 JUL 1869	
074	Vigrel, Henry	85y	C	Md.	22 MAR 1857	Young Mens
117	Vigsel, Edward	4y	C	D.C.	25 JUN 1858	Young Mens
696	Viland, Morgan, watchman	28y	W	Ire.	09 JUN 1873	Holyrood
688	Vincent, Joseph	13y	C	U.S.	13 MAY 1873	
694	Vincent, Nellie J.	7m	W	D.C.	24 JUN 1873	
596	Vineberger, Marg.	86y	W	U.S.	12 APR 1872	Glenwood
537	Virginia, Caroline				22 SEP 1871	
541	Virgins, Elisabeth	9m	C	D.C.	14 OCT 1871	
500	Vitall, Amanda	36y	C		08 JAN 1871	Harmony
244	Vivans, Louis	74y	W	Fra.	15 NOV 1866	Mt. Olivet*
749	Vodray, Millie	2y	C	U.S.	12 FEB 1874	Harmony
447	Vogel, Charlie	10m	W		16 MAR 1870	Glenwood
543	Vogel, Christian	1y	W	D.C.	26 OCT 1871	Glenwood
376	Vogel, Jacob, infant of	Still	W		16 FEB 1869	Prospect Hill
768	Vogt, Margaretha D.S.	10d	W	U.S.	22 MAY 1874	Prospect Hill
548	Vogues, Lenhort, mechanic	26y	W	Ger.	15 DEC 1871	Prospect Hill
366	Voigt, Emil	6y	W	D.C.	12 DEC 1868	German Catholic
697	Voigt, John	5m	W	U.S.	30 JUN 1873	St. Marys
067	Volger, Fridericke	66y	W	Ger.	31 DEC 1856	Glenwood
450	Volkert, Chas. Herman	11m	W		20 APR 1870	Prospect Hill
768	Volkmann, Christine	64y	W	Ger.	02 MAY 1874	Prospect Hill
356	Volland, Anna Mary	1y	W	D.C.	04 OCT 1868	Prospect Hill
522	Volland, Otto Chas.	1y	W	U.S.	11 JUN 1871	Prospect Hill
361	Voltz, Jas., Mr., infant of	Still	W		23 NOV 1868	
532	Von DeHeitz, Caroline	1y	W	D.C.	14 AUG 1871	Prospect Hill
695	Von Gluemer, Louise	51y	W	Prus.	20 JUN 1873	Glenwood
032	Von Herringen, Ernest, music tea.	55y	W	Prus.	24 DEC 1855	Congressional
453	Von Kammerhueber, J.W., arch.	45y	W	Bav.	27 MAY 1870	Congressional
018	Von, Webster	4m	C	D.C.	10 AUG 1855	Young Mens
339	Vondelher, Ann	1y	W	D.C.	11 AUG 1868	Mt. Olivet

District of Columbia Interments (Index to Deaths), 1855-1874

Page	Name	Age	Race	Birth	Death Date	Burial Ground
593	Vondelher, [blank]	1d	W	U.S.	11 APR 1872	
041	Vonderlehr, Cathe.	56y	W	Ger.	06 APR 1856	St. Patricks
755	Vose, Bertha M.	13y	W	U.S.	27 MAR 1874	Bangor, Me.
220	Voss, Lucy	30y	W	D.C.	01 MAY 1866	Oak Hill
070	Voss, Lucy A.	25y	W	D.C.	06 FEB 1857	Oak Hill
090	Voss, William L., watch maker	21y	W	Ger.	09 SEP 1857	Oak Hill
029	Vowlings, Hanorah	2y	W	D.C.	07 NOV 1855	St. Patricks

District of Columbia Interments (Index to Deaths), 1855-1874

Page	Name	Age	Race	Birth	Death Date	Burial Ground
W						
033	Wach, Lizette	30y	W	Ger.	05 JAN 1856	Asylum
241	Wachsmuth, Mrs.	62y	W	Rus.	21 OCT 1866	Prospect Hill
087	Wackenfil, John	6m	W	D.C.	14 AUG 1857	Catholic
031	Wade, Aldy B.	3y			06 DEC 1855	Oak Hill
475	Wade, Emily, servant	23y	C	Va.	11 SEP 1870	Freedmen's Hospital
062	Wade, Georgiana	34y	W		09 NOV 1856	Oak Hill
139	Wade, John C.	38y	W		17 JAN 1859	
047	Wade, John T.T.	11y	W	D.C.	28 JUN 1856	Oak Hill
663	Wade, Laura	16y	C	U.S.	27 JAN 1873	Small Pox
162	Wade, Mary	43y	C	Va.	29 SEP 1859	Harmony
465	Wade, Sayles	2m	C	D.C.	17 JUL 1870	Young Mens
061	Waer, [blank]	42y	C	Md.	30 OCT 1856	St. Peters
314	Waggoner, Emma Lester	8m	W	D.C.	01 MAY 1868	Congressional
039	Wagler, Joseph C., music printer		W	D.C.	04 MAR 1856	St. Matthews
128	Wagner, Anton	2d	W	D.C.	19 SEP 1858	German Catholic
454	Wagner, Barbara	60y	W	Ger.	03 MAY 1870	German Catholic
637	Wagner, Barbara	7y	W	U.S.	01 NOV 1872	St. Marys
344	Wagner, Catharina	33y	W	Ger.	30 AUG 1868	Prospect Hill
021	Wagner, Emma T.	1y	W		24 AUG 1855	Oak Hill
713	Wagner, Fredk., musician	58y	W	Ger.	23 AUG 1873	
477	Wagner, John G.	3y	W	D.C.	06 SEP 1870	Prospect Hill
534	Wagner, Margret A.E.	1y	W	D.C.	31 AUG 1871	
601	Wagner, Thomas, laborer	45y	C	U.S.	24 MAY 1872	Young Mens
232	Wagner, Wm. E.	3y	W	D.C.	24 AUG 1866	Oak Hill
642	Wahler, Chas.	10d	W	U.S.	05 DEC 1872	Mt. Olivet
090	Wailes, Isaac H.	11m	W	D.C.	05 SEP 1857	Glenwood
004	Wailes, Isaac H., guard	56y	W	Md.	15 MAR 1855	Glenwood
203	Wailes, S.C., Mrs.	28y	W	D.C.	25 MAY 1861	Glenwood
506	Waite, Edward, printer	56y	W	N.Y.	01 FEB 1871	Congressional
010	Waite, Henry Clay	11m	W	D.C.	10 JUN 1855	Congressional
292	Wakefield, Jane W.	72y	W		26 JAN 1868	Congressional
553	Wakes, Minetta I.	6y	W	U.S.	11 JAN 1872	Washington
465	Walas, Walter	10m	C	D.C.	16 JUL 1870	Young Mens
352	Walber, B.J.	1y	W	D.C.	03 SEP 1868	Holmead
744	Walbridge, Jane M.	56y	W	U.S.	29 JAN 1874	Glenwood
010	Walch, Mrs.		W		— JUN 1855	Bording Town, N.J.
301	Walch, Thomas L.	1m	C	U.S.	02 MAR 1868	Freedmen's Hospital
496	Waldo, Martha Bacon	2y	W	D.C.	31 DEC 1870	Glenwood
668	Waldon, Annie	30y	W	U.S.	24 FEB 1873	Washington Asylum
386	Waldon, William	2m	C	D.C.	10 APR 1869	Mt. Olivet
786	Waldron, Margaret, domestic	75y	W	Ire.	22 JUL 1874	Mt. Olivet
252	Wale, Mary	65y	W	Ire.	23 FEB 1867	Mt. Olivet
616	Waley, Conrad	16m	W	U.S.	18 JUL 1872	
463	Waley, Ida	1y	W	D.C.	19 JUL 1870	German Catholic
331	Walkens, Susanna	24y			18 JUL 1868	Glenwood
366	Walker, Alfred A.	21m	W	Amer.	31 DEC 1868	Glenwood
351	Walker, Andrew	1y	C	D.C.	12 SEP 1868	Ebenezer
530	Walker, Ann, servant	26y	C	Va.	31 JUL 1871	Washington
272	Walker, Benj.	1y	W	D.C.	04 AUG 1867	Congressional
550	Walker, Bertha	5y	W	D.C.	31 DEC 1871	Prospect Hill
375	Walker, Caroline C., Mrs.	39y	W	Va.	20 FEB 1869	Oak Hill
370	Walker, Carrie Lee	3y	W	D.C.	20 JAN 1869	Oak Hill
740	Walker, Catherine S.	40y	W	Ire.	02 JAN 1874	Mt. Olivet
543	Walker, Chas. E.	1y	W	D.C.	26 OCT 1871	Washington
489	Walker, Clara	30y	C	Va.	06 NOV 1870	Ebenezer
538	Walker, Cornelia	3m	W	D.C.	24 SEP 1871	Prospect Hill
547	Walker, Edw. Howard	4m	W	D.C.	03 DEC 1871	Congressional

Page	Name	Age	Race	Birth	Death Date	Burial Ground
029	Walker, Elizabeth	43y	W	Ger.	09 NOV 1855	
633	Walker, Elizabeth	25y	C	U.S.	22 OCT 1872	
121	Walker, Eugene M.	1y	W	Ohio	16 JUL 1858	Congressional
778	Walker, Fannie	3m	W	U.S.	28 JUN 1874	Glenwood
029	Walker, Flora	94y	C	Md.	20 NOV 1855	Foundry
449	Walker, George H., policeman	51y	W	Va.	01 APR 1870	Congressional
743	Walker, George, laborer	24y	C	U.S.	27 JAN 1874	Ebenezer
547	Walker, Harry, laborer	28y		Va.	04 DEC 1871	
427	Walker, Henry, whitewasher	70y	C	Md.	29 NOV 1869	
401	Walker, J.	10m	C		16 JUL 1869	Young Mens
405	Walker, J.	10m	C		26 JUL 1869	Young Mens
635	Walker, Jacob	42y	C	U.S.	30 NOV 1872	Small Pox
438	Walker, James C.	38y	W		08 JAN 1870	
434	Walker, James C.	38y	W		08 JAN 1870	Congressional
235	Walker, Jennie	53y	W	Mass.	22 SEP 1866	Congressional
068	Walker, John, butcher	48y	W		13 JAN 1857	Glenwood
039	Walker, John, farmer		W		15 MAR 1856	Piscataway, Md.
552	Walker, Josephine	28y	W	Mich.	02 JAN 1872	Prospect Hill
469	Walker, Josephine, scholar	19y	W	Pa.	10 AUG 1870	Oak Hill
637	Walker, Kate E.	19m	W	U.S.	12 NOV 1872	Glenwood
733	Walker, Louis	4m	C	U.S.	21 NOV 1873	
256	Walker, Louis	1y	C	D.C.	14 MAR 1867	Young Mens
479	Walker, Lucy A.	2y	C	Va.	03 SEP 1870	Washington Asylum
499	Walker, M.M.	2y	W	D.C.	19 JAN 1871	Congressional
389	Walker, Maria	3d	C	D.C.	06 APR 1869	Washington Asylum
725	Walker, Maria F.	30y	W	U.S.	22 OCT 1873	Glenwood
297	Walker, Martha	49y	W	Pa.	26 FEB 1868	Oak Hill
427	Walker, Martha	48y	C	Va.	23 NOV 1869	Washington Asylum
385	Walker, Martha	6m	C		06 APR 1869	Young Mens
156	Walker, Mary	47y	W	Md.	19 JUL 1859	Congressional
197	Walker, Mary	63y	W	Md.	27 JAN 1861	Mt. Olivet
018	Walker, Mary Ann	33y	W	Md.	30 AUG 1855	Congressional
660	Walker, Mary B.	65y	W	U.S.	19 JAN 1873	Oak Hill
042	Walker, Mary Ellen	23y	W	Md.	17 APR 1856	Methodist
442	Walker, Mary Jane	9m	C		22 FEB 1870	Washington Asylum
289	Walker, Mary, prostitute	43y	W	Va.	14 JAN 1868	Alms House
604	Walker, Netty	7m	C	D.C.	03 JUN 1872	Ebenezer
250	Walker, Philip	4m	C		16 JAN 1867	Young Mens
280	Walker, Richard		C		04 OCT 1867	Freedmen's Hospital
426	Walker, Robert J., Hon., lawyer	68y	W	Pa.	11 NOV 1869	Oak Hill
689	Walker, Rosa	32y	C	U.S.	29 MAY 1873	
415	Walker, Samuel, laborer	45y	W	Ire.	23 SEP 1869	
187	Walker, Sarah, chlid of	Still	C	D.C.	03 AUG 1860	Washington Asylum
429	Walker, Thomas Claude	3m	W		24 DEC 1869	Congressional
673	Walker, Thos.	2y	W	U.S.	10 MAR 1873	Congressional
516	Walker, Thos. T.	7m	W	U.S.	06 MAR 1871	Congressional
756	Walker, William T.	2y	W	U.S.	25 MAR 1874	
778	Walker, Wm. H., merchant	59y	W	U.S.	22 JUN 1874	Glenwood
485	Walker, Wm. J.	1y	C	D.C.	28 OCT 1870	Western
261	Walker, [blank]	6y	W	D.C.	19 MAY 1867	Congressional
011	Walker, [blank]	10m	W	D.C.	03 JUN 1855	Presbyterian
262	Walkins, Anna	5m	C	D.C.	28 JUN 1867	
226	Walkins, Sarah	3m	C	D.C.	25 JUN 1866	Alexandria, Va.
744	Wall, Henry	1y	W	U.S.	30 JAN 1874	
300	Wall, Henry	2m	C	D.C.	22 MAR 1868	Alms House
135	Wall, Mary A.	75y	W		08 DEC 1858	Glenwood
310	Wall, Michael	50y	W		c.16 APR 1868	Mt. Olivet
507	Wall, [blank]	36y	W	Md.	14 FEB 1871	Mt. Olivet

Page	Name	Age	Race	Birth	Death Date	Burial Ground
661	Wallace, Annie C.	27y	W	U.S.	27 JAN 1873	Mt. Olivet
070	Wallace, Charles, slave	4y	C	D.C.	06 FEB 1857	Western
182	Wallace, Chas. Douglass	1y	W	D.C.	29 JUN 1860	Glenwood
350	Wallace, Effie	8d	C	D.C.	21 SEP 1868	Young Mens
375	Wallace, Frances Ella	20y	W	Mass.	08 FEB 1869	Glenwood
616	Wallace, Geo. W., laborer	35y	C	U.S.	23 JUL 1872	
458	Wallace, George	10m	C	D.C.	29 JUN 1870	Potters Field
403	Wallace, Georgianna	30y	C		22 JUL 1869	Harmony
004	Wallace, H. Ann	28d	C	D.C.	10 MAR 1855	Harmony
704	Wallace, Henry		C		11 JUL 1873	Beckett's
246	Wallace, Joseph H.		C		15 DEC 1866	Harmony
674	Wallace, Julius	35y	C	U.S.	18 MAR 1873	
412	Wallace, Louisa	6d	C	D.C.	04 AUG 1869	Washington Asylum
744	Wallace, Mariah, servant	65y	C	U.S.	10 JAN 1874	
778	Wallace, Mary, Mrs.	90y	W	U.S.	12 JUN 1874	Congressional
778	Wallace, Maud M.	2y	W	U.S.	22 JUN 1874	Glenwood
322	Wallace, Mike	20y	C	S.C.	13 JUN 1868	Freedmen's Hospital
628	Wallace, R., sailor	50y	W	Ire.	12 SEP 1872	
366	Wallace, Richard	7m	B	Amer.	24 DEC 1868	Ebenezer
743	Wallace, Rose	3y	W	U.S.	25 JAN 1874	Glenwood
342	Wallace, Rose	8m	C	D.C.	15 AUG 1868	Young Mens
741	Wallace, Samuel, laborer	107y	C	U.S.	11 JAN 1874	Washington Asylum
302	Wallace, Susie	10m	C	D.C.	10 MAR 1868	Ebenezer
642	Wallace, Thos.	89y	W	U.S.	04 DEC 1872	Congressional
554	Wallace, Walter	4y	W	D.C.	17 JAN 1872	
555	Wallace, Walter, bookbinder	40y	W	U.S.	22 JAN 1872	
604	Wallace, Wm.	2m	C	D.C.	05 JUN 1872	Ebenezer
609	Wallace, Wm. B.	1y	W	U.S.	29 JUN 1872	
786	Wallace, Wm. H.	14y	C	U.S.	12 JUL 1874	Mt. Pleasant
523	Wallace, Wm. Henson	2m	W	D.C.	17 JUN 1871	Congressional*
147	Wallace, Wm. Thomas	6m	W	D.C.	27 APR 1859	Congressional
515	Wallach, Anna D.	23y	W	D.C.	17 MAR 1871	Congressional
557	Wallach, Chas. S., lawyer	55y	W	D.C.	03 FEB 1872	Congressional
778	Walleck, Mary Jane	45y	W	U.S.	02 JUN 1874	Glenwood
712	Wallen, Wm. Henry	8y	C	Va.	18 AUG 1873	Beckett's
231	Waller, James	11m	W	D.C.	18 AUG 1866	Mt. Olivet
756	Waller, Jerome	63y	W	Prus.	29 MAR 1874	
706	Waller, Marcellus, laborer	25y	C	Va.	29 JUL 1873	Beckett's
067	Waller, Wliliam, laborer	66y	W	Va.	31 DEC 1856	Holmead
258	Wallin, May	6m	W	Ill.	15 APR 1867	Chicago, Ill.
768	Walling, Blanche	21d	W	U.S.	07 MAY 1874	Glenwood
355	Walling, Joseph C.	2y	W		26 OCT 1868	Mt. Olivet
419	Walling, Mary	Still	W		28 OCT 1869	Glenwood
253	Wallingsford, Amelia	88y	W		07 FEB 1867	Congressional
499	Wallingsford, M., claim agent	35y	W	D.C.	19 JAN 1871	Congressional
548	Wallingsford, Malcolm	4m	W	D.C.	09 DEC 1871	Congressional*
278	Wallingsford, Wash., shoemaker	52y	W		01 OCT 1867	Oak Hill
392	Wallis, Annie	2y	C	D.C.	19 MAY 1869	Young Mens
255	Wallis, J.R., sailor	38y	W	Va.	08 MAR 1867	Alexandria, Va.
382	Wallis, Josephine	11m	C		03 MAR 1869	Young Mens
547	Walllach, Wm. D., editor	59y	W	Md.	04 DEC 1871	Congressional
762	Walls, Ann Pauline	2m	W	U.S.	02 APR 1874	
530	Walls, Elisabeth	38y		Md.	31 JUL 1871	Ebenezer
607	Walls, John	4y	C	D.C.	20 JUN 1872	Eastern
020	Walls, [blank]	9m	W	D.C.	04 AUG 1855	St. Patricks
341	Walmsley, Aaron, private marine	68y	W	Pa.	11 AUG 1868	Congressional
227	Walmsley, Emma E.	3y	W	D.C.	08 JUL 1866	Glenwood
103	Walmsley, Frank	28y	W	Md.	09 JAN 1858	St. Patricks

Page	Name	Age	Race	Birth	Death Date	Burial Ground
636	Walpole, Edward, printer	25y	W	Ire.	16 NOV 1872	
266	Walsh, Albert	15y	W	D.C.	18 JUL 1867	Mt. Olivet
730	Walsh, Charles, seaman	47y	W	For.	17 NOV 1873	
133	Walsh, Daniel, clerk	40y	W	Ire.	18 NOV 1858	St. Peters
618	Walsh, Felix A.	23m	W	U.S.	14 AUG 1872	
548	Walsh, James	3y	W	D.C.	12 DEC 1871	Mt. Olivet
261	Walsh, John, laborer	38y	W	Ire.	23 MAY 1867	Baltimore, Md.
142	Walsh, Joseph	3y	W		26 FEB 1859	Congressional
658	Walsh, Mary Elizabeth	7y	W	U.S.	05 JAN 1873	Mt. Olivet
273	Walsh, Michael, merchant	51y	W	Ire.	23 SEP 1867	Mt. Olivet
234	Walsh, Thomas, laborer	45y	W	Ire.	03 SEP 1866	Mt. Olivet
266	Walstern, Claria Anna	1y	W	D.C.	08 JUL 1867	Glenwood
769	Walston, Infant	1d	C	U.S.	19 MAY 1874	Holyrood
323	Walter, Alice E.	5m	W	Amer.	27 JUL 1868	Mt. Olivet
636	Walter, Cath.	52y	W	U.S.	06 NOV 1872	
421	Walter, Edward	1y	W		23 OCT 1869	German Catholic
376	Walter, Henry W.	2y	W		22 FEB 1869	Prospect Hill
661	Walter, Lizzie	9d	W	U.S.	29 JAN 1873	German
756	Walter, Mary	21d	W	U.S.	31 MAR 1874	
182	Walter, Mary A.	58y	W	Ger.	24 JUN 1860	German Catholic
073	Walter, Philip E.F.	3y	W	D.C.	06 MAR 1857	St. Patricks
434	Walter, Philopena	34y	W		02 JAN 1870	Congressional
457	Walter, Robert A., musician	23y	W	D.C.	29 JUN 1870	Congressional
230	Walter, Rosa	2y	W	D.C.	28 JUL 1866	Prospect Hill
532	Walter, Rosalia	1y	W	D.C.	14 AUG 1871	St. Marys
223	Walter, William, asst. engineer	30y	W	Ire.	08 JUN 1866	Mt. Olivet*
608	Walter, Wm.	2m	W	D.C.	12 JUN 1872	
025	Walter, Wm.	27y	W	Ger.	12 SEP 1855	German
157	Walters, Charles	1m	C	D.C.	09 AUG 1859	Young Mens
725	Walters, Elizabeth	57y	W	Ire.	22 OCT 1873	Mt. Olivet
786	Walters, Jno. & Eliza, infant of		C	U.S.	12 JUL 1874	
159	Walters, L. Durbin, Rev.	27y	W	D.C.	24 AUG 1859	Glenwood
621	Walters, Lullin	15m	W	U.S.	03 AUG 1872	Glenwood
296	Walters, Sarah	45y	C	Va.	29 FEB 1868	Young Mens
355	Walton, Susie M.	8m	W	D.C.	13 OCT 1868	Congressional
161	Wander, Paul Henry	1y	W	D.C.	06 SEP 1859	German Catholic
743	Wane, Alexander, laborer	62y	C	U.S.	24 JAN 1874	Mt. Pleasant
191	Waner, Lydia	88y	W	Conn.	23 OCT 1860	Troy, N.Y.
430	Wannall, J., Mr., infant of	5m	W		23 DEC 1869	Glenwood
271	Wannall, Jennie	10m	W	D.C.	07 AUG 1867	Glenwood
161	Wannell, Emma	18y	W	Md.	06 SEP 1859	Congressional
550	Wannell, Joseph	55y	W	D.C.	31 DEC 1871	Glenwood
483	Wanton, John S., clerk	23y	W	Mo.	05 OCT 1870	Congressional
658	Wanton, Wm. R., clerk	39y	W	U.S.	09 JAN 1873	Congressional
533	Wanzer, Elisabeth	3d	C	D.C.	26 AUG 1871	Young Mens
524	Wanzer, Sylvia	75y	C	Va.	21 JUN 1871	
581	Warbarre, Maria M.	75y	W	D.C.	16 FEB 1872	Oak Hill
329	Ward, Ann	78y	W	Eng.	18 JUL 1868	Oak Hill
053	Ward, Ann M.	8y	W	D.C.	27 AUG 1856	Congressional
645	Ward, Anna E.	4y	C	U.S.	27 DEC 1872	
393	Ward, Anne	24y	W	N.J.	02 MAY 1869	Washington Asylum
167	Ward, Carrie	6y	W	D.C.	02 DEC 1859	Congressional*
778	Ward, Carrie	5m	W	U.S.	24 JUN 1874	Congressional
007	Ward, Catharine J.	77y	W	Ire.	11 APR 1855	St. Matthews
240	Ward, Catherine	65y	W	Va.	28 OCT 1866	Alexandria, Va.
786	Ward, Clender	87y	W	U.S.	20 JUL 1874	Glenwood
599	Ward, Coltalt, laborer	42y	C	U.S.	20 MAY 1872	Ebenezer
608	Ward, Edw.	6m	C	D.C.	22 JUN 1872	

Page	Name	Age	Race	Birth	Death Date	Burial Ground
361	Ward, Elmer	7y	W	D.C.	17 NOV 1868	Glenwood
077	Ward, F.	60y	W	Ire.	13 MAY 1857	St. Patricks
749	Ward, George E.	2y	C	U.S.	26 FEB 1874	Mt. Pleasant
130	Ward, Inda May	2m	W	D.C.	12 OCT 1858	Glenwood
189	Ward, James	50y	W	Ire.	12 SEP 1860	Washington Asylum
718	Ward, Jno. B., lumberman	45y	W	D.C.	14 SEP 1873	Glenwood
235	Ward, John	10m	W	D.C.	18 SEP 1866	Mt. Olivet
690	Ward, John	30y	C	U.S.	02 MAY 1873	Small Pox
724	Ward, John O.	7m	W	D.C.	11 OCT 1873	Mt. Olivet
050	Ward, Joseph D., ex clerk	60y	W	N.C.	16 JUL 1856	Congressional
228	Ward, Joseph J., laborer		W	Ire.	17 JUL 1866	Mt. Olivet
588	Ward, Lizzie C.	30y	W	Pa.	25 MAR 1872	Pa.
105	Ward, Mary	30y	W	Ire.	21 FEB 1858	St. Patricks
143	Ward, Millard Dodd	1y	W	D.C.	15 MAR 1859	Congressional
786	Ward, Moses	2m	C	unk.	18 JUL 1874	Potters Field
215	Ward, Nancy	5y	C	D.C.	18 MAR 1866	Holmead
629	Ward, Penelope	34y	C	U.S.	11 OCT 1872	
255	Ward, Perry	40y	C		24 MAR 1867	Young Mens
062	Ward, Rachael	60y	C		18 NOV 1856	Western
635	Ward, Ralph	54y	C	U.S.	11 NOV 1872	Small Pox
428	Ward, Reuben, laborer	87y	C	Va.	23 NOV 1869	Washington Asylum
299	Ward, Revd. Ulysses, Mutual Fire	76y	W	Md.	30 MAR 1868	Glenwood
362	Ward, Robert	6m	C	D.C.	16 NOV 1868	Mt. Olivet
623	Ward, Robt.	52y	C	U.S.	29 AUG 1872	Catholic
221	Ward, Roy F.	11m	W	D.C.	18 MAY 1866	Harrisburg, Pa.
044	Ward, Samuel	1y	C	D.C.	12 MAY 1856	Navy Yard, Colored
203	Ward, Sarah L.	2y	W	D.C.	21 MAY 1861	Mt. Olivet
187	Ward, Thomas	8m	W	D.C.	13 AUG 1860	Rock Creek
627	Ward, W.H.	30y	W	U.S.	30 SEP 1872	Small Pox
050	Ward, William B.	12y	C	D.C.	17 JUL 1856	St. Patricks
263	Ward, William E., laborer	50y	W	Md.	20 JUN 1867	Glenwood
114	Ward, Wm. F.	2m	C	D.C.	28 MAY 1858	Young Mens
175	Ward, [blank]	Still	W	D.C.	17 MAR 1860	Md.
474	Warden, James	2y	C		27 AUG 1870	Washington Asylum
106	Warder, Anna E.	9y	W		26 FEB 1858	Glenwood
108	Warder, Florence	1y	W		25 MAR 1858	Glenwood
636	Warder, J.H.	2y	W	U.S.	26 NOV 1872	
105	Warder, Millard F.	7y	W		20 FEB 1858	Glenwood
105	Warder, Susan F.	11y	W		18 FEB 1858	Glenwood
112	Warder, Walter, merchant	53y	W	Va.	26 APR 1858	Congressional
016	Warder, [blank]	10m	W	D.C.	18 JUL 1855	Methodist
535	Wardwell Mary	25y	W	Ire.	04 SEP 1871	Mt. Olivet
634	Ware, Addison, clerk	70y	W	U.S.	12 OCT 1872	Congressional*
627	Ware, Chas.	3y	C	U.S.	26 SEP 1872	Small Pox
666	Ware, Cornelia	25y	C	U.S.	02 FEB 1873	Washington Asylum
769	Ware, Joseph A., lawyer	42y	W	U.S.	25 MAY 1874	Portland, Me.
301	Ware, Rose	40y	C	Va.	15 MAR 1868	Young Mens
235	Ware, Wm.	1y	C	D.C.	20 SEP 1866	Young Mens
719	Warfield, Carrie Isabel	11m	W	D.C.	15 SEP 1873	Congressional
633	Warfield, Emma	25y	C	U.S.	17 OCT 1872	
622	Warfield, Margaret	6m	C	U.S.	05 AUG 1872	
707	Warfield, Mary	9m	C	D.C.	21 JUL 1873	Beckett's
291	Warfield, William	3y	C	D.C.	05 JAN 1868	Western
268	Warham, Cora Liona	11m	W	D.C.	20 AUG 1867	Congressional
082	Waring, Ruth, cook	38y	C	Md.	06 JUL 1857	
786	Warmer, Benj. H.	10m	W	U.S.	24 JUL 1874	Methodist
436	Warmer, Eddy	4m	C		19 JAN 1870	Washington Asylum
786	Warmuth, Maggie A.	2y	W	U.S.	23 JUL 1874	Mt. Olivet*

Page	Name	Age	Race	Birth	Death Date	Burial Ground
629	Warnell, Mary A.	67y	W	U.S.	07 OCT 1872	
217	Warner, A.A., housekeeper	24y	W	Pa.	02 APR 1866	Philadelphia, Pa.
640	Warner, Benj. K.	24y	W	U.S.	24 DEC 1872	Small Pox*
090	Warner, Mary	87y	W		11 SEP 1857	Congressional
363	Warner, Mary L.		C	U.S.	27 NOV 1868	Washington Asylum
705	Warner, Mary W.	16m	W	D.C.	23 JUL 1873	
328	Warner, Rosa	1y	C	D.C.	22 JUL 1868	Western
177	Warner, Saml., child of	Still	W	D.C.	28 APR 1860	Congressional
343	Warner, Samuel	2y	C	D.C.	30 AUG 1868	
217	Warner, Sarah C.	3y	C	D.C.	03 APR 1866	Congressional
183	Warner, [blank]	34y	W	Md.	29 JUN 1860	Congressional
368	Warrell, Grace	9m	W		17 DEC 1868	Glenwood
762	Warren, Abraham, plasterer	63y	C	U.S.	11 APR 1874	
541	Warren, Columbus	4y	W	D.C.	13 OCT 1871	Congressional
138	Warren, Ellen	3m	W	D.C.	28 JAN 1859	Western
193	Warren, Emily	1y	W	D.C.	01 NOV 1860	Glenwood
350	Warren, Emily	1y	C	D.C.	18 SEP 1868	Young Mens
120	Warren, Emma G.	11m	W	D.C.	09 JUL 1858	Glenwood
264	Warren, Henry	28y	C	D.C.	15 JUL 1867	Harmony
769	Warren, James	6d	C	U.S.	27 MAY 1874	Mt. Olivet
427	Warren, John, laborer	72y	C	Md.	10 NOV 1869	Mt. Olivet
643	Warren, Lena, Mrs.	21y	W	U.S.	08 DEC 1872	Congressional
309	Warren, Louisa, nurse	78y	C	Md.	27 APR 1868	Harmony
364	Warren, Mrs. [Josephine]	30y	W	Tenn.	02 DEC 1868	Congressional*
515	Warren, Patrick K., Rev.	55y	W	Va.	12 MAR 1871	Congressional
456	Warren, Robert	4d	C	U.S.	11 JUN 1870	Young Mens
459	Warren, Robert	4d	C	U.S.	11 JUN 1870	Young Mens
220	Warren, Robert, huckster	39y	W	D.C.	06 MAY 1866	Glenwood
307	Warren, Thaddeus S., clerk	30y	W	Pa.	18 APR 1868	Gettysburgh, Pa.
218	Warren, W.L.	2d	W	D.C.	28 APR 1866	Holmead
316	Warren, Zach		C		c.16 MAY 1868	Alms House
055	Warren, [blank]	6d	W		06 AUG 1856	Western
021	Warren, [blank]	1y	C		08 AUG 1855	West
736	Warring, John P., farmer	62y	W	U.S.	17 DEC 1873	Mt. Olivet*
248	Warrington, Mary E.	42y	W	Md.	13 DEC 1866	Oak Hill
088	Warters, Sarah, cook	40y	W	Eng.	16 AUG 1857	Oak Hill
127	Warthington, Wm. B., printer	28y	W	Va.	02 SEP 1858	Glenwood
454	Washburn, Esther, servant	26y	C	Md.	21 MAY 1870	Washington Asylum
555	Washburn, John J.	10y	W	D.C.	22 JAN 1872	Congressional
449	Washburn, John Jay	11m	W		06 APR 1870	Congressional
662	Washburn, M., merchant	50y	W	U.S.	16 JAN 1873	
120	Washburn, Samuel	3d	W	D.C.	03 JUL 1858	St. Peters
786	Washington, Addry	10m	C	U.S.	11 JUL 1874	
544	Washington, Agnes	1y	C	D.C.	02 NOV 1871	
681	Washington, Allice	18y	C	U.S.	12 APR 1873	Harmony
631	Washington, Alx.	10y	C	U.S.	19 OCT 1872	
689	Washington, Anna	1m	C	U.S.	29 MAY 1873	
441	Washington, Armenia Augusta	10m	C		05 FEB 1870	Harmony
179	Washington, Catharine	60y	W	Ire.	03 MAY 1860	Mt. Olivet
426	Washington, Celia	60y	C	Va.	09 NOV 1869	Ebenezer
357	Washington, Charles	Still	B	D.C.	20 OCT 1868	Washington Asylum
437	Washington, Charlotte	19y	C	Va.	05 JAN 1870	Washington Asylum
030	Washington, Chs. H.	4m	C	D.C.	24 NOV 1855	Young Mens
670	Washington, Daniel	2y	C	U.S.	19 FEB 1873	Small Pox
225	Washington, Eleanor	1m	C	D.C.	18 JUN 1866	Harmony
478	Washington, Elizabeth	2y			02 SEP 1870	Ebenezer
141	Washington, Emma L.	2y	C	D.C.	24 FEB 1859	Foundry
333	Washington, Feitia	1y	C	D.C.	22 JUL 1868	Alms House

District of Columbia Interments (Index to Deaths), 1855-1874

Page	Name	Age	Race	Birth	Death Date	Burial Ground
335a	Washington, Felitia				22 JUL 1868	Washington Asylum
475	Washington, Frank, laborer	1y	C	Va.	18 SEP 1870	Freedmen's Hospital
291	Washington, Geo.		C		08 JAN 1868	Alms House
286	Washington, Geo.	2y	C		18 DEC 1867	Freedmen's Hospital
674	Washington, Geo. H.	1½m	C	U.S.	18 MAR 1873	
638	Washington, Geo., laborer	37y	C	U.S.	19 NOV 1872	Washington Asylum
063	Washington, George	16y	C	D.C.	21 NOV 1856	Foundry
283	Washington, George	2y	C		18 NOV 1867	Freedmen's Hospital
264	Washington, George	1y	C	D.C.	25 JUL 1867	Mt. Olivet
473	Washington, George	12y	C		24 AUG 1870	Mt. Olivet
363	Washington, George	2m	C	Conn.	27 NOV 1868	Washington Asylum
674	Washington, George	12y	C	U.S.	16 MAR 1873	Washington Asylum
673	Washington, George	4m	C	U.S.	02 MAR 1873	Washington Asylum
535	Washington, George	4y		D.C.	04 SEP 1871	Young Mens
378	Washington, George, laborer	30y	C	Md.	09 FEB 1869	Freedmen's Hospital
601	Washington, George, laborer	50y	C	U.S.	17 MAY 1872	Unknown
597	Washington, George, laborer	50y	C	U.S.	17 MAY 1872	Washington
247	Washington, Georgeanna	5m	C	D.C.	03 DEC 1866	Colored
452	Washington, Harris, laborer	65y	C	Va.	13 APR 1870	Washington Asylum
106	Washington, Henry A., prof.	36y	W	Va.	28 FEB 1858	Winchester, Va.
297	Washington, Henry Slade	7m	C	D.C.	25 FEB 1868	Harmony
580	Washington, I.H.	3y	C	D.C.	06 FEB 1872	Asylum
350	Washington, Ida	7m	C	D.C.	18 SEP 1868	Washington Asylum
635	Washington, Isaac	70y	C	U.S.	05 NOV 1872	Small Pox
161	Washington, J. Henry	17y	W	D.C.	07 SEP 1859	Oak Hill
410	Washington, Jackson	22d	C	D.C.	21 AUG 1869	Young Mens
287	Washington, James		C		c.27 DEC 1867	Alms House
286	Washington, James	2d	C		25 DEC 1867	Alms House
010	Washington, James	17y	C	Md.	11 JUN 1855	Harmony
460	Washington, James H.	5m	C	D.C.	04 JUN 1870	Ebenezer
253	Washington, Jane	3m	C	D.C.	02 FEB 1867	Moore's
151	Washington, Jane, washerwoman	56y	C	U.S.	20 JUN 1859	Young Mens
627	Washington, Jno. F.	7y	C	U.S.	07 SEP 1872	Small Pox
768	Washington, John	40y	C	U.S.	10 MAY 1874	Washington Asylum
670	Washington, Laurance	65y	C	U.S.	22 FEB 1873	Small Pox
465	Washington, Lilly H.	3m	C		25 JUL 1870	Ebenezer
337	Washington, Manuel	8m	C	U.S.	11 AUG 1868	Washington Asylum
296	Washington, Margaret	23y	C	Va.	16 FEB 1868	Young Mens
337	Washington, Maria	13y	C		15 AUG 1868	Washington Asylum
778	Washington, Marie alias Johnson	17y	C		15 JUN 1874	Washington Asylum
528	Washington, Martha	18d	C	D.C.	17 JUL 1871	Ebenezer
621	Washington, Martha A.	22y	C	U.S.	22 AUG 1872	
619	Washington, Mary	11m	C	U.S.	16 AUG 1872	
292	Washington, Mary		C		27 JAN 1868	Alms House
289	Washington, Mary	30y	C	Va.	20 JAN 1868	Alms House
292a	Washington, Mary, cook	80y	C	Va.	12 FEB 1868	Mt. Zion
768	Washington, Mary D.	3m	C	U.S.	01 MAY 1874	Mt. Olivet
377	Washington, Mary E.	4y	C		01 FEB 1869	Mt. Olivet
738	Washington, Mary, infant of	5d	C	U.S.	05 DEC 1873	
535	Washington, Mary J.	2y	C	D.C.	06 SEP 1871	Union
291	Washington, Millie	3y	C	D.C.	27 JAN 1868	Potters Field
097	Washington, Perrin, clerk	65y	W	Va.	29 NOV 1857	Congressional
613	Washington, Robt.	2y	C	U.S.	07 JUL 1872	
412	Washington, Ross E.	7m	C	D.C.	10 AUG 1869	Washington Asylum
532	Washington, Sally	73y	W	Md.	16 AUG 1871	Congressional
489	Washington, Sarah	15y	C		11 NOV 1870	Ebenezer
696	Washington, Spencer, laborer	19y	C	Va.	10 JUN 1873	
613	Washington, Wm.	4m	C	U.S.	26 JUL 1872	

Page	Name	Age	Race	Birth	Death Date	Burial Ground
768	Washington, Wm.	3m	C	U.S.	05 MAY 1874	
691	Washington, Wm. H.	5y	C	U.S.	17 MAY 1873	Small Pox*
452	Washington, Wm. Henry	1y	C		13 APR 1870	Ebenezer
320	Wassner, Catherine	97y	W	D.C.	05 JUN 1868	German, Georgetown
738	Waterhalter, W.	45y	W	Ger.	26 DEC 1873	
663	Waters, Abraham	3y	C	U.S.	02 JAN 1873	Small Pox*
282	Waters, Alexander	28y	C	Md.	26 NOV 1867	Union
428	Waters, Edwin	1y	C	D.C.	23 NOV 1869	Harmony
354	Waters, Elizabeth	50y	C	Md.	03 OCT 1868	Harmony
282	Waters, Elizabeth, dressmaker	50y	C	Va.	24 NOV 1867	Harmony
398	Waters, Henry	6m	B	D.C.	17 JUN 1869	Washington Asylum
697	Waters, Ida	1½m	C	D.C.	08 JUN 1873	Harmony
316	Waters, Isaiah	1y	C	D.C.	24 MAY 1868	Ebenezer
601	Waters, John, painter	57y	W	U.S.	01 MAY 1872	Glenwood
227	Waters, Kennard	10m	W	D.C.	07 JUL 1866	Glenwood
185	Waters, Laura F.	10d	C	D.C.	20 JUL 1860	Methodist
005	Waters, Laura Jane	2y	C		30 MAR 1855	Foundry
707	Waters, Laura M.	28y	C	Md.	15 JUL 1873	Harmony
660	Waters, Lizzie, nurse	80y	C	U.S.	20 JAN 1873	Congressional
286	Waters, Margaret	26y	C	D.C.	08 DEC 1867	Young Mens
269	Waters, Margaret E.	10y	C	D.C.	16 AUG 1867	Harmony
778	Waters, Mary	1y	W	U.S.	28 JUN 1874	Glenwood
619	Waters, Mary A.	37y	C	U.S.	15 AUG 1872	
643	Waters, Mary S.	41y	W	U.S.	06 DEC 1872	Glenwood
023	Waters, Mr., servant of		C		15 SEP 1855	Western
708	Waters, Mrs., lady	47y	W	D.C.	14 JUL 1873	
640	Waters, Noah	8y	C	U.S.	20 DEC 1872	Small Pox*
282	Waters, Oliver	8m	C	D.C.	02 NOV 1867	Mt. Olivet
390	Waters, Phebe	72y	W	Va.	23 MAY 1869	Congressional
377	Waters, Rachel	Still	C	D.C.	13 FEB 1869	Washington Asylum
066	Waters, Rebecca A.	35y	C	Va.*	17 DEC 1856	Harmony
274	Waters, Saml.	9m	W	D.C.	07 SEP 1867	Glenwood
264	Waters, Saml., laborer	50y	C	Md.	14 JUL 1867	Harmony
158	Waters, Sarah	3m	C	D.C.	18 AUG 1859	Foundry
070	Waters, Sarah, housewife	64y	W	Md.	12 FEB 1857	Foundry
320	Waters, Susannah G., washwm.	21y	C	D.C.	18 JUN 1868	Harmony
120	Waters, Tabitha	65y	W	Md.	09 JUL 1858	Glenwood
233	Waters, Thomas	83y	C	Md.	30 AUG 1866	Beckett's
212	Waters, William, formerly soldier	30y	C	Md.	07 FEB 1866	
471	Wather, Rachel	54y	W	Md.	26 AUG 1870	Congressional
417	Watkins, Henrietta, housekeeper	25y	C	Md.	12 SEP 1869	
786	Watkins, Jno. H.	6m	C	U.S.	15 JUL 1874	Mt. Pleasant
604	Watkins, March	5d	C	D.C.	07 JUN 1872	Ebenezer
337	Watkins, Mary E.	1m	C	U.S.	12 AUG 1868	Washington Asylum
428	Watkins, Mary, servant	20y	C	Md.	08 NOV 1869	Washington Asylum
418	Watkins, Rebecca	75y	C	Md.	28 SEP 1869	
413	Watkins, Rose	1m	C	D.C.	22 AUG 1869	Washington Asylum
030	Watkins, Tobias	75y	W	Md.	14 NOV 1855	Glenwood
389	Watkins, Wm.	4y	C	D.C.	30 APR 1869	Washington Asylum
416	Watkins, [blank]	Still	C		06 SEP 1869	
386	Watson, Adeline, servant	17y	C	U.S.	13 APR 1869	Mt. Olivet
306	Watson, Ann Elizabeth	1y	C	D.C.	17 APR 1868	Young Mens
736	Watson, Ann P.	14y	W	U.S.	18 DEC 1873	Glenwood
391	Watson, Annie E.	7y	C		15 MAY 1869	Young Mens
353	Watson, Ben	70y	C	Va.	01 SEP 1868	Freedmen's Hospital
011	Watson, Charles	14y	W	N.C.	10 JUN 1855	Congressional
778	Watson, Chas. J.	7m	W	U.S.	30 JUN 1874	Glenwood
659	Watson, Edward	24y	C	U.S.	10 JAN 1873	Washington Asylum

Page	Name	Age	Race	Birth	Death Date	Burial Ground
385	Watson, Eling	19y	C		04 APR 1869	Mt. Olivet
554	Watson, Elmore W.	1y	W	D.C.	14 JAN 1872	Congressional*
584	Watson, George	4m	C	D.C.	04 MAR 1872	Western
174	Watson, George	61y	W	Scot.	11 MAR 1860	Washington Asylum
044	Watson, Hannah, midwife	57y	W	Va.	18 MAY 1856	Congressional
439	Watson, Harry C.	2d	W		02 FEB 1870	Congressional
634	Watson, Jas., fireman	40y	W	Ire.	27 OCT 1872	
523	Watson, John Wallace	7m	W	D.C.	15 JUN 1871	Glenwood
379	Watson, Lewis	35y	W	Va.	21 MAR 1869	Congressional
489	Watson, Lizzie C.	34y	W	Pa.	04 NOV 1870	Glenwood
330	Watson, Malinda	2y	C	D.C.	29 JUL 1868	Young Mens
041	Watson, Mary E.	2m	W	D.C.	01 APR 1856	Congressional
492	Watson, Melinda B.	34y	C	La.	03 DEC 1870	Young Mens
660	Watson, Milton J.	2y	W	U.S.	19 JAN 1873	Mt. Olivet
616	Watson, Minnie	17m	C	U.S.	29 JUL 1872	
382	Watson, Reubin, brickmaker	26y	C		22 MAR 1869	Young Mens
035	Watson, Saml. N.	35y		Md.	23 FEB 1856	Glenwood
269	Watson, W.C.	10m	C		18 AUG 1867	Young Mens
299	Watson, William H., agent	53y	W	D.C.	01 MAR 1868	Rock Creek
183	Watson, [blank]	28y	W	U.S.	30 JUN 1860	Western
190	Watson, [blank]	3y	C		10 SEP 1860	Young Mens
054	Watters, David S., auctioneer	66y	W	Md.	23 AUG 1856	Foundry
092	Watterston, Eliza H.	38y	W	D.C.	27 SEP 1857	Congressional
547	Watts, Eliza	74y	W	D.C.	03 DEC 1871	
712	Watts, Eliza	18m	C	Va.	19 AUG 1873	Alms House
622	Watts, Martha	3m	W	U.S.	21 AUG 1872	
683	Watts, Maurice	65y	W	U.S.	19 APR 1873	
325	Watts, Reginia	Still	W	D.C.	04 JUL 1868	Congressional
071	Watts, Samuel, cook	32y	C	unk.	26 FEB 1857	Young Mens
439	Watwell, James, child of	Still	W		23 FEB 1870	Congressional
019	Waugh, Cathn.	1y	W	Md.	27 AUG 1855	Methodist
054	Waulk, Lise	9m	W	D.C.	25 AUG 1856	
314	Waverly, Gertrude	6m	W	Va.	20 MAY 1868	Mt. Olivet
762	Way, Edward, clerk Treas.	32y	W	U.S.	30 APR 1874	Congressional*
325	Way, George B., lawyer	56y	W	Md.	08 JUL 1868	Congressional
695	Waylen, Richard A.	2y	C	Pa.	16 JUN 1873	Holmead
176	Wayman, Sarah A.	26y	C	Mo.	02 APR 1860	Harmony
157	Waymen, Thos.	1y	C	D.C.	12 AUG 1859	Georgetown
265	Wayne, James M., Hon.	76y	W	Ga.	05 JUL 1867	Oak Hill
492	Wayne, Mary	16d	C	D.C.	13 DEC 1870	Ebenezer
132	Wayne, Mary C.	8y	C	D.C.	02 NOV 1858	Methodist
455	Wayne, Walter P.	2m	W		29 MAY 1870	Mt. Olivet
330	Wayne, Willie	5m	C	D.C.	27 JUL 1868	
335a	Wayne, Willie	5m	B	U.S.	27 JUL 1868	Washington Asylum
487	Wayson, Edward, carpenter	52y	W	Md.	27 NOV 1870	Congressional
061	Wayson, John	3y	W	D.C.	21 OCT 1856	Congressional
493	Weaks, Mary	73y	W	Va.	25 DEC 1870	Glenwood
640	Wealacher, Conrad	27y	W	Ger.	24 DEC 1872	Small Pox*
331	Weat, Ben	70y	C		31 JUL 1868	Freedmen's Hospital
591	Weathers, Winnie	11y	C	Va.	06 APR 1872	
671	Weaver, Addie	3y	C	U.S.	15 FEB 1873	Small Pox*
598	Weaver, Annie	9y	C	U.S.	05 MAY 1872	Unknown
069	Weaver, Catharine, servant	21y	W	Ger.	24 JAN 1857	Methodist
209	Weaver, Charles James	4m	W	Va.	01 JAN 1866	Prospect Hill
450	Weaver, Frank	9m	C		25 APR 1870	Union
592	Weaver, Henry	6y	W	D.C.	09 APR 1872	
021	Weaver, Jesse, Mrs.	30y	W	Pa.	24 AUG 1855	Congressional*
377	Weaver, Perry	50y	C		26 FEB 1869	Washington Asylum

Page	Name	Age	Race	Birth	Death Date	Burial Ground
020	Weaver, Sally	1y	W		20 AUG 1855	
769	Weaver, Wm. H.	1m	W	U.S.	22 MAY 1874	Glenwood
118	Weaver, [blank]	4m	W		26 JUN 1858	German
720	Webb, Andrew J.	2y	W	D.C.	29 SEP 1873	Congressional
417	Webb, Chas.	10y	W		13 SEP 1869	Mt. Olivet
500	Webb, Clara, laudness	80y	C	Va.	13 JAN 1871	Union
737	Webb, John H.	2y	C	U.S.	22 DEC 1873	
704	Webb, Mary Ann	11m	C	D.C.	03 JUL 1873	
777a	Webb, Mary E.	1m	C	U.S.	19 JUN 1874	
167	Webb, Pollard, agent	60y	W	Va.	11 DEC 1859	Congressional
488	Webb, Wm. Alex.	1y	C	U.S.	19 NOV 1870	Beckett's
230	Webber, Lydia A.	33y	W	Va.	18 JUL 1866	Congressional
778	Webel, E., Mrs.	44y	W	Ger.	07 JUN 1874	Prospect Hill
724	Webent, Guy	2y	M	D.C.	16 OCT 1873	Washington Asylum
778	Weber, Caroline	70y	W	Ger.	16 JUN 1874	Prospect Hill
430	Weber, H., infant of	Still	W	D.C.	31 DEC 1869	Prospect Hill
189	Weber, Jos. Valentine, laborer	73y	W	Ger.	19 SEP 1860	Congressional*
726	Webster, A.C.H., claim agt./atty.	41y	W	Eng.	27 OCT 1873	Congressional*
713	Webster, Ann	26y	W	Ire.	25 AUG 1873	Mt. Olivet
534	Webster, Ann, housekeeper	66y	W	U.S.	27 AUG 1871	Washington
619	Webster, Caroline	9m	C	U.S.	25 AUG 1872	Asylum
582	Webster, Caroline, servant	15y	C	D.C.	20 FEB 1872	
411	Webster, Charles	58y	W	Md.	04 AUG 1869	Glenwood
304	Webster, Charles Edward	1y	W	U.S.	19 MAR 1868	Congressional
336	Webster, Daniel	14d	C	D.C.	04 AUG 1868	
671	Webster, Daniel	24y	C	U.S.	28 FEB 1873	Small Pox*
708	Webster, Daniel	13y	C	D.C.	28 JUL 1873	Washington Asylum
054	Webster, Daniel, carpenter	20y	W	Md.	12 AUG 1856	Glenwood
598	Webster, Danl., white washer	52y	C	U.S.	09 MAY 1872	Unknown
418	Webster, Eliza, servant	19y	C	Va.	08 SEP 1869	
409	Webster, Elizabeth	63y	W	Md.	24 AUG 1869	Georgetown
408	Webster, Ella M.	1y	W		26 AUG 1869	Glenwood
384	Webster, George	3y	C	Md.	25 MAR 1869	Washington Asylum
755	Webster, Georgeanna	6d	C	D.C.	09 MAR 1874	Ebenezer
228	Webster, Hellen	2y	C	D.C.	17 JUL 1866	Harmony
676	Webster, Isaac	22y	C	U.S.	02 MAR 1873	Small Pox
436	Webster, James	10y	C		03 JAN 1870	Glenwood
523	Webster, James K., laborer	17y	W		17 JUN 1871	Methodist
711	Webster, Jas.	9m	W	D.C.	09 AUG 1873	Mt. Olivet
026	Webster, John		W		22 OCT 1855	Congressional
276	Webster, Jonas, laborer	20y	C	D.C.	14 SEP 1867	
587	Webster, Julia	24y	C	D.C.	21 MAR 1872	
495	Webster, Martha J.	1y	C	D.C.	28 DEC 1870	Potters Field
445	Webster, Rebecca G.	90y	W	Me.	31 MAR 1870	Oak Hill
087	Webster, Sandy, hackman	40y	C	Va.	14 AUG 1857	St. Matthews
554	Webster, T.E., butcher	47y	W	Mass.	14 JAN 1872	Congressional*
179	Webster, Thomas W., cabinet mkr.	36y	W	Va.*	04 MAY 1860	Congressional
749	Webster, Virginia M.	1y	W	U.S.	26 FEB 1874	
248	Webster, William, laborer	52y	W	Md.	25 DEC 1866	Congressional
609	Webster, Wm. W., upholsterer	73y	W	U.S.	12 JUN 1872	
533	Webster, [blank]	9m	C	D.C.	25 AUG 1871	Prospect Hill
584	Weddock, John W., white washer	32y	C	U.S.	01 MAR 1872	
527	Wedfield, Fritz	26y	W	Ger.	07 JUL 1871	Prospect Hill
412	Wedge, Perry	1m	C		25 AUG 1869	
428	Wedlock, Mary		C		02 NOV 1869	Harmony
285	Wedstrand, Mary E.	8d	W	D.C.	20 DEC 1867	Glenwood
234	Weed, Florence	6m	W	D.C.	07 SEP 1866	Glenwood
295	Weeden, Charles C.	29y	W	D.C.	28 FEB 1868	Congressional

Page	Name	Age	Race	Birth	Death Date	Burial Ground
635	Weeden, Francis	22y	W	U.S.	26 NOV 1872	Small Pox
364	Weeden, Henry A., coach maker	58y	W	Md.	11 DEC 1868	Congressional
394	Weedon, Lewis B., merchant	10h	W	D.C.	26 JUN 1869	Mt. Olivet
597	Weeks, Eliza	33y	W	U.S.	02 MAY 1872	Glenwood
267	Weeks, James	3m	C	D.C.	22 JUL 1867	Young Mens
268	Weeks, Joseph, watchman	61y	W	Va.	15 AUG 1867	Glenwood
096	Weeks, Mary	82y	W	Md.	04 NOV 1857	Foundry
630	Weeks, Mary E.	13m	C	U.S.	— OCT 1872	
112	Weeks, Mary Frances	1y	W	D.C.	22 APR 1858	Glenwood
640	Weens, Joseph	24y	C	U.S.	20 DEC 1872	Small Pox*
707	Weichhorn, Theo., butcher	19y	W	Ger.	22 JUL 1873	St. Marys
440	Weiderman, Catharina S.	5d			10 FEB 1870	Prospect Hill
456	Weidmeir, Anna	7½m	W	D.C.	30 JUN 1870	Prospect Hill
732	Weightman, Chas. H.	18y	W	U.S.	27 NOV 1873	Congressional*
282	Weightman, John, clerk	32y	W	Ire.	05 NOV 1867	Glenwood
414	Weightman, Susan, Mrs.	49y	W	D.C.	04 SEP 1869	Congressional
094	Weigle, Sophia	6y	W	Va.	27 OCT 1857	Congressional
345	Weilacker, Elenora	5m	W	D.C.	13 AUG 1868	German Catholic
384	Weir, Mathew	6y	C	Va.	22 MAR 1869	Washington Asylum
310	Weir, [blank], fisherman	25y	C	Va.	05 APR 1868	Harmony
082	Weirman, Susan	46y	W	Pa.	05 JUL 1857	Oak Hill
580	Weisenborn, Johanna	11y	W	D.C.	08 FEB 1872	Prospect Hill
786	Weisman, John	14m	W	U.S.	16 JUL 1874	Glenwood
723	Weisonborn, John H., grocer	57y	W	Ger.	09 OCT 1873	Prospect Hill
342	Weiss, Charles Henry	1y	W	D.C.	25 AUG 1868	Congressional
755	Weiss, Frederick C.	11m	W	U.S.	11 MAR 1874	Prospect Hill
350	Weiss, Gustave C., restaurant kpr.	36y	W	Ger.	04 SEP 1868	Mt. Olivet
317	Weissenger, Mr., child of	7m	W		29 JUN 1868	Prospect Hill
344	Weissinger, William H.	6m	W	D.C.	04 AUG 1868	Prospect Hill
083	Welch, Ann	3m	W	D.C.	11 JUL 1857	St. Patricks
659	Welch, Bridget	35y	W	U.S.	11 JAN 1873	Mt. Olivet
639	Welch, Frank	1m	W	U.S.	11 NOV 1872	
224	Welch, Henry	5y	W	D.C.	12 JUN 1866	Alms House
306	Welch, John	2y	C	D.C.	12 APR 1868	Young Mens
071	Welch, Joseph, clerk	61y	W	Pa.	25 FEB 1857	Congressional
459	Welch, Margaret	64y	W	Ire.	22 JUN 1870	Potters Field
736	Welch, Martin, Mrs.	25y	W	U.S.	15 DEC 1873	Mt. Olivet
609	Welch, Mary	18d	W	U.S.	23 JUN 1872	
401	Welch, Mary A.	5m	W		28 JUL 1869	Mt. Olivet
412	Welch, Mary Francis	11m	C		10 AUG 1869	
646	Welch, Pat, laborer	40y	W	Ire.	22 DEC 1872	
593	Welch, Richd., carpenter	36y	C	Va.	26 APR 1872	Mt. Pleasant
616	Welch, Tim, student	9y	W	U.S.	23 JUL 1872	
623	Welch, Timothy	9m	W	U.S.	23 JUL 1872	Holy Rood
623	Welch, Winni	4y	W	U.S.	04 JUL 1872	Catholic
400	Welcker, Barbara C.F.	7m	W		09 JUL 1869	N.Y. City
427	Welcome, Benj.	26y	C	Va.	18 NOV 1869	Washington Asylum
373	Welcome, Caroline, servant	16y	C		21 JAN 1869	
628	Welcome, Maria	30y	C	U.S.	29 SEP 1872	
585	Welden, Lizzie	32y	C	Md.	07 MAR 1872	Mt. Olivet
408	Weldon, Annie	30y	C	Md.	31 AUG 1869	Mt. Olivet
684	Weldon, Henry	2m	C	U.S.	02 APR 1873	Small Pox*
319	Weller, Rose E.	8y	W	Md.	28 JUN 1868	Congressional
723	Wells, D., real estate broker	48y	W	N.H.	10 OCT 1873	Congressional*
328	Wells, George	75y	C	Va.	13 JUL 1868	Alms House
132	Wells, George, brick maker	22y	W	Eng.	02 NOV 1858	Ebenezer
258	Wells, George H., Jr.	2m	W	D.C.	15 APR 1867	Congressional
755	Wells, Georgeanna D.	51y	W	U.S.	06 MAR 1874	Glenwood

Page	Name	Age	Race	Birth	Death Date	Burial Ground
397	Wells, James, clerk	74y	W	Pa.	15 JUN 1869	Philadelphia, Pa.
301	Wells, James H.	12d	C	D.C.	26 MAR 1868	Young Mens
607	Wells, Joseph, teamster	65y	W	Eng.	22 JUN 1872	Methodist
386	Wells, Liley D.	1y	W	U.S.	28 APR 1869	Congressional
616a	Wells, Lilly W.	3m	W	D.C.	05 JUL 1872	Congressional
551	Wells, Lizzie	1y	W	D.C.	— DEC 1871	
515	Wells, Maria	1y	C	D.C.	15 MAR 1871	Union
294	Wells, Richard	1y	C	D.C.	17 FEB 1868	Mt. Olivet
477	Wells, Samuel, carpenter	90y	W	Md.	27 SEP 1870	Rock Creek
488	Wells, Sarah	9m	C	U.S.	12 NOV 1870	Beckett's
644	Wells, Sarah E.	44y	W	U.S.	14 DEC 1872	Methodist
272	Wells, Sarah Elizabeth	1y	W	D.C.	12 AUG 1867	Holmead
004	Wells, Sarah Lavinia	8m	W	D.C.	17 MAR 1855	Foundry
340	Wells, Sarah, repairs cane chairs	53y	W	Va.	28 AUG 1868	Congressional
079	Wells, Thos., plasterer	22y	W	Md.	04 JUN 1857	Marlboro, Md.
481	Wells, William	2m	C	D.C.	09 OCT 1870	Ebenezer
026	Wells, Wm., chain maker	33y	W	Va.*	09 OCT 1855	Holmead
516	Welsh, Anna L.	1y	W		24 MAR 1871	Congressional
012	Welsh, Bridget	26y	W	Ire.	07 JUN 1855	St. Patricks
317	Welsh, Charles, tinner	28y	W	Md.	24 JUN 1868	Congressional
281	Welsh, James	2y	W		05 OCT 1867	Mt. Olivet
447	Welsh, James	2y	W		17 MAR 1870	Mt. Olivet
593	Welsh, John, plumber	22y	W	Va.	07 APR 1872	Mt. Olivet*
158	Welsh, Mary, domestic	40y	W	Ire.	20 AUG 1859	Mt. Olivet
034	Welsh, Michael, laborer	55y	W	Ire.	09 JAN 1856	Alms House
280	Welsh, Timothy	5m	W		01 OCT 1867	Mt. Olivet
140	Welsh, William, clerk	35y	W	Ire.	05 FEB 1859	Mt. Olivet
694	Welsh, William, laborer	28y	W	Ire.	11 JUN 1873	Mt. Olivet
437	Weltz, [blank]	Still	C	D.C.	13 JAN 1870	Washington Asylum
085	Wengle, A., child of	10m	W	D.C.	30 JUL 1857	German
344	Wentworth, Martha	3y	W	D.C.	02 AUG 1868	St. Aloysius
527	Wenzel, Anna C.	11y	W	D.C.	11 JUL 1871	Prospect Hill
636	Wenzel, J.I.	1y	W	U.S.	07 NOV 1872	
027	Werden, Sarah	46y	W	Va.*	10 OCT 1855	Foundry
712	Werheman, Anna E.	1y	W	D.C.	13 AUG 1873	Prospect Hill
786	Werner, Catharine	62y	W	Ger.	14 JUL 1874	Glenwood
136	Werner, John T.H., locksmith	55y	W	Ger.	28 DEC 1858	German
644	Werner, Kate, housekeeper	47y	W	Ger.	21 DEC 1872	Prospect Hill
730	Wertz, Addie	8m	C	U.S.	17 NOV 1873	Beckett's
283	Werwick, Lily	1y	W	Md.	20 NOV 1867	Baltimore, Md.
595	Wesburg, John W.	10d	W	D.C.	01 APR 1872	Oak Hill
727	Wesbury, Margaret	14d	C	U.S.	15 OCT 1873	Oak Hill
019	Wesenthal, Lize		W	D.C.	22 AUG 1855	German Lutheran
249	Weser, Helena		W	D.C.	22 JAN 1867	Mt. Olivet
531	Weshke, Catharine	43y	W		06 AUG 1871	Prospect Hill
412	Wesley, John	26y	C	Va.	17 AUG 1869	Washington Asylum
294	Wesley, John	2y	C	D.C.	05 FEB 1868	Western
591	Wesley, John A.	29y	C	Md.	06 APR 1872	Washington
260	Wesley, Winny	Still			28 MAY 1867	Young Mens
624	Wesley, Wm.	4y	C	U.S.	29 SEP 1872	
333	Wess, William	18y	C		21 JUL 1868	Harmony
508	West, Ann E.	6m	C	D.C.	12 FEB 1871	Holmead
335b	West, Anne	2y	C	D.C.	12 JUL 1868	Washington Asylum
665	West, Annie	7y	W	U.S.	26 JAN 1873	Small Pox*
065	West, B.O., clerk	32y	W	Md.	03 DEC 1856	Glenwood
675	West, Bessie	9m	W	U.S.	29 MAR 1873	Prince Wm. Co., Va.
264	West, Catherine L.	30y			07 JUL 1867	Glenwood
664	West, Daisey B.	2y	W	U.S.	18 JAN 1873	Small Pox*

Page	Name	Age	Race	Birth	Death Date	Burial Ground
060	West, Eleanor	56y	W	Md.	15 OCT 1856	Glenwood
179	West, Elizabeth O.	67y	W	Md.	22 MAY 1860	Glenwood
612	West, Geo.	7m	W	U.S.	26 JUL 1872	
663	West, George	5y	C	U.S.	28 JAN 1873	Small Pox
109	West, Gertrude	38y	W	Va.	26 MAR 1858	Washington
050	West, Harriet	1y	W	D.C.	18 JUL 1856	Methodist
329	West, Henry	3m	C	D.C.	14 JUL 1868	Mt. Olivet
342	West, Irene	7m	C	D.C.	26 AUG 1868	Harmony
449	West, J. Douglas	46y	W	Va.	06 APR 1870	Mt. Olivet
374	West, James Douglass	9m	W		07 FEB 1869	Congressional
762	West, James, laborer	36y	C	U.S.	24 APR 1874	
756	West, John, laborer	29y	C	U.S.	24 MAR 1874	
147	West, John P.	53y	W		21 APR 1859	
271	West, Leonard Laurance	1y	C	D.C.	28 AUG 1867	Harmony
201	West, Margaret	10y	C	D.C.	16 MAR 1861	Washington Asylum
010	West, Maria L.	23y	W	Md.	17 JUN 1855	Glenwood
589	West, Mary C.	4m	C	D.C.	28 MAR 1872	Asylum
261	West, Mary Ellen	2y	C		06 MAY 1867	Mt. Olivet
528	West, Roderwick	1y	C	D.C.	c.21 JUL 1871	
681	West, S.H., Mrs.	40y	W	U.S.	19 APR 1873	
099	West, Sarah	42y	C	Md.	25 DEC 1857	St. Patricks
704	West, Susan	3y	C	D.C.	11 JUL 1873	Harmony
330	West, Susan	60y	C	Va.	20 JUL 1868	Young Mens
762	West, William	4m	C	U.S.	03 APR 1874	Harmony
334	West, Willie L.	4y	W	D.C.	14 JUL 1868	Glenwood
600	West, Wm.	1y	C	U.S.	09 MAY 1872	Young Mens
258	West, [blank]	3m	C		10 APR 1867	Western
162	West, [blank]		C	D.C.	25 SEP 1859	Washington Asylum
011	West, [blank]	4m	C		03 JUN 1855	Western
603	Westely, Elisabeth	6m	W	D.C.	14 JUN 1872	
456	Westemein, Rosa	8m	W	D.C.	10 JUN 1870	Prospect Hill
161	Westerfield, David	77y	W	N.J.	01 SEP 1859	
127	Westerfold, Sarah	4y	W	D.C.	15 SEP 1858	Methodist, Western
267	Westerlinck, Henry, child of	6m	W		14 JUL 1867	Western
366	Western, Helen	23y	W	N.Y.	11 DEC 1868	Boston, Mass.
459	Westgate, Mary E.	3m	W	D.C.	13 JUN 1870	Holmead
524	Westle, Charles	10m	D	D.C.	21 JUN 1871	
130	Westly, James F.	1y	W	D.C.	16 OCT 1858	Laurel Factory
016	Westly, Mary Jane	1y	W	D.C.	08 JUL 1855	Laurel Factory, Md.
043	Weston, Elizabeth	75y	W	Md.	24 APR 1856	Methodist
226	Weston, William	6m	C	D.C.	29 JUN 1866	
326	Westwood, Charles G.	5m	W	D.C.	07 JUL 1868	Congressional
265	Westwood, Wm. Ferguson	5m	W	D.C.	15 JUL 1867	Congressional
223	Wetherall, Charles S.	10m	W	D.C.	06 JUN 1866	Glenwood
276	Wetherall, Elizabeth N.	28y	W	D.C.*	28 SEP 1867	Oak Hill
546	Wetmore, Henry G.	30y	W	Eng.	26 NOV 1871	Congressional
073	Wettie, George	1y	W	D.C.	10 MAR 1857	
450	Wetzel, William	5y	W		21 APR 1870	Prospect Hill
034	Weylich, Catharine	14y	W	D.C.	08 JAN 1856	German
075	Weyville, Maria Anne	7m	C	D.C.	09 APR 1857	Foundry
234	Weywich, Elizabeth	2y	W	D.C.	07 SEP 1866	Glenwood
786	Whalen, C. Elizabeth	51y	W	U.S.	09 JUL 1874	Oak Hill
768	Whalen, Eliza	73y	W	U.S.	10 MAY 1874	Congressional*
117	Whalen, John		W	Ire.	26 JUN 1858	
236	Whalen, Michael, r.r. contractor	34y	W	Ire.	23 SEP 1866	Mt. Olivet
015	Whalen, [blank]	18m	W	D.C.	11 JUL 1855	St. Patricks
434	Whaples, Mary	82y	W	N.Y.	24 JAN 1870	Congressional
557	Wharton, Francis Q.	8d	W	D.C.	02 FEB 1872	Congressional

Page	Name	Age	Race	Birth	Death Date	Burial Ground
167	Wharton, [blank]	35y	W	D.C.	10 DEC 1859	Congressional
135	Wheat, Eliza	35y	W	Md.	08 DEC 1858	Congressional
143	Wheat, Mary A., lady	78y	W	Va.	05 MAR 1859	Congressional
051	Wheat, William, cnty. constable	75y	W	Md.	25 JUL 1856	Methodist
184	Wheat, Wm. Henry	27y	W	D.C.	10 JUL 1860	Congressional
349	Wheatley, Anna	56y	W	Md.	23 SEP 1868	Mt. Olivet
327	Wheatley, Bridget, housekeeper	76y	W	Ire.	11 JUL 1868	Mt. Olivet
024	Wheatley, John H.	1y	C	D.C.	13 SEP 1855	
042	Wheatly, Ignaceous, porter	13y	C	Md.	19 APR 1856	Harmony
749	Wheatly, Lillian M.	6m	W	U.S.	20 FEB 1874	
299	Wheelan, Mary Adeline	24y	W		18 MAR 1868	Mt. Olivet
033	Wheeler, Alice	2y	W	Va.	27 JAN 1856	Congressional
704	Wheeler, Andrew, laborer	28y	W	Ire.	09 JUL 1873	
125	Wheeler, Catharine	52y	C	Md.	21 AUG 1858	Harmony
349	Wheeler, Catherine Irene	7m	W	D.C.	07 SEP 1868	Annapolis, Md.
456	Wheeler, Chas. H.	9m	C	D.C.	15 JUN 1870	Young Mens
162	Wheeler, Clara Alberta	1y	W	D.C.	22 SEP 1859	Congressional
769	Wheeler, Daniel M., clerk	35y	W	U.S.	15 MAY 1874	Oak Hill
102	Wheeler, Eli	28y	C	Va.	19 JAN 1858	Foundry
282	Wheeler, Emma	1y	W	D.C.	06 NOV 1867	Congressional
207	Wheeler, Geo. W.	49y	W		09 JUL 1862	Congressional
133	Wheeler, George D.	19y	W		26 NOV 1858	Congressional*
538	Wheeler, George H., merchant	31y	W	Ver.	24 SEP 1871	Ver.
435	Wheeler, Gracy	19y	C	Md.	27 JAN 1870	Ebenezer
347	Wheeler, James H., paper hanger	48y	W	Conn.	28 SEP 1868	Congressional
736	Wheeler, Jarriot, laborer	70y	C	U.S.	20 DEC 1873	Mt. Olivet
719	Wheeler, John Osborn	2y	C	D.C.	22 SEP 1873	
382	Wheeler, Julia	1y	C		23 MAR 1869	Young Mens
607	Wheeler, Leroy G.	1m	W	D.C.	12 JUN 1872	Congressional
719	Wheeler, Mary	20y	C		22 SEP 1873	
136	Wheeler, Mary	80y	W	Md.	24 DEC 1858	Congressional
153	Wheeler, Mary C.	2y	C	D.C.	12 JUL 1859	Mt. Olivet
244	Wheeler, Mary Charlotte	8m	W	Md.	12 NOV 1866	Annapolis, Md.
332	Wheeler, Mary G.	1y	W	D.C.	16 JUL 1868	Methodist
379	Wheeler, Mary Isabel	5m	W		10 MAR 1869	Congressional
352	Wheeler, Thos.	1y	C		25 SEP 1868	Washington Asylum
103	Wheeler, [blank]	4y	C		09 JAN 1858	
514	Wheeler, [blank]	Still	W		17 MAR 1871	Glenwood
241	Wheeler, [blank]	22y	C		30 OCT 1866	Md.
359	Wheelock, Olive	51y	W	N.Y.	30 NOV 1868	Congressional
496	Wheelon, Harrison E.	1y	W	Amer.	30 DEC 1870	Glenwood
542	Whelan, Bridget	33y	W	Ire.	25 OCT 1871	Mt. Olivet
265	Whelan, John H.	10m	W	D.C.	06 JUL 1867	Mt. Olivet
292a	Whelan, Martha, storekeeper	49y	W	D.C.*	06 FEB 1868	Pettit's Vault
334	Whelan, Susan	3y	W	D.C.	09 JUL 1868	Mt. Olivet
428	Whelan, William, soldier	28y	W		02 NOV 1869	Mt. Olivet
345	Whelter, James	3y	C	D.C.	14 AUG 1868	
721	Whey, Rose, infant of	7d	C	D.C.	17 SEP 1873	
172	Whillden, Mary	3m	W	D.C.	03 FEB 1860	Glenwood
091	Whilldin, Susan W., lady	45y	W	Pa.	14 SEP 1857	Glenwood
195	Whillen, Wm., child of	1d	W	D.C.	04 DEC 1860	Glenwood
712	Whipple, Georgeana	22y	W	D.C.	20 AUG 1873	Congressional
711	Whipple, Georgeanna	2m	W	D.C.	11 AUG 1873	Congressional
594	Whipple, Milton C.	3m	W	D.C.	05 APR 1872	Congressional
554	Whitaker, John T., painter	74y	W	Eng.	19 JAN 1872	
473	Whitby, William	1y	C	D.C.	29 AUG 1870	Western
598	White, Abraham, laborer	55y	C	U.S.	05 MAY 1872	Mt. Pleasant
597	White, Abraham, laborer	55y	C	U.S.	02 MAY 1872	Washington

District of Columbia Interments (Index to Deaths), 1855-1874

Page	Name	Age	Race	Birth	Death Date	Burial Ground
485	White, Adeline	3y	C	U.S.	20 OCT 1870	Ebenezer
442	White, Ann King	20y	W	Va.	12 FEB 1870	Washington Asylum
786	White, Anne	86y	W	U.S.	09 JUL 1874	Congressional
606	White, Archy	2m	C	D.C.	17 JUN 1872	
541	White, Catharine C.	29y	W	Can.	10 OCT 1871	Glenwood
740	White, Cauler		C	U.S.	06 JAN 1874	
555	White, Celia	5m	W	D.C.	27 JAN 1872	Mt. Olivet
482	White, Charles, clerk	70y	W	Ohio	12 OCT 1870	Congressional
010	White, Chas. W.	1m	W	D.C.	12 JUN 1855	St. Patricks
786	White, Cornelius, farmer	71y	W	U.S.	24 JUL 1874	
402	White, Elizabeth	89y	W	Ky.	25 JUL 1869	Glenwood
220	White, Elizabeth A., dressmaker	74y	W	Va.*	10 MAY 1866	Glenwood
631	White, Ella, housewife	40y	W	Ire.	08 OCT 1872	Mt. Olivet
778	White, Elmira	81y	W	U.S.	27 JUN 1874	Rock Creek
224	White, Emma	8m	W		12 JUN 1866	Mt. Olivet
365	White, Eva	3y	W	N.J.	30 DEC 1868	Congressional*
515	White, Gabriel, carpenter	60y	C		10 MAR 1871	Ebenezer
549	White, Geo. C.	7y	W	D.C.	21 DEC 1871	Congressional
710	White, George H.	25y	C		07 AUG 1873	Washington Asylum
711	White, H.W., laborer	25y	C	Va.	09 AUG 1873	Washington Asylum
378	White, Hannah, servant	21y	C	Va.	18 FEB 1869	Freedmen's Hospital
101	White, Harriet	45y	W		07 JAN 1858	
439	White, Hattie	2y	W		22 FEB 1870	Congressional
413	White, Henry	1y	C	D.C.	25 AUG 1869	Washington Asylum
318	White, Howard	5m	W	D.C.	23 JUN 1868	Congressional
007	White, Infant	c.3h	W		17 APR 1855	Congressional
711	White, Irene	7m	W	D.C.	10 AUG 1873	Mt. Olivet
297	White, Isabella	44y	W	Eng.	25 FEB 1868	Glenwood
664	White, Isabella	23y	C	U.S.	23 JAN 1873	Small Pox*
299	White, James	14y	C		04 MAR 1868	Ebenezer
690	White, James	35y	C	U.S.	08 MAY 1873	Small Pox
150	White, James Marion	10m	W	D.C.	06 JUN 1859	Mt. Olivet
445	White, James, plumber	21y	W	Ire.	17 MAR 1870	Mt. Olivet
658	White, John, barber	30y	C	U.S.	09 JAN 1873	
726	White, John D., laborer	40y	W	U.S.	29 OCT 1873	Mt. Olivet
548	White, John Frank	3y	W	Md.	17 DEC 1871	Congressional
097	White, Joseph, clerk	20y	W	Eng.	29 NOV 1857	Congressional
202	White, Joseph M.	2y	W		23 APR 1861	Mt. Olivet
258	White, Julia	20y	W	D.C.	15 APR 1867	Congressional
411	White, Julia	4m	C		18 AUG 1869	Methodist
723	White, Katie	2y	W	D.C.	04 OCT 1873	Congressional*
296	White, Landy	35y	C	Va.	19 FEB 1868	Freedmen's Hospital
695	White, Lizzie	4m	C	D.C.	24 JUN 1873	
368	White, Lucinda	43y	C	Va.	11 DEC 1868	Mt. Olivet
482	White, Lucy	18y	C	Va.*	25 OCT 1870	Ebenezer
109	White, Luther H.	1y	W	D.C.	29 MAR 1858	Methodist
202	White, Mary	15y	W	D.C.	04 APR 1861	Glenwood
786	White, Mary	4m	W	U.S.	09 JUL 1874	Mt. Olivet
525	White, Mary Ann	40y	W	Pa.	30 JUN 1871	Oak Hill
727	White, Mary C.	29y	W	U.S.	31 OCT 1873	Mt. Olivet
360	White, Mary, housekeeper	50y	W	Ire.	09 NOV 1868	Mt. Olivet*
185	White, Mary Magdalen	67y	W	Md.	22 JUL 1860	Carroll Chapel
318	White, Mathias M., undertaker	55y	W	Md.	05 JUN 1868	Congressional
677	White, Milly	27y	C	U.S.	c.24 MAR 1873	Small Pox
720	White, Miss, chambermaid	55y	C	Va.	27 SEP 1873	Harmony
706	White, Mr., child of	Still	W	D.C.	24 JUL 1873	
691	White, Mrs. [Elizabeth]	68y	W		12 MAY 1873	Congressional*
484	White, Rebecca S.	1y	W	N.J.	06 OCT 1870	Congressional

District of Columbia Interments (Index to Deaths), 1855-1874

Page	Name	Age	Race	Birth	Death Date	Burial Ground
489	White, Richard, carpenter	47y	C	Va.	28 NOV 1870	Ebenezer
226	White, Robert, clerk	24y	W	Pa.	27 JUN 1866	Pa.
300	White, Rose	40y	C	Va.	12 MAR 1868	Alms House
604	White, Sallie	9y	C	D.C.	23 JUN 1872	Small Pox
035	White, Saml. E.	6m	W	D.C.	17 FEB 1856	Congressional
319	White, Simeon				13 JUN 1868	
335	White, Susan, house servant	22y	C	D.C.	15 JUL 1868	Ebenezer
461	White, Thomas	1y	W	D.C.	13 JUL 1870	Congressional
155	White, Thomas	8m	W	D.C.	20 JUL 1859	Rock Creek
662	White, Thomas	19y	C	U.S.	05 JAN 1873	Small Pox
720	White, W.W.		W	D.C.	23 SEP 1873	Glenwood
318	White, Walter	1y	W	D.C.	28 JUN 1868	Congressional
139	White, Zaphy	52y	W	Va.	27 JAN 1859	Ebenezer
094	White, [blank], laborer	50y	W	Md.	26 OCT 1857	
009	Whiteman, Elizabeth	11y	W	Md.	09 MAY 1855	
003	Whiteman, Wm., gardener	36y	W	Eng.	09 FEB 1855	
444	Whitemore, Hester O'Neal	30y	W		28 MAR 1870	Holmead
218	Whitemore, Humphrey O'Neil	14y	W	D.C.	14 APR 1866	Holmead
255	Whitemore, Humphrey, shoemaker	70y	W	Md.	21 MAR 1867	Alexandria, Va.
269	Whitemore, Zach., child of	Still	W	D.C.	30 AUG 1867	Holmead
734	Whithalt, Dora	43y	W	Ger.	01 DEC 1873	Glenwood
276	Whiting, Geo. C., clerk	50y	W	Va.	03 SEP 1867	Oak Hill
346	Whiting, Johanna	25y	C		16 AUG 1868	Freedmen's Hospital
290	Whiting, Lewis		C		18 JAN 1868	Freedmen's Hospital
508	Whitlow, Jas. E.	7m	C	D.C.	10 FEB 1871	Young Mens
266	Whitman, Elvin E.	1y	W	D.C.	20 JUL 1867	Congressional
778	Whitmen, Margaret E.	1m	W	U.S.	02 JUN 1874	Graceland
002	Whitmore, Catharine P.	26y	W	Md.	— JAN 1855	
622	Whitmore, [blank]	2y	W	U.S.	21 AUG 1872	
121	Whitney, Geo. W.	1m	W	D.C.	10 JUL 1858	Methodist
161	Whitney, Jas. O., carpenter	34y	W	D.C.	08 SEP 1859	Congressional
585	Whitney, Joey H.	1y	W	D.C.	10 MAR 1872	Congressional*
264	Whitney, Joseph, scavenger	65y	W	Conn.	19 JUL 1867	Congressional
513	Whitney, Joshua	33y	W		27 MAR 1871	Glenwood
583	Whitney, Laura	4y	W	D.C.	29 FEB 1872	Glenwood
769	Whitney, Louisa F., clerk	58y	W	Can.	27 MAY 1874	Oak Hill
325	Whitney, Margaret	57y	W		19 JUL 1868	Congressional
381	Whitney, Maria	71y	W	Pa.	26 MAR 1869	Pa.
585	Whitney, Willie R.	6y		U.S.	07 MAR 1872	Congressional*
422	Whitrow, Judie	2y	C		10 OCT 1869	Holmead
429	Whitter, Wm. E.	8d	W		26 DEC 1869	Congressional
215	Whittier, Ella	3y	W	D.C.	14 MAR 1866	Congressional
542	Whittin, Sarah Ann	21y	C	Md.	23 OCT 1871	
744	Whittington, Thos. F.	4m	C	U.S.	11 JAN 1874	
134	Whittlesey, Elisha M., clerk	36y	W	Ohio	30 NOV 1858	Ohio
710	Whittlesey, Henry M., Br.B.G.	51y	W	U.S.	08 AUG 1873	Oswego, N.Y.
385	Whittlessy, Frederick	15y	W	D.C.	14 APR 1869	Congressional
544	Whittman, Moses	29y	C	Md.	04 NOV 1871	Washington
103	Whitwell, Anna W.	58y	W	Pa.	27 JAN 1858	Congressional
274	Whonohan, Mary	35y	W	Ire.	08 SEP 1867	Mt. Olivet
419	Whyte, Eliza Mary	70y	W	Eng.	14 OCT 1869	Congressional
732	Whyte, L.J.	20y	W	U.S.	30 NOV 1873	Congressional*
179	Wiber, Annie Bell	11m	W	U.S.	09 MAY 1860	Glenwood
274	Wiber, David, printer	33y	W	Pa.	03 SEP 1867	Glenwood
199	Wickmueller, Mary	66y	W	N.C.	02 FEB 1861	Mt. Olivet
536	Widerman, L.P.	Still	W	D.C.	17 SEP 1871	
344	Widman, Francis	3m	W	D.C.	04 AUG 1868	Prospect Hill
706	Widmeyer, George	8m	W	U.S.	22 JUL 1873	Prospect Hill

District of Columbia Interments (Index to Deaths), 1855-1874

Page	Name	Age	Race	Birth	Death Date	Burial Ground
620	Widmeyer, Rosina	18m	W	U.S.	22 AUG 1872	
391	Widmeyer, Rosina Christina	9m	W	D.C.	08 MAY 1869	Prospect Hill
628	Widmyer, John, butcher	46y	W	Ger.	04 SEP 1872	
111	Widmyer, Lewis C.	7m	W	D.C.	12 APR 1858	German
612	Widners, Geo.	1d	W	U.S.	21 JUL 1872	
713	Wiebking, Fred.	14m	W	D.C.	22 AUG 1873	Prospect Hill
318	Wiedersheim, [blank]	Still	W	D.C.	25 JUN 1868	Congressional
632	Wiegman, Ph.	48y	W	U.S.	20 OCT 1872	
704	Wier, Ada	3y	C	D.C.	03 JUL 1873	
154	Wiesenthal, Charles	6m	W	D.C.	19 JUL 1859	Lutheran
515	Wiggens, Matilda	70y	C	Va.	12 MAR 1871	Ebenezer
456	Wiggin, Clementine D.	7d	W	D.C.	17 JUN 1870	Glenwood
265	Wiggin, Isaac B., clerk	44y	W	N.H.	25 JUL 1867	Philadelphia, Pa.
376	Wiggins, Ernest W.	3d	W		16 FEB 1869	Glenwood
495	Wigginson, Henry	30y	W	Eng.	18 DEC 1870	Potters Field
645	Wilacher, Geo. Conrad, merchant	25y	W	Ger.	24 DEC 1872	Congressional*
318	Wilber, Elizabeth J.	22y	W	D.C.	02 JUN 1868	Congressional
187	Wilburn, Maggie G.	10m	W	D.C.	10 AUG 1860	Congressional
595	Wilburn, Martha	29y	W	Md.	21 APR 1872	Congressional*
591	Wilburn, Martha A.	25y	C	U.S.	22 APR 1872	Congressional
044	Wilburn, Mr., miller	49y	W	Md.	01 MAY 1856	Catholic
195	Wilburn, Rezin, laborer	74y	W		21 DEC 1860	Mt. Olivet
742	Wild, Magdelene	63y	W	Bav.	19 JAN 1874	Baltimore, Md.
481	Wild, Sarah E.	21y	W	Amer.	31 OCT 1870	Oak Hill
031	Wilde, Xavier, blacksmith	42y	W	Ger.	10 DEC 1855	Not Reported
002	Wildman, Mary	7m	W	D.C.	— JAN 1855	Removed from City
256	Wilds, James Ed.	2y		D.C.	24 MAR 1867	Congressional
150	Wiley, Casper	1y	W	D.C.	09 JUN 1859	Glenwood
090	Wiley, Fritrisk	2y		D.C.	10 SEP 1857	German Lutheran
151	Wiley, John C.	4y	W	D.C.	21 JUN 1859	Glenwood
524	Wiliams, Else Y.	2y	C	D.C.	23 JUN 1871	Union
530	Wilke, D.	5y	W	N.Y.	31 JUL 1871	Prospect Hill
630	Wilkenson, Ida	16y	W	U.S.	11 OCT 1872	Small Pox
319	Wilker, William	53y	W	Ger.	15 JUN 1868	Congressional
148	Wilkerson, Julia A., lady	26y	W	Pa.	14 MAY 1859	N.Y.
320	Wilkerson, Louisa	40y	W	Va.	15 JUN 1868	Va.
599	Wilkerson, Rosa	1y	C	U.S.	15 MAY 1872	Unknown
041	Wilkerson, Winnian	3m	W	D.C.	09 APR 1856	Methodist
148	Wilkerson, [blank]	1y	W	D.C.	11 MAY 1859	Methodist
227	Wilkey, Walter B.	3m	W	D.C.	05 JUL 1866	Mt. Olivet
606	Wilkins, E.J.	38y	W	Va.	18 JUN 1872	Congressional*
279	Wilkins, Eliza	58y	W	Pa.	28 OCT 1867	Glenwood
681	Wilkins, Frank	16m	W	U.S.	12 APR 1873	
588	Wilkins, Percy S.	2m	W	D.C.	26 MAR 1872	Oak Hill
615	Wilkins, Robt.	58y	C	U.S.	13 JUL 1872	
278	Wilkinson, Edward Barry	1y	W	D.C.	03 OCT 1867	Congressional
236	Wilkinson, Edward, waiter	21y	C		27 SEP 1866	Harmony (new)
606	Wilkinson, John, carpenter	24y	W	D.C.	23 JUN 1872	Congressional*
606	Wilkinson, John, carpenter	24y	W	D.C.	23 JUN 1872	Congressional*
730	Wilkinson, John, carpenter	84y	W	Eng.	11 NOV 1873	Glenwood
522	Wilkinson, Mahlon, lawyer	46y	W		10 JUN 1871	Mt. Pleasant
595	Wilkinson, Mary E.	2y	W	D.C.	25 APR 1872	Congressional*
290	Wilkinson, Mary J.	27y	W		18 JAN 1868	Albany, N.Y.
283	Wilkinson, Nany	42y	W	Md.	23 NOV 1867	Methodist
601	Wilkinson, Robt.	100y	C	U.S.	23 MAY 1872	Mt. Olivet*
195	Wilkinson, T., Miss	52y	W	Md.	16 DEC 1860	Congressional*
244	Will, Mary E.	27y	W	N.H.	28 NOV 1866	Congressional
778	Willard, A.C., Mrs.	37y	W	U.S.	09 JUN 1874	Oak Hill

Page	Name	Age	Race	Birth	Death Date	Burial Ground
507	Willard, Antonia, Mrs.	32y	W	Va.	14 FEB 1871	Oak Hill
518	Willard, Mary			Va.	10 MAY 1871	
047	Wille, Hellen L.	4m	W	D.C.	30 JUN 1856	Glenwood
612	Willenbucher, Pauline	3y	W	U.S.	06 JUL 1872	
608	Willenbucker, Ferdinand	2y	W	D.C.	18 JUN 1872	
276	Willes, Benjamin, gardener	60y	W	Va.	10 SEP 1867	
026	Willet, Birnah, carpenter	57y	W		24 OCT 1855	Glenwood/Rock Creek
501	Willet, Estelle	14d	W	D.C.	05 JAN 1871	Glenwood/Rock Creek
251	Willett, Clinton Beall	2y	W		20 JAN 1867	Rock Creek*
248	Willett, Emmeline	59y	W	D.C.	19 DEC 1866	Rock Creek
082	Willett, Florence	1m	W	D.C.	10 JUL 1857	Glenwood
131	Willett, Joseph R.	80y	W	Pa.	30 OCT 1858	Glenwood
415	Willett, Voltaire	65y	W	Pa.	23 SEP 1869	Glenwood
330	Willey, George	1y	C	D.C.	28 JUL 1868	Young Mens
405	Willey, Margaret	35y	W	Ger.	27 JUL 1869	Washington Asylum
580	Willey, Maria	76y	W	Md.	11 FEB 1872	Congressional
215	William, Camilla, servant	15y	C	Va.	20 MAR 1866	Union B[torn]
466	William, Emma	1y	C	D.C.	30 JUL 1870	Young Mens
545	William, Mary	6y	C	D.C.	21 NOV 1871	Washington
749	Williamon, Ann	81y	W	Eng.	24 FEB 1874	Glenwood
392	Williams, A.	1d	C		07 MAY 1869	Washington Asylum
607	Williams, A.A.	23y	W	D.C.	29 JUN 1872	Congressional
354	Williams, Ada E.	3d	W	D.C.	05 OCT 1868	Glenwood
152	Williams, Addison	6m	C	D.C.	26 JUN 1859	Young Mens
532	Williams, Albert	6m	W	D.C.	15 AUG 1871	Young Mens
681	Williams, Amelia	64y	C	U.S.	19 APR 1873	Young Mens
260	Williams, Ann	25y	C	Md.	01 MAY 1867	Beckett's
437	Williams, Ann A.	61y	W		15 JAN 1870	Glenwood
756	Williams, Ann, infant of	1d	C	U.S.	08 MAR 1874	
386	Williams, Anna	8m	W	D.C.	15 APR 1869	Congressional
667	Williams, Anna	45y	C	U.S.	15 FEB 1873	Washington Asylum
127	Williams, Anne	57y	C	Md.	06 SEP 1858	Young Mens
688	Williams, Annie	22y	C	U.S.	14 MAY 1873	
769	Williams, Annie	21y	C	U.S.	19 MAY 1874	Washington Asylum
108	Williams, Archibald, cartman	60y	C	Va.	13 MAR 1858	Western
272	Williams, Archie	4m	C		26 AUG 1867	Freedmen's Bureau
428	Williams, Arnold, laborer	24y	C	Va.	04 NOV 1869	Washington Asylum
242	Williams, Betsy, Miss	80y	W	Va.	02 OCT 1866	Congressional
006	Williams, Billy, slave & waiter	40y	C	Md.	05 APR 1855	Corporation
644	Williams, Blanche	14m	C	U.S.	17 DEC 1872	Harmony
315	Williams, C.J.	18y	C		c.25 MAY 1868	Mt. Olivet
327	Williams, Caroline	1y	C		21 JUL 1868	Holmead
635	Williams, Cath.	1m	C	U.S.	30 NOV 1872	Small Pox
034	Williams, Charles	62y	C		06 JAN 1856	Alms House
296	Williams, Charles	59y	C	Md.	03 FEB 1868	Freedmen's Hospital
750	Williams, Charles, laborer	45y	C	U.S.	05 FEB 1874	
326	Williams, Charles M.	3y	W	D.C.	01 JUL 1868	Congressional
158	Williams, Charles, slave	38y	C	Va.	15 AUG 1859	Harmony
583	Williams, Charlotte	103y	C	Va.	25 FEB 1872	Ebenezer
749	Williams, Chary	50y	C	U.S.	18 FEB 1874	
543	Williams, Christopher	10m	W	D.C.	26 OCT 1871	Mt. Olivet
769	Williams, Daniel	35y	C	U.S.	17 MAY 1874	
144	Williams, Daniel, laborer	35y	C		16 MAR 1859	Western
066	Williams, Daniel, porter	17y	C	D.C.	17 DEC 1856	St. Matthews
516	Williams, Doras A.	11m	W	D.C.	20 MAR 1871	Congressional
416	Williams, Elijah	7y	C	Va.	12 SEP 1869	
391	Williams, Eliza Ann, housekeeper	32y	W	Md.	18 MAY 1869	Mt. Olivet
351	Williams, Eliza, child of	Still	C	D.C.	20 SEP 1868	

District of Columbia Interments (Index to Deaths), 1855-1874

Page	Name	Age	Race	Birth	Death Date	Burial Ground
620	Williams, Elizab.	6m	W	U.S.	01 AUG 1872	Congressional*
291	Williams, Ellen		C		09 JAN 1868	Alms House
670	Williams, Ellen	14y	C	U.S.	17 FEB 1873	Small Pox
382	Williams, Ellen, laundress	26y	C	Va.	31 MAR 1869	Union
591	Williams, Ellinor	5y	C	U.S.	30 APR 1872	Small Pox
545	Williams, Elmira	8y	C	Md.	12 NOV 1871	Young Mens
474	Williams, Emma	1y	C		13 AUG 1870	Washington Asylum
417	Williams, Emma	2m	C		13 SEP 1869	Washington Asylum
168	Williams, Eva	30y	C	D.C.	29 DEC 1859	Harmony
607	Williams, F.W.	6m	W	D.C.	14 JUN 1872	Congressional
724	Williams, Frances R.	24y	W	D.C.	12 OCT 1873	Congressional
324	Williams, Frederick B., plasterer	34y	W	D.C.	04 JUL 1868	Glenwood
303	Williams, Geo.	11y	W		10 MAR 1868	Congressional
397	Williams, George	7d	B		12 JUN 1869	
590	Williams, George L.	3y	W	D.C.	01 APR 1872	Congressional
286	Williams, H., Mr.	26y	W	D.C.	25 DEC 1867	Glenwood
451	Williams, Hannah	3m	C	D.C.	08 APR 1870	Union
516	Williams, Harland, painter	26y	W	Md.	01 MAR 1871	Congressional
306	Williams, Harriet	60y	C	Md.	27 APR 1868	Young Mens
690	Williams, Henry	59y	C	U.S.	07 MAY 1873	Small Pox
581	Williams, Henry S.	2y	W	D.C.	15 FEB 1872	Congressional*
778	Williams, Henry, sailor	24y	C	U.S.	08 JUN 1874	Mt. Olivet
697	Williams, Hill	42y	C	U.S.	05 JUN 1873	
641	Williams, Ida	8m	C	U.S.	27 DEC 1872	Small Pox*
549	Williams, Irene	1y	W	U.S.	21 DEC 1871	Congressional
762	Williams, Isabella, housekeeper	28y	C	U.S.	02 APR 1874	
047	Williams, Israel	5m	W	D.C.	29 JUN 1856	Oak Hill
153	Williams, J.	2m	C	U.S.	06 JUL 1859	Western
058	Williams, J.B., capt. USMC	58y	W		26 SEP 1856	Congressional
713	Williams, J.B., painter	53y	W	Va.	24 AUG 1873	Congressional*
342	Williams, J.H.	7m	C	D.C.	17 AUG 1868	Union
235	Williams, Jacob	60y	C		13 SEP 1866	
235	Williams, Jak	2y	C	D.C.	13 SEP 1866	
639	Williams, James	4y	C	U.S.	11 DEC 1872	Small Pox*
278	Williams, James Edward	1y	C		18 OCT 1867	Union, Georgetown
644	Williams, James, laborer	23y	C	U.S.	21 DEC 1872	Young Mens
044	Williams, Jane	56y	C	D.C.	06 MAY 1856	Harmony
756	Williams, Jane E.	26y	C	U.S.	27 MAR 1874	
749	Williams, Jane, servant	30y	C	U.S.	26 FEB 1874	Mt. Pleasant
427	Williams, Jas.	2y	C	Va.	06 NOV 1869	Washington Asylum
711	Williams, Jas. M.	10m	C	D.C.	10 AUG 1873	Young Mens
453	Williams, Jessie	1y	W		21 MAY 1870	Congressional
144	Williams, Jno. Fred.		C	D.C.	21 MAR 1859	Harmony
664	Williams, Jno. H.	19y	C	U.S.	17 JAN 1873	Small Pox*
609	Williams, John	9y	C	U.S.	14 JUN 1872	
613	Williams, John	16d	C	U.S.	26 JUL 1872	
501	Williams, John	35y	W		25 JAN 1871	Catholic
016	Williams, John	3m	C	D.C.	08 JUL 1855	Holmead
005	Williams, John	1y	C	D.C.	24 MAR 1855	Holmead
591	Williams, John	25y	C	U.S.	23 APR 1872	Small Pox
591	Williams, John	25y	C	U.S.	24 APR 1872	Small Pox
640	Williams, John	3y	W	U.S.	16 DEC 1872	Small Pox*
036	Williams, John	65y	W		19 FEB 1856	West
451	Williams, John	4m	C	D.C.	04 APR 1870	Washington Asylum
298	Williams, John	28y	C	Va.	14 FEB 1868	Young Mens
333	Williams, John, Capt., waterman	51y	W	Va.	17 JUL 1868	Congressional
731	Williams, John, cook	30y	C	U.S.	22 NOV 1873	
266	Williams, John Edward	8m	W	D.C.*	06 JUL 1867	Oak Hill

District of Columbia Interments (Index to Deaths), 1855-1874

Page	Name	Age	Race	Birth	Death Date	Burial Ground
099	Williams, John, machinist	25y	C	D.C.	23 DEC 1857	Ebenezer
455	Williams, John Roland	1y	W		20 MAY 1870	Glenwood
322	Williams, John S., clerk	83y	W	U.S.	14 JUN 1868	Glenwood
530	Williams, Joseph	6m	W	U.S.	28 JUL 1871	
477	Williams, Joseph	9m	C	Va.*	12 SEP 1870	Holmead
273	Williams, Julius, laborer	22y	C	Va.	20 SEP 1867	Union
377	Williams, Katy	3m	C		06 FEB 1869	Md.
295	Williams, Lang, infant of		C	D.C.	14 FEB 1868	Ebenezer
390	Williams, Laura	25y	W		27 MAY 1869	Congressional
412	Williams, Laura	6m	C	D.C.	18 AUG 1869	Washington Asylum
507	Williams, Laura S., housekeeper	47y	W	Conn.	20 FEB 1871	Middleton, Conn.
226	Williams, Lea Jane	20y	W	D.C.	30 JUN 1866	Rock Creek
357	Williams, Lewis	1y	B	D.C.	18 OCT 1868	Washington Asylum
737	Williams, Louisa	22y	C	U.S.	23 DEC 1873	Mt. Olivet
531	Williams, Louise	76y	W	Mass.	01 AUG 1871	Congressional
003	Williams, Lucy	55y	C	Va.	03 FEB 1855	Freedmen's
142	Williams, Lucy, servant	22y	C	Va.	28 FEB 1859	Colored Methodist
410	Williams, Ludwel	1m	C		09 AUG 1869	
216	Williams, Lydia	22y	C		24 MAR 1866	Alms House
525	Williams, Maggie	1y	C	D.C.	26 JUN 1871	Ebenezer
417	Williams, Maria Martha	3m	C		12 SEP 1869	Harmony
762	Williams, Mariah, cook	62y	C	U.S.	03 APR 1874	Young Mens
337	Williams, Martha	2y	C	D.C.	13 AUG 1868	Ebenezer
251	Williams, Martha	93y	W	Md.	24 JAN 1867	Glenwood
370	Williams, Mary	50y	W		31 JAN 1869	Baltimore, Md.
272	Williams, Mary	25y	C		31 AUG 1867	Freedmen's Bureau
239	Williams, Mary	4y	C	D.C.	04 OCT 1866	Mt. Olivet
021	Williams, Mary	35y	W		15 AUG 1855	Poor House
525	Williams, Mary	1y	C	D.C.	28 JUN 1871	Potters Field
663	Williams, Mary	unk.	C	U.S.	02 JAN 1873	Small Pox*
683	Williams, Mary	14y	C	U.S.	16 APR 1873	Small Pox
337	Williams, Mary	1y	C	U.S.	17 AUG 1868	Washington Asylum
477	Williams, Mary	9m	C	Va.	10 SEP 1870	Western
343	Williams, Mary A.	1y	C	D.C.	23 AUG 1868	
481	Williams, Mary Ann	11d	C	D.C.	19 OCT 1870	Ebenezer
441	Williams, Mary Ann	5y	C	Va.	02 FEB 1870	Potters Field
379	Williams, Mary E.	5y	W	D.C.	19 MAR 1869	Congressional
300	Williams, Mary E., Mrs.	51y	W	Del.	15 MAR 1868	Glenwood
684	Williams, Mary E.	14y	C	U.S.	16 APR 1873	Small Pox*
591	Williams, Mary E.	3y	C	U.S.	29 APR 1872	Small Pox
019	Williams, Mary E.	9m		D.C.	09 AUG 1855	St. Patricks
382	Williams, Mary Emily	3m	C	Va.	08 MAR 1869	Holmead
223	Williams, Mary S.	62y	W	Va.	02 JUN 1866	Congressional
483	Williams, Mary, servant	20y	C	Va.	01 OCT 1870	Freedmen's Hospital
466	Williams, Mary, servant	27y	C	Va.	29 JUL 1870	Young Mens
492	Williams, Mary, servant	23y	C	Va.	02 DEC 1870	Young Mens
203	Williams, Matilda, washerwoman	63y	C	Md.	17 MAY 1861	Holmead
455	Williams, Melvin	30y	C	Va.	08 MAY 1870	
137	Williams, Miles	21y	C		11 JAN 1859	Western
315	Williams, Mrs., child of	9d	W		c.27 MAY 1868	Mt. Olivet
401	Williams, Myriam	7m	C	D.C.	31 JUL 1869	Young Mens
708	Williams, Nancy, servant	73y	C	Va.	27 JUL 1873	
255	Williams, Nat., laborer	70y	C	Va.	17 MAR 1867	Ebenezer
489	Williams, Nellie	2m	C	U.S.	28 NOV 1870	Georgetown
392	Williams, Ottoway, child of	Still			26 MAY 1869	
447	Williams, Peter	70y	C		28 MAR 1870	Ebenezer
732	Williams, Peter	7y	W	U.S.	29 NOV 1873	Mt. Olivet
216	Williams, Peter, baker	17y	C	Va.	26 MAR 1866	Young Mens

Page	Name	Age	Race	Birth	Death Date	Burial Ground
473	Williams, Polly	70y	C	D.C.	28 AUG 1870	Western
741	Williams, Priscella E.	2m	C	U.S.	07 JAN 1874	
455	Williams, R., painter	25y	W	Va.	22 MAY 1870	
401	Williams, R.A.	8m	C		20 JUL 1869	Holmead
128	Williams, Rebecca	1y	C		24 SEP 1858	Western
769	Williams, Richard	5y	C	U.S.	20 MAY 1874	Young Mens
539	Williams, Richd.	11m	C	D.C.	30 SEP 1871	Young Mens
621	Williams, Richd., laborer	13y	C	U.S.	10 AUG 1872	
507	Williams, Rigdon, clerk	30y	W	Ohio	14 FEB 1871	Cincinnati, Ohio
470	Williams, Robert	35y	W	N.Y.	12 AUG 1870	Rock Creek
294	Williams, Robert Gilbert	3½m	C		08 FEB 1868	
038	Williams, Rose	9y	W		14 MAR 1856	Va.
059	Williams, S.J.	38y	W	Pa.	29 SEP 1856	St. Patricks
248	Williams, Saml.	1y	C	D.C.	25 DEC 1866	Beckett's
032	Williams, Saml., ostler	35y	W	Md.	26 DEC 1855	St. Matthews
423	Williams, Samuel	1y	C		22 OCT 1869	Ebenezer
055	Williams, Samuel, laborer	21y	C	D.C.	24 AUG 1856	Holmead
603	Williams, Sarah	7d	C	D.C.	22 JUN 1872	Ebenezer
466	Williams, Sarah	1y	C	D.C.	13 JUL 1870	Union
458	Williams, Sarah C.	5m	C	D.C.	27 JUN 1870	Potters Field
136	Williams, Sarah, child of	Still	C	D.C.	27 DEC 1858	Western
096	Williams, Sarah J.	2y	W	D.C.	11 NOV 1857	Congressional
332	Williams, Sarah J.E.	8m	C	D.C.	18 JUL 1868	Brick Church, Bennings
545	Williams, Sarah, servant	88y	C	Md.	14 NOV 1871	
705	Williams, Seymore	1h	C	D.C.	03 JUL 1873	Beckett's
638	Williams, Solomon	2y	C	U.S.	08 NOV 1872	Washington Asylum
498	Williams, Sophia	45y	W	Md.	04 JAN 1871	Washington Asylum
786	Williams, Sophia B.	50y	W	U.S.	14 JUL 1874	Glenwood
146	Williams, Susan, servant	23y	C	Va.	02 APR 1859	Colored Methodist
394	Williams, Susie	3m	W	D.C.	29 JUN 1869	Mt. Olivet
553	Williams, Thomas	80y	C	Va.	08 JAN 1872	Washington
306	Williams, Thomas	1y	C	D.C.	16 APR 1868	Young Mens
343	Williams, Thomas J., clerk	59y	W	D.C.	30 AUG 1868	Congressional
255	Williams, Thornton	47y	C		23 MAR 1867	Young Mens
117	Williams, W. Henry	1y	C		24 JUN 1858	Harmony
073	Williams, W.G., bricklayer	22y	W	Va.	16 MAR 1857	Glenwood
398	Williams, William	14y	W	D.C.	19 JUN 1869	
682	Williams, William	11m	C	U.S.	28 APR 1873	
316	Williams, William E., bricklayer	62y	W	Va.	10 MAY 1868	Glenwood
327	Williams, Willie	8m	W	D.C.	26 JUL 1868	Holmead
111	Williams, Wm. H., farmer	56y	W	Va.	18 APR 1858	Glenwood
361	Williams, Wm. H.	1y	C	D.C.	23 NOV 1868	Young Mens
031	Williams, Wm., machinist	72y	W	Wales	18 DEC 1855	St. Patricks
172	Williams, [blank]	Still	W	D.C.	08 FEB 1860	Congressional
456	Williams, [blank]	6d	C	D.C.	23 JUN 1870	Harmony
459	Williams, [blank]	6d	C	D.C.	23 JUN 1870	Harmony
293	Williams, [blank]	24y	C		07 MAR 1868	Methodist
246	Williams, [blank]		W	Md.	27 DEC 1866	Md.
047	Williams, [blank]	27y	W	D.C.	24 JUN 1856	Oak Hill
140	Williams, [blank]	4y	C		10 FEB 1859	Western
141	Williams, [blank]	2y	C		12 FEB 1859	Western
357	Williams, [blank]	Still	B	D.C.	28 OCT 1868	Washington Asylum
018	Williams, [blank]	11m	C		30 AUG 1855	West
584	Williamson, A.V.	6y	W	D.C.	04 MAR 1872	Congressional*
379	Williamson, Benjamin	1y	W	D.C.	27 MAR 1869	Congressional
240	Williamson, Geo. P., clerk	64y	W		20 OCT 1866	Glenwood
221	Williamson, George M.	10m	W	D.C.	15 MAY 1866	Congressional
092	Williamson, John Thos.	2y	W	D.C.	30 SEP 1857	Congressional

District of Columbia Interments (Index to Deaths), 1855-1874

Page	Name	Age	Race	Birth	Death Date	Burial Ground
289	Williamson, Joseph, messenger	73y	W	Eng.	23 JAN 1868	Glenwood
638	Williamson, Sister M., teacher	49y	W	U.S.	11 NOV 1872	Convent
057	Williamson, Wm.	1y	W	D.C.	11 SEP 1856	Washington
193	Williamson, [blank]	10m	W		06 NOV 1860	Methodist
661	Williamson, [blank]	1m	W	U.S.	29 JAN 1873	Mt. Olivet
489	Willian, Catharine S.L.	39y	W	Ger.	02 NOV 1870	Glenwood
478	Willian, Geo.	7y	C	D.C.	03 SEP 1870	Mt. Olivet
473	Willian, Mary A.	9m	C	D.C.	15 AUG 1870	Holmead
417	Willis, Ann, servant	26y	C		01 SEP 1869	Washington Asylum
301	Willis, Betsey	32y	C	Va.	17 MAR 1868	Young Mens
399	Willis, Charles, merchant	75y	W	Rus.	29 JUL 1869	Congressional
613	Willis, Chas.	2y	C	U.S.	22 JUL 1872	
360	Willis, Emma	8m	W		17 NOV 1868	
430	Willis, Hale, clerk		W		29 DEC 1869	Oak Hill
768	Willis, Helen	2y	C	U.S.	03 MAY 1874	Washington Asylum
272	Willis, Henry M.	1m	W	D.C.	27 AUG 1867	Glenwood
353	Willis, Hiland	4m	C	D.C.	12 SEP 1868	Western
356	Willis, James, farmer	70y	B	Va.	02 OCT 1868	Union
667	Willis, James, laborer	40y	C	U.S.	15 FEB 1873	Washington Asylum
417	Willis, Jennie V.	2y	C	D.C.	23 SEP 1869	Harmony
443	Willis, Judy	50y	C	Va.	28 FEB 1870	Washington Asylum
399	Willis, Margaret	45y	C		24 JUL 1869	Congressional
778	Willis, Michael J., grocer	33y	W	Ire.	19 JUN 1874	Holyrood
278	Willison, Nancy, domestic	20y	C	D.C.	11 OCT 1867	Harmony
537	Willman, Martha J.	31y	W	Md.	21 SEP 1871	Congressional
661	Willner, Margaret A.	29y	W	U.S.	25 JAN 1873	Glenwood
734	Wills, Annie E.	15y	W	U.S.	01 DEC 1873	Congressional
513	Wills, Gertrude	1y	C	Amer.	20 MAR 1871	Harmony
530	Wills, John	63y	W	Md.	31 JUL 1871	Congressional
300	Wills, John W., Indian agent	50y	W	Md.	14 MAR 1868	Glenwood
762	Wills, Kate, infant of	2m	C	U.S.	05 APR 1874	Washington Asylum
545	Wills, Mary Ann	3y	C	D.C.	19 NOV 1871	
260	Wills, Robert, laborer	55y	C	Md.	26 MAY 1867	Mt. Olivet
527	Wills, Wm. H.	1y	C	D.C.	11 JUL 1871	Ebenezer
247	Wills, [blank]		W		10 DEC 1866	Congressional
466	Willson, Emma	11m	C	D.C.	11 JUL 1870	Union
197	Willson, George, block mker	63y	W	Md.	18 JAN 1861	Congressional
319	Willy, Martha, washerwoman	30y	C	D.C.	— JUN 1868	
267	Wilmer, Edward	1y	W		07 JUL 1867	Mt. Olivet
616a	Wilmuth, Mrs. [Deborah]	65y	W	U.S.	11 JUL 1872	Congressional*
626	Wilner, Frances	10y	W	U.S.	04 SEP 1872	
747	Wilobe, James, laborer	55y	W	U.S.	01 FEB 1874	Potters Field
289	Wilsey, Abram S.	6m	W	N.Y.	19 JAN 1868	Congressional
312	Wilsie, Catherine May	2y	W	Mich.	03 MAY 1868	Western
360	Wilson, Alice	5y	W	Md.	08 NOV 1868	Pr. Geo. Co., Md.
271	Wilson, Andrew	7m	W	D.C.	02 AUG 1867	Young Mens
250	Wilson, Ann E.	63y	W	Va.	18 JAN 1867	Congressional
426	Wilson, Anna, domestic	37y	C	Md.	25 NOV 1869	Union
393	Wilson, Anne	8m	C		10 MAY 1869	Beckett's
769	Wilson, Annie, domestic	15y	C	U.S.	16 MAY 1874	Harmony
288	Wilson, Biddy, Mrs.	67y	W	Md.	05 DEC 1867	Glenwood
042	Wilson, C.M.	46y	W		22 APR 1856	Oak Hill
598	Wilson, Carrie L.	5y	W	U.S.	10 MAY 1872	Glenwood
296	Wilson, Celia	25y	C	Md.	14 FEB 1868	Alms House
278	Wilson, Charles H.	1m	W	D.C.	09 OCT 1867	Congressional
501	Wilson, Charlotte	21d	C	D.C.	20 JAN 1871	Young Mens
755	Wilson, Columbus	33y	C	U.S.	09 MAR 1874	Young Mens
485	Wilson, Cora V.	3m	C	D.C.	03 OCT 1870	Beckett's

District of Columbia Interments (Index to Deaths), 1855-1874

Page	Name	Age	Race	Birth	Death Date	Burial Ground
528	Wilson, Danl. F.S.	5m	C	D.C.	13 JUL 1871	Union
035	Wilson, David M., agt. UB Society	59y	W	Md.	29 FEB 1856	Glenwood
324	Wilson, Dewitt C., Dr., real estate	45y	W	Ire.	20 JUL 1868	Middleton, N.Y.
098	Wilson, Dr., physician	25y	W		09 DEC 1857	Oak Hill
007	Wilson, Edwin	17y	W	D.C.	21 APR 1855	Episcopal
670	Wilson, Eliza	13y	C	U.S.	24 FEB 1873	Small Pox
073	Wilson, Eliza M.	46y	W	N.J.	07 MAR 1857	Glenwood
154	Wilson, Elizabeth	1y	W	D.C.	19 JUL 1859	Congressional
304	Wilson, Elizabeth	4y	C	D.C.	14 MAR 1868	Congressional
477	Wilson, Elizabeth	14y	C	Md.	11 SEP 1870	Holmead
552	Wilson, Emanuel, laborer	71y	C	D.C.	05 JAN 1872	Mt. Olivet
661	Wilson, Emma	22y	C	U.S.	28 JAN 1873	Washington Asylum
047	Wilson, Esebella F.	3m	W		28 JUN 1856	Foundry
520	Wilson, Eva Rebecca	10m	C	D.C.	26 MAY 1871	Young Mens
459	Wilson, Fanny, servant	22y	C	Md.	05 JUN 1870	
035	Wilson, Frances	23y	W		14 FEB 1856	Congressional
478	Wilson, Frances	48y	C		20 SEP 1870	Harmony
033	Wilson, Frank B.	1y	W		13 JAN 1856	Congressional
524	Wilson, George	11y	C	Md.	20 JUN 1871	Western
373	Wilson, George, shoemaker	35y	C		05 JAN 1869	Georgetown
366	Wilson, Harriet H.P.	4y	W	D.C.	05 DEC 1868	Glenwood
335b	Wilson, Henrietta	2m	B		04 JUL 1868	Washington Asylum
258	Wilson, Henry	57y	C		12 APR 1867	Alms House
720	Wilson, Henry T.L.	62y	W	Md.	27 SEP 1873	
423	Wilson, HEster	4y	C	D.C.	11 OCT 1869	Washington Asylum
342	Wilson, James Albert	11m	C	D.C.	18 AUG 1868	Union
598	Wilson, James B.	4m	W	U.S.	16 MAY 1872	Glenwood
154	Wilson, James H., gunner	28y	W	N.Y.	14 JUL 1859	Congressional
036	Wilson, James, waiter	45y	C		14 FEB 1856	Harmony
169	Wilson, Jessie	3m	W	D.C.	11 JAN 1860	Congressional
604	Wilson, Jno. H.	10m	C	D.C.	02 JUN 1872	
738	Wilson, John, farmer	37y	W	U.S.	02 DEC 1873	
146	Wilson, John M., gun carriage mkr.	59y	W	Md.	12 APR 1859	Methodist
065	Wilson, John Quincy, blacksmith		W	D.C.	17 DEC 1856	Congressional
039	Wilson, John T.R.	10y	W	D.C.	17 MAR 1856	Bladensburg, Md.
778	Wilson, Jos. Shields	68y	W	U.S.	23 JUN 1874	Glenwood
440	Wilson, Josephine Shidds	3y	W		15 FEB 1870	Glenwood
706	Wilson, Kate B.		C	Md.	— JUL 1873	
501	Wilson, Keziah	14y	C	Va.	30 JAN 1871	Holmead
508	Wilson, Laura	2y	C	D.C.	24 FEB 1871	Young Mens
181	Wilson, Laura E.	3y	W	D.C.	08 JUN 1860	Glenwood
371	Wilson, Lewis	1d	W	U.S.	04 JAN 1869	Washington Asylum
397	Wilson, Lizzi	3y	C	D.C.	15 JUN 1869	Holmead
611	Wilson, Lizzie	4m	C	U.S.	14 JUL 1872	
060	Wilson, Louisa, seamstress	23y	W	Md.	08 OCT 1856	Washington Asylum
681	Wilson, Lucy B.	2m	C	U.S.	19 APR 1873	
177	Wilson, Margaret	85y	W	Md.	22 APR 1860	Glenwood
783	Wilson, Margaret	51y	W	Ire.	28 JUL 1874	Mt. Olivet
442	Wilson, Margaret	1m	C		02 FEB 1870	Washington Asylum
660	Wilson, Margaret, servant	80y	C	U.S.	21 JAN 1873	
366	Wilson, Mark H.	1y	W	Md.	08 DEC 1868	Md.
027	Wilson, Martha E.	1y	W	D.C.	18 OCT 1855	St. Peters
520	Wilson, Mary	6y	C		25 MAY 1871	Young Mens
631	Wilson, Mary A.	7y	C	U.S.	11 OCT 1872	
528	Wilson, Mary A.	14y	C	Md.	15 JUL 1871	Union
170	Wilson, Mary, alias Thomas	56y	C	Md.	28 JAN 1860	Washington Asylum
280	Wilson, Mary Ann	9y	C	Ky.	15 OCT 1867	Young Mens
492	Wilson, Mary E.	8y	C	D.C.	24 DEC 1870	Young Mens

Page	Name	Age	Race	Birth	Death Date	Burial Ground
580	Wilson, Mary G.	72y	W	U.S.	07 FEB 1872	Congressional*
291	Wilson, Mary R.	60y	W	Md.	20 JAN 1868	Glenwood
550	Wilson, Mary Scott	3m	W	D.C.	28 DEC 1871	Washington
506	Wilson, Mattie E.	1y	W	D.C.	03 FEB 1871	Congressional
246	Wilson, Montania	1y	W	D.C.	23 DEC 1866	Congressional
008	Wilson, Mrs., child of		W	D.C.	13 MAY 1855	Foundry
709	Wilson, Nathaniel, confectioner	65y	W	N.J.	20 JUL 1873	Congressional*
703	Wilson, Noah, lgthse kpr. Piney Pt.	77y	W	Md.	07 JUL 1873	Glenwood
606	Wilson, Patrick	42d	C	D.C.	13 JUN 1872	
605	Wilson, Patrick	42d	C	U.S.	13 JUN 1872	
585	Wilson, Peter F., clerk		W	Ohio	06 MAR 1872	Oak Hill
552	Wilson, Priscilla	47y	C	Va.	07 JAN 1872	Young Mens
150	Wilson, Rachel	2m	W	D.C.	03 JUN 1859	Congressional
313	Wilson, Rebecca	27y	C	Va.	07 MAY 1868	Freedmen's Hospital
525	Wilson, Rhoda Ann	14m	W	D.C.	30 JUN 1871	Congressional*
735	Wilson, Richard, laborer	12y	C	U.S.	13 DEC 1873	Mt. Pleasant
738	Wilson, Robt. W.	2m	W	U.S.	30 DEC 1873	Congressional*
372	Wilson, S.	Still	C		25 JAN 1869	Washington Asylum
057	Wilson, S. Jane	56y	W	Md.	11 SEP 1856	Holmead
036	Wilson, Sarah A.	24y	C	Md.	12 FEB 1856	Harmony
661	Wilson, Susan	20y	C	U.S.	28 JAN 1873	Washington Asylum
494	Wilson, Susan H.O.	33y	W	D.C.	29 DEC 1870	Glenwood
552	Wilson, Thaddeus S.	3y	W	D.C.	05 JAN 1872	Congressional*
663	Wilson, Thomas	19y	C	U.S.	27 JAN 1873	Small Pox
658	Wilson, William	28y	W	U.S.	06 JAN 1873	
207	Wilson, William	10m	C		27 JUL 1862	Methodist
274	Wilson, William	1d	W	D.C.	02 SEP 1867	Mt. Olivet
382	Wilson, William	5y	C		09 MAR 1869	Young Mens
269	Wilson, William D.	21d	C	D.C.	24 AUG 1867	Young Mens
257	Wilson, William M., wood dealer	24y	W	D.C.	11 MAR 1867	Oak Hill
262	Wilson, William R., clerk	35y	W	Md.	02 JUN 1867	Congressional
658	Wilson, Wm.	27y	W	Eng.	05 JAN 1873	Methodist, Georgetown
375	Wilson, Wm.	64y	W	D.C.	20 FEB 1869	Oak Hill
042	Wilson, Wm.	1y	C	D.C.	14 APR 1856	Young Mens
168	Wilson, Wm. A., cartman	49y	W	U.S.	20 DEC 1859	Congressional*
184	Wilson, Wm. Lowe	11m	W	D.C.	03 JUL 1860	Oak Hill
161	Wilson, [blank]		W	D.C.	12 SEP 1859	Congressional
167	Wilson, [blank]	5m	C	D.C.	15 DEC 1859	Young Mens
374	Wilt, Mrs. [Eliza]	59y	W	Pa.	02 FEB 1869	Congressional*
786	Wiltse, Gilbert S.	1y	W	U.S.	11 JUL 1874	
273	Wimsatt, Richard	69y	W	Md.	20 SEP 1867	Congressional
233	Wimsatt, Richard D.	13y	W	D.C.	30 AUG 1866	Congressional
089	Wimsatt, Rose A.	7y	W	D.C.	13 AUG 1857	Congressional
203	Winans, John, play actor	19y	W		24 MAY 1861	Congressional
016	Winans, Rev.	29y	W		17 JUL 1855	Glenwood
416	Winate, George	1d	C		19 SEP 1869	
372	Winchester, Mary A.	65y	C	Miss.	24 JAN 1869	Young Mens
185	Windaw, Florence	2m	W	D.C.	26 JUL 1860	Glenwood
730	Windeler, Henry H., painter	40y	W	U.S.	13 NOV 1873	Cincinnati, Ohio
328	Winder, Rosa	1y	C	D.C.	21 JUL 1868	Holmead
632	Winders, Salley	18y	W	U.S.	30 OCT 1872	
115	Wineberry, Jacob, waiter	16y	C	D.C.	11 JUN 1858	St. Patricks
102	Wineberry, Jacob, wood sawyer	85y	C	Md.	25 JAN 1858	St. Patricks
416	Winfield, Ann	24y	W	Va.	05 SEP 1869	Methodist
159	Winfield, George		W	D.C.	27 AUG 1859	Md.
404	Winfield, Mary A.	3y	C	D.C.	12 JUL 1869	Washington Asylum
331	Winfield, [blank]	2y	C	D.C.	05 JUL 1868	
224	Wingate, Mrs., child of	Still			18 JUN 1866	Western

Page	Name	Age	Race	Birth	Death Date	Burial Ground
531	Wingfield, Flemming, laborer	29y	C	Va.	08 AUG 1871	Washington
397	Wingfield, Lucinda	39y	B	Va.	16 JUN 1869	
282	Wingfield, Robert	1y	C	D.C.	06 NOV 1867	Union
280	Winkerman, Ada	2m	W	D.C.	22 OCT 1867	Glenwood
473	Winkfield, Charles	1y	C		06 AUG 1870	Ebenezer
336	Winkfield, William	2y	C	D.C.	16 AUG 1868	Ebenezer
662	Winkler, Morritz, gunsmith	75y	W	Aust.	25 JAN 1873	
328	Winn, Alice Matilda	8m	C	D.C.	20 JUL 1868	Young Mens
663	Winn, Isaiah	29y	C	U.S.	01 JAN 1873	Small Pox*
328	Winn, Jennie	1y	W	Va.	17 JUL 1868	Warrenton, Va.
495	Winn, Lizzie	35y	C	Va.	16 DEC 1870	Potters Field
146	Winnebaga Prophet	52y	I	Nebr.	15 APR 1859	Congressional
272	Winns, Ellen	25y	C		20 AUG 1867	Freedmen's Bureau
768	Wins, Ann Maria	6m	C	U.S.	08 MAY 1874	Mt. Pleasant
659	Winslow, Carrol F., merchant	24y	W	U.S.	13 JAN 1873	Oak Hill
382	Winslow, Joseph Lorenzo	5m	C		12 MAR 1869	Mt. Olivet
600	Winstead, Ab.	12y	C	U.S.	25 MAY 1872	Young Mens
202	Winstead, George W.	5m	W	D.C.	08 APR 1861	Washington Asylum
769	Winstead, Nancy	1m	C	U.S.	23 MAY 1874	
768	Winster, Charles, laborer	38y	C	U.S.	05 MAY 1874	
591	Winston, Wm.	22y	C	Va.	04 APR 1872	Washington
545	Winter, Harry	4m	W	D.C.	16 NOV 1871	Prospect Hill
762	Winter, Homer, G.	4m	W	U.S.	10 APR 1874	Oak Hill
372	Winter, John F.	6d	C		06 JAN 1869	Washington Asylum
146	Winter, William H., capitol contr.	47y	W	Md.	07 APR 1859	Congressional
713	Winters, Harry St. Clair	27y	W	D.C.	22 AUG 1873	Congressional*
080	Winters, Henry, laborer	60y	C	Md.	19 JUN 1857	Harmony
618	Winters, Wm.	18m	C	U.S.	— AUG 1872	
387	Wipple, Susan C.	1y	W	Pa.	13 APR 1869	Pa.
097	Wirt, John L., police officer	47y	W	D.C.	26 NOV 1857	Congressional
340	Wise, Catherine Ann	6m	W	D.C.	03 AUG 1868	Congressional
541	Wise, Elisabeth J.	46y	W	D.C.	13 OCT 1871	Congressional
585	Wise, George, laborer	75y	C	D.C.	09 MAR 1872	Asylum
531	Wise, John H., detective	51y	W	Md.	05 AUG 1871	Congressional*
786	Wise, John Henry	1y	W	U.S.	08 JUL 1874	Congressional*
321	Wise, John W., child of	Still	W	D.C.	19 JUN 1868	Mt. Olivet
243	Wise, Lida A.	5m	W	D.C.	05 NOV 1866	Congressional
120	Wise, Mary	56y	W	Ire.	06 JUL 1858	Glenwood
786	Wise, Mary R.	4m	C	U.S.	09 JUL 1874	Mt. Olivet
239	Wise, Patrick	6m	W	D.C.	07 OCT 1866	Mt. Olivet
036	Wise, Servant of Mrs.	63y			04 FEB 1856	Young Mens
111	Wise, Wurden	5y	W	D.C.	17 APR 1858	Alexandria, Va.
047	Wiseman, Mary		W		27 JUN 1856	St. Patricks
324	Wisewall, J.	1y	W	D.C.	11 JUL 1868	Oak Hill
749	Wishall, [blank]	P.B.	C	U.S.	11 FEB 1874	
144	Wisher, Caroline	30y	C	Md.	30 MAR 1859	Washington Asylum
004	Wissenbecker, Infant	Still	W	D.C.	24 MAR 1855	St. Patricks
318	Withaff, August, wheelwright	75y	W	Ger.	03 JUN 1868	Congressional
376	Witherow, Samuel, clerk	60y	W	Pa.	12 FEB 1869	Glenwood
067	Withnoure, Mary	7y	W	D.C.	29 DEC 1856	St. Patricks
450	Witmyer, Rose	1m	W		03 APR 1870	Prospect Hill
523	Wittig, Charles	3y	W	D.C.	16 JUN 1871	
274	Wivel, Francis	2m	W	Pa.	11 SEP 1867	Baltimore, Md.
271	Wivel, Mary	1m	W	D.C.	26 AUG 1867	Baltimore, Md.
355	Wodward, Catharine	11m	C	D.C.	15 OCT 1868	Harmony
527	Wokling, George	2y	W	D.C.	10 JUL 1871	German Catholic
241	Wolcott, Dr.	42y	W		05 OCT 1866	N.Y.
762	Wolf, Catherine, housekeeper	50y	W	Ire.	15 APR 1874	

Page	Name	Age	Race	Birth	Death Date	Burial Ground
536	Wolf, Herbert L.	6y	W	U.S.	18 SEP 1871	Pa.
496	Wolf, John P., clerk	57y	W	Pa.	08 DEC 1870	Harrisburg, Pa.
360	Wolf, Sarah Ellen	24y	W	U.S.	07 NOV 1868	Mt. Olivet
207	Wolfe, Ellen	14d	W	D.C.	14 JUL 1862	Holmead
737	Wolfe, John	50y	W	Ger.	27 DEC 1873	Washington Asylum
327	Wolfe, John Ernest	4m	W		11 JUL 1868	Mt. Olivet
207	Wolfe, Mary	13d	W	D.C.	13 JUL 1862	Holmead
249	Wolfe, Wm. Thomas	5m	W	D.C.	22 JAN 1867	Mt. Olivet
681	Wolff, Mary	19y	W	U.S.	13 APR 1873	Mt. Olivet
105	Wollard, Mary	36y	W	D.C.	17 FEB 1858	Glenwood
467	Woltz, Henry Jessler	11m	W	Md.	25 JUL 1870	Glenwood
714	Woltz, Lotta A.	9y	W	D.C.	27 AUG 1873	Glenwood
636	Womer, A.L.	9m	W	U.S.	20 NOV 1872	Congressional*
731	Wonderlick, Mary M.	21y	W	U.S.	22 NOV 1873	
749	Wonderly, Harry G.	3y	W	U.S.	21 FEB 1874	Glenwood
313	Wonn, William W.	7m	W	D.C.	14 MAY 1868	Glenwood
299	Wood, Annie, ladies maid	35y	C	Md.	29 MAR 1868	Mt. Olivet
051	Wood, Caroline L.	3m	W	D.C.	28 JUL 1856	Methodist
075	Wood, Charles	6m	W	D.C.	05 APR 1857	Methodist, East
476	Wood, Charles	1y	C	D.C.	12 SEP 1870	Mt. Olivet
536	Wood, Chas. E.	2y	W	D.C.	17 SEP 1871	Washington
390	Wood, Cora Alice	6y	W		12 MAY 1869	Windham Co., Conn.
068	Wood, Dennis, laborer	43y	W	Ire.	02 JAN 1857	St. Patricks
162	Wood, Dr., servant child of	3m	C	D.C.	19 SEP 1859	Harmony
362	Wood, E., shoemaker	75y	C	Md.	04 NOV 1868	Western
285	Wood, Ellen Francis	38y	W	Va.	19 DEC 1867	Ebenezer
370	Wood, Ellen Rebecca, housekeeper	22y	W	U.S.	02 JAN 1869	Baltimore, Md.
703	Wood, Franklin F.	7m	C	D.C.	03 JUL 1873	
297	Wood, Geo. Washington, printer	35y	W	Ind.	21 FEB 1868	Richmond, Ind.
437	Wood, George Jeffries	5y	W		17 JAN 1870	Baltimore, Md.
720	Wood, Henderson, laborer	57y	C	Va.	27 SEP 1873	Washington Asylum
523	Wood, Henrietta	17y	C		19 JUN 1871	Ebenezer
594	Wood, Henry	65y	C	Va.	13 APR 1872	Washington
580	Wood, Henry	27y	C	Va.	10 FEB 1872	Washington
457	Wood, Herbert C.	1y	W	D.C.	04 JUN 1870	Congressional
348	Wood, J.F.	8m	W	Va.	06 SEP 1868	Congressional
506	Wood, Jacob	1m	W	D.C.	04 FEB 1871	Congressional
024	Wood, James F.	1y	W	Md.	03 SEP 1855	Methodist, East
261	Wood, James H.	1y	C	D.C.	08 MAY 1867	Young Mens
756	Wood, James, laborer	29y	C	U.S.	21 MAR 1874	
493	Wood, Jane	70y	W	D.C.	16 DEC 1870	Glenwood
293	Wood, Jas. Sidney	1y	W	D.C.*	20 MAR 1868	Oak Hill
305	Wood, Jesse, hackman	26y	C		26 MAR 1868	Rockville, Md.
719	Wood, Jno. P., farmer		W	Md.	20 SEP 1873	Congressional
421	Wood, John	85y	C	Md.	27 OCT 1869	Mt. Olivet*
515	Wood, John, upholsterer	31y	C	D.C.	02 MAR 1871	Union
532	Wood, Joseph H.	8m	W	D.C.	12 AUG 1871	Oak Hill
214	Wood, Joseph, laborer	21y	C	D.C.	10 MAR 1866	Mt. Olivet*
130	Wood, L.B., officer USA	36y	W	Va.	19 OCT 1858	Congressional
527	Wood, Leonora	2y	C	D.C.	07 JUL 1871	Young Mens
741	Wood, Levi W.	1y	W	U.S.	14 JAN 1874	Glenwood
084	Wood, Louisa	60y	W	Md.	21 JUL 1857	Foundry
738	Wood, Malenda, infant of	9m	C	U.S.	07 DEC 1873	
359	Wood, Margaret Emma	23y	W	D.C.	24 NOV 1868	Congressional
616a	Wood, Mary L.	7d	W	U.S.	07 JUL 1872	Congressional*
216	Wood, Mary L.	30y	W		29 MAR 1866	Glenwood
756	Wood, Mitty	75y	C	U.S.	21 MAR 1874	
273	Wood, P.J.	36y	W	Md.	17 SEP 1867	Glenwood

District of Columbia Interments (Index to Deaths), 1855-1874

Page	Name	Age	Race	Birth	Death Date	Burial Ground
412	Wood, Phillis, laundress	87y	C	Md.	17 AUG 1869	Mt. Olivet*
291	Wood, Rebah		W		07 JAN 1868	Alms House
050	Wood, Richard J.	1y	W	D.C.	18 JUL 1856	Congressional
614	Wood, Richd.	11y	W	U.S.	03 JUL 1872	
745	Wood, Robert M., restaurant	37y	C	U.S.	22 JAN 1874	
227	Wood, Saml. Wheeler, express drvr.	36y	W	D.C.	07 JUL 1866	Mt. Olivet
329	Wood, Susan	3m	C	D.C.	03 JUL 1868	Young Mens
756	Wood, Willie	2d	W	U.S.	29 MAR 1874	Congressional*
501	Wood, Wm., laborer	50y	C	D.C.	05 JAN 1871	Gardner's
523	Wood, [blank]		C		18 JUN 1871	Cemetery Vault
522	Woodall, Wm. Joseph, plasterer	30y	W	Amer.	10 JUN 1871	Baltimore, Md.
756	Woodard, Amon, pump maker	81y	W	U.S.	31 MAR 1874	
247	Woodard, Ann	62y	C		04 DEC 1866	Mt. Olivet
296	Woodard, Catherine	30y	C	Md.	20 FEB 1868	Freedmen's Hospital
214	Woodard, Jane	75y	C	Md.	04 MAR 1866	Ebenezer
290	Woodard, Nathan C., clerk	53y	W	Me.	17 JAN 1868	Bangor, Me.
295	Woodard, William, tailor	40y	W	Va.	13 FEB 1868	Congressional
540	Woodard, Wm., printer	69y	W		05 OCT 1871	Congressional
028	Woodbury, Elisha, contractor	55y	W	N.Y.	19 OCT 1855	Oak Hill
724	Woodend, Wm. R.	70y	W	Va.	15 OCT 1873	Congressional*
453	Woodfield, Benjamin, watchman	64y	W		10 MAY 1870	Congressional
356	Woodfield, Mary A.	2y	W	D.C.	30 OCT 1868	Methodist
697	Woodland, Annie	70y	C	Md.	16 JUN 1873	Washington Asylum
469	Woodland, Nancy	75y	C	Va.	07 AUG 1870	Harmony
161	Woodland, [blank]	1y	C	D.C.	11 SEP 1859	Western
164	Woodley, Emma	1y	W	D.C.	30 OCT 1859	Holmead
352	Woodro, John Henry	1y	C	Md.	04 SEP 1868	Washington Asylum
356	Woodro, Rosetta	10y	C	Md.	21 OCT 1868	Young Mens
351	Woodrow, Walter	3m	C		03 SEP 1868	
535	Woodruff, Marcia	33y	W	D.C.	03 SEP 1871	Congressional
150	Woods, Dr., servant of	22y	C	U.S.	14 JUN 1859	Harmony
053	Woods, Ida Ann	1y	W	D.C.	28 AUG 1856	Congressional
120	Woods, John, laborer	58y	W	Ire.	02 JUL 1858	St. Patricks
243	Woods, Margaret, grocer		W	Ire.	13 NOV 1866	Mt. Olivet
240	Woods, Mary	48y	W	Ire.	03 OCT 1866	Mt. Olivet
068	Woods, Richard J.	77y	W	Md.	02 JAN 1857	St. Peters
199	Woods, Sarah	35y	C		11 FEB 1861	Pr. Geo. Co., Md.
786	Woods, Thomas	7m	W	U.S.	21 JUL 1874	Mt. Olivet
464	Woodward, Clara Isabella	4m	W	Amer.	23 JUL 1870	Glenwood
526	Woodward, Clement	68y	W	U.S.	07 JUL 1871	Congressional
694	Woodward, Fred	23y	W		02 JUN 1873	Bangor, Me.
167	Woodward, Geo. C., clerk	26y	W	D.C.	03 DEC 1859	Congressional
185	Woodward, Henry	11m	W	D.C.	26 JUL 1860	Congressional
616a	Woodward, Lily M.	5m	W	U.S.	11 JUL 1872	Congressional*
118	Woodward, [blank]		W		24 JUN 1858	German
249	Woodyard, [blank]	1y	C	D.C.	— JAN 1867	Young Mens
778	Wooldridge, Valentine H.	1y	W	U.S.	11 JUN 1874	Glenwood
786	Wooley, [blank]	22d	W	U.S.	13 JUL 1874	Congressional*
101	Woolland, Edwin, seaman	31y	W	Eng.	09 JAN 1858	Marine
612	Woolly, Frank E.	1y	W	U.S.	15 JUL 1872	
071	Worden, James	45y	W	Conn.	19 FEB 1857	Washington Asylum
778	Wordley, Lucy, servant	52y	C	U.S.	07 JUN 1874	Young Mens
474	Wormley, Anne	3m	C		20 AUG 1870	Washington Asylum
307	Wormley, Mary	21d	W	D.C.	03 APR 1868	Glenwood
004	Wormley, Wm., hackney owner	55y	W	Va.	— MAR 1855	Harmony
128	Wormley, [blank]	1m	W	D.C.	16 SEP 1858	Washington
050	Wormsley, Frank, painter	30y	W	Ire.	13 JUL 1856	Congressional*
006	Worster, Tapley	2y		D.C.	29 APR 1855	Va.

District of Columbia Interments (Index to Deaths), 1855-1874

Page	Name	Age	Race	Birth	Death Date	Burial Ground
195	Worth, Mary	81y	W		30 DEC 1860	Congressional
167	Worthen, Cathrian	38y	W	U.S.	12 DEC 1859	Congressional*
197	Worthing, Mr., col. woman of	40y	C		23 JAN 1861	Young Mens
127	Worthington, Louisa	48y	W	Md.	07 SEP 1858	Glenwood
349	Worthington, Mary M.	1y	W		29 SEP 1868	Pr. Geo. Co., Md.
092	Worthington, Mr., servant of	25y	C		28 SEP 1857	Young Mens
244	Worthington, Saml., planter	76y	W	Ky.	21 NOV 1866	Miss.
103	Worthington, [blank]	67y	W		09 JAN 1858	Baltimore, Md.
421	Wotton, Wm. F.	3y	C	Md.	08 OCT 1869	Mt. Olivet
737	Wren, Geo. W., hotel keeper	74y	W	U.S.	25 DEC 1873	Congressional
475	Wren, Margaret, housekeeper	35y	W	Ire.	01 SEP 1870	Mt. Olivet
401	Wren, Sony	10m	C		— JUL 1869	Young Mens
359	Wright, Albert C.	1y	W	D.C.	11 NOV 1868	Congressional
261	Wright, Benjamin C.	1y	W	D.C.	30 MAY 1867	Glenwood
542	Wright, Caroline	34y	W	N.Y.	25 OCT 1871	Glenwood
675	Wright, Chas. H., letter carrier	26y	W	U.S.	22 MAR 1873	Glenwood
499	Wright, Chas. V.	3m	W	D.C.	11 JAN 1871	Congressional
037	Wright, Elizabeth	58y	W	Md.	06 FEB 1856	Alms House
355	Wright, Elizabeth A., Mrs.	45y	W	D.C.*	10 OCT 1868	Congressional
680	Wright, Enos	89y	W	U.S.	05 APR 1873	Congressional
108	Wright, Fanny	1y	W	D.C.	23 MAR 1858	Congressional
187	Wright, Frank	7m	C	D.C.	09 AUG 1860	Harmony
538	Wright, Geo. W.	3y	W	D.C.	27 SEP 1871	Congressional*
049	Wright, George H.	8m	W	D.C.	02 JUL 1856	Congressional
407	Wright, Georgie	1y	W		21 AUG 1869	Congressional/Oak Hill
348	Wright, Harvey Clayton	1y	W	D.C.	25 SEP 1868	Congressional
457	Wright, Hiram, stable foreman	53y	W	Ver.	21 JUN 1870	Congressional
123	Wright, James	7y	W	D.C.	03 JUL 1858	St. Patricks
422	Wright, Julia	82y	C	Va.	13 OCT 1869	Holmead
370	Wright, Liby E.	9m	W		03 JAN 1869	Glenwood
117	Wright, Maria	64y	W	Va.	28 JUN 1858	Congressional
768	Wright, Mary	35y	W	U.S.	07 MAY 1874	Holyrood
217	Wright, Mary E.	28y	W	N.J.	07 APR 1866	Baltimore, Md.
112	Wright, Robert H., tailor	56y	W		29 APR 1858	Methodist
416	Wright, Robert, waiter	27y	C	Md.	07 SEP 1869	Harmony
049	Wright, Susan M.	23y	W	Va.*	01 JUL 1856	Glenwood
409	Wright, Susanna	14d	C		06 AUG 1869	Union
623	Wright, Theo.	23y	W	U.S.	02 JUL 1872	Holy Rood
096	Wright, Theresa F.	1y	W	D.C.	10 NOV 1857	Glenwood
301	Wright, Thomas, dairyman	43y	W	Ire.	29 MAR 1868	Mt. Olivet
346	Wright, Willie	3y	C		01 AUG 1868	Freedmen's Hospital
168	Wright, Willie H.	23y	W	N.Y.	28 DEC 1859	
199	Wroe, Samuel, bricklayer	75y	W		13 FEB 1861	Rock Creek
386	Wuillmer, Chas., cook	36y	W	Fra.	13 APR 1869	Glenwood
177	Wuirdig, Loi	17d	W	D.C.	19 APR 1860	Prospect Hill
641	Wullivan, Richard	4y	W	U.S.	17 DEC 1872	Small Pox
786	Wurdeman, Catherine E.	9m	W	U.S.	30 JUL 1874	Prospect Hill
096	Wurdermann, Amalie	72y	W	Ger.	09 NOV 1857	German
681	Wurts, Maurice	65y	W	U.S.	17 APR 1873	
217	Wycoff, David Elmer, clerk	22y	W	N.Y.	09 APR 1866	N.Y.
393	Wye, Fanny A.	2y	C		23 MAY 1869	Western
396	Wye, Fanny A.	2y	C	D.C.	22 JUN 1869	Western
125	Wyer, Edward	38y	W	Ire.	01 AUG 1858	
431	Wyer, Peter	20y	C		05 DEC 1869	
508	Wygalt, Charles	Still	W		28 FEB 1871	Glenwood
322	Wylie, David B.	29y	W	Scot.	08 JUN 1868	Mt. Olivet
343	Wylie, Mary E.	20y	W	Ill.	19 AUG 1868	Glenwood
299	Wylie, William Wynne	4m	W	D.C.	16 MAR 1868	Glenwood

Page	Name	Age	Race	Birth	Death Date	Burial Ground
680	Wyman, Asa A., editor	63y	W	U.S.	06 APR 1873	Glenwood
023	Wyman, Infant	13m			09 SEP 1855	Oak Hill
542	Wyndham, Mary	24y	W	Va.	21 OCT 1871	Va.
684	Wyner, Jas.	6m	C	U.S.	05 APR 1873	Small Pox*
462	Wynkoop, Benjamin M.	8m	W	Pa.	24 JUL 1870	Glenwood
070	Wynkoop, Katie Estelle	1y	W	Va.*	01 FEB 1857	Glenwood
719	Wyre, Hattie	5m	C	D.C.	20 SEP 1873	Beckett's
144	Wyvill, Amanda B.	21y	W	D.C.	29 MAR 1859	Congressional*

X

Page	Name	Age	Race	Birth	Death Date	Burial Ground
409	Xander, A.	1y	W		18 AUG 1869	Prospect Hill

Y

Page	Name	Age	Race	Birth	Death Date	Burial Ground
631	Yager, John H., carpenter	46y	W	U.S.	10 OCT 1872	Glenwood
521	Yarnell, Anna Ray	3m	W	Amer.	02 JUN 1871	Glenwood
151	Yateman, Margaret E.	8m	W	D.C.	15 JUN 1859	Glenwood
600	Yates, Allison, merchant	27y	W	U.S.	14 MAY 1872	Oak Hill
087	Yates, Anna	1y	C		10 AUG 1857	Ebenezer
113	Yates, Elizabeth	39y	W	Va.	14 MAY 1858	St. Patricks
642	Yates, Lizzie	20y	C	U.S.	28 DEC 1872	Small Pox
535	Yates, Mary E.	51y	W	Md.	03 SEP 1871	Congressional*
276	Yates, Sophia P.	73y	W	N.Y.	11 SEP 1867	Oak Hill
723	Yeabower, Geo. W.	1y	W	D.C.	06 OCT 1873	Prospect Hill
261	Yeabower, John, blacksmith	78y	W	Ger.	14 MAY 1867	Oak Hill
691	Yearly, John	14y	C	U.S.	04 MAY 1873	Small Pox*
278	Yeatman, Fredk. A.	10m	W	D.C.	09 OCT 1867	Glenwood
530	Yeatman, Gillian H.	1y	W	U.S.	30 JUL 1871	Congressional
426	Yeatman, Mollie	1y	W		12 NOV 1869	Oak Hill
586	Yeidy, David, bar keeper	29y	W	Ire.	17 MAR 1872	Mt. Olivet
616a	Yenney, Henry	2y	W	U.S.	15 JUL 1872	Baltimore Co., Md.
361	Yennon, Matilda, laundress	75y	C	Va.	06 NOV 1868	
201	Yeo, Annie	22y	W	Md.	31 MAR 1861	Baltimore, Md.
142	Yeo, Jas. Thomas	6y	W	Md.	20 FEB 1859	Baltimore, Md.
684	Yerly, Ella	16y	C	U.S.	27 APR 1873	Small Pox*
680	Yervell, Gustavus, merchant	68y	W	U.S.	07 APR 1873	Glenwood
786	Yoder, Charles T.	1y	W	U.S.	06 JUL 1874	Glenwood
681	Yoder, Chas. Wm.	4m	W	U.S.	17 APR 1873	Glenwood
020	Yodrer, Eliza	11m	W	N.Y.	28 AUG 1855	German
729	York, Annie C.	1y	W	U.S.	09 NOV 1873	Graceland
047	York, Gertrude	5d	C	D.C.	30 JUN 1856	Harmony
309	Yost, Albert Berlingham	9m	W	U.S.	12 APR 1868	Glenwood
125	Yost, Barbara S.	8m	W	D.C.	25 AUG 1858	German Lutheran
626	Yost, John	17d	W	U.S.	26 SEP 1872	
421	Yost, Lewis H., merchant	31y	W	Md.	21 OCT 1869	Glenwood
706	Yost, Stephen	56y	W	Ger.	05 JUL 1873	Prospect Hill
456	Yost, William	8d	W	D.C.	19 JUN 1870	Prospect Hill
352	Young, Alfred	4m	C		16 SEP 1868	Washington Asylum
023	Young, Alfred W.	7m	W	D.C.	28 SEP 1855	Rock Creek
143	Young, Amelia	85y	W	Md.	04 MAR 1859	Methodist
756	Young, Ammi B., architect	79y	W	U.S.	13 MAR 1874	Oak Hill*
541	Young, Ann	65y	W		09 OCT 1871	Congressional*
293	Young, Bennet A.	1y	W	D.C.*	26 FEB 1868	Holy Rood

Page	Name	Age	Race	Birth	Death Date	Burial Ground
108	Young, Caroine	17y	W	D.C.	18 MAR 1858	Foundry
046	Young, Catherine W.	2y	W	D.C.	20 JUN 1856	Foundry
011	Young, Charity	60y	C	D.C.	13 JUN 1855	Poor House
230	Young, E.	22y	C		21 JUL 1866	Young Mens
223	Young, Elizabeth	30y	C	D.C.	06 JUN 1866	Alms House
314	Young, Ellen	81y	W	Va.	17 MAY 1868	Congressional
664	Young, Feuge	13y	C	U.S.	13 JAN 1873	Small Pox*
769	Young, Frederick A.	6y	W	U.S.	09 MAY 1874	Glenwood
257	Young, Geo. Washington, farmer	71y	W	D.C.	10 MAR 1867	Mt. Olivet
404	Young, George Edward	4y	W		31 JUL 1869	
165	Young, H.A., printer	46y	W	Md.	04 NOV 1859	Greenmount, Balto.
168	Young, Hannah	57y	W	Mass.	23 DEC 1859	Oak Hill
408	Young, Henry, child of	1d	C	D.C.	22 AUG 1869	Holmead
726	Young, James Rodney, barkeeper	52y	W	U.S.	27 OCT 1873	Harmony
241	Young, John		C		28 OCT 1866	Western
691	Young, John M., coach maker	66y	W	U.S.	22 MAY 1873	Congressional
756	Young, Joseph	2m	W	U.S.	11 MAR 1874	
372	Young, Lenthe	80y	C		21 JAN 1869	Freedmen's Hospital
352	Young Levina	25y	C	Md.	14 SEP 1868	Washington Asylum
071	Young, Lydia L.	32y	W	Md.	17 FEB 1857	Baltimore, Md.
083	Young, M.	34y	W	Va.	17 JUL 1857	Congressional
642	Young, Maggie	16y	C	U.S.	26 DEC 1872	Small Pox
673	Young, Margaret	68y	W	U.S.	11 MAR 1873	Oak Hill
641	Young, Margaret	20y	C	U.S.	11 DEC 1872	Small Pox
420	Young, Maria A.	38y	C		01 OCT 1869	Harmony
529	Young, Mary	1y			25 JUL 1871	Prospect Hill
092	Young, Mary Ann	73y	W	Ire.	22 SEP 1857	St. Patricks
474	Young, Mary E.	6m	C		12 AUG 1870	Washington Asylum
502	Young, Matilda	69y	W	Mo.	31 JAN 1871	Congressional
047	Young, Melinda	20y	W	D.C.	26 JUN 1856	Foundry
230	Young, Mrs., child of	Still			11 JUL 1866	Western
181	Young, Rebecca D.	10m	W	D.C.	16 JUN 1860	Frederick, Md.
174	Young, Samuel H., wood merchant	26y	W	D.C.	09 MAR 1860	Glenwood
336	Young, Sarah	1m	C	D.C.	18 AUG 1868	Ebenezer
432	Young, Susan	35y	W		27 DEC 1869	Washington Asylum
420	Young, Susan B.	57y	W		13 OCT 1869	Oak Hill
255	Young, Susan E.	1y	W	Mass.	31 MAR 1867	Boston, Mass.
022	Young, Thos.	37y	W	Scot.	26 AUG 1855	Congressional
555	Young, Virginia	23y	W	D.C.	25 JAN 1872	Va.
292a	Young, Walter	6m	C	D.C.*	26 JAN 1868	Methodist
581	Young Wesley	2y	C	Va.	15 FEB 1872	Holy Rood
636	Young, Will	7y	W	U.S.	02 NOV 1872	
415	Young, William, mariner	80y	W	Eng.	08 SEP 1869	Baltimore, Md.
216	Young, William P., clerk	73y	W	N.C.	27 MAR 1866	Oak Hill
031	Young, Wm. F.	4y	C	D.C.	07 DEC 1855	Harmony
590	Young, Wm. H.	1y	C	D.C.	19 APR 1872	Asylum
149	Young, Wm. W., clerk	37y	W		28 MAY 1859	Oak Hill
660	Young, Wm., watchman	82y	W	U.S.	21 JAN 1873	Congressional
002	Young, [blank]	6d	W	D.C.	— JAN 1855	St. Matthews
181	Young, [blank]	38y	C		19 JUN 1860	Western
536	Young. [torn]	73y		Sea	19 SEP 1871	Md.
323	Younger, Solomon C.	10y	C	D.C.	06 JUL 1868	Harmony
102	Younker, Christine	41y	W	Ger.	20 JAN 1858	German Catholic
181	Yukes, Harmon, carpenter	64y	W	Pa.	15 JUN 1860	Glenwood
713	Yzuaga, Emma M.		W	U.S.	23 AUG 1873	

District of Columbia Interments (Index to Deaths), 1855-1874

Page	Name	Age	Race	Birth	Death Date	Burial Ground
Z						
736	Zachary, Ann, storekeeper	35y	W	Ire.	18 DEC 1873	Mt. Olivet*
786	Zachary, Edward	10m	W	U.S.	28 JUL 1874	Mt. Olivet
749	Zachary, Robert	2y	W	U.S.	19 FEB 1874	Mt. Olivet
453	Zanner, [blank]	1y	W		21 MAY 1870	Congressional
081	Zantzinger, Rosa	1y	W	D.C.	30 JUN 1857	Congressional
483	Zanwitzer, Christian, laborer	40y	W	Ger.	12 OCT 1870	Prospect Hill
135	Zappone, Americus	4y	W	D.C.	06 DEC 1858	Oak Hill
137	Zappone, Rufino	2y	W	D.C.	01 JAN 1859	Oak Hill
421	Zappony, Margaret	35y	W		11 OCT 1869	Oak Hill
155	Zearmann, Mary E.	1y	W	D.C.	22 JUL 1859	Prospect Hill
634	Zedrick, Harry, laborer	60y	C	U.S.	05 OCT 1872	
463	Zeh, [blank]	Still	W		05 JUL 1870	Prospect Hill
677	Zell, Raymond	12y	W	U.S.	17 MAR 1873	Mt. Olivet
734	Zeller, Clarabell	9y	W	U.S.	07 DEC 1873	St. Marys
120	Zengel, Philepina	31y	W	Bav.	01 JUL 1858	Glenwood
609	Zerga, John S.	25d	W	U.S.	30 JUN 1872	
610	Zerga, Lewis F.	22y	W	Italy	09 JUL 1872	
612	Zerine, Wm.	6m	W	U.S.	15 JUL 1872	
622a	Zevely, Virginia	24y	W	U.S.	12 AUG 1872	
596	Zevercy, A.T., Dr.	56y	W	N.C.	26 APR 1872	N.C.
212	Ziege, Robert	2m	W	D.C.	15 FEB 1866	Prospect Hill
317	Ziegler, Christian	42y	W	Ger.	12 JUN 1868	Rock Creek
409	Ziemer, Frederick	9m	W		22 AUG 1869	Prospect Hill
088	Zigler, John	7d	W	D.C.	16 AUG 1857	German Catholic
447	Zimmerman, A., Mr., confectioner	26y	W	Switz.	11 MAR 1870	Glenwood
762	Zimmerman, Archibald M., clerk	33y	W	U.S.	15 APR 1874	Congressional
603	Zimmerman, Archie	1y	W	D.C.	15 JUN 1872	Congressional
604	Zimmerman, Archie	1y	W	D.C.	15 JUN 1872	Congressional
381	Zimmerman, Joanna E.	43y	W	Ger.	22 MAR 1869	Prospect Hill
521	Zimmerman, Johana E.	15y	W	Md.	03 JUN 1871	Prospect Hill
546	Zimmerman, John G.	62y	W	Ger.	31 NOV 1871	Prospect Hill
704	Zimmerman, Mary M.	8m	W		14 JUL 1873	Congressional
240	Zimmerman, Virginia	36y	W	Ky.	17 OCT 1866	Glenwood
220	Zimmerman, Willie	9y	W	D.C.	03 MAY 1866	Glenwood
694	Zohr, John	4m	W	D.C.	17 JUN 1873	St. Marys
698	Zurhorst, Chas. F., undertaker	48y	W	Eng.	19 JUN 1873	Congressional
325	Zurhorst, Dora Belle	7m	W	D.C.	19 JUL 1868	Congressional

NAME NOT GIVEN

Page	Name	Age	Race	Birth	Death Date	Burial Ground
025	[blank]		W		08 SEP 1855	
044	[blank]		W		13 MAY 1856	
047	[blank], laborer		W		29 JUN 1856	
048	[blank], laborer	24y	W	Md.	29 JUN 1856	
048	[blank]		W		01 JUN 1856	
051	[blank], servant	22y	C	Md.	25 JUL 1856	
057	[blank]	30y	W	Ger.	09 SEP 1856	
101	[blank]	8y	C	D.C.	05 JAN 1858	
125	[blank]	9m	W	D.C.	05 AUG 1858	
126	[blank], laborer		W	Ire.	06 AUG 1858	
128	[blank]	1h	W		28 SEP 1858	
201	[blank]		W	D.C.	05 MAR 1861	
238	[blank]	30y	C		30 SEP 1866	
248	[blank]	27y			28 DEC 1866	
268	[blank]		C		20 AUG 1867	
269	[blank]	66y			02 AUG 1867	
275	[blank]	3h	W	D.C.	26 SEP 1867	
276	[blank]	22d	W	D.C.	24 SEP 1867	
278	[blank]	Still	C		02 OCT 1867	
279	[blank]	2y			— OCT 1867	
284	[blank]	2d	W		— NOV 1867	
345	[blank]	Still	C	D.C.	31 AUG 1868	
345	[blank]	10m	C	D.C.	14 AUG 1868	
345	[blank]	3m	C	D.C.	16 AUG 1868	
383	[blank]	17y	C	Md.	06 MAR 1869	
408	[blank]	77y	W	Va.	31 AUG 1869	
410	[blank]		W		24 AUG 1869	
422	[blank]	9m	C		07 OCT 1869	
441	[blank], Child	1m	C		10 FEB 1870	
442	[blank]	61y	C	Va.	05 FEB 1870	
514	[blank]	4h	C	D.C.	04 MAR 1871	
613	[blank]	2m	C	U.S.	08 JUL 1872	
615	[blank]	3y	C	U.S.	25 JUL 1872	
617	[blank]	1m	C	U.S.	20 AUG 1872	
646	[blank]	Still	C	D.C.	04 DEC 1872	
646	[blank]	Still	C	D.C.	03 DEC 1872	
667	[blank]		C	U.S.	10 FEB 1873	
667	[blank]		C	U.S.	07 FEB 1873	
667	[blank]	19y	C	U.S.	12 FEB 1873	
674	[blank]		C	U.S.	12 MAR 1873	
680	[blank]		C	U.S.	04 APR 1873	
688	[blank]	8d	C	U.S.	c.15 MAY 1873	
689	[blank]	misc.	C	U.S.	25 MAY 1873	
051	[blank]		W		23 JUL 1856	Alexandria, Va.
142	[blank]	3y	W	D.C.	07 FEB 1859	Alexandria, Va.
046	[blank]		C		07 JUN 1856	Alms House
210	[blank]		W		17 JAN 1866	Alms House
245	[blank]	Still			11 NOV 1866	Alms House
249	[blank]		W		01 JAN 1867	Alms House
302	[blank]	Still	C		02 MAR 1868	Alms House
302	[blank]	Still	C		23 MAR 1868	Alms House
302	[blank]	Still	C		20 MAR 1868	Alms House
302	[blank]	Still	C		18 MAR 1868	Alms House
302	[blank]	Still	C		17 MAR 1868	Alms House
302	[blank]	Still	C		18 MAR 1868	Alms House
302	[blank]	Still	C		07 MAR 1868	Alms House
302	[blank]	Still	C		14 MAR 1868	Alms House

District of Columbia Interments (Index to Deaths), 1855-1874

Page	Name	Age	Race	Birth	Death Date	Burial Ground
303	[blank]	Still	C		26 MAR 1868	Alms House
321	[blank]	Still	W		c.27 JUN 1868	Alms House
321	[blank]	3d	C	U.S.	08 JUN 1868	Alms House
321	[blank]	Still	C		c.26 JUN 1868	Alms House
321	[blank]	Still			c.22 JUN 1868	Alms House
321	[blank]	Still			c.20 JUN 1868	Alms House
271	[blank]	15y	W		29 AUG 1867	Baltimore, Md.
694	[blank]	Still	C	D.C.	02 JUN 1873	Beckett's
459	[blank]	4m	C		21 JUN 1870	by Gawer F.H.
141	[blank]	Still	W	D.C.	16 FEB 1859	Catholic
011	[blank]	2d	C	D.C.	01 JUN 1855	Colored
042	[blank]	31y	W	D.C.	16 APR 1856	Congressional
044	[blank]		W		09 MAY 1856	Congressional
053	[blank]	12d	W	D.C.	08 AUG 1856	Congressional
071	[blank]	8m	W		25 FEB 1857	Congressional
124	[blank]				10 AUG 1858	Congressional
130	[blank]	1d	W	D.C.	17 OCT 1858	Congressional
142	[blank]	14d	W	D.C.	04 FEB 1859	Congressional
148	[blank]	Still	W	D.C.	06 MAY 1859	Congressional
220	[blank]	6y	W	D.C.	12 MAY 1866	Congressional
235	[blank]	2y	W	D.C.	19 SEP 1866	Congressional
247	[blank]		W	N.Y.	23 DEC 1866	Congressional
259	[blank]	6m	W	D.C.	04 APR 1867	Congressional
264	[blank]	17d	W	D.C.	13 JUL 1867	Congressional
267	[blank]	27y	W	Ger.	28 JUL 1867	Congressional
282	[blank]	Still	W		08 NOV 1867	Congressional
286	[blank]				— DEC 1867	Congressional
325	[blank]		W	D.C.	29 JUL 1868	Congressional
340	[blank]	2y	W		29 AUG 1868	Congressional
347	[blank]	Still	W		22 SEP 1868	Congressional
359	[blank]	Still	W	D.C.	06 NOV 1868	Congressional
359	[blank]	40h	W	D.C.	27 NOV 1868	Congressional
359	[blank]	Still			18 NOV 1868	Congressional
369	[blank]	10m	W	D.C.	04 JAN 1869	Congressional
390	[blank]		W	D.C.	01 MAY 1869	Congressional
407	[blank]	Still	W		02 AUG 1869	Congressional
456	[blank]	Still	W	D.C.	14 JUN 1870	Congressional
461	[blank]	Still	W		07 JUL 1870	Congressional
461	[blank]	Still	W		24 JUL 1870	Congressional
470	[blank]	Still	W		14 AUG 1870	Congressional
484	[blank]	Still	W	D.C.	25 OCT 1870	Congressional
487	[blank]	Still	W	D.C.	24 NOV 1870	Congressional
506	[blank]	Still	W	D.C.	06 FEB 1871	Congressional
506	[blank]	Still	W	D.C.	23 FEB 1871	Congressional
723	[blank]	P.B.	W	D.C.	06 OCT 1873	Congressional
025	[blank]		C		05 SEP 1855	Darlins
055	[blank]	4m	C		22 AUG 1856	Donlin's
023	[blank]		C		03 SEP 1855	Eastern
233	[blank]	3d	C	D.C.	31 AUG 1866	Ebenezer
244	[blank], cook		C	W.Va.	25 NOV 1866	Ebenezer
268	[blank]		C		23 AUG 1867	Ebenezer
302	[blank]	5d	C		22 MAR 1868	Ebenezer
312	[blank]	18y	C	Va.	04 MAY 1868	Ebenezer
316	[blank]	5m	C		11 MAY 1868	Ebenezer
473	[blank]	3m	C		07 AUG 1870	Ebenezer
483	[blank]				03 OCT 1870	Ebenezer
490	[blank]	Still	C		23 NOV 1870	Ebenezer
490	[blank]	Still	C		15 NOV 1870	Ebenezer

Page	Name	Age	Race	Birth	Death Date	Burial Ground
644	[blank]	Still	C	U.S.	18 DEC 1872	Ebenezer
667	[blank]	1d	C	U.S.	15 FEB 1873	Ebenezer
042	[blank]	1m	W	D.C.	24 APR 1856	Foundry
044	[blank]		W		10 MAY 1856	Foundry
046	[blank]	8m	C	D.C.	21 JUN 1856	Foundry
026	[blank]	1y		D.C.	15 OCT 1855	German
044	[blank]	6d		D.C.	01 MAY 1856	German
053	[blank]	7d	W	D.C.	25 AUG 1856	German
086	[blank]	3m	W		— AUG 1857	German
132	[blank]	Still	W	D.C.	01 NOV 1858	German
255	[blank]		W		05 MAR 1867	German
153	[blank]	1y	W	D.C.	05 JUL 1859	German Catholic
086	[blank]	1y	W	D.C.	02 AUG 1857	Glenwood
122	[blank]	Still			22 JUL 1858	Glenwood
122	[blank]	2m	W	D.C.	18 JUL 1858	Glenwood
221	[blank]				15 MAY 1866	Glenwood
123	[blank]	5y	C	Md.	30 JUL 1858	Harmony
162	[blank]	Still	C	D.C.	26 SEP 1859	Harmony
234	[blank]	52y	C		04 SEP 1866	Harmony
316	[blank]	Still	C	D.C.	13 MAY 1868	Harmony
218	[blank]	77y	W	D.C.	28 APR 1866	Holmead
232	[blank]	Still	W	D.C.	23 AUG 1866	Holmead
258	[blank]	Still	W	D.C.	29 APR 1867	Holmead
476	[blank]	2m	C	D.C.	11 SEP 1870	Holmead
681	[blank]	Still	C	U.S.	12 APR 1873	Holmead
044	[blank]		W		04 MAY 1856	Methodist
154	[blank]	1y	W	D.C.	19 JUL 1859	Methodist
212	[blank]	15y	C	Md.	15 FEB 1866	Methodist
268	[blank]	11m	C	D.C.	12 AUG 1867	Methodist
066	[blank]	Still	W	D.C.	22 DEC 1856	Methodist, East
152	[blank], servant	17y	W	Ire.	10 JUN 1859	Mt. Olivet
153	[blank]	9m	W	D.C.	04 JUL 1859	Mt. Olivet
155	[blank]	14d	W	D.C.	29 JUL 1859	Mt. Olivet
160	[blank]		W	D.C.	03 AUG 1859	Mt. Olivet
223	[blank]	10m	W	D.C.	10 JUN 1866	Mt. Olivet
226	[blank]	6m	W	D.C.	25 JUN 1866	Mt. Olivet
235	[blank], laborer	75y	W	Ire.	13 SEP 1866	Mt. Olivet
238	[blank]	11y	C	Md.	19 SEP 1866	Mt. Olivet
262	[blank]	Still	C	D.C.	03 JUN 1867	Mt. Olivet
264	[blank]	2m	W		14 JUL 1867	Mt. Olivet
268	[blank]	1y	C	D.C.	14 AUG 1867	Mt. Olivet
269	[blank]	Still	W		11 AUG 1867	Mt. Olivet
271	[blank]	11m	W	D.C.	12 AUG 1867	Mt. Olivet
286	[blank]				— DEC 1867	Mt. Olivet
305	[blank]	Still			c.16 MAR 1868	Mt. Olivet
349	[blank]	1y	W	D.C.	19 SEP 1868	Mt. Olivet
245	[blank]	66y			10 NOV 1866	Oak Hill
496	[blank]	Still	W		03 DEC 1870	Oak Hill
696	[blank]	Still	W		12 JUN 1873	Oak Hill
262	[blank]	1y	W	D.C.	16 JUN 1867	Prospect Hill
267	[blank]	16y	W		23 JUL 1867	Prospect Hill
387	[blank]	Still			07 APR 1869	Prospect Hill
482	[blank]	Still			14 OCT 1870	Prospect Hill
485	[blank]	Still			14 OCT 1870	Prospect Hill
492	[blank]	3y	W		27 DEC 1870	Prospect Hill
098	[blank]		W	D.C.	11 DEC 1857	St. Matthews
055	[blank]	10m	W	D.C.	21 AUG 1856	St. Patricks
060	[blank], housewife	65y	W	Ire.	12 OCT 1856	St. Patricks

District of Columbia Interments (Index to Deaths), 1855-1874

Page	Name	Age	Race	Birth	Death Date	Burial Ground
061	[blank]	Still			31 OCT 1856	St. Patricks
132	[blank], slave	80y	C	Md.	08 NOV 1858	St. Patricks
136	[blank]	14d	W	D.C.	13 DEC 1858	St. Patricks
147	[blank]	7y	W	D.C.	28 APR 1859	St. Patricks
159	[blank]	3m	W	D.C.	01 AUG 1859	St. Patricks
021	[blank]		W	D.C.	21 AUG 1855	St. Peters
055	[blank]	8m	W	D.C.	22 AUG 1856	St. Peters
082	[blank]	3m	W		06 JUL 1857	St. Peters
356	[blank]	1d	B	D.C.	02 OCT 1868	Union
264	[blank]	6m	C	D.C.	01 JUL 1867	Union Beneficial
098	[blank]		W	D.C.	17 DEC 1857	Washington
336	[blank]	Still	W		02 AUG 1868	Washington
077	[blank]		W		18 MAY 1857	Washington Asylum
121	[blank]	12h	C	D.C.	14 JUL 1858	Washington Asylum
123	[blank]		W		06 JUL 1858	Washington Asylum
130	[blank]		C		13 OCT 1858	Washington Asylum
130	[blank]		C		16 OCT 1858	Washington Asylum
138	[blank]	Still	C		24 JAN 1859	Washington Asylum
146	[blank] (infant)		W		14 APR 1859	Washington Asylum
170	[blank]	1d	C	D.C.	30 JAN 1860	Washington Asylum
177	[blank]		W	D.C.	11 APR 1860	Washington Asylum
338	[blank]	Still			22 AUG 1868	Washington Asylum
383	[blank]		W	D.C.	06 MAR 1869	Washington Asylum
383	[blank]	2d	W	D.C.	08 MAR 1869	Washington Asylum
383	[blank]		C	D.C.	03 MAR 1869	Washington Asylum
384	[blank]			D.C.	29 MAR 1869	Washington Asylum
389	[blank]		W	D.C.	28 APR 1869	Washington Asylum
389	[blank]				08 APR 1869	Washington Asylum
389	[blank]	Still	C	D.C.	01 APR 1869	Washington Asylum
375	[blank]	Still	W		26 FEB 1869	Washington Hebrew
375	[blank]	Still	W		23 FEB 1869	Washington Hebrew
387	[blank]	Still	W		12 APR 1869	Washington Hebrew
159	[blank]	1y	C	D.C.	29 AUG 1859	Western
192	[blank]	6d	C	D.C.	28 OCT 1860	Western
209	[blank]		W		05 JAN 1866	Western
281	[blank]		W		18 OCT 1867	Western
302	[blank]	1d	C	D.C.	01 MAR 1868	Western
383	[blank]	4m	C		09 MAR 1869	Western
417	[blank]	5m	C		08 SEP 1869	Western
481	[blank]	1y	C	D.C.	28 OCT 1870	Western
485	[blank]	5m	C	D.C.	11 OCT 1870	Western
046	[blank], slave	5m	C	D.C.	17 JUN 1856	Young Mens
124	[blank]	1y	C	D.C.	09 AUG 1858	Young Mens
210	[blank]		C		19 JAN 1866	Young Mens
223	[blank]		C		09 JUN 1866	Young Mens
234	[blank]		C	D.C.	07 SEP 1866	Young Mens
265	[blank]	1y	C	D.C.	25 JUL 1867	Young Mens
281	[blank]		C		18 OCT 1867	Young Mens
286	[blank, scratched through]	2y	C	N.Y.	13 DEC 1867	Young Mens
301	[blank]	9m	C	D.C.	13 MAR 1868	Young Mens
319	[blank], washerwoman		C	Va.	20 JUN 1868	Young Mens
320	[blank]	10m	C	D.C.	10 JUN 1868	Young Mens
361	[blank]	1d	C	D.C.	17 NOV 1868	Young Mens
361	[blank]	Still	C	D.C.	13 NOV 1868	Young Mens
378	[blank]	9d	C		18 FEB 1869	Young Mens
382	[blank], servant	15y	C	W.I.	06 MAR 1869	Young Mens
422	[blank]	40y	C	Va.	03 OCT 1869	Young Mens
436	[blank]	Still	C		01 JAN 1870	Young Mens

District of Columbia Interments (Index to Deaths), 1855-1874

Page	Name	Age	Race	Birth	Death Date	Burial Ground
472	[blank]	Still	C		17 AUG 1870	Young Mens

Page	Name	Age	Race	Birth	Death Date	Burial Ground

SURNAME NOT GIVEN

Page	Name	Age	Race	Birth	Death Date	Burial Ground
440	[blank], Adell	1m	W		15 FEB 1870	Mt. Olivet
450	[blank], Agatha	2m	W	Va.	17 APR 1870	Mt. Olivet
023	[blank], Amanda	27y	C	Md.	02 SEP 1855	St. Matthews
168	[blank], Anna, slave	45y	C	Va.	21 DEC 1859	
460	[blank], Anthony	3m	W	D.C.	03 JUN 1870	Mt. Olivet
453	[blank], August	5m	W		30 MAY 1870	Mt. Olivet
629	[blank], Augustina	2m	C	U.S.	26 OCT 1872	
275	[blank], Aunt Fanny	52y	C		19 SEP 1867	Alms House
006	[blank], Becky	2y	C	Va.	16 APR 1855	Western
006	[blank], Belle		W	N.H.	— APR 1855	Glenwood
440	[blank], Bridgett	2y	W		17 FEB 1870	Mt. Olivet
153	[blank], Caroline, servant	55y	C	Md.	03 JUL 1859	Mt. Olivet
177	[blank], Caroline, servant	55y	C	Va.	25 APR 1860	Young Mens
460	[blank], Cecelia	1y	W	D.C.	05 JUN 1870	Mt. Olivet
014	[blank], Charles, slave	16y	C	Md.	09 JUL 1855	Pr. Geo. Co., Md.
093	[blank], Charles, servant		C		12 OCT 1857	Western
691	[blank], Charlie	7m	W	U.S.	21 MAY 1873	Mt. Olivet
691	[blank], Charlie	7d	W	U.S.	18 MAY 1873	Mt. Olivet
600	[blank], Charlie	16d	W	U.S.	14 MAY 1872	Unknown
124	[blank], Chloe	83y	C	Md.	09 AUG 1858	Harmony
260	[blank], Christine		W		26 MAY 1867	Mt. Olivet
373	[blank], Christine	1m	W		22 JAN 1869	Mt. Olivet
600	[blank], Clementine	14d	W	U.S.	— MAY 1872	Unknown
191	[blank], Columbus, slave	27y	C	Va.	02 OCT 1860	
446	[blank], Cornelia	1y	C		29 MAR 1870	Young Mens
023	[blank], Cornelius	1y		D.C.	22 SEP 1855	St. Patricks
264	[blank], Eliza	10m			21 JUL 1867	
163	[blank], Eliza, servant	17y	C	D.C.	03 OCT 1859	Washington Asylum
644	[blank], Ellen	8m	W	U.S.	17 DEC 1872	Mt. Olivet
127	[blank], Ellen, slave	17y	C	Va.	08 SEP 1858	Colored, East
142	[blank], Ellen, slave	72y	C	Md.	05 FEB 1859	Colored
233	[blank], Emma, child of	Still	C	D.C.	31 AUG 1866	
027	[blank], Emmaline	30y	C	Md.	19 OCT 1855	St. Matthews
267	[blank], Euphemia	14d	W		16 JUL 1867	Mt. Olivet
608	[blank], Fannie	8m	C	D.C.	01 JUN 1872	
213	[blank], Fanny	11y	C		24 FEB 1866	
327	[blank], Ferdinand	9d	W		18 JUL 1868	Mt. Olivet
467	[blank], Florence	14d	W		21 JUL 1870	Mt. Olivet
453	[blank], Florence	5m	W		26 MAY 1870	Mt. Olivet
029	[blank], Frances		C		02 NOV 1855	Alms House
269	[blank], Francis	22d	W		24 AUG 1867	Mt. Olivet
281	[blank], Francis	16d	W		14 OCT 1867	Mt. Olivet
765	[blank], Frank	65y	W	Ger.	10 MAY 1874	Prospect Hill
099	[blank], George, fortune teller		W	Eng.	25 DEC 1857	St. Matthews
332	[blank], Hanora	3d	W	D.C.	03 JUL 1868	Mt. Olivet
086	[blank], Harriet	35y	C	Md.	02 AUG 1857	St. Patricks
113	[blank], Harry, farmer	15y	C	Md.	13 MAY 1858	Foundry
529	[blank], Henry	6m			27 JUL 1871	
612	[blank], Henry	1m	W	U.S.	04 JUL 1872	
542	[blank], Henry	22y	C	Va.	18 OCT 1871	Washington
319	[blank], James	2m	W		28 JUN 1868	Mt. Olivet
608	[blank], Jennie	2m	W	D.C.	01 JUN 1872	
314	[blank], Jennie	5m	C	D.C.	20 MAY 1868	Mt. Olivet
610	[blank], Jenny	1y	W	U.S.	29 JUL 1872	
070	[blank], Jenny, servant	80y	C	unk.	08 FEB 1857	Washington Asylum
074	[blank], Jesse, laborer	89y	C	Md.	28 MAR 1857	Harmony
450	[blank], John	1m	W	D.C.	21 APR 1870	Mt. Olivet

Page	Name	Age	Race	Birth	Death Date	Burial Ground
639	[blank], John	8m	W	U.S.	25 NOV 1872	Mt. Olivet
202	[blank], John, slave		C		13 APR 1861	Harmony
447	[blank], Johnny	3y	C		29 MAR 1870	Mt. Olivet
600	[blank], Joseph	1y	W	U.S.	01 MAY 1872	Mt. Olivet
150	[blank], Josephine, servant	22y	C	D.C.	14 JUN 1859	
086	[blank], Jun.	2y	C	D.C.	02 AUG 1857	Western
659	[blank], Katie	6m	W	U.S.	16 JAN 1873	
448	[blank], Laura	4m	W	D.C.	01 MAR 1870	Mt. Olivet
008	[blank], Liddy, slave	9y	C	Ga.	02 MAY 1855	Harmony
356	[blank], Magdalene	1m	W	D.C.	18 OCT 1868	Prospect Hill
448	[blank], Maria	1m	W		03 MAR 1870	Mt. Olivet
188	[blank], Maria, cook	65y	C	Va.	27 AUG 1860	Foundry
086	[blank], Maria, servant	22y	C	Va.	05 AUG 1857	Methodist
378	[blank], Martina	1m	W		17 FEB 1869	Mt. Olivet
773	[blank], Mary Ann	21d	W	U.S.	15 JUN 1874	Mt. Olivet
267	[blank], Mary Catherine	29d	W		18 JUL 1867	Mt. Olivet
528	[blank], Mary E.	1y	W	D.C.	16 JUL 1871	Congressional
051	[blank], Mary Elizabeth	2m	W		27 JUL 1856	Congressional
478	[blank], Mary Ellen	1m	W	D.C.	13 SEP 1870	Mt. Olivet
164	[blank], Mary, servant	76y	C	Va.	03 OCT 1859	Ebenezer
467	[blank], Matilda	10d	C	D.C.	03 JUL 1870	Mt. Olivet
581	[blank], Moses, laborer	55y	C		16 FEB 1872	Young Mens
223	[blank], Mr., carpenter	40y	C	Md.	10 JUN 1866	Beckett's
221	[blank], Mr., laborer	38y	W	Md.	25 MAY 1866	Mt. Olivet
361	[blank], Nancy	1m	C	D.C.	— NOV 1868	Young Mens
078	[blank], Olivia, slave	45y	C	Md.	27 MAY 1857	Ebenezer
042	[blank], Olivia, slave	14y	C	Md.	23 APR 1856	St. Matthews
187	[blank], Patsy, cook	50y	C	Va.	03 AUG 1860	Young Mens
319	[blank], Peter	7m	W		16 JUN 1868	Mt. Olivet
440	[blank], Raphael	4m	W		09 FEB 1870	Mt. Olivet
441	[blank], Raphael	5m	W		09 FEB 1870	Mt. Olivet
184	[blank], Rebecca	12y	C	Va.	09 JUL 1860	Young Mens
639	[blank], Rosanna	7d	W	U.S.	25 NOV 1872	Mt. Olivet
629	[blank], Samuel	8m	W	U.S.	09 OCT 1872	
021	[blank], Samuel	1y	C	D.C.	31 AUG 1855	Foundry
507	[blank], Stephen	43y	W		07 FEB 1871	Mt. Olivet
111	[blank], Susan	9y	C	D.C.	13 APR 1858	Colored, East
319	[blank], Thomas	2m	W		26 JUN 1868	Mt. Olivet
082	[blank], Thomas	2m	C		07 JUL 1857	St. Matthews
060	[blank], Thomas, slave	16y	C	S.C.	26 OCT 1856	Harmony
006	[blank], Tom	14y	C	D.C.	08 APR 1855	Asylum
260	[blank], Victor		W		12 MAY 1867	Mt. Olivet
587	[blank], William	2y	C	D.C.	21 MAR 1872	Jones Chapel
600	[blank], William	6m	W	U.S.	23 MAY 1872	Unknown
540	[blank], William	1m	W	D.C.	01 OCT 1871	Washington
478	[blank], Willie	1m	W	D.C.	19 SEP 1870	Mt. Olivet
392	[illegible]	30y	C		20 MAY 1869	Washington Asylum
508	[illegible], female	73y	C	Md.	22 FEB 1871	Ebenezer
209	[Perkins?], [torn] H.	60y			— JAN 1866	[torn]
002	[torn]	2m	W	D.C.	— JAN 1855	
002	[torn]	14y	W	D.C.	— JAN 1855	
004	[torn]		W	Eng.	— MAR 1855	Congressional
004	[torn]	2d		D.C.	— MAR 1855	Glenwood
002	[torn]		C	Md.	— JAN 1855	Glenwood
004	[torn]	12y	W	D.C.	— MAR 1855	Methodist
002	[torn]		W	D.C.	— JAN 1855	Oak Hill
002	[torn]				— JAN 1855	Western
004	[torn], Eleanor H.W.			D.C.	— MAR 1855	Holmead

District of Columbia Interments (Index to Deaths), 1855-1874

Page	Name	Age	Race	Birth	Death Date	Burial Ground
002	[torn], James	23y	C	Va.	2_ JAN 1855	Young Mens
002	[torn], James, laborer	90y	C	Md.	1_ JAN 1855	Young Mens
008	[torn], John T.	1y	W	D.C.	— MAY 1855	
528	[torn], Mary Ann		C	D.C.	c.21 JUL 1871	Young Mens
212	[torn], saddler	40y	W	Ire.	21 FEB 1866	Mt. Olivet
006	[torn], Sally	4y	W	Va.	— APR 1855	Va.
006	[torn], W.	11m	W	D.C.	— APR 1855	
544	[twins]	5d	W	D.C.	08 NOV 1871	Methocist

ABOUT THE AUTHOR

Wesley E. Pippenger is an active member in a number of historical and genealogical societies in Virginia, and is past-President of the Board of Governors of the Virginia Genealogical Society. He has been employed by the Federal Government for over 27 years, and is a management analyst with the Office of Inspector General, National Aeronautics and Space Administration in Washington, D.C. He resides in Arlington, Virginia.

Mr. Pippenger has been active in genealogical research since 1970. Shortly after moving from Colorado to Virginia in 1982, he began to locate, study, catalog, and have data published about cemeteries in the Alexandria, Virginia area. Subsequent published works, now numbering upwards of 60 items, include abstracts of court records, vital records, acts of the Virginia Assembly, newspapers, land, probate, and legislative petition records, and more. His current landmark project, published in series by the Virginia Genealogical Society, is to inventory all estate-related documents for the period 1800-1865, for the entire state of Virginia.